MEANS RESIDENTIAL COST DATA 1991

TABLE OF CONTENTS

Foreword	ii
How To Use This Book	iii
Square Foot Cost Section	1
Assemblies Section	79
Unit Price Section	241
Reference Section	393
Appendix	
Crew Listings	424
Location Factors	444
Abbreviations	449
Index	452

Senior Editors
John H. Chiang
Phillip R. Waier

Chief Editor
Phillip R. Waier

Contributing Editors
Allan B. Cleveland
Donald D. Denzer
Jeffrey M. Goldman
Patricia Jackson
Alan E. Lew
Melville J. Mossman
John J. Moylan
Jeannene D. Murphy
Kenneth M. Randall
Kornelis Smit
Rory Woolsey
David M. Zuniga

Technical Coordinators
Marion Schofield
Wayne D. Anderson

Graphics
Carl W. Linde

Publisher
Roger J. Grant

Second Printing

FOREWORD

THE COMPANY AND THE EDITORS

Since 1942, R.S. Means Company, Inc. has been actively engaged in construction cost publishing and consulting throughout North America. The primary objective of the company is to provide the construction industry professional — the contractor, the owner, the architect, the engineer, the facilities manager — with current and comprehensive construction cost data.

A thoroughly experienced and highly qualified staff of professionals at R.S. Means works daily at collecting, analyzing and disseminating reliable cost information for your needs. These staff members have years of practical construction experience and engineering training prior to joining the firm. Each contributes to the maintenance of a complete, continually-updated construction cost data system.

With the constant flow of new construction methods and materials, the construction professional often cannot find enough time to examine and evaluate all the diverse construction cost possibilities. R.S. Means performs this function by analyzing all facets of the industry. Data is collected and organized into a format that is instantly accessible. The data is useful for all phases of construction cost determination — from the preliminary budget to the detailed unit price estimate.

The Means organization is always prepared to assist you and help in the solution of construction problems through the services of its four major divisions; Construction and Cost Data Publishing, Computer Data and Software Services, Consulting Services and Educational Seminars.

DEVELOPMENT OF COST DATA

The staff at R.S. Means Company, Inc. continuously monitors developments in the construction industry in order to ensure reliable, thorough and up-to-date cost information. While *overall* construction costs may vary relative to general economic conditions, price fluctuations within the industry are dependent upon many other factors. Individual price variations may, in fact, be opposite to overall economic trends. Therefore, costs are monitored and updated and new items are added in response to industry changes.

All costs represent U.S. national averages and are given in U.S. dollars. The Means City Cost Indexes can be used to convert costs to a particular location. The City Cost Indexes for Canada can be used to convert U.S. national averages to local costs in Canadian dollars.

Material Costs are determined by contacting manufacturers, dealers, distributors, and contractors throughout the United States. If current material costs are available for a specific location, adjustments can be made to reflect differences from the national average. Material costs do not include sales tax.

Labor Costs are based on the average of open shop wages from seven major U.S. regions for the current year. Rates are listed on the inside back cover of this book. If wage rates in your area vary from those used in this book, or if rate increases are expected within a given year, labor costs should be adjusted accordingly.

Labor costs reflect productivity based on actual working conditions. These figures include time spent during a normal work day on items other than actual installation such as material receiving and handling, mobilization, site movement, breaks, and cleanup. Productivity data is developed over an extended period so as not to be influenced by abnormal variations, and reflects a typical average.

Equipment Costs as presented include not only rental costs, but also operating costs. Equipment prices are obtained from industry sources throughout North America — contractors, suppliers, dealers, manufacturers, and distributors.

FACTORS AFFECTING COSTS

Quality: The prices for materials and the workmanship upon which productivity is based are in line with U.S. Government specifications and represent good sound construction.

Overtime: No allowance has been made for overtime. If premium time or work during other than normal working hours is anticipated, adjustments to labor costs should be made accordingly.

Productivity: The productivity, daily output and man-hour figures for each line item are based on working an eight hour day in daylight hours. For other than normal work hours, productivity may decrease.

Size of Project: The size and type of construction project can have a significant impact on cost. Economy of scale can reduce costs for large projects. Conversely, costs may be higher for small projects due to higher percentage overhead costs, small quantity material purchases and minimum labor and/or equipment charges. Costs in this book are intended for the size and type of project as described in the "How To Use This Book" pages. Costs for projects of a significantly different size or type should be adjusted accordingly.

Location: Material prices are for metropolitan areas. Beyond a 20 mile radius of large cities, extra trucking or other transportation charges will increase the material costs slightly. This material increase may be offset by lower wage rates. Both of these factors should be considered when preparing an estimate, especially if the job site is remote. Highly specialized subcontract items may require high travel and per diem expenses for mechanics.

Other factors affecting costs are season of year, contractor management, weather, local trade practices, building code requirements, and the availability of adequate energy, skilled labor, and building materials. General business conditions influence the "in-place" cost of all items. Substitute materials and construction methods may have to be employed, and these may increase the installed cost and/or life cycle costs. Such factors are difficult to evaluate and cannot be predicted on the basis of the job's location in a particular section of the country. Thus, there may be a significant, but unavoidable cost variation where these factors are concerned.

CSI MASTERFORMAT

Unit price data in this book is organized according to the MASTERFORMAT system of classification and numbering as developed by the Construction Specifications Institute (CSI) and Construction Specifications Canada. This system, widely accepted in the industry, is used extensively by architects and engineers for construction specifications, by contractors for estimating and record keeping, and by manufacturers and suppliers for categorization of construction materials and products. R.S. Means has organized unit price data in this system to help construction professionals categorize all aspects of the construction process.

HOW TO USE THIS BOOK

HOW THE BOOK IS ARRANGED

This book is divided into five sections: Square Foot, Assemblies, Unit Price, Reference and an Appendix.

Square Foot Section: This section lists Square Foot costs for typical residential construction projects. The organizational format used divides the projects into basic building classes. These classes are defined at the beginning of the section. The individual projects are further divided into ten common components of construction. An outline of a typical page layout, an explanation of Square Foot prices, and a Table of Contents are located at the beginning of the section.

Assemblies Section: This section uses an "Assemblies" (sometimes referred to as "systems") format grouping all the functional elements of a building into 9 construction divisions.

At the top of each "Assembly" cost table is an illustration, a brief description, and the design criteria used to develop the cost. Each of the components and its contributing cost to the system is shown.

Material These cost figures include a standard 10% mark-up for "handling". They are national average material costs as of January of the current year and include delivery to the jobsite.

Installation The installation costs include labor and equipment, plus a mark-up for the installing contractor's overhead and profit.

For a complete breakdown and explanation of a typical "Assemblies" page, see "How To Use Assemblies Cost Tables" at the beginning of this section.

Unit Price Section: All cost data has been divided into the 16 divisions of the Construction Specifications Institute's (CSI) MASTERFORMAT. A listing of these divisions and an outline of their subdivisions is shown in the Table of Contents page at the beginning of the Unit Price Section.

Numbering Each unit price line item has been assigned a unique 10 digit code. A graphic explanation of the numbering system is shown on the "How To Use Unit Price" page.

Descriptions Each line item number is followed by a description of the item. Sub-items and additional sizes are indented beneath appropriate line items. The first line or two after the main (bold face) item often contain descriptive information that pertains to all line items beneath this bold face listing.

Crew The "Crew" column designates the typical trade or crew to install the item. When an installation is done by one trade and requires no power equipment, that trade is listed. For example, "2 Carp" indicates that the installation is done with 2 carpenters. Where a composite crew is appropriate, a crew code designation is listed. For example, a "C-2" crew is made up of 1 foreman, 4 carpenters, 1 laborer plus power tools. All crews are listed in the crew section of the Appendix. Costs are shown both with bare labor rates, and with the contractor's overhead and profit. For each, the total crew cost per eight-hour day and the composite cost per man-hour are listed.

Equipment The power equipment required for each crew is included in the crew cost. The daily allowance for crew equipment is based on dividing the weekly bare rental rate by 5 (number of working days per week), and then adding the hourly operating cost times 8 (hours per day).

Page Layout An outline of a typical page layout and an explanation of the components that make up Unit Prices is located at the beginning of the Unit Price Section.

Reference Section: Along with the items on the "Unit Price" pages are larger numbers in circles. These "circle numbers" refer the reader to reference tables and systems in this section. The tables and systems show how the editors arrived at the figures and are often of value in listing materials for purchase. This section also includes information on design and economy in construction.

Appendix: Included in this section are crew listings, location factors, a list of abbreviations and a comprehensive index.

Crews A listing of all crews used in the unit price section is provided here.

Location Factors To adjust the prices in this book for a specific location, use the zip code factors in this section.

Abbreviations/Index A listing of the abbreviations used throughout this book along with the terms they represent is included. Following the abbreviations is an index for all sections.

Other Factors Affecting Costs:
General Conditions The "Assemblies" and "Square Foot" sections of this book use costs that include the installing contractor's overhead and profit (O&P). An allowance covering the general contractor's mark-up must be added to these figures. The general contractor can include this price in the bid with a normal mark-up ranging from 5% to 15%. The mark-up depends on economic conditions plus the supervision and troubleshooting expected by the general contractor. For purposes of this book, it is best for a general contractor to add an allowance of 10% to the figures in the Assemblies and Square Foot Cost sections.

In the Unit Price section, the extreme right-hand column of each chart gives the "Total Including O&P." These figures contain the original installing subcontractor's O&P (in other words, the contractor doing the work), therefore it is necessary for a general contractor to add a percentage of all subcontracted items. For a detailed breakdown of O&P see the inside back cover of the book.

Overhead & Profit Tables in the reference section give details on overhead. For systems costs and square foot costs, simply add 10% to the estimate for general contractor's profit.

For Unit Price costs, these tables can be used by the general contractor as a guide to determine the appropriate overhead and profit mark-ups.

PROJECT SIZE

This book is intended for use by those involved primarily in Residential construction costing less than $500,000. This includes the construction of homes, row houses, townhouses, condominiums and apartments. WITH REASONABLE EXERCISE OF JUDGMENT, THE FIGURES CAN BE USED FOR OTHER TYPES OF WORK. For other types of projects, such as repair and remodeling or commercial buildings, consult the appropriate MEANS publication for more information.

ROUNDING OF COSTS

In general, all unit prices in excess of $5.00 have been rounded to make them easier to use and still maintain adequate precision of the results. The rounding rules are as follows:
Price from $5.01 to $20.00 rounded to the nearest 5¢
Price from $20.01 to $100.00 rounded to the nearest $1
Price from $100.01 to $1,000.00 rounded to the nearest $5
Price from $1,000.01 to $10,000.00 rounded to the nearest $25
Price from $10,000.01 to $50,000.00 rounded to the nearest $100
Price over $50,000.01 rounded to the nearest $500

HOW TO USE SQUARE FOOT SECTION

Introduction The residential section of this manual contains costs per square foot for four classes of construction in seven building types. Costs are listed for various exterior wall materials which are typical of the class and building type. There are cost tables for Wings and Ells with modification tables to adjust the base cost of each class of building. Non-standard items can easily be added to the standard structures.

Accompanying each building type in each class is a list of components used in a typical residence. The components are divided into ten primary estimating divisions. The divisions correspond with the "Assemblies" section of this manual.

Cost estimating for a residence is a three step process:

(1) Identification
(2) Listing dimensions
(3) Calculations

Guidelines and a sample cost estimating form are shown on the following pages.

Identification To properly identify a residential building, the class of construction, type, and exterior wall material must be determined. Located at the beginning of this section are drawings and guidelines for determining the class of construction. There are also detailed specifications accompanying each type of building along with additional drawings at the beginning of each set of tables to further aid in proper building class and type identification.

Sketches for seven types of residential buildings and their configurations are shown along with definitions of living area next to each sketch. Sketches and definitions of garage types follow the residential buildings.

Living Area Base cost tables are prepared as costs per square foot of living area. The living area of a residence is that area which is suitable and normally designed for full time living. It does not include basement recreation rooms or finished attics, although these areas are often considered full time living areas by the owners.

Living area is calculated from the exterior dimensions without the need to adjust for exterior wall thickness. When calculating the living area of a 1-1/2 story, two story, three story or tri-level residence, overhangs and other differences in size and shape between floors must be considered.

Only the floor area with a ceiling height of six feet or more in a 1-1/2 story residence is considered living area. In bi-levels and tri-levels, the areas that are below grade are considered living area, even when these areas may not be completely finished.

Base Tables and Modifications Base cost tables show the base cost per square foot without a basement, with one full bath and one full kitchen. Adjustments for finished and unfinished basements are part of the base cost tables. Adjustments for multi-family residences, additional bathrooms, townhouses, alternate roofs, and air conditioning and heating systems are listed in modification tables below the base cost tables.

The component list for each residence type should also be consulted when preparing an estimate. If the components listed are not appropriate, modifications can be made by consulting the "Assemblies" section of this manual.

Costs for other modifications, including garages, breezeways and site improvements, are in the modification tables at the end of this section. For additional information on contractor overhead and architectural fees, consult the "Reference" section of this manual.

Listing of Dimensions To use this section of the manual only the dimensions used to calculate the horizontal area of the building and additions and modifications are needed. The dimensions, normally the length and width, can come from drawings or field measurements. For ease in calculation, consider measuring in tenths of feet, i.e., 9 ft. 6 in. = 9.5 ft., 9 ft. 4 in. = 9.3 ft.

In all cases, make a sketch of the building. Any protrusions or other variations in shape should be noted on the sketch with dimensions.

Calculations The calculations portion of the estimate is a two step activity:

(1) The selection of appropriate costs from the tables
(2) Computations.

Selection of Appropriate Costs To select the appropriate cost from the base the following information is needed:

(1) Class of construction
(2) Type of residence
(3) Occupancy
(4) Building configuration
(5) Exterior wall construction
(6) Living area

Consult the tables and accompanying information to make the appropriate selections. Modifications are classified by class, type and size. Further modifications can be made using the "Assemblies" Section.

Computations The computation process should take the following sequence:

(1) Multiply the base cost by the area
(2) Add or subtract the modifications
(3) Apply the location modifier

When selecting costs, interpolate or use the cost that most nearly matches the structure under study. This applies to size, exterior wall construction and class.

SQUARE FOOT

TABLE OF CONTENTS

How to Use S. F. Section .... iv, 2, 3	3 Story 32	2½ Story 66
Building Classes 4	Bi-Level 34	3 Story 68
Building Types 4, 5	Tri-Level 36	Bi-Level 70
Building Material 6	Solid Wall (log home) 1 Story 38	Tri-Level 72
Building Configuration 7	Solid Wall (log home) 2 Story 40	Wings and Ells 74
Garage Types 8	Wings and Ells 42	**Residential Modifications**
Estimate Form 9, 10	**Custom**	Breezeway 75
Residential Models 11	1 Story 44	Porches 75
Economy	1½ Story 46	Finished Attic 75
1 Story 12	2 Story 48	Fireplace & Chimney 75
1½ Story 14	2½ Story 50	Appliances 75
2 Story 16	3 Story 52	Kitchen Cabinets 76
Bi-Level 18	Bi-Level 54	Alarm System 76
Tri-Level 20	Tri-Level 56	Sauna, Prefabricated 76
Wings and Ells 22	Wings and Ells 58	Garages 77
Average	**Luxury**	Carports 77
1 Story 24	1 Story 60	Fencing 77
1½ Story 26	1½ Story 62	Site Improvements 77
2 Story 28	2 Story 64	Wood and Coal Stoves 77
2½ Story 30		

HOW TO USE SQUARE FOOT COST PAGES

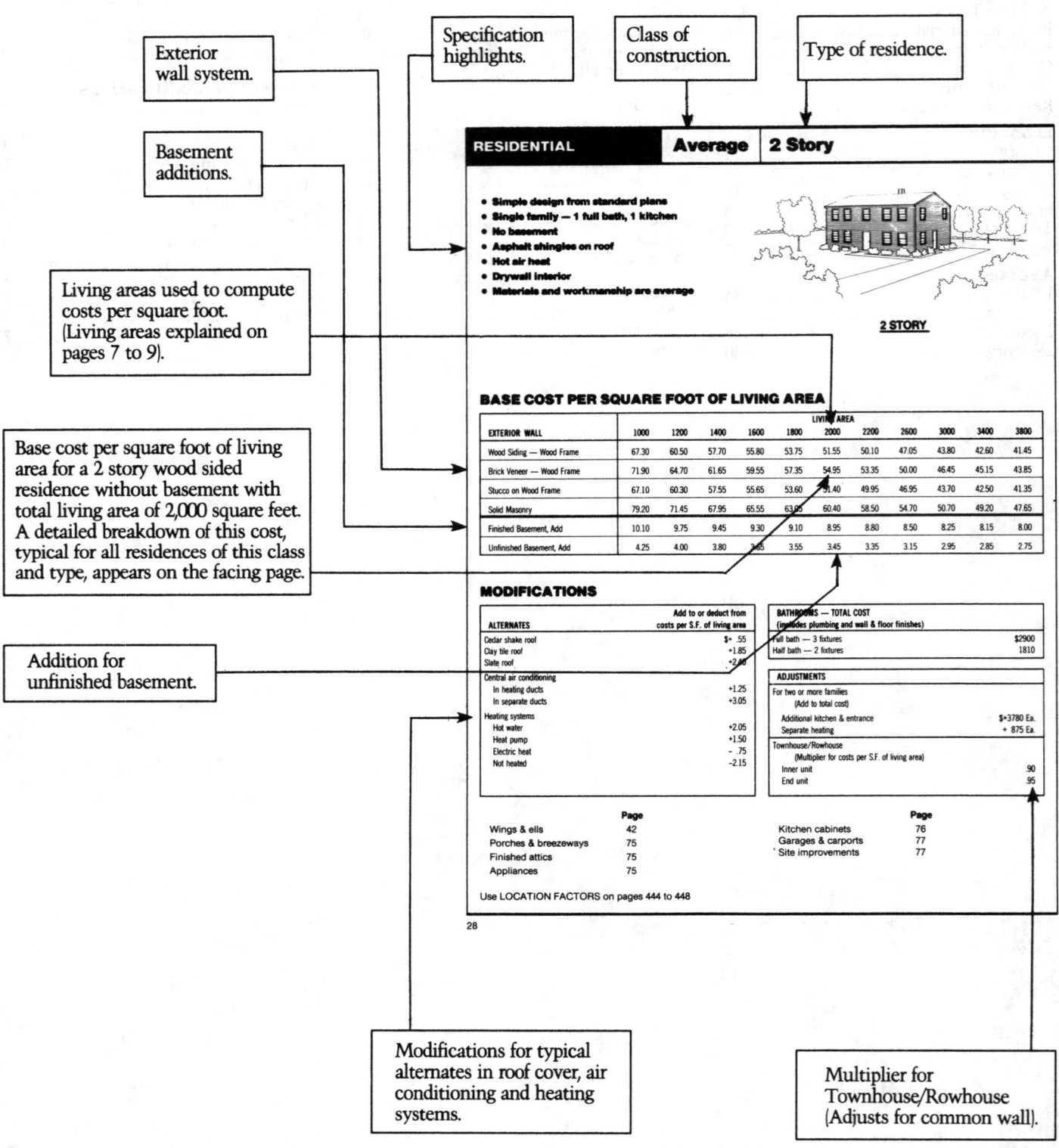

Components
This page contains the ten components needed to develop the complete square foot cost of the typical dwelling specified. All components are defined with a description of the materials and/or task involved. Use cost figures from each component to estimate the cost per square foot of that section of the project.

Specifications
The parameters for an example dwelling from the facing page are listed here. Included are the square foot dimensions of the proposed building. LIVING AREA takes into account the number of floors and other factors needed to define a building's TOTAL SQUARE FOOTAGE. Perimeter and partition dimensions are defined in terms of linear feet.

Line Totals
The extreme right-hand column lists the sum of two figures. Use this total to determine the sum of MATERIAL COST plus INSTALLATION COST. The result is a convenient total cost for each of the ten components.

Average 2 Story

Living Area: 2000 S.F.
Perimeter: 135 L.F.

#	Component	Description	MAN-HOURS	MAT.	LABOR	TOTAL
1	Site Work	Site preparation for slab; trench 4' deep for foundation wall.	.084		.67	.67
2	Foundations	Continuous concrete footing 8" deep x 18" wide; cast-in-place concrete wall, 8" thick, 4' deep, 4" concrete slab on 4" crushed stone base, trowel finish.	.066	1.77	1.87	3.64
3	Framing	2" x 4" wood studs, 16" O.C.; 1/2" plywood sheathing; 2" x 6" rafters 16" O.C. with 1/2" plywood sheathing, 4 in 12 pitch; 2" x 6" ceiling joists 16" O.C.; 2" x 8" floor joists 16" O.C. with bridging and 5/8" waferboard subfloor; 1/2" waferboard subfloor on 1" x 2" wood sleepers 16" O.C.	.131	3.62	4.15	7.77
4	Exterior Walls	Horizontal beveled wood siding; #15 felt building paper; 3-1/2" batt insulation; wood double hung windows; 3 flush solid core wood exterior doors; storms and screens.	.111	8.71	3.76	12.47
5	Roofing	240# asphalt shingles; #15 felt building paper; aluminum flashing; 6" attic insulation. Aluminum gutters and downspouts.	.024	.39	.59	.98
6	Interiors	1/2" drywall, taped and finished, painted with primer and 1 coat; softwood baseboard and trim, painted with primer and 1 coat; finished hardwood floor 40%, carpet with underlayment 40%, vinyl tile with underlayment 15%, ceramic tile with underlayment 5%; hollow core doors.	.232	9.28	7.90	17.18
7	Specialties	Kitchen cabinets - 14 L.F. wall and base cabinets with laminated plastic counter top; medicine cabinet, stairs.	.021	.93	.33	1.26
8	Mechanical	1 lavatory, white, wall hung; 1 water closet, white; 1 bathtub with shower, porcelain enamel steel, white; 1 kitchen sink, stainless steel, single; 1 water heater, gas fired, 30 gal.; gas fired warm air heat.	.060	1.57	1.34	2.91
9	Electrical	200 Amp. service; romex wiring; incandescent lighting fixtures, switches, receptacles.	.039	.50	.80	1.30
10	Overhead	Contractor's overhead and profit and plans.		1.87	1.50	3.37
	Total		28.64	22.91	51.55

Man-hours
Use this column to determine the unit of measure in MAN-HOURS needed to perform a task. This figure will give the builder MAN-HOURS PER SQUARE FOOT of building. The TOTAL MAN-HOURS PER COMPONENT are determined by multiplying the LIVING AREA times the MAN-HOURS listed on that line. (TOTAL MAN-HOURS PER COMPONENT=LIVING AREA × MAN-HOURS)

Installation
The labor rates included here incorporate the overhead and profit costs for the installing contractor. The average mark-up used to create these figures is 63.2% over and above BARE LABOR COST including fringe benefits.

Bottom Line Total
This figure is the complete square foot cost for the construction project. To determine TOTAL PROJECT COST, multiply the BOTTOM LINE TOTAL times the LIVING AREA. (TOTAL PROJECT COST = BOTTOM LINE TOTAL × LIVING AREA)

Materials
This column gives the unit needed to develop the COST OF MATERIALS. Note: The figures given here are not BARE COSTS. Ten percent has been added to BARE MATERIAL COST to cover handling.

*NOTE
The components listed on this page are typical of all the sizes of residences from the facing page. Specific quantities of components required would vary with the size of the dwelling and the exterior wall system.

BUILDING CLASSES

Given below are the four general definitions of building classes. Each building type — Economy, Average, Custom and Luxury — is common in residential construction. All four are used in this book to determine costs per square foot.

Economy Class
An economy class residence is usually mass-produced from stock plans. The materials and workmanship are sufficient only to satisfy minimum building codes. Low construction cost is more important than distinctive features. Design is seldom other than square or rectangular.

Average Class
An average class residence is simple in design and is built from standard designer plans. Materials and workmanship are average, but often exceed the minimum building codes. There are frequently special features that give the residence some distinctive characteristics.

Custom Class
A custom class residence is usually built from a designer's plans which have been modified to give the building a distinction of design. Material and workmanship are generally above average with obvious attention given to construction details. Construction normally exceeds building code requirements.

Luxury Class
A luxury class residence is built from an architect's plan for a specific owner. It is unique in design and workmanship. There are many special features, and construction usually exceeds all building codes. It is obvious that primary attention is placed on the owner's comfort and pleasure. Construction is supervised by an architect.

RESIDENTIAL BUILDING TYPES

One Story
This is an example of a one-story dwelling. The living area of this type of residence is confined to the ground floor. The headroom in the attic is usually too low for use as a living area.

One-and-a-half Story
The living area in the upper level of this type of residence is 50% to 90% of the ground floor. This is made possible by a combination of this design's high-peaked roof and/or dormers. Only the upper level area with a ceiling height of 6' or more is considered living area. The living area of this residence is the sum of the ground floor area plus the area on the second level with a ceiling height of 6' or more.

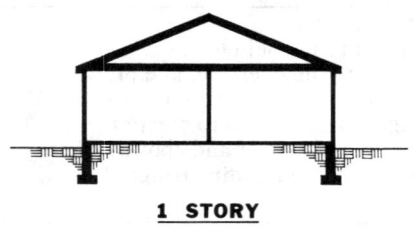

RESIDENTIAL BUILDING TYPES

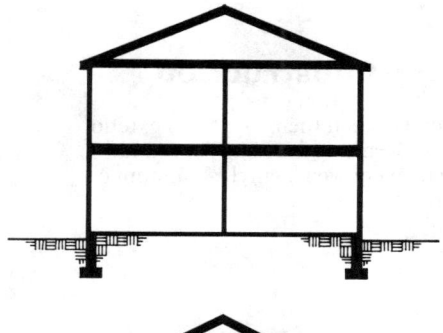

Two Story
This type of residence has a second floor or upper level area which is equal or nearly equal to the ground floor area. The upper level of this type of residence can range from 90% to 110% of the ground floor area, depending on setbacks or overhangs. The living area is the sum of the ground floor area and the upper level floor area.

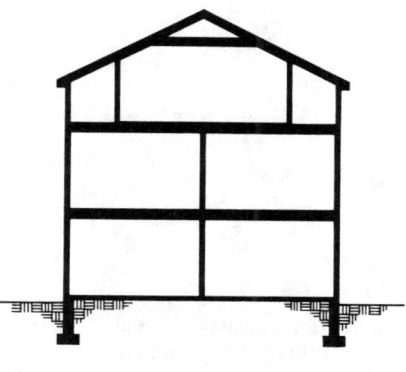

Two-and-one-half Story
This type of residence has two levels of equal or nearly equal area and a third level which has a living area that is 50% to 90% of the ground floor. This is made possible by a high peaked roof, extended wall heights and/or dormers. Only the upper level area with a ceiling height of 6 feet or more is considered living area. The living area of this residence is the sum of the ground floor area, the second floor area and the area on the third level with a ceiling height of 6 feet or more.

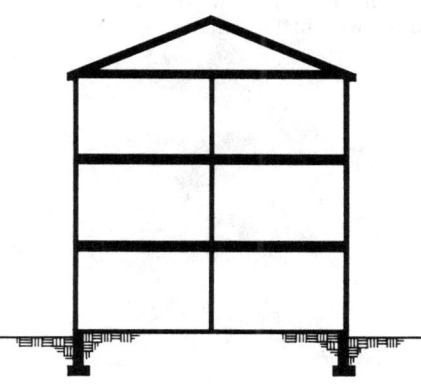

Three Story
This type of residence has three levels which are equal or nearly equal. As in the 2 story residence, the second and third floor areas may vary slightly depending on setbacks or overhangs. The living area is the sum of the ground floor area and the two upper level floor areas.

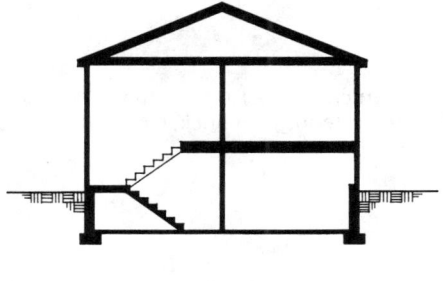

Bi-level
This type of residence has two living areas, one above the other. One area is about 4 feet below grade and the second is about 4 feet above grade. Both areas are equal in size. The lower level in this type of residence is originally designed and built to serve as a living area and not as a basement. Both levels have full ceiling heights. The living area is the sum of the lower level area and the upper level area.

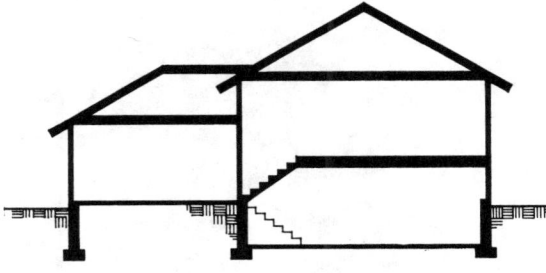

Tri-level
This type of residence has three levels of living area. One is at grade level, the second is about four feet below grade, and the third is about 4' above grade. All levels are originally designed to serve as living areas. All levels have full ceiling heights. The living area is the sum of the areas of each of the three levels.

EXTERIOR WALL CONSTRUCTION

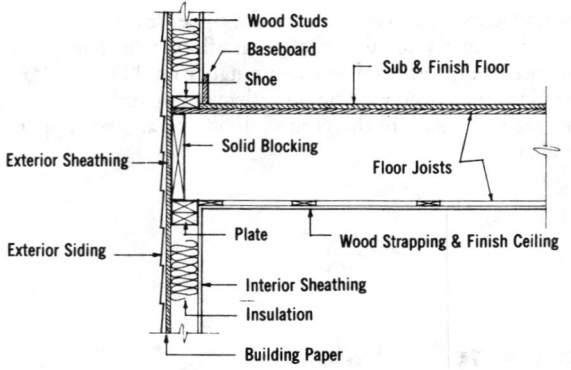

Typical Frame Construction
Typical wood frame construction consists of wood studs with insulation between them. A typical exterior surface is made up of sheathing, building paper and exterior siding consisting of wood, vinyl, aluminum or stucco over the wood sheathing.

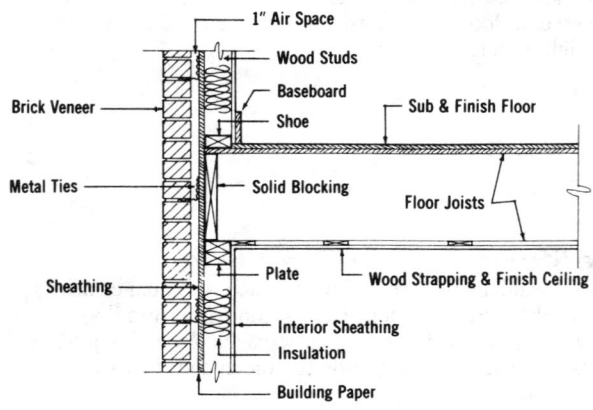

Brick Veneer
Typical brick veneer construction consists of wood studs with insulation between them. A typical exterior surface is sheathing, building paper and an exterior of brick tied to the sheathing with metal strips.

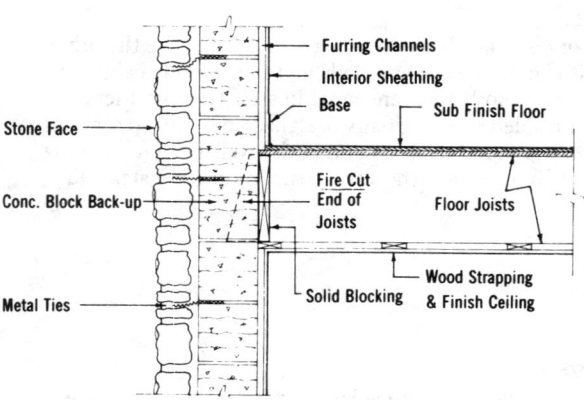

Stone
Typical solid masonry construction consists of a stone or block wall covered on the exterior with brick, stone or other masonry.

RESIDENTIAL CONFIGURATIONS

Detached House
This category of residence is a free standing separate building with or without an attached garage. It has four complete walls.

Town/Row House
This category of residence has a number of attached units made up of inner units and end units. The units are joined by common walls. The inner units have only two exterior walls. The common walls are fireproof. The end units have three walls and a common wall. Town houses/row houses can be any of the five types.

Semi-Detached House
This category of residence has two living units side-by-side. The common wall is a fireproof wall. Semi-detached residences can be treated as a row house with two end units. Semi-detached residences can be any of the five types.

RESIDENTIAL GARAGE TYPES

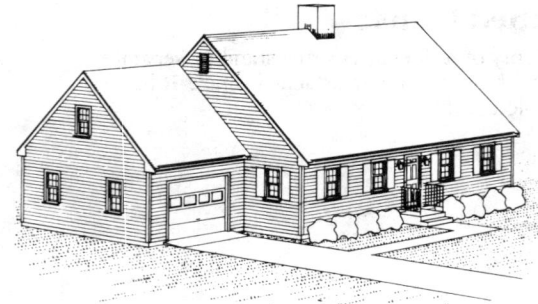

Attached Garage
Shares a common wall with the dwelling. Access is typically through a door between dwelling and garage.

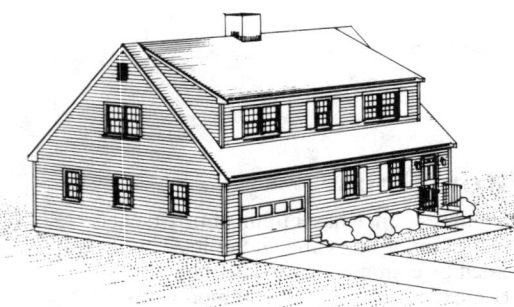

Built-In Garage
Constructed under the second floor living space and above basement level of dwelling. Reduces gross square feet of living area.

Basement Garage
Constructed under the roof of the dwelling but below the living area.

Detached Garage
Constructed apart from the main dwelling. Shares no common area or wall with the dwelling.

Means Forms
RESIDENTIAL COST ESTIMATE

OWNER'S NAME: _____   APPRAISER: _____

RESIDENCE ADDRESS: _____   PROJECT: _____

CITY, STATE, ZIP CODE: _____   DATE: _____

CLASS OF CONSTRUCTION	RESIDENCE TYPE	CONFIGURATION	EXTERIOR WALL SYSTEM
☐ ECONOMY	☐ 1 STORY	☐ DETACHED	☐ WOOD SIDING — WOOD FRAME
☐ AVERAGE	☐ 1½ STORY	☐ TOWN/ROW HOUSE	☐ BRICK VENEER — WOOD FRAME
☐ CUSTOM	☐ 2 STORY	☐ SEMI-DETACHED	☐ STUCCO ON WOOD FRAME
☐ LUXURY	☐ 2½ STORY		☐ PAINTED CONCRETE BLOCK
	☐ 3 STORY	OCCUPANCY	☐ SOLID MASONRY (AVERAGE & CUSTOM)
	☐ BI-LEVEL	☐ ONE STORY	☐ STONE VENEER — WOOD FRAME
	☐ TRI-LEVEL	☐ TWO FAMILY	☐ SOLID BRICK (LUXURY)
		☐ THREE FAMILY	☐ SOLID STONE (LUXURY)
		☐ OTHER _____	

*LIVING AREA (Main Building)
- First Level _____ S.F.
- Second Level _____ S.F.
- Third Level _____ S.F.
- Total _____ S.F.

*LIVING AREA (Wing or Ell) (   )
- First Level _____ S.F.
- Second Level _____ S.F.
- Third Level _____ S.F.
- Total _____ S.F.

*LIVING AREA (Wing or Ell) (   )
- First Level _____ S.F.
- Second Level _____ S.F.
- Third Level _____ S.F.
- Total _____ S.F.

*Basement Area is not part of living area.

MAIN BUILDING	COSTS PER S.F. LIVING AREA
Cost per Square Foot of Living Area, from Page _____	$
Basement Addition: _____ % Finished, _____ % Unfinished	+
Roof Cover Adjustment: _____ Type, Page _____ (Add or Deduct)	( )
Central Air Conditioning: ☐ Separate Ducts ☐ Heating Ducts, Page _____	+
Heating System Adjustment: _____ Type, Page _____ (Add or Deduct)	( )
Main Building: Adjusted Cost per S.F. of Living Area	$

MAIN BUILDING TOTAL COST: $ _____ /S.F. × _____ S.F. × _____ = $ _____
(Cost per S.F. Living Area) (Living Area) (Town/Row House Multiplier Use 1 for Detached) (TOTAL COST)

WING OR ELL ( ) _____ STORY	COSTS PER S.F. LIVING AREA
Cost per Square Foot of Living Area, from Page _____	$
Basement Addition: _____ % Finished, _____ % Unfinished	+
Roof Cover Adjustment: _____ Type, Page _____ (Add or Deduct)	( )
Central Air Conditioning: ☐ Separate Ducts ☐ Heating Ducts, Page _____	+
Heating System Adjustment: _____ Type, Page _____ (Add or Deduct)	( )
Wing or Ell ( ): Adjusted Cost per S.F. of Living Area	$

WING OR ELL (   ) TOTAL COST: $ _____ /S.F. × _____ S.F. = $ _____
(Cost per S.F. Living Area) (Living Area) (TOTAL COST)

WING OR ELL ( ) _____ STORY	COSTS PER S.F. LIVING AREA
Cost per Square Foot of Living Area, from Page _____	$
Basement Addition: _____ % Finished, _____ % Unfinished	+
Roof Cover Adjustment: _____ Type, Page _____ (Add or Deduct)	( )
Central Air Conditioning: ☐ Separate Ducts ☐ Heating Ducts, Page _____	+
Heating System Adjustment: _____ Type, Page _____ (Add or Deduct)	( )
Wing or Ell ( ): Adjusted Cost per S.F. of Living Area	$

WING OR ELL (   ) TOTAL COST: $ _____ /S.F. × _____ S.F. = $ _____
(Cost per S.F. Living Area) (Living Area) (TOTAL COST)

TOTAL THIS PAGE: _____

Means Forms
RESIDENTIAL COST ESTIMATE

Total Page 1			$
	QUANTITY	UNIT COST	
Additional Bathrooms: _____ Full, _____ Half			
Finished Attic: _____ Ft. x _____ Ft.	S.F.		+
Breezeway: ☐ Open ☐ Enclosed _____ Ft. x _____ Ft.	S.F.		+
Covered Porch: ☐ Open ☐ Enclosed _____ Ft. x _____ Ft.	S.F.		+
Fireplace: ☐ Interior Chimney ☐ Exterior Chimney ☐ No. of Flues ☐ Additional Fireplaces			+
Appliances:			+
Kitchen Cabinets Adjustment: (±)			
☐ Garage ☐ Carport: _____ Car(s) Description _____ (±)			
Miscellaneous:			+

ADJUSTED TOTAL BUILDING COST $ _____

REPLACEMENT COST
ADJUSTED TOTAL BUILDING COST	$ _____
Site Improvements	
(A) Paving & Sidewalks	$ _____
(B) Landscaping	$ _____
(C) Fences	$ _____
(D) Swimming Pool	$ _____
(E) Miscellaneous	$ _____
TOTAL	$ _____
Location Factor	× _____
Location Replacement Cost	$ _____
Depreciation	-$ _____
LOCAL DEPRECIATED COST	$ _____

INSURANCE COST
ADJUSTED TOTAL BUILDING COST	$ _____
Insurance Exclusions	
(A) Footings, Sitework, Underground Piping	-$ _____
(B) Architects Fees	-$ _____
Total Building Cost Less Exclusion	$ _____
Location Factor	× _____
LOCAL INSURABLE REPLACEMENT COST	$ _____

SKETCH AND ADDITIONAL CALCULATIONS

RESIDENTIAL Economy Illustrations

11

RESIDENTIAL — Economy | 1 Story

- Mass produced from stock plans
- Single family — 1 full bath, 1 kitchen
- No basement
- Asphalt shingles on roof
- Hot air heat
- Drywall interior
- Materials and workmanship are sufficient to meet codes

1 STORY

BASE COST PER SQUARE FOOT OF LIVING AREA

EXTERIOR WALL	600	800	1000	1200	1400	1600	1800	2000	2400	2800	3200
Wood Siding — Wood Frame	59.60	54.00	49.70	46.05	43.10	40.70	39.55	38.70	35.90	33.70	32.50
Brick Veneer — Wood Frame	63.10	57.15	52.55	48.65	45.50	42.85	41.65	40.70	37.75	35.35	34.05
Stucco on Wood Frame	57.90	52.55	48.35	44.85	42.00	39.70	38.60	37.75	35.05	32.95	31.75
Painted Concrete Block	60.25	54.60	50.20	46.55	43.55	41.10	39.95	39.10	36.25	34.05	32.75
Finished Basement, Add	13.50	12.50	12.35	11.85	11.50	11.15	11.00	10.90	10.60	10.35	10.15
Unfinished Basement, Add	6.75	6.10	5.70	5.25	4.95	4.65	4.50	4.40	4.15	3.90	3.75

MODIFICATIONS

ALTERNATES	Add to or deduct from costs per S.F. of living area
Composition roll roof	$– .55
Cedar shake roof	+1.45
Central air conditioning	
In heating ducts	+2.00
In separate ducts	+3.80
Heating systems	
Hot water	+2.40
Heat pump	+1.35
Electric heat	– .70
Not heated	–2.30

BATHROOMS — TOTAL COST
(includes plumbing and wall & floor finishes)

Full bath — 3 fixtures	$2310
Half bath — 2 fixtures	1440

ADJUSTMENTS

For two or more families (Add to total cost)	
Additional kitchen & entrance	+$2350 Ea.
Separate heating	+ 895 Ea.
Townhouse/Rowhouse (Multiplier for costs per S.F. of living area)	
Inner unit	.94
End unit	.97

	Page		Page
Wings & ells	22	Kitchen cabinets	76
Porches & breezeways	75	Garages & carports	77
Finished attics	75	Site improvements	77
Appliances	75		

Use LOCATION FACTORS on pages 444 to 448

Economy 1 Story

	Living Area	1200 S.F.
	Perimeter	146 L.F.

		MAN-HOURS	COST PER SQUARE FOOT OF LIVING AREA		
			MAT.	LABOR	TOTAL
1	**Site Work** — Site preparation for slab; trench 4' deep for foundation wall.	.060		1.09	1.09
2	**Foundations** — Continuous concrete footing 8" deep x 18" wide; 8" thick concrete block foundation wall, 4' deep; 4" concrete slab on 4" crushed stone base, trowel finish.	.131	3.19	3.36	6.55
3	**Framing** — 2" x 4" wood studs, 16" O.C.; 1/2" insulation board sheathing; 2" x 4" wood truss roof 24" O.C. with 3/8" plywood sheathing, 4 in 12 pitch.	.098	2.90	3.00	5.90
4	**Exterior Walls** — Stucco on wood frame; wood double hung windows; 2 flush solid core wood exterior doors.	.110	5.91	3.79	9.70
5	**Roofing** — 210-235# asphalt shingles; #15 felt building paper; aluminum flashing; 6" attic insulation.	.047	.76	1.14	1.90
6	**Interiors** — 1/2" drywall, taped and finished, painted with primer and 1 coat; softwood baseboard and trim, painted with primer and 1 coat; rubber backed carpeting 80%, asphalt tile 20%; hollow core wood interior doors.	.243	5.42	6.21	11.63
7	**Specialties** — Kitchen cabinets - 6 L.F. wall and base cabinets with laminated plastic counter top.	.004	.92	.43	1.35
8	**Mechanical** — 1 lavatory, white, wall hung; 1 water closet, white; 1 bathtub, porcelain enamel steel, white; 1 kitchen sink, stainless steel, single; 1 water heater, gas fired, 30 gal.; gas fired warm air heat.	.086	1.94	1.56	3.50
9	**Electrical** — 100 Amp. service; romex wiring; incandescent lighting fixtures, switches, receptacles.	.036	.40	.68	1.08
10	**Overhead** — Contractor's overhead and profit.		1.08	1.07	2.15
	Total		22.52	22.33	44.85

RESIDENTIAL | Economy | 1 ½ Story

- Mass produced from stock plans
- Single family — 1 full bath, 1 kitchen
- No basement
- Asphalt shingles on roof
- Hot air heat
- Drywall interior
- Materials and workmanship are sufficient to meet codes

1½ STORY

BASE COST PER SQUARE FOOT OF LIVING AREA

EXTERIOR WALL	600	800	1000	1200	1400	1600	1800	2000	2400	2800	3200
Wood Siding — Wood Frame	62.75	56.90	50.45	46.95	44.80	42.55	41.10	39.40	35.60	34.45	33.35
Brick Veneer — Wood Frame	66.70	60.55	53.75	49.95	47.60	45.25	43.65	41.80	37.65	36.45	35.25
Stucco on Wood Frame	60.85	55.20	48.90	45.55	43.50	41.30	39.90	38.25	34.60	33.55	32.50
Painted Concrete Block	63.50	57.60	51.05	47.50	43.35	43.05	41.60	39.85	36.00	34.85	33.75
Finished Basement, Add	9.25	8.80	8.45	8.05	7.85	7.70	7.55	7.40	7.05	6.95	6.85
Unfinished Basement, Add	4.95	4.55	4.20	3.85	3.65	3.55	3.40	3.30	2.95	2.85	2.75

MODIFICATIONS

ALTERNATES	Add to or deduct from costs per S.F. of living area
Composition roll roof	$– .35
Wood shake roof	+1.05
Central air conditioning	
In heating ducts	+1.50
In separate ducts	+3.28
Heating systems	
Hot water	+2.10
Heat pump	+1.55
Electric heat	– .50
Not heated	–2.15

BATHROOMS — TOTAL COST (includes plumbing and wall & floor finishes)	
Full bath — 3 fixtures	$2310
Half bath — 2 fixtures	1440

ADJUSTMENTS	
For two or more families (Add to total cost)	
Additional kitchen & entrance	+$2350 Ea.
Separate heating	+ 895 Ea.
Townhouse/Rowhouse (Multiplier for costs per S.F. of living area)	
Inner unit	.95
End unit	.97

	Page		Page
Wings & ells	22	Kitchen cabinets	76
Porches & breezeways	75	Garages & carports	77
Finished attics	75	Site improvements	77
Appliances	75		

Use LOCATION FACTORS on pages 444 to 448

Economy 1½ Story

	Living Area	1600 S.F.
	Perimeter	135 L.F.

	MAN-HOURS	COST PER SQUARE FOOT OF LIVING AREA		
		MAT.	LABOR	TOTAL
1 Site Work — Site preparation for slab; trench 4' deep for foundation wall.	.041		.81	.81
2 Foundations — Continuous concrete footing 8" deep x 18" wide, 8" thick concrete block foundation wall, 4' deep; 4" concrete slab on 4" crushed stone base, trowel finish.	.073	2.15	2.27	4.42
3 Framing — 2" x 4" wood studs, 16" O.C.; 1/2" insulation board sheathing; 2" x 6" rafters 16" O.C. with 3/8" plywood sheathing, 8 in 12 pitch; 2" x 8" floor joists 16" O.C. with bridging and 1/2" plywood subfloor.	.090	2.99	3.38	6.37
4 Exterior Walls — Beveled wood siding; #15 felt building paper; wood double hung windows; 2 flush solid core wood exterior doors.	.077	7.32	3.28	10.60
5 Roofing — 210-235# asphalt shingles; #15 felt building paper; aluminum flashing; 6" attic insulation.	.029	.48	.71	1.19
6 Interiors — 1/2" drywall, taped and finished, painted with primer and 1 coat; softwood baseboard and trim, painted with primer and 1 coat; rubber backed carpeting 80%, asphalt tile 20%; hollow core wood interior doors.	.204	5.68	6.48	12.16
7 Specialties — Kitchen cabinets - 6 L.F. wall and base cabinets with laminated plastic counter top; stairs.	.020	.68	.32	1.00
8 Mechanical — 1 lavatory, white, wall hung; 1 water closet, white; 1 bathtub, porcelain enamel steel, white; 1 kitchen sink, stainless steel, single; 1 water heater, gas fired, 30 gal.; gas fire warm air heat.	.079	1.61	1.41	3.02
9 Electrical — 100 Amp. service; romex wiring; incandescent lighting fixtures, switches, receptacles.	.033	.36	.61	.97
10 Overhead — Contractor's overhead and profit.		1.05	.96	2.01
Total		22.32	20.23	42.55

RESIDENTIAL — Economy 2 Story

- Mass produced from stock plans
- Single family — 1 full bath, 1 kitchen
- No basement
- Asphalt shingles on roof
- Hot air heat
- Drywall interior
- Materials and workmanship are sufficient to meet codes

2 STORY

BASE COST PER SQUARE FOOT OF LIVING AREA

EXTERIOR WALL	1000	1200	1400	1600	1800	2000	2200	2600	3000	3400	3800
Wood Siding — Wood Frame	54.95	49.30	46.90	45.30	43.60	41.65	40.35	37.85	35.00	34.05	33.00
Brick Veneer — Wood Frame	58.85	52.80	50.20	48.45	46.60	44.50	43.10	40.30	37.25	36.15	35.00
Stucco on Wood Frame	53.15	47.60	45.35	43.80	42.20	40.30	39.10	36.65	34.00	33.00	32.10
Painted Concrete Block	55.70	49.95	47.50	45.85	44.15	42.15	40.90	38.30	35.45	34.45	33.40
Finished Basement, Add	7.05	6.75	6.55	6.45	6.30	6.20	6.05	5.85	5.65	5.60	5.45
Unfinished Basement, Add	3.65	3.40	3.20	3.10	2.95	2.85	2.75	2.55	2.35	2.30	2.20

MODIFICATIONS

ALTERNATES	Add to or deduct from costs per S.F. of living area
Composition roll roof	$– .30
Wood shake roof	+ .75
Central air conditioning	
In heating ducts	+1.20
In separate ducts	+3.00
Heating systems	
Hot water	+1.95
Heat pump	+1.60
Electric heat	– .40
Not heated	–2.00

BATHROOMS — TOTAL COST (includes plumbing and wall & floor finishes)	
Full bath — 3 fixtures	$2310
Half bath — 2 fixtures	1440

ADJUSTMENTS	
For two or more families (Add to total cost)	
Additional kitchen & entrance	+$2350 Ea.
Separate heating	+ 895 Ea.
Townhouse/Rowhouse (Multiplier for costs per S.F. of living area)	
Inner unit	.93
End unit	.96

	Page		Page
Wings & ells	22	Kitchen cabinets	76
Porches & breezeways	75	Garages & carports	77
Finished attics	75	Site improvements	77
Appliances	75		

Use LOCATION FACTORS on pages 444 to 448

Economy 2 Story

	Living Area	2000 S.F.
	Perimeter	135 L.F.

			MAN-HOURS	COST PER SQUARE FOOT OF LIVING AREA		
				MAT.	LABOR	TOTAL
1	Site Work	Site preparation for slab; trench 4' deep for foundation wall.	.034		.65	.65
2	Foundations	Continuous concrete footing 8" deep x 18" wide; 8" thick concrete block foundation wall, 4' deep; 4" concrete slab on 4" crushed stone base, trowel finish.	.069	1.71	1.83	3.54
3	Framing	2" x 4" wood studs, 16" O.C.; 1/2" insulation board sheathing; 2" x 4" wood truss roof 24" O.C. with 3/8" plywood sheathing, 4 in 12 pitch; 2" x 8" floor joists 16" O.C. with bridging and 5/8" plywood subfloor.	.112	3.05	3.57	6.62
4	Exterior Walls	Beveled wood siding; #15 felt building paper; wood double hung windows; 2 flush solid core wood exterior doors.	.107	7.52	3.38	10.90
5	Roofing	210-235# asphalt shingles; #15 felt building paper; aluminum flashing; 6" attic insulation.	.024	.38	.57	.95
6	Interiors	1/2" drywall, taped and finished, painted with primer and 1 coat; softwood baseboard and trim, painted with primer and 1 coat; rubber backed carpeting 80%, asphalt tile 20%; hollow core wood doors.	.219	5.85	6.70	12.55
7	Specialties	Kitchen cabinets - 6 L.F. wall and base cabinets with laminated plastic counter top; stairs.	.017	.55	.26	.81
8	Mechanical	1 lavatory, white, wall hung; 1 water closet, white; 1 bathtub, porcelain enamel steel, white; 1 kitchen sink, stainless steel, single; 1 water heater, gas fired, 30 gal.; gas fired warm air heat.	.061	1.41	1.31	2.72
9	Electrical	100 Amp. service; romex wiring; incandescent lighting fixtures; switches, receptacles.	.030	.33	.58	.91
10	Overhead	Contractor's overhead and profit.		1.05	.95	2.00
		Total		21.85	19.80	41.65

RESIDENTIAL — Economy | Bi-level

- Mass produced from stock plans
- Single family — 1 full bath, 1 kitchen
- No basement
- Asphalt shingles on roof
- Hot air heat
- Drywall interior
- Materials and workmanship are sufficient to meet codes

BI-LEVEL

BASE COST PER SQUARE FOOT OF LIVING AREA

EXTERIOR WALL	1000	1200	1400	1600	1800	2000	2200	2600	3000	3400	3800
Wood Siding — Wood Frame	50.50	45.20	43.05	41.60	40.15	38.35	37.20	34.95	32.50	31.60	30.70
Brick Veneer — Wood Frame	53.40	47.85	45.55	44.00	42.40	40.45	39.25	36.80	34.15	33.20	32.20
Stucco on Wood Frame	49.15	43.95	41.90	40.50	39.10	37.30	36.25	34.10	31.70	30.85	30.00
Painted Concrete Block	51.05	45.70	43.55	42.10	40.55	38.70	37.60	35.35	32.80	31.90	31.00
Finished Basement, Add	7.05	6.75	6.55	6.45	6.30	6.20	6.05	5.85	5.65	5.60	5.45
Unfinished Basement, Add	3.65	3.40	3.20	3.10	2.95	2.85	2.75	2.55	2.35	2.30	2.20

MODIFICATIONS

ALTERNATES	Add to or deduct from costs per S.F. of living area
Composition roll roof	$– .30
Wood shake roof	+ .75
Central air conditioning	
In heating ducts	+1.20
In separate ducts	+3.00
Heating systems	
Hot water	+1.95
Heat pump	+1.60
Electric heat	– .40
Not heated	–2.00

BATHROOMS — TOTAL COST (includes plumbing and wall & floor finishes)	
Full bath — 3 fixtures	$2310
Half bath — 2 fixtures	1440

ADJUSTMENTS	
For two or more families (Add to total cost)	
Additional kitchen & entrance	+$2350 Ea.
Separate heating	+ 895 Ea.
Townhouse/Rowhouse (Multiplier for costs per S.F. of living area)	
Inner unit	.94
End unit	.97

	Page		Page
Wings & ells	22	Kitchen cabinets	76
Porches & breezeways	75	Garages & carports	77
Finished attics	75	Site improvements	77
Appliances	75		

Use LOCATION FACTORS on pages 444 to 448

Economy Bi-Level

	Living Area	2000 S.F.
	Perimeter	135 L.F.

			MAN-HOURS	COST PER SQUARE FOOT OF LIVING AREA		
				MAT.	LABOR	TOTAL
1	Site Work	Excavation for lower level, 4' deep. Site preparation for slab.	.029		.65	.65
2	Foundations	Continuous concrete footing 8" deep x 18" wide; 8" thick concrete block foundation wall 4' deep; 4" concrete slab on 4" crushed stone base, trowel finish.	.069	1.72	1.82	3.54
3	Framing	2" x 4" wood studs, 16" O.C.; 1/2" insulation board sheathing; 2" x 4" wood truss roof 24" O.C. with 1/2" plywood sheathing, 4 in 12 pitch; 2" x 8" floor joists 16" O.C. with bridging and 5/8" plywood subfloor.	.107	2.83	3.35	6.18
4	Exterior Walls	Beveled wood siding; #15 felt building paper; wood double hung windows; 2 flush solid core wood exterior doors.	.089	5.86	2.63	8.49
5	Roofing	210-235# asphalt shingles; #15 felt building paper; aluminum flashing; 6" attic insulation.	.024	.38	.57	.95
6	Interiors	1/2" drywall, taped and finished, painted with primer and 1 coat; softwood baseboard and trim, painted with primer and 1 coat; rubber backed carpeting 80%, asphalt tile 20%; hollow core wood interior doors.	.213	5.73	6.52	12.25
7	Specialties	Kitchen cabinets - base 6 L.F. with laminated plastic counter top, wall 30" high, 8 L.F.; stairs.	.018	.55	.26	.81
8	Mechanical	1 lavatory, white, wall hung; 1 water closet, white; 1 bathtub, porcelain enamel steel, white; 1 kitchen sink, stainless steel, single; 1 water heater, gas fired, 30 gal.; gas fired warm air heat.	.061	1.42	1.30	2.72
9	Electrical	100 Amp. service; romex wiring; incandescent lighting fixtures; switches, receptacles.	.030	.34	.57	.91
10	Overhead	Contractor's overhead and profit.		.96	.89	1.85
		Total		19.79	18.56	38.35

RESIDENTIAL — Economy Tri-Level

- Mass produced from stock plans
- Single family — 1 full bath, 1 kitchen
- No basement
- Asphalt shingles on roof
- Hot air heat
- Drywall interior
- Materials and workmanship are sufficient to meet codes

TRI-LEVEL

BASE COST PER SQUARE FOOT OF LIVING AREA

EXTERIOR WALL	1200	1500	1800	2000	2200	2400	2800	3200	3600	4000	4400
Wood Siding — Wood Frame	46.15	42.35	39.45	38.30	36.75	35.00	33.80	32.65	30.95	29.90	28.70
Brick Veneer — Wood Frame	48.80	44.75	41.60	40.35	38.70	36.80	35.55	34.30	32.45	31.35	30.05
Stucco on Wood Frame	44.90	41.25	38.40	37.35	35.80	34.15	33.00	31.90	30.20	29.20	28.05
Solid Masonry	46.65	42.80	39.85	38.70	37.10	35.35	34.15	32.95	31.20	30.15	28.95
Finished Basement, Add*	8.55	8.20	7.90	7.80	7.65	7.45	7.30	7.20	7.05	6.95	6.85
Unfinished Basement, Add*	4.10	3.80	3.50	3.40	3.30	3.10	3.00	2.90	2.75	2.70	2.60

*Basement under middle level only.

MODIFICATIONS

ALTERNATES	Add to or deduct from costs per S.F. of living area
Composition roll roof	$- .35
Wood shake roof	+1.05
Central air conditioning	
In heating ducts	+1.00
In separate ducts	+2.80
Heating systems	
Hot water	+2.10
Heat pump	+1.65
Electric heat	- .60
Not heated	-1.95

BATHROOMS — TOTAL COST (includes plumbing and wall & floor finishes)	
Full bath — 3 fixtures	$2310
Half bath — 2 fixtures	1440

ADJUSTMENTS	
For two or more families (Add to total cost)	
Additional kitchen & entrance	+$2350 Ea.
Separate heating	+ 895 Ea.
Townhouse/Rowhouse (Multiplier for costs per S.F. of living area)	
Inner unit	.93
End unit	.94

	Page		Page
Wings & ells	22	Kitchen cabinets	76
Porches & breezeways	75	Garages & carports	77
Finished attics	75	Site improvements	77
Appliances	75		

Use LOCATION FACTORS on pages 444 to 448

Economy Tri-Level

| | | Living Area | 2400 S.F. |
| | | Perimeter | 163 L.F. |

			MAN-HOURS	COST PER SQUARE FOOT OF LIVING AREA		
				MAT.	LABOR	TOTAL
1	Site Work	Site preparation for slab; excavation for lower level 4' deep; trench 4' deep for foundation wall.	.027		.54	.54
2	Foundations	Continuous concrete footing 8" deep x 18" wide; 8" concrete block foundation wall, 4' deep; 4" concrete slab on 4" crushed stone base, trowel finish.	.071	1.89	1.97	3.86
3	Framing	2" x 4" wood studs, 16" O.C.; 1/2" insulation board sheathing; 2" x 4" wood truss roof 24" O.C. with 1/2" plywood sheathing, 4 in 12 pitch; 2" x 8" floor joists 16" O.C. with bridging and 5/8" plywood subfloor.	.094	2.64	2.99	5.63
4	Exterior Walls	Beveled wood siding; #15 felt building paper; wood double hung windows; 2 flush solid core wood exterior doors.	.081	5.01	2.23	7.24
5	Roofing	210-235# asphalt shingles; #15 felt building paper; aluminum flashing; 6" attic insulation.	.032	.51	.76	1.27
6	Interiors	1/2" drywall, taped and finished, painted with primer and 1 coat; softwood baseboard and trim, painted with primer and 1 coat; rubber backed carpeting 80%, asphalt tile 20%; hollow core wood interior doors.	.177	5.03	5.72	10.75
7	Specialties	Kitchen cabinets - 6 L.F. wall and base cabinets with laminated plastic counter top; stairs.	.014	.45	.21	.66
8	Mechanical	1 lavatory, white, wall hung; 1 water closet, white; 1 bathtub, porcelain enamel steel, white; 1 kitchen sink, stainless steel, single; 1 water heater, gas fired, 30 gal; gas fired warm air heat.	.057	1.29	1.24	2.53
9	Electrical	100 Amp. service; romex wiring; incandescent lighting fixtures, switches, receptacles.	.029	.32	.54	.86
10	Overhead	Contractor's overhead and profit.		.86	.80	1.66
		Total		18.00	17.00	35.00

RESIDENTIAL   Economy | Wings & Ells

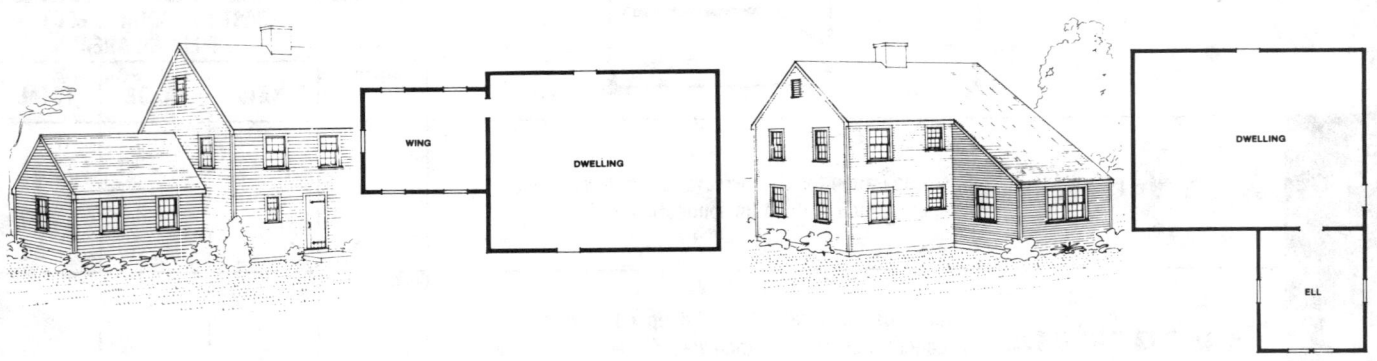

1 STORY — BASE COST PER SQUARE FOOT OF LIVING AREA

EXTERIOR WALL	50	100	200	300	400	500	600	700
Wood Siding — Wood Frame	82.45	62.60	54.10	43.80	41.00	39.35	38.20	38.25
Brick Veneer — Wood Frame	91.35	68.95	59.40	47.35	44.20	42.30	41.05	40.95
Stucco on Wood Frame	78.25	59.60	51.60	42.15	39.50	37.95	36.90	36.05
Painted Concrete Block	84.15	63.80	55.05	44.50	41.60	39.90	38.75	38.75
Finished Basement, Add	21.50	17.55	15.90	13.15	12.60	12.30	12.05	11.90
Unfinished Basement, Add	13.70	10.25	8.80	6.40	5.90	5.60	5.45	5.30

1½ STORY — BASE COST PER SQUARE FOOT OF LIVING AREA

EXTERIOR WALL	100	200	300	400	500	600	700	800
Wood Siding — Wood Frame	65.45	51.30	45.00	39.45	37.10	35.55	34.20	34.05
Brick Veneer — Wood Frame	73.40	57.65	50.35	43.60	40.90	39.15	37.60	37.40
Stucco on Wood Frame	61.70	48.30	42.55	37.50	35.30	33.85	32.60	32.45
Painted Concrete Block	66.95	52.50	46.00	40.25	37.80	36.25	34.85	34.65
Finished Basement, Add	14.35	12.75	11.65	10.45	10.10	9.90	9.70	9.65
Unfinished Basement, Add	8.50	7.05	6.10	5.00	4.75	4.55	4.35	4.35

2 STORY — BASE COST PER SQUARE FOOT OF LIVING AREA

EXTERIOR WALL	100	200	400	600	800	1000	1200	1400
Wood Siding — Wood Frame	67.45	50.05	42.55	34.00	31.50	30.05	29.05	29.20
Brick Veneer — Wood Frame	76.35	56.40	47.85	37.50	34.70	33.00	31.90	31.90
Stucco on Wood Frame	63.25	47.05	40.05	32.30	30.00	28.65	27.75	27.90
Painted Concrete Block	69.10	51.20	43.50	34.65	32.10	30.60	29.60	29.70
Finished Basement, Add	10.75	8.80	7.95	6.60	6.35	6.15	6.05	5.95
Unfinished Basement, Add	6.90	5.15	4.40	3.20	2.95	2.80	2.75	2.65

Base costs do not include bathroom or kitchen facilities. Use MODIFICATIONS on pages 75, 76, 77 where appropriate.

RESIDENTIAL — Average — Illustrations

RESIDENTIAL — Average — 1 Story

- Simple design from standard plans
- Single family — 1 full bath, 1 kitchen
- No basement
- Asphalt shingles on roof
- Hot air heat
- Drywall interior
- Materials and workmanship are average

1 STORY

BASE COST PER SQUARE FOOT OF LIVING AREA

EXTERIOR WALL	600	800	1000	1200	1400	1600	1800	2000	2400	2800	3200
Wood Siding — Wood Frame	74.10	67.40	62.20	57.85	54.50	51.65	50.25	49.20	45.95	43.40	41.95
Brick Veneer — Wood Frame	82.70	75.55	70.00	65.30	61.70	58.60	57.05	55.95	52.50	49.75	48.15
Stucco on Wood Frame	78.30	71.60	66.45	62.10	58.75	55.90	54.50	53.50	50.20	47.70	46.20
Solid Masonry	88.85	81.05	75.00	69.80	65.80	62.35	60.65	59.45	55.65	52.65	50.85
Finished Basement, Add	17.30	16.40	15.75	15.10	14.60	14.15	13.95	13.80	13.45	13.05	12.85
Unfinished Basement, Add	7.85	7.20	6.70	6.30	5.95	5.65	5.50	5.40	5.10	4.85	4.70

MODIFICATIONS

ALTERNATES	Add to or deduct from costs per S.F. of living area
Cedar shake roof	$+1.10
Clay tile roof	+3.65
Slate roof	+4.75
Central air conditioning	
In heating ducts	+2.05
In separate ducts	+3.85
Heating systems	
Hot water	+2.50
Heat pump	+1.45
Electric heat	− .80
Not heated	−2.20

BATHROOMS — TOTAL COST
(includes plumbing and wall & floor finishes)

Full bath — 3 fixtures	$2900
Half bath — 2 fixtures	1810

ADJUSTMENTS

For two or more families
(Add to total cost)

Additional kitchen & entrance	$+3780 Ea.
Separate heating	+ 875 Ea.

Townhouse/Rowhouse
(Multiplier for costs per S.F. of living area)

Inner unit	.92
End unit	.96

	Page		Page
Wings & ells	42	Kitchen cabinets	76
Porches & breezeways	75	Garages & carports	77
Finished attics	75	Site improvements	77
Appliances	75		

Use LOCATION FACTORS on pages 444 to 448

Average 1 Story

	Living Area	160 S.F.
	Perimeter	163 L.F.

			MAN-HOURS	COST PER SQUARE FOOT OF LIVING AREA		
				MAT.	LABOR	TOTAL
1	Site Work	Site preparation for slab; trench 4' deep for foundation wall.	.048		.83	.83
2	Foundations	Continuous concrete footing 8" deep x 18" wide, cast-in-place concrete wall, 8" thick, 4' deep; 4" concrete slab on 4" crushed stone base, trowel finish.	.113	2.91	3.03	5.94
3	Framing	2" x 4" wood studs, 16" O.C.; 1/2" plywood sheathing; 2" x 6" rafters 16" O.C. with 1/2" plywood sheathing, 4 in 12 pitch; 2" x 6" ceiling joists 16" O.C.; 1/2" wafer board subfloor on 1" x 2" wood sleepers 16" O.C.	.136	3.41	4.39	7.80
4	Exterior Walls	Horizontal beveled wood siding; #15 felt building paper; 3-1/2" batt insulation; wood double hung windows; 3 flush solid core wood exterior doors; storms and screens.	.098	7.19	3.07	10.26
5	Roofing	240 asphalt shingles; #15 felt building paper; aluminum flashing; 6" attic insulation. Aluminum gutters and downspouts.	047	.78	1.17	1.95
6	Interiors	1/2" drywall, taped and finished, painted with primer and 1 coat; softwood baseboard and trim, painted with primer and 1 coat; finished hardwood floor 40%, carpet with underlayment 40%, vinyl tile with underlayment 15%, ceramic tile with underlayment 5%; hollow core doors.	.251	8.35	6.92	15.27
7	Specialties	Kitchen cabinets - 14 L.F. wall and base cabinets with laminated plastic counter top; medicine cabinet.	.009	1.14	.41	1.55
8	Mechanical	1 lavatory, white, wall hung; 1 water closet, white; 1 bathtub with shower, porcelain enamel steel, white; 1 kitchen sink, stainless steel, single; 1 water heater, gas fired, 30 gal.; gas fired warm air heat.	.098	1.80	1.45	3.25
9	Electrical	200 Amp. service; romex wiring; incandescent lighting fixtures, switches, receptacles.	.041	.54	.87	1.41
10	Overhead	Contractor's overhead and profit and plans.		1.83	1.56	3.39
		Total		27.95	23.70	51.65

RESIDENTIAL — Average — 1½ Story

- Simple design from standard plans
- Single family — 1 full bath, 1 kitchen
- No basement
- Asphalt shingles on roof
- Hot air heat
- Drywall interior
- Materials and workmanship are average

1½ STORY

BASE COST PER SQUARE FOOT OF LIVING AREA

EXTERIOR WALL	600	800	1000	1200	1400	1600	1800	2000	2400	2800	3200
Wood Siding — Wood Frame	77.35	70.40	62.70	58.60	56.00	53.40	51.70	49.65	45.30	43.90	42.65
Brick Veneer — Wood Frame	82.10	74.75	66.65	62.15	59.30	56.60	54.75	52.55	47.80	46.30	44.90
Stucco on Wood Frame	77.15	70.25	62.55	58.45	55.85	53.25	51.55	49.50	45.20	43.80	42.55
Solid Masonry	89.00	81.05	72.40	67.30	64.15	61.30	59.15	56.75	51.35	49.75	48.15
Finished Basement, Add	12.70	12.10	11.60	11.10	10.80	10.65	10.45	10.25	9.75	9.60	9.45
Unfinished Basement, Add	5.70	5.30	4.95	4.55	4.40	4.25	4.10	4.00	3.60	3.55	3.40

MODIFICATIONS

ALTERNATES	Add to or deduct from costs per S.F. of living area
Cedar shake roof	$+ .80
Clay tile roof	+2.65
Slate roof	+3.45
Central air conditioning	
In heating ducts	+1.55
In separate ducts	+3.55
Heating systems	
Hot water	+2.15
Heat pump	+1.50
Electric heat	− .95
Not heated	−2.20

BATHROOMS — TOTAL COST (includes plumbing and wall & floor finishes)	
Full bath — 3 fixtures	$2900
Half bath — 2 fixtures	1810

ADJUSTMENTS	
For two or more families (Add to total cost)	
Additional kitchen & entrance	$+3780 Ea.
Separate heating	+ 875 Ea.
Townhouse/Rowhouse (Multiplier for costs per S.F. of living area)	
Inner unit	.92
End unit	.96

	Page		Page
Wings & ells	42	Kitchen cabinets	76
Porches & breezeways	75	Garages & carports	77
Finished attics	75	Site improvements	77
Appliances	75		

Use LOCATION FACTORS on pages 444 to 448

Average 1½ Story

	Living Area	1800 S.F.
	Perimeter	144 L.F.

			MAN-HOURS	COST PER SQUARE FOOT OF LIVING AREA		
				MAT.	LABOR	TOTAL
1	Site Work	Site preparation for slab; trench 4' deep for foundation wall.	.037		.74	.74
2	Foundations	Continuous concrete footing 8" deep x 18" wide, cast-in-place concrete wall, 8" thick, 4' deep; 4" concrete slab on 4" crushed stone base, trowel finish.	.073	2.13	2.24	4.37
3	Framing	2" x 4" wood studs, 16" O.C.; 1/2" plywood sheathing; 2" x 6" rafters 16" O.C. with 1/2" plywood sheathing, 8 in 12 pitch; 2" x 8" floor joists 16" O.C. with bridging and 5/8" plywood subfloor; 1/2" waferboard subfloor on 1" x 2" wood sleepers 16" O.C.	.098	3.50	4.04	7.54
4	Exterior Walls	Horizontal beveled wood siding; #15 felt building paper; 3-1/2" batt insulation; wood double hung windows; 3 flush solid core wood exterior doors; storms and screens.	.078	7.97	3.43	11.40
5	Roofing	240# asphalt shingles; #15 felt building paper; aluminum flashing; 6" attic insulation. Aluminum gutters and downspouts.	.029	.49	.73	1.22
6	Interiors	1/2" drywall, taped and finished, painted with primer and 1 coat; softwood baseboard and trim, painted with primer and 1 coat; finished hardwood floor 40%, carpet with underlayment 40%, vinyl tile with underlayment 15%, ceramic tile with underlayment 5%; hollow core doors.	.225	9.33	7.91	17.24
7	Specialties	Kitchen cabinets - 14 L.F. wall and base cabinets with laminated plastic counter top; medicine cabinet; stairs.	.022	1.03	.36	1.39
8	Mechanical	1 lavatory, white, wall hung; 1 water closet, white; 1 bathtub with shower, porcelain enamel steel, white; 1 kitchen sink, stainless steel, single; 1 water heater, gas fired, 30 gal.; gas fired warm air heat.	.049	1.68	1.39	3.07
9	Electrical	200 Amp. service; romex wiring; incandescent lighting fixtures, switches, receptacles.	.039	.52	.83	1.35
10	Overhead	Contractor's overhead and profit and plans.		1.86	1.52	3.38
		Total		28.51	23.19	51.70

RESIDENTIAL — Average 2 Story

- Simple design from standard plans
- Single family — 1 full bath, 1 kitchen
- No basement
- Asphalt shingles on roof
- Hot air heat
- Drywall interior
- Materials and workmanship are average

2 STORY

BASE COST PER SQUARE FOOT OF LIVING AREA

EXTERIOR WALL	1000	1200	1400	1600	1800	2000	2200	2600	3000	3400	3800
Wood Siding — Wood Frame	67.30	60.50	57.70	55.80	53.75	51.55	50.10	47.05	43.80	42.60	41.45
Brick Veneer — Wood Frame	71.90	64.70	61.65	59.55	57.35	54.95	53.35	50.00	46.45	45.15	43.85
Stucco on Wood Frame	67.10	60.30	57.55	55.65	53.60	51.40	49.95	46.95	43.70	42.50	41.35
Solid Masonry	79.20	71.45	67.95	65.55	63.05	60.40	58.50	54.70	50.70	49.20	47.65
Finished Basement, Add	10.10	9.75	9.45	9.30	9.10	8.95	8.80	8.50	8.25	8.15	8.00
Unfinished Basement, Add	4.25	4.00	3.80	3.65	3.55	3.45	3.35	3.15	2.95	2.85	2.75

MODIFICATIONS

ALTERNATES	Add to or deduct from costs per S.F. of living area
Cedar shake roof	$+ .55
Clay tile roof	+1.85
Slate roof	+2.40
Central air conditioning	
In heating ducts	+1.25
In separate ducts	+3.05
Heating systems	
Hot water	+2.05
Heat pump	+1.50
Electric heat	− .75
Not heated	−2.15

BATHROOMS — TOTAL COST (includes plumbing and wall & floor finishes)	
Full bath — 3 fixtures	$2900
Half bath — 2 fixtures	1810

ADJUSTMENTS	
For two or more families (Add to total cost)	
Additional kitchen & entrance	$+3780 Ea.
Separate heating	+ 875 Ea.
Townhouse/Rowhouse (Multiplier for costs per S.F. of living area)	
Inner unit	.90
End unit	.95

	Page		Page
Wings & ells	42	Kitchen cabinets	76
Porches & breezeways	75	Garages & carports	77
Finished attics	75	Site improvements	77
Appliances	75		

Use LOCATION FACTORS on pages 444 to 448

Average 2 Story

	Living Area	2000 S.F.
	Perimeter	135 L.F.

	MAN-HOURS	COST PER SQUARE FOOT OF LIVING AREA		
		MAT.	LABOR	TOTAL

#	Category	Description	MAN-HOURS	MAT.	LABOR	TOTAL
1	Site Work	Site preparation for slab; trench 4' deep for foundation wall.	.034		.67	.67
2	Foundations	Continuous concrete footing 8" deep x 18" wide; cast-in-place concrete wall, 8" thick, 4' deep, 4" concrete slab on 4" crushed stone base, trowel finish.	.066	1.77	1.87	3.64
3	Framing	2" x 4" wood studs, 16" O.C.; 1/2" plywood sheathing; 2" x 6" rafters 16" O.C. with 1/2" plywood sheathing, 4 in 12 pitch; 2" x 6" ceiling joists 16" O.C.; 2" x 8" floor joists 16" O.C. with bridging and 5/8" waferboard subfloor; 1/2" waferboard subfloor on 1" x 2" wood sleepers 16" O.C.	.131	3.62	4.15	7.77
4	Exterior Walls	Horizontal beveled wood siding; #15 felt building paper; 3-1/2" batt insulation; wood double hung windows; 3 flush solid core wood exterior doors; storms and screens.	.111	8.71	3.76	12.47
5	Roofing	240# asphalt shingles; #15 felt building paper; aluminum flashing; 6" attic insulation. Aluminum gutters and downspouts.	.024	.39	.59	.98
6	Interiors	1/2" drywall, taped and finished, painted with primer and 1 coat; softwood baseboard and trim, painted with primer and 1 coat; finished hardwood floor 40%, carpet with underlayment 40%, vinyl tile with underlayment 15%, ceramic tile with underlayment 5%; hollow core doors.	.232	9.28	7.90	17.18
7	Specialties	Kitchen cabinets - 14 L.F. wall and base cabinets with laminated plastic counter top; medicine cabinet, stairs.	.021	.93	.33	1.26
8	Mechanical	1 lavatory, white, wall hung; 1 water closet, white; 1 bathtub with shower, porcelain enamel steel, white; 1 kitchen sink, stainless steel, single; 1 water heater, gas fired, 30 gal.; gas fired warm air heat.	.060	1.57	1.34	2.91
9	Electrical	200 Amp. service; romex wiring; incandescent lighting fixtures, switches, receptacles.	.039	.50	.80	1.30
10	Overhead	Contractor's overhead and profit and plans.		1.87	1.50	3.37
	Total			28.64	22.91	51.55

RESIDENTIAL — Average 2½ Story

- Simple design from standard plans
- Single family — 1 full bath, 1 kitchen
- No basement
- Asphalt shingles on roof
- Hot air heat
- Drywall interior
- Materials and workmanship are average

2½ STORY

BASE COST PER SQUARE FOOT OF LIVING AREA

EXTERIOR WALL	1200	1400	1600	1800	2000	2400	2800	3200	3600	4000	4400
Wood Siding — Wood Frame	64.40	62.90	57.05	54.80	53.25	50.80	48.60	45.70	44.50	41.60	41.10
Brick Veneer — Wood Frame	68.85	67.35	61.15	58.60	56.90	54.20	51.90	48.65	47.35	44.15	43.60
Stucco on Wood Frame	64.20	62.70	56.90	54.60	53.15	50.65	48.45	45.55	44.40	41.50	41.00
Solid Masonry	75.30	73.80	67.05	64.10	62.20	59.20	56.70	53.00	51.45	47.85	47.20
Finished Basement, Add	8.25	8.25	8.00	7.75	7.65	7.45	7.35	7.10	7.00	6.80	6.75
Unfinished Basement, Add	3.30	3.30	3.10	2.95	2.85	2.75	2.65	2.50	2.40	2.30	2.25

MODIFICATIONS

ALTERNATES	Add to or deduct from costs per S.F. of living area
Cedar shake roof	$+ .45
Clay tile roof	+1.55
Slate roof	+2.05
Central air conditioning	
In heating ducts	+1.25
In separate ducts	+3.05
Heating systems	
Hot water	+2.00
Heat pump	+1.55
Electric heat	− .60
Not heated	−2.25

BATHROOMS — TOTAL COST (includes plumbing and wall & floor finishes)	
Full bath — 3 fixtures	$2900
Half bath — 2 fixtures	1810

ADJUSTMENTS	
For two or more families (Add to total cost)	
Additional kitchen & entrance	$+3780 Ea.
Separate heating	+ 875 Ea.
Townhouse/Rowhouse (Multiplier for costs per S.F. of living area)	
Inner unit	.91
End unit	.95

	Page		Page
Wings & ells	42	Kitchen cabinets	76
Porches & breezeways	75	Garages & carports	77
Finished attics	75	Site improvements	77
Appliances	75		

Use LOCATION FACTORS on pages 444 to 448

Average 2½ Story

	Living Area	1200 S.F.
	Perimeter	84 L.F.

			MAN-HOURS	COST PER SQUARE FOOT OF LIVING AREA		
				MAT.	LABOR	TOTAL
1	Site Work	Excavation for lower level 4' deep. Site preparation for slab.	.046		1.12	1.12
2	Foundations	Continuous concrete footing 8" deep x 18" wide, cast-in-place concrete wall, 8" thick, 4' deep; 4" concrete slab on 4" crushed stone base, trowel finish.	.061	1.71	1.82	3.53
3	Framing	2" x 4" wood studs, 16" O.C.; 1/2" plywood sheathing; 2" x 6" rafters 16" O.C. with 1/2" plywood sheathing 4 in 12 pitch; 2" x 6" ceiling joists 16" O.C.; 2" x 8" floor joists 16" O.C. with bridging and 5/8" waferbd. subfloor; 1/2" waferbd. subfloor on 1" x 2" wood sleepers 16" O.C.	.127	4.07	4.71	8.78
4	Exterior Walls	Horizontal beveled wood siding; #15 felt building paper; 3-1/2" batt insulation; wood double hung windows; 3 flush solid core wood exterior doors; storms and screens.	.136	11.04	4.79	15.83
5	Roofing	240# asphalt shingles; #15 felt building paper; aluminum flashing; 6" attic insulation. Aluminum gutters and downspouts.	.018	.30	.45	.75
6	Interiors	1/2" drywall, taped and finished, painted with primer and 1 coat; softwood baseboard and trim, painted with primer and 1 coat; finished hardwood floor 40%, carpet with underlayment 40%, vinyl tile with underlayment 15%, ceramic tile with underlayment 5%; hollow core doors.	.286	12.02	10.69	22.71
7	Specialties	Kitchen cabinets - 14 L.F. wall and base cabinets with laminated plastic counter top; medicine cabinet; stairs.	.030	1.52	.55	2.07
8	Mechanical	1 lavatory, white, wall hung; 1 water closet, white; 1 bathtub with shower, porcelain enamel steel, white; 1 kitchen sink, stainless steel, single; 1 water heater, gas fired, 30 gal.; gas fired warm air heat.	.072	2.20	1.60	3.80
9	Electrical	200 Amp. service; romex wiring; incandescent lighting fixtures, switches, receptacles.	.046	.64	.97	1.61
10	Overhead	Contractor's overhead and profit and plans.		2.34	1.86	4.20
		Total		35.84	28.56	64.40

31

RESIDENTIAL | Average | 3 Story

- Simple design from standard plans
- Single family — 1 full bath, 1 kitchen
- No basement
- Asphalt shingles on roof
- Hot air heat
- Drywall interior
- Materials and workmanship are average

3 STORY

BASE COST PER SQUARE FOOT OF LIVING AREA

EXTERIOR WALL	1500	1800	2100	2500	3000	3500	4000	4500	5000	5500	6000
Wood Siding — Wood Frame	62.40	56.20	53.80	51.95	48.20	46.70	44.15	41.15	40.60	39.45	38.95
Brick Veneer — Wood Frame	67.00	60.45	57.70	55.70	51.65	49.95	47.10	43.80	43.20	41.95	41.35
Stucco on Wood Frame	62.20	56.05	53.60	51.80	48.05	46.55	44.00	41.05	40.50	39.35	38.85
Solid Masonry	73.70	66.60	63.45	61.20	56.60	54.70	51.35	47.65	46.95	45.50	44.85
Finished Basement, Add	7.45	7.20	7.00	6.90	6.70	6.55	6.35	6.20	6.15	6.10	6.05
Unfinished Basement, Add	2.50	2.70	2.55	2.50	2.35	2.25	2.10	2.00	1.95	1.90	1.90

MODIFICATIONS

ALTERNATES	Add to or deduct from costs per S.F. of living area
Cedar shake roof	$+ .35
Clay tile roof	+1.20
Slate roof	+1.60
Central air conditioning	
In heating ducts	+1.05
In separate ducts	+2.85
Heating systems	
Hot water	+2.00
Heat pump	+1.60
Electric heat	- .75
Not heated	-2.30

BATHROOMS — TOTAL COST (includes plumbing and wall & floor finishes)	
Full bath — 3 fixtures	$2900
Half bath — 2 fixtures	1810

ADJUSTMENTS	
For two or more families (Add to total cost)	
Additional kitchen & entrance	$+3780 Ea.
Separate heating	+ 875 Ea.
Townhouse/Rowhouse (Multiplier for costs per S.F. of living area)	
Inner unit	.88
End unit	.94

	Page		Page
Wings & ells	42	Kitchen cabinets	76
Porches & breezeways	75	Garages & carports	77
Finished attics	75	Site improvements	77
Appliances	75		

Use LOCATION FACTORS on pages 444 to 448

Average 3 Story

| | | Living Area | 1500 S.F. |
| | | Perimeter | 91 L.F. |

			MAN-HOURS	COST PER SQUARE FOOT OF LIVING AREA		
				MAT.	LABOR	TOTAL
1	Site Work	Excavation for lower level 4' deep. Site preparation for slab.	.038		.89	.89
2	Foundations	Continuous concrete footing 8" deep x 18" wide, cast-in-place concrete wall, 8" thick, 4' deep; 4" concrete slab on 4" crushed stone base, trowel finish.	.053	1.47	1.57	3.04
3	Framing	2" x 4" wood studs, 16" O.C.; 1/2" plywood sheathing; 2" x 6" rafters 16" O.C. with 1/2" plywood sheathing 4 in 12 pitch; 2" x 6" ceiling joists 16" O.C.; 2" x 8" floor joists 16" O.C. with bridging and 5/8" waferbd. subfloor; 1/2" waferbd. subfloor on 1" x 2" wood sleepers 16" O.C.	.128	4.14	4.76	8.90
4	Exterior Walls	Horizontal beveled wood siding; #15 felt building paper; 3-1/2" batt insulation; wood double hung windows; 3 flush solid core wood exterior doors; storms and screens.	.139	11.25	4.90	16.15
5	Roofing	240# asphalt shingles; #15 felt building paper; aluminum flashing; 6" attic insulation. Aluminum gutters and downspouts.	.014	.26	.39	.65
6	Interiors	1/2" drywall, taped and finished, painted with primer and 1 coat; softwood baseboard and trim, painted with primer and 1 coat; finished hardwood floor 40%, carpet with underlayment 40%, vinyl tile with underlayment 15%, ceramic tile with underlayment 5%; hollow core doors.	.280	11.74	10.48	22.22
7	Specialties	Kitchen cabinets - 14 L.F. wall and base cabinets with laminated plastic counter top; medicine cabinet; stairs.	.025	1.22	.44	1.66
8	Mechanical	1 lavatory, white, wall hung; 1 water closet, white; 1 bathtub with shower, porcelain enamel steel, white; 1 kitchen sink, stainless steel, single; 1 water heater, gas fired, 30 gal.; gas fired warm air heat.	.065	1.88	1.47	3.35
9	Electrical	200 Amp. service; romex wiring; incandescent lighting fixtures, switches, receptacles.	.042	.57	.88	1.45
10	Overhead	Contractor's overhead and profit and plans.		2.29	1.80	4.09
		Total		34.82	27.58	62.40

RESIDENTIAL — Average Bi-Level

- Mass produced from stock plans
- Single family — 1 full bath, 1 kitchen
- No basement
- Asphalt shingles on roof
- Hot air heat
- Drywall interior
- Materials and workmanship are sufficient to meet codes

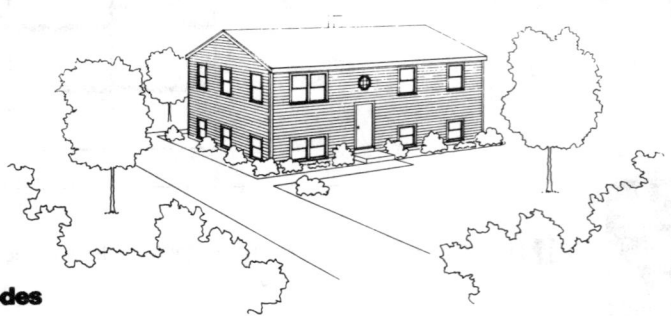

BI-LEVEL

BASE COST PER SQUARE FOOT OF LIVING AREA

EXTERIOR WALL	1000	1200	1400	1600	1800	2000	2200	2600	3000	3400	3800
Wood Siding — Wood Frame	62.15	55.80	53.30	51.60	49.80	47.75	46.45	43.75	40.90	39.80	38.80
Brick Veneer — Wood Frame	65.60	58.95	56.30	54.45	52.45	50.30	48.85	46.00	42.90	41.70	40.60
Stucco on Wood Frame	62.00	55.65	53.20	51.50	49.65	47.60	46.35	43.70	40.85	39.70	38.70
Solid Masonry	70.65	63.55	60.60	58.55	56.35	54.05	52.40	49.20	45.75	44.45	43.20
Finished Basement, Add	10.10	9.75	9.45	9.30	9.10	8.95	8.80	8.50	8.25	8.15	8.00
Unfinished Lower Level, Deduct	4.25	4.00	3.80	3.65	3.55	3.45	3.35	3.15	2.95	2.85	2.75

MODIFICATIONS

ALTERNATES	Add to or deduct from costs per S.F. of living area
Cedar shake roof	$+ .55
Clay tile roof	+1.85
Slate roof	+2.40
Central air conditioning	
In heating ducts	+1.25
In separate ducts	+3.05
Heating systems	
Hot water	+2.05
Heat pump	+1.55
Electric heat	- .75
Not heated	-2.15

BATHROOMS — TOTAL COST (includes plumbing and wall & floor finishes)	
Full bath — 3 fixtures	$2900
Half bath — 2 fixtures	1810

ADJUSTMENTS	
For two or more families (Add to total cost)	
Additional kitchen & entrance	$+3780 Ea.
Separate heating	+ 875 Ea.
Townhouse/Rowhouse (Multiplier for costs per S.F. of living area)	
Inner unit	.91
End unit	.96

	Page
Wings & ells	42
Porches & breezeways	75
Finished attics	75
Appliances	75

	Page
Kitchen cabinets	76
Garages & carports	77
Site improvements	77

Use LOCATION FACTORS on pages 444 to 448

Average Bi-level

	Living Area	2000 S.F.
	Perimeter	135 L.F.

			MAN-HOURS	COST PER SQUARE FOOT OF LIVING AREA		
				MAT.	LABOR	TOTAL
1	Site Work	Excavation for lower level 4' deep. Site preparation for slab.	.029		.67	.67
2	Foundations	Continuous concrete footing 8" deep x 18" wide, cast-in-place concrete wall, 8" thick, 4' deep; 4" concrete slab on 4" crushed stone base, trowel finish.	.066	1.77	1.87	3.64
3	Framing	2" x 4" wood studs, 16" O.C.; 1/2" plywood sheathing; 2" x 6" rafters 16" O.C. with 1/2" plywood sheathing 4 in 12 pitch; 2" x 6" ceiling joists 16" O.C.; 2" x 8" floor joists 16" O.C. with bridging and 5/8" waferbd. subfloor; 1/2" waferbd. subfloor on 1" x 2" wood sleepers 16" O.C.	.118	3.39	3.93	7.32
4	Exterior Walls	Horizontal beveled wood siding; #15 felt building paper; 3-1/2" batt insulation; wood double hung windows; 3 flush solid core wood exterior doors; storms and screens.	.091	6.76	2.92	9.68
5	Roofing	240# asphalt shingles; #15 felt building paper; aluminum flashing; 6" attic insulation. Aluminum gutters and downspouts.	.024	.39	.59	.98
6	Interiors	1/2" drywall, taped and finished, painted with primer and 1 coat; softwood baseboard and trim, painted with primer and 1 coat; finished hardwood floor 40%, carpet with underlayment 40%, vinyl tile with underlayment 15%, ceramic tile with underlayment 5%; hollow core doors.	.217	9.15	7.72	16.87
7	Specialties	Kitchen cabinets - 14 L.F. wall and base cabinets with laminated plastic counter top; medicine cabinet; stairs.	.021	.93	.32	1.25
8	Mechanical	1 lavatory, white, wall hung; 1 water closet, white; 1 bathtub with shower, porcelain enamel steel, white; 1 kitchen sink, stainless steel, single; 1 water heater, gas fired, 30 gal.; gas fired warm air heat.	.061	1.57	1.34	2.91
9	Electrical	200 Amp. service; romex wiring; incandescent lighting fixtures, switches, receptacles.	.039	.50	.80	1.30
10	Overhead	Contractor's overhead and profit and plans.		1.72	1.41	3.13
		Total		26.18	21.57	47.75

RESIDENTIAL — Average Tri-Level

- Simple design from standard plans
- Single family — 1 full bath, 1 kitchen
- No basement
- Asphalt shingles on roof
- Hot air heat
- Drywall interior
- Materials and workmanship are average

TRI-LEVEL

BASE COST PER SQUARE FOOT OF LIVING AREA

EXTERIOR WALL	1200	1500	1800	2100	2400	2700	3000	3400	3800	4200	4600
Wood Siding — Wood Frame	60.40	55.95	52.50	49.75	47.45	46.15	45.40	44.10	42.05	40.50	39.85
Brick Veneer — Wood Frame	63.55	58.80	55.10	52.10	49.60	48.20	47.40	46.00	43.80	42.15	41.45
Stucco on Wood Frame	60.30	55.95	52.40	49.65	47.35	46.10	45.30	44.00	41.95	40.45	39.80
Solid Masonry	68.10	62.95	58.80	55.50	52.70	51.20	50.30	48.80	46.35	44.55	43.85
Finished Basement, Add*	11.65	11.20	10.80	10.45	10.15	10.00	9.95	9.80	9.60	9.45	9.35
Unfinished Basement, Add*	4.85	4.55	4.25	4.00	3.80	3.70	3.65	3.55	3.40	3.30	3.25

*Basement under middle level only.

MODIFICATIONS

ALTERNATES	Add to or deduct from costs per S.F. of living area
Cedar shake roof	$+ .80
Clay tile roof	+2.65
Slate roof	+3.45
Central air conditioning	
In heating ducts	+1.05
In separate ducts	+2.85
Heating systems	
Hot water	+2.00
Heat pump	+1.60
Electric heat	- .75
Not heated	-2.30

BATHROOMS — TOTAL COST (includes plumbing and wall & floor finishes)	
Full bath — 3 fixtures	$2900
Half bath — 2 fixtures	1810

ADJUSTMENTS	
For two or more families (Add to total cost)	
Additional kitchen & entrance	$+3780 Ea.
Separate heating	+ 875 Ea.
Townhouse/Rowhouse (Multiplier for costs per S.F. of living area)	
Inner unit	.91
End unit	.92

	Page
Wings & ells	42
Porches & breezeways	75
Finished attics	75
Appliances	75

	Page
Kitchen cabinets	76
Garages & carports	77
Site improvements	77

Use LOCATION FACTORS on pages 444 to 448

Average Tri-Level

	Living Area	2400 S.F.
	Perimeter	163 L.F.

	MAN-HOURS	COST PER SQUARE FOOT OF LIVING AREA		
		MAT.	LABOR	TOTAL

#	Category	Description	Man-Hours	Mat.	Labor	Total
1	Site Work	Site preparation for slab; excavation for lower level 4' deep; trench 4' deep for foundation wall.	.029		.56	.56
2	Foundations	Continuous concrete footing 8" deep x 18" wide; cast-in-place concrete wall, 8" thick, 4' deep; 4" concrete slab on 4" crushed stone base, trowel finish.	.080	1.94	2.03	3.97
3	Framing	2" x 4" wood studs, 16" O.C.; 1/2" plywood sheathing; 2" x 6" rafters 16" O.C. with 1/2" plywood sheathing, 4 in 12 pitch; 2" x 6" ceiling joists 16" O.C.; 2" x 8" floor joists 16" O.C. with bridging and 5/8" waferbd. subfloor; 1/2" waferbd. subfloor on 1" x 2" wood sleepers 16" O.C.	.124	3.19	3.71	6.90
4	Exterior Walls	Horizontal beveled wood siding; #15 felt building paper; 3-1/2" batt insulation; wood double hung windows; 3 flush solid core wood exterior doors; storms and screens.	.083	5.77	2.47	8.24
5	Roofing	240# asphalt shingles; #15 felt building paper; aluminum flashing; 6" attic insulation. Aluminum gutters and downspouts.	.032	.52	.79	1.31
6	Interiors	1/2" drywall, taped and finished, painted with primer and 1 coat; softwood baseboard and trim, painted with primer and 1 coat; finished hardwood floor 40%, carpet with underlayment 40%, vinyl tile with underlayment 15%, ceramic tile with underlayment 5%; hollow core doors.	.186	11.08	7.37	18.45
7	Specialties	Kitchen cabinets - 14 L.F. wall and base cabinets with laminated plastic counter top; medicine cabinet.	.012	.77	.28	1.05
8	Mechanical	1 lavatory, white, wall hung; 1 water closet, white; 1 bathtub with shower, porcelain enamel steel, white; 1 kitchen sink, stainless steel, single; 1 water heater, gas fired, 30 gal.; gas fired warm air heat.	.059	1.38	1.26	2.64
9	Electrical	200 Amp. service; romex wiring; incandescent lighting fixtures, switches, receptacles.	.036	.46	.75	1.21
10	Overhead	Contractor's overhead and profit and plans.		1.76	1.36	3.12
	Total			26.87	20.58	47.45

RESIDENTIAL — Solid Wall | 1 Story

- Post and beam frame
- Log exterior walls
- Simple design from standard plans
- Single family — 1 full bath, 1 kitchen
- No basement
- Asphalt shingles on roof
- Hot air heat
- Drywall interior partitions
- Materials and workmanship are average

BASE COST PER SQUARE FOOT OF LIVING AREA

EXTERIOR WALL	600	800	1000	1200	1400	1600	1800	2000	2400	2800	3200
6" Log - Solid wall	69.60	62.90	57.65	53.50	50.20	47.50	46.10	45.05	42.00	39.60	38.25
8" Log - Solid wall	72.60	65.55	60.10	55.90	52.45	49.55	48.10	47.05	43.85	41.20	39.90
Finished Basement, Add	17.45	16.55	15.90	15.20	14.75	14.30	14.10	13.95	13.60	13.20	13.00
Unfinished Basement, Add	7.90	7.30	6.80	6.35	6.00	5.70	5.55	5.45	5.20	4.95	4.75

MODIFICATIONS

ALTERNATES	Add to or deduct from costs per S.F. of living area
Cedar shake roof	$+1.10
Central air conditioning	
In heating ducts	+2.05
In separate ducts	+3.85
Heating systems	
Hot water	+2.50
Heat pump	+1.45
Electric heat	− .80
Not heated	−2.20

BATHROOMS — TOTAL COST (includes plumbing and wall & floor finishes)	
Full bath — 3 fixtures	$2900
Half bath — 2 fixtures	1810

ADJUSTMENTS	
For two or more families (Add to total cost)	
Additional kitchen & entrance	+$3780 Ea.
Separate heating	+ 875 Ea.
Townhouse/Rowhouse (Multiplier for costs per S.F. of living area)	
Inner unit	.92
End unit	.96

	Page		Page
Wings & ells	42	Kitchen cabinets	76
Porches & breezeways	75	Garages & carports	77
Finished attics	75	Site improvements	77
Appliances	75		

Use LOCATION FACTORS on pages 444 to 448

Average Solid Wall 1 Story

Living Area	1600 S.F.
Perimeter	163 L.F.

			MAN-HOURS	COST PER SQUARE FOOT OF LIVING AREA		
				MAT.	LABOR	TOTAL
1	Site Work	Site preparation for slab; trench 4' deep for foundation wall.	.048		.83	83
2	Foundations	Continuous concrete footing 8" deep x 18" wide; cast-in-place concrete wall, 8" thick, 4' deep, 4" concrete slab on 4" crushed stone base, trowel finish.	.113	2.91	3.03	5.94
3	Framing	Precut traditional log home. Handicrafted white cedar or pine logs. Delivery included.				
4	Exterior Walls		.201	9.64	6.41	16.05
5	Roofing	240# asphalt shingles; #15 felt building paper; aluminum flashing; 6" attic insulation. Aluminum gutters and downspouts.	.047	.78	1.17	1.95
6	Interiors	1/2" drywall, taped and finished, painted with primer and 1 coat; softwood baseboard and trim, painted with primer and 1 coat; finished hardwood floor 40%, carpet with underlayment 40%, vinyl tile with underlayment 15%, ceramic tile with underlayment 5%; hollow core doors.	.232	7.01	6.40	13.41
7	Specialties	Kitchen cabinets - 14 L.F. wall and base cabinets with laminated plastic counter top; medicine cabinet, stairs.	.009	1.14	.41	1.55
8	Mechanical	1 lavatory, white, wall hung; 1 water closet, white; 1 bathtub with shower, porcelain enamel steel, white; 1 kitchen sink, stainless steel, single; 1 water heater, gas fired, 30 gal.; gas fired warm air heat.	.098	1.80	1.45	3.25
9	Electrical	200 Amp. service; romex wiring; incandescent lighting fixtures, switches, receptacles.	.041	.54	.87	1.41
10	Overhead	Contractor's overhead and profit and plans.		1.67	1.44	3.11
		Total		25.49	22.01	47.50

RESIDENTIAL — Solid Wall — 2 Story

- Post and beam frame
- Log exterior walls
- Simple design from standard plans
- Single family — 1 full bath, 1 kitchen
- No basement
- Asphalt shingles on roof
- Hot air heat
- Drywall interior partitions
- Materials and workmanship are average

BASE COST PER SQUARE FOOT OF LIVING AREA

EXTERIOR WALL	1000	1200	1400	1600	1800	2000	2200	2600	3000	3400	3800
6" Log - Solid wall	63.55	56.95	54.30	52.35	50.35	48.20	46.85	44.05	40.90	39.80	38.75
8" Log - Solid wall	66.30	59.45	56.60	54.65	52.50	50.30	48.90	45.85	42.75	41.55	40.40
Finished Basement, Add	10.30	9.90	9.60	9.40	9.20	9.05	8.90	8.65	8.35	8.25	8.15
Unfinished Basement, Add	4.35	4.10	3.85	3.75	3.60	3.50	3.40	3.15	2.95	2.90	2.80

MODIFICATIONS

ALTERNATES	Add to or deduct from costs per S.F. of living area
Cedar shake roof	$+ .55
Central air conditioning	
In heating ducts	+1.25
In separate ducts	+3.05
Heating systems	
Hot water	+2.05
Heat pump	+1.55
Electric heat	− .75
Not heated	−2.15

BATHROOMS — TOTAL COST (includes plumbing and wall & floor finishes)	
Full bath — 3 fixtures	$2900
Half bath — 2 fixtures	1810

ADJUSTMENTS	
For two or more families (Add to total cost)	
Additional kitchen & entrance	+$3780 Ea.
Separate heating	+ 875 Ea.
Townhouse/Rowhouse (Multiplier for costs per S.F. of living area)	
Inner unit	.90
End unit	.95

	Page
Wings & ells	42
Porches & breezeways	75
Finished attics	75
Appliances	75

	Page
Kitchen cabinets	76
Garages & carports	77
Site improvements	77

Use LOCATION FACTORS on pages 444 to 448

Average Solid Wall 2 Story

	Living Area	2000 S.F.
	Perimeter	135 L.F.

			MAN-HOURS	COST PER SQUARE FOOT OF LIVING AREA		
				MAT.	LABOR	TOTAL
1	Site Work	Site preparation for slab; trench 4' deep for foundation wall.	.034		.67	.67
2	Foundations	Continuous concrete footing 8" deep x 18" wide; cast-in-place concrete wall, 8" thick, 4' deep, 4" concrete slab on 4" crushed stone base, trowel finish.	.066	1.77	1.87	3.64
3	Framing	Precut traditional log home. Handicrafted white cedar or pine logs. Delivery included.				
4	Exterior Walls		.232	11.28	7.58	18.86
5	Roofing	240# asphalt shingles; #15 felt building paper; aluminum flashing; 6" attic insulation. Aluminum gutters and downspouts.	.024	.39	.59	.98
6	Interiors	1/2" drywall, taped and finished, painted with primer and 1 coat; softwood baseboard and trim, painted with primer and 1 coat; finished hardwood floor 40%, carpet with underlayment 40%, vinyl tile with underlayment 15%, ceramic tile with underlayment 5%; hollow core doors.	.225	7.77	7.66	15.43
7	Specialties	Kitchen cabinets - 14 L.F. wall and base cabinets with laminated plastic counter top; medicine cabinet, stairs.	.021	.93	.33	1.26
8	Mechanical	1 lavatory, white, wall hung; 1 water closet, white; 1 bathtub with shower, porcelain enamel steel, white; 1 kitchen sink, stainless steel, single; 1 water heater, gas fired, 30 gal.; gas fired warm air heat.	.060	1.57	1.34	2.91
9	Electrical	200 Amp. service; romex wiring; incandescent lighting fixtures, switches, receptacles.	.039	.50	.80	1.30
10	Overhead	Contractor's overhead and profit and plans.		1.69	1.46	3.15
		Total		25.90	22.30	48.20

RESIDENTIAL — Average — Wings & Ells

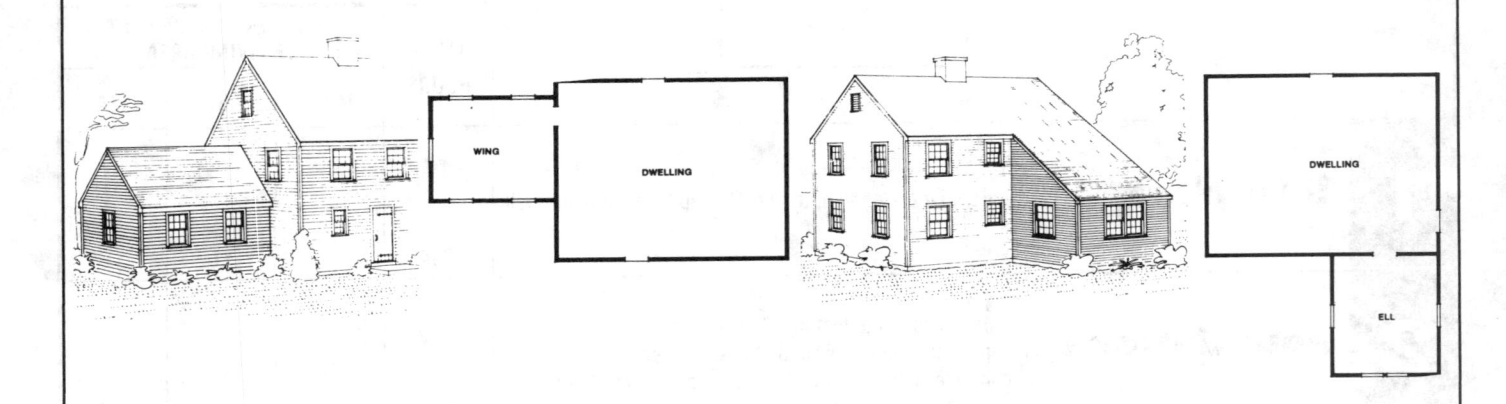

1 STORY — BASE COST PER SQUARE FOOT OF LIVING AREA

EXTERIOR WALL	\multicolumn{8}{c}{LIVING AREA}
	50	100	200	300	400	500	600	700
Wood Siding — Wood Frame	97.40	74.70	64.90	53.40	50.20	48.25	47.00	47.10
Brick Veneer — Wood Frame	103.65	77.90	66.85	53.25	49.60	47.45	46.00	46.00
Stucco on Wood Frame	96.85	74.30	64.55	53.15	49.95	48.00	46.75	46.90
Solid Masonry	158.65	110.90	89.20	69.65	63.90	60.50	58.20	57.60
Finished Basement, Add	28.25	22.90	20.65	16.95	16.20	15.75	15.45	15.25
Unfinished Basement, Add	15.15	11.50	10.00	7.45	6.95	6.65	6.45	6.30

1½ STORY — BASE COST PER SQUARE FOOT OF LIVING AREA

EXTERIOR WALL	\multicolumn{8}{c}{LIVING AREA}
	100	200	300	400	500	600	700	800
Wood Siding — Wood Frame	80.00	62.75	55.50	49.10	46.30	44.45	42.90	42.65
Brick Veneer — Wood Frame	104.30	77.75	66.75	57.75	53.80	51.25	49.05	48.55
Stucco on Wood Frame	94.40	69.85	60.15	52.60	49.05	46.75	44.85	44.35
Solid Masonry	118.10	88.80	75.95	64.95	60.45	57.50	55.00	54.40
Finished Basement, Add	19.20	16.95	15.50	13.85	13.40	13.10	12.80	12.75
Unfinished Basement, Add	9.55	8.05	7.00	5.90	5.60	5.40	5.20	5.20

2 STORY — BASE COST PER SQUARE FOOT OF LIVING AREA

EXTERIOR WALL	\multicolumn{8}{c}{LIVING AREA}
	100	200	400	600	800	1000	1200	1400
Wood Siding — Wood Frame	80.50	60.35	51.65	41.95	39.05	37.35	36.20	36.45
Brick Veneer — Wood Frame	107.15	75.95	62.00	48.85	44.85	42.50	40.95	40.85
Stucco on Wood Frame	96.05	68.05	55.35	44.45	40.90	38.80	37.40	37.45
Solid Masonry	122.65	87.00	71.20	55.00	50.40	47.65	45.85	45.60
Finished Basement, Add	15.20	12.55	11.40	9.55	9.20	8.95	8.80	8.70
Unfinished Basement, Add	7.65	5.85	5.10	3.80	3.55	3.40	3.30	3.25

Base costs do not include bathroom or kitchen facilities. Use MODIFICATIONS on pages 75, 76, 77 where appropriate.

RESIDENTIAL Custom Illustrations

43

RESIDENTIAL — Custom — 1 Story

- A distinct residence from designer's plans
- Single family — 1 full bath, 1 kitchen
- No basement
- Asphalt shingles on roof
- Forced hot air heat/air conditioning
- Drywall interior
- Materials and workmanship are above average

__1 STORY__

BASE COST PER SQUARE FOOT OF LIVING AREA

EXTERIOR WALL	800	1000	1200	1400	1600	1800	2000	2400	2800	3200	3600
Wood Siding — Wood Frame	87.95	80.25	73.95	69.15	65.15	63.00	61.40	56.95	53.60	51.45	48.60
Brick Veneer — Wood Frame	96.90	88.85	82.10	77.05	72.75	70.45	68.80	64.10	60.45	58.20	55.15
Stone Veneer — Wood Frame	101.85	93.30	86.15	80.75	76.15	73.70	71.95	66.95	63.10	60.65	57.40
Solid Masonry	100.95	92.50	85.40	80.05	75.50	73.10	71.35	66.40	62.60	60.20	57.00
Finished Basement, Add	24.00	22.85	21.80	21.00	20.30	19.95	19.70	19.10	18.50	18.15	17.75
Unfinished Basement, Add	10.95	10.40	9.80	9.40	9.00	8.80	8.70	8.35	8.00	7.80	7.55

MODIFICATIONS

ALTERNATES	Add to or deduct from costs per S.F. of living area
Cedar shake roof	$+ .60
Clay tile roof	+3.20
Slate roof	+4.25
Central air conditioning	
In heating ducts	+1.50
In separate ducts	+3.25
Heating systems	
Hot water	+2.15
Heat pump	+1.55
Electric heat	−1.10
Not heated	−2.20

BATHROOMS — TOTAL COST (includes plumbing and wall & floor finishes)	
Full bath — 3 fixtures	$3435
Half bath — 2 fixtures	1990

ADJUSTMENTS	
For two or more families (Add to total cost)	
Additional kitchen & entrance	$+6385 Ea.
Separate heating/Air conditioning	+2100 Ea.
Townhouse/Rowhouse (Multiplier for costs per S.F. of living area)	
Inner unit	.90
End unit	.95

	Page		Page
Wings & ells	58	Kitchen cabinets	76
Porches & breezeways	75	Garages & carports	77
Finished attics	75	Site improvements	77
Appliances	75		

Use LOCATION FACTORS on pages 444 to 448

Custom 1 Story

	Living Area	2400 S.F.
	Perimeter	207 L.F.

	MAN-HOURS	COST PER SQUARE FOOT OF LIVING AREA		
		MAT.	LABOR	TOTAL
1 Site Work — Site preparation for slab; trench 4' deep for foundation wall.	.028		.67	.67
2 Foundations — Continuous concrete footing 8" deep x 18" wide; cast-in-place concrete wall, 8" thick, 4' deep; 4" concrete slab on 4" crushed stone base, trowel finish.	.113	3.28	3.10	6.38
3 Framing — 2" x 6" wood studs, 16" O.C.; 1/2" plywood sheathing; 2" x 8" rafters 16" O.C. with 1/2" plywood sheathing, 4 in 12 pitch; 2" x 6" ceiling joists 16" O.C.; 5/8" plywood subfloor on 1" x 3" wood sleepers 16" O.C.; #15 felt building paper.	.190	2.98	3.29	6.27
4 Exterior Walls — Horizontal beveled wood siding; #15 felt building paper; 6" batt insulation; wood double hung windows; 3 solid core wood exterior doors; storms and screens.	.085	7.36	2.15	9.51
5 Roofing — 300# asphalt shingles; #15 felt building paper; copper flashing; 9" attic insulation. Aluminum gutters and downspouts.	.082	1.91	1.61	3.52
6 Interiors — 5/8" drywall, skim coat plaster painted with primer and 1 coat; hardwood baseboard and trim, sanded and finished; finished hardwood floor 70%, ceramic tile with underlayment 20%, vinyl tile with underlayment 10%; wood panel interior doors.	.292	10.76	6.67	17.43
7 Specialties — Kitchen cabinets - 20 L.F. wall and base cabinets with laminated plastic counter top; 4 L.F. bathroom vanity; medicine cabinet.	.019	1.95	.43	2.38
8 Mechanical — 1 kitchen sink, cast iron, double; 1 water heater, gas fired, 50 gal.; gas warm air heat/air conditioning; 1 full bath including: 1 bathtub, color; 1 corner shower; 1 lavatory, color, built in; 1 water closet, color. 1 half bath including: 1 lavatory, color, built in; 1 water closet, color.	.092	2.76	1.47	4.23
9 Electrical — 200 Amp. service; romex wiring; fluorescent and incandescent lighting fixtures, switches, receptacles.	.039	.52	.85	1.37
10 Overhead — Contractor's overhead and profit and design.		3.16	2.03	5.19
Total		34.68	22.27	56.95

RESIDENTIAL — Custom — 1½ Story

- A distinct residence from designer's plans
- Single family — 1 full bath, 1 kitchen
- No basement
- Asphalt shingles on roof
- Forced hot air heat/air conditioning
- Drywall interior
- Materials and workmanship are above average

1½ STORY

BASE COST PER SQUARE FOOT OF LIVING AREA

EXTERIOR WALL	1000	1200	1400	1600	1800	2000	2400	2800	3200	3600	4000
Wood Siding — Wood Frame	80.50	74.60	70.85	67.35	64.85	62.10	56.45	54.50	52.70	51.00	48.30
Brick Veneer — Wood Frame	85.10	78.80	74.75	71.10	68.45	65.45	59.35	57.25	55.35	53.50	50.60
Stone Veneer — Wood Frame	90.30	83.45	79.15	75.35	72.45	69.25	62.60	60.40	58.30	56.35	53.20
Solid Masonry	89.35	82.60	78.35	74.55	71.70	68.55	62.00	59.80	57.75	55.85	52.70
Finished Basement, Add	15.95	15.10	14.60	14.25	13.90	13.60	12.80	12.55	12.30	12.10	11.80
Unfinished Basement, Add	7.35	6.90	6.65	6.50	6.30	6.15	5.70	5.55	5.40	5.30	5.15

MODIFICATIONS

ALTERNATES	Add to or deduct from costs per S.F. of living area
Cedar shake roof	$+ .45
Clay tile roof	+2.30
Slate roof	+3.10
Central air conditioning	
In heating ducts	+1.35
In separate ducts	+3.30
Heating systems	
Hot water	+2.20
Heat pump	+1.55
Electric heat	− .85
Not heated	−2.15

BATHROOMS — TOTAL COST (includes plumbing and wall & floor finishes)	
Full bath — 3 fixtures	$3435
Half bath — 2 fixtures	1990

ADJUSTMENTS	
For two or more families (Add to total cost)	
Additional kitchen & entrance	$+6385 Ea.
Separate heating/Air conditioning	+2100 Ea.
Townhouse/Rowhouse (Multiplier for costs per S.F. of living area)	
Inner unit	.90
End unit	.95

	Page		Page
Wings & ells	58	Kitchen cabinets	76
Porches & breezeways	75	Garages & carports	77
Finished attics	75	Site improvements	77
Appliances	75		

Use LOCATION FACTORS on pages 444 to 448

Custom 1½ Story

Living Area: 2800 S.F.
Perimeter: 175 L.F.

#	Category	Description	Man-Hours	Mat.	Labor	Total
1	**Site Work**	Site preparation for slab; trench 4' deep for foundation wall.	.028		.58	.58
2	**Foundations**	Continuous concrete footing 8" deep x 18" wide; cast-in-place concrete wall, 8" thick, 4' deep; 4" concrete slab on 4" crushed stone base, trowel finish.	.065	2.28	2.16	4.44
3	**Framing**	2" x 6" wood studs, 16" O.C.; 1/2" plywood sheathing; 2" x 8" rafters 16" O.C. with 1/2" plywood sheathing, 8 in 12 pitch; 2" x 10" floor joists 16" O.C. with bridging and 5/8" plywood subfloor; 5/8" plywood subfloor on 1" x 3" wood sleepers 16" O.C.	.192	3.17	3.33	6.50
4	**Exterior Walls**	Horizontal beveled wood siding; #15 felt building paper; 6" batt insulation; wood double hung windows; 3 solid core wood exterior doors; storms and screens.	.064	7.74	2.27	10.01
5	**Roofing**	300# asphalt shingles; #15 felt building paper; copper flashing; 9" attic insulation. Aluminum gutters and downspouts.	.048	1.20	1.01	2.21
6	**Interiors**	5/8" drywall, skim coat plaster and finished, painted with primer and 1 coat; hardwood baseboard and trim, sanded and finished; finished hardwood floor 70%, ceramic tile with underlayment 20%, vinyl tile with underlayment 10%; wood panel interior doors.	.259	11.46	7.25	18.71
7	**Specialties**	Kitchen cabinets - 20 L.F. wall and base cabinets with laminated plastic counter top; 4 L.F. bathroom vanity; medicine cabinet; stairs.	.030	1.67	.38	2.05
8	**Mechanical**	1 kitchen sink, cast iron, double; 1 water heater, gas fired, 50 gal.; gas warm air heat/air conditioning; 1 full bath including: 1 bathtub, color; 1 corner shower; 1 lavatory, color, built in; 1 water closet, color. 1 half sink including: 1 lavatory, color, built in; 1 water closet, color.	.084	2.37	1.37	3.74
9	**Electrical**	200 Amp. service; romex wiring; fluorescent and incandescent lighting fixtures, switches, receptacles.	.038	.50	.81	1.31
10	**Overhead**	Contractor's overhead and profit and design.		3.04	1.91	4.95
	Total			33.43	21.07	54.50

RESIDENTIAL — Custom — 2 Story

- A distinct residence from designer's plans
- Single family — 1 full bath, 1 kitchen
- No basement
- Asphalt shingles on roof
- Forced hot air heat/air conditioning
- Drywall interior
- Materials and workmanship are above average

2 STORY

BASE COST PER SQUARE FOOT OF LIVING AREA

EXTERIOR WALL	1200	1400	1600	1800	2000	2400	2800	3200	3600	4000	4400
Wood Siding — Wood Frame	76.90	72.90	70.10	67.25	64.35	59.85	56.40	53.35	51.65	50.65	49.20
Brick Veneer — Wood Frame	81.90	77.50	74.50	71.45	68.35	63.45	59.70	56.40	54.55	53.50	51.90
Stone Veneer — Wood Frame	87.45	82.70	79.45	76.15	72.85	67.50	63.40	59.80	57.80	56.65	54.90
Solid Masonry	86.40	81.75	78.55	75.25	72.00	66.75	62.70	59.15	57.20	56.05	54.35
Finished Basement, Add	12.85	12.35	12.05	11.70	11.45	10.95	10.55	10.20	10.00	9.85	9.75
Unfinished Basement, Add	5.90	5.65	5.50	5.35	5.20	4.90	4.70	4.50	4.40	4.35	4.25

MODIFICATIONS

ALTERNATES	Add to or deduct from costs per S.F. of living area
Cedar shake roof	$+ .30
Clay tile roof	+1.60
Slate roof	+2.15
Central air conditioning	
In heating ducts	+1.20
In separate ducts	+2.40
Heating systems	
Hot water	+2.20
Heat pump	+1.60
Electric heat	–1.00
Not heated	–2.10

BATHROOMS — TOTAL COST (includes plumbing and wall & floor finishes)	
Full bath — 3 fixtures	$3435
Half bath — 2 fixtures	1990

ADJUSTMENTS	
For two or more families (Add to total cost)	
Additional kitchen & entrance	$+6385 Ea.
Separate heating/Air conditioning	+2100 Ea.
Townhouse/Rowhouse (Multiplier for costs per S.F. of living area)	
Inner unit	.87
End unit	.93

	Page		Page
Wings & ells	58	Kitchen cabinets	76
Porches & breezeways	75	Garages & carports	77
Finished attics	75	Site improvements	77
Appliances	75		

Use LOCATION FACTORS on pages 444 to 448

Custom 2 Story

	Living Area	2800 S.F.
	Perimeter	156 L.F.

		MAN-HOURS	COST PER SQUARE FOOT OF LIVING AREA		
			MAT.	LABOR	TOTAL
1	**Site Work** — Site preparation for slab; trench 4' deep for foundation wall.	.024		.58	.58
2	**Foundations** — Continuous concrete footing 8" deep x 18" wide; cast-in-place concrete wall, 8" thick, 4' deep; 4" concrete slab on 4" crushed stone base, trowel finish.	.058	1.98	1.88	3.86
3	**Framing** — 2" x 6" wood studs, 16" O.C.; 1/2" plywood sheathing; 2" x 8" rafters 16" O.C. with 1/2" plywood sheathing, 6 in 12 pitch; 2" x 8" ceiling joists 16" O.C.; 10" floor joists 16" O.C. with bridging and 5/8" plywood subfloor; 5/8" plywood subfloor on 1" x 3" wood sleepers 16" O.C.	.159	3.35	3.41	6.76
4	**Exterior Walls** — Horizontal beveled wood siding; #15 felt building paper; 6" batt insulation; wood double hung windows; 3 solid core wood exterior doors; storms and screens.	.091	8.75	2.59	11.34
5	**Roofing** — 300# asphalt shingles; #15 felt building paper; copper flashing; 9" attic insulation. Aluminum gutters and downspouts.	.042	.96	.81	1.77
6	**Interiors** — 5/8" drywall, skim coat plaster and finished, painted with primer and 1 coat; hardwood baseboard and trim, sanded and finished; finished hardwood floor 70%, ceramic tile with underlayment 20%, vinyl tile with underlayment 10%; wood panel interior doors.	.271	12.08	7.67	19.75
7	**Specialties** — Kitchen cabinets — 20 L.F. wall and base cabinets with laminated plastic counter top; 4 L.F. bathroom vanity; medicine cabinet; stairs.	.028	1.67	.38	2.05
8	**Mechanical** — 1 kitchen sink, cast iron, double; 1 water heater, gas fired, 50 gal.; gas warm air heat/air conditioning; 1 full bath including: 1 bathtub, color; 1 corner shower; 1 lavatory, color, built in; 1 water closet, color. 1 half bath including: 1 lavatory, color, built in; 1 water closet, color.	.078	2.47	1.39	3.86
9	**Electrical** — 200 Amp. service; romex wiring; fluorescent and incandescent lighting fixtures, switches, receptacles.	.038	.50	.81	1.31
10	**Overhead** — Contractor's overhead and profit and design.		3.17	1.95	5.12
	Total		34.93	21.47	56.40

RESIDENTIAL — Custom — 2½ Story

- A distinct residence from designer's plans
- Single family — 1 full bath, 1 kitchen
- No basement
- Asphalt shingles on roof
- Forced hot air heat/air conditioning
- Drywall interior
- Materials and workmanship are above average

2½ STORY

BASE COST PER SQUARE FOOT OF LIVING AREA

EXTERIOR WALL	1500	1800	2100	2400	2800	3200	3600	4000	4500	5000	5500
Wood Siding — Wood Frame	72.00	68.15	65.60	62.65	59.70	56.00	54.40	50.80	49.30	47.90	46.90
Brick Veneer — Wood Frame	76.75	72.65	69.85	66.65	63.60	59.50	57.70	53.80	52.15	50.60	49.55
Stone Veneer — Wood Frame	82.10	77.65	74.65	71.15	67.90	63.40	61.45	57.10	55.35	53.60	52.50
Solid Masonry	81.10	76.70	73.75	70.30	67.10	62.65	60.75	56.50	54.75	53.05	51.95
Finished Basement, Add	9.90	9.50	9.25	8.95	8.75	8.40	8.20	7.90	7.75	7.60	7.50
Unfinished Basement, Add	4.55	4.35	4.25	4.10	4.00	3.80	3.70	3.50	3.45	3.35	3.30

MODIFICATIONS

ALTERNATES	Add to or deduct from costs per S.F. of living area
Cedar shake roof	$+ .25
Clay tile roof	+1.40
Slate roof	+1.85
Central air conditioning	
In heating ducts	+1.25
In separate ducts	+2.30
Heating systems	
Hot water	+2.20
Heat pump	+1.60
Electric heat	− .75
Not heated	−2.15

BATHROOMS — TOTAL COST (includes plumbing and wall & floor finishes)	
Full bath — 3 fixtures	$3435
Half bath — 2 fixtures	1990

ADJUSTMENTS	
For two or more families (Add to total cost)	
Additional kitchen & entrance	$+6385 Ea.
Separate heating/Air conditioning	+2100 Ea.
Townhouse/Rowhouse (Multiplier for costs per S.F. of living area)	
Inner unit	.88
End unit	.94

	Page		Page
Wings & ells	58	Kitchen cabinets	76
Porches & breezeways	75	Garages & carports	77
Finished attics	75	Site improvements	77
Appliances	75		

Use LOCATION FACTORS on pages 444 to 448

Custom 2½ Story

	Living Area	1500 S.F.
	Perimeter	96 L.F.

		MAN-HOURS	COST PER SQUARE FOOT OF LIVING AREA		
			MAT.	LABOR	TOTAL
1	**Site Work** — Site preparation for slab; trench 4' deep for foundation wall.	.048		1.07	1.07
2	**Foundations** — Continuous concrete footing 8" deep x 18" wide; cast-in-place concrete wall, 8" thick, 4' deep; 4" concrete slab on 4" crushed stone base, trowel finish.	.063	2.08	1.99	4.07
3	**Framing** — 2" x 6" wood studs, 16" O.C.; 1/2" plywood sheathing; 2" x 8" rafters 16" O.C. with 1/2" plywood sheathing, 6 in 12 pitch; 2" x 8" ceiling joists 16" O.C.; 10" floor joists 16" O.C. with bridging and 5/8" plywood subfloor; 5/8" plywood subfloor on 1" x 3" wood sleepers 16" O.C.	.177	3.89	3.90	7.79
4	**Exterior Walls** — Horizontal beveled wood siding; #15 felt building paper; 6" batt insulation; wood double hung windows; 3 solid core wood exterior doors; storms and screens.	.134	12.44	3.65	16.09
5	**Roofing** — 300# asphalt shingles; #15 felt building paper; copper flashing; 9" attic insulation. Aluminum gutters and downspouts.	.032	.73	.62	1.35
6	**Interiors** — 5/8" drywall, skim coat plaster and finished, painted with primer and 1 coat; hardwood baseboard and trim, sanded and finished; finished hardwood floor 70%, ceramic tile with underlayment 20%, vinyl tile with underlayment 10%; wood panel interior doors.	.354	14.25	9.69	23.94
7	**Specialties** — Kitchen cabinets — 20 L.F. wall and base cabinets with laminated plastic counter top; 4 L.F. bathroom vanity; medicine cabinet; stairs.	.053	3.13	.68	3.81
8	**Mechanical** — 1 kitchen sink, cast iron, double; 1 water heater, gas fired, 50 gal.; gas warm air heat/air-conditioning; 1 full bath including: 1 bathtub, color; 1 corner shower; 1 lavatory color, built in; 1 water closet, color. 1 half bath including: 1 lavatory, color, built in; 1 water closet, color.	.104	3.95	1.77	5.72
9	**Electrical** — 200 Amp. service; romex wiring; fluorescent and incandescent lighting fixtures, switches, receptacles.	.048	.63	.98	1.61
10	**Overhead** — Contractor's overhead and profit and design.		4.11	2.44	6.55
	Total		45.21	26.79	72.00

RESIDENTIAL | Custom | 3 Story

- A distinct residence from designer's plans
- Single family — 1 full bath, 1 kitchen
- No basement
- Asphalt shingles on roof
- Forced hot air heat/air conditioning
- Drywall interior
- Materials and workmanship are above average

3 STORY

BASE COST PER SQUARE FOOT OF LIVING AREA

EXTERIOR WALL	1500	1800	2100	2500	3000	3500	4000	4500	5000	5500	6000
Wood Siding — Wood Frame	77.70	69.65	66.35	63.75	59.00	56.95	53.60	50.00	49.25	47.75	47.05
Brick Veneer — Wood Frame	83.10	74.60	71.00	68.15	63.00	60.80	57.10	53.10	52.25	50.65	49.85
Stone Veneer — Wood Frame	89.20	80.20	76.20	73.15	67.50	65.05	60.95	56.55	55.65	53.90	53.00
Solid Masonry	88.05	79.15	75.20	72.20	66.65	64.25	60.25	55.90	55.00	53.30	52.45
Finished Basement, Add	9.00	8.55	8.20	7.95	7.60	7.40	7.10	6.80	6.75	6.60	6.55
Unfinished Basement, Add	4.15	3.90	3.75	3.65	3.45	3.35	3.20	3.00	3.00	2.95	2.90

MODIFICATIONS

ALTERNATES	Add to or deduct from costs per S.F. of living area
Cedar shake roof	$+ .20
Clay tile roof	+1.05
Slate roof	+1.40
Central air conditioning	
In heating ducts	+1.25
In separate ducts	+2.30
Heating systems	
Hot water	+2.25
Heat pump	+1.65
Electric heat	–1.00
Not heated	–2.30

BATHROOMS — TOTAL COST (includes plumbing and wall & floor finishes)	
Full bath — 3 fixtures	$3435
Half bath — 2 fixtures	1990

ADJUSTMENTS	
For two or more families (Add to total cost)	
Additional kitchen & entrance	$+6385 Ea.
Separate heating/Air conditioning	+2100 Ea.
Townhouse/Rowhouse (Multiplier for costs per S.F. of living area)	
Inner unit	.85
End unit	.93

	Page		Page
Wings & ells	58	Kitchen cabinets	76
Porches & breezeways	75	Garages & carports	77
Finished attics	75	Site improvements	77
Appliances	75		

Use LOCATION FACTORS on pages 444 to 448

Custom 3 Story

	Living Area	1500 S.F.
	Perimeter	91 L.F.

			MAN-HOURS	COST PER SQUARE FOOT OF LIVING AREA		
				MAT.	LABOR	TOTAL
1	Site Work	Site preparation for slab; trench 4' deep for foundation wall.	.048		1.07	1.07
2	Foundations	Continuous concrete footing 8" deep x 18" wide; cast-in-place concrete wall, 8" thick, 4' deep; 4" concrete slab on 4" crushed stone base, trowel finish.	.060	1.93	1.85	3.78
3	Framing	2" x 6" wood studs, 16" O.C.; 1/2" plywood sheathing; 2" x 8" rafters 16" O.C. with 1/2" plywood sheathing, 6 in 12 pitch; 2" x 8" ceiling joists 16" O.C.; 10" floor joists 16" O.C. with bridging and 5/8" plywood subfloor; 5/8" plywood subfloor on 1" x 3" wood sleepers 16" O.C.	.191	4.17	4.19	8.36
4	Exterior Walls	Horizontal beveled wood siding; #15 felt building paper; 6" batt insulation; wood double hung windows; 3 solid core wood exterior doors; storms and screens.	.150	14.05	4.12	18.17
5	Roofing	300# asphalt shingles; #15 felt building paper; copper flashing; 9" attic insulation. Aluminum gutters and downspouts.	.028	.64	.53	1.17
6	Interiors	5/8" drywall, skim coat plaster and finished, painted with primer and 1 coat; hardwood baseboard and trim, sanded and finished; finished hardwood floor 70%, ceramic tile with underlayment 20%, vinyl tile with underlayment 10%; wood panel interior doors.	.409	15.91	11.04	26.95
7	Specialties	Kitchen cabinets — 20 L.F. wall and base cabinets with laminated plastic counter top; 4 L.F. bathroom vanity; medicine cabinet; stairs.	.053	3.13	.68	3.81
8	Mechanical	1 kitchen sink, cast iron, double; 1 water heater, gas fired, 50 gal.; gas warm air heat/air conditioning; 1 full bath including: 1 bathtub, color; 1 corner shower; 1 lavatory, color, built in; 1 water closet, color. 1 half bath including: 1 lavatory, color, built in; 1 water closet, color.	.105	3.95	1.77	5.72
9	Electrical	200 Amp. service; romex wiring; fluorescent and incandescent lighting fixtures, switches, receptacles.	.048	.63	.98	1.61
10	Overhead	Contractor's overhead and profit and design.		4.44	2.62	7.06
	Total			48.85	28.85	77.70

RESIDENTIAL Custom Bi-level

- A distinct residence from designer's plans
- Single family — 1 full bath, 1 kitchen
- No basement
- Asphalt shingles on roof
- Forced hot air heat/air conditioning
- Drywall interior
- Materials and workmanship are above average

BI-LEVEL

BASE COST PER SQUARE FOOT OF LIVING AREA

EXTERIOR WALL	1200	1400	1600	1800	2000	2400	2800	3200	3600	4000	4400
Wood Siding — Wood Frame	71.55	67.85	65.30	62.65	60.00	55.90	52.80	50.10	48.55	47.60	46.30
Brick Veneer — Wood Frame	75.30	71.35	68.60	65.80	63.00	58.65	55.30	52.35	50.70	49.70	48.30
Stone Veneer — Wood Frame	79.45	75.25	72.35	69.35	66.35	61.65	58.05	54.90	53.15	52.05	50.55
Solid Masonry	78.70	74.50	71.65	68.70	65.70	61.10	57.55	54.45	52.70	51.65	50.15
Finished Basement, Add	12.85	12.35	12.05	11.70	11.45	10.95	10.55	10.20	10.00	9.85	9.75
Unfinished Lower Level, Deduct	5.90	5.65	5.50	5.35	5.20	4.90	4.70	4.50	4.40	4.35	4.25

MODIFICATIONS

ALTERNATES	Add to or deduct from costs per S.F. of living area
Cedar shake roof	$+ .30
Clay tile roof	+1.60
Slate roof	+2.15
Central air conditioning	
In heating ducts	+1.25
In separate ducts	+2.35
Heating systems	
Hot water	+2.25
Heat pump	+1.65
Electric heat	−1.00
Not heated	−2.10

BATHROOMS — TOTAL COST (includes plumbing and wall & floor finishes)	
Full bath — 3 fixtures	$3435
Half bath — 2 fixtures	1990

ADJUSTMENTS	
For two or more families (Add to total cost)	
Additional kitchen & entrance	$+6385 Ea.
Separate heating/Air conditioning	+2100 Ea.
Townhouse/Rowhouse (Multiplier for costs per S.F. of living area)	
Inner unit	.89
End unit	.95

	Page
Wings & ells	58
Porches & breezeways	75
Finished attics	75
Appliances	75

	Page
Kitchen cabinets	76
Garages & carports	77
Site improvements	77

Use LOCATION FACTORS on pages 444 to 448

Custom Bi-level

| | | | Living Area | 2800 S.F. |
| | | | Perimeter | 156 L.F. |

			MAN-HOURS	COST PER SQUARE FOOT OF LIVING AREA		
				MAT.	LABOR	TOTAL
1	Site Work	Site preparation for slab; excavation for lower level 4' deep.	.024		.58	.58
2	Foundations	Continuous concrete footing 8" deep x 18" wide; cast-in-place concrete wall, 8" thick, 4' deep; 4" concrete slab on 4" crushed stone base, trowel finish.	.058	1.98	1.88	3.86
3	Framing	2" x 6" wood studs, 16" O.C.; 1/2" plywood sheathing; 2" x 8" rafters 16" O.C. with 1/2" plywood sheathing, 6 in 12 pitch; 2" x 8" ceiling joists 16" O.C.; 2" x 10" floor joists 16" O.C. with bridging and 5/8" plywood subfloor; 5/8" plywood subfloor on 1" x 3" wood sleepers 16" O.C.	.147	3.14	3.23	6.37
4	Exterior Walls	Horizontal beveled wood siding; #15 felt building paper; 6" batt insulation; wood double hung windows; 3 solid core wood exterior doors; storms and screens.	.079	6.75	1.98	8.73
5	Roofing	300# asphalt shingles; #15 felt building paper; copper flashing; 9" attic insulation. Aluminum gutters and downspouts.	.033	.96	.81	1.77
6	Interiors	5/8" drywall, skim coat plaster and finished, painted with primer and 1 coat; hardwood baseboard and trim, sanded and finished; finished hardwood floor 70%, ceramic tile with underlayment 20%, vinyl tile with underlayment 10%; wood panel interior doors.	.257	11.96	7.50	19.46
7	Specialties	Kitchen cabinets - 20 L.F. wall and base cabinets with laminated plastic counter top; 4 L.F. bathroom vanity; medicine cabinet; stairs.	.028	1.67	.38	2.05
8	Mechanical	1 kitchen sink, cast iron, double; 1 water heater, gas fired, 50 gal.; gas warm air heat/air conditioning; 1 full bath including: 1 bathtub, color; 1 corner shower; 1 lavatory, color, built in; 1 water closet, color. 1 half bath including: 1 lavatory, color, built in; 1 water closet, color.	.078	2.48	1.39	3.87
9	Electrical	200 Amp. service; romex wiring; fluorescent and incandescent lighting fixtures, switches, receptacles.	.038	.50	.81	1.31
10	Overhead	Contractor's overhead and profit and design.		2.94	1.86	4.80
		Total		32.38	20.42	52.80

55

RESIDENTIAL — Custom — Tri-level

- A distinct residence from designer's plans
- Single family — 1 full bath, 1 kitchen
- No basement
- Asphalt shingles on roof
- Forced hot air heat/air conditioning
- Drywall interior
- Materials and workmanship are above average

TRI—LEVEL

BASE COST PER SQUARE FOOT OF LIVING AREA

EXTERIOR WALL	1200	1500	1800	2100	2400	2800	3200	3600	4000	4500	5000
Wood Siding — Wood Frame	73.55	67.25	62.40	58.65	55.50	53.35	51.40	48.80	47.15	45.20	43.85
Brick Veneer — Wood Frame	77.20	70.60	65.40	61.40	58.00	55.80	53.70	50.95	49.15	47.10	45.65
Stone Veneer — Wood Frame	81.35	74.35	68.80	64.50	60.85	58.45	56.25	53.35	51.45	49.25	47.65
Solid Masonry	80.60	73.65	68.15	63.95	60.35	57.95	55.80	52.90	51.00	48.85	47.30
Finished Basement, Add*	16.00	15.25	14.55	14.00	13.55	13.25	13.05	12.75	12.50	12.25	12.10
Unfinished Basement, Add*	7.30	6.90	6.55	6.25	6.00	5.85	5.75	5.55	5.45	5.30	5.20

*Basement under middle level only.

MODIFICATIONS

ALTERNATES	Add to or deduct from costs per S.F. of living area
Cedar shake roof	$+ .45
Clay tile roof	+2.30
Slate roof	+3.10
Central air conditioning	
In heating ducts	+1.30
In separate ducts	+2.30
Heating systems	
Hot water	+2.25
Heat pump	+1.65
Electric heat	−1.00
Not heated	−2.30

BATHROOMS — TOTAL COST (includes plumbing and wall & floor finishes)	
Full bath — 3 fixtures	$3435
Half bath — 2 fixtures	1990

ADJUSTMENTS	
For two or more families (Add to total cost)	
Additional kitchen & entrance	$+6385 Ea.
Separate heating/Air conditioning	+2100 Ea.
Townhouse/Rowhouse (Multiplier for costs per S.F. of living area)	
Inner unit	.89
End unit	.91

	Page
Wings & ells	58
Porches & breezeways	75
Finished attics	75
Appliances	75

	Page
Kitchen cabinets	76
Garages & carports	77
Site improvements	77

Use LOCATION FACTORS on pages 444 to 448

Custom Tri-level

| | | Living Area | 3200 S.F. |
| | | Perimeter | 198 L.F. |

			MAN-HOURS	COST PER SQUARE FOOT OF LIVING AREA		
				MAT.	LABOR	TOTAL
1	**Site Work**	Site preparation for slab; excavation for lower level 4' deep; trench 4' deep for foundation wall.	.023		.50	.50
2	**Foundations**	Continuous concrete footing 8" deep x 18" wide; cast-in-place concrete wall, 8" thick, 4' deep; 4" concrete slab on 4" crushed stone base, trowel finish.	.073	2.31	2.19	4.50
3	**Framing**	2" x 6" wood studs, 16" O.C.; 1/2" plywood sheathing; 2" x 8" rafters 16" O.C. with 1/2" plywood sheathing, 6 in 12 pitch; 2" x 8" ceiling joists 16" O.C.; 2" x 10" floor joists 16" O.C. with bridging and 5/8" plywood subfloor; 5/8" plywood subfloor on 1" x 3" wood sleepers 16" O.C.	.162	3.04	3.24	6.28
4	**Exterior Walls**	Horizontal beveled wood siding; #15 felt building paper; 6" batt insulation; wood double hung windows; 3 solid core wood exterior doors; storms and screens.	.076	6.43	1.89	8.32
5	**Roofing**	300# asphalt shingles; #15 felt building paper; copper flashing; 9" attic insulation. Aluminum gutters and downspouts.	.045	1.28	1.07	2.35
6	**Interiors**	5/8" drywall, skim coat plaster and finished, painted with primer and 1 coat; hardwood baseboard and trim, sanded and finished; finished hardwood floor 70%, ceramic tile with underlayment 20%, vinyl tile with underlayment 10%; wood panel interior doors.	.242	11.13	7.00	18.13
7	**Specialties**	Kitchen cabinets - 20 L.F. wall and base cabinets with laminated plastic counter top; 4 L.F. bathroom vanity; medicine cabinet; stairs.	.026	1.47	.32	1.79
8	**Mechanical**	1 kitchen sink, cast iron, double; 1 water heater, gas fired, 50 gal.; gas warm air heat/air conditioning; 1 full bath including: 1 bathtub, color; 1 corner shower; 1 lavatory, color, built in; 1 water closet, color; 1 half bath including: 1 lavatory, color, built in; 1 water closet, color.	.073	2.26	1.33	3.59
9	**Electrical**	200 Amp. service; romex wiring; fluorescent and incandescent lighting fixtures, switches, receptacles.	.036	.48	.79	1.27
10	**Overhead**	Contractor's overhead and profit and design.		2.84	1.83	4.67
		Total		31.24	20.16	51.40

RESIDENTIAL — Custom — Wings & Ells

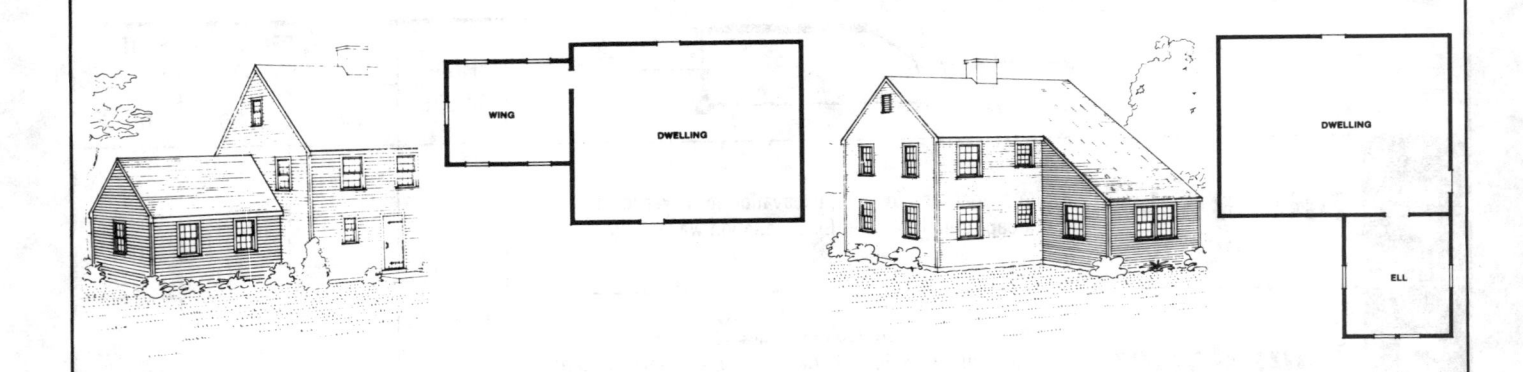

1 STORY — BASE COST PER SQUARE FOOT OF LIVING AREA

EXTERIOR WALL	\multicolumn{8}{c}{LIVING AREA}
	50	100	200	300	400	500	600	700
Wood Siding — Wood Frame	114.65	87.30	75.55	61.80	57.95	55.60	54.05	54.30
Brick Veneer — Wood Frame	127.15	96.25	82.95	66.75	62.40	59.75	58.00	58.10
Stone Veneer — Wood Frame	141.10	106.25	91.30	72.30	67.40	64.40	62.45	62.40
Solid Masonry	138.55	104.40	89.75	71.30	66.45	63.55	61.65	61.60
Finished Basement, Add	39.05	31.70	28.60	23.50	22.45	21.85	21.45	21.15
Unfinished Basement, Add	25.80	18.85	15.80	12.15	11.30	10.80	10.50	10.20

1½ STORY — BASE COST PER SQUARE FOOT OF LIVING AREA

EXTERIOR WALL	\multicolumn{8}{c}{LIVING AREA}
	100	200	300	400	500	600	700	800
Wood Siding — Wood Frame	93.10	73.10	64.75	57.35	54.05	51.90	50.05	49.85
Brick Veneer — Wood Frame	104.25	82.05	72.20	63.15	59.40	57.00	54.80	54.60
Stone Veneer — Wood Frame	116.75	92.00	80.50	69.60	65.40	62.65	60.15	59.90
Solid Masonry	114.45	90.15	78.95	68.45	64.30	61.60	59.20	58.90
Finished Basement, Add	25.95	22.90	20.85	18.60	17.95	17.55	17.20	17.10
Unfinished Basement, Add	15.95	12.85	11.20	9.55	9.05	8.70	8.40	8.35

2 STORY — BASE COST PER SQUARE FOOT OF LIVING AREA

EXTERIOR WALL	\multicolumn{8}{c}{LIVING AREA}
	100	200	400	600	800	1000	1200	1400
Wood Siding — Wood Frame	94.45	70.60	60.25	48.90	45.50	43.45	42.10	42.45
Brick Veneer — Wood Frame	107.00	79.55	67.70	53.85	49.95	47.60	46.10	46.30
Stone Veneer — Wood Frame	120.95	89.50	76.00	59.40	54.95	52.25	50.50	50.60
Solid Masonry	118.35	87.65	74.45	58.40	54.05	51.40	49.70	49.80
Finished Basement, Add	19.55	15.85	14.35	11.75	11.25	10.95	10.75	10.60
Unfinished Basement, Add	12.90	9.45	7.90	6.10	5.65	5.40	5.25	5.10

Base costs do not include bathroom or kitchen facilities. Use MODIFICATIONS on pages 75, 76, 77 where appropriate.

RESIDENTIAL — Luxury Illustrations

59

RESIDENTIAL — Luxury — 1 Story

- Unique residence built from an architect's plan
- Single family — 1 full bath, 1 kitchen
- No basement
- Cedar shakes on roof
- Forced hot air heat/air conditioning
- Double drywall interior
- Many special features
- Extraordinary materials and workmanship

1 STORY

BASE COST PER SQUARE FOOT OF LIVING AREA

EXTERIOR WALL	1000	1200	1400	1600	1800	2000	2400	2800	3200	3600	4000
Wood Siding — Wood Frame	99.00	91.65	86.20	81.55	79.00	77.10	72.00	68.10	65.70	62.40	60.55
Brick Veneer — Wood Frame	103.05	95.30	89.50	84.55	81.90	79.90	74.55	70.45	67.90	64.40	62.45
Solid Brick	109.35	100.95	94.65	89.30	86.40	84.30	78.55	74.10	71.30	67.55	65.45
Solid Stone	111.95	103.35	96.85	91.25	88.30	86.15	80.25	75.60	72.70	68.85	66.70
Finished Basement, Add	26.10	25.05	24.20	23.50	23.10	22.90	22.25	21.60	21.20	20.75	20.45
Unfinished Basement, Add	13.05	12.35	11.80	11.30	11.05	10.90	10.45	10.00	9.75	9.45	9.25

MODIFICATIONS

ALTERNATES	Add to or deduct from costs per S.F. of living area
Heavy weight asphalt shingles	$- .60
Clay tile roof	+2.60
Slate roof	+3.65
Central air conditioning	
In heating ducts	+1.55
In separate ducts	+3.45
Heating systems	
Hot water	+2.30
Heat pump	+1.70
Electric heat	-1.40
Not heated	-2.30

BATHROOMS — TOTAL COST (includes plumbing and wall & floor finishes)	
Full bath — 3 fixtures	$3985
Half bath — 2 fixtures	2310

ADJUSTMENTS	
For two or more families (Add to total cost)	
Additional kitchen & entrance	$+8615 Ea.
Separate heating/Air conditioning	+2255 Ea.
Townhouse/Rowhouse (Multiplier for costs per S.F. of living area)	
Inner unit	.89
End unit	.95

	Page		Page
Wings & ells	74	Kitchen cabinets	76
Porches & breezeways	75	Garages & carports	77
Finished attics	75	Site improvements	77
Appliances	75		

Use LOCATION FACTORS on pages 444 to 448

Luxury 1 Story

	Living Area	2800 S.F.
	Perimeter	219 L.F.

			MAN-HOURS	COST PER SQUARE FOOT OF LIVING AREA		
				MAT.	LABOR	TOTAL
1	Site Work	Site preparation for slab; trench 4' deep for foundation wall.	.028		.62	.62
2	Foundations	Continuous concrete footing 8" deep x 18" wide; cast-in-place concrete wall, 12" thick, 4' deep; vapor barrier; 4" concrete slab on 4" crushed stone base, trowel finish.	.098	3.75	3.22	6.97
3	Framing	2" x 6" wood studs, 16" O.C.; 5/8" plywood sheathing; 2" x 10" rafters 16" O.C. with 5/8" plywood sheathing, 6 in 12 pitch; 2" x 10" ceiling joists 16" O.C.; 5/8" plywood subfloor on 1" x 3" wood sleepers 16" O.C.	.260	7.05	6.54	13.59
4	Exterior Walls	Face brick veneer; #15 felt building paper; 6" batt insulation; wood double hung windows; 3 solid core wood exterior doors; storms and screens.	.204	6.24	2.29	8.53
5	Roofing	Wood cedar shingles; #15 felt building paper; copper flashing; 9" attic insulation. Aluminum gutters and downspouts.	.082	2.24	1.87	4.11
6	Interiors	5/8" drywall, thin coat plaster, painted with primer and 2 coats; hardwood baseboard and trim, sanded and finished; finished hardwood floor 70%, ceramic tile with underlayment 20%, vinyl tile with underlayment 10%; wood panel interior doors.	.287	9.46	7.39	16.85
7	Specialties	Kitchen cabinets - 25 L.F. wall and base cabinets with laminated plastic counter top; 6 L.F. bathroom vanity; medicine cabinet.	.052	2.17	.45	2.62
8	Mechanical	1 kitchen sink, cast iron, double; 1 water heater, gas fired, 75 gal.; gas warm air heat/air conditioning; 1 full bath including: 1 bathtub, color; 1 corner shower; 1 lavatory, color, built in; 1 water closet, color; 1 half bath including: 1 lavatory, color, built in; 1 water closet, color.	.078	2.85	1.52	4.37
9	Electrical	200 Amp. service; romex wiring; fluorescent and incandescent lighting fixtures; intercom, switches, receptacles.	.044	.60	.96	1.56
10	Overhead	Contractor's overhead and profit and architect's fees.		5.15	3.73	8.88
		Total		39.51	28.59	68.10

RESIDENTIAL — Luxury — 1½ Story

- Unique residence built from an architect's plan
- Single family — 1 full bath, 1 kitchen
- No basement
- Cedar shakes on roof
- Forced hot air heat/air conditioning
- Double drywall interior
- Many special features
- Extraordinary materials and workmanship

1½ STORY

BASE COST PER SQUARE FOOT OF LIVING AREA

EXTERIOR WALL	1000	1200	1400	1600	1800	2000	2400	2800	3200	3600	4000
Wood Siding — Wood Frame	92.85	86.00	81.50	77.40	74.50	71.25	64.85	62.50	60.40	58.40	55.35
Brick Veneer — Wood Frame	97.50	90.15	85.45	81.15	78.05	74.65	67.75	65.25	63.05	60.95	57.65
Solid Brick	104.80	96.70	91.55	87.05	83.65	79.95	72.30	69.65	67.15	64.95	61.30
Solid Stone	107.80	99.40	94.15	89.55	86.00	82.15	74.20	71.45	68.85	66.60	62.85
Finished Basement, Add	17.85	17.05	16.60	16.30	15.95	15.65	14.75	14.60	14.30	14.15	13.75
Unfinished Basement, Add	9.25	8.65	8.35	8.15	7.95	7.70	7.10	7.00	6.80	6.70	6.45

MODIFICATIONS

ALTERNATES	Add to or deduct from costs per S.F. of living area
Heavy weight asphalt shingles	$- .45
Clay tile roof	+1.85
Slate roof	+2.65
Central air conditioning	
In heating ducts	1.40
In separate ducts	+3.65
Heating systems	
Hot water	+2.25
Heat pump	+1.70
Electric heat	-1.10
Not heated	-2.35

BATHROOMS — TOTAL COST (includes plumbing and wall & floor finishes)	
Full bath — 3 fixtures	$3985
Half bath — 2 fixtures	2310

ADJUSTMENTS	
For two or more families (Add to total cost)	
Additional kitchen & entrance	$+8615 Ea.
Separate heating/Air conditioning	+2255 Ea.
Townhouse/Rowhouse (Multiplier for costs per S.F. of living area)	
Inner unit	.90
End unit	.95

	Page		Page
Wings & ells	74	Kitchen cabinets	76
Porches & breezeways	75	Garages & carports	77
Finished attics	75	Site improvements	77
Appliances	75		

Use LOCATION FACTORS on pages 444 to 448

Luxury 1½ Story

	Living Area	2800 S.F.
	Perimeter	175 L.F.

			MAN-HOURS	COST PER SQUARE FOOT OF LIVING AREA		
				MAT.	LABOR	TOTAL
1	Site Work	Site preparation for slab; trench 4' deep for foundation wall.	.025		.62	.62
2	Foundations	Continuous concrete footing 8" deep x 18" wide; cast-in-place concrete wall, 12" thick, 4' deep; vapor barrier; 4" concrete slab on 4" crushed stone base, trowel finish.	.066	2.74	2.39	5.13
3	Framing	2" x 6" wood studs, 16" O.C.; 5/8" plywood sheathing; 2" x 10" rafters 16" O.C. with 5/8" plywood sheathing, 8 in 12 pitch; 2" x 10" ceiling joists 16" O.C.; 2" x 12" floor joists 16" O.C. with bridging and 5/8" plywood subfloor; 5/8" plywood subfloor on 1" x 3" wood sleepers 16" O.C.	.189	4.36	4.26	8.62
4	Exterior Walls	Face brick veneer; #15 felt building paper; 6" batt insulation; wood double hung windows; 3 solid core wood exterior doors; storms and screens.	.174	7.26	2.69	9.95
5	Roofing	Wood cedar shingles; #15 felt building paper; copper flashing; 9" attic insulation. Aluminum gutters and downspouts.	.065	1.40	1.17	2.57
6	Interiors	5/8" drywall, thin coat plaster, painted with primer and 2 coats; hardwood baseboard and trim, sanded and finished; finished hardwood floor 70%, ceramic tile with underlayment 20%, vinyl tile with underlayment 10%; wood panel interior doors.	.260	10.56	8.34	18.90
7	Specialties	Kitchen cabinets - 25 L.F. wall and base cabinets with laminated plastic counter top; 6 L.F. bathroom vanity; medicine cabinet; stairs.	.062	2.16	.46	2.62
8	Mechanical	1 kitchen sink, cast iron, double; 1 water heater, gas fired, 75 gal.; gas warm air heat/air conditioning; 1 full bath including: 1 bathtub, color; 1 corner shower; 1 lavatory, color, built in; 1 water closet, color; 1 half bath including: 1 lavatory, color, built in; 1 water closet, color.	.080	2.85	1.53	4.38
9	Electrical	200 Amp. service; romex wiring; fluorescent and incandescent lighting fixtures; intercom, switches, receptacles.	.044	.60	.96	1.56
10	Overhead	Contractor's overhead and profit and architect's fees.		4.79	3.36	8.15
		Total		36.72	25.78	62.50

RESIDENTIAL — Luxury — 2 Story

- Unique residence built from an architect's plan
- Single family — 1 full bath, 1 kitchen
- No basement
- Cedar shakes on roof
- Forced hot air heat/air conditioning
- Double drywall interior
- Many special features
- Extraordinary materials and workmanship

2 STORY

BASE COST PER SQUARE FOOT OF LIVING AREA

EXTERIOR WALL	1200	1400	1600	1800	2000	2400	2800	3200	3600	4000	4400
Wood Siding — Wood Frame	87.65	83.00	79.70	76.40	73.05	67.95	64.05	60.60	58.65	57.45	55.80
Brick Veneer — Wood Frame	92.65	87.60	84.10	80.60	77.10	71.60	67.35	63.65	61.55	60.30	58.50
Solid Brick	100.40	94.90	91.05	87.20	83.35	77.25	72.50	68.40	66.05	64.70	62.75
Solid Stone	103.65	97.90	93.95	89.95	86.00	79.65	74.70	70.35	67.95	66.55	64.55
Finished Basement, Add	14.35	13.90	13.65	13.35	13.10	12.55	12.15	11.75	11.60	11.45	11.35
Unfinished Basement, Add	7.40	7.10	6.90	6.70	6.55	6.20	5.90	5.65	5.50	5.45	5.35

MODIFICATIONS

ALTERNATES	Add to or deduct from costs per S.F. of living area
Heavy weight asphalt shingles	$ – .30
Clay tile roof	+1.30
Slate roof	+1.85
Central air conditioning	
In heating ducts	+1.15
In separate ducts	+2.95
Heating systems	
Hot water	+2.20
Heat pump	+1.75
Electric heat	–1.20
Not heated	–2.30

BATHROOMS — TOTAL COST (includes plumbing and wall & floor finishes)	
Full bath — 3 fixtures	$3985
Half bath — 2 fixtures	2310

ADJUSTMENTS	
For two or more families (Add to total cost)	
Additional kitchen & entrance	$+8615 Ea.
Separate heating/Air conditioning	+2255 Ea.
Townhouse/Rowhouse (Multiplier for costs per S.F. of living area)	
Inner unit	.86
End unit	.93

	Page		Page
Wings & ells	74	Kitchen cabinets	76
Porches & breezeways	75	Garages & carports	77
Finished attics	75	Site improvements	77
Appliances	75		

Use LOCATION FACTORS on pages 444 to 448

Luxury 2 Story

	Living Area	3200 S.F.
	Perimeter	163 L.F.

	MAN-HOURS	COST PER SQUARE FOOT OF LIVING AREA		
		MAT.	LABOR	TOTAL
1 Site Work — Site preparation for slab; trench 4' deep for foundation wall.	.024		.54	.54
2 Foundations — Continuous concrete footing 8" deep x 18" wide; cast-in-place concrete wall, 12" thick, 4' deep; vapor barrier; 4" concrete slab on 4" crushed stone base, trowel finish.	.058	2.23	1.93	4.16
3 Framing — 2" x 6" wood studs, 16" O.C.; 5/8" plywood sheathing; 2" x 10" rafters 16" O.C. with 5/8" plywood sheathing, 6 in 12 pitch; 2" x 8" ceiling joists 16" O.C.; 2" x 12" floor joists 16" O.C. with bridging and 5/8" plywood subfloor; 5/8" plywood subfloor on 1" x 3" wood sleepers 16" O.C.	.193	4.39	4.19	8.58
4 Exterior Walls — Face brick veneer; #15 felt building paper; 6" batt insulation; wood double hung windows; 3 solid core wood exterior doors; storms and screens.	.247	7.41	2.82	10.23
5 Roofing — Wood cedar shingles; #15 felt building paper; copper flashing; 9" attic insulation. Aluminum gutters and downspouts.	.049	1.12	.94	2.06
6 Interiors — 5/8" drywall, thin coat plaster, painted with primer and 2 coats; hardwood baseboard and trim, sanded and finished; finished hardwood floor 70%, ceramic tile with underlayment 20%, vinyl tile with underlayment 10%; wood panel interior doors.	.252	10.79	8.49	19.28
7 Specialties — Kitchen cabinets - 25 L.F. wall and base cabinets with laminated plastic counter top; 6 L.F. bathroom vanity; medicine cabinet; stairs.	.057	1.90	.38	2.28
8 Mechanical — 1 kitchen sink, cast iron, double; 1 water heater, gas fired, 75 gal.; gas warm air heat/air conditioning; 1 full bath including: 1 bathtub, color; 1 corner shower; 1 lavatory, color, built in; 1 water closet, color; 1 half bath including: 1 lavatory, color, built in; 1 water closet, color.	.071	2.59	1.47	4.06
9 Electrical — 200 Amp. service; romex wiring; fluorescent and incandescent lighting fixtures; intercom, switches, receptacles.	.042	.58	.93	1.51
10 Overhead — Contractor's overhead and profit and architect's fee.		4.65	3.25	7.90
Total		35.66	24.94	60.60

RESIDENTIAL — Luxury — 2½ Story

- Unique residence built from an architect's plan
- Single family — 1 full bath, 1 kitchen
- No basement
- Cedar shakes on roof
- Forced hot air heat/air conditioning
- Double drywall interior
- Many special features
- Extraordinary materials and workmanship

2½ STORY

BASE COST PER SQUARE FOOT OF LIVING AREA

EXTERIOR WALL	1500	1800	2100	2500	3000	3500	4000	4500	5000	5500	6000
Wood Siding — Wood Frame	81.45	77.05	74.00	68.30	65.40	61.50	57.25	55.45	53.95	52.75	51.10
Brick Veneer — Wood Frame	86.25	81.50	78.25	72.15	69.10	64.85	60.20	58.35	56.65	55.40	53.65
Solid Brick	93.70	88.50	85.00	78.20	74.85	70.05	64.85	62.85	60.85	59.55	57.60
Solid Stone	96.80	91.40	87.80	80.75	77.25	72.25	66.80	64.70	62.60	61.30	59.25
Finished Basement, Add	11.00	10.70	10.50	10.05	9.85	9.50	9.10	9.00	8.80	8.75	8.60
Unfinished Basement, Add	5.70	5.50	5.35	5.05	4.90	4.65	4.40	4.30	4.20	4.15	4.05

MODIFICATIONS

ALTERNATES	Add to or deduct from costs per S.F. of living area
Heavy weight asphalt shingles	$+ .25
Clay tile roof	+1.10
Slate roof	+1.60
Central air conditioning	
In heating ducts	+1.05
In separate ducts	+2.75
Heating systems	
Hot water	+1.65
Heat pump	+1.75
Electric heat	-1.00
Not heated	-2.30

BATHROOMS — TOTAL COST (includes plumbing and wall & floor finishes)	
Full bath — 3 fixtures	$3985
Half bath — 2 fixtures	2310

ADJUSTMENTS	
For two or more families (Add to total cost)	
Additional kitchen & entrance	$+8615 Ea.
Separate heating/Air conditioning	+2255 Ea.
Townhouse/Rowhouse (Multiplier for costs per S.F. of living area)	
Inner unit	.84
End unit	.92

	Page		Page
Wings & ells	74	Kitchen cabinets	76
Porches & breezeways	75	Garages & carports	77
Finished attics	75	Site improvements	77
Appliances	75		

Use LOCATION FACTORS on pages 444 to 448

Luxury 2½ Story

	Living Area	1500 S.F.
	Perimeter	96 L.F.

	MAN-HOURS	COST PER SQUARE FOOT OF LIVING AREA		
		MAT.	LABOR	TOTAL
1 Site Work — Site preparation for slab; trench 4' deep for foundation wall.	.055		1.15	1.15
2 Foundations — Continuous concrete footing 8" deep x 18" wide; cast-in-place concrete wall, 12" thick, 4' deep; vapor barrier; 4" concrete slab on 4" crushed stone base, trowel finish.	.067	2.42	2.17	4.59
3 Framing — 2" x 6" wood studs, 16" O.C.; 5/8" plywood sheathing; 2" x 10" rafters 16" O.C. with 5/8" plywood sheathing, 6 in 12 pitch; 2" x 8" ceiling joists 16" O.C.; 2" x 12" floor joists 16" O.C. with bridging and 5/8" plywood subfloor; 5/8" plywood subfloor on 1" x 3" wood sleepers 16" O.C.	.209	5.00	4.73	9.73
4 Exterior Walls — Face brick veneer; #15 felt building paper; 6" batt insulation; wood double hung windows; 3 solid core wood exterior doors; storms and screens.	.405	11.55	4.35	15.90
5 Roofing — Wood cedar shingles; #15 felt building paper; copper flashing; 9" attic insulation. Aluminum gutters and downspouts.	.039	.86	.72	1.58
6 Interiors — 5/8" drywall, thin coat plaster, painted with primer and 2 coats; hardwood baseboard and trim, sanded and finished; finished hardwood floor 70%, ceramic tile with underlayment 20%, vinyl tile with underlayment 10%; wood panel interior doors.	.341	13.58	10.98	24.56
7 Specialties — Kitchen cabinets - 25 L.F. wall and base cabinets with laminated plastic counter top; 6 L.F. bathroom vanity; medicine cabinet; stairs.	.119	4.04	.83	4.87
8 Mechanical — 1 kitchen sink, cast iron, double; 1 water heater, gas fired, 75 gal.; gas warm air heat/air conditioning; 1 full bath including: 1 bathtub, color; 1 corner shower; 1 lavatory, color, built in; 1 water closet, color; 1 half bath including: 1 lavatory, color, built in; 1 water closet, color.	.103	4.58	1.99	6.57
9 Electrical — 200 Amp. service; romex wiring; fluorescent and incandescent lighting fixtures; intercom, switches, receptacles.	.054	.73	1.15	1.88
10 Overhead — Contractor's overhead and profit and architect's fee.		6.41	4.21	10.62
Total		49.17	32.28	81.45

RESIDENTIAL — Luxury — 3 Story

- Unique residence built from an architect's plan
- Single family — 1 full bath, 1 kitchen
- No basement
- Cedar shakes on roof
- Forced hot air heat/air conditioning
- Double drywall interior
- Many special features
- Extraordinary materials and workmanship

3 STORY

BASE COST PER SQUARE FOOT OF LIVING AREA

EXTERIOR WALL	1500	1800	2100	2500	3000	3500	4000	4500	5000	5500	6000
Wood Siding — Wood Frame	87.65	78.45	74.65	71.60	66.20	63.90	60.15	56.10	55.20	53.55	52.75
Brick Veneer — Wood Frame	93.05	83.40	79.30	76.00	70.25	67.75	63.60	59.20	58.25	56.45	55.55
Solid Brick	101.55	91.20	86.60	82.95	76.50	73.70	69.05	64.05	63.00	61.00	59.95
Solid Stone	105.10	94.40	89.60	85.85	79.15	76.20	71.30	66.10	65.00	62.85	61.80
Finished Basement, Add	9.95	9.55	9.25	9.05	8.70	8.55	8.20	7.90	7.85	7.70	7.65
Unfinished Basement, Add	5.25	4.95	4.75	4.60	4.35	4.25	4.00	3.80	3.75	3.70	3.65

MODIFICATIONS

ALTERNATES	Add to or deduct from costs per S.F. of living area
Heavy weight asphalt shingles	$− .20
Clay tile roof	+ .85
Slate roof	+1.20
Central air conditioning	
In heating ducts	+1.05
In separate ducts	+2.80
Heating systems	
Hot water	+1.70
Heat pump	+1.70
Electric heat	−1.20
Not heated	−2.25

BATHROOMS — TOTAL COST (includes plumbing and wall & floor finishes)	
Full bath — 3 fixtures	$3985
Half bath — 2 fixtures	2310

ADJUSTMENTS	
For two or more families (Add to total cost)	
Additional kitchen & entrance	$+8615 Ea.
Separate heating	+2255 Ea.
Townhouse/Rowhouse (Multiplier for costs per S.F. of living area)	
Inner unit	.84
End unit	.92

	Page		Page
Wings & ells	74	Kitchen cabinets	76
Porches & breezeways	75	Garages & carports	77
Finished attics	75	Site improvements	77
Appliances	75		

Use LOCATION FACTORS on pages 444 to 448

Luxury 3 Story

	Living Area	1500 S.F.
	Perimeter	91 L.F.

			MAN-HOURS	COST PER SQUARE FOOT OF LIVING AREA		
				MAT.	LABOR	TOTAL
1	**Site Work**	Site preparation for slab; trench 4' deep for foundation wall.	.055		1.15	1.15
2	**Foundations**	Continuous concrete footing 8" deep x 18" wide; cast-in-place concrete wall, 12" thick, 4' deep; vapor barrier; 4" concrete slab on 4" crushed stone base, trowel finish.	.063	2.24	2.03	4.27
3	**Framing**	2" x 6" wood studs, 16" O.C.; 5/8" plywood sheathing; 2" x 10" rafters 16" O.C. with 5/8" plywood sheathing, 6 in 12 pitch; 2" x 8" ceiling joists 16" O.C.; 2" x 12" floor joists 16" O.C. with bridging and 5/8" plywood subfloor; 5/8" plywood subfloor on 1" x 3" wood sleepers 16" O.C.	.225	5.29	5.03	10.32
4	**Exterior Walls**	Face brick veneer; #15 felt building paper; 6" batt insulation; wood double hung windows; 3 solid core wood exterior doors; storms and screens.	.454	13.03	4.93	17.96
5	**Roofing**	Wood cedar shingles; #15 felt building paper; copper flashing; 9" attic insulation. Aluminum gutters and downspouts.	.034	.75	.63	1.38
6	**Interiors**	5/8" drywall, thin coat plaster, painted with primer and 2 coats; hardwood baseboard and trim, sanded and finished; finished hardwood floor 70%, ceramic tile with underlayment 20%, vinyl tile with underlayment 10%; wood panel interior doors.	.390	15.37	12.45	27.82
7	**Specialties**	Kitchen cabinets - 25 L.F. wall and base cabinets with laminated plastic counter top; 6 L.F. bathroom vanity; medicine cabinet; stairs.	.119	4.04	.83	4.87
8	**Mechanical**	1 kitchen sink, cast iron, double; 1 water heater, gas fired, 75 gal.; gas warm air heat/air conditioning; 1 full bath including: 1 bathtub, color; 1 corner shower; 1 lavatory, color, built in; 1 water closet, color; 1 half bath including: 1 lavatory, color, built in; 1 water closet, color.	.103	4.58	1.99	6.57
9	**Electrical**	200 Amp. service; romex wiring; fluorescent and incandescent lighting fixtures; intercom, switches, receptacles.	.053	.73	1.15	1.88
10	**Overhead**	Contractor's overhead and profit and architect's fees.		6.90	4.53	11.43
		Total		52.93	34.72	87.65

RESIDENTIAL — Luxury Bi-level

- Unique residence built from an architect's plan
- Single family — 1 full bath, 1 kitchen
- No basement
- Cedar shakes on roof
- Forced hot air heat/air conditioning
- Double drywall interior
- Many special features
- Extraordinary materials and workmanship

BI-LEVEL

BASE COST PER SQUARE FOOT OF LIVING AREA

EXTERIOR WALL	1200	1400	1600	1800	2000	2400	2800	3200	3600	4000	4400
Wood Siding — Wood Frame	82.00	77.70	74.60	71.55	68.45	63.80	60.20	57.10	55.30	54.20	52.70
Brick Veneer — Wood Frame	85.70	81.15	77.95	74.65	71.45	66.50	62.65	59.40	57.50	56.35	54.75
Solid Brick	91.55	86.60	83.15	79.65	76.20	70.75	66.55	62.95	60.90	59.65	57.90
Solid Stone	93.95	88.85	85.30	81.70	78.15	72.50	68.15	64.45	62.30	61.00	59.25
Finished Basement, Add	14.35	13.90	13.65	13.35	13.10	12.55	12.15	11.75	11.60	11.45	11.35
Unfinished Lower Level, Deduct	7.40	7.10	6.90	6.70	6.55	6.20	5.90	5.65	5.50	5.45	5.35

MODIFICATIONS

ALTERNATES	Add to or deduct from costs per S.F. of living area
Heavy weight asphalt shingles	$– .30
Clay tile roof	+1.30
Slate roof	+1.85
Central air conditioning	
In heating ducts	+1.20
In separate ducts	+2.90
Heating systems	
Hot water	+2.20
Heat pump	+1.65
Electric heat	–1.20
Not heated	–2.25

BATHROOMS — TOTAL COST (includes plumbing and wall & floor finishes)	
Full bath — 3 fixtures	$3985
Half bath — 2 fixtures	2310

ADJUSTMENTS	
For two or more families (Add to total cost)	
Additional kitchen & entrance	$+8615 Ea.
Separate heating/Air conditioning	+2255 Ea.
Townhouse/Rowhouse (Multiplier for costs per S.F. of living area)	
Inner unit	.89
End unit	.94

	Page
Wings & ells	74
Porches & breezeways	75
Finished attics	75
Appliances	75

	Page
Kitchen cabinets	76
Garages & carports	77
Site improvements	77

Use LOCATION FACTORS on pages 444 to 448

Luxury Bi-level

| | | Living Area | 3200 S.F. |
| | | Perimeter | 163 L.F. |

		MAN-HOURS	COST PER SQUARE FOOT OF LIVING AREA		
			MAT.	LABOR	TOTAL
1	**Site Work** — Site preparation for slab; excavation for lower level 4' deep.	.024		.54	.54
2	**Foundations** — Continuous concrete footing 8" deep x 18" wide; cast-in-place concrete wall, 12" thick, 4' deep; vapor barrier; 4" concrete slab on 4" crushed stone base, trowel finish.	.058	2.23	1.93	4.16
3	**Framing** — 2" x 6" wood studs, 16" O.C.; 5/8" plywood sheathing; 2" x 10" rafters 16" O.C. with 5/8" plywood sheathing, 6 in 12 pitch; 2" x 8" ceiling joists 16" O.C.; 2" x 12" floor joists 16" O.C. with bridging and 5/8" plywood subfloor; 5/8" plywood subfloor on 1" x 3" wood sleepers 16" O.C.	.232	4.14	4.01	8.15
4	**Exterior Walls** — Face brick veneer, #15 felt building paper; 6" batt insulation; wood double hung windows; 3 solid core wood exterior doors; storms and screens.	.185	5.73	2.16	7.89
5	**Roofing** — Wood cedar shingles; #15 felt building paper; copper flashing; 9" attic insulation. Aluminum gutters and downspouts.	.042	1.12	.94	2.06
6	**Interiors** — 5/8" drywall, thin coat plaster, painted with primer and 2 coats; hardwood baseboard and trim, sanded and finished; finished hardwood floor 70%, ceramic tile with underlayment 20%; vinyl tile with underlayment 10%; wood panel interior doors.	.238	10.68	8.32	19.00
7	**Specialties** — Kitchen cabinets - 25 L.F. wall and base cabinets with laminated plastic counter top; 6 L.F. bathroom vanity; medicine cabinet; stairs.	.056	1.90	.38	2.28
8	**Mechanical** — 1 kitchen sink, cast iron, double; 1 water heater, gas fired, 75 gal.; gas warm air heat/air conditioning; 1 full bath including: 1 bathtub, color; 1 corner shower; 1 lavatory, color, built in; 1 water closet, color; 1 half bath including: 1 lavatory, color, built in; 1 water closet, color.	.071	2.59	1.47	4.06
9	**Electrical** — 200 Amp. service; romex wiring; fluorescent and incandescent lighting fixtures; intercom, switches, receptacles.	.042	.58	.93	1.51
10	**Overhead** — Contractor's overhead and profit and architect's fees.		4.35	3.10	7.45
	Total		33.32	23.78	57.10

RESIDENTIAL — Luxury Tri-level

- Unique residence built from an architect's plan
- Single family — 1 full bath, 1 kitchen
- No basement
- Cedar shakes on roof
- Forced hot air heat/air conditioning
- Double drywall interior
- Many special features
- Extraordinary materials and workmanship

TRI-LEVEL

BASE COST PER SQUARE FOOT OF LIVING AREA

EXTERIOR WALL	1500	1800	2100	2400	2800	3200	3600	4000	4500	5000	5500
Wood Siding — Wood Frame	77.30	71.70	67.40	63.80	61.30	59.00	56.05	54.15	51.95	50.45	48.25
Brick Veneer — Wood Frame	80.65	74.70	70.15	66.35	63.70	61.30	58.20	56.20	53.85	52.25	49.95
Solid Brick	85.90	79.45	74.50	70.30	67.45	64.90	61.55	59.35	56.85	55.05	52.55
Solid Stone	88.10	81.40	76.30	71.95	69.05	66.40	62.95	60.65	58.10	56.25	53.65
Finished Basement, Add*	17.40	16.65	16.15	15.65	15.35	15.15	14.80	14.55	14.30	14.10	13.85
Unfinished Basement, Add*	8.70	8.25	7.85	7.55	7.35	7.20	6.95	6.80	6.65	6.50	6.30

*Basement under middle level only.

MODIFICATIONS

ALTERNATES	Add to or deduct from costs per S.F. of living area
Heavy weight asphalt shingles	$– .45
Clay tile roof	+1.85
Slate roof	+2.65
Central air conditioning	
In heating ducts	+1.05
In separate ducts	+2.80
Heating systems	
Hot water	+2.25
Heat pump	+1.65
Electric heat	–1.20
Not heated	–2.25

BATHROOMS — TOTAL COST (includes plumbing and wall & floor finishes)	
Full bath — 3 fixtures	$3985
Half bath — 2 fixtures	2310

ADJUSTMENTS	
For two or more families (Add to total cost)	
Additional kitchen & entrance	$+8615 Ea.
Separate heating/Air conditioning	+2255 Ea.
Townhouse/Rowhouse (Multiplier for costs per S.F. of living area)	
Inner unit	.89
End unit	.91

	Page
Wings & ells	74
Porches & breezeways	75
Finished attics	75
Appliances	75

	Page
Kitchen cabinets	76
Garages & carports	77
Site improvements	77

Use LOCATION FACTORS on pages 444 to 448

Luxury Tri-level

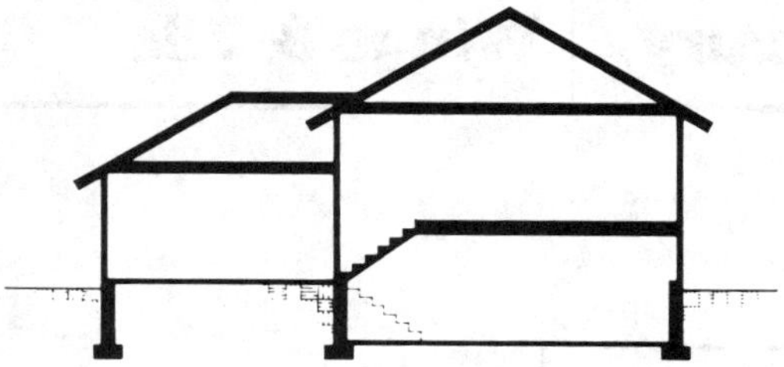

Living Area	3600 S.F.
Perimeter	207 L.F.

			MAN-HOURS	COST PER SQUARE FOOT OF LIVING AREA		
				MAT.	LABOR	TOTAL
1	**Site Work**	Site preparation for slab; excavation for lower level 4′ deep; trench 4′ deep for foundation wall.	.021		.47	.47
2	**Foundations**	Continuous concrete footing 8″ deep x 18″ wide; cast-in-place concrete wall, 12″ thick, 4′ deep; vapor barrier; 4″ concrete slab on 4″ crushed stone base, trowel finish.	.109	2.66	2.29	4.95
3	**Framing**	2″ x 6″ wood studs, 16″ O.C.; 5/8″ plywood sheathing; 2″ x 10″ rafters 16″ O.C. with 5/8″ plywood sheathing, 6 in 12 pitch; 2″ x 8″ ceiling joists 16″ O.C.; 2″ x 12″ floor joists 16″ O.C. with bridging and 5/8″ plywood subfloor; 5/8″ plywood subfloor on 1″ x 3″ wood sleepers 16″ O.C.	.204	4.13	4.04	8.17
4	**Exterior Walls**	Face brick veneer; #15 felt building paper; 6″ batt insulation; wood double hung windows; 3 solid core wood exterior doors; storms and screens.	.181	5.57	2.07	.64
5	**Roofing**	Wood cedar shingles; #15 felt building paper; copper flashing; 9″ attic insulation. Aluminum gutters and downspouts.	.056	1.50	1.25	2.75
6	**Interiors**	5/8″ drywall, thin coat plaster, painted with primer and 2 coats; hardwood baseboard and trim, sanded and finished; finished hardwood floor 70%, ceramic tile with underlayment 20%, vinyl tile with underlayment 10%; wood panel interior doors.	.217	9.78	7.66	17.44
7	**Specialties**	Kitchen cabinets - 25 L.F. wall and base cabinets with laminated plastic counter top; 6 L.F. bathroom vanity; medicine cabinet; stairs.	.048	1.68	.35	2.03
8	**Mechanical**	1 kitchen sink, cast iron, double; 1 water heater, gas fired, 75 gal.; gas warm air heat/air conditioning; 1 full bath including: 1 bathtub, color; 1 corner shower; 1 lavatory, color, built in; 1 water closet, color; 1 half bath including: 1 lavatory, color, built in; 1 water closet, color.	.057	2.38	1.43	3.81
9	**Electrical**	200 Amp. service; romex wiring; fluorescent and incandescent lighting fixtures; intercom, switches, receptacles.	.039	.57	.91	1.48
10	**Overhead**	Contractor's overhead and profit and architect's fee.		4.24	3.07	7.31
			Total	32.51	23.54	56.05

RESIDENTIAL — Luxury — Wings & Ells

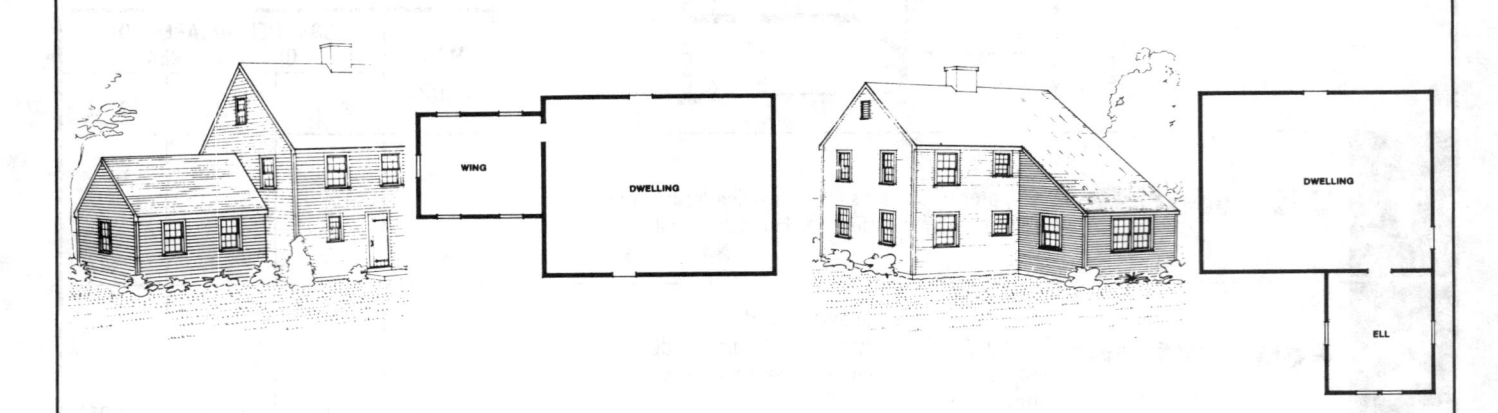

1 STORY — BASE COST PER SQUARE FOOT OF LIVING AREA

EXTERIOR WALL	50	100	200	300	400	500	600	700
Wood Siding — Wood Frame	129.35	99.45	86.55	71.70	67.50	64.95	63.25	63.55
Brick Veneer — Wood Frame	141.85	108.40	94.00	76.65	71.95	69.10	67.20	67.40
Solid Brick	161.45	122.40	105.70	84.45	79.00	75.65	73.45	73.40
Solid Stone	169.55	128.20	110.55	87.70	81.85	78.35	76.00	75.90
Finished Basement, Add	48.65	39.15	35.20	28.60	27.25	26.45	25.95	25.60
Unfinished Basement, Add	27.25	21.15	18.65	14.40	13.55	13.05	12.70	12.50

1½ STORY — BASE COST PER SQUARE FOOT OF LIVING AREA

EXTERIOR WALL	100	200	300	400	500	600	700	800
Wood Siding — Wood Frame	104.35	82.40	73.35	65.45	61.85	59.55	57.50	57.30
Brick Veneer — Wood Frame	115.50	91.30	80.80	71.25	67.20	64.60	62.30	62.00
Solid Brick	133.00	105.30	92.50	80.35	75.65	72.55	69.80	69.45
Solid Stone	140.30	111.10	97.35	84.15	79.10	75.85	72.90	72.55
Finished Basement, Add	32.10	28.15	25.50	22.60	21.85	21.30	20.80	20.75
Unfinished Basement, Add	17.45	14.90	13.20	11.35	10.85	10.50	10.20	10.15

2 STORY — BASE COST PER SQUARE FOOT OF LIVING AREA

EXTERIOR WALL	100	200	400	600	800	1000	1200	1400
Wood Siding — Wood Frame	104.70	78.75	67.45	55.30	51.65	49.40	47.95	48.40
Brick Veneer — Wood Frame	117.20	87.65	74.90	60.25	56.10	53.55	51.90	52.20
Solid Brick	136.80	101.65	86.55	68.05	63.10	60.10	58.10	58.20
Solid Stone	144.95	107.45	91.40	71.30	66.00	62.80	60.70	60.70
Finished Basement, Add	24.40	19.60	17.65	14.35	13.70	13.30	13.05	12.80
Unfinished Basement, Add	13.60	10.60	9.30	7.20	6.80	6.55	6.35	6.25

Base costs do not include bathroom or kitchen facilities. Use MODIFICATIONS on pages 75, 76, 77 where appropriate.

RESIDENTIAL | Adjustments | Modifications

BREEZEWAY (Cost per S.F.)

CLASS	TYPE	\multicolumn{4}{c}{AREA (S.F.)}
		50	100	150	200
Economy	Open	$11.70	$10.00	$ 8.35	$ 8.20
	Enclosed	56.40	43.55	36.20	31.70
Average	Open	14.80	13.05	11.40	10.40
	Enclosed	62.90	46.80	38.30	33.75
Custom	Open	20.20	17.80	15.55	14.20
	Enclosed	83.15	61.85	50.55	44.50
Luxury	Open	22.35	19.70	17.80	17.10
	Enclosed	90.25	66.90	54.20	48.45

PORCHES (Cost per S.F.)

CLASS	TYPE	\multicolumn{5}{c}{AREA (S.F.)}
		25	50	100	200	300
Economy	Open	$34.70	$23.30	$18.20	$15.35	$13.15
	Enclosed	69.40	48.40	36.60	28.50	24.45
Average	Open	42.05	26.80	20.50	17.10	17.10
	Enclosed	83.10	56.30	42.65	33.00	27.95
Custom	Open	52.35	34.75	26.15	22.80	20.50
	Enclosed	104.10	71.15	54.10	42.10	36.40
Luxury	Open	57.50	37.60	27.85	24.95	22.15
	Enclosed	112.60	79.15	58.65	45.60	39.25

FINISHED ATTIC (Cost per S.F.)

CLASS	\multicolumn{5}{c}{AREA (S.F.)}
	400	500	600	800	1000
Economy	$ 9.30	$ 8.95	$ 8.60	$ 8.48	$ 8.15
Average	14.15	13.75	13.50	13.25	12.95
Custom	16.70	16.35	16.05	15.80	15.45
Luxury	22.05	21.60	21.10	20.65	20.20

FIREPLACES & CHIMNEYS (Cost per unit)

	1-1½ Story	2 Story	3 Story
Economy (prefab metal)			
Exterior chimney - 1 fireplace	$2415	$2670	$2925
Interior chimney - 1 fireplace	2310	2565	2700
Average (masonry)			
Exterior chimney - 1 fireplace	2630	2930	3340
Interior chimney - 1 fireplace	2460	2760	3005
For more than 1 flue, add	200	335	570
For more than 1 fireplace, add	1865	1865	1865
Custom (masonry)			
Exterior chimney & 1 fireplace	2725	3075	3475
Interior chimney & 1 fireplace	2555	2895	3120
For more than 1 flue, add	220	375	525
For more than 1 fireplace, add	1955	1955	1955
Luxury (masonry)			
Exterior chimney & 1 fireplace	3970	4345	4770
Interior chimney & 1 fireplace	3795	4150	4390
For more than 1 flue, add	350	575	805
For more than 1 fireplace, add	3130	3130	3130

APPLIANCES (Cost per unit)

	Economy	Average	Custom	Luxury
Range				
30" free standing, 1 oven	$ 270	$ 645	$1020	$1400
2 oven	765	1055	1455	1725
30" built-in, 1 oven	570	800	1040	1275
2 oven	975	1200	1450	1725
21" free standing				
1 oven	360	410	475	525
Counter Top Ranges				
4 burner standard	255	350	475	585
As above with griddle	385	485	595	640
Microwave Oven	165	495	1130	1775
Combination Range, Refrigerator, Sink				
30" wide	850	1200	1525	1850
60" wide	2175	2375	2675	2750
72" wide	2525	2675	3095	3225
Combination Range, Refrig. Sink, Microwave Oven And Ice Maker	3700	4225	4575	4650
Compactor				
4 to 1 compaction	370	450	530	615
Deep Freeze				
15 to 23 C.F.	465	495	650	820
30 C.F.	755	835	915	955
Dehumidifier, portable, auto.				
15 pint	185	195	220	255
30 pint	280	295	310	325
Washing Machine, automatic	400	665	930	1200
Water Heater, Electric, glass lined				
30 gal.	235	300	375	490
80 gal.	460	685	895	1025
Water Heater, Gas, glass lined				
30 gal.	255	325	485	655
50 gal.	400	585	705	800
Water Softener, automatic				
30 grains/gal.	405	425	450	500
100 grains/gal.	795	850	875	925
Dishwasher, built-in				
2 cycles	360	490	585	645
4 or more cycles	435	620	800	985
Dryer, automatic	390	490	675	975
Garage Door Opener	225	275	310	355
Garbage Disposal	105	150	205	255
Heater, Electric Built-in				
1250 watt ceiling type	97	130	160	180
1250 watt wall type	97	105	120	155
Wall type w/blower				
1500 watt	125	135	140	150
3000 watt	195	215	225	240
Hood For Range, 2 speed				
30" wide	125	205	320	420
42" wide	250	315	380	465
Humidifier, portable				
7 gal. per day	85	88	95	100
15 gal. per day	165	175	185	195
Ice Maker, automatic				
13 lb. per day	475	505	530	565
51 lb. per day	850	935	970	1005
Refrigerator, no frost				
10-12 C.F.	360	490	620	700
14-16 C.F.	600	700	910	1025
18-20 C.F.	700	825	1050	1275
21-29 C.F.	870	1380	1995	2900
Sump Pump, 1/3 H.P.	170	260	350	440

RESIDENTIAL | Adjustments | Modifications

KITCHEN CABINETS

BASE UNITS, Hardwood *(Cost per unit)*

24" deep, 35" high, (Cost each)	Economy	Average	Custom	Luxury
One top drawer, one door below				
12" wide	$ 85	$120	$155	$205
15" wide	95	125	165	215
18" wide	100	130	175	225
21" wide	105	145	185	235
24" wide	110	155	190	260
four drawers				
12" wide	95	130	160	215
15" wide	100	140	165	220
18" wide	110	150	190	250
24" wide	120	170	200	270
Two top drawers, two doors below				
27" wide	145	195	250	325
30" wide	150	200	255	330
33" wide	155	210	270	340
36" wide	165	215	280	360
42" wide	175	235	305	390
48" wide	180	245	310	405
Range or sink base *(Cost per unit)* Two doors below				
30" wide	105	135	175	225
33" wide	120	155	210	270
36" wide	125	165	225	285
42" wide	140	180	235	300
48" wide	145	195	265	335
Corner Base Cabinet *(Cost per unit)*				
36" wide	130	170	215	275
Lazy Susan *(Cost per unit)*				
With revolving door	165	225	290	380
Counter tops *(Cost per L.F.)*				
Stock, 24" wide with backsplash	12.10	18	23	25
Custom plastic, no splash				
7/8" thick, alum. molding	22	23	28	38
1-1/4" thick, no splash	24	27	30	42
Marble 1/2" – 3/4" thick w/splash	43	52	74	96
Maple, laminated 1-1/2" thick w/splash	32	44	56	72
Stainless steel (per Sq. Ft.)	62	86	100	128
Cutting blocks, recessed 16" x 20" x 1" (Each)	48	66	90	120

WALL CABINETS, Hardwood *(Cost per unit)*

12" deep, 2 doors	Economy	Average	Custom	Luxury
12" high				
30" wide	$ 80	$105	$130	$170
36" wide	85	115	145	180
15" high				
30" wide	80	110	135	175
33" wide	85	115	145	185
36" wide	95	125	160	205
24" high				
30" wide	95	125	160	210
36" wide	110	150	190	255
42" wide	115	160	195	260
30" high, 1 door				
12" wide	80	105	130	165
15" wide	85	110	135	170
18" wide	90	125	145	185
24" wide	105	130	160	200
30" high, 2 doors				
27" wide	110	145	175	230
30" wide	120	150	195	260
36" wide	125	160	200	265
42" wide	140	170	210	275
48" wide	150	185	245	315
Corner wall, 30" high				
24" wide	115	155	200	260
30" wide	125	175	230	290
36" wide	140	195	255	325
Broom closet 84" high, 24" deep				
18" wide	130	190	235	315
Oven Cabinet 84" high, 24" deep				
27" wide	170	225	295	375
Vanity Bases, 2 doors 30" high, 21" deep				
24" wide	130	170	220	275
30" wide	150	210	255	300
36" wide	175	245	305	350
48" wide	200	275	360	450

SAUNA, PREFABRICATED
(Cost per unit, including heater & controls — 7' high)

Size	Cost
6' x 4'	$3325
6' x 5'	3700
6' x 6'	4100
6' x 9'	5300
8' x 10'	6475
8' x 12'	6650
10' x 12'	7450

ALARM SYSTEM *(Cost per system)*

	Burglar Alarm	Smoke Detector
Economy	$260	$ 38
Average	385	55
Custom	505	80
Luxury	785	140

RESIDENTIAL | Adjustments | Modifications

GARAGES
Costs include exterior wall systems comparable with the quality of the residence. Included in the cost is an allowance for one man door, manual overhead door(s) and electrical fixture.

CLASS	Detached One Car	Detached Two Car	Detached Three Car	Attached One Car	Attached Two Car	Attached Three Car	Built-in One Car	Built-in Two Car	Basement One Car	Basement Two Car
Economy										
Wood	$5900	$8045	$11,040	$5450	$7880	$11,435	$-1100	$-1875	$515	$855
Masonry	7670	10,195	13,515	6005	8745	12,045	-1250	-2415		
Average										
Wood	6445	8700	12,285	6010	8530	12,060	-1125	-2115	555	1050
Masonry	8200	10,880	13,595	7100	9400	12,675	-1295	-2860		
Custom										
Wood	7170	9710	12,825	6575	9340	13,205	-1195	-2210	650	1240
Masonry	9450	11,795	15,795	7635	10,120	14,245	-1525	-3010		
Luxury										
Wood	11,075	14,125	17,635	11,605	14,230	17,745	-1385	-2570	2995	4415
Masonry	17,135	21,600	25,880	15,160	19,770	24,285	-1830	-3495		

*See the Introduction to this section for definitions of garage types.

SITE IMPROVEMENTS

SIDEWALKS (Cost per S.F.)

Concrete, 3000 psi with wire mesh	4" thick	$1.87
	5" thick	2.15
	6" thick	2.42
Precast concrete patio blocks (natural)	2" thick	3.60
Precast concrete patio blocks (colors)	2" thick	4.10
Flagstone, bluestone (irregular)	1" thick	6.45
Flagstone, bluestone (snapped rectangular)	1" thick	6.50
Slate, (natural, irregular)	3/4" thick	5.50
Slate, (random rectangular)	1/2" thick	7.10
Redwood, prefabricated (4'x4' sections)		4.54
Redwood, planks (1" thick on sleepers)		3.82
Seeding		
Fine grading & seeding includes lime, fertilizer & seed	per S.Y.	1.35
Lawn Sprinkler System	per S.F.	.45

FENCING (Cost per L.F.)

Chain Link 4' high, galvanized	$6.90
Gate 4' high (each)	92.00
Cedar Picket 3' high, 2 rail	7.20
Gate (each)	90.00
3 Rail 4' high	7.75
Gate (each)	98.00
Cedar Stockade 3 Rail 6' high	8.20
Gate (each)	97.00
Board & battens 2 sides 6' high, pine	10.90
6' high, cedar	18.40
No. 1 Cedar basketweave 6' high	19.95
Gate 6' high (each)	100.00

SWIMMING POOLS (Cost per S.F.)

Residential (includes equipment)	
In-ground	$16-27
Deck equipment	1.30
Painting pool, preparation & 3 coats (epoxy)	2.06
Rubber base paint	1.88
Pool cover	.29
Swimming Pool Heaters (Cost per unit)	
(Not including wiring, external piping, base or pad)	
Gas	
120 MBH	$1100
170 MBH	1450
500 MBH	4125
Electric	
18 KW 7200 gallon pool	1450
24 KW 9600 gallon pool	1575
54 KW 24,000 gallon pool	2300

WOOD AND COAL STOVES

Wood Only	
Free Standing (minimum)	$915
Fireplace Insert (minimum)	1030
Coal Only	
Free Standing	1160
Fireplace Insert	1270
Wood and Coal	
Free Standing	2380
Fireplace Insert	2440

CARPORT (Cost per S.F.)

Economy	$4.55
Average	6.85
Custom	9.95
Luxury	11.65

HOW TO USE ASSEMBLIES SECTION

Illustration
Each building assembly system is accompanied by a detailed, illustrated description. Each individual component is labeled. Every element involved in the total system function is shown.

Quantities
Each material in a system is shown with the quantity required for the system unit. For example, the rafters in this system have 1.170 L.F. per S.F. of ceiling area.

Unit of Measure
In the three right-hand columns, each cost figure is adjusted to agree with the unit of measure for the entire system. In this case, COST PER SQUARE FOOT (S.F.) is the common unit of measure. NOTE: In addition, under the UNIT heading, all the elements of each system are defined in relation to the product as a selling commodity. For example, "fascia board" is defined in linear feet, instead of in board feet.

Description
Each page includes a brief outline of any special conditions to be used when pricing a system. All units of measure are defined here.

System Definition
Not only are all components broken down for each system, but alternative components can be found on the page opposite. Simply insert any chosen new element into the chart to develop a custom system.

Man-hours
Total man-hours for a system can be found by simply multiplying the quantity of the system required times MAN-HOURS. The resulting figure is the total man-hours needed to complete the system.
(QUANTITY OF SYSTEM x MAN-HOURS = TOTAL SYSTEM MAN-HOURS)

Materials
This column contains the MATERIAL COST of each element. These cost figures include 10% for handling.

Installation
Labor rates include both the INSTALLATION COST of the contractor and the standard contractor's O&P. On the average, the LABOR COST will be 67.6% over the above BARE LABOR COST.

Totals
This row provides the necessary system cost totals. TOTAL SYSTEM COST can be derived by multiplying the TOTAL times each system's SQUARE FOOT ESTIMATE. (TOTAL × SQUARE FEET = TOTAL SYSTEM COST)

Work Sheet
Using the SELECTIVE PRICE SHEET on the page opposite each system, it is possible to create estimates with alternative items for any number of systems.

Total
MATERIAL COST + INSTALLATION COST = TOTAL. Work on table from left to right across cost columns to derive totals.

Note:
Throughout this section, the words assembly and system are used interchangeably.

---

3 FRAMING | 12 Gable End Roof Framing Systems

SYSTEM DESCRIPTION	QUAN.	UNIT	MAN-HOURS	MAT.	INST.	TOTAL
2" X 8" RAFTERS, 16" O.C., 5/12 PITCH						
Rafters, 2" x 8", 16" O.C., 5/12 pitch	1.170	L.F.	.019	.71	.50	1.21
Ceiling joists, 2" x 6", 16" O.C.	1.000	L.F.	.013	.44	.32	.76
Ridge board, 2" x 8"	.050	L.F.	.001	.03	.05	.08
Fascia board, 2" x 8"	.100	L.F.	.007	.06	.18	.24
Rafter tie, 1" x 4", 4' O.C.	.060	L.F.	.001	.01	.03	.04
Soffit nailer (outrigger), 2" x 4", 24" O.C.	.170	L.F.	.004	.05	.11	.16
Sheathing, exterior, plywood, CDX, ½" thick	1.170	S.F.	.012	.41	.34	.75
Furring strips, 1" x 3", 16" O.C.	1.000	L.F.	.023	.15	.55	.70
TOTAL			.080	1.86	2.08	3.94
2" X 6" RAFTERS, 16" O.C., 5/12 PITCH						
Rafters, 2" x 6", 16" O.C., 5/12 pitch	1.170	L.F.	.018	.50	.47	.97
Ceiling joists, 2" x 4", 16" O.C.	1.000	L.F.	.013	.29	.32	.61
Ridge board, 2" x 6"	.050	L.F.	.001	.02	.04	.06
Fascia board, 2" x 6"	.100	L.F.	.005	.05	.13	.18
Rafter tie, 1" x 4", 4' O.C.	.060	L.F.	.001	.01	.03	.04
Soffit nailer (outrigger), 2" x 4", 24" O.C.	.170	L.F.	.004	.05	.11	.16
Sheathing, exterior, plywood, CDX, ½" thick	1.170	S.F.	.012	.41	.34	.75
Furring strips, 1" x 3", 16" O.C.	1.000	L.F.	.023	.15	.55	.70
TOTAL			.077	1.48	1.99	3.47

The cost of this system is based on the square foot of plan area. All quantities have been adjusted accordingly.

DESCRIPTION	QUAN.	UNIT	MAN-HOURS	MAT.	INST.	TOTAL

ASSEMBLIES SECTION

This section of this book provides the costs of construction "assemblies" made up by combining unit prices, including overhead and profit, from the Unit Price Section.

The System Components at the head of each table show typical unit price elements that are combined to create the single total cost for each assembly in the table.

By choosing the assembly with characteristics nearest to those required by your job, an accurate estimate can be compiled quickly.

Assemblies estimates are especially useful for preparing budget estimates, preparing feasibility studies, comparing the cost of optional construction methods, and checking the accuracy of unit price estimates.

TABLE OF CONTENTS

ASSEMBLY NO.		PAGE
1-04	Footing Excavation	80
1-08	Foundation Excavation	82
1-12	Utility Trenching	84
1-16	Sidewalk	86
1-20	Driveway	88
1-24	Septic	90
1-60	Chain Link Fence	92
1-64	Wood Fence	93
2-04	Footing	94
2-08	Block Wall	96
2-12	Concrete Wall	98
2-16	Wood Wall Foundation	100
2-20	Floor Slab	102
3-04	Floor (Wood)	104
3-08	Exterior Wall	106
3-12	Gable End Roof	108
3-16	Truss Roof	110
3-20	Hip Roof	112
3-24	Gambrel Roof	114
3-28	Mansard Roof	116
3-32	Shed/Flat Roof	118
3-40	Gable Dormer	120
3-44	Shed Dormer	122
3-48	Partition	124
4-02	Masonry Block Wall	126
4-04	Brick/Stone Veneer	128
4-08	Wood Siding	130
4-12	Shingle Siding	132
4-16	Metal & Plastic Siding	134

ASSEMBLY NO.		PAGE
4-20	Insulation	136
4-28	Double Hung Window	138
4-32	Casement Window	140
4-36	Awning Window	142
4-40	Sliding Window	144
4-44	Bow/Bay Window	146
4-48	Fixed Window	148
4-52	Entrance Door	150
4-53	Sliding Door	152
4-56	Residential Overhead Door	154
4-58	Aluminum Window	156
4-60	Storm Door & Window	158
4-64	Shutters/Blinds	159
5-04	Gable End Roofing	160
5-08	Hip Roof Roofing	162
5-12	Gambrel Roofing	164
5-16	Mansard Roofing	166
5-20	Shed Roofing	168
5-24	Gable Dormer Roofing	170
5-28	Shed Dormer Roofing	172
5-32	Skylight/Skywindow	174
5-34	Built-up Roofing	176
6-04	Drywall & Thincoat Wall	178
6-08	Drywall & Thincoat Ceiling	180
6-12	Plaster & Stucco Wall	182
6-16	Plaster & Stucco Ceiling	184
6-18	Suspended Ceiling	186
6-20	Interior Door	188
6-24	Closet Door	190

ASSEMBLY NO.		PAGE
6-60	Carpet	192
6-64	Flooring	193
6-90	Stairways	194
7-08	Kitchen	196
7-12	Appliances	198
7-16	Bath Accessories	199
7-24	Masonry Fireplace	200
7-30	Prefabricated Fireplace	202
7-32	Greenhouse	204
7-36	Swimming Pool	205
7-40	Wood Deck	206
8-04	Two Fixture Lavatory	208
8-12	Three Fixture Bathroom	210
8-16	Three Fixture Bathroom	212
8-20	Three Fixture Bathroom	214
8-24	Three Fixture Bathroom	216
8-28	Three Fixture Bathroom	218
8-32	Three Fixture Bathroom	220
8-36	Four Fixture Bathroom	222
8-40	Four Fixture Bathroom	224
8-44	Five Fixture Bathroom	226
8-60	Gas Fired Heating/Cooling	228
8-64	Oil Fired Heating/Cooling	230
8-68	Hot Water Heating	232
8-80	Rooftop Heating/Cooling	234
9-10	Electric Service	236
9-20	Electric Heating	237
9-30	Wiring Devices	238
9-40	Light Fixtures	239

1 | SITE WORK   04 | Footing Excavation Systems

SYSTEM DESCRIPTION	QUAN.	UNIT	MAN-HOURS	COST EACH MAT.	COST EACH INST.	COST EACH TOTAL
BUILDING, 24' X 38', 4' DEEP						
Clear and strip, dozer, light trees, 30' from building	.190	Acre	11.400		513.00	513.00
Excavate, backhoe	174.000	C.Y.	7.656		476.76	476.76
Backfill, dozer, 4" lifts, no compaction	87.000	C.Y.	.870		80.91	80.91
Rough grade, dozer, 30' from building	87.000	C.Y.	.870		80.91	80.91
TOTAL			20.796		1151.58	1151.58
BUILDING, 26' X 46', 4' DEEP						
Clear and strip, dozer, light trees, 30' from building	.210	Acre	12.600		567.00	567.00
Excavate, backhoe	201.000	C.Y.	8.844		550.74	550.74
Backfill, dozer, 4" lifts, no compaction	100.000	C.Y.	1.000		93.00	93.00
Rough grade, dozer, 30' from building	100.000	C.Y.	1.000		93.00	93.00
TOTAL			23.444		1303.74	1303.74
BUILDING, 26' X 60', 4' DEEP						
Clear and strip, dozer, light trees, 30' from building	.240	Acre	14.400		648.00	648.00
Excavate, backhoe	240.000	C.Y.	10.560		657.60	657.60
Backfill, dozer, 4" lifts, no compaction	120.000	C.Y.	1.200		111.60	111.60
Rough grade, dozer, 30' from building	120.000	C.Y.	1.200		111.60	111.60
TOTAL			27.360		1528.80	1528.80
BUILDING, 30' X 66', 4' DEEP						
Clear and strip, dozer, light trees, 30' from building	.260	Acre	15.600		702.00	702.00
Excavate, backhoe	268.000	C.Y.	11.792		734.32	734.32
Backfill, dozer, 4" lifts, no compaction	134.000	C.Y.	1.340		124.62	124.62
Rough grade, dozer, 30' from building	134.000	C.Y.	1.340		124.62	124.62
TOTAL			30.072		1685.56	1685.56

The costs in this system are on a cost each basis.
Quantities are based on 1'-0" clearance on each side of footing.

DESCRIPTION	QUAN.	UNIT	MAN-HOURS	COST EACH MAT.	COST EACH INST.	COST EACH TOTAL

Footing Excavation Price Sheet

	QUAN.	UNIT	MAN-HOURS	MAT.	INST.	TOTAL
Clear and grub, medium brush, 30' from building, 24' x 38'	.190	Acre	11.400		513.00	513.00
26' x 46'	.210	Acre	12.600		567.00	567.00
26' x 60'	.240	Acre	14.400		648.00	648.00
30' x 66'	.260	Acre	15.600		702.00	702.00
Light trees, to 6" dia. cut & chip, 24' x 38'	.190	Acre	11.400		513.00	513.00
26' x 46'	.210	Acre	12.600		567.00	567.00
26' x 60'	.240	Acre	14.400		648.00	648.00
30' x 66'	.260	Acre	15.600		702.00	702.00
Medium trees, to 10" dia. cut & chip, 24' x 38'	.190	Acre	13.028		584.25	584.25
26' x 46'	.210	Acre	14.399		645.75	645.75
26' x 60'	.240	Acre	16.456		738.00	738.00
30' x 66'	.260	Acre	17.828		799.50	799.50
Excavation, footing, 24' x 38', 2' deep	68.000	C.Y.	2.992		186.32	186.32
4' deep	174.000	C.Y.	7.656		476.76	476.76
8' deep	384.000	C.Y.	16.896		1052.16	1052.16
26' x 46', 2' deep	79.000	C.Y.	3.476		216.46	216.46
4' deep	201.000	C.Y.	8.844		550.74	550.74
8' deep	404.000	C.Y.	17.776		1106.96	1106.96
26' x 60', 2' deep	94.000	C.Y.	4.136		257.56	257.56
4' deep	240.000	C.Y.	10.560		657.60	657.60
8' deep	483.000	C.Y.	21.252		1323.42	1323.42
30' x 66', 2' deep	105.000	C.Y.	4.620		287.70	287.70
4' deep	268.000	C.Y.	11.792		734.32	734.32
8' deep	539.000	C.Y.	23.716		1476.86	1476.86
Backfill, 24' x 38', 2" lifts, no compaction	34.000	C.Y.	.340		31.62	31.62
Compaction, air tamped	34.000	C.Y.	2.278		204.00	204.00
4" lifts, no compaction	87.000	C.Y.	.870		80.91	80.91
Compaction, air tamped	87.000	C.Y.	5.829		522.00	522.00
8" lifts, no compaction	192.000	C.Y.	1.920		178.56	178.56
Compaction, air tamped	192.000	C.Y.	12.864		1152.00	1152.00
26' x 46', 2" lifts, no compaction	40.000	C.Y.	.400		37.20	37.20
Compaction, air tamped	40.000	C.Y.	2.680		240.00	240.00
4" lifts, no compaction	100.000	C.Y.	1.000		93.00	93.00
Compaction, air tamped	100.000	C.Y.	6.700		600.00	600.00
8" lifts, no compaction	202.000	C.Y.	2.020		187.86	187.86
Compaction, air tamped	202.000	C.Y.	13.534		1212.00	1212.00
26' x 60', 2" lifts, no compaction	47.000	C.Y.	.470		43.71	43.71
Compaction, air tamped	47.000	C.Y.	3.149		282.00	282.00
4" lifts, no compaction	120.000	C.Y.	1.200		111.60	111.60
Compaction, air tamped	120.000	C.Y.	8.040		720.00	720.00
8" lifts, no compaction	242.000	C.Y.	2.420		225.06	225.06
Compaction, air tamped	242.000	C.Y.	16.214		1452.00	1452.00
30' x 66', 2" lifts, no compaction	53.000	C.Y.	.530		49.29	49.29
Compaction, air tamped	53.000	C.Y.	3.551		318.00	318.00
4" lifts, no compaction	134.000	C.Y.	1.340		124.62	124.62
Compaction, air tamped	134.000	C.Y.	8.978		804.00	804.00
8" lifts, no compaction	269.000	C.Y.	2.690		250.17	250.17
Compaction, air tamped	269.000	C.Y.	18.023		1614.00	1614.00
Rough grade, 30' from building, 24' x 38'	87.000	C.Y.	.870		80.91	80.91
26' x 46'	100.000	C.Y.	1.000		93.00	93.00
26' x 60'	120.000	C.Y.	1.200		111.60	111.60
30' x 66'	134.000	C.Y.	1.340		124.62	124.62

1 | SITE WORK — 08 Foundation Excavation Systems

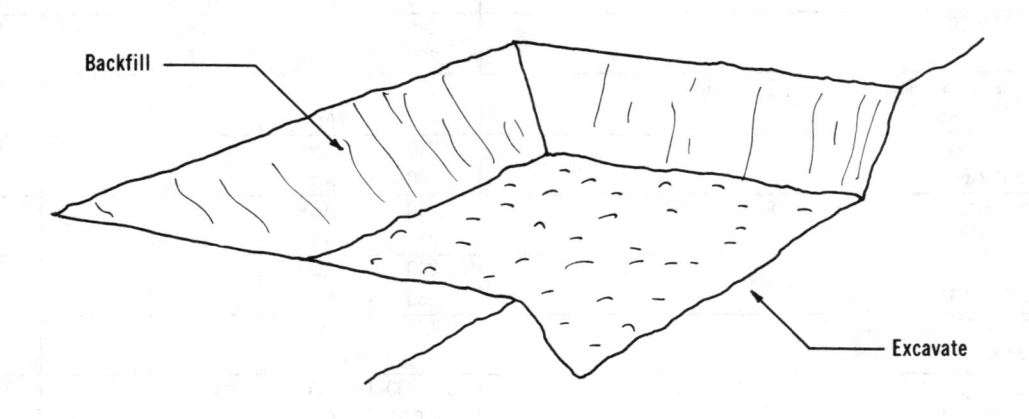

SYSTEM DESCRIPTION	QUAN.	UNIT	MAN-HOURS	COST EACH MAT.	COST EACH INST.	COST EACH TOTAL
BUILDING, 24' X 38', 8' DEEP						
Clear & grub, dozer, medium brush, 30' from building	.190	Acre	2.027		152.00	152.00
Excavate, track loader, 1-½ C.Y. bucket	550.000	C.Y.	11.550		632.50	632.50
Backfill, dozer, 8" lifts, no compaction	180.000	C.Y.	1.800		167.40	167.40
Rough grade, dozer, 30' from building	280.000	C.Y.	2.800		260.40	260.40
TOTAL			18.177		1212.30	1212.30
BUILDING, 26' X 46', 8' DEEP						
Clear & grub, dozer, medium brush, 30' from building	.210	Acre	2.240		168.00	168.00
Excavate, track loader, 1-½ C.Y. bucket	672.000	C.Y.	14.112		772.80	772.80
Backfill, dozer, 8" lifts, no compaction	220.000	C.Y.	2.200		204.60	204.60
Rough grade, dozer, 30' from building	340.000	C.Y.	3.400		316.20	316.20
TOTAL			21.952		1461.60	1461.60
BUILDING, 26' X 60', 8' DEEP						
Clear & grub, dozer, medium brush, 30' from building	.240	Acre	2.560		192.00	192.00
Excavate, track loader, 1-½ C.Y. bucket	829.000	C.Y.	17.409		953.35	953.35
Backfill, dozer, 8" lifts, no compaction	270.000	C.Y.	2.700		251.10	251.10
Rough grade, dozer, 30' from building	420.000	C.Y.	4.200		390.60	390.60
TOTAL			26.869		1787.05	1787.05
BUILDING, 30' X 66', 8' DEEP						
Clear & grub, dozer, medium brush, 30' from building	.260	Acre	2.774		208.00	208.00
Excavate, track loader, 1-½ C.Y. bucket	990.000	C.Y.	20.790		1138.50	1138.50
Backfill dozer, 8" lifts, no compaction	320.000	C.Y.	3.200		297.60	297.60
Rough grade, dozer, 30' from building	500.000	C.Y.	5.000		465.00	465.00
TOTAL			31.764		2109.10	2109.10

The costs in this system are on a cost each basis.
Quantities are based on 1'-0" clearance beyond footing projection.

DESCRIPTION	QUAN.	UNIT	MAN-HOURS	COST EACH MAT.	COST EACH INST.	COST EACH TOTAL

Foundation Excavation Price Sheet

	QUAN.	UNIT	MAN-HOURS	MAT.	INST.	TOTAL
Clear & grub, medium brush, 30' from building, 24' x 38'	.190	Acre	2.027		152.00	152.00
26' x 46'	.210	Acre	2.240		168.00	168.00
26' x 60'	.240	Acre	2.560		192.00	192.00
30' x 66'	.260	Acre	2.774		208.00	208.00
Light trees, to 6" dia. cut & chip, 24' x 38'	.190	Acre	11.400		513.00	513.00
26' x 46'	.210	Acre	12.600		567.00	567.00
26' x 60'	.240	Acre	14.400		648.00	648.00
30' x 66'	.260	Acre	15.600		702.00	702.00
Medium trees, to 10" dia. cut & chip, 24' x 38'	.190	Acre	13.028		584.25	584.25
26' x 46'	.210	Acre	14.399		645.75	645.75
26' x 60'	.240	Acre	16.456		738.00	738.00
30' x 66'	.260	Acre	17.828		799.50	799.50
Excavation, basement, 24' x 38', 2' deep	98.000	C.Y.	2.058		112.70	112.70
4' deep	220.000	C.Y.	4.620		253.00	253.00
8' deep	550.000	C.Y.	11.550		632.50	632.50
26' x 46', 2' deep	123.000	C.Y.	2.583		141.45	141.45
4' deep	274.000	C.Y.	5.754		315.10	315.10
8' deep	672.000	C.Y.	14.112		772.80	772.80
26' x 60', 2' deep	157.000	C.Y.	3.297		180.55	180.55
4' deep	345.000	C.Y.	7.245		396.75	396.75
8' deep	829.000	C.Y.	17.409		953.35	953.35
30' x 66', 2' deep	192.000	C.Y.	4.032		220.80	220.80
4' deep	419.000	C.Y.	8.799		481.85	481.85
8' deep	990.000	C.Y.	20.790		1138.50	1138.50
Backfill, 24' x 38', 2" lifts, no compaction	32.000	C.Y.	.320		29.76	29.76
Compaction, air tamped	32.000	C.Y.	2.144		192.00	192.00
4" lifts, no compaction	72.000	C.Y.	.720		66.96	66.96
Compaction, air tamped	72.000	C.Y.	4.824		432.00	432.00
8" lifts, no compaction	180.000	C.Y.	1.800		167.40	167.40
Compaction, air tamped	180.000	C.Y.	12.060		1080.00	1080.00
26' x 46', 2" lifts, no compaction	40.000	C.Y.	.400		37.20	37.20
Compaction, air tamped	40.000	C.Y.	2.680		240.00	240.00
4" lifts, no compaction	90.000	C.Y.	.900		83.70	83.70
Compaction, air tamped	90.000	C.Y.	6.030		540.00	540.00
8" lifts, no compaction	220.000	C.Y.	2.200		204.60	204.60
Compacton, air tamped	220.000	C.Y.	14.740		1320.00	1320.00
26' x 60', 2" lifts, no compaction	50.000	C.Y.	.500		46.50	46.50
Compaction, air tamped	50.000	C.Y.	3.350		300.00	300.00
4" lifts, no compaction	110.000	C.Y.	1.100		102.30	102.30
Compaction, air tamped	110.000	C.Y.	7.370		660.00	660.00
8" lifts, no compaction	270.000	C.Y.	2.700		251.10	251.10
Compaction, air tamped	270.000	C.Y.	18.090		1620.00	1620.00
30' x 66', 2" lifts, no compaction	60.000	C.Y.	.600		55.80	55.80
Compaction, air tamped	60.000	C.Y.	4.020		360.00	360.00
4" lifts, no compaction	130.000	C.Y.	1.300		120.90	120.90
Compaction, air tamped	130.000	C.Y.	8.710		780.00	780.00
8" lifts, no compaction	320.000	C.Y.	3.200		297.60	297.60
Compaction, air tamped	320.000	C.Y.	21.440		1920.00	1920.00
Rough grade, 30' from building, 24' x 38'	280.000	C.Y.	2.800		260.40	260.40
26' x 46'	340.000	C.Y.	3.400		316.20	316.20
26' x 60'	420.000	C.Y.	4.200		390.60	390.60
30' x 66'	500.000	C.Y.	5.000		465.00	465.00

1 | SITE WORK 12 | Utility Trenching Systems

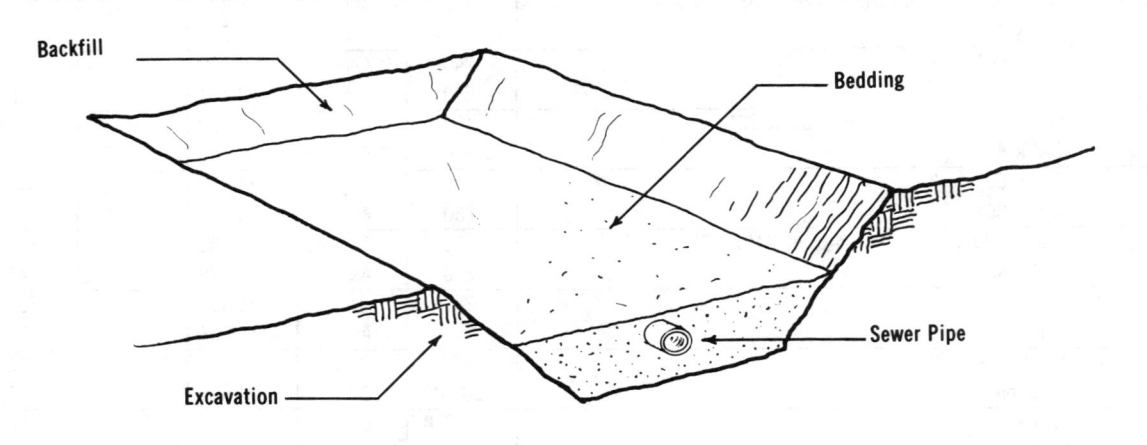

SYSTEM DESCRIPTION	QUAN.	UNIT	MAN-HOURS	COST PER L.F. MAT.	COST PER L.F. INST.	COST PER L.F. TOTAL
2' DEEP						
Excavation, backhoe	.296	C.Y.	.031		1.09	1.09
Bedding, sand	.111	C.Y.	.044	1.13	1.02	2.15
Utility, sewer, 6" cast iron	1.000	L.F.	.282	5.79	7.11	12.90
Backfill, incl. compaction	.185	C.Y.	.043		.83	.83
TOTAL			.400	6.92	10.05	16.97
4' DEEP						
Excavation, backhoe	.889	C.Y.	.095		3.28	3.28
Bedding, sand	.111	C.Y.	.044	1.13	1.02	2.15
Utility, sewer, 6" cast iron	1.000	L.F.	.282	5.79	7.11	12.90
Backfill, incl. compaction	.778	C.Y.	.182		3.48	3.48
TOTAL			.603	6.92	14.89	21.81
6' DEEP						
Excavation, backhoe	1.770	C.Y.	.189		6.53	6.53
Bedding, sand	.111	C.Y.	.044	1.13	1.02	2.15
Utility, sewer, 6" cast iron	1.000	L.F.	.282	5.79	7.11	12.90
Backfill, incl. compaction	1.660	C.Y.	.390		7.42	7.42
TOTAL			.905	6.92	22.08	29.00
8' DEEP						
Excavation, backhoe	2.960	C.Y.	.316		10.92	10.92
Bedding, sand	.111	C.Y.	.044	1.13	1.02	2.15
Utility, sewer, 6" cast iron	1.000	L.F.	.282	5.79	7.11	12.90
Backfill, incl. compaction	2.850	C.Y.	.669		12.74	12.74
TOTAL			1.311	6.92	31.79	38.71

The costs in this system are based on a cost per linear foot of trench, and based on 2' wide at bottom of trench up to 6' deep.

DESCRIPTION	QUAN.	UNIT	MAN-HOURS	COST PER L.F. MAT.	COST PER L.F. INST.	COST PER L.F. TOTAL

Utility Trenching Price Sheet

	QUAN.	UNIT	MAN-HOURS	COST PER L.F. MAT.	COST PER L.F. INST.	COST PER L.F. TOTAL
Excavation, bottom of trench 2' wide, 2' deep	.296	C.Y.	.031		1.09	1.09
4' deep	.889	C.Y.	.095		3.28	3.28
6' deep	1.770	C.Y.	.141		5.82	5.82
8' deep	2.960	C.Y.	.210		11.40	11.40
Bedding, sand, bottom of trench 2' wide, no compaction, pipe, 2" diameter	.070	C.Y.	.028	.71	.64	1.35
4" diameter	.084	C.Y.	.033	.86	.77	1.63
6" diameter	.105	C.Y.	.042	1.07	.96	2.03
8" diameter	.122	C.Y.	.048	1.24	1.12	2.36
Compacted, pipe, 2" diameter	.074	C.Y.	.029	.75	.68	1.43
4" diameter	.092	C.Y.	.036	.94	.84	1.78
6" diameter	.111	C.Y.	.044	1.13	1.02	2.15
8" diameter	.129	C.Y.	.051	1.31	1.19	2.50
¾" stone, bottom of trench 2' wide, pipe, 4" diameter	.082	C.Y.	.032	.83	.76	1.59
6" diameter	.099	C.Y.	.039	1.01	.91	1.92
⅜" stone, bottom of trench 2' wide, pipe, 4" diameter	.084	C.Y.	.033	.86	.77	1.63
6" diameter	.102	C.Y.	.040	1.04	.93	1.97
Utilities, drainage & sewerage, asbestos cement, 6" diameter	1.000	L.F.	.047	3.09	.89	3.98
8" diameter	1.000	L.F.	.053	7.26	.99	8.25
Bituminous fiber, 4" diameter	1.000	L.F.	.042	1.63	.80	2.43
6" diameter	1.000	L.F.	.047	3.09	.89	3.98
8" diameter	1.000	L.F.	.053	7.26	.99	8.25
Concrete, non-reinforced, 6" diameter	1.000	L.F.	.160	3.25	3.50	6.75
8" diameter	1.000	L.F.	.140	3.58	3.72	7.30
PVC, SDR 35, 4" diameter	1.000	L.F.	.064	.75	1.41	2.16
6" diameter	1.000	L.F.	.069	1.82	1.51	3.33
8" diameter	1.000	L.F.	.072	2.59	1.58	4.17
Vitrified clay, 4" diameter	1.000	L.F.	.091	1.16	1.99	3.15
6" diameter	1.000	L.F.	.120	1.93	2.64	4.57
8" diameter	1.000	L.F.	.140	3.03	3.72	6.75
Gas & service, polyethylene, 1-¼" diameter	1.000	L.F.	.060	.61	1.32	1.93
Steel sched.40, 1" diameter	1.000	L.F.	.107	3.26	2.89	6.15
2" diameter	1.000	L.F.	.114	3.71	3.09	6.80
Sub-drainage, asbestos cement pipe class 4000 perf., 4" diameter	1.000	L.F.	.062	2.26	1.29	3.55
6" diameter	1.000	L.F.	.063	3.58	1.32	4.90
Bituminous fiber, perforated, 3" diameter	1.000	L.F.	.030	1.32	.66	1.98
4" diameter	1.000	L.F.	.032	1.65	.69	2.34
5" diameter	1.000	L.F.	.033	2.86	.73	3.59
6" diameter	1.000	L.F.	.035	3.19	.78	3.97
Porous wall concrete, 4" diameter	1.000	L.F.	.072	1.65	1.58	3.23
Vitrified clay, perforated, 4" diameter	1.000	L.F.	.060	1.27	1.32	2.59
6" diameter	1.000	L.F.	.076	1.85	1.68	3.53
Water service, copper, type K, ¾"	1.000	L.F.	.083	2.02	2.25	4.27
1" diameter	1.000	L.F.	.093	3.23	2.51	5.74
PVC, ¾"	1.000	L.F.	.120	.62	3.27	3.89
1" diameter	1.000	L.F.	.180	.78	4.88	5.66
Backfill, bottom of trench 2' wide no compact, 2' deep, pipe, 2" diameter	.226	C.Y.	.053		1.01	1.01
4" diameter	.212	C.Y.	.049		.95	.95
6" diameter	.185	C.Y.	.043		.83	.83
4' deep, pipe, 2" diameter	.819	C.Y.	.192		3.66	3.66
4" diameter	.805	C.Y.	.189		3.60	3.60
6" diameter	.778	C.Y.	.182		3.48	3.48
6' deep, pipe, 2" diameter	1.700	C.Y.	.399		7.60	7.60
4" diameter	1.690	C.Y.	.397		7.55	7.55
6" diameter	1.660	C.Y.	.390		7.42	7.42
8' deep, pipe, 2" diameter	2.890	C.Y.	.679		12.92	12.92
4" diameter	2.870	C.Y.	.674		12.83	12.83
6" diameter	2.850	C.Y.	.669		12.74	12.74

1 | SITE WORK — 16 | Sidewalk Systems

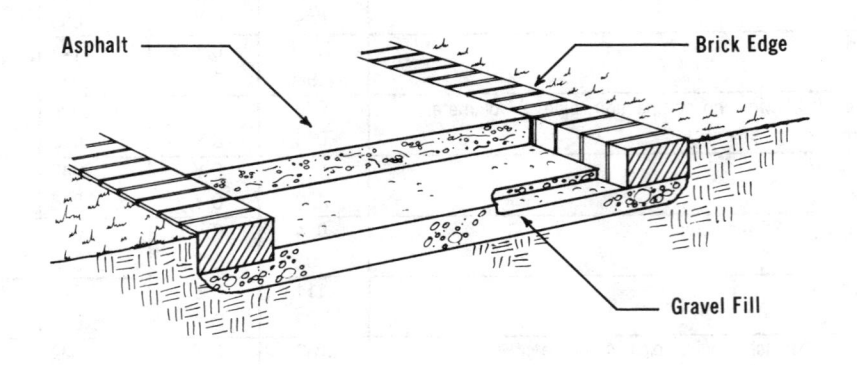

Asphalt · Brick Edge · Gravel Fill

SYSTEMS DESCRIPTION	QUAN.	UNIT	MAN-HOURS	MAT.	INST.	TOTAL
ASPHALT SIDEWALK SYSTEM, 3' WIDE WALK						
Gravel fill, 4" deep	1.000	S.F.		.13	.02	.15
Compact fill	.012	C.Y.			.01	.01
Handgrade	1.000	S.F.			.01	.01
Walking surface, bituminous paving, 2" thick	1.000	S.F.	.007	.39	.17	.56
Edging, brick, laid on edge	.670	L.F.	.079	1.12	1.71	2.83
TOTAL			.086	1.64	1.92	3.56
CONCRETE SIDEWALK SYSTEM, 3' WIDE WALK						
Gravel fill, 4" deep	1.000	S.F.		.13	.02	.15
Compact fill	.012	C.Y.			.01	.01
Handgrade	1.000	S.F.			.01	.01
Walking surface, concrete, 4" thick	1.000	S.F.	.040	1.00	.87	1.87
Edging, brick, laid on edge	.670	L.F.	.079	1.12	1.71	2.83
TOTAL			.119	2.25	2.62	4.87
PAVERS, BRICK SIDEWALK SYSTEM, 3' WIDE WALK						
Sand base fill, 4" deep	1.000	S.F.		.19	.05	.24
Compact fill	.012	C.Y.			.01	.01
Handgrade	1.000	S.F.			.01	.01
Walking surface, brick pavers	1.000	S.F.	.145	2.59	3.16	5.75
Edging, redwood, untreated, 1" x 4"	.670	L.F.	.031	.59	.81	1.40
TOTAL			.176	3.37	4.04	7.41

The costs in this system are based on a cost per square foot of sidewalk area. Concrete used is 3000 p.s.i.

DESCRIPTION	QUAN.	UNIT	MAN-HOURS	MAT.	INST.	TOTAL

Sidewalk Price Sheet

	QUAN.	UNIT	MAN-HOURS	COST PER S.F. MAT.	COST PER S.F. INST.	COST PER S.F. TOTAL
Base, crushed stone, 3" deep	1.000	S.F.	.001	.26	.06	.32
6" deep	1.000	S.F.	.001	.53	.06	.59
9" deep	1.000	S.F.	.002	.79	.08	.87
12" deep	1.000	S.F.	.002	1.05	.09	1.14
Bank run gravel, 6" deep	1.000	S.F.	.001	.19	.04	.23
9" deep	1.000	S.F.	.001	.29	.06	.35
12" deep	1.000	S.F.	.001	.37	.07	.44
Compact base, 3" deep	.009	C.Y.			.01	.01
6" deep	.019	C.Y.			.02	.02
9" deep	.028	C.Y.	.001		.03	.03
Handgrade	1.000	S.F.			.01	.01
Surface, brick, pavers dry joints, laid flat, running bond	1.000	S.F.	.145	2.59	3.16	5.75
Basket weave	1.000	S.F.	.168	2.59	3.61	6.20
Herringbone	1.000	S.F.	.174	2.59	3.76	6.35
Laid on edge, running bond	1.000	S.F.	.229	4.07	4.93	9.00
Mortar jts. laid flat, running bond	1.000	S.F.	.174	3.11	3.79	6.90
Basket weave	1.000	S.F.	.201	3.11	4.33	7.44
Herringbone	1.000	S.F.	.208	3.11	4.51	7.62
Laid on edge, running bond	1.000	S.F.	.274	4.88	5.92	10.80
Bituminous paving, 1-½" thick	1.000	S.F.	.005	.29	.13	.42
2" thick	1.000	S.F.	.007	.39	.17	.56
2-½" thick	1.000	S.F.	.008	.47	.18	.65
Sand finish, ¾" thick	1.000	S.F.	.002	.14	.07	.21
1" thick	1.000	S.F.	.003	.21	.10	.31
Concrete, reinforced, broom finish, 4" thick	1.000	S.F.	.040	1.00	.87	1.87
5" thick	1.000	S.F.	.044	1.19	.96	2.15
6" thick	1.000	S.F.	.047	1.39	1.03	2.42
Crushed stone, white marble, 3" thick	1.000	S.F.	.009	.41	.18	.59
Bluestone, 3" thick	1.000	S.F.	.009	.10	.18	.28
Flagging, bluestone, 1"	1.000	S.F.	.198	2.18	4.27	6.45
1-½"	1.000	S.F.	.188	3.33	4.07	7.40
Slate, natural cleft, ¾"	1.000	S.F.	.174	1.77	3.73	5.50
Random rect., ½"	1.000	S.F.	.152	3.83	3.27	7.10
Granite blocks	1.000	S.F.	.174	5.12	3.73	8.85
Edging, corrugated aluminum, 4", 3' wide walk	.666	L.F.	.007	.11	.21	.32
4' wide walk	.500	L.F.	.006	.09	.15	.24
6", 3' wide walk	.666	L.F.	.009	.14	.24	.38
4' wide walk	.500	L.F.	.007	.11	.18	.29
Redwood-cedar-cypress, 1" x 4", 3' wide walk	.666	L.F.	.021	.64	.53	1.17
4' wide walk	.500	L.F.	.016	.48	.40	.88
2" x 4", 3' wide walk	.666	L.F.	.031	.59	.81	1.40
4' wide walk	.500	L.F.	.024	.45	.60	1.05
Brick, dry joints, 3' wide walk	.666	L.F.	.079	1.12	1.71	2.83
4' wide walk	.500	L.F.	.059	.84	1.28	2.12
Mortar joints, 3' wide walk	.666	L.F.	.095	1.34	2.06	3.40
4' wide walk	.500	L.F.	.071	1.00	1.54	2.54

1 | SITE WORK — 20 | Driveway Systems

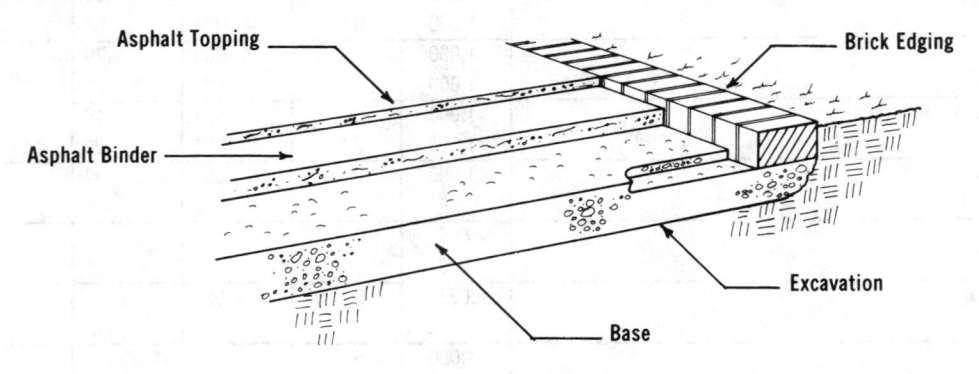

SYSTEMS DESCRIPTION	QUAN.	UNIT	MAN-HOURS	COST PER S.F. MAT.	COST PER S.F. INST.	COST PER S.F. TOTAL
ASPHALT DRIVEWAY TO 10' WIDE						
Excavation, driveway to 10' wide, 6" deep	.019	C.Y.			.03	.03
Base, 6" crushed stone	1.000	S.F.	.001	.53	.06	.59
Handgrade base	1.000	S.F.			.01	.01
Surface, asphalt, 2" thick base, 1" topping	1.000	S.F.	.007	.57	.27	.84
Edging, brick pavers	.200	L.F.	.023	.33	.52	.85
TOTAL			.031	1.43	.89	2.32
CONCRETE DRIVEWAY TO 10' WIDE						
Excavation, driveway to 10' wide, 6" deep	.019	C.Y.			.03	.03
Base, 6" crushed stone	1.000	S.F.	.001	.53	.06	.59
Handgrade base	1.000	S.F.			.01	.01
Surface, concrete, 4" thick	1.000	S.F.	.040	1.00	.87	1.87
Edging, brick pavers	.200	L.F.	.023	.33	.52	.85
TOTAL			.064	1.86	1.49	3.35
PAVERS, BRICK DRIVEWAY TO 10' WIDE						
Excavation, driveway to 10' wide, 6" deep	.019	C.Y.			.03	.03
Base, 6" sand	1.000	S.F.		.31	.07	.38
Handgrade base	1.000	S.F.			.01	.01
Surface, pavers, brick laid flat, running bond	1.000	S.F.	.145	2.59	3.16	5.75
Edging, redwood, untreated, 2" x 4"	.200	L.F.	.009	.18	.24	.42
TOTAL			.154	3.08	3.51	6.59

Driveway Price Sheet

	QUAN.	UNIT	MAN-HOURS	COST PER S.F. MAT.	COST PER S.F. INST.	TOTAL
Excavation, by machine, 10' wide, 6" deep	.019	C.Y.			.03	.03
12" deep	.037	C.Y.	.001		.05	.05
18" deep	.055	C.Y.	.001		.08	.08
20' wide, 6" deep	.019	C.Y.			.03	.03
12" deep	.037	C.Y.	.001		.05	.05
18" deep	.055	C.Y.	.001		.08	.08
Base, crushed stone, 10' wide, 3" deep	1.000	S.F.		.27	.03	.30
6" deep	1.000	S.F.	.001	.53	.06	.59
9" deep	1.000	S.F.	.002	.79	.08	.87
20' wide, 3" deep	1.000	S.F.		.27	.03	.30
6" deep	1.000	S.F.	.001	.53	.06	.59
9" deep	1.000	S.F.	.002	.79	.08	.87
Bank run gravel, 10' wide, 3" deep	1.000	S.F.		.10	.02	.12
6" deep	1.000	S.F.	.001	.19	.04	.23
9" deep	1.000	S.F.	.001	.29	.06	.35
20' wide, 3" deep	1.000	S.F.		.10	.02	.12
6" deep	1.000	S.F.	.001	.19	.04	.23
9" deep	1.000	S.F.	.001	.29	.06	.35
Handgrade, 10' wide	1.000	S.F.			.01	.01
20' wide	1.000	S.F.			.01	.01
Surface, asphalt, 10' wide, ¾" topping, 1" base	1.000	S.F.	.004	.42	.15	.57
2" base	1.000	S.F.	.006	.50	.24	.74
1" topping, 1" base	1.000	S.F.	.005	.49	.18	.67
2" base	1.000	S.F.	.007	.57	.27	.84
20' wide, ¾" topping, 1" base	1.000	S.F.	.004	.42	.15	.57
2" base	1.000	S.F.	.006	.50	.24	.74
1" topping, 1" base	1.000	S.F.	.005	.49	.18	.67
2" base	1.000	S.F.	.007	.57	.27	.84
Concrete, 10' wide, 4" thick	1.000	S.F.	.040	1.00	.87	1.87
6" thick	1.000	S.F.	.047	1.39	1.03	2.42
20' wide, 4" thick	1.000	S.F.	.040	1.00	.87	1.87
6" thick	1.000	S.F.	.047	1.39	1.03	2.42
Paver, brick 10' wide dry joints, running bond, laid flat	1.000	S.F.	.145	2.59	3.16	5.75
Laid on edge	1.000	S.F.	.229	4.07	4.93	9.00
Mortar joints, laid flat	1.000	S.F.	.174	3.11	3.79	6.90
Laid on edge	1.000	S.F.	.274	4.88	5.92	10.80
20' wide, running bond, dry jts., laid flat	1.000	S.F.	.145	2.59	3.16	5.75
Laid on edge	1.000	S.F.	.229	4.07	4.93	9.00
Mortar joints, laid flat	1.000	S.F.	.174	3.11	3.79	6.90
Laid on edge	1.000	S.F.	.274	4.88	5.92	10.80
Crushed stone, 10' wide, white marble, 3"	1.000	S.F.	.009	.41	.18	.59
Bluestone, 3"	1.000	S.F.	.009	.10	.18	.28
20' wide, white marble, 3"	1.000	S.F.	.009	.41	.18	.59
Bluestone, 3"	1.000	S.F.	.009	.10	.18	.28
Soil cement, 10' wide	1.000	S.F.	.006	.19	.47	.66
20' wide	1.000	S.F.	.006	.19	.47	.66
Granite blocks, 10' wide	1.000	S.F.	.174	5.12	3.73	8.85
20' wide	1.000	S.F.	.174	5.12	3.73	8.85
Asphalt block, solid 1-¼" thick	1.000	S.F.	.119	2.79	2.56	5.35
Solid 3" thick	1.000	S.F.	.123	4.05	2.65	6.70
Edging, brick, 10' wide	.200	L.F.	.023	.33	.52	.85
20' wide	.100	L.F.	.011	.17	.25	.42
Redwood, untreated 2" x 4", 10' wide	.200	L.F.	.009	.18	.24	.42
20' wide	.100	L.F.	.004	.09	.12	.21
Granite, 4 ½" x 12" straight, 10' wide	.200	L.F.	.037	1.39	1.17	2.56
20' wide	.100	L.F.	.018	.69	.59	1.28
Finishes, asphalt sealer, 10' wide	1.000	S.F.	.023	.36	.46	.82
20' wide	1.000	S.F.	.023	.36	.46	.82
Concrete, exposed aggregate 10' wide	1.000	S.F.	.013	.39	.28	.67
20' wide	1.000	S.F.	.013	.39	.28	.67

1 | SITE WORK — 24 | Septic Systems

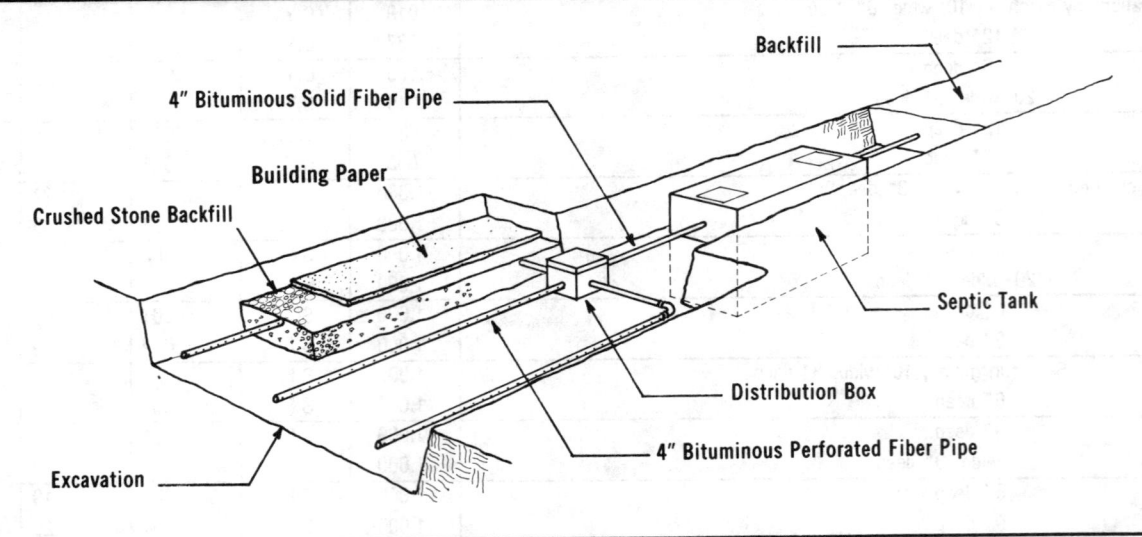

Diagram labels: Backfill, 4" Bituminous Solid Fiber Pipe, Building Paper, Crushed Stone Backfill, Septic Tank, Distribution Box, 4" Bituminous Perforated Fiber Pipe, Excavation

SYSTEM DESCRIPTION	QUAN.	UNIT	MAN-HOURS	MAT.	INST.	TOTAL
SEPTIC SYSTEM WITH 1000 S.F. LEACHING FIELD, 1000 GALLON TANK						
Tank, 1000 gallon, concrete	1.000	Ea.	3.500	473.00	92.00	565.00
Distribution box, concrete	1.000	Ea.	1.000	56.10	26.90	83.00
4" bituminous fiber pipe	25.000	L.F.	1.050	40.75	20.00	60.75
Tank and field excavation	119.000	C.Y.	13.090		708.05	708.05
Crushed stone backfill	76.000	C.Y.	12.160	1200.04	319.96	1520.00
Backfill with excavated material	36.000	C.Y.	.360		33.48	33.48
Building paper	125.000	S.Y.	2.250	33.76	56.24	90.00
4" bituminous fiber perforated pipe	145.000	L.F.	4.640	239.25	100.05	339.30
4" pipe fittings	2.000	Ea.	2.280	10.02	55.98	66.00
TOTAL			40.330	2052.92	1412.66	3465.58
SEPTIC SYSTEM WITH 2 LEACHING PITS, 1000 GALLON TANK						
Tank, 1000 gallon, concrete	1.000	Ea.	3.500	473.00	92.00	565.00
Distribution box, concrete	1.000	Ea.	1.000	56.10	26.90	83.00
4" bituminous fiber pipe	75.000	L.F.	3.150	122.25	60.00	182.25
Excavation for tank only	20.000	C.Y.	2.200		119.00	119.00
Crushed stone backfill	10.000	C.Y.	1.600	157.90	42.10	200.00
Backfill with excavated material	55.000	C.Y.	.550		51.15	51.15
Pits, 6' diameter, including excavation and stone backfill	2.000	Ea.		1150.00		1150.00
TOTAL			12.000	1959.25	391.15	2350.40

The costs in this system include all necessary piping and excavation.

DESCRIPTION	QUAN.	UNIT	MAN-HOURS	MAT.	INST.	TOTAL

Septic Systems Price Sheet

	QUAN.	UNIT	MAN-HOURS	COST EACH MAT.	COST EACH INST.	TOTAL
Tank, precast concrete, 1000 gallon	1.000	Ea.	3.500	473.00	92.00	565.00
2000 gallon	1.000	Ea.	5.600	891.00	159.00	1050.00
Distribution box, concrete, 5 outlets	1.000	Ea.	1.000	56.10	26.90	83.00
12 outlets	1.000	Ea.	2.000	330.00	40.00	370.00
4" pipe, bituminous fiber, solid	25.000	L.F.	1.050	40.75	20.00	60.75
Tank and field excavation, 1000 S.F. field	119.000	C.Y.	13.090		708.05	708.05
2000 S.F. field	190.000	C.Y.	20.900		1130.50	1130.50
Tank excavation only, 1000 gallon tank	20.000	C.Y.	2.200		119.00	119.00
2000 gallon tank	32.000	C.Y.	3.520		190.40	190.40
Backfill, crushed stone 1000 S.F. field	76.000	C.Y.	12.160	1200.04	319.96	1520.00
2000 S.F. field	140.000	C.Y.	22.400	2210.60	589.40	2800.00
Backfill with excavated material, 1000 S.F. field	36.000	C.Y.	.360		33.48	33.48
2000 S.F. field	60.000	C.Y.	.600		55.80	55.80
6' diameter pits	55.000	C.Y.	.550		51.15	51.15
3' diameter pits	42.000	C.Y.	.420		39.06	39.06
Building paper, 1000 S.F. field	125.000	S.Y.	2.200	33.00	55.00	88.00
2000 S.F. field	250.000	S.Y.	4.500	67.50	112.50	180.00
4" pipe, bituminous fiber, perforated, 1000 S.F. field	145.000	L.F.	4.640	239.25	100.05	339.30
2000 S.F. field	265.000	L.F.	8.480	437.25	182.85	620.10
Pipe fittings, bituminous fiber, 1000 S.F. field	2.000	Ea.	2.280	10.02	55.98	66.00
2000 S.F. field	4.000	Ea.	4.560	20.04	111.96	132.00
Leaching pit, including excavation and stone backfill, 3' diameter	1.000	Ea.		431.25		431.25
6' diameter	1.000	Ea.		575.00		575.00

1 | SITE WORK — 60 | Chain Link Fence Price Sheet

SYSTEM DESCRIPTION	QUAN.	UNIT	MAN-HOURS	MAT.	INST.	TOTAL
Chain link fence						
Galv. 9ga. wire, 1-⅝"post 10'O.C., 1-⅜"top rail, 2"corner post, 3'hi	1.000	L.F.	.130	3.37	2.63	6.00
4' high	1.000	L.F.	.141	4.08	2.82	6.90
6' high	1.000	L.F.	.209	5.12	4.18	9.30
Add for gate 3' wide 1-⅜" frame 3' high	1.000	Ea.	2.000	35.20	39.80	75.00
4' high	1.000	Ea.	2.400	44.00	48.00	92.00
6' high	1.000	Ea.	2.400	67.10	47.90	115.00
Add for gate 4' wide 1-⅜" frame 3' high	1.000	Ea.	2.670	44.00	54.00	98.00
4' high	1.000	Ea.	2.670	58.30	51.70	110.00
6' high	1.000	Ea.	3.000	86.90	58.10	145.00
Alum. 9ga. wire, 1-⅝"post, 10'O.C., 1-⅜"top rail, 2"corner post, 3'hi	1.000	L.F.	.130	4.07	2.63	6.70
4' high	1.000	L.F.	.141	4.80	2.85	7.65
6' high	1.000	L.F.	.209	6.16	4.19	10.35
Add for gate 3' wide 1-⅜" frame 3' high	1.000	Ea.	2.000	40.70	40.30	81.00
4' high	1.000	Ea.	2.400	55.00	50.00	105.00
6' high	1.000	Ea.	2.400	80.30	49.70	130.00
Add for gate 4' wide 1-⅜" frame 3' high	1.000	Ea.	2.400	55.00	50.00	105.00
4' high	1.000	Ea.	2.670	71.50	53.50	125.00
6' high	1.000	Ea.	3.000	108.90	61.10	170.00
Vinyl 9ga. wire, 1-⅝"post 10'O.C., 1-⅜"top rail, 2"corner post, 3'hi	1.000	L.F.	.130	3.76	2.59	6.35
4' high	1.000	L.F.	.141	4.53	2.82	7.35
6' high	1.000	L.F.	.209	5.70	4.20	9.90
Add for gate 3' wide 1-⅜" frame 3' high	1.000	Ea.	2.000	44.00	40.00	84.00
4' high	1.000	Ea.	2.400	58.30	46.70	105.00
6' high	1.000	Ea.	2.400	88.00	47.00	135.00
Add for gate 4' wide 1-⅜" frame 3' high	1.000	Ea.	2.400	58.30	46.70	105.00
4' high	1.000	Ea.	2.670	78.10	51.90	130.00
6' high	1.000	Ea.	3.000	115.50	59.50	175.00
Tennis court, chain link fence, 10' high						
Galv. 11ga. wire, 2"post 10'O.C., 1-⅜"top rail, 2-½"corner post	1.000	L.F.	.253	9.35	5.10	14.45
Add for gate 3' wide 1-⅜" frame	1.000	Ea.	2.400	115.50	49.50	165.00
Alum. 11ga. wire, 2"post 10'O.C., 1-⅜"top rail, 2-½"corner post	1.000	L.F.	.253	11.39	5.06	16.45
Add for gate 3' wide 1-⅜" frame	1.000	Ea.	2.400	148.50	46.50	195.00
Vinyl 11ga. wire, 2"post 10' O.C., 1-⅜"top rail, 2-½"corner post	1.000	L.F.	.253	10.40	5.10	15.50
Add for gate 3' wide 1-⅜" frame	1.000	Ea.	2.400	165.00	50.00	215.00
Railings, commercial						
Aluminum balcony rail, 1-½" posts with pickets	1.000	L.F.	.164	21.89	5.11	27.00
With expanded metal panels	1.000	L.F.	.164	37.51	5.49	43.00
With porcelain enamel panel inserts	1.000	L.F.	.164	50.71	5.29	56.00
Mild steel, ornamental rounded top rail	1.000	L.F.	.164	20.46	5.54	26.00
As above, but pitch down stairs	1.000	L.F.	.183	20.24	5.76	26.00
Steel pipe, welded, 1-½" round, painted	1.000	L.F.	.160	12.10	5.25	17.35
Galvanized	1.000	L.F.	.160	16.94	5.06	22.00
Residential, stock units, mild steel, deluxe	1.000	L.F.	.102	6.60	3.35	9.95
Economy	1.000	L.F.	.102	4.84	3.36	8.20

1 | SITE WORK — 64 | Wood Fence Price Sheet

SYSTEM DESCRIPTION	QUAN.	UNIT	MAN-HOURS	MAT.	INST.	TOTAL
Basketweave, ⅜"x4" boards, 2"x4" stringers on spreaders, 4"x4" posts						
No. 1 cedar, 6' high	1.000	L.F.	.150	19.14	2.86	22.00
Treated pine, 6' high	1.000	L.F.	.160	8.53	3.22	11.75
Board fence, 1"x4" boards, 2"x4" rails, 4"x4" posts						
Preservative treated, 2 rail, 3' high	1.000	L.F.	.166	5.08	3.32	8.40
4' high	1.000	L.F.	.178	5.94	3.56	9.50
3 rail, 5' high	1.000	L.F.	.185	7.26	3.69	10.95
6' high	1.000	L.F.	.192	7.98	3.87	11.85
Western cedar, No. 1, 2 rail, 3' high	1.000	L.F.	.166	5.94	3.31	9.25
3 rail, 4' high	1.000	L.F.	.178	11.33	3.57	14.90
5' high	1.000	L.F.	.185	14.63	3.72	18.35
6' high	1.000	L.F.	.192	17.55	3.45	21.00
No. 1 cedar, 2 rail, 3' high	1.000	L.F.	.166	14.25	3.35	17.60
4' high	1.000	L.F.	.178	16.34	3.56	19.90
3 rail, 5' high	1.000	L.F.	.185	17.99	4.01	22.00
6' high	1.000	L.F.	.192	19.69	4.31	24.00
Shadow box, 1"x6" boards, 2"x4" rails, 4"x4" posts						
Fir, pine or spruce, treated, 3 rail, 6' high	1.000	L.F.	.150	7.87	3.03	10.90
No. 1 cedar, 3 rail, 4' high	1.000	L.F.	.178	16.12	3.58	19.70
6' high	1.000	L.F.	.185	18.04	3.96	22.00
Open rail, split rails, No. 1 cedar, 2 rail, 3' high	1.000	L.F.	.150	4.03	3.02	7.05
3 rail, 4' high	1.000	L.F.	.160	5.32	3.23	8.55
No. 2 cedar, 2 rail, 3' high	1.000	L.F.	.150	2.13	3.02	5.15
3 rail, 4' high	1.000	L.F.	.160	2.37	3.23	5.60
Open rail, rustic rails, No. 1 cedar, 2 rail, 3' high	1.000	L.F.	.150	3.54	3.01	6.55
3 rail, 4' high	1.000	L.F.	.160	4.39	3.21	7.60
No. 2 cedar, 2 rail, 3' high	1.000	L.F.	.150	2.11	3.04	5.15
3 rail, 4' high	1.000	L.F.	.160	2.64	3.21	5.85
Rustic picket, molded pine pickets, 2 rail, 3' high	1.000	L.F.	.171	3.06	3.44	6.50
3 rail, 4' high	1.000	L.F.	.196	3.52	3.96	7.48
No. 1 cedar, 2 rail, 3' high	1.000	L.F.	.171	6.82	3.43	10.25
3 rail,	1.000	L.F.	.196	7.84	3.95	11.79
Picket fence, fir, pine or spruce, preserved, treated						
2 rail, 3' high	1.000	L.F.	.171	3.61	3.44	7.05
3 rail, 4' high	1.000	L.F.	.185	4.19	3.71	7.90
Western cedar, 2 rail, 3' high	1.000	L.F.	.171	4.19	3.46	7.65
3 rail, 4' high	1.000	L.F.	.185	4.61	3.69	8.30
No. 1 cedar, 2 rail, 3' high	1.000	L.F.	.171	9.52	3.43	12.95
3 rail, 4' high	1.000	L.F.	.185	10.84	3.71	14.55
Stockade, No. 1 cedar, 3-¼" rails, 6' high	1.000	L.F.	.150	8.42	3.03	11.45
8' high	1.000	L.F.	.155	11.17	3.13	14.30
No. 2 cedar, treated rails, 6' high	1.000	L.F.	.150	8.36	3.04	11.40
Treated pine, treated rails, 6' high	1.000	L.F.	.150	8.20	3.00	11.20
Gates, No. 2 cedar, picket, 3'-6" wide 4' high	1.000	Ea.	2.670	44.00	54.00	98.00
No. 2 cedar, rustic round, 3' wide, 3' high	1.000	Ea.	2.670	55.00	55.00	110.00
No. 2 cedar, stockade screen, 3'-6" wide, 6' high	1.000	Ea.	3.000	46.20	58.80	105.00
General, wood, 3'-6" wide, 4' high	1.000	Ea.	2.400	42.24	49.76	92.00
6' high	1.000	Ea.	3.000	52.80	62.20	115.00

2 | FOUNDATIONS — 04 Footing Systems

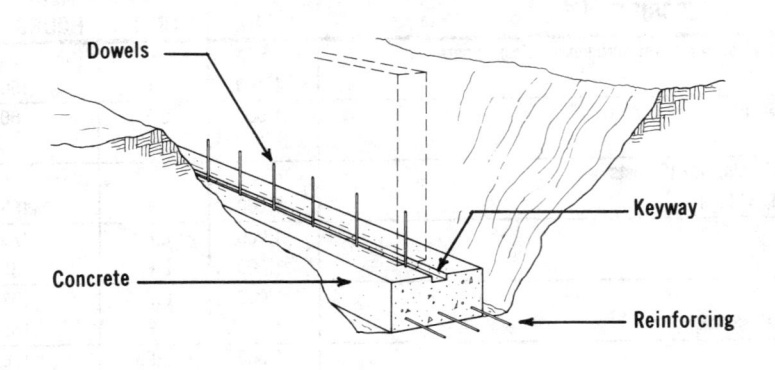

SYSTEM DESCRIPTION	QUAN.	UNIT	MAN-HOURS	COST PER L.F. MAT.	COST PER L.F. INST.	COST PER L.F. TOTAL
8" THICK BY 18" WIDE FOOTING						
Concrete, 3000 psi	.040	C.Y.		2.24		2.24
Place concrete, direct chute	.040	C.Y.	.016		.35	.35
Forms, footing, 4 uses	1.330	SFCA	.102	.56	2.41	2.97
Reinforcing, ½" diameter bars, 2 each	1.380	Lb.	.011	.41	.29	.70
Keyway, 2" x 4", beveled, 4 uses	1.000	L.F.	.015	.08	.36	.44
Dowels, ½" diameter bars, 2' long, 6' O.C.	.166	Ea.	.021	.18	.60	.78
TOTAL			.165	3.47	4.01	7.48
12" THICK BY 24" WIDE FOOTING						
Concrete, 3000 psi	.070	C.Y.		3.92		3.92
Place concrete, direct chute	.070	C.Y.	.028		.61	.61
Forms, footing, 4 uses	2.000	SFCA	.154	.84	3.62	4.46
Reinforcing, ½" diameter bars, 2 each	1.380	Lb.	.011	.41	.29	.70
Keyway, 2" x 4", beveled, 4 uses	1.000	L.F.	.015	.08	.36	.44
Dowels, ½" diameter bars, 2' long, 6' O.C.	.166	Ea.	.021	.18	.60	.78
TOTAL			.229	5.43	5.48	10.91
12" THICK BY 36" WIDE FOOTING						
Concrete, 3000 psi	.110	C.Y.		6.16		6.16
Place concrete, direct chute	.110	C.Y.	.044		.95	.95
Forms, footing, 4 uses	2.000	SFCA	.154	.84	3.62	4.46
Reinforcing, ½" diameter bars, 2 each	1.380	Lb.	.011	.41	.29	.70
Keyway, 2" x 4", beveled, 4 uses	1.000	L.F.	.015	.08	.36	.44
Dowels, ½" diameter bars, 2' long, 6' O.C.	.166	Ea.	.021	.18	.60	.78
TOTAL			.245	7.67	5.82	13.49

The footing costs in this system are on a cost per linear foot basis

DESCRIPTION	QUAN.	UNIT	MAN-HOURS	COST PER S.F. MAT.	COST PER S.F. INST.	COST PER S.F. TOTAL

Footing Price Sheet

	QUAN.	UNIT	MAN-HOURS	COST PER L.F. MAT.	COST PER L.F. INST.	COST PER L.F. TOTAL
Concrete, 8" thick by 18" wide footing						
2000 psi concrete	.040	C.Y.		2.12		2.12
2500 psi concrete	.040	C.Y.		2.16		2.16
3000 psi concrete	.040	C.Y.		2.24		2.24
3500 psi concrete	.040	C.Y.		2.32		2.32
4000 psi concrete	.040	C.Y.		2.40		2.40
12" thick by 24" wide footing						
2000 psi concrete	.070	C.Y.		3.71		3.71
2500 psi concrete	.070	C.Y.		3.78		3.78
3000 psi concrete	.070	C.Y.		3.92		3.92
3500 psi concrete	.070	C.Y.		4.06		4.06
4000 psi concrete	.070	C.Y.		4.20		4.20
12" thick by 36" wide footing						
2000 psi concrete	.110	C.Y.		5.83		5.83
2500 psi concrete	.110	C.Y.		5.94		5.94
3000 psi concrete	.110	C.Y.		6.16		6.16
3500 psi concrete	.110	C.Y.		6.38		6.38
4000 psi concrete	.110	C.Y.		6.60		6.60
Place concrete, 8" thick by 18" wide footing, direct chute	.040	C.Y.	.016		.35	.35
Pumped concrete	.040	C.Y.	.025		.78	.78
Crane & bucket	.040	C.Y.	.028		.96	.96
12" thick by 24" wide footing, direct chute	.070	C.Y.	.028		.61	.61
Pumped concrete	.070	C.Y.	.044		1.36	1.36
Crane & bucket	.070	C.Y.	.049		1.68	1.68
12" thick by 36" wide footing, direct chute	.110	C.Y.	.044		.95	.95
Pumped concrete	.110	C.Y.	.070		2.14	2.14
Crane & bucket	.110	C.Y.	.078		2.64	2.64
Forms, 8" thick footing, 1 use	1.330	SFCA	.139	1.54	3.29	4.83
4 uses	1.330	SFCA	.102	.56	2.41	2.97
12" thick footing, 1 use	2.000	SFCA	.210	2.32	4.94	7.26
4 uses	2.000	SFCA	.154	.84	3.62	4.46
Reinforcing, ⅜" diameter bar, 1 each	.400	Lb.	.003	.12	.08	.20
2 each	.800	Lb.	.006	.24	.17	.41
3 each	1.200	Lb.	.009	.36	.25	.61
½" diameter bar, 1 each	.700	Lb.	.005	.21	.15	.36
2 each	1.380	Lb.	.011	.41	.29	.70
3 each	2.100	Lb.	.016	.63	.44	1.07
⅝" diameter bar, 1 each	1.040	Lb.	.008	.31	.22	.53
2 each	2.080	Lb.	.016	.62	.44	1.06
Keyway, beveled, 2" x 4", 1 use	1.000	L.F.	.030	.16	.72	.88
2 uses	1.000	L.F.	.022	.12	.54	.66
2" x 6", 1 use	1.000	L.F.	.032	.22	.76	.98
2 uses	1.000	L.F.	.024	.17	.57	.74
Dowels, 2 feet long, 6' O.C., ⅜" bar	.166	Ea.	.018	.15	.53	.68
½" bar	.166	Ea.	.021	.18	.60	.78
⅝" bar	.166	Ea.	.024	.22	.68	.90
¾" bar	.166	Ea.	.024	.22	.68	.90

2 | FOUNDATIONS — 08 Block Wall Systems

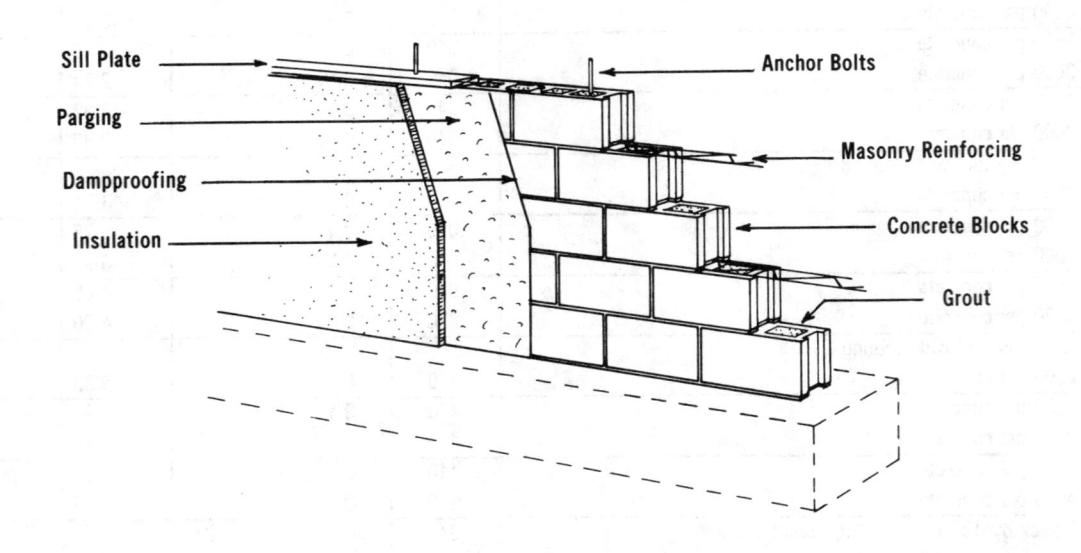

SYSTEM DESCRIPTION	QUAN.	UNIT	MAN-HOURS	COST PER S.F. MAT.	COST PER S.F. INST.	COST PER S.F. TOTAL
8" WALL, GROUTED, FULL HEIGHT						
Concrete block, 8" x 16" x 8"	1.000	S.F.	.093	1.76	2.06	3.82
Masonry reinforcing, every second course	.750	L.F.	.002	.15	.05	.20
Parging, plastering with portland cement plaster, 1 coat	1.000	S.F.	.014	.23	.32	.55
Dampproofing, bituminous coating, 1 coat	1.000	S.F.	.012	.09	.28	.37
Insulation, 1" rigid polystyrene	1.000	S.F.	.010	.45	.24	.69
Grout, solid, pumped	1.000	S.F.	.038	.92	.96	1.88
Anchor bolts, ½" diameter, 8" long, 4' O.C.	.060	Ea.	.002	.02	.06	.08
Sill plate, 2" x 4", treated	.250	L.F.	.007	.10	.19	.29
TOTAL			.178	3.72	4.16	7.88
12" WALL, GROUTED, FULL HEIGHT						
Concrete block, 8" x 16" x 12"	1.000	S.F.	.122	2.39	2.61	5.00
Masonry reinforcing, every second course	.750	L.F.	.003	.16	.07	.23
Parging, plastering with portland cement plaster, 1 coat	1.000	S.F.	.014	.23	.32	.55
Dampproofing, bituminous coating, 1 coat	1.000	S.F.	.012	.09	.28	.37
Insulation, 1" rigid polystyrene	1.000	S.F.	.010	.45	.24	.69
Grout, solid, pumped	1.000	S.F.	.040	1.52	1.01	2.53
Anchor bolts, ½" diameter, 8" long, 4' O.C.	.060	Ea.	.002	.02	.06	.08
Sill plate, 2" x 4", treated	.250	L.F.	.007	.10	.19	.29
TOTAL			.210	4.96	4.78	9.74

The costs in this system are based on a square foot of wall. Do not subtract for window or door openings.

DESCRIPTION	QUAN.	UNIT	MAN-HOURS	COST PER S.F. MAT.	COST PER S.F. INST.	COST PER S.F. TOTAL

Block Wall Systems

	QUAN.	UNIT	MAN-HOURS	MAT.	INST.	TOTAL
Concrete, block, 8" x 16" x, 6" thick	1.000	S.F.	.089	1.38	1.97	3.35
8" thick	1.000	S.F.	.093	1.76	2.06	3.82
10" thick	1.000	S.F.	.095	2.32	2.11	4.43
12" thick	1.000	S.F.	.122	2.39	2.61	5.00
Solid block, 8" x 16" x, 6" thick	1.000	S.F.	.091	1.93	2.01	3.94
8" thick	1.000	S.F.	.096	2.38	2.13	4.51
10" thick	1.000	S.F.	.096	2.38	2.13	4.51
12" thick	1.000	S.F.	.126	3.50	2.75	6.25
Masonry reinforcing, wire strips, to 8" wide, every course	1.500	L.F.	.004	.30	.09	.39
Every 2nd course	.750	L.F.	.002	.15	.05	.20
Every 3rd course	.500	L.F.	.001	.10	.03	.13
Every 4th course	.400	L.F.	.001	.08	.02	.10
Wire strips to 12" wide, every course	1.500	L.F.	.006	.32	.15	.47
Every 2nd course	.750	L.F.	.003	.16	.07	.23
Every 3rd course	.500	L.F.	.002	.11	.05	.16
Every 4th course	.400	L.F.	.001	.08	.04	.12
Parging, plastering with portland cement plaster, 1 coat	1.000	S.F.	.014	.23	.32	.55
2 coats	1.000	S.F.	.022	.35	.50	.85
Dampproofing, bituminous, brushed on, 1 coat	1.000	S.F.	.012	.09	.28	.37
2 coats	1.000	S.F.	.016	.18	.38	.56
Sprayed on, 1 coat	1.000	S.F.	.010	.18	.22	.40
2 coats	1.000	S.F.	.016	.23	.38	.61
Troweled on, 1/16" thick	1.000	S.F.	.016	.15	.38	.53
1/8" thick	1.000	S.F.	.020	.29	.47	.76
1/2" thick	1.000	S.F.	.023	1.21	.54	1.75
Insulation, rigid, fiberglass, 1.5#/C.F., unfaced						
1-1/2" thick R 6.2	1.000	S.F.	.008	.32	.19	.51
2" thick R 8.5	1.000	S.F.	.008	.42	.19	.61
3" thick R 13	1.000	S.F.	.010	.65	.24	.89
Foamglass, 1-1/2" thick R 2.64	1.000	S.F.	.010	1.74	.24	1.98
2" thick R 5.26	1.000	S.F.	.011	2.43	.26	2.69
Perlite, 1" thick R 2.77	1.000	S.F.	.010	.44	.24	.68
2" thick R 5.55	1.000	S.F.	.011	.83	.26	1.09
Polystyrene, extruded, 1" thick R 5.4	1.000	S.F.	.010	.45	.24	.69
2" thick R 10.8	1.000	S.F.	.011	.97	.26	1.23
Molded 1" thick R 3.85	1.000	S.F.	.010	.19	.24	.43
2" thick R 7.7	1.000	S.F.	.011	.37	.27	.64
Urethane, 1" thick, R 5.8	1.000	S.F.	.010	.55	.24	.79
2" thick R 11.7	1.000	S.F.	.011	1.10	.26	1.36
Grout, concrete block cores, 6" thick	1.000	S.F.	.028	.69	.72	1.41
8" thick	1.000	S.F.	.038	.92	.96	1.88
10" thick	1.000	S.F.	.039	1.22	.98	2.20
12" thick	1.000	S.F.	.040	1.52	1.01	2.53
Anchor bolts, 2' on center, 1/2" diameter, 8" long	.120	Ea.	.004	.04	.12	.16
12" long	.120	Ea.	.005	.06	.12	.18
3/4" diameter, 8" long	.120	Ea.	.006	.18	.15	.33
12" long	.120	Ea.	.006	.22	.16	.38
4' on center, 1/2" diameter, 8" long	.060	Ea.	.002	.02	.06	.08
12" long	.060	Ea.	.002	.03	.06	.09
3/4" diameter, 8" long	.060	Ea.	.003	.09	.07	.16
12" long	.060	Ea.	.003	.11	.08	.19
Sill plates, treated, 2" x 4"	.250	L.F.	.007	.10	.19	.29
4" x 4"	.250	L.F.	.006	.31	.17	.48

2 | FOUNDATIONS 12 | Concrete Wall Systems

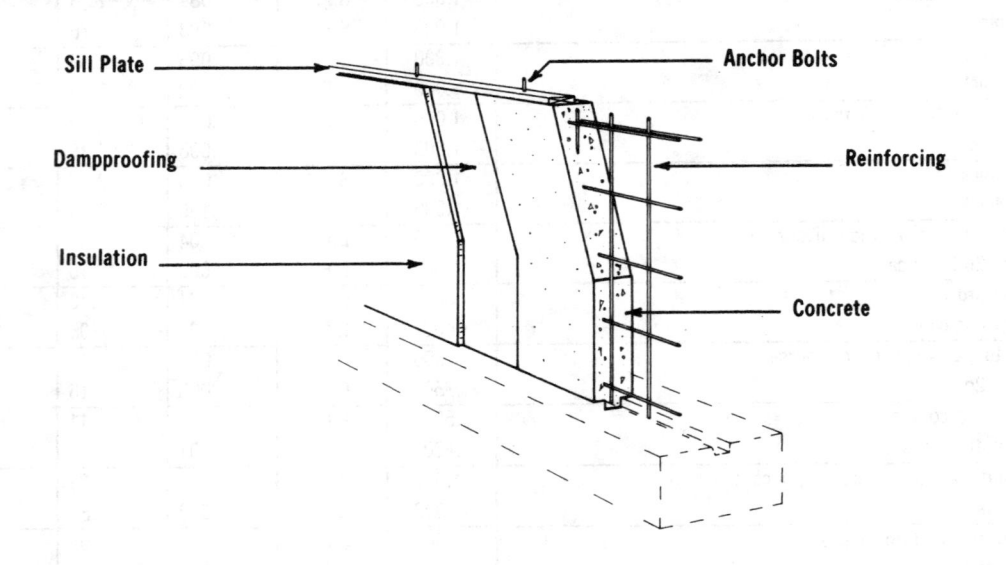

Labeled diagram: Sill Plate, Anchor Bolts, Dampproofing, Reinforcing, Insulation, Concrete

SYSTEM DESCRIPTION	QUAN.	UNIT	MAN-HOURS	MAT.	INST.	TOTAL
8" THICK, POURED CONCRETE WALL						
Concrete, 8" thick, 3000 psi	.025	C.Y.		1.40		1.40
Forms, prefabricated plywood, 4 uses per month	2.000	SFCA	.098	.62	2.42	3.04
Reinforcing, light	.670	Lb.	.003	.21	.10	.31
Placing concrete, direct chute	.025	C.Y.	.013		.29	.29
Dampproofing, brushed on, 2 coats	1.000	S.F.	.016	.18	.38	.56
Rigid insulation, 1" polystyrene	1.000	S.F.	.010	.45	.24	.69
Anchor bolts, ½" diameter, 12" long, 4' O.C.	.060	Ea.	.002	.03	.06	.09
Sill plates, 2" x 4", treated	.250	L.F.	.007	.10	.19	.29
TOTAL			.149	2.99	3.68	6.67
12" THICK, POURED CONCRETE WALL						
Concrete, 12" thick, 3000 psi	.040	C.Y.		2.24		2.24
Forms, prefabricated plywood, 4 uses per month	2.000	SFCA	.098	.62	2.42	3.04
Reinforcing, light	1.000	Lb.	.005	.31	.15	.46
Placing concrete, direct chute	.040	C.Y.	.019		.41	.41
Dampproofing, brushed on, 2 coats	1.000	S.F.	.016	.18	.38	.56
Rigid insulation, 1" polystyrene	1.000	S.F.	.010	.45	.24	.69
Anchor bolts, ½" diameter, 12" long, 4' O.C.	.060	Ea.	.002	.03	.06	.09
Sill plates, 2" x 4" treated	.250	L.F.	.007	.10	.19	.29
TOTAL			.157	3.93	3.85	7.78

The costs in this system are based on sq. ft. of wall. Do not subtract for window and door openings. The costs assume a 4' high wall.

DESCRIPTION	QUAN.	UNIT	MAN-HOURS	MAT.	INST.	TOTAL

Concrete Wall Price Sheet

	QUAN.	UNIT	MAN-HOURS	COST PER S.F. MAT.	COST PER S.F. INST.	COST PER S.F. TOTAL
Concrete, 8" wall, concrete, 2500 psi	.025	C.Y.		1.35		1.35
3000 psi	.025	C.Y.		1.40		1.40
3500 psi	.025	C.Y.		1.45		1.45
4500 psi	.025	C.Y.		1.53		1.53
10" wall, concrete, 2500 psi	.030	C.Y.		1.62		1.62
3000 psi	.030	C.Y.		1.68		1.68
3500 psi	.030	C.Y.		1.74		1.74
4500 psi	.030	C.Y.		1.83		1.83
12" wall, concrete, 2500 psi	.040	C.Y.		2.16		2.16
3000 psi	.040	C.Y.		2.24		2.24
3500 psi	.040	C.Y.		2.32		2.32
4500 psi	.040	C.Y.		2.44		2.44
Formwork, prefabricated plywood, 1 use per month	2.000	SFCA	.106	1.82	2.58	4.40
4 uses per month	2.000	SFCA	.098	.62	2.42	3.04
Job built forms, 1 use per month	2.000	SFCA	.260	3.30	6.32	9.62
4 uses per month	2.000	SFCA	.190	1.36	4.64	6.00
Reinforcing, 8" wall, light reinforcing	.670	Lb.	.003	.21	.10	.31
Heavy reinforcing	1.500	Lb.	.007	.47	.22	.69
10" wall, light reinforcing	.850	Lb.	.004	.26	.13	.39
Heavy reinforcing	2.000	Lb.	.010	.62	.30	.92
12" wall light reinforcing	1.000	Lb.	.005	.31	.15	.46
Heavy reinforcing	2.250	Lb.	.011	.70	.34	1.04
Placing concrete, 8" wall, direct chute	.025	C.Y.	.013		.29	.29
Pumped concrete	.025	C.Y.	.018		.58	.58
Crane & bucket	.025	C.Y.	.020		.68	.68
10" wall, direct chute	.030	C.Y.	.015		.35	.35
Pumped concrete	.030	C.Y.	.022		.69	.69
Crane & bucket	.030	C.Y.	.024		.81	.81
12" wall, direct chute	.040	C.Y.	.019		.41	.41
Pumped concrete	.040	C.Y.	.026		.80	.80
Crane & bucket	.040	C.Y.	.028		.96	.96
Dampproofing, bituminous, brushed on, 1 coat	1.000	S.F.	.012	.09	.28	.37
2 coats	1.000	S.F.	.016	.18	.38	.56
Sprayed on, 1 coat	1.000	S.F.	.010	.18	.22	.40
2 coats	1.000	S.F.	.016	.23	.38	.61
Troweled on, 1/16" thick	1.000	S.F.	.016	.15	.38	.53
1/8" thick	1.000	S.F.	.020	.29	.47	.76
1/2" thick	1.000	S.F.	.023	1.21	.54	1.75
Insulation rigid, fiberglass, 1.5#/C.F., unfaced						
1-1/2" thick, R 6.2	1.000	S.F.	.008	.32	.19	.51
2" thick, R 8.3	1.000	S.F.	.008	.42	.19	.61
3" thick, R 12.4	1.000	S.F.	.010	.65	.24	.89
Foamglass, 1-1/2" thick R 2.64	1.000	S.F.	.010	1.74	.24	1.98
2" thick R 5.26	1.000	S.F.	.011	2.43	.26	2.69
Perlite, 1" thick R 2.77	1.000	S.F.	.010	.44	.24	.68
2" thick R 5.55	1.000	S.F.	.011	.83	.26	1.09
Polystyrene, extruded, 1" thick R 5.40	1.000	S.F.	.010	.45	.24	.69
2" thick R 10.8	1.000	S.F.	.011	.97	.26	1.23
Molded, 1" thick R 3.85	1.000	S.F.	.010	.19	.24	.43
2" thick R 7.70	1.000	S.F.	.011	.37	.27	.64
Anchor bolts, 2' on center, 1/2" diameter, 8" long	.120	Ea.	.004	.04	.12	.16
12" long	.120	Ea.	.005	.06	.12	.18
3/4" diameter, 8" long	.120	Ea.	.006	.18	.15	.33
12" long	.120	Ea.	.006	.22	.16	.38
Sill plates, treated lumber, 2" x 4"	.250	L.F.	.007	.10	.19	.29
4" x 4"	.250	L.F.	.006	.31	.17	.48

2 | FOUNDATIONS 16 | Wood Wall Foundation Systems

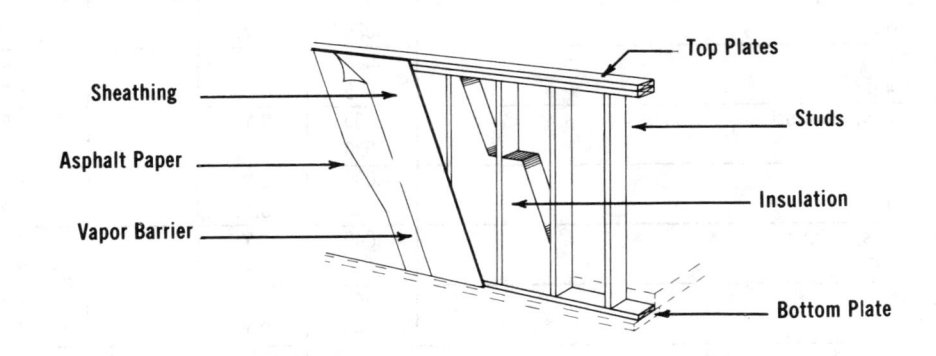

Diagram labels: Sheathing, Asphalt Paper, Vapor Barrier, Top Plates, Studs, Insulation, Bottom Plate

SYSTEM DESCRIPTION	QUAN.	UNIT	MAN-HOURS	MAT.	INST.	TOTAL
2" X 4" STUDS, 16" O.C., WALL						
Studs, 2" x 4", 16" O.C., treated	1.000	L.F.	.015	.39	.38	.77
Plates, double top plate, single bottom plate, treated, 2" x 4"	.750	L.F.	.011	.29	.29	.58
Sheathing, ½", exterior grade, CDX, treated	1.000	S.F.	.014	.57	.35	.92
Asphalt paper, 15# roll	1.100	S.F.	.002	.03	.06	.09
Vapor barrier, 4 mil polyethylene	1.000	S.F.	.002	.03	.05	.08
Insulation, batts, fiberglass, 3-½" thick, R 11	1.000	S.F.	.005	.28	.11	.39
TOTAL			.049	1.59	1.24	2.83
2" X 6" STUDS, 16" O.C., WALL						
Studs, 2" x 6", 16" O.C., treated	1.000	L.F.	.017	.53	.42	.95
Plates, double top plate, single bottom plate, treated, 2" x 6"	.750	L.F.	.012	.40	.31	.71
Sheathing, ⅝" exterior grade, CDX, treated	1.000	S.F.	.015	.66	.37	1.03
Asphalt paper, 15# roll	1.100	S.F.	.002	.03	.06	.09
Vapor barrier, 4 mil polyethylene	1.000	S.F.	.002	.03	.05	.08
Insulation, batts, fiberglass, 6" thick, R 19	1.000	S.F.	.006	.43	.14	.57
TOTAL			.054	2.08	1.35	3.43
2" X 8" STUDS, 16" O.C., WALL						
Studs, 2" x 8", 16" O.C. treated	1.000	L.F.	.020	.39	.50	.89
Plates, double top plate, single bottom plate, treated, 2" x 8"	.750	L.F.	.015	.29	.38	.67
Sheathing, ¾" exterior grade, CDX, treated	1.000	S.F.	.016	.81	.40	1.21
Asphalt paper, 15# roll	1.100	S.F.	.002	.03	.06	.09
Vapor barrier, 4 mil polyethylene	1.000	S.F.	.002	.03	.05	.08
Insulation, batts, fiberglass, 9" thick, R 30	1.000	S.F.	.006	.66	.14	.80
TOTAL			.061	2.21	1.53	3.74

The costs in this system are based on a sq. ft. of wall area. Do not Subtract for window or door openings. The costs assume a 4' high wall.

DESCRIPTION	QUAN.	UNIT	MAN-HOURS	MAT.	INST.	TOTAL

Wood Wall Foundation Price Sheet

	QUAN.	UNIT	MAN-HOURS	COST PER S.F. MAT.	COST PER S.F. INST.	COST PER S.F. TOTAL
Studs, treated, 2" x 4", 12" O.C.	1.250	L.F.	.018	.49	.47	.96
16" O.C.	1.000	L.F.	.015	.39	.38	.77
2" x 6", 12" O.C.	1.250	L.F.	.021	.66	.53	1.19
16" O.C.	1.000	L.F.	.017	.53	.42	.95
2" x 8", 12" O.C.	1.250	L.F.	.025	.49	.62	1.11
16" O.C.	1.000	L.F.	.020	.39	.50	.89
Plates, treated double top single bottom, 2" x 4"	.750	L.F.	.011	.29	.29	.58
2" x 6"	.750	L.F.	.012	.40	.31	.71
2" x 8"	.750	L.F.	.015	.29	.38	.67
Sheathing, treated exterior grade CDX, ½" thick	1.000	S.F.	.014	.57	.35	.92
⅝" thick	1.000	S.F.	.015	.66	.37	1.03
¾" thick	1.000	S.F.	.016	.81	.40	1.21
Asphalt paper, 15# roll	1.100	S.F.	.002	.03	.06	.09
Vapor barrier, polyethylene, 4 mil	1.000	S.F.	.002	.02	.05	.07
10 mil	1.000	S.F.	.002	.04	.06	.10
Insulation, rigid, fiberglass, 1.5#/C.F., unfaced			.008	.20	.19	.39
1-½" thick, R 6.2	1.000	S.F.	.008	.32	.19	.51
2" thick, R 8.3	1.000	S.F.	.008	.42	.19	.61
3" thick, R 12.4	1.000	S.F.	.010	.66	.25	.91
Foamglass 1 ½" thick, R 2.64	1.000	S.F.	.010	1.74	.24	1.98
2" thick, R 5.26	1.000	S.F.	.011	2.43	.26	2.69
Perlite 1" thick, R 2.77	1.000	S.F.	.010	.44	.24	.68
2" thick, R 5.55	1.000	S.F.	.011	.83	.26	1.09
Polystyrene, extruded, 1" thick, R 5.40	1.000	S.F.	.010	.45	.24	.69
2" thick, R 10.8	1.000	S.F.	.011	.97	.26	1.23
Molded 1" thick, R 3.85	1.000	S.F.	.010	.19	.24	.43
2" thick, R 7.7	1.000	S.F.	.011	.37	.27	.64
Urethane 1" thick, R 5.8	1.000	S.F.	.010	.55	.24	.79
2" thick, R 11.7	1.000	S.F.	.011	1.10	.26	1.36
Non rigid, batts, fiberglass, paper backed, 3-½" thick roll, R 11	1.000	S.F.	.005	.28	.11	.39
6", R 19	1.000	S.F.	.006	.43	.14	.57
9", R 30	1.000	S.F.	.006	.66	.14	.80
12", R 38	1.000	S.F.	.006	.86	.14	1.00
Mineral fiber, paper backed, 3-½", R 13	1.000	S.F.	.005	.31	.12	.43
6", R 19	1.000	S.F.	.005	.48	.12	.60
10", R 30	1.000	S.F.	.006	.77	.14	.91

2 | FOUNDATIONS — 20 Floor Slab Systems

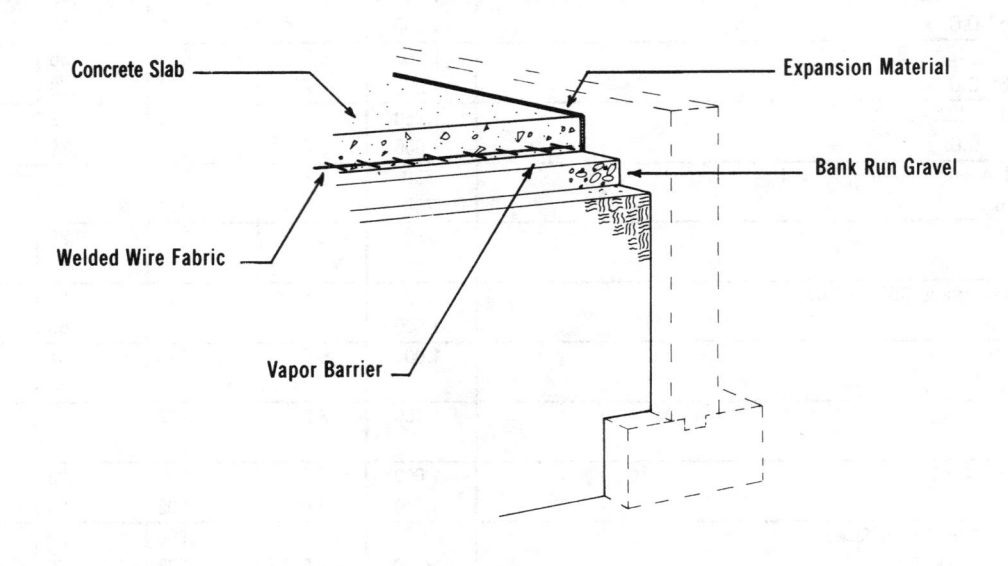

SYSTEM DESCRIPTION	QUAN.	UNIT	MAN-HOURS	MAT.	INST.	TOTAL
4" THICK SLAB						
Concrete, 4" thick, 3000 psi concrete	.012	C.Y.		.67		.67
Place concrete, direct chute	.012	C.Y.	.005		.11	.11
Bank run gravel, 4" deep	1.000	S.F.		.14	.03	.17
Polyethylene vapor barrier, .006" thick	1.000	S.F.	.002	.03	.05	.08
Edge forms, expansion material	.100	L.F.	.005	.03	.12	.15
Welded wire fabric, 6 x 6, 10/10 (W1.4/W1.4)	1.100	S.F.	.005	.09	.14	.23
Steel trowel finish	1.000	S.F.	.015		.40	.40
TOTAL			.032	.96	.85	1.81
6" THICK SLAB						
Concrete, 6" thick, 3000 psi concrete	.019	C.Y.		1.06		1.06
Place concrete, direct chute	.019	C.Y.	.008		.18	.18
Bank run gravel, 4" deep	1.000	S.F.		.14	.03	.17
Polyethylene vapor barrier, .006" thick	1.000	S.F.	.002	.03	.05	.08
Edge forms, expansion material	.100	L.F.	.005	.03	.12	.15
Welded wire fabric, 6 x 6, 10/10 (W1.4/W1.4)	1.100	S.F.	.005	.09	.14	.23
Steel trowel finish	1.000	S.F.	.015		.40	.40
TOTAL			.035	1.35	.92	2.27

The slab costs in this section are based on a cost per square foot of floor area.

DESCRIPTION	QUAN.	UNIT	MAN-HOURS	MAT.	INST.	TOTAL

Floor Slab Price Sheet

	QUAN.	UNIT	MAN-HOURS	COST PER S.F. MAT.	COST PER S.F. INST.	COST PER S.F. TOTAL
Concrete, 4" thick slab, 2000 psi concrete	.012	C.Y.		.64		.64
2500 psi concrete	.012	C.Y.		.65		.65
3000 psi concrete	.012	C.Y.		.67		.67
3500 psi concrete	.012	C.Y.		.70		.70
4000 psi concrete	.012	C.Y.		.72		.72
4500 psi concrete	.012	C.Y.		.73		.73
5" thick slab, 2000 psi concrete	.015	C.Y.		.80		.80
2500 psi concrete	.015	C.Y.		.81		.81
3000 psi concrete	.015	C.Y.		.84		.84
3500 psi concrete	.015	C.Y.		.87		.87
4000 psi concrete	.015	C.Y.		.90		.90
4500 psi concrete	.015	C.Y.		.92		.92
6" thick slab, 2000 psi concrete	.019	C.Y.		1.01		1.01
2500 psi concrete	.019	C.Y.		1.03		1.03
3000 psi concrete	.019	C.Y.		1.06		1.06
3500 psi concrete	.019	C.Y.		1.10		1.10
4000 psi concrete	.019	C.Y.		1.14		1.14
4500 psi concrete	.019	C.Y.		1.16		1.16
Place concrete, 4" slab, direct chute	.012	C.Y.	.005		.11	.11
Pumped concrete	.012	C.Y.	.006		.19	.19
Crane & bucket	.012	C.Y.	.006		.24	.24
5" slab, direct chute	.015	C.Y.	.006		.14	.14
Pumped concrete	.015	C.Y.	.007		.24	.24
Crane & bucket	.015	C.Y.	.008		.30	.30
6" slab, direct chute	.019	C.Y.	.008		.18	.18
Pumped concrete	.019	C.Y.	.010		.31	.31
Crane & bucket	.019	C.Y.	.011		.38	.38
Gravel, bank run, 4" deep	1.000	S.F.		.14	.03	.17
6" deep	1.000	S.F.	.001	.19	.04	.23
9" deep	1.000	S.F.	.001	.29	.06	.35
12" deep	1.000	S.F.	.001	.37	.07	.44
¾" crushed stone, 3" deep	1.000	S.F.		.27	.03	.30
6" deep	1.000	S.F.	.001	.53	.06	.59
9" deep	1.000	S.F.	.002	.79	.08	.87
12" deep	1.000	S.F.	.002	1.05	.09	1.14
Vapor barrier polyethylene, .004" thick	1.000	S.F.	.002	.02	.05	.07
.006" thick	1.000	S.F.	.002	.03	.05	.08
Edge forms, expansion material, 4" thick slab	.100	L.F.	.003	.02	.08	.10
6" thick slab	.100	L.F.	.005	.03	.12	.15
Welded wire fabric 6 x 6, 10/10 (W1.4/W1.4)	1.100	S.F.	.005	.09	.14	.23
6 x 6, ⅝ (W2.9/W2.9)	1.100	S.F.	.006	.17	.17	.34
4 x 4, 10/10 (W1.4/W1.4)	1.100	S.F.	.005	.14	.17	.31
Finish concrete, screed finish	1.000	S.F.	.009		.20	.20
Float finish	1.000	S.F.	.011		.30	.30
Steel trowel, for resilient floor	1.000	S.F.	.013		.35	.35
For finished floor	1.000	S.F.	.015		.40	.40

3 | FRAMING 04 | Floor Framing Systems (Wood)

Labels on diagram: Box Sill, Sheathing, Bridging, Furring, Girder, Box Sill, Wood Joists

SYSTEM DESCRIPTION	QUAN.	UNIT	MAN-HOURS	COST PER S.F. MAT.	COST PER S.F. INST.	COST PER S.F. TOTAL
2" X 8", 16" O.C.						
Wood joists, 2" x 8", 16" O.C.	1.000	L.F.	.017	.62	.43	1.05
Bridging, 1" x 3", 6' O.C.	.080	Pr.	.004	.03	.12	.15
Box sills, 2" x 8"	.150	L.F.	.002	.09	.07	.16
Girder, including lally columns, 3- 2" x 8"	.125	L.F.	.015	.30	.40	.70
Sheathing, plywood, subfloor, ⅝" CDX	1.000	S.F.	.012	.43	.30	.73
Furring, 1" x 3", 16" O.C.	1.000	L.F.	.023	.15	.55	.70
TOTAL			.073	1.62	1.87	3.49
2" X 10", 16" O.C.						
Wood joists, 2" x 10", 16" O.C.	1.000	L.F.	.018	.92	.44	1.36
Bridging, 1" x 3", 6' O.C.	.080	Pr.	.004	.03	.12	.15
Box sills, 2" x 10"	.150	L.F.	.002	.14	.06	.20
Girder, including lally columns, 3-2" x 10"	.125	L.F.	.016	.42	.41	.83
Sheathing, plywood, subfloor, ⅝" CDX	1.000	S.F.	.012	.43	.30	.73
Furring, 1" x 3",16" O.C.	1.000	L.F.	.023	.15	.55	.70
TOTAL			.075	2.09	1.88	3.97
2" X 12", 16" O.C.						
Wood joists, 2" x 12", 16" O.C.	1.000	L.F.	.018	1.12	.46	1.58
Bridging, 1" x 3", 6' O.C.	.080	Pr.	.004	.03	.12	.15
Box sills, 2" x 12"	.150	L.F.	.002	.17	.07	.24
Girder, including lally columns, 3-2" x 12"	.125	L.F.	.017	.49	.44	.93
Sheathing, plywood, subfloor, ⅝" CDX	1.000	S.F.	.012	.43	.30	.73
Furring, 1" x 3", 16" O.C.	1.000	L.F.	.023	.15	.55	.70
TOTAL			.076	2.39	1.94	4.33

Floor costs on this page are given on a cost per square foot basis.

DESCRIPTION	QUAN.	UNIT	MAN-HOURS	COST PER S.F. MAT.	COST PER S.F. INST.	COST PER S.F. TOTAL

Floor Framing Price Sheet (Wood)

	QUAN.	UNIT	MAN-HOURS	COST PER S.F. MAT.	COST PER S.F. INST.	COST PER S.F. TOTAL
Joists, #2 or better, pine, 2" x 4", 12" O.C.	1.250	L.F.	.016	.36	.40	.76
16" O.C.	1.000	L.F.	.013	.29	.32	.61
2" x 6", 12" O.C.	1.250	L.F.	.016	.55	.40	.95
16" O.C.	1.000	L.F.	.013	.44	.32	.76
2" x 8", 12" O.C.	1.250	L.F.	.021	.78	.53	1.31
16" O.C.	1.000	L.F.	.017	.62	.43	1.05
2" x 10", 12" O.C.	1.250	L.F.	.022	1.15	.55	1.70
16" O.C.	1.000	L.F.	.018	.92	.44	1.36
2" x 12", 12" O.C.	1.250	L.F.	.022	1.40	.58	1.98
16" O.C.	1.000	L.F.	.018	1.12	.46	1.58
Bridging, wood 1" x 3", joists 12" O.C.	.100	Pr.	.006	.03	.16	.19
16" O.C.	.080	Pr.	.004	.03	.12	.15
Metal, galvanized, joists 12" O.C.	.100	Pr.	.006	.09	.14	.23
16" O.C.	.080	Pr.	.004	.07	.12	.19
Compression type, joists 12" O.C.	.100	Pr.	.004	.13	.09	.22
16" O.C.	.080	Pr.	.003	.10	.08	.18
Box sills, #2 or better pine, 2" x 4"	.150	L.F.	.001	.04	.05	.09
2" x 6"	.150	L.F.	.001	.07	.04	.11
2" x 8"	.150	L.F.	.002	.09	.07	.16
2" x 10"	.150	L.F.	.002	.14	.06	.20
2" x 12"	.150	L.F.	.002	.17	.07	.24
Girders, including lally columns, 3 pieces spiked together, 2" x 8"	.125	L.F.	.015	.30	.40	.70
2" x 10"	.125	L.F.	.016	.42	.41	.83
2" x 12"	.125	L.F.	.017	.49	.44	.93
Solid girders, 3" x 8"	.040	L.F.	.003	.14	.10	.24
3" x 10"	.040	L.F.	.003	.15	.11	.26
3" x 12"	.040	L.F.	.004	.17	.11	.28
4" x 8"	.040	L.F.	.003	.16	.11	.27
4" x 10"	.040	L.F.	.004	.18	.11	.29
4" x 12"	.040	L.F.	.004	.19	.12	.31
Steel girders, bolted & including fabrication, wide flange shapes 12" deep, 14#/l.f.	1.000	L.F.	.071	8.05	3.52	11.57
10" deep, 15#/l.f.	1.000	L.F.	.078	8.80	3.85	12.65
8" deep, 10#/l.f.	1.000	L.F.	.078	7.70	3.85	11.55
6" deep, 9#/l.f.	1.000	L.F.	.078	6.60	3.85	10.45
5" deep, 16#/l.f.	1.000	L.F.	.075	8.51	3.72	12.23
Sheathing, plywood exterior grade CDX, ½" thick	1.000	S.F.	.015	.11	.35	.46
⅝" thick	1.000	S.F.	.012	.43	.30	.73
¾" thick	1.000	S.F.	.013	.51	.32	.83
Boards, 1" x 8" laid regular	1.000	S.F.	.016	.74	.40	1.14
Laid diagonal	1.000	S.F.	.019	.76	.47	1.23
1" x 10" laid regular	1.000	S.F.	.015	.75	.36	1.11
Laid diagonal	1.000	S.F.	.018	.77	.44	1.21
Furring, 1" x 3", 12" O.C.	1.250	L.F.	.028	.19	.69	.88
16" O.C.	1.000	L.F.	.023	.15	.55	.70
24" O.C.	.750	L.F.	.017	.11	.42	.53

3 | FRAMING — 08 | Exterior Wall Framing Systems

Diagram labels: Sheathing, Top Plates, Studs, Bottom Plate, Corner Bracing

SYSTEM DESCRIPTION	QUAN.	UNIT	MAN-HOURS	MAT.	INST.	TOTAL
2" X 4", 16" O.C.						
2" x 4" studs, 16" O.C.	1.000	L.F.	.015	.28	.38	.66
Plates, 2" x 4", double top, single bottom	.375	L.F.	.005	.11	.14	.25
Corner bracing, let-in, 1" x 6"	.063	L.F.	.003	.02	.08	.10
Sheathing, ½" plywood, CDX	1.000	S.F.	.013	.51	.33	.84
TOTAL			.036	.92	.93	1.85
2" X 4", 24" O.C.						
2" x 4" studs, 24" O.C.	.750	L.F.	.011	.21	.29	.50
Plates, 2" x 4", double top, single bottom	.375	L.F.	.005	.11	.14	.25
Corner bracing, let-in, 1" x 6"	.063	L.F.	.002	.02	.05	.07
Sheathing, ½" plywood, CDX	1.000	S.F.	.013	.51	.33	.84
TOTAL			.031	.85	.81	1.66
2" X 6", 16" O.C.						
2" x 6" studs, 16" O.C.	1.000	L.F.	.016	.44	.40	.84
Plates, 2" x 6", double top, single bottom	.375	L.F.	.006	.17	.15	.32
Corner bracing, let-in, 1" x 6"	.063	L.F.	.003	.02	.08	.10
Sheathing, ½" plywood, CDX	1.000	S.F.	.013	.51	.33	.84
TOTAL			.038	1.14	.96	2.10
2" X 6", 24" O.C.						
2" x 6" studs, 24" O.C.	.750	L.F.	.012	.33	.30	.63
Plates, 2" x 6", double top, single bottom	.375	L.F.	.006	.17	.15	.32
Corner bracing, let-in, 1" x 6"	.063	L.F.	.002	.02	.05	.07
Sheathing, ½" plywood, CDX	1.000	S.F.	.013	.51	.33	.84
TOTAL			.033	1.03	.83	1.86

The wall costs on this page are given in cost per square foot of wall.
For window and door openings see next page.

DESCRIPTION	QUAN.	UNIT	MAN-HOURS	MAT.	INST.	TOTAL

Exterior Wall Framing Price Sheet

	QUAN.	UNIT	MAN-HOURS	COST PER S.F. MAT.	COST PER S.F. INST.	COST PER S.F. TOTAL
Studs, #2 or better, 2" x 4", 12" O.C.	1.250	L.F.	.018	.35	.48	.83
16" O.C.	1.000	L.F.	.015	.28	.38	.66
24" O.C.	.750	L.F.	.011	.21	.29	.50
32" O.C.	.600	L.F.	.009	.17	.23	.40
2" x 6", 12" O.C.	1.250	L.F.	.020	.55	.50	1.05
16" O.C.	1.000	L.F.	.016	.44	.40	.84
24" O.C.	.750	L.F.	.012	.33	.30	.63
32" O.C.	.600	L.F.	.009	.26	.24	.50
2" x 8", 12" O.C.	1.250	L.F.	.025	.85	.63	1.48
16" O.C.	1.000	L.F.	.020	.68	.50	1.18
24" O.C.	.750	L.F.	.015	.51	.38	.89
32" O.C.	.600	L.F.	.012	.41	.30	.71
Plates, #2 or better, double top, single bottom, 2" x 4"	.375	L.F.	.005	.11	.14	.25
2" x 6"	.375	L.F.	.006	.17	.15	.32
2" x 8"	.375	L.F.	.007	.26	.18	.44
Corner bracing, let-in 1" x 6" boards, studs, 12" O.C.	.070	L.F.	.003	.02	.09	.11
16" O.C.	.063	L.F.	.003	.02	.08	.10
24" O.C.	.063	L.F.	.002	.02	.05	.07
32" O.C.	.057	L.F.	.001	.02	.05	.07
Let-in steel ("T" shape), studs, 12" O.C.	.070	L.F.		.05	.02	.07
16" O.C.	.063	L.F.		.04	.02	.06
24" O.C.	.063	L.F.		.04	.02	.06
32" O.C.	.057	L.F.		.04	.02	.06
Sheathing, plywood CDX, 3/8" thick	1.000	S.F.	.013	.51	.33	.84
1/2" thick	1.000	S.F.	.013	.51	.33	.84
5/8" thick	1.000	S.F.	.013	.51	.33	.84
3/4" thick	1.000	S.F.	.013	.51	.33	.84
Boards, 1" x 6", laid regular	1.000	S.F.	.025	.74	.62	1.36
Laid diagonal	1.000	S.F.	.027	.76	.68	1.44
1" x 8", laid regular	1.000	S.F.	.021	.74	.52	1.26
Laid diagonal	1.000	S.F.	.025	.76	.62	1.38
Wood fiber, regular, no vapor barrier, 1/2" thick	1.000	S.F.	.013	.39	.33	.72
5/8" thick	1.000	S.F.	.013	.51	.33	.84
Asphalt impregnated 25/32" thick	1.000	S.F.	.013	.33	.33	.66
1/2" thick	1.000	S.F.	.013	.29	.33	.62
Polystyrene, regular, 3/4" thick	1.000	S.F.	.010	.45	.24	.69
2" thick	1.000	S.F.	.011	.97	.26	1.23
Fiberglass, foil faced, 1" thick	1.000	S.F.	.008	.87	.19	1.06
2" thick	1.000	S.F.	.009	1.60	.21	1.81

Window & Door Openings

	QUAN.	UNIT	MAN-HOURS	COST EACH MAT.	COST EACH INST.	COST EACH TOTAL
The following costs are to be added to the total costs of the wall for each opening. Do not subtract the area of the openings.						
Headers, 2" x 6" double, 2' long	4.000	L.F.	.124	1.72	3.08	4.80
3' long	6.000	L.F.	.186	2.58	4.62	7.20
4' long	8.000	L.F.	.248	3.44	6.16	9.60
5' long	10.000	L.F.	.310	4.30	7.70	12.00
2" x 8" double, 4' long	8.000	L.F.	.376	4.88	9.44	14.32
5' long	10.000	L.F.	.470	6.10	11.80	17.90
6' long	12.000	L.F.	.564	7.32	14.16	21.48
8' long	16.000	L.F.	.752	9.76	18.88	28.64
2" x 10" double, 4' long	8.000	L.F.	.400	7.36	10.00	17.36
6' long	12.000	L.F.	.600	11.04	15.00	26.04
8' long	16.000	L.F.	.800	14.72	20.00	34.72
10' long	20.000	L.F.	1.000	18.40	25.00	43.40
2" x 12" double, 8' long	16.000	L.F.	.896	16.80	22.40	39.20
12' long	24.000	L.F.	1.344	25.20	33.60	58.80

3 | FRAMING — 12 | Gable End Roof Framing Systems

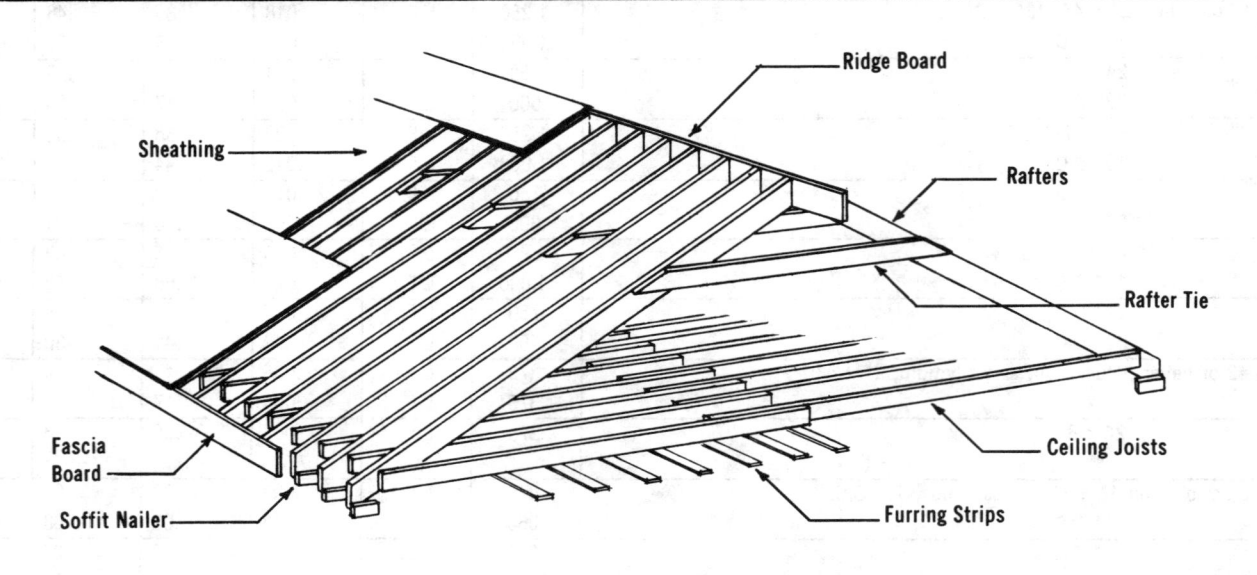

Diagram labels: Sheathing, Ridge Board, Rafters, Rafter Tie, Ceiling Joists, Furring Strips, Soffit Nailer, Fascia Board

SYSTEM DESCRIPTION	QUAN.	UNIT	MAN-HOURS	MAT.	INST.	TOTAL
2" X 8" RAFTERS, 16" O.C., 4/12 PITCH						
Rafters, 2" x 8", 16" O.C., 4/12 pitch	1.170	L.F.	.019	.71	.50	1.21
Ceiling joists, 2" x 6", 16" O.C.	1.000	L.F.	.013	.44	.32	.76
Ridge board, 2" x 8"	.050	L.F.	.001	.03	.05	.08
Fascia board, 2" x 8"	.100	L.F.	.007	.06	.18	.24
Rafter tie, 1" x 4", 4' O.C.	.060	L.F.	.001	.01	.03	.04
Soffit nailer (outrigger), 2" x 4", 24" O.C.	.170	L.F.	.004	.05	.11	.16
Sheathing, exterior, plywood, CDX, ½" thick	1.170	S.F.	.012	.41	.34	.75
Furring strips, 1" x 3", 16" O.C.	1.000	L.F.	.023	.15	.55	.70
TOTAL			.080	1.86	2.08	3.94
2" X 6" RAFTERS, 16" O.C., 4/12 PITCH						
Rafters, 2" x 6", 16" O.C., 4/12 pitch	1.170	L.F.	.018	.50	.47	.97
Ceiling joists, 2" x 4", 16" O.C.	1.000	L.F.	.013	.29	.32	.61
Ridge board, 2" x 6"	.050	L.F.	.001	.02	.04	.06
Fascia board, 2" x 6"	.100	L.F.	.005	.05	.13	.18
Rafter tie, 1" x 4", 4' O.C.	.060	L.F.	.001	.01	.03	.04
Soffit nailer (outrigger), 2" x 4", 24" O.C.	.170	L.F.	.004	.05	.11	.16
Sheathing, exterior, plywood, CDX, ½" thick	1.170	S.F.	.012	.41	.34	.75
Furring strips, 1" x 3", 16" O.C.	1.000	L.F.	.023	.15	.55	.70
TOTAL			.077	1.48	1.99	3.47

The cost of this system is based on the square foot of plan area. All quantities have been adjusted accordingly.

DESCRIPTION	QUAN.	UNIT	MAN-HOURS	MAT.	INST.	TOTAL

Gable End Roof Framing Price Sheet

	QUAN.	UNIT	MAN-HOURS	COST PER S.F. MAT.	COST PER S.F. INST.	COST PER S.F. TOTAL
Rafters, #2 or better, 16" O.C., 2" x 6", 4/12 pitch	1.170	L.F.	.018	.50	.47	.97
8/12 pitch	1.330	L.F.	.026	.57	.67	1.24
2" x 8", 4/12 pitch	1.170	L.F.	.019	.71	.50	1.21
8/12 pitch	1.330	L.F.	.027	.81	.71	1.52
2" x 10", 4/12 pitch	1.170	L.F.	.029	1.05	.74	1.79
8/12 pitch	1.330	L.F.	.042	1.20	1.07	2.27
24" O.C., 2" x 6", 4/12 pitch	.940	L.F.	.015	.40	.38	.78
8/12 pitch	1.060	L.F.	.021	.46	.53	.99
2" x 8", 4/12 pitch	.940	L.F.	.015	.57	.40	.97
8/12 pitch	1.060	L.F.	.022	.65	.56	1.21
2" x 10", 4/12 pitch	.940	L.F.	.023	.85	.59	1.44
8/12 pitch	1.060	L.F.	.033	.95	.86	1.81
Ceiling joist, #2 or better, 2" x 4", 16" O.C.	1.000	L.F.	.013	.29	.32	.61
24" O.C.	.750	L.F.	.009	.22	.24	.46
2" x 6", 16" O.C.	1.000	L.F.	.013	.44	.32	.76
24" O.C.	.750	L.F.	.009	.33	.24	.57
2" x 8", 16" O.C.	1.000	L.F.	.017	.62	.43	1.05
24" O.C.	.750	L.F.	.012	.47	.32	.79
2" x 10", 16" O.C.	1.000	L.F.	.018	.92	.44	1.36
24" O.C.	.750	L.F.	.013	.69	.33	1.02
Ridge board, #2 or better, 1" x 6"	.050	L.F.	.001	.02	.03	.05
1" x 8"	.050	L.F.	.001	.02	.04	.06
1" x 10"	.050	L.F.	.001	.03	.04	.07
2" x 6"	.050	L.F.	.001	.02	.04	.06
2" x 8"	.050	L.F.	.001	.03	.05	.08
2" x 10"	.050	L.F.	.002	.05	.05	.10
Fascia board, #2 or better, 1" x 6"	.100	L.F.	.003	.03	.10	.13
1" x 8"	.100	L.F.	.004	.04	.11	.15
1" x 10"	.100	L.F.	.005	.04	.13	.17
2" x 6"	.100	L.F.	.005	.05	.14	.19
2" x 8"	.100	L.F.	.007	.06	.18	.24
2" x 10"	.100	L.F.	.003	.18	.09	.27
Rafter tie, #2 or better, 4' O.C., 1" x 4"	.060	L.F.	.001	.01	.03	.04
1" x 6"	.060	L.F.	.001	.01	.04	.05
2" x 4"	.060	L.F.	.001	.02	.04	.06
2" x 6"	.060	L.F.	.002	.02	.05	.07
Soffit nailer (outrigger), 2" x 4", 16" O.C.	.220	L.F.	.005	.07	.14	.21
24" O.C.	.170	L.F.	.004	.05	.11	.16
2" x 6", 16" O.C.	.220	L.F.	.006	.08	.16	.24
24" O.C.	.170	L.F.	.005	.06	.13	.19
Sheathing, plywood CDX, 4/12 pitch, 3/8" thick.	1.170	S.F.	.011	.34	.30	.64
1/2" thick	1.170	S.F.	.012	.41	.34	.75
5/8" thick	1.170	S.F.	.014	.51	.37	.88
8/12 pitch, 3/8"	1.330	S.F.	.013	.39	.34	.73
1/2" thick	1.330	S.F.	.014	.47	.38	.85
5/8" thick	1.330	S.F.	.015	.59	.41	1.00
Boards, 4/12 pitch roof, 1" x 6"	1.170	S.F.	.025	.87	.64	1.51
1" x 8"	1.170	S.F.	.021	.87	.53	1.40
8/12 pitch roof, 1" x 6"	1.330	S.F.	.029	.98	.74	1.72
1" x 8"	1.330	S.F.	.023	.98	.62	1.60
Furring, 1" x 3", 12" O.C.	1.200	L.F.	.027	.18	.66	.84
16" O.C.	1.000	L.F.	.023	.15	.55	.70
24" O.C.	.800	L.F.	.018	.12	.44	.56

3 | FRAMING — 16 | Truss Roof Framing Systems

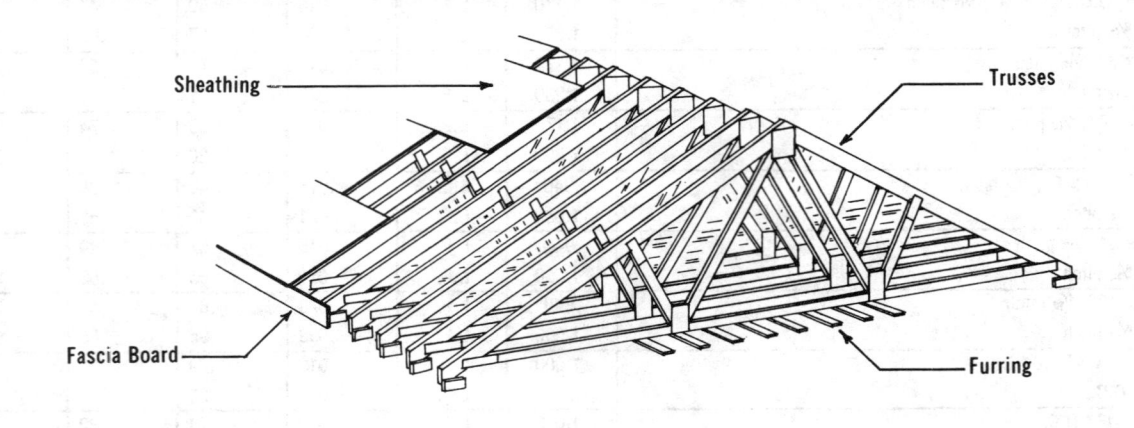

Labels on illustration: Sheathing, Trusses, Fascia Board, Furring

SYSTEM DESCRIPTION	QUAN.	UNIT	MAN-HOURS	MAT.	INST.	TOTAL
TRUSS, 16" O.C., 4/12 PITCH, INCLUDING 1' OVERHANG, 26' SPAN						
Truss, 40# loading, 16" O.C., 4/12 pitch, 26' span	.030	Ea.	.021	1.55	.70	2.25
Fascia board, 2" x 6"	.100	L.F.	.005	.05	.13	.18
Sheathing, exterior, plywood, CDX, ½" thick	1.170	S.F.	.012	.41	.34	.75
Furring, 1" x 3", 16" O.C.	1.000	L.F.	.023	.15	.55	.70
TOTAL			.061	2.16	1.72	3.88
TRUSS, 16" O.C., 8/12 PITCH, INCLUDING 1' OVERHANG, 26' SPAN						
Truss, 40# loading, 16" O.C., 8/12 pitch, 26' span	.030	Ea.	.023	1.49	.76	2.25
Fascia board, 2" x 6"	.100	L.F.	.005	.05	.13	.18
Sheathing, exterior, plywood, CDX, ½" thick	1.330	S.F.	.014	.47	.38	.85
Furring, 1" x 3", 16" O.C.	1.000	L.F.	.023	.15	.55	.70
TOTAL			.065	2.16	1.82	3.98
TRUSS, 24" O.C., 4/12 PITCH, INCLUDING 1' OVERHANG, 26' SPAN						
Truss, 40# loading, 24" O.C., 4/12 pitch, 26' span	.020	Ea.	.014	1.03	.47	1.50
Fascia board, 2" x 6"	.100	L.F.	.005	.05	.13	.18
Sheathing, exterior, plywood, CDX, ½" thick	1.170	S.F.	.012	.41	.34	.75
Furring, 1" x 3", 16" O.C.	1.000	L.F.	.023	.15	.55	.70
TOTAL			.054	1.64	1.49	3.13
TRUSS, 24" O.C., 8/12 PITCH, INCLUDING 1' OVERHANG, 26' SPAN						
Truss, 40# loading, 24" O.C., 8/12 pitch, 26' span	.020	Ea.	.015	.99	.51	1.50
Fascia board, 2" x 6"	.100	L.F.	.005	.05	.13	.18
Sheathing, exterior, plywood, CDX, ½" thick	1.330	S.F.	.014	.47	.38	.85
Furring, 1" x 3", 16" O.C.	1.000	L.F.	.023	.15	.55	.70
TOTAL			.057	1.66	1.57	3.23

The cost of this system is based on the square foot of plan area.
A one foot overhang is included.

DESCRIPTION	QUAN.	UNIT	MAN-HOURS	MAT.	INST.	TOTAL

Truss Roof Framing Price Sheet

	QUAN.	UNIT	MAN-HOURS	MAT.	INST.	TOTAL
Truss, 40# load including 1' overhang, 5/12 pitch, 24' span, 16" O.C.	.033	Ea.	.022	1.60	.71	2.31
24" O.C.	.022	Ea.	.014	1.06	.48	1.54
26' span, 16" O.C.	.030	Ea.	.021	1.55	.70	2.25
24" O.C.	.020	Ea.	.014	1.03	.47	1.50
28' span, 16" O.C.	.027	Ea.	.020	1.51	.68	2.19
24" O.C.	.019	Ea.	.014	1.07	.47	1.54
32' span, 16" O.C.	.024	Ea.	.019	1.53	.63	2.16
24" O.C.	.016	Ea.	.012	1.02	.42	1.44
36' span, 16" O.C.	.022	Ea.	.019	1.60	.60	2.20
24" O.C.	.015	Ea.	.013	1.09	.41	1.50
9/12 pitch, 24' span, 16" O.C.	.033	Ea.	.023	1.49	.79	2.28
24" O.C.	.022	Ea.	.015	.99	.53	1.52
26' span, 16" O.C.	.030	Ea.	.023	1.49	.76	2.25
24" O.C.	.020	Ea.	.015	.99	.51	1.50
28' span, 16" O.C.	.027	Ea.	.022	1.43	.70	2.13
24" O.C.	.019	Ea.	.015	1.00	.50	1.50
32' span, 16" O.C.	.024	Ea.	.021	1.45	.69	2.14
24" O.C.	.016	Ea.	.014	.97	.45	1.42
36' span, 16" O.C.	.022	Ea.	.021	1.72	.70	2.42
24" O.C.	.015	Ea.	.014	1.17	.48	1.65
Fascia board, #2 or better, 1" x 6"	.100	L.F.	.003	.03	.10	.13
1" x 8"	.100	L.F.	.004	.04	.11	.15
1" x 10"	.100	L.F.	.005	.04	.13	.17
2" x 6"	.100	L.F.	.005	.05	.14	.19
2" x 8"	.100	L.F.	.007	.06	.18	.24
2" x 10"	.100	L.F.	.008	.09	.22	.31
Sheathing, plywood CDX, 5/12 pitch, 3/8" thick	1.170	S.F.	.011	.34	.30	.64
1/2" thick	1.170	S.F.	.012	.41	.34	.75
5/8" thick	1.170	S.F.	.014	.51	.37	.88
9/12 pitch, 3/8" thick	1.330	S.F.	.013	.39	.34	.73
1/2" thick	1.330	S.F.	.014	.47	.38	.85
5/8" thick	1.330	S.F.	.015	.59	.41	1.00
Boards, 5/12 pitch, 1" x 6"	1.170	S.F.	.025	.87	.64	1.51
1" x 8"	1.170	S.F.	.021	.87	.53	1.40
9/12 pitch, 1" x 6"	1.330	S.F.	.029	.98	.74	1.72
1" x 8"	1.330	S.F.	.023	.98	.62	1.60
Furring, 1" x 3", 12" O.C.	1.200	L.F.	.027	.18	.66	.84
16" O.C.	1.000	L.F.	.023	.15	.55	.70
24" O.C.	.800	L.F.	.018	.12	.44	.56

3 | FRAMING — 20 | Hip Roof Framing System

Labels on illustration: Ceiling Joists, Sheathing, Fascia Board, Jack Rafters, Hip Rafter

SYSTEM DESCRIPTION	QUAN.	UNIT	MAN-HOURS	COST PER S.F. MAT.	COST PER S.F. INST.	TOTAL
2" X 8", 16" O.C., 4/12 PITCH						
Hip rafters, 2" x 8", 4/12 pitch	.160	L.F.	.003	.10	.09	.19
Jack rafters, 2" x 8", 16" O.C., 4/12 pitch	1.430	L.F.	.047	.87	1.17	2.04
Ceiling joists, 2" x 6", 16" O.C.	1.000	L.F.	.013	.44	.32	.76
Fascia board, 2" x 8"	.220	L.F.	.015	.13	.40	.53
Soffit nailer (outrigger), 2" x 4", 24" O.C.	.220	L.F.	.005	.07	.14	.21
Sheathing, ½" exterior plywood, CDX	1.570	S.F.	.017	.55	.45	1.00
Furring strips, 1" x 3", 16" O.C.	1.000	L.F.	.023	.15	.55	.70
TOTAL			.123	2.31	3.12	5.43
2" X 6", 16" O.C., 4/12 PITCH						
Hip rafters, 2" x 6", 4/12 pitch	.160	L.F.	.003	.07	.08	.15
Jack rafters, 2" x 6", 16" O.C., 4/12 pitch	1.430	L.F.	.038	.61	.96	1.57
Ceiling joists, 2" x 4", 16" O.C.	1.000	L.F.	.013	.29	.32	.61
Fascia board, 2" x 6"	.220	L.F.	.012	.10	.31	.41
Soffit nailer (outrigger), 2" x 4", 24" O.C.	.220	L.F.	.005	.07	.14	.21
Sheathing, ½" exterior plywood, CDX	1.570	S.F.	.017	.55	.45	1.00
Furring strips, 1" x 3", 16" O.C.	1.000	L.F.	.023	.15	.55	.70
TOTAL			.111	1.84	2.81	4.65

The cost of this system is based on S.F. of plan area. Measurement is -area under the hip roof only. See gable roof system for added costs.

DESCRIPTION	QUAN.	UNIT	MAN-HOURS	COST PER S.F. MAT.	COST PER S.F. INST.	TOTAL

Hip Roof Framing Price Sheet

	QUAN.	UNIT	MAN-HOURS	COST PER S.F. MAT.	COST PER S.F. INST.	COST PER S.F. TOTAL
Hip rafters, #2 or better, 2" x 6", 4/12 pitch	.160	L.F.	.003	.07	.08	.15
8/12 pitch	.210	L.F.	.005	.09	.14	.23
2" x 8", 4/12 pitch	.160	L.F.	.003	.10	.09	.19
8/12 pitch	.210	L.F.	.006	.13	.15	.28
2" x 10", 4/12 pitch	.160	L.F.	.004	.14	.12	.26
8/12 pitch roof	.210	L.F.	.007	.19	.19	.38
Jack rafters, #2 or better, 16" O.C., 2" x 6", 4/12 pitch	1.430	L.F.	.038	.61	.96	1.57
8/12 pitch	1.800	L.F.	.061	.77	1.52	2.29
2" x 8", 4/12 pitch	1.430	L.F.	.047	.87	1.17	2.04
8/12 pitch	1.800	L.F.	.075	1.10	1.87	2.97
2" x 10", 4/12 pitch	1.430	L.F.	.051	1.29	1.27	2.56
8/12 pitch	1.800	L.F.	.082	1.62	2.05	3.67
24" O.C., 2" x 6", 4/12 pitch	1.150	L.F.	.031	.49	.78	1.27
8/12 pitch	1.440	L.F.	.048	.62	1.21	1.83
2" x 8", 4/12 pitch	1.150	L.F.	.037	.70	.94	1.64
8/12 pitch	1.440	L.F.	.060	.88	1.50	2.38
2" x 10", 4/12 pitch	1.150	L.F.	.041	1.04	1.02	2.06
8/12 pitch	1.440	L.F.	.066	1.30	1.64	2.94
Ceiling joists, #2 or better, 2" x 4", 16" O.C.	1.000	L.F.	.013	.29	.32	.61
24" O.C.	.750	L.F.	.009	.22	.24	.46
2" x 6", 16" O.C.	1.000	L.F.	.013	.44	.32	.76
24" O.C.	.750	L.F.	.009	.33	.24	.57
2" x 8", 16" O.C.	1.000	L.F.	.017	.62	.43	1.05
24" O.C.	.750	L.F.	.012	.47	.32	.79
2" x 10", 16" O.C.	1.000	L.F.	.018	.92	.44	1.36
24" O.C.	.750	L.F.	.013	.69	.33	1.02
Fascia board, #2 or better, 1" x 6"	.220	L.F.	.008	.07	.22	.29
1" x 8"	.220	L.F.	.010	.09	.25	.34
1" x 10"	.220	L.F.	.011	.10	.28	.38
2" x 6"	.220	L.F.	.012	.11	.31	.42
2" x 8"	.220	L.F.	.015	.13	.40	.53
2" x 10"	.220	L.F.	.019	.20	.49	.69
Soffit nailer (outrigger), 2" x 4", 16" O.C.	.280	L.F.	.007	.08	.19	.27
24" O.C.	.220	L.F.	.005	.07	.14	.21
2" x 8", 16" O.C.	.280	L.F.	.006	.13	.17	.30
24" O.C.	.220	L.F.	.005	.11	.13	.24
Sheathing, plywood CDX, 4/12 pitch, 3/8" thick	1.570	S.F.	.015	.46	.40	.86
1/2" thick	1.570	S.F.	.017	.55	.45	1.00
5/8" thick	1.570	S.F.	.018	.69	.49	1.18
8/12 pitch, 3/8" thick	1.900	S.F.	.019	.55	.50	1.05
1/2" thick	1.900	S.F.	.020	.67	.55	1.22
5/8" thick	1.900	S.F.	.022	.84	.59	1.43
Boards, 4/12 pitch, 1" x 6" boards	1.450	S.F.	.031	1.07	.80	1.87
1" x 8" boards	1.450	S.F.	.026	1.07	.67	1.74
8/12 pitch, 1" x 6" boards	1.750	S.F.	.038	1.30	.96	2.26
1" x 8" boards	1.750	S.F.	.031	1.30	.80	2.10
Furring, 1" x 3", 12" O.C.	1.200	L.F.	.027	.18	.66	.84
16" O.C.	1.000	L.F.	.023	.15	.55	.70
24" O.C.	.800	L.F.	.018	.12	.44	.56

3 | FRAMING — 24 | Gambrel Roof Framing System

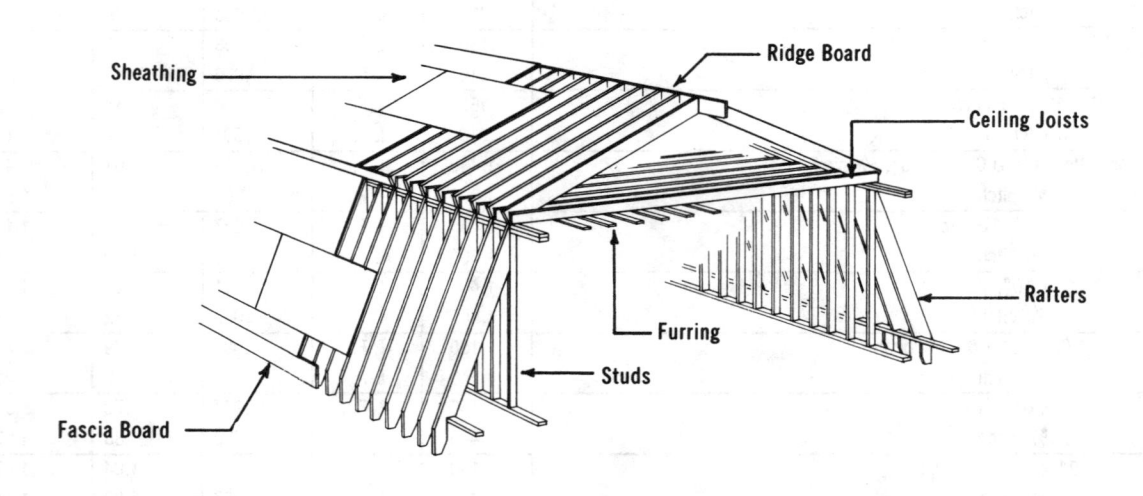

Labels on illustration: Sheathing, Ridge Board, Ceiling Joists, Rafters, Furring, Studs, Fascia Board

SYSTEM DESCRIPTION	QUAN.	UNIT	MAN-HOURS	MAT.	INST.	TOTAL
2" X 6" RAFTERS, 16" O.C.						
Roof rafters, 2" x 6", 16" O.C.	1.430	L.F.	.028	.61	.72	1.33
Ceiling joists, 2" x 6", 16" O.C.	.710	L.F.	.009	.31	.23	.54
Stud wall, 2" x 4", 16" O.C., including plates	.790	L.F.	.012	.24	.31	.55
Furring strips, 1" x 3", 16" O.C.	.710	L.F.	.016	.11	.39	.50
Ridge board, 2" x 8"	.050	L.F.	.001	.03	.05	.08
Fascia board, 2" x 6"	.100	L.F.	.005	.05	.14	.19
Sheathing, exterior grade plywood, ½" thick	1.450	S.F.	.015	.51	.42	.93
TOTAL			.086	1.86	2.26	4.12
2" X 8" RAFTERS, 16" O.C.						
Roof rafters, 2" x 8", 16" O.C.	1.430	L.F.	.030	.87	.76	1.63
Ceiling joists, 2" x 6", 16" O.C.	.710	L.F.	.009	.31	.23	.54
Stud wall, 2" x 4", 16" O.C., including plates	.790	L.F.	.012	.24	.31	.55
Furring strips, 1" x 3", 16" O.C.	.710	L.F.	.016	.11	.39	.50
Ridge board, 2" x 8"	.050	L.F.	.001	.03	.05	.08
Fascia board, 2" x 8"	.100	L.F.	.007	.06	.18	.24
Sheathing, exterior grade plywood, ½" thick	1.450	S.F.	.015	.51	.42	.93
TOTAL			.090	2.13	2.34	4.47

The cost of this system is based on the square foot of plan area on the First floor.

DESCRIPTION	QUAN.	UNIT	MAN-HOURS	MAT.	INST.	TOTAL

Gambrel Roof Framing Price Sheet

	QUAN.	UNIT	MAN-HOURS	COST PER S.F. MAT.	COST PER S.F. INST.	COST PER S.F. TOTAL
Roof rafters, #2 or better, 2" x 6", 16" O.C.	1.430	L.F.	.028	.61	.72	1.33
24" O.C.	1.140	L.F.	.022	.49	.57	1.06
2" x 8", 16" O.C.	1.430	L.F.	.030	.87	.76	1.63
24" O.C.	1.140	L.F.	.023	.70	.60	1.30
2" x 10", 16" O.C.	1.430	L.F.	.045	1.29	1.16	2.45
24" O.C.	1.140	L.F.	.036	1.03	.92	1.95
Ceiling joist, #2 or better, 2" x 4", 16" O.C.	.710	L.F.	.009	.21	.22	.43
24" O.C.	.570	L.F.	.007	.17	.18	.35
2" x 6", 16" O.C.	.710	L.F.	.009	.31	.23	.54
24" O.C.	.570	L.F.	.007	.25	.18	.43
2" x 8", 16" O.C.	.710	L.F.	.012	.44	.31	.75
24" O.C.	.570	L.F.	.009	.35	.25	.60
Stud wall, #2 or better, 2" x 4", 16" O.C.	.790	L.F.	.012	.24	.31	.55
24" O.C.	.630	L.F.	.010	.19	.24	.43
2" x 6", 16" O.C.	.790	L.F.	.014	.35	.35	.70
24" O.C.	.630	L.F.	.011	.28	.28	.56
Furring, 1" x 3", 16" O.C.	.710	L.F.	.016	.11	.39	.50
24" O.C.	.590	L.F.	.013	.09	.32	.41
Ridge board, #2 or better, 1" x 6"	.050	L.F.	.001	.02	.03	.05
1" x 8"	.050	L.F.	.001	.02	.04	.06
1" x 10"	.050	L.F.	.001	.03	.04	.07
2" x 6"	.050	L.F.	.001	.02	.04	.06
2" x 8"	.050	L.F.	.001	.03	.05	.08
2" x 10"	.050	L.F.	.002	.05	.05	.10
Fascia board, #2 or better, 1" x 6"	.100	L.F.	.003	.03	.10	.13
1" x 8"	.100	L.F.	.004	.04	.11	.15
1" x 10"	.100	L.F.	.005	.04	.13	.17
2" x 6"	.100	L.F.	.005	.05	.14	.19
2" x 8"	.100	L.F.	.007	.06	.18	.24
2" x 10"	.100	L.F.	.008	.09	.22	.31
Sheathing, plywood, exterior grade CDX, ⅜" thick	1.450	S.F.	.014	.42	.38	.80
½" thick	1.450	S.F.	.015	.51	.42	.93
⅝" thick	1.450	S.F.	.017	.64	.45	1.09
¾" thick	1.450	S.F.	.018	.74	.48	1.22
Boards, 1" x 6", laid regular	1.450	S.F.	.031	1.07	.80	1.87
Laid diagonal	1.450	S.F.	.036	1.10	.90	2.00
1" x 8", laid regular	1.450	S.F.	.026	1.07	.67	1.74
Laid diagonal	1.450	S.F.	.031	1.10	.80	1.90

3 | FRAMING — 28 Mansard Roof Framing System

SYSTEM DESCRIPTION	QUAN.	UNIT	MAN-HOURS	MAT.	INST.	TOTAL
2" X 6" RAFTERS, 16" O.C.						
Roof rafters, 2" x 6", 16" O.C.	1.210	L.F.	.032	.52	.82	1.34
Rafter plates, 2" x 6", double top, single bottom	.364	L.F.	.009	.16	.24	.40
Ceiling joists, 2" x 4", 16" O.C.	.920	L.F.	.011	.27	.29	.56
Hip rafter, 2" x 6"	.070	L.F.	.002	.03	.05	.08
Jack rafter, 2" x 6", 16" O.C.	1.000	L.F.	.039	.43	.98	1.41
Ridge board, 2" x 6"	.018	L.F.		.01	.01	.02
Sheathing, exterior grade plywood, ½" thick	2.210	S.F.	.024	.77	.64	1.41
Furring strips, 1" x 3", 16" O.C.	.920	L.F.	.021	.14	.50	.64
TOTAL			.138	2.33	3.53	5.86
2" X 8" RAFTERS, 16" O.C.						
Roof rafters, 2" x 8", 16" O.C.	1.210	L.F.	.036	.74	.89	1.63
Rafter plates, 2" x 8", double top, single bottom	.364	L.F.	.010	.22	.27	.49
Ceiling joists, 2" x 6", 16" O.C.	.920	L.F.	.011	.40	.30	.70
Hip rafter, 2" x 8"	.070	L.F.	.002	.04	.06	.10
Jack rafter, 2" x 8", 16" O.C.	1.000	L.F.	.048	.61	1.19	1.80
Ridge board, 2" x 8"	.018	L.F.		.01	.02	.03
Sheathing, exterior grade plywood, ½" thick	2.210	S.F.	.024	.77	.64	1.41
Furring strips, 1" x 3", 16" O.C.	.920	L.F.	.021	.14	.50	.64
TOTAL			.152	2.93	3.87	6.80

The cost of this system is based on the square foot of plan area.

DESCRIPTION	QUAN.	UNIT	MAN-HOURS	MAT.	INST.	TOTAL

Mansard Roof Framing Price Sheet

	QUAN.	UNIT	MAN-HOURS	COST PER S.F. MAT.	COST PER S.F. INST.	COST PER S.F. TOTAL
Roof rafters, #2 or better, 2" x 6", 16" O.C.	1.210	L.F.	.032	.52	.82	1.34
24" O.C.	.970	L.F.	.026	.42	.66	1.08
2" x 8", 16" O.C.	1.210	L.F.	.036	.74	.89	1.63
24" O.C.	.970	L.F.	.029	.59	.72	1.31
2" x 10", 16" O.C.	1.210	L.F.	.045	1.09	1.14	2.23
24" O.C.	.970	L.F.	.036	.87	.91	1.78
Rafter plates, #2 or better double top single bottom, 2" x 6"	.364	L.F.	.009	.16	.24	.40
2" x 8"	.364	L.F.	.010	.22	.27	.49
2" x 10"	.364	L.F.	.013	.33	.34	.67
Ceiling joist, #2 or better, 2" x 4", 16" O.C.	.920	L.F.	.011	.27	.29	.56
24" O.C.	.740	L.F.	.009	.21	.24	.45
2" x 6", 16" O.C.	.920	L.F.	.011	.40	.30	.70
24" O.C.	.740	L.F.	.009	.33	.23	.56
2" x 8", 16" O.C.	.920	L.F.	.015	.57	.40	.97
24" O.C.	.740	L.F.	.012	.46	.32	.78
Hip rafter, #2 or better, 2" x 6"	.070	L.F.	.002	.03	.05	.08
2" x 8"	.070	L.F.	.002	.04	.06	.10
2" x 10"	.070	L.F.	.002	.06	.08	.14
Jack rafter, #2 or better, 2" x 6", 16" O.C.	1.000	L.F.	.039	.43	.98	1.41
24" O.C.	.800	L.F.	.031	.34	.79	1.13
2" x 8", 16" O.C.	1.000	L.F.	.048	.61	1.19	1.80
24" O.C.	.800	L.F.	.038	.49	.95	1.44
Ridge board, #2 or better, 1" x 6"	.018	L.F.		.01	.01	.02
1" x 8"	.018	L.F.		.01	.01	.02
1" x 10"	.018	L.F.		.01	.01	.02
2" x 6"	.018	L.F.		.01	.01	.02
2" x 8"	.018	L.F.		.01	.02	.03
2" x 10"	.018	L.F.		.02	.01	.03
Sheathing, plywood exterior grade CDX, 3/8" thick	2.210	S.F.	.022	.64	.58	1.22
1/2" thick	2.210	S.F.	.024	.77	.64	1.41
5/8" thick	2.210	S.F.	.026	.97	.69	1.66
3/4" thick	2.210	S.F.	.028	1.13	.73	1.86
Boards, 1" x 6", laid regular	2.210	S.F.	.048	1.64	1.21	2.85
Laid diagonal	2.210	S.F.	.055	1.68	1.37	3.05
1" x 8", laid regular	2.210	S.F.	.039	1.64	1.01	2.65
Laid diagonal	2.210	S.F.	.048	1.68	1.22	2.90
Furring, 1" x 3", 12" O.C.	1.150	L.F.	.026	.17	.64	.81
24" O.C.	.740	L.F.	.017	.11	.41	.52

3 | FRAMING

32 Shed/Flat Roof Framing System

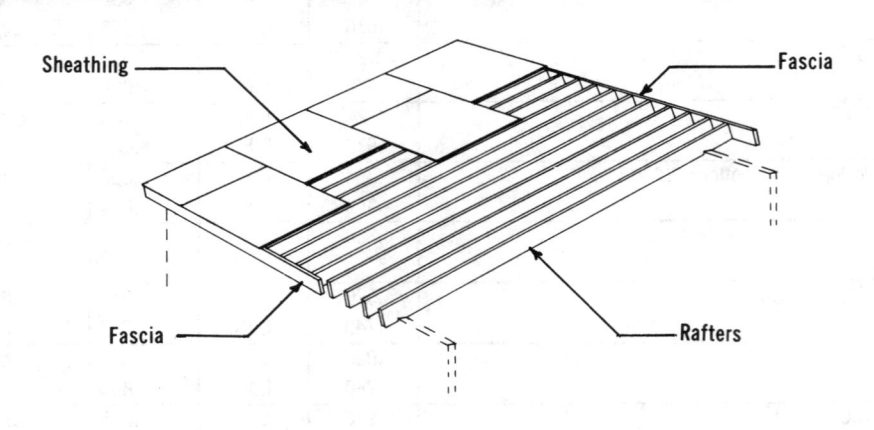

Diagram labels: Sheathing, Fascia, Fascia, Rafters

SYSTEM DESCRIPTION	QUAN.	UNIT	MAN-HOURS	COST PER S.F. MAT.	COST PER S.F. INST.	COST PER S.F. TOTAL
2" X 6", 16" O.C., 4/12 PITCH						
Rafters, 2" x 6", 16" O.C., 4/12 pitch	1.170	L.F.	.018	.50	.47	.97
Fascia, 2" x 6"	.100	L.F.	.005	.05	.14	.19
Bridging, 1" x 3", 6' O.C.	.080	Pr.	.004	.03	.12	.15
Sheathing, exterior grade plywood, ½" thick	1.230	S.F.	.013	.43	.36	.79
TOTAL			.040	1.01	1.09	2.10
2" X 6", 24" O.C., 4/12 PITCH						
Rafters, 2" x 6", 24" O.C., 4/12 pitch	.940	L.F.	.015	.40	.38	.78
Fascia, 2" x 6"	.100	L.F.	.005	.05	.14	.19
Bridging, 1" x 3", 6' O.C.	.060	Pr.	.003	.02	.09	.11
Sheathing, exterior grade plywood, ½" thick	1.230	S.F.	.013	.43	.36	.79
TOTAL			.036	.90	.97	1.87
2" X 8", 16" O.C., 4/12 PITCH						
Rafters, 2" x 8", 16" O.C., 4/12 pitch	1.170	L.F.	.019	.71	.50	1.21
Fascia, 2" x 8"	.100	L.F.	.007	.06	.18	.24
Bridging, 1" x 3", 6' O.C.	.080	Pr.	.004	.03	.12	.15
Sheathing, exterior grade plywood, ½" thick	1.230	S.F.	.013	.43	.36	.79
TOTAL			.043	1.23	1.16	2.39
2" X 8", 24" O.C., 4/12 PITCH						
Rafters, 2" x 8", 24" O.C., 4/12 pitch	.940	L.F.	.015	.57	.40	.97
Fascia, 2" x 8"	.100	L.F.	.007	.06	.18	.24
Bridging, 1" x 3", 6' O.C.	.060	Pr.	.003	.02	.09	.11
Sheathing, exterior grade plywood, ½" thick	1.230	S.F.	.013	.43	.36	.79
TOTAL			.038	1.08	1.03	2.11

The cost of this system is based on the square foot of plan area.
A 1' overhang is assumed. No ceiling joists or furring are included.

DESCRIPTION	QUAN.	UNIT	MAN-HOURS	COST PER S.F. MAT.	COST PER S.F. INST.	COST PER S.F. TOTAL

Shed/Flat Roof Framing Price Sheet

	QUAN.	UNIT	MAN-HOURS	COST PER S.F. MAT.	COST PER S.F. INST.	COST PER S.F. TOTAL
Rafters, #2 or better, 16" O.C., 2" x 4", 0 - 4/12 pitch	1.170	L.F.	.013	.37	.35	.72
5/12 - 9/12 pitch	1.330	L.F.	.020	.43	.50	.93
2" x 6", 0 - 4/12 pitch	1.170	L.F.	.018	.50	.47	.97
5/12 - 9/12 pitch	1.330	L.F.	.026	.57	.67	1.24
2" x 8", 0 - 4/12 pitch	1.170	L.F.	.019	.71	.50	1.21
5/12 - 9/12 pitch	1.330	L.F.	.027	.81	.71	1.52
2" x 10", 0 - 4/12 pitch	1.170	L.F.	.029	1.05	.74	1.79
5/12 - 9/12 pitch	1.330	L.F.	.042	1.20	1.07	2.27
24" O.C., 2" x 4", 0 - 4/12 pitch	.940	L.F.	.011	.31	.28	.59
5/12 - 9/12 pitch	1.060	L.F.	.021	.46	.53	.99
2" x 6", 0 - 4/12 pitch	.940	L.F.	.015	.40	.38	.78
5/12 - 9/12 pitch	1.060	L.F.	.021	.46	.53	.99
2" x 8", 0 - 4/12 pitch	.940	L.F.	.015	.57	.40	.97
5/12 - 9/12 pitch	1.060	L.F.	.022	.65	.56	1.21
2" x 10", 0 - 4/12 pitch	.940	L.F.	.023	.85	.59	1.44
5/12 - 9/12 pitch	1.060	L.F.	.033	.95	.86	1.81
Fascia, #2 or better,, 1" x 4"	.100	L.F.	.002	.02	.08	.10
1" x 6"	.100	L.F.	.003	.03	.10	.13
1" x 8"	.100	L.F.	.004	.04	.11	.15
1" x 10"	.100	L.F.	.005	.04	.13	.17
2" x 4"	.100	L.F.	.004	.04	.12	.16
2" x 6"	.100	L.F.	.005	.05	.14	.19
2" x 8"	.100	L.F.	.007	.06	.18	.24
2" x 10"	.100	L.F.	.008	.09	.22	.31
Bridging, wood 6' O.C., 1" x 3", rafters, 16" O.C.	.080	Pr.	.004	.03	.12	.15
24" O.C.	.060	Pr.	.003	.02	.09	.11
Metal, galvanized, rafters, 16" O.C.	.080	Pr.	.004	.07	.12	.19
24" O.C.	.060	Pr.	.003	.08	.08	.16
Compression type, rafters, 16" O.C.	.080	Pr.	.003	.10	.08	.18
24" O.C.	.060	Pr.	.002	.08	.05	.13
Sheathing, plywood, exterior grade, 3/8" thick, flat 0 - 4/12 pitch	1.230	S.F.	.012	.36	.32	.68
5/12 - 9/12 pitch	1.330	S.F.	.013	.39	.34	.73
1/2" thick, flat 0 - 4/12 pitch	1.230	S.F.	.013	.43	.36	.79
5/12 - 9/12 pitch	1.330	S.F.	.014	.47	.38	.85
5/8" thick, flat 0 - 4/12 pitch	1.230	S.F.	.014	.54	.38	.92
5/12 - 9/12 pitch	1.330	S.F.	.015	.59	.41	1.00
3/4" thick, flat 0 - 4/12 pitch	1.230	S.F.	.015	.63	.40	1.03
5/12 - 9/12 pitch	1.330	S.F.	.017	.68	.44	1.12
Boards, 1" x 6", laid regular, flat 0 - 4/12 pitch	1.230	S.F.	.027	.91	.68	1.59
5/12 - 9/12 pitch	1.330	S.F.	.041	.98	1.03	2.01
Laid diagonal, flat 0 - 4/12 pitch	1.230	S.F.	.030	.93	.77	1.70
5/12 - 9/12 pitch	1.330	S.F.	.043	.98	1.11	2.09
1" x 8", laid regular, flat 0 - 4/12 pitch	1.230	S.F.	.022	.91	.57	1.48
5/12 - 9/12 pitch	1.330	S.F.	.033	.98	.84	1.82
Laid diagonal, flat 0 - 4/12 pitch	1.230	S.F.	.027	.93	.68	1.61
5/12 - 9/12 pitch	1.330	S.F.	.043	.98	1.11	2.09

3 | FRAMING

40 | Gable Dormer Framing Systems

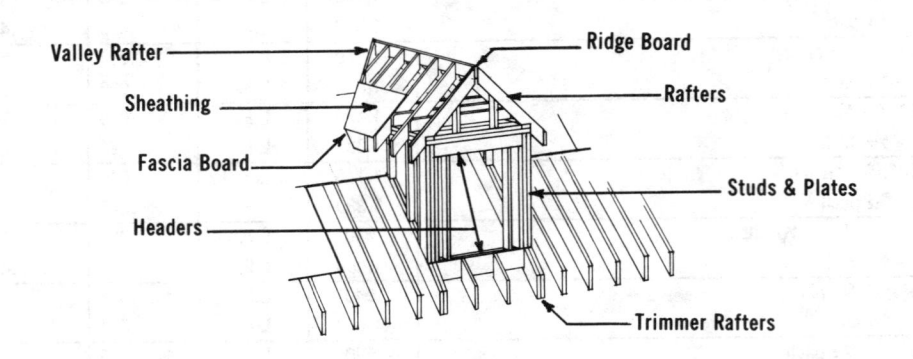

Diagram labels: Valley Rafter, Sheathing, Fascia Board, Headers, Ridge Board, Rafters, Studs & Plates, Trimmer Rafters

SYSTEM DESCRIPTION	QUAN.	UNIT	MAN-HOURS	MAT.	INST.	TOTAL
2" X 6", 16" O.C.						
Dormer rafter, 2" x 6", 16" O.C.	1.330	L.F.	.035	.57	.91	1.48
Ridge board, 2" x 6"	.280	L.F.	.008	.12	.22	.34
Trimmer rafters, 2" x 6"	.880	L.F.	.014	.38	.35	.73
Wall studs & plates, 2" x 4", 16" O.C.	3.160	L.F.	.056	.95	1.39	2.34
Fascia, 2" x 6"	.220	L.F.	.012	.10	.31	.41
Valley rafter, 2" x 6", 16" O.C.	.280	L.F.	.008	.12	.22	.34
Cripple rafter, 2" x 6", 16" O.C.	.560	L.F.	.021	.24	.55	.79
Headers, 2" x 6", doubled	.670	L.F.	.020	.29	.51	.80
Ceiling joist, 2" x 4", 16" O.C.	1.000	L.F.	.013	.29	.32	.61
Sheathing, exterior grade plywood, ½" thick	3.610	S.F.	.046	1.84	1.19	3.03
TOTAL			.233	4.90	5.97	10.87
2" X 8", 16" O.C.						
Dormer rafter, 2" x 8", 16" O.C.	1.330	L.F.	.039	.81	.99	1.80
Ridge board, 2" x 8"	.280	L.F.	.010	.17	.25	.42
Trimmer rafter, 2" x 8"	.880	L.F.	.014	.54	.37	.91
Wall studs & plates, 2" x 4", 16" O.C.	3.160	L.F.	.056	.95	1.39	2.34
Fascia, 2" x 8"	.220	L.F.	.015	.13	.40	.53
Valley rafter, 2" x 8", 16" O.C.	.280	L.F.	.009	.17	.24	.41
Cripple rafter, 2" x 8", 16" O.C.	.560	L.F.	.026	.34	.67	1.01
Headers, 2" x 8", doubled	.670	L.F.	.031	.41	.79	1.20
Ceiling joist, 2" x 4", 16" O.C.	1.000	L.F.	.013	.29	.32	.61
Sheathing,, exterior grade plywood, ½" thick	3.610	S.F.	.046	1.84	1.19	3.03
TOTAL			.259	5.65	6.61	12.26

The cost in this system is based on the square foot of plan area.
The measurement being the plan area of the dormer only.

DESCRIPTION	QUAN.	UNIT	MAN-HOURS	MAT.	INST.	TOTAL

Gable Dormer Framing Price Sheet

	QUAN.	UNIT	MAN-HOURS	COST PER S.F. MAT.	COST PER S.F. INST.	COST PER S.F. TOTAL
Dormer rafters, #2 or better, 2" x 4", 16" O.C.	1.330	L.F.	.028	.46	.72	1.18
24" O.C.	1.060	L.F.	.022	.37	.57	.94
2" x 6", 16" O.C.	1.330	L.F.	.035	.57	.91	1.48
24" O.C.	1.060	L.F.	.028	.46	.72	1.18
2" x 8", 16" O.C.	1.330	L.F.	.039	.81	.99	1.80
24" O.C.	1.060	L.F.	.031	.65	.78	1.43
Ridge board, #2 or better, 1" x 4"	.280	L.F.	.006	.07	.15	.22
1" x 6"	.280	L.F.	.007	.09	.19	.28
1" x 8"	.280	L.F.	.008	.12	.20	.32
2" x 4"	.280	L.F.	.007	.10	.18	.28
2" x 6"	.280	L.F.	.008	.12	.22	.34
2" x 8"	.280	L.F.	.010	.17	.25	.42
Trimmer rafters, #2 or better, 2" x 4"	.880	L.F.	.011	.30	.28	.58
2" x 6"	.880	L.F.	.014	.38	.35	.73
2" x 8"	.880	L.F.	.014	.54	.37	.91
2" x 10"	.880	L.F.	.022	.79	.56	1.35
Wall studs & plates, #2 or better, 2" x 4" studs, 16" O.C.	3.160	L.F.	.056	.95	1.39	2.34
24" O.C.	2.800	L.F.	.050	.84	1.23	2.07
2" x 6" studs, 16" O.C.	3.160	L.F.	.063	1.42	1.58	3.00
24" O.C.	2.800	L.F.	.056	1.26	1.40	2.66
Fascia, #2 or better, 1" x 4"	.220	L.F.	.006	.05	.17	.22
1" x 6"	.220	L.F.	.007	.07	.19	.26
1" x 8"	.220	L.F.	.009	.08	.23	.31
2" x 4"	.220	L.F.	.010	.09	.27	.36
2" x 6"	.220	L.F.	.013	.12	.33	.45
2" x 8"	.220	L.F.	.015	.13	.40	.53
Valley rafter, #2 or better, 2" x 4"	.280	L.F.	.006	.10	.17	.27
2" x 6"	.280	L.F.	.008	.12	.22	.34
2" x 8"	.280	L.F.	.009	.17	.24	.41
2" x 10"	.280	L.F.	.011	.25	.30	.55
Cripple rafter, #2 or better, 2" x 4", 16" O.C.	.560	L.F.	.017	.19	.44	.63
24" O.C.	.450	L.F.	.014	.15	.36	.51
2" x 6", 16" O.C.	.560	L.F.	.021	.24	.55	.79
24" O.C.	.450	L.F.	.017	.19	.44	.63
2" x 8", 16" O.C.	.560	L.F.	.026	.34	.67	1.01
24" O.C.	.450	L.F.	.021	.27	.54	.81
Headers, #2 or better double header, 2" x 4"	.670	L.F.	.016	.23	.42	.65
2" x 6"	.670	L.F.	.020	.29	.51	.80
2" x 8"	.670	L.F.	.031	.41	.79	1.20
2" x 10"	.670	L.F.	.033	.62	.83	1.45
Ceiling joist, #2 or better, 2" x 4", 16" O.C.	1.000	L.F.	.013	.29	.32	.61
24" O.C.	.800	L.F.	.010	.23	.26	.49
2" x 6", 16" O.C.	1.000	L.F.	.013	.44	.32	.76
24" O.C.	.800	L.F.	.010	.35	.26	.61
Sheathing, plywood exterior grade, ⅜" thick	3.610	S.F.	.046	1.84	1.19	3.03
½" thick	3.610	S.F.	.046	1.84	1.19	3.03
⅝" thick	3.610	S.F.	.046	1.84	1.19	3.03
¾" thick	3.610	S.F.	.046	1.84	1.19	3.03
Boards, 1" x 6", laid regular	3.610	S.F.	.090	2.67	2.24	4.91
Laid diagonal	3.610	S.F.	.097	2.74	2.46	5.20
1" x 8", laid regular	3.610	S.F.	.075	2.67	1.88	4.55
Laid diagonal	3.610	S.F.	.090	2.74	2.24	4.98

3 | FRAMING

44 | Shed Dormer Framing Systems

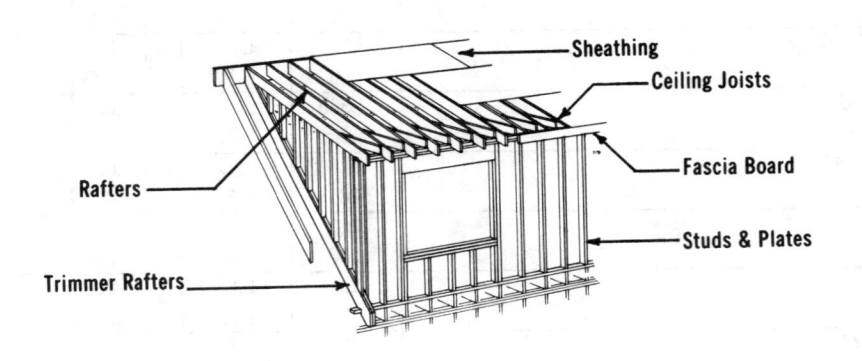

Labels on illustration: Sheathing, Ceiling Joists, Fascia Board, Studs & Plates, Rafters, Trimmer Rafters

SYSTEM DESCRIPTION	QUAN.	UNIT	MAN-HOURS	COST PER S.F. MAT.	COST PER S.F. INST.	TOTAL
2" X 6" RAFTERS, 16" O.C.						
Dormer rafter, 2" x 6", 16" O.C.	1.080	L.F.	.029	.46	.74	1.20
Trimmer rafter, 2" x 6"	.400	L.F.	.006	.17	.16	.33
Studs & plates, 2" x 4", 16" O.C.	2.750	L.F.	.049	.83	1.21	2.04
Fascia, 2" x 6"	.250	L.F.	.013	.12	.33	.45
Ceiling joist, 2" x 4", 16" O.C.	1.000	L.F.	.013	.29	.32	.61
Sheathing, exterior grade plywood, CDX, ½" thick	2.940	S.F.	.038	1.50	.97	2.47
TOTAL			.148	3.37	3.73	7.10
2" X 8" RAFTERS, 16" O.C.						
Dormer rafter, 2" x 8", 16" O.C.	1.080	L.F.	.032	.66	.80	1.46
Trimmer rafter, 2" x 8"	.400	L.F.	.006	.24	.17	.41
Studs & plates, 2" x 4", 16" O.C.	2.750	L.F.	.049	.83	1.21	2.04
Fascia, 2" x 8"	.250	L.F.	.017	.15	.45	.60
Ceiling joist, 2" x 6", 16" O.C.	1.000	L.F.	.013	.44	.32	.76
Sheathing, exterior grade plywood, CDX, ½" thick	2.940	S.F.	.038	1.50	.97	2.47
TOTAL			.155	3.82	3.92	7.74
2" X 10" RAFTERS, 16" O.C.						
Dormer rafter, 2" x 10", 16" O.C.	1.080	L.F.	.041	.97	1.02	1.99
Trimmer rafter, 2" x 10"	.400	L.F.	.010	.36	.25	.61
Studs & plates, 2" x 4", 16" O.C.	2.750	L.F.	.049	.83	1.21	2.04
Fascia, 2" x 10"	.250	L.F.	.022	.23	.55	.78
Ceiling joist, 2" x 6", 16" O.C.	1.000	L.F.	.013	.44	.32	.76
Sheathing, exterior grade plywood, CDX, ½" thick	2.940	S.F.	.038	1.50	.97	2.47
TOTAL			.173	4.33	4.32	8.65

The cost in this system is based on the square foot of plan area.
The measurement is the plan area of the dormer only.

DESCRIPTION	QUAN.	UNIT	MAN-HOURS	COST PER S.F. MAT.	COST PER S.F. INST.	TOTAL

Shed Dormer Framing Price Sheet

	QUAN.	UNIT	MAN-HOURS	COST PER S.F. MAT.	COST PER S.F. INST.	COST PER S.F. TOTAL
Dormer rafters, #2 or better, 2" x 4", 16" O.C.	1.080	L.F.	.023	.37	.59	.96
24" O.C.	.860	L.F.	.018	.30	.46	.76
2" x 6", 16" O.C.	1.080	L.F.	.029	.46	.74	1.20
24" O.C.	.860	L.F.	.023	.37	.58	.95
2" x 8", 16" O.C.	1.080	L.F.	.032	.66	.80	1.46
24" O.C.	.860	L.F.	.025	.52	.64	1.16
2" x 10", 16" O.C.	1.080	L.F.	.041	.97	1.02	1.99
24" O.C.	.860	L.F.	.032	.77	.81	1.58
Trimmer rafter, #2 or better, 2" x 4"	.400	L.F.	.005	.14	.13	.27
2" x 6"	.400	L.F.	.006	.17	.16	.33
2" x 8"	.400	L.F.	.006	.24	.17	.41
2" x 10"	.400	L.F.	.010	.36	.25	.61
Studs & plates, #2 or better, 2" x 4", 16" O.C.	2.750	L.F.	.049	.83	1.21	2.04
24" O.C.	2.200	L.F.	.039	.66	.97	1.63
2" x 6", 16" O.C.	2.750	L.F.	.055	1.24	1.37	2.61
24" O.C.	2.200	L.F.	.044	.99	1.10	2.09
Fascia, #2 or better, 1" x 4"	.250	L.F.	.006	.05	.17	.22
1" x 6"	.250	L.F.	.007	.07	.19	.26
1" x 8"	.250	L.F.	.009	.08	.23	.31
2" x 4"	.250	L.F.	.010	.09	.27	.36
2" x 6"	.250	L.F.	.013	.12	.33	.45
2" x 8"	.250	L.F.	.017	.15	.45	.60
Ceiling joist, #2 or better, 2" x 4", 16" O.C.	1.000	L.F.	.013	.29	.32	.61
24" O.C.	.800	L.F.	.010	.23	.26	.49
2" x 6", 16" O.C.	1.000	L.F.	.013	.44	.32	.76
24" O.C.	.800	L.F.	.010	.35	.26	.61
2" x 8", 16" O.C.	1.000	L.F.	.017	.62	.43	1.05
24" O.C.	.800	L.F.	.013	.50	.34	.84
Sheathing, plywood exterior grade, ⅜" thick	2.940	S.F.	.038	1.50	.97	2.47
½" thick	2.940	S.F.	.038	1.50	.97	2.47
⅝" thick	2.940	S.F.	.038	1.50	.97	2.47
¾" thick	2.940	S.F.	.038	1.50	.97	2.47
Boards, 1" x 6", laid regular	2.940	S.F.	.073	2.18	1.82	4.00
Laid diagonal	2.940	S.F.	.079	2.23	2.00	4.23
1" x 8", laid regular	2.940	S.F.	.061	2.18	1.52	3.70
Laid diagonal	2.940	S.F.	.073	2.23	1.83	4.06

Window Openings

	QUAN.	UNIT	MAN-HOURS	COST EACH MAT.	COST EACH INST.	COST EACH TOTAL
The following are to be added to the total cost of the dormers for window -openings. Do not subtract window area from the stud wall quantities.						
Headers, 2" x 6" doubled, 2' long	4.000	L.F.	.124	1.72	3.08	4.80
3' long	6.000	L.F.	.186	2.58	4.62	7.20
4' long	8.000	L.F.	.248	3.44	6.16	9.60
5' long	10.000	L.F.	.310	4.30	7.70	12.00
2" x 8" doubled, 4' long	8.000	L.F.	.376	4.88	9.44	14.32
5' long	10.000	L.F.	.470	6.10	11.80	17.90
6' long	12.000	L.F.	.564	7.32	14.16	21.48
8' long	16.000	L.F.	.752	9.76	18.88	28.64
2" x 10" doubled, 4' long	8.000	L.F.	.400	7.36	10.00	17.36
6' long	12.000	L.F.	.600	11.04	15.00	26.04
8' long	16.000	L.F.	.800	14.72	20.00	34.72
10' long	20.000	L.F.	1.000	18.40	25.00	43.40

3 | FRAMING   48 | Partition Framing System

Bracing, Top Plates, Studs, Bottom Plate

SYSTEM DESCRIPTION	QUAN.	UNIT	MAN-HOURS	MAT.	INST.	TOTAL
2" X 4", 16" O.C.						
2" x 4" studs, #2 or better, 16" O.C.	1.000	L.F.	.015	.28	.38	.66
Plates, double top, single bottom	.375	L.F.	.005	.11	.14	.25
Cross bracing, let-in, 1" x 6"	.080	L.F.	.004	.02	.11	.13
TOTAL			.024	.41	.63	1.04
2" X 4", 24" O.C.						
2" x 4" studs, #2 or better, 24" O.C.	.800	L.F.	.012	.22	.31	.53
Plates, double top, single bottom	.375	L.F.	.005	.11	.14	.25
Cross bracing, let-in, 1" x 6"	.080	L.F.	.002	.02	.07	.09
TOTAL			.019	.35	.52	.87
2" X 6", 16" O.C.						
2" x 6" studs, #2 or better, 16" O.C.	1.000	L.F.	.016	.44	.40	.84
Plates, double top, single bottom	.375	L.F.	.006	.17	.15	.32
Cross bracing, let-in, 1" x 6"	.080	L.F.	.004	.02	.11	.13
TOTAL			.026	.63	.66	1.29
2" X 6", 24" O.C.						
2" x 6" studs, #2 or better, 24" O.C.	.800	L.F.	.012	.35	.32	.67
Plates, double top, single bottom	.375	L.F.	.006	.17	.15	.32
Cross bracing, let-in, 1" x 6"	.080	L.F.	.002	.02	.07	.09
TOTAL			.020	.54	.54	1.08

The costs in this system are based on a square foot of wall area. Do not subtract for door or window openings. For openings see next page.

DESCRIPTION	QUAN.	UNIT	MAN-HOURS	MAT.	INST.	TOTAL

Partition Framing Price Sheet

	QUAN.	UNIT	MAN-HOURS	COST PER S.F. MAT.	COST PER S.F. INST.	COST PER S.F. TOTAL
Wood studs, #2 or better, 2" x 4", 12" O.C.	1.250	L.F.	.018	.35	.48	.83
16" O.C.	1.000	L.F.	.015	.28	.38	.66
24" O.C.	.800	L.F.	.012	.22	.31	.53
32" O.C.	.650	L.F.	.009	.18	.25	.43
2" x 6", 12" O.C.	1.250	L.F.	.020	.55	.50	1.05
16" O.C.	1.000	L.F.	.016	.44	.40	.84
24" O.C.	.800	L.F.	.012	.35	.32	.67
32" O.C.	.650	L.F.	.010	.29	.26	.55
Plates, #2 or better double top single bottom, 2" x 4"	.375	L.F.	.005	.11	.14	.25
2" x 6"	.375	L.F.	.006	.17	.15	.32
2" x 8"	.375	L.F.	.006	.23	.16	.39
Cross bracing, let-in, 1" x 6" boards studs, 12" O.C.	.080	L.F.	.005	.03	.13	.16
16" O.C.	.080	L.F.	.004	.02	.11	.13
24" O.C.	.080	L.F.	.002	.02	.07	.09
32" O.C.	.080	L.F.	.002	.02	.05	.07
Let-in steel (T shaped) studs, 12" O.C.	.080	L.F.	.001	.07	.03	.10
16" O.C.	.080	L.F.	.001	.05	.03	.08
24" O.C.	.080	L.F.	.001	.05	.03	.08
32" O.C.	.080	L.F.		.04	.02	.06
Steel straps studs, 12" O.C.	.080	L.F.	.001	.05	.03	.08
16" O.C.	.080	L.F.	.001	.05	.02	.07
24" O.C.	.080	L.F.	.001	.05	.02	.07
32" O.C.	.080	L.F.		.04	.03	.07
Metal studs, load bearing 24" O.C., 20 ga. galv., 2-½" wide	1.000	S.F.	.033	.80	.80	1.60
3-⅝" wide	1.000	S.F.	.035	.92	.84	1.76
4" wide	1.000	S.F.	.036	.97	.87	1.84
6" wide	1.000	S.F.	.038	1.18	.91	2.09
16 ga., 2-½" wide	1.000	S.F.	.036	1.01	.87	1.88
3-⅝" wide	1.000	S.F.	.038	1.13	.91	2.04
4" wide	1.000	S.F.	.040	1.22	.96	2.18
6" wide	1.000	S.F.	.042	1.50	1.00	2.50
Non-load bearing 24" O.C., 25 ga. galv., 1-⅝" wide	1.000	S.F.	.015	.21	.37	.58
2-½" wide	1.000	S.F.	.016	.24	.38	.62
3-⅝" wide	1.000	S.F.	.016	.29	.38	.67
4" wide	1.000	S.F.	.016	.32	.39	.71
6" wide	1.000	S.F.	.017	.41	.40	.81
20 ga., 2-½" wide	1.000	S.F.	.016	.43	.37	.80
3-⅝" wide	1.000	S.F.	.016	.51	.38	.89
4" wide	1.000	S.F.	.016	.54	.39	.93
6" wide	1.000	S.F.	.017	.67	.40	1.07

Window & Door Openings

	QUAN.	UNIT	MAN-HOURS	COST EACH MAT.	COST EACH INST.	COST EACH TOTAL
The following costs are to be added to the total costs of the walls. Do not subtract openings from total wall area.						
Headers, 2" x 6" double, 2' long	4.000	L.F.	.124	1.72	3.08	4.80
3' long	6.000	L.F.	.186	2.58	4.62	7.20
4' long	8.000	L.F.	.248	3.44	6.16	9.60
5' long	10.000	L.F.	.310	4.30	7.70	12.00
2" x 8" double, 4' long	8.000	L.F.	.376	4.88	9.44	14.32
5' long	10.000	L.F.	.470	6.10	11.80	17.90
6' long	12.000	L.F.	.564	7.32	14.16	21.48
8' long	16.000	L.F.	.752	9.76	18.88	28.64
2" x 10" double, 4' long	8.000	L.F.	.400	7.36	10.00	17.36
6' long	12.000	L.F.	.600	11.04	15.00	26.04
8' long	16.000	L.F.	.800	14.72	20.00	34.72
10' long	20.000	L.F.	1.000	18.40	25.00	43.40
2" x 12" double, 8' long	16.000	L.F.	.848	17.92	21.28	39.20
12' long	24.000	L.F.	1.272	26.88	31.92	58.80

4 | EXTERIOR WALLS — 02 Block Masonry Systems

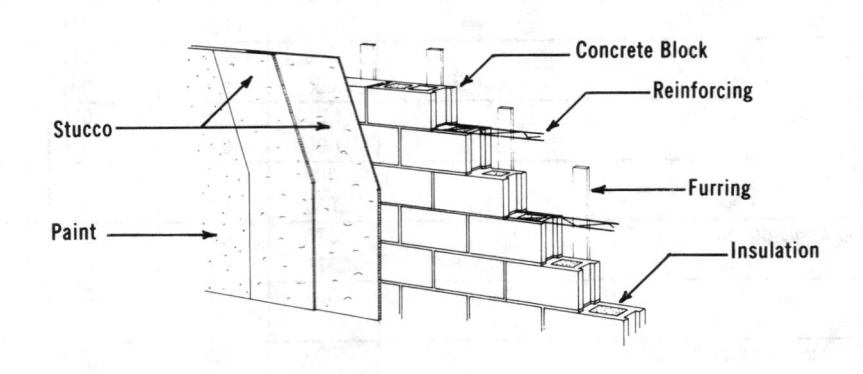

SYSTEM DESCRIPTION	QUAN.	UNIT	MAN-HOURS	MAT.	INST.	TOTAL
6" THICK CONCRETE BLOCK WALL						
6" thick concrete block, 6" x 8" x 16"	1.000	S.F.	.100	1.12	2.21	3.33
Masonry reinforcing, truss strips every other course	.625	L.F.	.001	.13	.03	.16
Furring, 1" x 3", 16" O.C.	1.000	L.F.	.016	.17	.38	.55
Masonry insulation, poured vermiculite	1.000	S.F.	.013	.65	.32	.97
Stucco, 2 coats	1.000	S.F.	.068	.20	1.54	1.74
Masonry paint, 2 coats	1.000	S.F.	.016	.18	.35	.53
TOTAL			.214	2.45	4.83	7.28
8" THICK CONCRETE BLOCK WALL						
8" thick concrete block, 8" x 8" x 16"	1.000	S.F.	.107	1.43	2.36	3.79
Masonry reinforcing, truss strips every other course	.625	L.F.	.001	.13	.03	.16
Furring, 1" x 3", 16" O.C.	1.000	L.F.	.016	.17	.38	.55
Masonry insulation, poured vermiculite	1.000	S.F.	.017	.86	.42	1.28
Stucco, 2 coats	1.000	S.F.	.068	.20	1.54	1.74
Masonry paint, 2 coats	1.000	S.F.	.016	.18	.35	.53
TOTAL			.225	2.97	5.08	8.05
12" THICK CONCRETE BLOCK WALL						
12" thick concrete block, 12" x 8" x 16"	1.000	S.F.	.141	2.04	3.06	5.10
Masonry reinforcing, truss strips every other course	.625	L.F.	.002	.13	.06	.19
Furring, 1" x 3", 16" O.C.	1.000	L.F.	.016	.17	.38	.55
Masonry insulation, poured vermiculite	1.000	S.F.	.026	1.27	.62	1.89
Stucco, 2 coats	1.000	S.F.	.068	.20	1.54	1.74
Masonry paint, 2 coats	1.000	S.F.	.016	.18	.35	.53
TOTAL			.269	3.99	6.01	10.00

Costs for this system are based on a square foot of wall area. Do not subtract for window openings.

DESCRIPTION	QUAN.	UNIT	MAN-HOURS	MAT.	INST.	TOTAL

Masonry Block Price Sheet

	QUAN.	UNIT	MAN-HOURS	COST PER S.F. MAT.	COST PER S.F. INST.	COST PER S.F. TOTAL
Block concrete, 8" x 16" regular, 4" thick	1.000	S.F.	.093	.91	2.06	2.97
6" thick	1.000	S.F.	.100	1.12	2.21	3.33
8" thick	1.000	S.F.	.107	1.43	2.36	3.79
10" thick	1.000	S.F.	.111	1.98	2.46	4.44
12" thick	1.000	S.F.	.141	2.04	3.06	5.10
Solid block, 4" thick	1.000	S.F.	.096	1.18	2.13	3.31
6" thick	1.000	S.F.	.104	1.64	2.30	3.94
8" thick	1.000	S.F.	.111	2.00	2.46	4.46
10" thick	1.000	S.F.	.133	2.75	2.88	5.63
12" thick	1.000	S.F.	.148	3.06	3.19	6.25
Lightweight, 4" thick	1.000	S.F.	.093	.91	2.06	2.97
6" thick	1.000	S.F.	.100	1.12	2.21	3.33
8" thick	1.000	S.F.	.107	1.43	2.36	3.79
10" thick	1.000	S.F.	.111	1.98	2.46	4.44
12" thick	1.000	S.F.	.141	2.04	3.06	5.10
Split rib profile, 4" thick	1.000	S.F.	.116	2.06	2.57	4.63
6" thick	1.000	S.F.	.123	2.56	2.74	5.30
8" thick	1.000	S.F.	.131	3.28	2.92	6.20
10" thick	1.000	S.F.	.157	3.57	3.41	6.98
12" thick	1.000	S.F.	.175	3.97	3.78	7.75
Masonry reinforcing, wire truss strips, every course, 8" block	1.375	L.F.	.004	.28	.08	.36
12" block	1.375	L.F.	.005	.29	.14	.43
Every other course, 8" block	.625	L.F.	.001	.13	.03	.16
12" block	.625	L.F.	.002	.13	.06	.19
Furring, wood, 1" x 3", 12" O.C.	1.250	L.F.	.020	.21	.48	.69
16" O.C.	1.000	L.F.	.016	.17	.38	.55
24" O.C.	.800	L.F.	.012	.14	.30	.44
32" O.C.	.640	L.F.	.010	.11	.24	.35
Steel, ¾" channels, 12" O.C.	1.250	L.F.	.034	.28	.78	1.06
16" O.C.	1.000	L.F.	.030	.22	.69	.91
24" O.C.	.800	L.F.	.023	.18	.52	.70
32" O.C.	.640	L.F.	.018	.14	.42	.56
Masonry insulation, vermiculite or perlite poured 4" thick	1.000	S.F.	.008	.42	.20	.62
6" thick	1.000	S.F.	.013	.64	.32	.96
8" thick	1.000	S.F.	.017	.86	.42	1.28
10" thick	1.000	S.F.	.021	1.04	.51	1.55
12" thick	1.000	S.F.	.026	1.27	.62	1.89
Block inserts polystyrene, 6" thick	1.000	S.F.		.72		.72
8" thick	1.000	S.F.		.72		.72
10" thick	1.000	S.F.		.87		.87
12" thick	1.000	S.F.		.87		.87
Stucco, 1 coat	1.000	S.F.	.056	.16	1.28	1.44
2 coats	1.000	S.F.	.068	.20	1.54	1.74
3 coats	1.000	S.F.	.081	.23	1.82	2.05
Painting, 1 coat	1.000	S.F.	.011	.13	.25	.38
2 coats	1.000	S.F.	.016	.18	.35	.53
Primer & 1 coat	1.000	S.F.	.013	.23	.29	.52
2 coats	1.000	S.F.	.018	.29	.40	.69
Lath, metal lath expanded 2.5 lb/S.Y., painted	1.000	S.F.	.010	.20	.24	.44
Galvanized	1.000	S.F.	.011	.22	.26	.48

4 | EXTERIOR WALLS 04 | Brick/Stone Veneer Systems

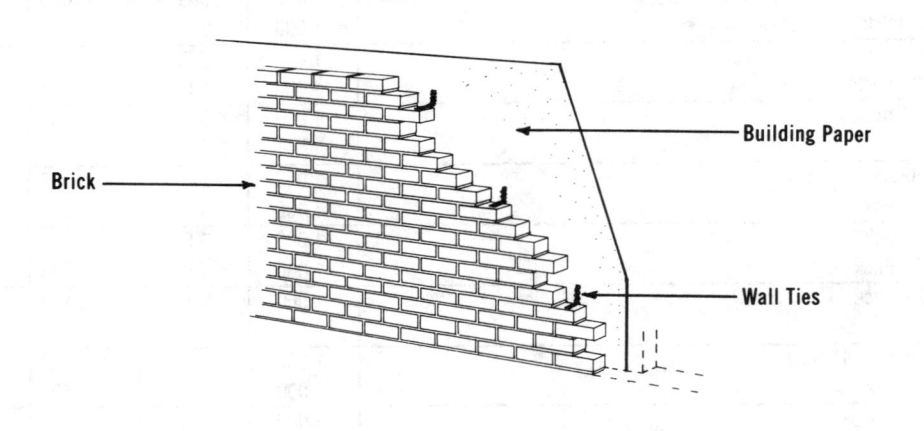

Brick — Building Paper — Wall Ties

SYSTEM DESCRIPTION	QUAN.	UNIT	MAN-HOURS	MAT.	INST.	TOTAL
COMMON BRICK $220 PER THOUSAND						
Brick, select common, running bond, brick $220 per thousand	1.000	S.F.	.174	2.11	3.84	5.95
Wall ties, 7/8" x 7", 22 gauge	1.000	Ea.	.008	.04	.19	.23
Building paper, #15 asphalt	1.100	S.F.	.002	.03	.06	.09
Trim, pine, painted	.125	L.F.	.004	.04	.09	.13
TOTAL			.188	2.22	4.18	6.40
COMMON BRICK $245 PER THOUSAND						
Brick, common, red faced, running bond, brick $245 per thousand	1.000	S.F.	.182	2.34	4.01	6.35
Wall ties, 7/8" x 7", 22 gauge	1.000	Ea.	.008	.04	.19	.23
Building paper, #15 asphalt	1.100	S.F.	.002	.03	.06	.09
Trim, pine, painted	.125	L.F.	.004	.04	.09	.13
TOTAL			.196	2.45	4.35	6.80
BUFF OR GREY FACE BRICK $280 PER THOUSAND						
Brick, buff or grey $280 per thousand	1.000	S.F.	.182	2.94	4.01	6.95
Wall ties, 7/8" x 7", 22 gauge	1.000	Ea.	.008	.04	.19	.23
Building paper, #15 asphalt	1.100	S.F.	.002	.03	.06	.09
Trim, pine, painted	.125	L.F.	.004	.04	.09	.13
TOTAL			.196	3.05	4.35	7.40
STONE WORK, ROUGH STONE, AVERAGE						
Stone work, rough stone, average	1.000	S.F.	.178	7.19	3.87	11.06
Wall ties, 7/8" x 7", 22 gauge	1.000	Ea.	.008	.04	.19	.23
Building paper, #15 asphalt	1.000	S.F.	.002	.03	.06	.09
Trim, pine, painted	.125	L.F.	.004	.04	.09	.13
TOTAL			.192	7.30	4.21	11.51

The costs in this system are based on a square foot of wall area. Do not subtract area for window & door openings.

DESCRIPTION	QUAN.	UNIT	MAN-HOURS	MAT.	INST.	TOTAL

Brick/Stone Veneer Price Sheet

	QUAN.	UNIT	MAN-HOURS	MAT.	INST.	TOTAL
Brick, standard, running bond						
Select common, $220 per thousand	1.000	S.F.	.174	2.11	3.84	5.95
Red faced, $245 per thousand	1.000	S.F.	.182	2.34	4.01	6.35
Buff or grey faced, brick $280 per thousand, running bond	1.000	S.F.	.182	2.94	4.01	6.95
Header every 6th course	1.000	S.F.	.216	2.73	4.77	7.50
English bond	1.000	S.F.	.286	3.51	6.34	9.85
Flemish bond	1.000	S.F.	.195	2.48	4.32	6.80
Common bond	1.000	S.F.	.267	3.12	5.88	9.00
Stack bond	1.000	S.F.	.182	2.94	4.01	6.95
Jumbo, $975 per thousand, running bond	1.000	S.F.	.092	3.56	2.04	5.60
Norman, $425 per thousand, running bond	1.000	S.F.	.125	2.99	2.76	5.75
Norwegian, $490 per thousand, running bond	1.000	S.F.	.107	2.71	2.34	5.05
Economy, $405 per thousand, running bond	1.000	S.F.	.129	2.65	2.85	5.50
Engineer, $280 per thousand, running bond	1.000	S.F.	.154	2.70	3.40	6.10
Roman, $510 per thousand, running bond	1.000	S.F.	.160	4.16	3.54	7.70
Utility, $715 per thousand, running bond	1.000	S.F.	.089	2.84	1.97	4.81
Glazed, $765 per thousand, running bond	1.000	S.F.	.190	6.99	4.21	11.20
Stone work, rough stone, average	1.000	S.F.	.178	7.19	3.87	11.06
Maximum	1.000	S.F.	.267	10.73	5.77	16.50
Wall ties, galvanized, corrugated ⅞" x 7", 22 gauge	1.000	Ea.	.008	.04	.19	.23
16 gauge	1.000	Ea.	.008	.12	.19	.31
Cavity wall, every 3rd course 6" long Z type, ¼" diameter	1.330	L.F.	.010	.25	.24	.49
3/16" diameter	1.330	L.F.	.010	.11	.24	.35
8" long, Z type, ¼" diameter	1.330	L.F.	.010	.29	.26	.55
3/16" diameter	1.330	L.F.	.010	.12	.24	.36
Building paper, aluminum and craft laminated foil, 1 side	1.000	S.F.	.004	.46	.10	.56
2 sides	1.000	S.F.	.004	.09	.10	.19
#15 asphalt paper	1.100	S.F.	.002	.03	.06	.09
Polyethylene, .002" thick	1.000	S.F.	.002	.01	.05	.06
.004" thick	1.000	S.F.	.002	.02	.05	.07
.006" thick	1.000	S.F.	.002	.03	.05	.08
.008" thick	1.000	S.F.	.002	.03	.05	.08
.010" thick	1.000	S.F.	.002	.04	.06	.10
Trim, 1" x 4", cedar	.125	L.F.	.005	.09	.12	.21
Fir	.125	L.F.	.005	.02	.12	.14
Redwood	.125	L.F.	.005	.09	.12	.21
White pine	.125	L.F.	.005	.02	.12	.14

4 | EXTERIOR WALLS — 08 | Wood Siding Systems

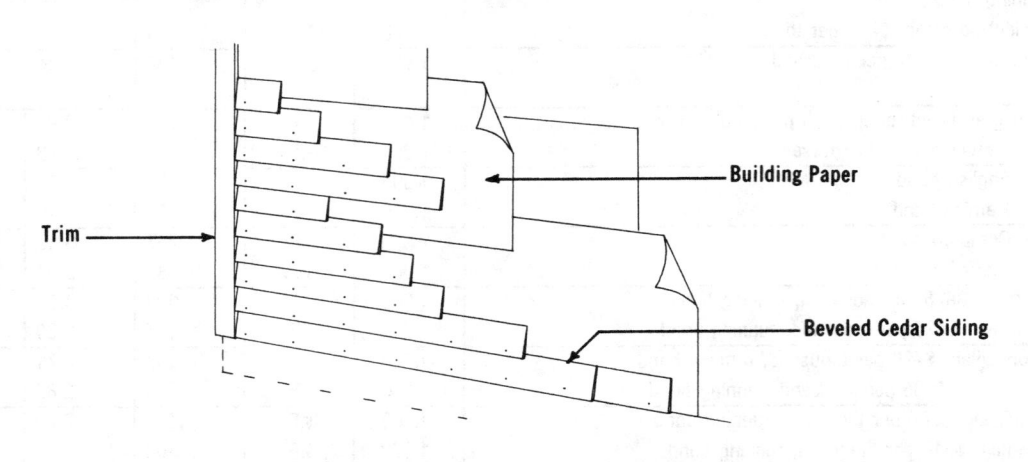

Building Paper
Trim
Beveled Cedar Siding

SYSTEM DESCRIPTION	QUAN.	UNIT	MAN-HOURS	COST PER S.F. MAT.	COST PER S.F. INST.	TOTAL
½" X 6" BEVELED CEDAR SIDING, "A" GRADE						
½" x 6" beveled cedar siding	1.000	S.F.	.032	1.58	.77	2.35
#15 asphalt felt paper	1.100	S.F.	.002	.03	.06	.09
Trim, cedar	.125	L.F.	.005	.09	.12	.21
Paint, primer & 2 coats	1.000	S.F.	.017	.19	.38	.57
TOTAL			.056	1.89	1.33	3.22
½" X 8" BEVELED CEDAR SIDING, "A" GRADE						
½" x 8" beveled cedar siding	1.000	S.F.	.029	1.97	.69	2.66
#15 asphalt felt paper	1.100	S.F.	.002	.03	.06	.09
Trim, cedar	.125	L.F.	.005	.09	.12	.21
Paint, primer & 2 coats	1.000	S.F.	.017	.19	.38	.57
TOTAL			.053	2.28	1.25	3.53
1" X 4" TONGUE & GROOVE, VERTICAL, REDWOOD, VERTICAL GRAIN						
1" x 4" tongue & groove, vertical, redwood	1.000	S.F.	.033	2.62	.80	3.42
#15 asphalt felt paper	1.100	S.F.	.002	.03	.06	.09
Trim, redwood	.125	L.F.	.005	.09	.12	.21
Sealer, 1 coat, stain, 1 coat	1.000	S.F.	.013	.13	.30	.43
TOTAL			.053	2.87	1.28	4.15
1" X 6" TONGUE & GROOVE, VERTICAL, REDWOOD, VERTICAL GRAIN						
1" x 6" tongue & groove, vertical, redwood	1.000	S.F.	.024	2.43	.56	2.99
#15 asphalt felt paper	1.100	S.F.	.002	.03	.06	.09
Trim, redwood	.125	L.F.	.005	.09	.12	.21
Sealer, 1 coat, stain, 1 coat	1.000	S.F.	.013	.13	.30	.43
TOTAL			.044	2.68	1.04	3.72

The costs in this system are based on a square foot of wall area. Do not subtract area for door or window openings.

DESCRIPTION	QUAN.	UNIT	MAN-HOURS	COST PER S.F. MAT.	COST PER S.F. INST.	TOTAL

Wood Siding Price Sheet

	QUAN.	UNIT	MAN-HOURS	MAT.	INST.	TOTAL
Siding, beveled cedar, "B" grade, ½" x 6"	1.000	S.F.	.028	1.18	.66	1.84
½" x 8"	1.000	S.F.	.023	1.20	.55	1.75
"A" grade, ½" x 6"	1.000	S.F.	.032	1.58	.77	2.35
½" x 8"	1.000	S.F.	.029	1.97	.69	2.66
Clear grade, ½" x 6"	1.000	S.F.	.028	1.87	.66	2.53
½" x 8"	1.000	S.F.	.023	1.60	.54	2.14
Redwood, clear vertical grain, ½" x 6"	1.000	S.F.	.028	1.49	.65	2.14
½" x 8"	1.000	S.F.	.032	1.42	.76	2.18
Clear all heart vertical grain, ½" x 6"	1.000	S.F.	.028	1.49	.65	2.14
½" x 8"	1.000	S.F.	.023	1.28	.54	1.82
Siding board & batten, cedar, "B" grade, 1" x 10"	1.000	S.F.	.031	1.21	.74	1.95
1" x 12"	1.000	S.F.	.031	1.21	.74	1.95
Redwood, clear vertical grain, 1" x 10"	1.000	S.F.	.043	2.27	1.07	3.34
1" x 12"	1.000	S.F.	.018	1.35	.43	1.78
White pine, #2 & better, 1" x 10"	1.000	S.F.	.029	.57	.70	1.27
1" x 12"	1.000	S.F.	.029	.57	.70	1.27
Siding vertical, tongue & groove, cedar "B" grade, 1" x 4"	1.000	S.F.	.033	1.18	.79	1.97
1" x 6"	1.000	S.F.	.024	1.08	.56	1.64
1" x 8"	1.000	S.F.	.024	1.01	.56	1.57
1" x 10"	1.000	S.F.	.021	1.29	.50	1.79
"A" grade, 1" x 4"	1.000	S.F.	.033	1.24	.80	2.04
1" x 6"	1.000	S.F.	.024	1.23	.56	1.79
1" x 8"	1.000	S.F.	.024	1.21	.56	1.77
1" x 10"	1.000	S.F.	.021	1.17	.50	1.67
Clear vertical grain, 1" x 4"	1.000	S.F.	.033	1.90	.80	2.70
1" x 6"	1.000	S.F.	.024	1.79	.57	2.36
1" x 8"	1.000	S.F.	.024	1.68	.57	2.25
1" x 10"	1.000	S.F.	.021	1.65	.50	2.15
Redwood, clear vertical grain, 1" x 4"	1.000	S.F.	.033	2.62	.80	3.42
1" x 6"	1.000	S.F.	.024	2.43	.56	2.99
1" x 8"	1.000	S.F.	.024	2.35	.57	2.92
1" x 10"	1.000	S.F.	.021	2.26	.50	2.76
Clear all heart vertical grain, 1" x 4"	1.000	S.F.	.033	2.62	.80	3.42
1" x 6"	1.000	S.F.	.024	2.92	.56	3.48
1" x 8"	1.000	S.F.	.024	2.70	.56	3.26
1" x 10"	1.000	S.F.	.021	2.61	.50	3.11
White pine, 1" x 8"	1.000	S.F.	.024	.75	.56	1.31
Siding plywood, texture 1-11 cedar, ⅜" thick	1.000	S.F.	.024	1.27	.59	1.86
⅝" thick	1.000	S.F.	.024	1.07	.59	1.66
Redwood, ⅜" thick	1.000	S.F.	.024	1.27	.59	1.86
⅝" thick	1.000	S.F.	.024	1.27	.59	1.86
Fir, ⅜" thick	1.000	S.F.	.024	.46	.59	1.05
⅝" thick	1.000	S.F.	.024	.57	.59	1.16
Southern yellow pine, ⅜" thick	1.000	S.F.	.024	.46	.59	1.05
⅝" thick	1.000	S.F.	.024	.63	.59	1.22
Hard board, ⁷⁄₁₆" thick primed, plain finish	1.000	S.F.	.021	.45	.53	.98
Board finish	1.000	S.F.	.021	.73	.53	1.26
Polyvinyl coated, ⅜" thick	1.000	S.F.	.021	.87	.53	1.40
⅝" thick	1.000	S.F.	.024	.63	.59	1.22
Paper, #15 asphalt felt	1.100	S.F.	.002	.03	.06	.09
Trim, cedar	.125	L.F.	.005	.09	.12	.21
Fir	.125	L.F.	.005	.02	.12	.14
Redwood	.125	L.F.	.005	.09	.12	.21
White pine	.125	L.F.	.005	.02	.12	.14
Painting, primer, & 1 coat	1.000	S.F.	.013	.13	.30	.43
2 coats	1.000	S.F.	.017	.19	.38	.57
Stain, sealer, & 1 coat	1.000	S.F.	.017	.12	.38	.50
2 coats	1.000	S.F.	.019	.17	.41	.58

4 | EXTERIOR WALLS 12 | Shingle Siding Systems

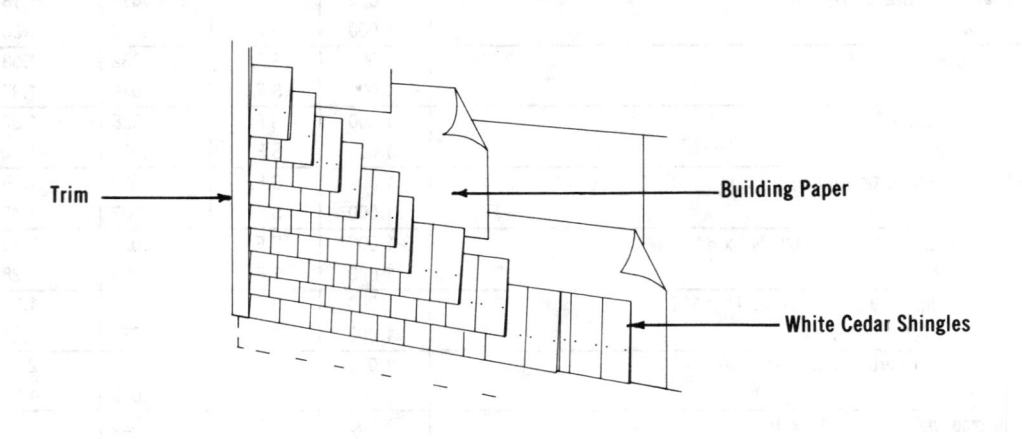

Trim → ← Building Paper
← White Cedar Shingles

SYSTEM DESCRIPTION	QUAN.	UNIT	MAN-HOURS	MAT.	INST.	TOTAL
WHITE CEDAR SHINGLES, 5" EXPOSURE						
White cedar shingles, 16" long, grade "A", 5" exposure	1.000	S.F.	.033	1.16	.79	1.95
#15 asphalt felt paper	1.100	S.F.	.002	.03	.06	.09
Trim, cedar	.125	S.F.	.005	.09	.12	.21
Paint, primer & 1 coat	1.000	S.F.	.017	.12	.38	.50
TOTAL			.057	1.40	1.35	2.75
NO. 1 PERFECTIONS, 5-½" EXPOSURE						
No. 1 perfections, red cedar, 5-½" exposure	1.000	S.F.	.029	1.22	.68	1.90
#15 asphalt felt paper	1.100	S.F.	.002	.03	.06	.09
Trim, cedar	.125	S.F.	.005	.09	.12	.21
Stain, sealer & 1 coat	1.000	S.F.	.017	.12	.38	.50
TOTAL			.053	1.46	1.24	2.70
RESQUARED & REBUTTED PERFECTIONS, 5-½" EXPOSURE						
Resquared & rebutted perfections, 5-½" exposure	1.000	S.F.	.026	.96	.64	1.60
#15 asphalt felt paper	1.100	S.F.	.002	.03	.06	.09
Trim, cedar	.125	S.F.	.005	.09	.12	.21
Stain, sealer & 1 coat	1.000	S.F.	.017	.12	.38	.50
TOTAL			.050	1.20	1.20	2.40
HAND-SPLIT SHAKES, 8-½" EXPOSURE						
Hand-split red cedar shakes, 18" long, 8-½"	1.000	S.F.	.040	.88	.97	1.85
#15 asphalt felt paper	1.100	S.F.	.002	.03	.06	.09
Trim, cedar	.125	S.F.	.005	.09	.12	.21
Stain, sealer & 1 coat	1.000	S.F.	.017	.12	.38	.50
TOTAL			.064	1.12	1.53	2.65

The costs in this system are based on a square foot of wall area. Do not subtract area for door or window openings.

DESCRIPTION	QUAN.	UNIT	MAN-HOURS	MAT.	INST.	TOTAL

Shingle Siding Price Sheet

	QUAN.	UNIT	MAN-HOURS	MAT.	INST.	TOTAL
Shingles wood, white cedar 16" long, "A" grade, 5" exposure	1.000	S.F.	.033	1.16	.79	1.95
7" exposure	1.000	S.F.	.029	1.04	.72	1.76
8-½" exposure	1.000	S.F.	.032	.67	.77	1.44
10" exposure	1.000	S.F.	.028	.59	.67	1.26
"B" grade, 5" exposure	1.000	S.F.	.033	.73	.77	1.50
7" exposure	1.000	S.F.	.023	.51	.54	1.05
8-½" exposure	1.000	S.F.	.019	.44	.46	.90
10" exposure	1.000	S.F.	.016	.36	.39	.75
Fire retardant, "A" grade, 5" exposure	1.000	S.F.	.033	1.49	.79	2.28
7" exposure	1.000	S.F.	.029	1.34	.72	2.06
8-½" exposure	1.000	S.F.	.026	1.18	.64	1.82
10" exposure	1.000	S.F.	.023	1.04	.56	1.60
"B" grade, 5" exposure	1.000	S.F.	.033	1.06	.77	1.83
7" exposure	1.000	S.F.	.023	.74	.54	1.28
8-½" exposure	1.000	S.F.	.019	.64	.46	1.10
10" exposure	1.000	S.F.	.016	.53	.39	.92
No. 1 perfections red cedar, 18" long, 5-½" exposure	1.000	S.F.	.029	1.22	.68	1.90
7" exposure	1.000	S.F.	.035	.89	.86	1.75
8-½" exposure	1.000	S.F.	.032	.80	.78	1.58
10" exposure	1.000	S.F.	.024	.62	.61	1.23
Fire retardant, 5" exposure	1.000	S.F.	.029	1.55	.68	2.23
7" exposure	1.000	S.F.	.035	1.22	.86	2.08
8-½" exposure	1.000	S.F.	.032	1.10	.78	1.88
10" exposure	1.000	S.F.	.024	.85	.61	1.46
Resquared & rebutted, 5-½" exposure	1.000	S.F.	.026	.96	.64	1.60
7" exposure	1.000	S.F.	.024	.86	.58	1.44
8-½" exposure	1.000	S.F.	.021	.77	.51	1.28
10" exposure	1.000	S.F.	.018	.67	.45	1.12
Fire retardant, 5" exposure	1.000	S.F.	.026	1.29	.64	1.93
7" exposure	1.000	S.F.	.024	1.16	.58	1.74
8-½" exposure	1.000	S.F.	.021	1.03	.51	1.54
10" exposure	1.000	S.F.	.022	.71	.54	1.25
Hand-split, red cedar, 24" long, 7" exposure	1.000	S.F.	.044	1.42	1.10	2.52
8-½" exposure	1.000	S.F.	.038	1.21	.95	2.16
10" exposure	1.000	S.F.	.032	1.01	.79	1.80
12" exposure	1.000	S.F.	.025	.81	.63	1.44
Fire retardant, 7" exposure	1.000	S.F.	.088	3.39	2.14	5.53
8-½" exposure	1.000	S.F.	.038	1.68	.95	2.63
10" exposure	1.000	S.F.	.032	1.40	.79	2.19
12" exposure	1.000	S.F.	.025	1.12	.63	1.75
18" long, 5" exposure	1.000	S.F.	.068	1.50	1.65	3.15
7" exposure	1.000	S.F.	.048	1.06	1.16	2.22
8-½" exposure	1.000	S.F.	.040	.88	.97	1.85
10" exposure	1.000	S.F.	.036	.79	.88	1.67
Fire retardant, 5" exposure	1.000	S.F.	.068	2.06	1.65	3.71
7" exposure	1.000	S.F.	.048	1.46	1.16	2.62
8-½" exposure	1.000	S.F.	.040	1.21	.97	2.18
10" exposure	1.000	S.F.	.036	1.09	.88	1.97
Paper, #15 asphalt felt	1.100	S.F.	.002	.03	.05	.08
Trim, cedar	.125	S.F.	.005	.09	.12	.21
Fir	.125	S.F.	.005	.02	.12	.14
Redwood	.125	S.F.	.005	.09	.12	.21
White pine	.125	S.F.	.005	.02	.12	.14
Painting, primer, & 1 coat	1.000	S.F.	.013	.13	.30	.43
2 coats	1.000	S.F.	.017	.19	.38	.57
Staining, sealer, & 1 coat	1.000	S.F.	.017	.12	.38	.50
2 coats	1.000	S.F.	.019	.17	.41	.58

4 | EXTERIOR WALLS — 16 | Metal & Plastic Siding

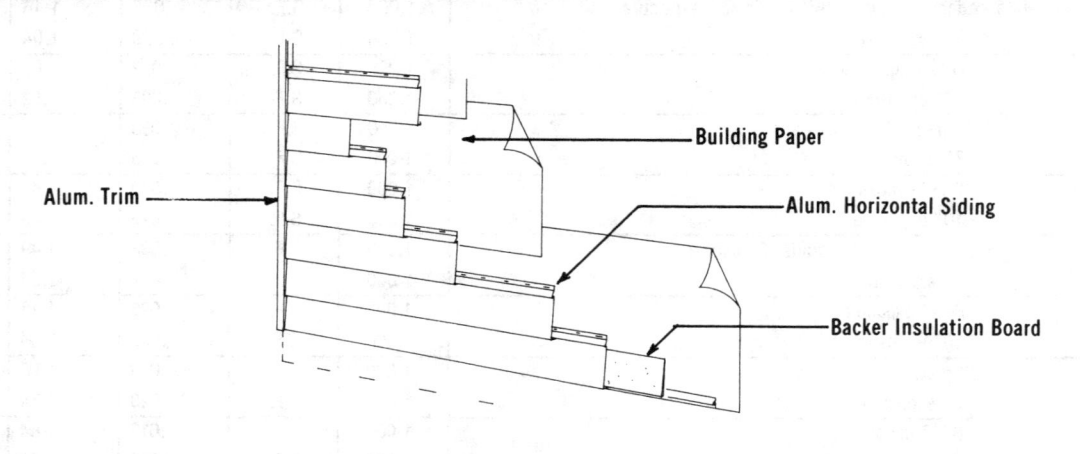

Diagram labels: Alum. Trim, Building Paper, Alum. Horizontal Siding, Backer Insulation Board

SYSTEM DESCRIPTIION	QUAN.	UNIT	MAN-HOURS	MAT.	INST.	TOTAL
ALUMINUM CLAPBOARD SIDING, 8" WIDE, WHITE						
Aluminum horizontal siding, 8" clapboard	1.000	S.F.	.031	.94	.78	1.72
Backer, insulation board	1.000	S.F.	.008	.32	.19	.51
Trim, aluminum	.600	L.F.	.015	.50	.39	.89
Paper, #15 asphalt felt	1.100	S.F.	.002	.03	.06	.09
TOTAL			.056	1.79	1.42	3.21
ALUMINUM VERTICAL BOARD & BATTEN, WHITE						
Aluminum vertical board & batten	1.000	S.F.	.027	1.10	.68	1.78
Backer insulation board	1.000	S.F.	.008	.32	.19	.51
Trim, aluminum	.600	L.F.	.015	.50	.39	.89
Paper, #15 asphalt felt	1.100	S.F.	.002	.03	.06	.09
TOTAL			.052	1.95	1.32	3.27
VINYL CLAPBOARD SIDING, 8" WIDE, WHITE						
PVC vinyl horizontal siding, 8" clapboard	1.000	S.F.	.032	.64	.81	1.45
Backer, insulation board	1.000	S.F.	.008	.32	.19	.51
Trim, vinyl	.600	L.F.	.013	.32	.35	.67
Paper, #15 asphalt felt	1.100	S.F.	.002	.03	.06	.09
TOTAL			.055	1.31	1.41	2.72
VINYL VERTICAL BOARD & BATTEN, WHITE						
PVC vinyl vertical board & batten	1.000	S.F.	.029	.75	.73	1.48
Backer, insulation board	1.000	S.F.	.008	.32	.19	.51
Trim, vinyl	.600	L.F.	.013	.32	.35	.67
Paper, #15 asphalt felt	1.100	S.F.	.002	.03	.06	.09
TOTAL			.052	1.42	1.33	2.75

The costs in this system are on a square foot of wall basis. Do not subtract openings from wall area.

DESCRIPTION	QUAN.	UNIT	MAN-HOURS	MAT.	INST.	TOTAL

Metal & Plastic Siding Price Sheet

	QUAN.	UNIT	MAN-HOURS	COST PER S.F. MAT.	COST PER S.F. INST.	COST PER S.F. TOTAL
Siding, aluminum, .024" thick, smooth, 8" wide, white	1.000	S.F.	.031	.94	.78	1.72
Color	1.000	S.F.	.031	1.00	.78	1.78
Double 4" pattern, 8" wide, white	1.000	S.F.	.031	.98	.78	1.76
Color	1.000	S.F.	.031	1.04	.78	1.82
Double 5" pattern, 10" wide, white	1.000	S.F.	.029	1.05	.73	1.78
Color	1.000	S.F.	.029	1.11	.73	1.84
Embossed, single, 8" wide, white	1.000	S.F.	.031	.94	.78	1.72
Color	1.000	S.F.	.031	1.00	.78	1.78
Double 4" pattern, 8" wide, white	1.000	S.F.	.031	.99	.78	1.77
Color	1.000	S.F.	.031	1.05	.78	1.83
Double 5" pattern, 10" wide, white	1.000	S.F.	.029	1.06	.73	1.79
Color	1.000	S.F.	.029	1.12	.73	1.85
Alum siding with insulation board, smooth, 8" wide, white	1.000	S.F.	.031	1.05	.78	1.83
Color	1.000	S.F.	.031	1.11	.78	1.89
Double 4" pattern, 8" wide, white	1.000	S.F.	.031	1.07	.78	1.85
Color	1.000	S.F.	.031	1.13	.78	1.91
Double 5" pattern, 10" wide, white	1.000	S.F.	.029	1.09	.73	1.82
Color	1.000	S.F.	.029	1.15	.73	1.88
Embossed, single, 8" wide, white	1.000	S.F.	.031	1.07	.78	1.85
Color	1.000	S.F.	.031	1.13	.78	1.91
Double 4" pattern, 8" wide, white	1.000	S.F.	.031	1.08	.78	1.86
Color	1.000	S.F.	.031	1.14	.78	1.92
Double 5" pattern, 10" wide, white	1.000	S.F.	.029	1.12	.73	1.85
Color	1.000	S.F.	.029	1.18	.73	1.91
Aluminum, shake finish, 10" wide, white	1.000	S.F.	.029	1.16	.73	1.89
Color	1.000	S.F.	.029	1.22	.73	1.95
Aluminum, vertical, 12" wide, white	1.000	S.F.	.027	1.10	.68	1.78
Color	1.000	S.F.	.027	1.16	.68	1.84
Vinyl siding, 8" wide, smooth, white	1.000	S.F.	.032	.64	.81	1.45
Color	1.000	S.F.	.032	.70	.81	1.51
10" wide, smooth, white	1.000	S.F.	.029	.69	.73	1.42
Color	1.000	S.F.	.029	.75	.73	1.48
Double 4" pattern, 8" wide, white	1.000	S.F.	.032	.72	.81	1.53
Color	1.000	S.F.	.032	.78	.81	1.59
Double 5" pattern, 10" wide, white	1.000	S.F.	.029	.75	.73	1.48
Color	1.000	S.F.	.029	.81	.73	1.54
Embossed, single, 8" wide, white	1.000	S.F.	.032	.68	.81	1.49
Color	1.000	S.F.	.032	.74	.81	1.55
10" wide, white	1.000	S.F.	.029	.73	.73	1.46
Color	1.000	S.F.	.029	.79	.73	1.52
Double 4" pattern, 8" wide, white	1.000	S.F.	.032	.75	.81	1.56
Color	1.000	S.F.	.032	.81	.81	1.62
Double 5" pattern, 10" wide, white	1.000	S.F.	.029	.77	.73	1.50
Color	1.000	S.F.	.029	.83	.73	1.56
Vinyl, shake finish, 10" wide, white	1.000	S.F.	.029	.75	.73	1.48
Color	1.000	S.F.	.029	.81	.73	1.54
Vinyl, vertical, double 5" pattern, 10" wide, white	1.000	S.F.	.029	.75	.73	1.48
Color	1.000	S.F.	.029	.81	.73	1.54
Backer board, installed in siding panels 8" or 10" wide	1.000	S.F.	.008	.32	.19	.51
4' x 8' sheets, polystyrene, ¾" thick	1.000	S.F.	.010	.45	.24	.69
4' x 8' fiberboard, plain	1.000	S.F.	.008	.32	.19	.51
Foil faced	1.000	S.F.	.012	.24	.29	.53
Trim, aluminum, white	.600	L.F.	.015	.50	.39	.89
Color	.600	L.F.	.015	.54	.39	.93
Vinyl, white	.600	L.F.	.013	.32	.35	.67
Color	.600	L.F.	.014	.33	.35	.68
Paper, #15 asphalt felt	1.100	S.F.	.002	.03	.06	.09
Kraft paper, plain	1.100	S.F.	.004	.51	.11	.62
Foil backed	1.100	S.F.	.004	.10	.11	.21

4 EXTERIOR WALLS — 20 Insulation Systems

DESCRIPTION	QUAN.	UNIT	MAN-HOURS	MAT.	INST.	TOTAL
Poured insulation, cellulose fiber, R3.8 per inch	1.000	S.F.	.003	.04	.08	.12
Fiberglass, R4.0 per inch	1.000	S.F.	.003	.03	.08	.11
Mineral wool, R3.0 per inch	1.000	S.F.	.003	.07	.08	.15
Polystyrene, R4.0 per inch	1.000	S.F.	.003	.15	.08	.23
Vermiculite, R2.7 per inch	1.000	S.F.	.003	.16	.08	.24
Perlite, R2.7 per inch	1.000	S.F.	.003	.16	.08	.24
Reflective, aluminum foil on kraft paper, foil one side R9	1.000	S.F.	.004	.03	.10	.13
Multilayered with air spaces, 2 ply, R14	1.000	S.F.	.004	.17	.10	.27
3 ply, R17	1.000	S.F.	.005	.21	.13	.34
5 ply, R22	1.000	S.F.	.005	.31	.13	.44
Rigid insulation, fiberglass, unfaced,						
1-½" thick, R6.2	1.000	S.F.	.008	.32	.19	.51
2" thick, R8.3	1.000	S.F.	.008	.42	.19	.61
2-½" thick, R10.3	1.000	S.F.	.010	.65	.24	.89
3" thick, R12.4	1.000	S.F.	.010	.65	.24	.89
Foil faced, 1" thick, R4.3	1.000	S.F.	.008	.87	.19	1.06
1-½" thick, R6.2	1.000	S.F.	.008	1.25	.20	1.45
2" thick, R8.7	1.000	S.F.	.009	1.60	.21	1.81
2-½" thick, R10.9	1.000	S.F.	.010	1.87	.24	2.11
3" thick, R13.0	1.000	S.F.	.010	2.37	.23	2.60
Foam glass, 1-½" thick R2.64	1.000	S.F.	.010	1.74	.24	1.98
2" thick R5.26	1.000	S.F.	.011	2.43	.26	2.69
Perlite, 1" thick R2.77	1.000	S.F.	.010	.44	.24	.68
2" thick R5.55	1.000	S.F.	.011	.83	.26	1.09
Polystyrene, extruded, blue, 2.2#/C.F., ¾" thick R4	1.000	S.F.	.010	.45	.24	.69
1-½" thick R8.1	1.000	S.F.	.011	.74	.26	1.00
2" thick R10.8	1.000	S.F.	.011	.97	.26	1.23
Molded bead board, white, 1" thick R3.85	1.000	S.F.	.010	.19	.24	.43
1-½" thick, R5.6	1.000	S.F.	.011	.30	.26	.56
2" thick, R7.7	1.000	S.F.	.011	.37	.27	.64
Urethane, no backing, ½" thick, R2.9	1.000	S.F.	.010	.31	.24	.55
1" thick, R5.8	1.000	S.F.	.010	.55	.24	.79
1-½" thick, R8.7	1.000	S.F.	.011	.83	.26	1.09
2" thick, R11.7	1.000	S.F.	.011	1.10	.26	1.36
Fire resistant, ½" thick, R2.9	1.000	S.F.	.010	.39	.23	.62
1" thick, R5.8	1.000	S.F.	.010	.76	.24	1.00
1-½" thick, R8.7	1.000	S.F.	.011	1.07	.26	1.33
2" thick, R11.7	1.000	S.F.	.011	1.36	.27	1.63
Non-rigid insulation, batts						
Fiberglass, kraft faced, 3-½" thick, R11, 11" wide	1.000	S.F.	.005	.28	.11	.39
15" wide	1.000	S.F.	.005	.28	.11	.39
23" wide	1.000	S.F.	.005	.28	.11	.39
6" thick, R19, 11" wide	1.000	S.F.	.006	.43	.14	.57
15" wide	1.000	S.F.	.006	.43	.14	.57
23" wide	1.000	S.F.	.006	.43	.14	.57
9" thick, R30, 15" wide	1.000	S.F.	.006	.66	.14	.80
23" wide	1.000	S.F.	.006	.66	.14	.80
12" thick, R38, 15" wide	1.000	S.F.	.006	.86	.14	1.00
23" wide	1.000	S.F.	.006	.86	.14	1.00
Fiberglass, foil faced, 3-½" thick, R11, 15" wide	1.000	S.F.	.005	.30	.12	.42
23" wide	1.000	S.F.	.005	.30	.12	.42
6" thick, R19, 15" thick	1.000	S.F.	.005	.43	.12	.55
23" wide	1.000	S.F.	.005	.43	.12	.55
9" thick, R30, 15" wide	1.000	S.F.	.006	.62	.14	.76
23" wide	1.000	S.F.	.006	.62	.14	.76

Insulation Systems

	QUAN.	UNIT	MAN-HOURS	COST PER S.F. MAT.	COST PER S.F. INST.	COST PER S.F. TOTAL
Non-rigid insulation batts						
Fiberglass unfaced, 3-½" thick, R11, 15" wide	1.000	S.F.	.005	.23	.12	.35
23" wide	1.000	S.F.	.005	.23	.12	.35
6" thick, R19, 15" wide	1.000	S.F.	.006	.40	.14	.54
23" wide	1.000	S.F.	.006	.40	.14	.54
9" thick, R19, 15" wide	1.000	S.F.	.007	.59	.17	.76
23" wide	1.000	S.F.	.007	.59	.17	.76
12" thick, R38, 15" wide	1.000	S.F.	.007	.87	.17	1.04
23" wide	1.000	S.F.	.007	.87	.17	1.04
Mineral fiber batts, 3" thick, R11	1.000	S.F.	.005	.31	.12	.43
3-½" thick, R13	1.000	S.F.	.005	.31	.12	.43
6" thick, R19	1.000	S.F.	.005	.48	.12	.60
6-½" thick, R22	1.000	S.F.	.005	.48	.12	.60
10" thick, R30	1.000	S.F.	.006	.77	.14	.91

137

4 | EXTERIOR WALLS — 28 Double Hung Window Systems

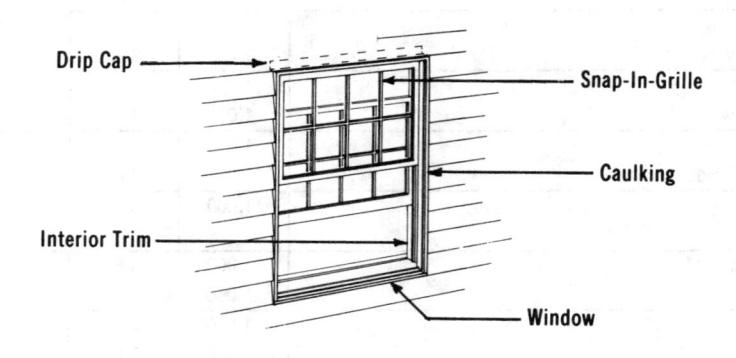

SYSTEM DESCRIPTION	QUAN.	UNIT	MAN-HOURS	MAT.	INST.	TOTAL
BUILDER'S QUALITY WOOD WINDOW 2' X 3', DOUBLE HUNG						
Window, wood primed, builder's quality, 2' x 3', insulating glass	1.000	Ea.	.800	134.20	20.80	155.00
Trim, interior casing	11.000	L.F.	.363	7.15	8.80	15.95
Paint, interior & exterior, primer & 2 coats	2.000	Face	1.600	2.46	35.24	37.70
Caulking	10.000	L.F.	.310	.80	7.50	8.30
Snap-in grille	1.000	Set	.333	14.30	7.70	22.00
Drip cap, metal	2.000	L.F.	.040	.28	.96	1.24
TOTAL			3.446	159.19	81.00	240.19
PLASTIC CLAD WOOD WINDOW 3' X 4', DOUBLE HUNG						
Window, wood, plastic clad, premium, 3' x 4', insulating glass	1.000	Ea.	.889	253.00	22.00	275.00
Trim, interior casing	15.000	L.F.	.495	9.75	12.00	21.75
Paint, interior, primer & 2 coats	1.000	Face	.800	3.83	17.17	21.00
Caulking	14.000	L.F.	.434	1.12	10.50	11.62
Snap-in grille	1.000	Set	.333	14.30	7.70	22.00
TOTAL			2.951	282.00	69.37	351.37
METAL CLAD WOOD WINDOW, 3' X 5', DOUBLE HUNG						
Window, wood, metal clad, deluxe, 3' x 5', insulating glass	1.000	Ea.	1.000	185.90	24.10	210.00
Trim, interior casing	17.000	L.F.	.561	11.05	13.60	24.65
Paint, interior, primer & 2 coats	1.000	Face	.800	3.83	17.17	21.00
Caulking	16.000	L.F.	.496	1.28	12.00	13.28
Snap-in grille	1.000	Set	.235	17.88	6.12	24.00
Drip cap, metal	3.000	L.F.	.060	.42	1.44	1.86
TOTAL			3.152	220.36	74.43	294.79

The cost of this system is on a cost per each window basis.

DESCRIPTION	QUAN.	UNIT	MAN-HOURS	MAT.	INST.	TOTAL

Double Hung Window Price Sheet

	QUAN.	UNIT	MAN-HOURS	COST EACH MAT.	COST EACH INST.	TOTAL
Windows, double-hung, builder's quality, 2' x 3', single glass	1.000	Ea.	.800	93.50	21.50	115.00
Insulating glass	1.000	Ea.	.800	134.20	20.80	155.00
3' x 4', single glass	1.000	Ea.	.889	116.60	23.40	140.00
Insulating glass	1.000	Ea.	.889	155.10	19.90	175.00
4' x 4'-6", single glass	1.000	Ea.	1.000	132.00	23.00	155.00
Insulating glass	1.000	Ea.	1.000	187.00	23.00	210.00
Plastic clad premium insulating glass, 2'-6" x 3'	1.000	Ea.	.800	192.50	17.50	210.00
3' x 3'-6"	1.000	Ea.	.800	232.10	17.90	250.00
3' x 4'	1.000	Ea.	.889	253.00	22.00	275.00
3' x 4'-6"	1.000	Ea.	.889	266.20	18.80	285.00
3' x 5'	1.000	Ea.	1.000	277.20	22.80	300.00
3'-6" x 6'	1.000	Ea.	1.000	333.30	21.70	355.00
Metal clad deluxe insulating glass, 2'-6" x 3'	1.000	Ea.	.800	118.80	21.20	140.00
3' x 3'-6"	1.000	Ea.	.800	143.00	17.00	160.00
3' x 4'	1.000	Ea.	.889	156.20	18.80	175.00
3' x 4'-6"	1.000	Ea.	.889	163.90	21.10	185.00
3' x 5'	1.000	Ea.	1.000	185.90	24.10	210.00
3'-6" x 6'	1.000	Ea.	1.000	207.90	22.10	230.00
Trim, interior casing, window 2' x 3'	11.000	L.F.	.363	7.15	8.80	15.95
2'-6" x 3'	12.000	L.F.	.396	7.80	9.60	17.40
3' x 3'-6"	14.000	L.F.	.462	9.10	11.20	20.30
3' x 4'	15.000	L.F.	.495	9.75	12.00	21.75
3' x 4'-6"	16.000	L.F.	.528	10.40	12.80	23.20
3' x 5'	17.000	L.F.	.561	11.05	13.60	24.65
3'-6" x 6'	20.000	L.F.	.660	13.00	16.00	29.00
4' x 4'-6"	18.000	L.F.	.594	11.70	14.40	26.10
Paint or stain, interior or exterior, 2' x 3' window, 1 coat	1.000	Face	.381	1.01	8.39	9.40
2 coats	1.000	Face	.615	1.09	13.56	14.65
Primer & 1 coat	1.000	Face	.615	1.17	13.53	14.70
Primer & 2 coats	1.000	Face	.800	1.23	17.62	18.85
3' x 4' window, 1 coat	1.000	Face	.533	1.32	11.73	13.05
2 coats	1.000	Face	.533	1.60	11.75	13.35
Primer & 1 coat	1.000	Face	.615	2.54	13.56	16.10
Primer & 2 coats	1.000	Face	.800	3.83	17.17	21.00
4' x 4'-6" window, 1 coat	1.000	Face	.533	1.32	11.73	13.05
2 coats	1.000	Face	.533	1.60	11.75	13.35
Primer & 1 coat	1.000	Face	.615	2.54	13.56	16.10
Primer & 2 coats	1.000	Face	.800	3.83	17.17	21.00
Caulking, window, 2' x 3'	10.000	L.F.	.310	.80	7.50	8.30
2'-6" x 3'	11.000	L.F.	.341	.88	8.25	9.13
3' x 3'-6"	13.000	L.F.	.403	1.04	9.75	10.79
3' x 4'	14.000	L.F.	.434	1.12	10.50	11.62
3' x 4'-6"	15.000	L.F.	.465	1.20	11.25	12.45
3' x 5'	16.000	L.F.	.496	1.28	12.00	13.28
3'-6" x 6'	19.000	L.F.	.589	1.52	14.25	15.77
4' x 4'-6"	17.000	L.F.	.527	1.36	12.75	14.11
Grilles, glass size to, 16" x 24" per sash	1.000	Set	.333	14.30	7.70	22.00
32" x 32" per sash	1.000	Set	.235	17.88	6.12	24.00
Drip cap, aluminum, 2' long	2.000	L.F.	.040	.28	.96	1.24
3' long	3.000	L.F.	.060	.42	1.44	1.86
4' long	4.000	L.F.	.080	.56	1.92	2.48
Wood, 2' long	2.000	L.F.	.066	1.30	1.60	2.90
3' long	3.000	L.F.	.099	1.95	2.40	4.35
4' long	4.000	L.F.	.132	2.60	3.20	5.80

4 | EXTERIOR WALLS — 32 | Casement Window Systems

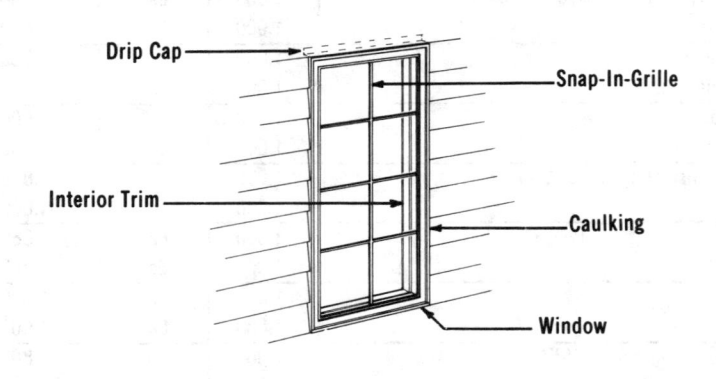

SYSTEM DESCRIPTION	QUAN.	UNIT	MAN-HOURS	MAT.	INST.	TOTAL
BUILDER'S QUALITY WINDOW, WOOD, 2' BY 3', CASEMENT						
Window, wood, primed, builder's quality, 2' x 3', insulating glass	1.000	Ea.	.800	184.80	20.20	205.00
Trim, interior casing	11.000	L.F.	.363	7.15	8.80	15.95
Paint, interior & exterior, primer & 2 coats	2.000	Face	1.600	2.46	35.24	37.70
Caulking	10.000	L.F.	.310	.80	7.50	8.30
Snap-in grille	1.000	Ea.	.267	10.62	6.38	17.00
Drip cap, metal	2.000	L.F.	.040	.28	.96	1.24
TOTAL			3.380	206.11	79.08	285.19
PLASTIC CLAD WOOD WINDOW, 2' X 4', CASEMENT						
Window, wood, plastic clad, premium, 2' x 4', insulating glass	1.000	Ea.	.889	170.50	19.50	190.00
Trim, interior casing	13.000	L.F.	.429	8.45	10.40	18.85
Paint, interior, primer & 2 coats	1.000	Ea.	.800	1.23	17.62	18.85
Caulking	12.000	L.F.	.372	.96	9.00	9.96
Snap-in grille	1.000	Ea.	.267	10.62	6.38	17.00
TOTAL			2.757	191.76	62.90	254.66
METAL CLAD WOOD WINDOW, 2' X 5', CASEMENT						
Window, wood, metal clad, deluxe, 2' x 5', insulating glass	1.000	Ea.	1.000	253.00	22.00	275.00
Trim, interior casing	15.000	L.F.	.495	9.75	12.00	21.75
Paint, interior, primer & 2 coats	1.000	Ea.	.800	3.83	17.17	21.00
Caulking	14.000	L.F.	.434	1.12	10.50	11.62
Snap-in grille	1.000	Ea.	.250	14.91	6.09	21.00
Drip cap, metal	12.000	L.F.	.040	.28	.96	1.24
TOTAL			3.019	282.89	68.72	351.61

The cost of this system is on a cost per each window basis.

DESCRIPTION	QUAN.	UNIT	MAN-HOURS	MAT.	INST.	TOTAL

Casement Window Price Sheet

	QUAN.	UNIT	MAN-HOURS	MAT.	INST.	TOTAL
Window, casement, builders quality, 2' x 3', single glass	1.000	Ea.	.800	143.00	17.00	160.00
Insulating glass	1.000	Ea.	.800	184.80	20.20	205.00
2' x 4'-6", single glass	1.000	Ea.	.727	324.50	15.50	340.00
Insulating glass	1.000	Ea.	.727	462.00	18.00	480.00
2' x 6', single glass	1.000	Ea.	.889	544.50	20.50	565.00
Insulating glass	1.000	Ea.	.889	698.50	21.50	720.00
Plastic clad premium insulating glass, 2' x 3'	1.000	Ea.	.800	269.50	20.50	290.00
2' x 4'	1.000	Ea.	.889	170.50	19.50	190.00
2' x 5'	1.000	Ea.	1.000	203.50	21.50	225.00
2' x 6'	1.000	Ea.	1.000	242.00	23.00	265.00
Metal clad deluxe insulating glass, 2' x 3'	1.000	Ea.	.800	467.50	17.50	485.00
2' x 4'	1.000	Ea.	.889	247.50	22.50	270.00
2' x 5'	1.000	Ea.	1.000	253.00	22.00	275.00
2' x 6'	1.000	Ea.	1.000	297.00	23.00	320.00
Trim, interior casing, window 2' x 3'	11.000	L.F.	.363	7.15	8.80	15.95
2' x 4'	13.000	L.F.	.429	8.45	10.40	18.85
2' x 4'-6"	14.000	L.F.	.462	9.10	11.20	20.30
2' x 5'	15.000	L.F.	.495	9.75	12.00	21.75
2' x 6'	17.000	L.F.	.561	11.05	13.60	24.65
Paint or stain, interior or exterior, 2' x 3' window, 1 coat	1.000	Face	.381	1.01	8.39	9.40
2 coats	1.000	Face	.615	1.09	13.56	14.65
Primer & 1 coat	1.000	Face	.615	1.17	13.53	14.70
Primer & 2 coats	1.000	Face	.800	1.23	17.62	18.85
2' x 4' window, 1 coat	1.000	Face	.381	1.01	8.39	9.40
2 coats	1.000	Face	.615	1.09	13.56	14.65
Primer & 1 coat	1.000	Face	.615	1.17	13.53	14.70
Primer & 2 coats	1.000	Face	.800	1.23	17.62	18.85
2' x 6' window, 1 coat	1.000	Face	.533	1.32	11.73	13.05
2 coats	1.000	Face	.533	1.60	11.75	13.35
Primer & 1 coat	1.000	Face	.615	2.54	13.56	16.10
Primer & 2 coats	1.000	Face	.800	3.83	17.17	21.00
Caulking, window, 2' x 3'	10.000	L.F.	.310	.80	7.50	8.30
2' x 4'	12.000	L.F.	.372	.96	9.00	9.96
2' x 4'-6"	13.000	L.F.	.403	1.04	9.75	10.79
2' x 5'	14.000	L.F.	.434	1.12	10.50	11.62
2' x 6'	16.000	L.F.	.496	1.28	12.00	13.28
Grilles, glass size, to 20" x 36"	1.000	Ea.	.267	10.62	6.38	17.00
To 20" x 56"	1.000	Ea.	.250	14.91	6.09	21.00
Drip cap, metal, 2' long	2.000	L.F.	.040	.28	.96	1.24
Wood, 2' long	2.000	L.F.	.066	1.30	1.60	2.90

4 | EXTERIOR WALLS — 36 | Awning Window System

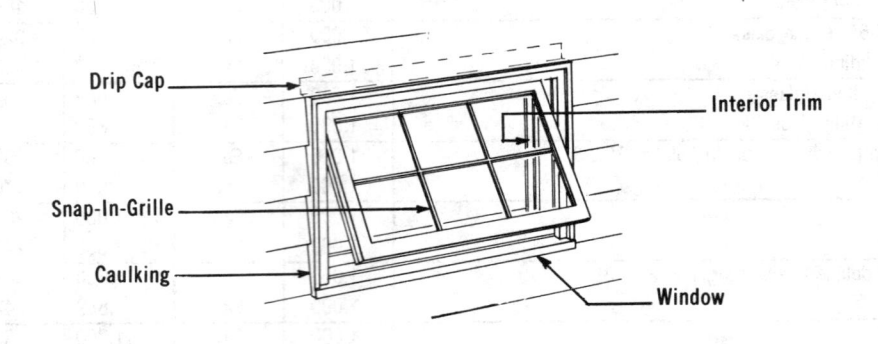

Drip Cap, Interior Trim, Snap-In-Grille, Caulking, Window

SYSTEM DESCRIPTION	QUAN.	UNIT	MAN-HOURS	MAT.	INST.	TOTAL
BUILDER'S QUALITY WINDOW, WOOD, 34" X 22", AWNING						
Window, wood, primed, builder quality, 34" x 22", insul. glass	1.000	Ea.	.800	165.00	20.00	185.00
Trim, interior casing	10.500	L.F.	.346	6.83	8.40	15.23
Paint, interior & exterior, primer & 2 coats	2.000	Face	1.600	2.46	35.24	37.70
Caulking	9.500	L.F.	.294	.76	7.13	7.89
Snap-in grille	1.000	Ea.	.267	10.18	6.37	16.55
Drip cap, metal	3.000	L.F.	.060	.42	1.44	1.86
TOTAL			3.367	185.65	78.58	264.23
PLASTIC CLAD WOOD WINDOW, 40" X 28", AWNING						
Window, wood, plastic clad, premium, 40" x 28", insulating glass	1.000	Ea.	.889	275.00	20.00	295.00
Trim interior casing	13.500	L.F.	.445	8.78	10.80	19.58
Paint, interior, primer & 2 coats	1.000	Face	.800	1.23	17.62	18.85
Caulking	12.500	L.F.	.387	1.00	9.38	10.38
Snap-in grille	1.000	Ea.	.267	10.18	6.37	16.55
TOTAL			2.788	296.19	64.17	360.36
METAL CLAD WOOD WINDOW, 48" X 36", AWNING						
Window, wood, metal clad, deluxe, 48" x 36", insulating glass	1.000	Ea.	1.000	319.00	26.00	345.00
Trim, interior casing	15.000	L.F.	.495	9.75	12.00	21.75
Paint, interior, primer & 2 coats	1.000	Face	.800	3.83	17.17	21.00
Caulking	14.000	L.F.	.434	1.12	10.50	11.62
Snap-in grille	1.000	Ea.	.250	13.81	5.99	19.80
Drip cap, metal	4.000	L.F.	.080	.56	1.92	2.48
TOTAL			3.059	348.07	73.58	421.65

The cost of this system is on a cost per each window basis.

DESCRIPTION	QUAN.	UNIT	MAN-HOURS	MAT.	INST.	TOTAL

Awning Window Price Sheet

	QUAN.	UNIT	MAN-HOURS	MAT.	INST.	TOTAL
Windows, awning, builder's quality, 34" x 22", single glass	1.000	Ea.	.800	148.50	21.50	170.00
Insulating glass	1.000	Ea.	.800	165.00	20.00	185.00
40" x 28", single glass	1.000	Ea.	.889	170.50	19.50	190.00
Insulating glass	1.000	Ea.	.889	198.00	22.00	220.00
48" x 36", single glass	1.000	Ea.	1.000	198.00	22.00	220.00
Insulating glass	1.000	Ea.	1.000	237.60	22.40	260.00
Plastic clad premium insulating glass, 34" x 22"	1.000	Ea.	.800	193.60	21.40	215.00
40" x 22"	1.000	Ea.	.800	211.20	18.80	230.00
36" x 28"	1.000	Ea.	.889	229.90	20.10	250.00
36" x 36"	1.000	Ea.	.889	275.00	20.00	295.00
48" x 28"	1.000	Ea.	1.000	299.20	25.80	325.00
60" x 36"	1.000	Ea.	1.000	473.00	22.00	495.00
Metal clad deluxe insulating glass, 34" x 22"	1.000	Ea.	.800	159.50	20.50	180.00
40" x 22"	1.000	Ea.	.800	172.70	17.30	190.00
36" x 25"	1.000	Ea.	.889	184.80	20.20	205.00
40" x 30"	1.000	Ea.	.889	187.00	23.00	210.00
48" x 28"	1.000	Ea.	1.000	209.00	26.00	235.00
60" x 36"	1.000	Ea.	1.000	319.00	26.00	345.00
Trim, interior casing window, 34" x 22"	10.500	L.F.	.346	6.83	8.40	15.23
40" x 22"	11.500	L.F.	.379	7.48	9.20	16.68
36" x 28"	12.500	L.F.	.412	8.13	10.00	18.13
40" x 28"	13.500	L.F.	.445	8.78	10.80	19.58
48" x 28"	14.500	L.F.	.478	9.43	11.60	21.03
48" x 36"	15.000	L.F.	.495	9.75	12.00	21.75
Paint or stain, interior or exterior, 34" x 22", 1 coat	1.000	Face	.381	1.01	8.39	9.40
2 coats	1.000	Face	.615	1.09	13.56	14.65
Primer & 1 coat	1.000	Face	.615	1.17	13.53	14.70
Primer & 2 coats	1.000	Face	.800	1.23	17.62	18.85
36" x 28", 1 coat	1.000	Face	.381	1.01	8.39	9.40
2 coats	1.000	Face	.615	1.09	13.56	14.65
Primer & 1 coat	1.000	Face	.615	1.17	13.53	14.70
Primer & 2 coats	1.000	Face	.800	1.23	17.62	18.85
48" x 36", 1 coat	1.000	Face	.533	1.32	11.73	13.05
2 coats	1.000	Face	.533	1.60	11.75	13.35
Primer & 1 coat	1.000	Face	.615	2.54	13.56	16.10
Primer & 2 coats	1.000	Face	.800	3.83	17.17	21.00
Caulking, window, 34" x 22"	9.500	L.F.	.294	.76	7.13	7.89
40" x 22"	10.500	L.F.	.325	.84	7.88	8.72
36" x 28"	11.500	L.F.	.356	.92	8.63	9.55
40" x 28"	12.500	L.F.	.387	1.00	9.38	10.38
48" x 28"	13.500	L.F.	.418	1.08	10.13	11.21
48" x 36"	14.000	L.F.	.434	1.12	10.50	11.62
Grilles, glass size, to 28" by 16"	1.000	Ea.	.267	10.18	6.37	16.55
To 44" by 24"	1.000	Ea.	.250	13.81	5.99	19.80
Drip cap, aluminum, 3' long	3.000	L.F.	.060	.42	1.44	1.86
3'-6" long	3.500	L.F.	.070	.49	1.68	2.17
4' long	4.000	L.F.	.080	.56	1.92	2.48
Wood, 3' long	3.000	L.F.	.099	1.95	2.40	4.35
3'-6" long	3.500	L.F.	.115	2.28	2.80	5.08
4' long	4.000	L.F.	.132	2.60	3.20	5.80

4 | EXTERIOR WALLS | 40 | Sliding Window Systems

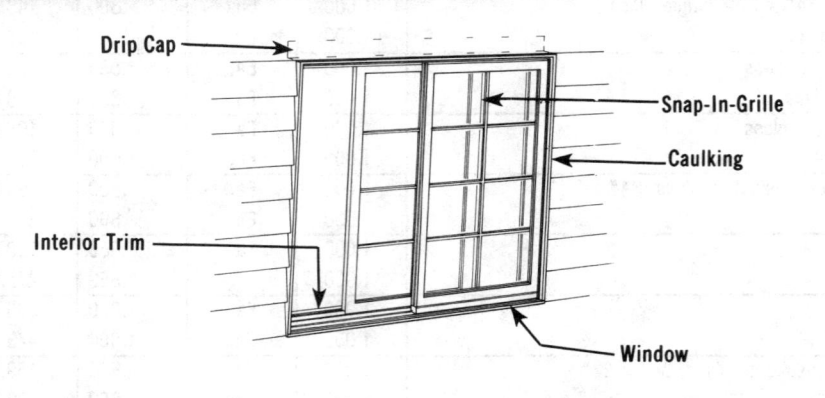

Diagram labels: Drip Cap, Snap-In-Grille, Caulking, Interior Trim, Window

SYSTEM DESCRIPTION	QUAN.	UNIT	MAN-HOURS	MAT.	INST.	TOTAL
BUILDER'S QUALITY WOOD WINDOW, 3' X 2', SLIDING						
Window, wood, primed, builder's quality, 3' x 2', insulating glass	1.000	Ea.	.800	144.10	20.90	165.00
Trim, interior casing	11.000	L.F.	.363	7.15	8.80	15.95
Paint, interior & exterior, primer & 2 coats	2.000	Face	1.600	2.46	35.24	37.70
Caulking	10.000	L.F.	.310	.80	7.50	8.30
Snap-in grille	1.000	Set	.333	38.50	7.50	46.00
Drip cap, metal	3.000	L.F.	.060	.42	1.44	1.86
TOTAL			3.466	193.43	81.38	274.81
PLASTIC CLAD WOOD WINDOW, 4' X 3'-6", SLIDING						
Window, wood, plastic clad, premium, 4' x 3'-6", insulating glass	1.000	Ea.	.889	333.30	21.70	355.00
Trim, interior casing	16.000	L.F.	.528	10.40	12.80	23.20
Paint, interior, primer & 2 coats	1.000	Face	.800	3.83	17.17	21.00
Caulking	17.000	L.F.	.527	1.36	12.75	14.11
Snap-in grille	1.000	Set	.333	38.50	7.50	46.00
TOTAL			3.077	387.39	71.92	459.31
METAL CLAD WOOD WINDOW, 6' X 5', SLIDING						
Window, wood, metal clad, deluxe, 6' x 5', insulating glass	1.000	Ea.	1.000	583.00	22.00	605.00
Trim, interior casing	23.000	L.F.	.759	14.95	18.40	33.35
Paint, interior, primer & 2 coats	1.000	Face	1.600	3.92	35.08	39.00
Caulking	22.000	L.F.	.682	1.76	16.50	18.26
Snap-in grille	1.000	Set	.364	60.50	8.50	69.00
Drip cap, metal	6.000	L.F.	.120	.84	2.88	3.72
TOTAL			4.525	664.97	103.36	768.33

The cost of this system is on a cost per each window basis.

DESCRIPTION	QUAN.	UNIT	MAN-HOURS	MAT.	INST.	TOTAL

Sliding Window Price Sheet

	QUAN.	UNIT	MAN-HOURS	COST EACH MAT.	COST EACH INST.	TOTAL
Windows, sliding, builder's quality, 3' x 2', single glass	1.000	EA	.800	467.50	17.50	485.00
Insulating glass	1.000	EA	.800	144.10	20.90	165.00
4' x 3'-6", single glass	1.000	Ea.	.889	207.90	22.10	230.00
Insulating glass	1.000	Ea.	.889	205.70	19.30	225.00
6' x 5', single glass	1.000	Ea.	1.000	214.50	25.50	240.00
Insulating glass	1.000	Ea.	1.000	335.50	24.50	360.00
Plastic clad premium insulating glass, 3' x 3'	1.000	Ea.	.800	269.50	20.50	290.00
4' x 3'-6"	1.000	Ea.	.889	333.30	21.70	355.00
5' x 4'	1.000	Ea.	.889	402.60	22.40	425.00
6' x 5'	1.000	Ea.	1.000	574.20	25.80	600.00
Metal clad deluxe insulating glass, 3' x 3'	1.000	Ea.	.800	271.70	18.30	290.00
4' x 3'-6"	1.000	Ea.	.889	337.70	22.30	360.00
5' x 4'	1.000	Ea.	.889	405.90	19.10	425.00
6' x 5'	1.000	Ea.	1.000	583.00	22.00	605.00
Trim, interior casing, window 3' x 2'	11.000	L.F.	.363	7.15	8.80	15.95
3' x 3'	13.000	L.F.	.429	8.45	10.40	18.85
4' x 3'-6"	16.000	L.F.	.528	10.40	12.80	23.20
5' x 4'	19.000	L.F.	.627	12.35	15.20	27.55
6' x 5'	23.000	L.F.	.759	14.95	18.40	33.35
Paint or stain, interior or exterior, 3' x 2' window, 1 coat	1.000	Face	.381	1.01	8.39	9.40
2 coats	1.000	Face	.615	1.09	13.56	14.65
Primer & 1 coat	1.000	Face	.615	1.17	13.53	14.70
Primer & 2 coats	1.000	Face	.800	1.23	17.62	18.85
4' x 3'-6" window, 1 coat	1.000	Face	.533	1.32	11.73	13.05
2 coats	1.000	Face	.533	1.60	11.75	13.35
Primer & 1 coat	1.000	Face	.615	2.54	13.56	16.10
Primer & 2 coats	1.000	Face	.800	3.83	17.17	21.00
6' x 5' window, 1 coat	1.000	Face	.800	3.49	17.51	21.00
2 coats	1.000	Face	1.330	3.63	29.37	33.00
Primer & 1 coat	1.000	Face	1.330	3.77	29.23	33.00
Primer & 2 coats	1.000	Face	1.600	3.92	35.08	39.00
Caulking, window, 3' x 2'	10.000	L.F.	.310	.80	7.50	8.30
3' x 3'	12.000	L.F.	.372	.96	9.00	9.96
4' x 3'-6"	15.000	L.F.	.465	1.20	11.25	12.45
5' x 4'	18.000	L.F.	.558	1.44	13.50	14.94
6' x 5'	22.000	L.F.	.682	1.76	16.50	18.26
Grilles, glass size, to 14" x 36"	1.000	Set	.333	38.50	7.50	46.00
To 36" x 36"	1.000	Set	.364	60.50	8.50	69.00
Drip cap, aluminum, 3' long	3.000	L.F.	.060	.42	1.44	1.86
4' long	4.000	L.F.	.080	.56	1.92	2.48
5' long	5.000	L.F.	.100	.70	2.40	3.10
6' long	6.000	L.F.	.120	.84	2.88	3.72
Wood, 3' long	3.000	L.F.	.099	1.95	2.40	4.35
4' long	4.000	L.F.	.132	2.60	3.20	5.80
5' long	5.000	L.F.	.165	3.25	4.00	7.25
6' long	6.000	L.F.	.198	3.90	4.80	8.70

4 | EXTERIOR WALLS   44 | Bow/Bay Window Systems

Diagram labels: Drip Cap, Caulking, Window, Snap-In-Grille

SYSTEM DESCRIPTION	QUAN.	UNIT	MAN-HOURS	MAT.	INST.	TOTAL
AWNING TYPE BOW WINDOW, BUILDER'S QUALITY, 8' X 5'						
Window, wood primed, builder's quality, 8' x 5', insulating glass	1.000	Ea.	1.600	842.60	37.40	880.00
Trim, interior casing	27.000	L.F.	.891	17.55	21.60	39.15
Paint, interior & exterior, primer & 1 coat	2.000	Face	3.200	7.84	70.16	78.00
Drip cap, vinyl	1.000	Ea.	.533	63.80	13.20	77.00
Caulking	26.000	L.F.	.806	2.08	19.50	21.58
Snap-in grilles	1.000	Set	1.068	42.48	25.52	68.00
TOTAL			8.098	976.35	187.38	1163.73
CASEMENT TYPE BOW WINDOW, PLASTIC CLAD, 10' X 6'						
Window, wood, plastic clad, premium, 10' x 6', insulating glass	1.000	Ea.	2.290	1996.50	53.50	2050.00
Trim, interior casing	33.000	L.F.	1.089	21.45	26.40	47.85
Paint, interior, primer & 1 coat	1.000	Face	1.600	7.66	34.34	42.00
Drip cap, vinyl	1.000	Ea.	.615	69.30	14.70	84.00
Caulking	32.000	L.F.	.992	2.56	24.00	26.56
Snap-in grilles	1.000	Set	1.335	53.10	31.90	85.00
TOTAL			7.921	2150.57	184.84	2335.41
DOUBLE HUNG TYPE, METAL CLAD, 9' X 5'						
Window, wood, metal clad, deluxe, 9' x 5', insulating glass	1.000	Ea.	2.670	913.00	62.00	975.00
Trim, interior casing	29.000	L.F.	.957	18.85	23.20	42.05
Paint, interior, primer & 1 coat	1.000	Face	1.600	7.66	34.34	42.00
Drip cap, vinyl	1.000	Set	.615	69.30	14.70	84.00
Caulking	28.000	L.F.	.868	2.24	21.00	23.24
Snap-in grilles	1.000	Set	1.068	42.48	25.52	68.00
TOTAL			7.778	1053.53	180.76	1234.29

The cost of this system is on a cost per each window basis.

DESCRIPTION	QUAN.	UNIT	MAN-HOURS	MAT.	INST.	TOTAL

Bow/Bay Window Price Sheet

	QUAN.	UNIT	MAN-HOURS	COST EACH MAT.	COST EACH INST.	TOTAL
Windows, bow awning type, builder's quality, 8' x 5', single glass	1.000	Ea.	1.600	737.00	38.00	775.00
Insulating glass	1.000	Ea.	1.600	842.60	37.40	880.00
12' x 6', single glass	1.000	Ea.	2.670	916.30	63.70	980.00
Insulating glass	1.000	Ea.	2.670	1028.50	71.50	1100.00
Plastic clad premium insulating glass, 6' x 4'	1.000	Ea.	1.600	1232.00	43.00	1275.00
9' x 4'	1.000	Ea.	2.000	1661.00	39.00	1700.00
10' x 5'	1.000	Ea.	2.290	2172.50	52.50	2225.00
12' x 6'	1.000	Ea.	2.670	2706.00	69.00	2775.00
Metal clad deluxe insulating glass, 6' x 4'	1.000	Ea.	1.600	739.20	35.80	775.00
9' x 4'	1.000	Ea.	2.000	1144.00	56.00	1200.00
10' x 5'	1.000	Ea.	2.290	1573.00	52.00	1625.00
12' x 6'	1.000	Ea.	2.670	2238.50	61.50	2300.00
Bow casement type, builder's quality, 8' x 5', single glass	1.000	Ea.	1.600	957.00	38.00	995.00
Insulating glass	1.000	Ea.	1.600	1160.50	39.50	1200.00
12' x 6', single glass	1.000	Ea.	2.670	1441.00	59.00	1500.00
Insulating glass	1.000	Ea.	2.670	2293.50	56.50	2350.00
Plastic clad premium insulating glass, 8' x 5'	1.000	Ea.	1.600	1309.00	41.00	1350.00
10' x 5'	1.000	Ea.	2.000	1738.00	37.00	1775.00
10' x 6'	1.000	Ea.	2.290	1996.50	53.50	2050.00
12' x 6'	1.000	Ea.	2.670	2530.00	70.00	2600.00
Metal clad deluxe insulating glass, 8' x 5'	1.000	Ea.	1.600	957.00	38.00	995.00
10' x 5'	1.000	Ea.	2.000	1215.50	59.50	1275.00
10' x 6'	1.000	Ea.	2.290	1468.50	56.50	1525.00
12' x 6'	1.000	Ea.	2.670	2656.50	68.50	2725.00
Bow, double hung type, builder's quality, 8' x 4', single glass	1.000	Ea.	1.600	891.00	39.00	930.00
Insulating glass	1.000	Ea.	1.600	1006.50	43.50	1050.00
9' x 5', single glass	1.000	Ea.	2.670	962.50	62.50	1025.00
Insulating glass	1.000	Ea.	2.670	1094.50	55.50	1150.00
Plastic clad premium insulating glass, 7' x 4'	1.000	Ea.	1.600	1089.00	36.00	1125.00
8' x 4'	1.000	Ea.	2.000	1188.00	37.00	1225.00
8' x 5'	1.000	Ea.	2.290	1215.50	59.50	1275.00
9' x 5'	1.000	Ea.	2.670	1320.00	55.00	1375.00
Metal clad deluxe insulating glass, 7' x 4'	1.000	Ea.	1.600	753.50	36.50	790.00
8' x 4'	1.000	Ea.	2.000	797.50	47.50	845.00
8' x 5'	1.000	Ea.	2.290	869.00	56.00	925.00
9' x 5'	1.000	Ea.	2.670	913.00	62.00	975.00
Trim, interior casing, window 7' x 4'	1.000	Ea.	.759	14.95	18.40	33.35
8' x 5'	1.000	Ea.	.891	17.55	21.60	39.15
10' x 6'	1.000	Ea.	1.089	21.45	26.40	47.85
12' x 6'	1.000	Ea.	1.221	24.05	29.60	53.65
Paint or stain, interior, or exterior, 7' x 4' window, 1 coat	1.000	Face	.800	3.49	17.51	21.00
Primer & 1 coat	1.000	Face	1.330	3.77	29.23	33.00
8' x 5' window, 1 coat	1.000	Face	.800	3.49	17.51	21.00
Primer & 1 coat	1.000	Face	1.330	3.77	29.23	33.00
10' x 6' window, 1 coat	1.000	Face	1.066	2.64	23.46	26.10
Primer & 1 coat	1.000	Face	1.600	7.66	34.34	42.00
12' x 6' window, 1 coat	1.000	Face	1.600	6.98	35.02	42.00
Primer & 1 coat	1.000	Face	2.660	7.54	58.46	66.00
Drip cap, vinyl moulded window, 7' long	1.000	Ea.	.533	63.80	13.20	77.00
8' long	1.000	Ea.	.533	63.80	13.20	77.00
10' long	1.000	Ea.	.615	69.30	14.70	84.00
12' long	1.000	Ea.	.615	69.30	14.70	84.00
Caulking, window, 7' x 4'	1.000	Ea.	.682	1.76	16.50	18.26
8' x 5'	1.000	Ea.	.806	2.08	19.50	21.58
10' x 6'	1.000	Ea.	.992	2.56	24.00	26.56
12' x 6'	1.000	Ea.	1.116	2.88	27.00	29.88
Grilles, window, 7' x 4'	1.000	Set	.801	31.86	19.14	51.00
8' x 5'	1.000	Set	1.068	42.48	25.52	68.00
10' x 6'	1.000	Set	1.335	53.10	31.90	85.00
12' x 6'	1.000	Set	1.602	63.72	38.28	102.00

4 | EXTERIOR WALLS — 48 | Fixed Window System

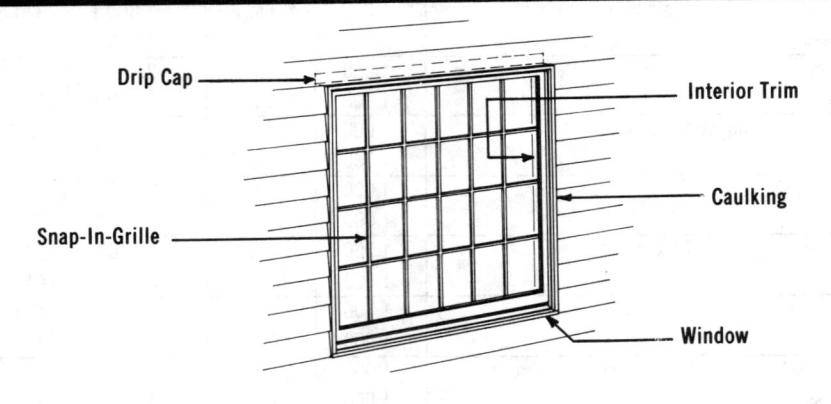

Diagram labels: Drip Cap, Interior Trim, Caulking, Snap-In-Grille, Window

SYSTEM DESCRIPTION	QUAN.	UNIT	MAN-HOURS	MAT.	INST.	TOTAL
BUILDER'S QUALITY PICTURE WINDOW, 4' X 4'						
Window, wood, primed, builder's quality, 4' x 4', insulating glass	1.000	Ea.	1.330	211.20	33.80	245.00
Trim, interior casing	17.000	L.F.	.561	11.05	13.60	24.65
Paint, interior & exterior, primer & 2 coats	2.000	Face	1.600	7.66	34.34	42.00
Caulking	16.000	L.F.	.496	1.28	12.00	13.28
Snap-in grille	1.000	Ea.	.267	67.10	5.90	73.00
Drip cap, metal	4.000	L.F.	.080	.56	1.92	2.48
TOTAL			4.334	298.85	101.56	400.41
PLASTIC CLAD WOOD WINDOW, 4'-6" X 6'-6"						
Window, wood, plastic clad, premium, 4'-6" x 6'-6", insul. glass	1.000	Ea.	1.450	489.50	35.50	525.00
Trim, interior casing	23.000	L.F.	.759	14.95	18.40	33.35
Paint, interior, primer & 2 coats	1.000	Face	.800	3.83	17.17	21.00
Caulking	22.000	L.F.	.682	1.76	16.50	18.26
Snap-in grille	1.000	Ea.	.267	67.10	5.90	73.00
TOTAL			3.958	577.14	93.47	670.61
METAL CLAD WOOD WINDOW, 6'-6" X 6'-6"						
Window, wood, metal clad, deluxe, 6'-6" x 6'-6", insulating glass	1.000	Ea.	1.600	456.50	38.50	495.00
Trim interior casing	27.000	L.F.	.891	17.55	21.60	39.15
Paint, interior, primer & 2 coats	1.000	Face	1.600	3.92	35.08	39.00
Caulking	26.000	L.F.	.806	2.08	19.50	21.58
Snap-in grille	1.000	Ea.	.267	67.10	5.90	73.00
Drip cap, metal	6.500	L.F.	.130	.91	3.12	4.03
TOTAL			5.294	548.06	123.70	671.76

The cost of this system is on a cost per each window basis.

DESCRIPTION	QUAN.	UNIT	MAN-HOURS	MAT.	INST.	TOTAL

Fixed Window Price Sheet

	QUAN.	UNIT	MAN-HOURS	COST EACH MAT.	COST EACH INST.	TOTAL
Window-picture, builder's quality, 4' x 4', single glass	1.000	Ea.	1.330	170.50	29.50	200.00
Insulating glass	1.000	Ea.	1.330	211.20	33.80	245.00
4' x 4'-6", single glass	1.000	Ea.	1.450	194.70	35.30	230.00
Insulating glass	1.000	Ea.	1.450	242.00	33.00	275.00
5' x 4', single glass	1.000	Ea.	1.450	225.50	34.50	260.00
Insulating glass	1.000	EA	1.450	260.70	34.30	295.00
6' x 4'-6", single glass	1.000	Ea.	1.600	284.90	40.10	325.00
Insulating glass	1.000	Ea.	1.600	293.70	36.30	330.00
Plastic clad premium insulating glass, 4' x 4'	1.000	Ea.	1.330	368.50	31.50	400.00
4'-6" x 6'-6"	1.000	Ea.	1.450	489.50	35.50	525.00
5'-6" x 6'-6"	1.000	Ea.	1.600	623.70	36.30	660.00
6'-6" x 6'-6"	1.000	Ea.	1.600	726.00	39.00	765.00
Metal clad deluxe insulating glass, 4' x 4'	1.000	Ea.	1.330	202.40	32.60	235.00
4'-6" x 6'-6"	1.000	Ea.	1.450	294.80	35.20	330.00
5'-6" x 6'-6"	1.000	Ea.	1.600	374.00	36.00	410.00
6'-6" x 6'-6"	1.000	Ea.	1.600	456.50	38.50	495.00
Trim, interior casing, window 4' x 4'	17.000	L.F.	.561	11.05	13.60	24.65
4'-6" x 4'-6"	19.000	L.F.	.627	12.35	15.20	27.55
5'-0" x 4'-0"	19.000	L.F.	.627	12.35	15.20	27.55
4'-6" x 6'-6"	23.000	L.F.	.759	14.95	18.40	33.35
5'-6" x 6'-6"	25.000	L.F.	.825	16.25	20.00	36.25
6'-6" x 6'-6"	27.000	L.F.	.891	17.55	21.60	39.15
Paint or stain, interior or exterior, 4' x 4' window, 1 coat	1.000	Face	.533	1.32	11.73	13.05
2 coats	1.000	Face	.533	1.60	11.75	13.35
Primer & 1 coat	1.000	Face	.615	2.54	13.56	16.10
Primer & 2 coats	1.000	Face	.800	3.83	17.17	21.00
4'-6" x 6'-6" window, 1 coat	1.000	Face	.533	1.32	11.73	13.05
2 coats	1.000	Face	.533	1.60	11.75	13.35
Primer & 1 coat	1.000	Face	.615	2.54	13.56	16.10
Primer & 2 coats	1.000	Face	.800	3.83	17.17	21.00
6'-6" x 6'-6" window, 1 coat	1.000	Face	.800	3.49	17.51	21.00
2 coats	1.000	Face	1.330	3.63	29.37	33.00
Primer & 1 coat	1.000	Face	1.330	3.77	29.23	33.00
Primer & 2 coats	1.000	Face	1.600	3.92	35.08	39.00
Caulking, window, 4' x 4'	1.000	Ea.	.496	1.28	12.00	13.28
4'-6" x 4'-6"	1.000	Ea.	.558	1.44	13.50	14.94
5'-0" x 4'-0"	1.000	Ea.	.558	1.44	13.50	14.94
4'-6" x 6'-6"	1.000	Ea.	.682	1.76	16.50	18.26
5'-6" x 6'-6"	1.000	Ea.	.744	1.92	18.00	19.92
6'-6" x 6'-6"	1.000	Ea.	.806	2.08	19.50	21.58
Grilles, glass size, to 48" x 48"	1.000	Ea.	.267	67.10	5.90	73.00
To 60" x 68"	1.000	Ea.	.286	78.54	6.46	85.00
Drip cap, aluminum, 4' long	4.000	L.F.	.080	.56	1.92	2.48
4'-6" long	4.500	L.F.	.090	.63	2.16	2.79
5' long	5.000	L.F.	.100	.70	2.40	3.10
6' long	6.000	L.F.	.120	.84	2.88	3.72
Wood, 4' long	4.000	L.F.	.132	2.60	3.20	5.80
4'-6" long	4.500	L.F.	.148	2.93	3.60	6.53
5' long	5.000	L.F.	.165	3.25	4.00	7.25
6' long	6.000	L.F.	.198	3.90	4.80	8.70

4 | EXTERIOR WALLS 52 | Entrance Door Systems

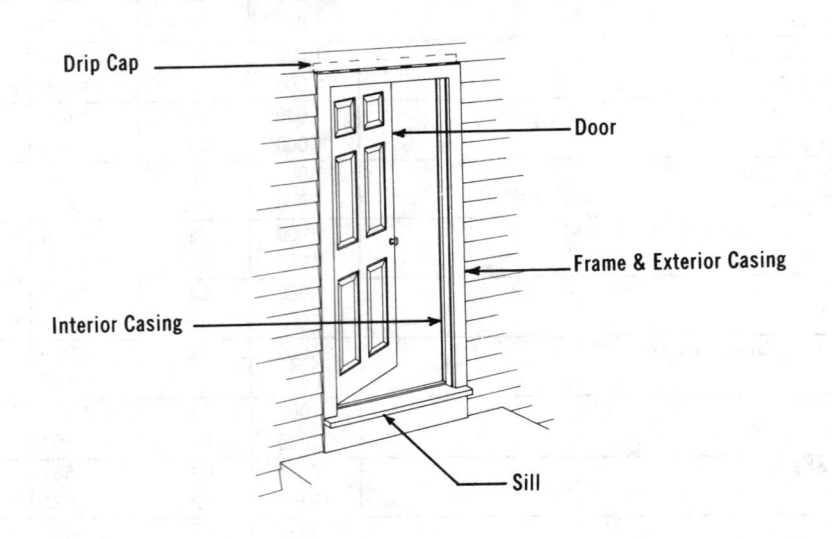

Diagram labels: Drip Cap, Door, Frame & Exterior Casing, Interior Casing, Sill

SYSTEM DESCRIPTION	QUAN.	UNIT	MAN-HOURS	MAT.	INST.	TOTAL
COLONIAL, 6 PANEL, 3' X 6'-8", WOOD						
Door, 3' x 6'-8" x 1-¾" thick, pine, 6 panel colonial	1.000	Ea.	1.070	297.00	28.00	325.00
Frame, pine, 5-13/16" deep, including exterior casing & drip cap	17.000	L.F.	.731	57.29	18.19	75.48
Interior casing, 2-½" wide	18.000	L.F.	.594	11.70	14.40	26.10
Sill, ¾ x 8" deep	3.000	L.F.	.480	29.04	12.06	41.10
Butt hinges, brass, 4-½" x 4-½"	1.500	Pr.		17.33		17.33
Lockset	1.000	Ea.	.571	24.20	13.80	38.00
Weatherstripping, metal, spring type, bronze	1.000	Set	1.050	7.59	25.41	33.00
Paint, interior & exterior, primer & 2 coats	2.000	Face	1.778	17.72	38.28	56.00
TOTAL			6.274	461.87	150.14	612.01
SOLID CORE BIRCH, FLUSH, 3' X 6'-8"						
Door, 3' x 6'-8", 1-¾" thick, birch, flush solid core	1.000	Ea.	1.070	93.50	26.50	120.00
Frame, pine, 5-13/16" deep, including exterior casing & drip cap	17.000	L.F.	.731	57.29	18.19	75.48
Interior casing, 2-½" wide	18.000	L.F.	.594	11.70	14.40	26.10
Sill, ¾ x 8" deep	3.000	L.F.	.480	29.04	12.06	41.10
Butt hinges, brass, 4-½" x 4-½"	1.500	Pr.		17.33		17.33
Lockset	1.000	Ea.	.571	24.20	13.80	38.00
Weatherstripping, metal, spring type, bronze	1.000	Set	1.050	7.59	25.41	33.00
Paint, interior & exterior, primer & 2 coats	2.000	Face	1.778	8.98	39.02	48.00
TOTAL			6.274	249.63	149.38	399.01

These systems are on a cost per each door basis.

DESCRIPTION	QUAN.	UNIT	MAN-HOURS	MAT.	INST.	TOTAL

Entrance Door Price Sheet

	QUAN.	UNIT	MAN-HOURS	MAT.	INST.	TOTAL
Door exterior wood 1-¾" thick, pine, dutch door, 2'-8" x 6'-8" minimum	1.000	Ea.	1.330	345.40	34.60	380.00
Maximum	1.000	Ea.	1.600	380.60	39.40	420.00
3'-0" x 6'-8", minimum	1.000	Ea.	1.330	361.90	33.10	395.00
Maximum	1.000	Ea.	1.600	399.30	40.70	440.00
Colonial, 6 panel, 2'-8" x 6'-8"	1.000	Ea.	1.000	286.00	24.00	310.00
3'-0" x 6'-8"	1.000	Ea.	1.070	297.00	28.00	325.00
8 panel, 2'-6" x 6'-8"	1.000	Ea.	1.000	313.50	26.50	340.00
3'-0" x 6'-8"	1.000	Ea.	1.070	319.00	26.00	345.00
Flush, birch, solid core, 2'-8" x 6'-8"	1.000	Ea.	1.000	88.00	27.00	115.00
3'-0" x 6'-8"	1.000	Ea.	1.070	93.50	26.50	120.00
Porch door, 2'-8" x 6'-8"	1.000	Ea.	1.000	181.50	23.50	205.00
3'-0" x 6'-8"	1.000	Ea.	1.070	192.50	27.50	220.00
Hand carved mahogany, 2'-8" x 6'-8"	1.000	Ea.	1.070	209.00	26.00	235.00
3'-0" x 6'-8"	1.000	Ea.	1.070	231.00	29.00	260.00
Rosewood, 2'-8" x 6'-8"	1.000	Ea.	1.070	566.50	28.50	595.00
3'-0" x 6-8"	1.000	Ea.	1.070	572.00	28.00	600.00
Door, metal clad wood 1-⅜" thick raised panel, 2'-8" x 6'-8"	1.000	Ea.	1.070	176.00	29.00	205.00
3'-0" x 6'-8"	1.000	Ea.	1.070	176.00	29.00	205.00
Deluxe metal door, 2'-8" x 6'-8"	1.000	Ea.	1.230	275.00	30.00	305.00
3'-0" x 6'-8"	1.000	Ea.	1.230	286.00	29.00	315.00
Frame, pine, including exterior trim & drip cap, ¾ x 4-9/16" deep	17.000	L.F.	.731	52.36	18.19	70.55
5-13/16" deep	17.000	L.F.	.731	57.29	18.19	75.48
6-9/16" deep	17.000	L.F.	.731	66.47	18.19	84.66
Safety glass lites, add	1.000	Ea.		23.00		23.00
Interior casing, 2'-8" x 6'-8" door	18.000	L.F.	.594	11.70	14.40	26.10
3'-0" x 6'-8" door	19.000	L.F.	.627	12.35	15.20	27.55
Sill, oak, ¾ x 8" deep	3.000	L.F.	.480	29.04	12.06	41.10
¾ x 10" deep	3.000	L.F.	.534	34.83	13.32	48.15
Butt hinges, steel plated, 4-½" x 4-½", plain	1.500	Pr.		17.33		17.33
Ball bearing	1.500	Pr.		31.50		31.50
Bronze, 4-½" x 4-½", plain	1.500	Pr.		60.00		60.00
Ball bearing	1.500	Pr.		87.00		87.00
Lockset, minimum	1.000	Ea.	.571	24.20	13.80	38.00
Maximum	1.000	Ea.	1.000	105.60	24.40	130.00
Weatherstripping, metal, interlocking, zinc	1.000	Set	2.670	11.00	64.00	75.00
Bronze	1.000	Set	2.670	16.50	63.50	80.00
Spring type, bronze	1.000	Set	1.050	7.59	25.41	33.00
Rubber, minimum	1.000	Set	1.050	4.29	24.71	29.00
Maximum	1.000	Set	1.140	4.90	27.10	32.00
Felt minimum	1.000	Set	.571	1.87	13.68	15.55
Maximum	1.000	Set	.615	2.15	14.70	16.85
Paint or stain, flush door, interior or exterior, 1 coat	2.000	Face	1.000	5.48	22.02	27.50
2 coats	2.000	Face	1.524	7.86	34.14	42.00
Primer & 1 coat	2.000	Face	1.454	7.86	32.04	39.90
Primer & 2 coats	2.000	Face	1.778	8.98	39.02	48.00
Paneled door, interior & exterior, 1 coat	2.000	Face	1.142	5.92	25.18	31.10
2 coats	2.000	Face	2.000	11.78	44.22	56.00
Primer & 1 coat	2.000	Face	1.454	11.78	32.22	44.00
Primer & 2 coats	2.000	Face	1.778	17.72	38.28	56.00

4 | EXTERIOR WALLS — 53 | Sliding Door Systems

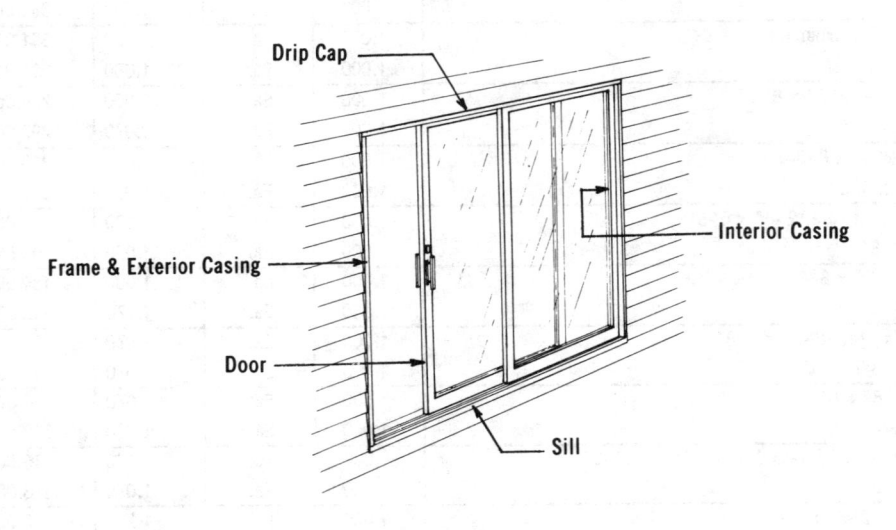

Diagram labels: Drip Cap, Interior Casing, Frame & Exterior Casing, Door, Sill

SYSTEM DESCRIPTION	QUAN.	UNIT	MAN-HOURS	MAT.	INST.	TOTAL
WOOD SLIDING DOOR, 8' WIDE, PREMIUM						
Wood, ⅝" thick tempered insul. glass, 8' wide, premium	1.000	Ea.	5.330	1100.00	125.00	1225.00
Interior casing	22.000	L.F.	.726	14.30	17.60	31.90
Exterior casing	22.000	L.F.	.726	14.30	17.60	31.90
Sill, oak, ¾ x 8" deep	8.000	L.F.	1.280	77.44	32.16	109.60
Drip cap	8.000	L.F.	.160	1.12	3.84	4.96
Paint, interior & exterior, primer & 2 coats	2.000	Face	2.816	9.68	61.60	71.28
TOTAL			11.038	1216.84	257.80	1474.64
ALUMINUM SLIDING DOOR, 8' WIDE, PREMIUM						
Aluminum, ⅝" thick tempered insul. glass, 8' wide, premium	1.000	Ea.	5.330	506.00	129.00	635.00
Interior casing	22.000	L.F.	.726	14.30	17.60	31.90
Exterior casing	22.000	L.F.	.726	14.30	17.60	31.90
Sill, oak, ¾ x 8" deep	8.000	L.F.	1.280	77.44	32.16	109.60
Drip cap	8.000	L.F.	.160	1.12	3.84	4.96
Paint, interior & exterior, primer & 2 coats	2.000	Face	1.408	4.84	30.80	35.64
TOTAL			9.630	618.00	231.00	849.00

The cost of this system is on a cost per each door basis.

DESCRIPTION	QUAN.	UNIT	MAN-HOURS	MAT.	INST.	TOTAL

Sliding Door Price Sheet

	QUAN.	UNIT	MAN-HOURS	MAT.	INST.	TOTAL
Sliding door, wood, ⅝" thick, tempered insul. glass, 6' wide, premium	1.000	Ea.	4.000	852.50	97.50	950.00
Economy	1.000	Ea.	4.000	517.00	98.00	615.00
8' wide, wood premium	1.000	Ea.	5.330	1100.00	125.00	1225.00
Economy	1.000	Ea.	5.330	660.00	130.00	790.00
12' wide, wood premium	1.000	Ea.	6.400	1639.00	161.00	1800.00
Economy	1.000	Ea.	6.400	1056.00	144.00	1200.00
Aluminum, ⅝" thick, tempered insul. glass, 6' wide, premium	1.000	Ea.	4.000	484.00	96.00	580.00
Economy	1.000	Ea.	4.000	319.00	96.00	415.00
8' wide, premium	1.000	Ea.	5.330	506.00	129.00	635.00
Economy	1.000	Ea.	5.330	407.00	128.00	535.00
12' wide, premium	1.000	Ea.	6.400	616.00	154.00	770.00
Economy	1.000	Ea.	6.400	510.40	154.60	665.00
Interior casing, 6' wide door	20.000	L.F.	.660	13.00	16.00	29.00
8' wide door	22.000	L.F.	.726	14.30	17.60	31.90
12' wide door	26.000	L.F.	.858	16.90	20.80	37.70
Exterior casing, 6' wide door	20.000	L.F.	.660	13.00	16.00	29.00
8' wide door	22.000	L.F.	.726	14.30	17.60	31.90
12' wide door	26.000	L.F.	.858	16.90	20.80	37.70
Sill, oak, ¾ x 8" deep, 6' wide door	6.000	L.F.	.960	58.08	24.12	82.20
8' wide door	8.000	L.F.	1.280	77.44	32.16	109.60
12' wide door	12.000	L.F.	1.920	116.16	48.24	164.40
¾ x 10" deep, 6' wide door	6.000	L.F.	1.068	69.66	26.64	96.30
8' wide door	8.000	L.F.	1.424	92.88	35.52	128.40
12' wide door	12.000	L.F.	2.136	139.32	53.28	192.60
Drip cap, 6' wide door	6.000	L.F.	.120	.84	2.88	3.72
8' wide door	8.000	L.F.	.160	1.12	3.84	4.96
12' wide door	12.000	L.F.	.240	1.68	5.76	7.44
Paint or stain, interior & exterior, 6' wide door, 1 coat	2.000	Face	1.600	3.20	35.20	38.40
2 coats	2.000	Face	1.600	3.20	35.20	38.40
Primer & 1 coat	2.000	Face	1.760	6.40	39.20	45.60
Primer & 2 coats	2.000	Face	2.560	8.80	56.00	64.80
8' wide door, 1 coat	2.000	Face	1.760	3.52	38.72	42.24
2 coats	2.000	Face	1.760	3.52	38.72	42.24
Primer & 1 coat	2.000	Face	1.936	7.04	43.12	50.16
Primer & 2 coats	2.000	Face	2.816	9.68	61.60	71.28
12' wide door, 1 coat	2.000	Face	2.080	4.16	45.76	49.92
2 coats	2.000	Face	2.080	4.16	45.76	49.92
Primer & 1 coat	2.000	Face	2.288	8.32	50.96	59.28
Primer & 2 coats	2.000	Face	3.328	11.44	72.80	84.24
Aluminum door, trim only, interior & exterior, 6' door, 1 coat	2.000	Face	.800	1.60	17.60	19.20
2 coats	2.000	Face	.800	1.60	17.60	19.20
Primer & 1 coat	2.000	Face	.880	3.20	19.60	22.80
Primer & 2 coats	2.000	Face	1.280	4.40	28.00	32.40
8' wide door, 1 coat	2.000	Face	.880	1.76	19.36	21.12
2 coats	2.000	Face	.880	1.76	19.36	21.12
Primer & 1 coat	2.000	Face	.968	3.52	21.56	25.08
Primer & 2 coats	2.000	Face	1.408	4.84	30.80	35.64
12' wide door, 1 coat	2.000	Face	1.040	2.08	22.88	24.96
2 coats	2.000	Face	1.040	2.08	22.88	24.96
Primer & 1 coat	2.000	Face	1.144	4.16	25.48	29.64
Primer & 2 coats	2.000	Face	1.664	5.72	36.40	42.12

4 | EXTERIOR WALLS — 56 | Resi Garage Door Systems

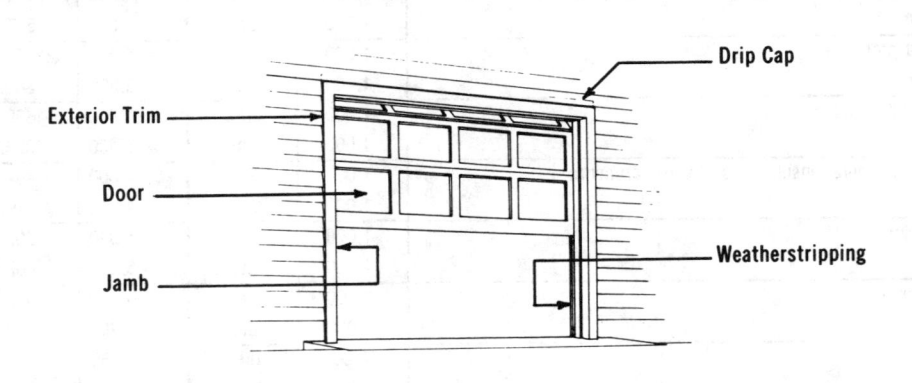

SYSTEM DESCRIPTION	QUAN.	UNIT	MAN-HOURS	MAT.	INST.	TOTAL
OVERHEAD, SECTIONAL GARAGE DOOR, 9' X 7'						
Wood, overhead sectional door, standard, incl. hardware, 9' x 7'	1.000	Ea.	2.000	291.50	48.50	340.00
Jamb & header blocking, 2" x 6"	25.000	L.F.	.900	11.25	22.50	33.75
Exterior trim	25.000	L.F.	.825	16.25	20.00	36.25
Paint, interior & exterior, primer & 2 coats	2.000	Face	3.556	35.44	76.56	112.00
Weatherstripping, molding type	1.000	Set	.759	14.95	18.40	33.35
Drip cap	9.000	L.F.	.180	1.26	4.32	5.58
TOTAL			8.220	370.65	190.28	560.93
OVERHEAD, SECTIONAL GARAGE DOOR, 16' X 7'						
Wood, overhead sectional door, standard, incl. hardware 16' x 7'	1.000	Ea.	2.670	583.00	62.00	645.00
Jamb & header blocking, 2" x 6"	30.000	L.F	1.080	13.50	27.00	40.50
Exterior trim	30.000	L.F.	.990	19.50	24.00	43.50
Paint, interior & exterior, primer & 2 coats	2.000	Face	5.334	53.16	114.84	168.00
Weatherstripping, molding type	1.000	Set	.990	19.50	24.00	43.50
Drip cap	16.000	L.F.	.320	2.24	7.68	9.92
TOTAL			11.384	690.90	259.52	950.42
OVERHEAD, SWING-UP TYPE, GARAGE DOOR, 16' X 7'						
Wood, overhead, swing-up type, standard, incl. hardware, 16' x 7'	1.000	Ea.	2.670	429.00	61.00	490.00
Jamb & header blocking, 2" x 6"	30.000	L.F.	1.080	13.50	27.00	40.50
Exterior trim	30.000	L.F.	.990	19.50	24.00	43.50
Paint, interior & exterior, primer & 2 coats	2.000	Face	5.334	53.16	114.84	168.00
Weatherstripping, molding type	1.000	Set	.990	19.50	24.00	43.50
Drip cap	16.000	L.F.	.320	2.24	7.68	9.92
TOTAL			11.384	536.90	258.52	795.42

This system is on a cost per each door basis.

DESCRIPTION	QUAN.	UNIT	MAN-HOURS	MAT.	INST.	TOTAL

Resi Garage Door Price Sheet

	QUAN.	UNIT	MAN-HOURS	COST EACH MAT.	COST EACH INST.	TOTAL
Overhead, sectional, including hardware, fiberglass, 9' x 7', standard	1.000	Ea.	2.000	390.50	49.50	440.00
Deluxe	1.000	Ea.	2.000	453.20	46.80	500.00
16' x 7', standard	1.000	Ea.	2.670	654.50	65.50	720.00
Deluxe	1.000	Ea.	2.670	819.50	65.50	885.00
Hardboard, 9' x 7', standard	1.000	Ea.	2.000	280.50	49.50	330.00
Deluxe	1.000	Ea.	2.000	357.50	47.50	405.00
16' x 7', standard	1.000	Ea.	2.670	495.00	65.00	560.00
Deluxe	1.000	Ea.	2.670	561.00	64.00	625.00
Metal, 9' x 7', standard	1.000	Ea.	2.000	297.00	48.00	345.00
Deluxe	1.000	Ea.	2.000	418.00	47.00	465.00
16' x 7', standard	1.000	Ea.	2.670	467.50	62.50	530.00
Deluxe	1.000	Ea.	2.670	704.00	66.00	770.00
Wood, 9' x 7', standard	1.000	Ea.	2.000	291.50	48.50	340.00
Deluxe	1.000	Ea.	2.000	836.00	49.00	885.00
16' x 7', standard	1.000	Ea.	2.670	583.00	62.00	645.00
Deluxe	1.000	Ea.	2.670	1265.00	60.00	1325.00
Overhead swing-up type including hardware, fiberglass, 9' x 7', standard	1.000	Ea.	2.000	500.50	49.50	550.00
Deluxe	1.000	Ea.	2.000	357.50	47.50	405.00
16' x 7', standard	1.000	Ea.	2.670	621.50	63.50	685.00
Deluxe	1.000	Ea.	2.670	495.00	60.00	555.00
Hardboard, 9' x 7', standard	1.000	Ea.	2.000	236.50	43.50	280.00
Deluxe	1.000	Ea.	2.000	313.50	46.50	360.00
16' x 7', standard	1.000	Ea.	2.670	330.00	60.00	390.00
Deluxe	1.000	Ea.	2.670	478.50	61.50	540.00
Metal, 9' x 7', standard	1.000	Ea.	2.000	253.00	47.00	300.00
Deluxe	1.000	Ea.	2.000	396.00	44.00	440.00
16' x 7', standard	1.000	Ea.	2.670	396.00	59.00	455.00
Deluxe	1.000	Ea.	2.670	682.00	63.00	745.00
Wood, 9' x 7', standard	1.000	Ea.	2.000	247.50	47.50	295.00
Deluxe	1.000	Ea.	2.000	396.00	44.00	440.00
16' x 7', standard	1.000	Ea.	2.670	429.00	61.00	490.00
Deluxe	1.000	Ea.	2.670	605.00	60.00	665.00
Jamb & header blocking, 2" x 6", 9' x 7' door	25.000	L.F.	.900	11.25	22.50	33.75
16' x 7' door	30.000	L.F.	1.080	13.50	27.00	40.50
2" x 8", 9' x 7' door	25.000	L.F.	1.000	15.25	25.00	40.25
16' x 7' door	30.000	L.F.	1.200	18.30	30.00	48.30
Exterior trim, 9' x 7' door	25.000	L.F.	.825	16.25	20.00	36.25
16' x 7' door	30.000	L.F.	.990	19.50	24.00	43.50
Paint or stain, interior & exterior, 9' x 7' door, 1 coat	1.000	Face	2.284	11.84	50.36	62.20
2 coats	1.000	Face	4.000	23.56	88.44	112.00
Primer & 1 coat	1.000	Face	2.908	23.56	64.44	88.00
Primer & 2 coats	1.000	Face	3.556	35.44	76.56	112.00
16' x 7' door, 1 coat	1.000	Face	3.426	17.76	75.54	93.30
2 coats	1.000	Face	6.000	35.34	132.66	168.00
Primer & 1 coat	1.000	Face	4.362	35.34	96.66	132.00
Primer & 2 coats	1.000	Face	5.334	53.16	114.84	168.00
Weatherstripping, molding type, 9' x 7' door	1.000	Set	.759	14.95	18.40	33.35
16' x 7' door	1.000	Set	.990	19.50	24.00	43.50
Drip cap, 9' door	9.000	L.F.	.180	1.26	4.32	5.58
16' door	16.000	L.F.	.320	2.24	7.68	9.92
Garage door opener, economy	1.000	Ea.	1.000	203.50	21.50	225.00
Deluxe, including remote control	1.000	Ea.	1.000	330.00	25.00	355.00

4 | EXTERIOR WALLS — 58 | Aluminum Window Systems

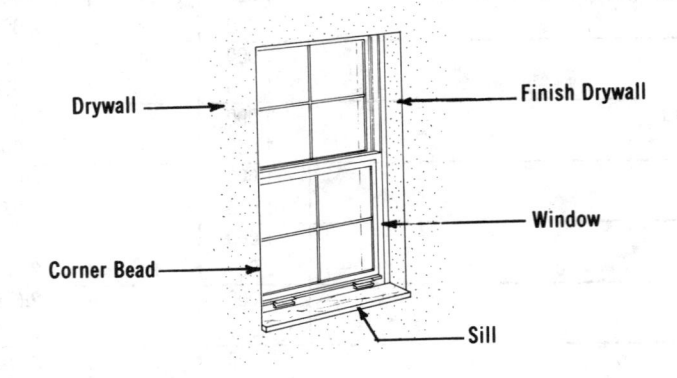

Drywall, Finish Drywall, Corner Bead, Window, Sill

SYSTEM DESCRIPTION	QUAN.	UNIT	MAN-HOURS	MAT.	INST.	TOTAL
SINGLE HUNG, 2' X 3' OPENING						
Window, single hung, 2' x 3' opening, enameled, insulating glass	1.000	Ea.	1.600	121.00	49.00	170.00
Blocking, 1" x 3" furring strip nailers	10.000	L.F.	.150	1.50	3.50	5.00
Drywall, ½" thick, standard	5.000	S.F.	.040	.95	.95	1.90
Corner bead, 1" x 1", galvanized steel	8.000	L.F.	.160	.72	3.84	4.56
Finish drywall, tape and finish corners inside and outside	16.000	L.F.	.240	.96	5.44	6.40
Sill, slate	2.000	L.F.	.400	14.86	8.94	23.80
TOTAL			2.590	139.99	71.67	211.66
SLIDING, 3' X 2' OPENING						
Window, sliding, 3' x 2' opening, enameled, insulating glass	1.000	Ea.	1.600	110.00	45.00	155.00
Blocking, 1" x 3" furring strip nailers	10.000	L.F.	.150	1.50	3.50	5.00
Drywall, ½" thick, standard	5.000	S.F.	.040	.95	.95	1.90
Corner bead, 1" x 1", galvanized steel	7.000	L.F.	.140	.63	3.36	3.99
Finish drywall, tape and finish corners inside and outside	14.000	L.F.	.210	.84	4.76	5.60
Sill, slate	3.000	L.F.	.600	22.29	13.41	35.70
TOTAL			2.740	136.21	70.98	207.19
AWNING, 3'-1" X 3'-2"						
Window awning, 3'-1" x 3'-2" opening, enameled, insulating glass	1.000	Ea.	1.600	147.40	47.60	195.00
Blocking, 1" x 3" furring strip, nailers	12.500	L.F.	.187	1.88	4.37	6.25
Drywall, ½" thick, standard	4.500	S.F.	.036	.86	.85	1.71
Corner bead, 1" x 1", galvanized steel	9.250	L.F.	.185	.83	4.44	5.27
Finish drywall, tape and finish corners, inside and outside	18.500	L.F.	.277	1.11	6.29	7.40
Sill, slate	3.250	L.F.	.650	24.15	14.53	38.68
TOTAL			2.935	176.23	78.08	254.31

DESCRIPTION	QUAN.	UNIT	MAN-HOURS	MAT.	INST.	TOTAL

Aluminum Window Price Sheet

	QUAN.	UNIT	MAN-HOURS	MAT.	INST.	TOTAL
Window, aluminum, awning, 3'-1" x 3'-2", standard glass	1.000	Ea.	1.600	147.40	47.60	195.00
Insulating glass	1.000	Ea.	1.600	147.40	47.60	195.00
4'-5" x 5'-3", standard glass	1.000	Ea.	2.000	209.00	61.00	270.00
Insulating glass	1.000	Ea.	2.000	275.00	60.00	335.00
Casement, 3'-1" x 3'-2", standard glass	1.000	Ea.	1.600	213.40	46.60	260.00
Insulating glass	1.000	Ea.	1.600	220.00	45.00	265.00
Single hung, 2' x 3', standard glass	1.000	Ea.	1.600	101.20	48.80	150.00
Insulating glass	1.000	Ea.	1.600	121.00	49.00	170.00
2'-8" x 6'-8", standard glass	1.000	Ea.	2.000	213.40	61.60	275.00
Insulating glass	1.000	Ea.	2.000	272.80	57.20	330.00
3'-4" x 5'-0", standard glass	1.000	Ea.	1.780	136.40	53.60	190.00
Insulating glass	1.000	Ea.	1.780	192.50	52.50	245.00
Sliding, 3' x 2', standard glass	1.000	Ea.	1.600	99.00	46.00	145.00
Insulating glass	1.000	Ea.	1.600	110.00	45.00	155.00
5' x 3', standard glass	1.000	Ea.	1.780	123.20	51.80	175.00
Insulating glass	1.000	Ea.	1.780	176.00	54.00	230.00
8' x 4', standard glass	1.000	Ea.	2.670	181.50	78.50	260.00
Insulating glass	1.000	Ea.	2.670	291.50	78.50	370.00
Blocking, 1" x 3" furring, opening 3' x 2'	10.000	L.F.	.150	1.50	3.50	5.00
3' x 3'	12.500	L.F.	.187	1.88	4.37	6.25
3' x 5'	16.000	L.F.	.240	2.40	5.60	8.00
4' x 4'	16.000	L.F.	.240	2.40	5.60	8.00
4' x 5'	18.000	L.F.	.270	2.70	6.30	9.00
4' x 6'	20.000	L.F.	.300	3.00	7.00	10.00
4' x 8'	24.000	L.F.	.360	3.60	8.40	12.00
6'-8" x 2'-8"	19.000	L.F.	.285	2.85	6.65	9.50
Drywall, ½" thick, standard, opening 3' x 2'	5.000	S.F.	.040	.95	.95	1.90
3' x 3'	6.000	S.F.	.048	1.14	1.14	2.28
3' x 5'	8.000	S.F.	.064	1.52	1.52	3.04
4' x 4'	8.000	S.F.	.064	1.52	1.52	3.04
4' x 5'	9.000	S.F.	.072	1.71	1.71	3.42
4' x 6'	10.000	S.F.	.080	1.90	1.90	3.80
4' x 8'	12.000	S.F.	.096	2.28	2.28	4.56
6'-8" x 2'	9.500	S.F.	.076	1.81	1.80	3.61
Corner bead, 1" x 1", galvanized steel, opening 3' x 2'	7.000	L.F.	.140	.63	3.36	3.99
3' x 3'	9.000	L.F.	.180	.81	4.32	5.13
3' x 5'	11.000	L.F.	.220	.99	5.28	6.27
4' x 4'	12.000	L.F.	.240	1.08	5.76	6.84
4' x 5'	13.000	L.F.	.260	1.17	6.24	7.41
4' x 6'	14.000	L.F.	.280	1.26	6.72	7.98
4' x 8'	16.000	L.F.	.320	1.44	7.68	9.12
6'-8" x 2'	15.000	L.F.	.300	1.35	7.20	8.55
Tape and finish corners, inside and outside, opening 3' x 2'	14.000	L.F.	.210	.84	4.76	5.60
3' x 3'	18.000	L.F.	.270	1.08	6.12	7.20
3' x 5'	22.000	L.F.	.330	1.32	7.48	8.80
4' x 4'	24.000	L.F.	.360	1.44	8.16	9.60
4' x 5'	26.000	L.F.	.390	1.56	8.84	10.40
4' x 6'	28.000	L.F.	.420	1.68	9.52	11.20
4' x 8'	32.000	L.F.	.480	1.92	10.88	12.80
6'-8" x 2'	30.000	L.F.	.450	1.80	10.20	12.00
Sill, slate, 2' long	2.000	L.F.	.400	14.86	8.94	23.80
3' long	3.000	L.F.	.600	22.29	13.41	35.70
4' long	4.000	L.F.	.800	29.72	17.88	47.60
Wood, 1-⅝" x 5-⅛", 2' long	2.000	L.F.	.128	3.66	3.06	6.72
3' long	3.000	L.F.	.192	5.49	4.59	10.08
4' long	4.000	L.F.	.256	7.32	6.12	13.44

4 | EXTERIOR WALLS 60 | Storm Door & Window Systems

Aluminum Window
Aluminum Door

SYSTEM DESCRIPTION	QUAN.	UNIT	MAN-HOURS	MAT.	INST.	TOTAL
Storm door, aluminum, combination, storm & screen, anodized, 2'-6" x 6'-8"	1.000	Ea.	1.070	203.50	26.50	230.00
2'-8" x 6'-8"	1.000	Ea.	1.140	203.50	26.50	230.00
3'-0" x 6'-8"	1.000	Ea.	1.140	209.00	31.00	240.00
Mill finish, 2'-6" x 6'-8"	1.000	Ea.	1.070	189.20	25.80	215.00
2'-8" x 6'-8"	1.000	Ea.	1.140	200.20	29.80	230.00
3'-0" x 6'-8"	1.000	Ea.	1.140	200.20	29.80	230.00
Painted, 2'-6" x 6'-8"	1.000	Ea.	1.070	209.00	26.00	235.00
2'-8" x 6'-8"	1.000	Ea.	1.140	209.00	31.00	240.00
3'-0" x 6'-8"	1.000	Ea.	1.140	220.00	30.00	250.00
Wood, combination, storm & screen, crossbuck, 2'-6" x 6'-9"	1.000	Ea.	1.450	187.00	38.00	225.00
2'-8" x 6'-9"	1.000	Ea.	1.600	190.30	39.70	230.00
3'-0" x 6'-9"	1.000	Ea.	1.780	195.80	44.20	240.00
Full lite, 2'-6" x 6'-9"	1.000	Ea.	1.450	165.00	35.00	200.00
2'-8" x 6'-9"	1.000	Ea.	1.600	176.00	39.00	215.00
3'-0" x	1.000	Ea.	1.780	181.50	43.50	225.00
Windows, aluminum, combination storm & screen, basement, 1'-10" x 1'-0"	1.000	Ea.	.533	17.60	13.40	31.00
2'-9" x 1'-6"	1.000	Ea.	.533	20.90	13.10	34.00
3'-4" x 2'-0"	1.000	Ea.	.533	26.40	13.60	40.00
Double hung, anodized, 2'-0" x 3'-5"	1.000	Ea.	.533	77.00	13.00	90.00
2'-6" x 5'-0"	1.000	Ea.	.571	116.60	13.40	130.00
4'-0" x 6'-0"	1.000	Ea.	.640	209.00	16.00	225.00
Painted, 2'-0" x 3'-5"	1.000	Ea.	.533	72.60	13.40	86.00
2'-6" x 5'-0"	1.000	Ea.	.571	116.60	13.40	130.00
4'-0" x 6'-0"	1.000	Ea.	.640	209.00	16.00	225.00
Fixed window, anodized, 4'-6" x 4'-6"	1.000	Ea.	.640	90.20	14.80	105.00
5'-8" x 4'-6"	1.000	Ea.	.800	92.40	17.60	110.00
Painted, 4'-6" x 4'-6"	1.000	Ea.	.640	79.20	15.80	95.00
5'-8" x 4'-6"	1.000	Ea.	.800	83.60	21.40	105.00

4 | EXTERIOR WALLS | 64 | Shutters/Blinds Systems

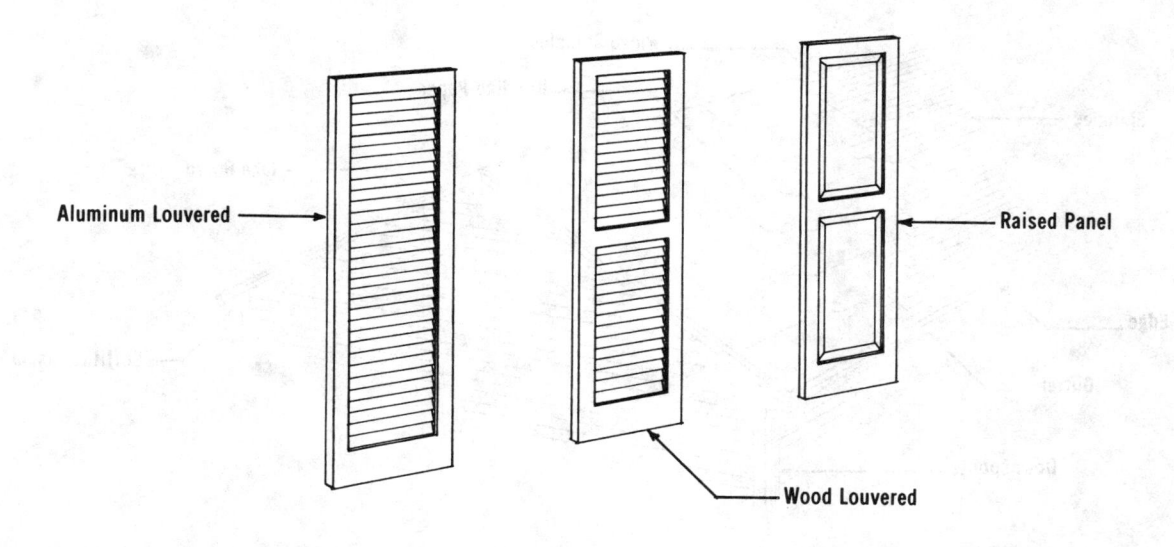

Aluminum Louvered

Wood Louvered

Raised Panel

SYSTEM DESCRIPTION	QUAN.	UNIT	MAN-HOURS	COST PER PAIR MAT.	COST PER PAIR INST.	COST PER PAIR TOTAL
Shutters, exterior blinds, aluminum, louvered, 1'-4" wide, 3"-0" long	1.000	Set	.800	34.10	18.90	53.00
4'-0" long	1.000	Set	.800	36.30	18.70	55.00
5'-4" long	1.000	Set	.800	39.60	19.40	59.00
6'-8" long	1.000	Set	.889	53.90	21.10	75.00
Wood, louvered, 1'-2" wide, 3'-3" long	1.000	Set	.800	45.10	18.90	64.00
4'-7" long	1.000	Set	.800	63.80	19.20	83.00
5'-3" long	1.000	Set	.800	57.20	18.80	76.00
1'-6" wide, 3'-3" long	1.000	Set	.800	53.90	19.10	73.00
4'-7" long	1.000	Set	.800	71.50	19.50	91.00
Polystyrene, solid raised panel, 3'-3" wide, 3'-0" long	1.000	Set	.800	68.20	18.80	87.00
3'-11" long	1.000	Set	.800	78.10	18.90	97.00
5'-3" long	1.000	Set	.800	94.60	20.40	115.00
6'-8" long	1.000	Set	.889	126.50	23.50	150.00
Polystyrene, louvered, 1'-2" wide, 3'-3" long	1.000	Set	.800	28.60	19.40	48.00
4'-7" long	1.000	Set	.800	36.30	18.70	55.00
5'-3" long	1.000	Set	.800	40.70	19.30	60.00
6'-8" long	1.000	Set	.889	55.00	21.00	76.00
Vinyl, louvered, 1'-2" wide, 4'-7" long	1.000	Set	.720	31.68	16.92	48.60
1'-4" x 6'-8" long	1.000	Set	.889	53.90	21.10	75.00

5 | ROOFING — 04 Gable End Roofing Systems

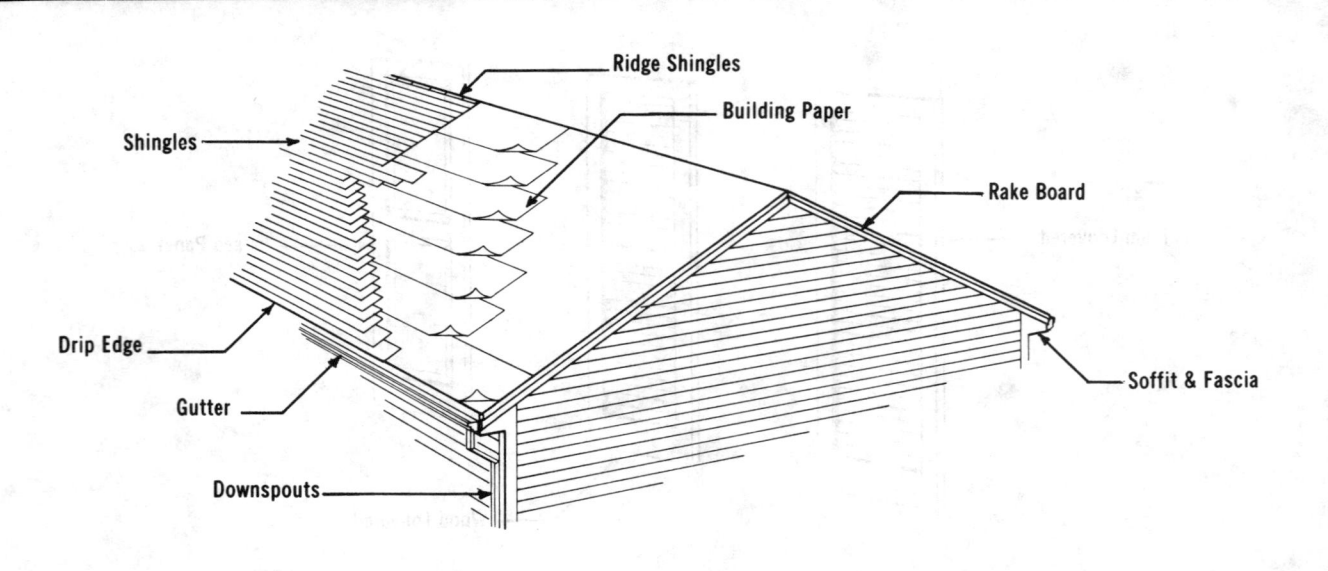

Diagram labels: Ridge Shingles, Building Paper, Shingles, Rake Board, Drip Edge, Soffit & Fascia, Gutter, Downspouts

SYSTEM DESCRIPTION	QUAN.	UNIT	MAN-HOURS	MAT.	INST.	TOTAL
ASPHALT, ROOF SHINGLES, CLASS A						
Shingles, asphalt std., inorganic class A, 210-235 lb./sq., 4/12 pitch	1.160	S.F.	.017	.42	.42	.84
Drip edge, metal, 5" girth	.150	L.F.	.003	.03	.08	.11
Building paper, #15 felt	1.300	S.F.	.001	.04	.05	.09
Ridge shingles, asphalt	.042	L.F.	.001	.03	.02	.05
Soffit & fascia, white painted aluminum, 1' overhang	.083	L.F.	.012	.12	.30	.42
Rake trim, painted, 1" x 6"	.040	L.F.	.002	.02	.08	.10
Gutter, seamless, aluminum painted	.083	L.F.	.005	.08	.15	.23
Downspouts, aluminum painted	.035	L.F.	.001	.02	.04	.06
TOTAL			.042	.76	1.14	1.90
WOOD, CEDAR SHINGLES NO. 1 PERFECTIONS, 18" LONG						
Shingles, wood, cedar, No. 1 perfections, 4/12 pitch	1.160	S.F.	.034	1.47	.81	2.28
Drip edge, metal, 5" girth	.150	L.F.	.003	.03	.08	.11
Building paper, #15 felt	1.300	S.F.	.001	.04	.05	.09
Ridge shingles, cedar	.042	L.F.	.001	.05	.03	.08
Soffit & fascia, white painted aluminum, 1' overhang	.083	L.F.	.012	.12	.30	.42
Rake trim, painted, 1" x 6"	.040	L.F.	.002	.02	.08	.10
Gutter, seamless, aluminum, painted	.083	L.F.	.005	.08	.15	.23
Downspouts, aluminum, painted	.035	L.F.	.001	.02	.04	.06
TOTAL			.059	1.83	1.54	3.37

The prices in these systems are based on a square foot of plan area.
All quantities have been adjusted accordingly.

DESCRIPTION	QUAN.	UNIT	MAN-HOURS	MAT.	INST.	TOTAL

Gable End Roofing Price Sheet

	QUAN.	UNIT	MAN-HOURS	COST PER S.F. MAT.	COST PER S.F. INST.	COST PER S.F. TOTAL
Shingles, asphalt, inorganic, class A, 210-235 lb./sq., 4/12 pitch	1.160	S.F.	.017	.42	.42	.84
9/12 pitch	1.330	S.F.	.018	.46	.45	.91
Laminated, multi-layered, 240-260 lb./sq., 4/12 pitch	1.160	S.F.	.021	.69	.51	1.20
9/12 pitch	1.330	S.F.	.023	.75	.55	1.30
Premium laminated, multi-layered, 260-300 lb./sq., 4/12 pitch	1.160	S.F.	.027	1.03	.65	1.68
9/12 pitch	1.330	S.F.	.029	1.11	.71	1.82
Clay tile, Spanish tile, red, 4/12 pitch	1.160	S.F.	.053	3.56	1.30	4.86
9/12 pitch	1.330	S.F.	.057	3.86	1.41	5.27
Mission tile, red, 4/12 pitch	1.160	S.F.	.083	5.35	1.97	7.32
9/12 pitch	1.330	S.F.	.090	5.79	2.14	7.93
French tile, red, 4/12 pitch	1.160	S.F.	.071	5.15	1.69	6.84
9/12 pitch	1.330	S.F.	.077	5.58	1.83	7.41
Slate, Buckingham, Virginia, black, 4/12 pitch	1.160	S.F.	.054	4.62	1.32	5.94
9/12 pitch	1.330	S.F.	.059	5.01	1.43	6.44
Vermont, black or grey, 4/12 pitch	1.160	S.F.	.054	4.75	1.31	6.06
9/12 pitch	1.330	S.F.	.059	5.15	1.42	6.57
Wood, No. 1 red cedar, 5X, 16" long, 5" exposure, 4/12 pitch	1.160	S.F.	.038	1.39	.89	2.28
9/12 pitch	1.330	S.F.	.041	1.50	.97	2.47
Fire retardant, 4/12 pitch	1.160	S.F.	.038	1.79	.89	2.68
9/12 pitch	1.330	S.F.	.041	1.93	.97	2.90
18" long, No.1 perfections, 5" exposure, 4/12 pitch	1.160	S.F.	.034	1.47	.81	2.28
9/12 pitch	1.330	S.F.	.037	1.59	.88	2.47
Fire retardant, 4/12 pitch	1.160	S.F.	.034	1.87	.81	2.68
9/12 pitch	1.330	S.F.	.037	2.02	.88	2.90
Resquared & rebutted, 18" long, 6" exposure, 4/12 pitch	1.160	S.F.	.032	1.15	.77	1.92
9/12 pitch	1.330	S.F.	.034	1.24	.84	2.08
Fire retardant, 4/12 pitch	1.160	S.F.	.032	1.55	.77	2.32
9/12 pitch	1.330	S.F.	.034	1.67	.84	2.51
Wood shakes hand split, 24" long, 10" exposure, 4/12 pitch	1.160	S.F.	.038	1.21	.95	2.16
9/12 pitch	1.330	S.F.	.041	1.32	1.02	2.34
Fire retardant, 4/12 pitch	1.160	S.F.	.038	1.68	.95	2.63
9/12 pitch	1.330	S.F.	.041	1.83	1.02	2.85
18" long, 8" exposure, 4/12 pitch	1.160	S.F.	.048	1.06	1.16	2.22
9/12 pitch	1.330	S.F.	.052	1.14	1.27	2.41
Fire retardant, 4/12 pitch	1.160	S.F.	.048	1.46	1.16	2.62
9/12 pitch	1.330	S.F.	.052	1.57	1.27	2.84
Drip edge, metal, 5" girth	.150	L.F.	.003	.03	.08	.11
8" girth	.150	L.F.	.003	.04	.07	.11
Building paper, #15 asphalt felt	1.300	S.F.	.001	.04	.05	.09
Ridge shingles, asphalt	.042	L.F.	.001	.03	.02	.05
Clay	.042	L.F.	.001	.18	.04	.22
Slate	.042	L.F.	.001	.18	.04	.22
Wood, shingles	.042	L.F.	.001	.05	.03	.08
Shakes	.042	L.F.	.001	.05	.03	.08
Soffit & fascia, aluminum, vented, 1' overhang	.083	L.F.	.012	.12	.30	.42
2' overhang	.083	L.F.	.013	.18	.33	.51
Vinyl, vented, 1' overhang	.083	L.F.	.011	.13	.27	.40
2' overhang	.083	L.F.	.012	.23	.31	.54
Wood, board fascia, plywood soffit, 1' overhang	.083	L.F.	.003	.01	.08	.09
2' overhang	.083	L.F.	.005	.02	.12	.14
Rake trim, painted, 1" x 6"	.040	L.F.	.002	.02	.08	.10
1" x 8"	.040	L.F.	.002	.03	.08	.11
Gutter, 5" box, aluminum, seamless, painted	.083	L.F.	.005	.08	.15	.23
Vinyl	.083	L.F.	.006	.09	.15	.24
Downspout, 2" x 3", aluminum, one story house	.035	L.F.	.001	.02	.04	.06
Two story house	.060	L.F.	.002	.04	.06	.10
Vinyl, one story house	.035	L.F.	.001	.02	.04	.06
Two story house	.060	L.F.	.002	.04	.06	.10

5 | ROOFING   08 | Hip Roof - Roofing Systems

SYSTEM DESCRIPTION	QUAN.	UNIT	MAN-HOURS	MAT.	INST.	TOTAL
ASPHALT, ROOF SHINGLES, CLASS A						
Shingles, asphalt, inorganic, class A, 210-235 lb./sq. 4/12 pitch	1.570	S.F.	.023	.56	.56	1.12
Drip edge, metal, 5" girth	.122	L.F.	.002	.03	.06	.09
Building paper, #15 asphalt felt	1.800	S.F.	.002	.06	.06	.12
Ridge shingles, asphalt	.075	L.F.	.001	.05	.05	.10
Soffit & fascia, white painted aluminum, 1' overhang	.120	L.F.	.017	.17	.44	.61
Gutter, seamless, aluminum, painted	.120	L.F.	.008	.12	.21	.33
Downspouts, aluminum, painted	.035	L.F.	.001	.02	.04	.06
TOTAL			.054	1.01	1.42	2.43
WOOD, CEDAR SHINGLES, NO. 1 PERFECTIONS, 18" LONG						
Shingles, wood, red cedar, No. 1 perfections, 5" exposure, 4/12 pitch	1.570	S.F.	.046	1.95	1.09	3.04
Drip edge, metal, 5" girth	.122	L.F.	.002	.03	.06	.09
Building paper, #15 asphalt felt	1.800	S.F.	.002	.06	.06	.12
Ridge shingles, wood, cedar	.075	L.F.	.002	.10	.05	.15
Soffit & fascia, white painted aluminum, 1' overhang	.120	L.F.	.017	.17	.44	.61
Gutter, seamless, aluminum, painted	.120	L.F.	.008	.12	.21	.33
Downspouts, aluminum, painted	.035	L.F.	.001	.02	.04	.06
TOTAL			.078	2.45	1.95	4.40

The prices in these systems are based on a square foot of plan area. All quantities have been adjusted accordingly.

DESCRIPTION	QUAN.	UNIT	MAN-HOURS	MAT.	INST.	TOTAL

Hip Roof - Roofing Price Sheet

Description	QUAN.	UNIT	MAN-HOURS	COST PER S.F. MAT.	COST PER S.F. INST.	COST PER S.F. TOTAL
Shingles, asphalt, inorganic, class A, 210-235 lb./sq., 4/12 pitch	1.570	S.F.	.023	.56	.56	1.12
9/12 pitch	1.850	S.F.	.027	.67	.66	1.33
Laminated, multi-layered, 240-260 lb./sq., 4/12 pitch	1.570	S.F.	.028	.92	.68	1.60
9/12 pitch	1.850	S.F.	.033	1.10	.80	1.90
Prem. laminated, multi-layered, 260-300 lb./sq., 4/12 pitch	1.570	S.F.	.036	1.37	.87	2.24
9/12 pitch	1.850	S.F.	.043	1.63	1.03	2.66
Clay tile, Spanish tile, red, 4/12 pitch	1.570	S.F.	.071	4.75	1.73	6.48
9/12 pitch	1.850	S.F.	.084	5.64	2.06	7.70
Mission tile, red, 4/12 pitch	1.570	S.F.	.111	7.13	2.63	9.76
9/12 pitch	1.850	S.F.	.132	8.46	3.13	11.59
French tile, red, 4/12 pitch	1.570	S.F.	.094	6.86	2.26	9.12
9/12 pitch	1.850	S.F.	.112	8.15	2.68	10.83
Slate, Buckingham, Virginia, black, 4/12 pitch	1.570	S.F.	.073	6.16	1.76	7.92
9/12 pitch	1.850	S.F.	.086	7.32	2.09	9.41
Vermont, black or grey, 4/12 pitch	1.570	S.F.	.073	6.34	1.74	8.08
9/12 pitch	1.850	S.F.	.086	7.52	2.08	9.60
Wood, red cedar, No.1 5X, 16" long, 5" exposure, 4/12 pitch	1.570	S.F.	.051	1.85	1.19	3.04
9/12 pitch	1.850	S.F.	.060	2.19	1.42	3.61
Fire retardant, 4/12 pitch	1.570	S.F.	.051	2.38	1.19	3.57
9/12 pitch	1.850	S.F.	.060	2.82	1.42	4.24
18" long, No.1 perfections, 5" exposure, 4/12 pitch	1.570	S.F.	.046	1.95	1.09	3.04
9/12 pitch	1.850	S.F.	.055	2.32	1.29	3.61
Fire retardant, 4/12 pitch	1.570	S.F.	.046	2.48	1.09	3.57
9/12 pitch	1.850	S.F.	.055	2.95	1.29	4.24
Resquared & rebutted, 18" long, 6" exposure, 4/12 pitch	1.570	S.F.	.042	1.53	1.03	2.56
9/12 pitch	1.850	S.F.	.050	1.82	1.22	3.04
Fire retardant, 4/12 pitch	1.570	S.F.	.042	2.06	1.03	3.09
9/12 pitch	1.850	S.F.	.050	2.45	1.22	3.67
Wood shakes hand split, 24" long, 10" exposure, 4/12 pitch	1.570	S.F.	.051	1.62	1.26	2.88
9/12 pitch	1.850	S.F.	.060	1.92	1.50	3.42
Fire retardant, 4/12 pitch	1.570	S.F.	.051	2.24	1.26	3.50
9/12 pitch	1.850	S.F.	.060	2.66	1.50	4.16
18" long, 8" exposure, 4/12 pitch	1.570	S.F.	.064	1.41	1.55	2.96
9/12 pitch	1.850	S.F.	.076	1.67	1.85	3.52
Fire retardant, 4/12 pitch	1.570	S.F.	.064	1.94	1.55	3.49
9/12 pitch	1.850	S.F.	.076	2.30	1.85	4.15
Drip edge, metal, 5" girth	.122	L.F.	.002	.03	.06	.09
8" girth	.122	L.F.	.002	.04	.05	.09
Building paper, #15 asphalt felt	1.800	S.F.	.002	.06	.06	.12
Ridge shingles, asphalt	.075	L.F.	.001	.05	.05	.10
Clay	.075	L.F.	.003	.33	.07	.40
Slate	.075	L.F.	.003	.31	.08	.39
Wood, shingles	.075	L.F.	.002	.10	.05	.15
Shakes	.075	L.F.	.002	.10	.05	.15
Soffit & fascia, aluminum, vented, 1' overhang	.120	L.F.	.017	.17	.44	.61
2' overhang	.120	L.F.	.019	.26	.48	.74
Vinyl, vented, 1' overhang	.120	L.F.	.015	.18	.40	.58
2' overhang	.120	L.F.	.017	.33	.44	.77
Wood, board fascia, plywood soffit, 1' overhang	.120	L.F.	.003	.01	.08	.09
2' overhang	.120	L.F.	.005	.02	.12	.14
Gutter, 5" box, aluminum, seamless, painted	.120	L.F.	.008	.12	.21	.33
Vinyl	.120	L.F.	.008	.14	.21	.35
Downspout, 2" x 3", aluminum, one story house	.035	L.F.	.001	.02	.04	.06
Two story house	.060	L.F.	.002	.04	.06	.10
Vinyl, one story house	.035	L.F.	.001	.02	.04	.06
Two story house	.060	L.F.	.002	.04	.06	.10

Hip Roof - Roofing Price Sheet

5 | ROOFING   12 | Gambrel Roofing Systems

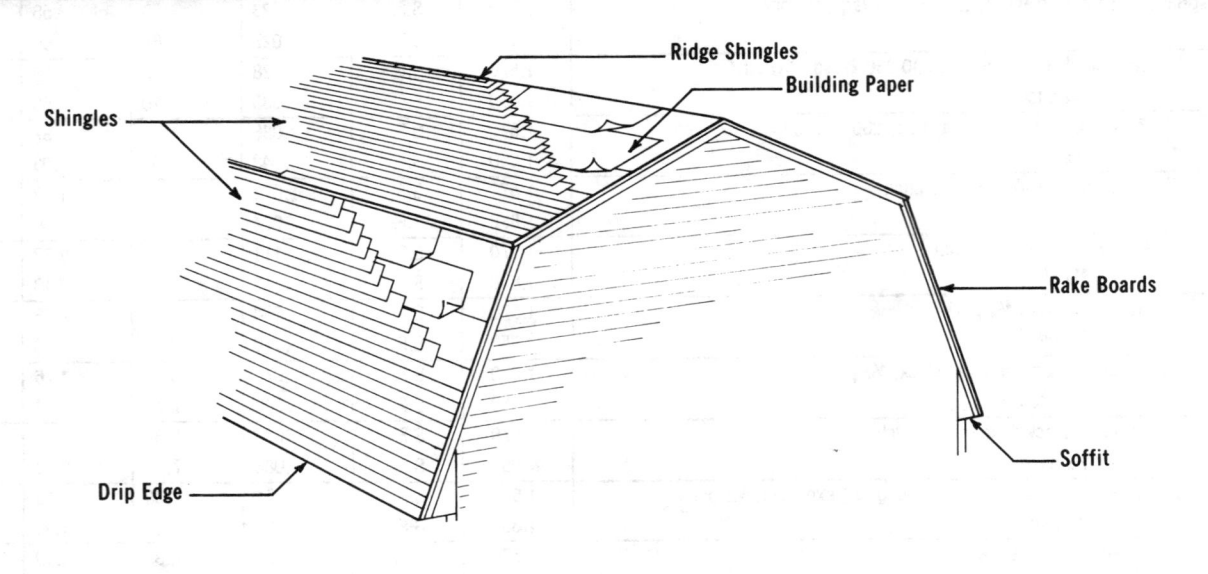

SYSTEM DESCRIPTION	QUAN.	UNIT	MAN-HOURS	MAT.	INST.	TOTAL
ASPHALT, ROOF SHINGLES, CLASS A						
Shingles, asphalt, inorganic, class A, 210-235 lb./sq.	1.450	S.F.	.021	.53	.52	1.05
Drip edge, metal, 5″ girth	.146	L.F.	.002	.03	.07	.10
Building paper, #15 asphalt felt	1.500	S.F.	.002	.05	.05	.10
Ridge shingles, asphalt	.042	L.F.	.001	.03	.02	.05
Soffit & fascia, painted aluminum, 1′ overhang	.083	L.F.	.012	.12	.30	.42
Rake, trim, painted, 1″ x 6″	.063	L.F.	.004	.03	.12	.15
Gutter, seamless, alumunum, painted	.083	L.F.	.005	.08	.15	.23
Downspouts, aluminum, painted	.042	L.F.	.001	.02	.05	.07
TOTAL			.048	.89	1.28	2.17
WOOD, CEDAR SHINGLES, NO. 1 PERFECTIONS, 18″ LONG						
Shingles, wood, red cedar, No. 1 perfections, 5″ exposure	1.450	S.F.	.043	1.83	1.02	2.85
Drip edge, metal, 5″ girth	.146	L.F.	.002	.03	.07	.10
Building paper, #15 asphalt felt	1.500	S.F.	.002	.05	.05	.10
Ridge shingles, wood	.042	L.F.	.001	.05	.03	.08
Soffit & fascia, white painted aluminum, 1′ overhang	.083	L.F.	.012	.12	.30	.42
Rake, trim, painted, 1″ x 6″	.063	L.F.	.002	.03	.08	.11
Gutter, seamless, aluminum, painted	.083	L.F.	.005	.08	.15	.23
Downspouts, aluminum, painted	.042	L.F.	.001	.02	.05	.07
TOTAL			.068	2.21	1.75	3.96

The prices in this system are based on a square foot of plan area.
All quantities have been adjusted accordingly.

DESCRIPTION	QUAN.	UNIT	MAN-HOURS	MAT.	INST.	TOTAL

Gambrel Roofing Price Sheet

	QUAN.	UNIT	MAN-HOURS	COST PER S.F. MAT.	COST PER S.F. INST.	COST PER S.F. TOTAL
Shingles, asphalt, standard, inorganic, class A, 210-235 lb./sq.	1.450	S.F.	.021	.53	.52	1.05
Laminated, multi-layered, 240-260 lb./sq.	1.450	S.F.	.026	.87	.63	1.50
Premium laminated, multi-layered, 260-300 lb./sq.	1.450	S.F.	.034	1.28	.82	2.10
Slate, Buckingham, Virginia, black	1.450	S.F.	.068	5.78	1.65	7.43
Vermont, black or grey	1.450	S.F.	.068	5.94	1.64	7.58
Wood, red cedar,	1.450	S.F.	.048	1.73	1.12	2.85
Fire retardant	1.450	S.F.	.048	2.23	1.12	3.35
18" long, No.1 perfections, 6" exposure, plain	1.450	S.F.	.043	1.83	1.02	2.85
Fire retardant	1.450	S.F.	.043	2.33	1.02	3.35
Resquared & rebutted, 18" long, 6" exposure, plain	1.450	S.F.	.040	1.44	.96	2.40
Fire retardant	1.450	S.F.	.040	2.31	.99	3.30
Shakes, hand split, 24" long, 10" exposure, plain	1.450	S.F.	.048	1.52	1.18	2.70
Fire retardant	1.450	S.F.	.048	2.11	1.18	3.29
18" long, 8" exposure, plain	1.450	S.F.	.060	1.32	1.46	2.78
Fire retardant	1.450	S.F.	.060	1.82	1.46	3.28
Drip edge, metal, 5" girth	.146	L.F.	.002	.03	.07	.10
8" girth	.146	L.F.	.002	.04	.07	.11
Building paper, #15 asphalt felt	1.500	S.F.	.002	.05	.05	.10
Ridge shingles, asphalt	.042	L.F.	.001	.03	.02	.05
Slate	.042	L.F.	.001	.18	.04	.22
Wood, shingles	.042	L.F.	.001	.05	.03	.08
Shakes	.042	L.F.	.001	.05	.03	.08
Soffit & fascia, aluminum, vented, 1' overhang	.083	L.F.	.012	.12	.30	.42
2' overhang	.083	L.F.	.013	.18	.33	.51
Vinyl vented, 1' overhang	.083	L.F.	.011	.13	.27	.40
2' overhang	.083	L.F.	.012	.23	.31	.54
Wood board fascia, plywood soffit, 1' overhang	.083	L.F.	.003	.01	.08	.09
2' overhang	.083	L.F.	.005	.02	.12	.14
Rake trim, painted, 1" x 6"	.063	L.F.	.004	.03	.12	.15
1" x 8"	.063	L.F.	.006	.03	.16	.19
Gutter, 5" box, aluminum, seamless, painted	.083	L.F.	.005	.08	.15	.23
Vinyl	.083	L.F.	.006	.09	.15	.24
Downspout 2" x 3", aluminum, one story house	.042	L.F.	.001	.03	.04	.07
Two story house	.070	L.F.	.002	.04	.08	.12
Vinyl, one story house	.042	L.F.	.001	.03	.04	.07
Two story house	.070	L.F.	.002	.04	.08	.12

5 | ROOFING — 16 Mansard Roofing Systems

SYSTEM DESCRIPTION	QUAN.	UNIT	MAN-HOURS	MAT.	INST.	TOTAL
ASPHALT, ROOF SHINGLES, CLASS A						
Shingles, asphalt standard inorganic class A 210-235 lb./sq.	2.210	S.F.	.031	.77	.77	1.54
Drip edge, metal, 5″ girth	.122	L.F.	.002	.03	.06	.09
Building paper, #15 asphalt felt	2.300	S.F.	.003	.08	.07	.15
Ridge shingles, asphalt	.090	L.F.	.002	.06	.06	.12
Soffit & fascia, white painted aluminum, 1′ overhang	.122	L.F.	.017	.17	.45	.62
Gutter, seamless, aluminum, painted	.122	L.F.	.008	.12	.22	.34
Downspouts, aluminum, painted	.042	L.F.	.001	.02	.05	.07
TOTAL			.064	1.25	1.68	2.93
WOOD, CEDAR SHINGLES, NO. 1 PERFECTIONS, 18″ LONG						
Shingles, wood, red cedar, No. 1 perfections, 5″ exposure	2.210	S.F.	.064	2.69	1.49	4.18
Drip edge, metal, 5″ girth	.122	L.F.	.002	.03	.06	.09
Building paper, #15 asphalt felt	2.300	S.F.	.003	.08	.07	.15
Ridge shingles, wood	.090	L.F.	.002	.11	.07	.18
Soffit & fascia, white painted aluminum, 1′ overhang	.122	L.F.	.017	.17	.45	.62
Gutter, seamless, aluminum, painted	.122	L.F.	.008	.12	.22	.34
Downspouts, aluminum, painted	.042	L.F.	.001	.02	.05	.07
TOTAL			.097	3.22	2.41	5.63

The prices in these systems are based on a square foot of plan area.
All quantities have been adjusted accordingly.

DESCRIPTION	QUAN.	UNIT	MAN-HOURS	MAT.	INST.	TOTAL

Mansard Roofing Price Sheet

	QUAN.	UNIT	MAN-HOURS	COST PER S.F. MAT.	COST PER S.F. INST.	COST PER S.F. TOTAL
Shingles, asphalt, standard, inorganic, class A, 210-235 lb./sq.	2.210	S.F.	.031	.77	.77	1.54
Laminated, multi-layered, 240-260 lb./sq.	2.210	S.F.	.039	1.27	.93	2.20
Premium laminated, multi-layered, 260-300 lb./sq.	2.210	S.F.	.050	1.88	1.20	3.08
Slate Buckingham, Virginia, black	2.210	S.F.	.100	8.47	2.42	10.89
Vermont, black or grey	2.210	S.F.	.100	8.71	2.40	11.11
Wood, red cedar, No.1 5X, 16" long, 5" exposure, plain	2.210	S.F.	.070	2.54	1.64	4.18
Fire retardant	2.210	S.F.	.070	3.27	1.64	4.91
18" long, No.1 perfections 6" exposure, plain	2.210	S.F.	.064	2.69	1.49	4.18
Fire retardant	2.210	S.F.	.064	3.42	1.49	4.91
Resquared & rebutted, 18" long, 6" exposure, plain	2.210	S.F.	.058	2.11	1.41	3.52
Fire retardant	2.210	S.F.	.058	2.84	1.41	4.25
Shakes, hand split, 24" long 10" exposure, plain	2.210	S.F.	.070	2.23	1.73	3.96
Fire retardant	2.210	S.F.	.070	3.09	1.73	4.82
18" long, 8" exposure, plain	2.210	S.F.	.088	1.94	2.13	4.07
Fire retardant	2.210	S.F.	.088	2.67	2.13	4.80
Drip edge, metal, 5" girth	.122	S.F.	.002	.03	.06	.09
8" girth	.122	S.F.	.002	.04	.05	.09
Building paper, #15 asphalt felt	2.300	S.F.	.003	.08	.07	.15
Ridge shingles, asphalt	.090	L.F.	.002	.06	.06	.12
Slate	.090	L.F.	.003	.38	.08	.46
Wood, shingles	.090	L.F.	.002	.11	.07	.18
Shakes	.090	L.F.	.002	.11	.07	.18
Soffit & fascia, aluminum vented, 1' overhang	.122	L.F.	.017	.17	.45	.62
2' overhang	.122	L.F.	.019	.27	.49	.76
Vinyl vented, 1' overhang	.122	L.F.	.016	.19	.40	.59
2' overhang	.122	L.F.	.017	.34	.45	.79
Wood board fascia, plywood soffit, 1' overhang	.122	L.F.	.011	.11	.30	.41
2' overhang	.122	L.F.	.018	.17	.45	.62
Gutter, 5" box, aluminum, seamless, painted	.122	L.F.	.008	.12	.22	.34
Vinyl	.122	L.F.	.008	.14	.21	.35
Downspout 2" x 3", aluminum, one story house	.042	L.F.	.001	.03	.04	.07
Two story house	.070	L.F.	.002	.04	.08	.12
Vinyl, one story house	.042	L.F.	.001	.03	.04	.07
Two story house	.070	L.F.	.002	.04	.08	.12

5 | ROOFING — 20 Shed Roofing Systems

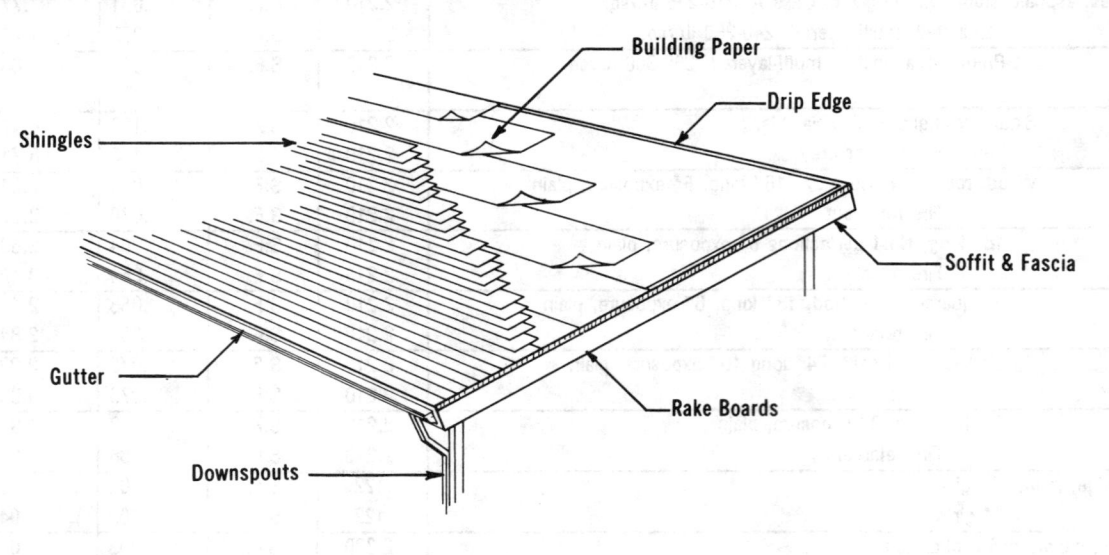

SYSTEM DESCRIPTION	QUAN.	UNIT	MAN-HOURS	MAT.	INST.	TOTAL
ASPHALT, ROOF SHINGLES, CLASS A						
Shingles, asphalt inorganic class A 210-235 lb./sq. 4/12 pitch	1.230	S.F.	.018	.46	.45	.91
Drip edge, metal, 5" girth	.100	L.F.	.002	.02	.05	.07
Building paper, #15 asphalt felt	1.300	S.F.	.001	.04	.05	.09
Soffit & fascia, white painted aluminum, 1' overhang	.080	L.F.	.011	.11	.29	.40
Rake trim, painted, 1" x 6"	.043	L.F.	.002	.02	.08	.10
Gutter, seamless, aluminum, painted	.040	L.F.	.002	.04	.07	.11
Downspouts, painted aluminum	.020	L.F.		.01	.02	.03
TOTAL			.036	.70	1.01	1.71
WOOD, CEDAR SHINGLES, NO. 1 PERFECTIONS, 18" LONG						
Shingles, wood, red cedar, No. 1 perfections, 5" exposure, 4/12 pitch	1.230	S.F.	.034	1.47	.81	2.28
Drip edge, metal, 5" girth	.100	L.F.	.002	.02	.05	.07
Building paper, #15 asphalt felt	1.300	S.F.	.001	.04	.05	.09
Soffit & fascia, white painted aluminum, 1' overhang	.080	L.F.	.011	.11	.29	.40
Rake trim, painted, 1" x 6"	.043	L.F.	.001	.02	.05	.07
Gutter, seamless, aluminum, painted	.040	L.F.	.002	.04	.07	.11
Downspouts, painted aluminum	.020	L.F.		.01	.02	.03
TOTAL			.051	1.71	1.34	3.05

The prices in these systems are based on a square foot of plan area.
All quantities have been adjusted accordingly.

DESCRIPTION	QUAN.	UNIT	MAN-HOURS	MAT.	INST.	TOTAL

Shed Roofing Price Sheet

	QUAN.	UNIT	MAN-HOURS	COST PER S.F. MAT.	COST PER S.F. INST.	COST PER S.F. TOTAL
Shingles, asphalt, inorganic, class A, 210-235 lb./sq., 4/12 pitch	1.230	S.F.	.017	.42	.42	.84
9/12 pitch	1.330	S.F.	.018	.46	.45	.91
Laminated, multi-layered, 240-260 lb./sq. 4/12 pitch	1.230	S.F.	.021	.69	.51	1.20
9/12 pitch	1.330	S.F.	.023	.75	.55	1.30
Premium laminated, multi-layered, 260-300 lb./sq. 4/12 pitch	1.230	S.F.	.027	1.03	.65	1.68
9/12 pitch	1.330	S.F.	.029	1.11	.71	1.82
Clay tile, Spanish tile, red, 4/12 pitch	1.230	S.F.	.053	3.56	1.30	4.86
9/12 pitch	1.330	S.F.	.057	3.86	1.41	5.27
Mission tile, red, 4/12 pitch	1.230	S.F.	.083	5.35	1.97	7.32
9/12 pitch	1.330	S.F.	.090	5.79	2.14	7.93
French tile, red, 4/12 pitch	1.230	S.F.	.071	5.15	1.69	6.84
9/12 pitch	1.330	S.F.	.077	5.58	1.83	7.41
Slate, Buckingham, Virginia, black, 4/12 pitch	1.230	S.F.	.054	4.62	1.32	5.94
9/12 pitch	1.330	S.F.	.059	5.01	1.43	6.44
Vermont, black or grey, 4/12 pitch	1.230	S.F.	.054	4.75	1.31	6.06
9/12 pitch	1.330	S.F.	.059	5.15	1.42	6.57
Wood, red cedar, No.1 5X, 16" long, 5" exposure, 4/12 pitch	1.230	S.F.	.038	1.39	.89	2.28
9/12 pitch	1.330	S.F.	.041	1.50	.97	2.47
Fire retardant, 4/12 pitch	1.230	S.F.	.038	1.79	.89	2.68
9/12 pitch	1.330	S.F.	.041	1.93	.97	2.90
18" long, 6" exposure, 4/12 pitch	1.230	S.F.	.034	1.47	.81	2.28
9/12 pitch	1.330	S.F.	.037	1.59	.88	2.47
Fire retardant, 4/12 pitch	1.230	S.F.	.034	1.87	.81	2.68
9/12 pitch	1.330	S.F.	.037	2.02	.88	2.90
Resquared & rebutted, 18" long, 6" exposure, 4/12 pitch	1.230	S.F.	.032	1.15	.77	1.92
9/12 pitch	1.330	S.F.	.034	1.24	.84	2.08
Fire retardant, 4/12 pitch	1.230	S.F.	.032	1.55	.77	2.32
9/12 pitch	1.330	S.F.	.034	1.67	.84	2.51
Wood shakes, hand split, 24" long, 10" exposure, 4/12 pitch	1.230	S.F.	.038	1.21	.95	2.16
9/12 pitch	1.330	S.F.	.041	1.32	1.02	2.34
Fire retardant, 4/12 pitch	1.230	S.F.	.038	1.68	.95	2.63
9/12 pitch	1.330	S.F.	.041	1.83	1.02	2.85
18" long, 8" exposure, 4/12 pitch	1.230	S.F.	.048	1.06	1.16	2.22
9/12 pitch	1.330	S.F.	.052	1.14	1.27	2.41
Fire retardant, 4/12 pitch	1.230	S.F.	.048	1.46	1.16	2.62
9/12 pitch	1.330	S.F.	.052	1.57	1.27	2.84
Drip edge, metal, 5" girth	.100	L.F.	.002	.02	.05	.07
8" girth	.100	L.F.	.002	.03	.05	.08
Building paper, #15 asphalt felt	1.300	S.F.	.001	.04	.05	.09
Soffit & fascia, aluminum vented, 1' overhang	.080	L.F.	.011	.11	.29	.40
2' overhang	.080	L.F.	.012	.18	.32	.50
Vinyl vented, 1' overhang	.080	L.F.	.010	.12	.27	.39
2' overhang	.080	L.F.	.011	.22	.30	.52
Wood board fascia, plywood soffit, 1' overhang	.080	L.F.	.008	.07	.23	.30
2' overhang	.080	L.F.	.013	.12	.34	.46
Rake, trim, painted, 1" x 6"	.043	L.F.	.002	.02	.08	.10
1" x 8"	.043	L.F.	.002	.02	.08	.10
Gutter, 5" box, aluminum, seamless, painted	.040	L.F.	.002	.04	.07	.11
Vinyl	.040	L.F.	.002	.05	.07	.12
Downspout 2" x 3", aluminum, one story house	.020	L.F.		.01	.02	.03
Two story house	.020	L.F.	.001	.02	.04	.06
Vinyl, one story house	.020	L.F.		.01	.02	.03
Two story house	.020	L.F.	.001	.02	.04	.06

5 | ROOFING — 24 | Gable Dormer Roofing Systems

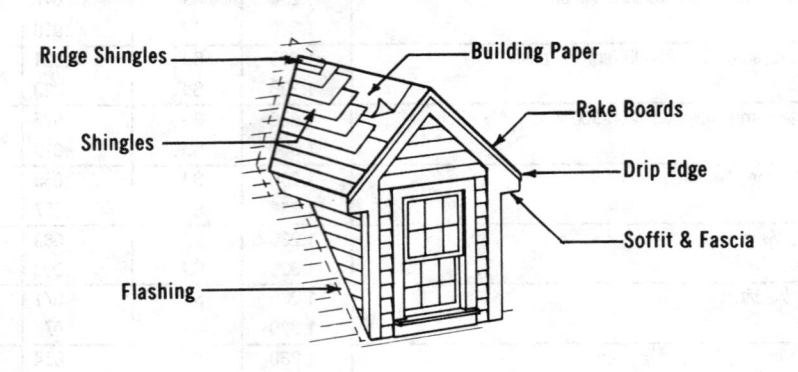

SYSTEM DESCRIPTION	QUAN.	UNIT	MAN-HOURS	MAT.	INST.	TOTAL
ASPHALT, ROOF SHINGLES, CLASS A						
Shingles, asphalt standard inorganic class A 210-235 lb./sq	1.400	S.F.	.020	.49	.49	.98
Drip edge, metal, 5" girth	.220	L.F.	.004	.05	.11	.16
Building paper, #15 asphalt felt	1.500	S.F.	.002	.05	.05	.10
Ridge shingles, asphalt	.280	L.F.	.006	.20	.16	.36
Soffit & fascia, aluminum, vented	.220	L.F.	.031	.31	.80	1.11
Flashing, aluminum, mill finish, .013" thick	1.500	S.F.	.082	.44	2.22	2.66
TOTAL			.145	1.54	3.83	5.37
WOOD, CEDAR, NO. 1 PERFECTIONS						
Shingles, wood, red cedar, No.1 perfections, 18" long, 5" exp.	1.400	S.F.	.040	1.71	.95	2.66
Drip edge, metal, 5" girth	.220	L.F.	.004	.05	.11	.16
Building paper, #15 asphalt felt	1.500	S.F.	.002	.05	.05	.10
Ridge shingles, wood	.280	L.F.	.008	.36	.19	.55
Soffit & fascia, aluminum, vented	.220	L.F.	.031	.31	.80	1.11
Flashing, aluminum, mill finish, .013" thick	1.500	S.F.	.082	.44	2.22	2.66
TOTAL			.167	2.92	4.32	7.24
SLATE, BUCKINGHAM, BLACK						
Shingles, Buckingham, Virginia, black	1.400	S.F.	.063	5.39	1.54	6.93
Drip edge, metal, 5" girth	.220	L.F.	.004	.05	.11	.16
Building paper, #15 asphalt felt	1.500	S.F.	.002	.05	.05	.10
Ridge shingles, slate	.280	L.F.	.011	1.17	.27	1.44
Soffit & fascia, aluminum, vented	.220	L.F.	.031	.31	.80	1.11
Flashing, copper, 16 oz.	1.500	S.F.	.105	4.29	2.81	7.10
TOTAL			.216	11.26	5.58	16.84

The prices in these systems are based on a square foot of plan area under the dormer roof.

DESCRIPTION	QUAN.	UNIT	MAN-HOURS	MAT.	INST.	TOTAL

Gable Dormer Roofing Price Sheet

	QUAN.	UNIT	MAN-HOURS	COST PER S.F. MAT.	COST PER S.F. INST.	COST PER S.F. TOTAL
Shingles, asphalt, standard, inorganic, class A, 210-235 lb./sq.	1.400	S.F.	.020	.49	.49	.98
Laminated, multi-layered, 240-260 lb./sq.	1.400	S.F.	.024	.81	.59	1.40
Premium laminated, multi-layered, 260-300 lb./sq.	1.400	S.F.	.032	1.20	.76	1.96
Clay tile, Spanish tile, red	1.400	S.F.	.062	4.16	1.51	5.67
Mission tile, red	1.400	S.F.	.097	6.24	2.30	8.54
French tile, red	1.400	S.F.	.083	6.01	1.97	7.98
Slate Buckingham, Virginia, black	1.400	S.F.	.063	5.39	1.54	6.93
Vermont, black or grey	1.400	S.F.	.063	5.54	1.53	7.07
Wood, red cedar, No.1 5X, 16" long, 5" exposure	1.400	S.F.	.044	1.62	1.04	2.66
Fire retardant	1.400	S.F.	.044	2.08	1.04	3.12
18" long, No.1 perfections, 5" exposure	1.400	S.F.	.040	1.71	.95	2.66
Fire retardant	1.400	S.F	.040	2.17	.95	3.12
Resquared & rebutted, 18" long, 5" exposure	1.400	S.F.	.037	1.34	.90	2.24
Fire retardant	1.400	S.F.	.037	1.80	.90	2.70
Shakes hand split, 24" long, 10" exposure	1.400	S.F.	.044	1.42	1.10	2.52
Fire retardant	1.400	S.F.	.044	1.97	1.10	3.07
18" long, 8" exposure	1.400	S.F.	.056	1.23	1.36	2.59
Fire retardant	1.400	S.F.	.056	1.69	1.36	3.05
Drip edge, metal, 5" girth	.220	L.F.	.004	.05	.11	.16
8" girth	.220	L.F.	.004	.06	.11	.17
Building paper, #15 asphalt felt	1.500	S.F.	.002	.05	.05	.10
Ridge shingles, asphalt	.280	L.F.	.006	.20	.16	.36
Clay	.280	L.F.	.011	1.23	.27	1.50
Slate	.280	L.F.	.011	1.17	.27	1.44
Wood	.280	L.F.	.008	.36	.19	.55
Soffit & fascia, aluminum, vented	.220	L.F.	.031	.31	.80	1.11
Vinyl, vented	.220	L.F.	.029	.34	.73	1.07
Wood, board fascia, plywood soffit	.220	L.F.	.024	.22	.61	.83
Flashing, aluminum, .013" thick	1.500	S.F.	.082	.44	2.22	2.66
.032" thick	1.500	S.F.	.082	1.29	2.22	3.51
.040" thick	1.500	S.F.	.082	2.18	2.23	4.41
.050" thick	1.500	S.F.	.082	2.64	2.24	4.88
Copper, 16 oz.	1.500	S.F.	.105	4.29	2.81	7.10
20 oz.	1.500	S.F.	.109	5.37	2.96	8.33
24 oz.	1.500	S.F.	.114	6.44	3.09	9.53
32 oz.	1.500	S.F.	.120	8.34	3.21	11.55

5 | ROOFING

28 | Shed Dormer Roofing Systems

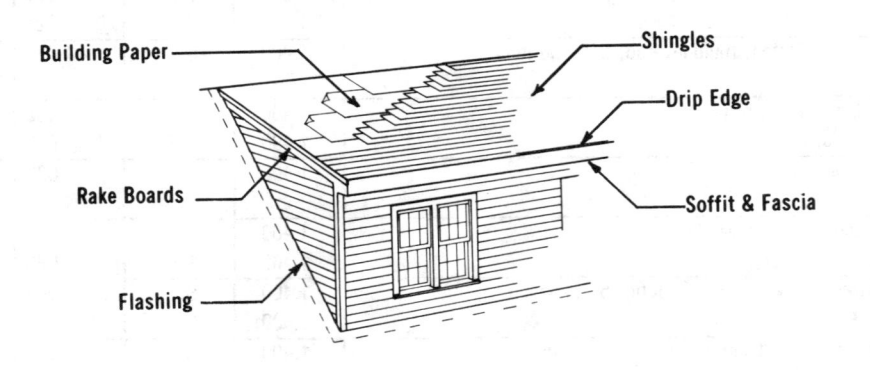

Diagram labels: Building Paper, Shingles, Drip Edge, Soffit & Fascia, Rake Boards, Flashing

SYSTEM DESCRIPTION	QUAN.	UNIT	MAN-HOURS	MAT.	INST.	TOTAL
ASPHALT, ROOF SHINGLES, CLASS A						
Shingles, asphalt standard inorganic class A 210-235 lb./sq.	1.100	S.F.	.015	.39	.38	.77
Drip edge, aluminum, 5" girth	.250	L.F.	.005	.04	.12	.16
Building paper, #15 asphalt felt	1.200	S.F.	.001	.04	.04	.08
Soffit & fascia, aluminum, vented, 1' overhang	.250	L.F.	.036	.36	.90	1.26
Flashing, aluminum, mill finish, 0.013" thick	.800	L.F.	.044	.23	1.19	1.42
TOTAL			.101	1.06	2.63	3.69
WOOD, CEDAR, NO. 1 PERFECTIONS, 18" LONG						
Shingles, wood, red cedar, #1 perfections, 5" exposure	1.100	S.F.	.032	1.34	.75	2.09
Drip edge, aluminum, 5" girth	.250	L.F.	.005	.04	.12	.16
Building paper, #15 asphalt felt	1.200	S.F.	.001	.04	.04	.08
Soffit & fascia, aluminum, vented, 1' overhang	.250	L.F.	.036	.36	.90	1.26
Flashing, aluminum, mill finish, 0.013" thick	.800	L.F.	.044	.23	1.19	1.42
TOTAL			.118	2.01	3.00	5.01
SLATE, BUCKINGHAM, BLACK						
Shingles, slate, Buckingham, black	1.100	S.F.	.050	4.24	1.21	5.45
Drip edge, aluminum, 5" girth	.250	L.F.	.005	.04	.12	.16
Building paper, #15 asphalt felt	1.200	S.F.	.001	.04	.04	.08
Soffit & fascia, aluminum, vented, 1' overhang	.250	L.F.	.036	.36	.90	1.26
Flashing, copper, 16 oz.	.800	L.F.	.056	2.29	1.49	3.78
TOTAL			.148	6.97	3.76	10.73

The prices in this system are based on a square foot of plan area under the dormer roof.

DESCRIPTION	QUAN.	UNIT	MAN-HOURS	MAT.	INST.	TOTAL

Shed Dormer Roofing Price Sheet

	QUAN.	UNIT	MAN-HOURS	COST PER S.F. MAT.	COST PER S.F. INST.	COST PER S.F. TOTAL
Shingles, asphalt, standard, inorganic, class A, 210-235 lb./sq.	1.100	S.F.	.015	.39	.38	.77
Laminated, multi-layered, 240-260 lb./sq.	1.100	S.F.	.019	.64	.46	1.10
Premium laminated, multi-layered, 260-300 lb./sq.	1.100	S.F.	.025	.94	.60	1.54
Clay tile, Spanish tile, red	1.100	S.F.	.048	3.27	1.19	4.46
Mission tile, red	1.100	S.F.	.076	4.90	1.81	6.71
French tile, red	1.100	S.F.	.065	4.72	1.55	6.27
Slate Buckingham, Virginia, black	1.100	S.F.	.050	4.24	1.21	5.45
Vermont, black or grey	1.100	S.F.	.050	4.36	1.20	5.56
Wood, red cedar, No. 1 5X, 16" long, 5" exposure	1.100	S.F.	.035	1.27	.82	2.09
Fire retardant	1.100	S.F.	.035	1.63	.82	2.45
18" long, No.1 perfections, 5" exposure	1.100	S.F.	.032	1.34	.75	2.09
Fire retardant	1.100	S.F.	.032	1.70	.75	2.45
Resquared & rebutted, 18" long, 5" exposure	1.100	S.F.	.029	1.05	.71	1.76
Fire retardant	1.100	S.F.	.029	1.41	.71	2.12
Shakes hand split, 24" long, 10" exposure	1.100	S.F.	.035	1.11	.87	1.98
Fire retardant	1.100	S.F.	.035	1.54	.87	2.41
18" long, 8" exposure	1.100	S.F.	.044	.97	1.07	2.04
Fire retardant	1.100	S.F.	.044	1.33	1.07	2.40
Drip edge, metal, 5" girth	.250	L.F.	.005	.04	.12	.16
8" girth	.250	L.F.	.005	.07	.12	.19
Building paper, #15 asphalt felt	1.200	S.F.	.001	.04	.04	.08
Soffit & fascia, aluminum, vented	.250	L.F.	.036	.36	.90	1.26
Vinyl, vented	.250	L.F.	.033	.39	.83	1.22
Wood, board fascia, plywood soffit	.250	L.F.	.029	.25	.69	.94
Flashing, aluminum, .013" thick	.800	L.F.	.044	.23	1.19	1.42
.032" thick	.800	L.F.	.044	.69	1.18	1.87
.040" thick	.800	L.F.	.044	1.16	1.19	2.35
.050" thick	.800	L.F.	.044	1.41	1.19	2.60
Copper, 16 oz.	.800	L.F.	.056	2.29	1.49	3.78
20 oz.	.800	L.F.	.058	2.86	1.58	4.44
24 oz.	.800	L.F.	.060	3.43	1.65	5.08
32 oz.	.800	L.F.	.064	4.45	1.71	6.16

5 | ROOFING — 32 | Skylight/Skywindow Systems

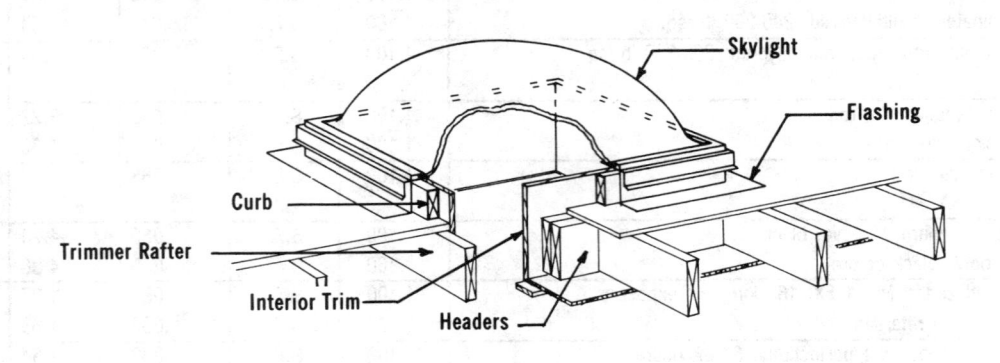

SYSTEM DESCRIPTION	QUAN.	UNIT	MAN-HOURS	MAT.	INST.	TOTAL
SKYLIGHT, FIXED, 32" X 32"						
Skylight, fixed bubble, insulating, 32" x 32"	1.000	Ea.	1.422	121.24	35.20	156.44
Trimmer rafters, 2" x 6"	28.000	L.F.	.448	12.04	11.20	23.24
Headers, 2" x 6"	6.000	L.F.	.186	2.58	4.62	7.20
Curb, 2" x 4"	12.000	L.F.	.156	3.48	3.84	7.32
Flashing, aluminum, .013" thick	13.500	S.F.	.742	3.92	19.98	23.90
Trim, interior casing, painted	12.000	L.F.	.612	8.40	14.40	22.80
TOTAL			3.566	151.66	89.24	240.90
SKYLIGHT, FIXED, 48" X 48"						
Skylight, fixed bubble, insulating, 48" x 48"	1.000	Ea.	1.296	217.44	30.56	248.00
Trimmer rafters, 2" x 6"	28.000	L.F.	.448	12.04	11.20	23.24
Headers, 2" x 6"	8.000	L.F.	.248	3.44	6.16	9.60
Curb, 2" x 4"	16.000	L.F.	.208	4.64	5.12	9.76
Flashing, aluminum, .013" thick	16.000	S.F.	.880	4.64	23.68	28.32
Trim, interior casing, painted	16.000	L.F.	.816	11.20	19.20	30.40
TOTAL			3.896	253.40	95.92	349.32
SKYWINDOW, OPERATING, 24" X 48"						
Skywindow, operating, thermopane glass, 24" x 48"	1.000	Ea.	3.200	385.00	75.00	460.00
Trimmer rafters, 2" x 6"	28.000	L.F.	.448	12.04	11.20	23.24
Headers, 2" x 6"	8.000	L.F.	.186	2.58	4.62	7.20
Curb, 2" x 4"	14.000	L.F.	.182	4.06	4.48	8.54
Flashing, aluminum, .013" thick	14.000	S.F.	.770	4.06	20.72	24.78
Trim, interior casing, painted	14.000	L.F.	.714	9.80	16.80	26.60
TOTAL			5.500	417.54	132.82	550.36

The prices in these systems are on a cost each basis.

Skylight/Skywindow Price Sheet

	QUAN.	UNIT	MAN-HOURS	COST EACH MAT.	COST EACH INST.	TOTAL
Skylight, fixed bubble insulating, 24" x 24"	1.000	Ea.	.800	68.20	19.80	88.00
32" x 32"	1.000	Ea.	1.422	121.24	35.20	156.44
32" x 48"	1.000	Ea.	.863	144.95	20.37	165.32
48" x 48"	1.000	Ea.	1.296	217.44	30.56	248.00
Ventilating bubble insulating, 36" x 36"	1.000	Ea.	2.670	330.00	65.00	395.00
52" x 52"	1.000	Ea.	2.670	495.00	65.00	560.00
28" x 52"	1.000	Ea.	3.200	385.00	75.00	460.00
36" x 52"	1.000	Ea.	3.200	418.00	77.00	495.00
Skywindow, operating, thermopane glass, 24" x 48"	1.000	Ea.	3.200	484.00	76.00	560.00
32" x 48"	1.000	Ea.	3.560	506.00	84.00	590.00
Trimmer rafters, 2" x 6"	28.000	L.F.	.448	12.04	11.20	23.24
2" x 8"	28.000	L.F.	.476	17.08	11.76	28.84
2" x 10"	28.000	L.F.	.700	25.20	17.64	42.84
Headers, 24" window, 2" x 6"	4.000	L.F.	.124	1.72	3.08	4.80
2" x 8"	4.000	L.F.	.188	2.44	4.72	7.16
2" x 10"	4.000	L.F.	.200	3.68	5.00	8.68
32" window, 2" x 6"	6.000	L.F.	.186	2.58	4.62	7.20
2" x 8"	6.000	L.F.	.282	3.66	7.08	10.74
2" x 10"	6.000	L.F.	.300	5.52	7.50	13.02
48" window, 2" x 6"	8.000	L.F.	.248	3.44	6.16	9.60
2" x 8"	8.000	L.F.	.376	4.88	9.44	14.32
2" x 10"	8.000	L.F.	.400	7.36	10.00	17.36
Curb, 2" x 4", skylight, 24" x 24"	8.000	L.F.	.104	2.32	2.56	4.88
32" x 32"	12.000	L.F.	.156	3.48	3.84	7.32
32" x 48"	14.000	L.F.	.182	4.06	4.48	8.54
48" x 48"	16.000	L.F.	.208	4.64	5.12	9.76
Flashing, aluminum .013" thick, skylight, 24" x 24"	9.000	S.F.	.495	2.61	13.32	15.93
32" x 32"	13.500	S.F.	.742	3.92	19.98	23.90
32" x 48"	14.000	S.F.	.770	4.06	20.72	24.78
48" x 48"	16.000	S.F.	.880	4.64	23.68	28.32
Copper 16 oz., skylight, 24" x 24"	9.000	S.F.	.630	25.74	16.83	42.57
32" x 32"	13.500	S.F.	.945	38.61	25.25	63.86
32" x 48"	14.000	S.F.	.980	40.04	26.18	66.22
48" x 48"	16.000	S.F.	1.120	45.76	29.92	75.68
Trim, interior casing painted, 24" x 24"	8.000	L.F.	.320	5.76	7.68	13.44
32" x 32"	12.000	L.F.	.480	8.64	11.52	20.16
32" x 48"	14.000	L.F.	.560	10.08	13.44	23.52
48" x 48"	16.000	L.F.	.640	11.52	15.36	26.88

5 | ROOFING — 34 | Built-up Roofing Systems

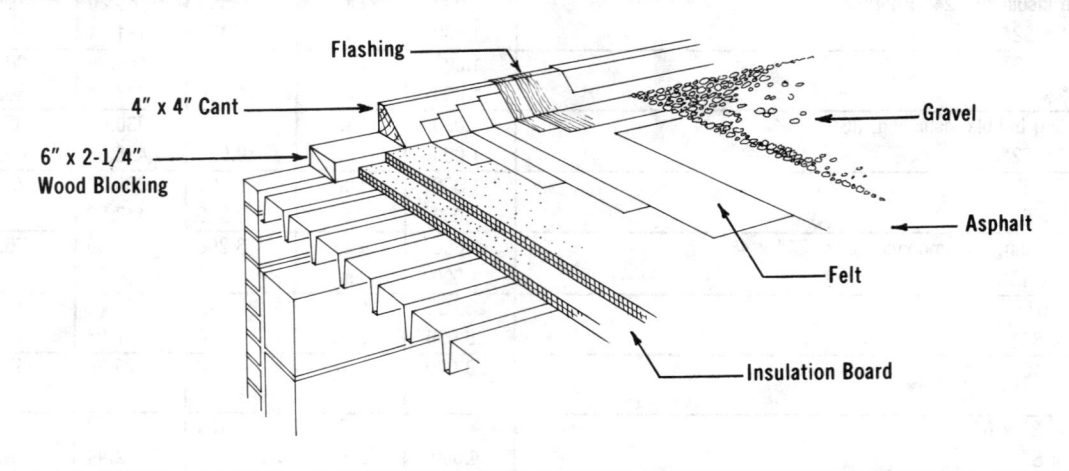

Diagram labels: Flashing; 4" x 4" Cant; 6" x 2-1/4" Wood Blocking; Gravel; Asphalt; Felt; Insulation Board

SYSTEM DESCRIPTION	QUAN.	UNIT	MAN-HOURS	MAT.	INST.	TOTAL
ASPHALT, ORGANIC, 4-PLY, INSULATED DECK						
Membrane, asphalt, 4-plies #15 felt, gravel surfacing	1.000	S.F.	.025	.41	.64	1.05
Insulation board, 2-layers of 1-1/16" glass fiber	2.000	S.F.	.016	1.10	.38	1.48
Wood blocking, treated, 6" x 2-1/4" & 4" x 4" cant	.040	L.F.	.005	.10	.14	.24
Flashing, aluminum, 0.040" thick	.050	S.F.	.002	.07	.08	.15
TOTAL			.048	1.68	1.24	2.92
ASPHALT, INORGANIC, 3-PLY, INSULATED DECK						
Membrane, asphalt, 3-plies type IV glass felt, gravel surfacing	1.000	S.F.	.025	.43	.62	1.05
Insulation board, 2-layers of 1-1/16" glass fiber	2.000	S.F.	.016	1.10	.38	1.48
Wood blocking, treated, 6" x 2-1/4" & 4" x 4" cant	.040	L.F.	.005	.10	.14	.24
Flashing, aluminum, 0.040" thick	.050	S.F.	.002	.07	.08	.15
TOTAL			.048	1.70	1.22	2.92
COAL TAR, ORGANIC, 4-PLY, INSULATED DECK						
Membrane, coal tar, 4-plies #15 felt, gravel surfacing	1.000	S.F.	.025	.68	.62	1.30
Insulation board, 2-layers of 1-1/16" glass fiber	2.000	S.F.	.016	1.10	.38	1.48
Wood blocking, treated, 6" x 2-1/4" & 4" x 4" cant	.040	L.F.	.005	.10	.14	.24
Flashing, aluminum, 0.040" thick	.050	S.F.	.002	.07	.08	.15
TOTAL			.048	1.95	1.22	3.17
COAL TAR, INORGANIC, 3-PLY, INSULATED DECK						
Membrane, coal tar, 3-plies type IV glass felt, gravel surfacing	1.000	S.F.	.028	.54	.71	1.25
Insulation board, 2-layers of 1-1/16" glass fiber	2.000	S.F.	.016	1.10	.38	1.48
Wood blocking, treated, 6" x 2-1/4" & 4" x 4" cant	.040	L.F.	.005	.10	.14	.24
Flashing, aluminum, 0.040" thick	.050	S.F.	.002	.07	.08	.15
TOTAL			.051	1.81	1.31	3.12

DESCRIPTION	QUAN.	UNIT	MAN-HOURS	MAT.	INST.	TOTAL

Built-up Roofing Price Sheet

	QUAN.	UNIT	MAN-HOURS	COST PER S.F. MAT.	COST PER S.F. INST.	COST PER S.F. TOTAL
Membrane, asphalt, 4-plies #15 organic felt, gravel surfacing	1.000	S.F.	.025	.41	.64	1.05
Asbestos base sheet & 3-plies #15 asbestos felt	1.000	S.F.	.025	.37	.62	.99
3-plies type IV glass fiber felt	1.000	S.F.	.025	.43	.62	1.05
4-plies type IV glass fiber felt	1.000	S.F.	.028	.53	.67	1.20
Coal tar, 4-plies #15 organic felt, gravel surfacing	1.000	S.F.	.025	.68	.62	1.30
4-plies asbestos felt	1.000	S.F.	.025	.66	.64	1.30
3-plies type IV glass fiber felt	1.000	S.F.	.028	.54	.71	1.25
4-plies type IV glass fiber felt	1.000	S.F.	.025	.77	.63	1.40
Roll, asphalt, 1-ply #15 organic felt, 2-plies mineral surfaced	1.000	S.F.	.020	.36	.51	.87
3-plies type IV glass fiber, 1-ply mineral surfaced	1.000	S.F.	.022	.56	.54	1.10
Insulation boards, glass fiber, 1-1/16" thick	1.000	S.F.	.008	.55	.19	.74
1-5/8" thick	1.000	S.F.	.008	.78	.19	.97
1-7/8" thick	1.000	S.F.	.008	.84	.19	1.03
2-1/4" thick	1.000	S.F.	.010	.84	.23	1.07
Expanded perlite, 1" thick	1.000	S.F.	.010	.41	.23	.64
1-1/2" thick	1.000	S.F.	.010	.65	.24	.89
2" thick	1.000	S.F.	.011	.83	.27	1.10
Fiberboard, 1" thick	1.000	S.F.	.010	.30	.23	.53
1-1/2" thick	1.000	S.F.	.010	.48	.24	.72
2" thick	1.000	S.F.	.010	.67	.24	.91
Phenolic foam, 1-3/16" thick	1.000	S.F.	.008	.56	.19	.75
1-3/4" thick	1.000	S.F.	.019	1.13	.45	1.58
2" thick	1.000	S.F.	.010	.88	.24	1.12
3" thick	1.000	S.F.	.010	1.16	.23	1.39
Urethane, 1" thick	1.000	S.F.	.008	.62	.19	.81
1-1/2" thick	1.000	S.F.	.008	.79	.19	.98
2" thick	1.000	S.F.	.010	.88	.24	1.12
2-1/2" thick	1.000	S.F.	.010	1.03	.24	1.27
Glass fiber/urethane composite, 1-11/16" thick	1.000	S.F.	.008	.70	.19	.89
2" thick	1.000	S.F.	.010	.83	.23	1.06
2-5/8" thick	1.000	S.F.	.010	1.06	.23	1.29
Perlite/urethane composite, 1-1/4" thick	1.000	S.F.	.008	.78	.19	.97
1-1/2" thick	1.000	S.F.	.008	.84	.19	1.03
2-1/2" thick	1.000	S.F.	.011	1.05	.25	1.30
3" thick	1.000	S.F.	.011	1.23	.27	1.50
Extruded polystyrene, 1" thick	1.000	S.F.	.005	.55	.13	.68
2" thick	1.000	S.F.	.006	1.03	.16	1.19
3" thick	1.000	S.F.	.008	1.54	.19	1.73
Wood blocking, treated, 6" x 2" & 4" x 4" cant	.040	L.F.	.002	.07	.06	.13
6" x 4-1/2" & 4" x 4" cant	.040	L.F.	.005	.10	.14	.24
6" x 5" & 4" x 4" cant	.040	L.F.	.006	.13	.18	.31
Flashing, aluminum, 0.019" thick	.050	S.F.	.002	.04	.07	.11
0.032" thick	.050	S.F.	.002	.04	.08	.12
0.040" thick	.050	S.F.	.002	.07	.08	.15
Copper sheets, 16 oz., under 500 lbs.	.050	S.F.	.003	.14	.10	.24
Over 500 lbs.	.050	S.F.	.002	.14	.07	.21
20 oz., under 500 lbs.	.050	S.F.	.003	.18	.10	.28
Over 500 lbs.	.050	S.F.	.002	.18	.07	.25
Lead-coated copper, 16 oz.	.050	S.F.	.009	.55	.25	.80
20 oz.	.050	S.F.	.004	.32	.13	.45
Galvanized steel, 25 gauge	.050	S.F.	.002	.07	.07	.14
24 gauge	.050	S.F.	.002	.10	.07	.17
20 gauge	.050	S.F.	.002	.12	.07	.19
16 gauge	.050	S.F.	.002	.14	.07	.21
Stainless steel, 32 gauge	.050	S.F.	.002	.10	.07	.17
28 gauge	.050	S.F.	.002	.13	.07	.20
26 gauge	.050	S.F.	.002	.16	.07	.23
24 gauge	.050	S.F.	.002	.19	.07	.26

6 | INTERIORS — 04 Drywall & Thincoat Wall Systems

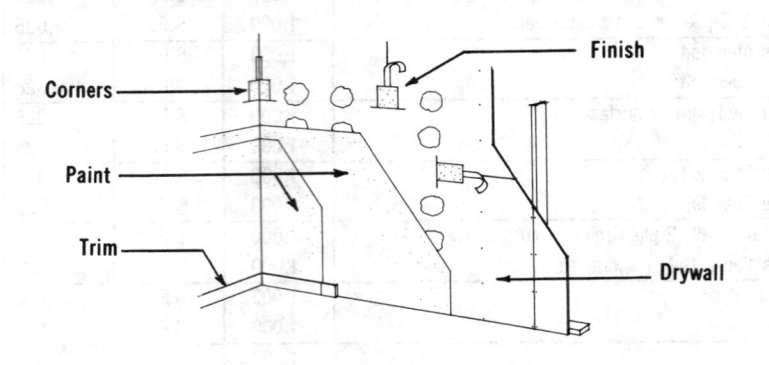

SYSTEM DESCRIPTION	QUAN.	UNIT	MAN-HOURS	MAT.	INST.	TOTAL
½" SHEETROCK, TAPED & FINISHED						
Drywall, ½" thick, standard	1.000	S.F.	.008	.19	.19	.38
Finish, taped & finished joints	1.000	S.F.	.008	.06	.19	.25
Corners, taped & finished, 32 L.F. per 12' x 12' room	.083	L.F.	.001	.01	.02	.03
Painting, primer & 2 coats	1.000	S.F.	.010	.10	.22	.32
Trim, baseboard, painted	.125	L.F.	.005	.14	.14	.28
TOTAL			.032	.50	.76	1.26
THINCOAT, SKIM-COAT, ON ½" BACKER DRYWALL						
Drywall, ½" thick, thincoat backer	1.000	S.F.	.008	.19	.19	.38
Thincoat plaster	1.000	S.F.	.011	.10	.25	.35
Corners, taped & finished, 32 L.F. per 12' x 12' room	.083	L.F.	.001	.01	.02	.03
Painting, primer & 2 coats	1.000	S.F.	.010	.10	.22	.32
Trim, baseboard, painted	.125	L.F.	.005	.14	.14	.28
TOTAL			.035	.54	.82	1.36
⅝" SHEETROCK, TAPED & FINISHED						
Drywall, ⅝" thick, standard	1.000	S.F.	.008	.23	.19	.42
Finish, taped & finished joints	1.000	S.F.	.008	.06	.19	.25
Corners, taped & finished, 32 L.F. per 12' x 12' room	.083	L.F.	.001	.01	.02	.03
Painting, primer & 2 coats	1.000	S.F.	.010	.10	.22	.32
Trim, baseboard, painted	.125	L.F.	.005	.14	.14	.28
TOTAL			.032	.54	.76	1.30

The costs in this system are based on a square foot of wall.
Do not deduct for openings.

DESCRIPTION	QUAN.	UNIT	MAN-HOURS	MAT.	INST.	TOTAL

Drywall & Thincoat Wall Price Sheet

	QUAN.	UNIT	MAN-HOURS	MAT.	INST.	TOTAL
Drywall-sheetrock, ½" thick, standard	1.000	S.F.	.008	.19	.19	.38
Fire resistant	1.000	S.F.	.008	.23	.19	.42
Water resistant	1.000	S.F.	.008	.30	.19	.49
⅝" thick, standard	1.000	S.F.	.008	.23	.19	.42
Fire resistant	1.000	S.F.	.008	.25	.19	.44
Water resistant	1.000	S.F.	.008	.34	.19	.53
Drywall backer for thincoat system, ½" thick	1.000	S.F.	.008	.19	.19	.38
⅝" thick	1.000	S.F.	.008	.23	.19	.42
Finish drywall, taped & finished	1.000	S.F.	.008	.06	.19	.25
Texture spray	1.000	S.F.	.015	.11	.33	.44
Thincoat plaster, including tape	1.000	S.F.	.011	.10	.25	.35
Corners drywall, taped & finished, 32 L.F. per 4' x 4' room	.250	L.F.	.003	.02	.08	.10
6' x 6' room	.110	L.F.	.001	.01	.03	.04
10' x 10' room	.100	L.F.	.001	.01	.03	.04
12' x 12' room	.083	L.F.	.001	.01	.02	.03
16' x 16' room	.063	L.F.		.01	.02	.03
Thincoat system, 32 L.F. per 4' x 4' room	.250	L.F.	.002	.03	.06	.09
6' x 6' room	.110	L.F.	.001	.01	.03	.04
10' x 10' room	.100	L.F.	.001	.01	.03	.04
12' x 12' room	.083	L.F.		.01	.02	.03
16' x 16' room	.063	L.F.		.01	.01	.02
Painting, primer, & 1 coat	1.000	S.F.	.007	.07	.14	.21
& 2 coats	1.000	S.F.	.010	.10	.22	.32
Wallpaper, $7/double roll	1.000	S.F.	.013	.24	.28	.52
$17/double roll	1.000	S.F.	.015	.42	.33	.75
$40/double roll	1.000	S.F.	.018	.84	.40	1.24
Tile, ceramic adhesive thin set, 4 ¼" x 4 ¼" tiles	1.000	S.F.	.089	2.04	1.82	3.86
6" x 6" tiles	1.000	S.F.	.080	2.53	1.64	4.17
Pregrouted sheets	1.000	S.F.	.067	3.91	1.39	5.30
Trim, painted or stained, baseboard	.125	L.F.	.005	.14	.14	.28
Base shoe	.125	L.F.	.004	.14	.12	.26
Chair rail	.125	L.F.	.003	.10	.11	.21
Cornice molding	.125	L.F.	.003	.07	.10	.17
Cove base, vinyl	.125	L.F.	.003	.06	.07	.13
Paneling, not including furring or trim						
Plywood, prefinished, ¼" thick, 4' x 8' sheets, vert. grooves						
Birch faced, minimum	1.000	S.F.	.032	.66	.80	1.46
Average	1.000	S.F.	.038	.99	.95	1.94
Maximum	1.000	S.F.	.046	1.38	1.14	2.52
Mahogany, African	1.000	S.F.	.040	1.71	1.00	2.71
Philippine (lauan)	1.000	S.F.	.032	.55	.80	1.35
Oak or cherry, minimum	1.000	S.F.	.032	1.49	.80	2.29
Maximum	1.000	S.F.	.040	2.64	1.00	3.64
Rosewood	1.000	S.F.	.050	10.45	1.25	11.70
Teak	1.000	S.F.	.040	2.64	1.00	3.64
Chestnut	1.000	S.F.	.043	3.96	1.09	5.05
Pecan	1.000	S.F.	.040	1.71	1.00	2.71
Walnut, minimum	1.000	S.F.	.032	2.26	.80	3.06
Maximum	1.000	S.F.	.040	4.24	1.01	5.25

6 | INTERIORS   08 | Drywall & Thincoat Ceiling Systems

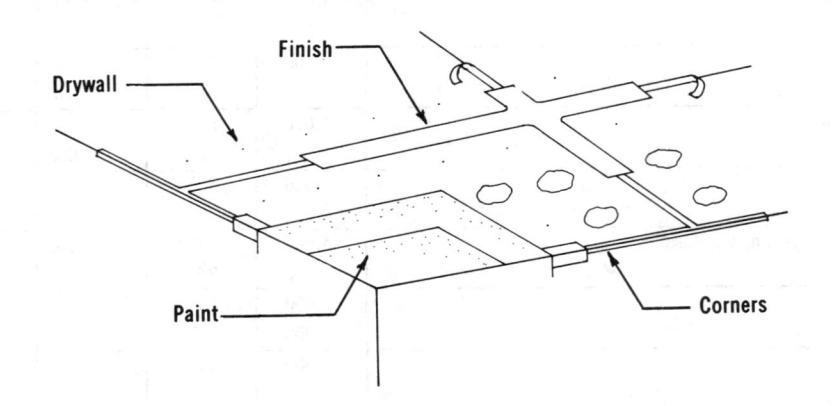

Labels on diagram: Drywall, Finish, Paint, Corners

SYSTEM DESCRIPTION	QUAN.	UNIT	MAN-HOURS	MAT.	INST.	TOTAL
½" SHEETROCK, TAPED & FINISHED						
Drywall, ½" thick, standard	1.000	S.F.	.008	.19	.19	.38
Finish, taped & finished	1.000	S.F.	.008	.06	.19	.25
Corners, taped & finished, 12' x 12' room	.333	L.F.	.004	.02	.11	.13
Paint, primer & 2 coats	1.000	S.F.	.010	.10	.22	.32
TOTAL			.030	.37	.71	1.08
THINCOAT, SKIM COAT ON ½" BACKER DRYWALL						
Drywall, ½" thick, thincoat backer	1.000	S.F.	.008	.19	.19	.38
Thincoat plaster	1.000	S.F.	.011	.10	.25	.35
Corners, taped & finished, 12' x 12' room	.333	L.F.	.004	.02	.11	.13
Paint, primer & 2 coats	1.000	S.F.	.010	.10	.22	.32
TOTAL			.033	.41	.77	1.18
WATER-RESISTANT SHEETROCK, ½" THICK, TAPED & FINISHED						
Drywall, ½" thick, water-resistant	1.000	S.F.	.008	.30	.19	.49
Finish, taped & finished	1.000	S.F.	.008	.06	.19	.25
Corners, taped & finished, 12' x 12' room	.333	L.F.	.004	.02	.11	.13
Paint, primer & 2 coats	1.000	S.F.	.010	.10	.22	.32
TOTAL			.030	.48	.71	1.19
⅝" SHEETROCK, TAPED & FINISHED						
Drywall, ⅝" thick, standard	1.000	S.F.	.008	.23	.19	.42
Finish, taped & finished	1.000	S.F.	.008	.06	.19	.25
Corners, taped & finished, 12' x 12' room	.333	L.F.	.004	.02	.11	.13
Paint, primer & 2 coats	1.000	S.F.	.010	.10	.22	.32
TOTAL			.030	.41	.71	1.12

The costs in this system are based on a square foot of ceiling.

DESCRIPTION	QUAN.	UNIT	MAN-HOURS	MAT.	INST.	TOTAL

Drywall & Thincoat Ceilings

	QUAN.	UNIT	MAN-HOURS	MAT.	INST.	TOTAL
Drywall-sheetrock, ½" thick, standard	1.000	S.F.	.008	.19	.19	.38
Fire resistant	1.000	S.F.	.008	.23	.19	.42
Water resistant	1.000	S.F.	.008	.30	.19	.49
⅝" thick, standard	1.000	S.F.	.008	.23	.19	.42
Fire resistant	1.000	S.F.	.008	.25	.19	.44
Water resistant	1.000	S.F.	.008	.34	.19	.53
Drywall backer for thincoat system, ½" thick	1.000	S.F.	.016	.42	.38	.80
⅝" thick	1.000	S.F.	.016	.46	.38	.84
Finish drywall, taped & finished	1.000	S.F.	.008	.06	.19	.25
Texture spray	1.000	S.F.	.015	.11	.33	.44
Thincoat plaster	1.000	S.F.	.011	.10	.25	.35
Corners taped & finished, 4' x 4' room	1.000	L.F.	.015	.06	.34	.40
6' x 6' room	.667	L.F.	.010	.04	.23	.27
10' x 10' room	.400	L.F.	.006	.02	.14	.16
12' x 12' room	.333	L.F.	.004	.02	.11	.13
16' x 16' room	.250	L.F.	.002	.01	.06	.07
Thincoat system, 4' x 4' room	1.000	L.F.	.011	.10	.25	.35
6' x 6' room	.667	L.F.	.007	.07	.16	.23
10' x 10' room	.400	L.F.	.004	.04	.10	.14
12' x 12' room	.333	L.F.	.003	.03	.09	.12
16' x 16' room	.250	L.F.	.002	.02	.05	.07
Painting, primer & 1 coat	1.000	S.F.	.007	.07	.14	.21
& 2 coats	1.000	S.F.	.010	.10	.22	.32
Wallpaper, $9.70/double roll	1.000	S.F.	.013	.24	.28	.52
$20.00/double roll	1.000	S.F.	.015	.42	.33	.75
$44.00/double roll	1.000	S.F.	.018	.84	.40	1.24
Tile, ceramic adhesive thin set, 4 ¼" x 4 ¼" tiles	1.000	S.F.	.089	2.04	1.82	3.86
6" x 6" tiles	1.000	S.F.	.080	2.53	1.64	4.17
Pregrouted sheets	1.000	S.F.	.067	3.91	1.39	5.30

6 | INTERIORS — 12 | Plaster & Stucco Wall Systems

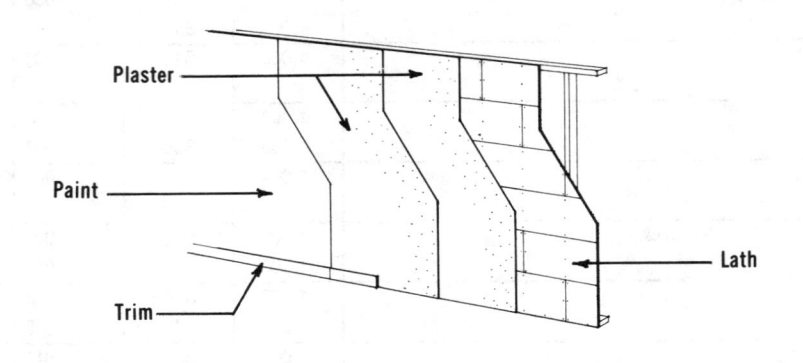

SYSTEM DESCRIPTION	QUAN.	UNIT	MAN-HOURS	MAT.	INST.	TOTAL
PLASTER ON GYPSUM LATH						
Plaster, gypsum or perlite, 2 coats	1.000	S.F.	.042	.37	.95	1.32
Lath, ⅜" gypsum	1.000	S.F.	.010	.40	.24	.64
Corners, expanded metal, 32 L.F. per 12' x 12' room	.083	L.F.	.001	.01	.04	.05
Painting, primer & 2 coats	1.000	S.F.	.010	.10	.22	.32
Trim, baseboard, painted	.125	L.F.	.005	.14	.14	.28
TOTAL			.068	1.02	1.59	2.61
PLASTER ON METAL LATH						
Plaster, gypsum or perlite, 2 coats	1.000	S.F.	.042	.37	.95	1.32
Lath, 2.5 Lb. diamond, metal	1.000	S.F.	.010	.20	.24	.44
Corners, expanded metal, 32 L.F. per 12' x 12' room	.083	L.F.	.001	.01	.04	.05
Painting, primer & 2 coats	1.000	S.F.	.010	.10	.22	.32
Trim, baseboard, painted	.125	L.F.	.005	.14	.14	.28
TOTAL			.068	.82	1.59	2.41
STUCCO ON METAL LATH						
Stucco, 2 coats	1.000	S.F.	.041	.63	.92	1.55
Lath, 2.5 Lb. diamond, metal	1.000	S.F.	.010	.20	.24	.44
Corners, expanded metal, 32 L.F. per 12' x 12' room	.083	L.F.	.001	.01	.04	.05
Painting, primer & 2 coats	1.000	S.F.	.010	.10	.22	.32
Trim, baseboard, painted	.125	L.F.	.005	.14	.14	.28
TOTAL			.067	1.08	1.56	2.64

The costs in these systems are based on a per square foot of wall area.
Do not deduct for openings.

DESCRIPTION	QUAN.	UNIT	MAN-HOURS	MAT.	INST.	TOTAL

Plaster & Stucco Wall Price Sheet

	QUAN.	UNIT	MAN-HOURS	COST PER S.F. MAT.	COST PER S.F. INST.	COST PER S.F. TOTAL
Plaster, gypsum or perlite, 2 coats	1.000	S.F.	.042	.37	.95	1.32
3 coats	1.000	S.F.	.051	.52	1.15	1.67
Lath, gypsum, standard, ⅜″ thick	1.000	S.F.	.010	.40	.24	.64
½″ thick	1.000	S.F.	.013	.47	.29	.76
Fire resistant, ⅜″ thick	1.000	S.F.	.013	.45	.29	.74
½″ thick	1.000	S.F.	.014	.48	.32	.80
Metal, diamond, 2.5 Lb.	1.000	S.F.	.010	.20	.24	.44
3.4 Lb.	1.000	S.F.	.012	.22	.27	.49
Rib, 2.75 Lb.	1.000	S.F.	.012	.21	.27	.48
3.4 Lb.	1.000	S.F.	.013	.24	.29	.53
Corners, expanded metal, 32 L.F. per 4′ x 4′ room	.250	L.F.	.005	.02	.12	.14
6′ x 6′ room	.110	L.F.	.002	.01	.05	.06
10′ x 10′ room	.100	L.F.	.002	.01	.05	.06
12′ x 12′ room	.083	L.F.	.001	.01	.04	.05
16′ x 16′ room	.063	L.F.	.001	.01	.03	.04
Painting, primer & 1 coats	1.000	S.F.	.007	.07	.14	.21
Primer & 2 coats	1.000	S.F.	.010	.10	.22	.32
Wallpaper, $7.00/double roll	1.000	S.F.	.013	.24	.28	.52
$17.00/double roll	1.000	S.F.	.015	.42	.33	.75
$40.00/double roll	1.000	S.F.	.018	.84	.40	1.24
Tile, ceramic thin set, 4-¼″ x 4-¼″ tiles	1.000	S.F.	.089	2.04	1.82	3.86
6″ x 6″ tiles	1.000	S.F.	.080	2.53	1.64	4.17
Pregrouted sheets	1.000	S.F.	.067	3.91	1.39	5.30
Trim, painted or stained, baseboard	.125	L.F.	.005	.14	.14	.28
Base shoe	.125	L.F.	.004	.14	.12	.26
Chair rail	.125	L.F.	.003	.10	.11	.21
Cornice molding	.125	L.F.	.003	.07	.10	.17
Cove base, vinyl	.125	L.F.	.003	.06	.07	.13
Paneling not including furring or trim						
Plywood, prefinished, ¼″ thick, 4′ x 8′ sheets, vert. grooves						
Birch faced, minimum	1.000	S.F.	.032	.66	.80	1.46
Average	1.000	S.F.	.038	.99	.95	1.94
Maximum	1.000	S.F.	.046	1.38	1.14	2.52
Mahogany, African	1.000	S.F.	.040	1.71	1.00	2.71
Philippine (lauan)	1.000	S.F.	.032	.55	.80	1.35
Oak or cherry, minimum	1.000	S.F.	.032	1.49	.80	2.29
Maximum	1.000	S.F.	.040	2.64	1.00	3.64
Rosewood	1.000	S.F.	.050	10.45	1.25	11.70
Teak	1.000	S.F.	.040	2.64	1.00	3.64
Chestnut	1.000	S.F.	.043	3.96	1.09	5.05
Pecan	1.000	S.F.	.040	1.71	1.00	2.71
Walnut, minimum	1.000	S.F.	.032	2.26	.80	3.06
Maximum	1.000	S.F.	.040	4.24	1.01	5.25

6 | INTERIORS — 16 | Plaster & Stucco Ceiling Systems

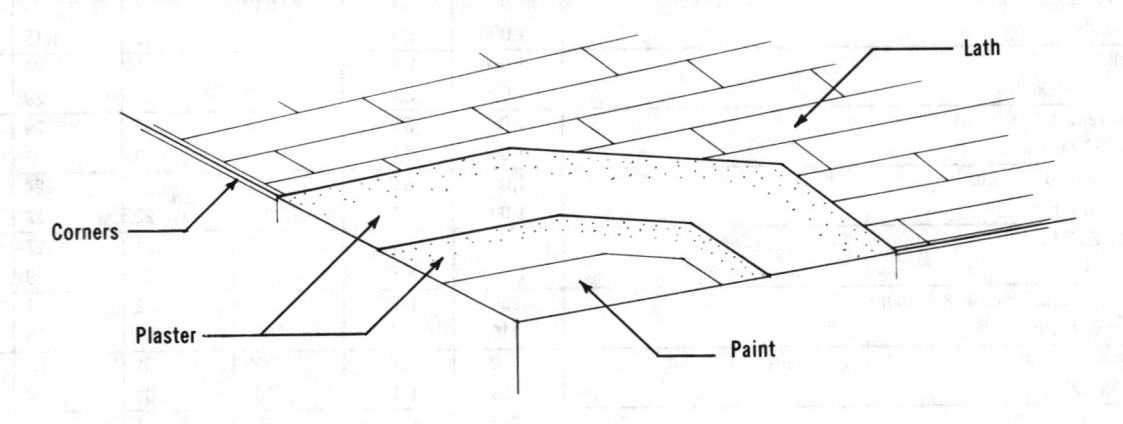

SYSTEM DESCRIPTION	QUAN.	UNIT	MAN-HOURS	MAT.	INST.	TOTAL
PLASTER ON GYPSUM LATH						
Plaster, gypsum or perlite,	1.000	S.F.	.048	.37	1.09	1.46
Lath, ⅜" gypsum	1.000	S.F.	.014	.40	.33	.73
Corners, expanded metal, 12' x 12' room	.330	L.F.	.006	.03	.16	.19
Painting, primer & 2 coats	1.000	S.F.	.010	.10	.22	.32
TOTAL			.078	.90	1.80	2.70
PLASTER ON METAL LATH						
Plaster, gypsum or perlite, 2 coats	1.000	S.F.	.048	.37	1.09	1.46
Lath, 2.5 Lb. diamond, metal	1.000	S.F.	.012	.20	.27	.47
Corners, expanded metal, 12' x 12' room	.330	L.F.	.006	.03	.16	.19
Painting, primer & 2 coats	1.000	S.F.	.010	.10	.22	.32
TOTAL			.076	.70	1.74	2.44
STUCCO ON GYPSUM LATH						
Stucco, 2 coats	1.000	S.F.	.041	.63	.92	1.55
Lath, ⅜" gypsum	1.000	S.F.	.014	.40	.33	.73
Corners, expanded metal, 12' x 12' room	.330	L.F.	.006	.03	.16	.19
Painting, primer & 2 coats	1.000	S.F.	.010	.10	.22	.32
TOTAL			.071	1.16	1.63	2.79
STUCCO ON METAL LATH						
Stucco, 2 coats	1.000	S.F.	.041	.63	.92	1.55
Lath, 2.5 Lb. diamond, metal	1.000	S.F.	.012	.20	.27	.47
Corners, expanded metal, 12' x 12' room	.330	L.F.	.006	.03	.16	.19
Painting, primer & 2 coats	1.000	S.F.	.010	.10	.22	.32
TOTAL			.069	.96	1.57	2.53

The costs in these systems are based on a square foot of ceiling area.

DESCRIPTION	QUAN.	UNIT	MAN-HOURS	MAT.	INST.	TOTAL

Plaster & Stucco Ceiling Price Sheet

	QUAN.	UNIT	MAN-HOURS	MAT.	INST.	TOTAL
Plaster, gypsum or perlite, 2 coats	1.000	S.F.	.048	.37	1.09	1.46
3 coats	1.000	S.F.	.051	.52	1.15	1.67
Lath, gypsum, standard, ⅜" thick	1.000	S.F.	.014	.40	.33	.73
½" thick	1.000	S.F.	.015	.43	.34	.77
Fire resistant, ⅜" thick	1.000	S.F.	.017	.45	.38	.83
½" thick	1.000	S.F.	.018	.48	.41	.89
Metal, diamond, 2.5 Lb.	1.000	S.F.	.012	.20	.27	.47
3.4 Lb.	1.000	S.F.	.015	.22	.34	.56
Rib, 2.75 Lb.	1.000	S.F.	.012	.21	.27	.48
3.4 Lb.	1.000	S.F.	.013	.24	.29	.53
Corners expanded metal, 4' x 4' room	1.000	L.F.	.020	.09	.48	.57
6' x 6' room	.667	L.F.	.013	.06	.32	.38
10' x 10' room	.400	L.F.	.008	.04	.19	.23
12' x 12' room	.333	L.F.	.006	.03	.16	.19
16' x 16' room	.250	L.F.	.003	.02	.09	.11
Painting, primer & 1 coat	1.000	S.F.	.007	.07	.14	.21
Primer & 2 coats	1.000	S.F.	.010	.10	.22	.32

Plaster & Stucco Ceiling Price Sheet

6 | INTERIORS — 18 Suspended Ceiling Systems

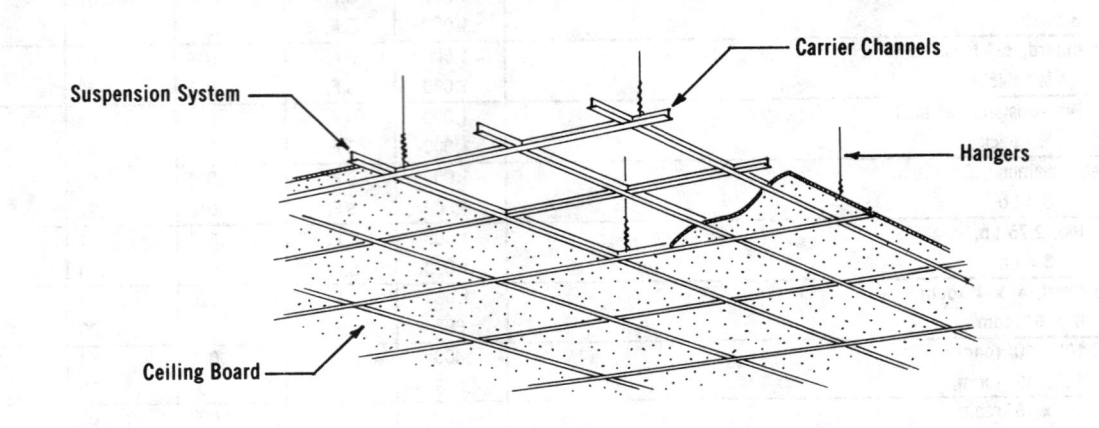

Diagram labels: Suspension System, Carrier Channels, Hangers, Ceiling Board

SYSTEM DESCRIPTION	QUAN.	UNIT	MAN-HOURS	MAT.	INST.	TOTAL
2' X 2' GRID, FILM FACED FIBERGLASS, ⅝" THICK						
Suspension system, 2' x 2' grid, T bar	1.000	S.F.	.012	.54	.29	.83
Ceiling board, film faced fiberglass, ⅝" thick	1.000	S.F.	.013	.43	.31	.74
Carrier channels, 1-½" x ¾"	1.000	S.F.	.017	.15	.41	.56
Hangers, #12 wire	1.000	S.F.	.001	.02	.04	.06
TOTAL			.043	1.14	1.05	2.19
2' X 4' GRID, FILM FACED FIBERGLASS, ⅝" THICK						
Suspension system, 2' x 4' grid, T bar	1.000	S.F.	.010	.41	.24	.65
Ceiling board, film faced fiberglass, ⅝" thick	1.000	S.F.	.013	.43	.31	.74
Carrier channels, 1-½" x ¾"	1.000	S.F.	.017	.15	.41	.56
Hangers, #12 wire	1.000	S.F.	.001	.02	.04	.06
TOTAL			.041	1.01	1.00	2.01
2' X 2' GRID, MINERAL FIBER, REVEAL EDGE, 1" THICK						
Suspension system, 2' x 2' grid, T bar	1.000	S.F.	.012	.54	.29	.83
Ceiling board, mineral fiber, reveal edge, 1" thick	1.000	S.F.	.013	.98	.32	1.30
Carrier channels, 1-½" x ¾"	1.000	S.F.	.017	.15	.41	.56
Hangers, #12 wire	1.000	S.F.	.001	.02	.04	.06
TOTAL			.043	1.69	1.06	2.75
2' X 4' GRID, MINERAL FIBER, REVEAL EDGE, 1" THICK						
Suspension system, 2' x 4' grid, T bar	1.000	S.F.	.010	.41	.24	.65
Ceiling board, mineral fiber, reveal edge, 1" thick	1.000	S.F.	.013	.98	.32	1.30
Carrier channels, 1-½" x ¾"	1.000	S.F.	.017	.15	.41	.56
Hangers, #12 wire	1.000	S.F.	.001	.02	.04	.06
TOTAL			.041	1.56	1.01	2.57

DESCRIPTION	QUAN.	UNIT	MAN-HOURS	MAT.	INST.	TOTAL

Suspended Ceiling Price Sheet

	QUAN.	UNIT	MAN-HOURS	COST PER S.F. MAT.	COST PER S.F. INST.	COST PER S.F. TOTAL
Suspension systems, T bar, 2' x 2' grid	1.000	S.F.	.012	.54	.29	.83
2' x 4' grid	1.000	S.F.	.010	.41	.24	.65
Concealed Z bar, 12" module	1.000	S.F.	.015	.62	.36	.98
Ceiling boards, fiberglass, film faced, 2' x 2' or 2' x 4', 5/8" thick	1.000	S.F.	.013	.43	.31	.74
3/4" thick	1.000	S.F.	.013	.50	.31	.81
3" thick thermal R11	1.000	S.F.	.016	1.05	.38	1.43
Glass cloth faced, 3/4" thick	1.000	S.F.	.016	1.36	.39	1.75
1" thick	1.000	S.F.	.016	1.52	.38	1.90
1-1/2" thick, nubby face	1.000	S.F.	.016	1.85	.38	2.23
Mineral fiber boards, 5/8" thick, aluminum face 2' x 2'	1.000	S.F.	.013	1.16	.31	1.47
2' x 4'	1.000	S.F.	.012	1.12	.30	1.42
Standard faced, 2' x 2' or 2' x 4'	1.000	S.F.	.012	.50	.28	.78
Plastic coated face, 2' x 2' or 2' x 4'	1.000	S.F.	.020	.77	.48	1.25
Fire rated, 2 hour rating, 5/8" thick	1.000	S.F.	.012	.72	.28	1.00
Reveal edge, 2' x 2' or 2' x 4', painted, 1" thick	1.000	S.F.	.013	.98	.32	1.30
2" thick	1.000	S.F.	.015	1.60	.34	1.94
2-1/2" thick	1.000	S.F.	.016	2.18	.38	2.56
3" thick	1.000	S.F.	.018	2.51	.42	2.93
Luminous panels, prismatic, acrylic	1.000	S.F.	.020	1.36	.48	1.84
Polystyrene	1.000	S.F.	.020	.72	.47	1.19
Flat or ribbed, acrylic	1.000	S.F.	.020	2.42	.48	2.90
Polystyrene	1.000	S.F.	.020	1.65	.48	2.13
Drop pan, white, acrylic	1.000	S.F.	.020	3.58	.47	4.05
Polystyrene	1.000	S.F.	.020	2.97	.48	3.45
Carrier channels, 4'-0" on center, 3/4" x 1-1/2"	1.000	S.F.	.017	.15	.41	.56
1-1/2" x 3-1/2"	1.000	S.F.	.017	.39	.40	.79
Hangers, #12 wire	1.000	S.F.	.001	.02	.04	.06

6 | INTERIORS

20 | Interior Door Systems

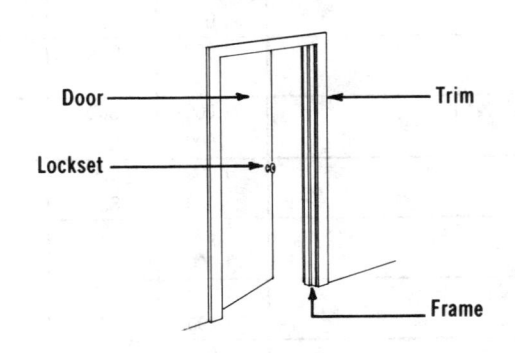

SYSTEM DESCRIPTION	QUAN.	UNIT	MAN-HOURS	MAT.	INST.	TOTAL
LAUAN, FLUSH DOOR, HOLLOW CORE						
Door, flush, lauan, hollow core, 2'-8" wide x 6'-8" high	1.000	Ea.	.889	31.90	22.10	54.00
Frame, pine, 4-⅝" jamb	17.000	L.F.	.731	26.18	18.19	44.37
Trim, casing, painted	34.000	L.F.	1.360	24.48	32.64	57.12
Butt hinges, chrome, 3-½" x 3-½"	1.500	Pr.		31.50		31.50
Lockset, passage	1.000	Ea.	.500	11.28	11.72	23.00
Paint, door & frame, primer & 2 coats	2.000	Face	2.466	8.26	54.24	62.50
TOTAL			5.946	133.60	138.89	272.49
BIRCH, FLUSH DOOR, HOLLOW CORE						
Door, flush, birch, hollow core, 2'-8" wide x 6'-8" high	1.000	Ea.	.889	38.50	22.50	61.00
Frame, pine, 4-⅝" jamb	17.000	L.F.	.731	26.18	18.19	44.37
Trim, casing, painted	34.000	L.F.	1.360	24.48	32.64	57.12
Butt hinges, chrome, 3-½" x 3-½"	1.500	Pr.		31.50		31.50
Lockset, passage	1.000	Ea.	.500	11.28	11.72	23.00
Paint, door & frame, primer & 2 coats	2.000	Face	2.466	8.26	54.24	62.50
TOTAL			5.946	140.20	139.29	279.49
RAISED PANEL, SOLID, PINE DOOR						
Door, pine, raised panel, 2'-8" wide x 6'-8" high	1.000	Ea.	.889	117.70	22.30	140.00
Frame, pine, 4-⅝" jamb	17.000	L.F.	.731	26.18	18.19	44.37
Trim, casing, painted	34.000	L.F.	1.360	24.48	32.64	57.12
Butt hinges, bronze, 3-½" x 3-½"	1.500	Pr.		63.00		63.00
Lockset, passage	1.000	Ea.	.500	11.28	11.72	23.00
Paint, door & frame, primer & 2 coats	2.000	Face	3.066	8.60	67.30	75.90
TOTAL			6.546	251.24	152.15	403.39

The costs in these systems are based on a cost per each door.

DESCRIPTION	QUAN.	UNIT	MAN-HOURS	MAT.	INST.	TOTAL

Interior Door Price Sheet

	QUAN.	UNIT	MAN-HOURS	COST EACH MAT.	COST EACH INST.	TOTAL
Door, hollow core, lauan 1-⅜" thick, 6'-8" high x 1'-6" wide	1.000	Ea.	.842	30.80	21.20	52.00
2'-0" wide	1.000	Ea.	.889	30.80	22.20	53.00
2'-6" wide	1.000	Ea.	.889	31.90	22.10	54.00
2'-8" wide	1.000	Ea.	.889	31.90	22.10	54.00
3'-0" wide	1.000	Ea.	.941	34.10	23.90	58.00
Birch 1-⅜" thick, 6'-8" high x 1'-6" wide	1.000	Ea.	.842	34.10	20.90	55.00
2'-0" wide	1.000	Ea.	.889	34.10	21.90	56.00
2'-6" wide	1.000	Ea.	.889	38.50	22.50	61.00
2'-8" wide	1.000	Ea.	.889	38.50	22.50	61.00
3'-0" wide	1.000	Ea.	.941	41.80	23.20	65.00
Louvered pine 1-⅜" thick, 6'-8" high x 1'-6" wide	1.000	Ea.	.842	82.50	22.50	105.00
2'-0" wide	1.000	Ea.	.889	88.00	22.00	110.00
2'-6" wide	1.000	Ea.	.889	99.00	21.00	120.00
2'-8" wide	1.000	Ea.	.889	121.00	24.00	145.00
3'-0" wide	1.000	Ea.	.941	121.00	24.00	145.00
Paneled pine 1-⅜" thick, 6'-8" high x 1'-6" wide	1.000	Ea.	.842	93.50	21.50	115.00
2'-0" wide	1.000	Ea.	.889	97.90	22.10	120.00
2'-6" wide	1.000	Ea.	.889	111.10	23.90	135.00
2'-8" wide	1.000	Ea.	.889	117.70	22.30	140.00
3'-0" wide	1.000	Ea.	.941	126.50	23.50	150.00
Frame, pine, 1'-6" thru 2'-0" wide door, 3-⅝" deep	16.000	L.F.	.688	20.32	17.12	37.44
4-⅝" deep	16.000	L.F.	.688	24.64	17.12	41.76
5-⅝" deep	16.000	L.F.	.688	34.88	17.12	52.00
2'-6" thru 3'0" wide door, 3-⅝" deep	17.000	L.F.	.731	21.59	18.19	39.78
4-⅝" deep	17.000	L.F.	.731	26.18	18.19	44.37
5-⅝" deep	17.000	L.F.	.731	37.06	18.19	55.25
Trim, casing, painted, both sides, 1'-6" thru 2'-6" wide door	32.000	L.F.	1.632	22.40	38.40	60.80
2'-6" thru 3'-0" wide door	34.000	L.F.	1.734	23.80	40.80	64.60
Butt hinges 3-½" x 3-½", steel plated, chrome	1.500	Pr.		31.50		31.50
Bronze	1.500	Pr.		63.00		63.00
Locksets, passage, minimum	1.000	Ea.	.500	11.28	11.72	23.00
Maximum	1.000	Ea.	.575	12.97	13.48	26.45
Privacy, miniumum	1.000	Ea.	.625	14.10	14.65	28.75
Maximum	1.000	Ea.	.675	15.23	15.82	31.05
Paint 2 sides, primer & 2 cts., flush door, 1'-6" to 2'-0" wide	2.000	Face	2.353	7.05	51.67	58.72
2'-6" thru 3'-0" wide	2.000	Face	2.942	8.82	64.58	73.40
Louvered door, 1'-6" thru 2'-0" wide	2.000	Face	2.452	6.88	53.84	60.72
2'-6" thru 3'-0" wide	2.000	Face	3.066	8.60	67.30	75.90
Paneled door, 1'-6" thru 2'-0" wide	2.000	Face	2.452	6.88	53.84	60.72
2'-6" thru 3'-0" wide	2.000	Face	3.066	8.60	67.30	75.90

6 | INTERIORS — 24 Closet Door Systems

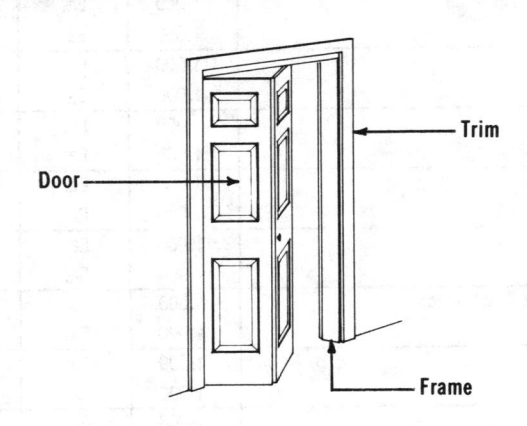

SYSTEM DESCRIPTION	QUAN.	UNIT	MAN-HOURS	MAT.	INST.	TOTAL
BI-PASSING, FLUSH, LAUAN, HOLLOW CORE, 4'-0" X 6'-8"						
Door, flush, lauan, hollow core, 4'-0" x 6'-8" opening	1.000	Ea.	1.330	82.50	32.50	115.00
Frame, pine, 4-5/8" jamb	18.000	L.F.	.774	27.72	19.26	46.98
Trim, both sides, casing, painted	36.000	L.F.	1.836	25.20	43.20	68.40
Paint, door & frame, primer & 2 coats	2.000	Face	2.466	8.26	54.24	62.50
TOTAL			6.406	143.68	149.20	292.88
BI-PASSING, FLUSH, BIRCH, HOLLOW CORE, 6'-0" X 6'-8"						
Door, flush, birch, hollow core, 6'-0" x 6'-8" opening	1.000	Ea.	1.600	118.80	41.20	160.00
Frame, pine, 4-5/8" jamb	19.000	L.F.	.817	29.26	20.33	49.59
Trim, both sides, casing, painted	38.000	L.F.	1.938	26.60	45.60	72.20
Paint, door & frame, primer & 2 coats	2.000	Face	3.082	10.33	67.80	78.13
TOTAL			7.437	184.99	174.93	359.92
BI-FOLD, PINE, PANELED, 3'-0" X 6'-8"						
Door, pine, paneled, 3'-0" x 6'-8" opening	1.000	Ea.	1.230	83.60	31.40	115.00
Frame, pine, 4-5/8" jamb	17.000	L.F.	.731	26.18	18.19	44.37
Trim, both sides, casing, painted	34.000	L.F.	1.734	23.80	40.80	64.60
Paint, door & frame, primer & 2 coats	2.000	Face	3.066	8.60	67.30	75.90
TOTAL			6.761	142.18	157.69	299.87
BI-FOLD, PINE, LOUVERED, 6'-0" X 6'-8"						
Door, pine, louvered, 6'-0" x 6'-8" opening	1.000	Ea.	1.600	165.00	40.00	205.00
Frame, pine, 4-5/8" jamb	19.000	L.F.	.817	29.26	20.33	49.59
Trim, both sides, casing, painted	38.000	L.F.	1.938	26.60	45.60	72.20
Paint, door & frame, primer & 2 coats	2.000	Face	3.832	10.76	84.12	94.88
TOTAL			8.187	231.62	190.05	421.67

The costs in this system are based on a cost per each door.

DESCRIPTION	QUAN.	UNIT	MAN-HOURS	MAT.	INST.	TOTAL

Closet Door Price Sheet

	QUAN.	UNIT	MAN-HOURS	COST EACH MAT.	COST EACH INST.	TOTAL
Doors, bi-passing, pine, louvered, 4'-0" x 6'-8" opening	1.000	Ea.	1.330	112.20	32.80	145.00
6'-0" x 6'-8" opening	1.000	Ea.	1.600	139.70	40.30	180.00
Paneled, 4'-0" x 6'-8" opening	1.000	Ea.	1.330	201.30	33.70	235.00
6'-0" x 6'-8" opening	1.000	Ea.	1.600	253.00	42.00	295.00
Flush, birch, hollow core, 4'-0" x 6'-8" opening	1.000	Ea.	1.330	93.50	31.50	125.00
6'-0" x 6'-8" opening	1.000	Ea.	1.600	118.80	41.20	160.00
Flush, lauan, hollow core, 4'-0" x 6'-8" opening	1.000	Ea.	1.330	82.50	32.50	115.00
6'-0" x 6'-8" opening	1.000	Ea.	1.600	99.00	41.00	140.00
Bi-fold, pine, louvered, 3'-0" x 6'-8" opening	1.000	Ea.	1.230	83.60	31.40	115.00
6'-0" x 6'-8" opening	1.000	Ea.	1.600	165.00	40.00	205.00
Paneled, 3'-0" x 6'-8" opening	1.000	Ea.	1.230	83.60	31.40	115.00
6'-0" x 6'-8" opening	1.000	Ea.	1.600	165.00	40.00	205.00
Flush, birch, hollow core, 3'-0" x 6'-8" opening	1.000	Ea.	1.230	60.50	30.50	91.00
6'-0" x 6'-8" opening	1.000	Ea.	1.600	115.50	39.50	155.00
Flush, lauan, hollow core, 3'-0" x 6'8" opening	1.000	Ea.	1.230	126.50	28.50	155.00
6'-0" x 6'-8" opening	1.000	Ea.	1.600	242.00	38.00	280.00
Frame pine, 3'-0" door, 3-5/8" deep	17.000	L.F.	.731	21.59	18.19	39.78
4-5/8" deep	17.000	L.F.	.731	26.18	18.19	44.37
5-5/8" deep	17.000	L.F.	.731	37.06	18.19	55.25
4'-0" door, 3-5/8" deep	18.000	L.F.	.774	22.86	19.26	42.12
4-5/8" deep	18.000	L.F.	.774	27.72	19.26	46.98
5-5/8" deep	18.000	L.F.	.774	39.24	19.26	58.50
6'-0" door, 3-5/8" deep	19.000	L.F.	.817	24.13	20.33	44.46
4-5/8" deep	19.000	L.F.	.817	29.26	20.33	49.59
5-5/8" deep	19.000	L.F.	.817	41.42	20.33	61.75
Trim both sides, painted 3'-0" x 6'-8" door	34.000	L.F.	1.734	23.80	40.80	64.60
4'-0" x 6'-8" door	36.000	L.F.	1.836	25.20	43.20	68.40
6'-0" x 6'-8" door	38.000	L.F.	1.938	26.60	45.60	72.20
Paint 2 sides, primer & 2 cts., flush door & frame, 3' x 6'-8" opng	2.000	Face	1.849	6.20	40.68	46.88
4'-0" x 6'-8" opening	2.000	Face	2.466	8.26	54.24	62.50
6'-0" x 6'-8" opening	2.000	Face	3.082	10.33	67.80	78.13
Paneled door & frame, 3'-0" x 6'-8" opening	2.000	Face	2.299	6.46	50.47	56.93
4'-0" x 6'-8" opening	2.000	Face	3.066	8.60	67.30	75.90
6'-0" x 6'-8" opening	2.000	Face	3.832	10.76	84.12	94.88
Louvered door & frame, 3'-0" x 6'-8" opening	2.000	Face	2.299	6.46	50.47	56.93
4'-0" x 6'-8" opening	2.000	Face	3.066	8.60	67.30	75.90
6'-0" x 6'-8" opening	2.000	Face	3.832	10.76	84.12	94.88

6 | INTERIORS — 60 | Carpet Systems

SYSTEM DESCRIPTION	QUAN.	UNIT	MAN-HOURS	MAT.	INST.	TOTAL
Carpet, direct glue-down, nylon, level loop, 26 oz.	1.000	S.F.	.018	1.68	.41	2.09
32 oz.	1.000	S.F.	.018	2.00	.41	2.41
40 oz.	1.000	S.F.	.018	2.54	.41	2.95
Nylon, plush, 20 oz.	1.000	S.F.	.018	1.03	.42	1.45
24 oz.	1.000	S.F.	.018	1.20	.41	1.61
30 oz.	1.000	S.F.	.018	1.50	.41	1.91
36 oz.	1.000	S.F.	.018	1.83	.41	2.24
42 oz.	1.000	S.F.	.022	2.18	.49	2.67
48 oz.	1.000	S.F.	.022	2.63	.49	3.12
54 oz.	1.000	S.F.	.022	2.99	.50	3.49
Needle bonded, 20 oz.	100.0	S.F.				
Olefin, 15 oz.	1.000	S.F.	.018	.51	.41	.92
22 oz.	1.000	S.F.	.018	.63	.41	1.04
Scrim installed nylon spongeback carpet, 20 oz.	1.000	S.F.	.018	1.84	.39	2.23
60 oz.	1.000	S.F.	.018	2.56	.40	2.96
Tile, foam backed, needle punch	1.000	S.F.	.017	2.20	.40	2.60
Tufted loop or shag	1.000	S.F.	.017	1.93	.39	2.32
Wool, 36 oz., level loop	1.000	S.F.	.018	3.72	.41	4.13
32 oz., patterned	1.000	S.F.	.020	3.48	.45	3.93
48 oz., patterned	1.000	S.F.	.020	4.75	.45	5.20
Padding, sponge rubber cushion, minimum	1.000	S.F.	.006	.28	.13	.41
Maximum	1.000	S.F.	.006	.73	.13	.86
Felt, 32 oz. to 56 oz., minimum	1.000	S.F.	.006	.31	.13	.44
Maximum	1.000	S.F.	.006	.48	.14	.62
Bonded urethane, ⅜" thick, minimum	1.000	S.F.	.006	.34	.14	.48
Maximum	1.000	S.F.	.006	.58	.14	.72
Prime urethane, ¼" thick, minimum	1.000	S.F.	.006	.21	.13	.34
Maximum	1.000	S.F.	.006	.36	.14	.50
Stairs, for stairs, add to above carpet prices	1.000	Riser	.267		6.10	6.10
Underlayment plywood, ⅜" thick	1.000	S.F.	.011	.35	.27	.62
½" thick	1.000	S.F.	.011	.40	.28	.68
⅝" thick	1.000	S.F.	.011	.48	.29	.77
¾" thick	1.000	S.F.	.012	.56	.31	.87
Particle board, ⅜" thick	1.000	S.F.	.011	.29	.27	.56
½" thick	1.000	S.F.	.011	.31	.28	.59
⅝" thick	1.000	S.F.	.011	.34	.29	.63
¾" thick	1.000	S.F.	.012	.39	.31	.70
Hardboard, 4' x 4', 0.215" thick	1.000	S.F.	.011	.31	.27	.58

6 INTERIORS — 64 Flooring Systems

SYSTEM DESCRIPTION	QUAN.	UNIT	MAN-HOURS	MAT.	INST.	TOTAL
Resilient flooring, asphalt tile on concrete, 1/8" thick						
Color group B	1.000	S.F.	.020	.88	.46	1.34
Color group C & D	1.000	S.F.	.020	.94	.45	1.39
Asphalt tile on wood subfloor, 1/8" thick						
Color group B	1.000	S.F.	.020	1.05	.46	1.51
Color group C & D	1.000	S.F.	.020	1.11	.45	1.56
Vinyl composition tile, 12" x 12", 1/16" thick	1.000	S.F.	.016	.61	.36	.97
Embossed	1.000	S.F.	.016	.77	.37	1.14
Marbleized	1.000	S.F.	.016	.77	.37	1.14
Plain	1.000	S.F.	.016	.88	.37	1.25
.080" thick, embossed	1.000	S.F.	.016	.83	.36	1.19
Marbleized	1.000	S.F.	.016	1.05	.36	1.41
Plain	1.000	S.F.	.016	1.38	.36	1.74
1/8" thick, marbleized	1.000	S.F.	.016	.94	.36	1.30
Plain	1.000	S.F.	.016	1.60	.36	1.96
Vinyl tile, 12" x 12", .050" thick, minimum	1.000	S.F.	.016	1.49	.36	1.85
Maximum	1.000	S.F.	.016	2.86	.37	3.23
1/8" thick, minimum	1.000	S.F.	.016	1.93	.36	2.29
Maximum	1.000	S.F.	.016	2.48	.36	2.84
1/8" thick, solid colors	1.000	S.F.	.016	2.92	.36	3.28
Florentine pattern	1.000	S.F.	.016	3.74	.37	4.11
Marbleized or travertine pattern	1.000	S.F.	.016	7.43	.37	7.80
Vinyl sheet goods, backed, .070" thick, minimum	1.000	S.F.	.032	1.27	.73	2.00
Maximum	1.000	S.F.	.040	2.31	.92	3.23
.093" thick, minimum	1.000	S.F.	.035	1.43	.80	2.23
Maximum	1.000	S.F.	.040	2.59	.91	3.50
.125" thick, minimum	1.000	S.F.	.035	1.65	.80	2.45
Maximum	1.000	S.F.	.040	3.58	.91	4.49
.250" thick, minimum	1.000	S.F.	.035	2.59	.79	3.38
Maximum	1.000	S.F.	.040	4.79	.91	5.70
Wood, oak, finished in place, 25/32" x 2-1/2" clear	1.000	S.F.	.074	2.97	1.76	4.73
Select	1.000	S.F.	.074	3.47	1.75	5.22
No. 1 common	1.000	S.F.	.070	3.25	1.66	4.91
Prefinished, oak, 2-1/2" wide	1.000	S.F.	.047	5.34	1.11	6.45
3-1/4" wide	1.000	S.F.	.043	6.44	1.01	7.45
Ranch plank, oak, random width	1.000	S.F.	.055	6.44	1.31	7.75
Parquet, 5/16" thick, finished in place, oak, minimum	1.000	S.F.	.077	2.31	1.83	4.14
Maximum	1.000	S.F.	.107	6.05	2.53	8.58
Teak, minimum	1.000	S.F.	.077	4.40	1.83	6.23
Maximum	1.000	S.F.	.107	7.15	2.53	9.68
Sleepers, treated, 16" O.C., 1" x 2"	1.000	S.F.	.007	.10	.17	.27
1" x 3"	1.000	S.F.	.008	.14	.20	.34
2" x 4"	1.000	S.F.	.011	.36	.27	.63
2" x 6"	1.000	S.F.	.012	.53	.31	.84
Subfloor, plywood, 1/2" thick	1.000	S.F.	.011	.35	.27	.62
5/8" thick	1.000	S.F.	.012	.43	.30	.73
3/4" thick	1.000	S.F.	.013	.51	.32	.83
Ceramic tile, color group 2, 1" x 1"	1.000	S.F.	.087	3.80	1.80	5.60
2" x 2" or 2" x 1"	1.000	S.F.	.087	3.96	1.79	5.75

6 | INTERIORS — 90 | Stairways

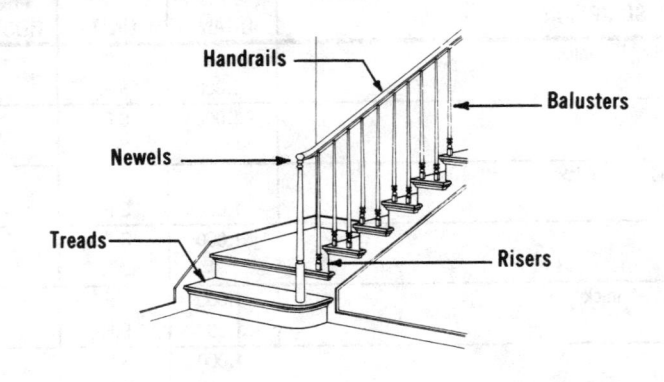

SYSTEM DESCRIPTION	QUAN.	UNIT	MAN-HOURS	MAT.	INST.	TOTAL
7 RISERS, OAK TREADS, BOX STAIRS						
Treads, oak, 9-½" x 1-1/16" thick	6.000	Ea.	2.664	113.88	66.12	180.00
Risers, ¾" thick, beech	7.000	Ea.	2.625	98.28	62.37	160.65
Balusters, birch, 30" high	12.000	Ea.	3.432	73.92	82.08	156.00
Newels, 3-¼" wide	2.000	Ea.	2.280	74.80	55.20	130.00
Handrails, oak laminated	7.000	L.F.	.931	32.76	22.19	54.95
Stringers, 2" x 10", 3 each	21.000	L.F.	2.583	19.74	64.68	84.42
TOTAL			14.515	413.38	352.64	766.02
14 RISERS, OAK TREADS, BOX STAIRS						
Treads, oak, 9-½" x 1-1/16" thick	13.000	Ea.	5.772	246.74	143.26	390.00
Risers, ¾" thick, beech	14.000	Ea.	5.250	196.56	124.74	321.30
Balusters, birch, 30" high	26.000	Ea.	7.436	160.16	177.84	338.00
Newels, 3-¼" wide	2.000	Ea.	2.280	74.80	55.20	130.00
Handrails, oak, laminated	14.000	L.F.	1.862	65.52	44.38	109.90
Stringers, 2" x 10", 3 each	42.000	L.F.	5.166	39.48	129.36	168.84
TOTAL			27.766	783.26	674.78	1458.04
14 RISERS, PINE TREADS, BOX STAIRS						
Treads, pine, 9-½" x ¾" thick	13.000	Ea.	5.772	112.97	137.93	250.90
Risers, ¾" thick, pine	14.000	Ea.	5.082	55.44	121.80	177.24
Balusters, pine, 30" high	26.000	Ea.	7.436	111.54	177.06	288.60
Newels, 3-¼" wide	2.000	Ea.	2.280	74.80	55.20	130.00
Handrails, oak, laminated	14.000	L.F.	1.862	65.52	44.38	109.90
Stringers, 2" x 10", 3 each	42.000	L.F.	5.166	39.48	129.36	168.84
TOTAL			27.598	459.75	665.73	1125.48

DESCRIPTION	QUAN.	UNIT	MAN-HOURS	MAT.	INST.	TOTAL

Stairway Price Sheet

	QUAN.	UNIT	MAN-HOURS	COST EACH MAT.	COST EACH INST.	TOTAL
Treads, oak, 1-1/16" x 9-1/2", 3' long, 7 riser stair	6.000	Ea.	2.664	113.88	66.12	180.00
14 riser stair	13.000	Ea.	5.772	246.74	143.26	390.00
1-1/16" x 11-1/2", 3' long, 7 riser stair	6.000	Ea.	2.664	143.58	66.42	210.00
14 riser stair	13.000	Ea.	5.772	311.09	143.91	455.00
Pine, 3/4" x 9-1/2", 3' long, 7 riser stair	6.000	Ea.	2.664	52.14	63.66	115.80
14 riser stair	13.000	Ea.	5.772	112.97	137.93	250.90
3/4" x 11-1/4", 3' long, 7 riser stair	6.000	Ea.	2.664	60.06	65.94	126.00
14 riser stair	13.000	Ea.	5.772	130.13	142.87	273.00
Risers, oak, 3/4" x 7-1/2" high, 7 riser stair	7.000	Ea.	2.625	90.09	63.21	153.30
14 riser stair	14.000	Ea.	5.250	180.18	126.42	306.60
Beech, 3/4" x 7-1/2" high, 7 riser stair	7.000	Ea.	2.625	98.28	62.37	160.65
14 riser stair	14.000	Ea.	5.250	196.56	124.74	321.30
Baluster, turned, 30" high, pine, 7 riser stair	12.000	Ea.	3.432	51.48	81.72	133.20
14 riser stair	26.000	Ea.	7.436	111.54	177.06	288.60
30" birch, 7 riser stair	12.000	Ea.	3.432	73.92	82.08	156.00
14 riser stair	26.000	Ea.	7.436	160.16	177.84	338.00
42" pine, 7 riser stair	12.000	Ea.	3.552	62.76	84.84	147.60
14 riser stair	26.000	Ea.	7.696	135.98	183.82	319.80
42" birch, 7 riser stair	12.000	Ea.	3.552	79.20	85.20	164.40
14 riser stair	26.000	Ea.	7.696	171.60	184.60	356.20
Newels, 3-1/4" wide, starting, 7 riser stair	2.000	Ea.	2.280	74.80	55.20	130.00
14 riser stair	2.000	Ea.	2.280	74.80	55.20	130.00
Landing, 7 riser stair	2.000	Ea.	3.200	143.00	77.00	220.00
14 riser stair	2.000	Ea.	3.200	143.00	77.00	220.00
Handrails, oak, laminated, 7 riser stair	7.000	L.F.	.931	32.76	22.19	54.95
14 riser stair	14.000	L.F.	1.862	65.52	44.38	109.90
Stringers, fir, 2" x 10" 7 riser stair	21.000	L.F.	2.583	19.74	64.68	84.42
14 riser stair	42.000	L.F.	5.166	39.48	129.36	168.84
2" x 12", 7 riser stair	21.000	L.F.	2.583	23.94	64.68	88.62
14 riser stair	42.000	L.F.	5.166	47.88	129.36	177.24

Special Stairways

	QUAN.	UNIT	MAN-HOURS	COST EACH MAT.	COST EACH INST.	TOTAL
Basement stairs, prefabricated, open risers	1.000	Flight	4.000	99.00	96.00	195.00
Curved stairways, 3'-3" wide, prefabricated oak, 9' high	1.000	Flight	22.860	4950.00	550.00	5500.00
10' high	1.000	Flight	22.860	5390.00	535.00	5925.00
Open two sides, 9' high	1.000	Flight	32.000	8140.00	760.00	8900.00
10' high	1.000	Flight	32.000	8800.00	775.00	9575.00
Spiral stairs, oak, 4'-6" diameter, prefabricated, 9' high	1.000	Flight	10.670	3300.00	250.00	3550.00
Aluminum, 5'-0" diameter stock unit	1.000	Flight	9.954	3157.00	343.00	3500.00
Custom unit	1.000	Flight	9.954	4774.00	336.00	5110.00
Cast iron, 4'-0" diameter, minimum	1.000	Flight	9.954	2464.00	336.00	2800.00
Maximum	1.000	Flight	17.920	3619.00	581.00	4200.00
Steel, industrial, pre-erected, 3'-6" wide, bar rail	1.000	Flight	9.016	2849.00	441.00	3290.00
Picket rail	1.000	Flight	9.016	3927.00	413.00	4340.00

7 SPECIALTIES — 08 Kitchen Systems

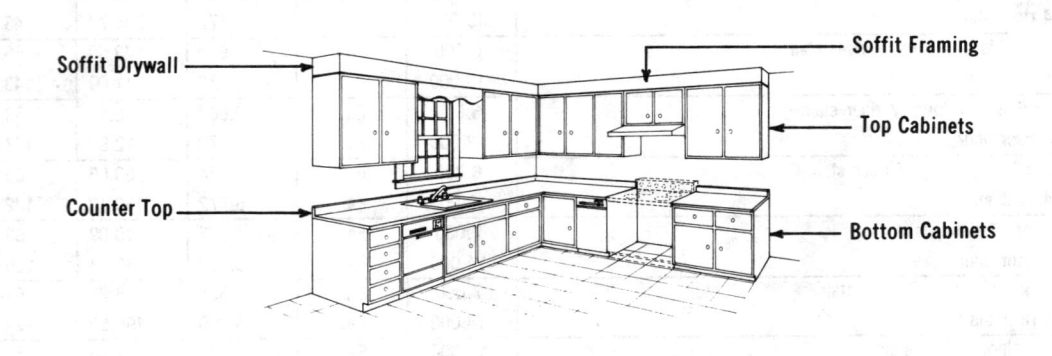

SYSTEM DESCRIPTION	QUAN.	UNIT	MAN-HOURS	MAT.	INST.	TOTAL
KITCHEN, ECONOMY GRADE						
Top cabinets, economy grade	1.000	L.F.	.170	21.12	4.16	25.28
Bottom cabinets, economy grade	1.000	L.F.	.255	31.68	6.24	37.92
Counter top, laminated plastic, post formed	1.000	L.F.	.267	8.86	6.39	15.25
Blocking, wood, 2" x 4"	1.000	L.F.	.032	.30	.80	1.10
Soffit, framing, wood, 2" x 4"	4.000	L.F.	.072	1.20	1.76	2.96
Soffit drywall, painted	2.000	S.F.	.062	.80	1.44	2.24
TOTAL			.858	63.96	20.79	84.75
AVERAGE GRADE						
Top cabinets, average grade	1.000	L.F.	.213	26.40	5.20	31.60
Bottom cabinets, average grade	1.000	L.F.	.319	39.60	7.80	47.40
Counter top, laminated plastic, square edge, incl. backsplash	1.000	L.F.	.267	27.50	6.50	34.00
Blocking, wood, 2" x 4"	1.000	L.F.	.032	.30	.80	1.10
Soffit framing, wood, 2" x 4"	4.000	L.F.	.072	1.20	1.76	2.96
Soffit drywall, painted	2.000	S.F.	.062	.80	1.44	2.24
TOTAL			.965	95.80	23.50	119.30
CUSTOM GRADE						
Top cabinets, custom grade	1.000	L.F.	.256	57.20	6.80	64.00
Bottom cabinets, custom grade	1.000	L.F.	.384	85.80	10.20	96.00
Counter top, laminated plastic, square edge, incl. backsplash	1.000	L.F.	.267	27.50	6.50	34.00
Blocking, wood, 2" x 4"	1.000	L.F.	.032	.30	.80	1.10
Soffit framing, wood, 2" x 4"	4.000	L.F.	.072	1.20	1.76	2.96
Soffit drywall, painted	2.000	S.F.	.062	.80	1.44	2.24
TOTAL			1.073	172.80	27.50	200.30

Kitchen Price Sheet

	QUAN.	UNIT	MAN-HOURS	MAT.	INST.	TOTAL
Top cabinets, economy grade	1.000	L.F.	.170	21.12	4.16	25.28
Average grade	1.000	L.F.	.213	26.40	5.20	31.60
Custom grade	1.000	L.F.	.256	57.20	6.80	64.00
Bottom cabinets, economy grade	1.000	L.F.	.255	31.68	6.24	37.92
Average grade	1.000	L.F.	.319	39.60	7.80	47.40
Custom grade	1.000	L.F.	.384	85.80	10.20	96.00
Counter top, laminated plastic, 7/8" thick, no splash	1.000	L.F.	.267	16.78	6.22	23.00
With backsplash	1.000	L.F.	.267	21.89	6.11	28.00
1-1/4" thick, no splash	1.000	L.F.	.286	19.75	7.25	27.00
With backsplash	1.000	L.F.	.286	24.75	7.25	32.00
Post formed, laminated plastic	1.000	L.F.	.267	8.86	6.39	15.25
Marble, with backsplash, minimum	1.000	L.F.	.471	31.90	11.10	43.00
Maximum	1.000	L.F.	.615	81.40	14.60	96.00
Maple, solid laminated, no backsplash	1.000	L.F.	.286	33.00	7.00	40.00
With backsplash	1.000	L.F.	.286	37.40	6.60	44.00
Blocking, wood, 2" x 4"	1.000	L.F.	.032	.30	.80	1.10
2" x 6"	1.000	L.F.	.036	.45	.90	1.35
2" x 8"	1.000	L.F.	.040	.61	1.00	1.61
Soffit framing, wood, 2" x 3"	4.000	L.F.	.064	.96	1.60	2.56
2" x 4"	4.000	L.F.	.072	1.20	1.76	2.96
Soffit, drywall, painted	2.000	S.F.	.062	.80	1.44	2.24
Paneling, standard	2.000	S.F.	.064	1.32	1.60	2.92
Deluxe	2.000	S.F.	.092	2.76	2.28	5.04
Sinks, porcelain on cast iron, single bowl, 21" x 24"	1.000	Ea.	10.340	292.23	247.77	540.00
21" x 30"	1.000	Ea.	10.340	317.53	247.47	565.00
Double bowl, 20" x 32"	1.000	Ea.	10.810	345.03	259.97	605.00
Stainless steel, single bowl, 16" x 20"	1.000	Ea.	10.340	361.53	248.47	610.00
22" x 25"	1.000	Ea.	10.340	392.33	247.67	640.00
Double bowl, 20" x 32"	1.000	Ea.	10.810	231.73	263.27	495.00

12 Appliance Systems

SYSTEM DESCRIPTION	QUAN.	UNIT	MAN-HOURS	COST EACH MAT.	COST EACH INST.	COST EACH TOTAL
All appliances include plumbing and electrical rough-in & hook-ups						
Range, free standing, minimum	1.000	Ea.	3.600	333.26	80.74	414.00
Maximum	1.000	Ea.	6.000	1356.26	132.74	1489.00
Built-in, minimum	1.000	Ea.	6.000	509.26	149.74	659.00
Maximum	1.000	Ea.	10.000	1125.26	238.74	1364.00
Counter top range, 4-burner, minimum	1.000	Ea.	3.330	256.26	87.74	344.00
Maximum	1.000	Ea.	4.670	553.26	120.74	674.00
Compactor, built-in, minimum	1.000	Ea.	2.215	339.70	56.30	396.00
Maximum	1.000	Ea.	3.285	559.70	81.30	641.00
Dishwasher, built-in, minimum	1.000	Ea.	8.235	318.81	222.19	541.00
Maximum	1.000	Ea.	12.235	494.81	331.19	826.00
Garbage disposer, minimum	1.000	Ea.	3.410	88.56	93.94	182.50
Maximum	1.000	Ea.	3.410	242.56	89.94	332.50
Microwave oven, minimum	1.000	Ea.	2.615	119.70	71.30	191.00
Maximum	1.000	Ea.	4.615	1687.20	113.80	1801.00
Range hood, ducted, minimum	1.000	Ea.	5.855	70.30	148.70	219.00
Maximum	1.000	Ea.	7.985	312.30	201.70	514.00
Ductless, minimum	1.000	Ea.	3.815	66.90	97.30	164.20
Maximum	1.000	Ea.	5.945	308.90	150.30	459.20
Refrigerator, 16 cu.ft., minimum	1.000	Ea.	2.000	412.50	37.50	450.00
Maximum	1.000	Ea.	3.200	660.00	60.00	720.00
16 cu.ft. with icemaker, minimum	1.000	Ea.	4.210	523.06	94.44	617.50
Maximum	1.000	Ea.	5.410	770.56	116.94	887.50
19 cu.ft., minimum	1.000	Ea.	2.670	649.00	51.00	700.00
Maximum	1.000	Ea.	4.672	1135.75	89.25	1225.00
19 cu.ft. with icemaker, minimum	1.000	Ea.	5.147	839.31	113.19	952.50
Maximum	1.000	Ea.	7.150	1326.06	151.44	1477.50
Sinks, porcelain on cast iron single bowl, 21″ x 24″	1.000	Ea.	10.340	292.23	247.77	540.00
21″ x 30″	1.000	Ea.	10.340	317.53	247.47	565.00
Double bowl, 20″ x 32″	1.000	Ea.	10.810	345.03	259.97	605.00
Stainless steel, single bowl 16″ x 20″	1.000	Ea.	10.340	361.53	248.47	610.00
22″ x 25″	1.000	Ea.	10.340	392.33	247.67	640.00
Double bowl, 20″ x 32″	1.000	Ea.	10.810	231.73	263.27	495.00
Water heater, electric, 30 gallon	1.000	Ea.	3.640	222.20	97.80	320.00
40 gallon	1.000	Ea.	4.000	243.10	106.90	350.00
Gas, 30 gallon	1.000	Ea.	4.000	207.90	107.10	315.00
75 gallon	1.000	Ea.	5.330	546.70	143.30	690.00
Wall, packaged terminal heater/air conditioner cabinet, wall sleeve, -louver, electric heat, thermostat, manual changeover, 208V						
6000 BTUH cooling, 8800 BTU heating	1.000	Ea.	2.670	737.00	63.00	800.00
9000 BTUH cooling, 13,900 BTU heating	1.000	Ea.	3.200	748.00	77.00	825.00
12,000 BTUH cooling, 13,900 BTU heating	1.000	Ea.	4.000	770.00	95.00	865.00
15,000 BTUH cooling, 13,900 BTU heating	1.000	Ea.	5.330	836.00	129.00	965.00

7 | SPECIALTIES — 16 | Bath Accessories

SYSTEM DESCRIPTION	QUAN.	UNIT	MAN-HOURS	MAT.	INST.	TOTAL
Curtain rods, stainless, 1" diameter, 3' long	1.000	Ea.	.615	22.00	15.00	37.00
5' long	1.000	Ea.	.615	22.00	15.00	37.00
Grab bar, 1" diameter, 12" long	1.000	Ea.	.283	19.64	6.71	26.35
36" long	1.000	Ea.	.340	25.25	7.90	33.15
1-¼" diameter, 12" long	1.000	Ea.	.333	23.10	7.90	31.00
36" long	1.000	Ea.	.400	29.70	9.30	39.00
1-½" diameter, 12" long	1.000	Ea.	.382	26.57	9.08	35.65
36" long	1.000	Ea.	.460	34.16	10.69	44.85
Mirror, 18" x 24"	1.000	Ea.	.400	77.00	10.00	87.00
72" x 24"	1.000	Ea.	1.330	231.00	34.00	265.00
Medicine chest with mirror, 18" x 24"	1.000	Ea.	.400	99.00	11.00	110.00
36" x 24"	1.000	Ea.	.600	148.50	16.50	165.00
Toilet tissue dispenser, surface mounted, minimum	1.000	Ea.	.267	17.60	6.40	24.00
Maximum	1.000	Ea.	.400	26.40	9.60	36.00
Flush mounted, minimum	1.000	Ea.	.293	19.36	7.04	26.40
Maximum	1.000	Ea.	.427	28.16	10.24	38.40
Towel bar, 18" long, minimum	1.000	Ea.	.278	15.49	6.91	22.40
Maximum	1.000	Ea.	.348	19.36	8.64	28.00
24" long, minimum	1.000	Ea.	.313	17.42	7.78	25.20
Maximum	1.000	Ea.	.382	21.30	9.50	30.80
36" long, minimum	1.000	Ea.	.381	22.44	9.56	32.00
Maximum	1.000	Ea.	.419	24.68	10.52	35.20

7 SPECIALTIES | 24 Masonry Fireplace Systems

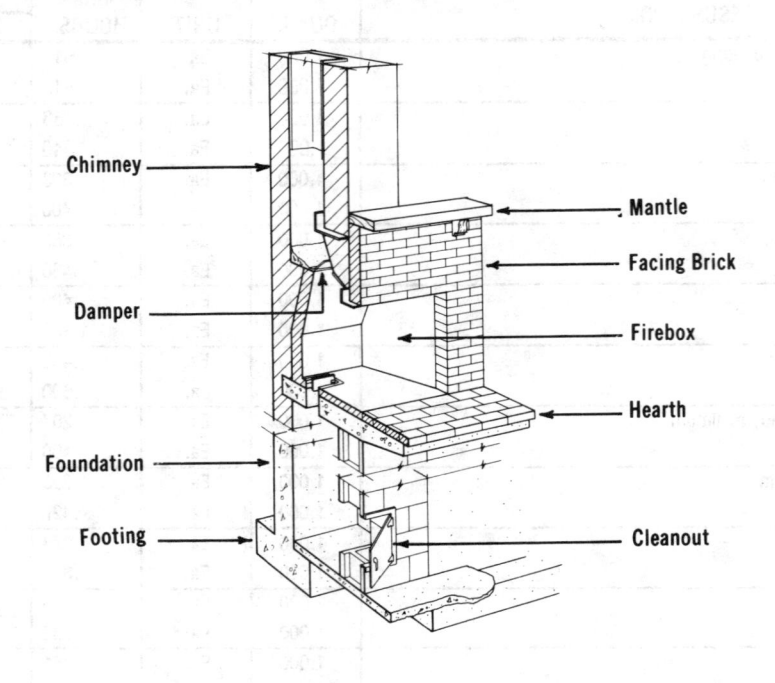

SYSTEM DESCRIPTION	QUAN.	UNIT	MAN-HOURS	COST EACH MAT.	COST EACH INST.	TOTAL
MASONRY FIREPLACE						
Footing, 8" thick, concrete, 4' x 7'	.700	C.Y.	1.596	64.68	47.32	112.00
Foundation, concrete block, 32" x 60" x 4' deep	1.000	Ea.	5.340	82.80	118.20	201.00
Fireplace, brick firebox, 30" x 29" opening	1.000	Ea.	40.000	363.00	862.00	1225.00
Damper, cast iron, 30" opening	1.000	Ea.	1.330	60.50	32.50	93.00
Facing brick, standard size brick, 6' x 5'	30.000	S.F.	5.220	63.30	115.20	178.50
Hearth, standard size brick, 3' x 6'	1.000	Ea.	8.000	110.00	175.00	285.00
Chimney, standard size brick, 8" x 12" flue, one story house	12.000	V.L.F.	12.000	192.72	263.28	456.00
Mantle, 4" x 8", wood	6.000	L.F.	1.332	24.12	31.98	56.10
Cleanout, cast iron, 8" x 8"	1.000	Ea.	.667	14.08	15.92	30.00
TOTAL			75.485	975.20	1661.40	2636.60

The costs in this system are on a cost each basis.

DESCRIPTION	QUAN.	UNIT	MAN-HOURS	COST EACH MAT.	COST EACH INST.	TOTAL

Masonry Fireplace Price Sheet

	QUAN.	UNIT	MAN-HOURS	COST EACH MAT.	COST EACH INST.	TOTAL
Footing 8" thick, 3' x 6'	.440	C.Y.	1.003	40.66	29.74	70.40
4' x 7'	.700	C.Y.	1.596	64.68	47.32	112.00
5' x 8'	1.000	C.Y.	2.280	92.40	67.60	160.00
1' thick, 3' x 6'	.670	C.Y.	1.527	61.91	45.29	107.20
4' x 7'	1.030	C.Y.	2.348	95.17	69.63	164.80
5' x 8'	1.480	C.Y.	3.374	136.75	100.05	236.80
Foundation-concrete block, 24" x 48", 4' deep	1.000	Ea.	4.272	66.24	94.56	160.80
8' deep	1.000	Ea.	8.544	132.48	189.12	321.60
24" x 60", 4' deep	1.000	Ea.	4.984	77.28	110.32	187.60
8' deep	1.000	Ea.	9.968	154.56	220.64	375.20
32" x 48", 4' deep	1.000	Ea.	4.717	73.14	104.41	177.55
8' deep	1.000	Ea.	9.434	146.28	208.82	355.10
32" x 60", 4' deep	1.000	Ea.	5.340	82.80	118.20	201.00
8' deep	1.000	Ea.	10.858	168.36	240.34	408.70
32" x 72", 4' deep	1.000	Ea.	6.141	95.22	135.93	231.15
8' deep	1.000	Ea.	12.282	190.44	271.86	462.30
Fireplace, brick firebox 30" x 29" opening	1.000	Ea.	40.000	363.00	862.00	1225.00
48" x 30" opening	1.000	Ea.	60.000	544.50	1293.00	1837.50
Steel fire box with registers, 25" opening	1.000	Ea.	26.670	602.80	582.20	1185.00
48" opening	1.000	Ea.	44.000	1226.50	958.50	2185.00
Damper, cast iron, 30" opening	1.000	Ea.	1.330	60.50	32.50	93.00
36" opening	1.000	Ea.	1.552	70.60	37.93	108.53
Steel, 30" opening	1.000	Ea.	1.330	55.00	32.00	87.00
36" opening	1.000	Ea.	1.552	64.19	37.34	101.53
Facing for fireplace, standard size brick, 6' x 5'	30.000	S.F.	5.220	63.30	115.20	178.50
7' x 5'	35.000	S.F.	6.090	73.85	134.40	208.25
8' x 6'	48.000	S.F.	8.352	101.28	184.32	285.60
Fieldstone, 6' x 5'	30.000	S.F.	5.220	340.80	115.20	456.00
7' x 5'	35.000	S.F.	6.090	397.60	134.40	532.00
8' x 6'	48.000	S.F.	8.352	545.28	184.32	729.60
Sheetrock on metal, studs, 6' x 5'	30.000	S.F.	1.050	18.90	24.90	43.80
7' x 5'	35.000	S.F.	1.225	22.05	29.05	51.10
8' x 6'	48.000	S.F.	1.680	30.24	39.84	70.08
Hearth, standard size brick, 3' x 6'	1.000	Ea.	8.000	110.00	175.00	285.00
3' x 7'	1.000	Ea.	9.280	127.60	203.00	330.60
3' x 8'	1.000	Ea.	10.640	146.30	232.75	379.05
Stone, 3' x 6'	1.000	Ea.	8.000	119.00	175.00	294.00
3' x 7'	1.000	Ea.	9.280	138.04	203.00	341.04
3' x 8'	1.000	Ea.	10.640	158.27	232.75	391.02
Chimney, standard size brick, 8" x 12" flue, one story house	12.000	V.L.F.	12.000	192.72	263.28	456.00
Two story house	20.000	V.L.F.	20.000	321.20	438.80	760.00
Mantle wood, beams, 4" x 8"	6.000	L.F.	1.332	24.12	31.98	56.10
4" x 10"	6.000	L.F.	1.374	27.72	32.88	60.60
Ornate, prefabricated, 6' x 3'-6" opening, minimum	1.000	Ea.	1.600	107.80	37.20	145.00
Maximum	1.000	Ea.	1.600	133.10	36.90	170.00
Cleanout, door and frame, cast iron, 8" x 8"	1.000	Ea.	.667	14.08	15.92	30.00
12" x 12"	1.000	Ea.	.800	31.46	19.54	51.00

7 SPECIALTIES — 30 Prefabricated Fireplace Systems

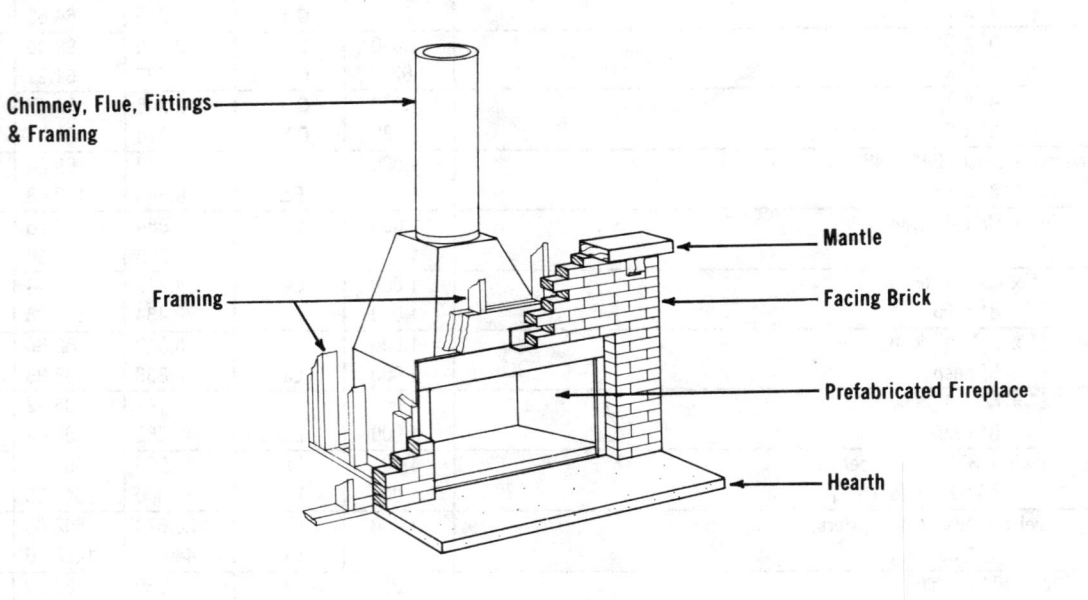

SYSTEM DESCRIPTION	QUAN.	UNIT	MAN-HOURS	MAT.	INST.	TOTAL
PREFABRICATED FIREPLACE						
Prefabricated fireplace, metal, minimum	1.000	Ea.	6.150	742.50	152.50	895.00
Framing, 2" x 4" studs, 6' x 5'	35.000	L.F.	.525	9.80	13.30	23.10
Sheetrock, ½" fire resistant, 6' x 5'	40.000	S.F.	.640	11.60	15.20	26.80
Facing, brick, standard size brick, 6' x 5'	30.000	S.F.	5.220	63.30	115.20	178.50
Hearth, standard size brick, 3' x 6'	1.000	Ea.	8.000	110.00	175.00	285.00
Chimney, one story house, framing, 2" x 4" studs	80.000	L.F.	1.200	22.40	30.40	52.80
Sheathing, plywood, ⅝" thick	32.000	S.F.	.768	34.24	18.88	53.12
Flue, 10" metal, insulated pipe	12.000	V.L.F.	3.996	186.84	101.16	288.00
Fittings, ceiling support	1.000	Ea.	.667	81.29	15.71	97.00
Fittings, joist shield	1.000	Ea.	.667	45.54	16.46	62.00
Fittings, roof flashing	1.000	Ea.	.667	92.51	17.49	110.00
Mantle beam, wood, 4" x 8"	6.000	L.F.	1.332	24.12	31.98	56.10
TOTAL			29.832	1424.14	703.28	2127.42

The costs in this system are on a cost each basis.

DESCRIPTION	QUAN.	UNIT	MAN-HOURS	MAT.	INST.	TOTAL

Prefabricated Fireplace Price Sheet

	QUAN.	UNIT	MAN-HOURS	COST EACH MAT.	COST EACH INST.	TOTAL
Prefabricated fireplace, minimum	1.000	Ea.	6.150	742.50	152.50	895.00
Average	1.000	Ea.	8.000	973.50	201.50	1175.00
Maximum	1.000	Ea.	8.890	2310.00	215.00	2525.00
Framing, 2" x 4" studs, fireplace, 6' x 5'	35.000	L.F.	.525	9.80	13.30	23.10
7' x 5'	40.000	L.F.	.600	11.20	15.20	26.40
8' x 6'	45.000	L.F.	.675	12.60	17.10	29.70
Sheetrock, ½" thick, fireplace, 6' x 5'	40.000	S.F.	.640	11.60	15.20	26.80
7' x 5'	45.000	S.F.	.720	13.05	17.10	30.15
8' x 6'	50.000	S.F.	.800	14.50	19.00	33.50
Facing for fireplace, brick, 6' x 5'	30.000	S.F.	5.220	63.30	115.20	178.50
7' x 5'	35.000	S.F.	6.090	73.85	134.40	208.25
8' x 6'	48.000	S.F.	8.352	101.28	184.32	285.60
Fieldstone, 6' x 5'	30.000	S.F.	5.220	333.30	115.20	448.50
7' x 5'	35.000	S.F.	6.090	388.85	134.40	523.25
8' x 6'	48.000	S.F.	8.352	533.28	184.32	717.60
Hearth, standard size brick, 3' x 6'	1.000	Ea.	8.000	110.00	175.00	285.00
3' x 7'	1.000	Ea.	9.280	127.60	203.00	330.60
3' x 8'	1.000	Ea.	10.640	146.30	232.75	379.05
Stone, 3' x 6'	1.000	Ea.	8.000	119.00	175.00	294.00
3' x 7'	1.000	Ea.	9.280	138.04	203.00	341.04
3' x 8'	1.000	Ea.	10.640	158.27	232.75	391.02
Chimney, framing, 2" x 4", one story house	80.000	L.F.	1.200	22.40	30.40	52.80
Two story house	120.000	L.F.	1.800	33.60	45.60	79.20
Sheathing, plywood, ⅝" thick	32.000	S.F.	.768	34.24	18.88	53.12
Stucco on plywood	32.000	S.F.	1.128	27.34	27.09	54.43
Flue, 10" metal pipe, insulated, one story house	12.000	V.L.F.	3.996	186.84	101.16	288.00
Two story house	20.000	V.L.F.	6.660	311.40	168.60	480.00
Fittings, ceiling support	1.000	Ea.	.667	81.29	15.71	97.00
Fittings joist sheild, one story house	1.000	Ea.	.667	45.54	16.46	62.00
Two story house	2.000	Ea.	1.334	91.08	32.92	124.00
Fittings roof flashing	1.000	Ea.	.667	92.51	17.49	110.00
Mantle, wood beam, 4" x 8"	6.000	L.F.	1.332	24.12	31.98	56.10
4" x 10"	6.000	L.F.	1.374	27.72	32.88	60.60
Ornate prefabricated, 6' x 3'-6" opening, minimum	1.000	Ea.	1.600	107.80	37.20	145.00
Maximum	1.000	Ea.	1.600	133.10	36.90	170.00

7 SPECIALTIES — 32 Greenhouse Systems

SYSTEM DESCRIPTION	QUAN.	UNIT	MAN-HOURS	MAT.	INST.	TOTAL
Economy, lean to, shell only, not incl. 2' stub wall, fndtn, flrs, heat 4'x10'	1.000	Ea.	18.840	1364.00	436.00	1800.00
4' x 16'	1.000	Ea.	26.234	1899.37	607.13	2506.50
4' x 24'	1.000	Ea.	30.285	2192.63	700.87	2893.50
6' x 10'	1.000	Ea.	16.560	1584.00	396.00	1980.00
6' x 16'	1.000	Ea.	23.046	2204.40	551.10	2755.50
6' x 24'	1.000	Ea.	29.808	2851.20	712.80	3564.00
8' x 10'	1.000	Ea.	22.080	2112.00	528.00	2640.00
8' x 16'	1.000	Ea.	38.419	3674.88	918.72	4593.60
8' x 24'	1.000	Ea.	49.680	4752.00	1188.00	5940.00
Free standing, 8' x 8'	1.000	Ea.	17.344	2464.00	416.00	2880.00
8' x 16'	1.000	Ea.	30.189	4288.90	724.10	5013.00
8' x 24'	1.000	Ea.	39.024	5544.00	936.00	6480.00
10' x 10'	1.000	Ea.	18.800	2970.00	430.00	3400.00
10' x 16'	1.000	Ea.	24.064	3801.60	550.40	4352.00
10' x 24'	1.000	Ea.	31.584	4989.60	722.40	5712.00
14' x 10'	1.000	Ea.	20.720	3696.00	504.00	4200.00
14' x 16'	1.000	Ea.	24.864	4435.20	604.80	5040.00
14' x 24'	1.000	Ea.	33.314	5942.64	810.36	6753.00
Standard, lean to, shell only, not incl. 2' stub wall, fndtn, flrs, heat 4'x10'	1.000	Ea.	28.260	2046.00	654.00	2700.00
4' x 16'	1.000	Ea.	39.375	2850.76	911.24	3762.00
4' x 24'	1.000	Ea.	45.451	3290.65	1051.85	4342.50
6' x 10'	1.000	Ea.	24.840	2376.00	594.00	2970.00
6' x 16'	1.000	Ea.	34.555	3305.28	826.32	4131.60
6' x 24'	1.000	Ea.	44.712	4276.80	1069.20	5346.00
8' x 10'	1.000	Ea.	33.120	3168.00	792.00	3960.00
8' x 16'	1.000	Ea.	57.628	5512.32	1378.08	6890.40
8' x 24'	1.000	Ea.	74.520	7128.00	1782.00	8910.00
Free standing, 8' x 8'	1.000	Ea.	26.016	3696.00	624.00	4320.00
8' x 16'	1.000	Ea.	45.284	6433.35	1086.15	7519.50
8' x 24'	1.000	Ea.	58.536	8316.00	1404.00	9720.00
10' x 10'	1.000	Ea.	28.200	4455.00	645.00	5100.00
10' x 16'	1.000	Ea.	36.096	5702.40	825.60	6528.00
10' x 24'	1.000	Ea.	47.376	7484.40	1083.60	8568.00
14' x 10'	1.000	Ea.	31.080	5544.00	756.00	6300.00
14' x 16'	1.000	Ea.	37.296	6652.80	907.20	7560.00
14' x 24'	1.000	Ea.	49.979	8915.28	1215.72	10131.00
Deluxe, lean to, shell only, not incl. 2' stub wall, fndtn, flrs or heat, 4'x10'	1.000	Ea.	20.640	3520.00	480.00	4000.00
4' x 16'	1.000	Ea.	33.024	5632.00	768.00	6400.00
4' x 24'	1.000	Ea.	49.536	8448.00	1152.00	9600.00
6' x 10'	1.000	Ea.	30.960	5280.00	720.00	6000.00
6' x 16'	1.000	Ea.	49.536	8448.00	1152.00	9600.00
6' x 24'	1.000	Ea.	74.304	12672.00	1728.00	14400.00
8' x 10'	1.000	Ea.	41.280	7040.00	960.00	8000.00
8' x 16'	1.000	Ea.	66.048	11264.00	1536.00	12800.00
8' x 24'	1.000	Ea.	99.072	16896.00	2304.00	19200.00
Freestanding, 8' x 8'	1.000	Ea.	18.624	4857.60	454.40	5312.00
8' x 16'	1.000	Ea.	37.248	9715.20	908.80	10624.00
8' x 24'	1.000	Ea.	55.872	14572.80	1363.20	15936.00
10' x 10'	1.000	Ea.	29.100	7590.00	710.00	8300.00
10' x 16'	1.000	Ea.	46.560	12144.00	1136.00	13280.00
10' x 24'	1.000	Ea.	69.840	18216.00	1704.00	19920.00
14' x 10'	1.000	Ea.	40.740	10626.00	994.00	11620.00
14' x 16'	1.000	Ea.	65.184	17001.60	1590.40	18592.00
14' x 24'	1.000	Ea.	97.776	25502.40	2385.60	27888.00

7 SPECIALTIES — 36 Swimming Pool Systems

SYSTEM DESCRIPTION	QUAN.	UNIT	MAN-HOURS	MAT.	INST.	TOTAL
Swimming pools, vinyl lined, metal sides, sand bottom, 12' x 28'	1.000	Ea.	50.265	2972.93	1516.03	4488.96
12' x 32'	1.000	Ea.	55.464	3280.40	1672.82	4953.22
12' x 36'	1.000	Ea.	60.167	3558.56	1814.67	5373.23
16' x 32'	1.000	Ea.	66.916	3957.71	2018.22	5975.93
16' x 36'	1.000	Ea.	71.316	4217.95	2150.93	6368.88
16' x 40'	1.000	Ea.	74.835	4426.10	2257.07	6683.17
20' x 36'	1.000	Ea.	77.997	4613.13	2352.44	6965.57
20' x 40'	1.000	Ea.	82.280	4866.40	2481.60	7348.00
20' x 44'	1.000	Ea.	90.508	5353.04	2729.76	8082.80
24' x 40'	1.000	Ea.	98.736	5839.68	2977.92	8817.60
24' x 44'	1.000	Ea.	108.609	6423.65	3275.71	9699.36
24' x 48'	1.000	Ea.	118.483	7007.62	3573.50	10581.12
Vinyl lined, concrete sides, 12' x 28'	1.000	Ea.	79.587	4707.14	2400.38	7107.52
12' x 32'	1.000	Ea.	88.974	5262.35	2683.51	7945.86
12' x 36'	1.000	Ea.	97.829	5786.04	2950.57	8736.61
16' x 32'	1.000	Ea.	111.590	6599.94	3365.62	9965.56
16' x 36'	1.000	Ea.	121.568	7190.11	3666.56	10856.67
16' x 40'	1.000	Ea.	130.675	7728.73	3941.23	11669.96
28' x 36'	1.000	Ea.	140.833	8329.51	4247.59	12577.10
20' x 40'	1.000	Ea.	149.600	8848.00	4512.00	13360.00
20' x 44'	1.000	Ea.	164.560	9732.80	4963.20	14696.00
24' x 40'	1.000	Ea.	179.520	10617.60	5414.40	16032.00
24' x 44'	1.000	Ea.	197.472	11679.36	5955.84	17635.20
24' x 48'	1.000	Ea.	215.424	12741.12	6497.28	19238.40
Gunite, bottom and sides, 12' x 28'	1.000	Ea.	129.696	5174.40	3897.60	9072.00
12' x 32'	1.000	Ea.	142.086	5668.74	4269.96	9938.70
12' x 36'	1.000	Ea.	152.944	6101.94	4596.27	10698.21
16' x 32'	1.000	Ea.	167.651	6688.68	5038.23	11726.91
16' x 36'	1.000	Ea.	176.324	7034.72	5298.88	12333.60
16' x 40'	1.000	Ea.	182.269	7271.88	5477.52	12749.40
20' x 36'	1.000	Ea.	187.846	7494.41	5645.14	13139.55
20' x 40'	1.000	Ea.	179.200	7040.00	5440.00	12480.00
20' x 44'	1.000	Ea.	197.120	7744.00	5984.00	13728.00
24' x 40'	1.000	Ea.	215.040	8448.00	6528.00	14976.00
24' x 44'	1.000	Ea.	273.095	10895.50	8207.00	19102.50
24' x 48'	1.000	Ea.	297.914	11885.72	8952.88	20838.60

7 | SPECIALTIES — 40 | Wood Deck Systems

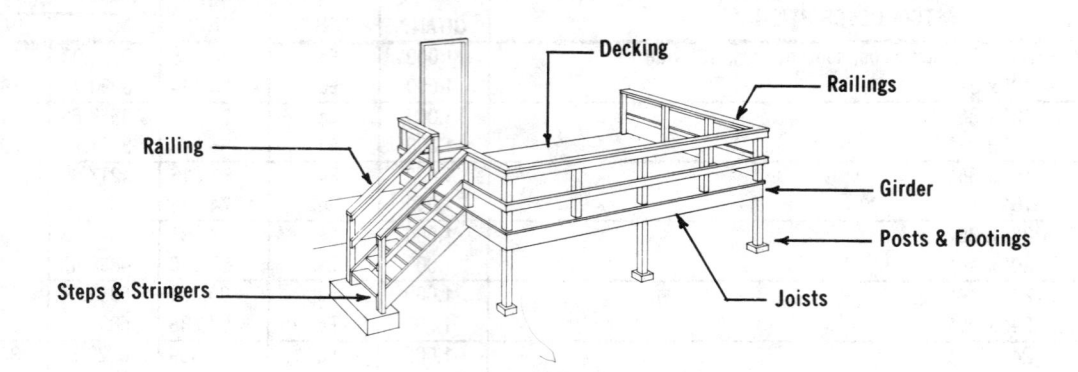

Diagram labels: Decking, Railings, Railing, Girder, Posts & Footings, Steps & Stringers, Joists

SYSTEM DESCRIPTION	QUAN.	UNIT	MAN-HOURS	MAT.	INST.	TOTAL
8' X 12' DECK, PRESSURE TREATED LUMBER, JOISTS 16" O.C.						
Decking, 2" x 6" lumber	2.080	L.F.	.027	1.17	.66	1.83
Joists, 2" x 8", 16" O.C.	1.000	L.F.	.017	.78	.43	1.21
Girder, 2" x 10"	.125	L.F.	.002	.15	.05	.20
Posts, 4" x 4", including concrete footing	.250	L.F.	.020	.48	.50	.98
Stairs, 2" x 10" stringers, 2" x 10" steps	1.000	Set	.020	.50	.48	.98
Railings, 2" x 4"	1.000	L.F.	.026	.38	.65	1.03
TOTAL			.112	3.46	2.77	6.23
12' X 16' DECK, PRESSURE TREATED LUMBER, JOISTS 24" O.C.						
Decking, 2" x 6"	2.080	L.F.	.027	1.17	.66	1.83
Joists, 2" x 10", 24" O.C.	.800	L.F.	.014	.90	.35	1.25
Girder, 2" x 10"	.083	L.F.	.001	.10	.03	.13
Posts, 4" x 4", including concrete footing	.122	L.F.	.015	.32	.38	.70
Stairs, 2" x 10" stringers, 2" x 10" steps	1.000	Set	.012	.30	.29	.59
Railings, 2" x 4"	.670	L.F.	.017	.25	.44	.69
TOTAL			.086	3.04	2.15	5.19
12' X 24' DECK, REDWOOD OR CEDAR, JOISTS 16" O.C.						
Decking, 2" x 6" redwood	2.080	L.F.	.027	2.12	.67	2.79
Joists, 2" x 10", 16" O.C.	1.000	L.F.	.018	1.83	.44	2.27
Girder, 2" x 10"	.083	L.F.	.001	.15	.04	.19
Post, 4" x 4", including concrete footing	.111	L.F.	.018	1.31	.46	1.77
Stairs, 2" x 10" stringers, 2" x 10" steps	1.000	Set	.012	1.30	.29	1.59
Railings, 2" x 4"	.540	L.F.	.004	.37	.11	.48
TOTAL			.080	7.08	2.01	9.09

The costs in this system are on a square foot basis.

DESCRIPTION	QUAN.	UNIT	MAN-HOURS	MAT.	INST.	TOTAL

Wood Deck Price Sheet

	QUAN.	UNIT	MAN-HOURS	COST PER S.F. MAT.	COST PER S.F. INST.	COST PER S.F. TOTAL
Decking, treated lumber, 1" x 4"	3.430	L.F.	.031	1.93	.75	2.68
1" x 6"	2.180	L.F.	.032	2.03	.78	2.81
2" x 4"	3.200	L.F.	.041	1.19	1.02	2.21
2" x 6"	2.080	L.F.	.027	1.17	.66	1.83
Redwood or cedar,, 1" x 4"	3.430	L.F.	.034	2.24	.83	3.07
1" x 6"	2.180	L.F.	.035	2.35	.86	3.21
2" x 4"	3.200	L.F.	.028	2.24	.71	2.95
2" x 6"	2.080	L.F.	.027	2.12	.67	2.79
Joists for deck, treated lumber, 2" x 8", 16" O.C.	1.000	L.F.	.017	.78	.43	1.21
24" O.C.	.800	L.F.	.013	.63	.34	.97
2" x 10", 16" O.C.	1.000	L.F.	.018	1.12	.44	1.56
24" O.C.	.800	L.F.	.014	.90	.35	1.25
Redwood or cedar, 2" x 8", 16" O.C.	1.000	L.F.	.015	1.39	.36	1.75
24" O.C.	.800	L.F.	.012	1.11	.29	1.40
2" x 10", 16" O.C.	1.000	L.F.	.018	1.83	.44	2.27
24" O.C.	.800	L.F.	.014	1.46	.36	1.82
Girder for joists, treated lumber, 2" x 10", 8' x 12' deck	.125	L.F.	.002	.15	.05	.20
12' x 16' deck	.083	L.F.	.001	.10	.03	.13
12' x 24' deck	.083	L.F.	.001	.10	.03	.13
Redwood or cedar, 2" x 10", 8' x 12' deck	.125	L.F.	.002	.23	.05	.28
12' x 16' deck	.083	L.F.	.001	.15	.04	.19
12' x 24' deck	.083	L.F.	.001	.15	.04	.19
Posts, 4" x 4", including concrete footing, 8' x 12' deck	.250	L.F.	.020	.48	.50	.98
12' x 16' deck	.122	L.F.	.015	.32	.38	.70
12' x 24' deck	.111	L.F.	.014	.31	.37	.68
Stairs 2" x 10" stringers, treated lumber, 8' x 12' deck	1.000	Set	.020	.50	.48	.98
12' x 16' deck	1.000	Set	.012	.30	.29	.59
12' x 24' deck	1.000	Set	.008	.20	.19	.39
Redwood or cedar, 8' x 12' deck	1.000	Set	.040	4.35	.95	5.30
12' x 16' deck	1.000	Set	.020	2.17	.48	2.65
12' x 24' deck	1.000	Set	.012	1.30	.29	1.59
Railings 2" x 4", treated lumber, 8' x 12' deck	1.000	L.F.	.026	.38	.65	1.03
12' x 16' deck	.670	L.F.	.017	.25	.44	.69
12' x 24' deck	.540	L.F.	.014	.20	.35	.55
Redwood or cedar, 8' x 12' deck	1.000	L.F.	.008	.68	.22	.90
12' x 16' deck	.670	L.F.	.005	.45	.14	.59
12' x 24' deck	.540	L.F.	.004	.37	.11	.48

8 | MECHANICAL 04 | Two Fixture Lavatory Systems

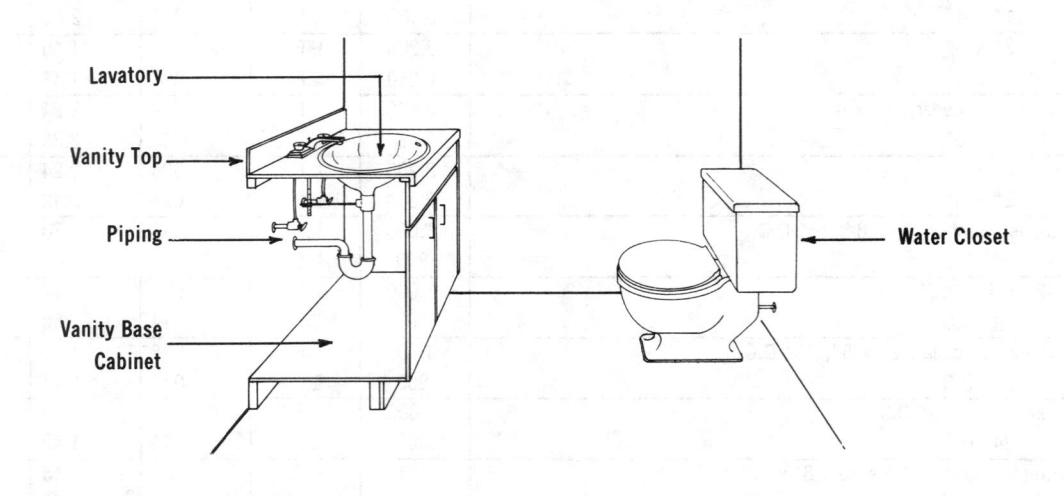

SYSTEM DESCRIPTION	QUAN.	UNIT	MAN-HOURS	MAT.	INST.	TOTAL
LAVATORY INSTALLED WITH VANITY, PLUMBING IN 2 WALLS						
Water closet, floor mounted, 2 piece, close coupled, white	1.000	Ea.	3.020	151.80	73.20	225.00
Rough-in supply, waste and vent for water closet	1.000	Ea.	2.378	34.81	59.40	94.21
Lavatory, 20" x 18", P.E. cast iron white	1.000	Ea.	2.500	147.40	62.60	210.00
Rough-in supply, waste and vent for lavatory	1.000	Ea.	2.846	36.28	71.72	108.00
Piping, supply, copper ½" diameter, type "L"	10.000	L.F.	.990	13.00	26.60	39.60
Waste, cast iron, 4" diameter, no-hub	7.000	L.F.	1.932	35.21	47.04	82.25
Vent, cast iron, 2" diameter, no-hub	12.000	L.F.	2.868	35.76	69.84	105.60
Vanity base cabinet, 2 door, 30" wide	1.000	Ea.	1.000	187.00	23.00	210.00
Vanity top, plastic & laminated, square edge	2.670	L.F.	.712	73.43	17.35	90.78
TOTAL			18.246	714.69	450.75	1165.44
LAVATORY WITH WALL-HUNG LAVATORY, PLUMBING IN 2 WALLS						
Water closet, floor mounted, 2 piece close coupled, white	1.000	Ea.	3.020	151.80	73.20	225.00
Rough-in supply, waste and vent for water closet	1.000	Ea.	2.378	34.81	59.40	94.21
Lavatory, 20" x 18", P.E. cast iron, wall hung, white	1.000	Ea.	2.000	121.00	49.00	170.00
Rough-in supply, waste and vent for lavatory	1.000	Ea.	2.846	36.28	71.72	108.00
Piping, supply, copper ½" diameter, type "L"	10.000	L.F.	.990	13.00	26.60	39.60
Waste, cast iron, 4" diameter, no-hub	7.000	L.F.	1.932	35.21	47.04	82.25
Vent, cast iron, 2" diameter, no hub	12.000	L.F.	2.868	35.76	69.84	105.60
Carrier, steel for studs, no arms	1.000	Ea.	1.140	15.62	30.38	46.00
TOTAL			17.174	443.48	427.18	870.66

DESCRIPTION	QUAN.	UNIT	MAN-HOURS	MAT.	INST.	TOTAL

Two Fixture Lavatory Price Sheet

	QUAN.	UNIT	MAN-HOURS	COST EACH MAT.	COST EACH INST.	TOTAL
Water closet, close coupled standard 2 piece, white	1.000	Ea.	3.020	151.80	73.20	225.00
Color	1.000	Ea.	3.020	187.00	73.00	260.00
One piece elongated bowl, white	1.000	Ea.	3.020	459.80	75.20	535.00
Color	1.000	Ea.	3.020	591.80	73.20	665.00
Low profile, one piece elongated bowl, white	1.000	Ea.	3.020	715.00	75.00	790.00
Color	1.000	Ea.	3.020	968.00	82.00	1050.00
Rough-in for water closet						
½" copper supply, 4" cast iron waste, 2" cast iron vent	1.000	Ea.	2.378	34.81	59.40	94.21
4" PVC waste, 2" PVC vent	1.000	Ea.	2.677	19.21	66.60	85.81
4" copper waste, 2" copper vent	1.000	Ea.	2.522	71.84	65.92	137.76
3" cast iron waste, 1-½" cast iron vent	1.000	Ea.	2.244	30.89	56.07	86.96
3" PVC waste, 1-½" PVC vent	1.000	Ea.	2.388	16.84	61.97	78.81
3" copper waste, 1-½" copper vent	1.000	Ea.	2.526	64.85	62.86	127.71
½" PVC supply, 4" PVC waste, 2" PVC vent	1.000	Ea.	2.971	19.81	74.64	94.45
3" PVC waste, 1-½" PVC vent	1.000	Ea.	2.682	17.44	70.01	87.45
½" steel supply, 4" cast iron waste, 2" cast iron vent	1.000	Ea.	2.546	34.51	64.02	98.53
4" cast iron waste, 2" steel vent	1.000	Ea.	2.590	38.11	65.02	103.13
4" PVC waste, 2" PVC vent	1.000	Ea.	2.845	18.91	71.22	90.13
Lavatory, vanity top mounted, P.E. on cast iron 20" x 18" white	1.000	Ea.	2.500	147.40	62.60	210.00
Color	1.000	Ea.	2.500	166.10	58.90	225.00
Steel, enameled 10" x 17" white	1.000	Ea.	2.500	89.10	60.90	150.00
Color	1.000	Ea.	2.500	93.50	61.50	155.00
Vitreous china 20" x 16", white	1.000	Ea.	2.500	190.30	59.70	250.00
Color	1.000	Ea.	2.500	190.30	59.70	250.00
Wall hung, P.E. on cast iron, 20" x 18", white	1.000	Ea.	2.000	121.00	49.00	170.00
Color	1.000	Ea.	2.000	181.50	48.50	230.00
Vitreous china 19" x 17", white	1.000	Ea.	2.000	115.50	49.50	165.00
Color	1.000	Ea.	2.000	132.00	48.00	180.00
Rough-in supply waste and vent for lavatory						
½" copper supply, 2" cast iron waste, 1-½" cast iron vent	1.000	Ea.	2.846	36.28	71.72	108.00
2" PVC waste, 1-½" PVC vent	1.000	Ea.	2.962	20.76	76.84	97.60
2" copper waste, 1-½" copper vent	1.000	Ea.	2.310	46.84	62.36	109.20
1-½" PVC waste, 1-¼" PVC vent	1.000	Ea.	2.638	20.08	71.12	91.20
1-½" copper waste, 1-¼" copper vent	1.000	Ea.	2.114	39.24	56.96	96.20
½" PVC supply, 2" PVC waste, 1-½" PVC vent	1.000	Ea.	3.452	21.76	90.24	112.00
1-½" PVC waste, 1-¼" PVC vent	1.000	Ea.	3.128	21.08	84.52	105.60
½" steel supply, 2" cast iron waste, 1-½" cast iron vent	1.000	Ea.	3.126	35.78	79.42	115.20
2" cast iron waste, 2" steel vent	1.000	Ea.	3.226	39.94	81.86	121.80
2" PVC waste, 1-½" PVC vent	1.000	Ea.	3.242	20.26	84.54	104.80
1-½" PVC waste, 1-¼" PVC vent	1.000	Ea.	2.918	19.58	78.82	98.40
Piping, supply, ½" copper, type "L"	10.000	L.F.	.990	13.00	26.60	39.60
½" steel	10.000	L.F.	1.270	12.50	34.30	46.80
½" PVC	10.000	L.F.	1.480	14.00	40.00	54.00
Waste, 4" cast iron	7.000	L.F.	1.932	35.21	47.04	82.25
4" copper	7.000	L.F.	2.800	104.44	70.56	175.00
4" PVC	7.000	L.F.	2.331	17.01	56.84	73.85
Vent, 2" cast iron	12.000	L.F.	2.868	35.76	69.84	105.60
2" copper	12.000	L.F.	2.184	57.84	59.16	117.00
2" PVC	12.000	L.F.	3.252	12.36	78.84	91.20
2" steel	12.000	Ea.	3.000	46.56	72.84	119.40
Vanity base cabinet, 2 door, 24" x 30"	1.000	Ea.	1.000	187.00	23.00	210.00
24" x 36"	1.000	Ea.	1.200	214.50	30.50	245.00
Vanity top, laminated plastic, square edge 25" x 32"	2.670	L.F.	.712	73.43	17.35	90.78
25" x 38"	3.170	L.F.	.846	87.18	20.60	107.78
Post formed, laminated plastic, 25" x 32"	2.670	L.F.	.712	23.66	17.06	40.72
25" x 38"	3.170	L.F.	.846	28.09	20.25	48.34
Cultured marble, 25" x 32" with bowl	1.000	Ea.	2.500	121.00	59.00	180.00
25" x 38" with bowl	1.000	Ea.	2.500	146.30	58.70	205.00
Carrier for lavatory, steel for studs	1.000	Ea.	1.140	15.62	30.38	46.00
Wood 2" x 8" blocking	1.330	L.F.	.053	.81	1.33	2.14

8 | MECHANICAL 12 | Three Fixture Bathroom Systems

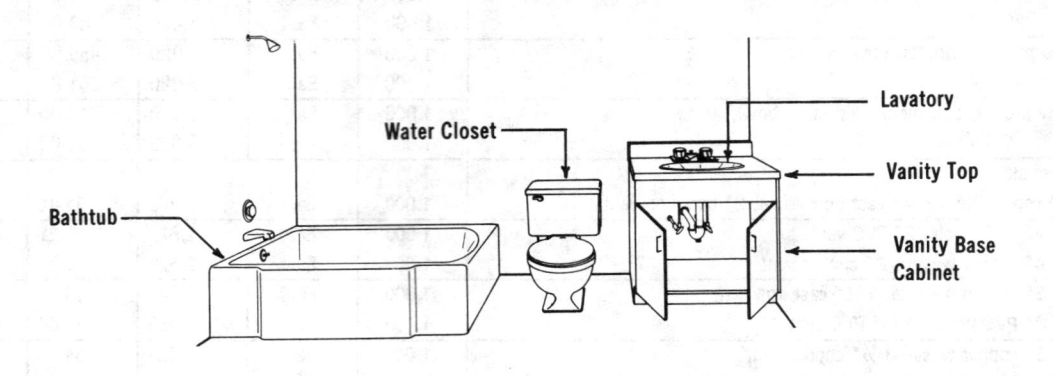

SYSTEM DESCRIPTION	QUAN.	UNIT	MAN-HOURS	MAT.	INST.	TOTAL
BATHROOM INSTALLED WITH VANITY						
Water closet, floor mounted, 2 piece, close coupled, white	1.000	Ea.	3.020	151.80	73.20	225.00
Rough-in supply, waste and vent for water closet	1.000	Ea.	2.378	34.81	59.40	94.21
Lavatory, 20" x 18", P.E. cast iron with accessories, white	1.000	Ea.	2.500	147.40	62.60	210.00
Rough-in supply, waste and vent for lavatory	1.000	Ea.	2.790	35.72	70.28	106.00
Bathtub, P.E. cast iron, 5' long with accessories, white	1.000	Ea.	3.640	309.10	85.90	395.00
Rough-in supply, waste and vent for bathtub	1.000	Ea.	2.410	42.65	62.80	105.45
Piping, supply, ½" copper	20.000	L.F.	1.980	26.00	53.20	79.20
Waste, 4" cast iron, no hub	9.000	L.F.	2.484	45.27	60.48	105.75
Vent, 2" galvanized steel	6.000	L.F.	1.500	23.28	36.42	59.70
Vanity base cabinet, 2 door, 30" wide	1.000	Ea.	1.000	187.00	23.00	210.00
Vanity top, plastic laminated square edge	2.670	L.F.	.712	56.39	18.37	74.76
TOTAL			24.414	1059.42	605.65	1665.07
BATHROOM WITH WALL HUNG LAVATORY						
Water closet, floor mounted, 2 piece, close coupled, white	1.000	Ea.	3.020	151.80	73.20	225.00
Rough-in supply, waste and vent for water closet	1.000	Ea.	2.378	34.81	59.40	94.21
Lavatory, 20" x 18" P.E. cast iron, wall hung, white	1.000	Ea.	2.000	121.00	49.00	170.00
Rough-in supply, waste and vent for lavatory	1.000	Ea.	2.790	35.72	70.28	106.00
Bathtub, P.E. cast iron, 5' long with accessories, white	1.000	Ea.	3.640	309.10	85.90	395.00
Rough-in supply, waste and vent for bathtub	1.000	Ea.	3.298	64.49	86.86	151.35
Piping, supply, ½" copper	20.000	L.F.	1.980	26.00	53.20	79.20
Waste, 4" cast iron, no hub	9.000	L.F.	2.484	45.27	60.48	105.75
Vent, 2" galvanized steel	6.000	L.F.	1.500	23.28	36.42	59.70
Carrier, steel, for studs, no arms	1.000	Ea.	1.140	15.62	30.38	46.00
TOTAL			24.230	827.09	605.12	1432.21

The costs in this system are a cost each basis, all necessary piping -is included

DESCRIPTION	QUAN.	UNIT	MAN-HOURS	MAT.	INST.	TOTAL

Three Fixture Bathroom Price Sheet

	QUAN.	UNIT	MAN-HOURS	COST EACH MAT.	COST EACH INST.	COST EACH TOTAL
Water closet, close coupled standard 2 piece, white	1.000	Ea.	3.020	151.80	73.20	225.00
Color	1.000	Ea.	3.020	187.00	73.00	260.00
One piece, elongated bowl, white	1.000	Ea.	3.020	459.80	75.20	535.00
Color	1.000	Ea.	3.020	591.80	73.20	665.00
Low profile, one piece elongated bowl, white	1.000	Ea.	3.020	715.00	75.00	790.00
Color	1.000	Ea.	3.020	968.00	82.00	1050.00
Rough-in, for water closet						
½" copper supply, 4" cast iron waste, 2" cast iron vent	1.000	Ea.	2.378	34.81	59.40	94.21
4" PVC/DWV waste, 2" PVC	1.000	Ea.	2.677	19.21	66.60	85.81
4" copper waste, 2" copper vent	1.000	Ea.	2.522	71.84	65.92	137.76
3" cast iron waste, 1-½" cast iron vent	1.000	Ea.	2.244	30.89	56.07	86.96
3" PVC waste, 1-½" PVC vent	1.000	Ea.	2.388	16.84	61.97	78.81
3" copper waste, 1-½" copper vent	1.000	Ea.	2.014	46.81	52.10	98.91
½" PVC supply, 4" PVC waste, 2" PVC vent	1.000	Ea.	2.971	19.81	74.64	94.45
3" PVC waste, 1-½" PVC supply	1.000	Ea.	2.682	17.44	70.01	87.45
½" steel supply, 4" cast iron waste, 2" cast iron vent	1.000	Ea.	2.546	34.51	64.02	98.53
4" cast iron waste, 2" steel vent	1.000	Ea.	2.590	38.11	65.02	103.13
4" PVC waste, 2" PVC vent	1.000	Ea.	2.845	18.91	71.22	90.13
Lavatory, wall hung, P.E. cast iron 20" x 18", white	1.000	Ea.	2.000	121.00	49.00	170.00
Color	1.000	Ea.	2.000	181.50	48.50	230.00
Vitreous china 19" x 17", white	1.000	Ea.	2.000	115.50	49.50	165.00
Color	1.000	Ea.	2.000	132.00	48.00	180.00
Lavatory, for vanity top, P.E. cast iron 20" x 18"', white	1.000	Ea.	2.500	147.40	62.60	210.00
Color	1.000	Ea.	2.500	166.10	58.90	225.00
Steel, enameled 20" x 17", white	1.000	Ea.	2.500	89.10	60.90	150.00
Color	1.000	Ea.	2.500	93.50	61.50	155.00
Vitreous china 20" x 16", white	1.000	Ea.	2.500	190.30	59.70	250.00
Color	1.000	Ea.	2.500	190.30	59.70	250.00
Rough-in, for lavatory						
½" copper supply, 1-½" C.I. waste, 1-½" C.I. vent	1.000	Ea.	2.790	35.72	70.28	106.00
1-½" PVC waste, 1-¼" PVC vent	1.000	Ea.	2.638	20.08	71.12	91.20
½" steel supply, 1-¼" cast iron waste, 1-¼" steel vent	1.000	Ea.	2.890	33.82	73.58	107.40
1-¼" PVC@ waste, 1-¼" PVC vent	1.000	Ea.	2.790	19.38	75.42	94.80
½" PVC supply, 1-½" PVC waste, 1-½" PVC vent	1.000	Ea.	3.256	21.28	87.92	109.20
Bathtub, P.E. cast iron, 5' long corner with fittings, white	1.000	Ea.	3.640	309.10	85.90	395.00
Color	1.000	Ea.	3.640	396.00	89.00	485.00
Rough-in, for bathtub						
½" copper supply, 4" cast iron waste, 1-½" copper vent	1.000	Ea.	2.410	42.65	62.80	105.45
4" PVC waste, 1-½" PVC vent	1.000	Ea.	2.877	23.93	74.92	98.85
½" steel supply, 4" cast iron waste, 1-½" steel vent	1.000	Ea.	2.898	39.63	73.82	113.45
4" PVC waste, 1-½" PVC vent	1.000	Ea.	3.157	23.43	82.62	106.05
½" PVC supply, 4" PVC waste, 1-½" PVC vent	1.000	Ea.	3.367	24.93	88.32	113.25
Piping, supply ½" copper	20.000	L.F.	1.980	26.00	53.20	79.20
½" steel	20.000	L.F.	2.540	25.00	68.60	93.60
½" PVC	20.000	L.F.	2.960	28.00	80.00	108.00
Piping, waste, 4" cast iron no hub	9.000	L.F.	2.484	45.27	60.48	105.75
4" PVC/DWV	9.000	L.F.	2.997	21.87	73.08	94.95
4" copper/DWV	9.000	L.F.	3.600	134.28	90.72	225.00
Piping, vent 2" cast iron no hub	6.000	L.F.	1.434	17.88	34.92	52.80
2" copper/DWV	6.000	L.F.	1.092	28.92	29.58	58.50
2" PVC/DWV	6.000	L.F.	1.626	6.18	39.42	45.60
2" steel, galvanized	6.000	L.F.	1.500	23.28	36.42	59.70
Vanity base cabinet, 2 door, 24" x 30"	1.000	Ea.	1.000	187.00	23.00	210.00
24" x 36"	1.000	Ea.	1.200	214.50	30.50	245.00
Vanity top, laminated plastic square edge 25" x 32"	2.670	L.F.	.712	56.39	18.37	74.76
25" x 38"	3.160	L.F.	.843	66.74	21.74	88.48
Cultured marble, 25" x 32", with bowl	1.000	Ea.	2.500	121.00	59.00	180.00
25" x 38", with bowl	1.000	Ea.	2.500	146.30	58.70	205.00
Carrier, for lavatory, steel for studs, no arms	1.000	Ea.	1.140	15.62	30.38	46.00
Wood, 2" x 8" blocking	1.300	L.F.	.052	.79	1.30	2.09

8 | MECHANICAL — 16 | Three Fixture Bathroom Systems

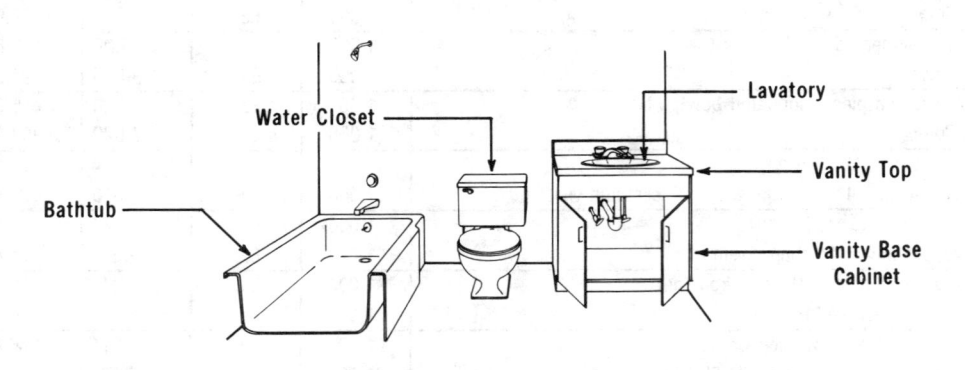

SYSTEM DESCRIPTION	QUAN.	UNIT	MAN-HOURS	MAT.	INST.	TOTAL
BATHROOM WITH LAVATORY INSTALLED IN VANITY						
Water closet, floor mounted, 2 piece, close coupled, white	1.000	Ea.	3.020	151.80	73.20	225.00
Rough-in supply, waste and vent for water closet	1.000	Ea.	2.378	34.81	59.40	94.21
Lavatory, 20" x 18", P.E. cast iron with accessories, white	1.000	Ea.	2.500	147.40	62.60	210.00
Rough-in supply, waste and vent for lavatory	1.000	Ea.	2.790	35.72	70.28	106.00
Bathtub, P.E. cast iron 5' long with accessories, white	1.000	Ea.	3.640	309.10	85.90	395.00
Rough-in supply, waste and vent for bathtub	1.000	Ea.	2.410	42.65	62.80	105.45
Piping, supply, ½" copper	10.000	L.F.	.990	13.00	26.60	39.60
Waste, 4" cast iron, no hub	6.000	L.F.	1.656	30.18	40.32	70.50
Vent, 2" galvanized steel	6.000	L.F.	1.500	23.28	36.42	59.70
Vanity base cabinet, 2 door, 30" wide	1.000	Ea.	1.000	187.00	23.00	210.00
Vanity top, plastic laminated square edge	2.670	L.F.	.712	56.39	18.37	74.76
TOTAL			22.596	1031.33	558.89	1590.22
BATHROOM WITH WALL HUNG LAVATORY						
Water closet, floor mounted, 2 piece, close coupled, white	1.000	Ea.	3.020	151.80	73.20	225.00
Rough-in supply, waste and vent for water closet	1.000	Ea.	2.378	34.81	59.40	94.21
Lavatory, 20" x 18" P.E. cast iron, wall hung, white	1.000	Ea.	2.000	121.00	49.00	170.00
Rough-in supply, waste and vent for lavatory	1.000	Ea.	2.790	35.72	70.28	106.00
Bathtub, P.E. cast iron, 5' long with accessories, white	1.000	Ea.	3.640	309.10	85.90	395.00
Rough-in supply, waste and vent for bathtub	1.000	Ea.	2.410	42.65	62.80	105.45
Piping, supply, ½" copper	10.000	L.F.	.990	13.00	26.60	39.60
Waste, 4" cast iron, no hub	6.000	L.F.	1.656	30.18	40.32	70.50
Vent, 2" galvanized steel	6.000	L.F.	1.500	23.28	36.42	59.70
Carrier, steel, for studs, no arms	1.000	Ea.	1.140	15.62	30.38	46.00
TOTAL			21.524	777.16	534.30	1311.46

The costs in this system are on a cost each basis. All necessary piping is included.

DESCRIPTION	QUAN.	UNIT	MAN-HOURS	MAT.	INST.	TOTAL

Three Fixture Bathroom Price Sheet

	QUAN.	UNIT	MAN-HOURS	MAT.	INST.	TOTAL
Water closet, close coupled standard 2 piece, white	1.000	Ea.	3.020	151.80	73.20	225.00
Color	1.000	Ea.	3.020	187.00	73.00	260.00
One piece elongated bowl, white	1.000	Ea.	3.020	459.80	75.20	535.00
Color	1.000	Ea.	3.020	591.80	73.20	665.00
Low profile, one piece elongated bowl, white	1.000	Ea.	3.020	715.00	75.00	790.00
Color	1.000	Ea.	3.020	968.00	82.00	1050.00
Rough-in for water closet						
½" copper supply, 4" cast iron waste, 2" cast iron vent	1.000	Ea.	2.378	34.81	59.40	94.21
4" PVC/DWV waste, 2" PVC vent	1.000	Ea.	2.677	19.21	66.60	85.81
4" carrier waste, 2" copper vent	1.000	Ea.	2.522	71.84	65.92	137.76
3" cast iron waste, 1-½" cast iron vent	1.000	Ea.	2.244	30.89	56.07	86.96
3" PVC waste, 1-½" PVC vent	1.000	Ea.	2.388	16.84	61.97	78.81
3" copper waste, 1-½" copper vent	1.000	Ea.	2.014	46.81	52.10	98.91
½" PVC supply, 4" PVC waste, 2" PVC vent	1.000	Ea.	2.971	19.81	74.64	94.45
3" PVC waste, 1-½" PVC supply	1.000	Ea.	2.682	17.44	70.01	87.45
½" steel supply, 4" cast iron waste, 2" cast iron vent	1.000	Ea.	2.546	34.51	64.02	98.53
4" cast iron waste, 2" steel vent	1.000	Ea.	2.590	38.11	65.02	103.13
4" PVC waste, 2" PVC vent	1.000	Ea.	2.845	18.91	71.22	90.13
Lavatory, wall hung, PE cast iron 20" x 18", white	1.000	Ea.	2.000	121.00	49.00	170.00
Color	1.000	Ea.	2.000	181.50	48.50	230.00
Vitreous china 19" x 17", white	1.000	Ea.	2.000	115.50	49.50	165.00
Color	1.000	Ea.	2.000	132.00	48.00	180.00
Lavatory, for vanity top, PE cast iron 20" x 18", white	1.000	Ea.	2.500	147.40	62.60	210.00
Color	1.000	Ea.	2.500	166.10	58.90	225.00
Steel enameled 20" x 17", white	1.000	Ea.	2.500	89.10	60.90	150.00
Color	1.000	Ea.	2.500	93.50	61.50	155.00
Vitreous china 20" x 16", white	1.000	Ea.	2.500	190.30	59.70	250.00
Color	1.000	Ea.	2.500	190.30	59.70	250.00
Rough-in for lavatory						
½" copper supply, 1-½" cast iron waste, 1-½" cast iron vent	1.000	Ea.	2.790	35.72	70.28	106.00
1-½" PVC waste, 1-¼" PVC vent	1.000	Ea.	2.638	20.08	71.12	91.20
½" steel supply, 1-¼" cast iron waste, 1-¼" steel vent	1.000	Ea.	2.890	33.82	73.58	107.40
1-¼" PVC waste, 1-¼" PVC vent	1.000	Ea.	2.790	19.38	75.42	94.80
½" PVC supply, 1-½" PVC waste, 1-½" PVC vent	1.000	Ea.	3.256	21.28	87.92	109.20
Bathtub, PE cast iron, 5' long corner with fittings, white	1.000	Ea.	3.640	309.10	85.90	395.00
Color	1.000	Ea.	3.640	396.00	89.00	485.00
Rough-in for bathtub						
½" copper supply, 4" cast iron waste, 1-½" copper vent	1.000	Ea.	2.410	42.65	62.80	105.45
4" PVC waste, ½" PVC vent	1.000	Ea.	2.877	23.93	74.92	98.85
½" steel supply, 4" cast iron waste, 1-½" steel vent	1.000	Ea.	2.898	39.63	73.82	113.45
4" PVC waste, 1-½" PVC vent	1.000	Ea.	3.157	23.43	82.62	106.05
½" PVC supply, 4" PVC waste, 1-½" PVC vent	1.000	Ea.	3.367	24.93	88.32	113.25
Piping supply, ½" copper	10.000	L.F.	.990	13.00	26.60	39.60
½" steel	10.000	L.F.	1.270	12.50	34.30	46.80
½" PVC	10.000	L.F.	1.480	14.00	40.00	54.00
Piping waste, 4" cast iron no hub	6.000	L.F.	1.656	30.18	40.32	70.50
4" PVC/DWV	6.000	L.F.	1.998	14.58	48.72	63.30
4" copper/DWV	6.000	L.F.	2.400	89.52	60.48	150.00
Piping vent 2" cast iron no hub	6.000	L.F.	1.434	17.88	34.92	52.80
2" copper/DWV	6.000	L.F.	1.092	28.92	29.58	58.50
2" PVC/DWV	6.000	L.F.	1.626	6.18	39.42	45.60
2" steel, galvanized	6.000	L.F.	1.500	23.28	36.42	59.70
Vanity base cabinet, 2 door, 24" x 30"	1.000	Ea.	1.000	187.00	23.00	210.00
24" x 36"	1.000	Ea.	1.200	214.50	30.50	245.00
Vanity top, laminated plastic square edge 25" x 32"	2.670	L.F.	.712	56.39	18.37	74.76
25" x 38"	3.160	L.F.	.843	66.74	21.74	88.48
Cultured marble, 25" x 32", with bowl	1.000	Ea.	2.500	121.00	59.00	180.00
25" x 38", with bowl	1.000	Ea.	2.500	146.30	58.70	205.00
Carrier, for lavatory, steel for studs, no arms	1.000	Ea.	1.140	15.62	30.38	46.00
Wood, 2" x 8" blocking	1.300	L.F.	.052	.79	1.30	2.09

8 | MECHANICAL   20 | Three Fixture Bathroom Systems

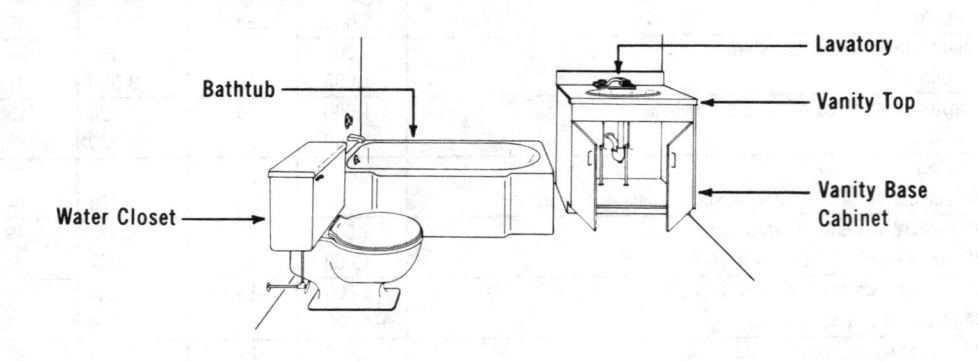

Diagram labels: Bathtub, Water Closet, Lavatory, Vanity Top, Vanity Base Cabinet

SYSTEM DESCRIPTION	QUAN.	UNIT	MAN-HOURS	MAT.	INST.	TOTAL
BATHROOM WITH LAVATORY INSTALLED IN VANITY						
Water closet, floor mounted, 2 piece, close coupled, white	1.000	Ea.	3.020	151.80	73.20	225.00
Rough-in supply, waste and vent for water closet	1.000	Ea.	2.378	34.81	59.40	94.21
Lavatory, 20" x 18", PE cast iron with accessories, white	1.000	Ea.	2.500	147.40	62.60	210.00
Rough-in supply, waste and vent for lavatory	1.000	Ea.	2.790	35.72	70.28	106.00
Bathtub, P.E. cast iron, 5' long with accessories, white	1.000	Ea.	3.640	309.10	85.90	395.00
Rough-in supply, waste and vent for bathtub	1.000	Ea.	2.410	42.65	62.80	105.45
Piping, supply, ½" copper	32.000	L.F.	3.168	41.60	85.12	126.72
Waste, 4" cast iron, no hub	12.000	L.F.	3.312	60.36	80.64	141.00
Vent, 2" galvanized steel	6.000	L.F.	1.500	23.28	36.42	59.70
Vanity base cabinet, 2 door, 30" wide	1.000	Ea.	1.000	187.00	23.00	210.00
Vanity top, plastic laminated square edge	2.670	L.F.	.712	56.39	18.37	74.76
TOTAL			26.430	1090.11	657.73	1747.84
BATHROOM WITH WALL HUNG LAVATORY						
Water closet, floor mounted, 2 piece, close coupled, white	1.000	Ea.	3.020	151.80	73.20	225.00
Rough-in supply, waste and vent for water closet	1.000	Ea.	2.378	34.81	59.40	94.21
Lavatory, 20" x 18" P.E. cast iron, wall hung, white	1.000	Ea.	2.000	121.00	49.00	170.00
Rough-in supply, waste and vent for lavatory	1.000	Ea.	2.790	35.72	70.28	106.00
Bathtub, P.E. cast iron, 5' long with accessories, white	1.000	Ea.	3.640	309.10	85.90	395.00
Rough-in supply, waste and vent for bathtub	1.000	Ea.	2.410	42.65	62.80	105.45
Piping, supply, ½" copper	32.000	L.F.	3.168	41.60	85.12	126.72
Waste, 4" cast iron, no hub	12.000	L.F.	3.312	60.36	80.64	141.00
Vent, 2" galvanized steel	6.000	L.F.	1.500	23.28	36.42	59.70
Carrier steel, for studs, no arms	1.000	Ea.	1.140	15.62	30.38	46.00
TOTAL			25.358	835.94	633.14	1469.08

The costs in this system are on a cost each basis. All necessary piping is included.

DESCRIPTION	QUAN.	UNIT	MAN-HOURS	MAT.	INST.	TOTAL

Three Fixture Bathroom Price Sheet

	QUAN.	UNIT	MAN-HOURS	COST EACH MAT.	COST EACH INST.	TOTAL
Water closet, close coupled, standard 2 piece, white	1.000	Ea.	3.020	151.80	73.20	225.00
Color	1.000	Ea.	3.020	187.00	73.00	260.00
One piece, elongated bowl, white	1.000	Ea.	3.020	459.80	75.20	535.00
Color	1.000	Ea.	3.020	591.80	73.20	665.00
Low profile, one piece, elongated bowl, white	1.000	Ea.	3.020	715.00	75.00	790.00
Color	1.000	Ea.	3.020	968.00	82.00	1050.00
Rough-in, for water closet						
½" copper supply, 4" cast iron waste, 2" cast iron vent	1.000	Ea.	2.378	34.81	59.40	94.21
4" PVC/DWV waste, 2" PVC vent	1.000	Ea.	2.677	19.21	66.60	85.81
4" copper waste, 2" copper vent	1.000	Ea.	2.522	71.84	65.92	137.76
3" cast iron waste, 1-½" cast iron vent	1.000	Ea.	2.244	30.89	56.07	86.96
3" PVC waste, 1-½" PVC vent	1.000	Ea.	2.388	16.84	61.97	78.81
3" copper waste, 1-½" copper vent	1.000	Ea.	2.014	46.81	52.10	98.91
½" PVC supply, 4" PVC waste, 2" PVC vent	1.000	Ea.	2.971	19.81	74.64	94.45
3" PVC waste, 1-½" PVC supply	1.000	Ea.	2.682	17.44	70.01	87.45
½" steel supply, 4" cast iron waste, 2" cast iron vent	1.000	Ea.	2.546	34.51	64.02	98.53
4" cast iron waste, 2" steel vent	1.000	Ea.	2.590	38.11	65.02	103.13
4" PVC waste, 2" PVC vent	1.000	Ea.	2.845	18.91	71.22	90.13
Lavatory wall hung, P.E. cast iron, 20" x 18", white	1.000	Ea.	2.000	121.00	49.00	170.00
Color	1.000	Ea.	2.000	181.50	48.50	230.00
Vitreous china, 19" x 17", white	1.000	Ea.	2.000	115.50	49.50	165.00
Color	1.000	Ea.	2.000	132.00	48.00	180.00
Lavatory, for vanity top, P.E., cast iron, 20" x 18", white	1.000	Ea.	2.500	147.40	62.60	210.00
Color	1.000	Ea.	2.500	166.10	58.90	225.00
Steel, enameled, 20" x 17", white	1.000	Ea.	2.500	89.10	60.90	150.00
Color	1.000	Ea.	2.500	93.50	61.50	155.00
Vitreous china, 20" x 16", white	1.000	Ea.	2.500	190.30	59.70	250.00
Color	1.000	Ea.	2.500	190.30	59.70	250.00
Rough-in, for lavatory						
½" copper supply, 1-½" C.I. waste, 1-½" C.I. vent	1.000	Ea.	2.790	35.72	70.28	106.00
1-½" PVC waste, 1-¼" PVC vent	1.000	Ea.	2.638	20.08	71.12	91.20
½" steel supply, 1-¼" cast iron waste, 1-¼" steel vent	1.000	Ea.	2.890	33.82	73.58	107.40
1-¼" PVC waste, 1-¼" PVC vent	1.000	Ea.	2.790	19.38	75.42	94.80
½" PVC supply, 1-½" PVC waste, 1-½" PVC vent	1.000	Ea.	3.256	21.28	87.92	109.20
Bathtub, P.E. cast iron, 5' long corner with fittings, white	1.000	Ea.	3.640	309.10	85.90	395.00
Color	1.000	Ea.	3.640	396.00	89.00	485.00
Rough-in, for bathtub						
½" copper supply, 4" cast iron waste, 1-½" copper vent	1.000	Ea.	2.410	42.65	62.80	105.45
4" PVC waste, ½" PVC vent	1.000	Ea.	2.877	23.93	74.92	98.85
½" steel supply, 4" cast iron waste, 1-½" steel vent	1.000	Ea.	2.898	39.63	73.82	113.45
4" PVC waste, 1-½" PVC vent	1.000	Ea.	3.157	23.43	82.62	106.05
½" PVC supply, 4" PVC waste, 1-½" PVC vent	1.000	Ea.	3.367	24.93	88.32	113.25
Piping, supply, ½" copper	32.000	L.F.	3.168	41.60	85.12	126.72
½" steel	32.000	L.F.	4.064	40.00	109.76	149.76
½" PVC	32.000	L.F.	4.736	44.80	128.00	172.80
Piping, waste, 4" cast iron no hub	12.000	L.F.	3.312	60.36	80.64	141.00
4" PVC/DWV	12.000	L.F.	3.996	29.16	97.44	126.60
4" copper/DWV	12.000	L.F.	4.800	179.04	120.96	300.00
Piping, vent, 2" cast iron no hub	6.000	L.F.	1.434	17.88	34.92	52.80
2" copper/DWV	6.000	L.F.	1.092	28.92	29.58	58.50
2" PVC/DWV	6.000	L.F.	1.626	6.18	39.42	45.60
2" steel, galvanized	6.000	L.F.	1.500	23.28	36.42	59.70
Vanity base cabinet, 2 door, 24" x 30"	1.000	Ea.	1.000	187.00	23.00	210.00
24" x 36"	1.000	Ea.	1.200	214.50	30.50	245.00
Vanity top, laminated plastic square edge, 25" x 32"	2.670	L.F.	.712	56.39	18.37	74.76
25" x 38"	3.160	L.F.	.843	66.74	21.74	88.48
Cultured marble, 25" x 32", with bowl	1.000	Ea.	2.500	121.00	59.00	180.00
25" x 38", with bowl	1.000	Ea.	2.500	146.30	58.70	205.00
Carrier, for lavatory, steel for studs, no arms	1.000	Ea.	1.140	15.62	30.38	46.00
Wood, 2" x 8" blocking	1.300	L.F.	.052	.79	1.30	2.09

8 | MECHANICAL — 24 | Three Fixture Bathroom Systems

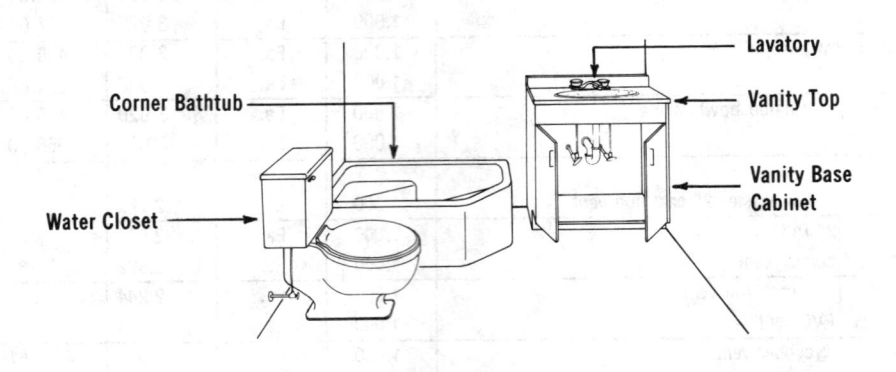

SYSTEM DESCRIPTION	QUAN.	UNIT	MAN-HOURS	MAT.	INST.	TOTAL
BATHROOM WITH LAVATORY INSTALLED IN VANITY						
Water closet, floor mounted, 2 piece, close coupled, white	1.000	Ea.	3.020	151.80	73.20	225.00
Rough-in supply waste and vent for water closet	1.000	Ea.	2.378	34.81	59.40	94.21
Lavatory, 20" x 18", P.E. cast iron with fittings, white	1.000	Ea.	2.500	147.40	62.60	210.00
Rough-in supply waste and vent for lavatory	1.000	Ea.	2.790	35.72	70.28	106.00
Bathtub, P.E. cast iron, 5' long corner with fittings, white	1.000	Ea.	3.640	309.10	85.90	395.00
Rough-in supply waste and vent for bathtub	1.000	Ea.	2.410	42.65	62.80	105.45
Piping supply, ½" copper	32.000	L.F.	3.168	41.60	85.12	126.72
Waste, 4" cast iron, no hub	12.000	L.F.	3.312	60.36	80.64	141.00
Vent, 2" steel, galvanized	6.000	L.F.	1.500	23.28	36.42	59.70
Vanity base cabinet, 2 door, 30" wide	1.000	Ea.	1.000	187.00	23.00	210.00
Vanity top, plastic laminated, square edge	2.670	L.F.	.712	73.43	17.35	90.78
TOTAL			26.430	1107.15	656.71	1763.86
BATHROOM WITH WALL HUNG LAVATORY						
Water closet, floor mounted, 2 piece, close coupled, white	1.000	Ea.	3.020	151.80	73.20	225.00
Rough-in supply waste and vent for water closet	1.000	Ea.	2.378	34.81	59.40	94.21
Lavatory, 20" x 18", P.E. cast iron, with fittings, white	1.000	Ea.	2.000	121.00	49.00	170.00
Rough-in supply, waste and vent, lavatory	1.000	Ea.	2.790	35.72	70.28	106.00
Bathtub, P.E. cast iron, 5' long corner, with fittings, white	1.000	Ea.	3.640	309.10	85.90	395.00
Rough-in supply, waste and vent, bathtub	1.000	Ea.	2.410	42.65	62.80	105.45
Piping, supply, ½" copper	32.000	L.F.	3.168	41.60	85.12	126.72
Waste, 4" cast iron, no hub	12.000	L.F.	3.312	60.36	80.64	141.00
Vent, 2" steel, galvanized	6.000	L.F.	1.500	23.28	36.42	59.70
Carrier, steel, for studs, no arms	1.000	Ea.	1.140	15.62	30.38	46.00
TOTAL			25.358	835.94	633.14	1469.08

The costs in this system are on a cost each basis. All necessary piping is included.

DESCRIPTION	QUAN.	UNIT	MAN-HOURS	MAT.	INST.	TOTAL

Three Fixture Bathroom Price Sheet

	QUAN.	UNIT	MAN-HOURS	COST EACH MAT.	COST EACH INST.	COST EACH TOTAL
Water closet, close coupled, standard 2 piece, white	1.000	Ea.	3.020	151.80	73.20	225.00
Color	1.000	Ea.	3.020	187.00	73.00	260.00
One piece elongated bowl, white	1.000	Ea.	3.020	459.80	75.20	535.00
Color	1.000	Ea.	3.020	591.80	73.20	665.00
Low profile, one piece elongated bowl, white	1.000	Ea.	3.020	732.60	72.40	805.00
Color	1.000	Ea.	3.020	1001.00	74.00	1075.00
Rough-in, for water closet						
½" copper supply, 4" cast iron waste, 2" cast iron vent	1.000	Ea.	2.378	34.81	59.40	94.21
4" PVC/DWV waste, 2" PVC vent	1.000	Ea.	2.677	19.21	66.60	85.81
4" copper waste, 2" copper vent	1.000	Ea.	2.522	71.84	65.92	137.76
3" cast iron waste, 1-½" cast iron vent	1.000	Ea.	2.244	30.89	56.07	86.96
3" PVC waste, 1-½" PVC vent	1.000	Ea.	2.388	16.84	61.97	78.81
3" copper waste, 1-½" copper vent	1.000	Ea.	2.014	46.81	52.10	98.91
½" PVC supply, 4" PVC waste, 2" PVC vent	1.000	Ea.	2.971	19.81	74.64	94.45
3" PVC waste, 1-½" PVC supply	1.000	Ea.	2.682	17.44	70.01	87.45
½" steel supply, 4" cast iron waste, 2" cast iron vent	1.000	Ea.	2.546	34.51	64.02	98.53
4" cast iron waste, 2" steel vent	1.000	Ea.	2.590	38.11	65.02	103.13
4" PVC waste, 2" PVC vent	1.000	Ea.	2.845	18.91	71.22	90.13
Lavatory, wall hung P.E. cast iron 20" x 18", white	1.000	Ea.	2.000	121.00	49.00	170.00
Color	1.000	Ea.	2.000	181.50	48.50	230.00
Vitreous china 19" x 17", white	1.000	Ea.	2.000	115.50	49.50	165.00
Color	1.000	Ea.	2.000	132.00	48.00	180.00
Lavatory, for vanity top, P.E., cast iron, 20" x 18", white	1.000	Ea.	2.500	147.40	62.60	210.00
Color	1.000	Ea.	2.500	166.10	58.90	225.00
Steel enameled 20" x 17", white	1.000	Ea.	2.500	89.10	60.90	150.00
Color	1.000	Ea.	2.500	93.50	61.50	155.00
Vitreous china 20" x 16", white	1.000	Ea.	2.500	190.30	59.70	250.00
Color	1.000	Ea.	2.500	190.30	59.70	250.00
Rough-in, for lavatory						
½" copper supply, 1-½" cast iron waste, 1-½" cast iron vent	1.000	Ea.	2.790	35.72	70.28	106.00
1-½" PVC waste, 1-¼" PVC vent	1.000	Ea.	2.638	20.08	71.12	91.20
½" steel supply, 1-¼" cast iron waste, 1-¼" steel vent	1.000	Ea.	2.890	33.82	73.58	107.40
1-¼" PVC waste, 1-¼" PVC vent	1.000	Ea.	2.790	19.38	75.42	94.80
½" PVC supply, 1-½" PVC waste, 1-½" PVC vent	1.000	Ea.	3.256	21.28	87.92	109.20
Bathtub, P.E. cast iron, 5' long corner with fittings, white	1.000	Ea.	3.640	309.10	85.90	395.00
Color	1.000	Ea.	3.640	396.00	89.00	485.00
Rough-in, for bathtub						
½" copper supply, 4" cast iron waste, 1-½" copper vent	1.000	Ea.	2.410	42.65	62.80	105.45
4" PVC waste, 1-½" PVC vent	1.000	Ea.	2.877	23.93	74.92	98.85
½" steel supply, 4" cast iron waste, 1-½" steel vent	1.000	Ea.	2.898	39.63	73.82	113.45
4" PVC waste, 1-½" PVC vent	1.000	Ea.	3.157	23.43	82.62	106.05
½" PVC supply, 4" PVC waste, 1-½" PVC vent	1.000	Ea.	3.367	24.93	88.32	113.25
Piping, supply, ½" copper	32.000	L.F.	3.168	41.60	85.12	126.72
½" steel	32.000	L.F.	4.064	40.00	109.76	149.76
½" PVC	32.000	L.F.	4.736	44.80	128.00	172.80
Piping, waste, 4" cast iron, no hub	12.000	L.F.	3.312	60.36	80.64	141.00
4" PVC/DWV	12.000	L.F.	3.996	29.16	97.44	126.60
4" copper/DWV	12.000	L.F.	4.800	179.04	120.96	300.00
Piping, vent 2" cast iron, no hub	6.000	L.F.	1.434	17.88	34.92	52.80
2" copper/DWV	6.000	L.F.	1.092	28.92	29.58	58.50
2" PVC/DWV	6.000	L.F.	1.626	6.18	39.42	45.60
2" steel, galvanized	6.000	L.F.	1.500	23.28	36.42	59.70
Vanity base cabinet, 2 door, 24" x 30"	1.000	Ea.	1.000	187.00	23.00	210.00
24" x 36"	1.000	Ea.	1.200	214.50	30.50	245.00
Vanity top, laminated plastic square edge 25" x 32"	2.670	L.F.	.712	73.43	17.35	90.78
25" x 38"	3.160	L.F.	.843	86.90	20.54	107.44
Cultured marble, 25" x 32", with bowl	1.000	Ea.	2.500	121.00	59.00	180.00
25" x 38", with bowl	1.000	Ea.	2.500	146.30	58.70	205.00
Carrier, for lavatory, steel for studs, no arms	1.000	Ea.	1.140	15.62	30.38	46.00
Wood, 2" x 8" blocking	1.300	L.F.	.053	.81	1.33	2.14

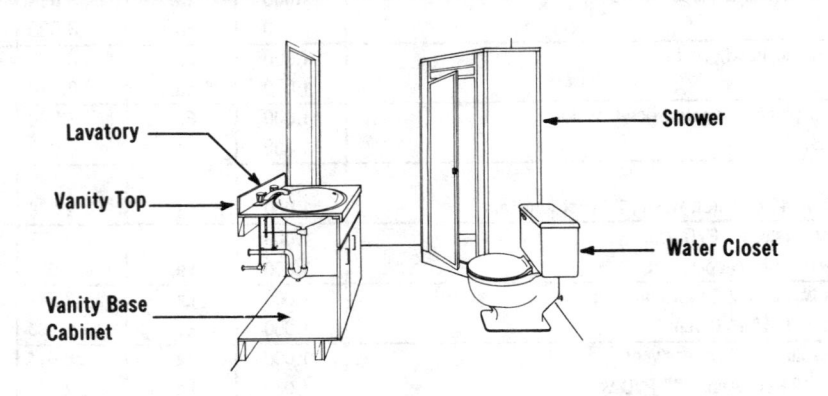

8 | MECHANICAL 28 | Three Fixture Bathroom Systems

SYSTEM DESCRIPTION	QUAN.	UNIT	MAN-HOURS	MAT.	INST.	TOTAL
BATHROOM WITH SHOWER, LAVATORY INSTALLED IN VANITY						
Water closet, floor mounted, 2 piece, close coupled, white	1.000	Ea.	3.020	151.80	73.20	225.00
Rough-in supply, waste and vent for water closet	1.000	Ea.	2.378	34.81	59.40	94.21
Lavatory, 20" x 18" P.E. cast iron with fittings, white	1.000	Ea.	2.500	147.40	62.60	210.00
Rough-in supply, waste and vent	1.000	Ea.	2.790	35.72	70.28	106.00
Shower, steel enameled, stone base	1.000	Ea.	8.000	347.60	192.40	540.00
Rough-in supply, waste and vent	1.000	Ea.	3.243	41.52	82.94	124.46
Piping supply, ½" copper	36.000	L.F.	4.158	54.60	111.72	166.32
Waste 4" cast iron, no hub	7.000	L.F.	2.760	50.30	67.20	117.50
Vent 2" steel galvanized	6.000	L.F.	2.250	34.92	54.63	89.55
Vanity base 2 door, 30" wide	1.000	Ea.	1.000	187.00	23.00	210.00
Vanity top, plastic laminated, square edge	2.170	L.F.	.712	58.45	16.31	74.76
TOTAL			32.811	1144.12	813.68	1957.80
BATHROOM WITH SHOWER, WALL HUNG LAVATORY						
Water closet, floor mounted, close coupled	1.000	Ea.	3.020	151.80	73.20	225.00
Rough-in supply, waste and vent for water closet	1.000	Ea.	2.378	34.81	59.40	94.21
Lavatory, 20" x 18" P.E. cast iron with fittings, white	1.000	Ea.	2.000	121.00	49.00	170.00
Rough-in supply, waste and vent for lavatory	1.000	Ea.	2.790	35.72	70.28	106.00
Shower, steel enameled, stone base, white	1.000	Ea.	8.000	347.60	192.40	540.00
Rough-in supply, waste and vent for shower	1.000	Ea.	3.243	41.52	82.94	124.46
Piping supply, ½" copper	36.000	L.F.	4.158	54.60	111.72	166.32
Waste, 4" cast iron, no hub	7.000	L.F.	2.760	50.30	67.20	117.50
Vent, 2" steel, galvanized	6.000	L.F.	2.250	34.92	54.63	89.55
Carrier, steel, for studs, no arms	1.000	Ea.	1.140	15.62	30.38	46.00
TOTAL			31.739	887.89	791.15	1679.04

The costs in this system are on a cost each basis. All necessary piping is included.

DESCRIPTION	QUAN.	UNIT	MAN-HOURS	MAT.	INST.	TOTAL

Three Fixture Bathroom Price Sheet

	QUAN.	UNIT	MAN-HOURS	COST EACH MAT.	COST EACH INST.	COST EACH TOTAL
Water closet, close coupled, standard 2 piece, white	1.000	Ea.	3.020	151.80	73.20	225.00
Color	1.000	Ea.	3.020	187.00	73.00	260.00
One piece elongated bowl, white	1.000	Ea.	3.020	459.80	75.20	535.00
Color	1.000	Ea.	3.020	591.80	73.20	665.00
Low profile, one piece elongated bowl, white	1.000	Ea.	3.020	715.00	75.00	790.00
Color	1.000	Ea.	3.020	968.00	82.00	1050.00
Rough-in, for water closet						
½" copper supply, 4" cast iron waste, 2" cast iron vent	1.000	Ea.	2.378	34.81	59.40	94.21
4" PVC/DWV waste, 2" PVC vent	1.000	Ea.	2.677	19.21	66.60	85.81
4" copper waste, 2" copper vent	1.000	Ea.	2.522	71.84	65.92	137.76
3" cast iron waste, 1-½" cast iron vent	1.000	Ea.	2.244	30.89	56.07	86.96
3" PVC waste, 1-½" PVC vent	1.000	Ea.	2.388	16.84	61.97	78.81
3" copper waste, 1-½" copper vent	1.000	Ea.	2.014	46.81	52.10	98.91
½" PVC supply, 4" PVC waste, 2" PVC vent	1.000	Ea.	2.971	19.81	74.64	94.45
3" PVC waste, 1-½" PVC supply	1.000	Ea.	2.682	17.44	70.01	87.45
½" steel supply, 4" cast iron waste, 2" cast iron vent	1.000	Ea.	2.546	34.51	64.02	98.53
4" cast iron waste, 2" steel vent	1.000	Ea.	2.590	38.11	65.02	103.13
4" PVC waste, 2" PVC vent	1.000	Ea.	2.845	18.91	71.22	90.13
Lavatory, wall hung, P.E. cast iron 20" x 18", white	1.000	Ea.	2.000	121.00	49.00	170.00
Color	1.000	Ea.	2.000	181.50	48.50	230.00
Vitreous china 19" x 17", white	1.000	Ea.	2.000	115.50	49.50	165.00
Color	1.000	Ea.	2.000	132.00	48.00	180.00
Lavatory, for vanity top, P.E. cast iron 20" x 18", white	1.000	Ea.	2.500	147.40	62.60	210.00
Color	1.000	Ea.	2.500	166.10	58.90	225.00
Steel enameled 20" x 17", white	1.000	Ea.	2.500	89.10	60.90	150.00
Color	1.000	Ea.	2.500	93.50	61.50	155.00
Vitreous china 20" x 16", white	1.000	Ea.	2.500	190.30	59.70	250.00
Color	1.000	Ea.	2.500	190.30	59.70	250.00
Rough-in, for lavatory						
½" copper supply, 1-½" cast iron waste, 1-½" cast iron vent	1.000	Ea.	2.790	35.72	70.28	106.00
1-½" PVC waste, 1-½" PVC vent	1.000	Ea.	2.638	20.08	71.12	91.20
½" steel supply, 1-¼" cast iron waste, 1-¼" steel vent	1.000	Ea.	2.890	33.82	73.58	107.40
1-¼" PVC waste, 1-¼" PVC vent	1.000	Ea.	2.918	19.58	78.82	98.40
½" PVC supply, 1-½" PVC waste, 1-½" PVC vent	1.000	Ea.	3.256	21.28	87.92	109.20
Shower, steel enameled stone base, 32" x 32", white	1.000	Ea.	8.000	347.60	192.40	540.00
Color	1.000	Ea.	7.823	569.18	192.02	761.20
36" x 36" white	1.000	Ea.	8.890	632.50	217.50	850.00
Color	1.000	Ea.	8.890	646.80	218.20	865.00
Rough-in, for shower						
½" copper supply, 4" cast iron waste, 1-½" copper vent	1.000	Ea.	3.243	41.52	82.94	124.46
4" PVC waste, 1-½" PVC vent	1.000	Ea.	3.432	27.89	87.97	115.86
½" steel supply, 4" cast iron waste, 1-½" steel vent	1.000	Ea.	3.666	40.89	94.64	135.53
4" PVC waste, 1-½" PVC vent	1.000	Ea.	3.880	27.09	100.29	127.38
½" PVC supply, 4" PVC waste, 1-½" PVC vent	1.000	Ea.	4.216	29.49	109.41	138.90
Piping, supply, ½" copper	36.000	L.F.	4.158	54.60	111.72	166.32
½" steel	36.000	L.F.	5.334	52.50	144.06	196.56
½" PVC	36.000	L.F.	6.216	58.80	168.00	226.80
Piping, waste, 4" cast iron no hub	7.000	L.F.	2.760	50.30	67.20	117.50
4" PVC/DWV	7.000	L.F.	3.330	24.30	81.20	105.50
4" copper/DWV	7.000	L.F.	4.000	149.20	100.80	250.00
Piping, vent, 2" cast iron no hub	6.000	L.F.	2.151	26.82	52.38	79.20
2" copper/DWV	6.000	L.F.	1.638	43.38	44.37	87.75
2" PVC/DWV	6.000	L.F.	2.439	9.27	59.13	68.40
2" steel, galvanized	6.000	L.F.	2.250	34.92	54.63	89.55
Vanity base cabinet, 2 door, 24" x 30"	1.000	Ea.	1.000	187.00	23.00	210.00
24" x 36"	1.000	Ea.	1.200	214.50	30.50	245.00
Vanity top, laminated plastic square edge, 25" x 32"	2.170	L.F.	.712	58.45	16.31	74.76
25" x 38"	2.670	L.F.	.846	69.39	19.37	88.76
Carrier, for lavatory, steel for studs, no arms	1.000	Ea.	1.140	15.62	30.38	46.00
Wood, 2" x 8" blocking	1.300	L.F.	.052	.79	1.30	2.09

8 | MECHANICAL 32 | Three Fixture Bathroom Systems

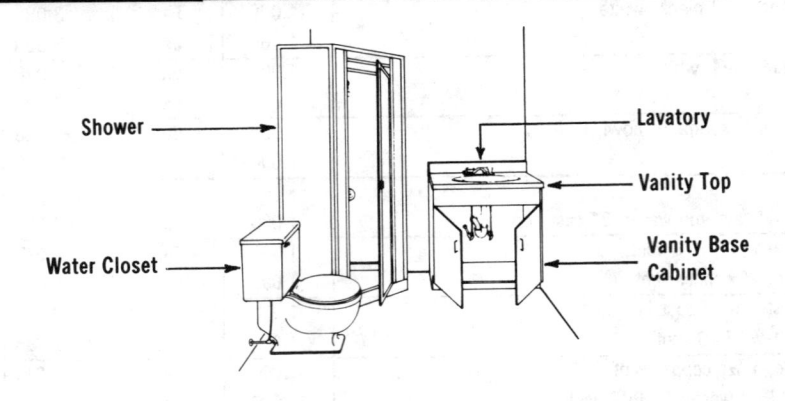

SYSTEM DESCRIPTION	QUAN.	UNIT	MAN-HOURS	MAT.	INST.	TOTAL
BATHROOM WITH LAVATORY INSTALLED IN VANITY						
Water closet, floor mounted, 2 piece, close coupled, white	1.000	Ea.	3.020	151.80	73.20	225.00
Rough-in supply, waste and vent for water closet	1.000	Ea.	2.378	34.81	59.40	94.21
Lavatory, 20" x 18", P.E. cast iron with fittings, white	1.000	Ea.	2.500	147.40	62.60	210.00
Rough-in supply, waste and vent for lavatory	1.000	Ea.	2.790	35.72	70.28	106.00
Shower, steel enameled, stone base, corner, white	1.000	Ea.	8.000	347.60	192.40	540.00
Rough-in supply, waste and vent for shower	1.000	Ea.	3.243	41.52	82.94	124.46
Piping, supply, ½" copper	36.000	L.F.	3.564	46.80	95.76	142.56
Waste, 4" cast iron, no hub	7.000	L.F.	1.932	35.21	47.04	82.25
Vent, 2" steel, galvanized	6.000	L.F.	1.500	23.28	36.42	59.70
Vanity base, 2 door, 30" wide	1.000	Ea.	1.000	187.00	23.00	210.00
Vanity top, plastic laminated, square edge	2.670	L.F.	.712	56.39	18.37	74.76
TOTAL			30.639	1107.53	761.41	1868.94
BATHROOM, WITH WALL HUNG LAVATORY						
Water closet, floor mounted, 2 piece, close coupled, white	1.000	Ea.	3.020	151.80	73.20	225.00
Rough-in supply, waste and vent for water closet	1.000	Ea.	2.378	34.81	59.40	94.21
Lavatory, wall hung, 20" x 18" P.E. cast iron with fittings, white	1.000	Ea.	2.000	121.00	49.00	170.00
Rough-in supply, waste and vent for lavatory	1.000	Ea.	2.790	35.72	70.28	106.00
Shower, steel enameled, stone base, corner, white	1.000	Ea.	8.000	347.60	192.40	540.00
Rough-in supply, waste and vent for shower	1.000	Ea.	3.243	41.52	82.94	124.46
Piping, supply, ½" copper	36.000	L.F.	3.564	46.80	95.76	142.56
Waste, 4" cast iron, no hub	7.000	L.F.	1.932	35.21	47.04	82.25
Vent, 2" steel, galvanized	6.000	L.F.	1.500	23.28	36.42	59.70
Carrier, steel, for studs, no arms	1.000	Ea.	1.140	15.62	30.38	46.00
TOTAL			29.567	853.36	736.82	1590.18

The costs in this system are on a cost each basis. All necessary piping is included.

DESCRIPTION	QUAN.	UNIT	MAN-HOURS	MAT.	INST.	TOTAL

Three Fixture Bathroom Price Sheet

Description	QUAN.	UNIT	MAN-HOURS	MAT.	INST.	TOTAL
Water closet, close coupled, standard 2 piece, white	1.000	Ea.	3.020	151.80	73.20	225.00
Color	1.000	Ea.	3.020	187.00	73.00	260.00
One piece elongated bowl, white	1.000	Ea.	3.020	459.80	75.20	535.00
Color	1.000	Ea.	3.020	591.80	73.20	665.00
Low profile one piece elongated bowl, white	1.000	Ea.	3.020	732.60	72.40	805.00
Color	1.000	Ea.	3.624	1201.20	88.80	1290.00
Rough-in, for water closet						
½" copper supply, 4" cast iron waste, 2" cast iron vent	1.000	Ea.	2.378	34.81	59.40	94.21
4" P.V.C./DWV waste, 2" PVC vent	1.000	Ea.	2.677	19.21	66.60	85.81
4" copper waste, 2" copper vent	1.000	Ea.	2.522	71.84	65.92	137.76
3" cast iron waste, 1-½" cast iron vent	1.000	Ea.	2.244	30.89	56.07	86.96
3" PVC waste, 1-½" PVC vent	1.000	Ea.	2.388	16.84	61.97	78.81
3" copper waste, 1-½" copper vent	1.000	Ea.	2.014	46.81	52.10	98.91
½" P.V.C. supply, 4" P.V.C. waste, 2" P.V.C. vent	1.000	Ea.	2.971	19.81	74.64	94.45
3" P.V.C. waste, 1-½" P.V.C. vent	1.000	Ea.	2.682	17.44	70.01	87.45
½" steel supply, 4" cast iron waste, 2" cast iron vent	1.000	Ea.	2.546	34.51	64.02	98.53
4" cast iron waste, 2" steel vent	1.000	Ea.	2.590	38.11	65.02	103.13
4" P.V.C. waste, 2" P.V.C. vent	1.000	Ea.	2.845	18.91	71.22	90.13
Lavatory, wall hung P.E. cast iron 20" x 18", white	1.000	Ea.	2.000	121.00	49.00	170.00
Color	1.000	Ea.	2.000	181.50	48.50	230.00
Vitreous china 19" x 17", white	1.000	Ea.	2.000	115.50	49.50	165.00
Color	1.000	Ea.	2.000	132.00	48.00	180.00
Lavatory, for vanity top P.E. cast iron 20" x 18", white	1.000	Ea.	2.500	147.40	62.60	210.00
Color	1.000	Ea.	2.500	166.10	58.90	225.00
Steel enameled 20" x 17", white	1.000	Ea.	2.500	89.10	60.90	150.00
Color	1.000	Ea.	2.500	93.50	61.50	155.00
Vitreous china 20" x 16", white	1.000	Ea.	2.500	190.30	59.70	250.00
Color	1.000	Ea.	2.500	190.30	59.70	250.00
Rough-in, for lavatory						
½" copper supply, 1-½" cast iron waste, 1-½" cast iron vent	1.000	Ea.	2.790	35.72	70.28	106.00
1-½" P.V.C. waste, 1-½" P.V.C. vent	1.000	Ea.	2.638	20.08	71.12	91.20
½" steel supply, 1-½" cast iron waste, 1-¼" steel vent	1.000	Ea.	2.890	33.82	73.58	107.40
1-½" P.V.C. waste, 1-¼" P.V.C. vent	1.000	Ea.	2.918	19.58	78.82	98.40
½" P.V.C. supply, 1-½" P.V.C. waste, 1-½" P.V.C. vent	1.000	Ea.	3.256	21.28	87.92	109.20
Shower, steel enameled stone base, 32" x 32", white	1.000	Ea.	8.000	347.60	192.40	540.00
Color	1.000	Ea.	7.823	569.18	192.02	761.20
36" x 36", white	1.000	Ea.	8.890	632.50	217.50	850.00
Color	1.000	Ea.	8.890	646.80	218.20	865.00
Rough-in, for shower						
½" copper supply, 2" cast iron waste, 1-½" copper vent	1.000	Ea.	3.166	42.32	81.49	123.81
2" P.V.C. waste, 1-½" P.V.C. vent	1.000	Ea.	3.432	27.89	87.97	115.86
½" steel supply, 2" cast iron waste, 1-½" steel vent	1.000	Ea.	3.888	53.19	100.04	153.23
2" P.V.C. waste, 1-½" P.V.C. vent	1.000	Ea.	3.880	27.09	100.29	127.38
	1.000	Ea.	4.216	29.49	109.41	138.90
Piping, supply, ½" copper	36.000	L.F.	3.564	46.80	95.76	142.56
½" steel	36.000	L.F.	4.572	45.00	123.48	168.48
½" P.V.C.	36.000	L.F.	5.328	50.40	144.00	194.40
Waste, 4" cast iron, no hub	7.000	L.F.	1.932	35.21	47.04	82.25
4" P.V.C./DWV	7.000	L.F.	2.331	17.01	56.84	73.85
4" copper/DWV	7.000	L.F.	2.800	104.44	70.56	175.00
Vent, 2" cast iron, no hub	6.000	L.F.	1.092	28.92	29.58	58.50
2" copper/DWV	6.000	L.F.	1.092	28.92	29.58	58.50
2" P.V.C./DWV	6.000	L.F.	1.626	6.18	39.42	45.60
2" steel, galvanized	6.000	L.F.	1.500	23.28	36.42	59.70
Vanity base cabinet, 2 door, 24" x 30"	1.000	Ea.	1.000	187.00	23.00	210.00
24" x 36"	1.000	Ea.	1.200	214.50	30.50	245.00
Vanity top, laminated plastic square edge, 25" x 32"	2.670	L.F.	.712	56.39	18.37	74.76
25" x 38"	3.170	L.F.	.846	66.95	21.81	88.76
Carrier, for lavatory, steel, for studs, no arms	1.000	Ea.	1.140	15.62	30.38	46.00
Wood, 2" x 8" blocking	1.300	L.F.	.052	.79	1.30	2.09

8 | MECHANICAL — 36 | Four Fixture Bathroom Systems

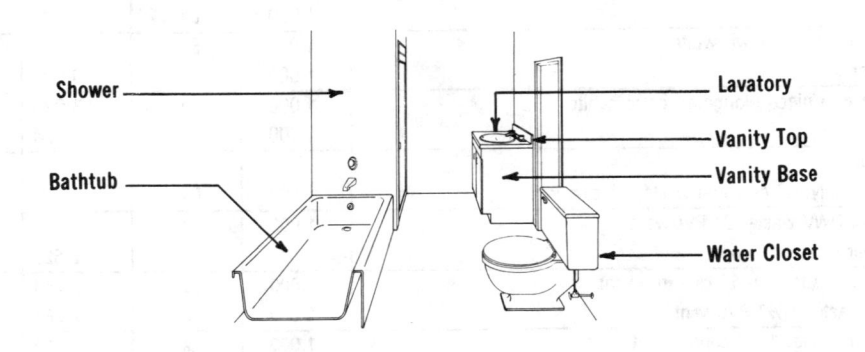

SYSTEM DESCRIPTION	QUAN.	UNIT	MAN-HOURS	MAT.	INST.	TOTAL
BATHROOM WITH LAVATORY INSTALLED IN VANITY						
Water closet, floor mounted, 2 piece, close coupled, white	1.000	Ea.	3.020	151.80	73.20	225.00
Rough-in supply, waste and vent for water closet	1.000	Ea.	2.378	34.81	59.40	94.21
Lavatory, 20" x 18" P.E. cast iron with fittings, white	1.000	Ea.	2.500	147.40	62.60	210.00
Shower, steel, enameled, stone base, corner, white	1.000	Ea.	8.890	643.50	216.50	860.00
Rough-in supply, waste and vent for lavatory and shower	2.000	Ea.	7.668	98.40	194.32	292.72
Bathtub, P.E. cast iron, 5' long with fittings, white	1.000	Ea.	3.640	309.10	85.90	395.00
Rough-in supply, waste and vent for bathtub	1.000	Ea.	2.410	42.65	62.80	105.45
Piping, supply, ½" copper	42.000	L.F.	4.158	54.60	111.72	166.32
Waste, 4" cast iron, no hub	10.000	L.F.	2.760	50.30	67.20	117.50
Vent, 2" steel galvanized	13.000	L.F.	3.250	50.44	78.91	129.35
Vanity base, 2 doors, 30" wide	1.000	Ea.	1.000	187.00	23.00	210.00
Vanity top, plastic laminated, square edge	2.670	L.F.	.712	56.39	18.37	74.76
TOTAL			42.386	1826.39	1053.92	2880.31
BATHROOM WITH WALL HUNG LAVATORY						
Water closet, floor mounted, 2 piece, close coupled, white	1.000	Ea.	3.020	151.80	73.20	225.00
Rough-in supply, waste and vent for water closet	1.000	Ea.	2.378	34.81	59.40	94.21
Lavatory, 20" x 18" P.E. cast iron with fittings, white	1.000	Ea.	2.000	121.00	49.00	170.00
Shower, steel enameled, stone base, corner, white	1.000	Ea.	8.890	643.50	216.50	860.00
Rough-in supply, waste and vent for lavatory and shower	2.000	Ea.	7.668	98.40	194.32	292.72
Bathtub, P.E. cast iron, 5' long with fittings, white	1.000	Ea.	3.640	309.10	85.90	395.00
Rough-in supply, waste and vent for bathtub	1.000	Ea.	2.410	42.65	62.80	105.45
Piping, supply, ½" copper	42.000	L.F.	4.158	54.60	111.72	166.32
Waste, 4" cast iron, no hub	10.000	L.F.	2.760	50.30	67.20	117.50
Vent, 2" steel galvanized	13.000	L.F.	3.250	50.44	78.91	129.35
Carrier, steel, for studs, no arms	1.000	Ea.	1.140	15.62	30.38	46.00
TOTAL			41.314	1572.22	1029.33	2601.55

The costs in this system are on a cost each basis. All necessary piping is included.

DESCRIPTION	QUAN.	UNIT	MAN-HOURS	MAT.	INST.	TOTAL

Four Fixture Bathroom Price Sheet

Description	QUAN.	UNIT	MAN-HOURS	MAT.	INST.	TOTAL
Water closet, close coupled, standard 2 piece, white	1.000	Ea.	3.020	151.80	73.20	225.00
Color	1.000	Ea.	3.020	187.00	73.00	260.00
One piece elongated bowl, white	1.000	Ea.	3.020	459.80	75.20	535.00
Color	1.000	Ea.	3.020	591.80	73.20	665.00
Low profile, one piece elongated bowl, white	1.000	Ea.	3.020	715.00	75.00	790.00
Color	1.000	Ea.	3.020	968.00	82.00	1050.00
Rough-in, for water closet						
½" copper supply, 4" cast iron waste, 2" cast iron vent	1.000	Ea.	2.378	34.81	59.40	94.21
4" PVC/DWV waste, 2" PVC vent	1.000	Ea.	2.677	19.21	66.60	85.81
4" copper waste, 2" copper vent	1.000	Ea.	2.522	71.84	65.92	137.76
3" cast iron waste, 1-½" cast iron vent	1.000	Ea.	2.244	30.89	56.07	86.96
3" P.V.C. waste, 1-½" P.V.C. vent	1.000	Ea.	2.388	16.84	61.97	78.81
3" copper waste, 1-½" copper vent	1.000	Ea.	2.014	46.81	52.10	98.91
½" P.V.C. supply, 4" P.V.C. waste, 2" P.V.C. vent	1.000	Ea.	2.971	19.81	74.64	94.45
3" P.V.C. waste, 1-½" P.V.C. vent	1.000	Ea.	2.682	17.44	70.01	87.45
½" steel supply, 4" cast iron waste, 2" cast iron vent	1.000	Ea.	2.546	34.51	64.02	98.53
4" cast iron waste, 2" steel vent	1.000	Ea.	2.590	38.11	65.02	103.13
4" P.V.C. waste, 2" P.V.C. vent	1.000	Ea.	2.845	18.91	71.22	90.13
Lavatory, wall hung P.E. cast iron 20" x 18", white	1.000	Ea.	2.000	121.00	49.00	170.00
Color	1.000	Ea.	2.000	181.50	48.50	230.00
Vitreous china 19" x 17", white	1.000	Ea.	2.000	115.50	49.50	165.00
Color	1.000	Ea.	2.000	132.00	48.00	180.00
Lavatory for vanity top, P.E. cast iron 20" x 18", white	1.000	Ea.	2.500	147.40	62.60	210.00
Color	1.000	Ea.	2.500	166.10	58.90	225.00
Steel enameled, 20" x 17", white	1.000	Ea.	2.500	89.10	60.90	150.00
Color	1.000	Ea.	2.500	93.50	61.50	155.00
Vitreous china 20" x 16", white	1.000	Ea.	2.500	190.30	59.70	250.00
Color	1.000	Ea.	2.500	190.30	59.70	250.00
Shower, steel enameled stone base, 36" square, white	1.000	Ea.	8.890	643.50	216.50	860.00
Color	1.000	Ea.	8.890	654.50	215.50	870.00
Rough-in, for lavatory or shower						
½" copper supply, 1-½" cast iron waste, 1-½" cast iron vent	1.000	Ea.	3.834	49.20	97.16	146.36
1-½" P.V.C. waste, 1-¼" P.V.C. vent	1.000	Ea.	3.676	29.70	99.06	128.76
½" steel supply, 1-¼" cast iron waste, 1-¼" steel vent	1.000	Ea.	4.102	47.00	105.08	152.08
1-¼" P.V.C. waste, 1-¼" P.V.C. vent	1.000	Ea.	3.932	28.60	106.28	134.88
½" P.V.C. supply, 1-½" P.V.C. waste, 1-½" P.V.C. vent	1.000	Ea.	4.588	31.50	123.90	155.40
Bathtub, P.E. cast iron, 5' long with fittings, white	1.000	Ea.	3.640	309.10	85.90	395.00
Color	1.000	Ea.	3.640	396.00	89.00	485.00
Steel, enameled 5' long with fittings, white	1.000	Ea.	2.910	211.20	68.80	280.00
Color	1.000	Ea.	2.910	220.00	70.00	290.00
Rough-in, for bathtub						
½" copper supply, 4" cast iron waste, 1-½" copper vent	1.000	Ea.	2.410	42.65	62.80	105.45
4" P.V.C. waste, 1-½" P.V.C. vent	1.000	Ea.	2.877	23.93	74.92	98.85
½" steel supply, 4" cast iron waste, 1-½" steel vent	1.000	Ea.	2.898	39.63	73.82	113.45
4" P.V.C. waste, 1-½" P.V.C. vent	1.000	Ea.	3.157	23.43	82.62	106.05
½" P.V.C. supply, 4" P.V.C. waste, 1-½" P.V.C. vent	1.000	Ea.	3.367	24.93	88.32	113.25
Piping, supply, ½" copper	42.000	L.F.	4.158	54.60	111.72	166.32
½" steel	42.000	L.F.	5.334	52.50	144.06	196.56
½" P.V.C.	42.000	L.F.	6.216	58.80	168.00	226.80
Waste, 4" cast iron, no hub	10.000	L.F.	2.760	50.30	67.20	117.50
4" P.V.C./DWV	10.000	L.F.	3.330	24.30	81.20	105.50
4" copper/DWV	10.000	Ea.	4.000	149.20	100.80	250.00
Vent 2" cast iron, no hub	13.000	L.F.	3.107	38.74	75.66	114.40
2" copper/DWV	13.000	L.F.	2.366	62.66	64.09	126.75
2" P.V.C./DWV	13.000	L.F.	3.523	13.39	85.41	98.80
2" steel, galvanized	13.000	L.F.	3.250	50.44	78.91	129.35
Vanity base cabinet, 2 doors, 30" wide	1.000	Ea.	1.000	187.00	23.00	210.00
Vanity top, plastic laminated, square edge	2.670	L.F.	.712	56.39	18.37	74.76
Carrier, steel for studs, no arms	1.000	Ea.	1.140	15.62	30.38	46.00
Wood, 2" x 8" blocking	1.300	L.F.	.052	.79	1.30	2.09

8 | MECHANICAL — 40 | Four Fixture Bathroom Systems

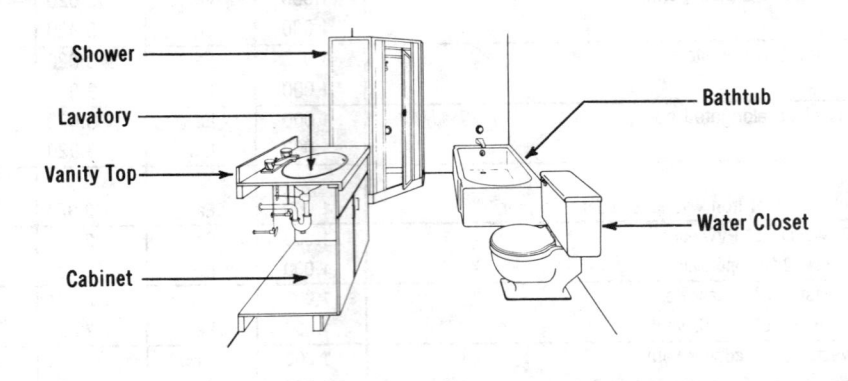

SYSTEM DESCRIPTION	QUAN.	UNIT	MAN-HOURS	MAT.	INST.	TOTAL
BATHROOM WITH LAVATORY INSTALLED IN VANITY						
Water closet, floor mounted, 2 piece, close coupled, white	1.000	Ea.	3.020	151.80	73.20	225.00
Rough-in supply, waste and vent for water closet	1.000	Ea.	2.378	34.81	59.40	94.21
Lavatory, 20" x 18" P.E. cast iron with fittings, white	1.000	Ea.	2.500	147.40	62.60	210.00
Shower, steel, enameled, stone base, corner, white	1.000	Ea.	8.890	643.50	216.50	860.00
Rough-in supply waste and vent for lavatory and shower	2.000	Ea.	7.668	98.40	194.32	292.72
Bathtub, P.E. cast iron, 5' long with fittings, white	1.000	Ea.	3.640	309.10	85.90	395.00
Rough-in supply waste and vent for bathtub	1.000	Ea.	2.410	42.65	62.80	105.45
Piping supply, ½" copper	42.000	L.F.	4.950	65.00	133.00	198.00
Waste, 4" cast iron, no hub	10.000	L.F.	4.140	75.45	100.80	176.25
Vent, 2" steel galvanized	13.000	L.F.	4.500	69.84	109.26	179.10
Vanity base, 2 doors, 30" wide	1.000	Ea.	1.000	187.00	23.00	210.00
Vanity top, plastic laminated, square edge	2.670	L.F.	.712	58.45	16.31	74.76
TOTAL			45.808	1883.40	1137.09	3020.49
BATHROOM WITH WALL HUNG LAVATORY						
Water closet, floor mounted, 2 piece, close coupled, white	1.000	Ea.	3.020	151.80	73.20	225.00
Rough-in supply, waste and vent for water closet	1.000	Ea.	2.378	34.81	59.40	94.21
Lavatory, 20" x 18" P.E. cast iron with fittings, white	1.000	Ea.	2.000	121.00	49.00	170.00
Shower, steel enameled, stone base, corner, white	1.000	Ea.	8.890	643.50	216.50	860.00
Rough-in supply, waste and vent for lavatory and shower	2.000	Ea.	7.668	98.40	194.32	292.72
Bathtub, P.E. cast iron, 5" long with fittings, white	1.000	Ea.	3.640	309.10	85.90	395.00
Rough-in supply, waste and vent for bathtub	1.000	Ea.	2.410	42.65	62.80	105.45
Piping, supply, ½" copper	42.000	L.F.	4.950	65.00	133.00	198.00
Waste, 4" cast iron, no hub	10.000	L.F.	4.140	75.45	100.80	176.25
Vent, 2" steel galvanized	13.000	L.F.	4.500	69.84	109.26	179.10
Carrier, steel for studs, no arms	1.000	Ea.	1.140	15.62	30.38	46.00
TOTAL			44.736	1627.17	1114.56	2741.73

The costs in this system are on a cost each basis. All necessary piping is included

DESCRIPTION	QUAN.	UNIT	MAN-HOURS	MAT.	INST.	TOTAL

Four Fixture Bathroom Price Sheet

Description	QUAN.	UNIT	MAN-HOURS	MAT.	INST.	TOTAL
Water closet, close coupled, standard 2 piece, white	1.000	Ea.	3.020	151.80	73.20	225.00
Color	1.000	Ea.	3.020	187.00	73.00	260.00
One piece, elongated bowl, white	1.000	Ea.	3.020	459.80	75.20	535.00
Color	1.000	Ea.	3.020	591.80	73.20	665.00
Low profile, one piece elongated bowl, white	1.000	Ea.	3.020	715.00	75.00	790.00
Color	1.000	Ea.	3.020	968.00	82.00	1050.00
Rough-in, for water closet						
½" copper supply, 4" cast iron waste, 2" cast iron vent	1.000	Ea.	2.378	34.81	59.40	94.21
4" PVC/DWV waste, 2" PVC vent	1.000	Ea.	2.677	19.21	66.60	85.81
4" copper waste, 2" copper vent	1.000	Ea.	2.522	71.84	65.92	137.76
3" cast iron waste, 1-½" cast iron vent	1.000	Ea.	2.244	30.89	56.07	86.96
3" PVC waste, 1-½" PVC vent	1.000	Ea.	2.388	16.84	61.97	78.81
3" PVC waste, 1-½" PVC vent	1.000	Ea.	2.014	46.81	52.10	98.91
½" PVC supply, 4" PVC waste, 2" PVC vent	1.000	Ea.	2.971	19.81	74.64	94.45
3" PVC waste, 1-½" PVC vent	1.000	Ea.	2.682	17.44	70.01	87.45
½" steel supply, 4" cast iron waste, 2" cast iron vent	1.000	Ea.	2.546	34.51	64.02	98.53
4" cast iron waste, 2" steel vent	1.000	Ea.	2.590	38.11	65.02	103.13
4" PVC waste, 2" PVC vent	1.000	Ea.	2.845	18.91	71.22	90.13
Lavatory wall hung, P.E. cast iron 20" x 18", white	1.000	Ea.	2.000	121.00	49.00	170.00
Color	1.000	Ea.	2.000	181.50	48.50	230.00
Vitreous china 19" x 17", white	1.000	Ea.	2.000	115.50	49.50	165.00
Color	1.000	Ea.	2.000	132.00	48.00	180.00
Lavatory for vanity top, P.E. cast iron, 20" x 18", white	1.000	Ea.	2.500	147.40	62.60	210.00
Color	1.000	Ea.	2.500	166.10	58.90	225.00
Steel, enameled 20" x 17", white	1.000	Ea.	2.500	89.10	60.90	150.00
Color	1.000	Ea.	2.500	93.50	61.50	155.00
Vitreous china 20" x 16", white	1.000	Ea.	2.500	190.30	59.70	250.00
Color	1.000	Ea.	2.500	190.30	59.70	250.00
Shower, steel enameled, stone base 36" square, white	1.000	Ea.	8.890	643.50	216.50	860.00
Color	1.000	Ea.	8.890	654.50	215.50	870.00
Rough-in, for lavatory and shower						
½" copper supply, 1-½" cast iron waste, 1-½" cast iron vent	1.000	Ea.	7.668	98.40	194.32	292.72
1-½" PVC waste, 1-¼" PVC vent	1.000	Ea.	7.352	59.40	198.12	257.52
½" steel supply, 1-¼" cast iron waste, 1-¼" steel vent	1.000	Ea.	8.204	94.00	210.16	304.16
1-¼" PVC waste, 1-¼" PVC vent	1.000	Ea.	7.864	57.20	212.56	269.76
½" PVC supply, 1-½" PVC waste, 1-½" PVC vent	1.000	Ea.	9.176	63.00	247.80	310.80
Bathtub, P.E. cast iron, 5' long with fittings, white	1.000	Ea.	3.640	309.10	85.90	395.00
Color	1.000	Ea.	3.640	396.00	89.00	485.00
Steel enameled, 5' long with fittings, white	1.000	Ea.	2.910	211.20	68.80	280.00
Color	1.000	Ea.	2.910	220.00	70.00	290.00
Rough-in, for bathtub						
½" copper supply, 4" cast iron waste, 1-½" copper vent	1.000	Ea.	2.410	42.65	62.80	105.45
4" PVC waste, 1-½" PVC vent	1.000	Ea.	2.877	23.93	74.92	98.85
½" steel supply, 4" cast iron waste, 1-½" steel vent	1.000	Ea.	2.898	39.63	73.82	113.45
4" PVC waste, 1-½" PVC vent	1.000	Ea.	3.157	23.43	82.62	106.05
½" PVC supply, 4" PVC waste, 1-½" PVC vent	1.000	Ea.	3.367	24.93	88.32	113.25
Piping supply, ½" copper	42.000	L.F.	4.158	54.60	111.72	166.32
½" steel	42.000	L.F.	5.334	52.50	144.06	196.56
½" PVC	42.000	L.F.	6.216	58.80	168.00	226.80
Piping, waste, 4" cast iron, no hub	10.000	L.F.	3.588	65.39	87.36	152.75
4" PVC/DWV	10.000	L.F.	4.329	31.59	105.56	137.15
4" copper/DWV	10.000	L.F.	5.200	193.96	131.04	325.00
Piping, vent, 2" cast iron, no hub	13.000	L.F.	3.107	38.74	75.66	114.40
2" copper/DWV	13.000	L.F.	2.366	62.66	64.09	126.75
2" PVC/DWV	13.000	L.F.	3.523	13.39	85.41	98.80
2" steel, galvanized	13.000	L.F.	3.250	50.44	78.91	129.35
Vanity base cabinet, 2 doors, 30" wide	1.000	Ea.	1.000	187.00	23.00	210.00
Vanity top, plastic laminated, square edge	3.160	L.F.	.843	66.74	21.74	88.48
Carrier, steel, for studs, no arms	1.000	Ea.	1.140	15.62	30.38	46.00
Wood, 2" x 8" blocking	1.300	L.F.	.052	.79	1.30	2.09

8 | MECHANICAL   44 Five Fixture Bathroom Systems

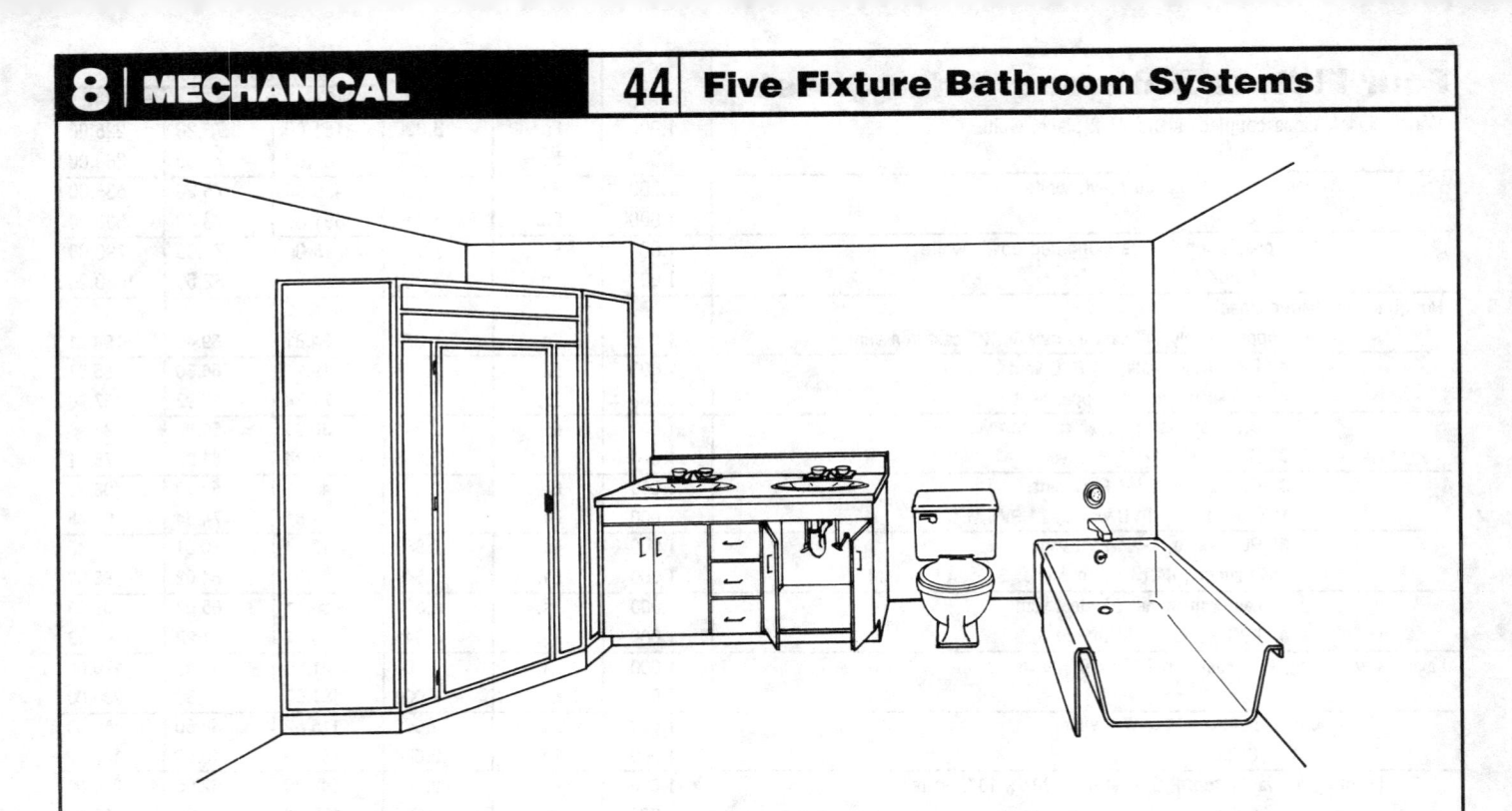

SYSTEM DESCRIPTION	QUAN.	UNIT	MAN-HOURS	MAT.	INST.	TOTAL
BATHROOM WITH SHOWER, BATHTUB, LAVATORIES IN VANITY						
Water closet, floor mounted, 1 piece combination, white	1.000	Ea.	3.020	715.00	75.00	790.00
Rough-in supply, waste and vent for water closet	1.000	Ea.	2.378	34.81	59.40	94.21
Lavatory, 20" x 16", vitreous china oval, with fittings, white	2.000	Ea.	5.000	380.60	119.40	500.00
Shower, steel enameled, stone base, corner, white	1.000	Ea.	8.890	643.50	216.50	860.00
Rough-in supply waste and vent for lavatory and shower	3.000	Ea.	8.370	107.16	210.84	318.00
Bathtub, P.E. cast iron, 5' long with fittings, white	1.000	Ea.	3.640	309.10	85.90	395.00
Rough-in supply, waste and vent for bathtub	1.000	Ea.	2.686	47.68	69.52	117.20
Piping, supply, ½" copper	42.000	L.F.	4.158	54.60	111.72	166.32
Waste, 4" cast iron, no hub	10.000	L.F.	2.760	50.30	67.20	117.50
Vent, 2" steel galvanized	13.000	L.F.	3.250	50.44	78.91	129.35
Vanity base, 2 door, 24" x 48"	1.000	Ea.	1.400	242.00	33.00	275.00
Vanity top, plastic laminated, square edge	4.170	L.F.	1.113	88.07	28.69	116.76
TOTAL			46.665	2723.26	1156.08	3879.34

The costs in this system are on a cost each basis. All necessary piping -is included

DESCRIPTION	QUAN.	UNIT	MAN-HOURS	MAT.	INST.	TOTAL

Five Fixture Bathroom Price Sheet

Description	QUAN.	UNIT	MAN-HOURS	MAT.	INST.	TOTAL
Water closet, close coupled, standard 2 piece, white	1.000	Ea.	3.020	151.80	73.20	225.00
Color	1.000	Ea.	3.020	187.00	73.00	260.00
One piece elongated bowl, white	1.000	Ea.	3.020	459.80	75.20	535.00
Color	1.000	Ea.	3.020	591.80	73.20	665.00
Low profile, one piece elongated bowl, white	1.000	Ea.	3.020	715.00	75.00	790.00
Color	1.000	Ea.	3.020	968.00	82.00	1050.00
Rough-in, supply, waste and vent for water closet						
½" copper supply, 4" cast iron waste, 2" cast iron vent	1.000	Ea.	2.378	34.81	59.40	94.21
4" P.V.C./DWV waste, 2" P.V.C. vent	1.000	Ea.	2.677	19.21	66.60	85.81
4" copper waste, 2" copper vent	1.000	Ea.	2.522	71.84	65.92	137.76
3" cast iron waste, 1-½" cast iron vent	1.000	Ea.	2.244	30.89	56.07	86.96
3" P.V.C. waste, 1-½" P.V.C. vent	1.000	Ea.	2.388	16.84	61.97	78.81
3" copper waste, 1-½" copper vent	1.000	Ea.	2.014	46.81	52.10	98.91
½" P.V.C. supply, 4" P.V.C. waste, 2" P.V.C. vent	1.000	Ea.	2.971	19.81	74.64	94.45
3" P.V.C. waste, 1-½" P.V.C. supply	1.000	Ea.	2.682	17.44	70.01	87.45
½" steel supply, 4" cast iron waste, 2" cast iron vent	1.000	Ea.	2.546	34.51	64.02	98.53
4" cast iron waste, 2" steel vent	1.000	Ea.	2.590	38.11	65.02	103.13
4" P.V.C. waste, 2" P.V.C. vent	1.000	Ea.	2.845	18.91	71.22	90.13
Lavatory, wall hung, P.E. cast iron 20" x 18", white	2.000	Ea.	4.000	242.00	98.00	340.00
Color	2.000	Ea.	4.000	363.00	97.00	460.00
Vitreous china, 19" x 17", white	2.000	Ea.	4.000	231.00	99.00	330.00
Color	2.000	Ea.	4.000	264.00	96.00	360.00
Lavatory, for vanity top, P.E. cast iron, 20" x 18", white	2.000	Ea.	5.000	294.80	125.20	420.00
Color	2.000	Ea.	5.000	332.20	117.80	450.00
Steel enameled 20" x 17", white	2.000	Ea.	5.000	178.20	121.80	300.00
Color	2.000	Ea.	5.000	187.00	123.00	310.00
Vitreous china 20" x 16", white	2.000	Ea.	5.000	380.60	119.40	500.00
Color	2.000	Ea.	5.000	380.60	119.40	500.00
Shower, steel enameled, stone base 36" square, white	1.000	Ea.	8.890	643.50	216.50	860.00
Color	1.000	Ea.	8.890	654.50	215.50	870.00
Rough-in, for lavatory or shower						
½" copper supply, 1-½" cast iron waste, 1-½" cast iron vent	3.000	Ea.	8.370	107.16	210.84	318.00
1-½" P.V.C. waste, 1-¼" P.V.C. vent	3.000	Ea.	7.914	60.24	213.36	273.60
½" steel supply, 1-¼" cast iron waste, 1-¼" steel vent	3.000	Ea.	8.670	101.46	220.74	322.20
1-¼" P.V.C. waste, 1-¼" P.V.C. vent	3.000	Ea.	8.370	58.14	226.26	284.40
½" P.V.C. supply, 1-½" P.V.C. waste, 1-½" P.V.C. vent	3.000	Ea.	9.768	63.84	263.76	327.60
Bathtub, P.E. cast iron 5' long with fittings, white	1.000	Ea.	3.640	309.10	85.90	395.00
Color	1.000	Ea.	3.640	396.00	89.00	485.00
Steel, enameled 5' long with fittings, white	1.000	Ea.	2.910	211.20	68.80	280.00
Color	1.000	Ea.	2.910	220.00	70.00	290.00
Rough-in, for bathtub						
½" copper supply, 4" cast iron waste, 1-½" copper vent	1.000	Ea.	2.686	47.68	69.52	117.20
4" P.V.C. waste, 1-½" P.V.C. vent	1.000	Ea.	3.210	26.36	83.04	109.40
½" steel supply, 4" cast iron waste, 1-½" steel vent	1.000	Ea.	3.174	44.66	80.54	125.20
4" P.V.C. waste, 1-½" P.V.C. vent	1.000	Ea.	3.490	25.86	90.74	116.60
½" P.V.C. supply, 4" P.V.C. waste, 1-½" P.V.C. vent	1.000	Ea.	3.700	27.36	96.44	123.80
Piping, supply, ½" copper	42.000	L.F.	4.158	54.60	111.72	166.32
½" steel	42.000	L.F.	5.334	52.50	144.06	196.56
½" P.V.C.	42.000	L.F.	6.216	58.80	168.00	226.80
Piping, waste, 4" cast iron, no hub	10.000	L.F.	2.760	50.30	67.20	117.50
4" P.V.C./DWV	10.000	L.F.	3.330	24.30	81.20	105.50
4" copper/DWV	10.000	L.F.	4.000	149.20	100.80	250.00
Piping, vent, 2" cast iron, no hub	13.000	L.F.	3.107	38.74	75.66	114.40
2" copper/DWV	13.000	L.F.	2.366	62.66	64.09	126.75
2" P.V.C./DWV	13.000	L.F.	3.523	13.39	85.41	98.80
2" steel, galvanized	13.000	L.F.	3.250	50.44	78.91	129.35
Vanity base cabinet, 2 doors, 24" x 48"	1.000	Ea.	1.400	242.00	33.00	275.00
Vanity top, plastic laminated, square edge	4.170	L.F.	1.113	88.07	28.69	116.76
Carrier, steel, for studs, no arms	1.000	Ea.	1.140	15.62	30.38	46.00
Wood, 2" x 8" blocking	1.300	L.F.	.052	.79	1.30	2.09

8 | MECHANICAL — 60 | Gas Heating/Cooling Systems

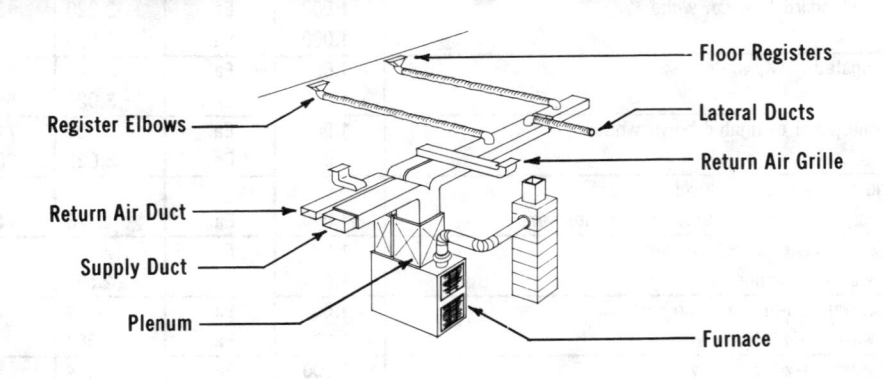

Diagram labels: Register Elbows, Floor Registers, Lateral Ducts, Return Air Grille, Return Air Duct, Supply Duct, Plenum, Furnace

SYSTEM DESCRIPTION	QUAN.	UNIT	MAN-HOURS	MAT.	INST.	TOTAL
HEATING ONLY, GAS FIRED HOT AIR, ONE ZONE, 1200 S.F. BUILDING						
Furnace, gas, up flow	1.000	Ea.	4.710	566.50	113.50	680.00
Intermittent pilot	1.000	Ea.		110.00		110.00
Supply duct, rigid fiberglass	176.000	L.F.	12.144	79.20	302.72	381.92
Return duct, sheet metal, galvanized	158.000	Lb.	16.116	131.14	406.06	537.20
Lateral ducts, 6" flexible fiberglass	144.000	L.F.	8.928	243.36	214.56	457.92
Register, elbows	12.000	Ea.	3.204	119.52	77.88	197.40
Floor registers, enameled steel	12.000	Ea.	3.000	141.96	80.64	222.60
Floor grille, return air	2.000	Ea.	.728	26.62	19.38	46.00
Thermostat	1.000	Ea.	1.000	17.93	27.07	45.00
Plenum	1.000	Ea.	1.000	60.50	24.50	85.00
TOTAL			50.830	1496.73	1266.31	2763.04
HEATING/COOLING, GAS FIRED FORCED AIR, ONE ZONE, 1200 S.F. BUILDING						
Furnace, including plenum, compressor, coil	1.000	Ea.	14.720	2671.68	364.32	3036.00
Intermittent pilot	1.000	Ea.		110.00		110.00
Supply duct, rigid fiberglass	176.000	L.F.	12.144	79.20	302.72	381.92
Return duct, sheet metal, galvanized	158.000	Lb.	16.116	131.14	406.06	537.20
Lateral duct, 6" flexible fiberglass	144.000	L.F.	8.928	243.36	214.56	457.92
Register elbows	12.000	Ea.	3.204	119.52	77.88	197.40
Floor registers, enameled steel	12.000	Ea.	3.000	141.96	80.64	222.60
Floor grille return air	2.000	Ea.	.728	26.62	19.38	46.00
Thermostat	1.000	Ea.	1.000	17.93	27.07	45.00
Refrigeration piping (precharged)	25.000	L.F.		130.00		130.00
TOTAL			59.840	3671.41	1492.63	5164.04

The costs in these systems are based on complete system basis. For larger buildings use the price sheet on the opposite page.

DESCRIPTION	QUAN.	UNIT	MAN-HOURS	MAT.	INST.	TOTAL

Gas Heating/Cooling Price Sheet

	QUAN.	UNIT	MAN-HOURS	MAT.	INST.	TOTAL
Furnace, heating only, 100 MBH, area to 1200 S.F.	1.000	Ea.	4.710	566.50	113.50	680.00
120 MBH, area to 1500 S.F.	1.000	Ea.	5.000	588.50	121.50	710.00
160 MBH, area to 2000 S.F.	1.000	Ea.	5.710	1171.50	128.50	1300.00
200 MBH, area to 2400 S.F.	1.000	Ea.	6.150	2915.00	160.00	3075.00
Heating/cooling, 100 MBH heat, 36 MBH cool, to 1200 S.F.	1.000	Ea.	16.000	2904.00	396.00	3300.00
120 MBH heat, 42 MBH cool, to 1500 S.F.	1.000	Ea.	18.460	3289.00	461.00	3750.00
144 MBH heat, 47	1.000	Ea.	20.000	3388.00	512.00	3900.00
200 MBH heat, 60 MBH cool, to 2400 S.F.	1.000	Ea.	34.290	3553.00	872.00	4425.00
Intermittent pilot, 100 MBH furnace	1.000	Ea.		110.00		110.00
200 MBH furnace	1.000	Ea.		110.00		110.00
Supply duct, rectangular, area to 1200 S.F., rigid fiberglass	176.000	S.F.	12.144	79.20	302.72	381.92
Sheet metal insulated	228.000	Lb.	31.352	277.24	783.08	1060.32
Area to 1500 S.F., rigid fiberglass	176.000	S.F.	12.144	79.20	302.72	381.92
Sheet metal insulated	228.000	Lb.	31.352	277.24	783.08	1060.32
Area to 2400 S.F., rigid fiberglass	205.000	S.F.	14.145	92.25	352.60	444.85
Sheet metal insulated	271.000	Lb.	37.072	327.43	926.07	1253.50
Round flexible, insulated 6" diameter, to 1200 S.F.	156.000	L.F.	9.672	263.64	232.44	496.08
To 1500 S.F.	184.000	L.F.	11.408	310.96	274.16	585.12
8" diameter, to 2000 S.F.	269.000	L.F.	23.941	586.42	581.04	1167.46
To 2400 S.F.	248.000	L.F.	22.072	540.64	535.68	1076.32
Return duct, sheet metal galvanized, to 1500 S.F.	158.000	Lb.	16.116	131.14	406.06	537.20
To 2400 S.F.	191.000	Lb.	19.482	158.53	490.87	649.40
Lateral ducts, flexible round 6" insulated, to 1200 S.F.	144.000	L.F.	8.928	243.36	214.56	457.92
To 1500 S.F.	172.000	L.F.	10.664	290.68	256.28	546.96
To 2000 S.F.	261.000	L.F.	16.182	441.09	388.89	829.98
To 2400 S.F.	300.000	L.F.	18.600	507.00	447.00	954.00
Spiral steel insulated, to 1200 S.F.	144.000	L.F.	20.122	645.02	490.24	1135.26
To 1500 S.F.	172.000	L.F.	24.018	770.26	585.16	1355.42
To 2000 S.F.	261.000	L.F.	36.451	1168.88	888.07	2056.95
To 2400 S.F.	300.000	L.F.	41.940	1344.00	1021.80	2365.80
Rectangular sheet metal galvanized insulated, to 1200 S.F.	228.000	Lb.	39.126	361.74	972.36	1334.10
To 1500 S.F.	344.000	Lb.	54.040	491.52	1345.52	1837.04
To 2000 S.F.	522.000	Lb.	82.040	746.26	2042.66	2788.92
To 2400 S.F.	600.000	Lb.	94.320	858.00	2348.40	3206.40
Register elbows, to 1500 S.F.	12.000	Ea.	3.204	119.52	77.88	197.40
To 2400 S.F.	14.000	Ea.	3.738	139.44	90.86	230.30
Floor registers, enameled steel w/damper, to 1500 S.F.	12.000	Ea.	3.000	141.96	80.64	222.60
To 2400 S.F.	14.000	Ea.	4.312	204.12	117.88	322.00
Return air grille, area to 1500 S.F. 12" x 12"	2.000	Ea.	.728	26.62	19.38	46.00
Area to 2400 S.F. 8" x 16"	2.000	Ea.	.444	24.20	11.80	36.00
Area to 2400 S.F. 8" x 16"	2.000	Ea.	.728	26.62	19.38	46.00
16" x 16"	1.000	Ea.	.364	19.97	10.03	30.00
Thermostat, manual, 1 set back	1.000	Ea.	1.000	17.93	27.07	45.00
Electric, timed, 1 set back	1.000	Ea.	1.000	65.40	26.60	92.00
2 set back	1.000	Ea.	1.000	65.40	26.60	92.00
Plenum, heating only, 100 M.B.H.	1.000	Ea.	1.000	60.50	24.50	85.00
120 MBH	1.000	Ea.	1.000	60.50	24.50	85.00
160 MBH	1.000	Ea.	1.000	60.50	24.50	85.00
200 MBH	1.000	Ea.	1.000	60.50	24.50	85.00
Refrigeration piping, ⅜"	25.000	L.F.		15.00		15.00
¾"	25.000	L.F.		30.50		30.50
⅞"	25.000	L.F.		35.56		35.56
Diffusers, ceiling, 6" diameter, to 1500 S.F.	10.000	Ea.	4.440	205.70	124.30	330.00
To 2400 S.F.	12.000	Ea.	6.000	269.28	162.72	432.00
Floor, aluminum, adjustable, 2-¼" x 12" to 1500 S.F.	12.000	Ea.	3.000	107.64	80.76	188.40
To 2400 S.F.	14.000	Ea.	3.500	125.58	94.22	219.80
Side wall, aluminum, adjustable, 8" x 4", to 1500 S.F.	12.000	Ea.	3.000	242.28	81.72	324.00
5" x 10" to 2400 S.F.	12.000	Ea.	3.696	323.40	96.60	420.00

8 | MECHANICAL — 64 | Oil Fired Heating/Cooling Systems

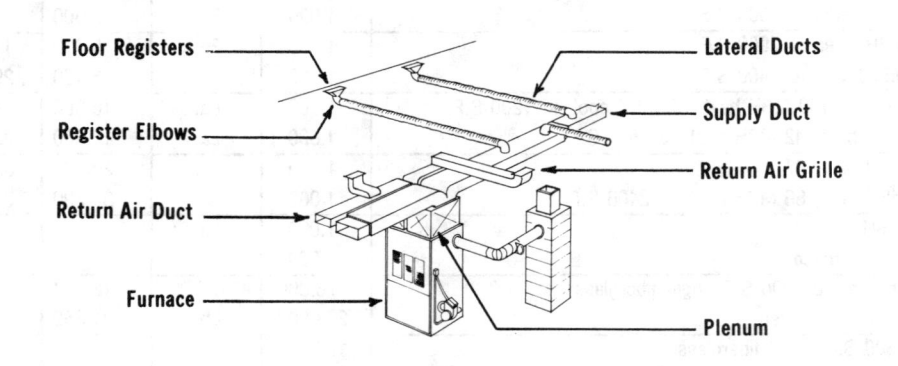

Diagram labels: Floor Registers, Register Elbows, Return Air Duct, Furnace, Lateral Ducts, Supply Duct, Return Air Grille, Plenum

SYSTEM DESCRIPTION	QUAN.	UNIT	MAN-HOURS	MAT.	INST.	TOTAL
HEATING ONLY, OIL FIRED HOT AIR, ONE ZONE, 1200 S.F. BUILDING						
Furnace, oil fired, atomizing gun type burner	1.000	Ea.	4.570	803.00	112.00	915.00
Oil piping to furnace	1.000	Ea.	3.181	41.45	85.55	127.00
Oil tank, 275 gallon, on legs	1.000	Ea.	3.200	247.50	77.50	325.00
Supply duct, rigid fiberglass	176.000	S.F.	12.144	79.20	302.72	381.92
Return duct, sheet metal, galvanized	158.000	Lb.	16.116	131.14	406.06	537.20
Lateral ducts, 6" flexible fiberglass	144.000	L.F.	8.928	243.36	214.56	457.92
Register elbows	12.000	Ea.	3.204	119.52	77.88	197.40
Floor register, enameled steel	12.000	Ea.	3.000	141.96	80.64	222.60
Floor grille, return air	2.000	Ea.	.728	26.62	19.38	46.00
Thermostat	1.000	Ea.	1.000	17.93	27.07	45.00
TOTAL			56.071	1851.68	1403.36	3255.04
HEATING/COOLING, OIL FIRED, FORCED AIR, ONE ZONE, 1200 S.F. BUILDING						
Furnace, including plenum, compressor, coil	1.000	Ea.	16.000	3047.00	378.00	3425.00
Oil piping to furnace	1.000	Ea.	3.413	91.94	90.96	182.90
Oil tank, 275 gallon on legs	1.000	Ea.	3.200	247.50	77.50	325.00
Supply duct, rigid fiberglass	176.000	S.F.	12.144	79.20	302.72	381.92
Return duct, sheet metal, galvanized	158.000	Lb.	16.116	131.14	406.06	537.20
Lateral ducts, 6" flexible fiberglass	144.000	L.F.	8.928	243.36	214.56	457.92
Register elbows	12.000	Ea.	3.204	119.52	77.88	197.40
Floor registers, enameled steel	12.000	Ea.	3.000	141.96	80.64	222.60
Floor grille, return air	2.000	Ea.	.728	26.62	19.38	46.00
Refrigeration piping (precharged)	25.000	L.F.		130.00		130.00
TOTAL			66.733	4258.24	1647.70	5905.94

DESCRIPTION	QUAN.	UNIT	MAN-HOURS	MAT.	INST.	TOTAL

Oil Fired Heating/Cooling

	QUAN.	UNIT	MAN-HOURS	COST EACH MAT.	COST EACH INST.	TOTAL
Furnace, heating, 95.2 MBH, area to 1200 S.F.	1.000	Ea.	4.570	803.00	112.00	915.00
123.2 MBH, area to 1500 S.F.	1.000	Ea.	5.000	990.00	110.00	1100.00
151.2 MBH, area to 2000 S.F.	1.000	Ea.	5.330	1226.50	123.50	1350.00
200 MBH, area to 2400 S.F.	1.000	Ea.	6.150	1941.50	158.50	2100.00
Heating/cooling, 95.2 MBH heat, 36 MBH cool, to 1200 S.F.	1.000	Ea.	16.000	3047.00	378.00	3425.00
112 MBH heat, 42 MBH cool, to 1500 S.F.	1.000	Ea.	24.000	4570.50	567.00	5137.50
151 MBH heat, 47 MBH cool, to 2000 S.F.	1.000	Ea.	20.800	3961.10	491.40	4452.50
184.8 MBH heat, 60 MBH cool, to 2400 S.F.	1.000	Ea.	24.000	3784.00	616.00	4400.00
Oil piping to furnace, ⅜" dia., copper	1.000	Ea.	3.413	91.94	90.96	182.90
Oil tank, on legs above ground, 275 gallons	1.000	Ea.	3.200	247.50	77.50	325.00
550 gallons	1.000	Ea.	4.000	1155.00	95.00	1250.00
Below ground, 275 gallons	1.000	Ea.	3.200	247.50	77.50	325.00
550 gallons	1.000	Ea.	4.000	1155.00	95.00	1250.00
1000 gallons	1.000	Ea.	8.000	1485.00	215.00	1700.00
Supply duct, rectangular, area to 1200 S.F., rigid fiberglass	176.000	S.F.	12.144	79.20	302.72	381.92
Sheet metal, insulated	228.000	Lb.	31.352	277.24	783.08	1060.32
Area to 1500 S.F., rigid fiberglass	176.000	S.F.	12.144	79.20	302.72	381.92
Sheet metal, insulated	228.000	Lb.	31.352	277.24	783.08	1060.32
Area to 2400 S.F., rigid fiberglass	205.000	S.F.	14.145	92.25	352.60	444.85
Sheet metal, insulated	271.000	Lb.	37.072	327.43	926.07	1253.50
Round flexible, insulated, 6" diameter to 1200 S.F.	156.000	L.F.	9.672	263.64	232.44	496.08
To 1500 S.F.	184.000	L.F.	11.408	310.96	274.16	585.12
8" diameter to 2000 S.F.	269.000	L.F.	23.941	586.42	581.04	1167.46
To 2400 S.F.	269.000	L.F.	22.072	540.64	535.68	1076.32
Return duct, sheet metal galvanized, to 1500 S.F.	158.000	Lb.	16.116	131.14	406.06	537.20
To 2400 S.F.	191.000	Lb.	19.482	158.53	490.87	649.40
Lateral ducts, flexible round, 6", insulated to 1200 S.F.	144.000	L.F.	8.928	243.36	214.56	457.92
To 1500 S.F.	172.000	L.F.	10.664	290.68	256.28	546.96
To 2000 S.F.	261.000	L.F.	16.182	441.09	388.89	829.98
To 2400 S.F.	300.000	L.F.	18.600	507.00	447.00	954.00
Spiral steel, insulated to 1200 S.F.	144.000	L.F.	20.122	645.02	490.24	1135.26
To 1500 S.F.	172.000	L.F.	24.018	770.26	585.16	1355.42
To 2000 S.F.	261.000	L.F.	36.451	1168.88	888.07	2056.95
To 2400 S.F.	300.000	L.F.	41.940	1344.00	1021.80	2365.80
Rectangular sheet metal galvanized insulated, to 1200 S.F.	288.000	Lb.	45.246	411.54	1126.56	1538.10
To 1500 S.F.	344.000	Lb.	54.040	491.52	1345.52	1837.04
To 2000 S.F.	522.000	Lb.	82.040	746.26	2042.66	2788.92
To 2400 S.F.	600.000	Lb.	94.320	858.00	2348.40	3206.40
Register elbows, to 1500 S.F.	12.000	Ea.	3.204	119.52	77.88	197.40
To 2400 S.F.	14.000	Ea.	3.738	139.44	90.86	230.30
Floor registers, enameled steel w/damper, to 1500 S.F.	12.000	Ea.	3.000	141.96	80.64	222.60
To 2400 S.F.	14.000	Ea.	4.312	204.12	117.88	322.00
Return air grille, area to 1500 S.F., 12" x 12"	2.000	Ea.	.728	26.62	19.38	46.00
12" x 24"	1.000	Ea.	.444	24.20	11.80	36.00
Area to 2400 S.F., 8" x 16"	2.000	Ea.	.728	26.62	19.38	46.00
16" x 16"	1.000	Ea.	.364	19.97	10.03	30.00
Thermostat, manual, 1 set back	1.000	Ea.	1.000	17.93	27.07	45.00
Electric, timed, 1 set back	1.000	Ea.	1.000	65.40	26.60	92.00
2 set back	1.000	Ea.	1.000	65.40	26.60	92.00
Refrigeration piping, ⅜"	25.000	L.F.		15.00		15.00
¾"	25.000	L.F.		30.50		30.50
Diffusers, ceiling, 6" diameter, to 1500 S.F.	10.000	Ea.	4.440	205.70	124.30	330.00
To 2400 S.F.	12.000	Ea.	6.000	269.28	162.72	432.00
Floor, aluminum, adjustable, 2-¼" x 12" to 1500 S.F.	12.000	Ea.	3.000	107.64	80.76	188.40
To 2400 S.F.	14.000	Ea.	3.500	125.58	94.22	219.80
Side wall, aluminum, adjustable, 8" x 4", to 1500 S.F.	12.000	Ea.	3.000	242.28	81.72	324.00
5" x 10" to 2400 S.F.	12.000	Ea.	3.696	323.40	96.60	420.00

8 | MECHANICAL — 68 | Hot Water Heating Systems

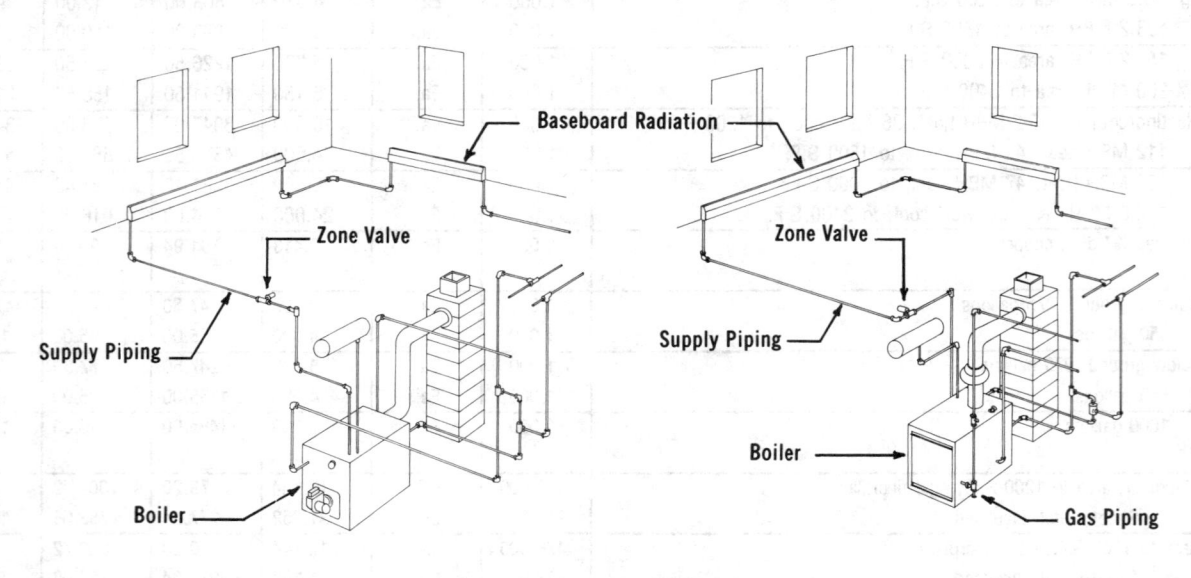

SYSTEM DESCRIPTION	QUAN.	UNIT	MAN-HOURS	MAT.	INST.	TOTAL
OIL FIRED HOT WATER HEATING SYSTEM, AREA TO 1200 S.F.						
Boiler package, oil fired, 97 MBH, area to 1200 S.F. building	1.000	Ea.	12.630	1914.00	311.00	2225.00
Oil piping, ¼" flexible copper tubing	1.000	Ea.	3.219	50.14	86.51	136.65
Oil tank, 275 gallon, with black iron filler pipe	1.000	Ea.	3.200	247.50	77.50	325.00
Supply piping, ¾" copper tubing	176.000	L.F.	18.480	343.20	499.84	843.04
Supply fittings, copper ¾"	36.000	Ea.	15.156	19.44	408.96	428.40
Supply valves, ¾"	2.000	Ea.	.800	36.42	21.58	58.00
Baseboard radiation, ¾"	106.000	L.F.	29.256	897.82	708.08	1605.90
Zone valve	1.000	Ea.	.400	37.51	10.49	48.00
TOTAL			83.141	3546.03	2123.96	5669.99
OIL FIRED HOT WATER HEATING SYSTEM, AREA TO 2400 S.F.						
Boiler package, oil fired, 225 MBH, area to 2400 S.F. building	1.000	Ea.	17.140	2909.50	440.50	3350.00
Oil piping, ⅜" flexible copper tubing	1.000	Ea.	3.264	60.10	87.80	147.90
Oil tank, 550 gallon, with black iron pipe filler pipe	1.000	Ea.	4.000	1155.00	95.00	1250.00
Supply piping, ¾" copper tubing	228.000	L.F.	23.940	444.60	647.52	1092.12
Supply fittings, copper	46.000	Ea.	19.366	24.84	522.56	547.40
Supply valves	2.000	Ea.	.800	36.42	21.58	58.00
Baseboard radiation	212.000	L.F.	58.512	1795.64	1416.16	3211.80
Zone valve	1.000	Ea.	.400	37.51	10.49	48.00
TOTAL			127.422	6463.61	3241.61	9705.22

The costs in this system are on a cost each basis. the costs represent -total cost for the system based on a gross square foot of plan area.

DESCRIPTION	QUAN.	UNIT	MAN-HOURS	MAT.	INST.	TOTAL

Hot Water Heating Price Sheet

	QUAN.	UNIT	MAN-HOURS	COST EACH MAT.	COST EACH INST.	TOTAL
Boiler, oil fired, 97 MBH, area to 1200 S.F.	1.000	Ea.	12.630	1914.00	311.00	2225.00
118 MBH, area to 1500 S.F.	1.000	Ea.	13.330	1947.00	328.00	2275.00
161 MBH, area to 2000 S.F.	1.000	Ea.	16.000	2464.00	411.00	2875.00
215 MBH, area to 2400 S.F.	1.000	Ea.	17.140	2909.50	440.50	3350.00
Oil piping, (valve & filter), 3/8" copper	1.000	Ea.	3.264	60.10	87.80	147.90
1/4" copper	1.000	Ea.	3.219	50.14	86.51	136.65
Oil tank, filler pipe and cap on legs, 275 gallon	1.000	Ea.	3.200	247.50	77.50	325.00
550 gallon	1.000	Ea.	4.000	1155.00	95.00	1250.00
Buried underground, 275 gallon	1.000	Ea.	3.200	247.50	77.50	325.00
550 gallon	1.000	Ea.	4.000	1155.00	95.00	1250.00
1000 gallon	1.000	Ea.	8.000	1485.00	215.00	1700.00
Supply piping copper, area to 1200 S.F., 1/2" tubing	176.000	L.F.	17.424	228.80	468.16	696.96
3/4" tubing	176.000	L.F.	18.480	343.20	499.84	843.04
Area to 1500 S.F., 1/2" tubing	186.000	L.F.	18.414	241.80	494.76	736.56
3/4" tubing	186.000	L.F.	19.530	362.70	528.24	890.94
Area to 2000 S.F., 1/2" tubing	204.000	L.F.	20.196	265.20	542.64	807.84
3/4" tubing	204.000	L.F.	21.420	397.80	579.36	977.16
Area to 2400 S.F., 1/2" tubing	228.000	L.F.	22.572	296.40	606.48	902.88
3/4" tubing	228.000	L.F.	23.940	444.60	647.52	1092.12
Supply pipe fittings copper, area to 1200 S.F., 1/2"	36.000	Ea.	14.400	11.52	388.08	399.60
3/4"	36.000	Ea.	15.156	19.44	408.96	428.40
Area to 1500 S.F., 1/2"	40.000	Ea.	16.000	12.80	431.20	444.00
3/4"	40.000	Ea.	16.840	21.60	454.40	476.00
Area to 2000 S.F., 1/2"	44.000	Ea.	17.600	14.08	474.32	488.40
3/4"	44.000	Ea.	18.524	23.76	499.84	523.60
Area to 2400, S.F., 1/2"	46.000	Ea.	18.400	14.72	495.88	510.60
3/4"	46.000	Ea.	19.366	24.84	522.56	547.40
Supply valves, 1/2" pipe size	2.000	Ea.	.666	30.58	17.42	48.00
3/4"	2.000	Ea.	.800	36.42	21.58	58.00
Baseboard radiation, area to 1200 S.F., 1/2" tubing	106.000	L.F.	28.302	857.54	684.76	1542.30
3/4" tubing	106.000	L.F.	29.256	897.82	708.08	1605.90
Area to 1500 S.F., 1/2" tubing	134.000	L.F.	35.778	1084.06	865.64	1949.70
3/4" tubing	134.000	L.F.	36.984	1134.98	895.12	2030.10
Area to 2000 S.F., 1/2" tubing	178.000	L.F.	47.526	1440.02	1149.88	2589.90
3/4" tubing	178.000	L.F.	49.128	1507.66	1189.04	2696.70
Area to 2400 S.F., 1/2" tubing	212.000	L.F.	56.604	1715.08	1369.52	3084.60
3/4" tubing	212.000	L.F.	58.512	1795.64	1416.16	3211.80
Zone valves, 1/2" tubing	1.000	Ea.	.400	37.51	10.49	48.00
3/4" tubing	1.000	Ea.	.400	37.51	10.49	48.00

8 | MECHANICAL — 80 | Rooftop Systems

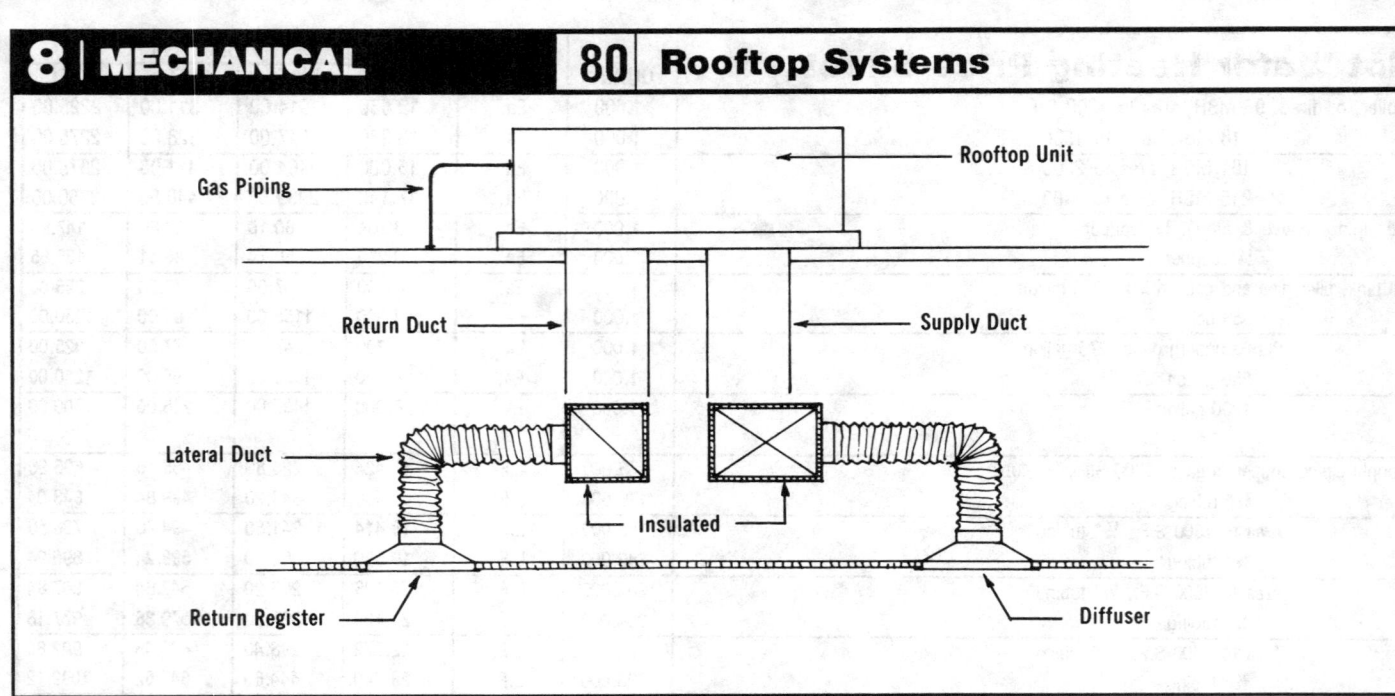

Diagram: Rooftop Unit with Gas Piping, Return Duct, Supply Duct, Lateral Duct (Insulated), Return Register, and Diffuser.

SYSTEM DESCRIPTION	QUAN.	UNIT	MAN-HOURS	MAT.	INST.	TOTAL
ROOFTOP HEATING/COOLING UNIT, AREA TO 2000 S.F.						
Rooftop unit, single zone, electric cool, gas heat, to 2000 s.f.	1.000	Ea.	28.570	3949.00	701.00	4650.00
Gas piping	34.500	L.F.	5.209	56.58	140.07	196.65
Duct, supply and return, galvanized steel	38.000	Lb.	3.876	31.54	97.66	129.20
Insulation, ductwork	33.000	S.F.	1.518	16.50	36.96	53.46
Lateral duct, flexible duct 12" diameter, insulated	72.000	L.F.	11.520	231.12	280.08	511.20
Diffusers	4.000	Ea.	4.560	668.80	131.20	800.00
Return registers	1.000	Ea.	1.000	64.13	26.87	91.00
TOTAL			56.253	5017.67	1413.84	6431.51
ROOFTOP HEATING/COOLING UNIT, AREA TO 5000 S.F.						
Rooftop unit, single zone, electric cool, gas heat, to 5000 s.f.	1.000	Ea.	77.420	10582.00	1918.00	12500.00
Gas piping	86.250	L.F.	13.023	141.45	350.18	491.63
Duct supply and return, galvanized steel	95.000	Lb.	9.690	78.85	244.15	323.00
Insulation, ductwork	82.000	S.F.	3.772	41.00	91.84	132.84
Lateral duct, flexible duct, 12" diameter, insulated	180.000	L.F.	28.800	577.80	700.20	1278.00
Diffusers	10.000	Ea.	11.400	1672.00	328.00	2000.00
Return registers	3.000	Ea.	3.000	192.39	80.61	273.00
TOTAL			147.105	13285.49	3712.98	16998.47

DESCRIPTION	QUAN.	UNIT	MAN-HOURS	MAT.	INST.	TOTAL

Rooftop Price Sheet

	QUAN.	UNIT	MAN-HOURS	COST EACH MAT.	COST EACH INST.	COST EACH TOTAL
Rooftop unit, single zone, electric cool, gas heat to 2000 S.F.	1.000	Ea.	28.570	3949.00	701.00	4650.00
Area to 3000 S.F.	1.000	Ea.	52.170	8008.00	1317.00	9325.00
Area to 5000 S.F.	1.000	Ea.	77.420	10582.00	1918.00	12500.00
Area to 10000 S.F.	1.000	Ea.	145.000	24585.00	3715.00	28300.00
Gas piping, area 2000 through 4000 S.F.	34.500	L.F.	5.209	56.58	140.07	196.65
Area 5000 to 10000 S.F.	86.250	L.F.	13.023	141.45	350.18	491.63
Duct, supply and return, galvanized steel, to 2000 S.F.	38.000	Lb.	3.876	31.54	97.66	129.20
Area to 3000 S.F.	57.000	Lb.	5.814	47.31	146.49	193.80
Area to 5000 S.F.	95.000	Lb.	9.690	78.85	244.15	323.00
Area to 10000 S.F.	190.000	Lb.	19.380	157.70	488.30	646.00
Rigid fiberglass, area to 2000 S.F.	33.000	S.F.	2.277	14.85	56.76	71.61
Area to 3000 S.F.	49.000	S.F.	3.381	22.05	84.28	106.33
Area to 5000 S.F.	82.000	S.F.	5.658	36.90	141.04	177.94
Area to 10000 S.F.	164.000	S.F.	11.316	73.80	282.08	355.88
Insulation, supply and return, blanket type, area to 2000 S.F.	33.000	S.F.	1.518	16.50	36.96	53.46
Area to 3000 S.F.	49.000	S.F.	2.254	24.50	54.88	79.38
Area to 5000 S.F.	82.000	S.F.	3.772	41.00	91.84	132.84
Area to 10000 S.F.	164.000	S.F.	7.544	82.00	183.68	265.68
Lateral ducts, flexible round, 12" insulated, to 2000 S.F.	72.000	L.F.	11.520	231.12	280.08	511.20
Area to 3000 S.F.	108.000	L.F.	17.280	346.68	420.12	766.80
Area to 5000 S.F.	180.000	L.F.	28.800	577.80	700.20	1278.00
Area to 10000 S.F.	360.000	L.F.	57.600	1155.60	1400.40	2556.00
Rectangular, galvanized steel, to 2000 S.F.	239.000	Lb.	24.378	198.37	614.23	812.60
Area to 3000 S.F.	360.000	Lb.	36.720	298.80	925.20	1224.00
Area to 5000 S.F.	599.000	Lb.	61.098	497.17	1539.43	2036.60
Area to 10000 S.F.	998.000	Lb.	101.796	828.34	2564.86	3393.20
Diffusers, ceiling, 1 to 4 way blow, 24" x 24", to 2000 S.F.	4.000	Ea.	4.560	668.80	131.20	800.00
Area to 3000 S.F.	6.000	Ea.	6.840	1003.20	196.80	1200.00
Area to 5000 S.F.	10.000	Ea.	11.400	1672.00	328.00	2000.00
Area to 10000 S.F.	20.000	Ea.	22.800	3344.00	656.00	4000.00
Return grilles, 24" x 24", to 2000 S.F.	1.000	Ea.	1.000	64.13	26.87	91.00
Area to 3000 S.F.	2.000	Ea.	2.000	128.26	53.74	182.00
Area to 5000 S.F.	3.000	Ea.	3.000	192.39	80.61	273.00
Area to 10000 S.F.	5.000	Ea.	5.000	320.65	134.35	455.00

9 | ELECTRICAL — 10 | Electric Service Systems

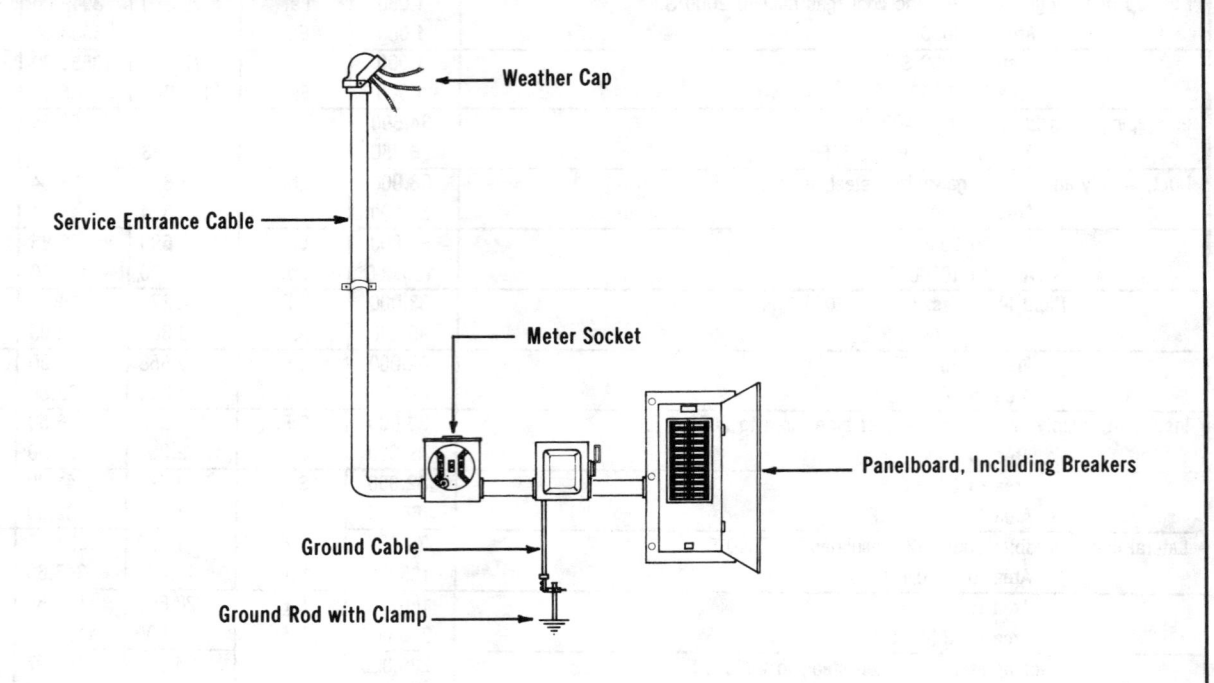

Diagram labels: Weather Cap, Service Entrance Cable, Meter Socket, Ground Cable, Ground Rod with Clamp, Panelboard, Including Breakers

SYSTEM DESCRIPTION	QUAN.	UNIT	MAN-HOURS	MAT.	INST.	TOTAL
100 AMP SERVICE						
Weather cap	1.000	Ea.	.667	4.68	17.32	22.00
Service entrance cable	10.000	L.F.	.760	29.70	20.10	49.80
Meter socket	1.000	Ea.	2.500	26.07	65.93	92.00
Ground rod with clamp	1.000	Ea.	1.510	11.17	39.83	51.00
Ground cable	5.000	L.F.	.250	6.60	6.60	13.20
Panel board, 12 circuit	1.000	Ea.	6.670	110.00	175.00	285.00
TOTAL			12.357	188.22	324.78	513.00
200 AMP SERVICE						
Weather cap	1.000	Ea.	1.000	13.86	26.14	40.00
Service entrance cable	10.000	L.F.	1.140	24.10	30.40	54.50
Meter socket	1.000	Ea.	4.210	40.70	109.30	150.00
Ground rod with clamp	1.000	Ea.	1.820	26.40	47.60	74.00
Ground cable	10.000	L.F.	.500	13.20	13.20	26.40
¾" EMT	5.000	L.F.	.310	2.60	8.10	10.70
Panel board, 24 circuit	1.000	Ea.	12.310	270.60	324.40	595.00
TOTAL			21.290	391.46	559.14	950.60
400 AMP SERVICE						
Weather cap	2.000	Ea.	12.500	232.52	329.48	562.00
Service entrance cable	180.000	L.F.	5.760	250.20	151.20	401.40
Meter socket	1.000	Ea.	4.210	40.70	109.30	150.00
Ground rod with clamp	1.000	Ea.	2.070	30.14	54.21	84.35
Ground cable	20.000	L.F.	.480	18.40	12.80	31.20
¾" greenfield	20.000	L.F.	1.000	8.20	26.40	34.60
Current transformer cabinet	1.000	Ea.	6.150	100.10	164.90	265.00
Panel board, 42 circuit	1.000	Ea.	33.330	2018.50	881.50	2900.00
TOTAL			65.500	2698.76	1729.79	4428.55

9 | ELECTRICAL — 20 | Electric Perimeter Heating Systems

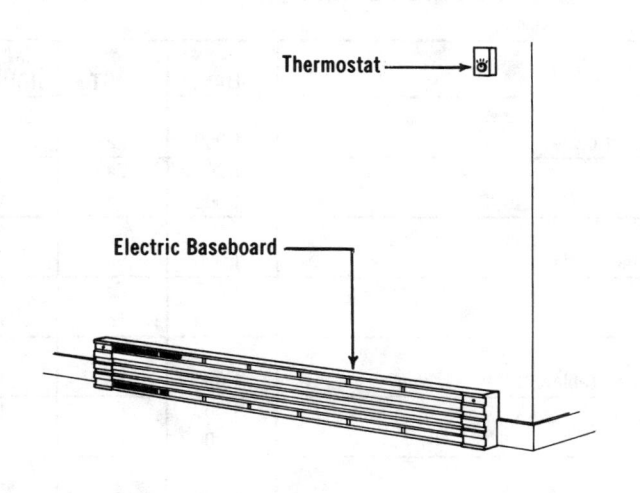

SYSTEM DESCRIPTION	QUAN.	UNIT	MAN-HOURS	MAT.	INST.	TOTAL
4' BASEBOARD HEATER						
Electric baseboard heater, 4' long	1.000	Ea.	1.190	50.19	31.81	82.00
Thermostat, integral	1.000	Ea.	.500	25.30	13.70	39.00
Romex, 12-3 with ground	40.000	L.F.	1.600	18.00	42.40	60.40
Panel board breaker, 20 Amp	1.000	Ea.	.300	5.30	7.90	13.20
TOTAL			3.590	98.79	95.81	194.60
6' BASEBOARD HEATER						
Electric baseboard heater, 6' long	1.000	Ea.	1.600	74.78	40.22	115.00
Thermostat, integral	1.000	Ea.	.500	25.30	13.70	39.00
Romex, 12-3 with ground	40.000	L.F.	1.600	18.00	42.40	60.40
Panel board breaker, 20 Amp	1.000	Ea.	.400	7.07	10.53	17.60
TOTAL			4.100	125.15	106.85	232.00
8' BASEBOARD HEATER						
Electric baseboard heater, 8' long	1.000	Ea.	2.000	99.70	55.30	155.00
Thermostat, integral	1.000	Ea.	.500	25.30	13.70	39.00
Romex, 12-3 with ground	40.000	L.F.	1.600	18.00	42.40	60.40
Panel board breaker, 20 Amp	1.000	Ea.	.500	8.84	13.16	22.00
TOTAL			4.600	151.84	124.56	276.40
10' BASEBOARD HEATER						
Electric baseboard heater, 10' long	1.000	Ea.	2.420	113.30	61.70	175.00
Thermostat, integral	1.000	Ea.	.500	25.30	13.70	39.00
Romex, 12-3 with ground	40.000	L.F.	1.600	18.00	42.40	60.40
Panel board breaker, 20 Amp	1.000	Ea.	.750	13.25	19.75	33.00
TOTAL			5.270	169.85	137.55	307.40

The costs in this system are on a cost each basis and include all
-necessary conduit fittings.

DESCRIPTION	QUAN.	UNIT	MAN-HOURS	MAT.	INST.	TOTAL

9 ELECTRICAL 30 Wiring Device Systems

The prices in this system are on a cost each basis and include 20 feet of wire and conduit (as necessary) for each device.

SYSTEM DESCRIPTION	QUAN.	UNIT	MAN-HOURS	MAT.	INST.	TOTAL
Air conditioning receptacles						
Using non-metallic sheathed cable	1.000	Ea.	.800	9.70	21.30	31.00
Using BX cable	1.000	Ea.	.964	14.56	25.44	40.00
Using EMT conduit	1.000	Ea.	1.190	17.00	32.00	49.00
Disposal wiring						
Using non-metallic sheathed cable	1.000	Ea.	.889	8.50	23.50	32.00
Using BX cable	1.000	Ea.	1.070	12.10	27.90	40.00
Using EMT conduit	1.000	Ea.	1.330	15.75	35.25	51.00
Dryer circuit						
Using non-metallic sheathed cable	1.000	Ea.	1.450	24.24	38.76	63.00
Using BX cable	1.000	Ea.	1.740	30.36	45.64	76.00
Using EMT conduit	1.000	Ea.	2.160	33.99	57.01	91.00
Duplex receptacles						
Using non-metallic sheathed cable	1.000	Ea.	.615	9.70	16.30	26.00
Using BX cable	1.000	Ea.	.741	14.56	19.44	34.00
Using EMT conduit	1.000	Ea.	.920	17.00	24.00	41.00
Exhaust fan wiring						
Using non-metallic sheathed cable	1.000	Ea.	.800	9.70	21.30	31.00
Using BX cable	1.000	Ea.	.964	14.56	25.44	40.00
Using EMT conduit	1.000	Ea.	1.190	18.13	31.87	50.00
Furnace circuit & switch						
Using non-metallic sheathed cable	1.000	Ea.	1.330	13.37	35.63	49.00
Using BX cable	1.000	Ea.	1.600	17.00	42.00	59.00
Using EMT conduit	1.000	Ea.	2.000	21.87	53.13	75.00
Ground fault						
Using non-metallic sheathed cable	1.000	Ea.	1.000	43.05	25.95	69.00
Using BX cable	1.000	Ea.	1.210	48.72	32.28	81.00
Using EMT conduit	1.000	Ea.	1.480	52.12	38.88	91.00
Heater circuits						
Using non-metallic sheathed cable	1.000	Ea.	1.000	9.70	26.30	36.00
Using BX cable	1.000	Ea.	1.210	13.37	31.63	45.00
Using EMT conduit	1.000	Ea.	1.480	17.00	39.00	56.00
Lighting wiring						
Using non-metallic sheathed cable	1.000	Ea.	.500	9.70	13.30	23.00
Using BX cable	1.000	Ea.	.602	14.56	15.44	30.00
Using EMT conduit	1.000	Ea.	.748	18.13	19.87	38.00
Range circuits						
Using non-metallic sheathed cable	1.000	Ea.	2.000	36.26	52.74	89.00
Using BX cable	1.000	Ea.	2.420	49.50	65.50	115.00
Using EMT conduit	1.000	Ea.	2.960	57.20	77.80	135.00
Switches, single pole						
Using non-metallic sheathed cable	1.000	Ea.	.500	9.70	13.30	23.00
Using BX cable	1.000	Ea.	.602	14.56	15.44	30.00
Using EMT conduit	1.000	Ea.	.748	17.00	20.00	37.00
Switches, 3-way						
Using non-metallic sheathed cable	1.000	Ea.	.667	12.10	17.90	30.00
Using BX cable	1.000	Ea.	.800	18.13	20.87	39.00
Using EMT conduit	1.000	Ea.	1.330	29.46	35.54	65.00
Water heater						
Using non-metallic sheathed cable	1.000	Ea.	1.600	12.10	41.90	54.00
Using BX cable	1.000	Ea.	1.900	17.00	50.00	67.00
Using EMT conduit	1.000	Ea.	2.350	20.63	62.37	83.00
Weatherproof receptacle						
Using non-metallic sheathed cable	1.000	Ea.	1.330	69.30	35.70	105.00
Using BX cable	1.000	Ea.	1.600	74.80	40.20	115.00
Using EMT conduit	1.000	Ea.	2.000	79.20	50.80	130.00

9 | ELECTRICAL — 40 | Light Fixture Systems

The costs for these fixtures are on an each basis and incl. installation of the fixt. only. For wiring & switches see sys. sheet 9-30.

DESCRIPTION	QUAN.	UNIT	MAN-HOURS	MAT.	INST.	TOTAL
Fluorescent strip, 4' long, 1 light, average	1.000	Ea.	.941	27.39	24.61	52.00
Deluxe	1.000	Ea.	1.129	32.87	29.53	62.40
2 lights, average	1.000	Ea.	1.000	28.60	26.40	55.00
Deluxe	1.000	Ea.	1.200	34.32	31.68	66.00
8' long, 1 light, average	1.000	Ea.	1.190	45.10	31.90	77.00
Deluxe	1.000	Ea.	1.428	54.12	38.28	92.40
2 lights, average	1.000	Ea.	1.290	51.70	34.30	86.00
Deluxe	1.000	Ea.	1.548	62.04	41.16	103.20
Surface mounted, 4' x 1', economy	1.000	Ea.	.912	44.00	24.00	68.00
Average	1.000	Ea.	1.140	55.00	30.00	85.00
Deluxe	1.000	Ea.	1.368	66.00	36.00	102.00
4' x 2', economy	1.000	Ea.	1.208	73.04	30.96	104.00
Average	1.000	Ea.	1.510	91.30	38.70	130.00
Deluxe	1.000	Ea.	1.812	109.56	46.44	156.00
Recessed, 4' x 1', 2 lamps, economy	1.000	Ea.	1.120	39.60	30.00	69.60
Average	1.000	Ea.	1.400	49.50	37.50	87.00
Deluxe	1.000	Ea.	1.680	59.40	45.00	104.40
4' x 2', 4' lamps, economy	1.000	Ea.	1.360	55.44	36.56	92.00
Average	1.000	Ea.	1.700	69.30	45.70	115.00
Deluxe	1.000	Ea.	2.040	83.16	54.84	138.00
Incandescent, exterior, 150W, single spot	1.000	Ea.	.500	18.70	13.30	32.00
Double spot	1.000	Ea.	1.167	53.90	31.10	85.00
Recessed, 100W, economy	1.000	Ea.	.800	42.24	20.96	63.20
Average	1.000	Ea.	1.000	52.80	26.20	79.00
Deluxe	1.000	Ea.	1.200	63.36	31.44	94.80
150W, economy	1.000	Ea.	.800	44.00	20.80	64.80
Average	1.000	Ea.	1.000	55.00	26.00	81.00
Deluxe	1.000	Ea.	1.200	66.00	31.20	97.20
Surface mounted, 60W, economy	1.000	Ea.	.800	34.10	20.90	55.00
Average	1.000	Ea.	1.000	38.50	26.50	65.00
Deluxe	1.000	Ea.	1.190	82.50	32.50	115.00
Mercury vapor, recessed, 2' x 2' with 250W DX lamp	1.000	Ea.	2.500	280.50	64.50	345.00
2' x 2' with 400W DX lamp	1.000	Ea.	2.760	291.50	73.50	365.00
Surface mounted, 2' x 2' with 250W DX lamp	1.000	Ea.	2.960	258.50	76.50	335.00
2' x 2' with 400W DX lamp	1.000	Ea.	3.330	280.50	89.50	370.00
High bay, single unit, 400W DX lamp	1.000	Ea.	3.480	269.50	90.50	360.00
Twin unit, 400W DX lamp	1.000	Ea.	5.000	539.00	131.00	670.00
Low bay, 250W DX lamp	1.000	Ea.	2.500	330.00	65.00	395.00
Metal halide, recessed 2' x 2' 250W	1.000	Ea.	2.500	308.00	67.00	375.00
2' x 2', 400W	1.000	Ea.	2.760	352.00	73.00	425.00
Surface mounted, 2' x 2', 250W	1.000	Ea.	2.960	286.00	79.00	365.00
2' x 2', 400W	1.000	Ea.	3.330	330.00	90.00	420.00
High bay, single, unit, 400W	1.000	Ea.	3.480	308.00	92.00	400.00
Twin unit, 400W	1.000	Ea.	5.000	616.00	134.00	750.00
Low bay, 250W	1.000	Ea.	2.500	385.00	65.00	450.00

HOW TO USE UNIT PRICE PAGES

Important
Prices in this section are listed in two ways: as bare costs and as costs including overhead and profit of the installing contractor. In most cases, if the work is to be subcontracted, it is best for a general contractor to add an additional 10% to the figures found in the column titled **"TOTAL INCL. O&P"**.

Unit
The unit of measure listed here reflects the material being used in the line item. For example: beam and girder framing is priced in lineal feet (L.F.).

Productivity
The daily output represents typical total daily amount of work that the designated crew will produce. Man-hours are a unit of measure for the labor involved in performing a task. To derive the total man-hours for a task, multiply the quantity of the item involved times the man-hour figure shown.

Line Number Determination
Each line item is identified by a unique ten-digit number.

MASTERFORMAT
Division
061 110 1040
Subdivision

MASTERFORMAT
Mediumscope
061 110
061 **110** 1040
Major Classification

061 110 **1040**
Individual Line Number

Description
This line item describes framing a beam and/or girder from a single 2" x 10" wood member by a F-2 crew at the rate of 600 L.F. per day or .027 man-hours per linear foot.

---

(86) Circle Reference Number
These reference numbers refer to charts, tables, estimating data, cost derivations and other information which may be useful to the user of this book. This information is located in the Reference Section of this book.

Bare Costs are developed as follows for line no. **061-110-1040**
Mat. is **Bare Material Cost ($0.87)**
Labor for Crew F2 = Man-hour Cost (**$14.30**) × Man-hour Units (**.027**) = **$0.38**
Equip. for Crew F2 = Equip. Hour Cost (**$1.00**) × Man-hour Units (**.027**) = **$0.03**
Total = **Mat. Cost ($0.82)** + **Labor Cost ($0.38)** + **Equip. Cost ($0.03)** = **$1.23** per square foot of contact area.
(**Note:** Where a crew is indicated, Equipment and Labor costs are derived from the Crew Tables. See example above.)

Total Costs Including O&P are developed as follows:
Mat. is **Bare Material Cost** + 10% = **$0.82** + **$0.08** = **$0.90**
Labor for Crew F2 = Man-hour Cost (**$23.90**) × Man-hour Units (**.027**) = **$0.64**
Equip. for Crew F2 = Equip. Hour Cost (**$1.10**) × Man-hour Units (**.027**) = **$0.03**
Total = **Mat. Cost ($0.90)** + **Labor Cost ($0.64)** + **Equip. Cost ($0.03)** = **$1.57**
(**Note:** Where a crew is indicated, Equipment and Labor costs are derived from the Crew Tables. See example above. **"Total incl. O&P"** costs may be rounded.)

Crew F-2

Crew No.	Bare Costs		Incl. Subs O & P		Cost Per Man-Hour	
Crew F-2	Hr.	Daily	Hr.	Daily	Bare Costs	Incl. O&P
2 Carpenters	$14.30	$228.80	$23.90	$382.40	$14.30	$23.90
Power Tools		16.00		17.60	1.00	1.10
16 M.H., Daily Totals		$244.80		$400.00	$15.30	$25.00

---

061 | Rough Carpentry

061 100 | Wood Framing

			CREW	DAILY OUTPUT	MAN-HOURS	UNIT	MAT.	LABOR	EQUIP.	TOTAL	TOTAL INCL O&P	
104	0010	BRACING Let-in, with 1" x 6" boards, studs @ 16" O.C.	F-1	150	.053	L.F.	.26	.76	.05	1.07	1.62	104
	0200	Studs @ 24" O.C.		230	.035	"	.26	.50	.03	.79	1.16	
106	0010	BRIDGING Wood, for joists 16" O.C., 1" x 3"		130	.062	Pr.	.31	.88	.06	1.25	1.88	106
	0100	2" x 3" bridging		130	.062		.57	.88	.06	1.51	2.17	
	0300	Steel, galvanized, 18 ga., for 2" x 10" joists at 12" O.C.	1 Carp	130	.062		.78	.88		1.66	2.33	
	0400	24" O.C.		140	.057		1.19	.82		2.01	2.68	
	0600	For 2" x 14" joists at 16" O.C.		1.30	6.150		1.45	88		89.45	150	
	0900	Compression type, 16" O.C., 2" x 8" joists		200	.040		1.15	.57		1.72	2.22	
	1000	2" x 12" joists		200	.040		1.23	.57		1.80	2.31	
110	0010	FRAMING, BEAMS & GIRDERS (86)										110
	0020											
	1000	Single, 2" x 6" (87)	F-2	700	.023	L.F.	.39	.33	.02	.74	1	
	1020	2" x 8"		650	.025		.55	.35	.02	.92	1.23	
	1040	2" x 10"		600	.027		.82	.38	.03	1.23	1.57	
	1060	2" x 12"		550	.029		1.03	.42	.03	1.48	1.86	
	1080	2" x 14"		500	.032		1.20	.46	.03	1.69	2.12	
	1100	3" x 8"		550	.029		1.17	.42	.03	1.62	2.02	
	1120	3" x 10"		500	.032		1.59	.46	.03	2.08	2.55	
	1140	3" x 12"		450	.036		1.80	.51	.04	2.35	2.87	
	1160	3" x 14"		400	.040		2.23	.57	.04	2.84	3.45	
	1180	4" x 8"	F-3	1,000	.040		1.65	.58	.38	2.61	3.20	
	1200	4" x 10"		950	.042		2.12	.61	.40	3.13	3.78	
	1220	4" x 12"		900	.044		2.55	.64	.42	3.61	4.34	
	1240	4" x 14"		850	.047		2.98	.68	.44	4.10	4.90	
	2000	Double, 2" x 6"	F-2	625	.026		.80	.37	.03	1.20	1.52	
	2020	2" x 8"		575	.028		1.10	.40	.03	1.53	1.91	
	2040	2" x 10"		550	.029		1.69	.42	.03	2.14	2.59	
	2060	2" x 12"		525	.030		2.06	.44	.03	2.53	3.03	
	2080	2" x 14"		475	.034		2.42	.48	.03	2.93	3.50	
	2100											
	3000	Triple, 2" x 6"	F-2	550	.029	L.F.	1.18	.42	.03	1.63	2.03	
	3060	2" x 12"		475	.034		3.10	.48	.03	3.61	4.25	
	3080	2" x 14"		450	.036		3.63	.51	.04	4.18	4.88	

240

UNIT PRICE SECTION

TABLE OF CONTENTS

DIV. NO.		PAGE
010	Overhead	242
013	Submittals	243
015	Construction Facilities & Temporary Controls	243
016	Material & Equipment	244
017	Contract Closeout	247
020	Subsurface Investigation & Demolition	248
021	Site Preparation	255
022	Earthwork	256
025	Paving & Surfacing	258
026	Piped Utilities	260
027	Sewerage & Drainage	260
028	Site Improvements	262
029	Landscaping	265
031	Concrete Formwork	267
032	Concrete Reinforcement	269
033	Cast-In-Place Concrete	270
034	Precast Concrete	271
041	Mortar & Masonry Accessories	272
042	Unit Masonry	272
044	Stone	276
045	Masonry Restoration & Cleaning/Refractories	277
050	Metal Materials, Finishes & Fastenings	278
051	Structural Metal Framing	280
052	Metal Joists	282
053	Metal Decking	282
055	Metal Fabrications	282
057	Ornamental Metal	283
060	Fasteners & Adhesives	283

DIV. NO.		PAGE
061	Rough Carpentry	285
062	Finish Carpentry	294
063	Wood Treatment	300
064	Architectural Woodwork	300
071	Waterproofing & Dampproofing	306
072	Insulation	307
073	Shingles & Roofing Tiles	309
074	Preformed Roofing & Siding	311
075	Membrane Roofing	313
076	Flashing & Sheet Metal	314
077	Roof Specialties & Accessories	317
078	Skylights	318
079	Joint Sealers	319
081	Metal Doors & Frames	319
082	Wood & Plastic Doors	321
083	Special Doors	326
085	Metal Windows	328
086	Wood & Plastic Windows	330
087	Hardware	333
088	Glazing	335
091	Metal Support Systems	336
092	Lath, Plaster & Gypsum Board	336
093	Tile	340
094	Terrazzo	341
095	Acoustical Treatment & Wood Flooring	342
096	Flooring & Carpet	344
098	Special Coatings	346
099	Painting & Wall Coverings	347

DIV. NO.		PAGE
101	Chalkboards, Compartments & Cubicles	352
102	Louvers, Corner Protection & Access Flooring	353
103	Fireplaces, Ext. Specialties & Flagpoles	354
105	Lockers, Protective Covers & Postal Specialties	355
106	Partitions & Storage Shelving	356
108	Toilet & Bath Accessories & Scales	357
110	Equipment	357
114	Food Service, Residential, Darkroom, Athletic Equipment	358
125	Window Treatment	360
130	Special Construction	361
131	Pre-Eng. Structures, Pools & Ice Rinks	362
142	Elevators	363
151	Pipe & Fittings	363
152	Plumbing Fixtures	370
153	Plumbing Appliances	372
154	Fire Extinguishing Systems	372
155	Heating	373
157	Air Conditioning/Ventilating	376
160	Raceways	379
161	Conductors & Grounding	381
162	Boxes & Wiring Devices	382
163	Starters, Boards, & Switches	383
165	Power Systems & Capacitors	384
166	Lighting	385
168	Special Systems	386

010 | Overhead

010 000 | Overhead

			CREW	DAILY OUTPUT	MAN-HOURS	UNIT	MAT.	LABOR	EQUIP.	TOTAL	TOTAL INCL O&P	
004	0011	**ARCHITECTURAL FEES**										004
	0020	For new construction										
	0060	Minimum				Project					4.90%	
	0090	Maximum									16%	
	0100	For alteration work, to $500,000, add to fee									50%	
	0150	Over $500,000, add to fee									25%	
016	0011	**CONSTRUCTION MANAGEMENT FEES**										016
	0060	For work to $10,000				Project					10%	
	0070	To $25,000									9%	
	0090	To $100,000									6%	
020	0010	**CONTINGENCIES** Allowance to add at conceptual stage									20%	020
	0150	Final working drawing stage									2%	
034	0010	**FIELD OFFICE EXPENSE**										034
	0100	Office equipment rental, average				Month	135				148.50	
	0120	Office supplies, average				"	250				275	
	0125	Office trailer rental, see division 015-904										
	0140	Telephone bill; avg. bill/month incl. long dist.				Month	225				247.50	
	0160	Field office lights & HVAC										
040	0010	**INSURANCE** Builders risk, standard, minimum				Job					.22%	040
	0050	Maximum									.59%	
	0200	All-risk type, minimum									.25%	
	0250	Maximum									.62%	
	0400	Contractor's equipment floater, minimum				Value					.90%	
	0450	Maximum				"					1.60%	
	0600	Public liability, average				Job					1.55%	
	0800	Workers' compensation & employer's liability, average										
	0850	by trade, carpentry, general				Payroll		16.64%				
	0900	Clerical						.53%				
	0950	Concrete						15.29%				
	1000	Electrical						5.97%				
	1050	Excavation						10.37%				
	1100	Glazing						11.90%				
	1150	Insulation						13.48%				
	1200	Lathing						10.22%				
	1250	Masonry						13.71%				
	1300	Painting & decorating						12.36%				
	1350	Pile driving						25.40%				
	1400	Plastering						13.39%				
	1450	Plumbing						7.45%				
	1500	Roofing						28.91%				
	1550	Sheet metal work (HVAC)						10.24%				
	1600	Steel erection, structural						35.36%				
	1650	Tile work, interior ceramic						8.28%				
	1700	Waterproofing, brush or hand caulking						7.09%				
	1800	Wrecking						35.54%				
	2000	Range of 35 trades in 50 states, excl. wrecking, minimum						2.20%				
	2100	Average						15.10%				
	2200	Maximum						162.50%				
070	0010	**PERMITS** Rule of thumb, most cities, minimum				Job					.50%	070
	0100	Maximum				"					2%	
082	0010	**SMALL TOOLS** As % of contractor's work, minimum				Total					.50%	082
	0100	Maximum				"					2%	
086	0010	**TAXES** Sales tax, State, County & City, average				%	4.44%					086
	0050	Maximum					7.50%					
	0200	Social Security, on first $51,300 of wages						7.65%				
	0210											
	0300	Unemployment, MA, combined Federal and State, minimum				%		2.60%				
	0350	Average				"		6.20%				

For expanded coverage of these items see *Means Building Construction Cost Data 1991*

010 | Overhead

010 000 | Overhead

		CREW	DAILY OUTPUT	MAN-HOURS	UNIT	BARE COSTS MAT.	BARE COSTS LABOR	BARE COSTS EQUIP.	BARE COSTS TOTAL	TOTAL INCL O&P	
086	0400 Maximum				%		6.80%				086
	0410										

013 | Submittals

013 300 | Survey Data

		CREW	DAILY OUTPUT	MAN-HOURS	UNIT	MAT.	LABOR	EQUIP.	TOTAL	INCL O&P	
306	0010 SURVEYING Conventional, topographical, minimum	A-7	3.30	7.270	Acre	13.25	91		104.25	165	306
	0100 Maximum	A-8	.60	53.330		41	650		691	1,125	
	0300 Lot location and lines, minimum, for large quantities	A-7	2	12		22	150		172	270	
	0320 Average	"	1.25	19.200		41	240		281	440	
	0400 Maximum, for small quantities	A-8	1	32		66	390		456	720	
	0600 Monuments, 3' long	A-7	10	2.400	Ea.	9.40	30		39.40	60	
	0800 Property lines, perimeter, cleared land	"	1,000	.024	L.F.	.03	.30		.33	.53	
	0900 Wooded land	A-8	875	.037	"	.03	.44		.47	.77	
	1100 Crew for building layout, 2 man crew	A-6	1	16	Day		210		210	345	
	1200 3 man crew	A-7	1	24	"		300		300	495	

013 400 | Shop Drawings

408	0010 RENDERINGS Water color, matted, 20" x 30", eye level,										408
	0050 Average				Ea.	925			925	1,025	

015 | Construction Facilities and Temporary Controls

015 250 | Construction Aids

		CREW	DAILY OUTPUT	MAN-HOURS	UNIT	MAT.	LABOR	EQUIP.	TOTAL	INCL O&P	
254	0014 SCAFFOLDING, STEEL TUBULAR Rent, 1 use per mo., no plank										254
	0090 Building exterior, 1 to 5 stories	3 Carp	16.80	1.430	C.S.F.	13	20		33	48	
	0200 To 12 stories	4 Carp	15	2.130		12.20	31		43.20	64	
	0310 13 to 20 stories ⑭	5 Carp	16.75	2.390		11.40	34		45.40	70	
	0460 Building interior walls, (area) up to 16' high	3 Carp	22.70	1.060		12.50	15.10		27.60	39	
	0560 16' to 40' high		18.70	1.280		12.75	18.35		31.10	45	
	0800 Building interior floor area, up to 30' high		90	.267	C.C.F.	3.90	3.81		7.71	10.65	
	0900 Over 30' high	4 Carp	100	.320	"	4.40	4.58		8.98	12.50	
	2000 Steel tubular regular, rent/mo.										
	2100 Frames 3' high 5' wide				Ea.	3.65			3.65	4.02	
	2150 5' high 5' wide					3.65			3.65	4.02	
	2200 6'-6" high 5' wide					3.65			3.65	4.02	
	2250 7'-6" high 6' wide					7.95			7.95	8.75	
	2500 Accessories cross braces					.75			.75	.83	
	2550 Guardrail post					1.10			1.10	1.21	
	2600 Guardrail 7' section					.80			.80	.88	
	2650 Screw jacks & plates					2			2	2.20	
	2700 Sidewalk brackets					1.60			1.60	1.76	
	2750 8" casters					5.75			5.75	6.35	
	2850 Plank 2"x10" x 16'-0" regular rent/mo.					5.10			5.10	5.60	
	3950 Erect frames, 1st tier	4 Clab	100	.320			3.63		3.63	6.05	
	3951 Erect frames (or dismantle) 2nd tier	"	144	.222			2.52		2.52	4.22	

For expanded coverage of these items see *Means Building Construction Cost Data 1991*

015 | Construction Facilities and Temporary Controls

015 250 | Construction Aids

			CREW	DAILY OUTPUT	MAN-HOURS	UNIT	MAT.	LABOR	EQUIP.	TOTAL	TOTAL INCL O&P	
254	3952	Erect frames (or dismantle) 3rd tier	4 Clab	134	.239	Ea.		2.71		2.71	4.53	254
	3953	Erect frames (or dismantle) 4th tier	"	124	.258	"		2.93		2.93	4.90	

015 600 | Temporary Controls

602	0010	TARPAULINS Cotton duck, 10 oz. to 13.13 oz. per S.Y., minimum				S.F.	.26			.26	.29	602
	0050	Maximum					.45			.45	.50	
	0200	Reinforced polyethylene 3 mils thick, white					.05			.05	.06	
	0300	4 mils thick, white, clear or black					.06			.06	.07	

016 | Material and Equipment

016 400 | Equipment Rental

			UNIT	HOURLY OPER. COST.	RENT PER DAY	RENT PER WEEK	RENT PER MONTH	CREW EQUIPMENT COST	
406	0010	**CONCRETE EQUIPMENT RENTAL**							406
	0100	without operators							
	0600	Cart, concrete, operator walking, 10 C.F.	Ea.	1	60	180	540	44	
	0700	Operator riding, 18 C.F.		2.35	145	435	1,300	105.80	
	0800	Conveyer for concrete, portable, gas, 16" wide, 26' long		2.73	115	350	1,050	91.85	
	0900	46' long		2.90	140	425	1,275	108.20	
	1100	Core drill, electric, 2-½ H.P., 1" to 8" bit diameter		.40	48	145	435	32.20	
	1200	Finisher, concrete floor, gas, riding trowel, 48" diameter		2.30	73	220	660	62.40	
	1300	Gas, manual, 3 blade, 36" trowel		.70	33	100	300	25.60	
	1400	4 blade, 48" trowel		1.10	43	130	390	34.80	
	1500	Float, hand-operated (Bull float) 48" wide		.12	6	18	55	4.55	
	1570	Curb builder, 14 H.P., gas, single screw		1.20	45	130	390	35.60	
	1590	Double screw		1.95	48	145	435	44.60	
	1600	Grinder, concrete and terrazzo, electric, floor		1.10	43	130	390	34.80	
	1700	Wall grinder		.39	23	70	210	17.10	
	1800	Mixer, powered, mortar and concrete, gas, 6 C.F., 18 H.P.		.90	43	130	390	33.20	
	1900	10 C.F., 25 H.P.		1.18	54	160	480	41.45	
	2000	16 C.F.		1.35	72	215	645	53.80	
	2120	Pump, concrete, truck mounted, 4" line, 80' boom		8.70	740	2,225	6,675	514.60	
	2600	Saw, concrete, manual, gas, 18 H.P.		2.55	57	170	510	54.40	
	2650	Self-propelled, gas, 30 H.P.		4.85	90	270	810	92.80	
	2700	Vibrators, concrete, electric, 60 cycle, 2 H.P.		.27	14.55	44	130	10.95	
	2800	3 H.P.		.43	16.65	50	150	13.45	
	2900	Gas engine, 5 H.P.		.64	26	77	230	20.50	
	3000	8 H.P.		1	38	115	345	31	
408	0010	**EARTHWORK EQUIPMENT RENTAL** Without operators							408
	0050	Augers for truck or trailer mounting, vertical drilling							
	0060	4" to 36" diam., 54 H.P., gas, 10' spindle travel	Ea.	13.20	485	1,450	4,350	395.60	
	0070	14' spindle travel		14.30	555	1,650	5,000	444.40	
	0100	Backhoe, diesel hydraulic, crawler mounted, ½ C.Y. cap.		9.55	435	1,300	3,900	336.40	
	0120	⅝ C.Y. capacity		13.30	410	1,225	3,675	351.40	
	0140	¾ C.Y. capacity		14.65	565	1,700	5,100	457.20	
	0350	Gradall type, truck mounted, 3 ton @ 15' radius, ⅝ C.Y.		22.45	625	1,880	5,650	555.60	
	0400	Backhoe-loader, wheel type, 40 to 45 H.P., ⅝ C.Y. capacity		6.20	190	565	1,700	162.60	
	0450	45 H.P. to 60 H.P., ¾ C.Y. capacity		7.30	220	660	2,000	190.40	
	0460	80 H.P., 1-¼ C.Y. capacity		10.95	330	995	2,975	286.60	
	0470	112 H.P., 1-¾ C.Y. loader, ½ C.Y. backhoe		13.15	320	970	2,900	299.20	
	0500	Brush chipper, gas engine, 6" cutter head, 35 H.P.		3.45	100	305	915	88.60	
	0550	12" cutter head, 130 H.P.		10.85	155	460	1,375	178.80	

For expanded coverage of these items see *Means Building Construction Cost Data 1991*

016 | Material and Equipment

016 400 | Equipment Rental

		UNIT	HOURLY OPER. COST.	RENT PER DAY	RENT PER WEEK	RENT PER MONTH	CREW EQUIPMENT COST	
408	0600	15" cutter head, 165 H.P.	Ea.	13.45	160	475	1,425	202.60	408
	1200	Compactor, roller, 2 drum, 2000 lb., operator walking		1.55	105	310	930	74.40	
	1250	Rammer compactor, gas, 1000 lb. blow		.35	35	105	315	23.80	
	1300	Vibratory plate, gas, 13" plate, 1000 lb. blow		.45	28	84	250	20.40	
	1350	24" plate, 5000 lb. blow		1.55	52	155	465	43.40	
	1860	Grader, self-propelled, 25,000 lb.		12.90	535	1,600	4,800	423.20	
	1910	30,000 lb.		14.50	675	2,025	6,075	521	
	4110	Tractor, crawler, with bulldozer, torque converter, diesel 75 H.P.		9.10	335	1,000	3,000	272.80	
	4150	105 H.P.		12.40	500	1,500	4,500	399.20	
	4200	140 H.P.		15.20	640	1,925	5,775	506.60	
	4260	200 H.P.		25.10	960	2,875	8,625	775.80	
	4400	Loader, crawler, torque conv., diesel, 1-½ C.Y., 80 H.P.		10.40	435	1,300	3,900	343.20	
	4450	1-½ to 1-¾ C.Y., 95 H.P.		12.65	450	1,350	4,050	371.20	
	4510	1-¾ to 2-¼ C.Y., 130 H.P.		15.80	515	1,550	4,650	436.40	
	4530	2-½ to 3-¼ C.Y., 190 H.P.		25.35	1,000	3,025	9,075	807.80	
	4610	Tractor loader, wheel, torque conv., 4 x 4, 1 to 1-¼ C.Y., 65 H.P.		7.70	275	820	2,450	225.60	
	4620	1-½ to 1-¾ C.Y., 80 H.P.		9.95	385	1,150	3,450	309.60	
	4650	1-¾ to 2 C.Y., 100 H.P.		11.05	435	1,300	3,900	348.40	
	4710	2-½ to 3-½ C.Y., 130 H.P.		15.65	540	1,620	4,850	449.20	
	4730	3 to 4-½ C.Y., 170 H.P.		18.50	690	2,075	6,225	563	
	4880	Wheeled, skid steer, 10 C.F., 30 H.P. gas		4.10	93	280	840	88.80	
	4890	1 C.Y., 78 H.P., diesel		6	315	940	2,825	236	
	4900	Trencher, chain, boom type, gas, operator walking, 12 H.P.		1.65	65	200	600	53.20	
	4910	Operator riding, 40 H.P.		5.40	155	460	1,375	135.20	
	5000	Wheel type, diesel, 4' deep, 12" wide		11.40	390	1,175	3,500	326.20	
	5100	Diesel, 6' deep, 20" wide		12.75	590	1,775	5,300	457	
	5150	Ladder type, diesel, 5' deep, 8" wide		8.05	295	875	2,650	239.40	
	5200	Diesel, 8' deep, 16" wide		15	500	1,500	4,500	420	
	5250	Truck, dump, tandem, 12 ton payload		15.10	295	890	2,675	298.80	
	5300	Three axle dump, 16 ton payload		16.90	385	1,150	3,450	365.20	
	5350	Dump trailer only, rear dump, 16-½ C.Y.		2.95	140	425	1,275	108.60	
	5400	20 C.Y.		2.95	145	430	1,300	109.60	
	5450	Flatbed, single axle, 1-½ ton rating		9.50	115	350	1,050	146	
	5500	3 ton rating		9.55	120	360	1,075	148.40	
420	0010	**GENERAL EQUIPMENT RENTAL**							420
	0150	Aerial lift, scissor type, to 15' high, 1000 lb. cap., electric	Ea.	.95	80	240	715	55.60	
	0160	To 25' high, 2000 lb. capacity		1.45	125	380	1,150	87.60	
	0170	Telescoping boom to 40' high, 750 lb. capacity, gas		5.60	345	1,025	3,100	249.80	
	0180	2000 lb. capacity		7.35	460	1,375	4,125	333.80	
	0190	To 60' high, 750 lb. capacity		7.80	535	1,625	4,825	387.40	
	0200	Air compressor, portable, gas engine, 60 C.F.M.		4.55	47	140	420	64.40	
	0300	160 C.F.M.		6.05	62	185	555	85.40	
	0400	Diesel engine, rotary screw, 250 C.F.M.		4.85	83	250	750	88.80	
	0500	365 C.F.M.		8.35	225	675	2,025	201.80	
	0800	For silenced models, small sizes, add		3%	5%	5%	5%		
	0920	Air tools and accessories							
	0930	Breaker, pavement, 60 lb.	Ea.	.10	22	65	195	13.80	
	0940	80 lb.		.12	21	71	195	15.15	
	0950	Drills, hand (jackhammer) 65 lb.		.18	22	65	195	14.45	
	0960	Wagon, swing boom, 4" drifter		9	240	725	2,175	217	
	0970	5" drifter		9.55	625	1,875	5,625	451.40	
	0980	Dust control per drill		.16	9	27	81	6.70	
	0990	Hammer, chipping, 12 lb.		.11	14	42	125	9.30	
	1000	Hose, air with couplings, 50' long, ¾" diameter		.39	3	8	25	4.70	
	1100	1" diameter		1	4	11	34	10.20	
	1200	1-½" diameter		.05	8	25	75	5.40	
	1300	2" diameter		.12	14	42	125	9.35	
	1400	2-½" diameter		.13	15	44	130	9.85	

For expanded coverage of these items see *Means Building Construction Cost Data 1991*

016 | Material and Equipment

016 400 | Equipment Rental

		UNIT	HOURLY OPER. COST.	RENT PER DAY	RENT PER WEEK	RENT PER MONTH	CREW EQUIPMENT COST	
420 1450	Drill, steel, 7/8" x 2'	Ea.		2.10	6.25	18.75	1.25	420
1520	Moil points		.75	1.05	4.15	12.50	6.80	
1530	Sheeting driver for 60 lb. breaker		.08	7.30	22	66	5.05	
1540	For 90 lb. breaker		.10	14	42	125	9.20	
1550	Spade, 25 lb.		.05	6.25	20	60	4.40	
1560	Tamper, single, 35 lb.		.10	21	62	185	13.20	
1580	Wrenches, impact, air powered, up to 3/4" bolt		.15	17	50	150	11.20	
1590	Up to 1-1/4" bolt		.35	42	125	375	27.80	
1600	Barricades, barrels, reflectorized, 1 to 50 barrels			.51	1.53	4.59	.30	
1620	Barrels with flashers, 1 to 50 barrels			.82	2.48	7.45	.50	
1640	Barrels with steady burn type C lights			.84	2.54	7.60	.50	
1850	Drill, rotary hammer, electric, 1-1/2" diameter		.10	19.10	57	170	12.20	
1860	Carbide bit for above			5.20	15.60	47	3.10	
1870	Emulsion sprayer, 65 gal., 5 H.P. gas engine		.45	42	125	375	28.60	
1880	200 gal., 5 H.P. engine		.43	49	145	435	32.45	
1920	Floodlight, mercury, vapor or quartz, on tripod							
1930	1000 watt	Ea.	.11	12	36	110	8.10	
1940	2000 watt		.09	35	105	310	21.70	
2020	Forklift, wheeled, for brick, 18', 3000 lb., 2 wheel drive, gas		8.25	165	500	1,500	166	
2100	Generator, electric, gas engine, 1.5 KW to 3 KW		.95	29	87	260	25	
2200	5 KW		1.18	47	140	420	37.45	
2300	10 KW		2.05	115	350	1,050	86.40	
2500	Diesel engine, 20 KW		3.65	81	245	735	78.20	
2850	Hammer, hydraulic, for mounting on boom, to 500 ft.-lb.		.80	110	325	985	71.40	
2860	500 to 1200 ft.-lb.		2.15	230	695	2,100	156.20	
2900	Heaters, space, oil or electric, 50 MBH		.10	20	61	185	13	
3000	100 MBH		.06	17	51	155	10.70	
3100	300 MBH		.11	42	125	375	25.90	
3150	500 MBH		.17	57	170	515	35.35	
3200	Hose, water, suction with coupling, 20' long, 2" diameter		.05	7	20	60	4.40	
3210	3" diameter		.05	11	32	95	6.80	
3220	4" diameter		.05	18	54	160	11.20	
3250	Discharge hose with coupling, 50' long, 2" diameter		.05	4	11	35	2.60	
3260	3" diameter		.05	5	16	50	3.60	
3270	4" diameter		.05	6	18	55	4	
3300	Ladders, extension type, 16' to 36' long			8.30	24	72	4.80	
3400	40' to 60' long			19.75	60	180	12	
3460	Builders level with tripod and rod			23	70	210	14	
3700	Mixer, powered, plaster and mortar, 6 C.F., 7 H.P.		.70	38	115	345	28.60	
3800	10 C.F., 9 H.P.		1.10	53	160	480	40.80	
3900	Paint sprayers complete, 8 CFM		.05	30	90	270	18.40	
4000	17 CFM		.05	42	125	375	25.40	
4100	Pump, centrifugal gas pump, 1-1/2", 4 MGPH		.37	19.05	57	170	14.35	
4200	2", 8 MGPH		.37	21	62	185	15.35	
4300	3", 15 MGPH		1	32	96	290	27.20	
4500	Submersible electric pump, 1-1/4", 55 GPM		.27	30	90	270	20.15	
4600	1-1/2", 83 GPM		.27	33	100	300	22.15	
4700	2", 120 GPM		.27	35	105	315	23.15	
4800	3", 300 GPM		.55	44	130	390	30.40	
4900	4", 560 GPM		1	59	180	535	44	
5100	Diaphragm pump, gas, single, 1-1/2" diameter		.43	16	48	145	13.05	
5200	2" diameter		.45	18	54	160	14.40	
5300	3" diameter		.60	31	94	280	23.60	
5400	Double, 4" diameter		1.40	65	195	585	50.20	
5500	Trash pump, self-priming, gas, 2" diameter		.95	27	80	240	23.60	
5600	Diesel, 4" diameter		1.50	81	245	735	61	
5660	Rollers, see division 016-408							
5700	Salamanders, L.P. gas fired, 100,000 B.T.U.	Ea.	.60	12	36	110	12	

For expanded coverage of these items see *Means Building Construction Cost Data 1991*

016 | Material and Equipment

016 400 | Equipment Rental

		Item	UNIT	HOURLY OPER. COST.	RENT PER DAY	RENT PER WEEK	RENT PER MONTH	CREW EQUIPMENT COST	
420	5720	Sandblaster, portable, open top, 3 C.F. capacity	Ea.	.15	37	110	330	23.20	420
	5740	Accessories for above		.05	16	47	140	9.80	
	5800	Saw, chain, gas engine, 18" long		.40	28	84	250	20	
	5900	36" long		.95	57	170	510	41.60	
	6000	Masonry, table mounted, 14" diameter, 5 H.P.		1.50	33	100	300	32	
	6100	Circular, hand held, electric, 7" diameter		.15	11	34	100	8	
	6200	12" diameter		.25	22	66	200	15.20	
	6300	Steam cleaner, 100 gallons per hour		.32	43	130	390	28.55	
	6310	200 gallons per hour		.60	45	135	405	31.80	
	6350	Torch, cutting, acetylene-oxygen, 150' hose		6.40	19	58	175	62.80	
	6360	Hourly operating cost includes tips and gas		6.75	16.65	50	150	64	
	6410	Toilet, portable chemical			8.30	25	75	5	
	6420	Recycle flush type			10.80	31	93	6.20	
	7020	Transit with tripod			27	80	240	16	
	7100	Truck, pickup, ¾ ton, 2 wheel drive		9.05	58	175	525	107.40	
	7200	4 wheel drive		10.25	60	175	530	117	
	7300	Tractor, 4 x 2, 30 ton capacity, 195 H.P.		9.05	325	980	2,950	268.40	
	7410	250 H.P.		12.50	360	1,075	3,225	315	
	7700	Welder, electric, 200 amp		.80	18	54	160	17.20	
	7800	300 amp		1.75	42	125	375	39	
	7900	Gas engine, 200 amp		4.05	35	105	315	53.40	
	8000	300 amp		4.30	57	170	510	68.40	
	8100	Wheelbarrow, any size	▼		6.65	20	60	4	
460	0010	**LIFTING & HOISTING EQUIPMENT RENTAL**							460
	0100	without operators							
	2400	Truck mounted, hydraulic, 12 ton capacity	Ea.	19	350	1,050	3,150	362	
	2500	25 ton capacity		19.55	550	1,650	4,950	486.40	
	2550	33 ton capacity		20.40	885	2,340	7,025	631.20	
	2600	55 ton capacity		28.40	835	2,500	7,500	727.20	
	2800	Self-propelled, 4 x 4, with telescoping boom, 5 ton		7.25	250	780	2,250	214	
	2900	12-½ ton capacity		13.65	515	1,550	4,650	419.20	
	3000	15 ton capacity		15.45	430	1,300	3,900	383.60	
	3100	25 ton capacity		17.65	640	1,925	5,775	526.20	
	3600	Hoists, chain type, overhead, manual, ¾ ton		.05	5.20	14.55	42.65	3.30	
	3900	10 ton		.25	22	66	200	15.20	
	5200	Jacks, hydraulic, 20 ton		.11	2	6	18	2.10	
	6350	For each added 10' jackrod section, add			3.12	9	27	1.80	
	6500	125 ton capacity			435	1,300	3,900	260	
	6550	For each added 10' jackrod section, add			22	65	195	13	
	6600	Cable jack, 10 ton capacity with 200' cable			74	225	670	45	
	6650	For each added 50' of cable, add	▼		4.50	13.50	41	2.70	

017 | Contract Closeout

017 100 | Final Cleaning

			CREW	DAILY OUTPUT	MAN-HOURS	UNIT	MAT.	LABOR	EQUIP.	TOTAL	TOTAL INCL O&P	
104	0011	**CLEANING UP** After job completion, minimum				Project					.30%	104
	0040	Maximum				"					1%	

020 | Subsurface Investigation and Demolition

020 120 | Std Penetration Tests

		Description	CREW	DAILY OUTPUT	MAN-HOURS	UNIT	MAT.	LABOR	EQUIP.	TOTAL	TOTAL INCL O&P	
123	0010	**BORINGS** Initial field stake out and determination of elevations	A-6	1	16	Day		210		210	345	123
	0100	Drawings showing boring details				Total		105		105	165	
	0200	Report and recommendations from P.E.						230		230	370	
	0300	Mobilization and demobilization, minimum	B-55	4	6			69	135	204	265	
	0350	For over 100 miles, per added mile		450	.053	Mile		.61	1.21	1.82	2.35	
	0600	Auger holes in earth, no samples, 2-½" diameter		78.60	.305	L.F.		3.51	6.90	10.41	13.45	
	0800	Cased borings in earth, with samples, 2-½" diameter		55.50	.432	"		4.97	9.80	14.77	19.05	
	1400	Drill rig and crew with light duty rig		1	24	Day		275	545	820	1,050	

020 550 | Site Demolition

		Description	CREW	DAILY OUTPUT	MAN-HOURS	UNIT	MAT.	LABOR	EQUIP.	TOTAL	TOTAL INCL O&P	
554	0010	**SITE DEMOLITION** No hauling, abandon catch basin or manhole	B-6	7	3.430	Ea.		42	27	69	99	554
	0020	Remove existing catch basin or manhole		4	6			73	48	121	175	
	0030	Catch basin or manhole frames and covers stored		14	1.710			21	13.60	34.60	50	
	0040	Remove and reset		7	3.430			42	27	69	99	
	0600	Fencing, barbed wire, 3 strand	2 Clab	430	.037	L.F.		.42		.42	.71	
	0650	5 strand		280	.057			.65		.65	1.08	
	0700	Chain link, remove only, 8' to 10' high		310	.052			.59		.59	.98	
	0750	Remove and reset		50	.320			3.63		3.63	6.05	
	1000	Masonry walls, block or tile, solid, remove	B-5	1,800	.036	C.F.		.46	.52	.98	1.34	
	1100	Cavity		2,200	.029			.38	.43	.81	1.09	
	1200	Brick, solid		900	.071			.92	1.04	1.96	2.67	
	1300	With block		1,130	.057			.73	.83	1.56	2.13	
	1400	Stone, with mortar		900	.071			.92	1.04	1.96	2.67	
	1500	Dry set		1,500	.043			.55	.62	1.17	1.60	
	1710	Pavement removal, bituminous, 3" thick	B-38	690	.058	S.Y.		.75	1.64	2.39	3.04	
	1750	4" to 6" thick		420	.095			1.23	2.69	3.92	5	
	1800	Bituminous driveways		680	.059			.76	1.66	2.42	3.09	
	1900	Concrete to 6" thick, mesh reinforced		255	.157			2.03	4.43	6.46	8.25	
	2000	Rod reinforced		200	.200			2.58	5.65	8.23	10.50	
	2300	With hand held air equipment, bituminous	B-39	1,900	.025	S.F.		.31	.07	.38	.58	
	2320	Concrete to 6" thick, no reinforcing		1,200	.040			.48	.11	.59	.92	
	2340	Mesh reinforced		830	.058			.70	.15	.85	1.34	
	2360	Rod reinforced		765	.063			.76	.17	.93	1.45	
	2400	Curbs, concrete, plain	B-6	325	.074	L.F.		.90	.59	1.49	2.14	
	2500	Reinforced		220	.109			1.33	.87	2.20	3.16	
	2600	Granite curbs		355	.068			.82	.54	1.36	1.96	
	2700	Bituminous curbs		830	.029			.35	.23	.58	.84	
	2900	Pipe removal, concrete, no excavation, 12" diameter		175	.137			1.67	1.09	2.76	3.98	
	2960	24" diameter		12	2			24	15.85	39.85	58	
	4000	Sidewalk removal, bituminous, 2-½" thick		325	.074	S.Y.		.90	.59	1.49	2.14	
	4050	Brick, set in mortar		185	.130			1.58	1.03	2.61	3.76	
	4100	Concrete, plain		160	.150			1.83	1.19	3.02	4.35	
	4200	Mesh reinforced		150	.160			1.95	1.27	3.22	4.64	
	5000	Slab on grade removal, plain	B-5	45	1.420	C.Y.		18.40	21	39.40	53	
	5100	Mesh reinforcing		33	1.940			25	28	53	73	
	5200	Rod reinforcing		25	2.560			33	37	70	96	
	5500	For congested sites or small quantities, add up to										
	5550	For disposal on site, add	B-11A	232	.069			.89	3.34	4.23	5.15	
	5600	To 5 miles, add	B-34D	76	.105			1.26	6.05	7.31	8.70	

020 600 | Building Demolition

		Description	CREW	DAILY OUTPUT	MAN-HOURS	UNIT	MAT.	LABOR	EQUIP.	TOTAL	TOTAL INCL O&P	
604	0011	**BUILDING DEMOLITION**										604
	0500	Small bldgs, or single bldgs, no salvage included, steel	B-3	14,800	.003	C.F.		.04	.10	.14	.18	
	0600	Concrete	"	11,300	.004	"		.05	.14	.19	.24	
	0605	Concrete foundations, plain	B-5	33	1.940	C.Y.		25	28	53	73	
	0610	Reinforced		25	2.560			33	37	70	96	
	0615	Concrete walls		34	1.880			24	28	52	71	

For expanded coverage of these items see *Means Site Work Cost Data 1991*

020 | Subsurface Investigation and Demolition

020 600 | Building Demolition

			CREW	DAILY OUTPUT	MAN-HOURS	UNIT	MAT.	LABOR	EQUIP.	TOTAL	TOTAL INCL O&P	
604	0620	Elevated slabs	B-5	26	2.460	C.Y.		32	36	68	92	604
	0650	Masonry	B-3	14,800	.003	C.F.		.04	.10	.14	.18	
	0700	Wood	"	14,800	.003	"		.04	.10	.14	.18	
	1000	Single family, one story house, wood, minimum				Ea.					1,950	
	1020	Maximum									3,350	
	1200	Two family, two story house, wood, minimum									2,525	
	1220	Maximum									5,025	
	1300	Three family, three story house, wood, minimum									3,250	
	1320	Maximum	↓								6,450	
	1400	Gutting building, see division 020-716										
612	0010	**DUMP CHARGES** Typical urban city, fees only										612
	0100	Building construction materials				C.Y.					25	
	0200	Demolition lumber, trees, brush									32	
	0300	Rubbish only									24	
	0500	Reclamation station, usual charge				Ton					55	
620	0010	**RUBBISH HANDLING** The following are to be added to the										620
	0020	selective demolition prices										
	0400	Chute, circular, prefabricated steel, 18" diameter	B-1	40	.600	L.F.	9.65	7.20		16.85	23	
	0440	30" diameter	"	30	.800	"	18.70	9.60		28.30	37	
	0600	Dumpster, (debris box container), 5 C.Y., rent per week				Ea.					170	
	0700	10 C.Y. capacity									210	
	0800	30 C.Y. capacity									290	
	0840	40 C.Y. capacity									345	
	1000	Dust partition, 6 mil polyethylene, 4' x 8' panels, 1" x 3" frame	2 Carp	2,000	.008	S.F.	.17	.11		.28	.38	
	1080	2" x 4" frame	"	2,000	.008	"	.29	.11		.40	.51	
	2000	Load, haul to chute & dumping into chute, 50' haul	2 Clab	24	.667	C.Y.		7.55		7.55	12.65	
	2040	100' haul		16.50	.970			11		11	18.40	
	2080	Over 100' haul, add per 100 L.F.		35.50	.451			5.10		5.10	8.55	
	2120	In elevators, per 10 floors, add	↓	140	.114	↓		1.30		1.30	2.17	
	3000	Loading & trucking, including 2 mile haul, chute loaded										
	3040	Hand loaded, 50' haul	2 Clab	21.50	.744	C.Y.		8.45		8.45	14.10	
	3080	Machine loaded	B-6	80	.300			3.66	2.38	6.04	8.70	
	3120	Wheeled 50' and ramp dump loaded	2 Clab	24	.667			7.55		7.55	12.65	
	5000	Haul, per mile, up to 8 C.Y. truck										
	5100	Over 8 C.Y. truck										

020 700 | Selective Demolition

			CREW	DAILY OUTPUT	MAN-HOURS	UNIT	MAT.	LABOR	EQUIP.	TOTAL	TOTAL INCL O&P	
702	0010	**CEILING DEMOLITION**										702
	0200	Drywall, on wood frame	2 Clab	800	.020	S.F.		.23		.23	.38	
	1000	Plaster, lime and horse hair, on wood lath, incl. lath		700	.023			.26		.26	.43	
	1500	Tile, wood fiber, 12" x 12", glued		900	.018			.20		.20	.34	
	1540	Stapled		1,500	.011			.12		.12	.20	
	2000	Wood, tongue and groove, 1" x 4"	↓	1,000	.016			.18		.18	.30	
	2040	1" x 8"	1 Clab	1,100	.007			.08		.08	.14	
	2400	Plywood or wood fiberboard, 4' x 8' sheets	2 Clab	1,200	.013	↓		.15		.15	.25	
704	0010	**CUTOUT DEMOLITION** Conc., elev. slab, light reinf., under 6 C.F.	B-9	65	.615	C.F.		7.25	1.96	9.21	14.25	704
	0050	Light reinforcing, over 6 C.F.		75	.533	"		6.25	1.70	7.95	12.35	
	0200	Slab on grade to 6" thick, not reinforced, under 8 S.F.		85	.471	S.F.		5.55	1.50	7.05	10.90	
	0250	Not reinforced, over 8 S.F.		175	.229	"		2.69	.73	3.42	5.30	
	0600	Walls, not reinforced, under 6 C.F.		60	.667	C.F.		7.85	2.12	9.97	15.45	
	0650	Not reinforced, over 6 C.F.		65	.615			7.25	1.96	9.21	14.25	
	1000	Concrete, elevated slab, bar reinforced, under 6 C.F.		45	.889			10.45	2.83	13.28	21	
	1050	Bar reinforced, over 6 C.F.		50	.800	↓		9.40	2.54	11.94	18.55	
	1200	Slab on grade to 6" thick, bar reinforced, under 8 S.F.		75	.533	S.F.		6.25	1.70	7.95	12.35	
	1250	Bar reinforced, over 8 S.F.		105	.381	"		4.48	1.21	5.69	8.85	
	1400	Walls, bar reinforced, under 6 C.F.		50	.800	C.F.		9.40	2.54	11.94	18.55	
	1450	Bar reinforced, over 6 C.F.	↓	55	.727	"		8.55	2.31	10.86	16.85	

For expanded coverage of these items see *Means Site Work Cost Data 1991*

020 | Subsurface Investigation and Demolition

020 700 | Selective Demolition

			CREW	DAILY OUTPUT	MAN-HOURS	UNIT	MAT.	LABOR	EQUIP.	TOTAL	TOTAL INCL O&P	
704	2000	Brick, to 4 S.F. opening, not including toothing										704
	2040	4" thick	B-9	30	1.330	Ea.		15.65	4.24	19.89	31	
	2060	8" thick		18	2.220			26	7.05	33.05	51	
	2080	12" thick		10	4			47	12.70	59.70	93	
	2400	Concrete block, to 4 S.F. opening, 2" thick		35	1.140			13.45	3.63	17.08	26	
	2420	4" thick		30	1.330			15.65	4.24	19.89	31	
	2440	8" thick		27	1.480			17.40	4.71	22.11	34	
	2460	12" thick		24	1.670			19.60	5.30	24.90	39	
	2600	Gypsum block, to 4 S.F. opening, 2" thick		80	.500			5.90	1.59	7.49	11.60	
	2620	4" thick		70	.571			6.70	1.82	8.52	13.25	
	2640	8" thick		55	.727			8.55	2.31	10.86	16.85	
	2800	Terra cotta, to 4 S.F. opening, 4" thick		70	.571			6.70	1.82	8.52	13.25	
	2840	8" thick		65	.615			7.25	1.96	9.21	14.25	
	2880	12" thick		50	.800			9.40	2.54	11.94	18.55	
	3000	Toothing masonry cutouts, brick, soft old mortar	1 Brhe	40	.200	V.L.F.		2.29		2.29	3.76	
	3100	Hard mortar		30	.267			3.05		3.05	5	
	3200	Block, soft old mortar		70	.114			1.31		1.31	2.15	
	3400	Hard mortar		50	.160			1.83		1.83	3.01	
	4000	For toothing masonry, see Division 045-290										
	4010											
	6000	Walls, interior, not including re-framing,										
	6010	openings to 5 S.F.										
	6100	Drywall to ⅝" thick	A-1	24	.333	Ea.		3.78	2.27	6.05	8.85	
	6200	Paneling to ¾" thick		20	.400			4.54	2.72	7.26	10.60	
	6300	Plaster, on gypsum lath		20	.400			4.54	2.72	7.26	10.60	
	6340	On wire lath		14	.571			6.50	3.89	10.39	15.15	
	7000	Wood frame, not including re-framing, openings to 5 S.F.										
	7200	Floors, sheathing and flooring to 2" thick	A-1	5	1.600	Ea.		18.15	10.90	29.05	42	
	7310	Roofs, sheathing to 1" thick, not including roofing		6	1.330			15.15	9.05	24.20	35	
	7410	Walls, sheathing to 1" thick, not including siding		7	1.140			12.95	7.75	20.70	30	
706	0010	**DOOR DEMOLITION**										706
	0020											
	0200	Doors, exterior, 1-¾" thick, single, 3' x 7' high	1 Clab	16	.500	Ea.		5.70		5.70	9.50	
	0220	Double, 6' x 7' high		12	.667			7.55		7.55	12.65	
	0500	Interior, 1-⅜" thick, single, 3' x 7' high		20	.400			4.54		4.54	7.60	
	0520	Double, 6' x 7' high		16	.500			5.70		5.70	9.50	
	0700	Bi-folding, 3' x 6'-8" high		20	.400			4.54		4.54	7.60	
	0720	6' x 6'-8" high		18	.444			5.05		5.05	8.45	
	0900	Bi-passing, 3' x 6'-8" high		16	.500			5.70		5.70	9.50	
	0940	6' x 6'-8" high		14	.571			6.50		6.50	10.85	
	1500	Remove and reset, minimum	1 Carp	8	1			14.30		14.30	24	
	1520	Maximum	"	6	1.330			19.05		19.05	32	
	2000	Frames, including trim, metal	A-1	8	1			11.35	6.80	18.15	26	
	2200	Wood		14	.571			6.50	3.89	10.39	15.15	
	2201	Alternate pricing method		200	.040	L.F.		.45	.27	.72	1.06	
	3000	Special doors, counter doors	F-2	6	2.670	Ea.		38	2.67	40.67	67	
	3300	Glass, sliding, including frames		12	1.330			19.05	1.33	20.38	33	
	3400	Overhead, commercial, 12' x 12' high		4	4			57	4	61	100	
	3500	Residential, 9' x 7' high		8	2			29	2	31	50	
	3540	16' x 7' high		7	2.290			33	2.29	35.29	57	
	3600	Remove and reset, minimum		4	4			57	4	61	100	
	3620	Maximum		2.50	6.400			92	6.40	98.40	160	
	3660	Remove and reset elec. garage door opener	1 Carp	8	1			14.30		14.30	24	
	4000	Residential lockset, exterior		30	.267			3.81		3.81	6.40	
	4200	Deadbolt lock		32	.250			3.58		3.58	6	
	9000	Minimum labor/equipment charge		4	2	Job		29		29	48	
708	0010	**ELECTRICAL DEMOLITION**										708
	0020	Conduit to 15' high, including fittings & hangers										

For expanded coverage of these items see *Means Site Work Cost Data 1991*

020 | Subsurface Investigation and Demolition

020 700 | Selective Demolition

			CREW	DAILY OUTPUT	MAN-HOURS	UNIT	MAT.	LABOR	EQUIP.	TOTAL	TOTAL INCL O&P	
708	0100	Rigid galvanized steel, ½" to 1" diameter	1 Elec	242	.033	L.F.		.54		.54	.87	708
	0120	1-¼" to 2"	"	200	.040			.65		.65	1.06	
	0271	Armored cable (BX)	2 Elec	1,200	.013			.22		.22	.35	
	0351	Non-metallic sheathed cable (Romex)	"	1,500	.011	↓		.17		.17	.28	
	1180	400 amp	1 Elec	3.40	2.350	Ea.		38		38	62	
	1210	Panel boards, incl. removal of all breakers,										
	1220	pipe terminations & wire connections										
	1720	Junction boxes, 4" sq. & oct.	1 Elec	80	.100	Ea.		1.64		1.64	2.64	
	1760	Switch box		107	.075			1.22		1.22	1.98	
	1780	Receptacle & switch plates		257	.031	↓		.51		.51	.82	
	1800	Wire, THW-THWN-THHN, removed from										
	1810	in place conduit, to 15' high										
	1830	#14	1 Elec	65	.123	C.L.F.		2.01		2.01	3.25	
	1840	#12		55	.145			2.38		2.38	3.84	
	1850	#10	↓	45.50	.176	↓		2.87		2.87	4.65	
	2000	Interior fluorescent fixtures, incl. supports										
	2010	& whips, to 15' high										
	2100	Recessed drop-in 2' x 2', 2 lamp	2 Elec	35	.457	Ea.		7.45		7.45	12.10	
	2140	2' x 4', 4 lamp	"	30	.533	"		8.70		8.70	14.10	
	2180	Surface mount, acrylic lens & hinged frame										
	2220	2' x 2', 2 lamp	2 Elec	44	.364	Ea.		5.95		5.95	9.60	
	2260	2' x 4', 4 lamp	"	33	.485	"		7.95		7.95	12.80	
	2300	Strip fixtures, surface mount										
	2320	4' long, 1 lamp	2 Elec	53	.302	Ea.		4.94		4.94	8	
	2380	8' long, 2 lamp	"	40	.400	"		6.55		6.55	10.55	
	2460	Interior incandescent, surface, ceiling										
	2470	or wall mount, to 12' high										
	2480	Metal cylinder type, 75 Watt	2 Elec	62	.258	Ea.		4.22		4.22	6.80	
	2600	Exterior fixtures, incandescent, wall mount										
	2620	100 Watt	2 Elec	50	.320	Ea.		5.25		5.25	8.45	
	3000	Ceiling fan, tear out and remove	1 Elec	18	.444	"		7.25		7.25	11.75	
	9000	Minimum labor/equipment charge	"	4	2	Job		33		33	53	
712	0010	**FLOORING DEMOLITION**										712
	0200	Brick with mortar	A-1	300	.027	S.F.		.30	.18	.48	.71	
	0400	Carpet, bonded, including surface scraping	2 Clab	2,000	.008			.09		.09	.15	
	0480	Tackless		9,000	.002			.02		.02	.03	
	0800	Resilient, sheet goods (linoleum)		1,400	.011			.13		.13	.22	
	0900	Tile, 12" x 12"		1,000	.016			.18		.18	.30	
	2000	Tile, ceramic, thin set	A-1	400	.020			.23	.14	.37	.53	
	2020	Mud set		350	.023			.26	.16	.42	.61	
	3000	Wood, block, on end		400	.020			.23	.14	.37	.53	
	3200	Parquet		450	.018			.20	.12	.32	.47	
	3400	Strip flooring, interior, 2-¼" x 25/32" thick		325	.025			.28	.17	.45	.65	
	3500	Exterior, porch flooring, 1" x 4"		400	.020			.23	.14	.37	.53	
	3800	Subfloor, tongue and groove, 1" x 6"		445	.018			.20	.12	.32	.48	
	3820	1" x 8"		535	.015			.17	.10	.27	.40	
	3840	1" x 10"		520	.015			.17	.10	.27	.41	
	4000	Plywood, nailed		600	.013			.15	.09	.24	.35	
	4100	Glued and nailed	↓	400	.020	↓		.23	.14	.37	.53	
714	0010	**FRAMING DEMOLITION**										714
	3000	Wood framing, beams, 6" x 8"	B-2	275	.145	L.F.		1.71		1.71	2.86	
	3040	6" x 10"		220	.182			2.14		2.14	3.58	
	3080	6" x 12"		185	.216			2.54		2.54	4.25	
	3120	8" x 12"		140	.286			3.36		3.36	5.60	
	3160	10" x 12"	↓	110	.364			4.27		4.27	7.15	
	3400	Fascia boards, 1" x 6"	1 Clab	500	.016			.18		.18	.30	
	3440	1" x 8"	"	450	.018	↓		.20		.20	.34	

For expanded coverage of these items see *Means Site Work Cost Data 1991*

020 | Subsurface Investigation and Demolition

020 700 | Selective Demolition

			CREW	DAILY OUTPUT	MAN-HOURS	UNIT	MAT.	LABOR	EQUIP.	TOTAL	TOTAL INCL O&P	
714	3480	1" x 10"	1 Clab	400	.020	L.F.		.23		.23	.38	714
	3800	Headers over openings, 2 @ 2" x 6"		110	.073			.83		.83	1.38	
	3840	2 @ 2" x 8"		100	.080			.91		.91	1.52	
	3880	2 @ 2" x 10"		90	.089			1.01		1.01	1.69	
	4230	Joists, 2" x 6"	2 Clab	970	.016			.19		.19	.31	
	4240	2" x 8"		940	.017			.19		.19	.32	
	4250	2" x 10"		910	.018			.20		.20	.33	
	4280	2" x 12"		880	.018			.21		.21	.35	
	5400	Posts, 4" x 4"		800	.020			.23		.23	.38	
	5440	6" x 6"		400	.040			.45		.45	.76	
	5480	8" x 8"		300	.053			.61		.61	1.01	
	5500	10" x 10"		240	.067			.76		.76	1.27	
	5800	Rafters, ordinary, 2" x 6"		850	.019			.21		.21	.36	
	5840	2" x 8"		720	.022			.25		.25	.42	
	6200	Stairs and stringers, minimum		40	.400	Riser		4.54		4.54	7.60	
	6240	Maximum		26	.615	"		7		7	11.70	
	6600	Studs, 2" x 4"		2,000	.008	L.F.		.09		.09	.15	
	6640	2" x 6"		1,600	.010	"		.11		.11	.19	
	7000	Trusses, 2" x 4" flat wood construction										
	7050	12' span	2 Clab	74	.216	Ea.		2.45		2.45	4.10	
	7150	24' span		66	.242			2.75		2.75	4.60	
	7200	26' span		64	.250			2.84		2.84	4.75	
	7250	28' span		62	.258			2.93		2.93	4.90	
	7300	30' span		56	.286			3.24		3.24	5.40	
	7350	32' span		56	.286			3.24		3.24	5.40	
	7400	34' span		54	.296			3.36		3.36	5.60	
	7450	36' span		52	.308			3.49		3.49	5.85	
	9000	Minimum labor/equipment charge	1 Clab	4	2	Job		23		23	38	
	9500	See Div. 020-620 for rubbish handling										
716	0010	**GUTTING** Building interior, including disposal										716
	0500	Residential building										
	0560	Minimum	B-16	400	.080	SF Flr.		.96	.91	1.87	2.60	
	0580	Maximum		360	.089			1.07	1.01	2.08	2.89	
	1000	Commercial building, minimum		350	.091			1.10	1.04	2.14	2.98	
	1020	Maximum		250	.128			1.54	1.46	3	4.17	
718	0010	**HVAC DEMOLITION**										718
	0100	Air conditioner, split unit, 3 ton	Q-5	2	8	Ea.		120		120	195	
	0150	Package unit, 3 ton	Q-6	3	8	"		125		125	200	
	0260	Baseboard, hydronic fin tube, ½"	Q-5	117	.137	L.F.		2.04		2.04	3.32	
	0300	Boiler, electric	Q-19	2	12	Ea.		185		185	300	
	0340	Gas or oil, steel, under 150 MBH	Q-6	3	8	"		125		125	200	
	1000	Ductwork, 4" high, 8" wide	1 Clab	200	.040	L.F.		.45		.45	.76	
	1100	6" high, 8" wide		165	.048			.55		.55	.92	
	1200	10" high, 12" wide		125	.064			.73		.73	1.21	
	1300	12" high, 18" wide		85	.094			1.07		1.07	1.79	
	1500	30" high, 36" wide		56	.143			1.62		1.62	2.71	
	2200	Furnace, electric	Q-20	2	10	Ea.		150		150	245	
	2300	Gas or oil, under 120 MBH	Q-9	4	4			59		59	97	
	2340	Over 120 MBH	"	3	5.330			78		78	130	
	2800	Heat pump, package unit, 3 ton	Q-5	2.40	6.670			99		99	160	
	2840	Split unit, 3 ton		2	8			120		120	195	
	2950	Tank, steel, oil, 275 gal., above ground		10	1.600			24		24	39	
	2960	Remove and reset		3	5.330			79		79	130	
	9000	Minimum labor/equipment charge	Q-6	3	8	Job		125		125	200	
720	0010	**MILLWORK AND TRIM DEMOLITION**										720
	1000	Cabinets, wood, base cabinets	2 Clab	80	.200	L.F.		2.27		2.27	3.80	

For expanded coverage of these items see *Means Site Work Cost Data 1991*

020 | Subsurface Investigation and Demolition

020 700 | Selective Demolition

			CREW	DAILY OUTPUT	MAN-HOURS	UNIT	MAT.	LABOR	EQUIP.	TOTAL	TOTAL INCL O&P	
720	1020	Wall cabinets	2 Clab	80	.200	L.F.		2.27		2.27	3.80	720
	1100	Steel, painted, base cabinets		60	.267			3.03		3.03	5.05	
	1500	Counter top, minimum		200	.080			.91		.91	1.52	
	1510	Maximum		120	.133			1.51		1.51	2.53	
	2000	Paneling, 4' x 8' sheets, ¼" thick		2,000	.008	S.F.		.09		.09	.15	
	2100	Boards, 1" x 4"		700	.023			.26		.26	.43	
	2120	1" x 6"		750	.021			.24		.24	.40	
	2140	1" x 8"		800	.020			.23		.23	.38	
	3000	Trim, baseboard, to 6" wide		1,200	.013	L.F.		.15		.15	.25	
	3040	12" wide		1,000	.016			.18		.18	.30	
	3100	Ceiling trim		1,000	.016			.18		.18	.30	
	3120	Chair rail		1,200	.013			.15		.15	.25	
	3140	Railings with balusters		240	.067			.76		.76	1.27	
	3160	Wainscoting		700	.023	S.F.		.26		.26	.43	
	4000	Curtain rod	1 Clab	80	.100	Ea.		1.14		1.14	1.90	
	9000	Minimum labor/equipment charge	"	4	2	Job		23		23	38	
724	0010	**PLUMBING DEMOLITION**										724
	1020	Fixtures, including 10' piping										
	1100	Bath tubs, cast iron	1 Plum	4	2	Ea.		33		33	54	
	1120	Fiberglass		6	1.330			22		22	36	
	1140	Steel		5	1.600			26		26	43	
	1200	Lavatory, wall hung		10	.800			13.25		13.25	22	
	1220	Counter top		8	1			16.55		16.55	27	
	1300	Sink, steel or cast iron, single		8	1			16.55		16.55	27	
	1320	Double		7	1.140			18.90		18.90	31	
	1400	Water closet, floor mounted		8	1			16.55		16.55	27	
	1420	Wall mounted		7	1.140			18.90		18.90	31	
	2000	Piping, metal, to 2" diameter		200	.040	L.F.		.66		.66	1.08	
	2050	To 4" diameter		150	.053			.88		.88	1.44	
	2100	To 8" diameter	2 Plum	100	.160			2.65		2.65	4.32	
	2250	Water heater, 40 gal.	1 Plum	6	1.330	Ea.		22		22	36	
	3000	Submersible sump pump		24	.333			5.50		5.50	9	
	6000	Remove and reset fixtures, minimum		6	1.330			22		22	36	
	6100	Maximum		4	2			33		33	54	
	9000	Minimum labor/equipment charge		2	4	Job		66		66	110	
726	0010	**ROOFING AND SIDING DEMOLITION**										726
	1200	Wood, boards, tongue and groove, 2" x 6"	2 Clab	960	.017	S.F.		.19		.19	.32	
	1220	2" x 10"		1,040	.015			.17		.17	.29	
	1280	Standard planks, 1" x 6"		1,080	.015			.17		.17	.28	
	1320	1" x 8"		1,160	.014			.16		.16	.26	
	1340	1" x 12"		1,200	.013			.15		.15	.25	
	1360	Flashing, aluminum	1 Clab	290	.028			.31		.31	.52	
	2000	Gutters, aluminum or wood, edge hung	"	240	.033	L.F.		.38		.38	.63	
	2010	Remove and reset, aluminum	1 Shee	100	.080			1.30		1.30	2.16	
	2020	Remove and reset, vinyl	1 Carp	100	.080			1.14		1.14	1.91	
	2100	Built-in	1 Clab	100	.080			.91		.91	1.52	
	2500	Roof accessories, plumbing vent flashing		14	.571	Ea.		6.50		6.50	10.85	
	2600	Adjustable metal chimney flashing		9	.889	"		10.10		10.10	16.85	
	3000	Roofing, built-up, 5 ply roof, no gravel	B-2	1,600	.025	S.F.		.29		.29	.49	
	3100	Gravel removal, minimum		5,000	.008			.09		.09	.16	
	3120	Maximum		2,000	.020			.24		.24	.39	
	3400	Roof insulation board		3,900	.010			.12		.12	.20	
	4000	Shingles, asphalt strip		3,500	.011			.13		.13	.22	
	4100	Slate		2,500	.016			.19		.19	.31	
	4300	Wood		2,200	.018			.21		.21	.36	
	4500	Skylight to 10 S.F.	1 Clab	8	1	Ea.		11.35		11.35	19	
	5000	Siding, metal, horizontal	"	444	.018	S.F.		.20		.20	.34	

For expanded coverage of these items see *Means Site Work Cost Data 1991*

020 | Subsurface Investigation and Demolition

020 700 | Selective Demolition

			CREW	DAILY OUTPUT	MAN-HOURS	UNIT	MAT.	LABOR	EQUIP.	TOTAL	TOTAL INCL O&P	
726	5020	Vertical	1 Clab	400	.020	S.F.		.23		.23	.38	726
	5200	Wood, boards, vertical		400	.020			.23		.23	.38	
	5220	Clapboards, horizontal		380	.021			.24		.24	.40	
	5240	Shingles		350	.023			.26		.26	.43	
	5260	Textured plywood		725	.011			.13		.13	.21	
	9000	Minimum labor/equipment charge		2	4	Job		45		45	76	
732	0010	**WALLS AND PARTITIONS DEMOLITION**										732
	1000	Drywall, nailed	1 Clab	1,000	.008	S.F.		.09		.09	.15	
	1500	Fiberboard, nailed	"	900	.009			.10		.10	.17	
	2200	Metal or wood studs, finish 2 sides, fiberboard	B-1	520	.046			.55		.55	.93	
	2250	Lath and plaster		260	.092			1.11		1.11	1.86	
	2300	Plasterboard (drywall)		520	.046			.55		.55	.93	
	2350	Plywood		450	.053			.64		.64	1.07	
	3000	Plaster, lime and horsehair, on wood lath	1 Clab	400	.020			.23		.23	.38	
	3020	On metal lath	"	335	.024			.27		.27	.45	
734	0010	**WINDOW DEMOLITION**										734
	0020											
	0200	Aluminum, including trim, to 12 S.F.	A-1A	16	.500	Ea.		5.70	1.86	7.56	11.55	
	0240	To 25 S.F.		11	.727			8.25	2.71	10.96	16.80	
	0280	To 50 S.F.		5	1.600			18.15	5.95	24.10	37	
	0320	Storm windows, to 12 S.F.		27	.296			3.36	1.10	4.46	6.85	
	0360	To 25 S.F.		21	.381			4.32	1.42	5.74	8.80	
	0400	To 50 S.F.		16	.500			5.70	1.86	7.56	11.55	
	0500	Screens, incl. aluminum frame, small	1 Clab	20	.400			4.54		4.54	7.60	
	0510	Large		16	.500			5.70		5.70	9.50	
	0600	Glass, minimum		200	.040	S.F.		.45		.45	.76	
	0620	Maximum		150	.053	"		.61		.61	1.01	
	2000	Wood, including trim, to 12 S.F.		22	.364	Ea.		4.13		4.13	6.90	
	2020	To 25 S.F.		18	.444			5.05		5.05	8.45	
	2060	To 50 S.F.		13	.615			7		7	11.70	
	5020	Remove and reset window, minimum	1 Carp	6	1.330			19.05		19.05	32	
	5040	Average		4	2			29		29	48	
	5080	Maximum		2	4			57		57	96	
	9100	Window awning, residential	1 Clab	80	.100	L.F.		1.14		1.14	1.90	
754	0010	**FOOTINGS AND FOUNDATIONS DEMOLITION**										754
	0200	Floors, concrete slab on grade,										
	0240	4" thick, plain concrete	B-9	500	.080	S.F.		.94	.25	1.19	1.85	
	0280	Reinforced, wire mesh		470	.085			1	.27	1.27	1.97	
	0300	Rods		400	.100			1.18	.32	1.50	2.32	
	0400	6" thick, plain concrete		375	.107			1.25	.34	1.59	2.47	
	0420	Reinforced, wire mesh		340	.118			1.38	.37	1.75	2.73	
	0440	Rods		300	.133			1.57	.42	1.99	3.09	
	1000	Footings, concrete, 1' thick, 2' wide	B-5	300	.213	L.F.		2.76	3.12	5.88	8	
	1080	1'-6" thick, 2' wide		250	.256			3.31	3.74	7.05	9.60	
	1120	3' wide		200	.320			4.14	4.68	8.82	12	
	1200	Average reinforcing, add								10%	10%	
	2000	Walls, block, 4" thick	A-1	200	.040	S.F.		.45	.27	.72	1.06	
	2040	6" thick		190	.042			.48	.29	.77	1.11	
	2080	8" thick		180	.044			.50	.30	.80	1.18	
	2100	12" thick		175	.046			.52	.31	.83	1.21	
	2400	Concrete, plain concrete, 6" thick	B-9	160	.250			2.94	.80	3.74	5.80	
	2420	8" thick		140	.286			3.36	.91	4.27	6.60	
	2440	10" thick		120	.333			3.92	1.06	4.98	7.70	
	2500	12" thick		100	.400			4.70	1.27	5.97	9.25	
	2600	For average reinforcing, add								10%	10%	
	4000	For congested sites or small quantities, add up to								200%	200%	

For expanded coverage of these items see *Means Site Work Cost Data 1991*

020 | Subsurface Investigation and Demolition

020 700 | Selective Demolition

			CREW	DAILY OUTPUT	MAN-HOURS	UNIT	MAT.	LABOR	EQUIP.	TOTAL	TOTAL INCL O&P	
754	4200	Add for disposal, on site	B-11A	232	.069	C.Y.		.89	3.34	4.23	5.15	754
	4250	To five miles	B-30	220	.109	"		1.40	6.40	7.80	9.35	
758	0010	**MASONRY DEMOLITION**										758
	1000	Chimney, 16" x 16", soft old mortar	A-1	24	.333	V.L.F.		3.78	2.27	6.05	8.85	
	1020	Hard mortar		18	.444			5.05	3.02	8.07	11.75	
	1080	20" x 20", soft old mortar		12	.667			7.55	4.53	12.08	17.65	
	1100	Hard mortar		10	.800			9.10	5.45	14.55	21	
	1140	20" x 32", soft old mortar		10	.800			9.10	5.45	14.55	21	
	1160	Hard mortar		8	1			11.35	6.80	18.15	26	
	1200	48" x 48", soft old mortar		5	1.600			18.15	10.90	29.05	42	
	1220	Hard mortar		4	2			23	13.60	36.60	53	
	2000	Columns, 8" x 8", soft old mortar		48	.167			1.89	1.13	3.02	4.41	
	2020	Hard mortar		40	.200			2.27	1.36	3.63	5.30	
	2060	16" x 16", soft old mortar		16	.500			5.70	3.40	9.10	13.25	
	2100	Hard mortar		14	.571			6.50	3.89	10.39	15.15	
	2140	24" x 24", soft old mortar		8	1			11.35	6.80	18.15	26	
	2160	Hard mortar		6	1.330			15.15	9.05	24.20	35	
	2200	36" x 36", soft old mortar		4	2			23	13.60	36.60	53	
	2220	Hard mortar		3	2.670			30	18.15	48.15	71	
	3000	Copings, precast or masonry, to 8" wide										
	3020	Soft old mortar	A-1	180	.044	L.F.		.50	.30	.80	1.18	
	3040	Hard mortar	"	160	.050	"		.57	.34	.91	1.32	
	3100	To 12" wide										
	3120	Soft old mortar	A-1	160	.050	L.F.		.57	.34	.91	1.32	
	3140	Hard mortar	"	140	.057	"		.65	.39	1.04	1.51	
	4000	Fireplace, brick, 30" x 24" opening										
	4020	Soft old mortar	A-1	2	4	Ea.		45	27	72	105	
	4040	Hard mortar		1.25	6.400			73	44	117	170	
	4100	Stone, soft old mortar		1.50	5.330			61	36	97	140	
	4120	Hard mortar		1	8			91	54	145	210	
	5000	Veneers, brick, soft old mortar		140	.057	S.F.		.65	.39	1.04	1.51	
	5020	Hard mortar		125	.064			.73	.44	1.17	1.69	
	5100	Granite and marble, 2" thick		180	.044			.50	.30	.80	1.18	
	5120	4" thick		170	.047			.53	.32	.85	1.25	
	5140	Stone, 4" thick		180	.044			.50	.30	.80	1.18	
	5160	8" thick		175	.046			.52	.31	.83	1.21	
	5400	Alternate pricing method, stone, 4" thick		60	.133	C.F.		1.51	.91	2.42	3.53	
	5420	8" thick		85	.094	"		1.07	.64	1.71	2.49	

021 | Site Preparation

021 100 | Site Clearing

			CREW	DAILY OUTPUT	MAN-HOURS	UNIT	MAT.	LABOR	EQUIP.	TOTAL	TOTAL INCL O&P	
104	0010	**CLEAR AND GRUB** Light, trees to 6" diam., cut & chip	B-7	.80	60	Acre		735	1,325	2,060	2,700	104
	0150	Grub stumps and remove	B-30	2	12			155	705	860	1,025	
	0200	Medium, trees to 12" diam., cut & chip	B-7	.70	68.570			840	1,525	2,365	3,075	
	0250	Grub stumps and remove	B-30	1	24			310	1,400	1,710	2,050	
	0300	Heavy, trees to 24" diam., cut & chip	B-7	.30	160			1,950	3,575	5,525	7,175	
	0350	Grub stumps and remove	B-30	.50	48			615	2,825	3,440	4,100	
	0400	If burning is allowed, reduce cut & chip									40%	
108	0010	**CLEARING** Brush with brush saw	A-1	.25	32	Acre		365	220	585	845	108
	0100	By hand	"	.12	66.670	"		755	455	1,210	1,775	

For expanded coverage of these items see *Means Site Work Cost Data 1991*

021 | Site Preparation

021 100 | Site Clearing

			CREW	DAILY OUTPUT	MAN-HOURS	UNIT	MAT.	LABOR	EQUIP.	TOTAL	TOTAL INCL O&P	
108	0300	With dozer, ball and chain, light clearing	B-11A	2	8	Acre		105	390	495	600	108
	0400	Medium clearing	"	1.50	10.670	"		140	515	655	800	

022 | Earthwork

022 100 | Grading

			CREW	DAILY OUTPUT	MAN-HOURS	UNIT	MAT.	LABOR	EQUIP.	TOTAL	TOTAL INCL O&P	
104	0010	GRADING Site excav. & fill, see div 022-200										104
	0020	Fine grading, see div 025-122										

022 200 | Excav, Backfill, Compact

			CREW	DAILY OUTPUT	MAN-HOURS	UNIT	MAT.	LABOR	EQUIP.	TOTAL	TOTAL INCL O&P	
204	0010	BACKFILL By hand, no compaction, light soil	1 Clab	14	.571	C.Y.		6.50		6.50	10.85	204
	0100	Heavy soil		11	.727			8.25		8.25	13.80	
	0300	Compaction in 6" layers, hand tamp, add to above	↓	20.60	.388			4.41		4.41	7.35	
	0500	Air tamp, add	B-9	190	.211			2.47	.67	3.14	4.88	
	0600	Vibrating plate, add	A-1	60	.133			1.51	.91	2.42	3.53	
	0800	Compaction in 12" layers, hand tamp, add to above	1 Clab	34	.235			2.67		2.67	4.47	
	1300	Dozer backfilling, bulk, up to 300' haul, no compaction	B-10B	1,200	.010			.14	.65	.79	.93	
	1400	Air tamped	B-11B	240	.067			.87	4.17	5.04	6	
212	0010	BORROW Buy and load at pit, haul 2 miles round trip										212
	0020	and spread, with 200 H.P. dozer, no compaction										
	0100	Bank run gravel	B-15	600	.047	C.Y.	3.95	.59	2.51	7.05	8.10	
	0200	Common borrow		600	.047		3.40	.59	2.51	6.50	7.45	
	0300	Crushed stone, 1-½"		600	.047		14.95	.59	2.51	18.05	20	
	0320	¾"		600	.047		15.20	.59	2.51	18.30	20	
	0340	½"		600	.047		15.75	.59	2.51	18.85	21	
	0360	⅜"		600	.047		16.25	.59	2.51	19.35	22	
	0400	Sand, washed, concrete		600	.047		14.70	.59	2.51	17.80	19.90	
	0500	Dead or bank sand	↓	600	.047		3.30	.59	2.51	6.40	7.35	
222	0010	COMPACTION Steel wheel tandem roller, 5 tons	B-10E	8	1.500	Hr.		20	14.80	34.80	50	222
	0050	Air tamp, 8" lifts, common fill	B-9	250	.160	C.Y.		1.88	.51	2.39	3.71	
	0060	Select fill	"	300	.133			1.57	.42	1.99	3.09	
	0600	Vibratory plate, 8" lifts, common fill	A-1	200	.040			.45	.27	.72	1.06	
	0700	Select fill	"	216	.037	↓		.42	.25	.67	.98	
238	0010	EXCAVATING, BULK BANK MEASURE Common earth piled										238
	0020	For loading onto trucks, add								15%	15%	
	0200	Backhoe, hydraulic, crawler mtd., 1 C.Y. cap. = 75 C.Y./hr.	B-12A	360	.044	C.Y.		.61	1.57	2.18	2.74	
	0310	Wheel mounted, ½ C.Y. cap. = 30 C.Y./hr.	B-12E	240	.067			.92	1.40	2.32	3.05	
	1200	Front end loader, track mtd., 1-½ C.Y. cap. = 70 C.Y./hr.	B-10N	560	.021			.29	.61	.90	1.15	
	1500	Wheel mounted, ¾ C.Y. cap. = 45 C.Y./hr.	B-10R	360	.033	↓		.45	.63	1.08	1.43	
	8000	For hauling excavated material, see div. 022-266										
246	0300	Common earth, 1500' haul										246
250	0010	EXCAVATING, STRUCTURAL Hand, pits to 6' deep, sandy soil	1 Clab	8	1	C.Y.		11.35		11.35	19	250
	0100	Heavy soil or clay		4	2			23		23	38	
	1100	Hand loading trucks from stock pile, sandy soil		12	.667			7.55		7.55	12.65	
	1300	Heavy soil or clay	↓	8	1	↓		11.35		11.35	19	
	1500	For wet or muck hand excavation, add to above				%				50%	50%	
254	0010	EXCAVATING, TRENCH or continuous footing, common earth										254
	0050	1' to 4' deep, ⅝ C.Y. tractor loader/backhoe	B-11C	150	.107	C.Y.		1.38	1.27	2.65	3.69	

For expanded coverage of these items see *Means Site Work Cost Data 1991*

022 | Earthwork

022 200 | Excav, Backfill, Compact

			CREW	DAILY OUTPUT	MAN-HOURS	UNIT	MAT.	LABOR	EQUIP.	TOTAL	TOTAL INCL O&P	
254	0060	½ C.Y. tractor loader/backhoe	B-11M	200	.080	C.Y.		1.04	1.43	2.47	3.29	254
	0090	4' to 6' deep, ½ C.Y. tractor loader/backhoe	"	200	.080			1.04	1.43	2.47	3.29	
	0100	⅝ C.Y. hydraulic backhoe	B-12Q	250	.064			.88	1.41	2.29	3	
	0300	½ C.Y. hydraulic excavator, truck mounted	B-12J	200	.080			1.11	2.78	3.89	4.87	
	1400	By hand with pick and shovel to 6' deep, light soil	1 Clab	8	1			11.35		11.35	19	
	1500	Heavy soil	"	4	2	↓		23		23	38	
258	0010	**EXCAVATING, UTILITY TRENCH** Common earth										258
	0050	Trenching with chain trencher, 12 H.P., operator walking										
	0100	4" wide trench, 12" deep	B-53	800	.010	L.F.		.14	.07	.21	.30	
	1000	Backfill by hand including compaction, add										
	1050	4" wide trench, 12" deep	A-1	800	.010	L.F.		.11	.07	.18	.26	
262	0010	**FILL** Spread dumped material, by dozer, no compaction	B-10B	1,000	.012	C.Y.		.16	.78	.94	1.12	262
	0100	By hand	1 Clab	12	.667	"		7.55		7.55	12.65	
	0500	Gravel fill, compacted, under floor slabs, 4" deep	B-37	10,000	.005	S.F.	.11	.06	.01	.18	.23	
	0600	6" deep		8,600	.006		.17	.07	.01	.25	.32	
	0700	9" deep		7,200	.007		.26	.08	.02	.36	.44	
	0800	12" deep		6,000	.008	↓	.35	.10	.02	.47	.57	
	1000	Alternate pricing method, 4" deep		120	.400	C.Y.	9.25	4.84	.99	15.08	19.35	
	1100	6" deep		160	.300		9.25	3.63	.74	13.62	17.05	
	1200	9" deep		200	.240		9.25	2.91	.59	12.75	15.70	
	1300	12" deep	↓	220	.218		9.25	2.64	.54	12.43	15.20	
266	0010	**HAULING** Earth 6 C.Y. dump truck, ¼ mile round trip, 5.0 loads/hr.	B-34A	240	.033			.40	1.25	1.65	2.02	266
	0200	4 mile round trip, 1.8 loads/hr.	"	85	.094			1.12	3.52	4.64	5.70	
	0300	12 C.Y. dump truck, 1 mile round trip, 2.7 loads/hr.	B-34B	260	.031			.37	1.40	1.77	2.15	
	0500	4 mile round trip, 1.6 loads/hr.	"	150	.053			.64	2.43	3.07	3.72	
274	0010	**MOBILIZATION AND DEMOBILIZATION** Up to 25 miles										274
	0020	Dozer or loader, 105 H.P.	B-34K	4	2	Ea.		24	175	199	230	
	0900	Shovel, backhoe or dragline, ¾ C.Y.		3.60	2.220			27	195	222	260	
	1200	Tractor shovel or front end loader, 1 C.Y.	↓	4.50	1.780	↓		21	155	176	205	
286	0010	**LOAM OR TOPSOIL** Remove and stockpile on site										286
	0700	Furnish and place, truck dumped @ $17.00 per C.Y., 4" deep	B-10S	12,000	.001	S.F.	.21	.01	.03	.25	.28	
	0800	6" deep	"	7,400	.002	"	.31	.02	.04	.37	.42	
	0900	Fine grading and seeding, incl. lime, fertilizer & seed,										
	1000	With equipment	B-14	9,000	.005	S.F.	.02	.06	.02	.10	.15	

022 300 | Pavement Base

			CREW	DAILY OUTPUT	MAN-HOURS	UNIT	MAT.	LABOR	EQUIP.	TOTAL	TOTAL INCL O&P	
304	0010	**BASE** Prepare and roll sub-base, small areas to 2500 S.Y.	B-32A	13,500	.002	S.F.		.02	.06	.08	.11	304
308	0010	**BASE COURSE** For roadways and large paved areas										308
	0050	¾" stone compacted to 3" deep	B-36	36,000	.001	S.F.	.24	.01	.03	.28	.32	
	0100	6" deep		35,100	.001		.48	.01	.03	.52	.59	
	0200	9" deep		25,875	.002		.72	.02	.04	.78	.87	
	0300	12" deep		21,150	.002		.95	.02	.05	1.02	1.14	
	0301	Crushed 1-½" stone base, compacted to 4" deep		47,000	.001		.28	.01	.02	.31	.35	
	0302	6" deep		35,100	.001		.44	.01	.03	.48	.54	
	0303	8" deep		27,000	.001		.56	.02	.04	.62	.69	
	0304	12" deep	↓	16,200	.002	↓	.87	.03	.06	.96	1.08	
	0350	Bank run gravel, spread and compacted										
	0370	6" deep	B-32	54,000	.001	S.F.	.17	.01	.03	.21	.23	
	0390	9" deep		39,600	.001		.26	.01	.04	.31	.35	
	0400	12" deep	↓	32,400	.001	↓	.34	.01	.05	.40	.44	
	8900	For small and irregular areas, add										

022 700 | Slope/Erosion Control

			CREW	DAILY OUTPUT	MAN-HOURS	UNIT	MAT.	LABOR	EQUIP.	TOTAL	TOTAL INCL O&P	
704	0010	**EROSION CONTROL** Jute mesh, 100 S.Y. per roll, 4' wide, stapled	B-1	2,500	.010	S.Y.	.62	.12		.74	.87	704
	0100	Plastic netting, stapled, 2" x 1" mesh, 20 mil	"	2,500	.010	"	.33	.12		.45	.55	

For expanded coverage of these items see *Means Site Work Cost Data 1991*

022 | Earthwork

022 700 | Slope/Erosion Control

			CREW	DAILY OUTPUT	MAN-HOURS	UNIT	MAT.	LABOR	EQUIP.	TOTAL	TOTAL INCL O&P	
704	0200	Polypropylene mesh, stapled, 6.5 oz./S.Y.	B-1	2,500	.010	S.Y.	1.63	.12		1.75	1.98	704
	0300	Tobacco netting, or jute mesh #2, stapled	"	2,500	.010	"	.03	.12		.15	.22	
708	1800	Gravity concrete with vertical face including										708
	1850	excavation and backfill, no reinforcing										
	1900	6' high, level embankment	C-17C	36	2.310	L.F.	38	35	12.10	85.10	115	
	2000	33° slope embankment	"	32	2.590	"	42	39	13.60	94.60	125	
	2800	Reinforced concrete cantilever, incl. excavation, backfill & reinf.										
	2900	6' high, 33° slope embankment	C-17C	35	2.370	L.F.	35	36	12.45	83.45	110	
716	0010	STONE WALL Including excavation, concrete footing and										716
	0020	stone 3' below grade. Price is exposed face area.										
	0200	Decorative random stone, to 6' high, 1'-6" thick, dry set	D-1	35	.457	S.F.	7.15	6		13.15	17.75	
	0300	Mortar set		40	.400		8.65	5.25		13.90	18.15	
	0500	Cut stone, to 6' high, 1'-6" thick, dry set		35	.457		11.45	6		17.45	22	
	0600	Mortar set		40	.400		12.30	5.25		17.55	22	
	0800	Retaining wall, random stone, 6' to 10' high, 2' thick, dry set		45	.356		8.90	4.67		13.57	17.45	
	0900	Mortar set		50	.320		10.90	4.20		15.10	18.90	
	1100	Cut stone, 6' to 10' high, 2' thick, dry set		45	.356		14.60	4.67		19.27	24	
	1200	Mortar set		50	.320		15.75	4.20		19.95	24	

022 800 | Soil Treatment

			CREW	DAILY OUTPUT	MAN-HOURS	UNIT	MAT.	LABOR	EQUIP.	TOTAL	TOTAL INCL O&P	
804	0010	TERMITE PRETREATMENT	1 Skwk	1,508	.005	SF Flr.	.11	.08		.19	.25	804
	0020	Slab and walls, residential	"	1,508	.005	"	.11	.08		.19	.25	
	0400	Insecticides for termite control, minimum				Gal.	10.50			10.50	11.55	
	0500	Maximum				"	17.25			17.25	19	

025 | Paving and Surfacing

025 100 | Walk/Rd/Parkng Paving

			CREW	DAILY OUTPUT	MAN-HOURS	UNIT	MAT.	LABOR	EQUIP.	TOTAL	TOTAL INCL O&P	
120	0010	CONCRETE PAVEMENT Including joints, finishing, and curing										120
	0020	Fixed form, 12' pass, unreinforced, 6" thick	B-26	18,000	.005	S.F.	1.39	.06	.09	1.54	1.74	
	0100	8" thick	"	13,500	.007		1.76	.08	.13	1.97	2.22	
	0700	Finishing, broom finish small areas	2 Cefi	1,215	.013			.19		.19	.30	
124	0010	PAVING Asphaltic concrete										124
	0020	6" stone base, 2" binder course, 1" topping ㊱	B-25	10,125	.009	S.F.	.97	.11	.15	1.23	1.41	
	0300	Binder course, 1-½" thick		41,400	.002		.25	.03	.04	.32	.36	
	0400	2" thick		20,700	.004		.33	.05	.07	.45	.53	
	0500	3" thick		14,850	.006		.50	.07	.10	.67	.78	
	0600	4" thick		10,800	.008		.66	.10	.14	.90	1.05	
	0800	Sand finish course, ¾" thick		51,300	.002		.13	.02	.03	.18	.21	
	0900	1" thick		34,650	.003		.19	.03	.04	.26	.31	
128	0010	SIDEWALKS, DRIVEWAYS, & PATIOS No base										128
	0020	Asphaltic concrete, 2" thick	B-37	6,480	.007	S.F.	.36	.09	.02	.47	.57	
	0100	2-½" thick	"	5,950	.008	"	.43	.10	.02	.55	.65	
	0300	Concrete, 3000 psi, cast in place with 6 x 6 - #10/10 mesh,										
	0310	broomed finish, no base, 4" thick	B-24	600	.040	S.F.	.91	.53		1.44	1.87	
	0350	5" thick		545	.044		1.08	.58		1.66	2.15	
	0400	6" thick		510	.047		1.26	.62		1.88	2.42	
	0450	For bank run gravel base, 4" thick, add	B-18	2,500	.010		.12	.12	.02	.26	.34	
	0520	8" thick, add	"	1,600	.015		.24	.18	.03	.45	.59	
	1000	Crushed stone, 1" thick, white marble	2 Clab	1,700	.009		.37	.11		.48	.59	
	1050	Bluestone	"	1,700	.009		.09	.11		.20	.28	
	1700	Redwood, prefabricated, 4' x 4' sections	F-2	316	.051		2.97	.72	.05	3.74	4.54	

For expanded coverage of these items see *Means Site Work Cost Data 1991*

025 | Paving and Surfacing

025 100 | Walk/Rd/Parkng Paving

			CREW	DAILY OUTPUT	MAN-HOURS	UNIT	MAT.	LABOR	EQUIP.	TOTAL	TOTAL INCL O&P	
128	1750	Redwood planks, 1" thick, on sleepers	F-2	240	.067	S.F.	1.95	.95	.07	2.97	3.82	128

025 150 | Unit Pavers

154	0010	ASPHALT BLOCKS Premold, 6"x12"x1-¼", w/bed & neopr. adhesive	D-1	135	.119	S.F.	2.54	1.56		4.10	5.35	154
	0100	3" thick		130	.123		3.68	1.62		5.30	6.70	
	0300	Hexagonal tile, 8" wide, 1-¼" thick		135	.119		2.81	1.56		4.37	5.65	
	0400	2" thick		130	.123		3.46	1.62		5.08	6.45	
	0500	Square, 8" x 8", 1-¼" thick		135	.119		2.80	1.56		4.36	5.65	
	0600	2" thick		130	.123		3.46	1.62		5.08	6.45	
158	0010	BRICK PAVING 4" x 8" x 1-½", without joints (4.5 brick/S.F.)		110	.145		2.32	1.91		4.23	5.70	158
	0100	Grouted, ⅜" joint (3.9 brick/S.F.)		90	.178		2.05	2.33		4.38	6.10	
	0200	4" x 8" x 2-¼", without joints (4.5 bricks/S.F.)		110	.145		2.51	1.91		4.42	5.90	
	0300	Grouted, ⅜" joint (3.9 brick/S.F.)		90	.178		2.19	2.33		4.52	6.25	
	1500	Brick on 4" thick sand bed laid flat, 4.5 per S.F.		110	.145		2.45	1.91		4.36	5.85	
	2000	Laid on edge, 7.2 per S.F.		70	.229		3.54	3		6.54	8.80	
166	0010	STONE PAVERS										166
	1100	Flagging, bluestone, irregular, 1" thick,	D-1	81	.198	S.F.	1.98	2.59		4.57	6.45	
	1150	Snapped random rectangular, 1" thick		92	.174		2.48	2.28		4.76	6.50	
	1200	1-½" thick		85	.188		3.03	2.47		5.50	7.40	
	1250	2" thick		83	.193		3.31	2.53		5.84	7.80	
	1300	Slate, natural cleft, irregular, ¾" thick		92	.174		1.61	2.28		3.89	5.50	
	1350	Random rectangular, gauged, ½" thick		105	.152		3.48	2		5.48	7.10	
	1400	Random rectangular, butt joint, gauged, ¼" thick		150	.107		3.75	1.40		5.15	6.45	
	1450	For sand rubbed finish, add					2.40			2.40	2.64	
	1550	Granite blocks, 3-½" x 3-½" x 3-½"	D-1	92	.174		4.65	2.28		6.93	8.85	

025 250 | Curbs

254	0010	CURBS Asphaltic, machine formed, 8" wide, 6" high, 40 L.F./ton	B-27	1,000	.032	L.F.	.70	.38	.06	1.14	1.47	254
	0150	Asphaltic berm, 12"W, 3"-6"H, 35 L.F./ton, before pavement	"	700	.046		.94	.54	.08	1.56	2.03	
	0200	12"W, 1-½" to 4" H, 60 L.F. per ton, laid with pavement	B-2	1,050	.038		.51	.45		.96	1.31	
	0300	Concrete, 6" x 18", wood forms, straight	C-2	500	.096		3.02	1.36	.06	4.44	5.65	
	0400	6" x 18", radius	"	200	.240		3.23	3.39	.16	6.78	9.40	
	0550	Precast, 6" x 18", straight	B-29	700	.080		5.15	.99	.79	6.93	8.20	
	0600	6" x 18", radius		325	.172		7.75	2.13	1.71	11.59	13.95	
	1000	Granite, split face, straight, 5" x 16"		500	.112		12.35	1.38	1.11	14.84	17.10	
	1100	6" x 18", see also division 044-651		450	.124		16.30	1.54	1.23	19.07	22	
	1300	Radius curbing, 6" x 18", over 10' radius		260	.215		19.95	2.66	2.14	24.75	29	
	1400	Corners, 2' radius		80	.700	Ea.	68	8.65	6.95	83.60	97	
	1600	Edging, 4-½" x 12", straight		300	.187	L.F.	6.30	2.30	1.85	10.45	12.80	
	1800	Curb inlets, (guttermouth) straight		41	1.370	Ea.	150	16.85	13.55	180.40	210	
256	0010	EDGING Redwood, untreated, 1" x 4"	F-2	500	.032	L.F.	.87	.46	.03	1.36	1.76	256
	0100	2" x 4"		330	.048		.81	.69	.05	1.55	2.10	
	0200	Steel edge strips, ¼" x 5" including stakes		330	.048		2.50	.69	.05	3.24	3.96	
	0300	3/16" x 4"		330	.048		1.86	.69	.05	2.60	3.26	
	0500	Brick edging, set vertically, 3 brick per L.F.	D-1	135	.119		1.52	1.56		3.08	4.23	
	0600	Set horizontally, 1-½ brick per L.F.	"	370	.043		.77	.57		1.34	1.78	

025 450 | Surfacing

458	0010	SEALCOATING 2 coal tar pitch emulsion over 10,000 S.Y.	B-45	5,000	.003	S.Y.	.33	.04	.12	.49	.57	458
	0100	Under 1000 S.Y.	B-1	1,050	.023		.33	.27		.60	.82	
	0300	Petroleum resistant, over 10,000 S.Y.	B-45	5,000	.003		.48	.04	.12	.64	.74	
	0400	Under 1000 S.Y.	B-1	1,050	.023		.48	.27		.75	.99	

For expanded coverage of these items see *Means Site Work Cost Data 1991*

026 | Piped Utilities

026 010 | Piped Utilities

			CREW	DAILY OUTPUT	MAN-HOURS	UNIT	MAT.	LABOR	EQUIP.	TOTAL	TOTAL INCL O&P	
012	0010	BEDDING For pipe and conduit, not incl. compaction										012
	0050	Crushed or screened bank run gravel	B-6	150	.160	C.Y.	11.05	1.95	1.27	14.27	16.80	
	0100	Crushed stone ¾" to ½"		150	.160		12.90	1.95	1.27	16.12	18.85	
	0200	Sand, dead or bank,		150	.160		3.45	1.95	1.27	6.67	8.45	
	0500	Compacting bedding in trench	A-1	90	.089			1.01	.60	1.61	2.35	

026 050 | Manholes And Cleanouts

054	0010	UTILITY VAULTS Precast concrete, 6" thick										054
	0050	5' x 10' x 6' high, I.D.	B-13	2	28	Ea.	1,600	345	245	2,190	2,600	
	0350	Hand hole, precast concrete, 1-½" thick										
	0400	1'-0" x 2'-0" x 1'-9", I.D., light duty	B-1	4	6	Ea.	255	72		327	400	
	0450	4'-6" x 3'-2" x 2'-0", O.D., heavy duty	B-6	3	8	"	540	98	63	701	825	

026 650 | Water Systems

686	0010	PIPING, WATER DISTRIBUTION SYSTEMS Pipe laid in trench, (129)										686
	0020	excavation and backfill not included										
	1400	Ductile Iron pipe, class 250 water piping, 18' lengths										
	1410	Mechanical joint, 4" diameter	B-20	144	.167	L.F.	6.50	2.19		8.69	10.80	
	2650	Polyvinyl chloride pipe, class 160, S.D.R.-26, 1-½" diameter		300	.080		.35	1.05		1.40	2.15	
	2700	2" diameter		250	.096		.55	1.26		1.81	2.72	
	2750	2-½" diameter		250	.096		.80	1.26		2.06	2.99	
	2800	3" diameter		200	.120		1.20	1.58		2.78	3.96	
	2850	4" diameter		200	.120		1.95	1.58		3.53	4.79	

026 700 | Water Wells

704	0010	WELLS Domestic water, drilled and cased, including casing										704
	0100	4" to 6" diameter	B-23	160	.250	V.L.F.	7.75	2.94	3.40	14.09	17.20	
	1500	Pumps, installed in wells to 100' deep, 4" submersible										
	1520	¾ H.P.	Q-1	2.66	6.020	Ea.	370	90		460	555	
	1600	1 H.P.	"	2.29	6.990	"	350	105		455	555	

026 850 | Gas Distribution System

852	0010	GAS SERVICE & DISTRIBUTION Not including excavation										852
	0050	or backfill										
	0100	Polyethylene, 60 psi, coils, ½" diameter, SDR 7	B-20	450	.053	L.F.	.15	.70		.85	1.34	
	0150	1-¼" diameter, SDR 10	"	400	.060	"	.55	.79		1.34	1.93	
	0500	Steel, schedule 40, plain end, tar coated & wrapped										
	0550	1" diameter	Q-4	300	.107	L.F.	2.96	1.69	.13	4.78	6.15	
	0600	2" diameter		280	.114		3.37	1.81	.14	5.32	6.80	
	0650	3" diameter		260	.123		6.50	1.95	.15	8.60	10.50	

027 | Sewerage & Drainage

027 100 | Subdrainage Systems

			CREW	DAILY OUTPUT	MAN-HOURS	UNIT	MAT.	LABOR	EQUIP.	TOTAL	TOTAL INCL O&P	
106	0010	PIPING, SUBDRAINAGE, BITUMINOUS (129)										106
	0021	Not including excavation and backfill										
	2000	Perforated underdrain, 3" diameter	B-20	800	.030	L.F.	1.20	.39		1.59	1.98	
	2020	4" diameter	"	760	.032	"	1.50	.41		1.91	2.34	

For expanded coverage of these items see *Means Site Work Cost Data 1991*

027 | Sewerage & Drainage

027 100 | Subdrainage Systems

			CREW	DAILY OUTPUT	MAN-HOURS	UNIT	MAT.	LABOR	EQUIP.	TOTAL	TOTAL INCL O&P	
106	2040	5" diameter	B-20	720	.033	L.F.	2.60	.44		3.04	3.59	106
	2060	6" diameter	"	680	.035	"	2.90	.46		3.36	3.97	
108	0010	**PIPING, SUBDRAINAGE, CONCRETE**										108
	0021	Not including excavation and backfill										
	3000	Porous wall concrete underdrain, std. strength, 4" diameter	B-20	335	.072	L.F.	1.50	.94		2.44	3.23	
	3020	6" diameter	"	315	.076		1.60	1		2.60	3.44	
	3040	8" diameter	B-21	310	.090	↓	2.60	1.21	.34	4.15	5.25	
110	0010	**PIPING, SUBDRAINAGE, CORRUGATED METAL**										110
	0021	Not including excavation and backfill										
	2010	Aluminum or steel, perforated, asphalt coated										
	2020	6" diameter, 18 ga.	B-20	380	.063	L.F.		.83		.83	1.39	
	2200	8" diameter, 16 ga.	"	370	.065		5.40	.85		6.25	7.35	
	2220	10" diameter, 16 ga.	B-21	360	.078	↓	6.65	1.04	.29	7.98	9.40	
	3000	Uncoated										
	3020	6" diameter, 18 ga.	B-20	380	.063	L.F.	4.46	.83		5.29	6.30	
	3200	8" diameter, 16 ga.	"	370	.065		4.83	.85		5.68	6.75	
	3220	10" diameter, 16 ga.	B-21	360	.078		6.14	1.04	.29	7.47	8.80	
	3240	12" diameter, 16 ga.	"	285	.098	↓	7.40	1.32	.36	9.08	10.75	
112	0010	**PIPING, SUBDRAINAGE, VITRIFIED CLAY**										112
	4000	Channel pipe, 4" diameter	B-20	430	.056	L.F.	1.36	.73		2.09	2.73	
	4060	8" diameter	"	295	.081	"	3.05	1.07		4.12	5.15	

027 150 | Sewage Systems

			CREW	DAILY OUTPUT	MAN-HOURS	UNIT	MAT.	LABOR	EQUIP.	TOTAL	TOTAL INCL O&P	
152	0010	**CATCH BASINS OR MANHOLES** Including footing & excavation,										152
	0020	not including frame and cover										
	0050	Brick, 4' inside diameter, 4' deep	D-1	1	16	Ea.	385	210		595	770	
	1110	Precast, 4' I.D., 4' deep	B-6	4.10	5.850		258	71	46	375	455	
	1600	Frames and covers, C.I., 24" square, 500 lb.	"	7.80	3.080	↓	172.20	38	24	234.20	280	
160	0010	**PIPING, DRAINAGE & SEWAGE, BITUMINOUS FIBER** (129)										160
	2000	Plain, 2" diameter	2 Clab	400	.040		.93	.45		1.38	1.78	
	2080	4" diameter		380	.042		1.48	.48		1.96	2.43	
	2240	8" diameter	↓	300	.053		6.60	.61		7.21	8.25	
162	0010	**PIPING, DRAINAGE & SEWAGE, CONCRETE**										162
	0020	Not including excavation or backfill										
	1020	8" diameter	B-21	200	.140	L.F.	3.25	1.88	.52	5.65	7.30	
	1030	10" diameter	"	173	.162	"	3.60	2.17	.60	6.37	8.25	
164	0020	Not including excavation or backfill										164
	2040	8" diameter 16 ga.	B-20	330	.073			.96		.96	1.60	
168	0010	**PIPING, DRAINAGE & SEWAGE, POLYVINYL CHLORIDE**										168
	0020	Not including excavation or backfill										
	2000	10' lengths, S.D.R. 35, 4" diameter	B-20	375	.064	L.F.	.68	.84		1.52	2.16	
	2040	6" diameter		350	.069		1.65	.90		2.55	3.33	
	2080	8" diameter	↓	335	.072		2.35	.94		3.29	4.17	
	2120	10" diameter	B-21	330	.085	↓	3.79	1.14	.32	5.25	6.40	
172	0010	**PIPING, DRAINAGE & SEWAGE, VITRIFIED CLAY** C700										172
	0020	Not including excavation or backfill, 4' & 5' lengths										
	4030	Extra strength, compression joints, C425										
	5000	4" diameter	B-20	265	.091	L.F.	1.05	1.19		2.24	3.15	
	5020	6" diameter	"	200	.120		1.75	1.58		3.33	4.57	
	5040	8" diameter	B-21	200	.140		2.75	1.88	.52	5.15	6.75	
	5060	10" diameter	"	190	.147	↓	4.50	1.98	.55	7.03	8.85	

For expanded coverage of these items see *Means Site Work Cost Data 1991*

027 | Sewerage & Drainage

027 400 | Septic Systems

			CREW	DAILY OUTPUT	MAN-HOURS	UNIT	MAT.	LABOR	EQUIP.	TOTAL	TOTAL INCL O&P	
404	0010	SEPTIC TANKS Not incl. excav. or piping, precast, 1,000 gallon	B-21	8	3.500	Ea.	430	47	13	490	565	404
	0100	2,000 gallon		5	5.600		810	75	21	906	1,050	
	0600	Fiberglass, 1,000 gallon		6	4.670		485	63	17.35	565.35	655	
	0700	1,500 gallon		4	7		610	94	26	730	855	
	1000	Distribution boxes, concrete, 7 outlets	2 Plum	16	1		51	16.55		67.55	83	
	1100	9 outlets	2 Clab	8	2		300	23		323	370	
	1150	Leaching field chambers, 13' x 3'-7" x 1'-4", standard	B-13	16	3.500		300	43	30	373	435	
	1420	Leaching pit, 6', dia, 3' deep complete									575	
	2200	Excavation for septic tank, ¾ C.Y. backhoe	B-12F	145	.110	C.Y.		1.53	3.15	4.68	5.95	
	2400	4' trench for disposal field, ¾ C.Y. backhoe	"	335	.048	L.F.		.66	1.36	2.02	2.58	
	2600	Gravel fill, run of bank	B-6	150	.160	C.Y.	10.85	1.95	1.27	14.07	16.60	
	2800	Crushed stone, ¾"	"	150	.160	"	14.35	1.95	1.27	17.57	20	

028 | Site Improvements

028 100 | Irrigation Systems

			CREW	DAILY OUTPUT	MAN-HOURS	UNIT	MAT.	LABOR	EQUIP.	TOTAL	TOTAL INCL O&P	
104	0010	SPRINKLER IRRIGATION SYSTEM For lawns										104
	0800	Residential system, custom, 1" supply	B-20	2,619	.009	S.F.	.22	.12		.34	.44	
	0900	1-½" supply	"	2,311	.010	"	.20	.14		.34	.45	

028 300 | Fences And Gates

			CREW	DAILY OUTPUT	MAN-HOURS	UNIT	MAT.	LABOR	EQUIP.	TOTAL	TOTAL INCL O&P	
304	0010	CHAIN LINK FENCE 11 ga. wire										304
	0020	1-⅝" post 10'O.C.,1-⅜" top rail,2" corner post galv. stl., 3' high	B-1	185	.130	L.F.	3.06	1.56		4.62	6	
	0050	4' high		170	.141		3.71	1.70		5.41	6.90	
	0100	6' high		115	.209		4.65	2.51		7.16	9.30	
	0150	Add for gate 3' wide, 1-⅜" frame 3' high		12	2	Ea.	32	24		56	75	
	0170	4' high		10	2.400		40	29		69	92	
	0190	6' high		10	2.400		61	29		90	115	
	0200	Add for gate 4' wide, 1-⅜" frame 3' high		9	2.670		40	32		72	98	
	0220	4' high		9	2.670		53	32		85	110	
	0240	6' high		8	3		79	36		115	145	
	0350	Aluminized steel, 9 ga. wire, 3' high		185	.130	L.F.	3.70	1.56		5.26	6.70	
	0380	4' high		170	.141		4.36	1.70		6.06	7.65	
	0400	6' high		115	.209		5.60	2.51		8.11	10.35	
	0450	Add for gate 3' wide, 1-⅜" frame 3' high		12	2	Ea.	37	24		61	81	
	0470	4' high		10	2.400		50	29		79	105	
	0490	6' high		10	2.400		73	29		102	130	
	0500	Add for gate 4' wide, 1-⅜" frame 3' high		10	2.400		50	29		79	105	
	0520	4' high		9	2.670		65	32		97	125	
	0540	6' high		8	3		99	36		135	170	
	0620	Vinyl covered 9 ga. wire, 3' high		185	.130	L.F.	3.42	1.56		4.98	6.35	
	0640	4' high		170	.141		4.12	1.70		5.82	7.35	
	0660	6' high		115	.209		5.18	2.51		7.69	9.90	
	0720	Add for gate 3' wide, 1-⅜" frame 3' high		12	2	Ea.	40	24		64	84	
	0740	4' high		10	2.400		53	29		82	105	
	0760	6' high		10	2.400		80	29		109	135	
	0780	Add for gate 4' wide, 1-⅜" frame 3' high		10	2.400		53	29		82	105	
	0800	4' high		9	2.670		71	32		103	130	
	0820	6' high		8	3		105	36		141	175	
	0860	Tennis courts, 11 ga. wire, 2 ½" post 10' O.C., 1-⅝" top rail										
	0900	2-½" corner post, 10' high	B-1	95	.253	L.F.	8.50	3.04		11.54	14.45	

For expanded coverage of these items see *Means Site Work Cost Data 1991*

028 | Site Improvements

028 300 | Fences And Gates

			CREW	DAILY OUTPUT	MAN-HOURS	UNIT	MAT.	LABOR	EQUIP.	TOTAL	TOTAL INCL O&P	
304	0920	12' high	B-1	80	.300	L.F.	10	3.61		13.61	17.05	304
	1000	Add for gate 3' wide, 1-5/8" frame 10' high		10	2.400	Ea.	105	29		134	165	
	1040	Aluminized, 11 ga. wire 10' high		95	.253	L.F.	10.35	3.04		13.39	16.45	
	1100	12' high		80	.300	"	12.10	3.61		15.71	19.35	
	1140	Add for gate 3' wide, 1-5/8" frame, 10' high		10	2.400	Ea.	135	29		164	195	
	1250	Vinyl covered 11 ga. wire, 10' high		95	.253	L.F.	9.45	3.04		12.49	15.50	
	1300	12' high		80	.300	"	11.20	3.61		14.81	18.35	
	1400	Add for gate 3' wide, 1-3/8" frame, 10' high		10	2.400	Ea.	150	29		179	215	
320	0010	FENCE, MISC. METAL Chicken wire, posts @ 4', 1" mesh, 4' high	B-80	410	.078	L.F.	.97	.98	.99	2.94	3.79	320
	0100	2" mesh, 6' high		350	.091		.86	1.15	1.16	3.17	4.13	
	0200	Galv. steel, 12 ga., 2" x 4" mesh, posts 5' O.C., 3' high		300	.107		1.22	1.34	1.35	3.91	5.05	
	0300	5' high		300	.107		1.83	1.34	1.35	4.52	5.70	
	0400	14 ga., 1" x 2" mesh, 3' high		300	.107		1.10	1.34	1.35	3.79	4.92	
	0500	5' high		300	.107		1.64	1.34	1.35	4.33	5.50	
	1000	Kennel fencing, 1-1/2" mesh, 6' long, 3'-6" wide, 6'-2" high	2 Clab	4	4	Ea.	220	45		265	320	
	1050	12' long		4	4		275	45		320	380	
	1200	Top covers, 1-1/2" mesh, 6' long		15	1.070		42	12.10		54.10	66	
	1250	12' long		12	1.330		76	15.15		91.15	110	
	1300	For kennel doors, see division 083-729										
	4800	Snow fence on steel posts 10' O.C., 4' high	B-1	500	.048	L.F.	.81	.58		1.39	1.86	
324	0010	FENCE, WOOD Picket, No. 2 cedar picket, Gothic, 2 rail, 3' high		160	.150	"	3.79	1.80		5.59	7.20	324
	0050	Gate, 3'-6" wide		9	2.670	Ea.	33	32		65	90	
	0400	3 rail, 4' high		150	.160	L.F.	4.12	1.92		6.04	7.75	
	0500	Gate, 3'-6" wide		9	2.670	Ea.	40	32		72	98	
	1200	Stockade, No. 2 cedar, treated wood rails, 6' high		160	.150	L.F.	4.69	1.80		6.49	8.20	
	1250	Gate, 3' wide		9	2.670	Ea.	39	32		71	97	
	1300	No. 1 cedar, 3-1/4" cedar rails, 6' high		160	.150	L.F.	11.60	1.80		13.40	15.80	
	1500	Gate, 3' wide		9	2.670	Ea.	96	32		128	160	
	2700	Prefabricated redwood or cedar, 4' high		160	.150	L.F.	8.95	1.80		10.75	12.85	
	2800	6' high		150	.160		11.90	1.92		13.82	16.30	
	3300	Board, shadow box, 1" x 6", treated pine, 6' high		160	.150		7.15	1.80		8.95	10.90	
	3400	No. 1 cedar, 6' high		150	.160		13.80	1.92		15.72	18.40	
	3900	Basket weave, No. 1 cedar, 6' high		160	.150		15.40	1.80		17.20	19.95	
	4200	Gate, 3'-6" wide		9	2.670	Ea.	44	32		76	100	
328	0010	FENCE, WOOD Basket weave, 3/8" x 4" boards, 2" x 4"										328
	0020	stringers on spreaders, 4" x 4" posts										
	0050	No. 1 cedar, 6' high	B-1	160	.150	L.F.	17.40	1.80		19.20	22	
	0070	Treated pine, 6' high		150	.160		7.75	1.92		9.67	11.75	
	0090	Vertical weave 6' high		145	.166		8.55	1.99		10.54	12.75	
	0200	Board fence, 1" x 4" boards, 2" x 4" rails, 4" x 4" post										
	0220	Preservative treated, 2 rail, 3' high	B-1	145	.166	L.F.	4.62	1.99		6.61	8.40	
	0240	4' high		135	.178		5.40	2.14		7.54	9.50	
	0260	3 rail, 5' high		130	.185		6.60	2.22		8.82	10.95	
	0300	6' high		125	.192		7.25	2.31		9.56	11.85	
	0320	No. 2 grade western cedar, 2 rail, 3' high		145	.166		5.40	1.99		7.39	9.25	
	0340	4' high		135	.178		10.30	2.14		12.44	14.90	
	0360	3 rail, 5' high		130	.185		13.30	2.22		15.52	18.35	
	0400	6' high		125	.192		15.95	2.31		18.26	21	
	0420	No. 1 grade cedar, 2 rail, 3' high		145	.166		12.95	1.99		14.94	17.60	
	0440	4' high		135	.178		14.85	2.14		16.99	19.90	
	0460	3 rail, 5' high		130	.185		16.35	2.22		18.57	22	
	0500	6' high		125	.192		17.90	2.31		20.21	24	
	0540	Shadow box, 1" x 6" board, 2" x 4" rail, 4" x 4" post										
	0560	Pine, pressure treated, 3 rail, 6' high	B-1	160	.150	L.F.	7.15	1.80		8.95	10.90	
	0600	Gate, 3'-6" wide		8	3	Ea.	48	36		84	115	
	0620	No. 1 cedar, 3 rail, 4' high		135	.178	L.F.	14.65	2.14		16.79	19.70	
	0640	6' high		130	.185		16.40	2.22		18.62	22	
	0860	Open rail fence, split rails, 2 rail 3' high, no. 1 cedar		160	.150		3.66	1.80		5.46	7.05	

For expanded coverage of these items see *Means Site Work Cost Data 1991*

028 | Site Improvements

028 300 | Fences And Gates

			CREW	DAILY OUTPUT	MAN-HOURS	UNIT	MAT.	LABOR	EQUIP.	TOTAL	TOTAL INCL O&P	
328	0870	No. 2 cedar	B-1	160	.150	L.F.	1.94	1.80		3.74	5.15	328
	0880	3 rail, 4' high, no. 1 cedar		150	.160		4.84	1.92		6.76	8.55	
	0890	No. 2 cedar		150	.160		2.15	1.92		4.07	5.60	
	0920	Rustic rails, 2 rail 3' high, no. 1 cedar		160	.150		3.22	1.80		5.02	6.55	
	0930	No. 2 cedar		160	.150		1.92	1.80		3.72	5.15	
	0940	3 rail, 4' high		150	.160		3.99	1.92		5.91	7.60	
	0950	No. 2 cedar	↓	150	.160	↓	2.40	1.92		4.32	5.85	
	0960	Picket fence, gothic, pressure treated pine										
	1000	2 rail, 3' high	B-1	140	.171	L.F.	3.28	2.06		5.34	7.05	
	1020	3 rail, 4' high		130	.185	"	3.81	2.22		6.03	7.90	
	1040	Gate, 3'-6" wide		9	2.670	Ea.	35	32		67	92	
	1060	No. 2 cedar, 2 rail, 3' high		140	.171	L.F.	3.81	2.06		5.87	7.65	
	1100	3 rail, 4' high		130	.185	"	4.19	2.22		6.41	8.30	
	1120	Gate, 3'-6" wide		9	2.670	Ea.	40	32		72	98	
	1140	No. 1 cedar, 2 rail 3' high		140	.171	L.F.	8.65	2.06		10.71	12.95	
	1160	3 rail, 4' high		130	.185		9.85	2.22		12.07	14.55	
	1200	Rustic picket, molded pine, 2 rail, 3' high		140	.171		2.78	2.06		4.84	6.50	
	1220	No. 1 cedar, 2 rail, 3' high		140	.171		6.20	2.06		8.26	10.25	
	1240	Stockade fence, no. 1 cedar, 3-¼" rails, 6' high		160	.150		7.65	1.80		9.45	11.45	
	1260	8' high		155	.155		10.15	1.86		12.01	14.30	
	1300	No. 2 cedar, treated wood rails, 6' high		160	.150	↓	7.60	1.80		9.40	11.40	
	1320	Gate, 3'-6" wide		8	3	Ea.	42	36		78	105	
	1360	Treated pine, treated rails, 6' high		160	.150		7.45	1.80		9.25	11.20	
	1400	8' high	↓	150	.160		11.45	1.92		13.37	15.80	

028 400 | Walk/Road/Parkg Appurt

416	0010	**STEPS** Incl. excav., borrow & concrete base, where applicable										416
	0100	Bricks	B-24	35	.686	LF Rsr	22	9.05		31.05	39	
	0200	Railroad ties	2 Clab	25	.640		7.90	7.25		15.15	21	
	0300	Bluestone treads, 12" x 2" or 12" x 1-½"	B-24	30	.800	↓	13	10.60		23.60	32	
	0600	Precast concrete, see division 034-804										
420	0010	**TERRACES** Compared to sidewalks, deduct				S.F.					10%	420

028 700 | Site/Street Furnishings

704	0010	**BENCHES** Park, precast concrete, w/backs, wood rails, 4' long	2 Clab	5	3.200	Ea.	230	36		266	315	704
	0100	8' long		4	4		395	45		440	510	
	0500	Steel barstock pedestals w/backs, 2" x 3" wood rails, 4' long		10	1.600		525	18.15		543.15	610	
	0510	8' long		7	2.290		625	26		651	730	
	0800	Cast iron pedestals, back & arms, wood slats, 4' long		8	2		450	23		473	535	
	0820	8' long		5	3.200		755	36		791	890	
	1700	Steel frame, fir seat, 10' long	↓	10	1.600	↓	130	18.15		148.15	175	
716	0010	**PLANTERS** Concrete, sandblasted, precast, 48" diameter, 24" high	2 Clab	15	1.070	Ea.	410	12.10		422.10	470	716
	0300	Fiberglass, circular, 36" diameter, 24" high		15	1.070		460	12.10		472.10	525	
	1200	Wood, square, 48" side, 24" high		15	1.070		575	12.10		587.10	655	
	1300	Circular, 48" diameter, 30" high		10	1.600		675	18.15		693.15	775	
	1600	Planter/bench, 72"	↓	5	3.200	↓	1,650	36		1,686	1,875	

For expanded coverage of these items see *Means Site Work Cost Data 1991*

029 | Landscaping

029 100 | Shrub/Tree Transplanting

		Crew	Daily Output	Man-Hours	Unit	Mat.	Labor	Equip.	Total	Total Incl O&P
104	0010 **TREE GUYING** Including stakes, guy wire and wrap										104
	0100 Less than 3" caliper, 2 stakes	2 Clab	35	.457	Ea.	6.65	5.20		11.85	16
	0200 3" to 4" caliper, 3 stakes	"	21	.762	"	12.20	8.65		20.85	28
	1000 Including arrowhead anchor, cable, turnbuckles and wrap									
	1100 Less than 3" caliper, 3" anchors	2 Clab	20	.800	Ea.	38	9.10		47.10	57
	1200 3" to 6" caliper, 4" anchors		15	1.070		48	12.10		60.10	73
	1300 6" caliper, 6" anchors		12	1.330		71	15.15		86.15	105
	1400 8" caliper, 8" anchors	↓	9	1.780	↓	85	20		105	125

029 200 | Soil Preparation

		Crew	Daily Output	Man-Hours	Unit	Mat.	Labor	Equip.	Total	Total Incl O&P
208	0010 **PLANT BED PREPARATION**										208
	0100 Backfill planting pit, by hand, on site topsoil	2 Clab	18	.889	C.Y.		10.10		10.10	16.85
	0200 Prepared planting mix	"	24	.667			7.55		7.55	12.65
	0300 Skid steer loader, on site topsoil	B-62	340	.071			.86	.26	1.12	1.72
	0400 Prepared planting mix	"	410	.059			.71	.22	.93	1.42
	1000 Excavate planting pit, by hand, sandy soil	2 Clab	16	1			11.35		11.35	19
	1100 Heavy soil or clay	"	8	2			23		23	38
	1200 ½ C.Y. backhoe, sandy soil	B-11C	150	.107			1.38	1.27	2.65	3.69
	1300 Heavy soil or clay	"	115	.139			1.81	1.66	3.47	4.81
	2000 Mix planting soil, incl. loam, manure, peat, by hand	2 Clab	60	.267		23	3.03		26.03	30
	2100 Skid steer loader	B-62	150	.160	↓	23	1.95	.59	25.54	29
	3000 Pile sod, skid steer loader	"	2,800	.009	S.Y.		.10	.03	.13	.21
	3100 By hand	2 Clab	400	.040			.45		.45	.76
	4000 Remove sod, F.E. loader	B-10S	2,000	.006			.08	.15	.23	.30
	4100 Sod cutter	B-12K	3,200	.005			.07	.24	.31	.38
	4200 By hand	2 Clab	240	.067	↓		.76		.76	1.27

029 300 | Lawns & Grasses

		Crew	Daily Output	Man-Hours	Unit	Mat.	Labor	Equip.	Total	Total Incl O&P
304	0010 **SEEDING** Mechanical seeding, $2.00/lb., 215 lb./acre (29)	A-1	.31	25.810	Acre	435	295	175	905	1,150	304
	0100 $2.00/lb., 44 lb./M.S.Y.	"	13,950	.001	S.F.	.01	.01		.02	.03
	0300 Fine grading and seeding incl. lime, fertilizer & seed,									
	0310 with equipment	B-14	1,000	.048	S.Y.	.15	.58	.19	.92	1.35
	0600 Limestone hand push spreader, 50 lbs. per M.S.F.	A-1	200	.040	M.S.F.	1.55	.45	.27	2.27	2.77
	0800 Grass seed hand push spreader, 4.5 lbs. per M.S.F.	"	200	.040	"	8.85	.45	.27	9.57	10.80
312	0010 **SODDING** In East, 1 inch deep, incl. fine grade, on level ground	B-14	9,000	.005	S.F.	.16	.06	.02	.24	.31	312
	0200 On slopes		7,200	.007		.17	.08	.03	.28	.35
	1200 In Midwest on level ground, prepared area, over 400 S.Y.		7,560	.006		.10	.08	.03	.21	.27
	1230 100 S.Y. area		7,200	.007		.15	.08	.03	.26	.33
	1260 50 S.Y. area		6,750	.007		.21	.09	.03	.33	.40
	1300 On slopes, 400 S.Y. area		6,480	.007		.11	.09	.03	.23	.30
	1700 Polyurethane with ceramic chips for median strip, minimum		1,153	.042		.58	.50	.17	1.25	1.66
	1800 Maximum	↓	875	.055	↓	.82	.66	.22	1.70	2.25

029 500 | Trees/Plants/Grnd Cover

		Crew	Daily Output	Man-Hours	Unit	Mat.	Labor	Equip.	Total	Total Incl O&P
504	0010 **GROUND COVER** Plants, pachysandra, in prepared beds	B-1	10	2.400	C	12.70	29		41.70	62	504
	0200 Vinca minor, 1 yr, bare root		10	2.400	"	47	29		76	100
	0600 Stone chips, in 50 lb. bags, Georgia marble		520	.046	Bag	2.75	.55		3.30	3.96
	0700 Onyx gemstone		260	.092		10.50	1.11		11.61	13.40
	0800 Quartz		260	.092	↓	4.68	1.11		5.79	7
	0900 Pea gravel, truckload lots		28	.857	C.Y.	16.70	10.30		27	36
516	0010 **MULCH**										516
	0100 Aged barks, 3" deep, hand spread	1 Clab	100	.080	S.Y.		.91		.91	1.52
	0150 Skid steer loader	B-63	13.50	2.960	M.S.F.		35	6.60	41.60	66
	0200 Hay, 1" deep, hand spread	1 Clab	475	.017	S.Y.		.19		.19	.32
	0250 Power mulcher, small	B-64	180	.089	M.S.F.		1.03	1.30	2.33	3.14
	0350 Large	B-65	530	.030	"		.35	.66	1.01	1.30
	0400 Humus peat, 1" deep, hand spread	1 Clab	700	.011	S.Y.	.13			.13	.22
	0450 Push spreader	A-1	2,500	.003	"	.04	.02		.06	.08

For expanded coverage of these items see *Means Site Work Cost Data 1991*

029 500 | Trees/Plants/Grnd Cover

		029 500 Trees/Plants/Grnd Cover	CREW	DAILY OUTPUT	MAN-HOURS	UNIT	BARE COSTS MAT.	LABOR	EQUIP.	TOTAL	TOTAL INCL O&P	
516	0550	Tractor spreader	B-66	700	.011	M.S.F.		.16	.23	.39	.52	516
	0600	Oat straw, 1" deep, hand spread	1 Clab	475	.017	S.Y.		.19		.19	.32	
	0650	Power mulcher, small	B-64	180	.089	M.S.F.		1.03	1.30	2.33	3.14	
	0700	Large	B-65	530	.030	"		.35	.66	1.01	1.30	
	0750	Add for asphaltic emulsion	B-45	1,770	.009	Gal.		.12	.35	.47	.58	
	0800	Peat moss, 1" deep, hand spread	1 Clab	900	.009	S.Y.		.10		.10	.17	
	0850	Push spreader	A-1	2,500	.003	"		.04	.02	.06	.08	
	0950	Tractor spreader	B-66	700	.011	M.S.F.		.16	.23	.39	.52	
	1000	Polyethylene film, 6 mil.	2 Clab	2,000	.008	S.Y.		.09		.09	.15	
	1100	Redwood nuggets, 3" deep, hand spread	1 Clab	150	.053	"		.61		.61	1.01	
	1150	Skid steer loader	B-63	13.50	2.960	M.S.F.		35	6.60	41.60	66	
	1200	Stone mulch, hand spread, ceramic chips, economy	B-14	125	.384	S.Y.		4.65	1.52	6.17	9.45	
	1250	Deluxe	"	95	.505	"		6.10	2	8.10	12.40	
	1300	Granite chips	B-1	10	2.400	C.Y.		29		29	48	
	1400	Marble chips		10	2.400			29		29	48	
	1500	Onyx gemstone		10	2.400			29		29	48	
	1600	Pea gravel		28	.857			10.30		10.30	17.25	
	1700	Quartz		10	2.400			29		29	48	
	1800	Tar paper, 15 Lb. felt	1 Clab	800	.010	S.Y.	.34	.11		.45	.56	
	1900	Wood chips, 2" deep, hand spread	"	220	.036	"	.83	.41		1.24	1.60	
	1950	Skid steer loader	B-63	20.30	1.970	M.S.F.	92	23	4.37	119.37	145	
520	0010	**PLANTING** Moving shrubs on site, 12" ball	B-1	28	.857	Ea.		10.30		10.30	17.25	520
	0100	24" ball	"	22	1.090			13.10		13.10	22	
	0300	Moving trees on site, 36" ball	B-6	3.75	6.400			78	51	129	185	
	0400	60" ball	"	1	24			295	190	485	695	
524	0010	**SHRUBS** Broadleaf evergreen, planted in prepared beds										524
	0100	Andromeda, 15"-18", container	B-1	96	.250	Ea.	16.45	3		19.45	23	
	0200	Azalea, 15"-18", container		96	.250		16.30	3		19.30	23	
	0300	Barberry, 9"-12", container		130	.185		5.80	2.22		8.02	10.10	
	0400	Boxwood, 15"-18", B & B		96	.250		22	3		25	29	
	0500	Euonymus, emerald gaiety, 12" to 15", container		115	.209		8.40	2.51		10.91	13.45	
	0600	Holly, 15"-18", B & B		96	.250		16.60	3		19.60	23	
	0900	Mount laurel, 18"-24", B & B		80	.300		18.75	3.61		22.36	27	
	1000	Privet, 18" to 24" high		130	.185		2.25	2.22		4.47	6.20	
	1100	Rhododendron, 18"-24", container		48	.500		18.50	6		24.50	30	
	1200	Rosemary, 1 gal container		600	.040		3.60	.48		4.08	4.76	
	2000	Deciduous, amelanchier, 2'-3', B & B		57	.421		14.65	5.05		19.70	25	
	2100	Azalea, 15"-18", B & B		96	.250		13.65	3		16.65	20	
	2300	Bayberry, 2'-3', B & B		57	.421		17.55	5.05		22.60	28	
	2600	Cotoneaster, 15"-18", B & B		80	.300		8.25	3.61		11.86	15.10	
	2800	Dogwood, 3'-4', B & B	B-17	40	.800		14.30	9.70	12.25	36.25	45	
	2900	Euonymus, alatus compacta, 15" to 18", container	B-1	80	.300		9.20	3.61		12.81	16.15	
	3200	Forsythia, 2'-3', container	"	60	.400		9.70	4.81		14.51	18.70	
	3300	Hibiscus, 3'-4', B & B	B-17	75	.427		25	5.20	6.50	36.70	43	
	3400	Honeysuckle, 3'-4', B & B	B-1	60	.400		25	4.81		29.81	36	
	3500	Hydrangea, 2'-3', B & B	"	57	.421		10.20	5.05		15.25	19.70	
	3600	Lilac, 3'-4', B & B	B-17	40	.800		20	9.70	12.25	41.95	52	
	3900	Privet, bare root, 18"-24"	B-1	80	.300		2.50	3.61		6.11	8.80	
	4100	Quince, 2'-3', B & B	"	57	.421		16.39	5.05		21.44	27	
	4200	Russian olive, 3'-4', B & B	B-17	75	.427		15.25	5.20	6.50	26.95	33	
	4400	Spirea, 3'-4', B & B	B-1	70	.343		16.20	4.12		20.32	25	
	4500	Viburnum, 3'-4', B & B	B-17	40	.800		16.20	9.70	12.25	38.15	47	
528	0010	**SHRUBS AND TREES** Evergreen, in prepared beds, B & B (30)										528
	0100	Arborvitae pyramidal, 4'-5'	B-17	30	1.070	Ea.	26	12.95	16.30	55.25	68	
	0150	Globe, 12"-15"	B-1	96	.250		8.65	3		11.65	14.55	
	0300	Cedar, blue, 8'-10'	B-17	18	1.780		105	22	27	154	180	

For expanded coverage of these items see *Means Site Work Cost Data 1991*

029 | Landscaping

029 500 | Trees/Plants/Grnd Cover

			CREW	DAILY OUTPUT	MAN-HOURS	UNIT	MAT.	LABOR	EQUIP.	TOTAL	TOTAL INCL O&P	
528	0500	Hemlock, canadian, 2-½'-3'	B-1	36	.667	Ea.	18.35	8		26.35	34	528
	0600	Juniper, andora, 18"-24"		80	.300		9.20	3.61		12.81	16.15	
	0620	Wiltoni, 15"-18"	↓	80	.300		13.60	3.61		17.21	21	
	0640	Skyrocket, 4-½'-5'	B-17	55	.582		33	7.05	8.90	48.95	58	
	0660	Blue pfitzer, 2'-2-½'	B-1	44	.545		14.30	6.55		20.85	27	
	0680	Ketleerie, 2-½'-3'										
	0700	Pine, black, 2-½'-3'	B-1	50	.480	Ea.	25	5.75		30.75	37	
	0720	Mugo, 18"-24"	"	60	.400		28	4.81		32.81	39	
	0740	White, 4'-5'	B-17	75	.427		31	5.20	6.50	42.70	50	
	0800	Spruce, blue, 18"-24"	B-1	60	.400		20	4.81		24.81	30	
	0840	Norway, 4'-5'	B-17	75	.427		39	5.20	6.50	50.70	59	
	0900	Yew, denisforma, 12"-15"	B-1	60	.400		10.35	4.81		15.16	19.45	
	1000	Capitata, 18"-24"		30	.800		15.30	9.60		24.90	33	
	1100	Hicksi, 2'-2-½'	↓	30	.800		16.35	9.60		25.95	34	
536	0010	**TREES** Deciduous, in prep. beds, balled & burlapped (B&B) (30)										536
	0100	Ash, 2" caliper	B-17	8	4	Ea.	76	49	61	186	230	
	0200	Beech, 5'-6'		50	.640		39	7.75	9.80	56.55	67	
	0300	Birch, 6'-8', 3 stems		20	1.600		45	19.40	24	88.40	110	
	0500	Crabapple, 6'-8'		20	1.600		40	19.40	24	83.40	105	
	0600	Dogwood, 4'-5'		40	.800		36	9.70	12.25	57.95	69	
	0700	Eastern redbud 4'-5'		40	.800		51	9.70	12.25	72.95	86	
	0800	Elm, 8'-10'		20	1.600		60	19.40	24	103.40	125	
	0900	Ginkgo, 6'-7'		24	1.330		51	16.20	20	87.20	105	
	1000	Hawthorn, 8'-10', 1" caliper		20	1.600		55	19.40	24	98.40	120	
	1100	Honeylocust, 10'-12', 1-½" caliper		10	3.200		43	39	49	131	165	
	1300	Larch, 8'		32	1		26	12.15	15.30	53.45	66	
	1400	Linden, 8'-10', 1" caliper		20	1.600		49	19.40	24	92.40	115	
	1500	Magnolia, 4'-5'		20	1.600		46	19.40	24	89.40	110	
	1600	Maple, red, 8'-10', 1-½" caliper		10	3.200		45	39	49	133	170	
	1700	Mountain ash, 8'-10', 1" caliper		16	2		50	24	31	105	130	
	1800	Oak, 2-½"-3" caliper		3	10.670		170	130	165	465	580	
	2100	Planetree, 9'-11', 1-¼" caliper		10	3.200		69	39	49	157	195	
	2200	Plum, 6'-8', 1" caliper		20	1.600		67	19.40	24	110.40	135	
	2300	Poplar, 9'-11', 1-¼" caliper		10	3.200		41	39	49	129	165	
	2500	Sumac, 2'-3'		75	.427		11.50	5.20	6.50	23.20	28	
	2700	Tulip, 5'-6'		40	.800		35	9.70	12.25	56.95	68	
	2800	Willow, 6'-8', 1" caliper	↓	20	1.600	↓	25	19.40	24	68.40	87	

031 | Concrete Formwork

031 100 | Struct C.I.P. Formwork

			CREW	DAILY OUTPUT	MAN-HOURS	UNIT	MAT.	LABOR	EQUIP.	TOTAL	TOTAL INCL O&P	
110	0010	**ACCESSORIES, ANCHOR BOLTS** incl. nut and washer										110
	0020	½" diameter, 6" long	1 Carp	90	.089	Ea.	.35	1.27		1.62	2.51	
	0050	10" long		85	.094		.50	1.35		1.85	2.80	
	0100	12" long		85	.094		.60	1.35		1.95	2.91	
	0200	⅝" diameter, 12" long		80	.100		1.25	1.43		2.68	3.77	
	0250	18" long		70	.114		1.80	1.63		3.43	4.71	
	0300	24" long		60	.133		1.95	1.91		3.86	5.35	
	0350	¾" diameter, 8" long		80	.100		1.30	1.43		2.73	3.82	
	0400	12" long		70	.114		1.55	1.63		3.18	4.44	
	0450	18" long	↓	60	.133	↓	1.95	1.91		3.86	5.35	

For expanded coverage of these items see *Means Concrete Cost Data 1991*

267

031 | Concrete Formwork

031 100 | Struct C.I.P. Formwork

			CREW	DAILY OUTPUT	MAN-HOURS	UNIT	MAT.	LABOR	EQUIP.	TOTAL	TOTAL INCL O&P	
110	0500	24" long	1 Carp	50	.160	Ea.	2.15	2.29		4.44	6.20	110
112	0010	**ACCESSORIES, CHAMFER STRIPS**										112
	5000	Wood ½" wide	1 Carp	535	.015	L.F.	.10	.21		.31	.47	
	5200	¾" wide		525	.015		.15	.22		.37	.53	
	5400	1" wide		515	.016		.17	.22		.39	.56	
114	0010	**ACCESSORIES, COLUMN FORM**										114
	1000	Column clamps, adjustable to 24" x 24", buy				Set	39.95			39.95	44	
	1400	Rent per month				"	5			5	5.50	
122	0010	**ACCESSORIES, INSERTS**										122
	1000	All size nut insert, ⅝" & ¾", incl. nut	1 Carp	84	.095	Ea.	2.65	1.36		4.01	5.20	
	2000	Continuous slotted, 1-⅝" x 1-⅜"										
	2100	3" long 12 ga.	1 Carp	65	.123	Ea.	2.40	1.76		4.16	5.60	
	2150	6" long 12 ga.		65	.123		3.20	1.76		4.96	6.45	
	2200	12" long 8 ga.		65	.123		7.90	1.76		9.66	11.65	
	2300	36" long 8 ga.		60	.133		17.15	1.91		19.06	22	
126	0010	**ACCESSORIES, SLEEVES AND CHASES**										126
	0100	Plastic type, 1 use, 9" long, 2" diameter	1 Carp	100	.080	Ea.	1.05	1.14		2.19	3.07	
	0150	4" diameter		90	.089		1.75	1.27		3.02	4.05	
	0200	6" diameter		75	.107		2.15	1.53		3.68	4.92	
128	0010	**ACCESSORIES, SNAP TIES, FLAT WASHER**										128
	0100	3000 lb. to 8"				C	41			41	45	
	0250	16"					51			51	56	
	0300	18"					53			53	58	
	0500	With plastic cone, to 8"					41			41	45	
	0600	11" & 12"					47			47	52	
	0650	16"					51			51	56	
	0700	18"					53			53	58	
130	0700	1-¼", 36,000 lb., to 8"					353			353	390	130
	1200	1-¼" dia. x 3" long					646			646	710	
	4200	30" long				Ea.	2.71			2.71	2.98	
	4250	36" long				"	3.10			3.10	3.41	
132	0010	**EXPANSION JOINT** Keyed cold joint, 24 ga., incl. stakes, 3-½" high	1 Carp	200	.040	L.F.	.82	.57		1.39	1.86	132
	0050	4-½" high		200	.040		.89	.57		1.46	1.94	
	0100	5-½" high		195	.041		1.08	.59		1.67	2.17	
	2000	Premolded, bituminous fiber, ½" x 6"		375	.021		.48	.31		.79	1.04	
	2050	1" x 12"		300	.027		2.15	.38		2.53	3	
	2500	Neoprene sponge, closed cell, ½" x 6"		375	.021		1.30	.31		1.61	1.94	
	2550	1" x 12"		300	.027		5	.38		5.38	6.15	
	5000	For installation in walls, add						75%				
	5250	For installation in boxouts, add						25%				
142	0010	**FORMS IN PLACE, COLUMNS**										142
	1500	Round fiber tube, 1 use, 8" diameter	C-1	155	.206	L.F.	1.76	2.80	.15	4.71	6.80	
	1550	10" diameter		155	.206		2.61	2.80	.15	5.56	7.70	
	1600	12" diameter		150	.213		3.05	2.89	.16	6.10	8.35	
	1700	16" diameter		140	.229		5.50	3.10	.17	8.77	11.40	
	5000	Plywood, 8" x 8" columns, 1 use		165	.194	SFCA	1.85	2.63	.15	4.63	6.60	
	5500	12" x 12" plywood columns, 1 use		180	.178		1.80	2.41	.13	4.34	6.15	
	7500	Steel framed plywood, 4 use per mo., rent, 8" x 8"		290	.110		.62	1.50	.08	2.20	3.27	
	7550	10" x 10"		300	.107		.48	1.45	.08	2.01	3.04	
	7600	12" x 12"		310	.103		.41	1.40	.08	1.89	2.88	
158	0010	**FORMS IN PLACE, FOOTINGS** Continuous wall, 1 use		375	.085		1.05	1.16	.06	2.27	3.17	158
	0150	4 use		485	.066		.35	.89	.05	1.29	1.94	
	1500	Keyway, 4 use, tapered wood, 2" x 4"	1 Carp	530	.015	L.F.	.07	.22		.29	.44	
	1550	2" x 6"	"	500	.016	"	.10	.23		.33	.49	

For expanded coverage of these items see *Means Concrete Cost Data 1991*

031 | Concrete Formwork

031 100 | Struct C.I.P. Formwork

			CREW	DAILY OUTPUT	MAN-HOURS	UNIT	MAT.	LABOR	EQUIP.	TOTAL	TOTAL INCL O&P	
158	5000	Spread footings, 1 use	C-1	305	.105	SFCA	1.05	1.42	.08	2.55	3.63	158
	5150	4 use	"	415	.077		.38	1.05	.06	1.49	2.23	
162	0010	FORMS IN PLACE, GRADE BEAM 1 use	C-2	530	.091		1.30	1.28	.06	2.64	3.64	162
	0150	4 use	"	605	.079		.50	1.12	.05	1.67	2.48	
170	0010	FORMS IN PLACE, SLAB ON GRADE										170
	1000	Bulkhead forms with keyway, 1 use, 2 piece	C-1	510	.063	L.F.	.44	.85	.05	1.34	1.95	
	2000	Curb forms, wood, 6" to 12" high, on grade, 1 use		215	.149	SFCA	1.34	2.02	.11	3.47	4.97	
	2150	4 use		275	.116	"	.44	1.58	.09	2.11	3.21	
	3000	Edge forms, to 6" high, 4 use, on grade		600	.053	L.F.	.23	.72	.04	.99	1.50	
	3050	7" to 12" high, 4 use, on grade		435	.074	SFCA	.70	1	.06	1.76	2.50	
	4000	For slab blockouts, 1 use to 12" high		200	.160	L.F.	.51	2.17	.12	2.80	4.32	
174	0010	FORMS IN PLACE, STAIRS (Slant length x width), 1 use	C-2	165	.291	S.F.	2.55	4.11	.19	6.85	9.90	174
	0150	4 use		190	.253		.94	3.57	.17	4.68	7.20	
	2000	Stairs, cast on sloping ground (length x width), 1 use		220	.218		1.80	3.09	.15	5.04	7.30	
	2100	4 use		240	.200		1.05	2.83	.13	4.01	6.05	
182	0010	FORMS IN PLACE, WALLS										182
	0100	Box out for wall openings, to 16" thick, to 10 S.F.	C-2	24	2	Ea.	14.70	28	1.33	44.03	65	
	0150	Over 10 S.F. (use perimeter)	"	280	.171	L.F.	1.35	2.42	.11	3.88	5.65	
	0250	Brick shelf, 4" wide, add to wall forms, use wall area										
	0260	above shelf, 1 use	C-2	240	.200	SFCA	1.44	2.83	.13	4.40	6.45	
	0350	4 use		300	.160	"	.58	2.26	.11	2.95	4.54	
	0500	Bulkhead forms for walls, with keyway, 1 use, 2 piece		265	.181	L.F.	1.75	2.56	.12	4.43	6.35	
	0550	3 piece		175	.274	"	2.20	3.88	.18	6.26	9.10	
	2000	Job built plyform wall forms, to 8' high, 1 use		370	.130	SFCA	1.50	1.83	.09	3.42	4.81	
	2150	4 use		505	.095		.62	1.34	.06	2.02	3	
	2400	Over 8' to 16' high, 1 use		280	.171		1.69	2.42	.11	4.22	6.05	
	2550	4 use		395	.122		.64	1.72	.08	2.44	3.66	
	3000	For architectural finish, add		1,820	.026		.41	.37	.02	.80	1.09	
	7800	Modular prefabricated plywood, to 8' high, 1 use per month		910	.053		.83	.75	.04	1.62	2.20	
	7860	4 use per month		970	.049		.28	.70	.03	1.01	1.52	
	8000	To 16' high, 1 use per month		550	.087		1.12	1.23	.06	2.41	3.36	
	8060	4 use per month		610	.079		.40	1.11	.05	1.56	2.36	
198	0010	WATERSTOP Polyvinyl chloride, ribbed 3/16" thick, 4" wide	1 Carp	155	.052	L.F.	1.29	.74		2.03	2.65	198
	0050	3/16" thick, 6" wide		145	.055		1.65	.79		2.44	3.13	
	0500	Ribbed, PVC, with center bulb, 3/16" thick, 9" wide		135	.059		2	.85		2.85	3.62	
	0550	3/8" thick		130	.062		3.20	.88		4.08	4.99	

032 | Concrete Reinforcement

032 100 | Reinforcing Steel

			CREW	DAILY OUTPUT	MAN-HOURS	UNIT	MAT.	LABOR	EQUIP.	TOTAL	TOTAL INCL O&P	
107	0010	REINFORCING IN PLACE A615 Grade 60										107
	0500	Footings, #4 to #7	4 Rodm	4,200	.008	Lb.	.27	.12		.39	.51	
	0550	#8 to #18		7,200	.004		.27	.07		.34	.42	
	0700	Walls, #3 to #7		6,000	.005		.28	.08		.36	.46	
	0750	#8 to #18		8,000	.004		.27	.06		.33	.41	
	2400	Dowels, 2 feet long, deformed, #3 bar	2 Rodm	140	.114	Ea.	.82	1.78		2.60	4.12	
	2410	#4 bar		125	.128		.97	1.99		2.96	4.68	
	2420	#5 bar		110	.145		1.18	2.26		3.44	5.40	
	2430	#6 bar		105	.152		1.59	2.37		3.96	6.05	

For expanded coverage of these items see *Means Concrete Cost Data 1991*

032 | Concrete Reinforcement

032 200 | Welded Wire Fabric

			CREW	DAILY OUTPUT	MAN-HOURS	UNIT	MAT.	LABOR	EQUIP.	TOTAL	TOTAL INCL O&P	
207	0010	WELDED WIRE FABRIC Rolls, 6 x 6 #10/10 (W1.4/W1.4) 21 lb.	2 Rodm	3,500	.005	S.F.	.07	.07		.14	.21	207
	0300	6 x 6 - #6/6 (W2.9/W2.9) 42 lb. per C.S.F.		2,900	.006		.14	.09		.23	.31	
	0500	4 x 4 - #10/10 (W1.4/W1.4) 31 lb. per C.S.F.		3,100	.005		.12	.08		.20	.28	
	0900	2 x 2 - #12 galv. for gunite reinforcing		650	.025		.18	.38		.56	.89	
	0950	Material prices for above include 10% lap										

033 | Cast-In-Place Concrete

033 100 | Structural Concrete

			CREW	DAILY OUTPUT	MAN-HOURS	UNIT	MAT.	LABOR	EQUIP.	TOTAL	TOTAL INCL O&P	
126	0010	CONCRETE, READY MIX Regular weight, 2000 psi				C.Y.	47.80			47.80	53	126
	0100	2500 psi					49.45			49.45	54	
	0150	3000 psi					51.05			51.05	56	
	0200	3500 psi					52.70			52.70	58	
	0250	3750 psi					53.50			53.50	59	
	0300	4000 psi					54.30			54.30	60	
	0350	4500 psi					55.90			55.90	61	
	0400	5000 psi					57.50			57.50	63	
	1000	For high early strength cement, add					10%					
	2000	For all lightweight aggregate, add					45%					
130	0010	CONCRETE IN PLACE Including forms (4 uses), reinforcing										130
	0050	steel, including finishing unless otherwise indicated										
	0500	Chimney foundations, industrial, minimum	C-17A	26.70	3.030	C.Y.	96	46	5.60	147.60	190	
	0510	Maximum	"	19.70	4.110		110	62	7.55	179.55	235	
	3800	Footings, spread under 1 C.Y.	C-17B	35.95	2.280		84	34	7.95	125.95	160	
	3850	Over 5 C.Y.	C-17C	73.91	1.120		70	16.95	5.90	92.85	110	
	3900	Footings, strip, 18" x 9", plain	C-17B	29.24	2.800		66	42	9.80	117.80	155	
	3950	36" x 12", reinforced		51.42	1.590		70	24	5.55	99.55	125	
	4000	Foundation mat, under 10 C.Y.		32.32	2.540		107	38	8.85	153.85	190	
	4050	Over 20 C.Y.		47.37	1.730		103	26	6.05	135.05	165	
	4750	Slab on grade, incl. troweled finish, not incl. forms										
	4760	or reinforcing, over 10,000 S.F., 4" thick slab	C-8	3,520	.016	S.F.	.65	.20	.15	1	1.22	
	4820	6" thick slab	"	3,610	.016	"	.98	.20	.14	1.32	1.57	
	6203	Retaining walls, gravity, 4' high	C-17B	19.10	4.290	C.Y.	64	65	15	144	195	
	6800	Stairs, not including safety treads, free standing	C-15	120	.600	LF Nose	4.85	8.15	.42	13.42	19.50	
	6850	Cast on ground		180	.400	"	3.66	5.45	.28	9.39	13.45	
	7000	Stair landings, free standing		285	.253	S.F.	2	3.44	.18	5.62	8.15	
	7050	Cast on ground		685	.105		1.18	1.43	.07	2.68	3.78	
134	0010	CURING With burlap, 4 uses assumed, 7.5 oz.	2 Clab	5,500	.003		.03	.03		.06	.09	134
	0100	12 oz.		5,500	.003		.04	.03		.07	.10	
	0200	With waterproof curing paper, 2 ply, reinforced		9,500	.002		.05	.02		.07	.09	
	0300	With sprayed membrane curing compound		9,500	.002		.02	.02		.04	.05	
152	0012	FLOOR PATCHING ¼" thick, small areas, regular	1 Cefi	170	.047		.80	.66		1.46	1.94	152
	0100	Epoxy	"	100	.080		3.50	1.12		4.62	5.65	
172	0010	PLACING CONCRETE and vibrating, including labor & equipment										172
	1900	Footings, continuous, shallow, direct chute	C-6	120	.400	C.Y.		4.85	.52	5.37	8.65	
	1950	Pumped	C-20	100	.640			7.90	5.75	13.65	19.45	
	2000	With crane and bucket	C-7	90	.711			8.80	8.95	17.75	24	
	2400	Footings, spread, under 1 C.Y., direct chute	C-6	55	.873			10.60	1.13	11.73	18.80	
	2600	Spread footings, over 5 C.Y., direct chute		110	.436			5.30	.56	5.86	9.40	
	2900	Foundation mats, over 20 C.Y., direct chute		350	.137			1.66	.18	1.84	2.96	
	4300	Slab on grade, 4" thick, direct chute		110	.436			5.30	.56	5.86	9.40	

For expanded coverage of these items see *Means Concrete Cost Data 1991*

033 | Cast-In-Place Concrete

033 100 | Structural Concrete

			CREW	DAILY OUTPUT	MAN-HOURS	UNIT	MAT.	LABOR	EQUIP.	TOTAL	TOTAL INCL O&P	
172	4350	Pumped	C-20	120	.533	C.Y.		6.60	4.81	11.41	16.20	172
	4400	With crane and bucket	C-7	110	.582			7.20	7.35	14.55	19.95	
	4900	Walls, 8" thick, direct chute	C-6	90	.533			6.45	.69	7.14	11.50	
	4950	Pumped	C-20	85	.753			9.30	6.80	16.10	23	
	5000	With crane and bucket	C-7	80	.800			9.90	10.10	20	27	
	5050	12" thick, direct chute	C-6	100	.480			5.80	.62	6.42	10.35	
	5100	Pumped	C-20	95	.674			8.30	6.05	14.35	20	
	5200	With crane and bucket	C-7	90	.711			8.80	8.95	17.75	24	
	5600	Wheeled concrete dumping, add to placing costs above										
	5610	Walking cart, 50' haul, add	A-1	31	.258	C.Y.		2.93	1.75	4.68	6.85	
	5620	150' haul, add		27	.296			3.36	2.01	5.37	7.85	
	5700	250' haul, add		23	.348			3.95	2.37	6.32	9.20	
	5800	Riding cart, 50' haul, add	B-9	320	.125			1.47	.40	1.87	2.90	
	5810	150' haul, add		230	.174			2.04	.55	2.59	4.03	
	5900	250' haul, add		200	.200			2.35	.64	2.99	4.63	
196	0010	WINTER PROTECTION For heated ready mix, add, minimum				C.Y.	3			3	3.30	196
	0050	Maximum				"	4			4	4.40	
	0100	Protecting concrete and temporary heat, add, minimum	2 Clab	6,000	.003	S.F.	.06	.03		.09	.12	
	0160	Maximum	"	2,000	.008	"	.46	.09		.55	.66	

033 450 | Concrete Finishing

			CREW	DAILY OUTPUT	MAN-HOURS	UNIT	MAT.	LABOR	EQUIP.	TOTAL	TOTAL INCL O&P	
454	0010	FINISHING FLOORS Monolithic, screed finish	1 Cefi	900	.009	S.F.		.12		.12	.20	454
	0050	Darby finish	"	750	.011			.15		.15	.24	
	0100	Float finish	C-9	725	.011			.16	.05	.21	.30	
	0150	Broom finish		675	.012			.17	.05	.22	.32	
	0200	Steel trowel finish, for resilient tile		625	.013			.18	.06	.24	.35	
	0250	For finish floor		550	.015			.20	.06	.26	.40	
	1600	Exposed local aggregate finish, minimum	1 Cefi	625	.013		.35	.18		.53	.67	
	1650	Maximum		465	.017		1.05	.24		1.29	1.54	
458	0010	FINISHING WALLS Break ties and patch voids		540	.015		.01	.21		.22	.34	458
	0050	Burlap rub with grout		450	.018		.05	.25		.30	.46	
	0300	Bush hammer, green concrete		170	.047		.01	.66		.67	1.07	
	0350	Cured concrete		110	.073		.02	1.02		1.04	1.66	

034 | Precast Concrete

034 800 | Precast Specialties

			CREW	DAILY OUTPUT	MAN-HOURS	UNIT	MAT.	LABOR	EQUIP.	TOTAL	TOTAL INCL O&P	
802	0010	LINTELS										802
	0800	Precast concrete, 4" x 8", stock units to 5' long	D-1	175	.091	L.F.	4.60	1.20		5.80	7.05	
	0850	To 12' long	D-4	190	.168		6	2.17	.64	8.81	10.85	
	1000	6" wide, 8" high, solid, stock units to 5' long		185	.173		7.05	2.23	.66	9.94	12.15	
	1050	To 12' long		190	.168		8.55	2.17	.64	11.36	13.70	
804	0010	STAIRS Concrete treads on steel stringers, 3' wide	C-12	75	.640	Riser	58	9.15	4.83	71.98	84	804
	0300	Front entrance, 5' wide with 48" platform, 2 risers		16	3	Flight	290	43	23	356	415	
	0350	5 risers		12	4		335	57	30	422	495	
	0500	6' wide, 2 risers		15	3.200		305	46	24	375	440	
	1200	Basement entrance stairs, steel bulkhead doors, minimum	B-51	22	2.180		485	26	6.65	517.65	585	
	1250	Maximum	"	11	4.360		725	51	13.25	789.25	900	

For expanded coverage of these items see *Means Concrete Cost Data 1991*

041 | Mortar and Masonry Accessories

041 000 | Mortar

			CREW	DAILY OUTPUT	MAN-HOURS	UNIT	MAT.	LABOR	EQUIP.	TOTAL	TOTAL INCL O&P	
008	0010	**CEMENT** Gypsum 80 lb. bag, T.L. lots				Bag	10.85			10.85	11.95	008
	0050	L.T.L. lots					11.05			11.05	12.15	
	0100	Masonry, 70 lb. bag, T.L. lots					5.60			5.60	6.15	
	0150	L.T.L. lots					5.85			5.85	6.45	
	0200	White masonry cement, 70 lb. bag, T.L. lots					13.85			13.85	15.25	
	0250	L.T.L. lots					14.10			14.10	15.50	
016	0010	**GROUTING** Bond bms. & lintels, 8" dp., pumped, not incl. block										016
	0200	Concrete block cores, solid, 4" thk., by hand, .067 C.F./S.F.	D-8	1,200	.033	S.F.	.22	.45		.67	.98	
	0250	8" thick, pumped .258 C.F. per S.F.	D-4	850	.038		.84	.49	.14	1.47	1.88	
	0300	10" thick, .340 C.F. per S.F.		825	.039		1.11	.50	.15	1.76	2.20	
	0350	12" thick, .422 C.F. per S.F.		800	.040		1.38	.52	.15	2.05	2.53	

041 500 | Masonry Accessories

			CREW	DAILY OUTPUT	MAN-HOURS	UNIT	MAT.	LABOR	EQUIP.	TOTAL	TOTAL INCL O&P	
504	0010	**ANCHOR BOLTS** Hooked type with nut, ½" diam., 8" long	1 Bric	200	.040	Ea.	.34	.59		.93	1.35	504
	0030	12" long		190	.042		.44	.62		1.06	1.51	
	0060	¾" diameter, 8" long		160	.050		1.38	.74		2.12	2.73	
	0070	12" long		150	.053		1.69	.79		2.48	3.16	
512	0010	**JOINT REINFORCING** Steel bars, placed horizontal, #3 & #4 bars		450	.018	Lb.	.30	.26		.56	.76	512
	0050	Placed vertical, #3 & #4 bars		800	.010		.30	.15		.45	.57	
	0060	#5 & #6 bars		650	.012		.30	.18		.48	.63	
	0200	Wire strips, regular truss, to 6" wide, galvanized		30	.267	C.L.F.	13	3.95		16.95	21	
	0250	12" wide		20	.400		15.50	5.90		21.40	27	
	0400	Cavity truss with drip section to 6" wide		30	.267		13.50	3.95		17.45	21	
	0450	12" wide		20	.400		16.50	5.90		22.40	28	
520	0010	**WALL TIES** To brick veneer, galv., corrugated, ⅞" x 7", 22 gauge	1 Bric	1,050	.008	Ea.	.04	.11		.15	.23	520
	0150	16 gauge		1,050	.008		.11	.11		.22	.31	
	0200	Buck anchors, galv., corrugated, 16 gauge, 2" bend, 8" x 2"		1,050	.008		.44	.11		.55	.67	
	0250	8" x 3"		1,050	.008		.58	.11		.69	.82	
	0600	Cavity wall, 6" long, Z type, galvanized, ¼" diameter		1,050	.008		.17	.11		.28	.37	
	0650	3/16" diameter		1,050	.008		.07	.11		.18	.26	
	0800	8" long, ¼" diameter, galvanized		1,050	.008		.20	.11		.31	.41	
	0850	3/16" diameter		1,050	.008		.08	.11		.19	.27	
	1000	Rectangular type, ¼" diameter, galv., 2" x 6"		1,050	.008		.24	.11		.35	.45	
	1050	2" x 8" or 4" x 6"		1,050	.008		.27	.11		.38	.48	
	1100	3/16" diameter, galv., 2" x 6"		1,050	.008		.15	.11		.26	.35	
	1150	2" x 8" or 4" x 6"		1,050	.008		.17	.11		.28	.37	
	1500	Rigid partition anchors, plain, 8" long, 1" x ⅛"		1,050	.008		.48	.11		.59	.71	
	1550	x ¼"		1,050	.008		.94	.11		1.05	1.22	
	1580	1-½" x ⅛"		1,050	.008		.66	.11		.77	.91	
	1600	x ¼"		1,050	.008		1.60	.11		1.71	1.95	
	1650	2" x ⅛"		1,050	.008		.85	.11		.96	1.12	
	1700	x ¼"		1,050	.008		2.25	.11		2.36	2.66	

042 | Unit Masonry

042 050 | Chimneys

			CREW	DAILY OUTPUT	MAN-HOURS	UNIT	MAT.	LABOR	EQUIP.	TOTAL	TOTAL INCL O&P	
054	0010	**CHIMNEY** For foundation, add to prices below, see div 033-130-0500										054
	0100	Brick @ $250/M, 16" x 16", 8" flue, scaff. not incl.	D-1	18.20	.879	V.L.F.	11.70	11.55		23.25	32	
	0150	16" x 20" with one 8" x 12" flue		16	1		14.60	13.15		27.75	38	
	0200	16" x 24" with two 8" x 8" flues		14	1.140		17.25	15		32.25	44	

For expanded coverage of these items see *Means Concrete Cost Data 1991*

042 | Unit Masonry

042 050 | Chimneys

			CREW	DAILY OUTPUT	MAN-HOURS	UNIT	MAT.	LABOR	EQUIP.	TOTAL	TOTAL INCL O&P	
054	0250	20" x 20" with one 12" x 12" flue	D-1	13.70	1.170	V.L.F.	17.10	15.35		32.45	44	054
	0300	20" x 24" with two 8" x 12" flues		12	1.330		23.20	17.50		40.70	54	
	0350	20" x 32" with two 12" x 12" flues	↓	10	1.600	↓	28.85	21		49.85	66	

042 100 | Brick Masonry

			CREW	DAILY OUTPUT	MAN-HOURS	UNIT	MAT.	LABOR	EQUIP.	TOTAL	TOTAL INCL O&P	
108	0010	**COLUMNS** Brick @ $250 per M, 8" x 8", 9 brick, scaff. not incl.	D-1	56	.286	V.L.F.	2.57	3.75		6.32	9	108
	0100	12" x 8", 13.5 brick		37	.432		3.85	5.70		9.55	13.55	
	0200	12" x 12", 20.3 brick		25	.640		5.80	8.40		14.20	20	
	0300	16" x 12", 27 brick		19	.842		7.70	11.05		18.75	27	
	0400	16" x 16", 36 brick		14	1.140		10.25	15		25.25	36	
	0500	20" x 16", 45 brick		11	1.450		12.85	19.10		31.95	46	
	0600	20" x 20", 56.3 brick	↓	9	1.780	↓	16.05	23		39.05	56	
110	0010	**COMMON BRICK** Standard size, material only, minimum ⑥¹				M	220			220	240	110
	0050	Average (select common)				"	250			250	275	
116	0010	**COPING** For 12" wall, stock units, aluminum	D-1	80	.200	L.F.	9	2.63		11.63	14.20	116
	0050	Precast concrete, special order, 8" wide		100	.160		12.50	2.10		14.60	17.20	
	0100	10" wide		90	.178		16.40	2.33		18.73	22	
	0150	14" wide		80	.200		22.75	2.63		25.38	29	
	0300	Limestone for 12" wall, 4" thick		90	.178		11.50	2.33		13.83	16.50	
	0350	6" thick		80	.200		13.75	2.63		16.38	19.45	
	0500	Marble to 4" thick, no wash, 9" wide		90	.178		16.80	2.33		19.13	22	
	0550	12" wide		80	.200		24.20	2.63		26.83	31	
	0700	Terra cotta, 9" wide		90	.178		3.95	2.33		6.28	8.20	
	0750	12" wide	↓	80	.200		6.75	2.63		9.38	11.75	
120	0010	**CORNICES** Brick cornice on existing building										120
	0020	Not including scaffolding										
	0110	Face bricks @ $280 per M, 12 brick/S.F., minimum	D-1	30	.533	S.F.Face	3.97	7		10.97	15.90	
	0150	15 brick/S.F., maximum	"	23	.696	"	4.81	9.15		13.96	20	
124	0010	**FACE BRICK** T.L. lots, material only, ⑥¹										124
	0020	Including truck delivery, red brick only										
	0300	Boston, standard size, 8" x 2-⅔" x 4", minimum				M	280			280	310	
	0350	Maximum					385			385	425	
	1200	Chicago, standard size, 8" x 2-⅔" x 4", minimum					340			340	375	
	1250	Maximum					365			365	400	
	2170	For less than truck load lots, add					5%			35	39	
	2180	For buff or gray brick, add				↓	10%					
134	0010	**LINTELS** See division 051-232										134
158	0010	**SCAFFOLDING & SWING STAGING** Div. 015-254, 255 & 256										158
184	0016	**WALLS**										184
	0800	Common 8" x 2-⅔" x 4" at $220/M, 4" wall, as face brick	D-8	215	.186	S.F.	1.72	2.50		4.22	6	
	0850	4" thick, as back up, 6.75 bricks per S.F. ⑤⁹		240	.167		1.72	2.24		3.96	5.60	
	0900	8" thick wall, 13.50 brick per S.F.		135	.296		3.51	3.99		7.50	10.40	
	1000	12" thick wall, 20.25 bricks per S.F.		95	.421		5.35	5.65		11	15.20	
	1050	16" thick wall, 27.00 bricks per S.F.		75	.533		7.15	7.20		14.35	19.65	
	1200	Reinf., straight hard, 8" x 2-⅔" x 4" at $250/M, 4" wall		205	.195		2.03	2.63		4.66	6.55	
	1250	8" thick wall, 13.50 brick per S.F.		130	.308		4.19	4.14		8.33	11.40	
	1300	12" thick wall, 20.25 bricks per S.F.		90	.444		6.30	6		12.30	16.75	
	1350	16" thick wall, 27.00 bricks per S.F.	↓	70	.571		8.50	7.70		16.20	22	
194	0010	**WINDOW SILL** Bluestone, natural cleft, 12" wide, 1-½" thick	D-1	85	.188		10.35	2.47		12.82	15.45	194
	0050	2" thick		85	.188	↓	10.75	2.47		13.22	15.90	
	0100	Cut stone, 5" x 8" plain		85	.188	L.F.	8.15	2.47		10.62	13.05	
	0200	Face brick on edge, brick @ $280 per M, 8" wide		80	.200		1.65	2.63		4.28	6.15	
	0400	Marble, 12" wide, ¾" thick		85	.188		12.40	2.47		14.87	17.70	
	0600	Precast concrete, special order, 6" wide		85	.188		13.50	2.47		15.97	18.90	

For expanded coverage of these items see *Means Concrete Cost Data 1991*

042 | Unit Masonry

042 100 | Brick Masonry

			CREW	DAILY OUTPUT	MAN-HOURS	UNIT	MAT.	LABOR	EQUIP.	TOTAL	TOTAL INCL O&P	
194	0650	10" wide	D-1	85	.188	L.F.	22	2.47		24.47	28	194
	0700	14" wide		85	.188		30	2.47		32.47	37	
	0900	Slate, colored, unfading, honed, 12" wide, 1" thick		85	.188		22.50	2.47		24.97	29	
	0950	2" thick	↓	85	.188	↓	32.50	2.47		34.97	40	

042 200 | Concrete Unit Masonry

			CREW	DAILY OUTPUT	MAN-HOURS	UNIT	MAT.	LABOR	EQUIP.	TOTAL	TOTAL INCL O&P	
216	0010	**CONCRETE BLOCK, BACK-UP,** Scaffolding not included (69)										216
	0020	Sand aggregate, tooled joint 1 side										
	1000	Reinforced, alternate courses, 4" thick	D-8	435	.092	S.F.	1	1.24		2.24	3.13	
	1100	6" thick		415	.096		1.19	1.30		2.49	3.44	
	1150	8" thick		395	.101		1.48	1.36		2.84	3.87	
	1200	10" thick	↓	385	.104		1.99	1.40		3.39	4.49	
	1250	12" thick	D-9	365	.132	↓	2.03	1.73		3.76	5.05	
220	0010	**CONCRETE BLOCK, DECORATIVE** Scaffolding not included										220
	5000	Split rib profile units, 1" deep ribs, 8 ribs										
	5100	8" x 16" x 4" thick	D-8	345	.116	S.F.	1.87	1.56		3.43	4.63	
	5150	6" thick		325	.123		2.33	1.66		3.99	5.30	
	5200	8" thick	↓	305	.131		2.98	1.77		4.75	6.20	
	5250	12" thick	D-9	275	.175	↓	3.61	2.29		5.90	7.75	
	5350											
	5400	For special deeper colors, 4" thick, add				S.F.	.15			.15	.17	
	5450	12" thick, add					.30			.30	.33	
	5600	For white, 4" thick, add					.60			.60	.66	
	5650	6" thick, add					.80			.80	.88	
	5700	8" thick, add					1			1	1.10	
	5750	12" thick, add				↓	1.40			1.40	1.54	
232	0010	**CONCRETE BLOCK, PARTITIONS** Scaffolding not included										232
	1000	Lightweight block, tooled joints, 2 sides, hollow										
	1100	Not reinforced, 8" x 16" x 4" thick	D-8	440	.091	S.F.	.92	1.22		2.14	3.02	
	1150	6" thick		410	.098		1.23	1.31		2.54	3.51	
	1200	8" thick		385	.104		1.61	1.40		3.01	4.07	
	1250	10" thick	↓	370	.108		2.39	1.46		3.85	5	
	1300	12" thick	D-9	350	.137	↓	2.44	1.80		4.24	5.65	
	4000	Regular block, tooled joints, 2 sides, hollow										
	4100	Not reinforced, 8" x 16" x 4" thick	D-8	430	.093	S.F.	.83	1.25		2.08	2.97	
	4150	6" thick		400	.100		1.02	1.35		2.37	3.33	
	4200	8" thick		375	.107		1.30	1.44		2.74	3.79	
	4250	10" thick	↓	360	.111		1.80	1.50		3.30	4.44	
	4300	12" thick	D-9	340	.141	↓	1.85	1.85		3.70	5.10	
252	0010	**INSULATION** See also division 072-108										252
	0100	Inserts, styrofoam, plant installed, add to block prices										
	0200	8" x 16" units, 6" thick				S.F.	.65			.65	.72	
	0250	8" thick					.65			.65	.72	
	0300	10" thick					.79			.79	.87	
	0350	12" thick				↓	.79			.79	.87	

042 300 | Reinforced Unit Masonry

			CREW	DAILY OUTPUT	MAN-HOURS	UNIT	MAT.	LABOR	EQUIP.	TOTAL	TOTAL INCL O&P	
304	0010	**CONCRETE BLOCK BOND BEAM** Scaffolding not included										304
	0020	Not including grout or reinforcing										
	0100	Regular block, 8" high, 8" thick	D-8	565	.071	L.F.	1.07	.95		2.02	2.75	
	0150	12" thick	D-9	510	.094	"	1.57	1.24		2.81	3.76	
310	0010	**CONCRETE BLOCK, EXTERIOR** Not including scaffolding										310
	0020	Reinforced, tooled joints 2 sides, styrofoam inserts										
	0100	Regular, 8" x 16" x 6" thick	D-8	390	.103	S.F.	1.77	1.38		3.15	4.22	
	0200	8" thick	"	365	.110	"	2.05	1.48		3.53	4.69	

For expanded coverage of these items see *Means Concrete Cost Data 1991*

042 | Unit Masonry

042 300	Reinforced Unit Masonry	CREW	DAILY OUTPUT	MAN-HOURS	UNIT	MAT.	LABOR	EQUIP.	TOTAL	TOTAL INCL O&P	
310	0250	10" thick	D-8	355	.113	S.F.	2.70	1.52		4.22	5.45	310
	0300	12" thick	D-9	330	.145	"	2.76	1.91		4.67	6.20	
320	0010	**CONCRETE BLOCK FOUNDATION WALL** Scaffolding not included										320
	0050	Sand aggregate, trowel cut joints, not reinf., parged ½" thick										
	0200	Regular, 8" x 16" x 6" thick	D-8	450	.089	S.F.	1.25	1.20		2.45	3.35	
	0250	8" thick		430	.093		1.60	1.25		2.85	3.82	
	0300	10" thick	↓	420	.095		2.11	1.28		3.39	4.43	
	0350	12" thick	D-9	395	.122		2.17	1.59		3.76	5	
	0500	Solid, 8" x 16" block, 6" thick	D-8	440	.091		1.75	1.22		2.97	3.94	
	0550	8" thick	"	415	.096		2.16	1.30		3.46	4.51	
	0600	12" thick	D-9	380	.126	↓	3.18	1.66		4.84	6.25	
330	0010	**CONCRETE BLOCK, LINTELS** Scaffolding not included										330
	0100	Including grout and reinforcing										
	0200	8" x 8" x 8", 1 #4 bar	D-4	300	.107	L.F.	2.33	1.38	.41	4.12	5.25	
	0250	2 #4 bars		295	.108		2.53	1.40	.41	4.34	5.55	
	1000	12" x 8" x 8", 1 #4 bar		275	.116		3.25	1.50	.44	5.19	6.55	
	1150	2 #5 bars	↓	270	.119	↓	3.67	1.53	.45	5.65	7.05	
042 550	**Masonry Veneer**											
554	0010	**BRICK VENEER** Scaffolding not included, truck load lots (59)										554
	0015	Material costs include a 3% brick waste allowance										
	2000	Standard, sel. common, 8" x 2-⅔" x 4", $250 per M (6.75/S.F.)	D-8	230	.174	S.F.	1.92	2.34		4.26	5.95	
	2020	Stnd, 8" x 2-⅔" x 4", running bond, red, (6.75/S.F.), $280/M		220	.182		2.13	2.45		4.58	6.35	
	2050	Full header every 6th course (7.88/S.F.) (60)		185	.216		2.48	2.91		5.39	7.50	
	2100	English, full header every 2nd course (10.13/S.F.)		140	.286		3.19	3.85		7.04	9.85	
	2150	Flemish, alternate header every course (9.00/S.F.) (61)		150	.267		2.84	3.59		6.43	9	
	2200	Flemish, alt. header every 6th course (7.13/S.F.)		205	.195		2.25	2.63		4.88	6.80	
	2250	Full headers throughout (13.50/S.F.) (62)		105	.381		4.25	5.15		9.40	13.10	
	2300	Rowlock course (13.50/S.F.)		100	.400		4.25	5.40		9.65	13.55	
	2350	Rowlock stretcher (4.50/S.F.)		310	.129		1.42	1.74		3.16	4.42	
	2400	Soldier course (6.75/S.F.) (63)		200	.200		2.13	2.69		4.82	6.75	
	2450	Sailor course (4.50/S.F.)		290	.138		1.42	1.86		3.28	4.61	
	2600	Running bond, buff or gray face at $355 per M (6.75/S.F.)		220	.182		2.67	2.45		5.12	6.95	
	2700	Glazed face, brick at $825 per M, running bond		210	.190		6.35	2.56		8.91	11.20	
	2750	Full header every 6th course (7.88/S.F.)		170	.235		6.95	3.17		10.12	12.85	
	3000	Jumbo, 12" x 4" x 6" running bond @ $985 per M (3.00/S.F.)		435	.092		3.24	1.24		4.48	5.60	
	3050	Norman, 12" x 2-⅔" x 4" running bond, $550/M (4.50/S.F.)		320	.125		2.72	1.68		4.40	5.75	
	3100	Norwegian, 12" x 3-⅛" x 4" at $595 per M (3.75/S.F.)		375	.107		2.46	1.44		3.90	5.05	
	3150	Economy, 8" x 4" x 4" at $490 per M (4.50/S.F.)		310	.129		2.41	1.74		4.15	5.50	
	3200	Engineer, 8" x 3-⅛" x 4" at $395 per M (5.63/S.F.)		260	.154		2.45	2.07		4.52	6.10	
	3250	Roman, 12" x 2" x 4" at $575 per M (6.00/S.F.)		250	.160		3.78	2.15		5.93	7.70	
	3300	SCR, 12" x 2-⅔" x 6" at $690 per M (4.50/S.F.)		310	.129		3.47	1.74		5.21	6.70	
	3350	Utility, 12" x 4" x 4" at $795 per M (3.00/S.F.)	↓	450	.089		2.58	1.20		3.78	4.81	
	3400	For cavity wall construction, add						15%				
	3450	For stacked bond, add						10%				
	3500	For interior veneer construction, add						15%				
	3550	For curved walls, add						30%				
704	0010	**GLASS BLOCK** Scaffolding not included (57)										704
	0150	8" x 8" block	D-8	160	.250	S.F.	14.70	3.37		18.07	22	
	0200	12" x 12" block	"	175	.229		18.50	3.08		21.58	25	
	0700	For solar reflective blocks, add					100%					
	0800	Plain, 4" x 8" blocks, under 1000 S.F.	D-8	145	.276		23.55	3.71		27.26	32	
	1000	3-⅛" thick thinline, plain, under 1000 S.F., 6" x 6" block		115	.348		17.35	4.68		22.03	27	
	1050	8" x 8" block		160	.250		11.05	3.37		14.42	17.70	
	1400	For cleaning block after installation (both sides), add	↓	1,000	.040		.08	.54		.62	.98	
904	0010	**ADOBE BRICK** Unstabilized, with adobe mortar (Southwestern States)										904
	0260	Brick, 4" x 3" x 8" @ $280 per M (6.0 per S.F.)	D-8	266	.150	S.F.	1.85	2.02		3.87	5.35	

For expanded coverage of these items see *Means Concrete Cost Data 1991*

042 | Unit Masonry

042 550 | Masonry Veneer

		CREW	DAILY OUTPUT	MAN-HOURS	UNIT	MAT.	LABOR	EQUIP.	TOTAL	TOTAL INCL O&P	
904	0280	4" x 4" x 8" @ $390 per M (4.5 per S.F.)	D-8	333	.120	S.F.	1.90	1.62		3.52	4.75	904
	0300	4" x 4" x 14" @ $490 per M (2.5 per S.F.)		540	.074		1.40	1		2.40	3.18	
	0320	8" x 3" x 16" @ $520 per M (3.0 per S.F.)		466	.086		1.70	1.16		2.86	3.77	
	0340	4" x 3" x 12" @ $420 per M (4.0 per S.F.)		362	.110		1.80	1.49		3.29	4.43	
	0360	6" x 3" x 12" @ $400 per M (4.0 per S.F.)		362	.110		1.75	1.49		3.24	4.38	
	0380	4" x 5" x 16" @ $490 per M (1.80 per S.F.)		600	.067		1	.90		1.90	2.58	
	0400	8" x 4" x 16" @ $580 per M (2.25 per S.F.)		577	.069		1.45	.93		2.38	3.13	
	0420	10" x 4" x 14" @ $540 per M (2.57 per S.F.)		555	.072		1.55	.97		2.52	3.30	
	0430											
	0440	Adobe, partially stabilized, add				S.F.	10%					
	0480	Fully stabilized, add				"	30%					

044 | Stone

044 100 | Rough Stone

		CREW	DAILY OUTPUT	MAN-HOURS	UNIT	MAT.	LABOR	EQUIP.	TOTAL	TOTAL INCL O&P	
104	0011	ROUGH STONE WALL Dry										104
	0100	Random fieldstone, under 18" thick	D-12	60	.533	C.F.	9.75	7.25		17	23	
	0150	Over 18" thick	"	63	.508	"	12.90	6.90		19.80	26	

044 550 | Marble

		CREW	DAILY OUTPUT	MAN-HOURS	UNIT	MAT.	LABOR	EQUIP.	TOTAL	TOTAL INCL O&P	
554	0010	MARBLE Base, ¾" thick, polished, group A, 4" thick	D-1	60	.267	L.F.	8.45	3.50		11.95	15.05	554
	1000	Facing, polished finish, cut to size, ¾" to ⅞" thick										
	1050	Average	D-10	130	.308	S.F.	16.50	4.29	3.22	24.01	29	
	1100	Maximum	"	130	.308	"	38.40	4.29	3.22	45.91	53	
	2200	Window sills, 6" x ¾" thick	D-1	85	.188	L.F.	4	2.47		6.47	8.45	
	2500	Flooring, polished tiles, 12" x 12" x ⅜" thick										
	2510	Thin set, average	D-11	90	.267	S.F.	7.20	3.83		11.03	14.20	
	2600	Maximum		90	.267		21.50	3.83		25.33	30	
	2700	Mortar bed, average		65	.369		7.20	5.30		12.50	16.65	
	2740	Maximum		65	.369		21.50	5.30		26.80	32	
	2780	Travertine, ⅜" thick, average	D-10	130	.308		10.10	4.29	3.22	17.61	22	
	2790	Maximum	"	130	.308		21.75	4.29	3.22	29.26	35	
	3500	Thresholds, 3' long, ⅞" thick, 4" to 5" wide, plain	D-12	24	1.330	Ea.	12.50	18.15		30.65	44	
	3550	Beveled		24	1.330	"	13.50	18.15		31.65	45	
	3700	Window stools, polished, ⅞" thick, 5" wide		85	.376	L.F.	10.50	5.15		15.65	20	

044 600 | Limestone

		CREW	DAILY OUTPUT	MAN-HOURS	UNIT	MAT.	LABOR	EQUIP.	TOTAL	TOTAL INCL O&P	
604	0012	LIMESTONE, Cut to size (68)										604
	0020	Veneer facing panels										
	0100	Sawn finish, 2" thick, to 3' x 5' panels	D-10	130	.308	S.F.	9.65	4.29	3.22	17.16	21	
	0150	Smooth finish, 2" thick, to 3' x 5' panels		130	.308		11.75	4.29	3.22	19.26	24	
	0300	3" thick, to 4' x 9' panels		225	.178		13.60	2.48	1.86	17.94	21	
	0350	4" thick, to 5' x 11' panels		275	.145		15.85	2.03	1.52	19.40	22	
	0500	Texture finish, light stick, 4-½" thick, 5' x 12'	D-4	300	.107		15.60	1.38	.41	17.39	19.85	
	0750	5" thick, to 5' x 14' panels	D-10	275	.145		18.60	2.03	1.52	22.15	25	
	1000	Medium ribbed, textured finish, 4-½" thick, to 5' x 12'		275	.145		16.50	2.03	1.52	20.05	23	
	1050	5" thick, to 5' x 14' panels		275	.145		19	2.03	1.52	22.55	26	
	1200	Deep ribbed, textured finish, 4-½" thick, to 5' x 10'		275	.145		17.50	2.03	1.52	21.05	24	
	1250	5" thick, to 5' x 14' panels		275	.145		19.85	2.03	1.52	23.40	27	

For expanded coverage of these items see *Means Concrete Cost Data 1991*

044 | Stone

044 600 | Limestone

			CREW	DAILY OUTPUT	MAN-HOURS	UNIT	MAT.	LABOR	EQUIP.	TOTAL	TOTAL INCL O&P	
604	1400	Sugar cube, textured finish, 4-½" thick, to 5' x 12'	D-10	275	.145	S.F.	16.50	2.03	1.52	20.05	23	604
	1450	5" thick, to 5' x 14' panels		275	.145	"	19	2.03	1.52	22.55	26	
	2000	Coping, smooth finish, top & 2 sides		30	1.330	C.F.	47	18.55	13.95	79.50	98	
	2050											
	2100	Sills, lintels, jambs, smooth finish, average	D-10	20	2	C.F.	51	28	21	100	125	
	2150	Detailed		20	2	"	65	28	21	114	140	
	2300	Steps, extra hard, 14" wide, 6" rise		50	.800	L.F.	32	11.15	8.40	51.55	63	

044 650 | Granite

			CREW	DAILY OUTPUT	MAN-HOURS	UNIT	MAT.	LABOR	EQUIP.	TOTAL	TOTAL INCL O&P	
651	0010	**GRANITE** Cut to size										651
	2450	For radius under 5', add				L.F.	100%					
	2500	Steps, copings, etc., finished on more than one surface										
	2550	Minimum	D-10	50	.800	C.F.	60	11.15	8.40	79.55	94	
	2600	Maximum	"	50	.800	"	90	11.15	8.40	109.55	125	
	2800	Pavers, 4" x 4" x 4" blocks, split face and joints										
	2850	Minimum	D-11	80	.300	S.F.	9.40	4.31		13.71	17.40	
	2900	Maximum	"	80	.300	"	17.40	4.31		21.71	26	
	3200											
	3500	Curbing, city street type, 6" x 18", split face,										
	3510	sawn top, radius nosing, 4' to 7' lengths	D-10	75	.533	L.F.	17.75	7.45	5.60	30.80	38	

044 700 | Sandstone

			CREW	DAILY OUTPUT	MAN-HOURS	UNIT	MAT.	LABOR	EQUIP.	TOTAL	TOTAL INCL O&P	
704	0011	**SANDSTONE OR BROWNSTONE**										704
	0100	Sawed face veneer, 2-½" thick, to 2' x 4' panels	D-10	130	.308	S.F.	10.80	4.29	3.22	18.31	22	
	0150	4" thick, to 3'-6" x 8' panels		100	.400		10.50	5.55	4.19	20.24	25	
	0300	Split face, random sizes		100	.400		7.65	5.55	4.19	17.39	22	
	0350	Cut stone trim (limestone)										
	0360	Ribbon stone, 4" thick, 5' pieces	D-8	120	.333	Ea.	97	4.49		101.49	115	
	0370	Cove stone, 4" thick, 5' pieces		105	.381		98	5.15		103.15	115	
	0380	Cornice stone, 10" to 12" wide		90	.444		120	6		126	140	
	0390	Band stone, 4" thick, 5' pieces		145	.276		65	3.71		68.71	78	
	0410	Window and door trim, 3" to 4" wide		160	.250		55	3.37		58.37	66	
	0420	Key stone, 18" long		60	.667		49	8.95		57.95	69	

044 750 | Slate

			CREW	DAILY OUTPUT	MAN-HOURS	UNIT	MAT.	LABOR	EQUIP.	TOTAL	TOTAL INCL O&P	
754	0010	**SLATE** Pennsylvania, blue gray to gray black; Vermont,										754
	3500	Stair treads, sand finish, 1" thick x 12" wide										
	3600	3 L.F. to 6 L.F.	D-10	120	.333	L.F.	15.25	4.64	3.49	23.38	28	
	3700	Ribbon, sand finish, 1" thick x 12" wide										
	3750	To 6 L.F.	D-10	120	.333	L.F.	10.90	4.64	3.49	19.03	23	

045 | Masonry Restoration and Cleaning/Refractories

045 100 | Masonry Cleaning

			CREW	DAILY OUTPUT	MAN-HOURS	UNIT	MAT.	LABOR	EQUIP.	TOTAL	TOTAL INCL O&P	
106	0010	**CLEAN AND POINT** Smooth brick	1 Bric	300	.027	S.F.	.20	.39		.59	.87	106
	0100	Rough brick		265	.030		.25	.45		.70	1.01	
108	0010	**WASHING BRICK** Acid wash, smooth brick (66)		560	.014		.08	.21		.29	.44	108
	0050	Rough brick		400	.020		.10	.30		.40	.60	

For expanded coverage of these items see *Means Concrete Cost Data 1991*

045 | Masonry Restoration and Cleaning/Refractories

045 550 | Flue Liners

			CREW	DAILY OUTPUT	MAN-HOURS	UNIT	MAT.	LABOR	EQUIP.	TOTAL	TOTAL INCL O&P	
554	0010	FLUE LINING Square, including mortar joints, 8" x 8"	D-1	125	.128	V.L.F.	2.95	1.68		4.63	6	554
	0100	8" x 12"		103	.155		4.60	2.04		6.64	8.40	
	0200	12" x 12"		93	.172		5.75	2.26		8.01	10.05	
	0300	12" x 18"		84	.190		12.95	2.50		15.45	18.35	
	0400	18" x 18"		75	.213		17.45	2.80		20.25	24	
	0500	20" x 20"		66	.242		27	3.18		30.18	35	
	0600	24" x 24"		56	.286		35	3.75		38.75	45	
	1000	Round, 18" diameter		66	.242		22	3.18		25.18	29	
	1100	24" diameter	↓	47	.340	↓	34.40	4.47		38.87	45	

045 650 | Fire Brick

			CREW	DAILY OUTPUT	MAN-HOURS	UNIT	MAT.	LABOR	EQUIP.	TOTAL	TOTAL INCL O&P	
656	0010	FIREPLACE For prefabricated fireplace, see div. 103-054										656
	0100	Brick fireplace, not incl. foundations or chimneys										
	0110	30" x 29" opening, incl. chamber, plain brickwork	D-1	.40	40	Ea.	330	525		855	1,225	
	0200	Fireplace box only (110 brick)	"	2	8		120	105		225	305	
	0300	For elaborate brickwork and details, add			80		35%	35%				
	0400	For hearth, brick & stone, add	D-1	2	8		100	105		205	285	
	0410	For steel angle, damper, cleanouts, add		4	4		75	53		128	170	
	0600	Plain brickwork, incl. metal circulator		.50	32		585	420		1,005	1,325	
	0800	Face brick only, standard size, 8" x 2-⅔" x 4"	↓	.30	53.330	M	330	700		1,030	1,525	
	0900	Stone fireplace, fieldstone, add				S.F.Face					9.25	
	1000	Cut stone, add				"					9	

050 | Metal Materials, Finishes and Fastenings

050 500 | Metal Fastening

			CREW	DAILY OUTPUT	MAN-HOURS	UNIT	MAT.	LABOR	EQUIP.	TOTAL	TOTAL INCL O&P	
508	0010	BOLTS & HEX NUTS Steel, A307										508
	0100	¼" diameter, ½" long				Ea.	.05			.05	.06	
	0200	1" long					.06			.06	.07	
	0300	2" long					.08			.08	.09	
	0400	3" long					.12			.12	.13	
	0500	4" long					.17			.17	.19	
	0600	⅜" diameter, 1" long					.12			.12	.13	
	0700	2" long					.17			.17	.19	
	0800	3" long					.22			.22	.24	
	0900	4" long					.28			.28	.31	
	1000	5" long					.41			.41	.45	
	1100	½" diameter, 1-½" long					.25			.25	.28	
	1200	2" long					.29			.29	.32	
	1300	4" long					.39			.39	.43	
	1400	6" long					.54			.54	.59	
	1500	8" long					.69			.69	.76	
	1600	⅝" diameter, 1-½" long					.44			.44	.48	
	1700	2" long					.51			.51	.56	
	1800	4" long					.66			.66	.73	
	1900	6" long					.84			.84	.92	
	2000	8" long					1.14			1.14	1.25	
	2100	10" long					1.31			1.31	1.44	
	2200	¾" diameter, 2" long					.66			.66	.73	
	2300	4" long				↓	.93			.93	1.02	

For expanded coverage of these items see *Means Building Construction Cost Data 1991*

050 | Metal Materials, Finishes and Fastenings

050 500 | Metal Fastening

			CREW	DAILY OUTPUT	MAN-HOURS	UNIT	MAT.	LABOR	EQUIP.	TOTAL	TOTAL INCL O&P	
508	2400	6" long				Ea.	1.13			1.13	1.24	508
	2500	8" long					1.52			1.52	1.67	
	2600	10" long					1.89			1.89	2.08	
	2700	12" long					2.60			2.60	2.86	
	2800	1" diameter, 3" long					2.12			2.12	2.33	
	2900	6" long					3.03			3.03	3.33	
	3000	12" long					5.17			5.17	5.70	
	3100	For galvanized, add					20%					
	3200	For stainless, add					150%					
515	0010	**DRILLING** And layout for anchors, per										515
	0050	inch of depth, concrete or brick walls										
	1000	For ceiling installations add						40%				
	1100	Drilling & layout for drywall or plaster walls										
	1200	Holes, ¼" diameter	1 Carp	150	.053	Ea.	.04	.76		.80	1.32	
	1300	⅜" diameter		140	.057		.05	.82		.87	1.42	
	1400	½" diameter		130	.062		.06	.88		.94	1.54	
	1500	¾" diameter		120	.067		.09	.95		1.04	1.69	
	1600	1" diameter		110	.073		.17	1.04		1.21	1.93	
	1700	1-¼" diameter		100	.080		.28	1.14		1.42	2.22	
	1800	1-½" diameter		90	.089		.45	1.27		1.72	2.62	
	1900	For ceiling installations add						40%				
520	0010	**EXPANSION ANCHORS** & shields										520
	0100	Bolt anchors for concrete, brick or stone, no layout and drilling										
	0200	Expansion shields, zinc, ¼" diameter, 1" long, single	1 Carp	90	.089	Ea.	.51	1.27		1.78	2.69	
	0300	1-⅜" long, double		85	.094		.58	1.35		1.93	2.89	
	0500	2" long, double		80	.100		1.08	1.43		2.51	3.58	
	0700	2-½" long, double		75	.107		1.41	1.53		2.94	4.10	
	0900	3" long, double		70	.114		2.14	1.63		3.77	5.10	
	1100	4" long, double		65	.123		4	1.76		5.76	7.35	
	1300	1" diameter, 6" long, double		60	.133		17.55	1.91		19.46	22	
	2100	Hollow wall anchors for gypsum board,										
	2200	plaster, tile or wall board										
	2500	3/16" diameter, short				Ea.	.38			.38	.42	
	3000	Toggle bolts, bright steel, ⅛" diameter, 2" long	1 Carp	85	.094		.24	1.35		1.59	2.52	
	3100	4" long		80	.100		.29	1.43		1.72	2.71	
	3200	3/16" diameter, 3" long		80	.100		.27	1.43		1.70	2.69	
	3300	6" long		75	.107		.40	1.53		1.93	2.99	
	3400	¼" diameter, 3" long		75	.107		.30	1.53		1.83	2.88	
	3500	6" long		70	.114		.44	1.63		2.07	3.22	
	3600	⅜" diameter, 3" long		70	.114		.67	1.63		2.30	3.47	
	3700	6" long		60	.133		.95	1.91		2.86	4.23	
	3800	½" diameter, 4" long		60	.133		1.97	1.91		3.88	5.35	
	3900	6" long		50	.160		2.62	2.29		4.91	6.70	
	4000	Nailing anchors										
	4100	Nylon anchor, standard nail, ¼" diameter, 1" long				C	10.80			10.80	11.90	
	4200	1-½" long					14.05			14.05	15.45	
	4300	2" long					21.25			21.25	23	
	4400	Zamac anchor, stainless nail, ¼" diameter, 1" long					20.55			20.55	23	
	4500	1-½" long					24.95			24.95	27	
	4600	2" long					37.90			37.90	42	
	5000	Screw anchors for concrete, masonry,										
	5100	stone & tile, no layout or drilling included										
	5200	Jute fiber, #6, #8, & #10, 1" long				Ea.	.09			.09	.10	
	5300	#12, 1-½" long					.12			.12	.13	
	5400	#14, 2" long					.19			.19	.21	
	5500	#16, 2" long					.23			.23	.25	
	5600	#20, 2" long					.30			.30	.33	

For expanded coverage of these items see *Means Building Construction Cost Data 1991*

050 | Metal Materials, Finishes and Fastenings

050 500 | Metal Fastening

			CREW	DAILY OUTPUT	MAN-HOURS	UNIT	MAT.	LABOR	EQUIP.	TOTAL	TOTAL INCL O&P	
520	5700	Lag screw shields, ¼" diameter, short				Ea.	.29			.29	.32	520
	5800	Long					.35			.35	.39	
	5900	⅜" diameter, short					.52			.52	.57	
	6000	Long					.62			.62	.68	
	6100	½" diameter, short					.80			.80	.88	
	6200	Long					1			1	1.10	
	6300	¾" diameter, short					1.59			1.59	1.75	
	6400	Long					1.98			1.98	2.18	
	6600	Lead, #6 & #8, ¾" long					.12			.12	.13	
	6700	#10 - #14, 1-½" long					.17			.17	.19	
	6800	#16 & #18, 1-½" long					.23			.23	.25	
	6900	Plastic, #6 & #8, ¾" long					.03			.03	.03	
	7000	#8 & #10, ⅞" long					.03			.03	.03	
	7100	#10 & #12, 1" long					.04			.04	.04	
	7200	#14 & #16, 1-½" long					.05			.05	.06	
530	0010	LAG SCREWS Steel, ¼" diameter, 2" long	1 Carp	140	.057	Ea.	.04	.82		.86	1.41	530
	0100	⅜" diameter, 3" long		105	.076		.12	1.09		1.21	1.95	
	0200	½" diameter, 3" long		95	.084		.21	1.20		1.41	2.25	
	0300	⅝" diameter, 3" long		85	.094		.36	1.35		1.71	2.65	
545	0010	RIVETS ½" grip length										545
	0020											
	0100	Aluminum rivet & mandrel, ⅛" diameter				C	3.40			3.40	3.74	
	0200	3/16" diameter					5.50			5.50	6.05	
	0300	Aluminum rivet, steel mandrel, ⅛" diameter					3.30			3.30	3.63	
	0400	3/16" diameter					4.95			4.95	5.45	
	0500	Copper rivet, steel mandrel, ⅛" diameter					3.90			3.90	4.29	
	0600	Monel rivet, steel mandrel, ⅛" diameter					11.20			11.20	12.30	
	0700	3/16" diameter					27.90			27.90	31	
	0800	Stainless rivet & mandrel, ⅛" diameter					15.05			15.05	16.55	
	0900	3/16" diameter					22.80			22.80	25	
	1000	Stainless rivet, steel mandrel, ⅛" diameter					9.30			9.30	10.25	
	1100	3/16" diameter					14.20			14.20	15.60	
	1200	Steel rivet and mandrel, ⅛" diameter					3.05			3.05	3.36	
	1300	3/16" diameter					5.25			5.25	5.80	
	1400	Hand riveting tool, minimum				Ea.	35			35	39	
	1500	Maximum					330			330	365	
	1600	Power riveting tool, minimum					150			150	165	
	1700	Maximum					650			650	715	
550	0010	STUDS .22 caliber stud driver, buy, minimum				Ea.	230			230	255	550
	0100	Maximum				"	375			375	415	
	0300	Powder charges for above, low velocity				C	12			12	13.20	
	0400	Standard velocity					20			20	22	
	0600	Drive pins & studs, ¼" & ⅜" diam., to 3" long, minimum					30			30	33	
	0700	Maximum					80			80	88	

051 | Structural Metal Framing

051 100 | Bracing

			CREW	DAILY OUTPUT	MAN-HOURS	UNIT	MAT.	LABOR	EQUIP.	TOTAL	TOTAL INCL O&P	
108	0010	BRACING										108
	0300	Let-in, "T" shaped, 20 ga. galv. steel, studs at 16" O.C.	F-1	580	.014	L.F.	.60	.20	.01	.81	1	

For expanded coverage of these items see *Means Building Construction Cost Data 1991*

051 | Structural Metal Framing

051 100 | Bracing

		CREW	DAILY OUTPUT	MAN-HOURS	UNIT	MAT.	LABOR	EQUIP.	TOTAL	TOTAL INCL O&P
0400	Studs at 24" O.C.	F-1	600	.013	L.F.	.60	.19	.01	.80	.99
0500	16 ga. galv. steel straps, studs at 16" O.C.		600	.013		.54	.19	.01	.74	.92
0600	Studs at 24" O.C.	↓	620	.013	↓	.54	.18	.01	.73	.91

051 200 | Structural Steel

		CREW	DAILY OUTPUT	MAN-HOURS	UNIT	MAT.	LABOR	EQUIP.	TOTAL	TOTAL INCL O&P
0010	**CEILING SUPPORTS**									
1000	Entrance door/folding partition supports	E-4	60	.533	L.F.	10.50	8.60	1.14	20.24	29
1100	Linear accelerator door supports		14	2.290		45	37	4.89	86.89	125
1200	Lintels or shelf angles, hung, exterior hot dipped galv.		267	.120		8	1.94	.26	10.20	12.75
1250	Two coats primer paint instead of galv.		267	.120	↓	6.50	1.94	.26	8.70	11.10
1400	Monitor support, ceiling hung, expansion bolted		4	8	Ea.	200	130	17.10	347.10	485
1450	Hung from pre-set inserts		6	5.330		200	86	11.40	297.40	395
1600	Motor supports for overhead doors		4	8	↓	115	130	17.10	262.10	390
1700	Partition support for heavy folding partitions, without pocket		24	1.330	L.F.	25	22	2.85	49.85	71
1750	Supports at pocket only		12	2.670		50	43	5.70	98.70	145
2000	Rolling grilles & fire door supports		34	.941	↓	20	15.20	2.01	37.21	53
2100	Spider-leg light supports, expansion bolted to ceiling slab		8	4	Ea.	68	65	8.55	141.55	205
2150	Hung from pre-set inserts		12	2.670	"	68	43	5.70	116.70	165
2400	Toilet partition support		36	.889	L.F.	30	14.35	1.90	46.25	62
2500	X-ray travel gantry support	↓	12	2.670	"	85	43	5.70	133.70	180
0011	**COLUMNS**									
0800	Steel, concrete filled, extra strong pipe, 3-½" diameter	E-2	660	.085	L.F.	10	1.31	1.62	12.93	15.20
0830	4" diameter		780	.072		12	1.11	1.37	14.48	16.75
0890	5" diameter		1,020	.055		16	.85	1.05	17.90	20
0930	6" diameter		1,210	.046		23	.71	.89	24.60	28
1000	Lightweight units, 3-½" diameter		780	.072		3	1.11	1.37	5.48	6.85
1050	4" diameter	↓	900	.062	↓	3.30	.96	1.19	5.45	6.70
1100	For galvanizing, add				Lb.	.40			.40	.44
1300	For web ties, angles, etc., add per added lb.	1 Sswk	945	.008		.70	.13		.83	1.02
1500	Steel pipe, extra strong, no concrete, 3" to 5" O.D.	E-2	12,960	.004		.80	.07	.08	.95	1.09
1600	6" to 12" O.D.	"	56,000	.001	↓	.70	.02	.02	.74	.82
2100	Square structural tubing, 4" x 4" x ¼"				L.F.				.50	.55
2400	Rectangular structural tubing, 5" to 6" wide, light section	E-2	11,200	.005	Lb.	.75	.08	.10	.93	1.08
2700	12" x 8" x ½"		28,000	.002		.75	.03	.04	.82	.93
2800	Heavy section	↓	56,000	.001	↓	.70	.02	.02	.74	.82
8000	Lally columns, to 8', 3 ½" diameter	F-2	24	.667	Ea.	21.50	9.55	.67	31.72	40
8080	4" diameter	"	20	.800	"	24.50	11.45	.80	36.75	47
0010	**LINTELS** Plain steel angles, under 500 lb.	1 Bric	500	.016	Lb.	.50	.24		.74	.94
0100	500 to 1000 lb.		600	.013	"	.46	.20		.66	.83
2000	Steel angles, 3-½" x 3", ¼" thick, 2'-6" long		50	.160	Ea.	6.75	2.37		9.12	11.30
2100	4'-6" long		45	.178		12.15	2.63		14.78	17.70
2600	4" x 3-½", ¼" thick, 5'-0" long		40	.200		15.50	2.96		18.46	22
2700	9'-0" long	↓	35	.229	↓	27.90	3.38		31.28	36
3500	For precast concrete lintels, see div. 034-802									
0010	**STRUCTURAL STEEL** Bolted, incl. fabrication, not incl. trucking									
0050	Beams, W 6 x 9	E-2	720	.078	L.F.	6	1.20	1.49	8.69	10.45
0100	W 8 x 10		720	.078		7	1.20	1.49	9.69	11.55
0200	Columns, W 6 x 15		540	.104		8	1.60	1.98	11.58	13.90
0250	W 8 x 31	↓	540	.104	↓	17	1.60	1.98	20.58	24

For expanded coverage of these items see *Means Building Construction Cost Data 1991*

052 | Metal Joists

052 100 | Steel Joists

			CREW	DAILY OUTPUT	MAN-HOURS	UNIT	MAT.	LABOR	EQUIP.	TOTAL	TOTAL INCL O&P	
108	0010	LIGHTGAGE JOISTS Punched, double nailable, 10" deep, 14 ga.	E-1	1,000	.024	L.F.	2.25	.38	.07	2.70	3.24	108
	0700	12 gauge		1,000	.024		3.75	.38	.07	4.20	4.89	
	0900	12" deep, 14 gauge		880	.027		2.55	.43	.08	3.06	3.68	
	1000	12 gauge		880	.027		3.75	.43	.08	4.26	5	

053 | Metal Decking

053 100 | Steel Deck

			CREW	DAILY OUTPUT	MAN-HOURS	UNIT	MAT.	LABOR	EQUIP.	TOTAL	TOTAL INCL O&P	
104	0010	METAL DECKING Steel floor panels, over 15,000 S.F.				S.F.						104
	1900	For congested site, add						50%				
	2100	Open type, galv., 1-½" deep, 22 ga., under 50 square	E-4	4,500	.007		.71	.11	.02	.84	1.01	
	2600	20 ga., under 50 square		3,865	.008		.86	.13	.02	1.01	1.22	
	2900	18 ga., under 50 square		3,800	.008		1.13	.14	.02	1.29	1.52	
	3700	4-½" deep, long span roof, 20 gauge		2,700	.012		1.90	.19	.03	2.12	2.48	
	6100	Slab form, steel 28 gauge, 9/16" deep, uncoated	E-1	4,000	.006		.32	.09	.02	.43	.54	
	6200	Galvanized		4,000	.006		.39	.09	.02	.50	.62	
	6300	24 gauge, 1-5/16" deep, uncoated		3,800	.006		.56	.10	.02	.68	.82	
	6400	Galvanized		3,800	.006		.64	.10	.02	.76	.90	
	6500	22 gauge, 1-5/16" deep, uncoated		3,700	.006		.68	.10	.02	.80	.96	
	6600	Galvanized		3,700	.006		.77	.10	.02	.89	1.06	

055 | Metal Fabrications

055 100 | Metal Stairs

			CREW	DAILY OUTPUT	MAN-HOURS	UNIT	MAT.	LABOR	EQUIP.	TOTAL	TOTAL INCL O&P	
104	0012	STAIR										104
	1700	Pre-erected, steel pan tread, 3'-6" wide, 2 line pipe rail	E-2	87	.644	Riser	185	9.90	12.30	207.20	235	
	1800	With flat bar picket rail	"	87	.644		255	9.90	12.30	277.20	310	
	1810	Spiral aluminum, 5'-0" diameter, stock units	E-4	45	.711		205	11.50	1.52	218.02	250	
	1820	Custom units		45	.711		310	11.50	1.52	323.02	365	
	1900	Spiral, cast iron, 4'-0" diameter, ornamental, minimum		45	.711		160	11.50	1.52	173.02	200	
	1920	Maximum		25	1.280		235	21	2.74	258.74	300	
156	0010	FIRE ESCAPE LADDERS One story, collapsible				Ea.	560			560	615	156
	0100	Portable				"	145			145	160	

055 200 | Handrails & Railings

			CREW	DAILY OUTPUT	MAN-HOURS	UNIT	MAT.	LABOR	EQUIP.	TOTAL	TOTAL INCL O&P	
203	0010	RAILING, PIPE Aluminum, 2 rail, 1-¼" diam., satin finish	E-4	160	.200	L.F.	9.50	3.23	.43	13.16	17.05	203
	0030	Clear anodized		160	.200		12.40	3.23	.43	16.06	20	
	0040	Dark anodized		160	.200		13.05	3.23	.43	16.71	21	
	0080	1-½" diameter, satin finish		160	.200		10.05	3.23	.43	13.71	17.65	
	0090	Clear anodized		160	.200		13.10	3.23	.43	16.76	21	
	0100	Dark anodized		160	.200		13.80	3.23	.43	17.46	22	
	0140	Aluminum, 3 rail, 1-¼" diam., satin finish		137	.234		14.10	3.77	.50	18.37	23	
	0150	Clear anodized		137	.234		19.10	3.77	.50	23.37	29	
	0160	Dark anodized		137	.234		19.50	3.77	.50	23.77	29	
	0200	1-½" diameter, satin finish		137	.234		14.95	3.77	.50	19.22	24	

For expanded coverage of these items see *Means Building Construction Cost Data 1991*

055 | Metal Fabrications

055 200 | Handrails & Railings

			Crew	Daily Output	Man-Hours	Unit	Mat.	Labor	Equip.	Total	Total Incl O&P	
203	0210	Clear anodized	E-4	137	.234	L.F.	19.40	3.77	.50	23.67	29	203
	0220	Dark anodized		137	.234		21.05	3.77	.50	25.32	31	
	0500	Steel, 2 rail, primed, 1-¼" diameter		160	.200		6.85	3.23	.43	10.51	14.10	
	0520	1-½" diameter		160	.200		7.50	3.23	.43	11.16	14.85	
	0540	Galvanized, 1-¼" diameter		160	.200		9.40	3.23	.43	13.06	16.90	
	0560	1-½" diameter		160	.200		10.60	3.23	.43	14.26	18.25	
	0580	Steel, 3 rail, primed, 1-¼" diameter		137	.234		10.15	3.77	.50	14.42	18.85	
	0600	1-½" diameter		137	.234		10.85	3.77	.50	15.12	19.60	
	0620	Galvanized, 1-¼" diameter		137	.234		14.10	3.77	.50	18.37	23	
	0640	1-½" diameter		137	.234		15.35	3.77	.50	19.62	25	
	0700	Stainless steel, 2 rail, 1-¼" diam. #4 finish		137	.234		22.05	3.77	.50	26.32	32	
	0720	High polish		137	.234		35.40	3.77	.50	39.67	47	
	0740	Mirror polish		137	.234		43.40	3.77	.50	47.67	55	
	0760	Stainless steel, 3 rail, 1-½" diam., #4 finish		120	.267		34.10	4.31	.57	38.98	46	
	0770	High polish		120	.267		54.20	4.31	.57	59.08	68	
	0780	Mirror finish		120	.267		65	4.31	.57	69.88	80	
	0900	Wall rail, alum. pipe, 1-¼" diam., satin finish		213	.150		6.50	2.43	.32	9.25	12.10	
	0905	Clear anodized		213	.150		8.15	2.43	.32	10.90	13.90	
	0910	Dark anodized		213	.150		8.85	2.43	.32	11.60	14.70	
	0915	1-½" diameter, satin finish		213	.150		7.40	2.43	.32	10.15	13.10	
	0920	Clear anodized		213	.150		9.50	2.43	.32	12.25	15.40	
	0925	Dark anodized		213	.150		10.05	2.43	.32	12.80	16	
	0930	Steel pipe, 1-¼" diameter, primed		213	.150		4.05	2.43	.32	6.80	9.40	
	0935	Galvanized		213	.150		5.65	2.43	.32	8.40	11.15	
	0940	1-½" diameter, primed		213	.150		4.30	2.43	.32	7.05	9.65	
	0945	Galvanized		213	.150		5.85	2.43	.32	8.60	11.40	
	0955	Stainless steel pipe, 1-½" diam., #4 finish		107	.299		21.10	4.83	.64	26.57	33	
	0960	High polish		107	.299		34.05	4.83	.64	39.52	47	
	0965	Mirror polish		107	.299		42.10	4.83	.64	47.57	56	

055 500 | Metal Specialties

			Crew	Daily Output	Man-Hours	Unit	Mat.	Labor	Equip.	Total	Total Incl O&P	
504	0010	LAMP POSTS Only, 7' high, stock units, aluminum	1 Carp	16	.500	Ea.	37	7.15		44.15	53	504
	0100	Mild steel, plain	"	16	.500	"	26	7.15		33.15	41	

057 | Ornamental Metal

057 250 | Ornamental Metal

			Crew	Daily Output	Man-Hours	Unit	Mat.	Labor	Equip.	Total	Total Incl O&P	
252	0010	WEATHERVANES Residential types, minimum	1 Carp	8	1	Ea.	25	14.30		39.30	51	252
	0100	Maximum	"	2	4	"	600	57		657	755	

060 | Fasteners and Adhesives

060 500 | Fasteners & Adhesives

			Crew	Daily Output	Man-Hours	Unit	Mat.	Labor	Equip.	Total	Total Incl O&P	
504	0010	NAILS Prices of material only, copper, plain				Lb.	3.75			3.75	4.13	504
	0400	Stainless steel, plain				"	5			5	5.50	

For expanded coverage of these items see *Means Building Construction Cost Data 1991*

060 | Fasteners and Adhesives

060 500 | Fasteners & Adhesives

			CREW	DAILY OUTPUT	MAN-HOURS	UNIT	MAT.	LABOR	EQUIP.	TOTAL	TOTAL INCL O&P	
504	0600	Common, 3d to 60d, plain				Lb.	.70			.70	.77	504
	0700	Galvanized					.90			.90	.99	
	0800	Aluminum					4.40			4.40	4.84	
	1000	Annular or spiral thread, 4d to 60d, plain					1			1	1.10	
	1200	Galvanized					1.10			1.10	1.21	
	1400	Drywall nails, plain					.98			.98	1.08	
	1600	Galvanized					1.20			1.20	1.32	
	1800	Finish nails, 4d to 10d, plain					.75			.75	.83	
	2000	Galvanized					.95			.95	1.05	
	2100	Aluminum					4.40			4.40	4.84	
	2300	Flooring nails, hardened steel, 2d to 10d, plain					1			1	1.10	
	2400	Galvanized					1.10			1.10	1.21	
	2500	Gypsum lath nails, 1-⅛", 13 ga. flathead, blued					1.20			1.20	1.32	
	2600	Masonry nails, hardened steel, ¾" to 3" long, plain					1			1	1.10	
	2700	Galvanized					1.15			1.15	1.27	
	2900	Roofing nails, threaded, galvanized					.90			.90	.99	
	3100	Aluminum					4.70			4.70	5.15	
	3300	Compressed lead head, threaded, galvanized					.98			.98	1.08	
	3600	Siding nails, plain shank, galvanized					.95			.95	1.05	
	3800	Aluminum					3.95			3.95	4.35	
	5000	Add to prices above for cement coating					.05			.05	.06	
	5200	Zinc or tin plating					.10			.10	.11	
508	0010	**SHEET METAL SCREWS** Steel, standard, #8 x ¾", plain				C	2.55			2.55	2.81	508
	0100	Galvanized					3.15			3.15	3.47	
	0300	#10 x 1", plain					3.45			3.45	3.80	
	0400	Galvanized					4.05			4.05	4.46	
	1500	Self-drilling, with washers, (pinch point) #8 x ¾", plain					4.45			4.45	4.90	
	1600	Galvanized					6			6	6.60	
	1800	#10 x ¾", plain					5.95			5.95	6.55	
	1900	Galvanized					6.80			6.80	7.50	
	3000	Stainless steel w/aluminum or neoprene washers, #14 x 1", plain					15.15			15.15	16.65	
	3100	#14 x 2", plain					22.55			22.55	25	
512	0010	**TIMBER CONNECTORS** Add up cost of each part for total										512
	0020	cost of connection										
	0100	Connector plates, steel, with bolts, straight	2 Carp	75	.213	Ea.	13.80	3.05		16.85	20	
	0110	Tee	"	50	.320		20.50	4.58		25.08	30	
	0200	Bolts, machine, sq. hd. with nut & washer, ½" diameter, 4" long	1 Carp	140	.057		.85	.82		1.67	2.30	
	0300	7-½" long		130	.062		1.05	.88		1.93	2.63	
	0500	¾" diameter, 7-½" long		130	.062		1.70	.88		2.58	3.34	
	0600	15" long		95	.084		2.05	1.20		3.25	4.27	
	0720	Machine bolts, sq. hd. w/nut & wash		150	.053	Lb.	1.79	.76		2.55	3.24	
	0800	Drilling bolt holes in timber, ½" diameter		450	.018	Inch		.25		.25	.43	
	0900	1" diameter		350	.023	"		.33		.33	.55	
	1100	Framing anchors, 2 or 3 dimensional, 10 gauge, no nails incl.		175	.046	Ea.	.38	.65		1.03	1.51	
	1250	Holdowns, 3 gauge base, 10 gauge body		8	1		12.10	14.30		26.40	37	
	1300	Joist and beam hangers, 18 ga. galv., for 2" x 4" joist		175	.046		.38	.65		1.03	1.51	
	1400	2" x 6" to 2" x 10" joist		165	.048		.55	.69		1.24	1.76	
	1600	16 ga. galv., 3" x 6" to 3" x 10" joist		160	.050		1.15	.72		1.87	2.46	
	1700	3" x 10" to 3" x 14" joist		160	.050		1.85	.72		2.57	3.23	
	1800	4" x 6" to 4" x 10" joist		155	.052		1.95	.74		2.69	3.38	
	1900	4" x 10" to 4" x 14" joist		155	.052		1.95	.74		2.69	3.38	
	2000	Two-2" x 6" to two-2" x 10" joists		150	.053		1.10	.76		1.86	2.49	
	2100	Two-2" x 10" to two-2" x 14" joists		150	.053		1.65	.76		2.41	3.09	
	2300	3/16" thick for 6" x 8" joist		145	.055		4.10	.79		4.89	5.85	
	2400	6" x 10" joist		140	.057		4.85	.82		5.67	6.70	
	2500	6" x 12" joist		135	.059		6.80	.85		7.65	8.90	
	2700	¼" thick, 6" x 14" joist		130	.062		7.25	.88		8.13	9.45	
	2800	Joist anchors, ¼" x 1-¼" x 18"		140	.057		2.80	.82		3.62	4.45	

For expanded coverage of these items see *Means Building Construction Cost Data 1991*

060 | Fasteners and Adhesives

060 500 | Fasteners & Adhesives

		CREW	DAILY OUTPUT	MAN-HOURS	UNIT	MAT.	LABOR	EQUIP.	TOTAL	TOTAL INCL O&P
512	2850									512
	2900	Plywood clips, extruded aluminum H clip, for ¾" panels				Ea.	.06			.06	.07
	3000	Galvanized 18 ga. back-up clip					.05			.05	.06
	3200	Post framing, 16 ga. galv. for 4" x 4" base, 2 piece	1 Carp	130	.062		2.95	.88		3.83	4.72
	3300	Cap		130	.062		1.85	.88		2.73	3.51
	3500	Rafter anchors, 18 ga. galv., 1-½" wide, 5-¼" long		145	.055		.40	.79		1.19	1.76
	3600	10-¾" long		145	.055		.70	.79		1.49	2.09
	3800	Shear plates, 2-⅝" diameter		120	.067		1.10	.95		2.05	2.80
	3900	4" diameter		115	.070		2.35	.99		3.34	4.25
	4000	Sill anchors, (embedded in concrete or block), 18-⅝" long		115	.070		.60	.99		1.59	2.32
	4100	Spike grids, 4" x 4", flat or curved		120	.067		3.60	.95		4.55	5.55
	4400	Split rings, 2-½" diameter		120	.067		.70	.95		1.65	2.36
	4500	4" diameter		110	.073		1.25	1.04		2.29	3.11
	4700	Strap ties, 16 ga., 1-⅜" wide, 12" long		180	.044		.85	.64		1.49	2
	4800	24" long		160	.050		1.20	.72		1.92	2.52
	5000	Toothed rings, 2-⅝" or 4" diameter		90	.089		.75	1.27		2.02	2.95
	5200	Truss plates, nailed, 20 gauge, up to 32' span	↓	17	.471	Truss	6.15	6.75		12.90	18
	5400	Washers, 2" x 2" x ⅛"				Ea.	.20			.20	.22
	5500	3" x 3" x 3/16"				"	.50			.50	.55
516	0010	**WOOD SCREWS** #8, 1" long, steel				Ea.	.03			.03	.03	516
	0100	Brass				"	.15			.15	.17
	0200	#8, 2" long, steel				C	5.50			5.50	6.05
	0300	Brass					27.10			27.10	30
	0400	#10, 1" long, steel					3.60			3.60	3.96
	0500	Brass				↓	18.85			18.85	21
	0600	#10, 2" long, steel				Ea.	.07			.07	.08
	0700	Brass				"	.34			.34	.37
	0800	#10, 3" long, steel				C	11.75			11.75	12.95
	1000	#12, 2" long, steel					8.50			8.50	9.35
	1100	Brass				↓	42.10			42.10	46
	1500	#12, 3" long, steel				Ea.	.14			.14	.15
	2000	#12, 4" long, steel				C	24			24	26

061 | Rough Carpentry

061 100 | Wood Framing

		CREW	DAILY OUTPUT	MAN-HOURS	UNIT	MAT.	LABOR	EQUIP.	TOTAL	TOTAL INCL O&P
102	0011	**BLOCKING**									102
	0020										
	1950	Miscellaneous, to wood construction									
	2000	2" x 4"	F-1	250	.032	L.F.	.27	.46	.03	.76	1.10
	2050	2" x 6"	↓	222	.036		.41	.52	.04	.97	1.35
	2100	2" x 8"		200	.040		.55	.57	.04	1.16	1.61
	2150	2" x 10"		178	.045		.86	.64	.04	1.54	2.07
	2200	2" x 12"	↓	151	.053	↓	1.02	.76	.05	1.83	2.44
	2300	To steel construction									
	2320	2" x 4"	F-1	208	.038	L.F.	.27	.55	.04	.86	1.26
	2340	2" x 6"		180	.044		.41	.64	.04	1.09	1.56
	2360	2" x 8"		158	.051		.55	.72	.05	1.32	1.88
	2380	2" x 10"		136	.059		.86	.84	.06	1.76	2.42
	2400	2" x 12"	↓	109	.073	↓	1.02	1.05	.07	2.14	2.95

For expanded coverage of these items see *Means Building Construction Cost Data 1991*

		061 100 | Wood Framing	CREW	DAILY OUTPUT	MAN-HOURS	UNIT	BARE COSTS MAT.	BARE COSTS LABOR	BARE COSTS EQUIP.	BARE COSTS TOTAL	TOTAL INCL O&P	
104	0010	**BRACING** Let-in, with 1″ x 6″ boards, studs @ 16″ O.C.	F-1	150	.053	L.F.	.26	.76	.05	1.07	1.62	104
	0200	Studs @ 24″ O.C.		230	.035	"	.26	.50	.03	.79	1.16	
106	0010	**BRIDGING** Wood, for joists 16″ O.C., 1″ x 3″		130	.062	Pr.	.31	.88	.06	1.25	1.88	106
	0100	2″ x 3″ bridging		130	.062		.57	.88	.06	1.51	2.17	
	0300	Steel, galvanized, 18 ga., for 2″ x 10″ joists at 12″ O.C.	1 Carp	130	.062		.78	.88		1.66	2.33	
	0400	24″ O.C.		140	.057		1.19	.82		2.01	2.68	
	0600	For 2″ x 14″ joists at 16″ O.C.		1.30	6.150		1.45	88		89.45	150	
	0900	Compression type, 16″ O.C., 2″ x 8″ joists		200	.040		1.15	.57		1.72	2.22	
	1000	2″ x 12″ joists		200	.040		1.23	.57		1.80	2.31	
110	0010	**FRAMING, BEAMS & GIRDERS** (86)										110
	0020											
	1000	Single, 2″ x 6″ (87)	F-2	700	.023	L.F.	.39	.33	.02	.74	1	
	1020	2″ x 8″		650	.025		.55	.35	.02	.92	1.23	
	1040	2″ x 10″		600	.027		.82	.38	.03	1.23	1.57	
	1060	2″ x 12″		550	.029		1.03	.42	.03	1.48	1.86	
	1080	2″ x 14″		500	.032		1.20	.46	.03	1.69	2.12	
	1100	3″ x 8″		550	.029		1.17	.42	.03	1.62	2.02	
	1120	3″ x 10″		500	.032		1.59	.46	.03	2.08	2.55	
	1140	3″ x 12″		450	.036		1.80	.51	.04	2.35	2.87	
	1160	3″ x 14″		400	.040		2.23	.57	.04	2.84	3.45	
	1180	4″ x 8″	F-3	1,000	.040		1.65	.58	.38	2.61	3.20	
	1200	4″ x 10″		950	.042		2.12	.61	.40	3.13	3.78	
	1220	4″ x 12″		900	.044		2.55	.64	.42	3.61	4.34	
	1240	4″ x 14″		850	.047		2.98	.68	.44	4.10	4.90	
	2000	Double, 2″ x 6″	F-2	625	.026		.80	.37	.03	1.20	1.52	
	2020	2″ x 8″		575	.028		1.10	.40	.03	1.53	1.91	
	2040	2″ x 10″		550	.029		1.69	.42	.03	2.14	2.59	
	2060	2″ x 12″		525	.030		2.06	.44	.03	2.53	3.03	
	2080	2″ x 14″		475	.034		2.42	.48	.03	2.93	3.50	
	2100											
	3000	Triple, 2″ x 6″	F-2	550	.029	L.F.	1.18	.42	.03	1.63	2.03	
	3020	2″ x 8″		525	.030		1.65	.44	.03	2.12	2.58	
	3040	2″ x 10″		500	.032		2.54	.46	.03	3.03	3.59	
	3060	2″ x 12″		475	.034		3.10	.48	.03	3.61	4.25	
	3080	2″ x 14″		450	.036		3.63	.51	.04	4.18	4.88	
112	0010	**FRAMING, CEILINGS**										112
	0020											
	6000	Suspended, 2″ x 3″	F-2	1,000	.016	L.F.	.22	.23	.02	.47	.64	
	6050	2″ x 4″		900	.018		.27	.25	.02	.54	.74	
	6100	2″ x 6″		800	.020		.40	.29	.02	.71	.94	
	6150	2″ x 8″		650	.025		.54	.35	.02	.91	1.21	
114	0010	**FRAMING, JOISTS**										114
	2000	Joists, 2″ x 4″	F-2	1,250	.013	L.F.	.27	.18	.01	.46	.62	
	2100	2″ x 6″		1,250	.013		.40	.18	.01	.59	.76	
	2150	2″ x 8″		1,100	.015		.54	.21	.01	.76	.95	
	2200	2″ x 10″		900	.018		.84	.25	.02	1.11	1.36	
	2250	2″ x 12″		875	.018		1.02	.26	.02	1.30	1.58	
	2300	2″ x 14″		770	.021		1.21	.30	.02	1.53	1.85	
	2350	3″ x 6″		925	.017		.92	.25	.02	1.19	1.44	
	2400	3″ x 10″		780	.021		1.54	.29	.02	1.85	2.20	
	2450	3″ x 12″		600	.027		1.85	.38	.03	2.26	2.71	
	2500	4″ x 6″		800	.020		1.25	.29	.02	1.56	1.88	
	2550	4″ x 10″		600	.027		2.09	.38	.03	2.50	2.97	
	2600	4″ x 12″		450	.036		2.51	.51	.04	3.06	3.65	
	2605	Sister joist, 2″ x 6″		800	.020		.40	.29	.02	.71	.94	
116	0010	**FRAMING, MISCELLANEOUS**										116
	0020											

For expanded coverage of these items see *Means Building Construction Cost Data 1991*

061 | Rough Carpentry

061 100 | Wood Framing

			CREW	DAILY OUTPUT	MAN-HOURS	UNIT	MAT.	LABOR	EQUIP.	TOTAL	TOTAL INCL O&P	
116	2000	Firestops, 2" x 4"	F-2	780	.021	L.F.	.27	.29	.02	.58	.81	116
	2100	2" x 6"		600	.027		.41	.38	.03	.82	1.12	
	5000	Nailers, treated, wood construction, 2" x 4"		800	.020		.37	.29	.02	.68	.91	
	5100	2" x 6"		750	.021		.53	.31	.02	.86	1.11	
	5120	2" x 8"		700	.023		.73	.33	.02	1.08	1.37	
	5200	Steel construction, 2" x 4"		750	.021		.37	.31	.02	.70	.94	
	5220	2" x 6"		700	.023		.53	.33	.02	.88	1.15	
	5240	2" x 8"		650	.025		.73	.35	.02	1.10	1.42	
	7000	Rough bucks, treated, for doors or windows, 2" x 6"		400	.040		.53	.57	.04	1.14	1.58	
	7100	2" x 8"		380	.042		.73	.60	.04	1.37	1.85	
	8000	Stair stringers, 2" x 10"		130	.123		.87	1.76	.12	2.75	4.04	
	8100	2" x 12"		130	.123		1.04	1.76	.12	2.92	4.22	
	8150	3" x 10"		125	.128		1.59	1.83	.13	3.55	4.95	
	8200	3" x 12"		125	.128		1.91	1.83	.13	3.87	5.30	
118	0010	**FRAMING, COLUMNS**										118
	0020											
	0100	4" x 4"	F-2	390	.041	L.F.	.85	.59	.04	1.48	1.97	
	0150	4" x 6"		275	.058		1.26	.83	.06	2.15	2.84	
	0200	4" x 8"		220	.073		1.64	1.04	.07	2.75	3.62	
	0250	6" x 6"		215	.074		2.15	1.06	.07	3.28	4.23	
	0300	6" x 8"		175	.091		2.86	1.31	.09	4.26	5.45	
	0350	6" x 10"		150	.107		3.60	1.53	.11	5.24	6.65	
120	0010	**FRAMING, ROOFS**										120
	2000	Fascia boards, 2" x 8"	F-2	225	.071	L.F.	.55	1.02	.07	1.64	2.39	
	2100	2" x 10"		180	.089		.82	1.27	.09	2.18	3.12	
	5000	Rafters, to 4 in 12 pitch, 2" x 6", ordinary		1,000	.016		.39	.23	.02	.64	.83	
	5020	On steep roofs		800	.020		.39	.29	.02	.70	.93	
	5040	On dormers or complex roofs		590	.027		.39	.39	.03	.81	1.11	
	5060	2" x 8", ordinary		950	.017		.55	.24	.02	.81	1.03	
	5080	On steep roofs		750	.021		.55	.31	.02	.88	1.14	
	5100	On dormers or complex roofs		540	.030		.55	.42	.03	1	1.35	
	5120	2" x 10", ordinary		630	.025		.82	.36	.03	1.21	1.53	
	5140	On steep roofs		495	.032		.82	.46	.03	1.31	1.71	
	5160	On dormers or complex roofs		425	.038		.82	.54	.04	1.40	1.84	
	5180	2" x 12", ordinary		575	.028		1.02	.40	.03	1.45	1.82	
	5200	On steep roofs		455	.035		1.02	.50	.04	1.56	2	
	5220	On dormers or complex roofs		395	.041		1.02	.58	.04	1.64	2.13	
	5300	Hip and valley rafters, 2" x 6", ordinary		760	.021		.39	.30	.02	.71	.96	
	5320	On steep roofs		585	.027		.39	.39	.03	.81	1.11	
	5340	On dormers or complex roofs		510	.031		.39	.45	.03	.87	1.21	
	5360	2" x 8", ordinary		720	.022		.55	.32	.02	.89	1.17	
	5380	On steep roofs		545	.029		.55	.42	.03	1	1.34	
	5400	On dormers or complex roofs		470	.034		.55	.49	.03	1.07	1.46	
	5420	2" x 10", ordinary		570	.028		.82	.40	.03	1.25	1.60	
	5440	On steep roofs		440	.036		.82	.52	.04	1.38	1.81	
	5460	On dormers or complex roofs		380	.042		.82	.60	.04	1.46	1.95	
	5470											
	5480	Hip and valley rafters, 2" x 12", ordinary	F-2	525	.030	L.F.	1.02	.44	.03	1.49	1.88	
	5500	On steep roofs		410	.039		1.02	.56	.04	1.62	2.10	
	5520	On dormers or complex roofs		355	.045		1.02	.64	.05	1.71	2.25	
	5540	Hip and valley jacks, 2" x 6", ordinary		600	.027		.39	.38	.03	.80	1.10	
	5560	On steep roofs		475	.034		.39	.48	.03	.90	1.27	
	5580	On dormers or complex roofs		410	.039		.39	.56	.04	.99	1.41	
	5600	2" x 8", ordinary		490	.033		.55	.47	.03	1.05	1.43	
	5620	On steep roofs		385	.042		.55	.59	.04	1.18	1.65	
	5640	On dormers or complex roofs		335	.048		.55	.68	.05	1.28	1.80	
	5660	2" x 10", ordinary		450	.036		.82	.51	.04	1.37	1.79	
	5680	On steep roofs		350	.046		.82	.65	.05	1.52	2.04	

For expanded coverage of these items see *Means Building Construction Cost Data 1991*

061 | Rough Carpentry

061 100 | Wood Framing

			CREW	DAILY OUTPUT	MAN-HOURS	UNIT	MAT.	LABOR	EQUIP.	TOTAL	TOTAL INCL O&P	
120	5700	On dormers or complex roofs	F-2	305	.052	L.F.	.82	.75	.05	1.62	2.21	120
	5720	2" x 12", ordinary		375	.043		1.02	.61	.04	1.67	2.19	
	5740	On steep roofs		295	.054		1.02	.78	.05	1.85	2.48	
	5760	On dormers or complex roofs		255	.063		1.02	.90	.06	1.98	2.69	
	5780	Rafter tie, 1" x 4", #3		800	.020		.19	.29	.02	.50	.71	
	5790	Rafter tie, 2" x 4", #3		800	.020		.27	.29	.02	.58	.80	
	5800	Ridge board, #2 or better, 1" x 6"		600	.027		.29	.38	.03	.70	.99	
	5820	1" x 8"		550	.029		.38	.42	.03	.83	1.15	
	5840	1" x 10"		500	.032		.48	.46	.03	.97	1.33	
	5860	2" x 6"		500	.032		.39	.46	.03	.88	1.23	
	5880	2" x 8"		450	.036		.55	.51	.04	1.10	1.50	
	5900	2" x 10"		400	.040		.82	.57	.04	1.43	1.90	
	5920	Roof cants, split, 4" x 4"		650	.025		1	.35	.02	1.37	1.72	
	5940	6" x 6"		600	.027		2.20	.38	.03	2.61	3.09	
	5960	Roof curbs, untreated, 2" x 6"		520	.031		.39	.44	.03	.86	1.20	
	5980	2" x 12"		400	.040		1.02	.57	.04	1.63	2.12	
	6000	Sister rafters, 2" x 6"		800	.020		.39	.29	.02	.70	.93	
	6020	2" x 8"		640	.025		.55	.36	.03	.94	1.24	
	6040	2" x 10"		535	.030		.82	.43	.03	1.28	1.65	
	6060	2" x 12"		455	.035		1.02	.50	.04	1.56	2	
122	0010	**FRAMING, SILLS**										122
	1810											
	2000	Ledgers, nailed, 2" x 4"	F-2	755	.021	L.F.	.27	.30	.02	.59	.83	
	2050	2" x 6"		600	.027		.41	.38	.03	.82	1.12	
	2100	Bolted, not including bolts, 3" x 6"		325	.049		.92	.70	.05	1.67	2.24	
	2150	3" x 12"		233	.069		1.85	.98	.07	2.90	3.76	
	2600	Mud sills, redwood, construction grade, 2" x 4"		895	.018		.70	.26	.02	.98	1.22	
	2620	2" x 6"		780	.021		1.03	.29	.02	1.34	1.64	
	4000	Sills, 2" x 4"		600	.027		.27	.38	.03	.68	.97	
	4050	2" x 6"		550	.029		.41	.42	.03	.86	1.18	
	4080	2" x 8"		500	.032		.55	.46	.03	1.04	1.41	
	4100	2" x 10"		450	.036		.86	.51	.04	1.41	1.84	
	4120	2" x 12"		400	.040		1.02	.57	.04	1.63	2.12	
	4200	Treated, 2" x 4"		550	.029		.37	.42	.03	.82	1.14	
	4220	2" x 6"		500	.032		.53	.46	.03	1.02	1.38	
	4240	2" x 8"		450	.036		.73	.51	.04	1.28	1.69	
	4260	2" x 10"		400	.040		1.10	.57	.04	1.71	2.21	
	4280	2" x 12"		350	.046		1.35	.65	.05	2.05	2.63	
	4400	4" x 4"		450	.036		1.11	.51	.04	1.66	2.11	
	4420	4" x 6"		350	.046		1.67	.65	.05	2.37	2.98	
	4460	4" x 8"		300	.053		2.18	.76	.05	2.99	3.73	
	4480	4" x 10"		260	.062		2.78	.88	.06	3.72	4.60	
124	0010	**FRAMING, SLEEPERS**										124
	0020											
	0100	On concrete, treated, 1" x 2"	F-2	2,350	.007	L.F.	.12	.10	.01	.23	.30	
	0150	1" x 3"		2,000	.008		.19	.11	.01	.31	.41	
	0200	2" x 4"		1,500	.011		.37	.15	.01	.53	.68	
	0250	2" x 6"		1,300	.012		.55	.18	.01	.74	.92	
126	0010	**FRAMING, SOFFITS & CANOPIES**										126
	1000	Canopy or soffit framing, 1" x 4"	F-2	900	.018	L.F.	.19	.25	.02	.46	.65	
	1020	1" x 6"		850	.019		.28	.27	.02	.57	.78	
	1040	1" x 8"		750	.021		.38	.31	.02	.71	.95	
	1100	2" x 4"		620	.026		.27	.37	.03	.67	.95	
	1120	2" x 6"		560	.029		.42	.41	.03	.86	1.17	
	1140	2" x 8"		500	.032		.56	.46	.03	1.05	1.42	
	1200	3" x 4"		500	.032		.62	.46	.03	1.11	1.48	
	1220	3" x 6"		400	.040		.92	.57	.04	1.53	2.01	
	1240	3" x 10"		300	.053		1.54	.76	.05	2.35	3.02	

For expanded coverage of these items see *Means Building Construction Cost Data 1991*

061 | Rough Carpentry

061 100 | Wood Framing

			CREW	DAILY OUTPUT	MAN-HOURS	UNIT	MAT.	LABOR	EQUIP.	TOTAL	TOTAL INCL O&P	
126	1250											126
128	0010	**FRAMING, WALLS** ⑧⑥										128
	0020											
	2000	Headers over openings, 2" x 6" ⑧⑦	F-2	360	.044	L.F.	.40	.64	.04	1.08	1.55	
	2050	2" x 8"		340	.047		.54	.67	.05	1.26	1.77	
	2100	2" x 10"		320	.050		.84	.72	.05	1.61	2.17	
	2150	2" x 12"		300	.053		1.02	.76	.05	1.83	2.45	
	2190	4" x 10"		100	.160		2.09	2.29	.16	4.54	6.30	
	2200	4" x 12"		190	.084		2.51	1.20	.08	3.79	4.87	
	2240	6" x 10"		73	.219		3.58	3.13	.22	6.93	9.40	
	2250	6" x 12"		70	.229		3.58	3.27	.23	7.08	9.65	
	5000	Plates, untreated, 2" x 3"		850	.019		.21	.27	.02	.50	.70	
	5020	2" x 4"		800	.020		.27	.29	.02	.58	.80	
	5040	2" x 6"		750	.021		.41	.31	.02	.74	.98	
	5060	Treated, 2" x 3"		750	.021		.27	.31	.02	.60	.83	
	5080	2" x 4"		700	.023		.37	.33	.02	.72	.98	
	5100	2" x 6"		650	.025		.55	.35	.02	.92	1.23	
	5120	Studs, 8' high wall, 2" x 3"		1,200	.013		.21	.19	.01	.41	.56	
	5140	2" x 4"		1,100	.015		.27	.21	.01	.49	.66	
	5160	2" x 6"		1,000	.016		.40	.23	.02	.65	.84	
	5180	3" x 4"		800	.020		.62	.29	.02	.93	1.18	
	5200	Installed on second story, 2" x 3"		1,170	.014		.21	.20	.01	.42	.57	
	5220	2" x 4"		1,015	.016		.27	.23	.02	.52	.69	
	5240	2" x 6"		890	.018		.40	.26	.02	.68	.89	
	5260	3" x 4"		800	.020		.62	.29	.02	.93	1.18	
	5280	Installed on dormer or gable, 2" x 3"		1,045	.015		.21	.22	.02	.45	.61	
	5300	2" x 4"		905	.018		.27	.25	.02	.54	.74	
	5320	2" x 6"		800	.020		.41	.29	.02	.72	.95	
	5340	3" x 4"		700	.023		.62	.33	.02	.97	1.25	
	5360	6' high wall, 2" x 3"		970	.016		.21	.24	.02	.47	.64	
	5380	2" x 4"		850	.019		.27	.27	.02	.56	.77	
	5400	2" x 6"		740	.022		.41	.31	.02	.74	.99	
	5420	3" x 4"		600	.027		.62	.38	.03	1.03	1.35	
	5440	Installed on second story, 2" x 3"		950	.017		.21	.24	.02	.47	.65	
	5460	2" x 4"		810	.020		.27	.28	.02	.57	.79	
	5480	2" x 6"		700	.023		.41	.33	.02	.76	1.02	
	5500	3" x 4"		550	.029		.62	.42	.03	1.07	1.41	
	5520	Installed on dormer or gable, 2" x 3"		850	.019		.21	.27	.02	.50	.70	
	5540	2" x 4"		720	.022		.27	.32	.02	.61	.86	
	5560	2" x 6"		620	.026		.41	.37	.03	.81	1.10	
	5580	3" x 4"		480	.033		.62	.48	.03	1.13	1.51	
	5600	3' high wall, 2" x 3"		740	.022		.21	.31	.02	.54	.77	
	5620	2" x 4"		640	.025		.27	.36	.03	.66	.93	
	5640	2" x 6"		550	.029		.41	.42	.03	.86	1.18	
	5660	3" x 4"		440	.036		.62	.52	.04	1.18	1.59	
	5680	Installed on second story, 2" x 3"		700	.023		.21	.33	.02	.56	.80	
	5700	2" x 4"		610	.026		.27	.38	.03	.68	.96	
	5720	2" x 6"		520	.031		.41	.44	.03	.88	1.22	
	5740	3" x 4"		430	.037		.62	.53	.04	1.19	1.61	
	5760	Installed on dormer or gable, 2" x 3"		625	.026		.21	.37	.03	.61	.87	
	5780	2" x 4"		545	.029		.27	.42	.03	.72	1.03	
	5800	2" x 6"		465	.034		.41	.49	.03	.93	1.31	
	5820	3" x 4"		380	.042		.62	.60	.04	1.26	1.73	
	8250	For second story & above, add					5%					
	8300	Dormer & gable, add					15%					
130	0010	**FURRING** Wood strips, on walls, 1" x 2", on wood	1 Carp	550	.015		.10	.21		.31	.46	130
	0300	On masonry	"	495	.016		.11	.23		.34	.51	

For expanded coverage of these items see *Means Building Construction Cost Data 1991*

289

061 | Rough Carpentry

061 100 | Wood Framing

			CREW	DAILY OUTPUT	MAN-HOURS	UNIT	MAT.	LABOR	EQUIP.	TOTAL	TOTAL INCL O&P	
130	0400	On concrete	1 Carp	260	.031	L.F.	.11	.44		.55	.86	130
	0600	1" x 3", wood strips, on walls, on wood		550	.015		.14	.21		.35	.50	
	0700	On masonry		495	.016		.15	.23		.38	.55	
	0800	On concrete		260	.031		.15	.44		.59	.90	
	0850	1" x 3", wood strips, on ceilings, on wood		350	.023		.14	.33		.47	.70	
	0900	On masonry		320	.025		.15	.36		.51	.76	
	0950	On concrete		210	.038		.15	.54		.69	1.08	
132	0010	GROUNDS For casework, 1" x 2" wood strips, on wood	1 Carp	330	.024	L.F.	.10	.35		.45	.69	132
	0100	On masonry		285	.028		.11	.40		.51	.79	
	0200	On concrete		250	.032		.11	.46		.57	.89	
	0400	For plaster, ¾" deep, on wood		450	.018		.10	.25		.35	.54	
	0500	On masonry		225	.036		.11	.51		.62	.97	
	0600	On concrete		175	.046		.11	.65		.76	1.21	
	0700	On metal lath		200	.040		.11	.57		.68	1.08	
134	0010	INSULATION See division 072										134
138	0010	PARTITIONS Wood stud with single bottom plate and										138
	0020	double top plate, no waste, std. & better lumber										
	0180	2" x 4" studs, 8' high, studs 12" O.C.	F-2	80	.200	L.F.	3.02	2.86	.20	6.08	8.30	
	0200	16" O.C.		100	.160		2.48	2.29	.16	4.93	6.75	
	0300	24" O.C.		125	.128		1.93	1.83	.13	3.89	5.30	
	0380	10' high, studs 12" O.C.		80	.200		3.58	2.86	.20	6.64	8.95	
	0400	16" O.C.		100	.160		2.89	2.29	.16	5.34	7.20	
	0500	24" O.C.		125	.128		2.20	1.83	.13	4.16	5.60	
	0580	12' high, studs 12" O.C.		65	.246		4.13	3.52	.25	7.90	10.70	
	0600	16" O.C.		80	.200		3.30	2.86	.20	6.36	8.65	
	0700	24" O.C.		100	.160		2.48	2.29	.16	4.93	6.75	
	0780	2" x 6" studs, 8' high, studs 12" O.C.		70	.229		4.48	3.27	.23	7.98	10.65	
	0800	16" O.C.		90	.178		3.66	2.54	.18	6.38	8.45	
	0900	24" O.C.		115	.139		2.85	1.99	.14	4.98	6.60	
	0980	10' high, studs 12" O.C.		70	.229		5.29	3.27	.23	8.79	11.55	
	1000	16" O.C.		90	.178		4.27	2.54	.18	6.99	9.15	
	1100	24" O.C.		115	.139		3.25	1.99	.14	5.38	7.05	
	1180	12' high, studs 12" O.C.		55	.291		6.10	4.16	.29	10.55	14	
	1200	16" O.C.		70	.229		4.88	3.27	.23	8.38	11.10	
	1300	24" O.C.		90	.178		3.66	2.54	.18	6.38	8.45	
	1400	For horizontal blocking, 2" x 4", add		600	.027		.27	.38	.03	.68	.97	
	1500	2" x 6", add		600	.027		.40	.38	.03	.81	1.11	
	1600	For openings, add		250	.064			.92	.06	.98	1.60	
	1700	Headers for above openings, material only, add				B.F.	.55			.55	.61	
140	0010	ROUGH HARDWARE Average % of carpentry material, minimum					.50%					140
	0200	Maximum					1.50%					

061 150 | Sheathing

			CREW	DAILY OUTPUT	MAN-HOURS	UNIT	MAT.	LABOR	EQUIP.	TOTAL	TOTAL INCL O&P	
154	0010	SHEATHING Plywood on roof, CDX (83)										154
	0030	5/16" thick	F-2	1,600	.010	S.F.	.24	.14	.01	.39	.51	
	0050	⅜" thick		1,525	.010		.26	.15	.01	.42	.55	
	0100	½" thick		1,400	.011		.32	.16	.01	.49	.64	
	0200	⅝" thick		1,300	.012		.40	.18	.01	.59	.75	
	0300	¾" thick		1,200	.013		.46	.19	.01	.66	.84	
	0500	Plywood on walls with exterior CDX, ⅜" thick		1,200	.013		.26	.19	.01	.46	.62	
	0600	½" thick		1,125	.014		.32	.20	.01	.53	.71	
	0700	⅝" thick		1,050	.015		.40	.22	.02	.64	.82	
	0800	¾" thick		975	.016		.46	.23	.02	.71	.92	
	1000	For shear wall construction, add						20%				
	1200	For structural 1 exterior plywood, add					10%					

For expanded coverage of these items see *Means Building Construction Cost Data 1991*

061 | Rough Carpentry

061 150 | Sheathing

			CREW	DAILY OUTPUT	MAN-HOURS	UNIT	MAT.	LABOR	EQUIP.	TOTAL	TOTAL INCL O&P	
154	1400	With boards, on roof 1" x 6" boards, laid horizontal	F-2	725	.022	S.F.	.67	.32	.02	1.01	1.29	154
	1500	Laid diagonal		650	.025		.69	.35	.02	1.06	1.38	
	1700	1" x 8" boards, laid horizontal		875	.018		.67	.26	.02	.95	1.20	
	1800	Laid diagonal		725	.022		.69	.32	.02	1.03	1.31	
	2000	For steep roofs, add						40%				
	2200	For dormers, hips and valleys, add					5%	50%				
	2400	Boards on walls, 1" x 6" boards, laid regular	F-2	650	.025		.67	.35	.02	1.04	1.36	
	2500	Laid diagonal		585	.027		.69	.39	.03	1.11	1.44	
	2700	1" x 8" boards, laid regular		765	.021		.67	.30	.02	.99	1.26	
	2800	Laid diagonal		650	.025		.69	.35	.02	1.06	1.38	
	2850	Gypsum, weatherproof, ½" thick		1,050	.015		.33	.22	.02	.57	.74	
	2900	Sealed, ⁴⁄₁₀" thick		1,100	.015		.31	.21	.01	.53	.70	
	3000	Wood fiber, regular, no vapor barrier, ½" thick		1,200	.013		.35	.19	.01	.55	.72	
	3100	⅝" thick		1,200	.013		.46	.19	.01	.66	.84	
	3300	No vapor barrier, in colors, ½" thick		1,200	.013		.49	.19	.01	.69	.87	
	3400	⅝" thick		1,200	.013		.60	.19	.01	.80	.99	
	3600	With vapor barrier one side, white, ½" thick		1,200	.013		.48	.19	.01	.68	.86	
	3700	Vapor barrier 2 sides		1,200	.013		.75	.19	.01	.95	1.16	
	3800	Asphalt impregnated, ²⁵⁄₃₂" thick		1,200	.013		.30	.19	.01	.50	.66	
	3850	Intermediate, ½" thick		1,200	.013		.26	.19	.01	.46	.62	
	4000	Wafer board on roof, ½" thick		1,455	.011		.24	.16	.01	.41	.53	
	4100	⅝" thick		1,330	.012		.31	.17	.01	.49	.64	

061 160 | Subfloor

			CREW	DAILY OUTPUT	MAN-HOURS	UNIT	MAT.	LABOR	EQUIP.	TOTAL	TOTAL INCL O&P	
161	0010	FLOORING, WOOD See division 095-604										161
164	0010	SUBFLOOR Plywood, CDX, ½" thick (83)	F-2	1,500	.011	SF Flr.	.32	.15	.01	.48	.62	164
	0100	⅝" thick		1,350	.012		.39	.17	.01	.57	.73	
	0200	¾" thick		1,250	.013		.46	.18	.01	.65	.83	
	0300	1-⅛" thick, 2-4-1 including underlayment		1,050	.015		1	.22	.02	1.24	1.48	
	0500	With boards, 1" x 10" S4S, laid regular		1,100	.015		.68	.21	.01	.90	1.11	
	0600	Laid diagonal		900	.018		.70	.25	.02	.97	1.21	
	0800	1" x 8" S4S, laid regular		1,000	.016		.67	.23	.02	.92	1.14	
	0900	Laid diagonal		850	.019		.69	.27	.02	.98	1.23	
	1100	Wood fiber, T&G, 2' x 8' planks, 1" thick		1,000	.016		.97	.23	.02	1.22	1.47	
	1200	1-⅜" thick		900	.018		1.28	.25	.02	1.55	1.85	
	1500	Wafer board, ⅝" thick		1,330	.012	S.F.	.30	.17	.01	.48	.63	
	1600	¾" thick		1,230	.013	"	.32	.19	.01	.52	.68	
168	0010	UNDERLAYMENT Plywood, underlayment grade, ⅜" thick		1,500	.011	SF Flr.	.32	.15	.01	.48	.62	168
	0100	½" thick		1,450	.011		.36	.16	.01	.53	.68	
	0200	⅝" thick		1,400	.011		.44	.16	.01	.61	.77	
	0300	¾" thick		1,300	.012		.51	.18	.01	.70	.87	
	0500	Particle board, ⅜" thick		1,500	.011		.26	.15	.01	.42	.56	
	0600	½" thick		1,450	.011		.28	.16	.01	.45	.59	
	0800	⅝" thick		1,400	.011		.31	.16	.01	.48	.63	
	0900	¾" thick		1,300	.012		.35	.18	.01	.54	.70	
	1100	Hardboard, underlayment grade, 4' x 4', .215" thick		1,500	.011		.28	.15	.01	.44	.58	

061 250 | Wood Decking

			CREW	DAILY OUTPUT	MAN-HOURS	UNIT	MAT.	LABOR	EQUIP.	TOTAL	TOTAL INCL O&P	
258	0011	ROOF DECKS										258
	0400	Cedar planks, 3.65 B.F. per S.F., 3" thick	F-2	320	.050	S.F.	3.86	.72	.05	4.63	5.50	
	0500	4.65 B.F. per S.F., 4" thick		250	.064		4.88	.92	.06	5.86	6.95	
	0700	Douglas fir, 3" thick		320	.050		1.85	.72	.05	2.62	3.29	
	0800	4" thick		250	.064		2.51	.92	.06	3.49	4.36	
	1000	Hemlock, 3" thick		320	.050		1.85	.72	.05	2.62	3.29	
	1100	4" thick		250	.064		2.51	.92	.06	3.49	4.36	
	1300	Western white spruce, 3" thick		320	.050		1.82	.72	.05	2.59	3.25	

For expanded coverage of these items see *Means Building Construction Cost Data 1991*

061 | Rough Carpentry

061 250 | Wood Decking

			CREW	DAILY OUTPUT	MAN-HOURS	UNIT	MAT.	LABOR	EQUIP.	TOTAL	TOTAL INCL O&P	
258	1400	4" thick	F-2	250	.064	S.F.	2.42	.92	.06	3.40	4.26	258

061 300 | Heavy Timber Const

			CREW	DAILY OUTPUT	MAN-HOURS	UNIT	MAT.	LABOR	EQUIP.	TOTAL	TOTAL INCL O&P	
304	0010	FRAMING, HEAVY Mill timber, beams, single 6" x 10"	F-2	220	.073	L.F.	3.25	1.04	.07	4.36	5.40	304
	0100	Single 8" x 16"		115	.139	"	7.04	1.99	.14	9.17	11.20	
	0200	Built from 2" lumber, multiple 2" x 14"		900	.018	B.F.	.52	.25	.02	.79	1.01	
	0210	Built from 3" lumber, multiple 3" x 6"		700	.023		.62	.33	.02	.97	1.25	
	0220	Multiple 3" x 8"		800	.020		.62	.29	.02	.93	1.18	
	0230	Multiple 3" x 10"		900	.018		.62	.25	.02	.89	1.12	
	0240	Multiple 3" x 12"		1,000	.016		.62	.23	.02	.87	1.08	
	0250	Built from 4" lumber, multiple 4" x 6"		800	.020		.63	.29	.02	.94	1.19	
	0260	Multiple 4" x 8"		900	.018		.63	.25	.02	.90	1.13	
	0270	Multiple 4" x 10"		1,000	.016		.63	.23	.02	.88	1.09	
	0280	Multiple 4" x 12"		1,100	.015		.63	.21	.01	.85	1.05	
	0290	Columns, structural grade, 1500f, 4" x 4"		450	.036	L.F.	.85	.51	.04	1.40	1.83	
	0300	6" x 6"		225	.071		2.20	1.02	.07	3.29	4.20	
	0400	8" x 8"		240	.067		3.95	.95	.07	4.97	6	
	0500	10" x 10"		90	.178		6.65	2.54	.18	9.37	11.75	
	0600	12" x 12"		70	.229		9.75	3.27	.23	13.25	16.45	
	0610											
	0800	Floor planks, 2" thick, T & G, 2" x 6"	F-2	1,050	.015	B.F.	.59	.22	.02	.83	1.03	
	0900	2" x 10"		1,100	.015		.61	.21	.01	.83	1.03	
	1100	3" thick, 3" x 6"		1,050	.015		.81	.22	.02	1.05	1.27	
	1200	3" x 10"		1,100	.015		.82	.21	.01	1.04	1.26	
	1400	Girders, structural grade, 12" x 12"		800	.020		.80	.29	.02	1.11	1.38	
	1500	10" x 16"		1,000	.016		.80	.23	.02	1.05	1.28	
	2050	Roof planks, see division 061-258										
	2300	Roof purlins, 4" thick, structural grade	F-2	1,050	.015	B.F.	.63	.22	.02	.87	1.07	
	2500	Roof trusses, add timber connectors, division 060-512	"	450	.036	"	.63	.51	.04	1.18	1.58	

061 500 | Wood-Metal Systems

			CREW	DAILY OUTPUT	MAN-HOURS	UNIT	MAT.	LABOR	EQUIP.	TOTAL	TOTAL INCL O&P	
508	0010	STRUCTURAL JOISTS Fabricated "I" joists with wood flanges,										508
	0100	Plywood webs, incl. bridging & blocking, panels 24" O.C.										
	1200	15' to 24' span, 50 psf live load	F-5	2,400	.013	SF Flr.	1.17	.20	.01	1.38	1.63	
	1300	55 psf live load		2,250	.014		1.24	.21	.01	1.46	1.72	
	1400	24' to 30' span, 45 psf live load		2,600	.012		1.41	.18	.01	1.60	1.86	
	1500	55 psf live load		2,400	.013		1.48	.20	.01	1.69	1.97	
	1600	Tubular steel open webs, 45 psf, 24" O.C., 40' span	F-3	6,250	.006		1.38	.09	.06	1.53	1.74	
	1700	55' span		5,150	.008		1.33	.11	.07	1.51	1.73	
	1800	70' span		9,250	.004		1.84	.06	.04	1.94	2.17	
	1900	85 psf live load, 26' span		2,300	.017		1.74	.25	.16	2.15	2.51	

061 800 | Glued-Laminated Const

			CREW	DAILY OUTPUT	MAN-HOURS	UNIT	MAT.	LABOR	EQUIP.	TOTAL	TOTAL INCL O&P	
804	0010	LAMINATED FRAMING Not including decking										804
	0020	30 lb., short term live load, 15 lb. dead load										
	0200	Straight roof beams, 20' clear span, beams 8' O.C.	F-3	2,560	.016	SF Flr.	1.20	.23	.15	1.58	1.86	
	0300	Beams 16' O.C.		3,200	.013		.82	.18	.12	1.12	1.33	
	0500	40' clear span, beams 8' O.C.		3,200	.013		2.26	.18	.12	2.56	2.92	
	0600	Beams 16' O.C.		3,840	.010		2.15	.15	.10	2.40	2.73	
	0800	60' clear span, beams 8' O.C.	F-4	2,880	.017		4.43	.24	.26	4.93	5.55	
	0900	Beams 16' O.C.	"	3,840	.013		2.65	.18	.19	3.02	3.43	
	1100	Tudor arches, 30' to 40' clear span, frames 8' O.C.	F-3	1,680	.024		5.20	.34	.23	5.77	6.55	
	1200	Frames 16' O.C.	"	2,240	.018		3.90	.26	.17	4.33	4.91	
	1400	50' to 60' clear span, frames 8' O.C.	F-4	2,200	.022		5.30	.31	.34	5.95	6.70	
	1500	Frames 16' O.C.		2,640	.018		4.55	.26	.28	5.09	5.75	
	1700	Radial arches, 60' clear span, frames 8' O.C.		1,920	.025		5	.35	.39	5.74	6.50	
	1800	Frames 16' O.C.		2,880	.017		3.85	.24	.26	4.35	4.92	

For expanded coverage of these items see *Means Building Construction Cost Data 1991*

061 | Rough Carpentry

061 800 | Glued-Laminated Const

			Crew	Daily Output	Man-Hours	Unit	Mat.	Labor	Equip.	Total	Total Incl O&P	
804	2000	100' clear span, frames 8' O.C.	F-4	1,600	.030	SF Flr.	5.15	.42	.46	6.03	6.90	804
	2100	Frames 16' O.C.		2,400	.020		4.60	.28	.31	5.19	5.85	
	2300	120' clear span, frames 8' O.C.		1,440	.033		6.90	.47	.52	7.89	8.95	
	2400	Frames 16' O.C.		1,920	.025		6.25	.35	.39	6.99	7.90	
	2600	Bowstring trusses, 20' O.C., 40' clear span	F-3	2,400	.017		3.10	.24	.16	3.50	3.98	
	2700	60' clear span	F-4	3,600	.013		2.80	.19	.21	3.20	3.62	
	2800	100' clear span		4,000	.012		3.95	.17	.19	4.31	4.84	
	2900	120' clear span		3,600	.013		4.25	.19	.21	4.65	5.20	
	3100	For premium appearance, add to S.F. prices					5%					
	3300	For industrial type, deduct					15%					
	3500	For stain and varnish, add					5%					
	3900	For ¾" laminations, add to straight					25%					
	4100	Add to curved					15%					
	4300	Alternate pricing method: (use nominal footage of										
	4310	components). Straight beams, camber less than 6"	F-3	3.50	11.430	M.B.F.	1,425	165	110	1,700	1,950	
	4400	Columns, including hardware		2	20		1,600	290	190	2,080	2,450	
	4600	Curved members, radius over 32'		2.50	16		1,625	230	150	2,005	2,350	
	4700	Radius 10' to 32'		3	13.330		1,750	195	125	2,070	2,375	
	4900	For complicated shapes, add maximum					100%					
	5100	For pressure treating, add to straight					35%					
	5200	Add to curved					45%					
806	0010	LAMINATED BEAMS Fb 2400 psi										806
	0050	3" x 15"	F-3	480	.083	L.F.	5.34	1.21	.79	7.34	8.75	
	0100	3" x 18"		450	.089		6.41	1.29	.84	8.54	10.10	
	0150	5" x 15"		360	.111		8.91	1.61	1.05	11.57	13.65	
	0200	5" x 18"		290	.138		10.69	2	1.30	13.99	16.50	
	0250	5" x 22-½"		220	.182		13.36	2.63	1.72	17.71	21	
	0300	6-¾" x 18"		320	.125		14.43	1.81	1.18	17.42	20	
	0350	6-¾" x 25-½"		260	.154		20.44	2.23	1.45	24.12	28	
	0400	6-¾" x 33"		210	.190		26.45	2.76	1.80	31.01	36	
	0450	8-¾" x 34-½"		160	.250		35.85	3.62	2.36	41.83	48	
	0500	For premium appearance, add to S.F. prices					5%					
	0550	For industrial type, deduct					15%					
	0600	For stain and varnish, add					5%					
	0650	For ¾" laminations, add					25%					
808	0010	LAMINATED ROOF DECK Pine or hemlock, 3" thick	F-2	425	.038	S.F.	2.31	.54	.04	2.89	3.48	808
	0100	4" thick		325	.049		2.69	.70	.05	3.44	4.19	
	0300	Cedar, 3" thick		425	.038		2.86	.54	.04	3.44	4.09	
	0400	4" thick		325	.049		3.41	.70	.05	4.16	4.98	
	0600	Fir, 3" thick		425	.038		2.53	.54	.04	3.11	3.72	
	0700	4" thick		325	.049		2.91	.70	.05	3.66	4.43	

061 900 | Wood Trusses

			Crew	Daily Output	Man-Hours	Unit	Mat.	Labor	Equip.	Total	Total Incl O&P	
908	0010	ROOF TRUSSES For timber connectors, see div. 060-512										908
	5000	Flat wood, 2" x 4" metal plate connected, 24" O.C., 4/12 slope										
	5010	1' overhang, 12' span ⑧⑤	F-5	55	.582	Ea.	28	8.60	.29	36.89	46	
	5050	20' span	F-6	62	.645		37	8.55	6.10	51.65	62	
	5100	24' span		60	.667		44	8.85	6.30	59.15	70	
	5150	26' span		57	.702		47	9.35	6.65	63	75	
	5200	28' span		53	.755		51	10.05	7.15	68.20	81	
	5240	30' span		51	.784		54	10.40	7.40	71.80	85	
	5250	32' span		50	.800		58	10.65	7.55	76.20	90	
	5280	34' span		48	.833		62	11.10	7.90	81	95	
	5350	8/12 pitch, 1' overhang, 20' span		57	.702		35	9.35	6.65	51	61	
	5400	24' span		55	.727		41	9.65	6.85	57.50	69	
	5450	26' span		52	.769		45	10.20	7.25	62.45	75	
	5500	28' span		49	.816		48	10.85	7.70	66.55	79	

For expanded coverage of these items see *Means Building Construction Cost Data 1991*

061 | Rough Carpentry

061 900 | Wood Trusses

			CREW	DAILY OUTPUT	MAN-HOURS	UNIT	MAT.	LABOR	EQUIP.	TOTAL	TOTAL INCL O&P	
908	5550	32' span	F-6	45	.889	Ea.	55	11.80	8.40	75.20	89	908
	5600	36' span	"	41	.976	"	71	12.95	9.20	93.15	110	

062 | Finish Carpentry

062 200 | Millwork Moldings

			CREW	DAILY OUTPUT	MAN-HOURS	UNIT	MAT.	LABOR	EQUIP.	TOTAL	TOTAL INCL O&P	
204	0010	MILLWORK Rule of thumb: Milled material cost										204
	0020	equals three times cost of lumber										
	1000	Typical finish hardwood milled material										
	1020	1" x 12", custom birch				L.F.	2.10			2.10	2.31	
	1040	Cedar					2.15			2.15	2.37	
	1060	Oak					4.45			4.45	4.90	
	1080	Redwood					3			3	3.30	
	1100	Southern yellow pine					.69			.69	.76	
	1120	Sugar pine					2.30			2.30	2.53	
	1140	Teak					8.31			8.31	9.15	
	1160	Walnut					4.34			4.34	4.77	
	1180	White pine					2.85			2.85	3.14	
208	0010	MOLDINGS, BASE										208
	0500	Base, stock pine, 9/16" x 3-1/2"	1 Carp	240	.033	L.F.	.80	.48		1.28	1.68	
	0501	Oak or birch		240	.033		1.22	.48		1.70	2.14	
	0550	9/16" x 4-1/2"		200	.040		.92	.57		1.49	1.97	
	0561	Base shoe, oak, 3/4" x 1"		240	.033		.92	.48		1.40	1.81	
	0570	2-1/2" x 9/16" prefinished base molding		242	.033		.80	.47		1.27	1.67	
	0580	3/8" x 5/8" prefinished shoe		266	.030		.32	.43		.75	1.07	
	0585	Flooring cand strip, 3/4" x 1/2"		500	.016		.19	.23		.42	.59	
212	0010	MOLDINGS, CASINGS										212
	0020											
	0090	Apron, stock pine, 5/8" x 2"	1 Carp	250	.032	L.F.	.61	.46		1.07	1.44	
	0110	5/8" x 3-1/2"		220	.036		1.28	.52		1.80	2.28	
	0300	Band, stock pine, 11/16" x 1-1/8"		270	.030		.37	.42		.79	1.12	
	0350	11/16" x 1-3/4"		250	.032		.48	.46		.94	1.29	
	0700	Casing, stock pine, 11/16" x 2-1/2"		240	.033		.59	.48		1.07	1.45	
	0701	Oak or birch		240	.033		.75	.48		1.23	1.62	
	0750	11/16" x 3-1/2"		215	.037		.81	.53		1.34	1.78	
	0760	Door & window casing, exterior, 1-1/4" x 2"		200	.040		1.07	.57		1.64	2.13	
	0770	Finger jointed, 1-1/4" x 2"		200	.040		.97	.57		1.54	2.02	
	4600	Mullion casing, stock pine, 5/16" x 2"		200	.040		.36	.57		.93	1.35	
	4601	Oak or birch		200	.040		.46	.57		1.03	1.46	
	4700	Teak, custom, nominal 1" x 1"		215	.037		.75	.53		1.28	1.72	
	4800	Nominal 1" x 3"		200	.040		2.29	.57		2.86	3.48	
216	0010	MOLDINGS, CEILINGS										216
	0020											
	0600	Bed, stock pine, 9/16" x 1-3/4"	1 Carp	270	.030	L.F.	.44	.42		.86	1.19	
	0650	9/16" x 2"		240	.033		.59	.48		1.07	1.45	
	1200	Cornice molding, stock pine, 9/16" x 1-3/4"		330	.024		.46	.35		.81	1.09	
	1300	9/16" x 2-1/4"		300	.027		.66	.38		1.04	1.36	
	2400	Cove scotia, stock pine, 9/16" x 1-3/4"		270	.030		.47	.42		.89	1.23	
	2401	Oak or birch		270	.030		.74	.42		1.16	1.52	
	2500	11/16" x 2-3/4"		255	.031		.77	.45		1.22	1.60	
	2600	Crown, stock pine, 9/16" x 3-5/8"		250	.032		1	.46		1.46	1.87	

For expanded coverage of these items see *Means Building Construction Cost Data 1991*

062 | Finish Carpentry

062 200 | Millwork Moldings

			CREW	DAILY OUTPUT	MAN-HOURS	UNIT	MAT.	LABOR	EQUIP.	TOTAL	TOTAL INCL O&P	
216	2700	11/16" x 4-5/8"	1 Carp	220	.036	L.F.	2.03	.52		2.55	3.10	216
220	0010	**MOLDINGS, EXTERIOR**										220
	1500	Cornice, boards, pine, 1" x 2"	1 Carp	330	.024	L.F.	.14	.35		.49	.73	
	1600	1" x 4"		250	.032		.28	.46		.74	1.07	
	1700	1" x 6"		200	.040		.55	.57		1.12	1.56	
	1800	1" x 8"		200	.040		.73	.57		1.30	1.76	
	1900	1" x 10"		180	.044		1.15	.64		1.79	2.33	
	2000	1" x 12"		180	.044		1.60	.64		2.24	2.82	
	2200	Three piece, built-up, pine, minimum		80	.100		1.20	1.43		2.63	3.71	
	2300	Maximum		65	.123		3.35	1.76		5.11	6.65	
	3000	Trim, exterior, sterling pine, corner board, 1" x 4"		200	.040		.17	.57		.74	1.14	
	3100	1" x 6"		200	.040		.27	.57		.84	1.25	
	3200	2" x 6"		165	.048		.39	.69		1.08	1.59	
	3300	2" x 8"		165	.048		.52	.69		1.21	1.73	
	3350	Fascia, 1" x 6"		250	.032		.27	.46		.73	1.06	
	3370	1" x 8"		225	.036		.36	.51		.87	1.25	
	3372	2" x 6"		225	.036		.38	.51		.89	1.27	
	3374	2" x 8"		200	.040		.52	.57		1.09	1.53	
	3376	2" x 10"		180	.044		.79	.64		1.43	1.93	
	3400	Moldings, back band		250	.032		.49	.46		.95	1.30	
	3500	Casing		250	.032		.26	.46		.72	1.05	
	3600	Crown		250	.032		1	.46		1.46	1.87	
	3700	Porch rail with balusters		22	.364		5.35	5.20		10.55	14.60	
	3800	Screen		395	.020		.19	.29		.48	.69	
	4100	Verge board, sterling pine, 1" x 4"		200	.040		.16	.57		.73	1.13	
	4200	1" x 6"		200	.040		.25	.57		.82	1.23	
	4300	2" x 6"		165	.048		.38	.69		1.07	1.58	
	4400	2" x 8"		165	.048		.51	.69		1.20	1.72	
	4700	For redwood trim, add					100%					
	5000	Trim, exterior, rough-sawn cedar casing/fascia										
	5100	1" x 2"	1 Carp	275	.029	L.F.	.30	.42		.72	1.03	
	5200	1" x 6"		250	.032		1.07	.46		1.53	1.94	
	5300	1" x 8"		230	.035		1.57	.50		2.07	2.56	
	5400	2" x 4"		220	.036		.82	.52		1.34	1.77	
	5500	2" x 6"		220	.036		1.22	.52		1.74	2.21	
	5600	2" x 8"		200	.040		1.58	.57		2.15	2.69	
	5700	2" x 10"		180	.044		2.40	.64		3.04	3.70	
	5800	2" x 12"		170	.047		2.85	.67		3.52	4.26	
224	0010	**MOLDINGS, TRIM**										224
	0200	Astragal, stock pine, 11/16" x 1-3/4"	1 Carp	255	.031	L.F.	.70	.45		1.15	1.52	
	0250	1-5/16" x 2-3/16"		240	.033		1.17	.48		1.65	2.08	
	0800	Chair rail, stock pine, 5/8" x 2-1/2"		270	.030		.66	.42		1.08	1.43	
	0900	5/8" x 3-1/2"		240	.033		1.18	.48		1.66	2.10	
	1000	Closet pole, stock pine, 1-1/8" diameter		200	.040		.83	.57		1.40	1.87	
	1100	Fir, 1-5/8" diameter		200	.040		.97	.57		1.54	2.02	
	1150	Corner, inside, 5/16" x 1"		225	.036		.21	.51		.72	1.08	
	1160	Outside, 1-1/16" x 1-1/16"		240	.033		.49	.48		.97	1.34	
	1161	1-5/16" x 1-5/16"		240	.033		.83	.48		1.31	1.71	
	3300	Half round, stock pine, 1/4" x 1/2"		270	.030		.10	.42		.52	.82	
	3350	1/2" x 1"		255	.031		.33	.45		.78	1.11	
	3400	Handrail, fir, single piece, stock, hardware not included										
	3450	1-1/2" x 1-3/4"	1 Carp	80	.100	L.F.	.90	1.43		2.33	3.38	
	3470	Pine, 1-1/2" x 1-3/4"		80	.100		.86	1.43		2.29	3.34	
	3500	1-1/2" x 2-1/2"		76	.105		1.22	1.51		2.73	3.86	
	3600	Lattice, stock pine, 1/4" x 1-1/8"		270	.030		.18	.42		.60	.91	
	3700	1/4" x 1-3/4"		250	.032		.22	.46		.68	1.01	

For expanded coverage of these items see *Means Building Construction Cost Data 1991*

062 | Finish Carpentry

062 200 | Millwork Moldings

		CREW	DAILY OUTPUT	MAN-HOURS	UNIT	MAT.	LABOR	EQUIP.	TOTAL	TOTAL INCL O&P	
224	3800 Miscellaneous, custom, pine or cedar, 1" x 1"	1 Carp	270	.030	L.F.	.14	.42		.56	.86	224
	3900 Nominal 1" x 3"		240	.033		.34	.48		.82	1.17	
	4100 Birch or oak, custom, nominal 1" x 1"		240	.033		.20	.48		.68	1.02	
	4200 Nominal 1" x 3"		215	.037		.56	.53		1.09	1.51	
	4400 Walnut, custom, nominal 1" x 1"		215	.037		.31	.53		.84	1.23	
	4500 Nominal 1" x 3"		200	.040		.86	.57		1.43	1.90	
	4700 Teak, custom, nominal 1" x 1"		215	.037		.77	.53		1.30	1.74	
	4800 Nominal 1" x 3"		200	.040		2.04	.57		2.61	3.20	
	4900 Quarter round, stock pine, ¼" x ¼"		275	.029		.10	.42		.52	.81	
	4950 ¾" x ¾"		255	.031		.21	.45		.66	.98	
	5600 Wainscot moldings, 1-⅛" x 9/16", 2' high, minimum		76	.105	S.F.	5.40	1.51		6.91	8.45	
	5700 Maximum		65	.123	"	10.70	1.76		12.46	14.70	
228	0010 **MOLDINGS, WINDOW AND DOOR**										228
	0020										
	2800 Door moldings, stock, decorative, 1-⅛" wide, plain	1 Carp	17	.471	Set	20	6.75		26.75	33	
	2900 Detailed		17	.471	"	50	6.75		56.75	66	
	3150 Door trim set, 1 head and 2 sides, pine, 2-½ wide		5.90	1.360	Opng.	8.50	19.40		27.90	42	
	3170 4-½" wide		5.30	1.510	"	37	22		59	77	
	3200 Glass beads, stock pine, ¼" x 11/16"		285	.028	L.F.	.17	.40		.57	.86	
	3250 ⅜" x ½"		275	.029		.24	.42		.66	.96	
	3270 ⅜" x ⅞"		270	.030		.28	.42		.70	1.02	
	4850 Parting bead, stock pine, ⅜" x ¾"		275	.029		.22	.42		.64	.94	
	4870 ½" x ¾"		255	.031		.27	.45		.72	1.05	
	5000 Stool caps, stock pine, 11/16" x 3-½"		200	.040		1.25	.57		1.82	2.33	
	5100 1-1/16" x 3-¼"		150	.053		2.45	.76		3.21	3.97	
	5300 Threshold, oak, 3' long, inside, ⅝" x 3-⅝"		32	.250	Ea.	4.80	3.58		8.38	11.25	
	5400 Outside, 1-½" x 7-⅝"		16	.500	"	18	7.15		25.15	32	
	5900 Window trim sets, including casings, header, stops,										
	5910 stool and apron, 2-½" wide, minimum	1 Carp	13	.615	Opng.	10.50	8.80		19.30	26	
	5950 Average		10	.800		15	11.45		26.45	36	
	6000 Maximum		6	1.330		20	19.05		39.05	54	

062 300 | Shelving

		CREW	DAILY OUTPUT	MAN-HOURS	UNIT	MAT.	LABOR	EQUIP.	TOTAL	TOTAL INCL O&P	
304	0010 **SHELVING** Pine, clear grade, no edge band, 1" x 8"	F-1	115	.070	L.F.	.96	.99	.07	2.02	2.80	304
	0100 1" x 10"		110	.073		1.22	1.04	.07	2.33	3.16	
	0200 1" x 12"		105	.076		1.50	1.09	.08	2.67	3.55	
	0400 For lumber edge band, by hand, add					1.30			1.30	1.43	
	0420 By machine, add					.85			.85	.94	
	0600 Plywood, ¾" thick with lumber edge, 12" wide	F-1	75	.107		1.04	1.53	.11	2.68	3.81	
	0700 24" wide		70	.114		1.95	1.63	.11	3.69	5	
	0900 Bookcase, pine, clear grade, 8" shelves, 12" O.C.		70	.114	S.F.	3.80	1.63	.11	5.54	7.05	
	1000 12" wide shelves		65	.123	"	4.50	1.76	.12	6.38	8.05	
	1200 Adjustable closet rod and shelf, 12" wide, 3' long		20	.400	Ea.	7.70	5.70	.40	13.80	18.45	
	1300 8' long		15	.533	"	13.90	7.65	.53	22.08	29	
	1500 Prefinished shelves with supports, stock, 8" wide		75	.107	L.F.	5.30	1.53	.11	6.94	8.50	
	1600 10" wide		70	.114	"	5.95	1.63	.11	7.69	9.40	
	1800 Custom, high quality dadoed pine shelving units, minimum				S.F.				23	28	
	1900 Maximum				"				31.50	40	
408	0010 **COUNTER TOP** Stock, plastic lam., 24" wide w/backsplash, min.	1 Carp	30	.267	L.F.	5.20	3.81		9.01	12.10	408
	0105 Maximum		25	.320		16	4.58		20.58	25	
	0300 Custom plastic, ⅞" thick, aluminum molding, no splash		30	.267		15.25	3.81		19.06	23	
	0400 Cove splash		30	.267		19.90	3.81		23.71	28	
	0600 1-¼" thick, no splash		28	.286		17.95	4.09		22.04	27	
	0700 Square splash		28	.286		22.50	4.09		26.59	32	
	0900 Square edge, plastic face, ⅞" thick, no splash		30	.267		19.20	3.81		23.01	28	
	1000 With splash		30	.267		25	3.81		28.81	34	

For expanded coverage of these items see *Means Building Construction Cost Data 1991*

062 | Finish Carpentry

062 300 | Shelving

			CREW	DAILY OUTPUT	MAN-HOURS	UNIT	MAT.	LABOR	EQUIP.	TOTAL	TOTAL INCL O&P	
408	1200	For stainless channel edge, ⅞" thick, add				L.F.	2.15			2.15	2.37	408
	1300	1-¼" thick, add					2.50			2.50	2.75	
	1500	For solid color suede finish, add				↓	1.85			1.85	2.04	
	1700	For end splash, add				Ea.	12			12	13.20	
	1900	For cut outs, standard, add, minimum	1 Carp	32	.250			3.58		3.58	6	
	2000	Maximum		8	1		3.05	14.30		17.35	27	
	2010	Cut out in blacksplash for elec. wall outlet		38	.211			3.01		3.01	5.05	
	2020	Cut out for sink		20	.400			5.70		5.70	9.55	
	2030	Cut out for stove top		18	.444			6.35		6.35	10.65	
	2100	Postformed, including backsplash and front edge		30	.267	L.F.	8.05	3.81		11.86	15.25	
	2110	Mitred, add		12	.667	Ea.		9.55		9.55	15.95	
	2200	Built-in place, 25" wide, plastic laminate		25	.320	L.F.	10.25	4.58		14.83	18.95	
	2300	Ceramic tile mosaic	↓	25	.320		24	4.58		28.58	34	
	2500	Marble, stock, with splash, ½" thick, minimum	1 Bric	17	.471		29	6.95		35.95	43	
	2700	¾" thick, maximum	"	13	.615		74	9.10		83.10	96	
	2900	Maple, solid, laminated, 1-½" thick, no splash	1 Carp	28	.286		30	4.09		34.09	40	
	3000	With square splash		28	.286	↓	34	4.09		38.09	44	
	3200	Stainless steel		24	.333	S.F.	71	4.77		75.77	86	
	3400	Recessed cutting block with trim, 16" x 20" x 1"		8	1	Ea.	38	14.30		52.30	66	
	3410	Replace cutting block only		16	.500	"	26.40	7.15		33.55	41	
	3600	Table tops, plastic laminate, square edge, ⅞" thick		45	.178	S.F.	6.80	2.54		9.34	11.75	
	3700	1-⅛" thick	↓	40	.200	"	7	2.86		9.86	12.50	

062 500 | Prefin. Wood Paneling

504	0010	**PANELING, PLYWOOD**										504
	2400	Plywood, prefinished, ¼" thick, 4' x 8' sheets										
	2410	with vertical grooves. Birch faced, minimum	F-2	500	.032	S.F.	.60	.46	.03	1.09	1.46	
	2420	Average		420	.038		.90	.54	.04	1.48	1.94	
	2430	Maximum		350	.046		1.25	.65	.05	1.95	2.52	
	2600	Mahogany, African		400	.040		1.55	.57	.04	2.16	2.71	
	2700	Philippine (Lauan)		500	.032		.50	.46	.03	.99	1.35	
	2900	Oak or Cherry, minimum		500	.032		1.35	.46	.03	1.84	2.29	
	3000	Maximum		400	.040		2.40	.57	.04	3.01	3.64	
	3200	Rosewood		320	.050		9.50	.72	.05	10.27	11.70	
	3400	Teak		400	.040		2.40	.57	.04	3.01	3.64	
	3600	Chestnut		375	.043		3.60	.61	.04	4.25	5.05	
	3800	Pecan		400	.040		1.55	.57	.04	2.16	2.71	
	3900	Walnut, minimum		500	.032		2.05	.46	.03	2.54	3.06	
	3950	Maximum		400	.040		3.85	.57	.04	4.46	5.25	
	4000	Plywood, prefinished, ¾" thick, stock grades, minimum		320	.050		.90	.72	.05	1.67	2.24	
	4100	Maximum		224	.071		4.15	1.02	.07	5.24	6.35	
	4300	Architectural grade, minimum		224	.071		3	1.02	.07	4.09	5.10	
	4400	Maximum		160	.100		4.60	1.43	.10	6.13	7.55	
	4600	Plywood, "A" face, birch, V.C., ½" thick, natural		450	.036		1.40	.51	.04	1.95	2.43	
	4700	Select		450	.036		1.50	.51	.04	2.05	2.54	
	4900	Veneer core, ¾" thick, natural		320	.050		1.50	.72	.05	2.27	2.90	
	5000	Select		320	.050		1.65	.72	.05	2.42	3.07	
	5200	Lumber core, ¾" thick, natural		320	.050		2.25	.72	.05	3.02	3.73	
	5500	Plywood, knotty pine, ¼" thick, A2 grade		450	.036		1	.51	.04	1.55	1.99	
	5600	A3 grade		450	.036		1.45	.51	.04	2	2.49	
	5800	¾" thick, veneer core, A2 grade		320	.050		1.50	.72	.05	2.27	2.90	
	5900	A3 grade		320	.050		1.70	.72	.05	2.47	3.12	
	6100	Aromatic cedar, ¼" thick, plywood		400	.040		1.45	.57	.04	2.06	2.60	
	6200	¼" thick, particle board		400	.040	↓	.70	.57	.04	1.31	1.77	

062 550 | Prefin. Hardboard Panel

554	0010	**PANELING, HARDBOARD**										554
	0050	Not incl. furring or trim, hardboard, tempered, ⅛" thick	F-2	500	.032	S.F.	.27	.46	.03	.76	1.10	

For expanded coverage of these items see *Means Building Construction Cost Data 1991*

062 | Finish Carpentry

062 550 | Prefin. Hardboard Panel

			CREW	DAILY OUTPUT	MAN-HOURS	UNIT	MAT.	LABOR	EQUIP.	TOTAL	TOTAL INCL O&P	
554	0100	¼" thick	F-2	500	.032	S.F.	.33	.46	.03	.82	1.16	554
	0300	Tempered pegboard, ⅛" thick		500	.032		.30	.46	.03	.79	1.13	
	0400	¼" thick		500	.032		.38	.46	.03	.87	1.22	
	0600	Untempered hardboard, natural finish, ⅛" thick		500	.032		.24	.46	.03	.73	1.06	
	0700	¼" thick		500	.032		.31	.46	.03	.80	1.14	
	0900	Untempered pegboard, ⅛" thick		500	.032		.27	.46	.03	.76	1.10	
	1000	¼" thick		500	.032		.33	.46	.03	.82	1.16	
	1200	Plastic faced hardboard, ⅛" thick		500	.032		.44	.46	.03	.93	1.28	
	1300	¼" thick		500	.032		.60	.46	.03	1.09	1.46	
	1500	Plastic faced pegboard, ⅛" thick		500	.032		.43	.46	.03	.92	1.27	
	1600	¼" thick		500	.032		.52	.46	.03	1.01	1.37	
	1800	Wood grained, plain or grooved, ¼" thick, minimum		500	.032		.40	.46	.03	.89	1.24	
	1900	Maximum		425	.038		.75	.54	.04	1.33	1.77	
	2100	Moldings for hardboard, wood or aluminum, minimum		500	.032	L.F.	.28	.46	.03	.77	1.11	
	2200	Maximum		425	.038	"	.75	.54	.04	1.33	1.77	

062 600 | Board Paneling

604	0010	PANELING, BOARDS										604
	6400	Wood board paneling, ¾" thick, knotty pine	F-2	300	.053	S.F.	.88	.76	.05	1.69	2.30	
	6500	Rough sawn cedar		300	.053		1.22	.76	.05	2.03	2.67	
	6700	Redwood, clear, 1" x 4" boards		300	.053		2.80	.76	.05	3.61	4.41	
	6900	Aromatic cedar, closet lining, boards		275	.058		1.90	.83	.06	2.79	3.54	

062 700 | Misc Finish Carpentry

704	0010	BEAMS, DECORATIVE Rough sawn cedar, non-load bearing, 4" x 4"	2 Carp	180	.089	L.F.	1.70	1.27		2.97	4	704
	0100	4" x 6"		170	.094		2.95	1.35		4.30	5.50	
	0200	4" x 8"		160	.100		3.65	1.43		5.08	6.40	
	0300	4" x 10"		150	.107		4.25	1.53		5.78	7.25	
	0400	4" x 12"		140	.114		5.50	1.63		7.13	8.80	
	0500	8" x 8"		130	.123		7.60	1.76		9.36	11.30	
	0600	Plastic beam, "hewn finish", 6" x 2"		240	.067		2.60	.95		3.55	4.45	
	0601	Plastic beam, "hewn finish", 6" x 4"		220	.073		3	1.04		4.04	5.05	
	1100	Beam connector plates see div 060-512										
720	0010	FIREPLACE MANTEL BEAMS Rough texture wood, 4" x 8"	1 Carp	36	.222	L.F.	3.65	3.18		6.83	9.35	720
	0100	4" x 10"		35	.229	"	4.20	3.27		7.47	10.10	
	0300	Laminated hardwood, 2-¼" x 10-½" wide, 6' long		5	1.600	Ea.	88	23		111	135	
	0400	8' long		5	1.600	"	122	23		145	170	
	0600	Brackets for above, rough sawn		12	.667	Pr.	8.15	9.55		17.70	25	
	0700	Laminated		12	.667	"	12.20	9.55		21.75	29	
725	0010	FIREPLACE MANTELS 6" molding, 6' x 3'-6" opening, minimum		5	1.600	Opng.	98	23		121	145	725
	0100	Maximum		5	1.600		121	23		144	170	
	0300	Prefabricated pine, colonial type, stock, deluxe		2	4		535	57		592	685	
	0400	Economy		3	2.670		200	38		238	285	
730	0010	GRILLES and Panels, hardwood, sanded										730
	0020	2' x 4' to 4' x 8', custom designs, unfinished, minimum	1 Carp	38	.211	S.F.	11.10	3.01		14.11	17.25	
	0050	Average		30	.267		17.30	3.81		21.11	25	
	0100	Maximum		19	.421		26.80	6		32.80	40	
	0300	As above, but prefinished, minimum		38	.211		13.85	3.01		16.86	20	
	0400	Maximum		19	.421		34	6		40	47	
735	0010	HARDWARE Finish, see divisions 064-108 & 087										735
	0100	Rough, see division 050										
740	0010	LOUVERS Redwood, 2'-0" opening, full circle	1 Carp	16	.500	Ea.	76	7.15		83.15	96	740
	0100	Half circle, 2'-0" diameter		16	.500		72	7.15		79.15	91	
	0200	Octagonal, 2'-0" diameter		16	.500		68	7.15		75.15	87	
	0300	Triangular, 5/12 pitch, 5'-0" at base		16	.500		70	7.15		77.15	89	

For expanded coverage of these items see *Means Building Construction Cost Data 1991*

062 | Finish Carpentry

062 700 | Misc Finish Carpentry

			CREW	DAILY OUTPUT	MAN-HOURS	UNIT	MAT.	LABOR	EQUIP.	TOTAL	TOTAL INCL O&P	
760	0010	**SHUTTERS, EXTERIOR** Aluminum, louvered, 1'-4" wide, 3'-0" long	1 Carp	10	.800	Pr.	25	11.45		36.45	47	760
	0200	4'-0" long		10	.800		28	11.45		39.45	50	
	0300	5'-4" long		10	.800		32	11.45		43.45	54	
	0400	6'-8" long		9	.889		42	12.70		54.70	67	
	1000	Pine, louvered, primed, each 1'-2" wide, 3'-3" long		10	.800		31	11.45		42.45	53	
	1100	4'-7" long		10	.800		39	11.45		50.45	62	
	1250	Each 1'-4" wide, 3'-0" long		10	.800		30	11.45		41.45	52	
	1350	5'-3" long		10	.800		42	11.45		53.45	65	
	1500	Each 1'-6" wide, 3'-3" long		10	.800		35	11.45		46.45	58	
	1600	4'-7" long		10	.800		48	11.45		59.45	72	
	1620	Hemlock, louvered, 1'-2" wide, 5'-7" long		10	.800		44	11.45		55.45	68	
	1630	Each 1'-4" wide, 2'-2" long		10	.800		28	11.45		39.45	50	
	1640	3'-0" long		10	.800		30	11.45		41.45	52	
	1650	3'-3" long		10	.800		31	11.45		42.45	53	
	1660	3'-11" long		10	.800		34	11.45		45.45	57	
	1670	4'-3" long		10	.800		36	11.45		47.45	59	
	1680	5'-3" long		10	.800		41	11.45		52.45	64	
	1690	5'-11" long		10	.800		45	11.45		56.45	69	
	1700	Door blinds, 6'-9" long, each 1'-3" wide		9	.889		53	12.70		65.70	80	
	1710	1'-6" wide		9	.889		66	12.70		78.70	94	
	1720	Hemlock, solid raised panel, each 1'-4" wide, 3'-3" long		10	.800		45	11.45		56.45	69	
	1730	3'-11" long		10	.800		55	11.45		66.45	80	
	1740	4'-3" long		10	.800		57	11.45		68.45	82	
	1750	4'-7" long		10	.800		60	11.45		71.45	85	
	1760	4'-11" long		10	.800		65	11.45		76.45	91	
	1770	5'-11" long		10	.800		79	11.45		90.45	105	
	1800	Door blinds, 6'-9" long, each 1'-3" wide		9	.889		88	12.70		100.70	120	
	1900	1'-6" wide		9	.889		92	12.70		104.70	120	
	2500	Polystyrene, solid raised panel, each 1'-4" wide, 3'-3" long		10	.800		40	11.45		51.45	63	
	2600	3'-11" long		10	.800		46	11.45		57.45	70	
	2700	4'-7" long		10	.800		50	11.45		61.45	74	
	2800	5'-3" long		10	.800		56	11.45		67.45	81	
	2900	6'-8" long		9	.889		77	12.70		89.70	105	
	4500	Polystyrene, louvered, each 1'-2" wide, 3'-3" long		10	.800		30	11.45		41.45	52	
	4600	4'-7" long		10	.800		38	11.45		49.45	61	
	4750	5'-3" long		10	.800		42	11.45		53.45	65	
	4850	6'-8" long		9	.889		68	12.70		80.70	96	
	6000	Vinyl, louvered, each 1'-2" x 4'-7" long		10	.800		40	11.45		51.45	63	
	6200	Each 1'-4" x 6'-8" long	↓	9	.889	↓	64	12.70		76.70	92	
775	0010	**SOFFITS** Wood fiber, no vapor barrier, 15/32" thick	F-2	525	.030	S.F.	.50	.44	.03	.97	1.31	775
	0100	5/8" thick		525	.030		.56	.44	.03	1.03	1.38	
	0300	As above, 5/8" thick, with factory finish		525	.030		.72	.44	.03	1.19	1.55	
	0500	Hardboard, 3/8" thick, slotted		525	.030		.70	.44	.03	1.17	1.53	
	1000	Exterior AC plywood, 1/4" thick		420	.038		.38	.54	.04	.96	1.37	
	1100	1/2" thick	↓	420	.038	↓	.50	.54	.04	1.08	1.50	
778	0010	**DOORS AND FRAMES** See division 081 & 082										778

For expanded coverage of these items see *Means Building Construction Cost Data 1991*

063 | Wood Treatment

063 100 | Preservative Treatment

			CREW	DAILY OUTPUT	MAN-HOURS	UNIT	MAT.	LABOR	EQUIP.	TOTAL	TOTAL INCL O&P	
102	0010	**LUMBER TREATMENT** Creosoted 8 lbs. per C.F., add				M.B.F.	210			210	230	102
	0200	For every added 2#/C.F., add per increment					25			25	28	
	0400	Fire retardant, wet					240			240	265	
	0500	KDAT					275			275	305	
	0700	Salt treated, water borne, .40 lb. retention					155			155	170	
	0800	Oil borne, 8 lb. retention					165			165	180	
	1000	Kiln dried lumber, 1" & 2" thick, soft woods					100			100	110	
	1100	Hard woods					105			105	115	
	1500	For small size 1" stock, add					10			10	11	
	1700	For full size rough lumber, add				↓	20%					
104	0010	**PLYWOOD TREATMENT** Fire retardant, ¼" thick				M.S.F.	220			220	240	104
	0030	⅜" thick					240			240	265	
	0050	½" thick					255			255	280	
	0070	⅝" thick					270			270	295	
	0100	¾" thick					300			300	330	
	0200	For KDAT, add					60			60	66	
	0500	Salt treated water borne, .25 lb., wet, ¼" thick					115			115	125	
	0530	⅜" thick					120			120	130	
	0550	½" thick					125			125	140	
	0570	⅝" thick					135			135	150	
	0600	¾" thick					145			145	160	
	0800	For KDAT add					60			60	66	
	0900	For .40 lb., per C.F. retention, add					40			40	44	
	1000	For certification stamp, add				↓	30			30	33	

064 | Architectural Woodwork

064 100 | Custom Casework

			CREW	DAILY OUTPUT	MAN-HOURS	UNIT	MAT.	LABOR	EQUIP.	TOTAL	TOTAL INCL O&P	
102	0010	**CABINETS** Corner china cabinets, stock pine,										102
	0020	80" high, unfinished, minimum	2 Carp	6.60	2.420	Ea.	240	35		275	320	
	0100	Maximum	"	4.40	3.640	"	560	52		612	705	
	0700	Kitchen base cabinets, hardwood, not incl. counter tops,										
	0710	24" deep, 35" high, prefinished										
	0800	One top drawer, one door below, 12" wide	2 Carp	24.80	.645	Ea.	95	9.25		104.25	120	
	0820	15" wide		24	.667		100	9.55		109.55	125	
	0840	18" wide		23.30	.687		105	9.80		114.80	130	
	0860	21" wide		22.70	.705		115	10.10		125.10	145	
	0880	24" wide	↓	22.30	.717	↓	125	10.25		135.25	155	
	0890											
	1000	Four drawers, 12" wide	2 Carp	24.80	.645	Ea.	105	9.25		114.25	130	
	1020	15" wide		24	.667		115	9.55		124.55	140	
	1040	18" wide		23.30	.687		120	9.80		129.80	150	
	1060	24" wide		22.30	.717		140	10.25		150.25	170	
	1200	Two top drawers, two doors below, 27" wide		22	.727		160	10.40		170.40	195	
	1220	30" wide		21.40	.748		165	10.70		175.70	200	
	1240	33" wide		20.90	.766		175	10.95		185.95	210	
	1260	36" wide		20.30	.788		180	11.25		191.25	215	
	1280	42" wide		19.80	.808		195	11.55		206.55	235	
	1300	48" wide		18.90	.847		205	12.10		217.10	245	
	1500	Range or sink base, two doors below, 30" wide		21.40	.748		105	10.70		115.70	135	
	1520	33" wide		20.90	.766		125	10.95		135.95	155	
	1540	36" wide		20.30	.788	↓	135	11.25		146.25	165	

For expanded coverage of these items see *Means Building Construction Cost Data 1991*

064 | Architectural Woodwork

064 100 | Custom Casework

			CREW	DAILY OUTPUT	MAN-HOURS	UNIT	MAT.	LABOR	EQUIP.	TOTAL	TOTAL INCL O&P	
102	1560	42" wide	2 Carp	19.80	.808	Ea.	145	11.55		156.55	180	102
	1580	48" wide	"	18.90	.847		160	12.10		172.10	195	
	1800	For sink front units, deduct					45			45	50	
	2000	Corner base cabinets, 36" wide, standard	2 Carp	18	.889		135	12.70		147.70	170	
	2100	Lazy Susan with revolving door	"	16.50	.970	↓	185	13.85		198.85	225	
	4000	Kitchen wall cabinets, hardwood, 12" deep with two doors										
	4050	12" high, 30" wide	2 Carp	24.80	.645	Ea.	80	9.25		89.25	105	
	4100	36" wide		24	.667		90	9.55		99.55	115	
	4400	15" high, 30" wide		24	.667		85	9.55		94.55	110	
	4420	33" wide		23.30	.687		90	9.80		99.80	115	
	4440	36" wide		22.70	.705		100	10.10		110.10	125	
	4450	42" wide		22.70	.705		100	10.10		110.10	125	
	4700	24" high, 30" wide		23.30	.687		100	9.80		109.80	125	
	4720	36" wide		22.70	.705		120	10.10		130.10	150	
	4740	42" wide		22.30	.717		130	10.25		140.25	160	
	5000	30" high, one door, 12" wide		22	.727		80	10.40		90.40	105	
	5020	15" wide		21.40	.748		85	10.70		95.70	110	
	5040	18" wide		20.90	.766		95	10.95		105.95	125	
	5060	24" wide		20.30	.788		100	11.25		111.25	130	
	5300	Two doors, 27" wide		19.80	.808		115	11.55		126.55	145	
	5320	30" wide		19.30	.829		120	11.85		131.85	150	
	5340	36" wide		18.80	.851		125	12.15		137.15	160	
	5360	42" wide		18.50	.865		135	12.35		147.35	170	
	5380	48" wide		18.40	.870		150	12.45		162.45	185	
	6000	Corner wall, 30" high, 24" wide		18	.889		120	12.70		132.70	155	
	6050	30" wide		17.20	.930		140	13.30		153.30	175	
	6100	36" wide		16.50	.970		155	13.85		168.85	195	
	6500	Revolving Lazy Susan		15.20	1.050		170	15.05		185.05	210	
	7000	Broom cabinet, 84" high, 24" deep, 18" wide		10	1.600		140	23		163	190	
	7500	Oven cabinets, 84" high, 24" deep, 27" wide		8	2	↓	160	29		189	225	
	7750	Valance board trim	↓	396	.040	L.F.	5	.58		5.58	6.45	
	7760											
	9000	For deluxe models of all cabinets, add to above				Ea.	40%					
	9500	For custom built in place, add to above				"	25%	10%				
	9550	Rule of thumb, kitchen cabinets not including										
	9560	appliances & counter top, minimum	2 Carp	30	.533	L.F.	60	7.65		67.65	79	
	9600	Maximum	"	25	.640	"	130	9.15		139.15	160	
104	0010	**CASEWORK, FRAMES**										104
	0050	Base cabinets, counter storage, 36" high, one bay										
	0100	18" wide	1 Carp	2.70	2.960	Ea.	70	42		112	150	
	0400	Two bay, 36" wide		2.20	3.640		110	52		162	210	
	1100	Three bay, 54" wide		1.50	5.330		140	76		216	280	
	2800	Book cases, one bay, 7' high, 18" wide		2.40	3.330		85	48		133	175	
	3500	Two bay, 36" wide		1.60	5		130	72		202	265	
	4100	Three bay, 54" wide		1.20	6.670		215	95		310	395	
	6100	Wall mounted cabinet, one bay, 24" high, 18" wide		3.60	2.220		40	32		72	97	
	6800	Two bay, 36" wide		2.20	3.640		65	52		117	160	
	7400	Three bay, 54" wide		1.70	4.710		85	67		152	205	
	8400	30" high, one bay, 18" wide		3.60	2.220		45	32		77	105	
	9000	Two bay, 36" wide		2.15	3.720		65	53		118	160	
	9400	Three bay, 54" wide		1.60	5		85	72		157	215	
	9800	Wardrobe, 7' high, single, 24" wide		2.70	2.960		95	42		137	175	
	9950	Partition, adjustable shelves & drawers, 48" wide	↓	1.40	5.710	↓	190	82		272	345	
106	0010	**CABINET DOORS**										106
	2000	Glass panel, hardwood frame										
	2200	12" wide, 18" high	1 Carp	34	.235	Ea.	5.60	3.36		8.96	11.80	
	2400	24" high	"	33	.242	"	6.50	3.47		9.97	12.95	

For expanded coverage of these items see *Means Building Construction Cost Data 1991*

064 | Architectural Woodwork

064 100 | Custom Casework

		CREW	DAILY OUTPUT	MAN-HOURS	UNIT	MAT.	LABOR	EQUIP.	TOTAL	TOTAL INCL O&P
2600	30" high	1 Carp	32	.250	Ea.	7.50	3.58		11.08	14.25
2800	36" high		30	.267		8.50	3.81		12.31	15.75
3000	48" high		23	.348		10.65	4.97		15.62	20
3200	60" high		17	.471		13	6.75		19.75	26
3400	72" high		15	.533		14.70	7.65		22.35	29
3600	15" wide x 18" high		33	.242		6.10	3.47		9.57	12.50
3800	24" high		32	.250		7.10	3.58		10.68	13.80
4000	30" high		30	.267		8.10	3.81		11.91	15.30
4250	36" high		28	.286		9.10	4.09		13.19	16.85
4300	48" high		22	.364		12.50	5.20		17.70	22
4350	60" high		16	.500		14.95	7.15		22.10	28
4400	72" high		14	.571		16.15	8.15		24.30	31
4450	18" wide, 18" high		32	.250		6.50	3.58		10.08	13.15
4500	24" high		30	.267		7.60	3.81		11.41	14.75
4550	30" high		29	.276		8.60	3.94		12.54	16.05
4600	36" high		27	.296		9.50	4.24		13.74	17.55
4650	48" high		21	.381		12.60	5.45		18.05	23
4700	60" high		15	.533		14.20	7.65		21.85	28
4750	72" high		13	.615		16.30	8.80		25.10	33
4800										
5000	Hardwood, raised panel									
5100	12" wide, 18" high	1 Carp	16	.500	Ea.	10.45	7.15		17.60	23
5150	24" high		15.50	.516		13.90	7.40		21.30	28
5200	30" high		15	.533		16.60	7.65		24.25	31
5250	36" high		14	.571		19.90	8.15		28.05	36
5300	48" high		11	.727		26.40	10.40		36.80	46
5320	60" high		8	1		33.10	14.30		47.40	60
5340	72" high		7	1.140		40	16.35		56.35	71
5360	15" wide x 18" high		15.50	.516		14.20	7.40		21.60	28
5380	24" high		15	.533		17.30	7.65		24.95	32
5400	30" high		14.50	.552		21.60	7.90		29.50	37
5420	36" high		13.50	.593		25.40	8.45		33.85	42
5440	48" high		10.50	.762		33.10	10.90		44	55
5460	60" high		7.50	1.070		41.90	15.25		57.15	72
5480	72" high		6.50	1.230		49.70	17.60		67.30	84
5500	18" wide, 18" high		15	.533		15.80	7.65		23.45	30
5550	24" high		14.50	.552		20	7.90		27.90	35
5600	30" high		14	.571		25.20	8.15		33.35	41
5650	36" high		13	.615		30.50	8.80		39.30	48
5700	48" high		10	.800		40.30	11.45		51.75	63
5750	60" high		7	1.140		48.90	16.35		65.25	81
5800	72" high		6	1.330		59.90	19.05		78.95	98
5900										
6000	Plastic laminate on particle board									
6100	12" wide, 18" high	1 Carp	25	.320	Ea.	3.35	4.58		7.93	11.35
6120	24" high		24	.333		4.65	4.77		9.42	13.10
6140	30" high		23	.348		6.15	4.97		11.12	15.10
6160	36" high		21	.381		7.10	5.45		12.55	16.90
6200	48" high		16	.500		9.50	7.15		16.65	22
6250	60" high		13	.615		12.10	8.80		20.90	28
6300	72" high		12	.667		14.40	9.55		23.95	32
6320	15" wide x 18" high		24.50	.327		4.90	4.67		9.57	13.20
6340	24" high		23.50	.340		6.05	4.87		10.92	14.80
6360	30" high		22.50	.356		7.30	5.10		12.40	16.55
6380	36" high		20.50	.390		9	5.60		14.60	19.25
6400	48" high		15.50	.516		11.75	7.40		19.15	25
6450	60" high		12.50	.640		15.10	9.15		24.25	32
6480	72" high		11.50	.696		17.70	9.95		27.65	36

For expanded coverage of these items see *Means Building Construction Cost Data 1991*

064 | Architectural Woodwork

064 100 | Custom Casework

			CREW	DAILY OUTPUT	MAN-HOURS	UNIT	MAT.	LABOR	EQUIP.	TOTAL	TOTAL INCL O&P	
106	6500	18" wide, 18" high	1 Carp	24	.333	Ea.	5.20	4.77		9.97	13.70	106
	6550	24" high		23	.348		6.80	4.97		11.77	15.80	
	6600	30" high		22	.364		8.60	5.20		13.80	18.15	
	6650	36" high		20	.400		9.75	5.70		15.45	20	
	6700	48" high		15	.533		13.10	7.65		20.75	27	
	6750	60" high		12	.667		16.70	9.55		26.25	34	
	6800	72" high	↓	11	.727	↓	19.90	10.40		30.30	39	
	6801											
	7000	Plywood, with edge band										
	7010	12" wide, 18" high	1 Carp	27	.296	Ea.	7.15	4.24		11.39	14.95	
	7100	24" high		26	.308		8.50	4.40		12.90	16.70	
	7120	30" high		25	.320		9.65	4.58		14.23	18.25	
	7140	36" high		23	.348		12	4.97		16.97	22	
	7180	48" high		18	.444		15.40	6.35		21.75	28	
	7200	60" high		15	.533		19.10	7.65		26.75	34	
	7250	72" high		14	.571		24.10	8.15		32.25	40	
	7300	15" wide x 18" high		26.50	.302		7.25	4.32		11.57	15.20	
	7350	24" high		25.50	.314		9.40	4.49		13.89	17.85	
	7400	30" high		24.50	.327		12.50	4.67		17.17	22	
	7450	36" high		22.50	.356		14.60	5.10		19.70	25	
	7500	48" high		17.50	.457		19.30	6.55		25.85	32	
	7550	60" high		14.50	.552		24.80	7.90		32.70	40	
	7600	72" high		13.50	.593		29.80	8.45		38.25	47	
	7650	18" wide, 18" high		26	.308		8.75	4.40		13.15	17	
	7700	24" high		25	.320		12.10	4.58		16.68	21	
	7750	30" high	↓	24	.333	↓	14.60	4.77		19.37	24	
108	0010	**CABINET HARDWARE**										108
	1000	Catches, minimum	1 Carp	235.29	.034	Ea.	.60	.49		1.09	1.47	
	1020	Average		119.40	.067		1.75	.96		2.71	3.53	
	1040	Maximum	↓	80	.100	↓	2.95	1.43		4.38	5.65	
	2000	Door/drawer pulls, handles										
	2200	Handles and pulls, projecting, metal, minimum	1 Carp	160	.050	Ea.	.90	.72		1.62	2.19	
	2220	Average		95.24	.084		2.30	1.20		3.50	4.54	
	2240	Maximum		68.83	.116		5.70	1.66		7.36	9.05	
	2300	Wood, minimum		160	.050		.80	.72		1.52	2.08	
	2320	Average		95.24	.084		1.25	1.20		2.45	3.38	
	2340	Maximum		68.38	.117		2.60	1.67		4.27	5.65	
	2600	Flush, metal, minimum		160	.050		1.40	.72		2.12	2.74	
	2620	Average		95.24	.084		2.85	1.20		4.05	5.15	
	2640	Maximum		68.38	.117		10	1.67		11.67	13.80	
	3000	Drawer tracks/glides, minimum		47.90	.167	↓	5.45	2.39		7.84	10	
	3020	Average		32	.250	Pr.	9.30	3.58		12.88	16.20	
	3040	Maximum		23.95	.334		15.50	4.78		20.28	25	
	4000	Cabinet hinges, minimum		160	.050		1.25	.72		1.97	2.57	
	4020	Average		95.24	.084		2.20	1.20		3.40	4.43	
	4040	Maximum	↓	68.38	.117	↓	5.70	1.67		7.37	9.05	
110	0010	**DRAWERS**										110
	0100	Solid hardwood front										
	1000	4" high, 12" wide										
	1200	18" wide	1 Carp	16	.500	Ea.	17.40	7.15		24.55	31	
	1400	24" wide		15	.533		23.10	7.65		30.75	38	
	1600	6" high x 12" wide		16	.500		17.75	7.15		24.90	31	
	1800	18" wide		15	.533		23	7.65		30.65	38	
	2000	24" wide		14	.571		29.15	8.15		37.30	46	
	2200	9" high x 12" wide		15	.533		23.20	7.65		30.85	38	
	2400	18" wide		14	.571		29.25	8.15		37.40	46	
	2600	24" wide	↓	13	.615	↓	35.50	8.80		44.30	54	
	2800	Plastic laminate on particle board front										

For expanded coverage of these items see *Means Building Construction Cost Data 1991*

064 | Architectural Woodwork

064 100 | Custom Casework

			CREW	DAILY OUTPUT	MAN-HOURS	UNIT	MAT.	LABOR	EQUIP.	TOTAL	TOTAL INCL O&P	
110	3000	4" high, 12" wide	1 Carp	17	.471	Ea.	13.40	6.75		20.15	26	110
	3200	18" wide		16	.500		16	7.15		23.15	30	
	3600	24" wide		15	.533		19.15	7.65		26.80	34	
	3800	6" high, x 12" wide		16	.500		15.90	7.15		23.05	29	
	4000	18" wide		15	.533		19.60	7.65		27.25	34	
	4500	24" wide		14	.571		24.50	8.15		32.65	41	
	4800	9" high x 12" wide		15	.533		17.50	7.65		25.15	32	
	5000	18" wide		14	.571		19.05	8.15		27.20	35	
	5200	24" wide	↓	13	.615	↓	30.80	8.80		39.60	49	
	5400	Plywood, flush panel front										
	6000	4" high, 12" wide										
	6200	18" wide	1 Carp	16	.500	Ea.	17.40	7.15		24.55	31	
140	0010	VANITIES										140
	0020											
	8000	Vanity bases, 2 doors, 30" high, 21" deep, 24" wide	2 Carp	20	.800	Ea.	135	11.45		146.45	170	
	8050	30" wide		16	1		170	14.30		184.30	210	
	8100	36" wide		13.33	1.200		195	17.15		212.15	245	
	8150	48" wide	↓	11.43	1.400		220	20		240	275	
	9000	For deluxe models of all vanities, add to above					40%					
	9500	For custom built in place, add to above				↓	25%	10%				

064 300 | Stairwork & Handrails

			CREW	DAILY OUTPUT	MAN-HOURS	UNIT	MAT.	LABOR	EQUIP.	TOTAL	TOTAL INCL O&P	
306	0011	STAIRS, PREFABRICATED (84)										306
	0100	Box stairs, prefabricated, 3'-0" wide										
	0110	Oak treads, no handrails, 2' high	2 Carp	5	3.200	Flight	105	46		151	190	
	0200	4' high		4	4		230	57		287	350	
	0300	6' high		3.50	4.570		370	65		435	515	
	0400	8' high		3	5.330		470	76		546	645	
	0600	With pine treads for carpet, 2' high		5	3.200		80	46		126	165	
	0700	4' high		4	4		145	57		202	255	
	0800	6' high		3.50	4.570		225	65		290	355	
	0900	8' high	↓	3	5.330		275	76		351	430	
	1100	For 4' wide stairs, add				↓	25%					
	1500	Prefabricated stair rail with balusters, 5 risers	2 Carp	15	1.070	Ea.	135	15.25		150.25	175	
	1600											
	1700	Basement stairs, prefabricated, soft wood,										
	1710	open risers, 3' wide, 8' high	2 Carp	4	4	Flight	90	57		147	195	
	1900	Open stairs, prefabricated prefinished poplar, metal stringers,										
	1910	treads 3'-6" wide, no railings										
	2000	3' high	2 Carp	5	3.200	Flight	320	46		366	430	
	2100	4' high		4	4		395	57		452	530	
	2200	6' high		3.50	4.570		695	65		760	875	
	2300	8' high	↓	3	5.330	↓	1,080	76		1,156	1,325	
	2500	For prefab. 3 piece wood railings & balusters, add for										
	2600	3' high stairs	2 Carp	15	1.070	Ea.	100	15.25		115.25	135	
	2700	4' high stairs		14	1.140		130	16.35		146.35	170	
	2800	6' high stairs		13	1.230		200	17.60		217.60	250	
	2900	8' high stairs		12	1.330		250	19.05		269.05	305	
	3100	For 3'-6" x 3'-6" platform, add	↓	4	4	↓	115	57		172	220	
	3300	Curved stairways, 3'-3" wide, prefabricated, oak, unfinished,										
	3310	incl. curved balustrade system, open one side										
	3400	9' high	2 Carp	.70	22.860	Flight	4,500	325		4,825	5,500	
	3500	10' high		.70	22.860		4,900	325		5,225	5,925	
	3700	Open two sides, 9' high		.50	32		7,400	460		7,860	8,900	
	3800	10' high		.50	32		8,000	460		8,460	9,575	
	4000	Residential, wood, oak treads, prefabricated		1.50	10.670		850	155		1,005	1,200	
	4200	Built in place	↓	.44	36.360	↓	984	520		1,504	1,950	

304

For expanded coverage of these items see *Means Building Construction Cost Data 1991*

064 | Architectural Woodwork

064 300 | Stairwork & Handrails

			CREW	DAILY OUTPUT	MAN-HOURS	UNIT	MAT.	LABOR	EQUIP.	TOTAL	TOTAL INCL O&P	
306	4400	Spiral, oak, 4'-6" diameter, unfinished, prefabricated,										306
	4500	incl. railing, 9' high	2 Carp	1.50	10.670	Flight	3,000	155		3,155	3,550	
308	0010	**STAIR PARTS** Balusters, turned, 30" high, pine, minimum	1 Carp	28	.286	Ea.	3.90	4.09		7.99	11.10	308
	0100	Maximum		26	.308		5.50	4.40		9.90	13.40	
	0300	30" high birch balusters, minimum		28	.286		5.60	4.09		9.69	13	
	0400	Maximum		26	.308		6.50	4.40		10.90	14.50	
	0600	42" high, pine balusters, minimum		27	.296		4.75	4.24		8.99	12.30	
	0700	Maximum		25	.320		6.50	4.58		11.08	14.80	
	0900	42" high birch balusters, minimum		27	.296		6	4.24		10.24	13.70	
	1000	Maximum		25	.320		8.50	4.58		13.08	17	
	1050	Baluster, stock pine, 1-1/16" x 1-1/16"		240	.033	L.F.	.65	.48		1.13	1.51	
	1100	1-5/8" x 1-5/8"		220	.036	"	1.20	.52		1.72	2.19	
	1200	Newels, 3-1/4" wide, starting, minimum		7	1.140	Ea.	34	16.35		50.35	65	
	1300	Maximum		6	1.330		250	19.05		269.05	305	
	1500	Landing, minimum		5	1.600		65	23		88	110	
	1600	Maximum		4	2		280	29		309	355	
	1800	Railings, oak, built-up, minimum		60	.133	L.F.	4.25	1.91		6.16	7.85	
	1900	Maximum		55	.145		10	2.08		12.08	14.50	
	2100	Add for sub rail		110	.073		3.30	1.04		4.34	5.35	
	2110											
	2300	Risers, Beech, 3/4" x 7-1/2" high	1 Carp	64	.125	L.F.	4.25	1.79		6.04	7.65	
	2400	Fir, 3/4" x 7-1/2" high		64	.125		1.20	1.79		2.99	4.31	
	2600	Oak, 3/4" x 7-1/2" high		64	.125		3.90	1.79		5.69	7.30	
	2800	Pine, 3/4" x 7-1/2" high		66	.121		1.20	1.73		2.93	4.22	
	2850	Skirt board, pine, 1" x 10"		55	.145		1.50	2.08		3.58	5.15	
	2900	1" x 12"		52	.154		1.80	2.20		4	5.65	
	3000	Treads, oak, 1-1/16" x 9-1/2" wide, 3' long		18	.444	Ea.	17.25	6.35		23.60	30	
	3100	4' long		17	.471		23	6.75		29.75	37	
	3300	1-1/16" x 11-1/2" wide, 3' long		18	.444		21.75	6.35		28.10	35	
	3400	6' long		14	.571		43.50	8.15		51.65	62	
	3600	Beech treads, add					40%					
	3800	For mitered return nosings, add				L.F.	2.35			2.35	2.59	
310	0010	**RAILING** Custom design, architectural grade, hardwood, minimum	1 Carp	38	.211		10.40	3.01		13.41	16.50	310
	0100	Maximum		30	.267		35	3.81		38.81	45	
	0300	Stock interior railing with spindles 6" O.C., 4' long		40	.200		25	2.86		27.86	32	
	0400	8' long		48	.167		23	2.38		25.38	29	

064 400 | Misc Ornamental Items

402	0011	**COLUMNS**										402
	0050	Aluminum, round colonial, 6" diameter	2 Carp	80	.200	V.L.F.	10.60	2.86		13.46	16.45	
	0100	8" diameter		62.25	.257		13.25	3.68		16.93	21	
	0200	10" diameter		55	.291		17.30	4.16		21.46	26	
	0250	Fir, stock units, hollow round, 6" diameter		80	.200		10.40	2.86		13.26	16.20	
	0300	8" diameter		80	.200		11.30	2.86		14.16	17.20	
	0350	10" diameter		70	.229		14.60	3.27		17.87	22	
	0400	Solid turned, to 8' high, 3-1/2" diameter		80	.200		4.10	2.86		6.96	9.30	
	0500	4-1/2" diameter		75	.213		6.10	3.05		9.15	11.80	
	0600	5-1/2" diameter		70	.229		7.90	3.27		11.17	14.15	
	0800	Square columns, built-up, 5" x 5"		65	.246		5.60	3.52		9.12	12.05	
	0900	Solid, 3-1/2" x 3-1/2"		130	.123		4.50	1.76		6.26	7.90	
	1600	Hemlock, tapered, T & G, 12" diam, 10' high		100	.160		25.50	2.29		27.79	32	
	1700	16' high		65	.246		38.75	3.52		42.27	49	
	1900	10' high, 14" diameter		100	.160		53	2.29		55.29	62	
	2000	18' high		65	.246		51	3.52		54.52	62	
	2200	18" diameter, 12' high		65	.246		71	3.52		74.52	84	
	2300	20' high		50	.320		65.25	4.58		69.83	79	
	2500	20" diameter, 14' high		40	.400		84.70	5.70		90.40	105	
	2600	20' high		35	.457		81.60	6.55		88.15	100	

For expanded coverage of these items see *Means Building Construction Cost Data 1991*

064 | Architectural Woodwork

064 400 | Misc Ornamental Items

			CREW	DAILY OUTPUT	MAN-HOURS	UNIT	MAT.	LABOR	EQUIP.	TOTAL	TOTAL INCL O&P	
402	2800	For flat pilasters, deduct				V.L.F.	33%					402
	3000	For splitting into halves, add				Ea.	52			52	57	
	4000	Rough sawn cedar posts, 4" x 4"	2 Carp	250	.064	V.L.F.	1.30	.92		2.22	2.96	
	4100	4" x 6"		235	.068		2	.97		2.97	3.83	
	4200	6" x 6"		220	.073		3.50	1.04		4.54	5.60	
	4300	8" x 8"		200	.080		9.10	1.14		10.24	11.90	

071 | Waterproofing and Dampproofing

071 600 | Bitum. Dampproofing

			CREW	DAILY OUTPUT	MAN-HOURS	UNIT	MAT.	LABOR	EQUIP.	TOTAL	TOTAL INCL O&P	
602	0010	BITUMINOUS ASPHALT COATING For foundation										602
	0030	Brushed on, below grade, 1 coat	1 Rofc	665	.012	S.F.	.08	.16		.24	.37	
	0100	2 coat		500	.016		.16	.21		.37	.56	
	0300	Sprayed on, below grade, 1 coat, 25.6 S.F./gal.		830	.010		.16	.13		.29	.40	
	0400	2 coat, 20.5 S.F./gal.		500	.016		.21	.21		.42	.61	
	0600	Troweled on, asphalt with fibers, 1/16" thick		500	.016		.14	.21		.35	.53	
	0700	1/8" thick		400	.020		.26	.26		.52	.76	
	1000	1/2" thick		350	.023		1.10	.30		1.40	1.75	

071 750 | Water Repellent Coat

			CREW	DAILY OUTPUT	MAN-HOURS	UNIT	MAT.	LABOR	EQUIP.	TOTAL	TOTAL INCL O&P	
754	0010	RUBBER COATING Water base liquid, roller applied	2 Rofc	7,000	.002	S.F.	.55	.03		.58	.66	754
	0200	Silicone or stearate, sprayed on masonry, 1 coat	1 Rofc	4,000	.002		.10	.03		.13	.16	
	0300	2 coats	"	2,000	.004		.18	.05		.23	.29	

071 800 | Cementitious Dampprfng

			CREW	DAILY OUTPUT	MAN-HOURS	UNIT	MAT.	LABOR	EQUIP.	TOTAL	TOTAL INCL O&P	
802	0010	CEMENT PARGING 2 coats, 1/2" thick, regular P.C.	D-1	250	.064	S.F.	.14	.84		.98	1.53	802
	0100	Waterproofed portland cement	"	250	.064	"	.16	.84		1	1.56	

071 920 | Vapor Retarders

			CREW	DAILY OUTPUT	MAN-HOURS	UNIT	MAT.	LABOR	EQUIP.	TOTAL	TOTAL INCL O&P	
922	0010	BUILDING PAPER Aluminum and kraft laminated, foil 1 side	1 Carp	1,900	.004	S.F.	.42	.06		.48	.56	922
	0100	Foil 2 sides		1,900	.004		.08	.06		.14	.19	
	0300	Asphalt, two ply, 30#, for subfloors		3,700	.002		.06	.03		.09	.12	
	0400	Asphalt felt sheathing paper, 15#		3,700	.002		.03	.03		.06	.08	
	0450	Housewrap, exterior, spun bonded polypropylene										
	0470	Small roll, 3' wide x 165'	1 Carp	3,800	.002	S.F.	.10	.03		.13	.16	
	0480	Large roll, 9' wide x 195'	"	4,000	.002	"	.09	.03		.12	.15	
	0500	Material only, 3' wide roll				Ea.	44			44	48	
	0520	9' wide roll				"	148			148	165	
	0600	Polyethylene vapor barrier, standard, .002" thick	1 Carp	3,700	.002	S.F.	.01	.03		.04	.06	
	0700	.004" thick		3,700	.002		.02	.03		.05	.07	
	0900	.006" thick		3,700	.002		.03	.03		.06	.08	
	1000	.008" thick		3,700	.002		.03	.03		.06	.08	
	1200	.010" thick		3,700	.002		.04	.03		.07	.10	
	1500	Red rosin paper, 5 sq. rolls, 4 lbs. per square		3,700	.002		.02	.03		.05	.07	
	1600	5 lbs. per square		3,700	.002		.03	.03		.06	.08	
	1800	Reinf. waterproof, .002" polyethylene backing, 1 side		3,700	.002		.04	.03		.07	.10	
	1900	2 sides		3,700	.002		.06	.03		.09	.12	
	3000	Building wrap, "TYVEK" type	2 Carp	8,000	.002		.06	.03		.09	.11	

For expanded coverage of these items see *Means Building Construction Cost Data 1991*

072 | Insulation

072 100 | Building Insulation

			CREW	DAILY OUTPUT	MAN-HOURS	UNIT	MAT.	LABOR	EQUIP.	TOTAL	TOTAL INCL O&P	
101	0010	**BLOWN-IN INSULATION** Ceilings, with open access										101
	0020	Cellulose, 3-½" thick, R13	G-4	5,000	.005	S.F.	.16	.06	.05	.27	.33	
	0030	5-³⁄₁₆" thick, R19		3,800	.006		.21	.08	.06	.35	.42	
	0050	6-½" thick, R22		3,000	.008		.28	.10	.08	.46	.56	
	1000	Fiberglass, 5" thick, R11		3,800	.006		.16	.08	.06	.30	.37	
	1050	6" thick, R13		3,000	.008		.19	.10	.08	.37	.46	
	1100	8-½" thick, R19		2,200	.011		.23	.13	.11	.47	.59	
	1300	12" thick, R26		1,500	.016		.38	.19	.15	.72	.91	
	2000	Mineral wool, 4" thick, R12		3,500	.007		.20	.08	.07	.35	.43	
	2050	6" thick, R17		2,500	.010		.31	.12	.09	.52	.63	
	2100	9" thick, R23	↓	1,750	.014	↓	.39	.16	.13	.68	.85	
	2500	Wall installation, incl. drilling & patching from outside, two 1"										
	2510	diam. holes @ 16" O.C., top & mid-point of wall										
	2700	For masonry	G-4	415	.058	S.F.	.05	.69	.56	1.30	1.84	
	2800	For wood siding		840	.029		.05	.34	.28	.67	.94	
	2900	For stucco/plaster		665	.036		.05	.43	.35	.83	1.17	
106	0010	**FLOOR INSULATION, NONRIGID** Including										106
	0020	spring type wire fasteners										
	2000	Fiberglass, blankets or batts, paper or foil backing										
	2100	1 side, 3-½" thick, R11	1 Carp	700	.011	S.F.	.22	.16		.38	.52	
	2150	6" thick, R19		600	.013		.37	.19		.56	.73	
	2200	8-½" thick, R30	↓	550	.015		.54	.21		.75	.94	
108	0010	**MASONRY INSULATION** Vermiculite or perlite, poured										108
	0100	In cores of concrete block, 4" thick wall, .115 C.F./S.F.	D-1	4,800	.003	S.F.	.17	.04		.21	.26	
	0700	Foamed in place, urethane in 2-⅝" cavity	G-2	1,035	.023		.18	.29	.22	.69	.92	
	0800	For each 1" added thickness, add	"	2,372	.010		.06	.13	.10	.29	.38	
109	0010	**PERIMETER INSULATION** Asphalt impregnated cork, ½" thick, R1.12	1 Carp	685	.012		.44	.17		.61	.76	109
	0100	1" thick, R2.24		685	.012		.65	.17		.82	.99	
	0600	Polystyrene, molded bead board, 1" thick, R4		685	.012		.27	.17		.44	.58	
	0700	2" thick, R8		685	.012	↓	.39	.17		.56	.71	
110	0010	**POURED INSULATION** Cellulose fiber, R3.8 per inch		200	.040	C.F.	.46	.57		1.03	1.46	110
	0080	Fiberglass wool, R4 per inch		200	.040		.32	.57		.89	1.31	
	0100	Mineral wool, R3 per inch		200	.040		.80	.57		1.37	1.84	
	0300	Polystyrene, R4 per inch		200	.040		1.64	.57		2.21	2.76	
	0400	Vermiculite or perlite, R2.7 per inch	↓	200	.040	↓	1.77	.57		2.34	2.90	
111	0010	**REFLECTIVE** Aluminum foil on 40 lb. kraft, foil 1 side, R9	1 Carp	1,900	.004	S.F.	.03	.06		.09	.13	111
	0100	Multilayered with air spaces, 2 ply, R14		1,900	.004		.15	.06		.21	.27	
	0500	3 ply, R17		1,500	.005		.19	.08		.27	.34	
	0600	5 ply, R22	↓	1,500	.005		.28	.08		.36	.44	
116	0010	**WALL INSULATION, RIGID**										116
	0040	Fiberglass, 1.5#/C.F., unfaced, 1" thick, R4.1	1 Carp	1,000	.008	S.F.	.18	.11		.29	.39	
	0060	1-½" thick, R6.2		1,000	.008		.29	.11		.40	.51	
	0080	2" thick, R8.3		1,000	.008		.38	.11		.49	.61	
	0120	3" thick, R12.4		800	.010		.59	.14		.73	.89	
	0370	3#/C.F., unfaced, 1" thick, R4.3		1,000	.008		.40	.11		.51	.63	
	0390	1-½" thick, R6.5		1,000	.008		.59	.11		.70	.84	
	0400	2" thick, R8.7		890	.009		.88	.13		1.01	1.18	
	0420	2-½" thick, R10.9		800	.010		1.05	.14		1.19	1.39	
	0440	3" thick, R13		800	.010		1.34	.14		1.48	1.71	
	0520	Foil faced, 1" thick, R4.3		1,000	.008		.79	.11		.90	1.06	
	0540	1-½" thick, R6.5		1,000	.008		1.14	.11		1.25	1.45	
	0560	2" thick, R8.7		890	.009		1.45	.13		1.58	1.81	
	0580	2-½" thick, R10.9		800	.010		1.70	.14		1.84	2.11	
	0600	3" thick, R13		800	.010		2.15	.14		2.29	2.60	
	0670	6#/C.F., unfaced, 1" thick, R4.3		1,000	.008		.75	.11		.86	1.02	
	0690	1-½" thick, R6.5		890	.009		1.14	.13		1.27	1.47	
	0700	2" thick, R8.7	↓	800	.010	↓	1.52	.14		1.66	1.91	

For expanded coverage of these items see *Means Building Construction Cost Data 1991*

072 | Insulation

072 100 | Building Insulation

			Crew	Daily Output	Man-Hours	Unit	Mat.	Labor	Equip.	Total	Total Incl O&P	
116	0721	2-½" thick, R10.9	1 Carp	800	.010	S.F.	1.91	.14		2.05	2.34	116
	0741	3" thick, R13		730	.011		2.30	.16		2.46	2.79	
	0821	Foil faced, 1" thick, R4.3		1,000	.008		.89	.11		1	1.17	
	0840	1-½" thick, R6.5		890	.009		1.12	.13		1.25	1.45	
	0850	2" thick, R8.7		800	.010		1.71	.14		1.85	2.12	
	0880	2-½" thick, R10.9		800	.010		2.20	.14		2.34	2.66	
	0900	3" thick, R13		730	.011		2.60	.16		2.76	3.12	
	1500	Foamglass, 1-½" thick, R2.64		800	.010		1.58	.14		1.72	1.98	
	1550	2" thick, R5.26	↓	730	.011	↓	2.21	.16		2.37	2.69	
	1600	Isocyanurate, 4' x 8' sheet, foil faced, both sides										
	1610	½" thick, R3.9	1 Carp	800	.010	S.F.	.27	.14		.41	.54	
	1620	⅝" thick, R4.5		800	.010		.32	.14		.46	.59	
	1630	¾" thick, R5.4		800	.010		.39	.14		.53	.67	
	1640	1" thick, R7.2		800	.010		.50	.14		.64	.79	
	1650	1-½" thick, R10.8		730	.011		.75	.16		.91	1.09	
	1660	2" thick, R14.4		730	.011		1	.16		1.16	1.36	
	1670	3" thick, R21.6		730	.011		1.49	.16		1.65	1.90	
	1680	4" thick, R28.8		730	.011		2	.16		2.16	2.46	
	1700	Perlite, 1" thick, R2.77		800	.010		.40	.14		.54	.68	
	1750	2" thick, R5.55		730	.011		.75	.16		.91	1.09	
	1900	Polystyrene, extruded blue, 2.2#/C.F., ¾" thick, R4		800	.010		.41	.14		.55	.69	
	1940	1-½" thick, R8.1		730	.011		.67	.16		.83	1	
	1960	2" thick, R10.8		730	.011		.88	.16		1.04	1.23	
	2100	Molded bead board, white, 1" thick, R3.85		800	.010		.17	.14		.31	.43	
	2120	1-½" thick, R5.6		730	.011		.27	.16		.43	.56	
	2140	2" thick, R7.7		730	.011		.34	.16		.50	.64	
	2350	Sheathing, insulating foil faced fiberboard, ⅜" thick	↓	670	.012	↓	.22	.17		.39	.53	
	2450											
	2510	Urethane, no paper backing, ½" thick, R2.9	1 Carp	800	.010	S.F.	.28	.14		.42	.55	
	2520	1" thick, R5.8		800	.010		.50	.14		.64	.79	
	2540	1-½" thick, R8.7		730	.011		.75	.16		.91	1.09	
	2560	2" thick, R11.7		730	.011		1	.16		1.16	1.36	
	2710	Fire resistant, ½" thick, R2.9		800	.010		.35	.14		.49	.62	
	2720	1" thick, R5.8		800	.010		.69	.14		.83	1	
	2740	1-½" thick, R8.7		730	.011		.97	.16		1.13	1.33	
	2760	2" thick, R11.7		730	.011		1.24	.16		1.40	1.63	
118	0010	**WALL OR CEILING INSUL., NON-RIGID**										118
	0040	Fiberglass, kraft faced, batts or blankets										
	0060	3-½" thick, R11, 11" wide	1 Carp	1,600	.005	S.F.	.25	.07		.32	.39	
	0140	6" thick, R19, 11" wide		1,350	.006		.39	.08		.47	.57	
	0200	9" thick, R30, 15" wide		1,350	.006		.60	.08		.68	.80	
	0240	12" thick, R38, 15" wide	↓	1,350	.006		.78	.08		.86	1	
	0400	Fiberglass, foil faced, batts or blankets										
	0420	3-½" thick, R11, 15" wide	1 Carp	1,600	.005	S.F.	.27	.07		.34	.42	
	0460	6" thick, R19, 15" wide		1,600	.005		.39	.07		.46	.55	
	0500	9" thick, R30, 15" wide		1,350	.006		.56	.08		.64	.76	
	0800	Fiberglass, unfaced, batts or blankets										
	0820	3-½" thick, R11, 15" wide	1 Carp	1,600	.005	S.F.	.21	.07		.28	.35	
	0860	6" thick, R19, 15" wide		1,350	.006		.36	.08		.44	.54	
	0900	9" thick, R30, 15" wide		1,150	.007		.54	.10		.64	.76	
	0940	12" thick, R38, 15" wide	↓	1,150	.007	↓	.79	.10		.89	1.04	
	1300	Mineral fiber batts, kraft faced										
	1320	3-½" thick, R13	1 Carp	1,600	.005	S.F.	.28	.07		.35	.43	
	1340	6" thick, R19		1,600	.005		.44	.07		.51	.60	
	1380	10" thick, R30	↓	1,350	.006	↓	.70	.08		.78	.91	
	1900	For foil backing, add						.04			.04	.04	

For expanded coverage of these items see *Means Building Construction Cost Data 1991*

072 | Insulation

072 200 | Roof & Deck Insulation

			CREW	DAILY OUTPUT	MAN-HOURS	UNIT	MAT.	LABOR	EQUIP.	TOTAL	TOTAL INCL O&P
203	0010	ROOF DECK INSULATION									
	0030	Fiberboard, mineral, 1" thick, R2.78	1 Rofc	800	.010	S.F.	.27	.13		.40	.53
	0080	1-½" thick, R4		800	.010		.44	.13		.57	.72
	0100	2" thick, R5.26		800	.010		.61	.13		.74	.91
	0300	Fiberglass, in 3' x 4' or 4' x 8' sheets									
	0400	15/16" thick, R3.3	1 Rofc	1,000	.008	S.F.	.39	.11		.50	.62
	0460	1-1/16" thick, R3.8		1,000	.008		.50	.11		.61	.74
	0600	1-5/16" thick, R5.3		1,000	.008		.62	.11		.73	.87
	0650	1-⅝" thick, R5.7		1,000	.008		.71	.11		.82	.97
	0700	1-⅞" thick, R7.7		1,000	.008		.76	.11		.87	1.03
	0800	2-¼" thick, R8		800	.010		.76	.13		.89	1.07
	1650	Perlite, 2' x 4' sheets									
	1655	¾" thick, R2.08	1 Rofc	800	.010	S.F.	.32	.13		.45	.59
	1660	1" thick, R2.78		800	.010		.37	.13		.50	.64
	1670	1-½" thick, R4.17		800	.010		.59	.13		.72	.89
	1680	2" thick, R5.26		700	.011		.75	.15		.90	1.10
	1700	Perlite/urethane composite									
	1711	1-¼" thick, R5.88	1 Rofc	1,000	.008	S.F.	.71	.11		.82	.97
	1721	1-½" thick, R7.2		1,000	.008		.76	.11		.87	1.03
	1730	1-¾" thick, R10		1,000	.008		.80	.11		.91	1.07
	1740	2" thick, R12.5		800	.010		.83	.13		.96	1.15
	1750	2-½" thick, R14.3		750	.011		.95	.14		1.09	1.30
	1760	3" thick, R20		700	.011		1.12	.15		1.27	1.50
	1900	Polystyrene									
	1910	Extruded, 2.3#/C.F., 1" thick, R5.26	1 Rofc	1,500	.005	S.F.	.50	.07		.57	.68
	1920	2" thick, R10		1,250	.006		.94	.08		1.02	1.19
	1930	3" thick, R15		1,000	.008		1.40	.11		1.51	1.73
	2010	Expanded bead board, 1" thick, R3.57		1,500	.005		.22	.07		.29	.37
	2100	2" thick, R7.14		1,250	.006		.33	.08		.41	.51

073 | Shingles and Roofing Tiles

073 100 | Shingles

			CREW	DAILY OUTPUT	MAN-HOURS	UNIT	MAT.	LABOR	EQUIP.	TOTAL	TOTAL INCL O&P
103	0010	MINERAL FIBER Strip shingles, 14" x 30", 325 lb. per square	1 Carp	4	2	Sq.	129	29		158	190
	0100	12" x 24", 167 lb. per square		3.50	2.290		65	33		98	125
	0200	Shakes, 9.35" x 16", 500 lb. per square (siding)		2.20	3.640		205	52		257	310
	0300	Hip & ridge shingles, 5-⅜" x 14"		100	.080	L.F.	3.15	1.14		4.29	5.40
	0400	Hexagonal shape, 16" x 16"		3	2.670	Sq.	130	38		168	205
	0500	Square, 16" x 16"		3	2.670		120	38		158	195
	2000	For steep roofs, add						50%			
104	0010	ASPHALT SHINGLES									
	0100	Standard strip shingles									
	0150	Inorganic, class A, 210-235 lb./square, 3 bundles/square	1 Rofc	5.50	1.450	Sq.	32	19.20		51.20	70
	0200	Organic, class C, 235-240 lb./square, 3 bundles/square	"	5	1.600	"	32.35	21		53.35	74
	0250	Standard, laminated multi-layered shingles									
	0300	Class A, 240-260 lb./square, 3 bundles/square	1 Rofc	4.50	1.780	Sq.	52.50	23		75.50	100
	0350	Class C, 260-300 lb./square, 4 bundles/square	"	4	2	"	47.85	26		73.85	100
	0400	Premium, laminated multi-layered shingles									
	0450	Class A, 260-300 lb./square, 4 bundles/square	1 Rofc	3.50	2.290	Sq.	77.80	30		107.80	140
	0500	Class C, 300-385 lb./square, 5 bundles/square	"	3	2.670	"	74.20	35		109.20	145

For expanded coverage of these items see *Means Building Construction Cost Data 1991*

073 | Shingles and Roofing Tiles

073 100 | Shingles

			CREW	DAILY OUTPUT	MAN-HOURS	UNIT	MAT.	LABOR	EQUIP.	TOTAL	TOTAL INCL O&P	
104	0700	Hip and ridge roll	1 Rofc	400	.020	L.F.	.57	.26		.83	1.10	104
	0900	Ridge shingles	"	330	.024	"	.65	.32		.97	1.29	
	1000	For steep roofs, add				Sq.		50%				
106	0010	**SLATE** Including felt underlay & nails, Buckingham, Virginia, black										106
	0100	3/16" thick	1 Rots	1.75	4.570	Sq.	350	61		411	495	
	0200	1/4" thick		1.75	4.570		350	61		411	495	
	0900	Pennsylvania black, Bangor, #1 clear		1.75	4.570		280	61		341	415	
	1200	Vermont, unfading colors, green, mottled green		1.75	4.570		390	61		451	540	
	1300	Semi-weathering green & gray		1.75	4.570		300	61		361	440	
	1400	Purple		1.75	4.570		450	61		511	605	
	1500	Black or gray		1.75	4.570		360	61		421	505	
	1510	For steep roofs, add to above						50%				
	1520											
	2700	Ridge shingles, slate	1 Rots	200	.040	L.F.	3.80	.53		4.33	5.15	
108	0010	**WOOD** 16" No. 1 red cedar shingles, 5X, 5" exposure, on roof	1 Carp	2.50	3.200	Sq.	105	46		151	190	108
	0200	7-1/2" exposure, on walls		2.05	3.900		76	56		132	175	
	0300	18" No. 1 red cedar perfections, 5-1/2" exposure, on roof		2.75	2.910		111	42		153	190	
	0500	7-1/2" exposure, on walls		2.25	3.560		81	51		132	175	
	0600	Resquared, and rebutted, 5-1/2" exposure, on roof		3	2.670		87	38		125	160	
	0900	7-1/2" exposure, on walls		2.45	3.270		62	47		109	145	
	1000	Add to above for fire retardant shingles, 16" long					30			30	33	
	1050	18" long					30			30	33	
	1100	Hand-split red cedar shakes, on roof, 24" long, 10" exposure	1 Carp	2.50	3.200		92	46		138	180	
	1200	18" long, 8-1/2" exposure	"	2	4		80	57		137	185	
	1700	Add to above for fire retardant shakes, 24" long					35			35	39	
	1800	18" long					30			30	33	
	2000	White cedar shingles, 16" long, extras, 5" exposure, on roof	1 Carp	2.40	3.330		105	48		153	195	
	2100	7-1/2" exposure, on walls		2	4		76	57		133	180	
	2150	"B" grade, 5" exposure on walls		2.40	3.330		66	48		114	150	
	2300	For #15 organic felt underlayment on roof, 1 layer, add		64	.125		2.80	1.79		4.59	6.05	
	2400	2 layers, add		32	.250		5.60	3.58		9.18	12.15	
	2600	For steep roofs, add to above						50%				
	3000	Ridge shakes or shingle wood	1 Carp	280	.029	L.F.	1.15	.41		1.56	1.95	

073 200 | Roofing Tile

			CREW	DAILY OUTPUT	MAN-HOURS	UNIT	MAT.	LABOR	EQUIP.	TOTAL	TOTAL INCL O&P	
202	0010	**CLAY TILE**										202
	0200	Lanai tile or Classic tile, 158 pcs. per sq.	1 Rots	1.65	4.850	Sq.	275	64		339	420	
	0300	Americana, 158 pcs. per sq., most colors		1.65	4.850		275	64		339	420	
	0350	Green, gray or brown		1.65	4.850		280	64		344	425	
	0400	Blue		1.65	4.850		650	64		714	830	
	0600	Spanish tile, 171 pcs. per sq., red		1.80	4.440		270	59		329	405	
	0800	Buff, green, gray, brown		1.80	4.440		380	59		439	525	
	0900	Blue		1.80	4.440		650	59		709	820	
	1100	Mission tile, 166 pcs. per sq., machine scored finish, red		1.15	6.960		405	93		498	610	
	1700	French tile, 133 pcs. per sq., smooth finish, red		1.35	5.930		390	79		469	570	
	1750	Blue or green		1.35	5.930		815	79		894	1,050	
	1800	Norman tile, 317 pcs. per sq.		1	8		890	105		995	1,175	
	2200	Williamsburg tile, 158 pcs. per sq., aged cedar		1.35	5.930		290	79		369	460	
	2250	Gray or green		1.35	5.930		290	79		369	460	
	2350	Ridge shingles, clay tile		200	.040	L.F.	4	.53		4.53	5.35	
	3000	For steep roofs, add to above				Sq.		50%				
204	0010	**CONCRETE TILE** Including installation of accessories	1 Rots	1.35	5.930	"	57	79		136	205	204
	0020	Corrugated, 13" x 16-1/2", 90 pcs. per sq., 950 lb. per sq.										
	0050	Earthtone colors, nailed to wood deck	1 Rots	1.35	5.930	Sq.	54	79		133	200	
	0150	Custom blues	"	1.35	5.930	"	200	79		279	360	

For expanded coverage of these items see *Means Building Construction Cost Data 1991*

073 | Shingles and Roofing Tiles

073 200 | Roofing Tile

		Crew	Daily Output	Man-Hours	Unit	Mat.	Labor	Equip.	Total	Total Incl O&P	
204	0200 Custom greens	1 Rots	1.35	5.930	Sq.	72	79		151	220	204
	0500 Shakes, 13" x 16-½", 90 per sq., 950 lb. per sq.										
	0600 All colors, nailed to wood deck	1 Rots	1.50	5.330	Sq.	73	71		144	210	
	1500 Accessory pieces, ridge & hip, 10" x 16-½", 8 lbs. each				Ea.	1.25			1.25	1.38	
	1700 Rake, 6-½" x 16-¾", 9 lbs. each					1.25			1.25	1.38	
	1800 Mansard hip, 10" x 16-½", 9.2 lbs. each					1.35			1.35	1.49	
	1900 Hip starter, 10" x 16-½", 10.5 lbs. each					2.75			2.75	3.03	
	2000 3 or 4 way apex, 10" each side, 11.5 lbs. each					5.75			5.75	6.35	

074 | Preformed Roofing and Siding

074 100 | Preformed Panels

		Crew	Daily Output	Man-Hours	Unit	Mat.	Labor	Equip.	Total	Total Incl O&P	
101	0010 **ALUMINUM ROOFING** Corrugated or ribbed, .0175" thick, natural	G-3	1,000	.032	S.F.	.58	.44	.03	1.05	1.40	101
	0300 Painted		1,000	.032		.73	.44	.03	1.20	1.56	
104	0010 **FIBERGLASS** Corrugated panels, roofing, 6 oz. per S.F.	↓	1,000	.032	↓	1.20	.44	.03	1.67	2.08	104
	0100 8 oz. per S.F.										
	0300 Corrugated siding, 4 oz. per S.F.	G-3	880	.036	S.F.	.95	.50	.03	1.48	1.92	
	0400 5 oz. per S.F.		880	.036		1.08	.50	.03	1.61	2.06	
	0600 8 oz. siding, textured		880	.036		1.55	.50	.03	2.08	2.58	
	0900 Flat panels, 6 oz. per S.F., clear or colors		880	.036		1.70	.50	.03	2.23	2.74	
	1300 8 oz. per S.F., clear or colors	↓	880	.036	↓	2.05	.50	.03	2.58	3.13	

074 600 | Cladding/Siding

		Crew	Daily Output	Man-Hours	Unit	Mat.	Labor	Equip.	Total	Total Incl O&P	
602	0011 **ALUMINUM SIDING**										602
	6040 .024 thick smooth white single 8" wide	F-2	515	.031	S.F.	.85	.44	.03	1.32	1.72	
	6060 Double 4" pattern 8" wide		515	.031		.89	.44	.03	1.36	1.76	
	6080 5" pattern 10" wide		550	.029		.95	.42	.03	1.40	1.78	
	6120 Embossed white single 8" wide		515	.031		.85	.44	.03	1.32	1.72	
	6140 Double 4" pattern 8" wide		515	.031		.90	.44	.03	1.37	1.77	
	6160 5" pattern 10" wide		550	.029		.96	.42	.03	1.41	1.79	
	6170 12" wide, embossed		590	.027		.95	.39	.03	1.37	1.73	
	6320 .019 thick insulated backed smooth white single 8" wide		515	.031		.95	.44	.03	1.42	1.83	
	6340 Double 4" pattern 8" wide		515	.031		.97	.44	.03	1.44	1.85	
	6360 5" pattern 10" wide		550	.029		.99	.42	.03	1.44	1.82	
	6400 Embossed white single 8" wide		515	.031		.97	.44	.03	1.44	1.85	
	6420 Double 4" pattern 8" wide		515	.031		.98	.44	.03	1.45	1.86	
	6440 5" pattern 10" wide		550	.029		1.02	.42	.03	1.47	1.85	
	6500 Shake finish 10" wide white		550	.029		1.05	.42	.03	1.50	1.89	
	6600 Vertical pattern 12" wide white	↓	590	.027		1	.39	.03	1.42	1.78	
	6640 For colors add				↓	.05			.05	.06	
	6700 Accessories white										
	6720 Starter strip 2-⅛"	F-2	610	.026	L.F.	.24	.38	.03	.65	.92	
	6740 Sill trim		450	.036		.26	.51	.04	.81	1.18	
	6760 Inside corner		610	.026		.75	.38	.03	1.16	1.49	
	6780 Outside corner post		610	.026		1.05	.38	.03	1.46	1.82	
	6800 Door & window trim	↓	440	.036		.25	.52	.04	.81	1.19	
	6820 For colors add					.05			.05	.06	
	6900 Soffit & fascia 1' overhang solid	F-2	110	.145		1.30	2.08	.15	3.53	5.05	
	6920 Vented		110	.145		1.30	2.08	.15	3.53	5.05	
	6940 2' overhang solid		100	.160		2	2.29	.16	4.45	6.20	
	6960 Vented	↓	100	.160		2	2.29	.16	4.45	6.20	

For expanded coverage of these items see *Means Building Construction Cost Data 1991*

074 | Preformed Roofing and Siding

074 600 | Cladding/Siding

			CREW	DAILY OUTPUT	MAN-HOURS	UNIT	MAT.	LABOR	EQUIP.	TOTAL	TOTAL INCL O&P	
606	0010	STEEL SIDING Beveled, vinyl coated, 8" wide	1 Carp	265	.030	S.F.	.69	.43		1.12	1.48	606
	0050	10" wide	"	270	.030		.66	.42		1.08	1.43	
	0100	28 gauge	G-3	775	.041		.52	.57	.03	1.12	1.55	
	0300	26 gauge		775	.041		.63	.57	.03	1.23	1.67	
	0400	24 gauge		775	.041		.75	.57	.03	1.35	1.81	
	0600	22 gauge		775	.041		.86	.57	.03	1.46	1.93	
	0700	Colored, corrugated/ribbed, on steel frame, 10 yr. fin., 28 ga.		775	.041		.70	.57	.03	1.30	1.75	
	0900	26 gauge		775	.041		.80	.57	.03	1.40	1.86	
	1000	24 gauge	↓	775	.041	↓	.92	.57	.03	1.52	1.99	
607	0010	VINYL SIDING Solid PVC panels, 8" to 10" wide, plain	1 Carp	255	.031	S.F.	.60	.45		1.05	1.41	607
	2000	Smooth, white, single, 8" wide	F-2	495	.032		.58	.46	.03	1.07	1.45	
	2020	10" wide		550	.029		.63	.42	.03	1.08	1.42	
	2100	Double 4" pattern, 8" wide		495	.032		.65	.46	.03	1.14	1.53	
	2120	5" pattern, 10" wide		550	.029		.68	.42	.03	1.13	1.48	
	2200	Embossed, white, single, 8" wide		495	.032		.62	.46	.03	1.11	1.49	
	2220	10" wide		550	.029		.66	.42	.03	1.11	1.46	
	2300	Double 4" pattern, 8" wide		495	.032		.68	.46	.03	1.17	1.56	
	2320	5" pattern, 10" wide		550	.029		.70	.42	.03	1.15	1.50	
	2400	Shake finish, 10" wide, white		550	.029		.68	.42	.03	1.13	1.48	
	2600	Vertical pattern, double 5", 10" wide, white	↓	550	.029	↓	.68	.42	.03	1.13	1.48	
	2620											
	2700	For colors, add				S.F.	.05			.05	.06	
	2720	For insulated backer, add	F-2	2,000	.008	"	.12	.11	.01	.24	.33	
	3000	Accessories, starter, strip		700	.023	L.F.	.21	.33	.02	.56	.80	
	3100	"J" channel, ½"		700	.023		.18	.33	.02	.53	.77	
	3120	⅝"		700	.023		.21	.33	.02	.56	.80	
	3140	¾"		695	.023		.22	.33	.02	.57	.82	
	3160	1"		690	.023		.23	.33	.02	.58	.83	
	3180	1-⅛"		685	.023		.25	.33	.02	.60	.86	
	3190	1-¼"		680	.024		.30	.34	.02	.66	.92	
	3200	Under sill trim		500	.032		.24	.46	.03	.73	1.06	
	3300	Outside corner post, 3" face, pocket ⅝"		700	.023		.85	.33	.02	1.20	1.51	
	3320	⅞"		690	.023		.88	.33	.02	1.23	1.55	
	3340	1-¼"		680	.024		.90	.34	.02	1.26	1.58	
	3400	Inside corner post, pocket ⅝"		700	.023		.45	.33	.02	.80	1.07	
	3420	⅞"		690	.023		.48	.33	.02	.83	1.11	
	3440	1-¼"		680	.024		.50	.34	.02	.86	1.14	
	3500	Door & window trim, 2-½" face, pocket ⅝"		510	.031		.45	.45	.03	.93	1.28	
	3520	⅞"		500	.032		.48	.46	.03	.97	1.33	
	3540	1-¼"		490	.033		.50	.47	.03	1	1.37	
	3600	Soffit & fascia, 1' overhang, solid		120	.133		1.35	1.91	.13	3.39	4.82	
	3620	Vented		120	.133		1.40	1.91	.13	3.44	4.87	
	3700	2' overhang, solid		110	.145		2.40	2.08	.15	4.63	6.30	
	3720	Vented	↓	110	.145	↓	2.54	2.08	.15	4.77	6.45	
609	0010	WOOD SIDING, BOARDS										609
	2000	Board & batten, cedar, "B" grade, 1" x 10"	1 Carp	400	.020	S.F.	.97	.29		1.26	1.55	
	2200	Redwood, clear, vertical grain, 1" x 10"		400	.020		1.55	.29		1.84	2.18	
	2400	White pine, #2 & better, 1" x 10"		400	.020		.64	.29		.93	1.18	
	2410	Board & batten siding, white pine #2, 1" x 12"		450	.018		.73	.25		.98	1.23	
	3200	Wood, cedar bevel, short lengths, A grade, ½" x 6"		250	.032		1.44	.46		1.90	2.35	
	3300	½" x 8"		275	.029		1.79	.42		2.21	2.66	
	3500	¾" x 10", clear grade, 3' to 16'		300	.027		1.59	.38		1.97	2.39	
	3600	"B" grade		300	.027		1.57	.38		1.95	2.36	
	3800	Cedar, rough sawn, 1" x 4", B & Btr., natural		240	.033		1.83	.48		2.31	2.81	
	3900	Stained		240	.033		1.88	.48		2.36	2.87	
	4100	1" x 12", board & batten, #3 & Btr., natural	↓	260	.031	↓	1.10	.44		1.54	1.95	

For expanded coverage of these items see *Means Building Construction Cost Data 1991*

074 | Preformed Roofing and Siding

074 600 | Cladding/Siding

			CREW	DAILY OUTPUT	MAN-HOURS	UNIT	MAT.	LABOR	EQUIP.	TOTAL	TOTAL INCL O&P	
609	4200	Stained	1 Carp	260	.031	S.F.	1.14	.44		1.58	1.99	609
	4400	1" x 8" channel siding, #3 & Btr., natural		250	.032		1.09	.46		1.55	1.96	
	4500	Stained		250	.032		1.14	.46		1.60	2.02	
	4700	Redwood, clear, beveled, vertical grain, ½" x 4"		200	.040		1.26	.57		1.83	2.34	
	4800	½" x 8"		250	.032		1.29	.46		1.75	2.18	
	5000	¾" x 10"		300	.027		1.73	.38		2.11	2.54	
	5200	Channel siding, 1" x 10", clear		285	.028		1.14	.40		1.54	1.93	
	5250	Redwood, T&G boards, clear, 1" x 4"	F-2	300	.053		2.29	.76	.05	3.10	3.85	
	5270	1" x 8"	"	375	.043		2.06	.61	.04	2.71	3.34	
	5400	White pine, rough sawn, 1" x 8", natural	1 Carp	275	.029		.52	.42		.94	1.27	
	5500	Stained	"	275	.029		.60	.42		1.02	1.36	
	5600	Tongue and groove, 1" x 8", horizontal	F-2	375	.043		.61	.61	.04	1.26	1.74	
611	0010	**WOOD SIDING, SHEETS**										611
	0030	Siding, hardboard, 7/16" thick, prime painted, lap,										
	0050	plain or grooved finish	F-2	750	.021	S.F.	.41	.31	.02	.74	.98	
	0100	Board finish, 7/16" thick, lap or grooved, primed		750	.021		.66	.31	.02	.99	1.26	
	0200	Stained		750	.021		.69	.31	.02	1.02	1.29	
	0700	Particle board, overlaid, ⅜" thick		750	.021		.55	.31	.02	.88	1.14	
	0900	Plywood, medium density overlaid, ⅜" thick		750	.021		.64	.31	.02	.97	1.23	
	1000	½" thick		700	.023		.70	.33	.02	1.05	1.34	
	1100	¾" thick		650	.025		.87	.35	.02	1.24	1.58	
	1600	Texture 1-11, cedar, ⅝" thick, natural		675	.024		.97	.34	.02	1.33	1.66	
	1700	Factory stained		675	.024		1.09	.34	.02	1.45	1.79	
	1900	Texture 1-11, fir, ⅝" thick, natural		675	.024		.52	.34	.02	.88	1.16	
	2000	Factory stained		675	.024		.59	.34	.02	.95	1.24	
	2050	Texture 1-11, S.Y.P., ⅝" thick, natural		675	.024		.57	.34	.02	.93	1.22	
	2100	Factory stained		675	.024		.64	.34	.02	1	1.29	
	2200	Rough sawn cedar, ⅜" thick, natural		675	.024		1.15	.34	.02	1.51	1.86	
	2300	Factory stained		675	.024		1.25	.34	.02	1.61	1.97	
	2500	Rough sawn fir, ⅜" thick, natural		675	.024		.42	.34	.02	.78	1.05	
	2600	Factory stained		675	.024		.49	.34	.02	.85	1.13	
	2800	Redwood, textured siding, ⅝" thick		675	.024		1.15	.34	.02	1.51	1.86	

075 | Membrane Roofing

075 100 | Built-Up Roofing

			CREW	DAILY OUTPUT	MAN-HOURS	UNIT	MAT.	LABOR	EQUIP.	TOTAL	TOTAL INCL O&P	
101	0010	**ASPHALT** Coated felt, #30, 2 sq. per roll, not mopped	1 Rofc	58	.138	Sq.	5	1.82		6.82	8.75	101
	0200	#15, 4 sq. per roll, plain or perforated, not mopped		58	.138		2.50	1.82		4.32	6	
	0250	Perforated		58	.138		2.50	1.82		4.32	6	
	0300	Roll roofing, smooth, #65		15	.533		10.25	7.05		17.30	24	
	0500	#90		15	.533		12	7.05		19.05	26	
	0520	Mineralized		15	.533		12.60	7.05		19.65	27	
	0540	D.C. (Double coverage), 19" selvage edge		10	.800		24	10.55		34.55	45	
	0580	Adhesive (lap cement)				Gal.	6.50			6.50	7.15	
102	0010	**BUILT-UP ROOFING**										102
	0120	Asphalt flood coat with gravel/slag surfacing, not including										
	0140	Insulation, flashing or wood nailers										
	0200	Asphalt base sheet, 3 plies #15 asphalt felt, mopped	G-1	22	2.550	Sq.	33.25	32	4.92	70.17	99	
	0350	On nailable decks		21	2.670		34.75	33	5.15	72.90	105	
	0500	4 plies #15 asphalt felt, mopped		20	2.800		36	35	5.40	76.40	110	
	0550	On nailable decks		19	2.950		34.75	37	5.70	77.45	110	
	2000	Asphalt flood coat, smooth surface										

For expanded coverage of these items see *Means Building Construction Cost Data 1991*

075 | Membrane Roofing

075 100 | Built-Up Roofing

			CREW	DAILY OUTPUT	MAN-HOURS	UNIT	MAT.	LABOR	EQUIP.	TOTAL	TOTAL INCL O&P	
102	2200	Asphalt base sheet & 3 plies #15 asphalt felt, mopped	G-1	24	2.330	Sq.	29	29	4.51	62.51	89	102
	2400	On nailable decks		23	2.430		28	30	4.70	62.70	91	
	2600	4 plies #15 asphalt felt, mopped		24	2.330		29.50	29	4.51	63.01	90	
	2700	On nailable decks		23	2.430		28	30	4.70	62.70	91	
	4500	Coal tar pitch with gravel/slag surfacing										
	4600	4 plies #15 tarred felt, mopped	G-1	22	2.550	Sq.	60	32	4.92	96.92	130	
	4800	3 plies glass fiber felt (type IV), mopped	"	20	2.800	"	49.20	35	5.40	89.60	125	
103	0010	CANTS 4" x 4" treated timber, cut diagonally	1 Rofc	325	.025	L.F.	.54	.32		.86	1.18	103
	0100	Foamglass		325	.025		.52	.32		.84	1.16	
	0300	Mineral or fiber, trapezoidal, 1"x 4" x 48"		325	.025		.15	.32		.47	.75	
	0400	1-½" x 5-⅝" x 48"		325	.025		.25	.32		.57	.86	

075 200 | Prepared Roll Roofing

			CREW	DAILY OUTPUT	MAN-HOURS	UNIT	MAT.	LABOR	EQUIP.	TOTAL	TOTAL INCL O&P	
204	0010	ROLL ROOFING										204
	0100	Asphalt, mineral surface										
	0200	1 ply #15 organic felt, 1 ply mineral surfaced										
	0300	selvage roofing, lap 19", nailed & mopped	G-1	27	2.070	Sq.	33	26	4.01	63.01	87	
	0400	3 plies glass fiber felt (type IV), 1 ply mineral surfaced										
	0500	selvage roofing, lapped 19", mopped	G-1	25	2.240	Sq.	51	28	4.33	83.33	110	
	0600	Coated glass fiber base sheet, 2 plies of glass fiber										
	0700	felt (type IV), 1 ply mineral surfaced selvage										
	0800	roofing, lapped 19", mopped	G-1	25	2.240	Sq.	52.50	28	4.33	84.83	115	
	0900	On nailable decks	"	24	2.330	"	50	29	4.51	83.51	110	
	1000	3 plies glass fiber felt (type III), 1 ply mineral surfaced										
	1100	selvage roofing, lapped 19", mopped	G-1	25	2.240	Sq.	47.80	28	4.33	80.13	110	

075 600 | Roof Maint. & Repairs

						UNIT	MAT.			TOTAL	TOTAL INCL O&P	
604	0010	ROOF COATINGS Asphalt				Gal.	2.75			2.75	3.03	604
	0800	Glass fibered roof & patching cement, 5 gallon					6.50			6.50	7.15	
	1100	Roof patch & flashing cement, 5 gallon					16.95			16.95	18.65	

076 | Flashing and Sheet Metal

076 100 | Sheet Metal Roofing

			CREW	DAILY OUTPUT	MAN-HOURS	UNIT	MAT.	LABOR	EQUIP.	TOTAL	TOTAL INCL O&P	
101	0010	COPPER ROOFING Batten seam, over 10 sq., 16 oz., 130 lb./sq.	1 Shee	1.10	7.270	Sq.	395	120		515	630	101
	0200	18 oz., 145 lb. per sq.		1	8		440	130		570	700	
	0400	Standing seam, over 10 squares, 16 oz., 125 lb. per sq.		1.30	6.150		395	100		495	600	
	0600	18 oz., 140 lb. per sq.		1.20	6.670		440	110		550	665	
	0900	Flat seam, over 10 squares, 16 oz., 115 lb. per sq.		1.20	6.670		365	110		475	580	
	1200	For abnormal conditions or small areas, add					25%	100%				
	1300	For lead-coated copper, add					20%					
103	0010	MONEL ROOFING Batten seam, over 10 squares, .018" thick	1 Shee	1.20	6.670	Sq.	400	110		510	620	103
	0100	.021" thick		1.15	6.960		420	115		535	650	
	0300	Standing seam, .018" thick		1.35	5.930		455	96		551	660	
	0400	.021" thick		1.30	6.150		495	100		595	710	
	0600	Flat seam, .018" thick		1.30	6.150		450	100		550	660	
	0700	.021" thick		1.20	6.670		500	110		610	730	
105	0010	ZINC Copper alloy roofing, batten seam, .020" thick		1.20	6.670		525	110		635	755	105
	0100	.027" thick		1.15	6.960		635	115		750	885	

For expanded coverage of these items see *Means Building Construction Cost Data 1991*

076 | Flashing and Sheet Metal

076 100 | Sheet Metal Roofing

			CREW	DAILY OUTPUT	MAN-HOURS	UNIT	MAT.	LABOR	EQUIP.	TOTAL	TOTAL INCL O&P	
105	0300	.032" thick	1 Shee	1.10	7.270	Sq.	715	120		835	985	105
	0400	.040" thick	"	1.05	7.620		845	125		970	1,125	
	0600	For standing seam construction, deduct					2%					
	0700	For flat seam construction, deduct					3%					

076 200 | Sheet Mtl Flash & Trim

			CREW	DAILY OUTPUT	MAN-HOURS	UNIT	MAT.	LABOR	EQUIP.	TOTAL	TOTAL INCL O&P	
201	0010	DOWNSPOUTS Aluminum 2" x 3", .020" thick, embossed	1 Shee	190	.042	L.F.	.52	.68		1.20	1.71	201
	0100	Enameled		190	.042		.55	.68		1.23	1.74	
	0300	Enameled, .024" thick, 2" x 3"		190	.042		.53	.68		1.21	1.72	
	0400	3" x 4"		140	.057		.85	.93		1.78	2.48	
	0600	Round, corrugated aluminum, 3" diameter, .020" thick		190	.042		.65	.68		1.33	1.85	
	0700	4" diameter, .025" thick		140	.057		.95	.93		1.88	2.59	
	0900	Wire strainer, round, 2" diameter		155	.052	Ea.	.76	.84		1.60	2.23	
	1000	4" diameter		155	.052		1.05	.84		1.89	2.55	
	1200	Rectangular, perforated, 2" x 3"		145	.055		1.45	.90		2.35	3.08	
	1300	3" x 4"		145	.055		2.35	.90		3.25	4.07	
	1500	Copper, round, 16 oz., stock, 2" diameter		190	.042	L.F.	3.15	.68		3.83	4.60	
	1600	3" diameter		190	.042		4.25	.68		4.93	5.80	
	1800	4" diameter		145	.055		5.40	.90		6.30	7.45	
	1900	5" diameter		130	.062		5.55	1		6.55	7.75	
	2100	Rectangular, corrugated copper, stock, 2" x 3"		190	.042		4.60	.68		5.28	6.20	
	2200	3" x 4"		145	.055		6.20	.90		7.10	8.30	
	2400	Rectangular, plain copper, stock, 2" x 3"		190	.042		4.75	.68		5.43	6.35	
	2500	3" x 4"		145	.055		5.80	.90		6.70	7.85	
	2700	Wire strainers, rectangular, 2" x 3"		145	.055	Ea.	2.40	.90		3.30	4.13	
	2800	3" x 4"		145	.055		3.80	.90		4.70	5.65	
	3000	Round, 2" diameter		145	.055		2.30	.90		3.20	4.02	
	3100	3" diameter		145	.055		3.30	.90		4.20	5.10	
	3300	4" diameter		145	.055		5.10	.90		6	7.10	
	3400	5" diameter		115	.070		7.05	1.13		8.18	9.65	
	3600	Lead-coated copper, round, stock, 2" diameter		190	.042	L.F.	4.10	.68		4.78	5.65	
	3700	3" diameter		190	.042		4.95	.68		5.63	6.60	
	3900	4" diameter		145	.055		6.10	.90		7	8.20	
	4300	Rectangular, corrugated, stock, 2" x 3"		190	.042		6.70	.68		7.38	8.50	
	4500	Plain, stock, 2" x 3"		190	.042		5.40	.68		6.08	7.05	
	4600	3" x 4"		145	.055		7	.90		7.90	9.20	
	4800	Steel, galvanized, round, corrugated, 2" or 3" diam., 28 ga.		190	.042		.45	.68		1.13	1.63	
	4900	4" diameter, 28 gauge		145	.055		.57	.90		1.47	2.11	
	5700	Rectangular, corrugated, 28 gauge, 2" x 3"		190	.042		.45	.68		1.13	1.63	
	5800	3" x 4"		145	.055		1.25	.90		2.15	2.86	
	6000	Rectangular, plain, 28 gauge, galvanized, 2" x 3"		190	.042		.45	.68		1.13	1.63	
	6100	3" x 4"		145	.055		1.25	.90		2.15	2.86	
	6300	Epoxy painted, 24 gauge, corrugated, 2" x 3"		190	.042		.80	.68		1.48	2.01	
	6400	3" x 4"		145	.055		1.33	.90		2.23	2.95	
	6600	Wire strainers, rectangular, 2" x 3"		145	.055	Ea.	1.35	.90		2.25	2.97	
	6700	3" x 4"		145	.055		2.18	.90		3.08	3.88	
	6900	Round strainers, 2" or 3" diameter		145	.055		.95	.90		1.85	2.53	
	7000	4" diameter		145	.055		1.18	.90		2.08	2.78	
	7200	5" diameter		145	.055		1.75	.90		2.65	3.41	
	7300	6" diameter		115	.070		2.15	1.13		3.28	4.24	
	8200	Vinyl, rectangular, 2" x 3"		210	.038	L.F.	.83	.62		1.45	1.94	
	8300	Round, 2-½"		220	.036		.83	.59		1.42	1.89	
202	0010	DRIP EDGE Aluminum, .016" thick, 5" girth, mill finish	1 Carp	400	.020		.13	.29		.42	.62	202
	0100	White finish		400	.020		.15	.29		.44	.64	
	0200	8" girth		400	.020		.27	.29		.56	.78	
	0300	28" girth		100	.080		1.18	1.14		2.32	3.21	
	0400	Galvanized, 5" girth		400	.020		.21	.29		.50	.71	
	0500	8" girth		400	.020		.26	.29		.55	.76	

For expanded coverage of these items see *Means Building Construction Cost Data 1991*

076 | Flashing and Sheet Metal

076 200 | Sheet Mtl Flash & Trim

			CREW	DAILY OUTPUT	MAN-HOURS	UNIT	MAT.	LABOR	EQUIP.	TOTAL	TOTAL INCL O&P	
203	0010	**ELBOWS** Aluminum, 2" x 3", embossed	1 Shee	100	.080	Ea.	.51	1.30		1.81	2.72	203
	0100	Enameled		100	.080		.51	1.30		1.81	2.72	
	0200	3" x 4", .025" thick, embossed		100	.080		.80	1.30		2.10	3.04	
	0300	Enameled		100	.080		.80	1.30		2.10	3.04	
	0400	Round corrugated, 3", embossed, .020" thick		100	.080		.75	1.30		2.05	2.98	
	0500	4", .025" thick		100	.080		.87	1.30		2.17	3.11	
	0600	Copper, 16 oz. round, 2" diameter		100	.080		4.25	1.30		5.55	6.85	
	0700	3" diameter		100	.080		5.30	1.30		6.60	8	
	0800	4" diameter		100	.080		9.40	1.30		10.70	12.50	
	1000	2" x 3" corrugated		100	.080		9	1.30		10.30	12.05	
	1100	3" x 4" corrugated		100	.080		12.70	1.30		14	16.15	
	1300	Vinyl, 2-½" diameter, 45° or 75°		100	.080		2.30	1.30		3.60	4.69	
	1400	Tee Y junction	↓	75	.107	↓	12.30	1.73		14.03	16.40	
204	0010	**FLASHING** Aluminum, mill finish, .013" thick	1 Shee	145	.055	S.F.	.26	.90		1.16	1.77	204
	0030	.016" thick		145	.055		.30	.90		1.20	1.82	
	0060	.019" thick		145	.055		.65	.90		1.55	2.20	
	0100	.032" thick		145	.055		.78	.90		1.68	2.34	
	0200	.040" thick		145	.055		1.32	.90		2.22	2.94	
	0300	.050" thick	↓	145	.055		1.60	.90		2.50	3.25	
	0400	Painted finish, add					.15			.15	.17	
	1600	Copper, 16 oz., sheets, under 6000 lbs.	1 Shee	115	.070		2.60	1.13		3.73	4.73	
	1900	20 oz. sheets, under 6000 lbs.		110	.073		3.25	1.18		4.43	5.55	
	2200	24 oz. sheets, under 6000 lbs.		105	.076		3.90	1.24		5.14	6.35	
	2500	32 oz. sheets, under 6000 lbs.		100	.080		5.05	1.30		6.35	7.70	
	2800	Copper, paperbacked 1 side, 2 oz.		330	.024		1	.39		1.39	1.75	
	2900	3 oz.		330	.024		1.35	.39		1.74	2.14	
	3100	Paperbacked 2 sides, copper, 2 oz.		330	.024		1	.39		1.39	1.75	
	3150	3 oz.		330	.024		1.45	.39		1.84	2.25	
	3200	5 oz.	↓	330	.024		2.25	.39		2.64	3.13	
	5800	Lead, 2.5 lb. per S.F., up to 12" wide	1 Rofc	135	.059		3.15	.78		3.93	4.87	
	5900	Over 12" wide	"	135	.059		3.15	.78		3.93	4.87	
	6100	Lead-coated copper, fabric-backed, 2 oz.	1 Shee	330	.024		1.25	.39		1.64	2.03	
	6200	5 oz.		330	.024		1.45	.39		1.84	2.25	
	6400	Mastic-backed 2 sides, 2 oz.		330	.024		.87	.39		1.26	1.61	
	6500	5 oz.		330	.024		1.40	.39		1.79	2.19	
	6700	Paperbacked 1 side, 2 oz.		330	.024		.80	.39		1.19	1.53	
	6800	3 oz.		330	.024		.98	.39		1.37	1.73	
	7000	Paperbacked 2 sides, 2 oz.		330	.024		.88	.39		1.27	1.62	
	7100	5 oz.		330	.024		1.45	.39		1.84	2.25	
	8500	Shower pan, bituminous membrane, 7 oz.		155	.052		1.05	.84		1.89	2.55	
	8550	3 ply copper and fabric, 3 oz.		155	.052		1.85	.84		2.69	3.43	
	8600	7 oz.		155	.052		3.40	.84		4.24	5.15	
	8650	Copper, 16 oz.		100	.080		2.70	1.30		4	5.15	
	8700	Lead on copper and fabric, 5 oz.		155	.052		2.15	.84		2.99	3.76	
	8800	7 oz.		155	.052		2.45	.84		3.29	4.09	
	8900	Stainless steel sheets, 32 ga., .010" thick		155	.052		1.85	.84		2.69	3.43	
	9000	28 ga., .015" thick		155	.052		2.30	.84		3.14	3.92	
	9100	26 ga., .018" thick		155	.052		2.85	.84		3.69	4.53	
	9200	24 ga., .025" thick	↓	155	.052		3.45	.84		4.29	5.20	
	9290	For mechanically keyed flashing, add					40%					
	9300	Stainless steel, paperbacked 2 sides, .005" thick	1 Shee	330	.024		1.15	.39		1.54	1.92	
	9320	Steel sheets, galvanized, 20 gauge		130	.062		.55	1		1.55	2.26	
	9340	30 gauge		160	.050		.22	.81		1.03	1.59	
	9400	Terne coated stainless steel, .015" thick, 28 ga.		155	.052		1.60	.84		2.44	3.15	
	9500	.018" thick, 26 ga.		155	.052		1.80	.84		2.64	3.37	
	9600	Zinc and copper alloy, .020" thick		155	.052		1.35	.84		2.19	2.88	
	9700	.027" thick	↓	155	.052	↓	1.80	.84		2.64	3.37	

For expanded coverage of these items see *Means Building Construction Cost Data 1991*

076 | Flashing and Sheet Metal

076 200 | Sheet Mtl Flash & Trim

			CREW	DAILY OUTPUT	MAN-HOURS	UNIT	MAT.	LABOR	EQUIP.	TOTAL	TOTAL INCL O&P	
204	9800	.032" thick	1 Shee	155	.052	S.F.	2.10	.84		2.94	3.70	204
	9900	.040" thick		155	.052	"	2.55	.84		3.39	4.20	
205	0010	GUTTERS Aluminum, stock units, 5" box, .027" thick, plain		120	.067	L.F.	.80	1.08		1.88	2.68	205
	0020	Inside corner		25	.320	Ea.	2.20	5.20		7.40	11.05	
	0030	Outside corner		25	.320	"	2.20	5.20		7.40	11.05	
	0100	Enameled		120	.067	L.F.	.90	1.08		1.98	2.79	
	0110	Inside corner		25	.320	Ea.	2.25	5.20		7.45	11.10	
	0120	Outside corner		25	.320	"	2.25	5.20		7.45	11.10	
	0300	5" box type, .032" thick, plain		120	.067	L.F.	1	1.08		2.08	2.90	
	0310	Inside corner		25	.320	Ea.	2.35	5.20		7.55	11.20	
	0320	Outside corner		25	.320	"	2.35	5.20		7.55	11.20	
	0400	Enameled		120	.067	L.F.	1	1.08		2.08	2.90	
	0410	Inside corner		25	.320	Ea.	2.45	5.20		7.65	11.30	
	0420	Outside corner		25	.320	"	2.45	5.20		7.65	11.30	
	0600	5" x 6" combination fascia & gutter, .032" thick, enameled		60	.133	L.F.	2.60	2.17		4.77	6.45	
	0700	Copper, half round, 16 oz., stock units, 4" wide		120	.067		4.05	1.08		5.13	6.25	
	0900	5" wide		120	.067		4.10	1.08		5.18	6.30	
	1000	6" wide		115	.070		4.55	1.13		5.68	6.90	
	1200	K type copper gutter, stock, 4" wide		120	.067		4.40	1.08		5.48	6.65	
	1300	5" wide		120	.067		4.80	1.08		5.88	7.10	
	1500	Lead coated copper, half round, stock, 4" wide		120	.067		4.70	1.08		5.78	6.95	
	1600	6" wide		115	.070		5.70	1.13		6.83	8.15	
	1800	K type lead coated copper, stock, 4" wide		120	.067		5.50	1.08		6.58	7.85	
	1900	5" wide		120	.067		6	1.08		7.08	8.40	
	2100	Stainless steel, half round or box, stock, 4" wide		120	.067		4.50	1.08		5.58	6.75	
	2200	5" wide		120	.067		4.90	1.08		5.98	7.20	
	2400	Steel, galv., half round or box, 28 ga., 5" wide, plain		120	.067		.62	1.08		1.70	2.48	
	2500	Enameled		120	.067		.66	1.08		1.74	2.52	
	2700	26 ga. galvanized steel, stock, 5" wide		120	.067		.75	1.08		1.83	2.62	
	2800	6" wide		120	.067		.95	1.08		2.03	2.84	
	3000	Vinyl, O.G., 4" wide	1 Carp	110	.073		.88	1.04		1.92	2.71	
	3100	5" wide		110	.073		1.04	1.04		2.08	2.88	
	3200	4" half round, stock units		110	.073		.63	1.04		1.67	2.43	
	3250	Joint connectors				Ea.	1.50			1.50	1.65	
	3300	Wood, clear treated cedar, fir or hemlock, 3" x 4"	1 Carp	100	.080	L.F.	3.85	1.14		4.99	6.15	
	3400	4" x 5"		100	.080		4.85	1.14		5.99	7.25	
206	0010	GUTTER GUARD 6" wide strip, aluminum mesh		500	.016		.39	.23		.62	.81	206
	0100	Vinyl mesh		500	.016		.15	.23		.38	.55	
217	0010	SOFFIT Aluminum, residential, stock units, .020" thick		210	.038	S.F.	.65	.54		1.19	1.63	217
	0100	Baked enamel on steel, 16 or 18 gauge		105	.076		3.95	1.09		5.04	6.15	
	0300	Polyvinyl chloride, white, solid		230	.035		.50	.50		1	1.38	
	0400	Perforated		230	.035		.51	.50		1.01	1.39	
	0500	For colors, add					.02			.02	.02	
219	0010	TERMITE SHIELDS Zinc, 10" wide, .012" thick	1 Carp	350	.023	L.F.	1	.33		1.33	1.65	219
	0100	.020" thick	"	350	.023	"	.70	.33		1.03	1.32	

077 | Roof Specialties and Accessories

077 100 | Prefab Roof Specialties

			CREW	DAILY OUTPUT	MAN-HOURS	UNIT	MAT.	LABOR	EQUIP.	TOTAL	TOTAL INCL O&P	
104	0010	FASCIA Aluminum, reverse board and batten,										104
	0100	.032" thick, colored, no furring included	1 Shee	145	.055	S.F.	1.70	.90		2.60	3.36	

For expanded coverage of these items see *Means Building Construction Cost Data 1991*

077 | Roof Specialties and Accessories

077 100 | Prefab Roof Specialties

		Crew	Daily Output	Man-Hours	Unit	Mat.	Labor	Equip.	Total	Total Incl O&P	
104	0200	Residential type, aluminum	1 Carp	200	.040	L.F.	1.15	.57		1.72	2.22	104
	0300	Steel, galv. and enameled, stock, no furring, long panels	1 Shee	145	.055	S.F.	1.90	.90		2.80	3.58	
	0600	Short panels	"	115	.070	"	3.05	1.13		4.18	5.25	
105	0010	GRAVEL STOP Aluminum, .050" thick, 4" height, mill finish	1 Shee	145	.055	L.F.	2.35	.90		3.25	4.07	105
	0080	Duranodic finish		145	.055		3.15	.90		4.05	4.95	
	0100	Painted		145	.055		3.60	.90		4.50	5.45	
	1350	Galv. steel, 24 ga., 4" leg, plain, with continuous cleat, 4" face		145	.055		1.70	.90		2.60	3.36	
	1500	Polyvinyl chloride, 6" face height		135	.059		2.65	.96		3.61	4.51	
	1800	Stainless steel, 24 ga., 6" face height		135	.059		6	.96		6.96	8.20	

078 | Skylights

078 100 | Plastic Skylights

		Crew	Daily Output	Man-Hours	Unit	Mat.	Labor	Equip.	Total	Total Incl O&P	
101	0010	SKYLIGHT Plastic roof domes, flush or curb mounted, ten or										101
	0100	more units, curb not included, "L" frames										
	0300	Nominal size under 10 S.F., double	G-3	130	.246	S.F.	20	3.40	.19	23.59	28	
	0400	Single		160	.200		15.50	2.76	.16	18.42	22	
	0600	10 S.F. to 20 S.F., double		315	.102		15.20	1.40	.08	16.68	19.15	
	0700	Single		395	.081		12.35	1.12	.06	13.53	15.50	
	0900	20 S.F. to 30 S.F., double		395	.081		14.30	1.12	.06	15.48	17.65	
	1000	Single		465	.069		11	.95	.05	12	13.75	
	1200	30 S.F. to 65 S.F., double		465	.069		13.40	.95	.05	14.40	16.40	
	1300	Single		610	.052		11	.72	.04	11.76	13.35	
	1500	For insulated 4" curbs, double, add					25%					
	1600	Single, add					30%					
	1800	For integral insulated 9" curbs, double, add					30%					
	1900	Single, add					40%					
	2120	Ventilating insulated plexiglass dome with										
	2130	curb mounting, 36" x 36"	G-3	12	2.670	Ea.	300	37	2.09	339.09	395	
	2150	52" x 52"		12	2.670		450	37	2.09	489.09	560	
	2160	28" x 52"		10	3.200		350	44	2.51	396.51	460	
	2170	36" x 52"		10	3.200		380	44	2.51	426.51	495	
	2180	For electric opening system, add					225			225	250	
	2210	Operating skylight, with thermopane glass, 24" x 48"	G-3	10	3.200		440	44	2.51	486.51	560	
	2220	32" x 48"	"	9	3.560		460	49	2.79	511.79	590	
	2310	Non venting insulated plexiglass dome skylight with										
	2320	Flush mount 22" x 46"	G-3	15.23	2.100	Ea.	255	29	1.65	285.65	330	
	2330	30" x 30"		16	2		235	28	1.57	264.57	305	
	2340	46" x 46"		13.91	2.300		430	32	1.81	463.81	530	
	2350	Curb mount 22" x 46"		15.23	2.100		215	29	1.65	245.65	285	
	2360	30" x 30"		16	2		205	28	1.57	234.57	275	
	2370	46" x 46"		13.91	2.300		385	32	1.81	418.81	480	
	2381	Non-insulated flush mount 22" x 46"		15.23	2.100		165	29	1.65	195.65	230	
	2382	30" x 30"		16	2		150	28	1.57	179.57	215	
	2383	46" x 46"		13.91	2.300		280	32	1.81	313.81	365	
	2384	Curb mount 22" x 46"		15.23	2.100		140	29	1.65	170.65	205	
	2385	30" x 30"		16	2		135	28	1.57	164.57	195	

For expanded coverage of these items see *Means Building Construction Cost Data 1991*

079 | Joint Sealers

079 204 | Sealants & Caulkings

		CREW	DAILY OUTPUT	MAN-HOURS	UNIT	MAT.	LABOR	EQUIP.	TOTAL	TOTAL INCL O&P
0010	CAULKING AND SEALANTS									
0020	Acoustical sealant, elastomeric				Gal.	14.50			14.50	15.95
0100	Caulking compound, oil base, bulk									
0200	Brilliant white color				Gal.	10.85			10.85	11.95
0300	Aluminum pigment and other colors				"	14			14	15.40
0500	Bulk, in place, ¼" x ½", 154 L.F./gal.	1 Bric	260	.031	L.F.	.07	.46		.53	.83
0600	½" x ½", 77 L.F./gal.		250	.032		.14	.47		.61	.93
0800	¾" x ¾", 34 L.F./gal.		230	.035		.32	.51		.83	1.20
0900	¾" x 1", 26 L.F./gal.		200	.040		.42	.59		1.01	1.44
1000	1" x 1", 19 L.F./gal.		180	.044		.57	.66		1.23	1.71
1100	Acrylic latex based, bulk				Gal.	12.50			12.50	13.75
1200	Cartridges					17.25			17.25	19
1400	Butyl based, bulk					13.50			13.50	14.85
1500	Cartridges					21			21	23
1700	Bulk, in place ¼" x ½", 154 L.F./gal.	1 Bric	230	.035	L.F.	.09	.51		.60	.95
1800	½" x ½", 77 L.F./gal.	"	180	.044	"	.18	.66		.84	1.28
2000	Latex acrylic based, bulk				Gal.	12.50			12.50	13.75
2100	Cartridges				"	17.25			17.25	19
2200	Bulk in place, ¼" x ½", 154 L.F./gal.	1 Bric	230	.035	L.F.	.11	.51		.62	.97
2300	Polysulfide compounds, 1 component, bulk				Gal.	27.50			27.50	30
2400	Cartridges				"	34.50			34.50	38
2600	1 or 2 component, in place, ¼" x ¼", 308 L.F./gal.	1 Bric	145	.055	L.F.	.10	.82		.92	1.45
2700	½" x ¼", 154 L.F./gal.		135	.059		.21	.88		1.09	1.67
2900	¾" x ⅜", 68 L.F./gal.		130	.062		.47	.91		1.38	2.01
3000	1" x ½", 38 L.F./gal.		130	.062		.82	.91		1.73	2.40
3200	Polyurethane, 1 or 2 component, bulk				Gal.	35.75			35.75	39
3300	Cartridges				"	42.50			42.50	47
3500	1 or 2 component, in place, ¼" x ¼", 308 L.F./gal.	1 Bric	150	.053	L.F.	.11	.79		.90	1.42
3600	½" x ¼", 154 L.F./gal.		145	.055		.24	.82		1.06	1.61
3800	¾" x ⅜", 68 L.F./gal.		130	.062		.54	.91		1.45	2.09
3900	1" x ½", 38 L.F./gal.		110	.073		.98	1.08		2.06	2.85
4100	Silicone rubber, bulk				Gal.	29.75			29.75	33
4200	Cartridges				"	40.15			40.15	44

081 | Metal Doors and Frames

081 100 | Steel Doors And Frames

		CREW	DAILY OUTPUT	MAN-HOURS	UNIT	MAT.	LABOR	EQUIP.	TOTAL	TOTAL INCL O&P
0010	FIRE DOOR Steel, flush, "B" label, 90 minute									
0020	Full panel, 20 ga., 2'-0" x 6'-8"	F-2	20	.800	Ea.	165	11.45	.80	177.25	200
0040	2'-8" x 6'-8"		18	.889		170	12.70	.89	183.59	210
0060	3'-0" x 6'-8"		17	.941		175	13.45	.94	189.39	215
0080	3'-0" x 7'-0"		17	.941		184	13.45	.94	198.39	225
0140	18 ga., 3'-0" x 6'-8"		16	1		198	14.30	1	213.30	245
0160	2'-8" x 7'-0"		17	.941		198	13.45	.94	212.39	240
0180	3'-0" x 7'-0"		16	1		205	14.30	1	220.30	250
0200	4'-0" x 7'-0"		15	1.070		240	15.25	1.07	256.32	290
0210										
0220	For "A" label, 3 hour, 18 ga., use same price as "B" label									
0240	For vision lite, add				Ea.	40			40	44
0520	Flush, "B" label 90 min., composite, 20 ga., 2'-0" x 6'-8"	F-2	18	.889		175	12.70	.89	188.59	215
0540	2'-8" x 6'-8"	"	17	.941		175	13.45	.94	189.39	215

For expanded coverage of these items see *Means Building Construction Cost Data 1991*

081 | Metal Doors and Frames

081 100 | Steel Doors And Frames

			Crew	Daily Output	Man-Hours	Unit	Mat.	Labor	Equip.	Total	Total Incl O&P	
110	0560	3'-0" x 6'-8"	F-2	16	1	Ea.	180	14.30	1	195.30	225	110
	0580	3'-0" x 7'-0"		16	1		185	14.30	1	200.30	230	
	0640	Flush, "A" label 3 hour, composite, 18 ga., 3'-0" x 6'-8"		15	1.070		200	15.25	1.07	216.32	245	
	0660	2'-8" x 7'-0"		16	1		200	14.30	1	215.30	245	
	0680	3'-0" x 7'-0"		15	1.070		210	15.25	1.07	226.32	260	
	0700	4'-0" x 7'-0"		14	1.140		250	16.35	1.14	267.49	305	
114	0010	**RESIDENTIAL STEEL DOOR** (95)										114
	0020	Prehung, insulated, exterior										
	0030	Embossed, full panel, 2'-8" x 6'-8"	F-2	16	1	Ea.	135	14.30	1	150.30	175	
	0040	3'-0" x 6'-8"		15	1.070		150	15.25	1.07	166.32	190	
	0060	3'-0" x 7'-0"		15	1.070		165	15.25	1.07	181.32	210	
	0070	5'-4" x 6'-8", double		8	2		330	29	2	361	415	
	0220	Half glass, 2'-8" x 6'-8"		17	.941		210	13.45	.94	224.39	255	
	0240	3'-0" x 6'-8"		16	1		210	14.30	1	225.30	255	
	0260	3'-0" x 7'-0"		16	1		225	14.30	1	240.30	275	
	0270	5'-4" x 6'-8", double		8	2		445	29	2	476	540	
	0720	Raised plastic face, full panel, 2'-8" x 6'-8"		16	1		165	14.30	1	180.30	205	
	0740	3'-0" x 6'-8"		15	1.070		170	15.25	1.07	186.32	215	
	0760	3'-0" x 7'-0"		15	1.070		185	15.25	1.07	201.32	230	
	0780	5'-4" x 6'-8", double		8	2		355	29	2	386	440	
	0820	Half glass, 2'-8" x 6'-8"		17	.941		205	13.45	.94	219.39	250	
	0840	3'-0" x 6'-8"		16	1		215	14.30	1	230.30	260	
	0860	3'-0" x 7'-0"		16	1		225	14.30	1	240.30	275	
	0880	5'-4" x 6'-8", double		8	2		425	29	2	456	520	
	1320	Flush face, full panel, 2'-6" x 6'-8"		16	1		135	14.30	1	150.30	175	
	1340	3'-0" x 6'-8"		15	1.070		145	15.25	1.07	161.32	185	
	1360	3'-0" x 7'-0"		15	1.070		155	15.25	1.07	171.32	195	
	1380	5'-4" x 6'-8", double		8	2		320	29	2	351	400	
	1420	Half glass, 2'-8" x 6'-8"		17	.941		185	13.45	.94	199.39	225	
	1440	3'-0" x 6'-8"		16	1		190	14.30	1	205.30	235	
	1460	3'-0" x 7'-0"		16	1		210	14.30	1	225.30	255	
	1480	5'-4" x 6'-8", double		8	2		405	29	2	436	495	
	2300	Interior, residential, closet, bi-fold, 6'-8" x 2'-0" wide		16	1		57	14.30	1	72.30	88	
	2330	3'-0" wide		16	1		65	14.30	1	80.30	97	
	2360	4'-0" wide		15	1.070		110	15.25	1.07	126.32	150	
	2400	5'-0" wide		14	1.140		115	16.35	1.14	132.49	155	
	2420	6'-0" wide		13	1.230		126	17.60	1.23	144.83	170	
	2510	Bi-passing closet, incl. hardware, no frame or trim incl.										
	2511	Mirrored, metal frame, 6'-8" x 4'-0" wide	F-2	10	1.600	Opng.	152	23	1.60	176.60	205	
	2512	5'-0" wide		10	1.600		190	23	1.60	214.60	250	
	2513	6'-0" wide		10	1.600		205	23	1.60	229.60	265	
	2514	7'-0" wide		9	1.780		245	25	1.78	271.78	315	
	2515	8'-0" wide		9	1.780		285	25	1.78	311.78	360	
	2611	Mirrored, metal, 8'-0" x 4'-0" wide		10	1.600		185	23	1.60	209.60	245	
	2612	5'-0" wide		10	1.600		220	23	1.60	244.60	280	
	2613	6'-0" wide		10	1.600		250	23	1.60	274.60	315	
	2614	7'-0" wide		9	1.780		295	25	1.78	321.78	370	
	2615	8'-0" wide		9	1.780		370	25	1.78	396.78	450	
118	0010	**STEEL FRAMES, KNOCK DOWN** 18 ga., up to 5-3/4" deep										118
	0020											
	0025	6'-8" high, 3'-0" wide, single	F-2	16	1	Ea.	66	14.30	1	81.30	98	
	0040	6'-0" wide, double		14	1.140		88	16.35	1.14	105.49	125	
	0100	7'-0" high, 3'-0" wide, single		16	1		66	14.30	1	81.30	98	
	0140	6'-0" wide, double		14	1.140		88	16.35	1.14	105.49	125	
	0150											
	2800	18 ga. drywall, up to 4-7/8" deep, 7'-0" high, 3'-0" wide, single	F-2	16	1	Ea.	66	14.30	1	81.30	98	
	2840	6'-0" wide, double		14	1.140		88	16.35	1.14	105.49	125	
	3600	16 ga., up to 5-3/4" deep, 7'-0" high, 4'-0" wide, single		15	1.070		71	15.25	1.07	87.32	105	

For expanded coverage of these items see *Means Building Construction Cost Data 1991*

081 | Metal Doors and Frames

081 100 | Steel Doors And Frames

			CREW	DAILY OUTPUT	MAN-HOURS	UNIT	MAT.	LABOR	EQUIP.	TOTAL	TOTAL INCL O&P	
118	3640	8'-0" wide, double	F-2	12	1.330	Ea.	106	19.05	1.33	126.38	150	118
	3700	8'-0" high, 4'-0" wide, single		15	1.070		85	15.25	1.07	101.32	120	
	3740	8'-0" wide, double		12	1.330		120	19.05	1.33	140.38	165	
	4000	6-¾" deep, 7'-0" high, 4'-0" wide, single		15	1.070		74	15.25	1.07	90.32	110	
	4040	8'-0" wide, double		12	1.330		105	19.05	1.33	125.38	150	
	4100	8'-0" high, 4'-0" wide, single		15	1.070		89	15.25	1.07	105.32	125	
	4140	8'-0" wide, double		12	1.330		108	19.05	1.33	128.38	150	
	4400	8-¾" deep, 7'-0" high, 4'-0" wide, single		15	1.070		81	15.25	1.07	97.32	115	
	4440	8'-0" wide, double		12	1.330		120	19.05	1.33	140.38	165	
	4500	8'-0" high, 4'-0" wide, single		15	1.070		100	15.25	1.07	116.32	135	
	4540	8'-0" wide, double		12	1.330		135	19.05	1.33	155.38	180	
	4800	16 ga. drywall, up to 3-⅞" deep, 7'-0" high, 3'-0" wide, single		16	1		66	14.30	1	81.30	98	
	4840	6'-0" wide, double		14	1.140		88	16.35	1.14	105.49	125	
	4900	For welded frames, add	(96)				30			30	33	
	5200											
	5400	16 ga. "B" label, up to 5-¾" deep, 7'-0" high, 4'-0" wide, single	F-2	15	1.070	Ea.	83	15.25	1.07	99.32	120	
	5440	8'-0" wide, double		12	1.330		120	19.05	1.33	140.38	165	
	5800	6-¾" deep, 7'-0" high, 4'-0" wide, single		15	1.070		92	15.25	1.07	108.32	130	
	5840	8'-0" wide, double		12	1.330		132	19.05	1.33	152.38	180	
	6200	8-¾" deep, 7'-0" high, 4'-0" wide, single		15	1.070		100	15.25	1.07	116.32	135	
	6240	8'-0" wide, double		12	1.330		136	19.05	1.33	156.38	185	
	6300	For "A" label use same price as "B" label										
	6400	For baked enamel finish, add					30%	60%				
	6500	For galvanizing, add					15%					
	6600	For porcelain enamel finish, add					125%	100%				
	7900	Transom lite frames, fixed, add	F-2	155	.103	S.F.	13	1.48	.10	14.58	16.90	
	8000	Movable, add	"	130	.123	"	17	1.76	.12	18.88	22	

082 | Wood and Plastic Doors

082 050 | Wood And Plastic Doors

			CREW	DAILY OUTPUT	MAN-HOURS	UNIT	MAT.	LABOR	EQUIP.	TOTAL	TOTAL INCL O&P	
054	0010	**WOOD FRAMES**										054
	0400	Exterior frame, incl. ext. trim, pine, ⁵⁄₄ x 4-⁹⁄₁₆" deep	F-2	375	.043	L.F.	2.80	.61	.04	3.45	4.15	
	0420	5-³⁄₁₆" deep		375	.043		3.06	.61	.04	3.71	4.44	
	0440	6-⁹⁄₁₆" deep		375	.043		3.55	.61	.04	4.20	4.98	
	0600	Oak, ⁵⁄₄ x 4-⁹⁄₁₆" deep		350	.046		3.75	.65	.05	4.45	5.25	
	0620	5-³⁄₁₆" deep		350	.046		4.05	.65	.05	4.75	5.60	
	0640	6-⁹⁄₁₆" deep		350	.046		4.80	.65	.05	5.50	6.40	
	0800	Walnut, ⁵⁄₄ x 4-⁹⁄₁₆" deep		350	.046		5.65	.65	.05	6.35	7.35	
	0820	5-³⁄₁₆" deep		350	.046		6.45	.65	.05	7.15	8.25	
	0840	6-⁹⁄₁₆" deep		350	.046		7.30	.65	.05	8	9.15	
	1000	Sills, ⁸⁄₄ x 8" deep, oak, no horns		100	.160		7.50	2.29	.16	9.95	12.25	
	1020	2" horns		100	.160		8.80	2.29	.16	11.25	13.70	
	1040	3" horns		100	.160		9.18	2.29	.16	11.63	14.10	
	1100	⁸⁄₄ x 10" deep, oak, no horns		90	.178		9.50	2.54	.18	12.22	14.90	
	1120	2" horns		90	.178		10.55	2.54	.18	13.27	16.05	
	1140	3" horns		90	.178		11.20	2.54	.18	13.92	16.75	
	1200	For casing, see division 062-212										
	1220											
	2000	Exterior, colonial, frame & trim, 3' opng., in-swing, minimum	F-2	22	.727	Ea.	230	10.40	.73	241.13	270	
	2020	Maximum	"	20	.800	"	520	11.45	.80	532.25	590	

For expanded coverage of these items see *Means Building Construction Cost Data 1991*

082 | Wood and Plastic Doors

082 050 | Wood And Plastic Doors

			CREW	DAILY OUTPUT	MAN-HOURS	UNIT	MAT.	LABOR	EQUIP.	TOTAL	TOTAL INCL O&P	
054	2100	5'-4" opening, in-swing, minimum	F-2	17	.941	Ea.	420	13.45	.94	434.39	485	054
	2120	Maximum		15	1.070		775	15.25	1.07	791.32	880	
	2140	Out-swing, minimum		17	.941		470	13.45	.94	484.39	540	
	2160	Maximum		15	1.070		825	15.25	1.07	841.32	935	
	2400	6'-0" opening, in-swing, minimum		16	1		430	14.30	1	445.30	500	
	2420	Maximum		10	1.600		815	23	1.60	839.60	935	
	2460	Out-swing, minimum		16	1		475	14.30	1	490.30	550	
	2480	Maximum		10	1.600		860	23	1.60	884.60	985	
	2600	For two sidelights, add, minimum		30	.533	Opng.	190	7.65	.53	198.18	220	
	2620	Maximum		20	.800	"	625	11.45	.80	637.25	710	
	2700	Custom birch frame, 3'-0" opening		16	1	Ea.	112	14.30	1	127.30	150	
	2750	6'-0" opening		16	1	"	160	14.30	1	175.30	200	
	3000	Interior frame, pine, 11/16" x 3-5/8" deep		375	.043	L.F.	1.15	.61	.04	1.80	2.34	
	3020	4-9/16" deep		375	.043		1.40	.61	.04	2.05	2.61	
	3040	5-3/16" deep		375	.043		1.98	.61	.04	2.63	3.25	
	3200	Oak, 11/16" x 3-5/8" deep		350	.046		2.10	.65	.05	2.80	3.45	
	3220	4-9/16" deep		350	.046		2.50	.65	.05	3.20	3.89	
	3240	5-3/16" deep		350	.046		2.85	.65	.05	3.55	4.28	
	3400	Walnut, 11/16" x 3-5/8" deep		350	.046		2.45	.65	.05	3.15	3.84	
	3420	4-9/16" deep		350	.046		3	.65	.05	3.70	4.44	
	3440	5-3/16" deep		350	.046		3.25	.65	.05	3.95	4.72	
	3600	Pocket door frame		16	1	Ea.	60	14.30	1	75.30	91	
	3800	Threshold, oak, 5/8" x 3-5/8" deep		200	.080	L.F.	2	1.14	.08	3.22	4.20	
	3820	4-5/8" deep		190	.084		2.57	1.20	.08	3.85	4.94	
	3840	5-5/8" deep		180	.089		3	1.27	.09	4.36	5.50	
	4000	For casing see division 062-212										
066	0010	**WOOD DOORS, DECORATOR**										066
	3000	Solid wood, stile and rail (97)										
	3020	Mahogany, 3'-0" x 7'-0", minimum	F-2	14	1.140	Ea.	330	16.35	1.14	347.49	390	
	3030	Maximum		10	1.600		635	23	1.60	659.60	740	
	3040	3'-6" x 8'-0", minimum		10	1.600		485	23	1.60	509.60	575	
	3050	Maximum		8	2		920	29	2	951	1,050	
	3100	Pine, 3'-0" x 7'-0", minimum		14	1.140		180	16.35	1.14	197.49	225	
	3110	Maximum		10	1.600		350	23	1.60	374.60	425	
	3120	3'-6" x 8'-0", minimum		10	1.600		255	23	1.60	279.60	320	
	3130	Maximum		8	2		475	29	2	506	575	
	3200	Red oak, 3'-0" x 7'-0", minimum		14	1.140		470	16.35	1.14	487.49	545	
	3210	Maximum		10	1.600		1,150	23	1.60	1,174	1,300	
	3220	3'-6" x 8'-0", minimum		10	1.600		670	23	1.60	694.60	775	
	3230	Maximum		8	2		1,395	29	2	1,426	1,575	
	4000	Hand carved door, mahogany										
	4020	3'-0" x 7'-0", minimum	F-2	14	1.140	Ea.	510	16.35	1.14	527.49	590	
	4030	Maximum		11	1.450		1,400	21	1.45	1,422	1,575	
	4040	3'-6" x 8'-0", minimum		10	1.600		820	23	1.60	844.60	940	
	4050	Maximum		8	2		1,750	29	2	1,781	1,975	
	4200	Red oak, 3'-0" x 7'-0", minimum		14	1.140		1,000	16.35	1.14	1,017	1,125	
	4210	Maximum		11	1.450		2,700	21	1.45	2,722	3,000	
	4220	3'-6" x 8'-0", minimum		10	1.600		1,300	23	1.60	1,324	1,475	
	4280	For 6'-8" high door, deduct from 7'-0" door					20			20	22	
	4400	For custom finish, add					95			95	105	
	4600	Side light, mahogany, 7'-0" x 1'-6" wide, minimum	F-2	18	.889		200	12.70	.89	213.59	240	
	4610	Maximum		14	1.140		630	16.35	1.14	647.49	720	
	4620	8'-0" x 1'-6" wide, minimum		14	1.140		250	16.35	1.14	267.49	305	
	4630	Maximum		10	1.600		730	23	1.60	754.60	845	
	4640	Side light, oak, 7'-0" x 1'-6" wide, minimum		18	.889		270	12.70	.89	283.59	320	
	4650	Maximum		14	1.140		725	16.35	1.14	742.49	825	
	4660	8'-0" x 1'-6" wide, minimum		14	1.140		330	16.35	1.14	347.49	390	
	4670	Maximum		10	1.600		850	23	1.60	874.60	975	

For expanded coverage of these items see *Means Building Construction Cost Data 1991*

082 | Wood and Plastic Doors

082 050 | Wood And Plastic Doors

			CREW	DAILY OUTPUT	MAN-HOURS	UNIT	MAT.	LABOR	EQUIP.	TOTAL	TOTAL INCL O&P	
066	6520	Interior cafe doors, 2'-6" opening, stock, panel pine	F-2	16	1	Ea.	98	14.30	1	113.30	135	066
	6540	3'-0" opening	"	16	1	"	109	14.30	1	124.30	145	
	6550	Custom hardwood or louvered pine										
	6560	2'-6" opening	F-2	16	1	Ea.	72	14.30	1	87.30	105	
	8000	3'-0" opening	"	16	1	"	82	14.30	1	97.30	115	
	8800	Pre-hung doors, see division 082-082										
074	0010	**WOOD DOORS, PANELED** Interior, six panel, hollow core, 1-3/8" thick										074
	0040	Molded hardboard, 2'-0" x 6'-8"	F-2	17	.941	Ea.	42	13.45	.94	56.39	70	
	0060	2'-6" x 6'-8"		17	.941		47	13.45	.94	61.39	75	
	0080	3'-0" x 6'-8"		17	.941		52	13.45	.94	66.39	81	
	0140	Embossed print, molded hardboard, 2'-0" x 6'-8"		17	.941		50	13.45	.94	64.39	79	
	0160	2'-6" x 6'-8"		17	.941		55	13.45	.94	69.39	84	
	0180	3'-0" x 6'-8"		17	.941		60	13.45	.94	74.39	90	
	0540	Six panel, solid, 1-3/8" thick, pine, 2'-0" x 6'-8"		15	1.070		98	15.25	1.07	114.32	135	
	0560	2'-6" x 6'-8"		14	1.140		103	16.35	1.14	120.49	140	
	0580	3'-0" x 6'-8"		13	1.230		122	17.60	1.23	140.83	165	
	1020	Two panel, bored rail, solid, 1-3/8" thick, pine, 1'-6" x 6'-8"		16	1		135	14.30	1	150.30	175	
	1040	2'-0" x 6'-8"		15	1.070		145	15.25	1.07	161.32	185	
	1060	2'-6" x 6'-8"		14	1.140		150	16.35	1.14	167.49	195	
	1340	Two panel, solid, 1-3/8" thick, fir, 2'-0" x 6'-8"		15	1.070		130	15.25	1.07	146.32	170	
	1360	2'-6" x 6'-8"		14	1.140		135	16.35	1.14	152.49	175	
	1380	3'-0" x 6'-8"		13	1.230		140	17.60	1.23	158.83	185	
	1740	Five panel, solid, 1-3/8" thick, fir, 2'-0" x 6'-8"		15	1.070		150	15.25	1.07	166.32	190	
	1760	2'-6" x 6'-8"		14	1.140		153	16.35	1.14	170.49	195	
	1780	3'-0" x 6'-8"		13	1.230		160	17.60	1.23	178.83	205	
078	0010	**WOOD DOORS, RESIDENTIAL**										078
	0200	Exterior, combination storm & screen, pine										
	0220	Cross buck, 6'-9" x 2'-6" wide	F-2	11	1.450	Ea.	170	21	1.45	192.45	225	
	0260	2'-8" wide		10	1.600		173	23	1.60	197.60	230	
	0280	3'-0" wide		9	1.780		178	25	1.78	204.78	240	
	0300	7'-1" x 3'-0" wide		9	1.780		190	25	1.78	216.78	255	
	0400	Full lite, 6'-9" x 2'-6" wide		11	1.450		150	21	1.45	172.45	200	
	0420	2'-8" wide		10	1.600		160	23	1.60	184.60	215	
	0440	3'-0" wide		9	1.780		165	25	1.78	191.78	225	
	0500	7'-1" x 3'-0" wide		9	1.780		175	25	1.78	201.78	235	
	0700	Dutch door, pine, 1-3/4" x 6'-8" x 2'-8" wide, minimum		12	1.330		314	19.05	1.33	334.38	380	
	0720	Maximum		10	1.600		346	23	1.60	370.60	420	
	0800	3'-0" wide, minimum		12	1.330		329	19.05	1.33	349.38	395	
	0820	Maximum		10	1.600		363	23	1.60	387.60	440	
	1000	Entrance door, colonial, 1-3/4" x 6'-8" x 2'-8" wide		16	1		260	14.30	1	275.30	310	
	1020	6 panel pine, 3'-0" wide		15	1.070		270	15.25	1.07	286.32	325	
	1100	8 panel pine, 2'-8" wide		16	1		285	14.30	1	300.30	340	
	1120	3'-0" wide		15	1.070		290	15.25	1.07	306.32	345	
	1200	For tempered safety glass lites, add					21			21	23	
	1220											
	1300	Flush, birch, solid core, 1-3/4" x 6'-8" x 2'-8" wide	F-2	16	1	Ea.	80	14.30	1	95.30	115	
	1320	3'-0" wide		15	1.070		85	15.25	1.07	101.32	120	
	1340	7'-0" x 2'-8" wide		16	1		88	14.30	1	103.30	120	
	1360	3'-0" wide		15	1.070		90	15.25	1.07	106.32	125	
	1700	Hand carved door, fir 2'-8" x 6'-8"		15	1.070		190	15.25	1.07	206.32	235	
	1720	3'-0" x 6'-8"		15	1.070		210	15.25	1.07	226.32	260	
	1740	Mahogany, 2'-8" x 6'-8"		15	1.070		515	15.25	1.07	531.32	595	
	1760	3'-0" x 6'-8"		15	1.070		520	15.25	1.07	536.32	600	
	2700	Interior closet, bi-fold, w/hardware, no frame or trim incl.										
	2720	Flush, birch, 6'-6" or 6'-8" x 2'-6" wide	F-2	13	1.230	Ea.	51	17.60	1.23	69.83	87	
	2740	3'-0" wide		13	1.230		55	17.60	1.23	73.83	91	
	2760	4'-0" wide		12	1.330		89	19.05	1.33	109.38	130	

For expanded coverage of these items see *Means Building Construction Cost Data 1991*

082 | Wood and Plastic Doors

082 050 | Wood And Plastic Doors

			CREW	DAILY OUTPUT	MAN-HOURS	UNIT	MAT.	LABOR	EQUIP.	TOTAL	TOTAL INCL O&P	
078	2780	5'-0" wide	F-2	11	1.450	Ea.	98	21	1.45	120.45	145	078
	2800	6'-0" wide		10	1.600		105	23	1.60	129.60	155	
	3000	Raised panel pine, 6'-6" or 6'-8" x 2'-6" wide		13	1.230		95	17.60	1.23	113.83	135	
	3020	3'-0" wide		13	1.230		115	17.60	1.23	133.83	155	
	3040	4'-0" wide		12	1.330		175	19.05	1.33	195.38	225	
	3060	5'-0" wide		11	1.450		200	21	1.45	222.45	255	
	3080	6'-0" wide		10	1.600		220	23	1.60	244.60	280	
	3200	Louvered, pine, 6'-6" or 6'-8" x 2'-6" wide		13	1.230		70	17.60	1.23	88.83	110	
	3220	3'-0" wide		13	1.230		76	17.60	1.23	94.83	115	
	3240	4'-0" wide		12	1.330		125	19.05	1.33	145.38	170	
	3260	5'-0" wide		11	1.450		145	21	1.45	167.45	195	
	3280	6'-0" wide	↓	10	1.600	↓	150	23	1.60	174.60	205	
	4400	Bi-passing closet, incl. hardware and frame, no trim incl.										
	4420	Flush, lauan, 6'-8" x 4'-0" wide	F-2	12	1.330	Opng.	75	19.05	1.33	95.38	115	
	4440	5'-0" wide		11	1.450		83	21	1.45	105.45	130	
	4460	6'-0" wide		10	1.600		90	23	1.60	114.60	140	
	4600	Flush, birch, 6'-8" x 4'-0" wide		12	1.330		85	19.05	1.33	105.38	125	
	4620	5'-0" wide		11	1.450		99	21	1.45	121.45	145	
	4640	6'-0" wide		10	1.600		108	23	1.60	132.60	160	
	4800	Louvered, pine, 6'-8" x 4'-0" wide		12	1.330		102	19.05	1.33	122.38	145	
	4820	5'-0" wide		11	1.450		116	21	1.45	138.45	165	
	4840	6'-0" wide		10	1.600		127	23	1.60	151.60	180	
	5000	Paneled, pine, 6'-8" x 4'-0" wide		12	1.330		183	19.05	1.33	203.38	235	
	5020	5'-0" wide		11	1.450		205	21	1.45	227.45	260	
	5040	6'-0" wide	↓	10	1.600	↓	230	23	1.60	254.60	295	
	5050											
	5061	Hardboard, 6'-8" x 4'-0" wide	F-2	10	1.600	Opng.	66	23	1.60	90.60	115	
	5062	5'-0" wide		10	1.600		73	23	1.60	97.60	120	
	5063	6'-0" wide	↓	10	1.600	↓	90	23	1.60	114.60	140	
	6100	Folding accordion, closet, not including frame										
	6120	Vinyl, 2 layer, stock (see also division 106-552)	F-2	400	.040	S.F.	4	.57	.04	4.61	5.40	
	6140	Woven mahogany and vinyl, stock		400	.040		1.60	.57	.04	2.21	2.76	
	6160	Wood slats with vinyl overlay, stock		400	.040		7.95	.57	.04	8.56	9.75	
	6180	Economy vinyl, stock		400	.040		1.10	.57	.04	1.71	2.21	
	6200	Rigid PVC	↓	400	.040		2.15	.57	.04	2.76	3.37	
	6220	For custom folding, add to above				Ea.	25%					
	6230											
	7400	Passage doors, flush, no frame included										
	7420	Lauan, hollow core, 1-⅜" x 6'-8" x 1'-6" wide	F-2	19	.842	Ea.	28	12.05	.84	40.89	52	
	7440	2'-0" wide		18	.889		28	12.70	.89	41.59	53	
	7460	2'-6" wide		18	.889		29	12.70	.89	42.59	54	
	7480	2'-8" wide		18	.889		29	12.70	.89	42.59	54	
	7500	3'-0" wide		17	.941		31	13.45	.94	45.39	58	
	7700	Birch, hollow core, 1-⅜" x 6'-8" x 1'-6" wide		19	.842		31	12.05	.84	43.89	55	
	7720	2'-0" wide		18	.889		31	12.70	.89	44.59	56	
	7740	2'-6" wide		18	.889		35	12.70	.89	48.59	61	
	7760	2'-8" wide		18	.889		35	12.70	.89	48.59	61	
	7780	3'-0" wide		17	.941		38	13.45	.94	52.39	65	
	8000	Pine louvered, 1-⅜" x 6'-8" x 1'-6" wide		19	.842		75	12.05	.84	87.89	105	
	8020	2'-0" wide		18	.889		80	12.70	.89	93.59	110	
	8040	2'-6" wide		18	.889		90	12.70	.89	103.59	120	
	8060	2'-8" wide		18	.889		110	12.70	.89	123.59	145	
	8080	3'-0" wide		17	.941		110	13.45	.94	124.39	145	
	8300	Pine paneled, 1-⅜" x 6'-8" x 1'-6" wide		19	.842		85	12.05	.84	97.89	115	
	8320	2'-0" wide		18	.889		89	12.70	.89	102.59	120	
	8340	2'-6" wide		18	.889		101	12.70	.89	114.59	135	
	8360	2'-8" wide		18	.889		107	12.70	.89	120.59	140	
	8380	3'-0" wide	↓	17	.941	↓	115	13.45	.94	129.39	150	

For expanded coverage of these items see *Means Building Construction Cost Data 1991*

082 | Wood and Plastic Doors

082 050 | Wood And Plastic Doors

			CREW	DAILY OUTPUT	MAN-HOURS	UNIT	MAT.	LABOR	EQUIP.	TOTAL	TOTAL INCL O&P	
078	8450	French door, pine, 15 lites, 1-3/8"x6'-8"x2'-6" wide	F-2	18	.889	Ea.	295	12.70	.89	308.59	345	078
	8470	2'x8" wide		18	.889		300	12.70	.89	313.59	350	
	8490	3'-0" wide	↓	17	.941	↓	315	13.45	.94	329.39	370	
	8550	For over 20 doors, deduct					15%					
082	0010	**PRE-HUNG DOORS**										082
	0300	Exterior, wood, combination storm & screen, 6'-9" x 2'-6" wide	F-2	15	1.070	Ea.	150	15.25	1.07	166.32	190	
	0320	2'-8" wide		15	1.070		157	15.25	1.07	173.32	200	
	0340	3'-0" wide	↓	15	1.070		165	15.25	1.07	181.32	210	
	0360	For 7'-0" high door, add				↓	7			7	7.70	
	0370	For aluminum storm doors, see division 083-900										
	1600	Entrance door, flush, birch, solid core										
	1620	4-5/8" solid jamb, 1-3/4" x 6'-8" x 2'-8" wide	F-2	16	1	Ea.	180	14.30	1	195.30	225	
	1640	3'-0" wide	"	16	1		200	14.30	1	215.30	245	
	1680	For 7'-0" high door, add				↓	10			10	11	
	2000	Entrance door, colonial, 6 panel pine										
	2020	4-5/8" solid jamb, 1-3/4" x 6'-8" x 2'-8" wide	F-2	16	1	Ea.	335	14.30	1	350.30	395	
	2040	3'-0" wide	"	16	1		365	14.30	1	380.30	425	
	2060	For 7'-0" high door, add					10			10	11	
	2200	For 5-5/8" solid jamb, add					14			14	15.40	
	2300	French door, 6'-8" x 6'-0" wide, 1/2" insul. glass and grille	F-2	7	2.290	↓	885	33	2.29	920.29	1,025	
	2500	Exterior, metal face, insulated, incl. jamb, brickmold and										
	2520	threshold, flush, 2'-8" x 6'-8"	F-2	16	1	Ea.	140	14.30	1	155.30	180	
	2550	3'-0" x 6'-8"	"	16	1	"	145	14.30	1	160.30	185	
	2990											
	3000	Raised molding, 6 panel, 2'-8" x 6'-8"	F-2	16	1	Ea.	160	14.30	1	175.30	200	
	3050	3'-0" x 6'-8"		16	1		165	14.30	1	180.30	205	
	3100	2 narrow lites, 2'-8" x 6'-8"		16	1		267	14.30	1	282.30	320	
	3150	3'-0" x 6'-8"		16	1		275	14.30	1	290.30	330	
	3200	Half glass, 2'-8" x 6'-8"		16	1		200	14.30	1	215.30	245	
	3250	3'-0" x 6'-8"		16	1		203	14.30	1	218.30	250	
	3300	2 top lites, 2'-8" x 6'-8"		16	1		190	14.30	1	205.30	235	
	3350	3'-0" x 6'-8"		16	1		195	14.30	1	210.30	240	
	3500	Embossed, 6 panel, 2'-8" x 6'-8"		16	1		144	14.30	1	159.30	185	
	3550	3'-0" x 6'-8"		16	1		150	14.30	1	165.30	190	
	3600	2 narrow lites, 2'-8" x 6'-8"		16	1		267	14.30	1	282.30	320	
	3650	3'-0" x 6'-8"		16	1		270	14.30	1	285.30	320	
	3700	Half glass, 2'-8" x 6'-8"		16	1		200	14.30	1	215.30	245	
	3750	3'-0" x 6'-8"		16	1		205	14.30	1	220.30	250	
	3800	2 top lites, 2'-8" x 6'-8"		16	1		205	14.30	1	220.30	250	
	3850	3'-0" x 6'-8"	↓	16	1	↓	210	14.30	1	225.30	255	
	4000	Interior, passage door, 4-5/8" solid jamb										
	4400	Lauan, flush, solid core, 1-3/8" x 6'-8" x 2'-6" wide	F-2	20	.800	Ea.	110	11.45	.80	122.25	140	
	4420	2'-8" wide		20	.800		112	11.45	.80	124.25	145	
	4440	3'-0" wide		19	.842		115	12.05	.84	127.89	150	
	4600	Hollow core, 1-3/8" x 6'-8" x 2'-6" wide		20	.800		78	11.45	.80	90.25	105	
	4620	2'-8" wide		20	.800		83	11.45	.80	95.25	110	
	4640	3'-0" wide	↓	19	.842		88	12.05	.84	100.89	120	
	4700	For 7'-0" high door, add					10			10	11	
	5000	Birch, flush, solid core, 1-3/8" x 6'-8" x 2'-6" wide	F-2	20	.800		145	11.45	.80	157.25	180	
	5020	2'-8" wide		20	.800		148	11.45	.80	160.25	185	
	5040	3'-0" wide		19	.842		153	12.05	.84	165.89	190	
	5200	Hollow core, 1-3/8" x 6'-8" x 2'-6" wide		20	.800		118	11.45	.80	130.25	150	
	5220	2'-8" wide		20	.800		122	11.45	.80	134.25	155	
	5240	3'-0" wide	↓	19	.842		127	12.05	.84	139.89	160	
	5280	For 7'-0" high door, add					10			10	11	
	5500	Hardboard paneled, 1-3/8" x 6'-8" x 2'-6" wide	F-2	20	.800		125	11.45	.80	137.25	160	
	5520	2'-8" wide		20	.800		128	11.45	.80	140.25	160	
	5540	3'-0" wide	↓	19	.842		133	12.05	.84	145.89	165	

For expanded coverage of these items see *Means Building Construction Cost Data 1991*

082 | Wood and Plastic Doors

082 050 | Wood And Plastic Doors

			CREW	DAILY OUTPUT	MAN-HOURS	UNIT	MAT.	LABOR	EQUIP.	TOTAL	TOTAL INCL O&P	
082	5600											082
	6000	Pine paneled, 1-3/8" x 6'-8" x 2'-6" wide	F-2	20	.800	Ea.	175	11.45	.80	187.25	215	
	6020	2'-8" wide		20	.800		185	11.45	.80	197.25	225	
	6040	3'-0" wide		20	.800		195	11.45	.80	207.25	235	
	6200											
	6500	For 5-5/8" solid jamb, add				Ea.	7			7	7.70	
	6520	For split jamb, deduct				"	22			22	24	

083 | Special Doors

083 100 | Sliding Doors

			CREW	DAILY OUTPUT	MAN-HOURS	UNIT	MAT.	LABOR	EQUIP.	TOTAL	TOTAL INCL O&P	
102	0010	GLASS, SLIDING Vinyl clad, 1" insulated glass, 6'-0" x 6'-10" high	2 Carp	4	4	Opng.	904	57		961	1,100	102
	0100	8'-0" x 6'-10" high		4	4		1,104	57		1,161	1,300	
	0500	3 leaf, 9'-0" x 6'-10" high		3	5.330		1,293	76		1,369	1,550	
	0600	12'-0" x 6'-10" high		3	5.330		1,588	76		1,664	1,875	
104	0010	GLASS, SLIDING Wood, 5/8" tempered insul. glass, 6' wide, premium		4	4	Ea.	775	57		832	950	104
	0100	Economy		4	4		470	57		527	615	
	0150	8' wide, wood, premium		3	5.330		1,000	76		1,076	1,225	
	0200	Economy		3	5.330		600	76		676	790	
	0250	12' wide, wood, premium		2.50	6.400		1,490	92		1,582	1,800	
	0300	Economy		2.50	6.400		960	92		1,052	1,200	
	0350	Aluminum sliding, 5/8" tempered insulated glass, 6' wide										
	0400	Premium	2 Carp	4	4	Ea.	440	57		497	580	
	0450	Economy	"	4	4	"	290	57		347	415	
	0460											
	0500	8' wide, premium	2 Carp	3	5.330	Ea.	460	76		536	635	
	0550	Economy		3	5.330		370	76		446	535	
	0600	12' wide, premium		2.50	6.400		560	92		652	770	
	0650	Economy		2.50	6.400		464	92		556	665	
	1000	Replacement doors, wood										
	1050	6' wide, premium	2 Carp	4	4	Ea.	425	57		482	565	

083 600 | Sectional Overhead Drs

			CREW	DAILY OUTPUT	MAN-HOURS	UNIT	MAT.	LABOR	EQUIP.	TOTAL	TOTAL INCL O&P	
606	0010	RESIDENTIAL GARAGE DOORS Including hardware, no frame										606
	0020											
	0050	Hinged, wood, custom, double door, 9' x 7'	2 Carp	3	5.330	Ea.	290	76		366	445	
	0070	16' x 7'		2	8		550	115		665	795	
	0200	Overhead, sectional, incl. hardware, fiberglass, 9' x 7', standard		8	2		355	29		384	440	
	0220	Deluxe		8	2		412	29		441	500	
	0300	16' x 7', standard		6	2.670		595	38		633	720	
	0320	Deluxe		6	2.670		745	38		783	885	
	0500	Hardboard, 9' x 7', standard		8	2		255	29		284	330	
	0520	Deluxe		8	2		325	29		354	405	
	0600	16' x 7', standard		6	2.670		450	38		488	560	
	0620	Deluxe		6	2.670		510	38		548	625	
	0700	Metal, 9' x 7', standard		8	2		270	29		299	345	
	0720	Deluxe		8	2		380	29		409	465	
	0800	16' x 7', standard		6	2.670		425	38		463	530	
	0820	Deluxe		6	2.670		640	38		678	770	
	0900	Wood, 9' x 7', standard		8	2		265	29		294	340	
	0920	Deluxe		8	2		760	29		789	885	

For expanded coverage of these items see *Means Building Construction Cost Data 1991*

083 | Special Doors

083 600 | Sectional Overhead Drs

			CREW	DAILY OUTPUT	MAN-HOURS	UNIT	MAT.	LABOR	EQUIP.	TOTAL	TOTAL INCL O&P	
606	1000	16' x 7', standard	2 Carp	6	2.670	Ea.	530	38		568	645	606
	1020	Deluxe	"	6	2.670		1,150	38		1,188	1,325	
	1800	Door hardware, sectional	1 Carp	4	2		105	29		134	165	
	1810	Door tracks only		4	2		55	29		84	110	
	1820	One side only	↓	7	1.140		39	16.35		55.35	70	
	3000	Swing-up, including hardware, metal, 9' x 7', standard	2 Carp	8	2		455	29		484	550	
	3100	16' x 7', standard	"	6	2.670		565	38		603	685	
	4000	For electric operator, economy, add	1 Carp	8	1		185	14.30		199.30	225	
	4100	Deluxe, including remote control	"	8	1	↓	300	14.30		314.30	355	
	4500	For transmitter/receiver control, add to operator				Total	65			65	72	
	4600	Transmitters, additional				"	20			20	22	
	6000	Replace section, on sectional door, fiberglass, 9' x 7'	1 Carp	4	2	Ea.	85	29		114	140	
	6020	16' x 7'		3.50	2.290		160	33		193	230	
	6200	Hardboard, 9' x 7'		4	2		87	29		116	145	
	6220	16' x 7'		3.50	2.290		145	33		178	215	
	6300	Metal, 9' x 7'		4	2		100	29		129	160	
	6320	16' x 7'		3.50	2.290		165	33		198	235	
	6500	Wood, 9' x 7'		4	2		95	29		124	150	
	6520	16' x 7'	↓	3.50	2.290		180	33		213	255	

083 720 | Special Purpose Doors

			CREW	DAILY OUTPUT	MAN-HOURS	UNIT	MAT.	LABOR	EQUIP.	TOTAL	TOTAL INCL O&P	
721	0010	BULKHEAD CELLAR DOORS Steel, not incl. sides, minimum	1 Carp	5.50	1.450	Ea.	210	21		231	265	721
	0100	Maximum		5.10	1.570		229	22		251	290	
	0500	With sides and foundation plates, minimum		4.70	1.700		212	24		236	275	
	0600	Maximum	↓	4.30	1.860	↓	268	27		295	340	

083 900 | Screen And Storm Doors

			CREW	DAILY OUTPUT	MAN-HOURS	UNIT	MAT.	LABOR	EQUIP.	TOTAL	TOTAL INCL O&P	
904	0010	STORM DOORS & FRAMES Aluminum, residential,										904
	0020	combination storm and screen										
	0400	Clear anodic coating, 6'-8" x 2'-6" wide	F-2	15	1.070	Ea.	185	15.25	1.07	201.32	230	
	0420	2'-8" wide		14	1.140		185	16.35	1.14	202.49	230	
	0440	3'-0" wide	↓	14	1.140		190	16.35	1.14	207.49	240	
	0500	For 7'-0" door, add					5%					
	1000	Mill finish, 6'-8" x 2'-6" wide	F-2	15	1.070		172	15.25	1.07	188.32	215	
	1020	2'-8" wide		14	1.140		182	16.35	1.14	199.49	230	
	1040	3'-0" wide	↓	14	1.140		182	16.35	1.14	199.49	230	
	1100	For 7'-0" door, add					5%					
	1500	White painted, 6'-8" x 2'-6" wide	F-2	15	1.070		190	15.25	1.07	206.32	235	
	1520	2'-8" wide		14	1.140		190	16.35	1.14	207.49	240	
	1540	3'-0" wide		14	1.140		200	16.35	1.14	217.49	250	
	1541	Storm door, painted, alum., insul., 6'-8" x 2'-6" wide		14	1.140		190	16.35	1.14	207.49	240	
	1545	2'-8" wide	↓	14	1.140		190	16.35	1.14	207.49	240	
	1600	For 7'-0" door, add					5%					
	1800	Aluminum screen door, minimum, 6'-8" x 2'-8" wide	F-2	14	1.140		82	16.35	1.14	99.49	120	
	1810	3'-0" wide		14	1.140		84	16.35	1.14	101.49	120	
	1820	Average, 6'-8" x 2'-8" wide		14	1.140		150	16.35	1.14	167.49	195	
	1830	3'-0" wide		14	1.140		156	16.35	1.14	173.49	200	
	1840	Maximum, 6'-8" x 2'-8" wide		14	1.140		202	16.35	1.14	219.49	250	
	1850	3'-0" wide	↓	14	1.140	↓	212	16.35	1.14	229.49	260	
	2000	Wood door & screen, see division 082-078										
	2020											

For expanded coverage of these items see *Means Building Construction Cost Data 1991*

085 | Metal Windows

085 200 | Aluminum Windows

			CREW	DAILY OUTPUT	MAN-HOURS	UNIT	MAT.	LABOR	EQUIP.	TOTAL	TOTAL INCL O&P	
204	0010	**ALUMINUM WINDOWS** Incl. frame and glazing, grade C										204
	1000	Stock units, casement, 3'-1" x 3'-2" opening	2 Sswk	10	1.600	Ea.	194	25		219	260	
	1040	Insulating glass	"	10	1.600		200	25		225	265	
	1050	Add for storms					39			39	43	
	1600	Projected, with screen, 3'-1" x 3'-2" opening	2 Sswk	10	1.600		134	25		159	195	
	1650	Insulating glass	"	10	1.600		134	25		159	195	
	1700	Add for storms					39			39	43	
	2000	4'-5" x 5'-3" opening	2 Sswk	8	2		190	31		221	270	
	2050	Insulating glass	"	8	2		250	31		281	335	
	2100	Add for storms					53			53	58	
	2500	Enamel finish windows, 3'-1" x 3'-2"	2 Sswk	10	1.600		124	25		149	185	
	2550	Insulating glass		10	1.600		151	25		176	215	
	2600	4'-5" x 5'-3"		8	2		212	31		243	290	
	2700	Insulating glass		8	2		270	31		301	355	
	3000	Single hung, 2' x 3' opening, enameled, standard glazed		10	1.600		92	25		117	150	
	3100	Insulating glass		10	1.600		110	25		135	170	
	3300	2'-8" x 6'-8" opening, standard glazed		8	2		194	31		225	275	
	3400	Insulating glass		8	2		248	31		279	330	
	3700	3'-4" x 5'-0" opening, standard glazed		9	1.780		124	28		152	190	
	3800	Insulating glass		9	1.780		175	28		203	245	
	4000	Sliding aluminum, 3' x 2' opening, standard glazed		10	1.600		90	25		115	145	
	4100	Insulating glass		10	1.600		100	25		125	155	
	4300	5' x 3' opening, standard glazed		9	1.780		112	28		140	175	
	4400	Insulating glass		9	1.780		160	28		188	230	
	4600	8' x 4' opening, standard glazed		6	2.670		165	42		207	260	
	4700	Insulating glass		6	2.670		265	42		307	370	
	5000	9' x 5' opening, standard glazed		4	4		250	63		313	395	
	5100	Insulating glass		4	4		400	63		463	560	
	5500	Sliding, with thermal barrier and screen, 6' x 4', 2 track		8	2		340	31		371	435	
	5700	4 track	↓	8	2		415	31		446	515	
	6000	For above units with bronze finish, add					12%					
	6200	For installation in concrete openings, add				↓	5%					

085 500 | Metal Jalousie Windows

			CREW	DAILY OUTPUT	MAN-HOURS	UNIT	MAT.	LABOR	EQUIP.	TOTAL	TOTAL INCL O&P	
502	0010	**JALOUSIES** Aluminum incl. glazing & screens, stock, 1'-7" x 3'-2"	2 Sswk	10	1.600	Ea.	75	25		100	130	502
	0100	2'-3" x 4'-0"		10	1.600		120	25		145	180	
	0200	3'-1" x 2'-0"		10	1.600		115	25		140	175	
	0300	3'-1" x 5'-3"		10	1.600		175	25		200	240	
	1000	Mullions for above, 2'-0" long		80	.200		7.20	3.13		10.33	13.85	
	1100	5'-3" long	↓	80	.200	↓	12.85	3.13		15.98	20	
504	0010	**LOUVERS** See division 041-524, 062-740 & 102-104										504

085 600 | Metal Storm Windows

			CREW	DAILY OUTPUT	MAN-HOURS	UNIT	MAT.	LABOR	EQUIP.	TOTAL	TOTAL INCL O&P	
601	0010	**STORM WINDOWS** Aluminum, residential										601
	0020											
	0300	Basement, mill finish, incl. fiberglass screen										
	0320	1'-10" x 1'-0" high	F-2	30	.533	Ea.	16	7.65	.53	24.18	31	
	0340	2'-9" x 1'-6" high		30	.533		19	7.65	.53	27.18	34	
	0360	3'-4" x 2'-0" high	↓	30	.533	↓	24	7.65	.53	32.18	40	
	1600	Double-hung, combination, storm & screen										
	1700	Custom, clear anodic coating, 2'-0" x 3'-5" high	F-2	30	.533	Ea.	70	7.65	.53	78.18	90	
	1720	2'-6" x 5'-0" high		28	.571		106	8.15	.57	114.72	130	
	1740	4'-0" x 6'-0" high		25	.640		190	9.15	.64	199.79	225	
	1800	White painted, 2'-0" x 3'-5" high		30	.533		66	7.65	.53	74.18	86	
	1820	2'-6" x 5'-0" high		28	.571		106	8.15	.57	114.72	130	
	1840	4'-0" x 6'-0" high		25	.640		190	9.15	.64	199.79	225	
	2000	Average quality, clear anodic coating, 2'-0" x 3'-5" high		30	.533		57	7.65	.53	65.18	76	

For expanded coverage of these items see *Means Building Construction Cost Data 1991*

085 | Metal Windows

085 600 | Metal Storm Windows

			CREW	DAILY OUTPUT	MAN-HOURS	UNIT	MAT.	LABOR	EQUIP.	TOTAL	TOTAL INCL O&P	
601	2020	2'-6" x 5'-0" high	F-2	28	.571	Ea.	72	8.15	.57	80.72	93	601
	2040	4'-0" x 6'-0" high		25	.640		80	9.15	.64	89.79	105	
	2400	White painted, 2'-0" x 3'-5" high		30	.533		54	7.65	.53	62.18	73	
	2420	2'-6" x 5'-0" high		28	.571		60	8.15	.57	68.72	80	
	2440	4'-0" x 6'-0" high		25	.640		65	9.15	.64	74.79	88	
	2600	Mill finish, 2'-0" x 3'-5" high		30	.533		50	7.65	.53	58.18	68	
	2620	2'-6" x 5'-0" high		28	.571		56	8.15	.57	64.72	76	
	2640	4'-0" x 6-8" high		25	.640		62	9.15	.64	71.79	84	
	4000	Picture window, storm, 1 lite, white or bronze finish										
	4020	4'-6" x 4'-6" high	F-2	25	.640	Ea.	82	9.15	.64	91.79	105	
	4040	5'-8" x 4'-6" high		20	.800		84	11.45	.80	96.25	110	
	4400	Mill finish, 4'-6" x 4'-6" high		25	.640		72	9.15	.64	81.79	95	
	4420	5'-8" x 4'-6" high		20	.800		76	11.45	.80	88.25	105	
	4600	3 lite, white or bronze finish										
	4620	4'-6" x 4'-6" high	F-2	25	.640	Ea.	96	9.15	.64	105.79	120	
	4640	5'-8" x 4'-6" high		20	.800		100	11.45	.80	112.25	130	
	4800	Mill finish, 4'-6" x 4'-6" high		25	.640		90	9.15	.64	99.79	115	
	4820	5'-8" x 4'-6" high		20	.800		93	11.45	.80	105.25	120	
	5000	Sliding glass door, storm 6' x 6'-8", standard	1 Glaz	2	4		260	59		319	380	
	5100	Economy	"	2	4		175	59		234	290	
	6000	Sliding window, storm, 2 lite, white or bronze finish										
	6020	3'-4" x 2'-7" high	F-2	28	.571	Ea.	52	8.15	.57	60.72	71	
	6040	4'-4" x 3'-3" high		25	.640		60	9.15	.64	69.79	82	
	6060	5'-4" x 6'-0" high		20	.800		90	11.45	.80	102.25	120	
	6400	3 lite, white or bronze finish										
	6420	4'-4" x 3'-3" high	F-2	25	.640	Ea.	80	9.15	.64	89.79	105	
	6440	5'-4" x 6'-0" high		20	.800		125	11.45	.80	137.25	160	
	6460	6'-0" x 6'-0" high		18	.889		130	12.70	.89	143.59	165	
	6800	Mill finish, 4'-4" x 3'-3" high		25	.640		72	9.15	.64	81.79	95	
	6820	5'-4" x 6'-0" high		20	.800		103	11.45	.80	115.25	135	
	6840	6'-0" x 6-0" high		18	.889		110	12.70	.89	123.59	145	
	9000	Magnetic interior storm window										
	9100	3/16" plate glass	1 Glaz	107	.075	S.F.	3.75	1.10		4.85	5.90	

085 700 | Screens

			CREW	DAILY OUTPUT	MAN-HOURS	UNIT	MAT.	LABOR	EQUIP.	TOTAL	TOTAL INCL O&P	
701	0010	SCREENS For metal sash, aluminum or bronze mesh, flat screen	2 Sswk	1,230	.013	S.F.	2.65	.20		2.85	3.30	701
	0500	Wicket screen, inside window	"	1,000	.016	"	4.10	.25		4.35	4.98	
	0600	Residential, aluminum mesh and frame, 2' x 3'	F-2	32	.500	Ea.	12	7.15	.50	19.65	26	
	0610	Rescreen		50	.320		2	4.58	.32	6.90	10.20	
	0620	3' x 5'		32	.500		19	7.15	.50	26.65	33	
	0630	Rescreen		45	.356		4.75	5.10	.36	10.21	14.10	
	0640	4' x 8'		25	.640		43	9.15	.64	52.79	63	
	0650	Rescreen		40	.400		9.75	5.70	.40	15.85	21	
	0660	Patio door		25	.640		34.80	9.15	.64	44.59	54	
	0680	Rescreening		1,600	.010	S.F.	.30	.14	.01	.45	.58	
	1000	For solar louvers, add	2 Sswk	160	.100	"	14.95	1.57		16.52	19.40	

For expanded coverage of these items see *Means Building Construction Cost Data 1991*

086 | Wood and Plastic Windows

086 100 | Wood Windows

			CREW	DAILY OUTPUT	MAN-HOURS	UNIT	MAT.	LABOR	EQUIP.	TOTAL	TOTAL INCL O&P	
104	0010	**AWNING WINDOW** Including frame, screen, and exterior trim										104
	0020											
	0100	Average quality, builders model, 34" x 22", standard glazed	1 Carp	10	.800	Ea.	135	11.45		146.45	170	
	0200	Insulating glass		10	.800		150	11.45		161.45	185	
	0300	40" x 28", standard glazed		9	.889		155	12.70		167.70	190	
	0400	Insulating glass		9	.889		180	12.70		192.70	220	
	0500	48" x 36", standard glazed		8	1		180	14.30		194.30	220	
	0600	Insulating glass		8	1		216	14.30		230.30	260	
	1000	Vinyl clad, premium, insulating glass, 34" x 22"		10	.800		176	11.45		187.45	215	
	1100	40" x 22"		10	.800		192	11.45		203.45	230	
	1200	36" x 28"		9	.889		209	12.70		221.70	250	
	1300	36" x 36"		9	.889		250	12.70		262.70	295	
	1400	48" x 28"		8	1		272	14.30		286.30	325	
	1500	60" x 36"		8	1		430	14.30		444.30	495	
	2000	Metal clad, deluxe, insulating glass, 34" x 22"		10	.800		145	11.45		156.45	180	
	2100	40" x 22"		10	.800		157	11.45		168.45	190	
	2200	36" x 25"		9	.889		168	12.70		180.70	205	
	2300	40" x 30"		9	.889		170	12.70		182.70	210	
	2400	48" x 28"		8	1		190	14.30		204.30	235	
	2500	60" x 36"		8	1		290	14.30		304.30	345	
108	0010	**BOW-BAY WINDOW** Including frame, screen and exterior trim,										108
	0020	end panels operable										
	1000	Awning type, builders model, 8' x 5' high, std. glazed, 4 panels	2 Carp	10	1.600	Ea.	670	23		693	775	
	1050	Insulating glass		10	1.600		766	23		789	880	
	1100	10'-0" x 5'-0" high, standard glazed		6	2.670		833	38		871	980	
	1200	Insulating glass, 6 panels		6	2.670		935	38		973	1,100	
	1300	Vinyl clad, premium, insulating glass, 6'-0" x 4'-0"		10	1.600		1,120	23		1,143	1,275	
	1340	9'-0" x 4'-0"		8	2		1,510	29		1,539	1,700	
	1380	10'-0" x 6'-0"		7	2.290		1,975	33		2,008	2,225	
	1420	12'-0" x 6'-0"		6	2.670		2,460	38		2,498	2,775	
	1600	Metal clad, deluxe, insul. glass, 6'-0" x 4'-0" high, 3 panels		10	1.600		672	23		695	775	
	1640	9'-0" x 4'-0" high, 4 panels		8	2		1,040	29		1,069	1,200	
	1680	10'-0" x 5'-0" high, 5 panels		7	2.290		1,430	33		1,463	1,625	
	1720	12'-0" x 6'-0" high, 6 panels		6	2.670		2,035	38		2,073	2,300	
	2000	Casement, builders model, bow, 8' x 5' high, std. glazed, 4 panels		10	1.600		870	23		893	995	
	2050	Insulating glass		10	1.600		1,055	23		1,078	1,200	
	2100	12'-0" x 6'-0" high, 6 panels, standard glazed		6	2.670		1,310	38		1,348	1,500	
	2200	Insulating glass		6	2.670		2,085	38		2,123	2,350	
	2300	Vinyl clad, premium, insulating glass, 8'-0" x 5'-0"		10	1.600		1,190	23		1,213	1,350	
	2340	10'-0" x 5'-0"		8	2		1,580	29		1,609	1,775	
	2380	10'-0" x 6'-0"		7	2.290		1,815	33		1,848	2,050	
	2420	12'-0" x 6'-0"		6	2.670		2,300	38		2,338	2,600	
	2600	Metal clad, deluxe, insul. glass, 8'-0" x 5'-0" high, 4 panels		10	1.600		870	23		893	995	
	2640	10'-0" x 5'-0" high, 5 panels		8	2		1,105	29		1,134	1,275	
	2680	10'-0" x 6'-0" high, 5 panels		7	2.290		1,335	33		1,368	1,525	
	2720	12'-0" x 6'-0" high, 6 panels		6	2.670		2,415	38		2,453	2,725	
	3000	Double hung, bldrs. model, bay, 8' x 4' high, std. glazed		10	1.600		810	23		833	930	
	3050	Insulating glass		10	1.600		915	23		938	1,050	
	3100	9'-0" x 5'-0" high, standard glazed		6	2.670		875	38		913	1,025	
	3200	Insulating glass		6	2.670		995	38		1,033	1,150	
	3300	Vinyl clad, premium, insulating glass, 7'-0" x 4'-6"		10	1.600		990	23		1,013	1,125	
	3340	8'-0" x 4'-6"		8	2		1,080	29		1,109	1,225	
	3380	8'-0" x 5'-0"		7	2.290		1,105	33		1,138	1,275	
	3420	9'-0" x 5'-0"		6	2.670		1,200	38		1,238	1,375	
	3600	Metal clad, deluxe, insul. glass, 7'-0" x 4'-0" high		10	1.600		685	23		708	790	
	3640	8'-0" x 4'-0" high		8	2		725	29		754	845	
	3680	8'-0" x 5'-0" high		7	2.290		790	33		823	925	
	3720	9'-0" x 5'-0" high		6	2.670		830	38		868	975	

For expanded coverage of these items see *Means Building Construction Cost Data 1991*

086 | Wood and Plastic Windows

086 100 | Wood Windows

			CREW	DAILY OUTPUT	MAN-HOURS	UNIT	MAT.	LABOR	EQUIP.	TOTAL	TOTAL INCL O&P	
108	7000	Drip cap, premolded vinyl, 8' long	2 Carp	30	.533	Ea.	58	7.65		65.65	77	108
	7040	12' long	"	26	.615	"	63	8.80		71.80	84	
120	0010	**CASEMENT WINDOW** Including frame, screen, and exterior trim (102)										120
	0020											
	0100	Average quality, bldrs. model, 2'-0" x 3'-0" high, standard glazed	1 Carp	10	.800	Ea.	130	11.45		141.45	160	
	0150	Insulating glass		10	.800		168	11.45		179.45	205	
	0200	2'-0" x 4'-6" high, standard glazed		9	.889		170	12.70		182.70	210	
	0250	Insulating glass		9	.889		217	12.70		229.70	260	
	0300	2'-3" x 6'-0" high, standard glazed		8	1		263	14.30		277.30	315	
	0350	Insulating glass		8	1		310	14.30		324.30	365	
	1000	Vinyl clad, premium, insulating glass, 2'-0" x 3'-0"		10	.800		197	11.45		208.45	235	
	1040	2'-0" x 4'-0"		9	.889		213	12.70		225.70	255	
	1080	2'-0" x 5'-0"		8	1		247	14.30		261.30	295	
	1120	2'-0" x 6'-0"		8	1		292	14.30		306.30	345	
	2000	Metal clad, deluxe, insulating glass, 2'-0" x 3'-0" high		10	.800		197	11.45		208.45	235	
	2040	2'-0" x 4'-0" high		9	.889		160	12.70		172.70	195	
	2080	2'-0" x 5'-0" high		8	1		182	14.30		196.30	225	
	2120	2'-0" x 6'-0" high		8	1		212	14.30		226.30	255	
	2200	For multiple leaf units, deduct for stationary sash										
	2210	2' high				Ea.	37			37	41	
	2300	4'-6" high					52			52	57	
	2400	6' high					51			51	56	
	3000	For installation, add per leaf						15%				
124	0010	**DOUBLE HUNG** Including frame, screen, and exterior trim										124
	0020											
	0100	Average quality, bldrs. model, 2'-0" x 3'-0" high, standard glazed	1 Carp	10	.800	Ea.	85	11.45		96.45	115	
	0150	Insulating glass		10	.800		122	11.45		133.45	155	
	0200	3'-0" x 4'-0" high, standard glazed		9	.889		106	12.70		118.70	140	
	0250	Insulating glass		9	.889		141	12.70		153.70	175	
	0300	4'-0" x 4'-6" high, standard glazed		8	1		120	14.30		134.30	155	
	0350	Insulating glass		8	1		170	14.30		184.30	210	
	1000	Vinyl clad, premium, insulating glass, 2'-6" x 3'-0"		10	.800		175	11.45		186.45	210	
	1100	3'-0" x 3'-6"		10	.800		211	11.45		222.45	250	
	1200	3'-0" x 4'-0"		9	.889		230	12.70		242.70	275	
	1300	3'-0" x 4'-6"		9	.889		242	12.70		254.70	285	
	1400	3'-0" x 5'-0"		8	1		252	14.30		266.30	300	
	1500	3'-6" x 6'-0"		8	1		303	14.30		317.30	355	
	2000	Metal clad, deluxe, insulating glass, 2'-6" x 3'-0" high		10	.800		108	11.45		119.45	140	
	2100	3'-0" x 3'-6" high		10	.800		130	11.45		141.45	160	
	2200	3'-0" x 4'-0" high		9	.889		142	12.70		154.70	175	
	2300	3'-0" x 4'-6" high		9	.889		149	12.70		161.70	185	
	2400	3'-0" x 5'-0" high		8	1		169	14.30		183.30	210	
	2500	3'-6" x 6'-0" high		8	1		189	14.30		203.30	230	
132	0010	**PICTURE WINDOW** Including frame and exterior trim										132
	0020											
	0100	Average quality, bldrs. model, 3'-6" x 4'-0" high, standard glazed	2 Carp	12	1.330	Ea.	155	19.05		174.05	200	
	0150	Insulating glass		12	1.330		192	19.05		211.05	245	
	0200	4'-0" x 4'-6" high, standard glazed		11	1.450		177	21		198	230	
	0250	Insulating glass		11	1.450		220	21		241	275	
	0300	5'-0" x 4'-0" high, standard glazed		11	1.450		205	21		226	260	
	0350	Insulating glass		11	1.450		237	21		258	295	
	0400	6'-0" x 4'-6" high, standard glazed		10	1.600		259	23		282	325	
	0450	Insulating glass		10	1.600		267	23		290	330	
	1000	Vinyl clad, premium, insulating glass, 4'-0" x 4'-0"		12	1.330		335	19.05		354.05	400	
	1100	4'-0" x 6'-0"		11	1.450		445	21		466	525	
	1200	5'-0" x 6'-0"		10	1.600		567	23		590	660	
	1300	6'-0" x 6'-0"		10	1.600		660	23		683	765	

For expanded coverage of these items see *Means Building Construction Cost Data 1991*

086 | Wood and Plastic Windows

086 100 | Wood Windows

			CREW	DAILY OUTPUT	MAN-HOURS	UNIT	MAT.	LABOR	EQUIP.	TOTAL	TOTAL INCL O&P	
132	2000	Metal clad, deluxe, insulating glass, 4'-0" x 4'-0" high	2 Carp	12	1.330	Ea.	184	19.05		203.05	235	132
	2100	4'-0" x 6'-0" high		11	1.450		268	21		289	330	
	2200	5'-0" x 6'-0" high		10	1.600		340	23		363	410	
	2300	6'-0" x 6'-0" high	↓	10	1.600	↓	415	23		438	495	
140	0010	**SLIDING WINDOW** Including frame, screen, and exterior trim										140
	0020											
	0100	Average quality, bldrs. model, 3'-0" x 3'-0" high, standard glazed	1 Carp	10	.800	Ea.	95	11.45		106.45	125	
	0120	Insulating glass		10	.800		131	11.45		142.45	165	
	0200	4'-0" x 3'-6" high, standard glazed		9	.889		121	12.70		133.70	155	
	0220	Insulating glass		9	.889		187	12.70		199.70	225	
	0300	6'-0" x 5'-0" high, standard glazed		8	1		205	14.30		219.30	250	
	0320	Insulating glass		8	1		305	14.30		319.30	360	
	1000	Vinyl clad, premium, insulating glass, 3'-0" x 3'-0"		10	.800		245	11.45		256.45	290	
	1050	4'-0" x 3'-6"		9	.889		303	12.70		315.70	355	
	1100	5'-0" x 4'-0"		9	.889		366	12.70		378.70	425	
	1150	6'-0" x 5'-0"		8	1		522	14.30		536.30	600	
	2000	Metal clad, deluxe, insulating glass, 3'-0" x 3'-0" high		10	.800		247	11.45		258.45	290	
	2050	4'-0" x 3'-6" high		9	.889		307	12.70		319.70	360	
	2100	5'-0" x 4'-0" high		9	.889		369	12.70		381.70	425	
	2150	6'-0" x 5'-0" high	↓	8	1	↓	530	14.30		544.30	605	
142	0010	**WEATHERSTRIPPING** See division 087-300										142
144	0010	**WINDOW GRILLE OR MUNTIN** Snap-in type										144
	0020	Colonial or diamond pattern										
	2000	Wood, awning window, glass size 28" x 16" high	1 Carp	30	.267	Ea.	9.25	3.81		13.06	16.55	
	2060	44" x 24" high		32	.250		12.55	3.58		16.13	19.80	
	2100	Casement, glass size, 20" x 36" high		30	.267		9.65	3.81		13.46	17	
	2180	20" x 56" high		32	.250	↓	13.55	3.58		17.13	21	
	2200	Double hung, glass size, 16" x 24" high		24	.333	Set	13	4.77		17.77	22	
	2280	32" x 32" high		34	.235	"	16.25	3.36		19.61	24	
	2500	Picture, glass size, 48" x 48" high		30	.267	Ea.	61	3.81		64.81	73	
	2580	60" x 68" high		28	.286	"	71.40	4.09		75.49	85	
	2600	Sliding, glass size, 14" x 36" high		24	.333	Set	35	4.77		39.77	46	
	2680	36" x 36" high	↓	22	.364	"	55	5.20		60.20	69	
148	0010	**WOOD SASH** Including glazing but not including trim										148
	0020											
	0050	Custom, 5'-0" x 4'-0", 1" dbl. glazed, 3/16" thick lites	2 Carp	3.20	5	Ea.	257	72		329	400	
	0100	¼" thick lites		5	3.200		273	46		319	375	
	0200	1" thick, triple glazed		5	3.200		394	46		440	510	
	0300	7'-0" x 4'-6" high, 1" double glazed, 3/16" thick lites		4.30	3.720		394	53		447	520	
	0400	¼" thick lites		4.30	3.720		445	53		498	580	
	0500	1" thick, triple glazed		4.30	3.720		499	53		552	640	
	0600	8'-6" x 5'-0" high, 1" double glazed, 3/16" thick lites		3.50	4.570		535	65		600	700	
	0700	¼" thick lites		3.50	4.570		588	65		653	755	
	0800	1" thick, triple glazed	↓	3.50	4.570	↓	588	65		653	755	
	0900	Window frames only, based on perimeter length				L.F.	1.95			1.95	2.15	
	0910											
	3000	Replacement sash, double hung, double glazing, to 12 S.F.	1 Carp	64	.125	S.F.	12.20	1.79		13.99	16.40	
	3100	12 S.F. to 20 S.F.		94	.085		11.20	1.22		12.42	14.35	
	3200	20 S.F. and over	↓	106	.075		10.50	1.08		11.58	13.35	
	3800	Triple glazing for above, add				↓	2.36			2.36	2.60	
	7000	Sash, single lite, 2'-0" x 2'-0" high	1 Carp	20	.400	Ea.	20.15	5.70		25.85	32	
	7050	2'-6" x 2'-0" high		19	.421		24.25	6		30.25	37	
	7100	2'-6" x 2'-6" high		18	.444		27.30	6.35		33.65	41	
	7150	3'-0" x 2'-0" high	↓	17	.471	↓	27.30	6.75		34.05	41	
152	0010	**WOOD SCREENS** Over 3 S.F., ¾" frames	2 Carp	375	.043	S.F.	2.42	.61		3.03	3.68	152
	0100	1-⅛" frames	"	375	.043	"	2.63	.61		3.24	3.91	

For expanded coverage of these items see *Means Building Construction Cost Data 1991*

087 | Hardware

087 100 | Finish Hardware

			CREW	DAILY OUTPUT	MAN-HOURS	UNIT	MAT.	LABOR	EQUIP.	TOTAL	TOTAL INCL O&P	
101	0010	**AVERAGE** Percentage for hardware, total job cost, minimum									.60%	101
	0050	Maximum									3%	
	0500	Total hardware for building, average distribution					85%	15%				
	1000	Door hardware, apartment, interior				Door	89			89	98	
	2100	Pocket door				Ea.	90			90	99	
110	0010	**DOORSTOPS** Holder and bumper, floor or wall	1 Carp	24	.333	Ea.	10	4.77		14.77	18.95	110
	1300	Wall bumper		24	.333		4.25	4.77		9.02	12.65	
	1600	Floor bumper, 1" high		24	.333		3.50	4.77		8.27	11.80	
	1900	Plunger type, door mounted		24	.333		24	4.77		28.77	34	
112	0010	**ENTRANCE LOCKS** Cylinder, grip handle, deadlocking latch		9	.889		88	12.70		100.70	120	112
	0020	Deadbolt		8	1		105	14.30		119.30	140	
	0100	Push and pull plate, dead bolt		8	1		97	14.30		111.30	130	
	0900	For handicapped lever, add					65			65	72	
116	0010	**HINGES** Full mortise, avg. freq., steel base, 4-½"x 4-½", USP				Pr.	18.50			18.50	20	116
	0100	5" x 5", USP					35			35	39	
	0200	6" x 6", USP					52			52	57	
	0400	Brass base, 4-½" x 4-½", US10					45			45	50	
	0500	5" x 5", US10					50			50	55	
	0600	6" x 6", US10					90			90	99	
	0800	Stainless steel base, 4-½" x 4-½", US32					60			60	66	
	0900	For non removable pin, add				Ea.	3.40			3.40	3.74	
	0910	For floating pin, driven tips, add					3.75			3.75	4.13	
	0930	For hospital type tip on pin, add					11			11	12.10	
	0940	For steeple type tip on pin, add					3.75			3.75	4.13	
	1000	Full mortise, high frequency, steel base, 4-½" x 4-½", USP				Pr.	45			45	50	
	1100	5" x 5", USP					50			50	55	
	1200	6" x 6", USP					75			75	83	
	1400	Brass base, 4-½" x 4-½", US10					70			70	77	
	1500	5" x 5", US10					85			85	94	
	1600	6" x 6", US10					95			95	105	
	1800	Stainless steel base, 4-½" x 4-½", US32					90			90	99	
	1930	For hospital type tip on pin, add				Ea.	12.50			12.50	13.75	
	2000	Full mortise low frequency, steel base, 4-½" x 4-½", USP				Pr.	10.85			10.85	11.95	
	2100	5" x 5", USP					24.50			24.50	27	
	2200	6" x 6", USP					38			38	42	
	2400	Brass base, 4-½" x 4-½", US10					35			35	39	
	2500	5" x 5", US10					46			46	51	
	2800	Stainless steel base, 4-½" x 4-½", US32					53			53	58	
118	0010	**KICK PLATE** 6" high, for 3' door, stainless steel	1 Carp	15	.533	Ea.	17	7.65		24.65	31	118
	0500	Bronze		15	.533		35	7.65		42.65	51	
120	0010	**LOCKSET** Standard duty, cylindrical, with sectional trim		12	.667		26.50	9.55		36.05	45	120
	0020	Non-keyed, passage		12	.667		29.50	9.55		39.05	48	
	0100	Privacy		12	.667		36	9.55		45.55	56	
	0400	Keyed, single cylinder function		10	.800		58	11.45		69.45	83	
	1700	Residential, interior door, minimum		16	.500		10.25	7.15		17.40	23	
	1720	Maximum		8	1		28	14.30		42.30	55	
	1800	Exterior, minimum		14	.571		22	8.15		30.15	38	
	1820	Maximum		8	1		96	14.30		110.30	130	
134	0010	**WINDOW HARDWARE**										134
	1000	Handles, surface mounted, aluminum	1 Carp	24	.333	Ea.	1.55	4.77		6.32	9.70	
	1020	Brass		24	.333		1.80	4.77		6.57	9.95	
	1040	Chrome		24	.333		1.65	4.77		6.42	9.80	
	1500	Recessed, aluminum		12	.667		.90	9.55		10.45	16.95	
	1520	Brass		12	.667		1	9.55		10.55	17.05	
	1540	Chrome		12	.667		.95	9.55		10.50	17	
	2000	Latches, aluminum		20	.400		1.30	5.70		7	11	

For expanded coverage of these items see *Means Building Construction Cost Data 1991*

087 | Hardware

087 100 | Finish Hardware

			CREW	DAILY OUTPUT	MAN-HOURS	UNIT	MAT.	LABOR	EQUIP.	TOTAL	TOTAL INCL O&P	
134	2020	Brass	1 Carp	20	.400	Ea.	1.55	5.70		7.25	11.25	134
	2040	Chrome	"	20	.400	"	1.45	5.70		7.15	11.15	

087 300 | Weatherstripping/Seals

304	0010	THRESHOLD 3' long door saddles, aluminum, minimum	1 Carp	20	.400	Ea.	22	5.70		27.70	34	304
	0100	Maximum		12	.667		68	9.55		77.55	91	
	0500	Bronze, minimum		20	.400		44	5.70		49.70	58	
	0600	Maximum		12	.667		120	9.55		129.55	150	
	0700	Rubber, ½" thick, 5-½" wide		20	.400		27	5.70		32.70	39	
	0800	2-¾" wide		20	.400		12.50	5.70		18.20	23	
306	0010	WEATHERSTRIPPING Window, double hung, 3' x 5', zinc		7.20	1.110	Opng.	8.50	15.90		24.40	36	306
	0100	Bronze		7.20	1.110		15.50	15.90		31.40	44	
	0200	Vinyl V strip		7	1.140		3	16.35		19.35	31	
	0500	As above but heavy duty, zinc		4.60	1.740		10.50	25		35.50	53	
	0600	Bronze		4.60	1.740		18.50	25		43.50	62	
	1000	Doors, wood frame, interlocking, for 3' x 7' door, zinc		3	2.670		10	38		48	75	
	1100	Bronze		3	2.670		15	38		53	80	
	1300	6' x 7' opening, zinc		2	4		11.50	57		68.50	110	
	1400	Bronze		2	4		17	57		74	115	
	1500	Vinyl V strip		6.40	1.250	Ea.	8.25	17.90		26.15	39	
	1700	Wood frame, spring type, bronze										
	1800	3' x 7' door	1 Carp	7.60	1.050	Opng.	6.90	15.05		21.95	33	
	1900	6' x 7' door		7	1.140		7.95	16.35		24.30	36	
	1920	Felt, 3' x 7' door		14	.571		1.70	8.15		9.85	15.55	
	1930	6' x 7' door		13	.615		1.95	8.80		10.75	16.85	
	1950	Rubber, 3' x 7' door		7.60	1.050		3.90	15.05		18.95	29	
	1960	6' x 7' door		7	1.140		4.45	16.35		20.80	32	
	2200	Metal frame, spring type, bronze										
	2300	3' x 7' door	1 Carp	2.80	2.860	Opng.	30	41		71	100	
	2400	6' x 7' door	"	2.30	3.480		35	50		85	120	
	2500	For stainless steel, spring type, add					133%					
	2510											
	2700	Metal frame, extruded sections, 3' x 7' door, aluminum	1 Carp	2	4	Opng.	30	57		87	130	
	2800	Bronze		2	4		68	57		125	170	
	3100	6' x 7' door, aluminum		1.20	6.670		36	95		131	200	
	3200	Bronze		1.20	6.670		80	95		175	245	
	3500	Threshold weatherstripping										
	3650	Door sweep, flush mounted, aluminum	1 Carp	32	.250	Ea.	8.50	3.58		12.08	15.35	
	3700	Vinyl		25	.320	"	9.80	4.58		14.38	18.45	
	4000	Astragal for double doors, aluminum		4	2	Opng.	16	29		45	65	
	4100	Bronze		4	2	"	26	29		55	76	
	5000	Garage door bottom weatherstrip, 12' aluminum, clear		14	.571	Ea.	12.60	8.15		20.75	28	
	5010	Bronze		14	.571		50	8.15		58.15	69	
	5050	Bottom protection, 12' aluminum, clear		14	.571		17.95	8.15		26.10	33	
	5100	Bronze		14	.571		62	8.15		70.15	82	

087 500 | Door/Window Acces.

504	0010	DETECTION SYSTEMS See division 168-120										504
506	0010	DOOR ACCESSORIES										506
	0020											
	1000	Knockers, brass, standard	1 Carp	16	.500	Ea.	32	7.15		39.15	47	
	1100	Deluxe		10	.800		100	11.45		111.45	130	
	4000	Security chain, standard		18	.444		5.50	6.35		11.85	16.70	
	4100	Deluxe		18	.444		33	6.35		39.35	47	

For expanded coverage of these items see *Means Building Construction Cost Data 1991*

088 | Glazing

088 100 | Glass

			CREW	DAILY OUTPUT	MAN-HOURS	UNIT	MAT.	LABOR	EQUIP.	TOTAL	TOTAL INCL O&P	
118	0010	FLOAT GLASS 3/16" thick, clear, plain	2 Glaz	130	.123	S.F.	3.05	1.80		4.85	6.30	118
	0200	Tempered, clear		130	.123		5.80	1.80		7.60	9.30	
	0300	Tinted		130	.123		6.95	1.80		8.75	10.60	
	0600	1/4" thick, clear, plain		120	.133		3.05	1.95		5	6.55	
	0700	Tinted		120	.133		4.10	1.95		6.05	7.70	
	0800	Tempered, clear		120	.133		5.45	1.95		7.40	9.15	
	0900	Tinted		120	.133		6.90	1.95		8.85	10.75	
	1200	5/16" thick, clear, plain		100	.160		5.90	2.34		8.24	10.30	
	1300	Tempered, clear		100	.160		9.85	2.34		12.19	14.65	
	1600	3/8" thick, clear, plain		75	.213		6.75	3.13		9.88	12.50	
	1700	Tinted		75	.213		8.65	3.13		11.78	14.60	
	1800	Tempered, clear		75	.213		14.10	3.13		17.23	21	
	1900	Tinted		75	.213		16.35	3.13		19.48	23	
	2200	1/2" thick, clear, plain		55	.291		11.05	4.26		15.31	19.10	
	2300	Tinted		55	.291		12.65	4.26		16.91	21	
	2400	Tempered, clear		55	.291		21.75	4.26		26.01	31	
	2500	Tinted		55	.291		24.65	4.26		28.91	34	
	2800	5/8" thick, clear, plain		45	.356		12.80	5.20		18	23	
	2900	Tempered, clear	↓	45	.356		24.15	5.20		29.35	35	
	4000	For low emissivity coating, add to above				↓	100%					
128	0010	GLAZING VARIABLES										128
	0600	For glass replacement, add				S.F.		100%				
	0700	For gasket settings, add				L.F.	2.35			2.35	2.59	
	0900	For sloped glazing, add				S.F.		25%				
	2000	Fabrication, polished edges, 1/4" thick				Inch	.22			.22	.24	
	2100	1/2" thick					.34			.34	.37	
	2500	Mitered edges, 1/4" thick					.78			.78	.86	
	2600	1/2" thick				↓	1.10			1.10	1.21	
132	0010	INSULATING GLASS 2 lites 1/8" float, 1/2" thk, under 15 S.F.										132
	0100	Tinted	2 Glaz	95	.168	S.F.	7.75	2.47		10.22	12.55	
	0204	Double glazed, 5/8" thk unit, 3/16" float, 15-30 S.F., clear		90	.178		7.15	2.60		9.75	12.10	
	0400	1" thick, double glazed, 1/4" float, 30 to 70 S.F., clear		75	.213		8.75	3.13		11.88	14.70	
	0500	Tinted		75	.213		9.50	3.13		12.63	15.55	
	2000	Both lites, light & heat reflective		85	.188		14.50	2.76		17.26	20	
	2500	Heat reflective, film inside, 1" thick unit, clear		85	.188		12.85	2.76		15.61	18.60	
	2600	Tinted		85	.188		13.60	2.76		16.36	19.45	
	3000	Film on weatherside, clear, 1/2" thick unit		95	.168		9.70	2.47		12.17	14.70	
	3100	5/8" thick unit		90	.178		10.95	2.60		13.55	16.30	
	3200	1" thick unit	↓	85	.188	↓	12.60	2.76		15.36	18.35	
144	0010	MIRRORS No frames, wall type, 1/4" plate glass, polished edge										144
	0100	Up to 5 S.F.	2 Glaz	125	.128	S.F.	6.45	1.88		8.33	10.15	
	0200	Over 5 S.F.		160	.100		6.05	1.47		7.52	9.05	
	0500	Door type, 1/4" plate glass, up to 12 S.F.		160	.100		5.85	1.47		7.32	8.80	
	1000	Float glass, up to 10 S.F., 1/8" thick		160	.100		4.60	1.47		6.07	7.45	
	1100	3/16" thick		150	.107		5.85	1.56		7.41	9	
	1500	12" x 12" wall tiles, square edge, clear		195	.082		1.85	1.20		3.05	3.99	
	1600	Veined		195	.082		2.60	1.20		3.80	4.81	
	2010	Bathroom, unframed, laminated	↓	160	.100		8.10	1.47		9.57	11.30	
176	0010	WINDOW GLASS Clear float, stops, putty bed, 1/8" thick	2 Glaz	480	.033	S.F.	2.85	.49		3.34	3.93	176
	0500	3/16" thick, clear		480	.033		2.95	.49		3.44	4.04	
	0600	Tinted		480	.033		3.60	.49		4.09	4.75	
	0700	Tempered	↓	480	.033	↓	5.65	.49		6.14	7	

For expanded coverage of these items see *Means Building Construction Cost Data 1991*

091 | Metal Support Systems

091 300 | Suspension Systems

			CREW	DAILY OUTPUT	MAN-HOURS	UNIT	MAT.	LABOR	EQUIP.	TOTAL	TOTAL INCL O&P	
304	0010	SUSPENSION SYSTEMS For boards and tile										304
	0050	Class A suspension system, T bar, 2' x 4' grid	1 Carp	800	.010	S.F.	.37	.14		.51	.65	
	0300	2' x 2' grid		650	.012		.49	.18		.67	.83	
	0400	Concealed Z bar suspension system, 12" module		520	.015		.56	.22		.78	.98	
	0600	1-½" carrier channels, 4' O.C., add		470	.017		.14	.24		.38	.56	
	0650	1-½" x 3-½" channels		470	.017		.35	.24		.59	.79	
	0700	Carrier channels for ceilings with										
	0900	recessed lighting fixtures, add	1 Carp	460	.017	S.F.	.30	.25		.55	.75	
	5000	Wire hangers, #12 wire	"	300	.027	Ea.	.30	.38		.68	.97	

092 | Lath, Plaster and Gypsum Board

092 050 | Furring & Lathing

			CREW	DAILY OUTPUT	MAN-HOURS	UNIT	MAT.	LABOR	EQUIP.	TOTAL	TOTAL INCL O&P	
052	0010	ACCESSORIES, PLASTER Casing bead, expanded flange, galvanized	1 Lath	2.70	2.960	C.L.F.	29	42		71	100	052
	0100	Zinc alloy	"	2.70	2.960		65	42		107	140	
	0900	Channels, cold rolled, 16 ga., ¾" deep, painted					20			20	22	
	1620	Corner bead, expanded bullnose, ¾" radius, #10 galvanized	1 Lath	2.60	3.080		40	44		84	115	
	1640	Zinc alloy		2.70	2.960		50	42		92	125	
	1650	#1, galvanized		2.55	3.140		27	45		72	100	
	1660	Zinc alloy		2.70	2.960		52	42		94	125	
	1670	Expanded wing, 2-¾" wide, galv. #1		2.65	3.020		42	43		85	115	
	1680	Zinc alloy		2.70	2.960		53	42		95	125	
	1700	Inside corner, (corner rite) 3" x 3", painted		2.60	3.080		22	44		66	95	
	1750	Strip-ex, 4" wide, painted		2.55			12			12	13.20	
	1800	Expansion joint, ¾" grounds, limited expansion, galv., 1 piece		2.70			38			38	42	
	1900	Zinc alloy		2.70			60			60	66	
	2100	Extreme expansion, galvanized, 2 piece		2.60			68			68	75	
	2300	Zinc alloy	L-ATH	2.70			115			115	125	
	2500	Joist clips for lath, 2-½" flange	1 Lath	1.90	4.210	M	55	60		115	155	
	2600	4-½" flange		1.80	4.440	"	63	63		126	170	
	2800	Metal base, galvanized and painted, 2-½" high		2.40	3.330	C.L.F.	35	48		83	115	
	2900	Stud clips for gypsum lath, field clip		2.35	3.400	M	55	49		104	140	
	3100	Resilient		2.30	3.480		85	50		135	175	
	3200	Starter/finisher		2.20	3.640		55	52		107	145	
054	0010	FURRING Beams & columns, ¾" galvanized channels,										054
	0030	12" O.C.	1 Lath	155	.052	S.F.	.25	.74		.99	1.46	
	0050	16" O.C.		170	.047		.20	.67		.87	1.30	
	0070	24" O.C.		185	.043		.16	.62		.78	1.17	
	0100	Ceilings, on steel, ¾" channels, galvanized, 12" O.C.		210	.038		.25	.54		.79	1.15	
	0300	16" O.C.		290	.028		.20	.39		.59	.85	
	0400	24" O.C.		420	.019		.16	.27		.43	.61	
	0600	1-½" channels, galvanized, 12" O.C.		190	.042		.34	.60		.94	1.34	
	0700	16" O.C.		260	.031		.27	.44		.71	1	
	0900	24" O.C.		390	.021		.22	.29		.51	.71	
	1000	Walls, galvanized, ¾" channels, 12" O.C.		235	.034		.25	.49		.74	1.06	
	1200	16" O.C.		265	.030		.20	.43		.63	.91	
	1300	24" O.C.		350	.023		.16	.33		.49	.70	
	1500	1-½" channels, galvanized, 12" O.C.,		210	.038		.34	.54		.88	1.25	
	1600	16" O.C.		240	.033		.27	.48		.75	1.06	
	1800	24" O.C.		305	.026		.22	.37		.59	.84	

For expanded coverage of these items see *Means Building Construction Cost Data 1991*

092 | Lath, Plaster and Gypsum Board

092 050 | Furring & Lathing

			CREW	DAILY OUTPUT	MAN-HOURS	UNIT	MAT.	LABOR	EQUIP.	TOTAL	TOTAL INCL O&P	
054	8000	Suspended ceilings, including carriers										054
	8200	1-½" carriers, 24" O.C. with:										
	8300	¾" channels, 16" O.C.	1 Lath	165	.048	S.F.	.37	.69		1.06	1.52	
	8320	24" O.C.		200	.040		.33	.57		.90	1.28	
	8400	1-½" channels, 16" O.C.		155	.052		.44	.74		1.18	1.67	
	8420	24" O.C.		190	.042		.39	.60		.99	1.39	
	8600	2" carriers, 24" O.C. with:										
	8700	¾" channels, 16" O.C.	1 Lath	155	.052	S.F.	.39	.74		1.13	1.61	
	8720	24" O.C.		190	.042		.35	.60		.95	1.35	
	8800	1-½" channels, 16" O.C.		145	.055		.46	.79		1.25	1.77	
	8820	24" O.C.		180	.044		.41	.63		1.04	1.47	
056	0010	**GYPSUM LATH** Plain or perforated, nailed, ⅜" thick	1 Lath	765	.010	S.F.	.36	.15		.51	.64	056
	0100	½" thick, nailed		720	.011		.39	.16		.55	.68	
	0300	Clipped to steel studs, ⅜" thick		675	.012		.40	.17		.57	.71	
	0400	½" thick		630	.013		.43	.18		.61	.76	
	0600	Firestop gypsum base, to steel studs, ⅜" thick		630	.013		.41	.18		.59	.74	
	0700	½" thick		585	.014		.44	.19		.63	.80	
	0900	Foil back, to steel studs, ⅜" thick		675	.012		.40	.17		.57	.71	
	1000	½" thick		630	.013		.43	.18		.61	.76	
	1500	For ceiling installations, add		1,950	.004			.06		.06	.09	
	1600	For columns and beams, add		1,550	.005			.07		.07	.12	
058	0011	**METAL LATH**										058
	0020											
	3600	2.5 lb. diamond painted, on wood framing, on walls	1 Lath	765	.010	S.F.	.18	.15		.33	.44	
	3700	On ceilings		675	.012		.18	.17		.35	.47	
	4200	3.4 lb. diamond painted, wired to steel framing, on walls		675	.012		.20	.17		.37	.49	
	4300	On ceilings		540	.015		.20	.21		.41	.56	
	5100	Rib lath, painted, wired to steel, on walls, 2.75 lb.		675	.012		.19	.17		.36	.48	
	5200	3.4 lb.		630	.013		.22	.18		.40	.53	
	5700	Suspended ceiling system, incl. 3.4 lb. diamond lath, painted		135	.059		.90	.84		1.74	2.35	
	5800	Galvanized		135	.059		.92	.84		1.76	2.37	

092 100 | Gypsum Plaster

			CREW	DAILY OUTPUT	MAN-HOURS	UNIT	MAT.	LABOR	EQUIP.	TOTAL	TOTAL INCL O&P	
108	0010	**GYPSUM PLASTER** 80# bag, less than 1 ton (110)				Bag	12.20			12.20	13.40	108
	0020											
	0300	2 coats, no lath included, on walls	J-1	945	.042	S.F.	.34	.56	.04	.94	1.32	
	0400	On ceilings		828	.048		.34	.64	.04	1.02	1.46	
	0900	3 coats, no lath included, on walls		783	.051		.47	.67	.04	1.18	1.67	
	1000	On ceilings		702	.057		.47	.75	.05	1.27	1.80	
	1600	For irregular or curved surfaces, add					30%			30%		
	1800	For columns and beams, add					50%			50%		
116	0010	**PERLITE OR VERMICULITE PLASTER** 100 lb. bags Under 200 bags				Bag	12.35			12.35	13.60	116
	0300	2 coats, no lath included, on walls	J-1	830	.048	S.F.	.38	.63	.04	1.05	1.50	
	0400	On ceilings		710	.056		.38	.74	.05	1.17	1.69	
	0900	3 coats, no lath included, on walls		665	.060		.60	.79	.05	1.44	2.01	
	1000	On ceilings		565	.071		.60	.93	.06	1.59	2.25	
	1700	For irregular or curved surfaces, add to above					30%			30%		
	1800	For columns and beams, add to above					50%			50%		
	1900	For soffits, add to ceiling prices						40%				

092 150 | Veneer Plaster

			CREW	DAILY OUTPUT	MAN-HOURS	UNIT	MAT.	LABOR	EQUIP.	TOTAL	TOTAL INCL O&P	
154	0010	**THIN COAT** Plaster, 1 coat veneer, not incl. lath	J-1	3,600	.011	S.F.	.09	.15	.01	.25	.35	154
	1000	In 50 lb. bags				Bag	8.50			8.50	9.35	

092 300 | Aggregate Coatings

			CREW	DAILY OUTPUT	MAN-HOURS	UNIT	MAT.	LABOR	EQUIP.	TOTAL	TOTAL INCL O&P	
304	0010	**STUCCO** 3 coats 1" thick, float finish, with mesh, on wood frame (111)	J-2	470	.102	S.F.	.64	1.36	.07	2.07	3	304
	0100	On masonry construction	J-1	495	.081	"	.21	1.06	.07	1.34	2.05	

For expanded coverage of these items see *Means Building Construction Cost Data 1991*

092 | Lath, Plaster and Gypsum Board

092 300 | Aggregate Coatings

		Description	CREW	DAILY OUTPUT	MAN-HOURS	UNIT	MAT.	LABOR	EQUIP.	TOTAL	TOTAL INCL O&P	
304	0150	2 coats, ¾" thick, float finish, no lath incl.	J-1	980	.041	S.F.	.57	.54	.03	1.14	1.55	304
	0300	For trowel finish, add	1 Plas	1,530	.005			.07		.07	.12	
	0600	For coloring and special finish, add, minimum					.03			.03	.03	
	0700	Maximum					.12			.12	.13	
	1000	Exterior stucco, with bonding agent, 3 coats, on walls	J-1	1,800	.022		.32	.29	.02	.63	.85	
	1200	Ceilings		1,620	.025		.32	.32	.02	.66	.90	
	1300	Beams		720	.056		.32	.73	.05	1.10	1.60	
	1500	Columns		900	.044		.32	.58	.04	.94	1.35	
	1600	Mesh, painted, nailed to wood, 1.8 lb.	1 Lath	540	.015		.28	.21		.49	.65	
	1800	3.6 lb.		495	.016		.32	.23		.55	.72	
	1900	Wired to steel, painted, 1.8 lb.		477	.017		.28	.24		.52	.69	
	2100	3.6 lb.		450	.018		.32	.25		.57	.76	

092 600 | Gypsum Board Systems

		Description	CREW	DAILY OUTPUT	MAN-HOURS	UNIT	MAT.	LABOR	EQUIP.	TOTAL	TOTAL INCL O&P	
602	0010	**BLUEBOARD** For use with thin coat										602
	0100	plaster application (see division 092-154)										
	1000	⅜" thick, on walls or ceilings, standard, no finish included	2 Carp	1,900	.008	S.F.	.16	.12		.28	.38	
	1100	With thin coat plaster finish		875	.018		.25	.26		.51	.71	
	1400	On beams, columns, or soffits, standard, no finish included		675	.024		.26	.34		.60	.85	
	1450	With thin coat plaster finish		475	.034		.35	.48		.83	1.19	
	3000	½" thick, on walls or ceilings, standard, no finish included		1,900	.008		.17	.12		.29	.39	
	3100	With thin coat plaster finish		875	.018		.26	.26		.52	.72	
	3300	Fire resistant, no finish included		1,900	.008		.21	.12		.33	.43	
	3400	With thin coat plaster finish		875	.018		.30	.26		.56	.77	
	3450	On beams, columns, or soffits, standard, no finish included		675	.024		.27	.34		.61	.86	
	3500	With thin coat plaster finish		475	.034		.36	.48		.84	1.20	
	3700	Fire resistant, no finish included		675	.024		.31	.34		.65	.91	
	3800	With thin coat plaster finish		475	.034		.40	.48		.88	1.25	
	5000	⅝" thick, on walls or ceilings, fire resistant, no finish included		1,900	.008		.21	.12		.33	.43	
	5100	With thin coat plaster finish		875	.018		.30	.26		.56	.77	
	5500	On beams, columns, or soffits, no finish included		675	.024		.31	.34		.65	.91	
	5600	With thin coat plaster finish		475	.034		.40	.48		.88	1.25	
	6000	For high ceilings, over 8' high, add		3,060	.005		.08	.07		.15	.21	
	6500	For over 3 stories high, add per story		6,100	.003		.04	.04		.08	.11	
608	0010	**DRYWALL** Gypsum plasterboard, nailed or screwed to studs,										608
	0100	unless otherwise noted										
	0150	⅜" thick, on walls, standard, no finish included	2 Carp	2,000	.008	S.F.	.16	.11		.27	.37	
	0200	On ceilings, standard, no finish included		1,800	.009		.16	.13		.29	.39	
	0250	On beams, columns, or soffits, no finish included		675	.024		.26	.34		.60	.85	
	0300	½" thick, on walls, standard, no finish included		2,000	.008		.17	.11		.28	.38	
	0350	Taped and finished		965	.017		.22	.24		.46	.64	
	0400	Fire resistant, no finish included		2,000	.008		.21	.11		.32	.42	
	0450	Taped and finished		965	.017		.26	.24		.50	.68	
	0500	Water resistant, no finish included		2,000	.008		.27	.11		.38	.49	
	0550	Taped and finished		965	.017		.32	.24		.56	.75	
	0600	Prefinished, vinyl, clipped to studs		900	.018		.55	.25		.80	1.03	
	0650											
	1000	On ceilings, standard, no finish included	2 Carp	1,800	.009	S.F.	.17	.13		.30	.40	
	1050	Taped and finished		765	.021		.22	.30		.52	.74	
	1100	Fire resistant, no finish included		1,800	.009		.21	.13		.34	.44	
	1150	Taped and finished		765	.021		.26	.30		.56	.79	
	1200	Water resistant, no finish included		1,800	.009		.27	.13		.40	.51	
	1250	Taped and finished		765	.021		.32	.30		.62	.85	
	1500	On beams, columns, or soffits, standard, no finish included		675	.024		.27	.34		.61	.86	
	1550	Taped and finished		475	.034		.32	.48		.80	1.16	
	1600	Fire resistant, no finish included		675	.024		.31	.34		.65	.91	
	1650	Taped and finished		475	.034		.36	.48		.84	1.20	
	1700	Water resistant, no finish included		675	.024		.37	.34		.71	.97	

For expanded coverage of these items see *Means Building Construction Cost Data 1991*

092 | Lath, Plaster and Gypsum Board

092 600 | Gypsum Board Systems

			CREW	DAILY OUTPUT	MAN-HOURS	UNIT	MAT.	LABOR	EQUIP.	TOTAL	TOTAL INCL O&P	
608	1750	Taped and finished	2 Carp	475	.034	S.F.	.42	.48		.90	1.27	608
	2000	5/8" thick, on walls, standard, no finish included		2,000	.008		.21	.11		.32	.42	
	2050	Taped and finished		965	.017		.26	.24		.50	.68	
	2100	Fire resistant, no finish included		2,000	.008		.23	.11		.34	.44	
	2150	Taped and finished		965	.017		.28	.24		.52	.70	
	2200	Water resistant, no finish included		2,000	.008		.31	.11		.42	.53	
	2250	Taped and finished		965	.017		.36	.24		.60	.79	
	2300	Prefinished, vinyl, clipped to studs		900	.018		.62	.25		.87	1.11	
	2350											
	3000	On ceilings, standard, no finish included	2 Carp	1,800	.009	S.F.	.21	.13		.34	.44	
	3050	Taped and finished		765	.021		.26	.30		.56	.79	
	3100	Fire resistant, no finish included		1,800	.009		.23	.13		.36	.47	
	3150	Taped and finished		765	.021		.28	.30		.58	.81	
	3200	Water resistant, no finish included		1,800	.009		.31	.13		.44	.55	
	3250	Taped and finished		765	.021		.36	.30		.66	.90	
	3500	On beams, columns, or soffits, standard, no finish included		675	.024		.31	.34		.65	.91	
	3550	Taped and finished		475	.034		.36	.48		.84	1.20	
	3600	Fire resistant, no finish included		675	.024		.33	.34		.67	.93	
	3650	Taped and finished		475	.034		.38	.48		.86	1.22	
	3700	Water resistant, no finish included		675	.024		.41	.34		.75	1.02	
	3750	Taped and finished		475	.034		.46	.48		.94	1.31	
	4000	Fireproofing, beams or columns, 2 layers, 1/2" thick, incl finish		330	.048		.52	.69		1.21	1.73	
	4050	5/8" thick		300	.053		.56	.76		1.32	1.89	
	4100	3 layers, 1/2" thick		225	.071		.78	1.02		1.80	2.56	
	4150	5/8" thick		210	.076		.84	1.09		1.93	2.75	
	5200	For high ceilings, over 8' high, add		3,060	.005		.08	.07		.15	.21	
	5270	For textured spray, add	2 Lath	1,100	.015		.10	.21		.31	.44	
	5350	For finishing corners, inside or outside, add	2 Carp	1,100	.015	L.F.	.05	.21		.26	.40	
	5500	For acoustical sealant, add per bead	1 Carp	500	.016	"	.02	.23		.25	.40	
	5550	Sealant, 1 quart tube				Ea.	4			4	4.40	
	5600	Sound deadening board, 1/4" gypsum	2 Carp	1,800	.009	S.F.	.15	.13		.28	.38	
	5650	1/2" wood fiber	"	1,800	.009	"	.20	.13		.33	.43	
612	0010	**METAL STUDS, DRYWALL** Partitions, 10' high, with runners										612
	2000	Non-load bearing, galvanized, 25 ga. 1-5/8", 16" O.C.	1 Carp	450	.018	S.F.	.23	.25		.48	.68	
	2100	24" O.C.		520	.015		.19	.22		.41	.58	
	2200	2-1/2" wide, 16" O.C.		440	.018		.27	.26		.53	.73	
	2250	24" O.C.		510	.016		.22	.22		.44	.62	
	2300	3-5/8" wide, 16" O.C.		430	.019		.31	.27		.58	.79	
	2350	24" O.C.		500	.016		.26	.23		.49	.67	
	2400	4" wide, 16" O.C.		420	.019		.35	.27		.62	.84	
	2450	24" O.C.		490	.016		.29	.23		.52	.71	
	2500	6" wide, 16" O.C.		410	.020		.45	.28		.73	.96	
	2550	24" O.C.		480	.017		.37	.24		.61	.81	
	2600	20 ga. studs, 1-5/8" wide, 16" O.C.		450	.018		.41	.25		.66	.88	
	2650	24" O.C.		520	.015		.34	.22		.56	.74	
	2700	2-1/2" wide, 16" O.C.		440	.018		.47	.26		.73	.95	
	2750	24" O.C.		510	.016		.39	.22		.61	.80	
	2800	3-5/8" wide, 16" O.C.		430	.019		.56	.27		.83	1.06	
	2850	24" O.C.		500	.016		.46	.23		.69	.89	
	2900	4" wide, 16" O.C.		420	.019		.59	.27		.86	1.10	
	2950	24" O.C.		490	.016		.49	.23		.72	.93	
	3000	6" wide, 16" O.C.		410	.020		.74	.28		1.02	1.28	
	3050	24" O.C.		480	.017		.61	.24		.85	1.07	
	4000	LB studs, light ga. structural, galv., 18 ga., 2-1/2", 16" O.C.		200	.040		.88	.57		1.45	1.92	
	4100	24" O.C.		240	.033		.73	.48		1.21	1.60	
	4200	3-5/8" wide, 16" O.C.		190	.042		1.01	.60		1.61	2.12	
	4250	24" O.C.		230	.035		.84	.50		1.34	1.76	
	4300	4" wide, 16" O.C.		180	.044		1.07	.64		1.71	2.24	

For expanded coverage of these items see *Means Building Construction Cost Data 1991*

092 | Lath, Plaster and Gypsum Board

092 600 | Gypsum Board Systems

			CREW	DAILY OUTPUT	MAN-HOURS	UNIT	MAT.	LABOR	EQUIP.	TOTAL	TOTAL INCL O&P	
612	4350	24" O.C.	1 Carp	220	.036	S.F.	.88	.52		1.40	1.84	612
	4400	6" wide, 16" O.C.		170	.047		1.29	.67		1.96	2.54	
	4450	24" O.C.		210	.038		1.07	.54		1.61	2.09	
	4600	16 ga. studs, 2-½", 16" O.C.		180	.044		1.10	.64		1.74	2.27	
	4650	24" O.C.		220	.036		.92	.52		1.44	1.88	
	4700	3-⅝" wide, 16" O.C.		170	.047		1.24	.67		1.91	2.49	
	4750	24" O.C.		210	.038		1.03	.54		1.57	2.04	
	4800	4" wide, 16" O.C.		160	.050		1.33	.72		2.05	2.66	
	4850	24" O.C.		200	.040		1.11	.57		1.68	2.18	
	4900	6" wide, 16" O.C.		150	.053		1.64	.76		2.40	3.08	
	4950	24" O.C.	↓	190	.042	↓	1.36	.60		1.96	2.50	

092 800 | Drywall Accessories

			CREW	DAILY OUTPUT	MAN-HOURS	UNIT	MAT.	LABOR	EQUIP.	TOTAL	TOTAL INCL O&P	
804	0010	ACCESSORIES, DRYWALL Casing bead, galvanized steel	1 Carp	290	.028	L.F.	.13	.39		.52	.80	804
	0100	Vinyl		290	.028		.19	.39		.58	.87	
	0300	Corner bead, galvanized steel, 1" x 1"		400	.020		.08	.29		.37	.57	
	0400	1-¼" x 1-¼"		350	.023		.11	.33		.44	.67	
	0600	Vinyl corner bead		400	.020		.13	.29		.42	.62	
	0700	Door casing, vinyl, for 2" wall systems		250	.032		.22	.46		.68	1.01	
	0900	Furring channel, galv. steel, ⅞" deep, standard		260	.031		.16	.44		.60	.91	
	1000	Resilient		260	.031		.16	.44		.60	.91	
	1100	J trim, galvanized steel, ½" wide		300	.027		.14	.38		.52	.79	
	1120	⅝" wide	↓	300	.027	↓	.14	.38		.52	.79	
	1160	Screws #6 x 1" A				M	5.80			5.80	6.40	
	1170	#6 x 1-⅝" A				"	8.90			8.90	9.80	
	1500	Z stud, galvanized steel, 1-½" wide	1 Carp	260	.031	L.F.	.22	.44		.66	.98	

093 | Tile

093 100 | Ceramic Tile

			CREW	DAILY OUTPUT	MAN-HOURS	UNIT	MAT.	LABOR	EQUIP.	TOTAL	TOTAL INCL O&P	
102	0010	CERAMIC TILE Base, using 1' x 5" hi pc. with 1" x 1" tiles, mud set	D-7	82	.195	L.F.	5.30	2.51		7.81	9.85	102
	0100	Thin set	"	128	.125		5.05	1.61		6.66	8.10	
	0300	For 6" high base, 1" x 1" tile face, add					.50			.50	.55	
	0400	For 2" x 2" tile face, add to above					.25			.25	.28	
	0600	Cove base, 4-¼" x 4-¼" high, mud set	D-7	91	.176		2.70	2.26		4.96	6.55	
	0700	Thin set		128	.125		2.50	1.61		4.11	5.30	
	0900	6" x 4-¼" high, mud set		100	.160		2.60	2.06		4.66	6.15	
	1000	Thin set		137	.117		2.40	1.50		3.90	5.05	
	1200	Sanitary cove base, 6" x 4-¼" high, mud set		93	.172		2.75	2.22		4.97	6.55	
	1300	Thin set		124	.129		2.45	1.66		4.11	5.35	
	1500	6" x 6" high, mud set		84	.190		3.30	2.45		5.75	7.55	
	1600	Thin set		117	.137		3	1.76		4.76	6.10	
	1800	Bathroom accessories, average		82	.195	Ea.	9	2.51		11.51	13.90	
	1900	Bathtub, 5', rec. 4-¼" x 4-¼" tile wainscot, adhesive set 6' high		2.90	5.520		230	71		301	365	
	2100	7' high wainscot		2.50	6.400		270	82		352	430	
	2200	8' high wainscot	↓	2.20	7.270	↓	305	94		399	485	
	2400	Bullnose trim, 4-¼" x 4-¼", mud set		82	.195	L.F.	2.70	2.51		5.21	6.95	
	2500	Thin set		128	.125		2.40	1.61		4.01	5.20	
	2700	6" x 4-¼" bullnose trim, mud set		84	.190		3.50	2.45		5.95	7.75	
	2800	Thin set		124	.129		3.30	1.66		4.96	6.25	

For expanded coverage of these items see *Means Building Construction Cost Data 1991*

093 | Tile

093 100 | Ceramic Tile

			Crew	Daily Output	Man-Hours	Unit	Mat.	Labor	Equip.	Total	Total Incl O&P	
102	3000	Floors, natural clay, random or uniform, thin set, color group 1	D-7	183	.087	S.F.	2.95	1.13		4.08	5.05	102
	3100	Color group 2		183	.087		3.15	1.13		4.28	5.25	
	3300	Porcelain type, 1 color, color group 2, 1" x 1"		183	.087		3.45	1.13		4.58	5.60	
	3400	2" x 2" or 2" x 1", thin set	↓	183	.087		3.60	1.13		4.73	5.75	
	3600	For random blend, 2 colors, add					.60			.60	.66	
	3700	4 colors, add					.85			.85	.94	
	4300	Specialty tile, 4-¼" x 4-¼" x ½", decorator finish	D-7	183	.087	↓	5.45	1.13		6.58	7.80	
	4310											
	4500	Add for epoxy grout, ¹⁄₁₆" joint, 1" x 1" tile	D-7	965	.017	S.F.	.45	.21		.66	.84	
	4600	2" x 2" tile	"	965	.017	"	.40	.21		.61	.78	
	4800	Pregrouted sheets, walls, 4-¼" x 4-¼", 6" x 4-¼"										
	4810	and 8-½" x 4-¼", 4 S.F. sheets, silicone grout	D-7	240	.067	S.F.	3.55	.86		4.41	5.30	
	5100	Floors, unglazed, 2 S.F. sheets,										
	5110	urethane adhesive	D-7	180	.089	S.F.	3.50	1.14		4.64	5.65	
	5400	Walls, interior, thin set, 4-¼" x 4-¼" tile		180	.089		1.85	1.14		2.99	3.86	
	5500	6" x 4-¼" tile		190	.084		2.15	1.08		3.23	4.09	
	5700	8-½" x 4-¼" tile		190	.084		2.80	1.08		3.88	4.80	
	5800	6" x 6" tile		200	.080		2.30	1.03		3.33	4.17	
	6000	Decorated wall tile, 4-¼" x 4-¼", minimum		180	.089		2.50	1.14		3.64	4.57	
	6100	Maximum		160	.100		9.50	1.29		10.79	12.50	
	6600	Crystalline glazed, 4-¼" x 4-¼", mud set, plain		100	.160		3.20	2.06		5.26	6.80	
	6700	4-¼" x 4-¼", scored tile		100	.160		3.30	2.06		5.36	6.90	
	6900	1-⅜" squares		93	.172		3.30	2.22		5.52	7.15	
	7000	For epoxy grout, ¹⁄₁₆" joints, 4-¼" tile, add		965	.017		.45	.21		.66	.84	
	7200	For tile set in dry mortar, add		1,735	.009			.12		.12	.19	
	7300	For tile set in portland cement mortar, add	↓	290	.055	↓		.71		.71	1.13	

093 300 | Quarry Tile

			Crew	Daily Output	Man-Hours	Unit	Mat.	Labor	Equip.	Total	Total Incl O&P	
304	0010	QUARRY TILE Base, cove or sanitary, 2" or 5" high, mud set										304
	0100	½" thick	D-7	110	.145	L.F.	2.50	1.87		4.37	5.75	
	0300	Bullnose trim, red, mud set, 6" x 6" x ½" thick		120	.133		2.50	1.72		4.22	5.50	
	0400	4" x 4" x ½" thick		110	.145		2.50	1.87		4.37	5.75	
	0600	4" x 8" x ½" thick, using 8" as edge	↓	130	.123	↓	2.60	1.58		4.18	5.40	
	0610											
	0700	Floors, mud set, 1000 S.F. lots, red, 4" x 4" x ½" thick	D-7	120	.133	S.F.	2.90	1.72		4.62	5.90	
	0900	6" x 6" x ½" thick		140	.114		2.90	1.47		4.37	5.55	
	1000	4" x 8" x ½" thick	↓	130	.123		3.05	1.58		4.63	5.90	
	1300	For waxed coating, add					.30			.30	.33	
	1500	For colors other than green, add					.40			.40	.44	
	1600	For abrasive surface, add					.45			.45	.50	
	1800	Brown tile, imported, 6" x 6" x ¾"	D-7	120	.133		3.50	1.72		5.22	6.60	
	1900	8" x 8" x 1"		110	.145		4.35	1.87		6.22	7.75	
	2100	For thin set mortar application, deduct	↓	700	.023	↓		.29		.29	.47	
	2500											
	2700	Stair tread & riser, 6" x 6" x ¾", plain	D-7	50	.320	S.F.	4.50	4.12		8.62	11.50	
	2800	Abrasive		50	.320		5.05	4.12		9.17	12.10	
	3000	Wainscot, 6" x 6" x ½", thin set, red		105	.152		2.75	1.96		4.71	6.15	
	3100	Colors other than green		105	.152	↓	2.95	1.96		4.91	6.35	
	3300	Window sill, 6" wide, ¾" thick		90	.178	L.F.	3.60	2.29		5.89	7.60	
	3400	Corners	↓	90	.178	Ea.	2.90	2.29		5.19	6.85	

093 700 | Metal Tile

			Crew	Daily Output	Man-Hours	Unit	Mat.	Labor	Equip.	Total	Total Incl O&P	
701	0010	METAL TILE 4' x 4' sheet, 24 ga., tile pattern, nailed										701
	0200	Stainless steel	2 Carp	512	.031	S.F.	14.75	.45		15.20	16.95	
	0400	Aluminized steel	"	512	.031	"	7.80	.45		8.25	9.35	

For expanded coverage of these items see *Means Building Construction Cost Data 1991*

094 | Terrazzo

094 200 | Precast Terrazzo

			CREW	DAILY OUTPUT	MAN-HOURS	UNIT	MAT.	LABOR	EQUIP.	TOTAL	TOTAL INCL O&P	
201	0010	**TERRAZZO, PRECAST** Base, 6" high, straight	1 Mstz	35	.229	L.F.	6	3.28		9.28	11.80	201
	0100	Cove		30	.267		7.20	3.83		11.03	14	
	0300	8" high base, straight		30	.267		6.60	3.83		10.43	13.35	
	0400	Cove	↓	25	.320		7.80	4.59		12.39	15.90	
	0600	For white cement, add					.25			.25	.28	
	0700	For 16 ga. zinc toe strip, add					.75			.75	.83	
	0900	Curbs, 4" x 4" high	1 Mstz	19	.421		12.45	6.05		18.50	23	
	1000	8" x 8" high	"	15	.533		13.60	7.65		21.25	27	
	1200	Floor tiles, non-slip, 1" thick, 12" x 12"	D-1	29	.552	S.F.	9	7.25		16.25	22	
	1300	1-¼" thick, 12" x 12"		29	.552		10	7.25		17.25	23	
	1500	16" x 16"		23	.696		11.20	9.15		20.35	27	
	1600	1-½" thick, 16" x 16"	↓	21	.762		13.50	10		23.50	31	
	4800	Wainscot, 12" x 12" x 1" tiles	1 Mstz	12	.667		9	9.55		18.55	25	
	4900	16" x 16" x 1-½" tiles	"	8	1	↓	13.50	14.35		27.85	38	

095 | Acoustical Treatment and Wood Flooring

095 100 | Acoustical Ceilings

			CREW	DAILY OUTPUT	MAN-HOURS	UNIT	MAT.	LABOR	EQUIP.	TOTAL	TOTAL INCL O&P	
102	0010	**CEILING TILE** Stapled, cemented or installed on suspension										102
	0100	system, 12" x 12" or 12" x 24", not including furring										
	0600	Mineral fiber, vinyl coated, ⅝" thick	1 Carp	200	.040	S.F.	.48	.57		1.05	1.48	
	0700	¾" thick		200	.040		.63	.57		1.20	1.65	
	0900	Fire rated, ¾" thick, plain faced		200	.040		.64	.57		1.21	1.66	
	1000	Plastic coated face		200	.040		.69	.57		1.26	1.72	
	1200	Aluminum faced, ⅝" thick, plain		200	.040	↓	.83	.57		1.40	1.87	
	1210		↓									
	3300	For flameproofing, add				S.F.	.06			.06	.07	
	3400	For sculptured 3 dimensional, add				↓	.18			.18	.20	
	3900	For ceiling primer, add					.09			.09	.10	
	4000	For ceiling cement, add					.24			.24	.26	
104	0010	**SUSPENDED ACOUSTIC CEILING BOARDS** Not including										104
	0100	suspension system										
	0300	Fiberglass boards, film faced, 2' x 2' or 2' x 4', ⅝" thick	1 Carp	625	.013	S.F.	.39	.18		.57	.74	
	0400	¾" thick		600	.013		.45	.19		.64	.81	
	0500	3" thick, thermal, R11		500	.016		.95	.23		1.18	1.43	
	0600	Glass cloth faced fiberglass, ¾" thick		500	.016		1.24	.23		1.47	1.75	
	0700	1" thick		500	.016		1.38	.23		1.61	1.90	
	0820	1-½" thick, nubby face		500	.016		1.68	.23		1.91	2.23	
	0900	Mineral fiber boards, ⅝" thick, aluminum faced, 24" x 24"		600	.013		1.05	.19		1.24	1.47	
	0930	24" x 48"		650	.012		1.02	.18		1.20	1.42	
	0960	Standard face		675	.012		.45	.17		.62	.78	
	1000	Plastic coated face		400	.020		.70	.29		.99	1.25	
	1200	Mineral fiber, 2 hour rating, ⅝" thick		675	.012		.65	.17		.82	1	
	1300	Mirror faced panels, ¹⁵⁄₁₆" thick, 2' x 2'		500	.016		4.50	.23		4.73	5.35	
	1900	Eggcrate, acrylic, ½" x ½" x ½" cubes		500	.016		1.05	.23		1.28	1.54	
	2100	Polystyrene eggcrate, ⅜" x ⅜" x ½" cubes		500	.016		.86	.23		1.09	1.33	
	2200	½" x ½" x ½" cubes		500	.016		1.18	.23		1.41	1.68	
	2400	Luminous panels, prismatic, acrylic		400	.020		1.24	.29		1.53	1.84	
	2500	Polystyrene		400	.020		.65	.29		.94	1.19	
	2700	Flat white acrylic		400	.020		2.20	.29		2.49	2.90	
	2800	Polystyrene		400	.020		1.50	.29		1.79	2.13	
	3000	Drop pan, white, acrylic		400	.020		3.25	.29		3.54	4.05	

For expanded coverage of these items see *Means Building Construction Cost Data 1991*

095 | Acoustical Treatment and Wood Flooring

095 100 | Acoustical Ceilings

			CREW	DAILY OUTPUT	MAN-HOURS	UNIT	MAT.	LABOR	EQUIP.	TOTAL	TOTAL INCL O&P	
104	3100	Polystyrene	1 Carp	400	.020	S.F.	2.70	.29		2.99	3.45	104
	3600	Perforated aluminum sheets, .024" thick, corrugated, painted		500	.016		1.30	.23		1.53	1.81	
	3700	Plain		500	.016		1.16	.23		1.39	1.66	
	3750	Wood fiber in cementitious binder, 2' x 2' or 4', painted, 1" thick		600	.013		.89	.19		1.08	1.30	
	3760	2" thick		550	.015		1.45	.21		1.66	1.94	
	3770	2-½" thick		500	.016		1.98	.23		2.21	2.56	
	3780	3" thick	↓	450	.018	↓	2.28	.25		2.53	2.93	
106	0010	SUSPENDED CEILINGS, COMPLETE Including standard										106
	0100	suspension system but not incl. 1-½" carrier channels										
	0600	Fiberglass ceiling board, 2' x 4' x ⅝", plain faced, supermarkets	1 Carp	500	.016	S.F.	.77	.23		1	1.23	
	0700	Offices, 2' x 4' x ¾"		380	.021		.86	.30		1.16	1.45	
	1800	Tile, Z bar suspension, ⅝" mineral fiber tile		150	.053		1.10	.76		1.86	2.49	
	1900	¾" mineral fiber tile	↓	150	.053	↓	1.18	.76		1.94	2.57	

095 600 | Wood Strip Flooring

			CREW	DAILY OUTPUT	MAN-HOURS	UNIT	MAT.	LABOR	EQUIP.	TOTAL	TOTAL INCL O&P	
604	0010	WOOD Fir, vertical grain, 1" x 4", not incl. finish, B & better	1 Carp	255	.031	S.F.	1.85	.45		2.30	2.79	604
	0100	C grade & better		255	.031		1.75	.45		2.20	2.68	
	0300	Flat grain, 1" x 4", not incl. finish, B & better		255	.031		2.05	.45		2.50	3.01	
	0400	C & better		255	.031		1.95	.45		2.40	2.90	
	4000	Maple, strip, 25/32" x 2-¼", not incl. finish, select		170	.047		2.35	.67		3.02	3.71	
	4100	#2 & better		170	.047		2.05	.67		2.72	3.38	
	4300	33/32" x 3-¼", not incl. finish, #1 grade		170	.047		2.55	.67		3.22	3.93	
	4400	#2 & better	↓	170	.047		2.35	.67		3.02	3.71	
	4600	Oak, white or red, 25/32" x 2-¼", not incl. finish										
	4700	Clear quartered	1 Carp	170	.047	S.F.	2.20	.67		2.87	3.55	
	4900	Clear/select, 2-¼" wide		170	.047		2.65	.67		3.32	4.04	
	5000	#1 common		185	.043		2.45	.62		3.07	3.73	
	5200	Parquetry, standard, 5/16" thick, not incl. finish, oak, minimum		160	.050		1.60	.72		2.32	2.96	
	5300	Maximum		100	.080		5	1.14		6.14	7.40	
	5500	Teak, minimum		160	.050		3.50	.72		4.22	5.05	
	5600	Maximum		100	.080		6	1.14		7.14	8.50	
	5650	13/16" thick, select grade oak, minimum		160	.050		7.50	.72		8.22	9.45	
	5700	Maximum		100	.080		10.85	1.14		11.99	13.85	
	5800	Custom parquetry, including finish, minimum		100	.080		10.80	1.14		11.94	13.80	
	5900	Maximum		50	.160		14.75	2.29		17.04	20	
	6100	Prefinished white oak, prime grade, 2-¼" wide		170	.047		4.85	.67		5.52	6.45	
	6200	3-¼" wide		185	.043		5.85	.62		6.47	7.45	
	6400	Ranch plank		145	.055		5.85	.79		6.64	7.75	
	6500	Hardwood blocks, 9" x 9", 25/32" thick		160	.050		3.70	.72		4.42	5.25	
	6700	Parquetry, 5/16" thick, oak, minimum		160	.050		2.85	.72		3.57	4.33	
	6800	Maximum		100	.080		8	1.14		9.14	10.70	
	7000	Walnut or teak, parquetry, minimum		160	.050		3.85	.72		4.57	5.45	
	7100	Maximum	↓	100	.080		6.45	1.14		7.59	9	
	7200	Acrylic wood parquet blocks, 12" x 12" x 5/16",										
	7210	irradiated, set in epoxy	1 Carp	160	.050	S.F.	5.10	.72		5.82	6.80	
	7400	Yellow pine, ¾" x 3-⅛", T & G, C & better, not incl. finish	"	200	.040		1.70	.57		2.27	2.83	
	7500	Refinish old floors, minimum	A-1A	400	.020		.50	.23	.07	.80	1.01	
	7600	Maximum		130	.062		.75	.70	.23	1.68	2.25	
	7800	Sanding and finishing, fill, polyurethane, wax	↓	295	.027	↓	.50	.31	.10	.91	1.18	
	7900	Subfloor and underlayment, see division 061-164 & 168										

For expanded coverage of these items see *Means Building Construction Cost Data 1991*

096 | Flooring and Carpet

096 150 | Marble Flooring

			CREW	DAILY OUTPUT	MAN-HOURS	UNIT	MAT.	LABOR	EQUIP.	TOTAL	TOTAL INCL O&P	
151	0010	MARBLE Thin gauge tile, 12" x 6", ⅜", White Carara	D-7	60	.267	S.F.	3.90	3.43		7.33	9.75	151
	0100	Filled Travertine		60	.267		3.90	3.43		7.33	9.75	
	0200	12" x 12" x ⅜", thin set, floors		60	.267		5.55	3.43		8.98	11.55	
	0300	On walls		52	.308		5.55	3.96		9.51	12.40	

096 250 | Slate Flooring

251	0010	SLATE TILE Vermont, 6" x 6" x ¼" thick, thin set	D-7	180	.089	S.F.	2.85	1.14		3.99	4.96	251
252	0010	SLATE & STONE FLOORS See division 025-166										252

096 350 | Brick Flooring

354	0010	FLOORING Acidproof shales, red, 8" x 3-¾" x 1-¼" thick	D-7	.43	37.210	M	495	480		975	1,300	354
	0050	2-¼" thick	D-1	.40	40		525	525		1,050	1,450	
	0200	Acid proof clay brick, 8" x 3-¾" x 2-¼" thick	"	.40	40		525	525		1,050	1,450	
	0260	Cast ceramic, pressed, 4" x 8" x ½", unglazed	D-7	100	.160	S.F.	4.10	2.06		6.16	7.80	
	0270	Glazed		100	.160		5.45	2.06		7.51	9.30	
	0280	Hand molded flooring, 4" x 8" x ¾", unglazed		95	.168		5.45	2.17		7.62	9.45	
	0290	Glazed		95	.168		6.55	2.17		8.72	10.65	
	0300	8" hexagonal, ¾" thick, unglazed		85	.188		5.85	2.42		8.27	10.30	
	0310	Glazed		85	.188		10.35	2.42		12.77	15.25	
	0450	Acid proof joints, ¼" wide	D-1	65	.246		.85	3.23		4.08	6.25	
	0500	Pavers, 8" x 4", 1" to 1-¼" thick, red	D-7	95	.168		2.40	2.17		4.57	6.10	
	0510	Ironspot	"	95	.168		3.85	2.17		6.02	7.70	
	0540	1-⅜" to 1-¾" thick, red	D-1	95	.168		2.60	2.21		4.81	6.50	
	0560	Ironspot		95	.168		3.60	2.21		5.81	7.60	
	0580	2-¼" thick, red		90	.178		2.60	2.33		4.93	6.70	
	0590	Ironspot		90	.178		3.60	2.33		5.93	7.80	
	0600	Sidewalk or patios, on sand bed, laid flat, no mortar, 4.5 per S.F.		110	.145		2.35	1.91		4.26	5.75	
	0650	Laid on edge, 7 per S.F.		70	.229		3.70	3		6.70	9	
	0800	For basket weave pattern, add						15%				
	0850	For herringbone pattern, add						20%				
	0870	For epoxy joints, add	D-1	600	.027		1.75	.35		2.10	2.51	
	0880	For Furan underlayment, add	"	600	.027		1.45	.35		1.80	2.18	
	0890	For waxed surface, steam cleaned, add	D-5	1,000	.008		.09	.12	.03	.24	.33	

096 600 | Resilient Tile Flooring

601	0010	RESILIENT Asphalt tile, on concrete, ⅛" thick (113)										601
	0050	Color group B	1 Tilf	400	.020	S.F.	.80	.29		1.09	1.34	
	0100	Color group C & D	"	400	.020		.85	.29		1.14	1.39	
	0300	For wood subfloor, add to above for felt underlayment					.15			.15	.17	
	0800	Base, cove, rubber or vinyl, .080" thick										
	1100	Standard colors, 2-½" high	1 Tilf	315	.025	L.F.	.40	.37		.77	1.02	
	1150	4" high		315	.025		.50	.37		.87	1.13	
	1200	6" high		315	.025		.70	.37		1.07	1.35	
	1450	⅛" thick, standard colors, 2-½" high		315	.025		.45	.37		.82	1.08	
	1500	4" high		315	.025		.66	.37		1.03	1.31	
	1550	6" high		315	.025		.70	.37		1.07	1.35	
	1600	Corners, 2-½" high		315	.025	Ea.	.70	.37		1.07	1.35	
	1630	4" high		315	.025		.80	.37		1.17	1.46	
	1660	6" high		315	.025		.90	.37		1.27	1.57	
	1700	Conductive flooring, rubber tile, ⅛" thick		315	.025	S.F.	2.45	.37		2.82	3.28	
	1800	Homogeneous vinyl tile, ⅛" thick		315	.025		2.70	.37		3.07	3.55	
	2200	Cork tile, standard finish, ⅛" thick		315	.025		1.80	.37		2.17	2.56	
	2250	3/16" thick		315	.025		2.10	.37		2.47	2.89	
	2300	5/16" thick		315	.025		2.85	.37		3.22	3.72	
	2350	½" thick		315	.025		3.45	.37		3.82	4.38	

For expanded coverage of these items see *Means Building Construction Cost Data 1991*

096 | Flooring and Carpet

096 600 | Resilient Tile Flooring

			CREW	DAILY OUTPUT	MAN-HOURS	UNIT	MAT.	LABOR	EQUIP.	TOTAL	TOTAL INCL O&P	
601	2500	Urethane finish, 1/8" thick	1 Tilf	315	.025	S.F.	2.75	.37		3.12	3.61	601
	2550	3/16" thick		315	.025		3.90	.37		4.27	4.87	
	2600	5/16" thick		315	.025		4.85	.37		5.22	5.90	
	2650	1/2" thick		315	.025		6.50	.37		6.87	7.75	
	3700	Polyethylene, in rolls, no base incl., landscape surfaces		275	.029		1.75	.42		2.17	2.59	
	3800	Nylon action surface, 1/8" thick		275	.029		1.90	.42		2.32	2.76	
	3900	1/4" thick		275	.029		2.75	.42		3.17	3.69	
	4000	3/8" thick		275	.029		3.65	.42		4.07	4.68	
	5900	Rubber, sheet goods, 36" wide, 1/8" thick		120	.067		2.45	.96		3.41	4.22	
	5950	3/16" thick		100	.080		3.15	1.15		4.30	5.30	
	6000	1/4" thick		90	.089		3.65	1.28		4.93	6.05	
	6050	Tile, marbleized colors, 12" x 12", 1/8" thick		400	.020		2.30	.29		2.59	2.99	
	6100	3/16" thick		400	.020		3.20	.29		3.49	3.98	
	6300	Special tile, plain colors, 1/8" thick		400	.020		2.85	.29		3.14	3.59	
	6350	3/16" thick		400	.020		3.80	.29		4.09	4.64	
	6500											
	7000	Vinyl composition tile, 12" x 12", 1/16" thick	1 Tilf	500	.016	S.F.	.55	.23		.78	.97	
	7050	Embossed		500	.016		.70	.23		.93	1.14	
	7100	Marbleized		500	.016		.70	.23		.93	1.14	
	7150	Solid		500	.016		.80	.23		1.03	1.25	
	7200	3/32" thick, embossed		500	.016		.75	.23		.98	1.19	
	7250	Marbleized		500	.016		.85	.23		1.08	1.30	
	7300	Solid		500	.016		1.25	.23		1.48	1.74	
	7310											
	7350	1/8" thick, marbleized	1 Tilf	500	.016	S.F.	.95	.23		1.18	1.41	
	7400	Solid		500	.016		1.45	.23		1.68	1.96	
	7500	Vinyl tile, 12" x 12", .050" thick, minimum		500	.016		1.35	.23		1.58	1.85	
	7550	Maximum		500	.016		2.60	.23		2.83	3.23	
	7600	1/8" thick, minimum		500	.016		1.75	.23		1.98	2.29	
	7650	Solid colors		500	.016		2.25	.23		2.48	2.84	
	7700	Marbleized or Travertine pattern		500	.016		2.65	.23		2.88	3.28	
	7750	Florentine pattern		500	.016		3.40	.23		3.63	4.11	
	7800	Maximum		500	.016		6.75	.23		6.98	7.80	
	7810											
	8000	Vinyl sheet goods, backed, .065" thick, minimum	1 Tilf	250	.032	S.F.	1.15	.46		1.61	2	
	8050	Maximum		200	.040		2.10	.58		2.68	3.23	
	8100	.080" thick, minimum		230	.035		1.30	.50		1.80	2.23	
	8150	Maximum		200	.040		2.35	.58		2.93	3.50	
	8200	.125" thick, minimum		230	.035		1.50	.50		2	2.45	
	8250	Maximum		200	.040		3.25	.58		3.83	4.49	
	8300	.250" thick, minimum		230	.035		2.35	.50		2.85	3.38	
	8350	Maximum		200	.040		4.35	.58		4.93	5.70	
	8700	Adhesive cement, 1 gallon does 200 to 300 S.F.				Gal.	11.40			11.40	12.55	
	8800	Asphalt primer, 1 gallon per 300 S.F.					7.45			7.45	8.20	
	8900	Emulsion, 1 gallon per 140 S.F.					7.45			7.45	8.20	
	8950	Latex underlayment					22.75			22.75	25	

096 850 | Sheet Carpet

			CREW	DAILY OUTPUT	MAN-HOURS	UNIT	MAT.	LABOR	EQUIP.	TOTAL	TOTAL INCL O&P	
852	0010	CARPET Commercial grades, direct cement										852
	0700	Nylon, level loop, 26 oz., light to medium traffic	1 Tilf	445	.018	S.F.	1.53	.26		1.79	2.09	
	0900	32 oz., medium traffic		445	.018		1.82	.26		2.08	2.41	
	1100	40 oz., medium to heavy traffic		445	.018		2.31	.26		2.57	2.95	
	2100	Nylon, plush, 20 oz., light traffic		445	.018		.94	.26		1.20	1.45	
	2800	24 oz., light to medium traffic		445	.018		1.09	.26		1.35	1.61	
	2900	30 oz., medium traffic		445	.018		1.36	.26		1.62	1.91	
	3000	36 oz., medium traffic		445	.018		1.66	.26		1.92	2.24	
	3100	42 oz., medium to heavy traffic		370	.022		1.98	.31		2.29	2.67	
	3200	46 oz., medium to heavy traffic		370	.022		2.39	.31		2.70	3.12	

For expanded coverage of these items see *Means Building Construction Cost Data 1991*

096 | Flooring and Carpet

096 850 | Sheet Carpet

			CREW	DAILY OUTPUT	MAN-HOURS	UNIT	MAT.	LABOR	EQUIP.	TOTAL	TOTAL INCL O&P	
852	3300	54 oz., heavy traffic	1 Tilf	370	.022	S.F.	2.72	.31		3.03	3.49	852
	3500	Olefin, 15 oz., light traffic		445	.018		.46	.26		.72	.92	
	3650	22 oz., light traffic		445	.018		.57	.26		.83	1.04	
	4500	50 oz., medium to heavy traffic, level loop		445	.018		3.38	.26		3.64	4.13	
	4700	32 oz., medium to heavy traffic, patterned		400	.020		3.16	.29		3.45	3.93	
	4900	48 oz., heavy traffic, patterned		400	.020		4.32	.29		4.61	5.20	
	4950											
	5000	For less than full roll, add					25%					
	5100	For small rooms, add						25%				
	5200	For large open areas, deduct						25%				
	5600	For bound carpet baseboard, add	1 Tilf	300	.027	L.F.	.85	.38		1.23	1.55	
	5610	For stairs, not incl. price of carpet, add	"	30	.267	Riser		3.84		3.84	6.10	
	8100											
	8950	For tackless, stretched installation, add padding to above										
	9000	Sponge rubber pad, minimum	1 Tilf	1,350	.006	S.F.	.25	.09		.34	.41	
	9100	Maximum		1,350	.006		.66	.09		.75	.86	
	9200	Felt pad, minimum		1,350	.006		.28	.09		.37	.44	
	9300	Maximum		1,350	.006		.44	.09		.53	.62	
	9400	Bonded urethane pad, minimum		1,350	.006		.31	.09		.40	.48	
	9500	Maximum		1,350	.006		.53	.09		.62	.72	
	9600	Prime urethane pad, minimum		1,350	.006		.19	.09		.28	.34	
	9700	Maximum		1,350	.006		.33	.09		.42	.50	

096 900 | Carpet Tile

			CREW	DAILY OUTPUT	MAN-HOURS	UNIT	MAT.	LABOR	EQUIP.	TOTAL	TOTAL INCL O&P	
901	0010	**CARPET TILE**										901
	1100	Tufted, 18" x 18" or 24" x 24", 24 oz. nylon	1 Tilf	80	.100	S.Y.	18.45	1.44		19.89	23	
	1180	35 oz.		80	.100		21.30	1.44		22.74	26	
	5060	42 oz.		80	.100		27.35	1.44		28.79	32	

098 | Special Coatings

098 150 | Glazed Coatings

			CREW	DAILY OUTPUT	MAN-HOURS	UNIT	MAT.	LABOR	EQUIP.	TOTAL	TOTAL INCL O&P	
150	0010	**WALL COATINGS** Acrylic glazed coatings, minimum	1 Pord	525	.015	S.F.	.18	.21		.39	.53	150
	0100	Maximum		305	.026		.35	.35		.70	.96	
	0300	Epoxy coatings, minimum		525	.015		.20	.21		.41	.56	
	0400	Maximum		170	.047		.65	.64		1.29	1.75	
	0600	Exposed aggregate, troweled on, 1/16" to 1/4", minimum		235	.034		.55	.46		1.01	1.35	
	0700	Maximum (epoxy or polyacrylate)		130	.062		.95	.83		1.78	2.40	
	0900	1/2" to 5/8" aggregate, minimum		130	.062		1	.83		1.83	2.45	
	1000	Maximum		80	.100		1.60	1.35		2.95	3.96	
	1200	1" aggregate size, minimum		90	.089		1.35	1.20		2.55	3.44	
	1300	Maximum		55	.145		2.05	1.96		4.01	5.45	
	1500	Exposed aggregate, sprayed on, 1/8" aggregate, minimum		295	.027		.45	.37		.82	1.09	
	1600	Maximum		145	.055		.75	.74		1.49	2.04	

For expanded coverage of these items see *Means Building Construction Cost Data 1991*

099 | Painting and Wall Coverings

099 100 | Exterior Painting

			CREW	DAILY OUTPUT	MAN-HOURS	UNIT	MAT.	LABOR	EQUIP.	TOTAL	TOTAL INCL O&P	
106	0010	**SIDING** Exterior										106
	0020	Labor cost includes protection of adjacent items not painted										
	0100	Steel siding, oil base, primer or sealer coat, brushwork (115)	2 Pord	2,800	.006	S.F.	.07	.08		.15	.20	
	0500	Spray		5,600	.003		.06	.04		.10	.13	
	0800	Paint 2 coats, brushwork (116)		1,850	.009		.14	.12		.26	.34	
	1000	Spray		3,600	.004		.12	.06		.18	.23	
	1200	Stucco, rough, oil base, paint 2 coats, brushwork		1,100	.015		.15	.20		.35	.49	
	1400	Roller		1,800	.009		.16	.12		.28	.37	
	1600	Spray		3,600	.004		.13	.06		.19	.24	
	1800	Texture 1-11 or clapboard, oil base, primer coat, brushwork		3,000	.005		.08	.07		.15	.21	
	2000	Spray		4,760	.003		.07	.05		.12	.15	
	2100	Paint 1 coat, brushwork		2,900	.006		.06	.07		.13	.19	
	2200	Spray		4,760	.003		.07	.05		.12	.15	
	2400	Paint 2 coats, brushwork		1,800	.009		.12	.12		.24	.33	
	2600	Spray		2,700	.006		.14	.08		.22	.28	
	3000	Stain 1 coat, brushwork		2,040	.008		.08	.11		.19	.26	
	3200	Spray		4,760	.003		.10	.05		.15	.18	
	3400	Stain 2 coats, brushwork		1,225	.013		.16	.18		.34	.46	
	4000	Spray		2,700	.006		.12	.08		.20	.26	
	4200	Wood shingles, oil base primer coat, brushwork		1,500	.011		.08	.14		.22	.32	
	4400	Spray		2,380	.007		.07	.09		.16	.22	
	4600	Paint 1 coat, brushwork		1,400	.011		.07	.15		.22	.33	
	4800	Spray		2,380	.007		.06	.09		.15	.21	
	5000	Paint 2 coats, brushwork		800	.020		.14	.27		.41	.59	
	5200	Spray		2,800	.006		.12	.08		.20	.26	
	5800	Stain 1 coat, brushwork		1,225	.013		.08	.18		.26	.38	
	6000	Spray		2,380	.007		.10	.09		.19	.26	
	6500	Stain 2 coats, brushwork		775	.021		.16	.28		.44	.63	
	7000	Spray	↓	2,800	.006		.11	.08		.19	.25	
	8000	For latex paint, deduct				↓	10%					

099 200 | Interior Painting

204	0010	**CABINETS AND CASEWORK**										204
	0020	Labor cost includes protection of adjacent items not painted										
	1000	Primer coat, oil base, brushwork	1 Pord	680	.012	S.F.	.05	.16		.21	.31	
	2000	Paint, oil base, brushwork, 1 coat		600	.013		.05	.18		.23	.35	
	2500	2 coats		428	.019		.10	.25		.35	.52	
	3000	Stain, brushwork, wipe off		400	.020		.05	.27		.32	.50	
	4000	Shellac, 1 coat, brushwork		600	.013		.05	.18		.23	.35	
	4500	Varnish, 3 coats, brushwork, sand after 1st coat	↓	235	.034		.16	.46		.62	.93	
	5000	For latex paint, deduct				↓	10%					
216	0010	**DOORS AND WINDOWS**										216
	0020	Labor cost includes protection of adjacent items not painted										
	0500	Flush door & frame, 3' x 7', per side, oil, primer, brushwork	1 Pord	17	.471	Ea.	1.20	6.35		7.55	11.70	
	1000	Paint, 1 coat		16	.500		1.40	6.75		8.15	12.55	
	1200	2 coats		10.50	.762		2.55	10.30		12.85	19.55	
	1400	Stain, brushwork, wipe off		18	.444		1.10	6		7.10	11	
	1600	Shellac, 1 coat, brushwork		25	.320		1.10	4.32		5.42	8.25	
	1800	Varnish, 3 coats, brushwork, sand after 1st coat		9	.889		3.15	12		15.15	23	
	2000	Panel door & frame, 3' x 7' per side, oil, primer, brushwork		15	.533		1.10	7.20		8.30	12.95	
	2200	Paint, 1 coat		14	.571		1.40	7.70		9.10	14.10	
	2400	2 coats		8	1		2.81	13.50		16.31	25	
	2600	Stain, brushwork, panel door, 3' x 7', per side, not incl. frame		16	.500		1.10	6.75		7.85	12.20	
	2800	Shellac, 1 coat, brushwork		22	.364		1.10	4.91		6.01	9.20	
	3000	Varnish, 3 coats, brushwork, sand after 1st coat	↓	7.50	1.070	↓	3.20	14.40		17.60	27	
	3020	French door, incl. 3' x 7', 6 lites, frame & trim, per side										
	3022	Paint, 1 coat, over existing paint	1 Pord	13	.615	Ea.	2.64	8.30		10.94	16.45	

For expanded coverage of these items see *Means Building Construction Cost Data 1991*

099 | Painting and Wall Coverings

099 200 | Interior Painting

			CREW	DAILY OUTPUT	MAN-HOURS	UNIT	MAT.	LABOR	EQUIP.	TOTAL	TOTAL INCL O&P	
216	3024	2 coats, over existing paint	1 Pord	7.50	1.070	Ea.	5.28	14.40		19.68	29	216
	3026	Primer & 1 coat		7.50	1.070		5.28	14.40		19.68	29	
	3028	Primer & 2 coats		6	1.330		7.92	18		25.92	38	
	3032	Varnish or polyurethane, 1 coat		13	.615		2.91	8.30		11.21	16.75	
	3034	2 coats, sanding between		4.50	1.780		5.82	24		29.82	46	
	4400	Windows, including frame and trim, per side										
	4600	Colonial type, ⅝ lites, 2' x 3', oil, primer, brushwork	1 Pord	21	.381	Ea.	.85	5.15		6	9.30	
	5800	Paint, 1 coat		21	.381		1	5.15		6.15	9.50	
	6000	2 coats		13	.615		1.95	8.30		10.25	15.70	
	6200	3' x 5' opening, ⅝ lites, primer coat, brushwork		15	.533		1.20	7.20		8.40	13.05	
	6400	Paint, 1 coat		15	.533		1.45	7.20		8.65	13.35	
	6600	2 coats		9	.889		2.70	12		14.70	23	
	6800	4' x 8' opening, ⅝ lites, primer coat, brushwork		10	.800		1.50	10.80		12.30	19.25	
	7000	Paint, 1 coat		10	.800		1.75	10.80		12.55	19.55	
	7200	2 coats		6	1.330		3.25	18		21.25	33	
	8000	Single lite type, 2' x 3', oil base, primer coat, brushwork		34	.235		.82	3.18		4	6.10	
	8200	Paint, 1 coat		34	.235		1	3.18		4.18	6.30	
	8400	2 coats		22	.364		1.95	4.91		6.86	10.15	
	8600	3' x 5' opening, primer coat, brushwork		17	.471		1.10	6.35		7.45	11.55	
	8800	Paint, 1 coat		17	.471		1.35	6.35		7.70	11.85	
	9000	2 coats		11	.727		2.60	9.80		12.40	18.85	
	9200	4' x 8' opening, primer coat, brushwork		12	.667		1.50	9		10.50	16.30	
	9400	Paint, 1 coat		12	.667		1.75	9		10.75	16.60	
	9600	2 coats		8	1		3.25	13.50		16.75	26	
	9800	For latex paint deduct					10%					
220	0010	**MISCELLANEOUS PAINTING**										220
	0020	Labor cost includes protection of adjacent items not painted										
	0700	Fence, chain link, oil base, primer coat, brushwork	2 Pord	1,450	.011	S.F.	.05	.15		.20	.30	
	1000	Spray		4,760	.003		.06	.05		.11	.14	
	1200	Paint 1 coat, brushwork		1,450	.011		.05	.15		.20	.30	
	1400	Spray		4,760	.003		.06	.05		.11	.14	
	1600	Picket, wood, one side, primer coat, brushwork		1,700	.009		.04	.13		.17	.25	
	1800	Spray		4,760	.003		.05	.05		.10	.13	
	2000	Paint 1 coat, brushwork		1,500	.011		.05	.14		.19	.29	
	2200	Spray		4,760	.003		.05	.05		.10	.13	
	2400	Floors, conc./wood, oil base, primer/sealer coat, brushwork		3,400	.005		.03	.06		.09	.14	
	2450	Roller		3,800	.004		.05	.06		.11	.15	
	2600	Spray		6,000	.003		.04	.04		.08	.10	
	2650	Paint 1 coat, brushwork		3,200	.005		.04	.07		.11	.15	
	2800	Roller		5,200	.003		.05	.04		.09	.12	
	2850	Spray		6,000	.003		.04	.04		.08	.10	
	3000	Stain, wood floor, brushwork, 1 coat		4,760	.003		.04	.05		.09	.12	
	3200	Roller		5,400	.003		.04	.04		.08	.11	
	3250	Spray		6,000	.003		.04	.04		.08	.10	
	3400	Varnish, wood floor, brushwork		4,760	.003		.04	.05		.09	.12	
	3450	Roller		5,400	.003		.04	.04		.08	.11	
	3600	Spray		6,000	.003		.04	.04		.08	.10	
	3800	Grilles, per side, oil base, primer coat, brushwork	1 Pord	550	.015		.04	.20		.24	.36	
	3850	Spray		1,100	.007		.04	.10		.14	.20	
	3880	Paint 1 coat, brushwork		540	.015		.04	.20		.24	.37	
	3900	Spray		1,100	.007		.04	.10		.14	.20	
	3920	Paint 2 coats, brushwork		340	.024		.06	.32		.38	.58	
	3940	Spray		680	.012		.06	.16		.22	.32	
	4200	Gutters and downspouts, oil base, primer coat, brushwork	2 Pord	1,200	.013	L.F.	.08	.18		.26	.38	
	4250	Paint 1 coat, brushwork		1,200	.013		.08	.18		.26	.38	
	4300	Paint 2 coats, brushwork		800	.020		.16	.27		.43	.62	
	4500	Louvers, one side, primer, brushwork	1 Pord	544	.015	S.F.	.05	.20		.25	.38	

For expanded coverage of these items see *Means Building Construction Cost Data 1991*

099 | Painting and Wall Coverings

099 200 | Interior Painting

			CREW	DAILY OUTPUT	MAN-HOURS	UNIT	MAT.	LABOR	EQUIP.	TOTAL	TOTAL INCL O&P	
220	4520	Paint one coat, brushwork	1 Pord	500	.016	S.F.	.05	.22		.27	.41	220
	4530	Spray		1,190	.007		.05	.09		.14	.20	
	4540	Paint two coats, brushwork		340	.024		.08	.32		.40	.61	
	4550	Spray		680	.012		.10	.16		.26	.37	
	4560	Paint three coats, brushwork		283	.028		.12	.38		.50	.75	
	4570	Spray		510	.016		.14	.21		.35	.50	
	5000	Pipe, to 4" diameter, primer or sealer coat, oil base, brushwork	2 Pord	1,360	.012	L.F.	.08	.16		.24	.35	
	5100	Spray		2,380	.007		.08	.09		.17	.24	
	5200	Paint 1 coat, brushwork		1,360	.012		.08	.16		.24	.35	
	5300	Spray		2,380	.007		.08	.09		.17	.24	
	5350	Paint 2 coats, brushwork		850	.019		.14	.25		.39	.57	
	5400	Spray		1,360	.012		.14	.16		.30	.41	
	5450	To 8" diameter, primer or sealer coat, brushwork		650	.025		.10	.33		.43	.65	
	5500	Spray		1,135	.014		.10	.19		.29	.42	
	5550	Paint 1 coat, brushwork		600	.027		.11	.36		.47	.71	
	5600	Spray		1,135	.014		.11	.19		.30	.43	
	5650	Paint 2 coats, brushwork		404	.040		.20	.53		.73	1.09	
	5700	Spray		647	.025		.20	.33		.53	.76	
	6600	Radiators, per side, primer, brushwork	1 Pord	550	.015	S.F.	.08	.20		.28	.41	
	6620	Paint one coat, brushwork		540	.015		.09	.20		.29	.43	
	6640	Paint two coats, brushwork		340	.024		.18	.32		.50	.72	
	6660	Paint three coats, brushwork		283	.028		.27	.38		.65	.92	
	7000	Trim, wood, incl. puttying, under 6" wide										
	7200	Primer coat, oil base, brushwork	1 Pord	900	.009	L.F.	.02	.12		.14	.22	
	7250	Paint, 1 coat, brushwork		875	.009		.03	.12		.15	.23	
	7400	2 coats		520	.015		.05	.21		.26	.39	
	7450	3 coats		370	.022		.09	.29		.38	.57	
	7500	Over 6" wide, primer coat, brushwork		600	.013		.03	.18		.21	.33	
	7550	Paint, 1 coat, brushwork		450	.018		.04	.24		.28	.44	
	7600	2 coats		265	.030		.08	.41		.49	.75	
	7650	3 coats		190	.042		.11	.57		.68	1.05	
	8000	Cornice, simple design, primer coat, oil base, brushwork		550	.015	S.F.	.04	.20		.24	.36	
	8250	Paint, 1 coat		500	.016		.05	.22		.27	.41	
	8300	2 coats		300	.027		.09	.36		.45	.69	
	8350	Ornate design, primer coat		300	.027		.04	.36		.40	.63	
	8400	Paint, 1 coat		280	.029		.05	.39		.44	.68	
	8450	2 coats		170	.047		.09	.64		.73	1.13	
	8600	Balustrades, primer coat, oil base, brushwork		598	.013		.04	.18		.22	.34	
	8650	Paint, 1 coat		544	.015		.05	.20		.25	.38	
	8700	2 coats		340	.024		.09	.32		.41	.62	
	8900	Trusses and wood frames, primer coat, oil base, brushwork		800	.010		.04	.14		.18	.26	
	8950	Spray		1,200	.007		.04	.09		.13	.19	
	9000	Paint 1 coat, brushwork		750	.011		.05	.14		.19	.29	
	9200	Spray		1,200	.007		.05	.09		.14	.20	
	9220	Paint 2 coats, brushwork		500	.016		.09	.22		.31	.45	
	9240	Spray		600	.013		.09	.18		.27	.39	
	9260	Stain, brushwork, wipe off		600	.013		.04	.18		.22	.34	
	9280	Varnish, 3 coats, brushwork		275	.029		.15	.39		.54	.81	
	9350	For latex paint, deduct					10%					
224	0010	**WALLS AND CEILINGS**										224
	0020	Labor cost includes protection of adjacent items not painted										
	0100	Concrete, dry wall or plaster, oil base, primer or sealer coat										
	0200	Smooth finish, brushwork	1 Pord	1,300	.006	S.F.	.04	.08		.12	.18	
	0240	Roller		2,040	.004		.04	.05		.09	.13	
	0300	Sand finish, brushwork		1,163	.007		.05	.09		.14	.21	
	0340	Roller		1,700	.005		.05	.06		.11	.16	
	0380	Spray		2,720	.003		.05	.04		.09	.12	

For expanded coverage of these items see *Means Building Construction Cost Data 1991*

099 | Painting and Wall Coverings

099 200 | Interior Painting

			CREW	DAILY OUTPUT	MAN-HOURS	UNIT	MAT.	LABOR	EQUIP.	TOTAL	TOTAL INCL O&P	
224	0400	Paint 1 coat, smooth finish, brushwork	1 Pord	1,200	.007	S.F.	.05	.09		.14	.20	224
	0440	Roller		2,000	.004		.05	.05		.10	.14	
	0480	Spray		2,200	.004		.05	.05		.10	.14	
	0500	Sand finish, brushwork		1,050	.008		.06	.10		.16	.23	
	0540	Roller		1,600	.005		.06	.07		.13	.18	
	0580	Spray		2,100	.004		.06	.05		.11	.15	
	0800	Paint 2 coats, smooth finish, brushwork		680	.012		.08	.16		.24	.35	
	0840	Roller		1,190	.007		.09	.09		.18	.25	
	0880	Spray		1,700	.005		.11	.06		.17	.22	
	0900	Sand finish, brushwork		605	.013		.10	.18		.28	.40	
	0940	Roller		1,020	.008		.11	.11		.22	.29	
	0980	Spray		1,700	.005		.13	.06		.19	.25	
	1200	Paint 3 coats, smooth finish, brushwork		510	.016		.13	.21		.34	.49	
	1240	Roller		790	.010		.14	.14		.28	.38	
	1280	Spray		1,133	.007		.15	.10		.25	.32	
	1300	Sand finish, brushwork		454	.018		.16	.24		.40	.56	
	1340	Roller		680	.012		.17	.16		.33	.45	
	1380	Spray		1,133	.007		.18	.10		.28	.35	
	1600	Glaze coating, 5 coats, spray, clear		900	.009		.50	.12		.62	.75	
	1640	Multicolor		900	.009		.60	.12		.72	.86	
	1700	For latex paint, deduct					10%					
	1800	For ceiling installations, add						25%				
	1900											
	2000	Masonry or concrete block, oil base, primer or sealer coat										
	2100	Smooth finish, brushwork	1 Pord	1,224	.007	S.F.	.04	.09		.13	.19	
	2180	Spray		2,400	.003		.09	.05		.14	.17	
	2200	Sand finish, brushwork		1,089	.007		.05	.10		.15	.22	
	2280	Spray		2,400	.003		.11	.05		.16	.19	
	2400	Paint 1 coat, smooth finish, brushwork		1,100	.007		.06	.10		.16	.23	
	2480	Spray		2,400	.003		.07	.05		.12	.15	
	2500	Sand finish, brushwork		979	.008		.07	.11		.18	.26	
	2580	Spray		2,400	.003		.12	.05		.17	.21	
	2800	Paint 2 coats, smooth finish, brushwork		756	.011		.08	.14		.22	.32	
	2880	Spray		1,360	.006		.11	.08		.19	.25	
	2900	Sand finish, brushwork		672	.012		.09	.16		.25	.36	
	2980	Spray		1,360	.006		.14	.08		.22	.28	
	3200	Paint 3 coats, smooth finish, brushwork		560	.014		.12	.19		.31	.45	
	3280	Spray		1,088	.007		.15	.10		.25	.33	
	3300	Sand finish, brushwork		498	.016		.13	.22		.35	.50	
	3380	Spray		1,088	.007		.17	.10		.27	.35	
	3600	Glaze coating, 5 coats, spray, clear		900	.009		.50	.12		.62	.75	
	3620	Multicolor		900	.009		.60	.12		.72	.86	
	4000	Block filler, 1 coat, brushwork		520	.015		.09	.21		.30	.44	
	4100	Silicone, water repellent, 2 coats, spray		2,000	.004		.12	.05		.17	.22	
	4120	For latex paint, deduct					10%					
228	0010	VARNISH 1 coat + sealer, on wood trim, no sanding included	1 Pord	400	.020	S.F.	.07	.27		.34	.52	228
	0100	Hardwood floors, 1 coat, no sanding included, 1 brushwork	"	2,380	.003	"	.07	.05		.12	.15	

099 700 | Wallpaper

701	0010	WALL COVERING (114)										701
	0050	Aluminum foil	1 Pape	275	.029	S.F.	.62	.39		1.01	1.32	
	0100	Copper sheets, .025" thick, vinyl backing		240	.033		3.10	.45		3.55	4.14	
	0300	Phenolic backing		240	.033		4.05	.45		4.50	5.20	
	0600	Cork tiles, light or dark, 12" x 12" x 3/16"		240	.033		1.80	.45		2.25	2.71	
	0700	5/16" thick		240	.033		1.90	.45		2.35	2.82	
	0900	1/4" basketweave		240	.033		2.85	.45		3.30	3.87	
	1000	1/2" natural, non-directional pattern		240	.033		2.75	.45		3.20	3.76	

For expanded coverage of these items see *Means Building Construction Cost Data 1991*

099 | Painting and Wall Coverings

099 700 | Wallpaper

			CREW	DAILY OUTPUT	MAN-HOURS	UNIT	MAT.	LABOR	EQUIP.	TOTAL	TOTAL INCL O&P	
701	1200	Granular surface, 12" x 36", ½" thick	1 Pape	385	.021	S.F.	.60	.28		.88	1.12	701
	1300	1" thick		385	.021		.80	.28		1.08	1.34	
	1500	Polyurethane coated, 12" x 12" x 3/16" thick		240	.033		1.78	.45		2.23	2.69	
	1600	5/16" thick		240	.033		2.48	.45		2.93	3.46	
	1800	Cork wallpaper, paperbacked, natural		480	.017		1.05	.23		1.28	1.52	
	1900	Colors		480	.017		1.25	.23		1.48	1.74	
	2100	Flexible wood veneer, 1/32" thick, plain woods		100	.080		1.30	1.08		2.38	3.19	
	2200	Exotic woods		100	.080		1.88	1.08		2.96	3.83	
	2400	Gypsum-based, fabric-backed, fire										
	2500	resistant for masonry walls, minimum	1 Pape	800	.010	S.F.	.58	.14		.72	.86	
	2600	Average		720	.011		.68	.15		.83	.99	
	2700	Maximum		640	.013		.80	.17		.97	1.16	
	2750	Acrylic, modified, semi-rigid PVC, .028" thick	2 Carp	330	.048		.69	.69		1.38	1.92	
	2800	.040" thick	"	320	.050		.89	.72		1.61	2.18	
	3000	Vinyl wall covering, fabric-backed, lightweight	1 Pape	640	.013		.62	.17		.79	.96	
	3300	Medium weight		480	.017		.75	.23		.98	1.19	
	3400	Heavy weight		435	.018		.98	.25		1.23	1.48	
	3600	Adhesive, 5 gal. lots				Gal.	6.95			6.95	7.65	
	3700	Wallpaper at $10.00 per double roll, average workmanship	1 Pape	640	.013	S.F.	.22	.17		.39	.52	
	3900	Paper at $20 per double roll, average workmanship		535	.015		.38	.20		.58	.75	
	4000	Paper at $44 per double roll, quality workmanship		435	.018		.76	.25		1.01	1.24	
	4010											
	4100	Linen wall covering, paper backed										
	4150	Flame treatment, minimum	1 Pape	400	.020	S.F.		.27		.27	.44	
	4180	Maximum		350	.023			.31		.31	.50	
	4200	Grass cloths with lining paper, minimum		400	.020		.55	.27		.82	1.05	
	4300	Maximum		350	.023		1.40	.31		1.71	2.04	

099 900 | Surface Preparation

902	0010	REMOVAL Existing lead paint, by chemicals,										902
	0020	refinish with 2 coats of paint										
	0050	Baseboard, to 6" wide	1 Pord	190	.042	L.F.	.07	.57		.64	1	
	0070	To 12" wide		150	.053	"	.14	.72		.86	1.33	
	0200	Balustrades, one side		90	.089	S.F.	.17	1.20		1.37	2.14	
	0220											
	1400	Cabinets, simple design	1 Pord	85	.094	S.F.	.14	1.27		1.41	2.23	
	1420	Ornate design		40	.200		.16	2.70		2.86	4.58	
	1600	Cornice, simple design		65	.123		.14	1.66		1.80	2.86	
	1620	Ornate design		35	.229		.16	3.09		3.25	5.20	
	2800	Doors, one side, flush		125	.064		.14	.86		1	1.56	
	2820	Two panel		110	.073		.14	.98		1.12	1.75	
	2840	Four panel		95	.084		.16	1.14		1.30	2.03	
	2880	For trim, one side, add		200	.040	L.F.	.14	.54		.68	1.03	
	3000	Fence, picket, one side		80	.100	S.F.	.14	1.35		1.49	2.36	
	3020											
	3200	Grilles, one side, simple design	1 Pord	95	.084	S.F.	.16	1.14		1.30	2.03	
	3220	Ornate design		45	.178	"	.19	2.40		2.59	4.12	
	4400	Pipes, to 4" diameter		200	.040	L.F.	.07	.54		.61	.96	
	4420	To 8" diameter		90	.089		.14	1.20		1.34	2.11	
	4440	To 12" diameter		65	.123		.24	1.66		1.90	2.97	
	4460	To 16" diameter		45	.178		.37	2.40		2.77	4.32	
	4500	For hangers, add		100	.080	Ea.	.21	1.08		1.29	1.99	
	4510											
	4800	Siding	1 Pord	170	.047	S.F.	.14	.64		.78	1.19	
	5000	Trusses, open		75	.107	S.F.Face	.14	1.44		1.58	2.50	
	6200	Windows, one side only, double hung, 1/1 light, 24" x 48" high		12	.667	Ea.	1.12	9		10.12	15.90	
	6220	30" x 60" high		9	.889	"	1.75	12		13.75	21	

For expanded coverage of these items see *Means Building Construction Cost Data 1991*

099 | Painting and Wall Coverings

099 900 | Surface Preparation

			CREW	DAILY OUTPUT	MAN-HOURS	UNIT	MAT.	LABOR	EQUIP.	TOTAL	TOTAL INCL O&P	
902	6240	36" x 72" high	1 Pord	8	1	Ea.	2.52	13.50		16.02	25	902
	6280	40" x 80" high		6	1.330		3.15	18		21.15	33	
	6400	Colonial window, 6/6 light, 24" x 48" high		7	1.140		1.39	15.45		16.84	27	
	6420	30" x 60" high		5	1.600		2.17	22		24.17	38	
	6440	36" x 72" high		4	2		2.95	27		29.95	47	
	6480	40" x 80" high		3.50	2.290		3.63	31		34.63	54	
	6600	9/9 light, 24" x 48" high		6	1.330		1.66	18		19.66	31	
	6620	40" x 80" high		3	2.670		4.14	36		40.14	63	
	6800	12/12 light, 24" x 48" high		5	1.600		2.12	22		24.12	38	
	6820	40" x 80" high		2.50	3.200		4.57	43		47.57	75	
	6840	For frame & trim, add	↓	150	.053	L.F.	.14	.72		.86	1.33	
904	0010	**SANDING** And puttying interior trim, compared to										904
	0100	painting 1 coat, on quality work				L.F.		100%				
	0300	Medium work						50%				
	0400	Industrial grade				↓		25%				
906	0010	**SCRAPE AFTER FIRE DAMAGE**										906
	0020											
	0050	Boards, 1" x 4"	1 Pord	336	.024	L.F.		.32		.32	.52	
	0060	1" x 6"		260	.031			.42		.42	.68	
	0070	1" x 8"		207	.039			.52		.52	.85	
	0080	1" x 10"		174	.046			.62		.62	1.01	
	0500	Framing, 2" x 4"		265	.030			.41		.41	.66	
	0510	2" x 6"		221	.036			.49		.49	.80	
	0520	2" x 8"		190	.042			.57		.57	.93	
	0530	2" x 10"		165	.048			.65		.65	1.07	
	0540	2" x 12"	↓	144	.056	↓		.75		.75	1.22	
	0550											
	1000	Heavy framing, 3" x 4"	1 Pord	226	.035	L.F.		.48		.48	.78	
	1010	4" x 4"		210	.038			.51		.51	.84	
	1020	4" x 6"		191	.042			.57		.57	.92	
	1030	4" x 8"		165	.048			.65		.65	1.07	
	1040	4" x 10"		144	.056			.75		.75	1.22	
	1060	4" x 12"		131	.061	↓		.82		.82	1.34	
	2900	For sealing, minimum		825	.010	S.F.	.08	.13		.21	.30	
	2920	Maximum	↓	460	.017	"	.08	.23		.31	.47	

101 | Chalkboards, Compartments and Cubicles

101 850 | Shower Compartments

			CREW	DAILY OUTPUT	MAN-HOURS	UNIT	MAT.	LABOR	EQUIP.	TOTAL	TOTAL INCL O&P	
852	0010	**PARTITIONS, SHOWER** Floor mounted, no plumbing										852
	0100	Cabinet, incl. base, no door, painted steel, 1" thick walls	2 Shee	5	3.200	Ea.	450	52		502	580	
	0300	With door, fiberglass		5	3.200		340	52		392	460	
	0600	Galvanized and painted steel, 1" thick walls		5	3.200		485	52		537	620	
	0800	Stall, 1" thick wall, no base, enameled steel		5	3.200		465	52		517	600	
	1500	Circular fiberglass, cabinet 36" diameter,		4	4		375	65		440	520	
	1700	One piece, 36" diameter, less door		4	4		325	65		390	465	
	1800	With door	↓	3.50	4.570	↓	510	74		584	685	
	1900											
	2400	Glass stalls, with doors, no receptors, chrome on brass	2 Shee	3	5.330	Ea.	805	87		892	1,025	
	2700	Anodized aluminum	"	4	4		540	65		605	700	
	3200	Receptors, precast terrazzo, 32" x 32"	2 Marb	14	1.140	↓	185	16.75		201.75	230	

For expanded coverage of these items see *Means Building Construction Cost Data 1991*

101 | Chalkboards, Compartments and Cubicles

101 850 | Shower Compartments

		CREW	DAILY OUTPUT	MAN-HOURS	UNIT	MAT.	LABOR	EQUIP.	TOTAL	TOTAL INCL O&P	
852	3300	48" x 34"	2 Marb	12	1.330	Ea.	245	19.55		264.55	300	852
	3500	Plastic, simulated terrazzo receptor, 32" x 32"		14	1.140		75	16.75		91.75	110	
	3600	32" x 48"		12	1.330		95	19.55		114.55	135	
	3800	Precast concrete, colors, 32" x 32"		14	1.140		119	16.75		135.75	160	
	3900	48" x 48"	↓	12	1.330		140	19.55		159.55	185	
	4100	Shower doors, economy plastic, 24" wide	1 Shee	9	.889		70	14.45		84.45	100	
	4200	Tempered glass door, economy		8	1		120	16.25		136.25	160	
	4400	Folding, tempered glass, aluminum frame		6	1.330		155	22		177	205	
	4700	Deluxe, tempered glass, chrome on brass frame, minimum		5	1.600		265	26		291	335	
	4800	Maximum		1	8		490	130		620	755	
	4850	On anodized aluminum frame, minimum		2	4		80	65		145	195	
	4900	Maximum	↓	1	8	↓	265	130		395	505	
	5100	Shower enclosure, tempered glass, anodized alum. frame										
	5120	2 panel & door, corner unit, 32" x 32"	1 Shee	2	4	Ea.	260	65		325	395	
	5140	Neo-angle corner unit, 16" x 24" x 16"	"	2	4		465	65		530	620	
	5200	Shower surround, 3 wall, polypropylene, 32" x 32"	1 Carp	4	2		145	29		174	205	
	5220	PVC, 32" x 32"		4	2		165	29		194	230	
	5240	Fiberglass		4	2		210	29		239	280	
	5250	2 wall, polypropylene, 32" x 32"		4	2		135	29		164	195	
	5270	PVC		4	2		175	29		204	240	
	5290	Fiberglass		4	2		195	29		224	260	
	5300	Tub doors, tempered glass & frame, minimum	1 Shee	8	1		105	16.25		121.25	140	
	5400	Maximum		6	1.330		245	22		267	305	
	5600	Chrome plated, brass frame, minimum		8	1		145	16.25		161.25	185	
	5700	Maximum		6	1.330		295	22		317	360	
	5900	Tub/shower enclosure, temp. glass, alum. frame, minimum		2	4		195	65		260	320	
	6200	Maximum		1.50	5.330		375	87		462	555	
	6500	On chrome-plated brass frame, minimum		2	4		275	65		340	410	
	6600	Maximum	↓	1.50	5.330		575	87		662	775	
	6800	Tub surround, 3 wall, polypropylene	1 Carp	4	2		105	29		134	165	
	6900	PVC		4	2		165	29		194	230	
	7000	Fiberglass, minimum		4	2		190	29		219	255	
	7100	Maximum	↓	3	2.670	↓	325	38		363	420	

102 | Louvers, Corner Protection and Access Flooring

102 100 | Metal Wall Louvers

		CREW	DAILY OUTPUT	MAN-HOURS	UNIT	MAT.	LABOR	EQUIP.	TOTAL	TOTAL INCL O&P	
104	0010	LOUVERS Aluminum with screen, residential, 8" x 8"	1 Carp	38	.211	Ea.	6	3.01		9.01	11.65	104
	0100	12" x 12"		38	.211		8.20	3.01		11.21	14.05	
	0200	12" x 18"		35	.229		10.65	3.27		13.92	17.20	
	0250	14" x 24"		30	.267		13.90	3.81		17.71	22	
	0300	18" x 24"		27	.296		16.35	4.24		20.59	25	
	0500	24" x 30"		24	.333		24	4.77		28.77	34	
	0700	Triangle, adjustable, small		20	.400		17.30	5.70		23	29	
	0800	Large		15	.533		82	7.65		89.65	105	
	2100	Midget, aluminum, ¾" deep, 1" diameter		85	.094		.51	1.35		1.86	2.81	
	2150	3" diameter		60	.133		1.34	1.91		3.25	4.66	
	2200	4" diameter		50	.160		1.69	2.29		3.98	5.70	
	2250	6" diameter	↓	30	.267		2.37	3.81		6.18	9	
	2300	Ridge vent strip, mill finish	1 Shee	155	.052	L.F.	2.51	.84		3.35	4.15	
	2400	Under eaves vent, aluminum, mill finish, 16" x 4"	1 Carp	75	.107	Ea.	1.67	1.53		3.20	4.39	

For expanded coverage of these items see *Means Building Construction Cost Data 1991*

102 | Louvers, Corner Protection and Access Flooring

102 100 | Metal Wall Louvers

		CREW	DAILY OUTPUT	MAN-HOURS	UNIT	MAT.	LABOR	EQUIP.	TOTAL	TOTAL INCL O&P	
2500	16" x 8"	1 Carp	75	.107	Ea.	1.89	1.53		3.42	4.63	104
7000	Vinyl gable vent, 8" x 8"		380	.021		5.25	.30		5.55	6.30	
7020	12" x 12"		38	.211		6.25	3.01		9.26	11.90	
7080	12" x 18"		35	.229		8.55	3.27		11.82	14.85	
7200	14" x 24"	↓	30	.267	↓	11.55	3.81		15.36	19.10	

103 | Fireplaces, Ext. Specialties and Flagpoles

103 050 | Prefabricated Fireplaces

		CREW	DAILY OUTPUT	MAN-HOURS	UNIT	MAT.	LABOR	EQUIP.	TOTAL	TOTAL INCL O&P	
0010	FIREPLACE, PREFABRICATED Free standing or wall hung										054
0100	with hood & screen, minimum	F-1	1.30	6.150	Ea.	675	88	6.15	769.15	895	
0150	Average		1	8		885	115	8	1,008	1,175	
0200	Maximum		.90	8.890		2,100	125	8.90	2,233	2,525	
0500	Chimney dbl. wall, all stainless, over 8'-6", 7" diam., add		33	.242	V.L.F.	19.50	3.47	.24	23.21	28	
0600	10" diameter, add		32	.250		32.20	3.58	.25	36.03	42	
0700	12" diameter, add		31	.258		42.50	3.69	.26	46.45	53	
0800	14" diameter, add		30	.267	↓	52.60	3.81	.27	56.68	65	
1000	Simulated brick chimney top, 4' high, 16" x 16"		10	.800	Ea.	130	11.45	.80	142.25	165	
1100	24" x 24"		7	1.140	"	260	16.35	1.14	277.49	315	
1500	Simulated logs, gas fired, 40,000 BTU, 2' long, minimum		7	1.140	Set	300	16.35	1.14	317.49	360	
1600	Maximum		6	1.330		500	19.05	1.33	520.38	585	
1700	Electric, 1,500 BTU, 1'-6" long, minimum		7	1.140		85	16.35	1.14	102.49	120	
1800	11,500 BTU, maximum		6	1.330	↓	190	19.05	1.33	210.38	240	
2000	Fireplace, built-in, 36" hearth, radiant		1.30	6.150	Ea.	385	88	6.15	479.15	575	
2100	Recirculating, small fan		1	8		530	115	8	653	785	
2150	Large fan		.90	8.890		1,035	125	8.90	1,168	1,350	
2200	42" hearth, radiant		1.20	6.670		490	95	6.65	591.65	705	
2300	Recirculating, small fan		.90	8.890		655	125	8.90	788.90	945	
2350	Large fan		.80	10		1,250	145	10	1,405	1,625	
2400	48" hearth, radiant		1.10	7.270		930	105	7.25	1,042	1,200	
2500	Recirculating, small fan		.80	10		1,125	145	10	1,280	1,500	
2550	Large fan		.70	11.430		1,780	165	11.45	1,956	2,250	
3000	See through, including doors		.80	10		1,435	145	10	1,590	1,825	
3200	Corner (2 wall)	↓	1	8	↓	700	115	8	823	970	

103 100 | Fireplace Accessories

		CREW	DAILY OUTPUT	MAN-HOURS	UNIT	MAT.	LABOR	EQUIP.	TOTAL	TOTAL INCL O&P	
0010	FIREPLACE ACCESSORIES Chimney screens, galv., 13" x 13" flue	1 Bric	8	1	Ea.	35	14.80		49.80	63	104
0050	Galv., 24" x 24" flue		5	1.600		95	24		119	145	
0200	Stainless steel, 13" x 13" flue		8	1		200	14.80		214.80	245	
0250	20" x 20" flue		5	1.600		280	24		304	345	
0400	Cleanout doors and frames, cast iron, 8" x 8"		12	.667		12.80	9.85		22.65	30	
0450	12" x 12"		10	.800		28.60	11.85		40.45	51	
0500	18" x 24"		8	1		80	14.80		94.80	110	
0550	Cast iron frame, steel door, 24" x 30"		5	1.600		175	24		199	230	
0800	Damper, rotary control, steel, 30" opening		6	1.330		50	19.75		69.75	87	
0850	Cast iron, 30" opening		6	1.330		55	19.75		74.75	93	
1200	Steel plate, poker control, 60" opening		8	1		165	14.80		179.80	205	
1250	84" opening		5	1.600		295	24		319	365	
1400	"Universal" type, chain operated, 32" x 20" opening		8	1		125	14.80		139.80	160	
1450	48" x 24" opening	↓	5	1.600	↓	195	24		219	255	

For expanded coverage of these items see *Means Building Construction Cost Data 1991*

103 | Fireplaces, Ext. Specialties and Flagpoles

103 100 | Fireplace Accessories

			CREW	DAILY OUTPUT	MAN-HOURS	UNIT	MAT.	LABOR	EQUIP.	TOTAL	TOTAL INCL O&P	
104	1600	Dutch Oven door and frame, cast iron, 12" x 15" opening	1 Bric	13	.615	Ea.	65	9.10		74.10	86	104
	1650	Copper plated, 12" x 15" opening		13	.615		125	9.10		134.10	150	
	1800	Fireplace forms with registers, 25" opening		3	2.670		350	39		389	450	
	1900	34" opening		2.50	3.200		425	47		472	545	
	2000	48" opening		2	4		785	59		844	960	
	2100	72" opening		1.50	5.330		1,100	79		1,179	1,350	
	2400	Squirrel and bird screens, galvanized, 8" x 8" flue		16	.500		32	7.40		39.40	47	
	2450	13" x 13" flue	↓	8	1	↓	38	14.80		52.80	66	

103 200 | Stoves

			CREW	DAILY OUTPUT	MAN-HOURS	UNIT	MAT.	LABOR	EQUIP.	TOTAL	TOTAL INCL O&P	
201	0010	WOODBURNING STOVES Cast iron, minimum	F-2	1.30	12.310	Ea.	550	175	12.30	737.30	915	201
	0020	Average		1	16		800	230	16	1,046	1,275	
	0030	Maximum	↓	.80	20		2,000	285	20	2,305	2,700	
	0050	For gas log lighter, add				↓	28			28	31	

103 460 | Cupolas

			CREW	DAILY OUTPUT	MAN-HOURS	UNIT	MAT.	LABOR	EQUIP.	TOTAL	TOTAL INCL O&P	
464	0010	CUPOLA Stock units, pine, painted, 18" sq., 28" high, alum. roof	1 Carp	4	2	Ea.	105	29		134	165	464
	0100	Copper roof		4	2		105	29		134	165	
	0300	23" square, 33" high, aluminum roof		3.50	2.290		167	33		200	240	
	0400	Copper roof		3.50	2.290		167	33		200	240	
	0600	30" square, 37" high, aluminum roof		3.50	2.290		266	33		299	345	
	0700	Copper roof		3.50	2.290		266	33		299	345	
	0900	Hexagonal, 31" wide, 46" high, copper roof		3	2.670		368	38		406	470	
	1000	36" wide, 50" high, copper roof	↓	3	2.670		431	38		469	540	
	1200	For deluxe stock units, add to above					25%					
	1400	For custom built units, add to above					50%	50%				
	1600	Fiberglass, 5'-0" base, 63" high minimum	F-3	6	6.670		1,000	96	63	1,159	1,325	
	1650	Maximum		4	10		2,500	145	95	2,740	3,100	
	1700	6'-0" base, 63" high, minimum		5	8		1,100	115	76	1,291	1,475	
	1750	Maximum	↓	3	13.330	↓	2,750	195	125	3,070	3,475	
524	0010	FLAGPOLE Not including base or foundation										524
	0100	Aluminum, tapered, ground set 20' high	K-1	2	8	Ea.	930	105	195	1,230	1,400	
	0200	25' high		1.70	9.410		1,150	125	230	1,505	1,725	
	0300	30' high		1.50	10.670		1,300	140	260	1,700	1,950	
	0500	40' high	↓	1.20	13.330		2,375	175	325	2,875	3,250	

105 | Lockers, Protective Covers and Postal Specialties

105 380 | Canopies

			CREW	DAILY OUTPUT	MAN-HOURS	UNIT	MAT.	LABOR	EQUIP.	TOTAL	TOTAL INCL O&P	
388	0010	CANOPIES, RESIDENTIAL Prefabricated										388
	0020											
	0500	Carport, free standing, baked enamel, alum., 40 psf										
	0520	16' x 8', 4 posts	2 Carp	3	5.330	Ea.	1,010	76		1,086	1,250	
	0600	20' x 10', 6 posts	"	2	8		1,350	115		1,465	1,675	
	1000	Door canopies, extruded alum., 42" projection, 4' wide	1 Carp	8	1		350	14.30		364.30	410	
	1020	6' wide	"	6	1.330		420	19.05		439.05	495	
	1040	8' wide	2 Carp	9	1.780		580	25		605	680	
	1060	10' wide		7	2.290		660	33		693	780	
	1080	12' wide	↓	5	3.200		785	46		831	940	
	1100											
	1200	54" projection, 4' wide	1 Carp	8	1	Ea.	440	14.30		454.30	510	

For expanded coverage of these items see *Means Building Construction Cost Data 1991*

105 | Lockers, Protective Covers and Postal Specialties

105 380 | Canopies

			CREW	DAILY OUTPUT	MAN-HOURS	UNIT	BARE COSTS MAT.	LABOR	EQUIP.	TOTAL	TOTAL INCL O&P	
388	1220	6' wide	1 Carp	6	1.330	Ea.	585	19.05		604.05	675	388
	1240	8' wide	2 Carp	9	1.780		790	25		815	910	
	1260	10' wide		7	2.290		885	33		918	1,025	
	1280	12' wide		5	3.200		995	46		1,041	1,175	
	1300	Painted, add					20%					
	1310	Bronze anodized, add					50%					
	3000	Window awnings, aluminum, window 3' high, 4' wide	1 Carp	10	.800		98	11.45		109.45	125	
	3020	6' wide	"	8	1		128	14.30		142.30	165	
	3040	9' wide	2 Carp	9	1.780		170	25		195	230	
	3060	12' wide	"	5	3.200		215	46		261	315	
	3100	Window, 4' high, 4' wide	1 Carp	10	.800		116	11.45		127.45	145	
	3120	6' wide	"	8	1		154	14.30		168.30	195	
	3140	9' wide	2 Carp	9	1.780		205	25		230	270	
	3160	12' wide	"	5	3.200		260	46		306	365	
	3200	Window, 6' high, 4' wide	1 Carp	10	.800		180	11.45		191.45	215	
	3220	6' wide	"	8	1		250	14.30		264.30	300	
	3240	9' wide	2 Carp	9	1.780		310	25		335	385	
	3260	12' wide	"	5	3.200		385	46		431	500	
	3400	Roll-up aluminum, 2'-6" wide	1 Carp	14	.571		72	8.15		80.15	93	
	3420	3' wide		12	.667		87	9.55		96.55	110	
	3440	4' wide		10	.800		110	11.45		121.45	140	
	3460	6' wide		8	1		133	14.30		147.30	170	
	3480	9' wide	2 Carp	9	1.780		185	25		210	245	
	3500	12' wide	"	5	3.200		240	46		286	340	
	3600	Window awnings, canvas, 24" drop, 3' wide	1 Carp	30	.267	L.F.	43	3.81		46.81	54	
	3620	4' wide		40	.200		40	2.86		42.86	49	
	3700	30" drop, 3' wide		30	.267		49	3.81		52.81	60	
	3720	4' wide		40	.200		43	2.86		45.86	52	
	3740	5' wide		45	.178		40	2.54		42.54	48	
	3760	6' wide		48	.167		38	2.38		40.38	46	
	3780	8' wide		48	.167		31	2.38		33.38	38	
	3800	10' wide		50	.160		28	2.29		30.29	35	

105 520 | Mail Boxes

			CREW	DAILY OUTPUT	MAN-HOURS	UNIT	MAT.	LABOR	EQUIP.	TOTAL	INCL O&P	
521	0011	MAIL BOXES										521
	1900	Letter slot, residential	1 Carp	20	.400	Ea.	26	5.70		31.70	38	
	2400	Residential, galv. steel, small 20" x 7" x 9"	1 Clab	16	.500		12	5.70		17.70	23	
	2410	With galv. steel post, 54" long		6	1.330		27	15.15		42.15	55	
	2420	Large, 24" x 12" x 15"		16	.500		28	5.70		33.70	40	
	2430	With galv. steel post, 54" long		6	1.330		43	15.15		58.15	73	
	2440	Decorative, polyethylene, 22" x 10" x 10"		16	.500		25	5.70		30.70	37	
	2450	With alum. post, decorative, 54" long		6	1.330		40	15.15		55.15	69	

106 | Partitions and Storage Shelving

106 750 | Storage & Shelving

			CREW	DAILY OUTPUT	MAN-HOURS	UNIT	MAT.	LABOR	EQUIP.	TOTAL	INCL O&P	
754	0010	SHELVING Metal, industrial, cross-braced, 3' wide, 12" deep	1 Sswk	175	.046	SF Shlf	5.90	.72		6.62	7.85	754
	0100	24" deep		330	.024		4.25	.38		4.63	5.40	
	2200	Wide span, 1600 lb. capacity per shelf, 6' wide, 24" deep		380	.021		4.60	.33		4.93	5.70	
	2400	36" deep		440	.018		3.75	.28		4.03	4.66	
	3000	Residential, adjustable metal, 12" deep										
	3100	23" to 37" wide	1 Carp	16	.500	Ea.	6.60	7.15		13.75	19.20	

For expanded coverage of these items see *Means Building Construction Cost Data 1991*

106 | Partitions and Storage Shelving

106 750 | Storage & Shelving

			CREW	DAILY OUTPUT	MAN-HOURS	UNIT	MAT.	LABOR	EQUIP.	TOTAL	TOTAL INCL O&P	
754	3200	47" to 61" wide	1 Carp	16	.500	Ea.	9.50	7.15		16.65	22	754
	3300	71" to 88" wide		16	.500		14	7.15		21.15	27	
	3400	95" to 109"	↓	16	.500		14	7.15		21.15	27	
	3500	For closet rod, add					22%	2%				
	3600	For 14" shelves, add				↓	12%	5%				

108 | Toilet and Bath Accessories and Scales

108 200 | Bath Accessories

			CREW	DAILY OUTPUT	MAN-HOURS	UNIT	MAT.	LABOR	EQUIP.	TOTAL	TOTAL INCL O&P	
204	0010	**BATHROOM ACCESSORIES**										204
	0200	Curtain rod, stainless steel, 5' long, 1" diameter	1 Carp	13	.615	Ea.	20	8.80		28.80	37	
	0300	1-¼" diameter		13	.615		25	8.80		33.80	42	
	0800	Grab bar, straight, 1-¼" diameter, stainless steel, 18" long		24	.333		21	4.77		25.77	31	
	1100	36" long		20	.400		27	5.70		32.70	39	
	3000	Mirror with stainless steel, ¾" square frame, 18" x 24"		20	.400		70	5.70		75.70	87	
	3100	36" x 24"		15	.533		110	7.65		117.65	135	
	3300	72" x 24"		6	1.330		210	19.05		229.05	265	
	4300	Robe hook, single, regular		36	.222		9.60	3.18		12.78	15.90	
	4400	Heavy duty, concealed mounting		36	.222		12	3.18		15.18	18.50	
	6400	Towel bar, stainless steel, 18" long		23	.348		17.60	4.97		22.57	28	
	6500	30" long		21	.381		20.40	5.45		25.85	32	
	7400	Tumbler holder, tumbler only		30	.267		10.35	3.81		14.16	17.75	
	7500	Soap, tumbler & toothbrush		30	.267		17.50	3.81		21.31	26	
208	0010	**MEDICINE CABINETS** With mirror, st. st. frame, 16" x 22", unlighted		14	.571		57	8.15		65.15	76	208
	0100	Wood frame		14	.571		61	8.15		69.15	81	
	0300	Sliding mirror doors, 20" x 16" x 4-¾", unlighted		7	1.140		56	16.35		72.35	89	
	0400	24" x 19" x 8-½", lighted		5	1.600		94	23		117	140	
	0600	Triple door, 30" x 32", unlighted, plywood body		7	1.140		183	16.35		199.35	230	
	0700	Steel body		7	1.140		243	16.35		259.35	295	
	0900	Oak door, wood body, beveled mirror, single door		7	1.140		102	16.35		118.35	140	
	1000	Double door	↓	6	1.330	↓	200	19.05		219.05	250	

110 | Equipment

110 100 | Maintenance Equipment

			CREW	DAILY OUTPUT	MAN-HOURS	UNIT	MAT.	LABOR	EQUIP.	TOTAL	TOTAL INCL O&P	
121	0010	**VACUUM CLEANING** Central, 3 inlet, residential	1 Skwk	.90	8.890	Total	600	130		730	880	121
	0400	5 inlet system, residential		.50	16		690	235		925	1,150	
	0600	7 inlet system	↓	.40	20		780	295		1,075	1,350	
	0800	9 inlet system	1 Sswk	.30	26.670	↓	870	415		1,285	1,750	

For expanded coverage of these items see *Means Building Construction Cost Data 1991*

114 | Food Service, Residential, Darkroom, Athletic Equipment

114 000 | Food Service Equipment

			CREW	DAILY OUTPUT	MAN-HOURS	UNIT	MAT.	LABOR	EQUIP.	TOTAL	TOTAL INCL O&P	
002	0010	APPLIANCES Cooking range, 30" free standing, 1 oven, minimum	2 Clab	10	1.600	Ea.	270	18.15		288.15	325	002
	0050	Maximum		4	4		1,200	45		1,245	1,400	
	0150	2 oven, minimum		10	1.600		670	18.15		688.15	765	
	0200	Maximum		4	4		1,500	45		1,545	1,725	
	0350	Built-in, 30" wide, 1 oven, minimum	2 Carp	4	4		430	57		487	570	
	0400	Maximum		2	8		990	115		1,105	1,275	
	0500	2 oven, conventional, minimum		4	4		800	57		857	975	
	0550	1 conventional, 1 microwave, maximum		2	8		1,400	115		1,515	1,725	
	0700	Free-standing, 21" wide range, 1 oven, minimum	2 Clab	10	1.600		300	18.15		318.15	360	
	0750	Maximum	"	4	4		410	45		455	525	
	0900	Counter top cook tops, 4 burner, standard, minimum	1 Elec	6	1.330		200	22		222	255	
	0950	Maximum		3	2.670		470	44		514	585	
	1050	As above, but with grille and griddle attachment, minimum		6	1.330		320	22		342	385	
	1100	Maximum		3	2.670		520	44		564	640	
	1250	Microwave oven, minimum		4	2		100	33		133	165	
	1300	Maximum		2	4		1,525	65		1,590	1,775	
	1570	60" wide, average	L-1	1.40	11.430		1,875	190		2,065	2,375	
	1590	72" wide, average	"	1.20	13.330		2,100	220		2,320	2,675	
	1750	Compactor, residential size, 4 to 1 compaction, minimum	1 Carp	5	1.600		300	23		323	370	
	1800	Maximum	"	3	2.670		500	38		538	615	
	2000	Deep freeze, 15 to 23 C.F., minimum	2 Clab	10	1.600		395	18.15		413.15	465	
	2050	Maximum		5	3.200		690	36		726	820	
	2200	30 C.F., minimum		8	2		650	23		673	755	
	2250	Maximum		3	5.330		775	61		836	955	
	2450	Dehumidifier, portable, automatic, 15 pint					175			175	195	
	2550	40 pint					270			270	295	
	2750	Dishwasher, built-in, 2 cycles, minimum	L-1	4	4		230	66		296	360	
	2800	Maximum		2	8		390	130		520	645	
	2950	4 or more cycles, minimum		4	4		300	66		366	435	
	3000	Maximum		2	8		700	130		830	985	
	3200	Dryer, automatic, minimum	L-2	3	5.330		250	68		318	390	
	3250	Maximum	"	2	8		730	100		830	975	
	3300	Garbage disposer, sink type, minimum	L-1	10	1.600		55	26		81	105	
	3350	Maximum	"	10	1.600		195	26		221	255	
	3550	Heater, electric, built-in, 1250 watt, ceiling type, minimum	1 Elec	4	2		40	33		73	97	
	3600	Maximum		3	2.670		100	44		144	180	
	3700	Wall type, minimum		4	2		40	33		73	97	
	3750	Maximum		3	2.670		75	44		119	155	
	3900	1500 watt wall type, with blower		4	2		75	33		108	135	
	3950	3000 watt		3	2.670		130	44		174	215	
	4150	Hood for range, 2 speed, vented, 30" wide, minimum	L-3	5	3.200		40	49		89	125	
	4200	Maximum		3	5.330		260	82		342	420	
	4300	42" wide, minimum		5	3.200		155	49		204	250	
	4350	Maximum		3	5.330		300	82		382	465	
	4500	For ventless hood, 2 speed, add					12			12	13.20	
	4650	For vented 1 speed, deduct from maximum					25			25	28	
	4850	Humidifier, portable, 7 gallons per day					80			80	88	
	5000	15 gallons per day					160			160	175	
	5200	Icemaker, automatic, 13 lb. per day	1 Plum	7	1.140		430	18.90		448.90	505	
	5350	51 lb. per day	"	2	4		750	66		816	935	
	5380	Oven, built in, standard	1 Elec	2	4		350	65		415	490	
	5390	Deluxe	"	2	4		680	65		745	855	
	5500	Refrigerator, no frost, 10 C.F. to 12 C.F. minimum	2 Clab	10	1.600		300	18.15		318.15	360	
	5600	Maximum		6	2.670		590	30		620	700	
	5750	14 C.F. to 16 C.F., minimum		9	1.780		515	20		535	600	
	5800	Maximum		5	3.200		875	36		911	1,025	
	5950	18 C.F. to 20 C.F., minimum		8	2		600	23		623	700	
	6000	Maximum		4	4		1,100	45		1,145	1,275	

For expanded coverage of these items see *Means Building Construction Cost Data 1991*

114 | Food Service, Residential, Darkroom, Athletic Equipment

114 000 | Food Service Equipment

			CREW	DAILY OUTPUT	MAN-HOURS	UNIT	MAT.	LABOR	EQUIP.	TOTAL	TOTAL INCL O&P	
002	6150	21 C.F. to 29 C.F., minimum	2 Clab	7	2.290	Ea.	750	26		776	870	002
	6200	Maximum	"	3	5.330		2,550	61		2,611	2,900	
	6400	Sump pump cellar drainer, ⅓ H.P., minimum	1 Plum	3	2.670		90	44		134	170	
	6450	Maximum	"	2	4		300	66		366	440	
	6460	Sump pump, see also division 152-480										
	6650	Washing machine, automatic, minimum	1 Plum	3	2.670	Ea.	300	44		344	400	
	6700	Maximum	"	1	8		890	130		1,020	1,200	
	6900	Water heater, electric, glass lined, 30 gallon, minimum	L-1	5	3.200		135	53		188	235	
	6950	Maximum		3	5.330		315	88		403	490	
	7100	80 gallon, minimum		2	8		225	130		355	460	
	7150	Maximum		1	16		535	265		800	1,025	
	7180	Water heater, gas, glass lined, 30 gallon, minimum	2 Plum	5	3.200		155	53		208	255	
	7220	Maximum		3	5.330		465	88		553	655	
	7260	50 gallon, minimum		2.50	6.400		205	105		310	400	
	7300	Maximum		1.50	10.670		465	175		640	800	
	7310	Water heater, see also division 153-110										
	7350	Water softener, automatic, to 30 grains per gallon	2 Plum	5	3.200	Ea.	310	53		363	425	
	7400	To 100 grains per gallon	"	4	4		675	66		741	850	
	7450	Vent kits for dryers	1 Carp	10	.800		12	11.45		23.45	32	
008	0010	**WINE VAULT** Redwood, air conditioned, walk-in type										008
	0020	6'-8" high, incl. racks, 2' x 4' for 156 bottles	2 Carp	2	8	Ea.	3,050	115		3,165	3,550	
	0200	4' x 6' for 614 bottles	"	1.50	10.670	"	4,975	155		5,130	5,725	

114 580 | Disappearing Stairs

			CREW	DAILY OUTPUT	MAN-HOURS	UNIT	MAT.	LABOR	EQUIP.	TOTAL	TOTAL INCL O&P	
581	0010	**DISAPPEARING STAIRWAY** No trim included										581
	0020	One piece, yellow pine, 8'-0" ceiling	2 Carp	4	4	Ea.	925	57		982	1,125	
	0030	9'-0" ceiling		4	4		950	57		1,007	1,150	
	0040	10'-0" ceiling		3	5.330		1,000	76		1,076	1,225	
	0050	11'-0" ceiling		3	5.330		1,175	76		1,251	1,425	
	0060	12'-0" ceiling		3	5.330		1,225	76		1,301	1,475	
	0080	For 90 minute mineral core fire door, add					180			180	200	
	0100	Custom grade, pine, 8'-6" ceiling, minimum	1 Carp	4	2		70	29		99	125	
	0150	Average		3.50	2.290		120	33		153	185	
	0200	Maximum		3	2.670		180	38		218	260	
	0500	Heavy duty, pivoted, from 7'7" to 12'10" floor to floor		3	2.670		195	38		233	280	
	0600	16'-0" ceiling		2	4		800	57		857	975	
	0800	Economy folding, pine, 8'-6" ceiling		4	2		50	29		79	105	
	0900	9'-6" ceiling		4	2		70	29		99	125	
	1000	Fire escape, galvanized steel, 8'-0" to 10'-4" ceiling	2 Carp	1	16		1,025	230		1,255	1,500	
	1010	10'-6" to 13'-6" ceiling		1	16		1,300	230		1,530	1,825	
	1100	Automatic electric, aluminum, floor to floor height, 8' to 9'		1	16		5,000	230		5,230	5,875	

123 900 | Residential Casework

			CREW	DAILY OUTPUT	MAN-HOURS	UNIT	MAT.	LABOR	EQUIP.	TOTAL	TOTAL INCL O&P	
905	0010	**IRONING CENTER** Including cabinet, board & light, minimum	1 Carp	2	4	Ea.	258	57		315	380	905
	0100	Maximum, see also division 111-101	"	1.50	5.330	"	452	76		528	625	

For expanded coverage of these items see *Means Building Construction Cost Data 1991*

125 | Window Treatment

125 100 | Blinds

			CREW	DAILY OUTPUT	MAN-HOURS	UNIT	MAT.	LABOR	EQUIP.	TOTAL	TOTAL INCL O&P	
101	0010	**BLINDS, EXTERIOR** Aluminum, louvered, 1'-4" wide, 3'-0" long	1 Carp	10	.800	Pr.	31	11.45		42.45	53	101
	0200	4'-0" long		10	.800		33	11.45		44.45	55	
	0300	5'-4" long		10	.800		36	11.45		47.45	59	
	0400	6'-8" long		9	.889		49	12.70		61.70	75	
	1000	Pine, louvered, primed, each 1'-2" wide, 3'-3" long		10	.800		41	11.45		52.45	64	
	1100	4'-7" long		10	.800		58	11.45		69.45	83	
	1250	Each 1'-4" wide, 3'-0" long		10	.800		43	11.45		54.45	66	
	1350	5'-3" long		10	.800		52	11.45		63.45	76	
	1500	Each 1'-6" wide, 3'-3" long		10	.800		49	11.45		60.45	73	
	1600	4'-7" long		10	.800		65	11.45		76.45	91	
	2500	Polystyrene, solid raised panel, each 3'-3" wide, 3'-0" long		10	.800		62	11.45		73.45	87	
	2600	3'-11" long		10	.800		71	11.45		82.45	97	
	2700	4'-7" long		10	.800		78	11.45		89.45	105	
	2800	5'-3" long		10	.800		86	11.45		97.45	115	
	2900	6'-8" long		9	.889		115	12.70		127.70	150	
	3500											
	4500	Polystyrene, louvered, each 1'-2" wide, 3'-3" long	1 Carp	10	.800	Pair	26	11.45		37.45	48	
	4600	4'-7" long		10	.800	Pr.	33	11.45		44.45	55	
	4750	5'-3" long		10	.800		37	11.45		48.45	60	
	4850	6'-8" long		9	.889		50	12.70		62.70	76	
	6000	Vinyl, louvered, each 1'-2" x 4'-7" long		10	.800		32	11.45		43.45	54	
	6200	Each 1'-4" x 6'-8" long		9	.889		49	12.70		61.70	75	
	8000	PVC exterior rolling shutters										
	8100	including crank control	1 Carp	8	1	Ea.	288	14.30		302.30	340	
	8500	Insulative - 6' x 6'8" stock unit	"	8	1	"	411	14.30		425.30	475	
103	0010	**BLINDS, INTERIOR** Solid colors	1 Carp	590	.014	S.F.	2	.19		2.19	2.52	103
	0090	Horizontal, 1" aluminum slats, custom, minimum		590	.014		2	.19		2.19	2.52	
	0100	Maximum		440	.018		6	.26		6.26	7.05	
	0450	Stock, minimum		590	.014		1	.19		1.19	1.42	
	0500	Maximum		440	.018		4	.26		4.26	4.83	
	3000	Wood folding panels with movable louvers, 7" x 20" each		17	.471	Pr.	18	6.75		24.75	31	
	3300	8" x 28" each		17	.471		26	6.75		32.75	40	
	3450	9" x 36" each		17	.471		34	6.75		40.75	49	
	3600	10" x 40" each		17	.471		37	6.75		43.75	52	
	4000	Fixed louver type, stock units, 8" x 20" each		17	.471		21	6.75		27.75	34	
	4150	10" x 28" each		17	.471		30	6.75		36.75	44	
	4300	12" x 36" each		17	.471		42	6.75		48.75	57	
	4450	18" x 40" each		17	.471		58	6.75		64.75	75	
	5000	Insert panel type, stock, 7" x 20" each		17	.471		11	6.75		17.75	23	
	5150	8" x 28" each		17	.471		20	6.75		26.75	33	
	5300	9" x 36" each		17	.471		26	6.75		32.75	40	
	5450	10" x 40" each		17	.471		28	6.75		34.75	42	
	5600	Raised panel type, stock, 10" x 24" each		17	.471		30	6.75		36.75	44	
	5650	12" x 26" each		17	.471		32	6.75		38.75	46	
	5700	14" x 30" each		17	.471		37	6.75		43.75	52	
	5750	16" x 36" each		17	.471		47	6.75		53.75	63	
	6000	For custom built pine, add										
	6500	For custom built hardwood blinds, add				Pr.	42%					
201	0011	**SHADES** Basswood roll-up, stain finish, ⅜" slats	1 Carp	300	.027	S.F.	11.80	.38		12.18	13.60	201
	5011	Insulative shades		125	.064		6.40	.92		7.32	8.55	
	6011	Solar screening, fiberglass		85	.094		3.20	1.35		4.55	5.75	
	8011	Interior insulative shutter										
	8111	Stock unit, 15" x 60"	1 Carp	17	.471	Pr.	6.40	6.75		13.15	18.30	

For expanded coverage of these items see *Means Building Construction Cost Data 1991*

125 | Window Treatment

125 300 | Drape/Curtain Hardware

			CREW	DAILY OUTPUT	MAN-HOURS	UNIT	MAT.	LABOR	EQUIP.	TOTAL	TOTAL INCL O&P	
301	0010	DRAPERY HARDWARE										301
	0020											
	0030	Standard traverse, per foot, minimum	1 Carp	59	.136	L.F.	1	1.94		2.94	4.34	
	0100	Maximum		51	.157	"	5.40	2.24		7.64	9.70	
	0200	Decorative traverse, 28"-48", minimum		22	.364	Ea.	21.50	5.20		26.70	32	
	0220	Maximum		21	.381		22.60	5.45		28.05	34	
	0300	48"-84", minimum		20	.400		34.40	5.70		40.10	47	
	0320	Maximum		19	.421		36.60	6		42.60	50	
	0400	66"-120", minimum		18	.444		40.90	6.35		47.25	56	
	0420	Maximum		17	.471		46.30	6.75		53.05	62	
	0500	84"-156", minimum		16	.500		47.30	7.15		54.45	64	
	0520	Maximum		15	.533		52.70	7.65		60.35	71	
	0600	130"-240", minimum		14	.571		68.80	8.15		76.95	89	
	0620	Maximum		13	.615		79.70	8.80		88.50	100	
	0700	Slide rings, each, minimum					.40			.40	.44	
	0720	Maximum					1			1	1.10	
	3000	Ripplefold, snap-a-pleat system, 3' or less, minimum	1 Carp	15	.533		23.80	7.65		31.45	39	
	3020	Maximum	"	14	.571		37.80	8.15		45.95	55	
	3200	Each additional foot, add, minimum				L.F.	3.20			3.20	3.52	
	3220	Maximum				"	3.20			3.20	3.52	
	4000	Traverse rods, adjustable, 28" to 48"	1 Carp	22	.364	Ea.	14.10	5.20		19.30	24	
	4020	48" to 84"		20	.400		21.60	5.70		27.30	33	
	4040	66" to 120"		18	.444		25.90	6.35		32.25	39	
	4060	84" to 156"		16	.500		29.20	7.15		36.35	44	
	4080	120" to 220"		14	.571		35.70	8.15		43.85	53	
	4100	228" to 312"		13	.615		49.70	8.80		58.50	69	
	4500	Curtain rod, 28" to 48", single		22	.364		3.20	5.20		8.40	12.20	
	4510	Double		22	.364		5.40	5.20		10.60	14.65	
	4520	48" to 86", single		20	.400		5.40	5.70		11.10	15.50	
	4530	Double		20	.400		8.70	5.70		14.40	19.15	
	4540	66" to 120", single		18	.444		8.70	6.35		15.05	20	
	4550	Double		18	.444		14.10	6.35		20.45	26	
	4600	Valance, pinch pleated fabric, 12" deep, up to 54" long, minimum					22.70			22.70	25	
	4610	Maximum					56.20			56.20	62	
	4620	Up to 77" long, minimum					34.60			34.60	38	
	4630	Maximum					89.80			89.80	99	
	5000	Stationary rods, first 2 feet					6.50			6.50	7.15	

130 | Special Construction

130 520 | Saunas

			CREW	DAILY OUTPUT	MAN-HOURS	UNIT	MAT.	LABOR	EQUIP.	TOTAL	TOTAL INCL O&P	
521	0010	SAUNA Prefabricated, incl. heater & controls, 7' high, 6' x 4'	L-7	2.20	12.730	Ea.	2,750	175		2,925	3,325	521
	0400	6' x 5'		2	14		3,075	195		3,270	3,700	
	0600	6' x 6'		1.80	15.560		3,400	215		3,615	4,100	
	0800	6' x 9'		1.60	17.500		4,450	240		4,690	5,300	
	1000	8' x 12'		1.10	25.450		5,525	350		5,875	6,650	
	1400	8' x 10'		1.20	23.330		5,400	320		5,720	6,475	
	1600	10' x 12'		1	28		6,200	385		6,585	7,450	
	1700	Door only, with tempered insulated glass window	2 Carp	3.40	4.710		160	67		227	290	
	1800	Prehung, incl. jambs, pulls & hardware	"	12	1.330		200	19.05		219.05	250	
	2500	Heaters only (incl. above), wall mounted, to 200 C.F.					375			375	415	

For expanded coverage of these items see *Means Building Construction Cost Data 1991*

130 | Special Construction

130 520 | Saunas

			CREW	DAILY OUTPUT	MAN-HOURS	UNIT	MAT.	LABOR	EQUIP.	TOTAL	TOTAL INCL O&P	
521	2750	To 300 C.F.				Ea.	480			480	530	521
	3000	Floor standing, to 720 C.F., 10,000 watts	1 Elec	3	2.670		720	44		764	860	
	3250	To 1,000 C.F., 12,500 watts	"	3	2.670	↓	780	44		824	930	

130 540 | Steam Baths

541	0010	STEAM BATH Heater, timer & head, single, to 140 C.F.	1 Plum	1.20	6.670	Ea.	790	110		900	1,050	541
	0500	To 300 C.F.	"	1.10	7.270		900	120		1,020	1,175	
	2700	Conversion unit for residential tub, including door				↓	950			950	1,050	

131 | Pre-Eng. Structures, Pools and Ice Rinks

131 230 | Greenhouses

			CREW	DAILY OUTPUT	MAN-HOURS	UNIT	MAT.	LABOR	EQUIP.	TOTAL	TOTAL INCL O&P	
231	0010	GREENHOUSE Shell only, stock units, not incl. 2' stub walls,										231
	0020	foundation, floors, heat or compartments										
	0300	Residential type, free standing, 8'-6" long x 7'-6" wide	2 Carp	59	.271	SF Flr.	35	3.88		38.88	45	
	0400	10'-6" wide		85	.188		27	2.69		29.69	34	
	0600	13'-6" wide		108	.148		24	2.12		26.12	30	
	0700	17'-0" wide		160	.100		27	1.43		28.43	32	
	0900	Lean-to type, 3'-10" wide		34	.471		31	6.75		37.75	45	
	1000	6'-10" wide	↓	58	.276	↓	24	3.94		27.94	33	
	1100	Wall mounted, to existing window, 3' x 3'	1 Carp	4	2	Ea.	335	29		364	415	
	1120	4' x 5'	"	3	2.670	"	500	38		538	615	
	1200	Deluxe quality, free standing, 7'-6" wide	2 Carp	55	.291	SF Flr.	69	4.16		73.16	83	
	1220	10'-6" wide		81	.198		64	2.82		66.82	75	
	1240	13'-6" wide		104	.154		60	2.20		62.20	70	
	1260	17'-0" wide		150	.107		51	1.53		52.53	59	
	1400	Lean-to type, 3'-10" wide		31	.516		80	7.40		87.40	100	
	1420	6'-10" wide		55	.291		75	4.16		79.16	89	
	1440	8'-0" wide	↓	97	.165	↓	70	2.36		72.36	81	

131 520 | Swimming Pools

521	0010	SWIMMING POOL ENCLOSURE Translucent, free standing,										521
	0020	not including foundations, heat or light										
	0200	Economy, minimum	2 Carp	200	.080	SF Hor.	7.25	1.14		8.39	9.90	
	0300	Maximum		100	.160		16	2.29		18.29	21	
	0400	Deluxe, minimum		100	.160		20	2.29		22.29	26	
	0600	Maximum		70	.229	↓	210	3.27		213.27	235	
523	0010	SWIMMING POOL EQUIPMENT Diving stand, stainless steel, 3 meter		.40	40	Ea.	3,050	570		3,620	4,300	523
	0600	Diving boards, 16' long, aluminum		2.70	5.930		1,125	85		1,210	1,375	
	0700	Fiberglass	↓	2.70	5.930		580	85		665	780	
	0900	Filter system, sand or diatomite type, incl. pump, 6000 gal./hr.	2 Plum	1.80	8.890	Total	815	145		960	1,125	
	1020	Add for chlorination system, 800 S.F. pool	"	3	5.330	Ea.	270	88		358	440	
	1200	Ladders, heavy duty, stainless steel, 2 tread	2 Carp	7	2.290		105	33		138	170	
	1500	4 tread	"	6	2.670		195	38		233	280	
	2100	Lights, underwater, 12 volt, with transformer, 300 watt	1 Elec	.40	20		205	325		530	755	
	2200	110 volt, 500 watt, standard	"	.40	20	↓	73	325		398	610	
	3000	Pool covers, reinforced vinyl				S.F.	.26			.26	.29	
	3100	Vinyl water tube, minimum					.39			.39	.43	
	3200	Maximum				↓	.93			.93	1.02	

For expanded coverage of these items see *Means Building Construction Cost Data 1991*

131 | Pre-Eng. Structures, Pools and Ice Rinks

131 520 | Swimming Pools

			CREW	DAILY OUTPUT	MAN-HOURS	UNIT	MAT.	LABOR	EQUIP.	TOTAL	TOTAL INCL O&P	
523	3300	Slides, fiberglass, aluminum handrails & ladder, 6'-0", straight	2 Carp	1.60	10	Ea.	240	145		385	505	523
	3320	7'-6", curved	"	3	5.330	"	355	76		431	520	
525	0010	SWIMMING POOLS Residential in-ground, vinyl lined, concrete sides										525
	0020	Sides including equipment, sand bottom	B-52	300	.187	SF Surf	10.05	2.50	1.35	13.90	16.70	
	0100	Metal or polystyrene sides	B-14	410	.117		8.40	1.42	.46	10.28	12.10	
	0200	Add for vermiculite bottom									1.65	
	0500	Gunite bottom and sides, white plaster finish										
	0600	12' x 30' pool	B-52	145	.386	SF Surf	14	5.15	2.79	21.94	27	
	0720	16' x 32' pool		155	.361		8.25	4.84	2.61	15.70	20	
	0750	20' x 40' pool		250	.224		8	3	1.62	12.62	15.60	
	0810	Concrete bottom and sides, tile finish										
	0820	12' x 30' pool	B-52	80	.700	SF Surf	16.80	9.40	5.05	31.25	40	
	0830	16' x 32' pool		95	.589		13.90	7.90	4.25	26.05	33	
	0840	20' x 40' pool		130	.431		11.05	5.75	3.11	19.91	25	
	1600	For water heating system, see division 155-150										
	1700	Filtration and deck equipment only, as % of total				Total				20%	20%	
	1800	Deck equipment, rule of thumb, 20' x 40' pool				SF Pool					1.30	
	3000	Painting pools, preparation + 3 coats, 20' x 40' pool, epoxy	2 Pord	.33	48.480	Total	525	655		1,180	1,650	
	3100	Rubber base paint, 18 gallons	"	.33	48.480	"	395	655		1,050	1,500	

142 | Elevators

142 010 | Elevators

			CREW	DAILY OUTPUT	MAN-HOURS	UNIT	MAT.	LABOR	EQUIP.	TOTAL	TOTAL INCL O&P	
011	0010	ELEVATORS For multi-story buildings, housing project, minimum										011
	7000	Residential, cab type, 1 floor, 2 stop, minimum	2 Elev	.20	80	Ea.	5,500	1,325		6,825	8,200	
	7100	Maximum		.10	160		10,000	2,625		12,625	15,300	
	7200	2 floor, 3 stop, minimum		.12	133		7,000	2,200		9,200	11,300	
	7300	Maximum		.06	267		17,000	4,375		21,375	25,900	
	7700	Stair climber (chair lift), single seat, minimum		1	16		3,850	265		4,115	4,675	
	7800	Maximum		.20	80		5,250	1,325		6,575	7,925	

151 | Pipe and Fittings

151 100 | Miscellaneous Fittings

			CREW	DAILY OUTPUT	MAN-HOURS	UNIT	MAT.	LABOR	EQUIP.	TOTAL	TOTAL INCL O&P	
105	0010	BACKFLOW PREVENTER Includes gate valves,										105
	0020	and four test cocks, corrosion resistant, automatic operation										
	4100	Threaded										
	4120	¾" pipe size	1 Plum	16	.500	Ea.	215	8.30		223.30	250	
110	0010	CLEANOUTS										110
	0080	Round or square, scoriated nickel bronze top										
	0100	2" pipe size	1 Plum	10	.800	Ea.	46	13.25		59.25	72	
	0140	4" pipe size	"	6	1.330	"	65	22		87	110	
115	0010	CLEANOUT TEE Cast iron with countersunk plug										115
	0220	3" pipe size	1 Plum	3.60	2.220	Ea.	21	37		58	83	

For expanded coverage of these items see *Means Mechanical Cost Data* or *Means Plumbing Cost Data 1991*

151 | Pipe and Fittings

151 100 | Miscellaneous Fittings

			CREW	DAILY OUTPUT	MAN-HOURS	UNIT	MAT.	LABOR	EQUIP.	TOTAL	TOTAL INCL O&P	
115	0240	4" pipe size	1 Plum	3.30	2.420	Ea.	32	40		72	100	115
	0500	For round smooth access cover, add				"	20%					
125	0010	**DRAINS**										125
	2000	Floor, medium duty, C.I., deep flange, 7" top										
	2040	2" and 3" pipe size	Q-1	12	1.330	Ea.	33	19.85		52.85	69	
	2080	For galvanized body, add					13.85			13.85	15.25	
	2120	For polished bronze top, add				↓	18			18	19.80	
	3860	Roof, flat metal deck, C.I. body, 10" aluminum dome										
	3890	3" pipe size	Q-1	14	1.140	Ea.	115	17		132	155	
141	0010	**FAUCETS/FITTINGS**										141
	0150	Bath, faucets, diverter spout combination, sweat	1 Plum	8	1	Ea.	48	16.55		64.55	80	
	0200	For integral stops, IPS unions, add					21.75			21.75	24	
	0500	Drain, central lift, 1-½" IPS male	1 Plum	20	.400		29	6.60		35.60	43	
	0600	Trip lever, 1-½" IPS male		20	.400		29	6.60		35.60	43	
	1000	Kitchen sink faucets, top mount, cast spout		10	.800		35	13.25		48.25	60	
	1100	For spray, add					10	10%				
	2000	Laundry faucets, shelf type, IPS or copper unions	1 Plum	12	.667	↓	30	11.05		41.05	51	
	2020											
	2100	Lavatory faucet, centerset, without drain	1 Plum	10	.800	Ea.	25	13.25		38.25	49	
	2200	For pop-up drain, add					11	15%				
	2800	Self-closing, center set	1 Plum	10	.800		75	13.25		88.25	105	
	3000	Service sink faucet, cast spout, pail hook, hose end		14	.571		51	9.45		60.45	72	
	4000	Shower by-pass valve with union		18	.444		37	7.35		44.35	53	
	4200	Shower thermostatic mixing valve, concealed	↓	8	1		180	16.55		196.55	225	
	4300	For inlet strainer, check, and stops, add					54	5%				
	5000	Sillcock, compact, brass, IPS or copper to hose	1 Plum	24	.333	↓	4.50	5.50		10	13.95	
165	0010	**SHOCK ABSORBERS**										165
	0500	¾" male I.P.S. For 1 to 11 fixtures	1 Plum	12	.667	Ea.	37	11.05		48.05	59	
170	0010	**SUPPORTS/CARRIERS** For plumbing fixtures										170
	0600	Plate type with studs, top back plate	1 Plum	7	1.140	Ea.	14.20	18.90		33.10	46	
	3000	Lavatory, concealed arm										
	3050	Floor mounted, single										
	3100	High back fixture	1 Plum	6	1.330	Ea.	72	22		94	115	
	3200	Flat slab fixture	"	6	1.330	"	85	22		107	130	
	8200	Water closet, residential										
	8220	Vertical centerline, floor mount										
	8240	Single, 3" caulk, 2" or 3" vent	1 Plum	6	1.330	Ea.	60	22		82	100	
	8260	4" caulk, 2" or 4" vent	"	6	1.330	"	83	22		105	125	
181	0010	**TRAPS**										181
	0030	Cast iron, service weight										
	0050	Long P trap, 2" pipe size										
	1100	12" long	Q-1	16	1	Ea.	9.05	14.90		23.95	34	
	3000	P trap, 2" pipe size		16	1		7.10	14.90		22	32	
	3040	3" pipe size	↓	14	1.140		9.05	17		26.05	38	
	3800	Drum trap, 4" x 5", 1-½" tapping	Q-2	17	1.410	↓	12.50	22		34.50	49	
	4700	Copper, drainage, drum trap										
	4840	3" x 6" swivel, 1-½" pipe size	1 Plum	16	.500	Ea.	40	8.30		48.30	58	
	5100	P trap, standard pattern										
	5200	1-¼" pipe size	1 Plum	18	.444	Ea.	24	7.35		31.35	38	
	5240	1-½" pipe size		17	.471		22	7.80		29.80	37	
	5260	2" pipe size		15	.533		43	8.85		51.85	62	
	5280	3" pipe size	↓	11	.727	↓	55	12.05		67.05	80	
	6710	ABS DWV P trap, solvent weld joint										
	6720	1-½" pipe size	1 Plum	18	.444	Ea.	3.33	7.35		10.68	15.65	
	6730	2" pipe size		17	.471		5.40	7.80		13.20	18.65	
	6740	3" pipe size	↓	15	.533		25	8.85		33.85	42	

For expanded coverage of these items see *Means Mechanical Cost Data* or *Means Plumbing Cost Data 1991*

151 | Pipe and Fittings

151 100 | Miscellaneous Fittings

			CREW	DAILY OUTPUT	MAN-HOURS	UNIT	MAT.	LABOR	EQUIP.	TOTAL	TOTAL INCL O&P	
181	6750	4" pipe size	1 Plum	14	.571	Ea.	51	9.45		60.45	72	181
	6860	PVC DWV hub x hub, basin trap, 1-¼" pipe size		18	.444		3.50	7.35		10.85	15.85	
	6870	Sink P trap, 1-½" pipe size		18	.444		3.73	7.35		11.08	16.10	
	6880	Tubular S trap, 1-½" pipe size		17	.471		4.30	7.80		12.10	17.45	
	6890	PVC sch. 40 DWV, drum trap										
	6900	1-½" pipe size	1 Plum	16	.500	Ea.	19.40	8.30		27.70	35	
	6910	P trap, 1-½" pipe size		18	.444		4.11	7.35		11.46	16.50	
	6920	2" pipe size		17	.471		5.60	7.80		13.40	18.85	
	6930	3" pipe size		15	.533		28	8.85		36.85	45	
	6940	4" pipe size		14	.571		67	9.45		76.45	89	
	6950	P trap w/clean out, 1-½" pipe size		18	.444		10	7.35		17.35	23	
	6960	2" pipe size		17	.471		17	7.80		24.80	31	
185	0010	**VACUUM BREAKERS** Hot or cold water										185
	1030	Anti-siphon, brass										
	1060	½" size	1 Plum	24	.333	Ea.	14.10	5.50		19.60	25	
	1080	¾" size		20	.400		16.75	6.60		23.35	29	
	1100	1" size		19	.421		26	6.95		32.95	40	

151 300 | Cast Iron Pipe

			CREW	DAILY OUTPUT	MAN-HOURS	UNIT	MAT.	LABOR	EQUIP.	TOTAL	TOTAL INCL O&P	
301	0010	**PIPE, CAST IRON** Soil, on hangers 5' O.C.										301
	0020	Single hub, service wt., lead & oakum joints 10' O.C. (129)										
	2120	2" diameter	Q-1	63	.254	L.F.	2.03	3.78		5.81	8.40	
	2140	3" diameter		60	.267		2.83	3.97		6.80	9.60	
	2160	4" diameter		55	.291		3.67	4.33		8	11.10	
	4000	No hub, couplings 10' O.C.										
	4100	1-½" diameter	Q-1	71	.225	L.F.	2.58	3.36		5.94	8.30	
	4120	2" diameter		67	.239		2.71	3.56		6.27	8.80	
	4140	3" diameter		64	.250		3.55	3.72		7.27	10	
	4160	4" diameter		58	.276		4.57	4.11		8.68	11.75	
320	0010	**PIPE, CAST IRON, FITTINGS,** Soil										320
	0040	Hub and spigot, service weight, lead & oakum joints										
	0080	¼ Bend, 2"	Q-1	16	1	Ea.	2.87	14.90		17.77	27	
	0120	3"		14	1.140		5.35	17		22.35	34	
	0140	4"		13	1.230		7.80	18.35		26.15	38	
	0340	⅛ Bend, 2"		16	1		2.32	14.90		17.22	27	
	0350	3"		14	1.140		4.18	17		21.18	32	
	0360	4"		13	1.230		6.25	18.35		24.60	37	
	0500	Sanitary Tee, 2"		10	1.600		4.95	24		28.95	44	
	0540	3"		9	1.780		9.15	26		35.15	53	
	0620	4"		8	2		11.15	30		41.15	61	
	5990	No hub										
	6000	Cplg. & labor required at joints not incl. in fitting										
	6010	price. Add 1 coupling per joint for installed price										
	6020	¼ Bend, 1-½"				Ea.	2.37			2.37	2.61	
	6060	2"					2.50			2.50	2.75	
	6080	3"					3.30			3.30	3.63	
	6120	4"					4.95			4.95	5.45	
	6200	⅛ Bend, 1-½"					1.90			1.90	2.09	
	6240	2"					1.95			1.95	2.15	
	6260	3"					2.70			2.70	2.97	
	6280	4"					3.60			3.60	3.96	
	6400	Sanitary Tee, 1-½"					3.15			3.15	3.47	
	6460	2"					3.50			3.50	3.85	
	6520	3"					4.20			4.20	4.62	
	6600	4"					6.55			6.55	7.20	
	8000	Coupling, standard (by CISPI Mfrs.)										
	8020	1-½"	Q-1	48	.333	Ea.	2.10	4.97		7.07	10.40	

For expanded coverage of these items see *Means Mechanical Cost Data* or *Means Plumbing Cost Data 1991*

365

151 | Pipe and Fittings

151 300 | Cast Iron Pipe

			CREW	DAILY OUTPUT	MAN-HOURS	UNIT	MAT.	LABOR	EQUIP.	TOTAL	TOTAL INCL O&P	
320	8040	2"	Q-1	44	.364	Ea.	2.10	5.40		7.50	11.15	320
	8080	3"		38	.421		2.55	6.25		8.80	13.05	
	8120	4"	↓	33	.485	↓	2.95	7.20		10.15	15.05	

151 400 | Copper Pipe & Tubing

			CREW	DAILY OUTPUT	MAN-HOURS	UNIT	MAT.	LABOR	EQUIP.	TOTAL	TOTAL INCL O&P	
401	0010	**PIPE, COPPER** Solder joints										401
	0020	Type K tubing, couplings & clevis hangers 10' O.C.										
	1180	¾" diameter	1 Plum	74	.108	L.F.	2.38	1.79		4.17	5.55	
	1200	1" diameter	"	66	.121	"	3.82	2.01		5.83	7.45	
	2000	Type L tubing, couplings & hangers 10' O.C.										
	2140	½" diameter	1 Plum	81	.099	L.F.	1.18	1.63		2.81	3.96	
	2160	⅝" diameter		79	.101		1.73	1.68		3.41	4.64	
	2180	¾" diameter		76	.105		1.77	1.74		3.51	4.79	
	2200	1" diameter		68	.118		2.45	1.95		4.40	5.85	
	2220	1-¼" diameter	↓	58	.138	↓	3.35	2.28		5.63	7.40	
	3000	Type M tubing, couplings & hangers 10' O.C.										
	3140	½" diameter	1 Plum	84	.095	L.F.	.89	1.58		2.47	3.55	
	3180	¾" diameter		78	.103		1.35	1.70		3.05	4.25	
	3200	1" diameter		70	.114		1.88	1.89		3.77	5.15	
	3220	1-¼" diameter		60	.133		2.72	2.21		4.93	6.60	
	3240	1-½" diameter		54	.148		3.76	2.45		6.21	8.15	
	3260	2" diameter	↓	44	.182	↓	5.73	3.01		8.74	11.20	
	4000	Type DWV tubing, couplings & hangers 10' O.C.										
	4100	1-¼" diameter	1 Plum	60	.133	L.F.	2.65	2.21		4.86	6.50	
	4120	1-½" diameter		54	.148		3.31	2.45		5.76	7.65	
	4140	2" diameter	↓	44	.182		4.38	3.01		7.39	9.75	
	4160	3" diameter	Q-1	58	.276		7.41	4.11		11.52	14.85	
	4180	4" diameter	"	40	.400	↓	13.56	5.95		19.51	25	
430	0010	**PIPE, COPPER, FITTINGS**, Wrought unless otherwise noted										430
	0040	Solder joints, copper x copper										
	0101	90° Elbow, ½"	1 Plum	20	.400	Ea.	.29	6.60		6.89	11.10	
	0120	¾"		19	.421		.49	6.95		7.44	11.90	
	0250	45° Elbow, ¼"		22	.364		1.73	6		7.73	11.70	
	0280	½"		20	.400		.53	6.60		7.13	11.40	
	0290	⅝"		19	.421		2.65	6.95		9.60	14.30	
	0300	¾"		19	.421		.90	6.95		7.85	12.35	
	0310	1"		16	.500		2.31	8.30		10.61	16.05	
	0320	1-¼"		15	.533		3.18	8.85		12.03	17.90	
	0450	Tee, ¼"		14	.571		2.15	9.45		11.60	17.80	
	0480	½"		13	.615		.49	10.20		10.69	17.15	
	0490	⅝"		12	.667		3.21	11.05		14.26	22	
	0500	¾"		12	.667		1.22	11.05		12.27	19.35	
	0510	1"		10	.800		3.55	13.25		16.80	26	
	0520	1-¼"		9	.889		6.60	14.70		21.30	31	
	0650	Coupling, ¼"		24	.333		.17	5.50		5.67	9.20	
	0680	½"		22	.364		.24	6		6.24	10.10	
	0690	⅝"		21	.381		.73	6.30		7.03	11.10	
	0700	¾"		21	.381		.49	6.30		6.79	10.80	
	0710	1"		18	.444		.99	7.35		8.34	13.10	
	0720	1-¼"	↓	17	.471		1.73	7.80		9.53	14.60	
	2000	DWV, solder joints, copper x copper										
	2030	90° Elbow, 1-¼"	1 Plum	13	.615	Ea.	2.84	10.20		13.04	19.75	
	2050	1-½"		12	.667		2.93	11.05		13.98	21	
	2070	2"	↓	10	.800		6.50	13.25		19.75	29	
	2090	3"	Q-1	10	1.600		13.30	24		37.30	54	
	2100	4"	"	9	1.780	↓	43	26		69	91	

For expanded coverage of these items see *Means Mechanical Cost Data* or *Means Plumbing Cost Data 1991*

151 | Pipe and Fittings

151 400 | Copper Pipe & Tubing

		CREW	DAILY OUTPUT	MAN-HOURS	UNIT	MAT.	LABOR	EQUIP.	TOTAL	TOTAL INCL O&P	
2250	Tee, Sanitary, 1-¼"	1 Plum	9	.889	Ea.	4.75	14.70		19.45	29	430
2270	1-½"		8	1		4.40	16.55		20.95	32	
2290	2"	↓	7	1.140		8.10	18.90		27	40	
2310	3"	Q-1	7	2.290		15.90	34		49.90	73	
2330	4"	"	6	2.670		46	40		86	115	
2400	Coupling, 1-¼"	1 Plum	14	.571		1.21	9.45		10.66	16.75	
2420	1-½"		13	.615		1.64	10.20		11.84	18.40	
2440	2"	↓	11	.727		2.26	12.05		14.31	22	
2460	3"	Q-1	11	1.450		3.77	22		25.77	40	
2480	4"	"	10	1.600		9.60	24		33.60	49	

151 550 | Plastic Pipe

		CREW	DAILY OUTPUT	MAN-HOURS	UNIT	MAT.	LABOR	EQUIP.	TOTAL	TOTAL INCL O&P	
0010	**PIPE, PLASTIC** See also division 151-451										551
1800	PVC, couplings 10' O.C., hangers 3 per 10'										
1820	Schedule 40										
1860	½" diameter	1 Plum	54	.148	L.F.	.62	2.45		3.07	4.68	
1870	¾" diameter		51	.157		.69	2.60		3.29	4.99	
1880	1" diameter		46	.174		.82	2.88		3.70	5.60	
1890	1-¼" diameter		42	.190		.96	3.15		4.11	6.20	
1900	1-½" diameter	↓	36	.222		1.04	3.68		4.72	7.15	
1910	2" diameter	Q-1	59	.271		1.32	4.04		5.36	8.05	
1920	2-½" diameter		56	.286		1.90	4.26		6.16	9.05	
1930	3" diameter		53	.302		2.40	4.50		6.90	10	
1940	4" diameter	↓	48	.333		3.29	4.97		8.26	11.70	
4100	DWV type, schedule 40, couplings 10' O.C., hangers 3 per 10'										
4120	ABS										
4140	1-¼" diameter	1 Plum	42	.190	L.F.	1.04	3.15		4.19	6.30	
4150	1-½" diameter	"	36	.222		1.12	3.68		4.80	7.25	
4160	2" diameter	Q-1	59	.271		1.33	4.04		5.37	8.05	
4400	PVC										
4410	1-¼" diameter	1 Plum	42	.190	L.F.	.78	3.15		3.93	6	
4420	1-½" diameter	"	36	.222		.83	3.68		4.51	6.90	
4460	2" diameter	Q-1	59	.271		.94	4.04		4.98	7.60	
4470	3" diameter		53	.302		1.64	4.50		6.14	9.15	
4480	4" diameter	↓	48	.333		2.21	4.97		7.18	10.55	
5360	CPVC, couplings 10' O.C., hangers 3 per 10'										
5380	Schedule 40										
5460	½" diameter	1 Plum	54	.148	L.F.	1.27	2.45		3.72	5.40	
5470	¾" diameter		51	.157		1.52	2.60		4.12	5.90	
5480	1" diameter		46	.174		1.94	2.88		4.82	6.85	
5490	1-¼" diameter		42	.190		2.71	3.15		5.86	8.10	
5500	1-½" diameter	↓	36	.222		3.47	3.68		7.15	9.80	
5510	2" diameter	Q-1	59	.271		4.03	4.04		8.07	11	

		CREW	DAILY OUTPUT	MAN-HOURS	UNIT	MAT.	LABOR	EQUIP.	TOTAL	TOTAL INCL O&P	
0010	**PIPE, PLASTIC, FITTINGS**										558
2700	PVC (white), Schedule 40, socket joints										
2760	Elbow 90°, ½"	1 Plum	22	.364	Ea.	.17	6		6.17	10	
2770	¾"		21	.381		.20	6.30		6.50	10.50	
2780	1"		18	.444		.34	7.35		7.69	12.35	
2790	1-¼"		17	.471		.58	7.80		8.38	13.35	
2800	1-½"	↓	16	.500		.62	8.30		8.92	14.20	
2810	2"	Q-1	28	.571		.97	8.50		9.47	14.95	
2820	2-½"		22	.727		2.94	10.85		13.79	21	
2830	3"		17	.941		3.52	14		17.52	27	
2840	4"	↓	14	1.140		6.30	17		23.30	35	
3181	Tee, ½"	1 Plum	14	.571		.21	9.45		9.66	15.65	
3190	¾"		13	.615		.23	10.20		10.43	16.85	
3200	1"		12	.667		.43	11.05		11.48	18.45	

For expanded coverage of these items see *Means Mechanical Cost Data* or *Means Plumbing Cost Data 1991*

151 | Pipe and Fittings

151 550 | Plastic Pipe

			CREW	DAILY OUTPUT	MAN-HOURS	UNIT	MAT.	LABOR	EQUIP.	TOTAL	TOTAL INCL O&P	
558	3210	1-¼"	1 Plum	11	.727	Ea.	.68	12.05		12.73	20	558
	3220	1-½"	"	10	.800		.83	13.25		14.08	23	
	3230	2"	Q-1	17	.941		1.20	14		15.20	24	
	3240	2-½"		14	1.140		3.93	17		20.93	32	
	3250	3"		11	1.450		5.60	22		27.60	42	
	3260	4"		9	1.780		9.35	26		35.35	53	
	3381	Coupling, ½"	1 Plum	22	.364		.11	6		6.11	9.95	
	3390	¾"		21	.381		.15	6.30		6.45	10.45	
	3400	1"		18	.444		.25	7.35		7.60	12.30	
	3410	1-¼"		17	.471		.35	7.80		8.15	13.10	
	3420	1-½"		16	.500		.37	8.30		8.67	13.90	
	3430	2"	Q-1	28	.571		.58	8.50		9.08	14.55	
	3440	2-½"		20	.800		1.28	11.90		13.18	21	
	3450	3"		19	.842		2	12.55		14.55	23	
	3460	4"		16	1		2.85	14.90		17.75	27	
	4500	DWV, ABS, non pressure, socket joints										
	4540	¼ Bend, 1-¼"	1 Plum	17	.471	Ea.	1.21	7.80		9.01	14.05	
	4560	1-½"	"	16	.500		.61	8.30		8.91	14.15	
	4570	2"	Q-1	28	.571		.80	8.50		9.30	14.75	
	4800	Tee, sanitary										
	4820	1-¼"	1 Plum	11	.727	Ea.	2.59	12.05		14.64	22	
	4830	1-½"	"	10	.800		.96	13.25		14.21	23	
	4840	2"	Q-1	17	.941		1.43	14		15.43	24	
	5000	PVC, Schedule 40, socket joints										
	5040	¼ Bend, 1-¼" diameter	1 Plum	17	.471	Ea.	1.31	7.80		9.11	14.15	
	5060	1-½"	"	16	.500		.55	8.30		8.85	14.10	
	5070	2"	Q-1	28	.571		.70	8.50		9.20	14.65	
	5080	3"		17	.941		2.15	14		16.15	25	
	5090	4"		14	1.140		4.55	17		21.55	33	
	5250	Tee, sanitary 1-¼"	1 Plum	11	.727		1.64	12.05		13.69	21	
	5270	1-½"	"	10	.800		.96	13.25		14.21	23	
	5280	2"	Q-1	17	.941		1.39	14		15.39	24	
	5290	3"		11	1.450		3.69	22		25.69	39	
	5300	4"		9	1.780		7.05	26		33.05	51	
	5500	CPVC, Schedule 80, threaded joints										
	5540	90° Elbow, ¼"	1 Plum	20	.400	Ea.	4.40	6.60		11	15.65	
	5560	½"		18	.444		1.95	7.35		9.30	14.15	
	5570	¾"		17	.471		2.48	7.80		10.28	15.45	
	5580	1"		15	.533		3.94	8.85		12.79	18.75	
	5590	1-¼"		14	.571		8.55	9.45		18	25	
	5600	1-½"		13	.615		9.50	10.20		19.70	27	
	5610	2"	Q-1	22	.727		14.50	10.85		25.35	34	
	6000	Coupling, ¼"	1 Plum	20	.400		5.30	6.60		11.90	16.65	
	6020	½"		18	.444		2.05	7.35		9.40	14.25	
	6030	¾"		17	.471		2.87	7.80		10.67	15.85	
	6040	1"		15	.533		3.87	8.85		12.72	18.65	
	6050	1-¼"		14	.571		5.75	9.45		15.20	22	
	6060	1-½"		13	.615		7.30	10.20		17.50	25	
	6070	2"	Q-1	22	.727		8.50	10.85		19.35	27	

151 700 | Steel Pipe

			CREW	DAILY OUTPUT	MAN-HOURS	UNIT	MAT.	LABOR	EQUIP.	TOTAL	TOTAL INCL O&P	
701	0010	**PIPE, STEEL**										701
	0050	Schedule 40, threaded, with couplings, and clevis type										
	0060	hangers sized for covering, 10' O.C.										
	0540	Black, ¼" diameter	1 Plum	66	.121	L.F.	.75	2.01		2.76	4.10	
	0570	¾" diameter		61	.131		1.06	2.17		3.23	4.71	
	0580	1" diameter		53	.151		1.49	2.50		3.99	5.70	

For expanded coverage of these items see *Means Mechanical Cost Data* or *Means Plumbing Cost Data 1991*

151 | Pipe and Fittings

151 700 | Steel Pipe

			CREW	DAILY OUTPUT	MAN-HOURS	UNIT	MAT.	LABOR	EQUIP.	TOTAL	TOTAL INCL O&P	
701	0590	1-¼" diameter	Q-1	89	.180	L.F.	1.85	2.68		4.53	6.40	701
	0600	1-½" diameter		80	.200		2.17	2.98		5.15	7.25	
	0610	2" diameter	↓	64	.250	↓	2.91	3.72		6.63	9.30	
716	0010	**PIPE, STEEL, FITTINGS,** Threaded										716
	5000	Malleable iron, 150 lb.										
	5020	Black										
	5040	90° Elbow, straight										
	5090	¾"	1 Plum	14	.571	Ea.	.64	9.45		10.09	16.15	
	5100	1"	"	13	.615		1.17	10.20		11.37	17.90	
	5120	1-½"	Q-1	20	.800		2.53	11.90		14.43	22	
	5130	2"	"	18	.889	↓	3.69	13.25		16.94	26	
	5450	Tee, straight										
	5500	¾"	1 Plum	9	.889	Ea.	1.03	14.70		15.73	25	
	5510	1"	"	8	1		1.82	16.55		18.37	29	
	5520	1-¼"	Q-1	14	1.140		2.96	17		19.96	31	
	5530	1-½"		13	1.230		3.65	18.35		22	34	
	5540	2"	↓	11	1.450	↓	5.35	22		27.35	41	
	5650	Coupling, straight										
	5700	¾"	1 Plum	16	.500	Ea.	.90	8.30		9.20	14.50	
	5710	1"	"	15	.533		1.35	8.85		10.20	15.90	
	5730	1-½"	Q-1	24	.667		2.25	9.95		12.20	18.70	
	5740	2"	"	21	.762	↓	3.26	11.35		14.61	22	

151 950 | Valves

			CREW	DAILY OUTPUT	MAN-HOURS	UNIT	MAT.	LABOR	EQUIP.	TOTAL	TOTAL INCL O&P	
955	0010	**VALVES, BRONZE**										955
	1750	Check, swing, class 150, regrinding disc, threaded										
	1860	¾" size	1 Plum	20	.400	Ea.	11	6.60		17.60	23	
	1870	1" size	"	19	.421	"	14.50	6.95		21.45	27	
	2850	Gate, N.R.S., soldered, 300 psi										
	2940	¾" size	1 Plum	20	.400	Ea.	14.40	6.60		21	27	
	2950	1" size	"	19	.421	"	17.50	6.95		24.45	31	
	5600	Relief, pressure & temperature, self-closing, ASME										
	5650	1" size	1 Plum	24	.333	Ea.	61	5.50		66.50	76	
	5660	1-¼" size	"	20	.400	"	125	6.60		131.60	150	
	6400	Pressure, water, ASME, threaded										
	6440	¾" size	1 Plum	28	.286	Ea.	33	4.73		37.73	44	
	6450	1" size	"	24	.333	"	56	5.50		61.50	71	
	6900	Reducing, water pressure										
	6940	½" size	1 Plum	24	.333	Ea.	56	5.50		61.50	71	
	6960	1" size	"	19	.421	"	100	6.95		106.95	120	
	8350	Tempering, water, sweat connections										
	8400	½" size	1 Plum	24	.333	Ea.	27	5.50		32.50	39	
	8440	¾" size	"	20	.400	"	31	6.60		37.60	45	
	8650	Threaded connections										
	8700	½" size	1 Plum	24	.333	Ea.	31	5.50		36.50	43	
	8740	¾" size	"	20	.400	"	38	6.60		44.60	53	

For expanded coverage of these items see *Means Mechanical Cost Data or Means Plumbing Cost Data 1991*

152 | Plumbing Fixtures

152 100 | Fixtures

			CREW	DAILY OUTPUT	MAN-HOURS	UNIT	MAT.	LABOR	EQUIP.	TOTAL	TOTAL INCL O&P
104	0010	**BATHS**									104
	0100	Tubs, recessed porcelain enamel on cast iron, with trim (130)									
	0180	48" x 42"	Q-1	4	4	Ea.	865	60		925	1,050
	0220	72" x 36"		3	5.330		925	79		1,004	1,150
	0300	Mat bottom, 4' long		5.50	2.910		705	43		748	845
	0380	5' long		4.40	3.640		281	54		335	395
	0480	Above floor drain, 5' long		4	4		520	60		580	670
	0560	Corner 48" x 44"		4	4		995	60		1,055	1,200
	2000	Enameled formed steel, 4'-6" long		5.80	2.760		207	41		248	295
	2200	5' long		5.50	2.910		192	43		235	280
	4600	Module tub & showerwall surround, molded fiberglass									
	4610	5' long x 34" wide x 76" high	Q-1	4	4	Ea.	540	60		600	690
	6000	Whirlpool, bath with vented overflow, molded fiberglass									
	6100	66" x 48" x 24"	Q-1	1	16	Ea.	1,930	240		2,170	2,500
	6400	72" x 36" x 24"		1	16		1,860	240		2,100	2,425
	6500	60" x 36" x 21"		1	16		1,520	240		1,760	2,050
	6600	72" x 42" x 22"		1	16		2,290	240		2,530	2,900
	6700	84" x 66"		.30	53.330		3,680	795		4,475	5,350
	7000	Redwood tub system									
	7050	4' diameter x 4' deep	Q-1	1	16	Ea.	690	240		930	1,150
	7150	6' diameter x 4' deep		.80	20		1,050	300		1,350	1,650
	7200	8' diameter x 4' deep		.80	20		1,430	300		1,730	2,050
	9600	Rough-in, supply, waste and vent, for all above tubs, add		2.07	7.730		97.19	115		212.19	295
136	0010	**LAVATORIES** With trim, white unless noted otherwise									136
	0500	Vanity top, porcelain enamel on cast iron									
	0600	20" x 18"	Q-1	6.40	2.500	Ea.	134	37		171	210
	0640	26" x 18" oval		6.40	2.500		167	37		204	245
	0720	18" round		6.40	2.500		126	37		163	200
	0860	For color, add					25%				
	1000	Cultured marble, 19" x 17", single bowl	Q-1	6.40	2.500		88	37		125	160
	1120	25" x 22", single bowl		6.40	2.500		110	37		147	180
	1160	37" x 22", single bowl		6.40	2.500		133	37		170	205
	1560										
	1900	Stainless steel, self-rimming, 25" x 22", single bowl, ledge	Q-1	6.40	2.500	Ea.	185	37		222	265
	1960	17" x 22", single bowl		6.40	2.500		93	37		130	165
	2600	Steel, enameled, 20" x 17", single bowl		6.40	2.500		81	37		118	150
	2900	Vitreous china, 20" x 16", single bowl		6.40	2.500		173	37		210	250
	3200	22" x 13", single bowl		6.40	2.500		149	37		186	225
	3580	Rough-in, supply, waste and vent for all above lavatories		2.30	6.960		88.75	105		193.75	265
	4000	Wall hung									
	4040	Porcelain enamel on cast iron, 16" x 14", single bowl	Q-1	8	2	Ea.	260	30		290	335
	4180	20" x 18", single bowl	"	8	2		110	30		140	170
	4580	For color, add					30%				
	6000	Vitreous china, 18" x 15", single bowl with backsplash	Q-1	8	2		155	30		185	220
	6060	19" x 17", single bowl		8	2		105	30		135	165
	6960	Rough-in, supply, waste and vent for above lavatories		1.66	9.640		130.10	145		275.10	375
140	0010	**LAUNDRY SINKS** With trim									140
	0020	Porcelain enamel on cast iron, black iron frame									
	0050	24" x 20", single compartment	Q-1	6	2.670	Ea.	288	40		328	380
	0100	24" x 23", single compartment	"	6	2.670	"	315	40		355	410
	3000	Plastic, on wall hanger or legs									
	3020	18" x 23", single compartment	Q-1	6.50	2.460	Ea.	102	37		139	170
	3100	20" x 24", single compartment		6.50	2.460		123	37		160	195
	3200	36" x 23", double compartment		5.50	2.910		135	43		178	220
	3300	40" x 24", double compartment		5.50	2.910		190	43		233	280
	5000	Stainless steel, counter top, 22" x 17" single compartment		6	2.670		232	40		272	320

For expanded coverage of these items see *Means Mechanical Cost Data* or *Means Plumbing Cost Data 1991*

152 | Plumbing Fixtures

152 100 | Fixtures

			CREW	DAILY OUTPUT	MAN-HOURS	UNIT	MAT.	LABOR	EQUIP.	TOTAL	TOTAL INCL O&P	
140	5100	19" x 22", single compartment	Q-1	6	2.670	Ea.	247	40		287	335	140
	5200	33" x 22", double compartment		5	3.200		295	48		343	400	
	9600	Rough-in, supply, waste and vent, for all laundry sinks	↓	2.14	7.480	↓	95.66	110		205.66	285	
148	0010	**SHOWERS**										148
	0030	Stall, galvanized steel, molded stone receptor, with door										
	0050	30" x 30" square	Q-1	2.20	7.270	Ea.	243	110		353	445	
	0100	32" x 32" square		2.20	7.270		257	110		367	460	
	0200	36" x 36" square	↓	2.20	7.270	↓	575	110		685	810	
	1500	Stall, with door and trim										
	1520	32" square	Q-1	2	8	Ea.	316	120		436	540	
	1540	Terrazzo receptor, 32" square		2	8		530	120		650	775	
	1560	36" square		1.80	8.890		575	130		705	850	
	1580	36" corner angle		1.80	8.890		585	130		715	860	
	3000	Fiberglass, one piece, with 3 walls, 32" x 32" square		2.40	6.670		338	99		437	535	
	3100	36" x 36" square		2.40	6.670		378	99		477	580	
	4960	Rough-in, supply, waste and vent for above showers	↓	2.05	7.800	↓	72.99	115		187.99	270	
	4970											
152	0010	**SINKS** With faucets and drain										152
	2000	Kitchen, counter top, P.E. on C.I., 24" x 21" single bowl	Q-1	5.60	2.860	Ea.	170	43		213	255	
	2100	30" x 21" single bowl		5.60	2.860		193	43		236	280	
	2200	32" x 21" double bowl		4.80	3.330		218	50		268	320	
	3000	Stainless steel, self rimming, 19" x 18" single bowl		5.60	2.860		233	43		276	325	
	3100	25" x 22" single bowl		5.60	2.860		261	43		304	355	
	3200	33" x 22" double bowl		4.80	3.330		365	50		415	485	
	3300	43" x 22" double bowl		4.80	3.330		450	50		500	575	
	4000	Steel, enameled, with ledge, 24" x 21" single bowl		5.60	2.860		104	43		147	185	
	4100	32" x 21" double bowl	↓	4.80	3.330		115	50		165	210	
	4960	For color sinks except stainless steel, add					10%					
	4980	For rough-in, supply, waste and vent, counter top sinks	Q-1	2.14	7.480		95.66	110		205.66	285	
	5000	Kitchen, raised deck, P.E. on C.I.										
	5100	32" x 21", dual level, double bowl	Q-1	2.60	6.150	Ea.	268	92		360	445	
	5790	For rough-in, supply, waste & vent, sinks		1.85	8.650		95.66	130		225.66	315	
	6650	Service, floor, corner, P.E. on C.I., 28" x 28"	↓	4.40	3.640		420	54		474	550	
	6750	Vinyl coated rim guard, add					46			46	51	
	6770	For stainless steel rim guard, front or side, add					28			28	31	
	6790	For rough-in, supply, waste & vent, floor service sinks	Q-1	1.64	9.760	↓	152.24	145		297.24	405	
180	0010	**WATER CLOSETS**										180
	0150	Tank type, vitreous china, incl. seat, supply pipe w/stop										
	0200	Wall hung, one piece	Q-1	5.30	3.020	Ea.	495	45		540	620	
	0400	Two piece, close coupled		5.30	3.020		339	45		384	445	
	0960	For rough-in, supply, waste, vent and carrier		2.60	6.150		147.31	92		239.31	310	
	1000	Floor mounted, one piece		5.30	3.020		418	45		463	535	
	1020	One piece, low profile		5.30	3.020		666	45		711	805	
	1100	Two piece, close coupled, water saver	↓	5.30	3.020		138	45		183	225	
	1960	For color, add					30%					
	1980	For rough-in, supply, waste and vent	Q-1	1.94	8.250	↓	85.65	125		210.65	295	
	3000	Bowl only, with flush valve, seat										
	3100	Wall hung	Q-1	5.80	2.760	Ea.	275	41		316	370	
	3200	For rough-in, supply, waste and vent, single WC		2.05	7.800		156.94	115		271.94	360	
	3300	Floor mounted	↓	5.80	2.760		275	41		316	370	
	3400	For rough-in, supply, waste and vent, single WC		1.80		↓	95.28			95.28	105	

152 400 | Pumps

410	0010	**PUMPS, CIRCULATING** Heated or chilled water application										410
	0600	Bronze, sweat connections, 1/40 HP, in line										

For expanded coverage of these items see *Means Mechanical Cost Data* or *Means Plumbing Cost Data 1991*

152 | Plumbing Fixtures

152 400 | Pumps

			CREW	DAILY OUTPUT	MAN-HOURS	UNIT	BARE COSTS MAT.	BARE COSTS LABOR	BARE COSTS EQUIP.	BARE COSTS TOTAL	TOTAL INCL O&P	
410	0640	¾″ size	Q-1	16	1	Ea.	94.60	14.90		109.50	130	410
	1000	Flange connection, ¾″ to 1-½″ size										
	1040	1/12 HP	Q-1	6	2.670	Ea.	230	40		270	320	
	1060	1/6 HP	"	6	2.670	"	385	40		425	490	
480	0010	**PUMPS, SUBMERSIBLE** Dewatering										480
	7000	Sump pump, 10′ head, automatic										
	7100	Bronze, 22 GPM., ¼ HP, 1-¼″ discharge	1 Plum	6	1.330	Ea.	230	22		252	290	
	7500	Cast iron, 23 GPM, ¼ HP, 1-¼″ discharge	"	6	1.330	"	109	22		131	155	

153 | Plumbing Appliances

153 100 | Water Appliances

			CREW	DAILY OUTPUT	MAN-HOURS	UNIT	BARE COSTS MAT.	BARE COSTS LABOR	BARE COSTS EQUIP.	BARE COSTS TOTAL	TOTAL INCL O&P	
110	0010	**WATER HEATERS**										110
	1000	Residential, electric, glass lined tank, 10 gal., single element	1 Plum	2.30	3.480	Ea.	144	58		202	250	
	1060	30 gallon, double element		2.20	3.640		202	60		262	320	
	1080	40 gallon, double element		2	4		221	66		287	350	
	1100	52 gallon, double element		2	4		244	66		310	375	
	1120	66 gallon, double element		1.80	4.440		314	74		388	465	
	1140	80 gallon, double element		1.60	5		363	83		446	535	
	2000	Gas fired, glass lined tank, vent not incl., 20 gallon		2.10	3.810		186	63		249	305	
	2040	30 gallon		2	4		189	66		255	315	
	2100	75 gallon		1.50	5.330		497	88		585	690	
	3000	Oil fired, glass lined tank, vent not included, 30 gallon		2	4		673	66		739	850	
	3040	50 gallon		1.80	4.440		910	74		984	1,125	
160	0010	**WATER SUPPLY METERS**										160
	2000	Domestic/commercial, bronze										
	2020	Threaded										
	2060	⅝″ diameter, to 20 GPM	1 Plum	16	.500	Ea.	45	8.30		53.30	63	
	2080	¾″ diameter, to 30 GPM		14	.571		86	9.45		95.45	110	
	2100	1″ diameter, to 50 GPM		12	.667		104	11.05		115.05	130	

154 | Fire Extinguishing Systems

154 100 | Fire Systems

			CREW	DAILY OUTPUT	MAN-HOURS	UNIT	BARE COSTS MAT.	BARE COSTS LABOR	BARE COSTS EQUIP.	BARE COSTS TOTAL	TOTAL INCL O&P	
125	0010	**FIRE EXTINGUISHERS**										125
	0120	CO2, portable with swivel horn, 5 lb.				Ea.	87.10			87.10	96	
	0140	With hose and "H" horn, 10 lb.				"	130			130	145	
	1000	Dry chemical, pressurized										
	1040	Standard type, portable, painted, 2-½ lb.				Ea.	18.25			18.25	20	
	1080	10 lb.					47.60			47.60	52	
	1100	20 lb.					69			69	76	
	2000	ABC all purpose type, portable, 2-½ lb.					18.25			18.25	20	
	2080	9-½ lb.					47.60			47.60	52	

For expanded coverage of these items see *Means Mechanical Cost Data or Means Plumbing Cost Data 1991*

155 | Heating

155 100 | Boilers

			CREW	DAILY OUTPUT	MAN-HOURS	UNIT	MAT.	LABOR	EQUIP.	TOTAL	TOTAL INCL O&P	
110	0010	**BOILERS, ELECTRIC, ASME** Standard controls and trim										110
	1000	Steam, 6 KW, 20.5 MBH	Q-19	1.20	20	Ea.	2,950	310		3,260	3,750	
	1160	60 KW, 205 MBH		1	24		4,240	370		4,610	5,275	
	2000	Hot water, 12 KW, 41 MBH		1.30	18.460		2,440	285		2,725	3,150	
	2040	24 KW, 82 MBH		1.20	20		2,610	310		2,920	3,375	
	2060	30 KW, 103 MBH	↓	1.20	20		2,670	310		2,980	3,425	
115	0010	**BOILERS, GAS FIRED** Natural or propane, standard controls										115
	1000	Cast iron, with insulated jacket										
	3000	Hot water, gross output, 80 MBH	Q-7	1.46	21.920	Ea.	935	345		1,280	1,600	
	3020	100 MBH	"	1.35	23.700	"	1,100	375		1,475	1,825	
	4000	Steel, insulating jacket										
	6000	Hot water, including burner & one zone valve, gross output										
	6010	51.2 MBH	Q-6	2.25	10.670	Ea.	1,090	165		1,255	1,475	
	6020	72 MBH		2	12		1,490	185		1,675	1,950	
	6040	89 MBH		1.90	12.630		1,530	195		1,725	2,000	
	6060	105 MBH		1.80	13.330		1,710	205		1,915	2,225	
	6080	132 MBH		1.70	14.120		1,960	220		2,180	2,500	
	6100	155 MBH	↓	1.50	16		2,270	245		2,515	2,900	
	7000	For tankless water heater on smaller gas units, add					10%					
	7050	For additional zone valves up to 312 MBH add				↓	70			70	77	
120	0010	**BOILERS, OIL FIRED** Standard controls, flame retention burner										120
	1000	Cast iron, with insulated flush jacket										
	2000	Steam, gross output, 109 MBH	Q-7	1.20	26.670	Ea.	1,400	425		1,825	2,225	
	2060	207 MBH	"	.90	35.560	"	1,810	565		2,375	2,900	
	3000	Hot water, same price as steam										
	7000	Hot water, gross output, 103 MBH	Q-6	1.90	12.630	Ea.	1,740	195		1,935	2,225	
	7020	122 MBH		1.80	13.330		1,770	205		1,975	2,275	
	7060	168 MBH		1.50	16		2,240	245		2,485	2,875	
	7080	225 MBH	↓	1.40	17.140	↓	2,645	265		2,910	3,350	
125	0010	**BOILERS, GAS/OIL** Combination with burners and controls										125
	1000	Cast Iron with insulated jacket										
	2000	Steam, gross output, 720 MBH	Q-7	.40	80	Ea.	9,900	1,275		11,175	13,000	
	3000	Hot water, gross output, 584 MBH	"	.54	59.260	"	6,840	940		7,780	9,050	
	4000	Steel, insulated jacket, skid base, tubeless										
	4500	Steam, 150 psi gross output, 335 MBH, 10 BHP	Q-6	.65	36.920	Ea.	7,720	570		8,290	9,425	
150	0010	**SWIMMING POOL HEATERS** Not including wiring, external										150
	0020	piping, base or pad,										
	0060	Gas fired, gross output, 50 MBH	Q-6	3	8	Ea.	475	125		600	725	
	0100	80 MBH		2	12		610	185		795	975	
	0160	120 MBH		1.50	16		635	245		880	1,100	
	0200	170 MBH		1	24		765	370		1,135	1,450	
	0280	500 MBH	↓	.40	60		2,370	925		3,295	4,125	
	2000	Electric, 12 KW, 4800 gallon pool	Q-19	3	8		1,100	125		1,225	1,400	
	2020	18 KW, 7200 gallon pool		2.80	8.570		1,130	130		1,260	1,450	
	2040	24 KW, 9600 gallon pool		2.40	10		1,200	155		1,355	1,575	
	2100	54 KW, 24,000 gallon pool	↓	1.20	20	↓	1,640	310		1,950	2,300	

155 200 | Boiler Accessories

			CREW	DAILY OUTPUT	MAN-HOURS	UNIT	MAT.	LABOR	EQUIP.	TOTAL	TOTAL INCL O&P	
230	0010	**BURNERS**										230
	0990	Residential, conversion, gas fired, LP or natural										
	1000	Gun type, atmospheric input 35 to 180 MBH	Q-1	2.50	6.400	Ea.	162	95		257	335	
	1020	50 to 240 MBH		2	8		187	120		307	400	
	1040	200 to 400 MBH	↓	1.70	9.410	↓	350	140		490	615	

For expanded coverage of these items see *Means Mechanical Cost Data* or *Means Plumbing Cost Data 1991*

155 | Heating

155 400 | Warm Air Systems

			CREW	DAILY OUTPUT	MAN-HOURS	UNIT	MAT.	LABOR	EQUIP.	TOTAL	TOTAL INCL O&P
420	0010	**FURNACES** Hot air heating, blowers, standard controls (134)										420
	0020	not including gas, oil or flue piping.									
	1000	Electric, UL listed, heat staging, 240 volt									
	1020	30 MBH	Q-20	4	5	Ea.	290	75		365	440
	1080	76 MBH		3.60	5.560		515	83		598	705
	1090	85.3 MBH		3.70	5.410		575	81		656	765
	1100	91 MBH		3.40	5.880		720	88		808	935
	3000	Gas, AGA certified, direct drive models									
	3020	42 MBH output	Q-9	4	4	Ea.	400	59		459	535
	3040	63 MBH output		3.80	4.210		420	62		482	565
	3060	79 MBH output		3.60	4.440		475	65		540	630
	3080	84 MBH output		3.40	4.710		515	69		584	680
	3100	105 MBH output		3.20	5		535	73		608	710
	3120	126 MBH output		3	5.330		690	78		768	890
	3130	160 MBH output		2.80	5.710		1,065	84		1,149	1,300
	3140	200 MBH output		2.60	6.150		2,650	90		2,740	3,075
	4000	For starter plenum, add		16	1		55	14.65		69.65	85
	6000	Oil, UL listed, atomizing gun type burner									
	6020	55 MBH output	Q-9	3.60	4.440	Ea.	705	65		770	885
	6030	84 MBH output		3.50	4.570		730	67		797	915
	6040	99 MBH output		3.40	4.710		790	69		859	985
	6060	125 MBH output		3.20	5		900	73		973	1,100
	6080	152 MBH output		3	5.330		1,115	78		1,193	1,350
	6100	200 MBH output		2.60	6.150		1,765	90		1,855	2,100
430	0010	**FURNACES, COMBINATION SYSTEMS** Heating, cooling, electric air										430
	0020	cleaner, humidification, dehumidification.									
	2000	Gas fired, 80 MBH heat output, 24 MBH cooling	Q-9	1.20	13.330	Ea.	2,330	195		2,525	2,875
	2020	80 MBH heat output, 36 MBH cooling		1.20	13.330		2,480	195		2,675	3,050
	2040	100 MBH heat output, 29 MBH cooling		1	16		2,520	235		2,755	3,150
	2060	100 MBH heat output, 36 MBH cooling		1	16		2,640	235		2,875	3,300
	2080	100 MBH heat output, 47 MBH cooling		.90	17.780		2,910	260		3,170	3,625
	2100	120 MBH heat output, 29 MBH cooling	Q-10	1.30	18.460		2,670	280		2,950	3,400
	2120	120 MBH heat output, 42 MBH cooling		1.30	18.460		2,990	280		3,270	3,750
	2140	120 MBH heat output, 47 MBH cooling		1.20	20		3,010	305		3,315	3,825
	2160	120 MBH heat output, 55 MBH cooling		1.10	21.820		3,180	330		3,510	4,050
	2180	144 MBH heat output, 42 MBH cooling		1.20	20		3,060	305		3,365	3,875
	2200	144 MBH heat output, 47 MBH cooling		1.20	20		3,080	305		3,385	3,900
	2220	144 MBH heat output, 58 MBH cooling		1	24		3,230	365		3,595	4,150
	2250	144 MBH heat, 60 MBH cool		.70	34.290		3,230	520		3,750	4,425
	3000	Oil fired, 84 MBH heat output, 24 MBH cooling	Q-9	1.20	13.330		2,500	195		2,695	3,075
	3020	84 MBH heat output, 36 MBH cooling		1.20	13.330		2,660	195		2,855	3,250
	3040	95.2 MBH heat output, 29 MBH cooling		1	16		2,680	235		2,915	3,325
	3060	95.2 MBH heat output, 36 MBH cooling		1	16		2,770	235		3,005	3,425
	3280	184.8 MBH heat, 60 MBH cooling	Q-10	1	24		3,440	365		3,805	4,400
	3500	For precharged tubing with connection, add									
	3520	15 feet				Ea.	88			88	97
	3540	25 feet					117			117	130
	3560	35 feet					147			147	160

155 600 | Heating System Access.

			CREW	DAILY OUTPUT	MAN-HOURS	UNIT	MAT.	LABOR	EQUIP.	TOTAL	TOTAL INCL O&P
630	0010	**HYDRONIC HEATING** Terminal units, not incl. main supply pipe										630
	1000	Radiation									
	1310	Baseboard, pkgd, ½" copper tube, alum. fin, 7" high	Q-5	60	.267	L.F.	7.35	3.97		11.32	14.55
	1320	¾" copper tube, alum. fin, 7" high		58	.276		7.70	4.11		11.81	15.15
	1340	1" copper tube, alum. fin, 8-⅞" high		56	.286		13.80	4.26		18.06	22
	1360	1-¼" copper tube, alum. fin, 8-⅞" high		54	.296		19.42	4.41		23.83	29
	3000	Radiators, cast iron									
	3100	Free standing or wall hung, 6 tube, 25" high	Q-5	96	.167	Section	20.16	2.48		22.64	26

For expanded coverage of these items see *Means Mechanical Cost Data* or *Means Plumbing Cost Data 1991*

155 | Heating

155 600 | Heating System Access.

			CREW	DAILY OUTPUT	MAN-HOURS	UNIT	MAT.	LABOR	EQUIP.	TOTAL	TOTAL INCL O&P	
640	0010	**HUMIDIFIERS**										640
	0030	Centrifugal atomizing										
	0100	10 lb. per hour	Q-5	10	1.600	Ea.	1,135	24		1,159	1,275	
651	0010	**INSULATION**										651
	2900	Domestic water heater wrap kit										
	2920	1-½" with vinyl jacket, 20-60 gal.	1 Plum	8	1	Ea.	23.50	16.55		40.05	53	
	3000	Ductwork										
	3020	Blanket type, fiberglass, flexible										
	3030	Fire resistant liner, black coating one side										
	3050	½" thick, 2 lb. density	Q-14	380	.042	S.F.	.34	.61		.95	1.40	
	3060	1" thick, 1-½ lb. density	"	350	.046	"	.45	.66		1.11	1.62	
	3140	FRK vapor barrier wrap, .75 lb. density										
	3160	1" thick	Q-14	350	.046	S.F.	.23	.66		.89	1.37	
	3170	1-½" thick	"	320	.050	"	.30	.72		1.02	1.55	
	3490	Board type, fiberglass, 3 lb. density										
	3500	Fire resistant, black pigmented, 1 side										
	3520	1" thick	Q-14	150	.107	S.F.	1.29	1.54		2.83	4.03	
	3540	1-½" thick	"	130	.123	"	1.50	1.78		3.28	4.66	
	4000	Pipe covering										
	6600	Fiberglass, with all service jacket										
	6840	1" wall, ½" iron pipe size	Q-14	240	.067	L.F.	.97	.96		1.93	2.70	
	6860	¾" iron pipe size		230	.070		1.12	1		2.12	2.93	
	6870	1" iron pipe size		220	.073		1.15	1.05		2.20	3.05	
	6900	2" iron pipe size	↓	200	.080	↓	1.51	1.16		2.67	3.62	
	7879	Rubber tubing, flexible closed cell foam										
	8100	½" wall, ¼" iron pipe size	1 Asbe	90	.089	L.F.	.34	1.43		1.77	2.79	
	8130	½" iron pipe size		90	.089		.42	1.43		1.85	2.88	
	8140	¾" iron pipe size		90	.089		.47	1.43		1.90	2.93	
	8150	1" iron pipe size		90	.089		.52	1.43		1.95	2.99	
	8170	1-½" iron pipe size		90	.089		.73	1.43		2.16	3.22	
	8180	2" iron pipe size		90	.089		.89	1.43		2.32	3.39	
	8300	¾" wall, ¼" iron pipe size		90	.089		.51	1.43		1.94	2.97	
	8330	½" iron pipe size		90	.089		.69	1.43		2.12	3.17	
	8340	¾" iron pipe size		90	.089		.85	1.43		2.28	3.35	
	8350	1" iron pipe size		90	.089		.97	1.43		2.40	3.48	
	8380	2" iron pipe size	↓	90	.089	↓	1.73	1.43		3.16	4.32	
671	0010	**TANKS**										671
	0020	Fiberglass, underground, U.L. listed, not including										
	0030	manway or hold-down strap										
	0100	1000 gallon capacity	Q-6	2	12	Ea.	1,570	185		1,755	2,025	
	0140	2000 gallon capacity	Q-7	2	16		2,290	255		2,545	2,925	
	0500	For manway, fittings and hold-downs, add					20%	15%				
	2000	Steel, liquid expansion, ASME, painted, 15 gallon capacity	Q-5	17	.941		244	14		258	290	
	2040	30 gallon capacity		12	1.330		278	19.85		297.85	340	
	3000	Steel ASME expansion, rubber diaphragm, 19 gal. cap. accept.		12	1.330		945	19.85		964.85	1,075	
	3020	31 gallon capacity	↓	8	2		1,050	30		1,080	1,200	
	4000	Steel, storage, above ground, including supports, coating,										
	4020	fittings, not including mat, pumps or piping										
	4040	275 gallon capacity	Q-5	5	3.200	Ea.	225	48		273	325	
	4060	550 gallon capacity	"	4	4	↓	1,050	60		1,110	1,250	
	4080	1000 gallon capacity	Q-7	4	8	↓	1,350	125		1,475	1,700	
	5000	Steel underground, sti-P3, set in place, incl. hold-down bars.										
	5500	Excavation, pad, pumps and piping not included										
	5520	1000 gallon capacity, 7 gauge shell	Q-7	4	8	Ea.	1,400	125		1,525	1,750	
680	0010	**VENT CHIMNEY** Prefab metal, U.L. listed										680
	0020	Gas, double wall, galvanized steel										

For expanded coverage of these items see *Means Mechanical Cost Data or Means Plumbing Cost Data 1991*

155 | Heating

155 600 | Heating System Access.

			CREW	DAILY OUTPUT	MAN-HOURS	UNIT	MAT.	LABOR	EQUIP.	TOTAL	TOTAL INCL O&P	
680	0080	3" diameter	Q-9	72	.222	V.L.F.	2.47	3.25		5.72	8.10	680
	0100	4" diameter		68	.235	"	3.01	3.44		6.45	9	
	5000	Vent damper bi-metal 6" flue		16	1	Ea.	59.30	14.65		73.95	89	
	5100	Gas, auto., electric	↓	8	2	"	115	29		144	175	

157 | Air Conditioning/Ventilating

157 100 | A.C. & Vent. Units

			CREW	DAILY OUTPUT	MAN-HOURS	UNIT	MAT.	LABOR	EQUIP.	TOTAL	TOTAL INCL O&P	
160	0010	**HEAT PUMPS**										160
	1000	Air to air, split system, not including curbs or pads										
	1020	2 ton cooling, 8.5 MBH heat @ 0°F	Q-5	1.20	13.330	Ea.	1,600	200		1,800	2,075	
	1500	Single package, not including curbs, pads, or plenums										
	1520	2 ton cooling, 6.5 MBH heat @ 0°F	Q-5	1.50	10.670	Ea.	1,930	160		2,090	2,375	
	2000	Water source to air, single package										
	2100	1 ton cooling, 13 MBH heat @ 75°F	Q-5	2	8	Ea.	860	120		980	1,150	
170	0010	**PACKAGED TERMINAL AIR CONDITIONER** Cabinet, wall sleeve,										170
	0100	louver, electric heat, thermostat, manual changeover, 208 V										
	0200	6,000 BTUH cooling, 8800 BTU heat	Q-5	6	2.670	Ea.	670	40		710	800	
	0220	9,000 BTUH cooling, 13,900 BTU heat		5	3.200		680	48		728	825	
	0240	12,000 BTUH cooling, 13,900 BTU heat		4	4		700	60		760	865	
	0260	15,000 BTUH cooling, 13,900 BTU heat	↓	3	5.330	↓	760	79		839	965	
180	0010	**ROOF TOP AIR CONDITIONERS** Standard controls, curb, economizer										180
	1000	Single zone, electric cool, gas heat										
	1140	5 ton cooling, 112 MBH heating	Q-5	.56	28.570	Ea.	3,590	425		4,015	4,650	
	1160	10 ton cooling, 200 MBH heating	Q-6	.46	52.170	"	7,280	805		8,085	9,325	
185	0010	**SELF-CONTAINED SINGLE PACKAGE**										185
	0100	Air cooled, for free blow or duct, including remote condenser										
	0200	3 ton cooling	Q-5	1	16	Ea.	3,300	240		3,540	4,025	
	0210	4 ton cooling	"	.90	17.780	"	3,940	265		4,205	4,775	
	1000	Water cooled for free blow or duct, not including tower										
	1100	3 ton cooling	Q-6	1	24	Ea.	2,310	370		2,680	3,150	
195	0010	**WINDOW UNIT AIR CONDITIONERS**										195
	4000	Portable, 15 amp 125V grounded receptacle required										
	4020	Standard models										
	4060	5000 BTUH, 1 speed fan	1 Carp	8	1	Ea.	245	14.30		259.30	295	
	4080	5000 BTUH, 3 speed fan	"	8	1	↓	253	14.30		267.30	300	
	4100	For high efficiency (EER rating), add					49			49	54	
	4250	Semi-permanent installation, 3 speed fan										
	4260	15 amp 125V grounded receptacle required										
	4280	Standard models, 2 way air direction										
	4320	5000 BTUH	1 Carp	8	1	Ea.	291	14.30		305.30	345	
	4340	6000 BTUH	"	8	1	"	334	14.30		348.30	390	
	4400	High efficiency models										
	4450	5900 BTUH, 2 way air direction	1 Carp	8	1	Ea.	355	14.30		369.30	415	
	4480	8000 BTUH, 4 way high thrust air		6	1.330		416	19.05		435.05	490	
	4500	10,000 BTUH, 4 way high thrust air	↓	6	1.330		520	19.05		539.05	605	
	4520	12,000 BTUH, 4 way high thrust air	L-2	8	2		575	25		600	675	
	4540	14,000 BTUH, 4 way high thrust air	"	8	2	↓	640	25		665	745	
	4600	15 amp 250V grounded receptacle required										
	4700	High efficiency, 4 way high thrust air										
	4740	15,000 BTUH	L-2	6	2.670	Ea.	585	34		619	700	

For expanded coverage of these items see *Means Mechanical Cost Data* or *Means Plumbing Cost Data 1991*

157 | Air Conditioning/Ventilating

157 100 | A.C. & Vent. Units

			CREW	DAILY OUTPUT	MAN-HOURS	UNIT	MAT.	LABOR	EQUIP.	TOTAL	TOTAL INCL O&P	
195	4780	18,000 BTUH	L-2	6	2.670	Ea.	680	34		714	805	195
	4820	20 amp 250V grounded receptacle required										
	4840	High efficiency, 4 way high thrust air										
	4860	21,000 BTUH	L-2	6	2.670	Ea.	775	34		809	910	
	4900	30 amp 250V grounded receptacle required										
	4901	Window unit AC, 30 amp 250 V grounded receptacle										
	4910	High efficiency, 4 way high thrust air										
	4940	25,000 BTUH	L-2	4	4	Ea.	840	51		891	1,000	
	4960	29,000 BTUH	"	4	4	"	940	51		991	1,125	

157 200 | System Components

			CREW	DAILY OUTPUT	MAN-HOURS	UNIT	MAT.	LABOR	EQUIP.	TOTAL	TOTAL INCL O&P	
250	0010	**DUCTWORK**										250
	0020	Fabricated rectangular, includes fittings, joints, supports,										
	0030	allowance for flexible connections, no insulation										
	0031	NOTE: Fabrication and installation are combined										
	0040	as LABOR cost.										
	0100	Aluminum, alloy 3003-H14, under 100 lb.	Q-10	80	.300	Lb.	2.45	4.55		7	10.25	
	0110	100 to 500 lb.		80	.300		1.69	4.55		6.24	9.40	
	0120	500 to 1000 lb.		95	.253		1.50	3.83		5.33	8	
	0140	1000 to 2000 lb.		120	.200		1.43	3.03		4.46	6.60	
	0500	Galvanized steel, under 200 lb.		235	.102		.75	1.55		2.30	3.40	
	0520	200 to 500 lb.		245	.098		.65	1.49		2.14	3.18	
	0540	500 to 1000 lb.		255	.094		.55	1.43		1.98	2.98	
	1300	Flexible, coated fiberglass fabric on corr. resist. metal helix										
	1400	pressure to 12" (WG) UL-181										
	1500	Non-insulated, 3" diameter	Q-9	400	.040	L.F.	.69	.59		1.28	1.73	
	1540	5" diameter		320	.050		.83	.73		1.56	2.12	
	1560	6" diameter		280	.057		.96	.84		1.80	2.45	
	1580	7" diameter		240	.067		1.13	.98		2.11	2.86	
	1900	Insulated, 1" thick with ¾ lb., PE jacket, 3" diameter		380	.042		1.18	.62		1.80	2.32	
	1910	4" diameter		340	.047		1.18	.69		1.87	2.44	
	1920	5" diameter		300	.053		1.40	.78		2.18	2.83	
	1940	6" diameter		260	.062		1.54	.90		2.44	3.18	
	1960	7" diameter		220	.073		1.84	1.06		2.90	3.78	
	1980	8" diameter		180	.089		1.98	1.30		3.28	4.34	
	2040	12" diameter		100	.160		2.92	2.34		5.26	7.10	
290	0010	**FANS**										290
	8000	Ventilation, residential										
	8020	Attic, roof type										
	8030	Aluminum dome, damper & curb										
	8040	6" diameter, 300 CFM	1 Elec	16	.500	Ea.	143	8.20		151.20	170	
	8050	7" diameter, 450 CFM		15	.533		160	8.70		168.70	190	
	8060	9" diameter, 900 CFM		14	.571		285	9.35		294.35	330	
	8080	12" diameter, 1000 CFM (gravity)		10	.800		200	13.10		213.10	240	
	8090	16" diameter, 1500 CFM (gravity)		9	.889		255	14.55		269.55	305	
	8100	20" diameter, 2500 CFM (gravity)		8	1		320	16.35		336.35	380	
	8160	Plastic, ABS dome										
	8180	1050 CFM	1 Elec	14	.571	Ea.	67	9.35		76.35	89	
	8200	1600 CFM	"	12	.667	"	101	10.90		111.90	130	
	8240	Attic, wall type, with shutter, one speed										
	8250	12" diameter, 1000 CFM	1 Elec	14	.571	Ea.	115	9.35		124.35	140	
	8260	14" diameter, 1500 CFM		12	.667		135	10.90		145.90	165	
	8270	16" diameter, 2000 CFM		9	.889		166	14.55		180.55	205	
	8290	Whole house, wall type, with shutter, one speed										
	8300	30" diameter, 4800 CFM	1 Elec	7	1.140	Ea.	290	18.70		308.70	350	
	8310	36" diameter, 7000 CFM	"	6	1.330	"	345	22		367	415	

For expanded coverage of these items see *Means Mechanical Cost Data* or *Means Plumbing Cost Data 1991*

157 | Air Conditioning/Ventilating

157 200 | System Components

			CREW	DAILY OUTPUT	MAN-HOURS	UNIT	MAT.	LABOR	EQUIP.	TOTAL	TOTAL INCL O&P	
290	8320	42" diameter, 10,000 CFM	1 Elec	5	1.600	Ea.	410	26		436	495	290
	8330	48" diameter, 16,000 CFM	"	4	2		495	33		528	595	
	8340	For two speed, add					11			11	12.10	
	8350	Whole house, lay-down type, with shutter, one speed										
	8360	30" diameter, 4500 CFM	1 Elec	8	1	Ea.	303	16.35		319.35	360	
	8370	36" diameter, 6500 CFM		7	1.140		355	18.70		373.70	420	
	8380	42" diameter, 9000 CFM		6	1.330		420	22		442	495	
	8390	48" diameter, 12,000 CFM		5	1.600		500	26		526	590	
	8440	For two speed, add					11			11	12.10	
	8450	For 12 hour timer switch, add	1 Elec	32	.250		16.50	4.09		20.59	25	

157 400 | Accessories

			CREW	DAILY OUTPUT	MAN-HOURS	UNIT	MAT.	LABOR	EQUIP.	TOTAL	TOTAL INCL O&P	
401	0010	**AIR FILTERS**										401
	0050	Activated charcoal type, full flow				MCFM	600			600	660	
	2000	Electronic air cleaner, self-contained										
	2150	500 CFM	1 Shee	2.30	3.480	Ea.	585	57		642	735	
	2200	1000 CFM		2.20	3.640		810	59		869	990	
	2250	1200 CFM		2.10	3.810		1,190	62		1,252	1,400	
	2300	2500 CFM		2	4		1,360	65		1,425	1,600	
	2950	Mechanical media filtration units										
	3000	High efficiency type, with frame, non-supported				MCFM	35			35	39	
	3100	Supported type					47			47	52	
	4000	Medium efficiency, extended surface					5			5	5.50	
	4500	Permanent washable					33			33	36	
	5000	Renewable disposable roll					85			85	94	
	5500	Throwaway glass or paper media type	1 Shee	32	.250	Ea.	2.65	4.06		6.71	9.65	
420	0010	**CONTROL COMPONENTS**										420
	5000	Thermostats										
	5030	1 set back, manual	1 Shee	8	1	Ea.	16.30	16.25		32.55	45	
	5040	1 set back, electric, timed		8	1		59.45	16.25		75.70	92	
	5050	2 set back, electric, timed		8	1		59.45	16.25		75.70	92	
450	0010	**DIFFUSERS** Aluminum, opposed blade damper unless noted										450
	0100	Ceiling, linear, also for sidewall										
	0120	2" wide	1 Shee	32	.250	L.F.	18.35	4.06		22.41	27	
	0160	4" wide		26	.308	"	24.50	5		29.50	35	
	0500	Perforated, 24" x 24", panel size 6" x 6"		16	.500	Ea.	50	8.15		58.15	68	
	0520	8" x 8"		15	.533		51.70	8.65		60.35	71	
	1000	Rectangular, 1 to 4 way blow, 6" x 6"		16	.500		29.70	8.15		37.85	46	
	1020	12" x 6"		15	.533		37.90	8.65		46.55	56	
	1040	12" x 9"		14	.571		45.60	9.30		54.90	66	
	1060	12" x 12"		12	.667		52.25	10.85		63.10	75	
	1100	24" x 12"		10	.800		89.10	13		102.10	120	
	1180	24" x 24"		7	1.140		152	18.55		170.55	200	
	1500	Round, butterfly damper, 6" diameter		18	.444		18.70	7.20		25.90	33	
	1520	8" diameter		16	.500		20.40	8.15		28.55	36	
	2000	T bar mounting, 24" x 24" lay-in frame, 6" x 6"		16	.500		47.85	8.15		56	66	
	2020	9" x 9"		14	.571		56.10	9.30		65.40	77	
	2040	12" x 12"		12	.667		71.50	10.85		82.35	97	
	2060	15" x 15"		11	.727		92.40	11.80		104.20	120	
	2080	18" x 18"		10	.800		93.40	13		106.40	125	
	6000	For steel diffusers instead of aluminum, deduct					10%					
460	0010	**GRILLES**										460
	0020	Aluminum										
	1000	Air return, 6" x 6"	1 Shee	26	.308	Ea.	7.15	5		12.15	16.15	
	1020	10" x 6"		24	.333		8.25	5.40		13.65	18.05	
	1080	16" x 8"		22	.364		12.10	5.90		18	23	
	1100	12" x 12"		22	.364		12.10	5.90		18	23	

For expanded coverage of these items see *Means Mechanical Cost Data* or *Means Plumbing Cost Data 1991*

157 | Air Conditioning/Ventilating

157 400 | Accessories

			CREW	DAILY OUTPUT	MAN-HOURS	UNIT	MAT.	LABOR	EQUIP.	TOTAL	TOTAL INCL O&P	
460	1120	24" x 12"	1 Shee	18	.444	Ea.	22	7.20		29.20	36	460
	1180	16" x 16"	"	22	.364	"	18.15	5.90		24.05	30	
470	0010	**REGISTERS**										470
	0980	Air supply										
	3000	Baseboard, hand adj. damper, enameled steel										
	3020	10" x 6"	1 Shee	24	.333	Ea.	6.55	5.40		11.95	16.20	
	3040	12" x 5"		22	.364		7.75	5.90		13.65	18.35	
	3060	12" x 6"	↓	23	.348	↓	7.15	5.65		12.80	17.25	
	4000	Floor, toe operated damper, enameled steel										
	4020	4" x 6"	1 Shee	32	.250	Ea.	10.75	4.06		14.81	18.55	
	4040	4" x 12"	"	26	.308	"	13.25	5		18.25	23	
480	0010	**DUCT ACCESSORIES**										480
	0050	Air extractors, 12" x 4"	1 Shee	24	.333	Ea.	7.70	5.40		13.10	17.45	
	0100	8" x 6"		22	.364		5.50	5.90		11.40	15.85	
	3000	Fire damper, curtain type, vertical, 8" x 4"		24	.333		15.40	5.40		20.80	26	
	3020	12" x 4"		22	.364		15.40	5.90		21.30	27	
	6000	Multi-blade dampers, opposed blade, 12" x 12"	↓	21	.381	↓	8	6.20		14.20	19.05	
	8000	Volume control, dampers										
	8100	8" x 8"	1 Shee	24	.333	Ea.	17.10	5.40		22.50	28	
	9200	Plenums, measured by panel surface				S.F.	8			8	8.80	
490	0010	**VENTILATORS** Base, damper & bird screen, CFM in 5 MPH wind										490
	0500	Rotary syphon, galvanized, 6" neck diameter, 185 CFM	Q-9	16	1	Ea.	38.30	14.65		52.95	66	
	0520	8" neck diameter, 215 CFM	"	14	1.140	"	41.85	16.70		58.55	74	

160 | Raceways

160 200 | Conduits

			CREW	DAILY OUTPUT	MAN-HOURS	UNIT	MAT.	LABOR	EQUIP.	TOTAL	TOTAL INCL O&P	
205	0010	**CONDUIT** To 15' high, includes 2 terminations, 2 elbows and										205
	0020	11 beam clamps per 100 L.F.										
	1750	Rigid galvanized steel, ½" diameter	1 Elec	90	.089	L.F.	1.08	1.45		2.53	3.54	
	1770	¾" diameter		80	.100		1.40	1.64		3.04	4.18	
	1800	1" diameter		65	.123		1.75	2.01		3.76	5.20	
	1830	1-¼" diameter		60	.133		2.30	2.18		4.48	6.05	
	1850	1-½" diameter		55	.145		2.85	2.38		5.23	7	
	1870	2" diameter		45	.178		3.60	2.91		6.51	8.65	
	5000	Electric metallic tubing (EMT), ½" diameter		170	.047		.33	.77		1.10	1.61	
	5020	¾" diameter		130	.062		.47	1.01		1.48	2.14	
	5040	1" diameter		115	.070		.70	1.14		1.84	2.61	
	5060	1-¼" diameter		100	.080		1	1.31		2.31	3.21	
	5080	1-½" diameter		90	.089		1.15	1.45		2.60	3.61	
	9100	PVC, #40, ½" diameter		190	.042		.41	.69		1.10	1.56	
	9110	¾" diameter		145	.055		.53	.90		1.43	2.04	
	9120	1" diameter		125	.064		.80	1.05		1.85	2.57	
	9130	1-¼" diameter		110	.073		1.07	1.19		2.26	3.10	
	9140	1-½" diameter		100	.080		1.30	1.31		2.61	3.54	
	9150	2" diameter	↓	90	.089	↓	1.70	1.45		3.15	4.22	
230	0010	**CONDUIT IN CONCRETE SLAB** Including terminations,										230
	0020	fittings and supports										

For expanded coverage of these items see *Means Electrical Cost Data 1991*

160 | Raceways

160 200 | Conduits

			CREW	DAILY OUTPUT	MAN-HOURS	UNIT	MAT.	LABOR	EQUIP.	TOTAL	TOTAL INCL O&P	
230	3230	PVC, schedule 40, ½" diameter	1 Elec	270	.030	L.F.	.34	.48		.82	1.16	230
	3250	¾" diameter		230	.035		.35	.57		.92	1.30	
	3270	1" diameter		200	.040		.48	.65		1.13	1.59	
	3300	1-¼" diameter		170	.047		.64	.77		1.41	1.95	
	3330	1-½" diameter		140	.057		.81	.93		1.74	2.40	
	3350	2" diameter		120	.067		1.07	1.09		2.16	2.94	
	4350	Rigid galvanized steel, ½" diameter		200	.040		1.01	.65		1.66	2.17	
	4400	¾" diameter		170	.047		1.26	.77		2.03	2.63	
	4450	1" diameter		130	.062		1.72	1.01		2.73	3.52	
	4500	1-¼" diameter		110	.073		2.23	1.19		3.42	4.38	
	4600	1-½" diameter		100	.080		2.75	1.31		4.06	5.15	
	4800	2" diameter		90	.089		3.55	1.45		5	6.25	
240	0010	**CONDUIT IN TRENCH** Includes terminations and fittings										240
	0200	Rigid galvanized steel, 2" diameter	1 Elec	150	.053	L.F.	3.40	.87		4.27	5.15	
	0400	2-½" diameter		100	.080		5.60	1.31		6.91	8.25	
	0600	3" diameter		80	.100		7.10	1.64		8.74	10.45	
	0800	3-½" diameter		70	.114		9.30	1.87		11.17	13.25	
250	0010	**CONDUIT FITTINGS** For RGS										250
	2280	LB, LR or LL fittings & covers, ½" diameter	1 Elec	16	.500	Ea.	5.10	8.20		13.30	18.85	
	2290	¾" diameter		13	.615		6.20	10.05		16.25	23	
	2300	1" diameter		11	.727		8.80	11.90		20.70	29	
	2330	1-¼" diameter		8	1		13.60	16.35		29.95	41	
	2350	1-½" diameter		6	1.330		16.75	22		38.75	54	
	2370	2" diameter		5	1.600		27.90	26		53.90	73	
	5280	Service entrance cap, ½" diameter		16	.500		4.30	8.20		12.50	17.95	
	5300	¾" diameter		13	.615		4.95	10.05		15	22	
	5320	1" diameter		10	.800		6.20	13.10		19.30	28	
	5340	1-¼" diameter		8	1		7.90	16.35		24.25	35	
	5360	1-½" diameter		6.50	1.230		11.85	20		31.85	46	
	5380	2" diameter		5.50	1.450		20.70	24		44.70	61	
270	0010	**FLEXIBLE METALLIC CONDUIT**										270
	0050	Greenfield, ⅜" diameter	1 Elec	200	.040	L.F.	.20	.65		.85	1.28	
	0100	½" diameter		200	.040		.29	.65		.94	1.38	
	0200	¾" diameter		160	.050		.37	.82		1.19	1.73	
	0250	1" diameter		100	.080		.70	1.31		2.01	2.88	
	0300	1-¼" diameter		70	.114		.88	1.87		2.75	3.99	
	0350	1-½" diameter		50	.160		1.13	2.62		3.75	5.45	
	0370	2" diameter		40	.200		1.48	3.27		4.75	6.90	
275	0010	**MOTOR CONNECTIONS**										275
	0020	Flexible conduit and fittings, up to 1 HP motor, 115 volt, 1 phase	1 Elec	8	1	Ea.	2.95	16.35		19.30	30	
290	0010	**WIREMOLD RACEWAY**										290
	0100	No. 500	1 Elec	100	.080	L.F.	.46	1.31		1.77	2.62	
	0200	No. 1000		90	.089		.75	1.45		2.20	3.17	
	0400	No. 1500, small pancake		90	.089		.76	1.45		2.21	3.19	
	0600	No. 2000, base & cover		90	.089		.80	1.45		2.25	3.23	
	0800	No. 3000, base & cover		75	.107		1.65	1.74		3.39	4.63	
	2400	Fittings, elbows, No. 500		40	.200	Ea.	.78	3.27		4.05	6.15	
	2800	Elbow cover, No. 2000		40	.200		1.60	3.27		4.87	7.05	
	3000	Switch box, No. 500		16	.500		6.25	8.20		14.45	20	
	3400	Telephone outlet, No. 1500		16	.500		5.43	8.20		13.63	19.20	
	3600	Junction box, No. 1500		16	.500		3.67	8.20		11.87	17.25	
	3800	Plugmold wired sections, No. 2000										
	4000	1 circuit, 6 outlets, 3 ft. long	1 Elec	8	1	Ea.	16.50	16.35		32.85	45	
	4100	2 circuits, 8 outlets, 6 ft. long	"	5.30	1.510	"	21.05	25		46.05	63	

For expanded coverage of these items see *Means Electrical Cost Data 1991*

161 | Conductors and Grounding

161 100 | Conductors

			Crew	Daily Output	Man-Hours	Unit	Mat.	Labor	Equip.	Total	Total Incl O&P	
105	0010	**ARMORED CABLE**										105
	0050	600 volt, copper (BX), #14, 2 wire	1 Elec	240	.033	L.F.	.27	.55		.82	1.18	
	0100	3 wire		200	.040		.33	.65		.98	1.42	
	0150	#12, 2 wire		210	.038		.32	.62		.94	1.36	
	0200	3 wire		180	.044		.42	.73		1.15	1.64	
	0250	#10, 2 wire		180	.044		.53	.73		1.26	1.76	
	0300	3 wire		150	.053		.66	.87		1.53	2.14	
	0350	#8, 3 wire		120	.067		1.10	1.09		2.19	2.97	
145	0010	**NON-METALLIC SHEATHED CABLE** 600 volt										145
	0100	Copper with ground wire, (Romex)										
	0150	#14, 2 wire	1 Elec	250	.032	L.F.	.16	.52		.68	1.02	
	0200	3 wire		230	.035		.30	.57		.87	1.25	
	0250	#12, 2 wire		220	.036		.25	.59		.84	1.24	
	0300	3 wire		200	.040		.41	.65		1.06	1.51	
	0350	#10, 2 wire		200	.040		.41	.65		1.06	1.51	
	0400	3 wire		140	.057		.63	.93		1.56	2.20	
	0450	#8, 3 wire		130	.062		1.34	1.01		2.35	3.10	
	0500	#6, 3 wire		120	.067		1.87	1.09		2.96	3.82	
	0550	SE type SER aluminum cable, 3 RHW and										
	0600	1 bare neutral, 3 #8 & 1 #8	1 Elec	150	.053	L.F.	.50	.87		1.37	1.96	
	0650	3 #6 & 1 #6		130	.062		.57	1.01		1.58	2.25	
	0700	3 #4 & 1 #6		110	.073		.73	1.19		1.92	2.73	
	0750	3 #2 & 1 #4		100	.080		.99	1.31		2.30	3.20	
	0800	3 #1/0 & 1 #2		90	.089		1.47	1.45		2.92	3.97	
	0850	3 #2/0 & 1 #1		80	.100		1.70	1.64		3.34	4.51	
	0900	3 #4/0 & 1 #2/0		70	.114		2.19	1.87		4.06	5.45	
	2400	SEU service entrance cable, copper 2 conductors, #8 + #8 neut.		150	.053		.90	.87		1.77	2.40	
	2600	#6 + #8 neutral		130	.062		1.27	1.01		2.28	3.02	
	2800	#6 + #6 neutral		130	.062		1.35	1.01		2.36	3.11	
	3000	#4 + #6 neutral		110	.073		2.19	1.19		3.38	4.33	
	3200	#4 + #4 neutral		110	.073		2.44	1.19		3.63	4.61	
	3400	#3 + #5 neutral		105	.076		2.70	1.25		3.95	4.98	
	6500	Service entrance cap for copper SEU										
	6600	100 amp	1 Elec	12	.667	Ea.	4.25	10.90		15.15	22	
	6700	150 amp		10	.800		9.20	13.10		22.30	31	
	6800	200 amp		8	1		12.60	16.35		28.95	40	
165	0010	**WIRE**										165
	0020	600 volt, type THW, copper, solid, #14	1 Elec	1,300	.006	L.F.	.04	.10		.14	.21	
	0030	#12		1,100	.007		.06	.12		.18	.26	
	0040	#10		1,000	.008		.09	.13		.22	.31	
	0160	#6		650	.012		.23	.20		.43	.58	
	0180	#4		530	.015		.36	.25		.61	.79	
	0200	#3		500	.016		.44	.26		.70	.91	
	0220	#2		450	.018		.54	.29		.83	1.06	
	0240	#1		400	.020		.71	.33		1.04	1.31	
	0260	1/0		330	.024		.84	.40		1.24	1.56	
	0280	2/0		290	.028		1.02	.45		1.47	1.85	
	0300	3/0		250	.032		1.26	.52		1.78	2.23	
	0350	4/0		220	.036		1.56	.59		2.15	2.68	

161 800 | Grounding

			Crew	Daily Output	Man-Hours	Unit	Mat.	Labor	Equip.	Total	Total Incl O&P	
810	0010	**GROUNDING**										810
	0030	Rod, copper clad, 8' long, ½" diameter	1 Elec	5.30	1.510	Ea.	10.15	25		35.15	51	
	0050	¾" diameter		5.30	1.510		19	25		44	61	
	0080	10' long, ½" diameter		4.80	1.670		12.55	27		39.55	58	
	0100	¾" diameter		4.40	1.820		24	30		54	74	
	0260	Wire, ground, bare armored, #8-1 conductor		200	.040	L.F.	.64	.65		1.29	1.76	

For expanded coverage of these items see *Means Electrical Cost Data 1991*

161 | Conductors and Grounding

161 800	Grounding	CREW	DAILY OUTPUT	MAN-HOURS	UNIT	MAT.	LABOR	EQUIP.	TOTAL	TOTAL INCL O&P	
810 0270	#6-1 conductor	1 Elec	180	.044	L.F.	.78	.73		1.51	2.03	810
0390	Bare copper wire #8 stranded		11	.727	C.L.F.	18.70	11.90		30.60	40	
0400	Bare copper, #6 wire		1,000	.008	L.F.	.24	.13		.37	.48	
0600	#2		500	.016	"	.54	.26		.80	1.02	
1800	Water pipe ground clamps, heavy duty										
2000	Bronze, ½" to 1" diameter	1 Elec	8	1	Ea.	5.75	16.35		22.10	33	

162 | Boxes and Wiring Devices

162 100	Boxes	CREW	DAILY OUTPUT	MAN-HOURS	UNIT	MAT.	LABOR	EQUIP.	TOTAL	TOTAL INCL O&P	
110 0010	OUTLET BOXES										110
0020	Pressed steel, octagon, 4"	1 Elec	18	.444	Ea.	1.06	7.25		8.31	12.90	
0100	Extension		40	.200		1.27	3.27		4.54	6.70	
0150	Square 4"		18	.444		1.30	7.25		8.55	13.20	
0200	Extension		40	.200		1.68	3.27		4.95	7.15	
0250	Covers, blank		64	.125		.50	2.04		2.54	3.85	
0300	Plaster rings		64	.125		.77	2.04		2.81	4.15	
0650	Switchbox		24	.333		1.10	5.45		6.55	10	
1100	Concrete, floor, 1 gang		4.80	1.670		42	27		69	90	
120 0010	OUTLET BOXES, PLASTIC										120
0050	4", round, with 2 mounting nails	1 Elec	23	.348	Ea.	1.02	5.70		6.72	10.30	
0100	Bar hanger mounted		23	.348		1.90	5.70		7.60	11.30	
0200	Square with 2 mounting nails		23	.348		1.30	5.70		7	10.60	
0300	Plaster ring		64	.125		.41	2.04		2.45	3.75	
0400	Switch box with 2 mounting nails, 1 gang		27	.296		.68	4.84		5.52	8.60	
0500	2 gang		23	.348		1.45	5.70		7.15	10.80	
0600	3 gang		18	.444		2.35	7.25		9.60	14.35	
130 0010	PULL BOXES & CABINETS										130
0100	Sheet metal, pull box, NEMA 1, type SC, 6"W x 6"H x 4"D	1 Elec	8	1	Ea.	6.10	16.35		22.45	33	
0200	8"W x 8"H x 4"D		8	1		8.35	16.35		24.70	36	
0300	10"W x 12"H x 6"D		5.30	1.510		14.70	25		39.70	56	

162 300	Wiring Devices										
310 0010	LOW VOLTAGE SWITCHING										310
3600	Relays, 120V or 277V standard	1 Elec	12	.667	Ea.	20.30	10.90		31.20	40	
3800	Flush switch, standard		40	.200		6.10	3.27		9.37	12	
4000	Interchangeable		40	.200		9.10	3.27		12.37	15.30	
4100	Surface switch, standard		40	.200		3	3.27		6.27	8.60	
4200	Transformer 115V to 25V		12	.667		67	10.90		77.90	91	
4400	Master control, 12 circuit, manual		4	2		53	33		86	110	
4500	25 circuit, motorized		4	2		58	33		91	115	
4600	Rectifier, silicon		12	.667		23.10	10.90		34	43	
4610											
4700											
4800	Switchplates, 1 gang, 1, 2 or 3 switch, plastic	1 Elec	80	.100	Ea.	1.75	1.64		3.39	4.57	
5000	Stainless steel		80	.100		5.20	1.64		6.84	8.35	
5400	2 gang, 3 switch, stainless steel		53	.151		10.45	2.47		12.92	15.50	
5500	4 switch, plastic		53	.151		3.70	2.47		6.17	8.05	
5600	2 gang, 4 switch, stainless steel		53	.151		10.45	2.47		12.92	15.50	
5700	6 switch, stainless steel		53	.151		25	2.47		27.47	31	
5800	3 gang, 9 switch, stainless steel		32	.250		34	4.09		38.09	44	

For expanded coverage of these items see *Means Electrical Cost Data 1991*

162 | Boxes and Wiring Devices

162 300 | Wiring Devices

			CREW	DAILY OUTPUT	MAN-HOURS	UNIT	MAT.	LABOR	EQUIP.	TOTAL	TOTAL INCL O&P
320	0010	**WIRING DEVICES**									320
	0200	Toggle switch, quiet type, single pole, 15 amp	1 Elec	40	.200	Ea.	3.20	3.27		6.47	8.80
	0600	3 way, 15 amp		23	.348		4.95	5.70		10.65	14.65
	0900	4 way, 15 amp		15	.533		14.10	8.70		22.80	30
	1650	Dimmer switch, 120 volt, incandescent, 600 watt, 1 pole		16	.500		9	8.20		17.20	23
	2200	Receptacle, duplex, 120 V grounded, 15 amp		40	.200		1.65	3.27		4.92	7.10
	2300	20 amp		27	.296		7.65	4.84		12.49	16.25
	2400	Dryer, 30 amp		15	.533		9.15	8.70		17.85	24
	2500	Range, 50 amp		11	.727		10.35	11.90		22.25	31
	2600	Wall plates, stainless steel, 1 gang		80	.100		1.50	1.64		3.14	4.29
	2800	2 gang		53	.151		3.75	2.47		6.22	8.10
	3200	Lampholder, keyless		26	.308		2.50	5.05		7.55	10.90
	3400	Pullchain with receptacle	↓	22	.364	↓	6.40	5.95		12.35	16.65

163 | Starters, Boards and Switches

163 200 | Boards

			CREW	DAILY OUTPUT	MAN-HOURS	UNIT	MAT.	LABOR	EQUIP.	TOTAL	TOTAL INCL O&P
205	0010	**CIRCUIT BREAKERS** (in enclosure)									205
	0100	Enclosed (NEMA 1), 600 volt, 3 pole, 30 amp	1 Elec	3.20	2.500	Ea.	220	41		261	310
	0200	60 amp		2.80	2.860		220	47		267	320
	0400	100 amp	↓	2.30	3.480	↓	270	57		327	390
225	0010	**FUSE CABINETS**									225
	0050	120/240 volts, 3 wire, 30 amp branches,									
	0100	plug fuse not included									
	0200	4 circuits	1 Elec	4	2	Ea.	30.30	33		63.30	86
	0300	6 circuits		3.20	2.500		48	41		89	120
	0400	8 circuits		2.70	2.960		58	48		106	140
	0500	12 circuits	↓	2	4	↓	80	65		145	195
230	0010	**LOAD CENTERS** (residential type)									230
	0100	3 wire, 120/240V, 1 phase, including 1 pole plug-in breakers									
	0200	100 amp main lugs, indoor, 8 circuits	1 Elec	1.40	5.710	Ea.	74	93		167	230
	0300	12 circuits		1.20	6.670		100	110		210	285
	0400	Rainproof, 8 circuits		1.40	5.710		85	93		178	245
	0500	12 circuits		1.20	6.670		109	110		219	295
	0600	200 amp main lugs, indoor, 16 circuits		.90	8.890		182	145		327	435
	0700	20 circuits		.75	10.670		223	175		398	525
	0800	24 circuits		.65	12.310		246	200		446	595
	1200	Rainproof, 16 circuits		.90	8.890		228	145		373	485
	1300	20 circuits		.75	10.670		250	175		425	555
	1400	24 circuits	↓	.65	12.310	↓	275	200		475	630
240	0010	**METER CENTERS AND SOCKETS**									240
	0100	Sockets, single position, 4 terminal, 100 amp	1 Elec	3.20	2.500	Ea.	23.70	41		64.70	92
	0200	150 amp		2.30	3.480		28.50	57		85.50	125
	0300	200 amp		1.90	4.210		37	69		106	150
	0500	Double position, 4 terminal, 100 amp		2.80	2.860		70.50	47		117.50	155
	0600	150 amp		2.10	3.810		86	62		148	195
	0700	200 amp	↓	1.70	4.710	↓	115	77		192	250
	2590	Basic meter device									
	2600	1P 3W 120/240V 4 jaw 125A sockets, 3 meter	1 Elec	.50	16	Ea.	255	260		515	705
	2620	5 meter	"	.40	20	"	410	325		735	980

For expanded coverage of these items see *Means Electrical Cost Data 1991*

163 | Starters, Boards and Switches

163 200 | Boards

			Crew	Daily Output	Man-Hours	Unit	Mat.	Labor	Equip.	Total	Total Incl O&P	
240	2640	7 meter	1 Elec	.28	28.570	Ea.	570	465		1,035	1,375	240
	2660	10 meter	"	.24	33.330	"	825	545		1,370	1,800	
	2680	Rainproof 1P 3W 120/240V 4 jaw 125A sockets										
	2690	3 meter	1 Elec	.50	16	Ea.	270	260		530	720	
	2710	6 meter		.30	26.670		540	435		975	1,300	
	2730	8 meter		.26	30.770		710	505		1,215	1,600	
	2750	1P 3W 120/240V 4 jaw sockets										
	2760	with 125A circuit breaker, 3 meter	1 Elec	.50	16	Ea.	525	260		785	1,000	
	2780	5 meter		.40	20		845	325		1,170	1,450	
	2800	7 meter		.28	28.570		1,175	465		1,640	2,050	
	2820	10 meter		.24	33.330		1,660	545		2,205	2,700	
	2830	Rainproof 1P 3W 120/240V 4 jaw sockets										
	2840	with 125A circuit breaker, 3 meter	1 Elec	.50	16	Ea.	535	260		795	1,000	
	2870	6 meter		.30	26.670		1,030	435		1,465	1,850	
	2890	8 meter		.26	30.770		1,390	505		1,895	2,350	
	3250	1P 3W 120/240V 4 jaw sockets										
	3260	with 200A circuit breaker, 3 meter	1 Elec	.50	16	Ea.	810	260		1,070	1,325	
	3290	6 meter		.30	26.670		1,545	435		1,980	2,400	
	3310	8 meter		.28	28.570		2,090	465		2,555	3,050	
	3330	Rainproof 1P 3W 120/240V 4 jaw sockets										
	3350	with 200A circuit breaker, 3 meter	1 Elec	.50	16	Ea.	830	260		1,090	1,325	
	3380	6 meter		.30	26.670		1,600	435		2,035	2,475	
	3400	8 meter		.26	30.770		2,140	505		2,645	3,175	

163 300 | Switches

			Crew	Daily Output	Man-Hours	Unit	Mat.	Labor	Equip.	Total	Total Incl O&P	
360	0010	**SAFETY SWITCHES**										360
	0100	General duty, 240 volt, 3 pole, fused, 30 amp	1 Elec	3.20	2.500	Ea.	38	41		79	110	
	0200	60 amp		2.30	3.480		65	57		122	165	
	0300	100 amp		1.90	4.210		114	69		183	235	
	0400	200 amp		1.30	6.150		230	100		330	415	
	0500	400 amp		.90	8.890		513	145		658	800	
	9010	Disc. switch, 600V, 3 pole, fused, 30 amp, to 10 HP motor		3.20	2.500		130	41		171	210	
	9050	60 amp, to 30 HP motor		2.30	3.480		130	57		187	235	
	9070	100 amp, to 60 HP motor		1.90	4.210		239	69		308	375	
370	0010	**TIME SWITCHES**										370
	0100	Single pole, single throw, 24 hour dial	1 Elec	4	2	Ea.	47	33		80	105	
	0200	24 hour dial with reserve power		3.60	2.220		239	36		275	320	
	0300	Astronomic dial		3.60	2.220		80	36		116	145	
	0400	Astronomic dial with reserve power		3.30	2.420		263	40		303	355	
	0500	7 day calendar dial		3.30	2.420		75	40		115	145	
	0600	7 day calendar dial with reserve power		3.20	2.500		250	41		291	340	
	0700	Photo cell 2000 watt		8	1		17	16.35		33.35	45	

165 | Power Systems and Capacitors

165 100 | Power Systems

			Crew	Daily Output	Man-Hours	Unit	Mat.	Labor	Equip.	Total	Total Incl O&P	
110	0010	**AUTOMATIC TRANSFER SWITCHES**										110
	0100	Switches, enclosed 480 volt, 3 pole, 30 amp	1 Elec	2.30	3.480	Ea.	1,180	57		1,237	1,400	
	0200	60 amp	"	1.90	4.210	"	1,715	69		1,784	2,000	

For expanded coverage of these items see *Means Electrical Cost Data 1991*

165 | Power Systems and Capacitors

165 100 | Power Systems

			CREW	DAILY OUTPUT	MAN-HOURS	UNIT	MAT.	LABOR	EQUIP.	TOTAL	TOTAL INCL O&P	
120	0010	**GENERATOR SET**										120
	0020	Gas or gasoline operated, includes battery,										
	0050	charger, muffler & transfer switch										
	0200	3 phase, 4 wire, 277/480 volt, 7.5 KW	R-3	.83	24.100	Ea.	5,480	395	125	6,000	6,800	
	0300	10 KW		.71	28.170		7,470	460	145	8,075	9,125	
	0400	15 KW	↓	.63	31.750	↓	8,860	520	165	9,545	10,800	

166 | Lighting

166 100 | Lighting

			CREW	DAILY OUTPUT	MAN-HOURS	UNIT	MAT.	LABOR	EQUIP.	TOTAL	TOTAL INCL O&P	
115	0010	**EXTERIOR FIXTURES** With lamps										115
	0400	Quartz, 500 watt	1 Elec	5.30	1.510	Ea.	80	25		105	130	
	0800	Wall pack, mercury vapor, 175 watt		4	2		235	33		268	310	
	1000	250 watt		4	2		250	33		283	330	
	1100	Low pressure sodium, 35 watt		4	2		166	33		199	235	
	1150	55 watt		4	2		250	33		283	330	
	6420	Wood pole, 4-½" x 5-⅛", 8' high		6	1.330		115	22		137	160	
	6440	12' high		5.70	1.400		190	23		213	245	
	6460	20' high	↓	4	2	↓	220	33		253	295	
	6500	Bollard light, lamp & ballast, 42" high with polycarbonate lens										
	6700	Mercury vapor, 175 watt	1 Elec	3	2.670	Ea.	400	44		444	510	
	7200	Incandescent, 150 watt	"	3	2.670	"	335	44		379	440	
	7380	Landscape recessed uplight, incl. housing, ballast, transformer										
	7390	& reflector										
	7420	Incandescent, 250 watt	1 Elec	5	1.600	Ea.	390	26		416	470	
	7440	Quartz, 250 watt	"	5	1.600	"	445	26		471	530	
130	0010	**INTERIOR LIGHTING FIXTURES** Including lamps, mounting										130
	0030	hardware and connections										
	0100	Fluorescent, C.W. lamps, troffer, recess mounted in grid, RS										
	0130	grid ceiling mount										
	0200	Acrylic lens, 1'W x 4'L, two 40 watt	1 Elec	5.70	1.400	Ea.	45	23		68	87	
	0300	2'W x 2'L, two U40 watt		5.70	1.400		58	23		81	100	
	0600	2'W x 4'L, four 40 watt	↓	4.70	1.700	↓	63	28		91	115	
	1000	Surface mounted, RS										
	1030	Acrylic lens with hinged & latched door frame										
	1100	1'W x 4'L, two 40 watt	1 Elec	7	1.140	Ea.	50	18.70		68.70	85	
	1200	2'W x 2'L, two U40 watt		7	1.140		80	18.70		98.70	120	
	1500	2'W x 4'L, four 40 watt		5.30	1.510		83	25		108	130	
	2100	Strip fixture										
	2200	4' long, one 40 watt RS	1 Elec	8.50	.941	Ea.	24.90	15.40		40.30	52	
	2300	4' long, two 40 watt RS		8	1		26	16.35		42.35	55	
	2600	8' long, one 75 watt, SL		6.70	1.190		41	19.50		60.50	77	
	2700	8' long, two 75 watt, SL	↓	6.20	1.290	↓	47	21		68	86	
	4450	Incandescent, high hat can, round alzak reflector, prewired										
	4470	100 watt	1 Elec	8	1	Ea.	48	16.35		64.35	79	
	4480	150 watt	"	8	1	"	50	16.35		66.35	81	
	5200	Ceiling, surface mounted, opal glass drum										
	5300	8", one 60 watt	1 Elec	10	.800	Ea.	31	13.10		44.10	55	
	5400	10", two 60 watt lamps		8	1		35	16.35		51.35	65	
	5500	12", four 60 watt lamps		6.70	1.190		75	19.50		94.50	115	
	6900	Mirror light, fluorescent, RS, acrylic enclosure, two 40 watt		8	1		61	16.35		77.35	94	
	6910	One 40 watt	↓	8	1		56	16.35		72.35	88	

For expanded coverage of these items see *Means Electrical Cost Data 1991*

166 | Lighting

166 100 | Lighting

			CREW	DAILY OUTPUT	MAN-HOURS	UNIT	MAT.	LABOR	EQUIP.	TOTAL	TOTAL INCL O&P	
130	6920	One 20 watt	1 Elec	12	.667	Ea.	49	10.90		59.90	72	130
140	0010	**LAMPS**										140
	0080	Fluorescent, rapid start, cool white, 2' long, 20 watt	1 Elec	100	.080	Ea.	3.85	1.31		5.16	6.35	
	0100	4' long, 40 watt		90	.089		2.24	1.45		3.69	4.81	
	1350	Sodium high pressure, 70 watt		30	.267		47.12	4.36		51.48	59	
	1370	150 watt	↓	30	.267	↓	50.59	4.36		54.95	63	
145	0010	**RESIDENTIAL FIXTURES**										145
	0200	Pendant globe with shade, 150 watt	1 Elec	20	.400	Ea.	62	6.55		68.55	79	
	0400	Fluorescent, interior, surface, circline, 32 watt & 40 watt		20	.400		49	6.55		55.55	64	
	0500	2' x 2', two U 40 watt		8	1		68	16.35		84.35	100	
	0700	Shallow under cabinet, two 20 watt		16	.500		46	8.20		54.20	64	
	0900	Wall mounted, 4'L, one 40 watt, with baffle		10	.800		42	13.10		55.10	67	
	2000	Incandescent, exterior lantern, wall mounted, 60 watt		16	.500		37	8.20		45.20	54	
	2100	Post light, 150W, with 7' post		4	2		108	33		141	170	
	2500	Lamp holder, weatherproof with 150W PAR		16	.500		17	8.20		25.20	32	
	2550	With reflector and guard		12	.667		32	10.90		42.90	53	
	2600	Interior pendent, globe with shade, 150 watt	↓	20	.400	↓	80	6.55		86.55	99	
150	0010	**TRACK LIGHTING**										150
	0100	8' section	1 Elec	5.30	1.510	Ea.	52	25		77	97	
	0300	3 circuits, 4' section		6.70	1.190		39	19.50		58.50	74	
	0400	8' section		5.30	1.510		52	25		77	97	
	0500	12' section	↓	4.40	1.820	↓	96	30		126	155	
	0750											
	1000	Feed kit, surface mounting	1 Elec	16	.500	Ea.	13	8.20		21.20	28	
	1100	End cover		24	.333		2.10	5.45		7.55	11.10	
	1200	Feed kit, stem mounting, 1 circuit		16	.500		17	8.20		25.20	32	
	1300	3 circuit		16	.500		17	8.20		25.20	32	
	2000	Electrical joiner for continuous runs, 1 circuit		32	.250		7.20	4.09		11.29	14.55	
	2100	3 circuit		32	.250		13	4.09		17.09	21	
	2200	Fixtures, spotlight, 150w PAR		16	.500		51	8.20		59.20	69	
	3000	Wall washer, 250 watt tungsten halogen		16	.500		110	8.20		118.20	135	
	3100	Low voltage, 25/50 watt, 1 circuit		16	.500		111	8.20		119.20	135	
	3120	3 circuit	↓	16	.500		117	8.20		125.20	140	

168 | Special Systems

168 100 | Special Systems

			CREW	DAILY OUTPUT	MAN-HOURS	UNIT	MAT.	LABOR	EQUIP.	TOTAL	TOTAL INCL O&P	
120	0010	**DETECTION SYSTEMS**										120
	0100	Burglar alarm, battery operated, mechanical trigger	1 Elec	4	2	Ea.	190	33		223	260	
	0200	Electrical trigger		4	2		229	33		262	305	
	0400	For outside key control, add		8	1		54	16.35		70.35	86	
	0600	For remote signaling circuitry, add		8	1		85	16.35		101.35	120	
	0800	Card reader, flush type, standard		2.70	2.960		643	48		691	785	
	1000	Multi-code		2.70	2.960		824	48		872	985	
	1200	Door switches, hinge switch		5.30	1.510		41	25		66	85	
	1400	Magnetic switch		5.30	1.510		48	25		73	93	
	2800	Ultrasonic motion detector, 12 volt		2.30	3.480		159	57		216	265	
	3000	Infrared photoelectric detector		2.30	3.480		128	57		185	235	
	3200	Passive infrared detector	↓	2.30	3.480	↓	195	57		252	305	

For expanded coverage of these items see *Means Electrical Cost Data 1991*

168 | Special Systems

168 100 | Special Systems

			CREW	DAILY OUTPUT	MAN-HOURS	UNIT	MAT.	LABOR	EQUIP.	TOTAL	TOTAL INCL O&P	
120	3420	Switchmats, 30" x 5'	1 Elec	5.30	1.510	Ea.	58	25		83	105	120
	3440	25'		4	2		138	33		171	205	
	3460	Police connect panel		4	2		170	33		203	240	
	3480	Telephone dialer		5.30	1.510		263	25		288	330	
	3500	Alarm bell		4	2		53	33		86	110	
	3520	Siren		4	2		100	33		133	165	
	5200	Smoke detector, ceiling type		6.20	1.290		49	21		70	88	
	5600	Light and horn		5.30	1.510		81	25		106	130	
	5800	Fire alarm horn		6.70	1.190		28	19.50		47.50	62	
	6600	Drill switch		8	1		66	16.35		82.35	99	
	6800	Master box		2.70	2.960		1,600	48		1,648	1,850	
	7800	Remote annunciator, 8 zone lamp		1.80	4.440		188	73		261	325	
	8000	12 zone lamp		1.30	6.150		234	100		334	420	
	8200	16 zone lamp		1.10	7.270		287	120		407	510	
	8400	Standpipe or sprinkler alarm, alarm device		8	1		100	16.35		116.35	135	
	8600	Actuating device		8	1		230	16.35		246.35	280	
125	0010	**DOORBELL SYSTEM** Incl. transformer, button & signal										125
	1000	Door chimes, 2 notes, minimum	1 Elec	16	.500	Ea.	21	8.20		29.20	36	
	1020	Maximum		12	.667		88	10.90		98.90	115	
	1100	Tube type, 3 tube system		12	.667		72	10.90		82.90	97	
	1180	4 tube system		10	.800		175	13.10		188.10	215	
	1900	For transformer & button, minimum add		5	1.600		21	26		47	65	
	1960	Maximum, add		4.50	1.780		45	29		74	96	
	3000	For push button only, minimum		24	.333		7.80	5.45		13.25	17.40	
	3100	Maximum		20	.400		19	6.55		25.55	31	
130	0010	**ELECTRIC HEATING**										130
	0400	Cable heating, radiant heat plaster, no controls, in South	1 Elec	130	.062	S.F.	5.67	1.01		6.68	7.85	
	0600	In North		90	.089		5.67	1.45		7.12	8.60	
	0800	Cable on ½" board, not incl. controls, tract housing		90	.089		4.68	1.45		6.13	7.50	
	1000	Custom housing		80	.100		5.35	1.64		6.99	8.55	
	1100	Rule of thumb: Baseboard units, including control		4.40	1.820	KW	58.50	30		88.50	110	
	1300	Baseboard heaters, 2' long, 375 watt		8	1	Ea.	29.70	16.35		46.05	59	
	1400	3' long, 500 watt		8	1		37	16.35		53.35	67	
	1600	4' long, 750 watt		6.70	1.190		45.63	19.50		65.13	82	
	1800	5' long, 935 watt		5.70	1.400		60.77	23		83.77	105	
	2000	6' long, 1125 watt		5	1.600		67.98	26		93.98	115	
	2400	8' long, 1500 watt		4	2		90.64	33		123.64	155	
	2800	10' long, 1875 watt		3.30	2.420		103	40		143	175	
	2950	Wall heaters with fan, 120 to 277 volt										
	2970	surface mounted, residential, 750 watt	1 Elec	7	1.140	Ea.	50	18.70		68.70	85	
	2980	1000 watt		7	1.140		64	18.70		82.70	100	
	2990	1250 watt		6	1.330		77	22		99	120	
	3000	1500 watt		4	2		82	33		115	145	
	3010	2000 watt		5	1.600		86	26		112	135	
	3050	2500 watt		4	2		143	33		176	210	
	3070	4000 watt		3.50	2.290		148	37		185	225	
	3600	Thermostats, integral		16	.500		23	8.20		31.20	39	
	3800	Line voltage, 1 pole		8	1		23	16.35		39.35	52	
	5000	Radiant heating ceiling panels, 2' x 4', 500 watt		16	.500		111	8.20		119.20	135	
	5050	750 watt		16	.500		124	8.20		132.20	150	
	5300	Infra-red quartz heaters, 120 volts, 1000 watts		6.70	1.190		76	19.50		95.50	115	
	5350	1500 watt		5	1.600		76	26		102	125	
	5400	240 volts, 1500 watt		5	1.600		76	26		102	125	
	5450	2000 watt		4	2		76	33		109	135	
	5500	3000 watt		3	2.670		109	44		153	190	
140	0010	**LIGHTNING PROTECTION**										140
	0200	Air terminals, copper										

For expanded coverage of these items see *Means Electrical Cost Data 1991*

168 | Special Systems

168 100 | Special Systems

			CREW	DAILY OUTPUT	MAN-HOURS	UNIT	MAT.	LABOR	EQUIP.	TOTAL	TOTAL INCL O&P	
140	0400	⅜" diameter x 10" (to 75' high)	1 Elec	8	1	Ea.	18.90	16.35		35.25	47	140
	1000	Aluminum, ½" diameter x 12" (to 75' high)		8	1	"	14.70	16.35		31.05	43	
	2000	Cable, copper, 220 lb. per thousand ft. (to 75' high)		320	.025	L.F.	1.03	.41		1.44	1.79	
	2500	Aluminum, 101 lb. per thousand ft. (to 75' high)		280	.029	"	.24	.47		.71	1.02	
	3000	Arrestor, 175 volt AC to ground	↓	8	1	Ea.	27.30	16.35		43.65	56	
160	0010	**T.V. SYSTEMS**										160
	0100	Master TV antenna system										
	0200	VHF reception & distribution, 12 outlets	1 Elec	6	1.330	Outlet	118	22		140	165	
	0800	VHF & UHF reception & distribution, 12 outlets		6	1.330	"	118	22		140	165	
	5000	T.V. Antenna only, minimum		6	1.330	Ea.	27	22		49	65	
	5100	Maximum	↓	4	2	"	115	33		148	180	
170	0010	**RESIDENTIAL WIRING**										170
	0020	20' avg. runs and #14/2 wiring incl. unless otherwise noted										
	1000	Service & panel, includes 24' SE-AL cable, service eye, meter,										
	1010	Socket, panel board, main bkr., ground rod, 15 or 20 amp										
	1020	1-pole circuit breakers, and misc. hardware										
	1100	100 amp, with 10 branch breakers	1 Elec	1.19	6.720	Ea.	270	110		380	475	
	1110	With PVC conduit and wire		.92	8.700		291	140		431	550	
	1120	With RGS conduit and wire		.73	10.960		384	180		564	710	
	1170	With PVC conduit and wire		.82	9.760		478	160		638	785	
	1180	With RGS conduit and wire		.67	11.940		587	195		782	960	
	1200	200 amp, with 18 branch breakers		.90	8.890		551	145		696	840	
	1220	With PVC conduit and wire		.73	10.960		587	180		767	935	
	1230	With RGS conduit and wire		.62	12.900		785	210		995	1,200	
	1800	Lightning surge suppressor for above services, add	↓	32	.250		30	4.09		34.09	40	
	2000	Switch devices										
	2100	Single pole, 15 amp, Ivory, with a 1-gang box, cover plate,										
	2110	Type NM (Romex) cable	1 Elec	17.10	.468	Ea.	5.72	7.65		13.37	18.65	
	2120	Type MC (BX) cable		14.30	.559		10.82	9.15		19.97	27	
	2130	EMT & wire		5.71	1.400		13.78	23		36.78	52	
	2150	3-way, #14/3, type NM cable		14.55	.550		9.46	9		18.46	25	
	2170	Type MC cable		12.31	.650		12.79	10.65		23.44	31	
	2180	EMT & wire		5	1.600		15	26		41	59	
	2200	4-way, #14/3, type NM cable		14.55	.550		18.56	9		27.56	35	
	2220	Type MC cable		12.31	.650		21.79	10.65		32.44	41	
	2230	EMT & wire		5	1.600		23.40	26		49.40	68	
	2250	S.P., 20 amp, #12/2, type NM cable		13.33	.600		10.60	9.80		20.40	28	
	2270	Type MC cable		11.43	.700		14.87	11.45		26.32	35	
	2280	EMT & wire		4.85	1.650		17.78	27		44.78	63	
	2300	S.P. rotary dimmer, 600W, type NM cable		14.55	.550		13.15	9		22.15	29	
	2320	Type MC cable		12.31	.650		18.35	10.65		29	37	
	2330	EMT & wire		5	1.600		21.26	26		47.26	66	
	2350	3-way rotary dimmer, type NM cable		13.33	.600		19.34	9.80		29.14	37	
	2370	Type MC cable		11.43	.700		23.20	11.45		34.65	44	
	2380	EMT & wire	↓	4.85	1.650		25.42	27		52.42	72	
	2400	Interval timer wall switch, 20 amp, 1-30 min., #12/2			.550							
	2410	Type NM cable	1 Elec	14.55	.550	Ea.	19.34	9		28.34	36	
	2420	Type MC cable		12.31	.650		24.28	10.65		34.93	44	
	2430	EMT & wire		5	1.600		27.56	26		53.56	73	
	2500	Decorator style										
	2510	S.P., 15 amp, type NM cable	1 Elec	17.10	.468	Ea.	8.11	7.65		15.76	21	
	2520	Type MC cable		14.30	.559		13.47	9.15		22.62	30	
	2530	EMT & wire		5.71	1.400		16.43	23		39.43	55	
	2550	3-way, #14/3, type NM cable		14.55	.550		11.28	9		20.28	27	
	2570	Type MC cable		12.31	.650		16.06	10.65		26.71	35	
	2580	EMT & wire		5	1.600		18.15	26		44.15	62	
	2600	4-way, #14/3, type NM cable		14.55	.550		20.80	9		29.80	37	

For expanded coverage of these items see *Means Electrical Cost Data 1991*

168 | Special Systems

168 100 | Special Systems

			CREW	DAILY OUTPUT	MAN-HOURS	UNIT	MAT.	LABOR	EQUIP.	TOTAL	TOTAL INCL O&P	
170	2620	Type MC cable	1 Elec	12.31	.650	Ea.	24.54	10.65		35.19	44	170
	2630	EMT & wire		5	1.600		26.73	26		52.73	72	
	2650	S.P., 20 amp, #12/2, type NM cable		13.33	.600		14.92	9.80		24.72	32	
	2670	Type MC cable		11.43	.700		19	11.45		30.45	39	
	2680	EMT & wire		4.85	1.650		22.15	27		49.15	68	
	2700	S.P., slide dimmer, type NM cable		17.10	.468		18.20	7.65		25.85	32	
	2720	Type MC cable		14.30	.559		23.60	9.15		32.75	41	
	2730	EMT & wire		5.71	1.400		27	23		50	67	
	2750	S.P., touch dimmer, type NM cable		17.10	.468		25	7.65		32.65	40	
	2770	Type MC cable		14.30	.559		30	9.15		39.15	48	
	2780	EMT & wire		5.71	1.400		33.28	23		56.28	74	
	2800	3-way touch dimmer, type NM cable		13.33	.600		35.36	9.80		45.16	55	
	2820	Type MC cable		11.43	.700		39.52	11.45		50.97	62	
	2830	EMT & wire	↓	4.85	1.650	↓	41.60	27		68.60	89	
	3000	Combination devices										
	3100	S.P. switch/15 amp recpt., Ivory, 1-gang box, plate										
	3110	Type NM cable	1 Elec	11.43	.700	Ea.	11.44	11.45		22.89	31	
	3120	Type MC cable		10	.800		20.43	13.10		33.53	44	
	3130	EMT & wire		4.40	1.820		23.60	30		53.60	74	
	3150	S.P. switch/pilot light, type NM cable		11.43	.700		11.33	11.45		22.78	31	
	3170	Type MC cable		10	.800		16	13.10		29.10	39	
	3180	EMT & wire		4.43	1.810		18.93	30		48.93	69	
	3200	2-S.P. switches, 2-#14/2, type NM cables		10	.800		14.71	13.10		27.81	37	
	3220	Type MC cable		8.89	.900		22.46	14.70		37.16	48	
	3230	EMT & wire		4.10	1.950		21.37	32		53.37	75	
	3250	3-way switch/15 amp recpt., #14/3, type NM cable		10	.800		20.33	13.10		33.43	44	
	3270	Type MC cable		8.89	.900		23.60	14.70		38.30	50	
	3280	EMT & wire		4.10	1.950		26	32		58	80	
	3300	2-3 way switches, 2-#14/3 type NM cables		8.89	.900		26	14.70		40.70	52	
	3320	Type MC cable		8	1		30.16	16.35		46.51	60	
	3330	EMT & wire		4	2		29.12	33		62.12	85	
	3350	S.P. switch/20 amp recpt., #12/2 type NM cable		10	.800		18.72	13.10		31.82	42	
	3370	Type MC cable		8.89	.900		23.60	14.70		38.30	50	
	3380	EMT & wire	↓	4.10	1.950		26	32		58	80	
	3400	Decorator style										
	3410	S.P. switch/15 amp recpt., type NM cable	1 Elec	11.43	.700	Ea.	19	11.45		30.45	39	
	3420	Type MC cable		10	.800		20.22	13.10		33.32	43	
	3430	EMT & wire		4.40	1.820		23.50	30		53.50	74	
	3450	S.P. switch/pilot light, type NM cable		11.43	.700		16.22	11.45		27.67	36	
	3470	Type MC cable		10	.800		20.75	13.10		33.85	44	
	3480	EMT & wire		4.40	1.820		25	30		55	76	
	3500	2-S.P. switches, 2-#14/2 type NM cables		10	.800		18.40	13.10		31.50	41	
	3520	Type MC cable		8.89	.900		26	14.70		40.70	52	
	3530	EMT & wire		4.10	1.950		25	32		57	79	
	3550	3-way/15 amp recpt., #14/3 type NM cable		10	.800		24	13.10		37.10	48	
	3570	Type MC cable		8.89	.900		27	14.70		41.70	53	
	3580	EMT & wire		4.10	1.950		29	32		61	83	
	3650	2-3 way switches, 2-3 #14/3 type NM cables		8.89	.900		31.20	14.70		45.90	58	
	3670	Type MC cable		8	1		35.36	16.35		51.71	65	
	3680	EMT & wire		4	2		34.32	33		67.32	91	
	3700	S.P. switch/20 amp recpt., #12/2 type NM cable		10	.800		21.84	13.10		34.94	45	
	3720	Type MC cable		8.89	.900		27	14.70		41.70	53	
	3730	EMT & wire	↓	4.10	1.950	↓	29	32		61	83	
	4000	Receptacle devices										
	4010	Duplex outlet, 15 amp recpt., Ivory, 1-gang box, plate										
	4015	Type NM cable	1 Elec	12.31	.650	Ea.	5.72	10.65		16.37	23	
	4020	Type MC cable		12.31	.650		10.30	10.65		20.95	29	
	4030	EMT & wire	↓	5.33	1.500		13.31	25		38.31	54	

For expanded coverage of these items see *Means Electrical Cost Data 1991*

168 | Special Systems

168 100 | Special Systems

		CREW	DAILY OUTPUT	MAN-HOURS	UNIT	MAT.	LABOR	EQUIP.	TOTAL	TOTAL INCL O&P	
4050	With #12/2 type NM cable	1 Elec	12.31	.650	Ea.	6.86	10.65		17.51	25	170
4070	Type MC cable		10.67	.750		12.32	12.25		24.57	33	
4080	EMT & wire		4.71	1.700		14.20	28		42.20	61	
4100	20 amp recpt., #12/2 type NM cable		12.31	.650		9.30	10.65		19.95	27	
4120	Type MC cable		10.67	.750		13.62	12.25		25.87	35	
4130	EMT & wire		4.71	1.700		16.60	28		44.60	63	
4140	For GFI see line 4300 below										
4150	Decorator style, 15 amp recpt., type NM cable	1 Elec	14.55	.550	Ea.	7	9		16	22	
4170	Type MC cable		12.31	.650		11.54	10.65		22.19	30	
4180	EMT & wire		5.33	1.500		14.45	25		39.45	56	
4200	With #12/2 type NM cable		12.31	.650		8.22	10.65		18.87	26	
4220	Type MC cable		10.67	.750		12.58	12.25		24.83	34	
4230	EMT & wire		4.71	1.700		15.50	28		43.50	62	
4250	20 amp recpt. #12/2 type NM cable		12.31	.650		11.75	10.65		22.40	30	
4270	Type MC cable		10.67	.750		15	12.25		27.25	36	
4280	EMT & wire		4.71	1.700		19.45	28		47.45	66	
4300	GFI, 15 amp recpt., type NM cable		12.31	.650		28	10.65		38.65	48	
4320	Type MC cable		10.67	.750		32.24	12.25		44.49	55	
4330	EMT & wire		4.71	1.700		35.36	28		63.36	84	
4350	GFI with #12/2 type NM cable		10.67	.750		29	12.25		41.25	52	
4370	Type MC cable		9.20	.870		33.28	14.20		47.48	60	
4380	EMT & wire		4.21	1.900		36.40	31		67.40	90	
4400	20 amp recpt., #12/2 type NM cable		10.67	.750		31.20	12.25		43.45	54	
4420	Type MC cable		9.20	.870		35.36	14.20		49.56	62	
4430	EMT & wire		4.21	1.900		37.44	31		68.44	91	
4500	Weather-proof cover for above receptacles, add		32	.250		3.54	4.09		7.63	10.50	
4550	Air conditioner outlet, 20 amp-240 volt recpt.										
4560	30' of #12/2, 2 pole circuit breaker										
4570	Type NM cable	1 Elec	10	.800	Ea.	26	13.10		39.10	50	
4580	Type MC cable		9	.889		31.20	14.55		45.75	58	
4590	EMT & wire		4	2		42.64	33		75.64	100	
4600	Decorator style, type NM cable		10	.800		28	13.10		41.10	52	
4620	Type MC cable		9	.889		33.28	14.55		47.83	60	
4630	EMT & wire		4	2		43.68	33		76.68	100	
4650	Dryer outlet, 30 amp-240 volt recpt., 20' of #10/3										
4660	2 pole circuit breaker										
4670	Type NM cable	1 Elec	6.41	1.250	Ea.	42.64	20		62.64	80	
4680	Type MC cable		5.71	1.400		43.68	23		66.68	85	
4690	EMT & wire		3.48	2.300		40.56	38		78.56	105	
4700	Range outlet, 50 amp-240 volt recpt., 30' of #8/3										
4710	Type NM cable	1 Elec	4.21	1.900	Ea.	71.76	31		102.76	130	
4720	Type MC cable		4	2		69.68	33		102.68	130	
4730	EMT & wire		2.96	2.700		58.24	44		102.24	135	
4750	Central vacuum outlet		6.40	1.250		53	20		73	91	
4770	Type MC cable		5.71	1.400		37.44	23		60.44	78	
4780	EMT & wire		3.48	2.300		47	38		85	110	
4800	30 amp-110 volt locking recpt., #10/2 circ. bkr.										
4810	Type NM cable	1 Elec	6.20	1.290	Ea.	45.76	21		66.76	84	
4820	Type MC cable		5.40	1.480		48.90	24		72.90	93	
4830	EMT & wire		3.20	2.500		44.72	41		85.72	115	
4900	Low voltage outlets										
4910	Telephone recpt., 20' of 4/C phone wire	1 Elec	26	.308	Ea.	5.20	5.05		10.25	13.85	
4920	TV recpt., 20' of RG59U coax wire, F type connector	"	16	.500	"	7.90	8.20		16.10	22	
4950	Door bell chime, transformer, 2 buttons, 60' of bellwire										
4970	Economy model	1 Elec	11.50	.696	Ea.	44.72	11.35		56.07	68	
4980	Custom model		11.50	.696		91.52	11.35		102.87	120	
4990	Luxury model, 3 buttons		9.50	.842		197	13.75		210.75	240	
6000	Lighting outlets										

For expanded coverage of these items see *Means Electrical Cost Data 1991*

168 | Special Systems

168 100 | Special Systems

		CREW	DAILY OUTPUT	MAN-HOURS	UNIT	MAT.	LABOR	EQUIP.	TOTAL	TOTAL INCL O&P	
170	6050	Wire only (for fixture) type NM cable	1 Elec	32	.250	Ea.	3.45	4.09		7.54	10.40	170
	6070	Type MC cable		24	.333		6.80	5.45		12.25	16.30	
	6080	EMT & wire		10	.800		9.15	13.10		22.25	31	
	6100	Box (4") and wire (for fixture), type NM cable		25	.320		5.93	5.25		11.18	15	
	6120	Type MC cable		20	.400		10.60	6.55		17.15	22	
	6130	EMT & wire	↓	11	.727	↓	12.85	11.90		24.75	33	
	6200	Fixtures (use with lines 6050 or 6100 above)										
	6210	Canopy style, economy grade	1 Elec	40	.200	Ea.	19.45	3.27		22.72	27	
	6220	Custom grade		40	.200		35.36	3.27		38.63	44	
	6250	Dining room chandelier, economy grade		19	.421		58.24	6.90		65.14	75	
	6260	Custom grade	↓	19	.421	↓	172	6.90		178.90	200	
	6270	Luxury grade										
	6310	Kitchen fixture (fluorescent), economy grade	1 Elec	30	.267	Ea.	39.52	4.36		43.88	51	
	6320	Custom grade										
	6350	Outdoor, wall mounted, economy grade	1 Elec	30	.267	Ea.	22.67	4.36		27.03	32	
	6360	Custom grade		30	.267		78	4.36		82.36	93	
	6370	Luxury grade		25	.320		176	5.25		181.25	200	
	6410	Outdoor Par floodlights, 1 lamp, 150 watt		20	.400		15.15	6.55		21.70	27	
	6420	2 lamp, 150 watt each	↓	20	.400	↓	25.22	6.55		31.77	38	
	6430	For infrared security sensor, add										
	6450	Outdoor, quartz-halogen, 300 watt flood	1 Elec	20	.400	Ea.	28	6.55		34.55	41	
	6600	Recessed downlight, round, pre-wired, 50 or 75 watt trim		30	.267		27	4.36		31.36	37	
	6610	With shower light trim		30	.267		32	4.36		36.36	42	
	6620	With wall washer trim		28	.286		40	4.67		44.67	52	
	6630	With eye-ball trim	↓	28	.286		37	4.67		41.67	48	
	6640	For direct contact with insulation, add					1.15			1.15	1.27	
	6700	Porcelain lamp holder	1 Elec	40	.200		2.70	3.27		5.97	8.25	
	6710	With pull switch		40	.200		3	3.27		6.27	8.60	
	6750	Fluorescent strip, 1-20 watt tube, wrap around diffuser, 24"		24	.333		40	5.45		45.45	53	
	6760	1-40 watt tube, 48"		24	.333		57	5.45		62.45	72	
	6770	2-40 watt tubes, 48"		20	.400		67	6.55		73.55	84	
	6780	With 0° ballast		20	.400		70	6.55		76.55	88	
	6800	Bathroom heat lamp, 1-250 watt		28	.286		23.80	4.67		28.47	34	
	6810	2-250 watt lamps	↓	28	.286	↓	39.52	4.67		44.19	51	
	6820	For timer switch, see line 2400										
	6900	Outdoor post lamp, incl. post, fixture, 35' of #14/2										
	6910	Type NMC cable	1 Elec	3.50	2.290	Ea.	140	37		177	215	
	6920	Photo-eye, add		27	.296		22.50	4.84		27.34	33	
	6950	Clock dial time switch, 24 hr., w/enclosure, type NM cable		11.43	.700		39	11.45		50.45	61	
	6970	Type MC cable		11	.727		44	11.90		55.90	68	
	6980	EMT & wire	↓	4.85	1.650	↓	46	27		73	94	
	7000	Alarm systems										
	7050	Smoke detectors, box, #14/3 type NM cable	1 Elec	14.55	.550	Ea.	21.63	9		30.63	38	
	7070	Type MC cable		12.31	.650		26	10.65		36.65	46	
	7080	EMT & wire	↓	5	1.600		38	26		64	84	
	7090	For relay output to security system, add					9			9	9.90	
	8000	Residential equipment										
	8050	Disposal hook-up, incl. switch, outlet box, 3' of flex										
	8060	20 amp-1 pole circ. bkr., and 25' of #12/2										
	8070	Type NM cable	1 Elec	10	.800	Ea.	17.50	13.10		30.60	40	
	8080	Type MC cable		8	1		20.95	16.35		37.30	49	
	8090	EMT & wire	↓	5	1.600	↓	22.67	26		48.67	67	
	8100	Trash compactor or dishwasher hook-up, incl. outlet box,										
	8110	3' of flex, 15 amp-1 pole circ. bkr., and 25' of #14/2										
	8130	Type MC cable	1 Elec	8	1	Ea.	14.66	16.35		31.01	43	
	8140	EMT & wire	"	5	1.600	"	17.57	26		43.57	62	
	8150	Hot water sink dispensor hook-up, use line 8100										
	8200	Vent/exhaust fan hook-up, type NM cable	1 Elec	32	.250	Ea.	3.43	4.09		7.52	10.40	

For expanded coverage of these items see *Means Electrical Cost Data 1991*

168 | Special Systems

168 100 | Special Systems

		CREW	DAILY OUTPUT	MAN-HOURS	UNIT	MAT.	LABOR	EQUIP.	TOTAL	TOTAL INCL O&P	
170	8220 Type MC cable	1 Elec	24	.333	Ea.	6.86	5.45		12.31	16.35	170
	8230 EMT & wire	"	10	.800	"	9.15	13.10		22.25	31	
	8250 Bathroom vent fan, 50 CFM (use with above hook-up)										
	8260 Economy model	1 Elec	15	.533	Ea.	18	8.70		26.70	34	
	8270 Low noise model		15	.533		23.71	8.70		32.41	40	
	8280 Custom model		12	.667		85	10.90		95.90	110	
	8300 Bathroom or kitchen vent fan, 110 CFM										
	8310 Economy model	1 Elec	15	.533	Ea.	45.45	8.70		54.15	64	
	8320 Low noise model	"	15	.533	"	59.28	8.70		67.98	79	
	8350 Paddle fan, variable speed (w/o lights)										
	8360 Economy model (AC motor)	1 Elec	10	.800	Ea.	70.72	13.10		83.82	99	
	8370 Custom model (AC motor)		10	.800		123	13.10		136.10	155	
	8380 Luxury model (DC motor)		8	1		251	16.35		267.35	305	
	8390 Remote speed switch for above, add		12	.667		16.22	10.90		27.12	35	
	8500 Whole house exhaust fan, ceiling mount, 36", variable speed										
	8510 Remote switch, incl. shutters, 20 amp-1 pole circ. bkr.										
	8520 30' of #12/2/ type NM cable	1 Elec	4	2	Ea.	368	33		401	460	
	8530 Type MC cable		3.50	2.290		376	37		413	475	
	8540 EMT & wire		3	2.670		392	44		436	500	
	8600 Whirlpool tub hook-up, incl. timer switch, outlet box										
	8610 3' of flex, 20 amp-1 pole GFI circ. bkr.										
	8620 30' of #12/2 type NM cable	1 Elec	10	.800	Ea.	60	13.10		73.10	87	
	8630 Type MC cable		8	1		63	16.35		79.35	96	
	8640 EMT & wire		4	2		65	33		98	125	
	8650 Hot water heater hook-up, incl. 1-2 pole circ. bkr. box;										
	8660 3' of flex, 20' of #10/2 type NM cable	1 Elec	10	.800	Ea.	11.85	13.10		24.95	34	
	8670 Type MC cable		8	1		14.56	16.35		30.91	42	
	8680 EMT & wire		5	1.600		17.26	26		43.26	61	
	9000 Heating/air conditioning										
	9050 Furnace/boiler hook-up, incl. firestat, local on-off switch										
	9060 Emergency switch, and 40' of type NM cable	1 Elec	4	2	Ea.	29	33		62	85	
	9070 Type MC cable		3.50	2.290		35.15	37		72.15	99	
	9080 EMT & wire		1.50	5.330		39.52	87		126.52	185	
	9100 Air conditioner hook-up, incl. local 60 amp disc. switch										
	9110 3' Sealtite, 40 amp, 2 pole circuit breaker										
	9130 40' of #8/2 type NM cable	1 Elec	3.50	2.290	Ea.	103	37		140	175	
	9140 Type MC cable		3	2.670		108	44		152	190	
	9150 EMT & wire		1.30	6.150		109	100		209	285	
	9200 Heat pump hook-up, 1-40 & 1-100 amp 2 pole circ. bkr.										
	9210 Local disconnect switch, 3' Sealtite										
	9220 40' of #8/2 & 30' of #3/2										
	9230 Type NM cable	1 Elec	1.30	6.150	Ea.	252	100		352	440	
	9240 Type MC cable		1.08	7.410		257	120		377	480	
	9250 EMT & wire		.94	8.510		247	140		387	495	
	9500 Thermostat hook-up, using low voltage wire										
	9520 Heating only	1 Elec	24	.333	Ea.	3.43	5.45		8.88	12.60	
	9530 Heating/cooling	"	20	.400	"	3.75	6.55		10.30	14.70	

For expanded coverage of these items see *Means Electrical Cost Data 1991*

REFERENCE SECTION

Along with the items in the "Unit Price" section, there frequently are larger numbers in circles. These "circle numbers" refer to reference tables, explanations and estimating information which explain the derivation of the unit price data. Also included is information which can be used for material lists, design and economy in construction.

CIRCLE REFERENCE NUMBERS

② Builder's Risk Insurance (Div. 010-040)

Builder's Risk Insurance is insurance on a building during construction. Premiums are paid by the owner or the contractor. Blasting, collapse and underground insurance would raise total insurance costs above those listed. Floater policy for materials delivered to the job runs $.75 to $1.25 per $100 value. Contractor equipment insurance runs $.50 to $1.50 per $100 value.

Tabulated below are New England Builder's Risk insurance rates in dollars per $100 value for $1,000 deductible. For $25,000 deductible, rates can be reduced 13% to 34%. On contracts over $1,000,000, rates may be lower than those tabulated. Policies are written annually for the total completed value in place. For "all risk" insurance (excluding flood, earthquake and certain other perils) add $.025 to total rates below.

Coverage	Frame Construction (Class 1)		Brick Construction (Class 4)		Fire Resistive (Class 6)	
	Range	Average	Range	Average	Range	Average
Fire Insurance	$.300 to .420	$.394	$.132 to .189	$.174	$.052 to .080	$.070
Extended Coverage	.115 to .150	.144	.080 to .105	.101	.081 to .105	.100
Vandalism	.012 to .016	.015	.008 to .011	.011	.008 to .011	.010
Total Annual Rate	$.427 to .586	$.553	$.220 to .305	$.286	$.141 to .196	$.180

④ General Contractor's Overhead (Div. 010)

The table below shows a contractor's overhead as a percentage of direct cost in two ways. The figures on the right are for the overhead, markup based on both material and labor. The figures on the left are based on the entire overhead applied only to the labor. This figure would be used if the owner supplied the materials or if a contract is for labor only.

Items of General Contractor's Indirect Costs	% of Direct Costs	
	As a Markup of Labor Only	As a Markup of Both Material and Labor
Field Supervision	6.0%	3.2%
Main Office Expense (see details below)	14.7	7.7
Tools and Minor Equipment	0.8	0.4
Workers' Compensation & Employers' Liability. See ⑦	15.1	7.9
Field Office, Sheds, Photos, Etc.	1.5	0.8
Performance and Payment Bond, 0.5% to 0.9%. See	0.7	0.7
Unemployment Tax See ⑤ (Combined Federal and State)	6.2	3.3
Social Security and Medicare (7.65% of first $51,300)	7.7	4.0
Sales Tax — add if applicable 38/80 x % as markup of total direct costs including both material and labor. See ⑧		
Sub Total	52.7%	28.0%
*Builder's Risk Insurance ranges from 0.141% to 0.586%. See ②	0.3	0.3
*Public Liability Insurance	1.5	1.5
Grand Total	54.5%	29.8%

*Paid by Owner or Contractor

CIRCLE REFERENCE NUMBERS

④ Main Office Expense

A General Contractor's main office expense consists of many items not detailed in the front portion of the book. The percentage of main office expense declines with increased annual volume of the contractor. Typical main office expense ranges from 2% to 20% with the median about 7.2% of total volume. This equals about 7.7% of direct costs. The following are approximate percentages of total overhead for different items usually included in a General Contractor's main office overhead. With different accounting procedures, these percentages may vary.

Item	Typical Range	Average
Managers', clerical and estimators' salaries	40% to 55%	48%
Profit sharing, pension and bonus plans	2 to 20	12
Insurance	5 to 8	6
Estimating and project management (not including salaries)	5 to 9	7
Legal, accounting and data processing	0.5 to 5	3
Automobile and light truck expense	2 to 8	5
Depreciation of overhead capital expenditures	2 to 6	4
Maintenance of office equipment	0.1 to 1.5	1
Office rental	3 to 5	4
Utilities including phone and light	1 to 3	2
Miscellaneous	5 to 15	8
Total		100%

⑤ Unemployment Taxes and Social Security Taxes (Div. 010-086)

Mass. State Unemployment tax ranges from 1.8% to 6.0% plus an experience rating assessment the following year, on the first $7,000 of wages. Federal Unemployment tax is 5.4% of the first $7,000 of wages. This is reduced by a credit for payment to the state. The minimum Federal Unemployment tax is .8% after all credits.

Combined rates in Mass. thus vary from 2.6% to 6.8% of the first $7,000 of wages. Combined average U.S. rate is about 6.2% of the first $7,000. Contractors with permanent workers will pay less since the average annual wages for skilled workers is $22.65 x 2,000 hours or about $45,300 per year. The average combined rate for U.S. would thus be 6.2% x $7,000 ÷ $45,300 = .96% of total wages for permanent employees.

Rates not only vary from state to state but also with the experience rating of the contractor.

Social Security (FICA) for 1991 is estimated at time of publication to be 7.65% of wages up to $53,400.

CIRCLE REFERENCE NUMBERS

⑥ Contractor's Overhead & Profit (Div. 010)

Listed below in the last two columns are **average** billing rates for the installing contractor's labor.

The Base Rates are averages for the building construction industry and include the usual negotiated fringe benefits. Workers' Compensation is a national average of state rates established for each trade. Average Fixed Overhead is a total of average rates for U.S. and State Unemployment, 6.2%; Social Security (FICA), 7.65%; Builders' Risk, 0.34%; and Public Liability, 1.55%. These are analyzed in ② and ⑤. All the rates except Social Security vary from state to state as well as from company to company. The installing contractor's overhead presumes annual billing of $500,000 and up. Overhead percentages may increase with smaller annual billing.

Overhead varies greatly within each trade. Some controlling factors are annual volume, job type, job size, location, local economic conditions, engineering and logistical support staff and equipment requirements. All factors should be examined carefully for each job.

Abbr.	Trade	Base Rate Incl. Fringes Hourly	Base Rate Incl. Fringes Daily	Workers' Comp. Ins.	Average Fixed Overhead	Overhead	Profit	Total Overhead & Profit %	Total Overhead & Profit Amount	Rate with O & P Hourly	Rate with O & P Daily
Skwk	Skilled Workers Average (35 trades)	$14.70	$117.60	15.1%	15.7%	26.8%	10%	67.6%	$ 9.95	$24.65	$197.20
	Helpers Average (5 trades)	11.10	88.80	16.2		27.0		68.9	7.65	18.75	150.00
	Foremen Average, Inside (50¢ over trade)	15.20	121.60	15.1		26.8		67.6	10.25	25.45	203.60
	Foremen Average, Outside ($2.00 over trade)	16.70	133.60	15.1		26.8		67.6	11.30	28.00	224.00
Clab	Common Building Laborers	11.35	90.80	16.6		25.0		67.3	7.65	19.00	152.00
Asbe	Asbestos Workers	16.05	128.40	13.5		30.0		69.2	11.10	27.15	217.20
Boil	Boilermakers	16.30	130.40	9.3		30.0		65.0	10.60	26.90	215.20
Bric	Bricklayers	14.80	118.40	13.7		25.0		64.4	9.55	24.35	194.80
Brhe	Bricklayer Helpers	11.45	91.60	13.7		25.0		64.4	7.35	18.80	150.40
Carp	Carpenters	14.30	114.40	16.6		25.0		67.3	9.60	23.90	191.20
Cefi	Cement Finishers	14.05	112.40	9.6		25.0		60.3	8.45	22.50	180.00
Elec	Electricians	16.35	130.80	6.0		30.0		61.7	10.10	26.45	211.60
Elev	Elevator Constructors	16.45	131.60	7.7		30.0		63.4	10.45	26.90	215.20
Eqhv	Equipment Operators, Crane or Shovel	15.15	121.20	10.4		28.0		64.1	9.70	24.85	198.80
Eqmd	Equipment Operators, Medium Equipment	14.60	116.80	10.4		28.0		64.1	9.35	23.95	191.60
Eqlt	Equipment Operators, Light Equipment	13.90	111.20	10.4		28.0		64.1	8.90	22.80	182.40
Eqol	Equipment Operators, Oilers	12.50	100.00	10.4		28.0		64.1	8.00	20.50	164.00
Eqmm	Equipment Operators, Master Mechanics	15.60	124.80	10.4		28.0		64.1	10.00	25.60	204.80
Glaz	Glaziers	14.65	117.20	11.9		25.0		62.6	9.15	23.80	190.40
Lath	Lathers	14.25	114.00	10.2		25.0		60.9	8.70	22.95	183.60
Marb	Marble Setters	14.65	117.20	13.7		25.0		64.4	9.45	24.10	192.80
Mill	Millwrights	14.90	119.20	9.9		25.0		60.6	9.05	23.95	191.60
Mstz	Mosaic and Terrazzo Workers	14.35	114.80	8.3		25.0		59.0	8.45	22.80	182.40
Pord	Painters, Ordinary	13.50	108.00	12.4		25.0		63.1	8.50	22.00	176.00
Psst	Painters, Structural Steel	13.95	111.60	42.9		25.0		93.6	13.05	27.00	216.00
Pape	Paper Hangers	13.50	108.00	12.4		25.0		63.1	8.50	22.00	176.00
Pile	Pile Drivers	14.45	115.60	25.4		30.0		81.1	11.70	26.15	209.20
Plas	Plasterers	14.15	113.20	13.4		25.0		64.1	9.05	23.20	185.60
Plah	Plasterer Helpers	11.65	93.20	13.4		25.0		64.1	7.45	19.10	152.80
Plum	Plumbers	16.55	132.40	7.5		30.0		63.2	10.45	27.00	216.00
Rodm	Rodmen (Reinforcing)	15.55	124.40	27.6		28.0		81.3	12.65	28.20	225.60
Rofc	Roofers, Composition	13.20	105.60	28.9		25.0		79.6	10.50	23.70	189.60
Rots	Roofers, Tile & Slate	13.30	106.40	28.9		25.0		79.6	10.60	23.90	191.20
Rohe	Roofer Helpers (Composition)	9.70	77.60	28.9		25.0		79.6	7.70	17.40	139.20
Shee	Sheet Metal Workers	16.25	130.00	10.2		30.0		65.9	10.70	26.95	215.60
Spri	Sprinkler Installers	17.15	137.20	7.7		30.0		63.4	10.85	28.00	224.00
Stpi	Steamfitters or Pipefitters	16.55	132.40	7.5		30.0		63.2	10.45	27.00	216.00
Ston	Stone Masons	14.70	117.60	13.7		25.0		64.4	9.45	24.15	193.20
Sswk	Structural Steel Workers	15.65	125.20	35.4		28.0		89.1	13.95	29.60	263.80
Tilf	Tile Layers (Floor)	14.40	115.20	8.3		25.0		59.0	8.50	22.90	183.20
Tilh	Tile Layer Helpers	11.35	90.80	8.3		25.0		59.0	6.70	18.05	144.40
Trlt	Truck Drivers, Light	11.75	94.00	13.5		25.0		64.2	7.55	19.30	154.40
Trhv	Truck Drivers, Heavy	11.95	95.60	13.5		25.0		64.2	7.65	19.60	156.80
Sswl	Welders, Structural Steel	15.65	125.20	35.4		28.0		89.1	13.95	29.60	236.80
Wrck	*Wrecking	11.35	90.80	35.5		25.0		86.2	9.80	21.15	169.20

*Not included in Averages.

396

CIRCLE REFERENCE NUMBERS

⑦ Workers' Compensation (Div. 010)

The table below tabulates the national averages for Workers' Compensation insurance rates by trade and type of building. The average "Insurance Rate" is multiplied by the "% of Building Cost" for each trade. This produces the "Workers' Compensation Cost" by % of total labor cost, to be added for each trade by building type to determine the weighted average Workers' Compensation rate for the building types analyzed.

Trade	Insurance Rate (% of Labor Cost) Range	Insurance Rate Average	% of Building Cost Office Bldgs.	% of Building Cost Schools & Apts.	% of Building Cost Mfg.	Workers' Compensation Cost Office Bldgs.	Workers' Compensation Cost Schools & Apts.	Workers' Compensation Cost Mfg.
Excavation, Grading, etc.	4.7% to 27.2%	10.4%	4.8%	4.9%	4.5%	.50%	.51%	.47%
Piles & Foundations	5.0 to 54.8	25.4	7.1	5.2	8.7	1.80	1.32	2.21
Concrete	5.0 to 44.3	15.3	5.0	14.8	3.7	.77	2.26	.57
Masonry	4.0 to 44.2	13.7	6.9	7.5	1.9	.95	1.03	.26
Structural Steel	5.0 to 162.5	35.4	10.7	3.9	17.6	3.79	1.38	6.23
Miscellaneous & Ornamental Metals	3.9 to 22.4	10.8	2.8	4.0	3.6	.30	.43	.39
Carpentry & Millwork	5.0 to 43.4	16.6	3.7	4.0	0.5	.61	.66	.08
Metal or Composition Siding	5.0 to 34.2	13.7	2.3	0.3	4.3	.32	.04	.59
Roofing	5.0 to 62.5	28.9	2.3	2.6	3.1	.66	.75	.90
Doors & Hardware	4.7 to 20.9	9.6	0.9	1.4	0.4	.09	.13	.04
Sash & Glazing	4.1 to 23.4	11.9	3.5	4.0	1.0	.42	.48	.12
Lath & Plaster	5.0 to 38.5	13.4	3.3	6.9	0.8	.44	.92	.11
Tile, Marble & Floors	3.2 to 23.1	8.3	2.6	3.0	0.5	.22	.25	.04
Acoustical Ceilings	3.7 to 26.9	10.2	2.4	0.2	0.3	.24	.02	.03
Painting	4.6 to 44.2	12.4	1.5	1.6	1.6	.19	.20	.20
Interior Partitions	5.0 to 43.4	16.6	3.9	4.3	4.4	.65	.71	.73
Miscellaneous Items	2.2 to 139.7	15.1	5.2	3.7	9.7	.79	.56	1.46
Elevators	2.5 to 16.2	7.7	2.1	1.1	2.2	.16	.08	.17
Sprinklers	2.2 to 15.1	7.7	0.5	—	2.0	.04	—	.15
Plumbing	2.7 to 16.0	7.5	4.9	7.2	5.2	.37	.54	.39
Heat., Vent., Air Conditioning	4.1 to 25.5	10.2	13.5	11.0	12.9	1.38	1.12	1.32
Electrical	2.4 to 12.9	6.0	10.1	8.4	11.1	.61	.50	.67
Total	2.2% to 162.5%	—	100.0%	100.0%	100.0%	15.30%	13.89%	17.13%

Overall Weighted Average 15.44%

The table below lists the weighted average Workers' Compensation base rate for each state with a factor comparing this with the national average of 15.1%.

State	Weighted Average	Factor	State	Weighted Average	Factor	State	Weighted Average	Factor
Alabama	13.2%	87	Kentucky	13.2%	87	North Dakota	13.5%	89
Alaska	22.2	147	Louisiana	12.8	85	Ohio	13.4	89
Arizona	15.8	105	Maine	24.1	160	Oklahoma	12.8	85
Arkansas	11.7	77	Maryland	15.4	102	Oregon	27.9	185
California	16.5	109	Massachusetts	25.3	168	Pennsylvania	15.2	101
Colorado	22.1	146	Michigan	15.1	100	Rhode Island	19.2	127
Connecticut	23.5	156	Minnesota	25.2	167	South Carolina	10.6	70
Delaware	12.1	80	Mississippi	10.0	66	South Dakota	10.3	68
District of Columbia	21.0	139	Missouri	8.2	54	Tennessee	10.5	70
Florida	30.4	201	Montana	37.5	248	Texas	19.2	127
Georgia	13.9	92	Nebraska	9.5	63	Utah	9.7	64
Hawaii	17.6	117	Nevada	16.2	107	Vermont	10.7	71
Idaho	12.8	85	New Hampshire	19.0	126	Virginia	9.1	60
Illinois	22.6	150	New Jersey	7.9	52	Washington	13.3	88
Indiana	6.5	43	New Mexico	18.5	123	West Virginia	10.1	67
Iowa	13.1	87	New York	11.7	77	Wisconsin	13.9	92
Kansas	9.5	63	North Carolina	7.3	48	Wyoming	5.5	36

Weighted Average for U.S. is 15.4% of payroll = 100

Rates in the following table are the base or manual costs per $100 of payroll for Workers' Compensation in each state. Rates are usually applied to straight time wages only and not to premium time wages and bonuses.

The weighted average skilled worker rate for 35 trades is 15.1%. For bidding purposes, apply the full value of Workers' Compensation directly to total labor costs, or if labor is 32%, materials 48% and overhead and profit 20% of total cost, carry 32/80 x 15.1% = 6.0% of cost (before overhead and profit) into overhead. Rates vary not only from state to state but also with the experience rating of the contractor.

Rates are the most current available at the time of publication.

CIRCLE REFERENCE NUMBERS

⑦ Workers' Compensation (cont.)

STATE	CARPENTRY – 3 stories or less	CARPENTRY – interior cab. work	CARPENTRY – general	CONCRETE WORK–NOC	CONCRETE WORK – flat (flr. sdwk.)	ELECTRICAL WIRING – inside	EXCAVATION – earth NOC	EXCAVATION – rock	GLAZIERS	INSULATION WORK	LATHING	MASONRY	PAINTING & DECORATING	PILE DRIVING	PLASTERING	PLUMBING	ROOFING	SHEET METAL WORK (HVAC)	STEEL ERECTION – door & sash	STEEL ERECTION – inter., ornam.	STEEL ERECTION – structure	STEEL ERECTION – NOC	TILE WORK – (interior ceramic)	WATERPROOFING	WRECKING
	5651	5437	5403	5213	5221	5190	6217	6217	5462	5479	5443	5022	5474	6003	5480	5183	5551	5538	5102	5102	5040	5057	5348	9014	5701
AL	14.97	8.55	14.18	11.06	7.25	5.86	8.68	8.68	11.20	11.17	8.35	10.59	11.54	32.21	9.38	6.53	25.13	13.57	7.78	7.78	23.21	20.90	8.16	3.60	20.90
AK	16.10	11.21	14.48	18.19	10.46	9.07	12.87	12.87	18.59	19.83	13.80	12.49	10.31	41.05	21.55	12.61	29.27	14.16	19.77	19.77	74.36	56.94	10.21	6.51	74.36
AZ	19.74	7.60	23.31	12.41	10.23	9.30	7.07	7.07	13.56	17.90	8.95	16.91	11.59	27.00	19.08	6.60	24.77	10.19	12.74	12.74	35.69	17.97	6.70	7.24	17.97
AR	11.85	6.30	15.05	12.20	6.23	4.71	8.50	8.50	8.80	8.61	8.14	10.02	10.68	16.64	10.01	4.49	13.70	7.62	6.18	6.18	44.38	16.97	5.54	5.34	44.38
CA	21.96	8.01	21.96	9.33	9.33	7.82	7.55	7.55	12.94	22.76	8.13	14.05	14.90	19.03	15.92	10.36	36.32	13.11	12.18	12.18	28.27	24.76	7.68	14.90	28.35
CO	22.81	13.43	19.38	20.39	14.20	6.56	13.75	13.75	11.58	20.41	10.43	26.22	17.00	36.16	38.54	11.54	48.70	12.88	12.23	12.23	52.23	30.77	10.81	9.24	30.77
CT	18.58	20.34	25.91	26.78	15.09	8.87	12.75	12.75	21.83	25.42	15.47	28.35	17.77	42.59	21.19	10.09	51.57	15.49	16.81	16.81	50.82	26.21	9.81	4.61	50.82
DE	11.44	13.73	11.44	9.20	6.25	5.71	8.49	8.49	11.11	11.44	10.45	9.77	13.30	11.50	10.45	5.32	22.88	10.11	10.09	10.09	26.31	10.09	7.46	9.77	25.47
DC	10.32	9.62	14.81	27.57	12.88	11.76	14.68	14.68	14.11	13.79	10.72	21.41	11.84	37.37	12.32	14.82	32.92	11.25	20.59	20.59	47.36	46.44	23.24	5.77	47.36
FL	25.21	18.82	30.26	44.32	18.17	12.89	20.27	20.27	23.43	25.66	26.91	26.88	30.18	46.97	31.60	16.01	55.77	19.12	22.40	22.40	48.03	58.10	12.70	10.32	48.03
GA	15.40	10.28	17.30	11.49	9.47	5.67	11.86	11.86	9.06	12.63	13.51	11.69	10.65	27.66	11.35	6.07	24.90	9.60	8.21	8.21	18.44	26.83	5.90	7.36	26.83
HI	11.66	9.32	39.81	13.93	9.03	8.89	10.81	10.81	14.08	20.18	9.51	17.35	7.68	28.43	19.16	5.36	40.64	8.32	14.10	14.10	27.94	26.82	7.72	10.50	27.94
ID	13.17	7.20	18.71	12.78	5.84	4.67	10.20	10.20	11.13	13.14	7.93	16.25	12.51	20.62	10.67	4.53	27.80	8.95	7.45	7.45	18.09	16.83	6.59	7.26	18.09
IL	16.54	11.14	17.49	26.51	12.88	8.75	10.19	10.19	21.11	17.72	13.22	18.01	15.60	31.52	13.46	12.20	31.86	15.94	13.72	13.72	61.21	84.88	12.92	5.22	84.88
IN	9.00	4.97	6.19	6.08	3.94	2.64	5.07	5.07	6.83	5.21	3.67	5.54	4.65	13.11	5.37	2.67	10.84	3.97	3.90	3.90	8.73	14.57	3.58	3.14	14.57
IA	9.23	7.01	10.64	17.71	4.89	5.38	9.85	9.85	8.25	12.47	6.76	10.58	8.30	17.54	8.92	7.78	18.49	8.41	9.80	9.80	38.15	37.61	6.25	4.27	37.61
KS	10.35	5.61	7.94	9.82	5.58	3.66	4.70	4.70	6.25	15.84	7.81	9.75	6.57	15.96	7.75	4.59	19.70	6.82	4.74	4.74	11.50	23.34	5.08	4.75	23.34
KY	14.27	6.19	14.56	11.42	7.61	4.67	7.40	7.40	8.65	10.16	10.07	13.10	12.37	28.02	9.53	5.21	23.87	9.76	9.85	9.85	30.22	23.44	7.65	4.39	30.22
LA	16.33	10.25	16.12	8.59	7.84	5.59	9.61	9.61	12.34	8.20	7.25	7.74	13.24	37.62	8.86	6.29	20.21	7.76	7.91	7.91	24.13	13.43	6.64	6.06	24.13
ME	12.13	10.90	38.36	24.84	10.99	8.38	16.53	16.53	18.35	19.96	13.34	19.36	19.26	43.24	19.49	12.27	44.12	13.43	17.46	17.46	52.06	57.53	13.46	7.99	52.06
MD	12.59	12.33	10.70	17.28	9.77	7.64	12.85	12.85	18.78	12.60	8.29	12.40	9.07	19.45	10.26	9.40	32.69	13.58	11.27	11.27	26.18	32.54	9.59	4.30	37.63
MA	14.16	12.04	30.31	33.73	15.36	6.21	9.34	9.34	21.21	16.86	15.19	23.65	14.05	26.22	15.99	9.21	79.41	13.85	16.23	16.23	83.51	48.66	13.21	9.81	65.27
MI	11.40	7.35	12.74	12.71	9.27	5.75	12.42	12.42	14.56	15.48	9.32	16.14	13.24	26.48	14.23	7.23	26.63	8.70	11.42	11.42	29.17	20.06	8.13	NA	29.17
MN	20.86	20.86	36.23	21.03	14.74	6.95	21.20	21.20	17.38	22.76	22.29	17.84	17.92	35.90	22.29	11.77	45.20	14.86	16.41	16.41	51.17	54.54	12.08	9.34	51.17
MS	10.19	6.87	12.79	8.41	4.70	4.93	8.18	8.18	8.45	6.92	7.85	6.29	6.64	22.56	9.94	3.36	15.30	7.80	6.98	6.98	22.27	13.33	6.72	3.86	22.27
MO	7.88	5.54	7.19	6.30	5.92	3.52	6.07	6.07	5.38	9.22	5.76	7.22	4.95	16.62	6.26	3.33	17.56	4.75	5.91	5.91	15.91	13.15	4.58	3.66	13.15
MT	23.27	13.56	43.40	38.99	21.88	8.30	27.19	27.19	19.61	25.49	23.34	44.23	44.16	54.83	28.08	15.32	62.45	16.29	17.94	17.94	162.26	55.63	14.05	16.25	162.26
NE	8.22	5.45	8.84	9.53	7.35	3.72	7.11	7.11	6.84	9.78	6.05	8.01	7.17	12.60	7.58	4.53	18.79	7.89	5.42	5.42	13.54	27.21	4.76	4.92	27.21
NV	14.25	14.25	14.25	11.31	11.31	7.21	10.61	10.61	11.46	13.98	13.68	11.93	12.97	10.90	13.68	8.97	23.39	25.48	13.01	13.01	33.81	33.81	9.98	10.90	N.A.
NH	15.51	9.63	18.51	26.18	13.21	5.16	12.90	12.90	10.28	14.57	11.62	14.47	13.26	52.73	18.31	9.06	60.55	11.19	11.94	11.94	31.55	16.57	8.96	6.26	31.55
NJ	6.83	5.66	6.83	5.78	4.90	2.43	6.26	6.26	4.91	6.54	6.43	7.98	7.58	10.12	6.43	3.18	15.67	4.20	7.66	7.66	22.64	10.49	3.16	3.51	27.74
NM	14.96	11.73	19.31	24.57	9.63	5.95	10.09	10.09	16.15	14.70	11.32	16.70	11.44	49.12	16.45	10.09	37.80	12.36	18.46	18.46	21.61	25.84	10.07	7.75	21.61
NY	9.63	4.67	9.88	12.46	9.73	5.00	10.17	10.17	8.89	8.52	8.23	12.36	9.56	17.49	9.18	7.53	22.73	9.75	7.68	7.68	17.83	24.06	7.13	5.44	19.97
NC	6.06	5.70	9.29	8.46	3.63	4.32	5.94	5.94	5.09	6.14	4.15	4.01	5.05	11.79	8.46	4.46	12.70	5.31	4.73	4.73	19.37	8.00	3.27	2.59	19.37
ND	12.86	12.86	12.86	9.98	9.98	4.54	8.28	8.28	14.60	7.64	5.87	6.34	9.54	27.52	5.87	10.27	15.98	10.27	12.86	12.86	27.52	27.52	5.69	15.98	NA
OH	9.93	9.93	9.93	10.32	10.32	3.87	10.32	10.32	11.36	8.83	8.83	10.48	11.36	10.32	8.83	5.69	20.00	12.71	N.A.	N.A.	58.93	N.A.	5.03	10.32	10.32
OK	14.20	7.38	11.62	10.27	8.38	3.78	9.39	9.39	8.02	9.81	7.80	9.85	8.30	24.54	10.73	5.06	20.50	8.02	7.74	7.74	37.18	29.25	5.53	6.60	37.18
OR	34.23	14.01	33.37	26.01	19.95	8.49	20.99	20.99	15.10	28.80	13.90	24.25	24.82	53.64	26.62	11.10	60.89	14.90	16.80	16.80	48.90	36.45	23.07	17.85	48.90
PA	12.32	11.41	12.32	18.08	8.25	5.50	9.57	9.57	10.58	12.32	13.37	12.19	12.85	17.01	13.37	7.30	27.01	9.87	16.25	16.25	41.51	16.25	8.23	12.19	64.42
RI	15.52	7.13	12.32	14.83	16.49	6.22	12.89	12.89	18.05	15.23	11.26	14.94	17.87	30.71	15.05	4.69	31.27	6.80	10.13	10.13	78.01	40.30	9.28	8.00	78.01
SC	14.28	7.39	15.32	7.64	6.55	6.30	7.43	7.43	11.77	11.46	6.85	10.01	9.36	14.13	9.58	3.44	17.21	8.84	4.23	4.23	11.28	24.72	8.80	4.44	11.28
SD	8.52	5.88	13.80	10.26	5.60	4.22	7.72	7.72	8.18	11.76	6.24	7.27	8.01	17.08	8.45	7.03	27.14	6.16	6.92	6.92	17.97	13.96	5.02	3.91	17.97
TN	11.89	6.11	11.70	9.84	5.61	4.17	7.59	7.59	7.91	9.44	6.15	8.76	8.99	21.90	7.96	5.32	18.61	8.59	8.03	8.03	20.93	15.57	4.73	4.33	20.93
TX	22.09	15.58	22.09	18.49	14.60	9.81	14.91	14.91	13.54	20.74	9.35	16.27	14.06	30.47	14.57	12.00	38.41	16.85	11.50	11.50	39.93	21.52	8.82	7.96	38.04
UT	NA	NA	8.79	9.82	4.93	5.05	6.25	6.25	6.84	6.73	8.06	13.07	9.18	15.75	8.37	5.67	20.31	5.72	5.90	5.90	NA	24.80	4.77	3.07	24.80
VT	7.62	5.25	12.12	12.62	5.63	3.63	6.85	6.85	8.04	8.22	7.31	12.12	8.01	19.05	9.67	5.05	19.24	6.31	6.66	6.66	20.53	26.40	5.90	5.02	20.53
VA	7.28	5.90	9.08	9.23	6.29	3.45	5.52	5.52	8.03	8.84	6.87	7.69	8.54	9.24	5.64	4.72	25.24	7.11	5.10	5.10	21.59	15.51	3.78	3.34	21.59
WA	12.37	12.37	12.37	10.52	8.78	3.12	8.18	8.18	13.15	10.10	12.37	12.99	10.69	21.35	13.05	4.47	11.99	5.92	10.52	10.52	29.26	29.26	7.92	11.94	14.80
WV	10.80	10.80	10.80	14.90	14.90	4.00	8.48	8.48	4.13	4.13	15.81	7.03	15.81	8.40	15.81	3.52	12.91	4.13	9.94	9.93	7.96	9.93	7.03	2.73	7.96
WI	10.26	7.57	17.21	11.12	6.31	5.41	8.58	8.58	10.62	12.79	8.28	11.77	11.34	28.37	12.80	7.34	28.44	8.70	9.19	9.19	29.73	24.92	10.03	5.38	63.36
WY	5.00	5.00	5.00	5.00	5.00	5.00	5.00	5.00	5.00	5.00	5.00	5.00	5.00	5.00	5.00	5.00	5.00	5.00	5.00	5.00	5.00	5.00	5.00	5.00	5.00
AVG.	13.72	9.61	16.64	15.29	9.55	5.97	10.37	10.37	11.90	13.48	10.22	13.71	12.36	25.40	13.39	7.45	28.91	10.24	10.79	10.79	35.36	27.59	8.28	7.09	35.54

CIRCLE REFERENCE NUMBERS

(7) Workers' Compensation (cont.) (Canada in Canadian dollars)

PROVINCE		Alberta	British Columbia	Manitoba	Ontario	New Brunswick	Newfndld. & Labrador	Northwest Territories	Nova Scotia	Prince Edward Island	Quebec	Saskatchewan	Yukon
CARPENTRY—3 stories or less	Rate	5.33	2.99	5.65	3.98	3.66	4.75	6.50	2.90	5.65	8.21	5.25	2.00
	Code	8-04	060412	401	062-08	403	403	4-41	4013	401	40010	B12-02	4-042
CARPENTRY—interior cab. work	Rate	5.33	2.99	5.65	3.98	3.66	4.75	6.50	2.90	5.65	8.21	4.50	2.00
	Code	8-04	060412	401	062-08	403	403	4-41	4013	401	40010	B11-25	4-042
CARPENTRY—general	Rate	5.33	2.99	5.65	3.98	3.66	4.75	6.50	2.90	5.65	8.21	5.25	2.00
	Code	8-04	060412	401	062-08	403	403	4-41	4013	401	40010	B12-02	4-042
CONCRETE WORK—NOC	Rate	6.48	5.36	5.65	8.23	3.66	4.75	6.50	2.90	5.65	11.36	8.65	2.50
	Code	6-01	070604	401	744-09	403	403	4-41	4222	401	40080	B14-04	2-032
CONCRETE WORK—flat (flr., sidewalk)	Rate	6.48	5.36	5.65	8.23	3.66	4.75	6.50	2.90	5.65	11.36	8.65	2.50
	Code	6-01	070604	401	744-09	403	403	4-41	4222	401	40080	B14-04	2-032
ELECTRICAL Wiring—inside	Rate	2.70	2.46	2.97	5.99	3.66	2.75	4.50	1.33	3.05	5.75	4.50	2.00
	Code	6-06	071100	402	864-07	403	400	4-46	4261	402	40150	B11-05	4-041
EXCAVATION—earth NOC	Rate	4.88	3.63	7.11	12.25	3.66	4.75	7.00	2.73	5.65	8.14	5.90	2.50
	Code	6-07	072607	407	753-13	403	403	4-43	4214	401	40021	R11-06	2-016
EXCAVATION—rock	Rate	4.88	3.63	7.11	12.25	3.66	4.75	7.00	2.73	5.65	8.14	5.90	2.50
	Code	6-07	072607	407	753-13	403	403	4-43	4214	401	40021	R11-06	2-016
GLAZIERS	Rate	3.65	1.52	5.65	8.64	3.66	2.60	6.50	2.90	3.05	6.83	7.35	2.00
	Code	6-03	060236	401	873-11	403	402	4-41	4233	402	40110	B13-04	4-042
INSULATION WORK	Rate	6.64	6.39	5.65	8.64	3.66	2.60	6.50	2.90	5.65	9.03	5.25	2.50
	Code	6-03	070504	401	873-11	403	402	4-41	4234	401	40170	B12-07	2-035
LATHING	Rate	6.53	6.39	5.65	9.81	3.66	2.60	6.50	2.90	3.05	9.03	7.35	2.50
	Code	6-03	070500	401	854-12	403	402	4-41	4271	402	40170	B13-02	2-036
MASONRY	Rate	7.56	5.36	5.65	9.81	3.66	4.75	6.50	2.90	5.65	11.36	11.50	2.50
	Code	6-04	070602	401	854-12	403	403	4-41	4231	401	40080	B15-01	2-032
PAINTING & DECORATING	Rate	4.91	6.39	5.65	8.64	3.66	2.60	4.50	2.90	3.05	9.03	5.25	2.50
	Code	6-03	070501	401	873-11	403	402	4-49	4275	402	40170	B12-01	2-036
PILE DRIVING	Rate	6.48	15.33	7.11	10.69	3.66	5.50	7.00	3.03	5.65	8.14	5.25	2.50
	Code	6-01	072502	407	836-13	403	404	4-43	4221	401	40021	B12-10	2-030
PLASTERING	Rate	6.53	6.39	5.65	9.68	3.66	2.60	6.50	2.90	3.05	9.03	7.35	2.50
	Code	6-03	070502	401	854-12	403	402	4-41	4271	402	40170	B13-02	2-036
PLUMBING	Rate	3.16	2.99	2.97	5.99	3.66	3.75	4.50	1.97	3.05	6.95	4.50	2.00
	Code	6-02	070712	402	864-07	403	401	4-46	4241	402	40130	B11-01	4-039
ROOFING	Rate	11.07	5.36	7.94	9.68	3.66	4.75	6.50	2.90	5.65	12.52	11.50	2.50
	Code	6-05	070600	404	854-12	403	403	4-41	4235	401	40121	B15-02	2-031
SHEET METAL WORK (HVAC)	Rate	2.20	2.99	7.94	5.99	3.66	3.75	4.50	2.90	3.05	6.95	4.50	2.00
	Code	6-02	070714	404	864-07	403	401	4-46	4236	402	40130	B11-07	4-040
STEEL ERECTION—door & sash	Rate	4.12	15.33	9.51	10.10	3.66	5.50	6.50	2.90	5.65	16.57	11.50	2.50
	Code	8-03	072509	405	827-09	403	404	4-41	4223	401	40100	B15-03	2-012
STEEL ERECTION—inter., ornam.	Rate	4.48	15.33	9.51	10.10	3.66	4.75	6.50	2.90	5.65	16.57	11.50	2.50
	Code	6-01	072509	405	827-09	403	403	4-41	4223	401	40100	B15-03	2-012
STEEL ERECTION—structure	Rate	11.40	15.33	9.51	23.26	3.66	5.50	4.25	5.48	5.65	16.57	11.50	2.50
	Code	6-08	072509	405	809-14	403	404	4-44	4227	401	40100	B15-04	2-012
STEEL ERECTION—NOC	Rate	11.40	15.33	9.51	10.10	3.66	5.50	6.50	5.48	5.65	16.57	11.50	2.50
	Code	6-08	072509	405	827-09	403	404	4-41	4227	401	40100	B15-03	2-012
TILE WORK—inter. (ceramic)	Rate	6.19	6.39	5.65	5.99	3.66	2.60	4.50	2.90	3.05	9.03	7.35	2.50
	Code	6-03	070506	401	864-07	403	402	4-49	4276	402	40170	B13-01	2-034
WATERPROOFING	Rate	5.39	1.52	7.11	8.64	3.66	4.75	6.50	2.90	3.05	11.38	4.50	2.50
	Code	6-02	060237	407	873-11	403	403	4-41	4239	402	40122	B11-17	2-030
WRECKING	Rate	17.18	5.36	5.65	23.28	3.66	4.75	7.00	2.90	5.65	11.36	8.65	2.50
	Code	6-08	070600	401	859-15	403	403	4-43	4211	401	40080	B14-07	2-030

CIRCLE REFERENCE NUMBERS

(8) Sales Tax (Div. 010-086)

State sales tax on materials is tabulated below (5 states have no sales tax). Many states allow local jurisdictions, such as a county or city, to levy additional sales tax.

Some projects may be sales tax exempt, particularly those constructed with public funds.

State	Tax	State	Tax	State	Tax	State	Tax
Alabama	4%	Illinois	5%	Montana	0%	Rhode Island	6%
Alaska	0	Indiana	5	Nebraska	4	South Carolina	5
Arizona	5	Iowa	4	Nevada	3.50	South Dakota	4
Arkansas	4	Kansas	4.25	New Hampshire	0	Tennessee	5.5
California	6	Kentucky	5	New Jersey	6	Texas	6
Colorado	3	Louisiana	4	New Mexico	4.75	Utah	6
Connecticut	7.5	Maine	5	New York	4	Vermont	4
Delaware	0	Maryland	5	North Carolina	5	Virginia	4.5
District of Columbia	6	Massachusetts	5	North Dakota	6	Washington	6.5
Florida	6	Michigan	4	Ohio	5.5	West Virginia	6
Georgia	3	Minnesota	6	Oklahoma	4	Wisconsin	6
Hawaii	4	Mississippi	6	Oregon	0	Wyoming	3
Idaho	5	Missouri	4.225	Pennsylvania	6	Average	4.44%

(10) Architectural Fees (Div. 010-004)

Tabulated below are typical percentage fees by project size, for good professional architectural service. Fees may vary from those listed depending upon degree of design difficulty and economic conditions in any particular area.

Rates can be interpolated horizontally and vertically. Various portions of the same project requiring different rates should be adjusted proportionately. For alterations, add 50% to the fee for the first $500,000 of project cost and add 25% to the fee for project cost over $500,000.

Architectural fees tabulated below include Engineering Fees.

Building Type	Total Project Size in Thousands of Dollars						
	100	250	500	1,000	5,000	10,000	50,000
Factories, garages, warehouses repetitive housing	9.0%	8.0%	7.0%	6.2%	5.3%	4.9%	4.5%
Apartments, banks, schools, libraries, offices, municipal buildings	11.7	10.8	8.5	7.3	6.4	6.0	5.6
Churches, hospitals, homes, laboratories, museums, research	14.0	12.8	11.9	10.9	8.5	7.8	7.2
Memorials, monumental work, decorative furnishings	—	16.0	14.5	13.1	10.0	9.0	8.3

CIRCLE REFERENCE NUMBERS

⑭ Steel Tubular Scaffolding (Div. 015-254)

On new construction, tubular scaffolding is efficient up to 60' high or five stories. Above this it is usually better to use a hung scaffolding if construction permits.

In repairing or cleaning the front of an existing building the cost of tubular scaffolding per S.F. of building front increases as the height increases above the first tier. The first tier cost is relatively high due to leveling and alignment. Swing scaffolding operations may interfere with tenants. In this case the tubular is more practical at all heights.

The minimum efficient crew for erection is three men. For heights over 50', a four-man crew is more efficient. Use two or more on top and two at the bottom for handing up or hoisting. Four men can erect and dismantle about nine frames per hour up to five stories. From five to eight stories they will average six frames per hour. With 7' horizontal spacing this will run about 300 S.F. and 200 S.F. of wall surface, respectively. Time for placing planks must be added to the above. On heights above 50', five planks can be placed per man-hour.

The cost per 1,000 S.F. of building front in the table below was developed by pricing the materials required for a typical tubular scaffolding system eleven frames long and two frames high. Planks were figured five wide for standing plus two wide for materials.

Frames are 2', 4' and 5' wide and usually spaced 7' O.C. horizontally. Sidewalk frames are 6' wide. Rental rates will be lower for jobs over three months duration.

For jobs under twenty-five frames, figure rental at $6.00 per frame. For jobs over one hundred frames, rental can go as low as $2.65 per frame. These figures do not include accessories which are listed separately below. Large quantities for long periods can reduce rental rates by 20%.

Item	Unit	Purchase, Each Regular	Purchase, Each Heavy Duty	Monthly Rent, Each Regular	Monthly Rent, Each Heavy Duty	Per 1,000 S.F. of Building Front No. of Frames	Per 1,000 S.F. of Building Front Rental per Mo.
5' Wide Frames, 3' High	Ea.	$55	$ —	$3.65	$ —	—	—
*5'-0" High		70	—	3.65	—	—	—
*6'-6" High		85	—	3.65	—	24	$ 87.60
2' & 4' Wide, 5' High		—	75	—	3.75	—	—
6'-0" High		—	85	—	3.75	—	—
6' Wide Frame, 7'-6" High		130	155	7.95	10	—	—
Sidewalk Bracket, 20"		20	—	1.60	—	12	19.20
Guardrail Post		15	—	1.10	—	12	13.20
Guardrail, 7' section		7	—	.80	—	11	8.80
Cross Braces		15	17	.75	.75	44	33.00
Screw Jacks & Plates		20	30	2.00	2.50	24	48.00
8" Casters		50	—	5.75	—	—	—
16' Plank, 2" x 10"		22	—	5.10	—	35	178.50
8' Plank, 2" x 10"		11	—	3.75	—	7	26.25
1' to 6' Extension Tube	↓	—	70	—	2.50	—	—
Shoring Stringers, steel, 10' to 12' long	L.F.	—	7	—	.40	—	—
Aluminum, 12' to 16' long		—	16	—	.60	—	—
Aluminum joists with nailers, 10' to 22' long		—	12.50	—	.50	—	—
Flying Truss System, Aluminum	S.F.C.A.	—	10	—	.60	—	—
						Total	$414.55
						2 Use/Mo.	$207.28

*Most commonly used

Scaffolding is often used as falsework over 15' high during construction of cast-in-place concrete beams and slabs. Two ft. wide scaffolding is generally used for heavy beam construction. The span between frames depends upon the load to be carried with a maximum span of 5'.

Heavy duty scaffolding with a capacity of 10,000#/leg can be spaced up to 10' O.C. depending upon form support design and loading.

Scaffolding used as horizontal shoring requires less than half the material required with conventional shoring.

On new construction, erection is done by carpenters.

Rolling towers supporting horizontal shores can reduce labor and speed the job. For maintenance work, catwalks with spans up to 70' can be supported by the rolling towers.

CIRCLE REFERENCE NUMBERS

(26) Bituminous Paving (Div. 025-100)

City	Bituminous Asphalt per Ton*	3" Thick Roads & Parking Areas (6.13 S.Y./ton) Cost per Square Yard	2" Thick Sidewalks (9.2 S.Y./ton) Cost per Square Yard
Atlanta	$23.45	$4.29	$3.09
Baltimore	31.20	5.61	4.15
Boston	31.50	5.81	4.63
Buffalo	33.60	6.11	4.75
Chicago	31.05	5.72	4.55
Cincinnati	27.75	5.13	4.09
Cleveland	27.15	5.10	4.25
Columbus	24.60	4.58	3.61
Dallas	30.90	5.49	3.84
Denver	24.75	4.53	3.34
Detroit	27.65	5.15	4.16
Houston	26.50	4.80	3.49
Indianapolis	27.55	5.05	3.86
Kansas City	25.00	4.66	3.69
Los Angeles	27.15	5.17	4.45
Memphis	26.20	4.72	3.41
Milwaukee	23.80	4.48	3.64
Minneapolis	23.65	4.47	3.64
Nashville	22.60	4.13	2.95
New Orleans	28.80	5.18	3.78
New York City	38.35	7.03	5.77
Philadelphia	34.15	6.22	4.95
Phoenix	26.80	4.93	3.81
Pittsburgh	34.25	6.16	4.62
St. Louis	24.65	4.67	3.87
San Antonio	31.65	5.60	3.92
San Diego	29.25	5.51	4.68
San Francisco	38.25	6.98	5.63
Seattle	28.25	5.23	4.20
Washington, D.C.	34.25	6.12	4.49
Average	$28.82	$5.29	$4.11

Assumed density is 145 lb. per C.F.
*Include delivery within 20 miles.

Table below shows quantities and bare costs for 1000 S.Y. of Bituminous Paving.

Item	Roads and Parking Areas, 3" Thick (025-104-0460) Quantities	Cost	Sidewalks, 2" Thick (025-128-0010) Quantities	Cost
Bituminous asphalt	163 tons @ $28.82 per ton	$4,697.66	109 tons @ $28.82 per ton	$3,141.38
Installation using	Crew B-25B @ $2,907.40/4900 SY/day x 1000	593.30	Crew B-37 @ $699.60/720 SY/day x 1000	971.67
Total per 1000 S.Y.		$5,290.96		$4,113.05
Total per S.Y.		$ 5.29		$ 4.11
Total per Ton		$ 32.46		$ 37.73

(29) Seeding (Div. 029-300)

The type of grass is determined by light, shade and moisture content of soil plus intended use. Fertilizer should be disked 4" before seeding. For steep slopes disk five tons of mulch and lay two tons of hay or straw on surface per acre after seeding. Surface mulch can be staked, lightly disked or tar emulsion sprayed. Material for mulch can be wood chips, peat moss, partially rotted hay or straw, wood fibers and sprayed emulsions. Hemp seed blankets with fertilizer are also available. For spring seeding, watering is necessary. Late fall seeding may have to be reseeded in the spring. Hydraulic seeding, power mulching, and aerial seeding can be used on large areas.

CIRCLE REFERENCE NUMBERS

㉚ Cost of Trees (Deciduous) (Div. 029-536)

Tree Diameter	Normal Height	Catalog List Price of Tree	Guying Material	Equipment Charge	Installation Labor	Total
2 to 3 inch	14 feet	$ 88	$12	$ 49	$ 39	$ 188
3 to 4 inch	16 feet	170	29	82	65	346
4 to 5 inch	18 feet	245	46	98	78	467
6 to 7 inch	22 feet	655	80	122	97	954
8 to 9 inch	26 feet	1300	98	163	129	1690

Installation Time & Cost for Planting Trees, Bare Costs

Ball Size Diam. x Depth Inches	Soil in Ball C.F.	Weight of Ball Lbs.	Hole Diam. Req'd. Feet	Hole Excavation C.F.	Amount of Soil Displ. C.F.	Topsoil Handled C.F.	Dig & Lace	Handle Ball	Dig Hole	Plant & Prune	Water & Guy	Total M.H.	Crew	Total per Tree
12x12	.7	56	2	4	3	11	.25	.17	.33	.25	.07	1.1	1 Clab	$ 12
18x16	2	160	2.5	8	6	21	.50	.33	.47	.35	.08	1.7	2 Clab	19
24x18	4	320	3	13	9	38	1.00	.67	1.08	.82	.20	3.8	3 Clab	43
30x21	7.5	600	4	27	19.5	76	.82	.71	.79	1.22	.26	3.8		$ 76
36x24	12.5	980	4.5	38	25.5	114	1.08	.95	1.11	1.32	.30	4.76		96
42x27	19	1520	5.5	64	45	185	1.90	1.27	1.87	1.43	.34	6.8	B-6	137
48x30	28	2040	6	85	57	254	2.41	1.60	2.06	1.55	.39	8.0	@	161
54x33	38.5	3060	7	127	88.5	370	2.86	1.90	2.39	1.76	.45	9.4	$20.13	189
60x36	52	4160	7.5	159	107	474	3.26	2.17	2.73	2.00	.51	10.7	per	215
66x39	68	5440	8	196	128	596	3.61	2.41	3.07	2.26	.58	11.9	man-	240
72x42	87	7160	9	267	180	785	3.90	2.60	3.71	2.78	.70	13.7	hour	276

CIRCLE REFERENCE NUMBERS

(56) Cement Mortar (material only) (Div. 041)

Type N — 1:1:6 mix by volume. Use everywhere above grade except as noted below.

Type M — 1:¼:3 mix by volume, or 1 part cement, 1/4 (10% by wt.) lime, 3 parts sand. Use for heavy loads and where earthquakes or hurricanes may occur. Also for reinforced brick, sewers, manholes and everywhere below grade.

Type N — 1:3 mix using conventional masonry cement which saves handling two separate bagged materials.

Cost and Mix Proportions of Various Types of Mortar and Grout

Components	M 1:1:6	M 1:¼:3	S ½:1:4	S 1:½:4	N 1:3	N 1:1:6	O 1:3	K 1:2:9	K 1:3:12	PM 1:1:6	PL 1:½:4
Portland cement @ $6.55 per bag	$6.55	$6.55	$3.28	$6.55	—	$6.55	—	$6.55	$6.55	$6.55	$6.55
Masonry cement @ $5.60 per bag	5.60	—	5.60	—	$5.60	—	$5.60	—	—	5.60	—
Lime @ $4.35 per 50 lb. bag	—	1.09	—	2.18	—	4.35	—	8.70	13.05	—	2.18
Masonry sand @ $20.75 per C.Y.*	4.61	2.31	3.07	3.07	2.31	4.61	2.31	6.92	9.22	4.61	3.07
Mixing machine incl. fuel**	1.22	.61	.82	.82	.61	1.22	.61	1.84	2.45	1.22	.82
Total for Materials	$17.98	$10.56	$12.77	$12.62	$8.52	$16.73	$8.52	$24.01	$31.27	$17.98	$12.62
Total C.F.	6	3	4	4	3	6	3	9	12	6	4
Approximate Cost per C.F.	$3.00	$3.52	$3.19	$3.15	$2.84	$2.79	$2.84	$2.67	$2.61	$3.00	$3.15

* Includes 10 mile haul
** Based on a daily rental, 10 C.F., 9 H.P. mixer, mix 200 C.F./Day

Mix Proportions by Volume, Compressive Strength and Cost of Mortar & Grout

Where Used	Mortar Type	Portland Cement	Masonry Cement	Hydrated Lime	Masonry Sand	Compressive Strength @28 days	Cost per Cubic Foot
Plain Masonry	M	1 / 1	1 / —	— / 1/4	6 / 3	2500 psi	$3.00 / 3.52
	S	1/2 / 1	1 / —	— / 1/4 to 1/2	4 / 4	1800 psi	3.19 / 3.15
	N	— / 1	1 / —	— / 1/2 to 1-1/4	3 / 6	750 psi	2.84 / 2.79
	O	— / 1	1 / —	— / 1-1/4 to 2-1/2	3 / 9		2.84 / 2.67
	K	1	—	2-1/2 to 4	12	75 psi	2.61
Reinforced Masonry	PM	1	1	—	6	2500 psi	3.00
	PL	1	—	1/4 to 1/2	4	2500 psi	3.15

Note: The total aggregate should be between 2.25 to 3 times the sum of the cement and lime used.

The labor cost to mix is included in the labor cost on brickwork, etc.

Machine mixing is usually specified on jobs of any size. There is a large price saving over hand mixing and mortar is more uniform.

There are two types of mortar color used. Prices in Section 041-012 are for the inert additive type with about 100 lbs. per M brick as the typical quantity required. These colors are also available in smaller batch size bags (1 lb. to 15 lb.) which can be placed directly into the mixer without measuring. The other type is premixed and replaces the masonry cement with ranges in price from $9 to $18 per 70 lb. bag. Dark green color has the highest cost.

(57) Miscellaneous Mortar (material only) (Div. 041)

Quantities	Glass Block Mortar		Gypsum Cement Mortar	
White waterproofed Portland cement at $15.80 per bag	7 bags	$110.60		
Gypsum cement at $10.85 per 80 lb. bag			11.25 bags	$122.06
Lime at $4.35 per 50 lb. bag	280 lbs.	24.36		
Sand at $20.75 per C.Y.*	1 C.Y.	20.75	1 C.Y.	20.75
Mixing machine and fuel		5.51		5.51
Total per C.Y.		$161.22		$148.32
Approximate Total per C.F.		$5.97		$5.49

* Includes 10 mile haul

CIRCLE REFERENCE NUMBERS

58 Masonry Reinforcing (Div. 041)

Reinforcing prevents wall cracks where there is earth movement due to freezing and thawing. Reinforcing strips come in 10' and 12' lengths. Field labor runs between 2.7 to 5.3 hours per 1000 L.F. for wall thicknesses up to 12". Table below is cost per 1000 L.F., material only, all galvanized. For hot dip galvanizing, add 65%.

Galvanized Reinforcing Size	Type	Wall Thickness						
		4"	6"	8"	10"	12"	14"	16"
9 ga. sides, 9 ga. ties	Regular truss	$125	$130	$135	$145	$155	$170	$185
3/16" sides, 9 ga. ties		170	175	180	185	190	210	235
3/16" sides, 3/16" ties		205	210	225	230	240	275	310
9 ga. sides, 9 ga. ties	Cavity truss	130	135	140	150	165	185	205
3/16" sides, 9 ga. ties		175	180	185	190	195	210	245
9 ga. sides, 9 ga. ties	Ladder	90	95	100	105	110	115	140
9 ga. sides, 9 ga. ties	Cavity Ladder	105	110	115	125	135	150	175
3/16" sides, 9 ga. ties		155	165	175	180	190	195	235

59 Brick, Block & Mortar Quantities (Div. 4)

Running Bond
Number of Brick per S.F. of Wall - Single Wythe with 3/8" Joints

Type Brick	Nominal Size (incl. mortar) L H W	Modular Coursing	Number of Brick per S.F.	C.F. of Mortar per M Bricks, Waste Included	
				3/8" Joint	1/2" Joint
Standard	8 x 2-2/3 x 4	3C=8"	6.75	10.3	12.9
Economy	8 x 4 x 4	1C=4"	4.50	11.4	14.6
Engineer	8 x 3-1/5 x 4	5C=16"	5.63	10.6	13.6
Fire	9 x 2-1/2 x 4-1/2	2C=5"	6.40	550 # Fireclay	—
Jumbo	12 x 4 x 6 or 8	1C=4"	3.00	23.8	30.8
Norman	12 x 2-2/3 x 4	3C=8"	4.50	14.0	17.9
Norwegian	12 x 3-1/5 x 4	5C=16"	3.75	14.6	18.6
Roman	12 x 2 x 4	2C=4"	6.00	13.4	17.0
SCR	12 x 2-2/3 x 6	3C=8"	4.50	21.8	28.0
Utility	12 x 4 x 4	1C=4"	3.00	15.4	19.6

For Other Bonds Standard Size Add to S.F. Quantities in Table to Left

Bond Type	Description	Factor
Common	full header every fifth course	+20%
	full header every sixth course	+16.7%
English	full header every second course	+50%
Flemish	alternate headers every course	+33.3%
	every sixth course	+5.6%
Header = W x H exposed		+100%
Rowlock = H x W exposed		+100%
Rowlock stretcher = L x W exposed		+33.3%
Soldier = H x L exposed		—
Sailor = W x L exposed		−33.3%

Concrete Blocks Nominal Size	Approximate Weight per S.F.		Blocks per 100 S.F.	Mortar per M block	
	Standard	Lightweight		Partitions	Back up
2" x 8" x 16"	20 PSF	15 PSF	113	16 C.F.	36 C.F.
4"	30	20		31	51
6"	42	30		46	66
8"	55	38		62	82
10"	70	47		77	97
12"	85	55		92	112

60 Economy in Bricklaying (Div. 4)

Have adequate supervision. Be sure bricklayers are always supplied with materials so there is no waiting. Place best bricklayers at corners and openings.

Use only screened sand for mortar. Otherwise, labor time will be wasted picking out pebbles. Use seamless metal tubs for mortar as they do not leak or catch trowel. Locate stack and mortar for easy wheeling.

Have brick delivered for stacking. This makes for faster handling, reduces chipping and breakage, and requires less storage space. Many dealers will deliver select common in 2' x 3' x 4' pallets or face brick packaged. This affords quick handling with a crane or forklift and easy tonging in units of ten, which reduces waste.

Use wider bricks for one wythe wall construction. Keep scaffolding away from wall to allow mortar to fall clear and not stain wall.

On large jobs develop specialized crews for each type of masonry unit.

Consider designing for prefabricated panel construction on high rise projects.

Avoid excessive corners or openings. Each opening adds about 50% to labor cost for area of opening.

Bolting stone panels and using window frames as stops reduces labor costs and speeds up erection.

405

CIRCLE REFERENCE NUMBERS

⑥¹ Common and Face Brick Prices (Div. 042)

Prices are truckload lots on Common, carloads on Face Brick. Prices are per M brick.

City	Material Brick per M Delivered Common	Face	City	Material Brick per M Delivered Common	Face	City	Material Brick per M Delivered Common	Face
Atlanta	$170	$210	Detroit	$215	$250	New York City	$300	$330
Baltimore	200	260	Houston	205	245	Philadelphia	210	270
Boston	255	325	Indianapolis	215	285	Phoenix	245	350
Buffalo	265	295	Kansas City	220	260	Pittsburgh	235	285
Chicago	210	320	Los Angeles	255	325	St. Louis	195	260
Cincinnati	185	225	Memphis	195	235	San Antonio	220	270
Cleveland	190	245	Milwaukee	210	280	San Diego	285	375
Columbus	175	250	Minneapolis	215	290	San Francisco	290	390
Dallas	195	230	Nashville	170	230	Seattle	285	350
Denver	160	215	New Orleans	175	215	Washington, D.C.	245	340
						Average	$220	$280

Subcontractors markup on material is normally 10%. A breakage allowance of 3% would also be added. If bricks are delivered palletized with 280 to 300 per pallet or packaged, allow only 1½% for breakage. This would add $10 per M to the cost of brick, but would save approximately two hours on helper's time. The net result is a savings of $20 to $30 per M in place. Packaged or palletized delivery is practical when a job is big enough to have a crane or other equipment to handle a true package of brick. This is true on all industrial work, but not always true on small commercial buildings.

There are many types of red face brick. The prices above are for the most usual type used in commercial, apartment house or industrial construction. If it is possible to obtain the price of the actual brick to be used, it should be done and then substituted in the table. The use of buff and gray face is increasing, and there is a continuing trend to the Norman, Roman, Jumbo and SCR brick.

See ㊾ for brick quantities per S.F. and mortar quantities per M brick. (Average prices for the various sizes are listed in the unit price section of this book.)

The use of common red clay brick for backup has decreased substantially. Concrete block is the most usual backup material, with occasional use of sand lime or cement brick. Sand lime costs about $15 per M less than red clay and cement brick are about $5 per M less than red clay. These figures may be substituted in the common brick breakdown for the cost of these items in place, as labor is about the same. Occasionally, common brick is being used in solid walls for strength and as a fire stop.

Several recent jobs have brick panels built on the ground floor and then crane erected to the upper floors. This allows the work to be done under cover and without scaffolding.

⑥² Brick in Place (Div. 042-184 & 554)

Table below is for common bond with 3/8" concave joints and includes 3% waste for brick and 25% waste for mortar.

Item	8" Common Brick Wall 8" x 2-2/3" x 4"		Select Common Face Veneer 8" x 2-2/3" x 4"		Red Face Brick Veneer 8" x 2-2/3" x 4"	
1030 brick delivered	$220 per M	$226.60	$250 per M	$257.50	$280 per M	$288.40
Type N mortar @ $2.79 per C.F.	12.5 C.F.	34.88	10.3 C.F.	28.74	10.3 C.F.	28.74
Installation using indicated crew (Bare Cost)	Crew D-2 @ 22.24 M.H.	299.35	Crew D-2 @ 25.80 M.H.	347.27	Crew D-2 @ 26.68 M.H.	359.11
Total per M in place		$560.83		$633.51		$676.25
Total per S.F. of wall	13.5 bricks/S.F.	$ 7.57	6.75 bricks/S.F.	$ 4.28	6.75 bricks/S.F.	$ 4.56

⑥³ Brick Veneer in Place (Div. 042-554)

Table below is for common bond with 3/8" concave joints and includes 3% waste for brick and 25% waste for mortar.

Item	Buff Face Brick Veneer 8" x 2-2/3" x 4"		Red Norman Face Brick Veneer 12" x 2-2/3" x 4"		Buff Roman Face Brick Veneer 12" x 2" x 4"	
1030 brick delivered	$355 per M	$365.65	$550 per M	$566.50	$575 per M	$592.25
Type N mortar @ $2.79 per C.F.	10.3 C.F.	28.74	14.0 C.F.	39.06	13.4 C.F.	37.39
Installation using indicated crew	Crew D-2 @ 26.68 M.H.	359.11	Crew D-2 @ 27.60 M.H.	371.50	Crew D-2 @ 26.68 M.H.	359.11
Total per M in place		$753.50		$977.06		$988.75
Total per S.F. of wall	6.75 brick/S.F.	$ 5.09	4.50 bricks/S.F.	$ 4.40	6.00 brick/S.F.	$ 5.93

CIRCLE REFERENCE NUMBERS

65) Brick Chimneys (Div. 042-054)

Quantities	16" x 16"		20" x 20"		20" x 24"		20" x 32"	
Brick at $250 per M	28 brick	$ 7.00	37 brick	$ 9.25	42 brick	$10.50	51 brick	$12.75
Type M mortar at $3.52 per C.F.	.5 C.F.	1.76	.6 C.F.	2.11	1.0 C.F.	3.52	1.3 C.F.	4.58
Flue tile	8" x 8"	2.95	12" x 12"	5.75	2 @ 8" x 12"	9.20	2 @ 12" x 12"	11.50
Install tile & brick, crew D-1	.88 M.H.	11.55	1.17 M.H.	15.35	1.33 M.H.	17.45	1.6 M.H.	20.99
Total per L.F. high		$23.26		$32.46		$40.67		$49.82

Only use 2/3 of the above figures if the chimney butts against a straight wall. Labor for chimney brick using D-1 crew is 31 hours per thousand brick or about $407 per thousand brick. An 8" x 12" flue takes 33 brick and two 8" x 8" flues take 37 brick.

66) Cleaning Face Brick (Div. 045-108)

On smooth brick a man can clean 70 S.F. an hour; on rough brick 50 S.F. per hour. Use one gallon muriatic acid to 20 gallons of water for 1000 S.F. Do not use acid solution until wall is at least seven days old, but a mild soap solution may be used after two days. Commercial cleaners cost from $10 to $15 per gallon.

Time has been allowed for clean-up in brick prices.

68) Ashlar Veneer (Div. 044-504)

Quantities	Medium Price Stone		High Price Stone	
4" Stone, random ashlar, 2.5 tons average	$130 per ton	$325.00	$210 per ton	$525.00
Type N mortar at $2.79 per C.F.	20 C.F.	55.80	20 C.F.	55.80
50 - 1" x 1/4" x 6" galv. stone anchors, at $.95 each		47.50		47.50
Using crew D-8 @ $13.46 per M.H.	30.80 M.H.	414.57	28.60 M.H.	384.96
Total per 1.00 S.F.		$842.87		$1013.26

Stone coverage varies from 30 S.F. to 50 S.F. per ton. Mortar quantities include 1" backing bed.

CIRCLE REFERENCE NUMBERS

(69) Concrete Block (Div. 042)

8" x 16" block, sand aggregate blocks with 3/8 joints for partitions.

City	Material Per Block, Delivered 4" Thick	Material Per Block, Delivered 8" Thick	113 Block, Delivered 4" Thick	113 Block, Delivered 8" Thick	City	Material Per Block, Delivered 4" Thick	Material Per Block, Delivered 8" Thick	113 Block, Delivered 4" Thick	113 Block, Delivered 8" Thick
Atlanta	$.59	$.90	$66.65	$101.70	Memphis	$.55	$.85	$62.15	$96.05
Baltimore	.60	.90	65.55	101.70	Milwaukee	.68	1.00	76.85	113.00
Boston	.68	.96	76.85	108.50	Minneapolis	.65	.95	73.45	107.35
Buffalo	.69	.95	77.95	107.35	Nashville	.65	.85	73.45	96.05
Chicago	.58	.85	65.55	96.05	New Orleans	.68	.95	76.85	107.35
Cincinnati	.55	.80	62.15	90.40	New York City	.70	1.05	79.10	118.65
Cleveland	.64	.95	72.30	107.35	Philadelphia	.60	.90	65.55	101.70
Columbus	.59	.90	66.65	101.70	Phoenix	.54	.95	61.00	107.35
Dallas	.65	.95	73.45	107.35	Pittsburgh	.65	.98	73.45	110.75
Denver	.68	1.00	76.85	113.00	St. Louis	.52	.94	58.75	106.20
Detroit	.68	1.00	76.85	113.00	San Antonio	.65	.95	73.45	107.35
Houston	.75	1.15	84.75	129.95	San Diego	.72	1.10	81.35	124.30
Indianapolis	.65	1.00	73.45	113.00	San Francisco	.80	1.28	90.40	144.65
Kansas City	.68	1.05	76.85	118.65	Seattle	.80	1.25	90.40	141.25
Los Angeles	.68	1.00	76.85	113.00	Washington D.C.	.65	.95	73.45	107.35
					Average	$.65	$.98	$73.45	$110.75

The cost of sand aggregate block is based on the delivered price of 113 blocks, which is the equivalent of a 100 S.F. wall area. Mortar for a 100 S.F. wall area will average $9.75 for 4" thick block and $19.55 for 8" thick block.

Cost for 100 S.F. of 8" x 16" Concrete Block Partitions to Four Stories High, Tooled Joint One Side

8" x 16" Sand Aggregate	4" Thick Block		8" Thick Block		12" Thick Block	
113 block delivered	$.65 ea.	$73.45	$.98 ea.	$110.74	$1.38 ea.	$155.94
Type N mortar at $2.79 per C.F.	3.5 C.F.	9.77	7.0 C.F.	19.53	10.4 C.F.	29.02
Installation crew (Bare Cost)	D-2 9.32 M.H.	125.45	D-2 10.68 M.H.	143.75	D-6 14.70 M.H.	192.86
Total per 100 S.F.		$208.67		$274.02		$377.82
Add for filling cores solid	6.7 C.F.	$91.00	25.8 C.F.	$173.00	42.2 C.F.	$233.00

Cost for 100 S.F. of 8" x 16" Concrete Block Backup with Trowel Cut Joints

8" x 16" Sand Aggregate	4" Thick Block		8" Thick Block		12" Thick Block	
113 block delivered	$.65 Ea.	$73.45	$.98 Ea.	$110.74	$1.38 Ea.	$155.94
Type N mortar at $2.79 per C.F.	5.8 C.F.	16.18	9.3 C.F.	25.95	12.7 C.F.	35.43
Installation crew (Bare Cost)	D-8 9.20 M.H.	123.83	D-8 10.10 M.H.	135.95	D-9 13.20 M.H.	173.18
Total per 100 S.F.		$213.46		$272.64		$364.55

Special block: corner, jamb and head block are same price as ordinary block of same size. Tabulated on the next page are national average prices per block. Labor on specials is about the same as equal sized regular block. Bond beam and 16" high lintel blocks cost 30% more than regular units of equal size.

Lintel blocks are 8" long and 8" or 16" high. Costs in individual cities may be factored from the table above.

Use of motorized mortar spreader box will speed construction of continuous walls.

CIRCLE REFERENCE NUMBERS

(69) Concrete Block (cont.)

Size in Inches	Type	\multicolumn{9}{c}{Net Area Strength in PSI, Material Cost per Block}	Lightweight	
		2000	2500	3000	3500	4000	4500	5000	5500	6000	Std.	Prem.
2 x 8 x 16	Solid	$ .53	$ .54	$ .57	$ .58	$ .59	$ .64	$ .66	$ .71	$ .74	$ .55	$ .76
3 x 8 x 16	Solid	.85	.90	.93	.94	.96	.99	1.00	1.03	1.07	1.08	1.48
4 x 8 x 16	Hollow	.65	.68	.70	.72	.75	.78	.79	.81	.84	.73	.97
	75% Solid	.81	.84	.87	.88	.91	.97	1.04	1.10	1.16	.98	1.31
	Solid	.86	.90	.94	.95	.98	1.00	1.05	1.12	1.18	1.08	1.48
6 x 8 x 16	Hollow	.77	.80	.85	.86	.91	.94	.99	1.04	1.10	.96	1.31
	75% Solid	1.01	1.05	1.12	1.13	1.20	1.23	1.30	1.38	1.43	1.39	1.53
	Solid	1.19	1.24	1.31	1.33	1.40	1.48	1.52	1.60	1.64	1.49	1.66
8 x 8 x 16	Hollow	.98	1.00	1.05	1.08	1.12	1.20	1.30	1.35	1.45	1.25	1.52
	75% Solid	1.19	1.25	1.33	1.35	1.43	1.46	1.48	1.54	1.62	1.69	2.05
	Solid	1.44	1.50	1.59	1.62	1.71	1.76	1.84	1.90	1.96	1.92	2.23
	Bond Beam	1.26	—	—	—	—	—	—	—	—	1.63	1.95
	Sash	1.00	—	—	—	—	—	—	—	—	1.37	1.53
	Interlocking	1.06	—	1.25	—	1.35	—	—	—	—	—	—
10 x 8 x 16	Hollow	1.38	1.40	1.48	1.51	1.60	1.70	1.84	1.88	2.00	1.90	2.25
	75% Solid	1.75	1.83	1.95	1.99	2.11	2.15	2.19	2.25	2.33	2.35	2.70
	Solid	2.15	2.24	2.38	2.42	2.56	2.58	2.64	2.70	2.82	2.85	3.35
12 x 8 x 16	Hollow	1.38	1.40	1.48	1.51	1.60	1.70	1.82	1.85	1.97	1.90	2.25
	75% Solid	1.85	1.93	2.05	2.09	2.30	2.34	2.40	2.52	2.60	2.50	2.85
	Solid	2.20	2.29	2.43	2.47	2.61	2.66	2.75	2.81	2.94	3.00	3.50
	Bond Beam	1.83	—	—	—	—	—	—	—	—	2.39	2.80
	Sash	1.45	—	—	—	—	—	—	—	—	2.00	2.40
	Fire Rated	1.95	—	—	—	—	—	—	—	—	2.60	3.20
	Interlocking	1.55	—	1.85	—	2.00	—	—	—	—	—	—
16 x 8 x 16	Interlocking	2.25	—	2.65	—	2.80	—	—	—	—	—	—

CIRCLE REFERENCE NUMBERS

(74) Pre-engineered Steel Buildings (Div. 051-235)

These buildings are manufactured by many companies and normally erected by franchised dealers throughout the U.S. The four basic types are: Rigid Frames, Truss type, Post and Beam and the Sloped Beam type. Most popular roof slope is low pitch of 1" in 12". The minimum economical area of these buildings is about 3000 S.F. of floor area. Bay sizes are usually 20' to 24' but can go as high as 30' with heavier girts and purlins. Eave heights are usually 12' to 24' with 18' to 20' most typical. Pre-engineered buildings become increasingly economical with higher eave heights.

Prices shown here are for the building shell only and do not include floors, foundations, interior finishes or utilities. Erection of the frame and insulated roof runs $1.05 to $1.35 per S.F. Insulated side wall installation runs about $1.10 per S.F. of skin. Typical erection cost including both siding and roofing depends on the building shape and runs $1.30 to $2.50 for one in twelve roof slope and $1.35 to $3.50 per S.F. of floor for four in twelve roof slope. Site, weather, labor source, shape and size of project will determine the erection cost of each job. Prices include erector's overhead and profit.

Table below is based on 30 psf roof load, 20 psf wind load and no unusual structural requirements. Costs assume at least three bays of 24' each. Material costs include the structural frame, 26 ga. colored steel roofing, 26 ga. colored steel siding, fasteners, closures and flashing but no allowance for doors, windows, gutters or skylights. Very large projects would generally cost less than the prices listed below. Typical budget figures for above material delivered to the job runs $1190 to $1420 per ton. Fasteners and flashings (included below) run $.45 to $.65 per S.F.

Material Costs per S.F. of Floor Area Above the Foundations

Type of Building	Total Width in Feet	Eave Height 10 Ft.	14 Ft.	16 Ft.	20 Ft.	24 Ft.
Rigid Frame Clear Span	30-40	$3.45	$3.75	$4.05	$4.45	$5.00
	50-100	3.50	3.55	3.85	4.05	4.45
	110	—	—	—	—	—
	120	—	—	—	3.80	—
	130	—	—	—	—	—
Tapered Beam Clear Span	30	3.70	4.10	4.50	4.80	—
	40	3.40	3.65	3.90	4.35	—
	50-80	3.30	3.45	3.65	3.90	—
Post & Beam 1 Post at Center	80	—	3.00	3.30	3.50	3.85
	100	—	2.90	3.10	3.45	3.75
	120	—	2.85	2.95	3.15	3.55
Post & Beam 2 Posts at 1/3 Points	120	—	—	—	—	—
	150	—	2.90	3.10	3.30	3.75
	180	—	—	—	—	—
Post & Beam 3 Posts at 1/4 points	160	—	2.85	2.95	3.30	3.60
	200	—	2.90	3.10	3.35	3.65
	240	—	—	—	—	—

Typical accessory items are listed in the front of the book. All normal interior work, floors, foundations, utilities and sitework should be figured the same as usual.

Costs in the table below include allowance for erection, normal doors, windows, gutters and erector's overhead and profit. Figures do not include foundations, floors, interior finishes, electrical, mechanical or installed equipment.

Total Cost per S.F. Above the Foundations, 16' Eave Height

Project Size: Rigid Frame 30' to 60' Spans 1 in 12 Roof Slope	Basic Building Using 26 ga. Galvanized Roof & Siding S.F. Floor Area	R20 Field Insulation S.F. Floor Area	Add to Basic Building Price Exterior Finish	S.F. of Skin
			Sandwich wall	$3.00 to $3.45
			Vinyl clad steel	—
4,000 S.F.	$5.30	$2.45	Corrugated fiberglass	1.00
10,000 S.F.	4.65	1.95	Corr. fiberglass-insulated	1.10
20,000 S.F.	4.30	1.80	20 year paint	.10

CIRCLE REFERENCE NUMBERS

(83) Plywood (Div. 061)

There are two types of plywood used in construction: interior, which is moisture resistant but not waterproofed, and exterior, which is waterproofed.

The grade of the exterior surface of the plywood sheets is designated by the first letter: A, for smooth surface with patches allowed; B, for solid surface with patches and plugs allowed; C, which may be surface plugged or may have knot holes up to 1" wide; and D, which is used only for interior type plywood and may have knot holes up to 2-1/2" wide. "Structural Grade" is specifically designed for engineered applications such as box beams. All CC & DD grades have roof and floor spans marked on them.

Underlayment grade plywood runs from 1/4" to 1-1/4" thick. Thicknesses 5/8" and over have optional tongue and groove joints which eliminates the need for blocking the edges. Underlayment 19/32" and over may be referred to as Sturd-i-Floor.

The price of plywood can fluctuate widely due to geographic and economic conditions. When one or two local prices are known, the relative prices for other types and sizes may be found by direct factoring of the prices in the table below.

Typical uses for various plywood grades are as follows:
AA-AD Interior — cupboards, shelving, paneling, furniture
B-B Plyform — concrete form plywood
CDX — wall and roof sheathing
Structural — box beams, girders, stressed skin panels
AA-AC Exterior — fences, signs, siding, soffits, etc.
Underlayment — base for resilient floor coverings
Overlaid HDO — high density for concrete forms & highway signs
Overlaid MDO — medium density for painting, siding, soffits & signs
303 siding — exterior siding, textured, striated, embossed, etc.

Grade	National Average Price in Lots of 10 MSF, per MSF-January 1991						
	Type	4'x8'	Type	4'x8'	4'x10'
Sanded Grade	1/4" Interior AD 3/8" 1/2" 5/8" 3/4" 1" 1-1/4" Interior AA, add	$330 385 480 525 565 675 810 105	1/4" Exterior AC 3/8" 1/2" 5/8" 3/4" 1" Exterior AA, add Exterior AB, add	$380 440 500 560 630 720 105 90	$390 450 510 570 640 730 100 90
			CD Structural 1		**Underlayment**	
Un-sanded Grade 4'x8' Sheets	5/16" CDX 3/8" 1/2" 5/8" 3/4" 3/4" T&G	$225 240 290 360 420 460	5/16", 4'x8' sheets 3/8" 1/2" 5/8" 3/4"	$230 260 325 375 425	3/8", 4'x8' sheets 1/2" 5/8" 3/4" 1-1/8" 2-4-1	$290 325 400 460 675
Form Plywood	5/8" Exterior, oiled BB, plyform 3/4" Exterior, oiled BB, plyform	$620 710	5/8" HDO (overlay 2 sides) 3/4" HDO (overlay 2 sides)		$1,325 1,700
Overlaid 4'x8' Sheets	Overlay 2 Sides MDO 3/8" thick 1/2" 5/8" 3/4"	$740 860 950 1,030	Overlay 1 Side MDO 3/8" thick 1/2" 5/8" 3/4"		$590 670 810 870
303 Siding	Fir, rough sawn, natural finish, 3/8" thick Redwood Cedar Southern Yellow Pine	$490 1,350 1,350 340	Texture 1-11 5/8" thick, Fir Redwood Cedar Southern Yellow		$630 1,785 1,785 460
Waferboard/O.S.B.	1/4" sheathing 7/16" sheathing	$175 225	19/32" T&G 23/32" T&G		$300 320

For 2 MSF to 10 MSF, add 10%. For less than 2 MSF, add 15%.

CIRCLE REFERENCE NUMBERS

(84) Wood Stair, Residential (Div. 064-308)

One Flight with 8'-6" Story Height, 3'-6" Wide Oak Treads Open One Side, Built in Place				
Item	Quantity	Unit Cost	Bare Costs	Costs Incl. Subs O & P
Treads 10-1/2" x 1-1/16" thick	11 Ea.	$ 20.00	$ 220.00	$ 242.00
Landing tread nosing, rabbeted	1 Ea.	7.00	7.00	7.70
Risers 3/4" thick	12 Ea.	10.10	121.20	133.32
Single end starting step (range $90 to $155)	1 Ea.	122.50	122.50	134.75
Balusters (range $3.50 to $9.00)	22 Ea.	6.25	137.50	151.25
Newels, starting & landing (range $36 to $85)	2 Ea.	60.50	121.00	133.10
Rail starter (range $29 to $80)	1 Ea.	54.50	54.50	59.95
Handrail (range $3.50 to $7.50)	26 L.F.	5.50	143.00	157.30
Cove trim	50 L.F.	.37	18.50	20.35
Rough stringers three - 2 x 12's, 14' long	84 B.F.	.46	38.64	42.50
Carpenters installation: Bare Cost Cost incl. Subs O & P	36 Hrs.	$ 14.30 23.90	$ 514.80	$ 860.40
	Total per Flight		$1,498.64	$1,942.62

Add for rail return on second floor and for varnishing or other finish. Adjoining walls or landings must be figured separately.

(85) Wood Roof Trusses (Div. 061-908)

Loading figures represent live load. An additional load of 10 psf on the top chord and 10 psf on the bottom chord is included in the truss design. Spacing is 24" O.C.

Span in Feet	Cost per Truss for Different Live Loads and Roof Pitches					
	Flat	4 in 12 Pitch		5 in 12 Pitch		8 in 12 Pitch
	40 psf	30 psf	40 psf	30 psf	40 psf	30 psf
20	$ 49.00	$32.00	$37.00	$31.00	$36.00	$35.00
22	54.00	34.00	40.00	34.00	39.00	38.00
24	58.00	36.00	44.00	37.00	42.00	41.00
26	63.00	42.00	47.00	40.00	46.00	45.00
28	67.00	44.00	51.00	42.00	49.00	48.00
30	72.00	46.00	54.00	45.00	53.00	52.00
32	87.00	51.00	58.00	55.00	56.00	55.00
34	93.00	52.00	62.00	55.00	60.00	67.00
36	99.00	58.00	66.00	57.00	64.00	71.00
38	113.00	59.00	70.00	61.00	71.00	84.00
40	120.00	69.00	83.00	64.00	80.00	102.00

CIRCLE REFERENCE NUMBERS

(86) Thirty City Lumber Prices (Jan. 1st, 1991) (Div. 061)

Prices for boards are for #2 or better or sterling, whichever is in best supply. Dimension lumber is "Standard or Better" either Southern Yellow Pine (S.Y.P.), Spruce-Pine-Fir (S.P.F.), Hem-Fir (H.F.) or Douglas Fir (D.F.). The species of lumber used in a geographic area is listed by city. Rough sawn lumber is Douglas Fir, Hem-Fir, or a variety of hardwood, sheathing or lagging grade. Plyform is 3/4" BB oil sealed fir or S.Y.P. whichever prevails locally, 5/8" CDX is S.Y.P. or Fir.

These are prices at the time of publication and should be checked against the current market price. Relative differences between cities will stay approximately constant.

City	Species	S4S Dimensions 2"x4"	2"x6"	2"x10"	Boards 1"x6"	1"x12"	Rough Sawn Lumber 3"x12"	6"x12"	12"x12"	3/4" Ext. Plyform	5/8" Thick CDX
Atlanta	S.Y.P.	$395	$370	$425	$515	$665	$575	$670	$720	$740	$375
Baltimore	S.P.F.	450	390	490	540	700	605	705	760	730	355
Boston	S.P.F.	350	350	420	490	635	600	700	755	730	350
Buffalo	S.P.F.	355	350	450	485	625	540	630	680	670	330
Chicago	S.P.F.	390	380	525	525	680	585	680	735	760	410
Cincinnati	S.Y.P.	345	325	430	450	585	510	595	640	700	355
Cleveland	S.P.F.	475	470	575	650	830	705	750	805	800	460
Columbus	S.P.F.	330	330	425	460	600	520	610	660	760	405
Dallas	S.Y.P.	430	400	510	560	725	625	725	780	790	405
Denver	H.F.	330	320	410	445	570	490	570	615	750	360
Detroit	S.P.F.	340	320	420	445	575	495	575	620	700	310
Houston	S.Y.P.	325	305	410	420	540	465	540	585	620	350
Indianapolis	S.P.F.	340	340	435	470	605	520	605	650	600	275
Kansas City	D.F.	385	380	460	520	670	575	670	720	650	360
Los Angeles	D.F.	410	405	500	560	725	625	725	780	770	375
Memphis	S.Y.P.	380	365	455	500	645	555	645	695	720	340
Milwaukee	S.P.F.	380	380	520	525	680	585	680	735	640	315
Minneapolis	S.P.F.	365	350	445	480	620	535	625	675	630	360
Nashville	S.Y.P.	305	305	395	420	545	470	545	590	680	345
New Orleans	S.Y.P.	355	350	450	485	630	545	635	685	600	295
New York City	H.F.	485	485	560	660	850	735	855	910	700	425
Philadelphia	H.F.	410	405	500	560	725	625	730	785	720	365
Phoenix	S.Y.P.	365	355	455	490	635	550	640	690	810	395
Pittsburgh	S.P.F.	390	385	485	530	690	595	695	750	640	305
St. Louis	S.Y.P.	345	340	380	470	610	525	610	660	800	330
San Antonio	S.Y.P.	350	340	445	470	610	530	615	665	600	310
San Diego	D.F.	330	325	405	450	590	545	640	690	750	375
San Francisco	D.F.	370	370	475	510	660	570	660	710	790	390
Seattle	D.F.	280	280	390	385	500	435	505	545	670	365
Washington, DC	H.F.	380	380	470	525	680	585	680	735	800	420
Average		$370	$360	$460	$500	$650	$560	$650	$700	$710	$360

To convert square feet of surface to board feet, 4% waste included

S4S Size	Multiply S.F. by	T & G Size	Multiply S.F. by	Flooring Size	Multiply S.F. by
1 x 4	1.18	1 x 4	1.27	25/32" x 2-1/4"	1.37
1 x 6	1.13	1 x 6	1.18	25/32" x 3-1/4"	1.29
1 x 8	1.11	1 x 8	1.14	15/32" x 1-1/2"	1.54
1 x 10	1.09	2 x 6	2.36	1" x 3"	1.28
				1" x 4"	1.24

CIRCLE REFERENCE NUMBERS

(87) Lumber Product Material Prices (Div. 061, 062, 073 & 096)

The price of forest products fluctuates widely from location to location and from season to season depending upon economic conditions. The table below indicates National Average material prices in effect Jan. 1, 1991. The table shows relative differences between various sizes, grades and species. These percentage differentials remain fairly constant even though lumber prices in general may change significantly during the year.

Availability of certain items depends upon geographic location and must be checked prior to firm price bidding.

National Average Contractor Price, Quantity Purchase

Dimension Lumber, S4S, #2 & Better, KD | Heavy Timbers, Fir

	Species	2"x4"	2"x6"	2"x8"	2"x10"	2"x12"		
Framing Lumber per MBF	Douglas Fir	$355	$350	$340	$450	$465	3"x4" thru 3"x12"	$560
	Spruce	335	370	365	470	475	4"x4" thru 4"x12"	560
	Southern Yellow Pine	360	345	345	435	450	6"x6" thru 6"x12"	650
	Hem-Fir	400	400	410	485	490	8"x8" thru 8"x12"	650
	Redwood	940	940	940	995	995	10"x10" and 10"x12"	700

S4S "D" Quality or Clear, KD | S4S #2 & Better or Sterling, KD

	Species	1"x4"	1"x6"	1"x8"	1"x10"	1"x12"	Species	1"x4"	1"x6"	1"x8"	1"x10"	1"x12"
Boards per MBF *see also Cedar Siding	Sugar Pine	$1,375	$1,375	$1,200	$1,300	$1,740	Sugar Pine	—	$440	$430	$430	$650
	Idaho Pine	695	1,100	1,000	1,435	1,650	Idaho Pine	$700	700	700	700	710
	Engleman Spruce	600	975	975	1,000	1,400	Engleman Spruce	400	475	405	400	630
	So. Yellow Pine	450	575	560	530	670	So. Yellow Pine	310	320	310	305	375
	Ponderosa Pine	740	1,040	870	1,450	1,710	Ponderosa Pine	445	440	425	410	650
	Redwood, CVG	1,990	2,300	2,350	2,800	3,000						
	Finger Jt. Heart	1,530	1,800	1,990	2,140	2,140						

Flooring per MSF	1"x4" Vertical grain, Fir "B" & better	$1,800	2-1/4"x25/32" Maple, select	$2,400
	2-1/4"x25/32", Oak, clear	2,300	#2 & better	2,000
	Select	2,200	2-1/4"x33/32" Maple, #2 & better	2,400
	#1 common	1,850	3-1/4"x33/32" Maple, #2 & better	2,300
	Oak, prefinished, standard & better	2,650	Parquet, unfinished, 5/16", minimum	1,450
	Standard	2,250	Maximum	4,600

Siding per MSF	Clapboard, Cedar, beveled		*Rough sawn, Cedar, T&G, "A" grade 1"x4"	$1,750
	1/2" x6" thru 1/2"x8", clear	$1,100	1"x6"	2,150
	"A" grade	930	"STK" grade, 1"x6"	1,200
	"B" grade	700	Board, "STK" grade, 1"x8"	1,150
	3/4"x10" "clear"	1,820	Board & Batten 1" x 12"	1,200
	"A" grade	1,680	Cedar channel siding 1"x8", #3 & better	$1,150
	Redwood, beveled		Factory stained	1,250
	1/2"x6" thru 1/2"x8", vertical grain, clear	910	White Pine siding, T&G, rough sawn	$390
	3/4"x10" vertical grain, clear	1,720	Factory stained	430

Shingles per CFS	Red Cedar		White Cedar shingles	
	5X—16" long #1 regular	$90	16" long, extra grade	$100
	#2	60	Clear, 1st grade	90
	18" long perfections #1	95		
	#2	60	Fire retardant Red Cedar	
	Resquared & Rebutted #1	70	5X — 16" long	$160
	#2	65	18" long perfections	175
	Handsplit shakes, resawn		Handsplit & resawn	
	24" long, 1/2" to 3/4"	90	24" long, 1/2" to 3/4"	175
	18" long, 1/2" to 3/4"	95	3/4" to 5/4"	185

CIRCLE REFERENCE NUMBERS

(88) Roof Slate (Div. 073-106)

16", 18" and 20" are standard lengths and slate usually comes in random widths. For standard 3/16" thickness use 1-1/4" copper nails. Allow for 3% breakage.

Quantities Per Square	Unfading Vermont Colored	Weathering Sea Green	Buckingham, Virginia Black, Clear
Slate delivered (incl. punching)	$377.50	$287.50	$337.50
# 30 Felt, copper nails	12.50	12.50	12.50
Slate roofer 4.6 hrs. @ $13.30 per M.H.	61.18	61.18	61.18
Total Bare Cost per Square	$451.18	$361.18	$411.18

(89) 1/2" Pargeting (rough dampproofing plaster) (Div. 071-802)

1:2-1/2 Mix, 4.5 C.F. Covers 100 S.F., 2 Coats, Waste Included	Regular Portland Cement		Waterproofed Portland Cement	
1.7 lbs. integral waterproofing admixture			80¢ per lb.	$ 1.35
1.7 bags portland cement	$6.55 per bag	$11.15	$6.55 per bag	11.15
4.25 C.F. sand at $20.75 per C.Y.		3.25		3.25
Labor mix, apply, crew D-1 at $13.12 per M.H.	6.4 M.H.	83.97	6.4 M.H.	83.97
Total Bare Cost per 100 S.F.		$98.37		$99.72

(94) Front Door, Residential (Div. 082-078)

Figures below do not include Subs O & P.

Size 3'-0" x 6'-8" x 1-3/4"	Item Location	Deluxe Colonial Design Pine		Modern Flush Solid Core Birch	
Door, glazed with small panels	082-078		$260.00		$120.00
Exterior frame and trim, stock unit	082-054		66.00		66.00
Entrance sill and interior trim (Colonial range $140 to $1,150)	082-054		255.00		140.00
Hardware (with brass cylinder set)	087-116+120		100.00		100.00
Install door, carpenter @ $14.30 per M.H.		1.0 M.H.	14.30	1.0 M.H.	14.30
Install hardware		1.0 M.H.	14.30	1.0 M.H.	14.30
Install entrance, frame and trim		3.0 M.H.	42.90	1.5 M.H.	21.45
Complete in place			$752.50		$476.05

(95) Hollow Metal Doors (Div. 081-103 & 110)

Table below lists material prices only, not including hardware or labor.

	Door Thickness and Size	Full Flush Doors, 18 Ga.				Flush Fire Doors			
		Hollow Core		Composite Core		Hollow Core "B"		Composite Core "A"	
		Plain	Glazed	Plain	Glazed	20 Ga.	18 Ga.	16 Ga.	18 Ga.
1-3/4"	3'-0" x 6'-8"	$181	$230	$198	$254	$175	$198	—	$200
	3'-0" x 7'-0"	188	238	205	265	184	205	$235	210
	3'-6" x 7'-0"	209	250	225	285	—	225	266	227
	3'-0" x 8'-0"	233	300	260	320	—	250	282	253
	4'-0" x 8'-0"	267	330	290	345	—	285	—	285
1-3/8"	2'-0" x 6'-8"	122*	163*	—	—	156	—	—	—
	2'-6" x 6'-8"	130*	173*	—	—	172	—	—	—
	3'-0" x 7'-0"	146*	184*	—	—	185	—	—	—

*Indicates 20 gauge doors.

CIRCLE REFERENCE NUMBERS

(96) Hollow Metal Frames (Div. 081-118)

Table below lists material prices only.

Frame for Opening Size	16 Ga. Frames 6-3/4" Deep	16 Ga. Frames 8-3/4" Deep	16 Ga. UL Frames 6-3/4" Deep	16 Ga. UL Frames 8-3/4" Deep	16 Ga. Drywall Frames 7-1/8" Deep	16 Ga. Drywall Frames 8-1/4" Deep	16 Ga. UL Drywall Frames 7-1/8" Deep	16 Ga. UL Drywall Frames 8-1/4" Deep
2'-0" x 6'-8"	$67	$78	$75	$82	$78	$97	$92	$109
2'-6" x 6'-8"	67	78	76	84	78	99	92	111
3'-0" x 7'-0"	69	80	77	89	79	103	94	113
3'-6" x 7'-0"	71	82	80	92	79	105	94	115
4'-0" x 7'-0"	74	81	92	100	83	107	98	117
6'-0" x 7'-0"	85	96	102	114	94	129	116	146
8'-0" x 8'-0"	108	135	132	136	113	142	136	162

For welded frames, add $30.00   For galvanized frames, add $22.00

(97) Wood Doors (Div. 082)

Table below lists price per door only, not including frame, hardware or labor. For pre-hung exterior door units up to 3' x 7', add $133 per door for wood frame and hardware for types not listed under pre-hung. Pricing is for ten or more doors. Doors are factory trimmed for butts and locksets.

Door Thickness and Size		Flush Type Doors Hollow Core Lauan	Flush Type Doors Hollow Core Birch	Flush Type Doors Solid Particle Core Lauan	Flush Type Doors Solid Particle Core Birch	Flush Type Doors Solid Particle Core Oak	Architectural Pine Panel	Architectural Pine Glazed	Architectural Fir Panel	Architectural Fir Glazed	Pre-hung Pine Panel	Pre-hung Flush Birch Solid Core
1-3/4"	2'-6" x 6'-8"	$32	$36	$46	$49*	$58	$218	$208	$145	$170	$320	$177
	3'-0" x 6'-8"	34	39	49	53*	64	235	224	150	176	355	190
	3'-0" x 7'-0"	41	47	54	58*	69	247	248	160	177	371	198
	3'-6" x 7'-0"	—	—	—	68*	82	—	—	—	—	—	—
	4'-0" x 7'-0"	—	—	—	73*	88	—	—	—	—	—	—
1-3/8"	2'-0" x 6'-8"	28	31	41	43	51	98	—	147	—	197	155
	2'-6" x 6'-8"	29	35	43	46	55	102	—	149	—	202	157
	3'-0" x 6'-8"	31	38	46	50	61	120	—	155	—	220	165
	3'-0" x 7'-0"	38	46	51	55	66	—	—	162	—	—	—

*Add to the above for the following birch face door types:

Solid wood core, add $35
3/4 hour label door, add $60
1 hour label door, add $70
1-1/2 hour label door, add 100%
8' high door, add 30%
Acoustical door, add 220%
Static shielded door, add 500%
Lead lined door, add 450%
Vinyl laminated door, add 100%

(98) Wood Interior Door, Residential (Div. 082-078)

Figures below do not include Subs Overhead & Profit.

Item	Item Location	6 Panel Pine	Flush Birch Hollow Core	Louvered Pine
Door 3'-0" x 6'-8" x 1-3/8" thick	082-078	$120.00	$ 38.00	$124.00
Frame 1-3/8" x 4-5/8", stock pine	082-054	35.00	35.00	35.00
Trim interior	062-208	24.48	24.48	24.48
Hardware incl. hinge & lockset	087-120	50.00	50.00	50.00
Install door, F-2 Crew @ $13.70 per M.H.	.94 M.H.	12.88	12.88	12.88
Install hardware, 1 Carp.	.7 M.H.	10.01	10.01	10.01
Install frame and trim, 1 Carp.	2.0 M.H.	28.60	28.60	28.60
Total in Place		$280.97	$198.97	$284.97

CIRCLE REFERENCE NUMBERS

(101) Hinges (Div. 087-116)

All closer equipped doors should have ball bearing hinges. Lead lined or extremely heavy doors require special strength hinges.

Usually 1-1/2 pair of hinges are used per door up to 7'-6" high openings. Table below shows typical hinge requirements.

Use Frequency	Type Hinge Required	Type of Opening	Type of Structure
High	Heavy weight ball bearing	Entrances Toilet Rooms	Banks, Office buildings, Schools, Stores & Theaters Office buildings and Schools
Average	Standard weight ball bearing	Entrances Corridors Toilet Rooms	Dwellings Office buildings and Schools Stores
Low	Plain bearing	Interior	Dwellings

Door Thickness	Weight of Doors in Pounds per Square Foot					
	White Pine	Oak	Hollow Core	Solid Core	Hollow Metal
1-3/8"	3 psf	6 psf	1-1/2 psf	3-1/2 — 4 psf	6-1/2 psf
1-3/4"	3-1/2	7	2	4-1/2 — 5-1/4	6-1/2
2-1/4"	4-1/2	9	—	5-1/2 — 6-3/4	6-1/2

(102) D. H. Wood Window (ready hung) (Div. 086-124)

Ponderosa pine sash, glazed and exterior primed.

Description	2'-0" x 3'-0"			3'-0" x 4'-0"		
	Plain Glazed		Insulating Glass		Plain Glazed		Insulating Glass
Window and frame, 2 lights		$ 75.00		$117.00		$105.00		$155.00
Removable grilles		10.00		10.00		14.00		14.00
Aluminum storm/screen		42.00		42.00		58.30		58.30
Interior trim set		10.00		10.00		13.50		13.50
Carpenter @ $14.30 per M.H.	2.5 M.H.	35.75	2.5 M.H.	35.75	3.2 M.H.	45.76	3.2 M.H.	45.76
Complete in place		$172.75		$214.75		$236.56		$286.56

Mullions for above windows are about $25 each. Vinyl clad double-hung windows run about $18 per square foot of glass.

Aluminum clad double-hung windows run about $20 per square foot of glass.

(109) Vermiculite or Perlite Plaster (Div. 092-116)

Proportions: Over lath, scratch coat and brown coat 100# gypsum plaster to 2 C.F. aggregate; over masonry, 100# gypsum plaster to 3 C.F. aggregate.

Quantities for 100 S.Y.	2 Coat, 5/8" Thick			3 Coat, 3/4" Thick		
	Quantities	Bare Cost	Incl. O & P	Quantities	Bare Cost	Incl. O & P
Gypsum plaster @ $12.20 per 80 lb. bag	1250 lb.	$190.65	$ 209.70	2250 lb.	$ 343.15	$ 377.45
Vermiculite or perlite @ $12.35 per bag	7.8 bags	96.35	106.00	11.3 bags	139.55	153.50
Finish hydrated lime @ $4.35 per 50 lb. bag	340 lb.	29.60	32.55	340 lb.	29.60	32.55
Gauging plaster @ $16.05 per 100 lb. bag	170 lb.	27.30	30.05	170 lb.	27.30	30.05
J-1 crew @ $13.98 & $22.47 per M.H.	40.0 M.H.	559.20	898.80	50.0 M.H.	699.00	1,123.50
Cleaning, staging, handling, patching	3.6 M.H.	50.35	80.90	4.0 M.H.	55.90	89.90
Total per 100 S.Y. in place		$ 953.45	$1,358.00		$1,294.50	$1,806.95

CIRCLE REFERENCE NUMBERS

⑩ Gypsum Plaster (Div. 092-108)

Quantities for 100 S.Y.	2 Coat, 5/8" Thick		3 Coat, 3/4" Thick		
	Base	Finish	Scratch	Brown	Finish
	1:3 Mix	2:1 Mix	1:2 Mix	1:3 Mix	2:1 Mix
Gypsum plaster	1300 lb.		1350 lb.	650 lb.	
Sand	2.6 C.Y.		1.85 C.Y.	1.35 C.Y.	
Finish hydrated lime		340 lb.			340 lb.
Gauging plaster		170 lb.			170 lb.

Total, in Place for 100 S.Y. on Walls	2 Coat, 5/8" Thick			3 Coat, 3/4" Thick		
	Quantities	Bare Cost	Incl. O & P	Quantities	Bare Cost	Incl. O & P
Gypsum plaster @ $12.20 per 80 lb. bag	1300 lb.	$198.25	$218.10	2000 lb.	$305.00	$335.50
Finish hydrated lime @ $4.35 per 50 lb. bag	340 lb.	29.60	32.55	340 lb.	29.60	32.55
Gauging plaster @ $16.05 per 100 lb. bag	170 lb.	27.30	30.05	170 lb.	27.30	30.05
Sand @ $18.00 per C.Y.	2.6 C.Y.	46.80	51.50	3.2 C.Y.	57.60	63.35
J-1 crew @ $13.98 & $22.47 per M.H.	34.8 M.H.	486.50	781.95	42.0 M.H.	587.15	943.75
Cleaning, staging, handling, patching	3.6 M.H.	50.35	80.90	4.0 M.H.	55.90	89.90
Total per 100 S.Y. in place		$838.80	$1,195.05		$1,062.55	$1,495.10

⑪ Stucco (Div. 092-304)

Quantities for 100 S.Y. 3 Coats, 1" Thick	On Wood Frame			On Masonry		
	Quantities	Bare Cost	Incl. O & P	Quantities	Bare Cost	Incl. O & P
Portland cement at $6.55 per bag	29 bags	$189.95	$208.95	21 bags	$137.55	$151.30
Sand at $18.00 per C.Y.	3.2 C.Y.	57.60	63.35	2.4 C.Y.	43.20	47.50
Hydrated lime at $4.35 per 50 lb. bag	180 lb.	15.65	17.20	120 lb.	10.45	11.50
Painted stucco mesh at $2.89 per S.Y., 3.6#	105 S.Y.	303.45	333.80	—	—	—
Furring nails and jute fiber		15.60	17.15		—	—
Mix and install with crew indicated	J-2 @ 87.4 M.H.	1,225.35	1,970.85	J-1 @ 68.8 M.H.	961.80	1,545.95
Cleaning, staging, handling, patching	4.8 M.H.	67.30	108.25	4.0 M.H.	55.90	89.90
Total per 100 S.Y. in place		$1,874.90	$2,719.55		$1,208.90	$1,846.15

⑬ Resilient Flooring and Base (Div. 096-600)

Description	12" x 12" x 3/32" V.C. Tile			4" x 1/8" Vinyl Base		
	Quantities	Bare Cost	Incl. O & P	Quantities	Bare Cost	Incl. O & P
Vinyl composition, tile, standard line	100 S.F.	$75.00	$82.50	100 L.F.	$60.00	$66.00
Vinyl cement at $11.85 per gallon	0.8 gallon	9.50	10.45	0.5 gallon	5.95	6.55
Tile layer at $14.40 and $22.90 per M.H.	1.5 M.H.	21.60	34.35	2.7 M.H.	38.90	61.85
Total per 100 S.F. in place		$106.10	$127.30	100 L.F.	$104.85	$134.40

⑭ Wall Covering (Div. 099-700)

Quantities for 100 S.F.	Medium Price Paper			Expensive Paper		
	Quantities	Bare Cost	Incl. O & P	Quantities	Bare Cost	Incl. O & P
Paper at $20.00 and $44.00 per double roll	1.6 dbl. rolls	$32.00	$35.20	1.6 dbl. rolls	$70.40	$77.45
Wall sizing at $12.95 per gal.	0.25 gal.	3.25	3.60	0.25 gal.	3.25	3.60
Vinyl wall paste at $6.95 per gal.	0.4 gal.	2.80	3.10	0.4 gal.	2.80	3.10
Apply sizing at $13.50 and $22.00 per M.H.	0.3 M.H.	4.05	6.60	0.3 M.H.	4.05	6.60
Apply paper at $13.50 and $22.00 per M.H.	1.2 M.H.	16.20	26.40	1.5 M.H.	20.25	33.00
Total including waste allowance per 100 S.F.		$58.30	$74.90		$100.75	$123.75

This is equivalent to about $46.80 and $77.35 per double roll complete in place. Most wallpapers now come in double rolls only. To remove old paper allow 1.3 hours per 100 S.F.

CIRCLE REFERENCE NUMBERS

(115) Paint (Div. 099)

Material prices per gallon in 5 gallon lots, up to 25 gallons. For 100 gallons, deduct 10%.

Exterior, Alkyd (oil base)		Masonry, Exterior		Rust inhibitor ferrous metal	$18.95
Flat	$20.50	Alkali resistant primer	$18.75	Zinc chromate	16.25
Gloss	19.95	Block filler, epoxy	18.50	**Heavy Duty Coatings**	
Primer	16.75	Block filler, latex	9.40	Acrylic urethane	48.95
		Latex, flat or semi-gloss	18.00	Chlorinated rubber	25.75
Exterior, Latex (water base)		**Masonry, Interior**		Coal tar epoxy	18.00
Acrylic stain	12.80	Alkali resistant primer	12.50	Metal pretreatment (polyvinyl butyral)	21.00
Gloss enamel	23.95	Block filler, epoxy	18.50	Polyamide epoxy finish	26.00
Flat	16.70	Block filler, latex	9.40	Polyamide epoxy primer	27.00
Primer	18.75	Floor, alkyd	17.25	Silicone alkyd	31.00
Semi-gloss	17.50	Floor, latex	17.30	2 component solvent based acrylic epoxy	25.00
		Latex, flat acrylic	10.25	2 component solvent based polyester epoxy	35.00
Interior, Alkyd (oil base)		Latex, flat emulsion	13.45	Vinyl	23.95
Enamel undercoater	16.80	Latex, sealer	9.95	Zinc rich primer	38.00
Flat	18.25	Latex, semi-gloss	18.65	**Special Coatings/Miscellaneous**	
Gloss	17.25	**Varnish and Stain**		Aluminum	13.55
Primer sealer	16.60	Alkyd clear	17.60	Creosote	7.00
Semi-gloss	19.95	Polyurethane, clear	17.95	Dry fall out, flat	8.50
		Primer sealer	15.40	Fire retardant, intumescent	24.00
Interior, Latex (water base)		Semi-transparent stain	13.95	Linseed oil	8.50
Enamel undercoater	13.95	Solid color stain	13.45	Shellac	12.00
Flat	13.95	**Metal Coatings**		Swimming pool, epoxy or urethane base	27.00
Floor and deck	17.25	Galvanized	18.75	Swimming pool, rubber base	25.75
Gloss	23.95	High heat	31.00	Texture paint	11.35
Primer sealer	9.95	Machinery enamel, alkyd	17.70	Turpentine	9.00
Semi-gloss	18.65	Normal heat	15.95	Water repellent 5% silicone	11.50

(116) Painting (Div. 099)

Item	Coat	One Gallon Covers			In 8 Hours Man Covers			Man Hours per 100 S.F.		
		Brush	Roller	Spray	Brush	Roller	Spray	Brush	Roller	Spray
Paint wood siding	prime	275 S.F.	250 S.F.	325 S.F.	1150 S.F.	1400 S.F.	4000 S.F.	.695	.571	.200
	others	300	275	325	1600	2200	4000	.500	.364	.200
Paint exterior trim	prime	450	—	—	650	—	—	1.230	—	—
	1st	525	—	—	700	—	—	1.143	—	—
	2nd	575	—	—	750	—	—	1.067	—	—
Paint shingle siding	prime	300	285	335	1050	1700	2800	.763	.470	.286
	others	400	375	425	1200	2000	3200	.667	.400	.250
Stain shingle siding	1st	200	190	220	1200	1400	3200	.667	.571	.250
	2nd	300	275	325	1300	1700	4000	.615	.471	.200
Paint brick masonry	prime	200	150	175	850	1700	4000	.941	.471	.200
	1st	300	250	320	1200	2200	4400	.364	.364	.182
	2nd	375	340	400	1300	2400	4400	.615	.333	.182
Paint interior plaster or drywall	prime	450	425	550	1600	2500	4000	.500	.320	.200
	others	500	475	550	1400	3000	4000	.571	.267	.200
Paint interior doors and windows	prime	450	—	—	1300	—	—	.333	—	—
	1st	475	—	—	1150	—	—	.696	—	—
	2nd	500	—	—	1000	—	—	.800	—	—

CIRCLE REFERENCE NUMBERS

(119) Swimming Pools (Div. 131-525)

Pool prices given per square foot of surface area include pool structure, filter and chlorination equipment where required, pumps, related piping, diving boards, ladders, maintenance kit, skimmer and vacuum system. Decks and electrical service to equipment are not included.

Residential in-ground pool construction can be divided into two categories: vinyl lined and gunite. Vinyl lined pool walls are constructed of different materials including wood, concrete, plastic or metal. The bottom is often graded with sand over which the vinyl liner is installed. Costs are generally in the $12 to $17 per S.F. range. Vermiculite or soil cement bottoms may be substituted for an added cost of $.72 per S.F. surface.

Gunite pool construction is used both in residential and municipal installations. These structures are steel reinforced for strength and finished with a white cement limestone plaster. Residential costs run from $16 to $28 per S.F. surface. Municipal costs vary from $35 to $51 because plumbing codes require more expensive materials, chlorination equipment and higher filtration rates.

Municipal pools greater than 1,600 S.F. require gutter systems to control waves. This gutter may be formed into the concrete wall. Often a vinyl, stainless steel gutter or gutter and wall system is specified, which will raise the pool cost an additional $51 to $180 per L.F. of gutter installed and up to $290 per L.F. if a gutter and wall system is installed.

Competition pools usually require tile bottoms and sides with contrasting lane striping. Add $12 per S.F. of wall or bottom to be tiled.

(129) Pipe Material Costs and Considerations (Div. 026, 027 & 151)

1. Malleable fittings should be used for gas service.
2. Malleable fittings are used where there are stresses/strains due to expansion and vibration.
3. Cast fittings may be broken as an aid to disassembling of heating lines frozen by long use, temperature and minerals.
4. Cast iron pipe is extensively used for underground and submerged service.
5. Type M (light wall) copper tubing is available in hard temper only and is used for nonpressure and less severe applications than K and L.
6. Type L (medium wall) copper tubing, available hard or soft for interior service.
7. Type K (heavy wall) copper tubing, available in hard or soft temper for use where conditions are severe. For underground and interior service.
8. Hard drawn tubing requires fewer hangers or supports but should not be bent. Silver brazed fittings are recommended, however soft solder is normally used.
9. Type DMV (very light wall) copper tubing designed for drainage, waste and vent plus other non-critical pressure services.

Domestic/Imported Pipe and Fittings Cost

The prices shown in this publication for steel/cast iron pipe and steel, cast iron, malleable iron fittings are based on domestic production sold at the normal trade discounts. The above listed items of foreign manufacture may be available at prices of 1/3 to 1/2 those shown. Some imported items after minor machining or finishing operations are being sold as domestic to further complicate the system.

Caution: Most pipe prices in this book also include a coupling and pipe hangers which for the larger sizes can add significantly to the per foot cost and should be taken into account when comparing "book cost" with quoted supplier's cost.

(130) Plumbing Fixtures (Div. 152)

Total labor hours to install fixtures.

Item	Rough-In	Set	Total Hours	Item	Rough-In	Set	Total Hours
Bath tub	5	5	10	Shower head only	2	1	3
Bath tub and shower, cast iron	6	6	12	Shower drain	3	1	4
Fire hose reel and cabinet	4	2	6	Shower stall, slate		15	15
Floor drain to 4 inch diameter	3	1	4	Slop sink	5	3	8
Grease trap, single, cast iron	5	3	8	Test 6 fixtures			14
Kitchen gas range		4	4	Urinal, wall	6	2	8
Kitchen sink, single	4	4	8	Urinal, pedestal or floor	6	4	10
Kitchen sink, double	6	6	12	Water closet and tank	4	3	7
Laundry tubs	4	2	6	Water closet and tank, wall hung	5	3	8
Lavatory wall hung	5	3	8	Water heater, 45 gals. gas, automatic	5	2	7
Lavatory pedestal	5	3	8	Water heaters, 65 gals. gas, automatic	5	2	7
Shower and stall	6	4	10	Water heaters, electric, plumbing only	4	2	6

Fixture prices in front of book are based on the cost per fixture set in place. The rough-in cost, which must be added for each fixture, includes carrier, if required, some supply, waste and vent pipe connecting fittings and stops. The lengths of rough-in pipe are nominal runs which would connect to the larger runs and stacks. The supply runs and DWV runs and stacks must be accounted for in separate entries. In the eastern half of the United States it is common for the plumber to carry these to a point 5' outside the building.

CIRCLE REFERENCE NUMBERS

(134) Solar Heating (basic requirements) (Div. 155-471)

Face collectors as close to due south as practical. Locate collectors so they are not shaded from sun's rays. Incline collectors at a slope of latitude minus 5° for domestic hot water and latitude plus 15° for space heating. Insulate piping and storage tank well to minimize heat losses. Size domestic water heating storage tanks to hold 20 gallons water per user, minimum, 30 gallons per user preferable. For domestic water heating an optimum collector size is approximately 3/4 square foot of area per gallon of water storage. For space heating of residences and small commercial applications the collector is commonly sized between 30% and 50% of the internal floor area. For space heating of large commercial applications, collector areas less than 30% of the internal floor area can still provide significant heating reductions.

The price of the collector varies from $18 to $40 per square foot of collector depending on the installation and includes all but the terminal pump, controls, thermostat and storage tank. See Divisions 155-471 and 155-671 for tanks. Size the tank 1-1/2 gallons capacity per square foot of collector area.

A supplementary heat source is recommended for Northern states for December through February. The solar energy transmission per square foot of collector surface varies greatly with the material used.

Initial cost, heat transmittance and useful life are obviously interrelated.

(143) Repair and Remodeling

Cost figures in MEANS RESIDENTIAL COST DATA are based on new construction utilizing the most cost-effective combination of labor, equipment and material with the work scheduled in proper sequence to allow the various trades to accomplish their work in an efficient manner.

The costs for repair and remodeling work must be modified due to the following factors that may be present in any given repair and remodeling project:

1. Equipment usage curtailment due to the physical limitations of the project, with only hand-operated equipment being used.
2. Increased requirement for shoring and bracing to hold up the building while structural changes are being made and to allow for temporary storage of construction materials on above-grade floors.
3. Material handling becomes more costly due to having to move within the confines of an enclosed building. For multi-story construction, low capacity elevators and stairwells may be the only access to the upper floors.
4. Large amount of cutting and patching and attempting to match the existing construction is required. It is often more economical to remove entire walls rather than create many new door and window openings. This sort of trade-off has to be carefully analyzed.
5. Cost of protection of completed work is increased since the usual sequence of construction usually can not be accomplished.
6. Economies of scale usually associated with new construction may not be present. If small quantities of components must be custom fabricated due to job requirements, unit costs will naturally increase. Also, if only small work areas are available at a given time, job scheduling between trades becomes difficult and subcontractor quotations may reflect the excessive start-up and shut-down phases of the job.
7. Work may have to be done on other than normal shifts and may have to be done around an existing production facility which has to stay in production during the course of the repair and remodeling.
8. Dust and noise protection of adjoining non-construction areas can involve substantial special protection and alter usual construction methods.
9. Job may be delayed due to unexpected conditions discovered during demolition or removal. These delays ultimately increase construction costs.
10. Piping and ductwork runs may not be as simple as for new construction. Wiring may have to be snaked through walls and floors.
11. Matching "existing construction" may be impossible because materials may no longer be manufactured. Substitutions may be expensive.
12. Weather protection of existing structure requires additional temporary structures to protect building at opening.
13. On small projects, because of local conditions, it may be necessary to pay a tradesman for a minimum of four hours for a task that is completed in one hour.

All of the above areas can contribute to increased costs for a repair and remodeling project. Each of the above factors should be considered in the planning, bidding and construction stage in order to minimize the increased costs associated with repair and remodeling jobs.

APPENDIX

TABLE OF CONTENTS

Crew Listings	424
Location Factors	444
Abbreviations	449
Index	452

CREWS

Crew No.		Bare Costs		Incl. Subs O & P		Cost Per Man-Hour	
Crew A-1	Hr.	Daily	Hr.	Daily	Bare Costs	Incl. O&P
1 Building Laborer	$11.35	$90.80	$19.00	$152.00	$11.35	$19.00
1 Gas Eng. Power Tool		54.40		59.85	6.80	7.48
8 M.H., Daily Totals		$145.20		$211.85	$18.15	$26.48
Crew A-1A	Hr.	Daily	Hr.	Daily	Bare Costs	Incl. O&P
1 Laborer	$11.35	$90.80	$19.00	$152.00	$11.35	$19.00
1 Power Equipment		29.80		32.80	3.72	4.10
8 M.H., Daily Totals		$120.60		$184.80	$15.07	$23.10
Crew A-2	Hr.	Daily	Hr.	Daily	Bare Costs	Incl. O&P
2 Building Laborers	$11.35	$181.60	$19.00	$304.00	$11.48	$19.10
1 Truck Driver (light)	11.75	94.00	19.30	154.40		
1 Light Truck, 1.5 Ton		146.00		160.60	6.08	6.69
24 M.H., Daily Totals		$421.60		$619.00	$17.56	$25.79
Crew A-3	Hr.	Daily	Hr.	Daily	Bare Costs	Incl. O&P
1 Truck Driver (heavy)	$11.95	$95.60	$19.60	$156.80	$11.95	$19.60
1 Dump Truck, 12 Ton		298.80		328.70	37.35	41.08
8 M.H., Daily Totals		$394.40		$485.50	$49.30	$60.68
Crew A-4	Hr.	Daily	Hr.	Daily	Bare Costs	Incl. O&P
2 Carpenters	$14.30	$228.80	$23.90	$382.40	$14.03	$23.26
1 Painter, Ordinary	13.50	108.00	22.00	176.00		
24 M.H., Daily Totals		$336.80		$558.40	$14.03	$23.26
Crew A-5	Hr.	Daily	Hr.	Daily	Bare Costs	Incl. O&P
2 Building Laborers	$11.35	$181.60	$19.00	$304.00	$11.39	$19.03
.25 Truck Driver (light)	11.75	23.50	19.30	38.60		
.25 Light Truck, 1.5 Ton		36.50		40.15	2.02	2.23
18 M.H., Daily Totals		$241.60		$382.75	$13.41	$21.26
Crew A-6	Hr.	Daily	Hr.	Daily	Bare Costs	Incl. O&P
1 Chief Of Party	$13.90	$111.20	$22.80	$182.40	$13.20	$21.65
1 Instrument Man	12.50	100.00	20.50	164.00		
16 M.H., Daily Totals		$211.20		$346.40	$13.20	$21.65
Crew A-7	Hr.	Daily	Hr.	Daily	Bare Costs	Incl. O&P
1 Chief Of Party	$13.90	$111.20	$22.80	$182.40	$12.50	$20.68
1 Instrument Man	12.50	100.00	20.50	164.00		
1 Rodman/Chainman	11.10	88.80	18.75	150.00		
24 M.H., Daily Totals		$300.00		$496.40	$12.50	$20.68
Crew A-8	Hr.	Daily	Hr.	Daily	Bare Costs	Incl. O&P
1 Chief Of Party	$13.90	$111.20	$22.80	$182.40	$12.15	$20.20
1 Instrument Man	12.50	100.00	20.50	164.00		
2 Rodmen/Chainmen	11.10	177.60	18.75	300.00		
32 M.H., Daily Totals		$388.80		$646.40	$12.15	$20.20
Crew A-9	Hr.	Daily	Hr.	Daily	Bare Costs	Incl. O&P
1 Asbestos Foreman	$16.55	$132.40	$28.00	$224.00	$16.11	$27.25
7 Asbestos Workers	16.05	898.80	27.15	1520.40		
4 Airless Sprayers		101.60		111.75		
3 HEPA Vacs., 16 Gal.		89.40		98.35	2.98	3.28
64 M.H., Daily Totals		$1222.20		$1954.50	$19.09	$30.53
Crew A-10	Hr.	Daily	Hr.	Daily	Bare Costs	Incl. O&P
1 Asbestos Foreman	$16.55	$132.40	$28.00	$224.00	$16.11	$27.25
7 Asbestos Workers	16.05	898.80	27.15	1520.40		
2 HEPA Vacs., 16 Gal.		59.60		65.55	.93	1.02
64 M.H., Daily Totals		$1090.80		$1809.95	$17.04	$28.27

Crew No.		Bare Costs		Incl. Subs O & P		Cost Per Man-Hour	
Crew A-11	Hr.	Daily	Hr.	Daily	Bare Costs	Incl. O&P
1 Asbestos Foreman	$16.55	$132.40	$28.00	$224.00	$16.11	$27.25
7 Asbestos Workers	16.05	898.80	27.15	1520.40		
4 Airless Sprayers		101.60		111.75		
2 HEPA Vacs., 16 Gal.		59.60		65.55		
2 Chipping Hammers		18.40		20.25	2.80	3.08
64 M.H., Daily Totals		$1210.80		$1941.95	$18.91	$30.33
Crew A-12	Hr.	Daily	Hr.	Daily	Bare Costs	Incl. O&P
1 Asbestos Foreman	$16.55	$132.40	$28.00	$224.00	$16.11	$27.25
7 Asbestos Workers	16.05	898.80	27.15	1520.40		
4 Airless Sprayers		101.60		111.75		
2 HEPA Vacs., 16 Gal.		59.60		65.55		
1 Large Prod. Vac. Loader		440.80		484.90	9.40	10.34
64 M.H., Daily Totals		$1633.20		$2406.60	$25.51	$37.59
Crew B-1	Hr.	Daily	Hr.	Daily	Bare Costs	Incl. O&P
1 Labor Foreman (outside)	$13.35	$106.80	$22.35	$178.80	$12.01	$20.11
2 Building Laborers	11.35	181.60	19.00	304.00		
24 M.H., Daily Totals		$288.40		$482.80	$12.01	$20.11
Crew B-2	Hr.	Daily	Hr.	Daily	Bare Costs	Incl. O&P
1 Labor Foreman (outside)	$13.35	$106.80	$22.35	$178.80	$11.75	$19.67
4 Building Laborers	11.35	363.20	19.00	608.00		
40 M.H., Daily Totals		$470.00		$786.80	$11.75	$19.67
Crew B-3	Hr.	Daily	Hr.	Daily	Bare Costs	Incl. O&P
1 Labor Foreman (outside)	$13.35	$106.80	$22.35	$178.80	$12.42	$20.58
2 Building Laborers	11.35	181.60	19.00	304.00		
1 Equip. Oper. (med.)	14.60	116.80	23.95	191.60		
2 Truck Drivers (heavy)	11.95	191.20	19.60	313.60		
F.E. Loader, T.M., 2.5 C.Y.		807.80		888.60		
2 Dump Trucks, 16 Ton		730.40		803.45	32.04	35.25
48 M.H., Daily Totals		$2134.60		$2680.05	$44.46	$55.83
Crew B-4	Hr.	Daily	Hr.	Daily	Bare Costs	Incl. O&P
1 Labor Foreman (outside)	$13.35	$106.80	$22.35	$178.80	$11.78	$19.65
4 Building Laborers	11.35	363.20	19.00	608.00		
1 Truck Driver (heavy)	11.95	95.60	19.60	156.80		
1 Tractor, 4 x 2, 195 H.P.		268.40		295.25		
1 Platform Trailer		130.60		143.65	8.31	9.14
48 M.H., Daily Totals		$964.60		$1382.50	$20.09	$28.79
Crew B-5	Hr.	Daily	Hr.	Daily	Bare Costs	Incl. O&P
1 Labor Foreman (outside)	$13.35	$106.80	$22.35	$178.80	$12.94	$21.48
4 Building Laborers	11.35	363.20	19.00	608.00		
2 Equip. Oper. (med.)	14.60	233.60	23.95	383.20		
1 Mechanic	15.60	124.80	25.60	204.80		
1 Air Compr., 250 C.F.M.		88.80		97.70		
Air Tools & Accessories		27.60		30.35		
2-50 Ft. Air Hoses, 1.5" Dia.		10.80		11.90		
F.E. Loader, T.M., 2.5 C.Y.		807.80		888.60	14.60	16.07
64 M.H., Daily Totals		$1763.40		$2403.35	$27.54	$37.55
Crew B-6	Hr.	Daily	Hr.	Daily	Bare Costs	Incl. O&P
2 Building Laborers	$11.35	$181.60	$19.00	$304.00	$12.20	$20.26
1 Equip. Oper. (light)	13.90	111.20	22.80	182.40		
1 Backhoe Loader, 48 H.P.		190.40		209.45	7.93	8.72
24 M.H., Daily Totals		$483.20		$695.85	$20.13	$28.98

CREWS

Crew B-7	Hr.	Daily	Hr.	Daily	Bare Costs	Incl. O&P
1 Labor Foreman (outside)	$13.35	$106.80	$22.35	$178.80	$12.22	$20.38
4 Building Laborers	11.35	363.20	19.00	608.00		
1 Equip. Oper. (med.)	14.60	116.80	23.95	191.60		
1 Chipping Machine		178.80		196.70		
F.E. Loader, T.M., 2.5 C.Y.		807.80		888.60		
2 Chain Saws		83.20		91.50	22.28	24.51
48 M.H., Daily Totals		$1656.60		$2155.20	$34.50	$44.89

Crew B-7A	Hr.	Daily	Hr.	Daily	Bare Costs	Incl. O&P
2 Laborers	$11.35	$181.60	$19.00	$304.00	$12.20	$20.26
1 Equip. Oper. (light)	13.90	111.20	22.80	182.40		
1 Rake w/Tractor		186.80		205.50		
2 Chain Saws		40.00		44.00	9.45	10.39
24 M.H., Daily Totals		$519.60		$735.90	$21.65	$30.65

Crew B-8	Hr.	Daily	Hr.	Daily	Bare Costs	Incl. O&P
1 Labor Foreman (outside)	$13.35	$106.80	$22.35	$178.80	$12.70	$20.99
2 Building Laborers	11.35	181.60	19.00	304.00		
2 Equip. Oper. (med.)	14.60	233.60	23.95	383.20		
1 Equip. Oper. Oiler	12.50	100.00	20.50	164.00		
2 Truck Drivers (heavy)	11.95	191.20	19.60	313.60		
1 Hyd. Crane, 25 Ton		486.40		535.05		
F.E. Loader, T.M., 2.5 C.Y.		807.80		888.60		
2 Dump Trucks, 16 Ton		730.40		803.45	31.63	34.79
64 M.H., Daily Totals		$2837.80		$3570.70	$44.33	$55.78

Crew B-9	Hr.	Daily	Hr.	Daily	Bare Costs	Incl. O&P
1 Labor Foreman (outside)	$13.35	$106.80	$22.35	$178.80	$11.75	$19.67
4 Building Laborers	11.35	363.20	19.00	608.00		
1 Air Compr., 250 C.F.M.		88.80		97.70		
Air Tools & Accessories		27.60		30.35		
2-50 Ft. Air Hoses, 1.5" Dia.		10.80		11.90	3.18	3.49
40 M.H., Daily Totals		$597.20		$926.75	$14.93	$23.16

Crew B-10	Hr.	Daily	Hr.	Daily	Bare Costs	Incl. O&P
1 Equip. Oper. (med.)	$14.60	$116.80	$23.95	$191.60	$13.51	$22.30
.5 Building Laborer	11.35	45.40	19.00	76.00		
12 M.H., Daily Totals		$162.20		$267.60	$13.51	$22.30

Crew B-10A	Hr.	Daily	Hr.	Daily	Bare Costs	Incl. O&P
1 Equip. Oper. (med.)	$14.60	$116.80	$23.95	$191.60	$13.51	$22.30
.5 Building Laborer	11.35	45.40	19.00	76.00		
1 Roll. Compact., 2K Lbs.		74.40		81.85	6.20	6.82
12 M.H., Daily Totals		$236.60		$349.45	$19.71	$29.12

Crew B-10B	Hr.	Daily	Hr.	Daily	Bare Costs	Incl. O&P
1 Equip. Oper. (med.)	$14.60	$116.80	$23.95	$191.60	$13.51	$22.30
.5 Building Laborer	11.35	45.40	19.00	76.00		
1 Dozer, 200 H.P.		775.80		853.40	64.65	71.11
12 M.H., Daily Totals		$938.00		$1121.00	$78.16	$93.41

Crew B-10C	Hr.	Daily	Hr.	Daily	Bare Costs	Incl. O&P
1 Equip. Oper. (med.)	$14.60	$116.80	$23.95	$191.60	$13.51	$22.30
.5 Building Laborer	11.35	45.40	19.00	76.00		
1 Dozer, 200 H.P.		775.80		853.40		
1 Vibratory Roller, Towed		90.40		99.45	72.18	79.40
12 M.H., Daily Totals		$1028.40		$1220.45	$85.69	$101.70

Crew B-10D	Hr.	Daily	Hr.	Daily	Bare Costs	Incl. O&P
1 Equip. Oper. (med.)	$14.60	$116.80	$23.95	$191.60	$13.51	$22.30
.5 Building Laborer	11.35	45.40	19.00	76.00		
1 Dozer, 200 H.P.		775.80		853.40		
1 Sheepsft. Roller, Towed		119.80		131.80	74.63	82.10
12 M.H., Daily Totals		$1057.80		$1252.80	$88.14	$104.40

Crew B-10E	Hr.	Daily	Hr.	Daily	Bare Costs	Incl. O&P
1 Equip. Oper. (med.)	$14.60	$116.80	$23.95	$191.60	$13.51	$22.30
.5 Building Laborer	11.35	45.40	19.00	76.00		
1 Tandem Roller, 5 Ton		118.40		130.25	9.86	10.85
12 M.H., Daily Totals		$280.60		$397.85	$23.37	$33.15

Crew B-10F	Hr.	Daily	Hr.	Daily	Bare Costs	Incl. O&P
1 Equip. Oper. (med.)	$14.60	$116.80	$23.95	$191.60	$13.51	$22.30
.5 Building Laborer	11.35	45.40	19.00	76.00		
1 Tandem Roller, 10 Ton		187.60		206.35	15.63	17.19
12 M.H., Daily Totals		$349.80		$473.95	$29.14	$39.49

Crew B-10G	Hr.	Daily	Hr.	Daily	Bare Costs	Incl. O&P
1 Equip. Oper. (med.)	$14.60	$116.80	$23.95	$191.60	$13.51	$22.30
.5 Building Laborer	11.35	45.40	19.00	76.00		
1 Sheepsft. Roll., 130 H.P.		487.00		535.70	40.58	44.64
12 M.H., Daily Totals		$649.20		$803.30	$54.09	$66.94

Crew B-10H	Hr.	Daily	Hr.	Daily	Bare Costs	Incl. O&P
1 Equip. Oper. (med.)	$14.60	$116.80	$23.95	$191.60	$13.51	$22.30
.5 Building Laborer	11.35	45.40	19.00	76.00		
1 Diaphr. Water Pump, 2"		14.40		15.85		
1-20 Ft. Suction Hose, 2"		4.40		4.85		
2-50 Ft. Disch. Hoses, 2"		5.20		5.70	2.00	2.20
12 M.H., Daily Totals		$186.20		$294.00	$15.51	$24.50

Crew B-10I	Hr.	Daily	Hr.	Daily	Bare Costs	Incl. O&P
1 Equip. Oper. (med.)	$14.60	$116.80	$23.95	$191.60	$13.51	$22.30
.5 Building Laborer	11.35	45.40	19.00	76.00		
1 Diaphr. Water Pump, 4"		50.20		55.20		
1-20 Ft. Suction Hose, 4"		11.20		12.30		
2-50 Ft. Disch. Hoses, 4"		8.00		8.80	5.78	6.35
12 M.H., Daily Totals		$231.60		$343.90	$19.29	$28.65

Crew B-10J	Hr.	Daily	Hr.	Daily	Bare Costs	Incl. O&P
1 Equip. Oper. (med.)	$14.60	$116.80	$23.95	$191.60	$13.51	$22.30
.5 Building Laborer	11.35	45.40	19.00	76.00		
1 Centr. Water Pump, 3"		27.20		29.90		
1-20 Ft. Suction Hose, 3"		6.80		7.50		
2-50 Ft. Disch. Hoses, 3"		7.20		7.90	3.43	3.77
12 M.H., Daily Totals		$203.40		$312.90	$16.94	$26.07

Crew B-10K	Hr.	Daily	Hr.	Daily	Bare Costs	Incl. O&P
1 Equip. Oper. (med.)	$14.60	$116.80	$23.95	$191.60	$13.51	$22.30
.5 Building Laborer	11.35	45.40	19.00	76.00		
1 Centr. Water Pump, 6"		146.20		160.80		
1-20 Ft. Suction Hose, 6"		23.40		25.75		
2-50 Ft. Disch. Hoses, 6"		26.00		28.60	16.30	17.92
12 M.H., Daily Totals		$357.80		$482.75	$29.81	$40.22

CREWS

Crew No.	Bare Costs Hr.	Daily	Incl. Subs O & P Hr.	Daily	Cost Per Man-Hour Bare Costs	Incl. O&P
Crew B-10L						
1 Equip. Oper. (med.)	$14.60	$116.80	$23.95	$191.60	$13.51	$22.30
.5 Building Laborer	11.35	45.40	19.00	76.00		
1 Dozer, 75 H.P.		272.80		300.10	22.73	25.00
12 M.H., Daily Totals		$435.00		$567.70	$36.24	$47.30
Crew B-10M						
1 Equip. Oper. (med.)	$14.60	$116.80	$23.95	$191.60	$13.51	$22.30
.5 Building Laborer	11.35	45.40	19.00	76.00		
1 Dozer, 300 H.P.		861.80		948.00	71.81	79.00
12 M.H., Daily Totals		$1024.00		$1215.60	$85.32	$101.30
Crew B-10N						
1 Equip. Oper. (med.)	$14.60	$116.80	$23.95	$191.60	$13.51	$22.30
.5 Building Laborer	11.35	45.40	19.00	76.00		
F.E. Loader, T.M., 1.5 C.Y		343.20		377.50	28.60	31.45
12 M.H., Daily Totals		$505.40		$645.10	$42.11	$53.75
Crew B-10O						
1 Equip. Oper. (med.)	$14.60	$116.80	$23.95	$191.60	$13.51	$22.30
.5 Building Laborer	11.35	45.40	19.00	76.00		
F.E. Loader, T.M., 2.25 C.Y.		436.40		480.05	36.36	40.00
12 M.H., Daily Totals		$598.60		$747.65	$49.87	$62.30
Crew B-10P						
1 Equip. Oper. (med.)	$14.60	$116.80	$23.95	$191.60	$13.51	$22.30
.5 Building Laborer	11.35	45.40	19.00	76.00		
F.E. Loader, T.M., 2.5 C.Y.		807.80		888.60	67.31	74.05
12 M.H., Daily Totals		$970.00		$1156.20	$80.82	$96.35
Crew B-10Q						
1 Equip. Oper. (med.)	$14.60	$116.80	$23.95	$191.60	$13.51	$22.30
.5 Building Laborer	11.35	45.40	19.00	76.00		
F.E. Loader, T.M., 5 C.Y.		1006.00		1106.60	83.83	92.21
12 M.H., Daily Totals		$1168.20		$1374.20	$97.34	$114.51
Crew B-10R						
1 Equip. Oper. (med.)	$14.60	$116.80	$23.95	$191.60	$13.51	$22.30
.5 Building Laborer	11.35	45.40	19.00	76.00		
F.E. Loader, W.M., 1 C.Y.		225.60		248.15	18.80	20.67
12 M.H., Daily Totals		$387.80		$515.75	$32.31	$42.97
Crew B-10S						
1 Equip. Oper. (med.)	$14.60	$116.80	$23.95	$191.60	$13.51	$22.30
.5 Building Laborer	11.35	45.40	19.00	76.00		
F.E. Loader, W.M., 1.5 C.Y.		309.60		340.55	25.80	28.37
12 M.H., Daily Totals		$471.80		$608.15	$39.31	$50.67
Crew B-10T						
1 Equip. Oper. (med.)	$14.60	$116.80	$23.95	$191.60	$13.51	$22.30
.5 Building Laborer	11.35	45.40	19.00	76.00		
F.E. Loader, W.M., 2.5 C.Y.		449.20		494.10	37.43	41.17
12 M.H., Daily Totals		$611.40		$761.70	$50.94	$63.47
Crew B-10U						
1 Equip. Oper. (med.)	$14.60	$116.80	$23.95	$191.60	$13.51	$22.30
.5 Building Laborer	11.35	45.40	19.00	76.00		
F.E. Loader, W.M., 5.5 C.Y.		927.40		1020.15	77.28	85.01
12 M.H., Daily Totals		$1089.60		$1287.75	$90.79	$107.31

Crew No.	Bare Costs Hr.	Daily	Incl. Subs O & P Hr.	Daily	Cost Per Man-Hour Bare Costs	Incl. O&P
Crew B-10V						
1 Equip. Oper. (med.)	$14.60	$116.80	$23.95	$191.60	$13.51	$22.30
.5 Building Laborer	11.35	45.40	19.00	76.00		
1 Dozer, 700 H.P.		2483.20		2731.50	206.93	227.62
12 M.H., Daily Totals		$2645.40		$2999.10	$220.44	$249.92
Crew B-10W						
1 Equip. Oper. (med.)	$14.60	$116.80	$23.95	$191.60	$13.51	$22.30
.5 Building Laborer	11.35	45.40	19.00	76.00		
1 Dozer, 105 H.P.		399.20		439.10	33.26	36.59
12 M.H., Daily Totals		$561.40		$706.70	$46.77	$58.89
Crew B-10X						
1 Equip. Oper. (med.)	$14.60	$116.80	$23.95	$191.60	$13.51	$22.30
.5 Building Laborer	11.35	45.40	19.00	76.00		
1 Dozer, 410 H.P.		1156.80		1272.50	96.40	106.04
12 M.H., Daily Totals		$1319.00		$1540.10	$109.91	$128.34
Crew B-10Y						
1 Equip. Oper. (med.)	$14.60	$116.80	$23.95	$191.60	$13.51	$22.30
.5 Building Laborer	11.35	45.40	19.00	76.00		
1 Vibratory Drum Roller		296.80		326.50	24.73	27.20
12 M.H., Daily Totals		$459.00		$594.10	$38.24	$49.50
Crew B-11						
1 Equipment Oper. (med.)	$14.60	$116.80	$23.95	$191.60	$12.97	$21.47
1 Building Laborer	11.35	90.80	19.00	152.00		
16 M.H., Daily Totals		$207.60		$343.60	$12.97	$21.47
Crew B-11A						
1 Equipment Oper. (med.)	$14.60	$116.80	$23.95	$191.60	$12.97	$21.47
1 Building Laborer	11.35	90.80	19.00	152.00		
1 Dozer, 200 H.P.		775.80		853.40	48.48	53.33
16 M.H., Daily Totals		$983.40		$1197.00	$61.45	$74.80
Crew B-11B						
1 Equipment Oper. (med.)	$14.60	$116.80	$23.95	$191.60	$12.97	$21.47
1 Building Laborer	11.35	90.80	19.00	152.00		
1 Dozer, 200 H.P.		775.80		853.40		
1 Air Powered Tamper		13.20		14.50		
1 Air Compr. 365 C.F.M.		201.80		222.00		
2-50 Ft. Air Hoses, 1.5" Dia.		10.80		11.90	62.60	68.86
16 M.H., Daily Totals		$1209.20		$1445.40	$75.57	$90.33
Crew B-11C						
1 Equipment Oper. (med.)	$14.60	$116.80	$23.95	$191.60	$12.97	$21.47
1 Building Laborer	11.35	90.80	19.00	152.00		
1 Backhoe Loader, 48 H.P.		190.40		209.45	11.90	13.09
16 M.H., Daily Totals		$398.00		$553.05	$24.87	$34.56
Crew B-11K						
1 Equipment Oper. (med.)	$14.60	$116.80	$23.95	$191.60	$12.97	$21.47
1 Building Laborer	11.35	90.80	19.00	152.00		
1 Trencher, 8' D., 16" W.		420.00		462.00	26.25	28.87
16 M.H., Daily Totals		$627.60		$805.60	$39.22	$50.34
Crew B-11L						
1 Equipment Oper. (med.)	$14.60	$116.80	$23.95	$191.60	$12.97	$21.47
1 Building Laborer	11.35	90.80	19.00	152.00		
1 Grader, 30,000 Lbs.		521.00		573.10	32.56	35.81
16 M.H., Daily Totals		$728.60		$916.70	$45.53	$57.28

CREWS

Crew No.	Bare Costs		Incl. Subs O & P		Cost Per Man-Hour	
Crew B-11M	Hr.	Daily	Hr.	Daily	Bare Costs	Incl. O&P
1 Equipment Oper. (med.)	$14.60	$116.80	$23.95	$191.60	$12.97	$21.47
1 Building Laborer	11.35	90.80	19.00	152.00		
1 Backhoe Loader, 80 H.P.		286.60		315.25	17.91	19.70
16 M.H., Daily Totals		$494.20		$658.85	$30.88	$41.17
Crew B-12	Hr.	Daily	Hr.	Daily	Bare Costs	Incl. O&P
1 Equip. Oper. (crane)	$15.15	$121.20	$24.85	$198.80	$13.82	$22.67
1 Equip. Oper. Oiler	12.50	100.00	20.50	164.00		
16 M.H., Daily Totals		$221.20		$362.80	$13.82	$22.67
Crew B-12A	Hr.	Daily	Hr.	Daily	Bare Costs	Incl. O&P
1 Equip. Oper. (crane)	$15.15	$121.20	$24.85	$198.80	$13.82	$22.67
1 Equip. Oper. Oiler	12.50	100.00	20.50	164.00		
1 Hyd. Excavator, 1 C.Y.		566.60		623.25	35.41	38.95
16 M.H., Daily Totals		$787.80		$986.05	$49.23	$61.62
Crew B-12B	Hr.	Daily	Hr.	Daily	Bare Costs	Incl. O&P
1 Equip. Oper. (crane)	$15.15	$121.20	$24.85	$198.80	$13.82	$22.67
1 Equip. Oper. Oiler	12.50	100.00	20.50	164.00		
1 Hyd. Excavator, 1.5 C.Y.		679.60		747.55	42.47	46.72
16 M.H., Daily Totals		$900.80		$1110.35	$56.29	$69.39
Crew B-12C	Hr.	Daily	Hr.	Daily	Bare Costs	Incl. O&P
1 Equip. Oper. (crane)	$15.15	$121.20	$24.85	$198.80	$13.82	$22.67
1 Equip. Oper. Oiler	12.50	100.00	20.50	164.00		
1 Hyd. Excavator, 2 C.Y.		947.00		1041.70	59.18	65.10
16 M.H., Daily Totals		$1168.20		$1404.50	$73.00	$87.77
Crew B-12D	Hr.	Daily	Hr.	Daily	Bare Costs	Incl. O&P
1 Equip. Oper. (crane)	$15.15	$121.20	$24.85	$198.80	$13.82	$22.67
1 Equip. Oper. Oiler	12.50	100.00	20.50	164.00		
1 Hyd. Excavator, 3.5 C.Y.		2017.00		2218.70	126.06	138.66
16 M.H., Daily Totals		$2238.20		$2581.50	$139.88	$161.33
Crew B-12E	Hr.	Daily	Hr.	Daily	Bare Costs	Incl. O&P
1 Equip. Oper. (crane)	$15.15	$121.20	$24.85	$198.80	$13.82	$22.67
1 Equip. Oper. Oiler	12.50	100.00	20.50	164.00		
1 Hyd. Excavator, .5 C.Y.		336.40		370.05	21.02	23.12
16 M.H., Daily Totals		$557.60		$732.85	$34.84	$45.79
Crew B-12F	Hr.	Daily	Hr.	Daily	Bare Costs	Incl. O&P
1 Equip. Oper. (crane)	$15.15	$121.20	$24.85	$198.80	$13.82	$22.67
1 Equip. Oper. Oiler	12.50	100.00	20.50	164.00		
1 Hyd. Excavator, .75 C.Y.		457.20		502.90	28.57	31.43
16 M.H., Daily Totals		$678.40		$865.70	$42.39	$54.10
Crew B-12G	Hr.	Daily	Hr.	Daily	Bare Costs	Incl. O&P
1 Equip. Oper. (crane)	$15.15	$121.20	$24.85	$198.80	$13.82	$22.67
1 Equip. Oper. Oiler	12.50	100.00	20.50	164.00		
1 Power Shovel, .5 C.Y.		376.40		414.05		
1 Clamshell Bucket, .5 C.Y.		46.80		51.50	26.45	29.09
16 M.H., Daily Totals		$644.40		$828.35	$40.27	$51.76
Crew B-12H	Hr.	Daily	Hr.	Daily	Bare Costs	Incl. O&P
1 Equip. Oper. (crane)	$15.15	$121.20	$24.85	$198.80	$13.82	$22.67
1 Equip. Oper. Oiler	12.50	100.00	20.50	164.00		
1 Power Shovel, 1 C.Y.		435.80		479.40		
1 Clamshell Bucket, 1 C.Y.		59.60		65.55	30.96	34.05
16 M.H., Daily Totals		$716.60		$907.75	$44.78	$56.72

Crew No.	Bare Costs		Incl. Subs O & P		Cost Per Man-Hour	
Crew B-12I	Hr.	Daily	Hr.	Daily	Bare Costs	Incl. O&P
1 Equip. Oper. (crane)	$15.15	$121.20	$24.85	$198.80	$13.82	$22.67
1 Equip. Oper. Oiler	12.50	100.00	20.50	164.00		
1 Power Shovel, .75 C.Y.		401.20		441.30		
1 Dragline Bucket, .75 C.Y.		29.60		32.55	26.92	29.61
16 M.H., Daily Totals		$652.00		$836.65	$40.74	$52.28
Crew B-12J	Hr.	Daily	Hr.	Daily	Bare Costs	Incl. O&P
1 Equip. Oper. (crane)	$15.15	$121.20	$24.85	$198.80	$13.82	$22.67
1 Equip. Oper. Oiler	12.50	100.00	20.50	164.00		
1 Gradall, 3 Ton, .5 C.Y.		555.60		611.15	34.72	38.19
16 M.H., Daily Totals		$776.80		$973.95	$48.54	$60.86
Crew B-12K	Hr.	Daily	Hr.	Daily	Bare Costs	Incl. O&P
1 Equip. Oper. (crane)	$15.15	$121.20	$24.85	$198.80	$13.82	$22.67
1 Equip. Oper. Oiler	12.50	100.00	20.50	164.00		
1 Gradall, 3 Ton, 1 C.Y.		768.00		844.80	48.00	52.80
16 M.H., Daily Totals		$989.20		$1207.60	$61.82	$75.47
Crew B-12L	Hr.	Daily	Hr.	Daily	Bare Costs	Incl. O&P
1 Equip. Oper. (crane)	$15.15	$121.20	$24.85	$198.80	$13.82	$22.67
1 Equip. Oper. Oiler	12.50	100.00	20.50	164.00		
1 Power Shovel, .5 C.Y.		376.40		414.05		
1 F.E. Attachment, .5 C.Y.		47.00		51.70	26.46	29.10
16 M.H., Daily Totals		$644.60		$828.55	$40.28	$51.77
Crew B-12M	Hr.	Daily	Hr.	Daily	Bare Costs	Incl. O&P
1 Equip. Oper. (crane)	$15.15	$121.20	$24.85	$198.80	$13.82	$22.67
1 Equip. Oper. Oiler	12.50	100.00	20.50	164.00		
1 Power Shovel, .75		401.20		441.30		
1 F.E. Attachment, .75 C.Y.		86.80		95.50	30.50	33.55
16 M.H., Daily Totals		$709.20		$899.60	$44.32	$56.22
Crew B-12N	Hr.	Daily	Hr.	Daily	Bare Costs	Incl. O&P
1 Equip. Oper. (crane)	$15.15	$121.20	$24.85	$198.80	$13.82	$22.67
1 Equip. Oper. Oiler	12.50	100.00	20.50	164.00		
1 Power Shovel, 1 C.Y.		435.80		479.40		
1 F.E. Attachment, 1 C.Y.		123.40		135.75	34.95	38.44
16 M.H., Daily Totals		$780.40		$977.95	$48.77	$61.11
Crew B-12O	Hr.	Daily	Hr.	Daily	Bare Costs	Incl. O&P
1 Equip. Oper. (crane)	$15.15	$121.20	$24.85	$198.80	$13.82	$22.67
1 Equip. Oper. Oiler	12.50	100.00	20.50	164.00		
1 Power Shovel, 1.5 C.Y.		659.00		724.90		
1 F.E. Attachment, 1.5 C.Y.		137.80		151.60	49.80	54.78
16 M.H., Daily Totals		$1018.00		$1239.30	$63.62	$77.45
Crew B-12P	Hr.	Daily	Hr.	Daily	Bare Costs	Incl. O&P
1 Equip. Oper. (crane)	$15.15	$121.20	$24.85	$198.80	$13.82	$22.67
1 Equip. Oper. Oiler	12.50	100.00	20.50	164.00		
1 Crawler Crane, 40 Ton		659.00		724.90		
1 Dragline Bucket, 1.5 C.Y.		42.20		46.40	43.82	48.20
16 M.H., Daily Totals		$922.40		$1134.10	$57.64	$70.87
Crew B-12Q	Hr.	Daily	Hr.	Daily	Bare Costs	Incl. O&P
1 Equip. Oper. (crane)	$15.15	$121.20	$24.85	$198.80	$13.82	$22.67
1 Equip. Oper. Oiler	12.50	100.00	20.50	164.00		
1 Hyd. Excavator, 5/8 C.Y.		351.40		386.55	21.96	24.15
16 M.H., Daily Totals		$572.60		$749.35	$35.78	$46.82

CREWS

Crew No.		Bare Costs		Incl. Subs O & P		Cost Per Man-Hour	
Crew B-12R	Hr.	Daily	Hr.	Daily	Bare Costs	Incl. O&P
1 Equip. Oper. (crane)	$15.15	$121.20	$24.85	$198.80	$13.82	$22.67
1 Equip. Oper. Oiler	12.50	100.00	20.50	164.00		
1 Hyd. Excavator, 1.5 C.Y.		679.60		747.55	42.47	46.72
16 M.H., Daily Totals		$900.80		$1110.35	$56.29	$69.39
Crew B-12S	Hr.	Daily	Hr.	Daily	Bare Costs	Incl. O&P
1 Equip. Oper. (crane)	$15.15	$121.20	$24.85	$198.80	$13.82	$22.67
1 Equip. Oper. Oiler	12.50	100.00	20.50	164.00		
1 Hyd. Excavator, 2.5 C.Y.		1614.20		1775.60	100.88	110.97
16 M.H., Daily Totals		$1835.40		$2138.40	$114.70	$133.64
Crew B-12T	Hr.	Daily	Hr.	Daily	Bare Costs	Incl. O&P
1 Equip. Oper. (crane)	$15.15	$121.20	$24.85	$198.80	$13.82	$22.67
1 Equip. Oper. Oiler	12.50	100.00	20.50	164.00		
1 Crawler Crane, 75 Ton		871.20		958.30		
1 F.E. Attachment, 3 C.Y.		255.00		280.50	70.38	77.42
16 M.H., Daily Totals		$1347.40		$1601.60	$84.20	$100.09
Crew B-12V	Hr.	Daily	Hr.	Daily	Bare Costs	Incl. O&P
1 Equip. Oper. (crane)	$15.15	$121.20	$24.85	$198.80	$13.82	$22.67
1 Equip. Oper. Oiler	12.50	100.00	20.50	164.00		
1 Crawler Crane, 75 Ton		871.20		958.30		
1 Dragline Bucket, 3 C.Y.		75.40		82.95	59.16	65.07
16 M.H., Daily Totals		$1167.80		$1404.05	$72.98	$87.74
Crew B-13	Hr.	Daily	Hr.	Daily	Bare Costs	Incl. O&P
1 Labor Foreman (outside)	$13.35	$106.80	$22.35	$178.80	$12.34	$20.52
4 Building Laborers	11.35	363.20	19.00	608.00		
1 Equip. Oper. (crane)	15.15	121.20	24.85	198.80		
1 Equip. Oper. Oiler	12.50	100.00	20.50	164.00		
1 Hyd. Crane, 25 Ton		486.40		535.05	8.68	9.55
56 M.H., Daily Totals		$1177.60		$1684.65	$21.02	$30.07
Crew B-14	Hr.	Daily	Hr.	Daily	Bare Costs	Incl. O&P
1 Labor Foreman (outside)	$13.35	$106.80	$22.35	$178.80	$12.10	$20.19
4 Building Laborers	11.35	363.20	19.00	608.00		
1 Equip. Oper. (light)	13.90	111.20	22.80	182.40		
1 Backhoe Loader, 48 H.P.		190.40		209.45	3.96	4.36
48 M.H., Daily Totals		$771.60		$1178.65	$16.06	$24.55
Crew B-15	Hr.	Daily	Hr.	Daily	Bare Costs	Incl. O&P
1 Equipment Oper. (med)	$14.60	$116.80	$23.95	$191.60	$12.62	$20.75
.5 Building Laborer	11.35	45.40	19.00	76.00		
2 Truck Drivers (heavy)	11.95	191.20	19.60	313.60		
2 Dump Trucks, 16 Ton		730.40		803.45		
1 Dozer, 200 H.P.		775.80		853.40	53.79	59.17
28 M.H., Daily Totals		$1859.60		$2238.05	$66.41	$79.92
Crew B-16	Hr.	Daily	Hr.	Daily	Bare Costs	Incl. O&P
1 Labor Foreman (outside)	$13.35	$106.80	$22.35	$178.80	$12.00	$19.98
2 Building Laborers	11.35	181.60	19.00	304.00		
1 Truck Driver (heavy)	11.95	95.60	19.60	156.80		
1 Dump Truck, 16 Ton		365.20		401.70	11.41	12.55
32 M.H., Daily Totals		$749.20		$1041.30	$23.41	$32.53

Crew No.		Bare Costs		Incl. Subs O & P		Cost Per Man-Hour	
Crew B-17	Hr.	Daily	Hr.	Daily	Bare Costs	Incl. O&P
2 Building Laborers	$11.35	$181.60	$19.00	$304.00	$12.13	$20.10
1 Equip. Oper. (light)	13.90	111.20	22.80	182.40		
1 Truck Driver (heavy)	11.95	95.60	19.60	156.80		
1 Backhoe Loader, 48 H.P.		190.40		209.45		
1 Dump Truck, 12 Ton		298.80		328.70	15.28	16.81
32 M.H., Daily Totals		$877.60		$1181.35	$27.41	$36.91
Crew B-18	Hr.	Daily	Hr.	Daily	Bare Costs	Incl. O&P
1 Labor Foreman (outside)	$13.35	$106.80	$22.35	$178.80	$12.01	$20.11
2 Building Laborers	11.35	181.60	19.00	304.00		
1 Vibrating Compactor		43.40		47.75	1.80	1.98
24 M.H., Daily Totals		$331.80		$530.55	$13.81	$22.09
Crew B-19	Hr.	Daily	Hr.	Daily	Bare Costs	Incl. O&P
1 Pile Driver Foreman	$16.45	$131.60	$29.80	$238.40	$14.63	$25.57
4 Pile Drivers	14.45	462.40	26.15	836.80		
2 Equip. Oper. (crane)	15.15	242.40	24.85	397.60		
1 Equip. Oper. Oiler	12.50	100.00	20.50	164.00		
1 Crane, 40 Ton & Access.		659.00		724.90		
60 L.F. Leads, 15K Ft. Lbs.		60.00		66.00		
1 Hammer, 15K Ft. Lbs.		258.40		284.25		
1 Air Compr., 600 C.F.M.		269.20		296.10		
2-50 Ft. Air Hoses, 3" Dia.		20.40		22.45	19.79	21.77
64 M.H., Daily Totals		$2203.40		$3030.50	$34.42	$47.34
Crew B-20	Hr.	Daily	Hr.	Daily	Bare Costs	Incl. O&P
1 Labor Foreman (out)	$13.35	$106.80	$22.35	$178.80	$13.13	$22.00
1 Skilled Worker	14.70	117.60	24.65	197.20		
1 Building Laborer	11.35	90.80	19.00	152.00		
24 M.H., Daily Totals		$315.20		$528.00	$13.13	$22.00
Crew B-21	Hr.	Daily	Hr.	Daily	Bare Costs	Incl. O&P
1 Labor Foreman (out)	$13.35	$106.80	$22.35	$178.80	$13.42	$22.40
1 Skilled Worker	14.70	117.60	24.65	197.20		
1 Building Laborer	11.35	90.80	19.00	152.00		
.5 Equip. Oper. (crane)	15.15	60.60	24.85	99.40		
.5 S.P. Crane, 5 Ton		104.00		114.40	3.71	4.08
28 M.H., Daily Totals		$479.80		$741.80	$17.13	$26.48
Crew B-22	Hr.	Daily	Hr.	Daily	Bare Costs	Incl. O&P
1 Labor Foreman (out)	$13.35	$106.80	$22.35	$178.80	$13.53	$22.57
1 Skilled Worker	14.70	117.60	24.65	197.20		
1 Building Laborer	11.35	90.80	19.00	152.00		
.75 Equip. Oper. (crane)	15.15	90.90	24.85	149.10		
.75 S.P. Crane, 5 Ton		156.00		171.60	5.20	5.72
30 M.H., Daily Totals		$562.10		$848.70	$18.73	$28.29
Crew B-23	Hr.	Daily	Hr.	Daily	Bare Costs	Incl. O&P
1 Labor Foreman (outside)	$13.35	$106.80	$22.35	$178.80	$11.75	$19.67
4 Building Laborers	11.35	363.20	19.00	608.00		
1 Drill Rig		395.60		435.15		
1 Light Truck, 3 Ton		148.40		163.25	13.60	14.96
40 M.H., Daily Totals		$1014.00		$1385.20	$25.35	$34.63
Crew B-24	Hr.	Daily	Hr.	Daily	Bare Costs	Incl. O&P
1 Cement Finisher	$14.05	$112.40	$22.50	$180.00	$13.23	$21.80
1 Building Laborer	11.35	90.80	19.00	152.00		
1 Carpenter	14.30	114.40	23.90	191.20		
24 M.H., Daily Totals		$317.60		$523.20	$13.23	$21.80

CREWS

Crew No.	Bare Costs		Incl. Subs O & P		Cost Per Man-Hour	
Crew B-25	Hr.	Daily	Hr.	Daily	Bare Costs	Incl. O&P
1 Labor Foreman	$13.35	$106.80	$22.35	$178.80	$12.41	$20.65
7 Laborers	11.35	635.60	19.00	1064.00		
3 Equip. Oper. (med.)	14.60	350.40	23.95	574.80		
1 Asphalt Paver, 130 H.P.		1086.40		1195.05		
1 Tandem Roller, 10 Ton		187.60		206.35		
1 Roller, Pneumatic Wheel		236.20		259.80	17.16	18.87
88 M.H., Daily Totals		$2603.00		$3478.80	$29.57	$39.52
Crew B-25B	Hr.	Daily	Hr.	Daily	Bare Costs	Incl. O&P
1 Labor Foreman	$13.35	$106.80	$22.35	$178.80	$12.60	$20.92
7 Laborers	11.35	635.60	19.00	1064.00		
4 Equip. Oper. (medium)	14.60	467.20	23.95	766.40		
1 Asphalt Paver, 130 H.P.		1086.40		1195.05		
2 Rollers, Steel Wheel		375.20		412.70		
1 Roller, Pneumatic Wheel		236.20		259.80	17.68	19.45
96 M.H., Daily Totals		$2907.40		$3876.75	$30.28	$40.37
Crew B-26	Hr.	Daily	Hr.	Daily	Bare Costs	Incl. O&P
1 Labor Foreman (outside)	$13.35	$106.80	$22.35	$178.80	$12.75	$21.35
6 Building Laborers	11.35	544.80	19.00	912.00		
2 Equip. Oper. (med.)	14.60	233.60	23.95	383.20		
1 Rodman (reinf.)	15.55	124.40	28.20	225.60		
1 Cement Finisher	14.05	112.40	22.50	180.00		
1 Grader, 30,000 Lbs.		521.00		573.10		
1 Paving Mach. & Equip.		1175.80		1293.40	19.28	21.21
88 M.H., Daily Totals		$2818.80		$3746.10	$32.03	$42.56
Crew B-27	Hr.	Daily	Hr.	Daily	Bare Costs	Incl. O&P
1 Labor Foreman (outside)	$13.35	$106.80	$22.35	$178.80	$11.85	$19.83
3 Building Laborers	11.35	272.40	19.00	456.00		
1 Berm Machine		58.20		64.00	1.81	2.00
32 M.H., Daily Totals		$437.40		$698.80	$13.66	$21.83
Crew B-28	Hr.	Daily	Hr.	Daily	Bare Costs	Incl. O&P
2 Carpenters	$14.30	$228.80	$23.90	$382.40	$13.31	$22.26
1 Building Laborer	11.35	90.80	19.00	152.00		
24 M.H., Daily Totals		$319.60		$534.40	$13.31	$22.26
Crew B-29	Hr.	Daily	Hr.	Daily	Bare Costs	Incl. O&P
1 Labor Foreman (outside)	$13.35	$106.80	$22.35	$178.80	$12.34	$20.52
4 Building Laborers	11.35	363.20	19.00	608.00		
1 Equip. Oper. (crane)	15.15	121.20	24.85	198.80		
1 Equip. Oper. Oiler	12.50	100.00	20.50	164.00		
1 Gradall, 3 Ton, 1/2 C.Y.		555.60		611.15	9.92	10.91
56 M.H., Daily Totals		$1246.80		$1760.75	$22.26	$31.43
Crew B-30	Hr.	Daily	Hr.	Daily	Bare Costs	Incl. O&P
1 Equip. Oper. (med.)	$14.60	$116.80	$23.95	$191.60	$12.83	$21.05
2 Truck Drivers (heavy)	11.95	191.20	19.60	313.60		
1 Hyd. Excavator, 1.5 C.Y.		679.60		747.55		
2 Dump Trucks, 16 Ton		730.40		803.45	58.75	64.62
24 M.H., Daily Totals		$1718.00		$2056.20	$71.58	$85.67

Crew No.	Bare Costs		Incl. Subs O & P		Cost Per Man-Hour	
Crew B-31	Hr.	Daily	Hr.	Daily	Bare Costs	Incl. O&P
1 Labor Foreman (outside)	$13.35	$106.80	$22.35	$178.80	$12.34	$20.65
3 Building Laborers	11.35	272.40	19.00	456.00		
1 Carpenter	14.30	114.40	23.90	191.20		
1 Air Compr., 250 C.F.M.		88.80		97.70		
1 Sheeting Driver		9.20		10.10		
2-50 Ft. Air Hoses, 1.5" Dia.		10.80		11.90	2.72	2.99
40 M.H., Daily Totals		$602.40		$945.70	$15.06	$23.64
Crew B-32	Hr.	Daily	Hr.	Daily	Bare Costs	Incl. O&P
1 Highway Laborer	$11.35	$90.80	$19.00	$152.00	$13.78	$22.71
3 Equip. Oper. (med.)	14.60	350.40	23.95	574.80		
1 Grader, 30,000 Lbs.		521.00		573.10		
1 Tandem Roller, 10 Ton		187.60		206.35		
1 Dozer, 200 H.P.		775.80		853.40	46.38	51.02
32 M.H., Daily Totals		$1925.60		$2359.65	$60.16	$73.73
Crew B-32A	Hr.	Daily	Hr.	Daily	Bare Costs	Incl. O&P
1 Laborer	$11.35	$90.80	$19.00	$152.00	$13.51	$22.30
2 Equip. Oper. (medium)	14.60	233.60	23.95	383.20		
1 Grader, 30,000 Lbs.		521.00		573.10		
1 Roller, Vbrtry, 29,000 Lbs.		341.60		375.75	35.94	39.53
24 M.H., Daily Totals		$1187.00		$1484.05	$49.45	$61.83
Crew B-32B	Hr.	Daily	Hr.	Daily	Bare Costs	Incl. O&P
1 Laborer	$11.35	$90.80	$19.00	$152.00	$13.51	$22.30
2 Equip. Oper. (medium)	14.60	233.60	23.95	383.20		
1 Dozer, 200 H.P.		775.80		853.40		
1 Roller, Vbrtry, 29,000 Lbs.		341.60		375.75	46.55	51.21
24 M.H., Daily Totals		$1441.80		$1764.35	$60.06	$73.51
Crew B-32C	Hr.	Daily	Hr.	Daily	Bare Costs	Incl. O&P
1 Labor Foreman	$13.35	$106.80	$22.35	$178.80	$13.30	$22.03
2 Laborers	11.35	181.60	19.00	304.00		
3 Equip. Oper. (medium)	14.60	350.40	23.95	574.80		
1 Grader, 30,000 Lbs.		521.00		573.10		
1 Roller, Steel Wheel		187.60		206.35		
1 Dozer, 200 H.P.		775.80		853.40	30.92	34.01
48 M.H., Daily Totals		$2123.20		$2690.45	$44.22	$56.04
Crew B-33	Hr.	Daily	Hr.	Daily	Bare Costs	Incl. O&P
1 Equip. Oper. (med.)	$14.60	$116.80	$23.95	$191.60	$13.67	$22.53
.5 Building Laborer	11.35	45.40	19.00	76.00		
.25 Equip. Oper. (med.)	14.60	29.20	23.95	47.90		
14 M.H., Daily Totals		$191.40		$315.50	$13.67	$22.53
Crew B-33A	Hr.	Daily	Hr.	Daily	Bare Costs	Incl. O&P
1 Equip. Oper. (med.)	$14.60	$116.80	$23.95	$191.60	$13.67	$22.53
.5 Building Laborer	11.35	45.40	19.00	76.00		
.25 Equip. Oper. (med.)	14.60	29.20	23.95	47.90		
1 Scraper, Towed, 7 C.Y.		61.60		67.75		
1 Dozer, 300 H.P.		861.80		948.00		
.25 Dozer, 300 H.P.		215.45		237.00	81.34	89.48
14 M.H., Daily Totals		$1330.25		$1568.25	$95.01	$112.01

CREWS

Crew No.		Bare Costs		Incl. Subs O & P		Cost Per Man-Hour	
Crew B-33B	Hr.	Daily	Hr.	Daily	Bare Costs	Incl. O&P
1 Equip. Oper. (med.)	$14.60	$116.80	$23.95	$191.60	$13.67	$22.53
.5 Building Laborer	11.35	45.40	19.00	76.00		
.25 Equip. Oper. (med.)	14.60	29.20	23.95	47.90		
1 Scraper, Towed, 10 C.Y.		170.00		187.00		
1 Dozer, 300 H.P.		861.80		948.00		
.25 Dozer, 300 H.P.		215.45		237.00	89.08	98.00
14 M.H., Daily Totals		$1438.65		$1687.50	$102.75	$120.53
Crew B-33C	Hr.	Daily	Hr.	Daily	Bare Costs	Incl. O&P
1 Equip. Oper. (med.)	$14.60	$116.80	$23.95	$191.60	$13.67	$22.53
.5 Building Laborer	11.35	45.40	19.00	76.00		
.25 Equip. Oper. (med.)	14.60	29.20	23.95	47.90		
1 Scraper, Towed, 12 C.Y.		170.00		187.00		
1 Dozer, 300 H.P.		861.80		948.00		
.25 Dozer, 300 H.P.		215.45		237.00	89.08	98.00
14 M.H., Daily Totals		$1438.65		$1687.50	$102.75	$120.53
Crew B-33D	Hr.	Daily	Hr.	Daily	Bare Costs	Incl. O&P
1 Equip. Oper. (med.)	$14.60	$116.80	$23.95	$191.60	$13.67	$22.53
.5 Building Laborer	11.35	45.40	19.00	76.00		
.25 Equip. Oper. (med.)	14.60	29.20	23.95	47.90		
1 S.P. Scraper, 14 C.Y.		1382.60		1520.85		
.25 Dozer, 300 H.P.		215.45		237.00	114.14	125.56
14 M.H., Daily Totals		$1789.45		$2073.35	$127.81	$148.09
Crew B-33E	Hr.	Daily	Hr.	Daily	Bare Costs	Incl. O&P
1 Equip. Oper. (med.)	$14.60	$116.80	$23.95	$191.60	$13.67	$22.53
.5 Building Laborer	11.35	45.40	19.00	76.00		
.25 Equip. Oper. (med.)	14.60	29.20	23.95	47.90		
1 S.P. Scraper, 24 C.Y.		1650.60		1815.65		
.25 Dozer, 300 H.P.		215.45		237.00	133.28	146.61
14 M.H., Daily Totals		$2057.45		$2368.15	$146.95	$169.14
Crew B-33F	Hr.	Daily	Hr.	Daily	Bare Costs	Incl. O&P
1 Equip. Oper. (med.)	$14.60	$116.80	$23.95	$191.60	$13.67	$22.53
.5 Building Laborer	11.35	45.40	19.00	76.00		
.25 Equip. Oper. (med.)	14.60	29.20	23.95	47.90		
1 Elev. Scraper, 11 C.Y.		589.20		648.10		
.25 Dozer, 300 H.P.		215.45		237.00	57.47	63.22
14 M.H., Daily Totals		$996.05		$1200.60	$71.14	$85.75
Crew B-33G	Hr.	Daily	Hr.	Daily	Bare Costs	Incl. O&P
1 Equip. Oper. (med.)	$14.60	$116.80	$23.95	$191.60	$13.67	$22.53
.5 Building Laborer	11.35	45.40	19.00	76.00		
.25 Equip. Oper. (med.)	14.60	29.20	23.95	47.90		
1 Elev. Scraper, 20 C.Y.		774.80		852.30		
.25 Dozer, 300 H.P.		215.45		237.00	70.73	77.80
14 M.H., Daily Totals		$1181.65		$1404.80	$84.40	$100.33
Crew B-34	Hr.	Daily	Hr.	Daily	Bare Costs	Incl. O&P
1 Truck Driver (heavy)	$11.95	$95.60	$19.60	$156.80	$11.95	$19.60
8 M.H., Daily Totals		$95.60		$156.80	$11.95	$19.60
Crew B-34A	Hr.	Daily	Hr.	Daily	Bare Costs	Incl. O&P
1 Truck Driver (heavy)	$11.95	$95.60	$19.60	$156.80	$11.95	$19.60
1 Dump Truck, 12 Ton		298.80		328.70	37.35	41.08
8 M.H., Daily Totals		$394.40		$485.50	$49.30	$60.68

Crew No.		Bare Costs		Incl. Subs O & P		Cost Per Man-Hour	
Crew B-34B	Hr.	Daily	Hr.	Daily	Bare Costs	Incl. O&P
1 Truck Driver (heavy)	$11.95	$95.60	$19.60	$156.80	$11.95	$19.60
1 Dump Truck, 16 Ton		365.20		401.70	45.65	50.21
8 M.H., Daily Totals		$460.80		$558.50	$57.60	$69.81
Crew B-34C	Hr.	Daily	Hr.	Daily	Bare Costs	Incl. O&P
1 Truck Driver (heavy)	$11.95	$95.60	$19.60	$156.80	$11.95	$19.60
1 Truck Tractor, 40 Ton		348.80		383.70		
1 Dump Trailer, 16.5 C.Y.		108.60		119.45	57.17	62.89
8 M.H., Daily Totals		$553.00		$659.95	$69.12	$82.49
Crew B-34D	Hr.	Daily	Hr.	Daily	Bare Costs	Incl. O&P
1 Truck Driver (heavy)	$11.95	$95.60	$19.60	$156.80	$11.95	$19.60
1 Truck Tractor, 40 Ton		348.80		383.70		
1 Dump Trailer, 20 C.Y.		109.60		120.55	57.30	63.03
8 M.H., Daily Totals		$554.00		$661.05	$69.25	$82.63
Crew B-34E	Hr.	Daily	Hr.	Daily	Bare Costs	Incl. O&P
1 Truck Driver (heavy)	$11.95	$95.60	$19.60	$156.80	$11.95	$19.60
1 Truck, Off Hwy., 25 Ton		549.00		603.90	68.62	75.48
8 M.H., Daily Totals		$644.60		$760.70	$80.57	$95.08
Crew B-34F	Hr.	Daily	Hr.	Daily	Bare Costs	Incl. O&P
1 Truck Driver (heavy)	$11.95	$95.60	$19.60	$156.80	$11.95	$19.60
1 Truck, Off Hwy., 22 C.Y.		836.00		919.60	104.50	114.95
8 M.H., Daily Totals		$931.60		$1076.40	$116.45	$134.55
Crew B-34G	Hr.	Daily	Hr.	Daily	Bare Costs	Incl. O&P
1 Truck Driver (heavy)	$11.95	$95.60	$19.60	$156.80	$11.95	$19.60
1 Truck, Off Hwy., 34 C.Y.		1096.80		1206.50	137.10	150.81
8 M.H., Daily Totals		$1192.40		$1363.30	$149.05	$170.41
Crew B-34H	Hr.	Daily	Hr.	Daily	Bare Costs	Incl. O&P
1 Truck Driver (heavy)	$11.95	$95.60	$19.60	$156.80	$11.95	$19.60
1 Truck, Off Hwy., 42 C.Y.		1368.80		1505.70	171.10	188.21
8 M.H., Daily Totals		$1464.40		$1662.50	$183.05	$207.81
Crew B-34J	Hr.	Daily	Hr.	Daily	Bare Costs	Incl. O&P
1 Truck Driver (heavy)	$11.95	$95.60	$19.60	$156.80	$11.95	$19.60
1 Truck, Off Hwy., 60 C.Y.		1860.40		2046.45	232.55	255.80
8 M.H., Daily Totals		$1956.00		$2203.25	$244.50	$275.40
Crew B-34K	Hr.	Daily	Hr.	Daily	Bare Costs	Incl. O&P
1 Truck Driver (heavy)	$11.95	$95.60	$19.60	$156.80	$11.95	$19.60
1 Truck Tractor, 240 H.P.		439.00		482.90		
1 Low Bed Trailer		262.20		288.40	87.65	96.41
8 M.H., Daily Totals		$796.80		$928.10	$99.60	$116.01
Crew B-35	Hr.	Daily	Hr.	Daily	Bare Costs	Incl. O&P
1 Laborer Foreman (out)	$13.35	$106.80	$22.35	$178.80	$13.93	$23.05
1 Skilled Worker	14.70	117.60	24.65	197.20		
1 Welder (plumber)	16.55	132.40	27.00	216.00		
1 Laborer	11.35	90.80	19.00	152.00		
1 Equip. Oper. (crane)	15.15	121.20	24.85	198.80		
1 Equip. Oper. Oiler	12.50	100.00	20.50	164.00		
1 Electric Welding Mach.		39.00		42.90		
1 Hyd. Excavator, .75 C.Y.		457.20		502.90	10.33	11.37
48 M.H., Daily Totals		$1165.00		$1652.60	$24.26	$34.42

CREWS

Crew No.	Bare Costs Hr.	Daily	Incl. Subs O & P Hr.	Daily	Cost Per Man-Hour Bare Costs	Incl. O&P
Crew B-36	Hr.	Daily	Hr.	Daily	Bare Costs	Incl. O&P
1 Labor Foreman (outside)	$13.35	$106.80	$22.35	$178.80	$13.05	$21.65
2 Highway Laborers	11.35	181.60	19.00	304.00		
2 Equip. Oper. (med.)	14.60	233.60	23.95	383.20		
1 Dozer, 200 H.P.		775.80		853.40		
1 Aggregate Spreader		58.60		64.45		
1 Tandem Roller, 10 Ton		187.60		206.35	25.55	28.10
40 M.H., Daily Totals		$1544.00		$1990.20	$38.60	$49.75
Crew B-36A	Hr.	Daily	Hr.	Daily	Bare Costs	Incl. O&P
1 Labor Foreman	$13.35	$106.80	$22.35	$178.80	$13.49	$22.30
2 Laborers	11.35	181.60	19.00	304.00		
4 Equip. Oper. (medium)	14.60	467.20	23.95	766.40		
1 Dozer, 200 H.P.		775.80		853.40		
1 Aggregate Spreader		58.60		64.45		
1 Roller, Steel Wheel		187.60		206.35		
1 Roller, Pneumatic Wheel		236.20		259.80	22.46	24.71
56 M.H., Daily Totals		$2013.80		$2633.20	$35.95	$47.01
Crew B-37	Hr.	Daily	Hr.	Daily	Bare Costs	Incl. O&P
1 Labor Foreman (outside)	$13.35	$106.80	$22.35	$178.80	$12.10	$20.19
4 Building Laborers	11.35	363.20	19.00	608.00		
1 Equip. Oper. (light)	13.90	111.20	22.80	182.40		
1 Tandem Roller, 5 Ton		118.40		130.25	2.46	2.71
48 M.H., Daily Totals		$699.60		$1099.45	$14.56	$22.90
Crew B-38	Hr.	Daily	Hr.	Daily	Bare Costs	Incl. O&P
1 Labor Foreman (outside)	$13.35	$106.80	$22.35	$178.80	$12.91	$21.42
2 Building Laborers	11.35	181.60	19.00	304.00		
1 Equip. Oper. (light)	13.90	111.20	22.80	182.40		
1 Equip. Oper. (medium)	14.60	116.80	23.95	191.60		
1 Backhoe Loader, 48 H.P.		190.40		209.45		
1 Hammer., Hyd. (1000 lb.)		337.80		371.60		
1 F.E. Loader (170 H.P.)		563.00		619.30		
1 Pavt. Rem. Bucket		38.20		42.00	28.23	31.05
40 M.H., Daily Totals		$1645.80		$2099.15	$41.14	$52.47
Crew B-39	Hr.	Daily	Hr.	Daily	Bare Costs	Incl. O&P
1 Labor Foreman (outside)	$13.35	$106.80	$22.35	$178.80	$12.10	$20.19
4 Building Laborers	11.35	363.20	19.00	608.00		
1 Equipment Oper. (light)	13.90	111.20	22.80	182.40		
1 Air Compr., 250 C.F.M.		88.80		97.70		
Air Tools & Accessories		27.60		30.35		
2-50 Ft. Air Hoses, 1.5" Dia.		10.80		11.90	2.65	2.91
48 M.H., Daily Totals		$708.40		$1109.15	$14.75	$23.10
Crew B-40	Hr.	Daily	Hr.	Daily	Bare Costs	Incl. O&P
1 Pile Driver Foreman	$16.45	$131.60	$29.80	$238.40	$14.63	$25.57
4 Pile Drivers	14.45	462.40	26.15	836.80		
2 Equip. Oper. (crane)	15.15	242.40	24.85	397.60		
1 Equip. Oper. Oiler	12.50	100.00	20.50	164.00		
1 Crane, 40 Ton		659.00		724.90		
Vibratory Hammer & Gen.		1059.80		1165.80	26.85	29.54
64 M.H., Daily Totals		$2655.20		$3527.50	$41.48	$55.11

Crew No.	Bare Costs Hr.	Daily	Incl. Subs O & P Hr.	Daily	Cost Per Man-Hour Bare Costs	Incl. O&P
Crew B-41	Hr.	Daily	Hr.	Daily	Bare Costs	Incl. O&P
1 Labor Foreman (outside)	$13.35	$106.80	$22.35	$178.80	$11.93	$19.94
4 Building Laborers	11.35	363.20	19.00	608.00		
.25 Equip. Oper. (crane)	15.15	30.30	24.85	49.70		
.25 Equip. Oper. Oiler	12.50	25.00	20.50	41.00		
.25 Crawler Crane, 40 Ton		164.75		181.25	3.74	4.11
44 M.H., Daily Totals		$690.05		$1058.75	$15.67	$24.05
Crew B-42	Hr.	Daily	Hr.	Daily	Bare Costs	Incl. O&P
1 Labor Foreman (outside)	$13.35	$106.80	$22.35	$178.80	$12.75	$21.66
4 Building Laborers	11.35	363.20	19.00	608.00		
1 Equip. Oper. (crane)	15.15	121.20	24.85	198.80		
1 Equip. Oper. Oiler	12.50	100.00	20.50	164.00		
1 Welder	15.65	125.20	29.60	236.80		
1 Hyd. Crane, 25 Ton		486.40		535.05		
1 Gas Welding Machine		68.40		75.25		
1 Horz. Boring Csg. Mch.		424.40		466.85	15.30	16.83
64 M.H., Daily Totals		$1795.60		$2463.55	$28.05	$38.49
Crew B-43	Hr.	Daily	Hr.	Daily	Bare Costs	Incl. O&P
1 Labor Foreman (outside)	$13.35	$106.80	$22.35	$178.80	$12.50	$20.78
3 Building Laborers	11.35	272.40	19.00	456.00		
1 Equip. Oper. (crane)	15.15	121.20	24.85	198.80		
1 Equip. Oper. Oiler	12.50	100.00	20.50	164.00		
1 Drill Rig & Augers		744.65		819.15	15.51	17.06
48 M.H., Daily Totals		$1345.05		$1816.75	$28.01	$37.84
Crew B-44	Hr.	Daily	Hr.	Daily	Bare Costs	Incl. O&P
1 Pile Driver Foreman	$16.45	$131.60	$29.80	$238.40	$14.48	$25.38
4 Pile Drivers	14.45	462.40	26.15	836.80		
2 Equip. Oper. (crane)	15.15	242.40	24.85	397.60		
1 Building Laborer	11.35	90.80	19.00	152.00		
1 Crane, 40 Ton, & Access.		1153.25		1268.60		
45 L.F. Leads, 15K Ft. Lbs.		45.00		49.50	18.72	20.59
64 M.H., Daily Totals		$2125.45		$2942.90	$33.20	$45.97
Crew B-45	Hr.	Daily	Hr.	Daily	Bare Costs	Incl. O&P
1 Equip. Oper. (med.)	$14.60	$116.80	$23.95	$191.60	$13.27	$21.77
1 Truck Driver (heavy)	11.95	95.60	19.60	156.80		
1 Dist. Tank Truck, 3K Gal.		308.20		339.00		
1 Tractor, 4 x 2, 250 H.P.		315.00		346.50	38.95	42.84
16 M.H., Daily Totals		$835.60		$1033.90	$52.22	$64.61
Crew B-46	Hr.	Daily	Hr.	Daily	Bare Costs	Incl. O&P
1 Pile Driver Foreman	$16.45	$131.60	$29.80	$238.40	$13.23	$23.18
2 Pile Drivers	14.45	231.20	26.15	418.40		
3 Building Laborers	11.35	272.40	19.00	456.00		
1 Chain Saw, 36" Long		41.60		45.75	.86	.95
48 M.H., Daily Totals		$676.80		$1158.55	$14.09	$24.13
Crew B-47	Hr.	Daily	Hr.	Daily	Bare Costs	Incl. O&P
1 Blast Foreman	$13.35	$106.80	$22.35	$178.80	$12.86	$21.38
1 Driller	11.35	90.80	19.00	152.00		
1 Equip. Oper. (light)	13.90	111.20	22.80	182.40		
1 Crawler Type Drill, 4"		217.00		238.70		
1 Air Compr., 600 C.F.M.		269.20		296.10		
2-50 Ft. Air Hoses, 3" Dia.		20.40		22.45	21.10	23.21
24 M.H., Daily Totals		$815.40		$1070.45	$33.96	$44.59

CREWS

Crew No.		Bare Costs	Incl. Subs O & P		Cost Per Man-Hour	
Crew B-47A	Hr.	Daily	Hr.	Daily	Bare Costs	Incl. O&P
1 Drilling Foreman	$13.35	$106.80	$22.35	$178.80	$13.66	$22.56
1 Equip. Oper. (heavy)	15.15	121.20	24.85	198.80		
1 Oiler	12.50	100.00	20.50	164.00		
1 Quarry Drill		451.40		496.55	18.80	20.68
24 M.H., Daily Totals		$779.40		$1038.15	$32.46	$43.24
Crew B-48	Hr.	Daily	Hr.	Daily	Bare Costs	Incl. O&P
1 Labor Foreman (outside)	$13.35	$106.80	$22.35	$178.80	$12.70	$21.07
3 Building Laborers	11.35	272.40	19.00	456.00		
1 Equip. Oper. (crane)	15.15	121.20	24.85	198.80		
1 Equip. Oper. Oiler	12.50	100.00	20.50	164.00		
1 Equip. Oper. (light)	13.90	111.20	22.80	182.40		
1 Centr. Water Pump, 6"		146.20		160.80		
1-20 Ft. Suction Hose, 6"		23.40		25.75		
1-50 Ft. Disch. Hose, 6"		13.00		14.30		
1 Drill Rig & Augers		744.65		819.15	16.55	18.21
56 M.H., Daily Totals		$1638.85		$2200.00	$29.25	$39.28
Crew B-49	Hr.	Daily	Hr.	Daily	Bare Costs	Incl. O&P
1 Labor Foreman (outside)	$13.35	$106.80	$22.35	$178.80	$13.22	$22.28
3 Building Laborers	11.35	272.40	19.00	456.00		
2 Equip. Oper. (crane)	15.15	242.40	24.85	397.60		
2 Equip. Oper. Oilers	12.50	200.00	20.50	328.00		
1 Equip. Oper. (light)	13.90	111.20	22.80	182.40		
2 Pile Drivers	14.45	231.20	26.15	418.40		
1 Hyd. Crane, 25 Ton		486.40		535.05		
1 Centr. Water Pump, 6"		146.20		160.80		
1-20 Ft. Suction Hose, 6"		23.40		25.75		
1-50 Ft. Disch. Hose, 6"		13.00		14.30		
1 Drill Rig & Augers		744.65		819.15	16.06	17.67
88 M.H., Daily Totals		$2577.65		$3516.25	$29.28	$39.95
Crew B-50	Hr.	Daily	Hr.	Daily	Bare Costs	Incl. O&P
2 Pile Driver Foremen	$16.45	$263.20	$29.80	$476.80	$14.03	$24.55
6 Pile Drivers	14.45	693.60	26.15	1255.20		
2 Equip. Oper. (crane)	15.15	242.40	24.85	397.60		
1 Equip. Oper. Oiler	12.50	100.00	20.50	164.00		
3 Building Laborers	11.35	272.40	19.00	456.00		
1 Crane, 40 Ton		659.00		724.90		
60 L.F. Leads, 15K Ft. Lbs.		60.00		66.00		
1 Hammer, 15K Ft. Lbs.		258.40		284.25		
1 Air Compr., 600 C.F.M.		269.20		296.10		
2-50 Ft. Air Hoses, 3" Dia.		20.40		22.45		
1 Chain Saw, 36" Long		41.60		45.75	11.68	12.85
112 M.H., Daily Totals		$2880.20		$4189.05	$25.71	$37.40
Crew B-51	Hr.	Daily	Hr.	Daily	Bare Costs	Incl. O&P
1 Labor Foreman (outside)	$13.35	$106.80	$22.35	$178.80	$11.75	$19.60
4 Building Laborers	11.35	363.20	19.00	608.00		
1 Truck Driver (light)	11.75	94.00	19.30	154.40		
1 Light Truck, 1.5 Ton		146.00		160.60	3.04	3.34
48 M.H., Daily Totals		$710.00		$1101.80	$14.79	$22.94

Crew No.		Bare Costs	Incl. Subs O & P		Cost Per Man-Hour	
Crew B-52	Hr.	Daily	Hr.	Daily	Bare Costs	Incl. O&P
1 Carpenter Foreman	$16.30	$130.40	$27.25	$218.00	$13.39	$22.38
1 Carpenter	14.30	114.40	23.90	191.20		
3 Building Laborers	11.35	272.40	19.00	456.00		
1 Cement Finisher	14.05	112.40	22.50	180.00		
.5 Rodman (reinf.)	15.55	62.20	28.20	112.80		
.5 Equip. Oper. (med.)	14.60	58.40	23.95	95.80		
.5 F.E. Ldr., T.M., 2.5 C.Y.		403.90		444.30	7.21	7.93
56 M.H., Daily Totals		$1154.10		$1698.10	$20.60	$30.31
Crew B-53	Hr.	Daily	Hr.	Daily	Bare Costs	Incl. O&P
1 Equip. Oper. (light)	$13.90	$111.20	$22.80	$182.40	$13.90	$22.80
1 Trencher, Chain, 12 H.P.		53.20		58.50	6.65	7.31
8 M.H., Daily Totals		$164.40		$240.90	$20.55	$30.11
Crew B-54	Hr.	Daily	Hr.	Daily	Bare Costs	Incl. O&P
1 Equip. Oper. (light)	$13.90	$111.20	$22.80	$182.40	$13.90	$22.80
1 Trencher, Chain, 40 H.P.		135.20		148.70	16.90	18.58
8 M.H., Daily Totals		$246.40		$331.10	$30.80	$41.38
Crew B-55	Hr.	Daily	Hr.	Daily	Bare Costs	Incl. O&P
2 Building Laborers	$11.35	$181.60	$19.00	$304.00	$11.48	$19.10
1 Truck Driver (light)	11.75	94.00	19.30	154.40		
1 Flatbed Truck w/Auger		395.60		435.15		
1 Truck, 3 Ton		148.40		163.25	22.66	24.93
24 M.H., Daily Totals		$819.60		$1056.80	$34.14	$44.03
Crew B-56	Hr.	Daily	Hr.	Daily	Bare Costs	Incl. O&P
1 Building Laborer	$11.35	$90.80	$19.00	$152.00	$12.62	$20.90
1 Equip. Oper. (light)	13.90	111.20	22.80	182.40		
1 Crawler Type Drill, 4"		217.00		238.70		
1 Air Compr., 600 C.F.M.		269.20		296.10		
1-50 Ft. Air Hose, 3" Dia.		10.20		11.20	31.02	34.12
16 M.H., Daily Totals		$698.40		$880.40	$43.64	$55.02
Crew B-57	Hr.	Daily	Hr.	Daily	Bare Costs	Incl. O&P
1 Labor Foreman (outside)	$13.35	$106.80	$22.35	$178.80	$12.93	$21.41
2 Building Laborers	11.35	181.60	19.00	304.00		
1 Equip. Oper. (crane)	15.15	121.20	24.85	198.80		
1 Equip. Oper. (light)	13.90	111.20	22.80	182.40		
1 Equip. Oper. Oiler	12.50	100.00	20.50	164.00		
1 Power Shovel, 1 C.Y.		435.80		479.40		
1 Clamshell Bucket, 1 C.Y.		59.60		65.55		
1 Centr. Water Pump, 6"		146.20		160.80		
1-20 Ft. Suction Hose, 6"		23.40		25.75		
20-50 Ft. Disch. Hoses, 6"		260.00		286.00	19.27	21.19
48 M.H., Daily Totals		$1545.80		$2045.50	$32.20	$42.60
Crew B-58	Hr.	Daily	Hr.	Daily	Bare Costs	Incl. O&P
2 Building Laborers	$11.35	$181.60	$19.00	$304.00	$12.20	$20.26
1 Equip. Oper. (light)	13.90	111.20	22.80	182.40		
1 Backhoe Loader, 48 H.P.		190.40		209.45		
1 Small Helicopter		2259.00		2484.90	102.05	112.26
24 M.H., Daily Totals		$2742.20		$3180.75	$114.25	$132.52
Crew B-59	Hr.	Daily	Hr.	Daily	Bare Costs	Incl. O&P
1 Truck Driver (heavy)	$11.95	$95.60	$19.60	$156.80	$11.95	$19.60
1 Truck, 30 Ton		268.40		295.25		
1 Water Tank, 5000 Gal.		184.80		203.30	56.65	62.31
8 M.H., Daily Totals		$548.80		$655.35	$68.60	$81.91

CREWS

Crew No.	Bare Costs		Incl. Subs O & P		Cost Per Man-Hour	
Crew B-60	Hr.	Daily	Hr.	Daily	Bare Costs	Incl. O&P
1 Labor Foreman (outside)	$13.35	$106.80	$22.35	$178.80	$13.07	$21.61
2 Building Laborers	11.35	181.60	19.00	304.00		
1 Equip. Oper. (crane)	15.15	121.20	24.85	198.80		
2 Equip. Oper. (light)	13.90	222.40	22.80	364.80		
1 Equip. Oper. Oiler	12.50	100.00	20.50	164.00		
1 Crawler Crane, 40 Ton		659.00		724.90		
45 L.F. Leads, 15K Ft. Lbs.		45.00		49.50		
1 Backhoe Loader, 48 H.P.		190.40		209.45	15.97	17.56
56 M.H., Daily Totals		$1626.40		$2194.25	$29.04	$39.17
Crew B-61	Hr.	Daily	Hr.	Daily	Bare Costs	Incl. O&P
1 Labor Foreman (outside)	$13.35	$106.80	$22.35	$178.80	$12.26	$20.43
3 Building Laborers	11.35	272.40	19.00	456.00		
1 Equip. Oper. (light)	13.90	111.20	22.80	182.40		
1 Cement Mixer, 2 C.Y.		230.60		253.65		
1 Air Compr., 160 C.F.M.		85.40		93.95	7.90	8.69
40 M.H., Daily Totals		$806.40		$1164.80	$20.16	$29.12
Crew B-62	Hr.	Daily	Hr.	Daily	Bare Costs	Incl. O&P
2 Building Laborers	$11.35	$181.60	$19.00	$304.00	$12.20	$20.26
1 Equip. Oper. (light)	13.90	111.20	22.80	182.40		
1 Loader, Skid Steer		88.80		97.70	3.70	4.07
24 M.H., Daily Totals		$381.60		$584.10	$15.90	$24.33
Crew B-63	Hr.	Daily	Hr.	Daily	Bare Costs	Incl. O&P
4 Building Laborers	$11.35	$363.20	$19.00	$608.00	$11.86	$19.76
1 Equip. Oper. (light)	13.90	111.20	22.80	182.40		
1 Loader, Skid Steer		88.80		97.70	2.22	2.44
40 M.H., Daily Totals		$563.20		$888.10	$14.08	$22.20
Crew B-64	Hr.	Daily	Hr.	Daily	Bare Costs	Incl. O&P
1 Building Laborer	$11.35	$90.80	$19.00	$152.00	$11.55	$19.15
1 Truck Driver (light)	11.75	94.00	19.30	154.40		
1 Power Mulcher (small)		88.60		97.45		
1 Light Truck, 1.5 Ton		146.00		160.60	14.66	16.12
16 M.H., Daily Totals		$419.40		$564.45	$26.21	$35.27
Crew B-65	Hr.	Daily	Hr.	Daily	Bare Costs	Incl. O&P
1 Building Laborer	$11.35	$90.80	$19.00	$152.00	$11.55	$19.15
1 Truck Driver (light)	11.75	94.00	19.30	154.40		
1 Power Mulcher (large)		202.60		222.85		
1 Light Truck, 1.5 Ton		146.00		160.60	21.78	23.96
16 M.H., Daily Totals		$533.40		$689.85	$33.33	$43.11
Crew B-66	Hr.	Daily	Hr.	Daily	Bare Costs	Incl. O&P
1 Equip. Oper. (light)	$13.90	$111.20	$22.80	$182.40	$13.90	$22.80
1 Backhoe Ldr. w/Attchmt.		162.60		178.85	20.32	22.35
8 M.H., Daily Totals		$273.80		$361.25	$34.22	$45.15
Crew B-67	Hr.	Daily	Hr.	Daily	Bare Costs	Incl. O&P
1 Millwright	$14.90	$119.20	$23.95	$191.60	$14.40	$23.37
1 Equip. Oper. (light)	13.90	111.20	22.80	182.40		
1 Forklift		183.00		201.30	11.43	12.58
16 M.H., Daily Totals		$413.40		$575.30	$25.83	$35.95
Crew B-68	Hr.	Daily	Hr.	Daily	Bare Costs	Incl. O&P
2 Millwrights	$14.90	$238.40	$23.95	$383.20	$14.56	$23.56
1 Equip. Oper. (light)	13.90	111.20	22.80	182.40		
1 Forklift		183.00		201.30	7.62	8.38
24 M.H., Daily Totals		$532.60		$766.90	$22.18	$31.94

Crew No.	Bare Costs		Incl. Subs O & P		Cost Per Man-Hour	
Crew B-69	Hr.	Daily	Hr.	Daily	Bare Costs	Incl. O&P
1 Labor Foreman (outside)	$13.35	$106.80	$22.35	$178.80	$12.50	$20.78
3 Highway Laborers	11.35	272.40	19.00	456.00		
1 Equip. Oper. (crane)	15.15	121.20	24.85	198.80		
1 Equip. Oper. Oiler	12.50	100.00	20.50	164.00		
1 Truck Crane, 80 Ton		1103.40		1213.75	22.98	25.28
48 M.H., Daily Totals		$1703.80		$2211.35	$35.48	$46.06
Crew B-69A	Hr.	Daily	Hr.	Daily	Bare Costs	Incl. O&P
1 Labor Foreman	$13.35	$106.80	$22.35	$178.80	$12.67	$20.96
3 Laborers	11.35	272.40	19.00	456.00		
1 Equip. Oper. (medium)	14.60	116.80	23.95	191.60		
1 Concrete Finisher	14.05	112.40	22.50	180.00		
1 Curb Paver		394.80		434.30	8.22	9.04
48 M.H., Daily Totals		$1003.20		$1440.70	$20.89	$30.00
Crew B-69B	Hr.	Daily	Hr.	Daily	Bare Costs	Incl. O&P
1 Labor Foreman	$13.35	$106.80	$22.35	$178.80	$12.67	$20.96
3 Laborers	11.35	272.40	19.00	456.00		
1 Equip. Oper. (medium)	14.60	116.80	23.95	191.60		
1 Cement Finisher	14.05	112.40	22.50	180.00		
1 Curb/Gutter Paver		858.00		943.80	17.87	19.66
48 M.H., Daily Totals		$1466.40		$1950.20	$30.54	$40.62
Crew B-70	Hr.	Daily	Hr.	Daily	Bare Costs	Incl. O&P
1 Labor Foreman (outside)	$13.35	$106.80	$22.35	$178.80	$13.02	$21.60
3 Highway Laborers	11.35	272.40	19.00	456.00		
3 Equip. Oper. (med.)	14.60	350.40	23.95	574.80		
1 Motor Grader, 30,000 Lb.		521.00		573.10		
1 Grader Attach., Ripper		51.60		56.75		
1 Road Sweeper, S.P.		148.60		163.45		
1 F.E. Loader, 1-3/4 C.Y.		309.60		340.55	18.40	20.24
56 M.H., Daily Totals		$1760.40		$2343.45	$31.42	$41.84
Crew B-71	Hr.	Daily	Hr.	Daily	Bare Costs	Incl. O&P
1 Labor Foreman (outside)	$13.35	$106.80	$22.35	$178.80	$13.02	$21.60
3 Highway Laborers	11.35	272.40	19.00	456.00		
3 Equip. Oper. (med.)	14.60	350.40	23.95	574.80		
1 Pvmt. Profiler, 450 H.P.		3455.60		3801.15		
1 Road Sweeper, S.P.		148.60		163.45		
1 F.E. Loader, 1-3/4 C.Y.		309.60		340.55	69.88	76.87
56 M.H., Daily Totals		$4643.40		$5514.75	$82.90	$98.47
Crew B-72	Hr.	Daily	Hr.	Daily	Bare Costs	Incl. O&P
1 Labor Foreman (outside)	$13.35	$106.80	$22.35	$178.80	$13.22	$21.89
3 Highway Laborers	11.35	272.40	19.00	456.00		
4 Equip. Oper. (med.)	14.60	467.20	23.95	766.40		
1 Pvmt. Profiler, 450 H.P.		3455.60		3801.15		
1 Hammermill, 250 H.P.		935.20		1028.70		
1 Windrow Loader		938.80		1032.70		
1 Mix Paver 165 H.P.		1230.20		1353.20		
1 Roller, Pneu. Tire, 12 T.		236.20		259.80	106.18	116.80
64 M.H., Daily Totals		$7642.40		$8876.75	$119.40	$138.69

CREWS

Crew B-73			Bare Costs		Incl. Subs O&P		Cost Per Man-Hour	
		Hr.	Daily	Hr.	Daily	Bare Costs	Incl. O&P
1 Labor Foreman (outside)		$13.35	$106.80	$22.35	$178.80	$13.63	$22.51
2 Highway Laborers		11.35	181.60	19.00	304.00		
5 Equip. Oper. (med.)		14.60	584.00	23.95	958.00		
1 Road Mixer, 310 H.P.			871.40		958.55		
1 Roller, Tandem, 12 Ton			187.60		206.35		
1 Hammermill, 250 H.P.			935.20		1028.70		
1 Motor Grader, 30,000 Lb.			521.00		573.10		
.5 F.E. Loader, 1-3/4 C.Y.			154.80		170.30		
.5 Truck, 30 Ton			134.20		147.60		
.5 Water Tank, 5000 Gal.			92.40		101.65	45.25	49.78
64 M.H., Daily Totals			$3769.00		$4627.05	$58.88	$72.29

Crew B-74		Hr.	Daily	Hr.	Daily	Bare Costs	Incl. O&P
1 Labor Foreman (outside)		$13.35	$106.80	$22.35	$178.80	$13.37	$22.04
1 Highway Laborer		11.35	90.80	19.00	152.00		
4 Equip. Oper. (med.)		14.60	467.20	23.95	766.40		
2 Truck Drivers (heavy)		11.95	191.20	19.60	313.60		
1 Motor Grader, 30,000 Lb.			521.00		573.10		
1 Grader Attach., Ripper			51.60		56.75		
2 Stabilizers, 310 H.P.			1198.00		1317.80		
1 Flatbed Truck, 3 Ton			148.40		163.25		
1 Chem. Spreader, Towed			89.00		97.90		
1 Vibr. Roller, 29,000 Lb.			341.60		375.75		
1 Water Tank, 5000 Gal.			184.80		203.30		
1 Truck, 30 Ton			268.40		295.25	43.79	48.17
64 M.H., Daily Totals			$3658.80		$4493.90	$57.16	$70.21

Crew B-75		Hr.	Daily	Hr.	Daily	Bare Costs	Incl. O&P
1 Labor Foreman (outside)		$13.35	$106.80	$22.35	$178.80	$13.57	$22.39
1 Highway Laborer		11.35	90.80	19.00	152.00		
4 Equip. Oper. (med.)		14.60	467.20	23.95	766.40		
1 Truck Driver (heavy)		11.95	95.60	19.60	156.80		
1 Motor Grader, 30,000 Lb.			521.00		573.10		
1 Grader Attach., Ripper			51.60		56.75		
2 Stabilizers, 310 H.P.			1198.00		1317.80		
1 Dist. Truck, 3000 Gal.			308.20		339.00		
1 Vibr. Roller, 29,000 Lb.			341.60		375.75	43.22	47.54
56 M.H., Daily Totals			$3180.80		$3916.40	$56.79	$69.93

Crew B-76		Hr.	Daily	Hr.	Daily	Bare Costs	Incl. O&P
1 Dock Builder Foreman		$16.45	$131.60	$29.80	$238.40	$14.61	$25.63
5 Dock Builders		14.45	578.00	26.15	1046.00		
2 Equip. Oper. (crane)		15.15	242.40	24.85	397.60		
1 Equip. Oper. Oiler		12.50	100.00	20.50	164.00		
1 Crawler Crane, 50 Ton			758.00		833.80		
1 Barge, 400 Ton			384.00		422.40		
1 Hammer, 15K. Ft. Lbs.			258.40		284.25		
60 L.F. Leads, 15K. Ft. Lbs.			60.00		66.00		
1 Air Compr., 600 C.F.M.			269.20		296.10		
2-50 Ft. Air Hoses, 3" Dia.			20.40		22.45	24.30	26.73
72 M.H., Daily Totals			$2802.00		$3771.00	$38.91	$52.36

Crew B-77		Hr.	Daily	Hr.	Daily	Bare Costs	Incl. O&P
1 Labor Foreman		$13.35	$106.80	$22.35	$178.80	$11.83	$19.73
3 Laborers		11.35	272.40	19.00	456.00		
1 Truck Driver (light)		11.75	94.00	19.30	154.40		
1 Crack Cleaner, 25 H.P.			71.20		78.30		
1 Crack Filler, Trailer Mtd.			126.40		139.05		
1 Flatbed Truck, 3 Ton			148.40		163.25	8.65	9.51
40 M.H., Daily Totals			$819.20		$1169.80	$20.48	$29.24

Crew B-78		Hr.	Daily	Hr.	Daily	Bare Costs	Incl. O&P
1 Labor Foreman		$13.35	$106.80	$22.35	$178.80	$11.75	$19.60
4 Laborers		11.35	363.20	19.00	608.00		
1 Truck Driver (light)		11.75	94.00	19.30	154.40		
1 Paint Striper, S.P.			180.40		198.45		
1 Flatbed Truck, 3 Ton			148.40		163.25		
1 Pickup Truck, 3/4 Ton			107.40		118.15	9.08	9.99
48 M.H., Daily Totals			$1000.20		$1421.05	$20.83	$29.59

Crew B-79		Hr.	Daily	Hr.	Daily	Bare Costs	Incl. O&P
1 Labor Foreman		$13.35	$106.80	$22.35	$178.80	$11.83	$19.73
3 Laborers		11.35	272.40	19.00	456.00		
1 Truck Driver (light)		11.75	94.00	19.30	154.40		
1 Thermo. Striper, T.M.			225.50		248.05		
1 Flatbed Truck, 3 Ton			148.40		163.25		
2 Pickup Trucks, 3/4 Ton			214.80		236.30	14.71	16.19
40 M.H., Daily Totals			$1061.90		$1436.80	$26.54	$35.92

Crew B-80		Hr.	Daily	Hr.	Daily	Bare Costs	Incl. O&P
1 Labor Foreman		$13.35	$106.80	$22.35	$178.80	$12.58	$20.86
1 Laborer		11.35	90.80	19.00	152.00		
1 Truck Driver (light)		11.75	94.00	19.30	154.40		
1 Equip. Oper. (light)		13.90	111.20	22.80	182.40		
1 Flatbed Truck, 3 Ton			148.40		163.25		
1 Post Driver, T.M.			256.80		282.50	12.66	13.92
32 M.H., Daily Totals			$808.00		$1113.35	$25.24	$34.78

Crew B-81		Hr.	Daily	Hr.	Daily	Bare Costs	Incl. O&P
1 Laborer		$11.35	$90.80	$19.00	$152.00	$12.63	$20.85
1 Equip. Oper. (med.)		14.60	116.80	23.95	191.60		
1 Truck Driver (heavy)		11.95	95.60	19.60	156.80		
1 Hydromulcher, T.M.			239.80		263.80		
1 Tractor Truck, 4x2			268.40		295.25	21.17	23.29
24 M.H., Daily Totals			$811.40		$1059.45	$33.80	$44.14

Crew B-82		Hr.	Daily	Hr.	Daily	Bare Costs	Incl. O&P
1 Highway Laborer		$11.35	$90.80	$19.00	$152.00	$12.62	$20.90
1 Equip. Oper. (light)		13.90	111.20	22.80	182.40		
1 Horiz. Borer, 6 H.P.			37.00		40.70	2.31	2.54
16 M.H., Daily Totals			$239.00		$375.10	$14.93	$23.44

Crew B-83		Hr.	Daily	Hr.	Daily	Bare Costs	Incl. O&P
1 Tugboat Captain		$14.60	$116.80	$23.95	$191.60	$12.97	$21.47
1 Tugboat Hand		11.35	90.80	19.00	152.00		
1 Tugboat, 250 H.P.			456.40		502.05	28.52	31.37
16 M.H., Daily Totals			$664.00		$845.65	$41.49	$52.84

Crew B-84		Hr.	Daily	Hr.	Daily	Bare Costs	Incl. O&P
1 Equip. Oper. (med.)		$14.60	$116.80	$23.95	$191.60	$14.60	$23.95
1 Rotary Mower/Tractor			227.40		250.15	28.42	31.26
8 M.H., Daily Totals			$344.20		$441.75	$43.02	$55.21

Crew B-85		Hr.	Daily	Hr.	Daily	Bare Costs	Incl. O&P
3 Highway Laborers		$11.35	$272.40	$19.00	$456.00	$12.12	$20.11
1 Equip. Oper. (med.)		14.60	116.80	23.95	191.60		
1 Truck Driver (heavy)		11.95	95.60	19.60	156.80		
1 Aerial Lift Truck			515.00		566.50		
1 Brush Chipper, 130 H.P.			178.80		196.70		
1 Pruning Saw, Rotary			15.20		16.70	17.72	19.49
40 M.H., Daily Totals			$1193.80		$1584.30	$29.84	$39.60

CREWS

Crew No.	Bare Costs		Incl. Subs O & P		Cost Per Man-Hour	
Crew B-86	Hr.	Daily	Hr.	Daily	Bare Costs	Incl. O&P
1 Equip. Oper. (med.)	$14.60	$116.80	$23.95	$191.60	$14.60	$23.95
1 Stump Chipper, S.P.		152.40		167.65	19.05	20.95
8 M.H., Daily Totals		$269.20		$359.25	$33.65	$44.90
Crew B-86A	Hr.	Daily	Hr.	Daily	Bare Costs	Incl. O&P
1 Equip. Oper. (medium)	$14.60	$116.80	$23.95	$191.60	$14.60	$23.95
1 Grader, 30,000 Lbs.		521.00		573.10	65.12	71.63
8 M.H., Daily Totals		$637.80		$764.70	$79.72	$95.58
Crew B-86B	Hr.	Daily	Hr.	Daily	Bare Costs	Incl. O&P
1 Equip. Oper. (medium)	$14.60	$116.80	$23.95	$191.60	$14.60	$23.95
1 Dozer, 200 H.P.		775.80		853.40	96.97	106.67
8 M.H., Daily Totals		$892.60		$1045.00	$111.57	$130.62
Crew B-87	Hr.	Daily	Hr.	Daily	Bare Costs	Incl. O&P
1 Laborer	$11.35	$90.80	$19.00	$152.00	$13.95	$22.96
4 Equip. Oper. (med.)	14.60	467.20	23.95	766.40		
2 Feller Bunchers, 50 H.P.		626.80		689.50		
1 Log Chipper, 22" Tree		1820.20		2002.20		
1 Dozer, 105 H.P.		272.80		300.10		
1 Chainsaw, Gas, 36" Long		41.60		45.75	69.03	75.93
40 M.H., Daily Totals		$3319.40		$3955.95	$82.98	$98.89
Crew B-88	Hr.	Daily	Hr.	Daily	Bare Costs	Incl. O&P
1 Laborer	$11.35	$90.80	$19.00	$152.00	$14.13	$23.24
6 Equip. Oper. (med.)	14.60	700.80	23.95	1149.60		
2 Feller Bunchers, 50 H.P.		626.80		689.50		
1 Log Chipper, 22" Tree		1820.20		2002.20		
2 Log Skidders, 50 H.P.		639.60		703.55		
1 Dozer, 105 H.P.		272.80		300.10		
1 Chainsaw, Gas, 36" Long		41.60		45.75	60.73	66.80
56 M.H., Daily Totals		$4192.60		$5042.70	$74.86	$90.04
Crew B-89	Hr.	Daily	Hr.	Daily	Bare Costs	Incl. O&P
1 Equip. Oper. (light)	$13.90	$111.20	$22.80	$182.40	$12.82	$21.05
1 Truck Driver (light)	11.75	94.00	19.30	154.40		
1 Truck, Stake Body, 3 Ton		148.40		163.25		
1 Concrete Saw		92.80		102.10		
1 Water Tank, 65 Gal.		6.60		7.25	15.48	17.03
16 M.H., Daily Totals		$453.00		$609.40	$28.30	$38.08
Crew B-89A	Hr.	Daily	Hr.	Daily	Bare Costs	Incl. O&P
1 Skilled Worker	$14.70	$117.60	$24.65	$197.20	$13.02	$21.82
1 Laborer	11.35	90.80	19.00	152.00		
1 Core Drill (large)		48.80		53.70	3.05	3.35
16 M.H., Daily Totals		$257.20		$402.90	$16.07	$25.17
Crew B-90	Hr.	Daily	Hr.	Daily	Bare Costs	Incl. O&P
1 Labor Foreman (outside)	$13.35	$106.80	$22.35	$178.80	$12.38	$20.51
3 Highway Laborers	11.35	272.40	19.00	456.00		
2 Equip. Oper. (light)	13.90	222.40	22.80	364.80		
2 Truck Drivers (heavy)	11.95	191.20	19.60	313.60		
1 Road Mixer, 310 H.P.		871.40		958.55		
1 Dist. Truck, 2000 Gal.		285.00		313.50	18.06	19.87
64 M.H., Daily Totals		$1949.20		$2585.25	$30.44	$40.38

Crew No.	Bare Costs		Incl. Subs O & P		Cost Per Man-Hour	
Crew B-90A	Hr.	Daily	Hr.	Daily	Bare Costs	Incl. O&P
1 Labor Foreman	$13.35	$106.80	$22.35	$178.80	$13.49	$22.30
2 Laborers	11.35	181.60	19.00	304.00		
4 Equip. Oper. (medium)	14.60	467.20	23.95	766.40		
2 Graders, 30,000 Lbs.		1042.00		1146.20		
1 Roller, Steel Wheel		187.60		206.35		
1 Roller, Pneumatic Wheel		236.20		259.80	26.17	28.79
56 M.H., Daily Totals		$2221.40		$2861.55	$39.66	$51.09
Crew B-90B	Hr.	Daily	Hr.	Daily	Bare Costs	Incl. O&P
1 Labor Foreman	$13.35	$106.80	$22.35	$178.80	$13.30	$22.03
2 Laborers	11.35	181.60	19.00	304.00		
3 Equip. Oper. (medium)	14.60	350.40	23.95	574.80		
1 Roller, Steel Wheel		187.60		206.35		
1 Roller, Pneumatic Wheel		236.20		259.80		
1 Road Mixer, 310 H.P.		871.40		958.55	26.98	29.68
48 M.H., Daily Totals		$1934.00		$2482.30	$40.28	$51.71
Crew B-91	Hr.	Daily	Hr.	Daily	Bare Costs	Incl. O&P
1 Labor Foreman (outside)	$13.35	$106.80	$22.35	$178.80	$13.30	$21.96
2 Highway Laborers	11.35	181.60	19.00	304.00		
4 Equip. Oper. (med.)	14.60	467.20	23.95	766.40		
1 Truck Driver (heavy)	11.95	95.60	19.60	156.80		
1 Dist. Truck, 3000 Gal.		308.20		339.00		
1 Aggreg. Spreader, S.P.		561.40		617.55		
1 Roller, Pneu. Tire, 12 Ton		236.20		259.80		
1 Roller, Steel, 10 Ton		187.60		206.35	20.20	22.22
64 M.H., Daily Totals		$2144.60		$2828.70	$33.50	$44.18
Crew B-92	Hr.	Daily	Hr.	Daily	Bare Costs	Incl. O&P
1 Labor Foreman (outside)	$13.35	$106.80	$22.35	$178.80	$11.85	$19.83
3 Highway Laborers	11.35	272.40	19.00	456.00		
1 Crack Cleaner, 25 H.P.		71.20		78.30		
1 Air Compressor		64.40		70.85		
1 Tar Kettle, T.M.		17.80		19.60		
1 Flatbed Truck, 3 Ton		148.40		163.25	9.43	10.37
32 M.H., Daily Totals		$681.00		$966.80	$21.28	$30.20
Crew B-93	Hr.	Daily	Hr.	Daily	Bare Costs	Incl. O&P
1 Equip. Oper. (med.)	$14.60	$116.80	$23.95	$191.60	$14.60	$23.95
1 Feller Buncher, 50 H.P.		313.40		344.75	39.17	43.09
8 M.H., Daily Totals		$430.20		$536.35	$53.77	$67.04
Crew C-1	Hr.	Daily	Hr.	Daily	Bare Costs	Incl. O&P
3 Carpenters	$14.30	$343.20	$23.90	$573.60	$13.56	$22.67
1 Building Laborer	11.35	90.80	19.00	152.00		
Power Tools		24.00		26.40	.75	.82
32 M.H., Daily Totals		$458.00		$752.00	$14.31	$23.49
Crew C-1A	Hr.	Daily	Hr.	Daily	Bare Costs	Incl. O&P
1 Carpenter	$14.30	$114.40	$23.90	$191.20	$14.30	$23.90
1 Circular Saw, 7"		8.00		8.80	1.00	1.10
8 M.H., Daily Totals		$122.40		$200.00	$15.30	$25.00
Crew C-2	Hr.	Daily	Hr.	Daily	Bare Costs	Incl. O&P
1 Carpenter Foreman (out)	$16.30	$130.40	$27.25	$218.00	$14.14	$23.64
4 Carpenters	14.30	457.60	23.90	764.80		
1 Building Laborer	11.35	90.80	19.00	152.00		
Power Tools		32.00		35.20	.66	.73
48 M.H., Daily Totals		$710.80		$1170.00	$14.80	$24.37

CREWS

Crew No.	Bare Costs Hr.	Daily	Incl. Subs O & P Hr.	Daily	Cost Per Man-Hour Bare Costs	Incl. O&P
Crew C-3						
1 Rodman Foreman	$17.55	$140.40	$31.80	$254.40	$14.54	$25.67
4 Rodmen (reinf.)	15.55	497.60	28.20	902.40		
1 Equip. Oper. (light)	13.90	111.20	22.80	182.40		
2 Building Laborers	11.35	181.60	19.00	304.00		
Stressing Equipment		36.00		39.60		
Grouting Equipment		115.20		126.70	2.36	2.59
64 M.H., Daily Totals		$1082.00		$1809.50	$16.90	$28.26
Crew C-4	Hr.	Daily	Hr.	Daily	Bare Costs	Incl. O&P
1 Rodman Foreman	$17.55	$140.40	$31.80	$254.40	$16.05	$29.10
3 Rodmen (reinf.)	15.55	373.20	28.20	676.80		
Stressing Equipment		36.00		39.60	1.12	1.23
32 M.H., Daily Totals		$549.60		$970.80	$17.17	$30.33
Crew C-5	Hr.	Daily	Hr.	Daily	Bare Costs	Incl. O&P
1 Rodman Foreman	$17.55	$140.40	$31.80	$254.40	$15.34	$27.13
4 Rodmen (reinf.)	15.55	497.60	28.20	902.40		
1 Equip. Oper. (crane)	15.15	121.20	24.85	198.80		
1 Equip. Oper. Oiler	12.50	100.00	20.50	164.00		
1 Hyd. Crane, 25 Ton		486.40		535.05	8.68	9.55
56 M.H., Daily Totals		$1345.60		$2054.65	$24.02	$36.68
Crew C-6	Hr.	Daily	Hr.	Daily	Bare Costs	Incl. O&P
1 Labor Foreman (outside)	$13.35	$106.80	$22.35	$178.80	$12.13	$20.14
4 Building Laborers	11.35	363.20	19.00	608.00		
1 Cement Finisher	14.05	112.40	22.50	180.00		
2 Gas Engine Vibrators		62.00		68.20	1.29	1.42
48 M.H., Daily Totals		$644.40		$1035.00	$13.42	$21.56
Crew C-7	Hr.	Daily	Hr.	Daily	Bare Costs	Incl. O&P
1 Labor Foreman (outside)	$13.35	$106.80	$22.35	$178.80	$12.34	$20.47
5 Building Laborers	11.35	454.00	19.00	760.00		
1 Cement Finisher	14.05	112.40	22.50	180.00		
1 Equip. Oper. (med.)	14.60	116.80	23.95	191.60		
2 Gas Engine Vibrators		62.00		68.20		
1 Concrete Bucket, 1 C.Y.		16.80		18.50		
1 Hyd. Crane, 55 Ton		727.20		799.90	12.59	13.85
64 M.H., Daily Totals		$1596.00		$2197.00	$24.93	$34.32
Crew C-8	Hr.	Daily	Hr.	Daily	Bare Costs	Incl. O&P
1 Labor Foreman (outside)	$13.35	$106.80	$22.35	$178.80	$12.87	$21.18
3 Building Laborers	11.35	272.40	19.00	456.00		
2 Cement Finishers	14.05	224.80	22.50	360.00		
1 Equip. Oper. (med.)	14.60	116.80	23.95	191.60		
1 Concrete Pump (small)		514.60		566.05	9.18	10.10
56 M.H., Daily Totals		$1235.40		$1752.45	$22.05	$31.28
Crew C-9	Hr.	Daily	Hr.	Daily	Bare Costs	Incl. O&P
1 Cement Finisher	$14.05	$112.40	$22.50	$180.00	$14.05	$22.50
1 Gas Finishing Mach.		34.80		38.30	4.35	4.78
8 M.H., Daily Totals		$147.20		$218.30	$18.40	$27.28
Crew C-10	Hr.	Daily	Hr.	Daily	Bare Costs	Incl. O&P
1 Building Laborer	$11.35	$90.80	$19.00	$152.00	$13.15	$21.33
2 Cement Finishers	14.05	224.80	22.50	360.00		
2 Gas Finishing Mach.		69.60		76.55	2.90	3.18
24 M.H., Daily Totals		$385.20		$588.55	$16.05	$24.51

Crew No.	Bare Costs Hr.	Daily	Incl. Subs O & P Hr.	Daily	Cost Per Man-Hour Bare Costs	Incl. O&P
Crew C-11						
1 Struc. Steel Foreman	$17.65	$141.20	$33.40	$267.20	$15.46	$28.48
6 Struc. Steel Workers	15.65	751.20	29.60	1420.80		
1 Equip. Oper. (crane)	15.15	121.20	24.85	198.80		
1 Equip. Oper. Oiler	12.50	100.00	20.50	164.00		
1 Truck Crane, 150 Ton		1387.80		1526.60	19.27	21.20
72 M.H., Daily Totals		$2501.40		$3577.40	$34.73	$49.68
Crew C-12	Hr.	Daily	Hr.	Daily	Bare Costs	Incl. O&P
1 Carpenter Foreman (out)	$16.30	$130.40	$27.25	$218.00	$14.28	$23.80
3 Carpenters	14.30	343.20	23.90	573.60		
1 Building Laborer	11.35	90.80	19.00	152.00		
1 Equip. Oper. (crane)	15.15	121.20	24.85	198.80		
1 Hyd. Crane, 12 Ton		362.00		398.20	7.54	8.29
48 M.H., Daily Totals		$1047.60		$1540.60	$21.82	$32.09
Crew C-13	Hr.	Daily	Hr.	Daily	Bare Costs	Incl. O&P
1 Struc. Steel Worker	$15.65	$125.20	$29.60	$236.80	$15.20	$27.70
1 Welder	15.65	125.20	29.60	236.80		
1 Carpenter	14.30	114.40	23.90	191.20		
1 Gas Welding Machine		68.40		75.25	2.85	3.13
24 M.H., Daily Totals		$433.20		$740.05	$18.05	$30.83
Crew C-14	Hr.	Daily	Hr.	Daily	Bare Costs	Incl. O&P
1 Carpenter Foreman (out)	$16.30	$130.40	$27.25	$218.00	$13.95	$23.66
5 Carpenters	14.30	572.00	23.90	956.00		
4 Building Laborers	11.35	363.20	19.00	608.00		
4 Rodmen (reinf.)	15.55	497.60	28.20	902.40		
2 Cement Finishers	14.05	224.80	22.50	360.00		
1 Equip. Oper. (crane)	15.15	121.20	24.85	198.80		
1 Equip. Oper. Oiler	12.50	100.00	20.50	164.00		
1 Crane, 80 Ton, & Tools		1103.40		1213.75		
Power Tools		24.00		26.40		
2 Gas Finishing Mach.		69.60		76.55	8.31	9.14
144 M.H., Daily Totals		$3206.20		$4723.90	$22.26	$32.80
Crew C-15	Hr.	Daily	Hr.	Daily	Bare Costs	Incl. O&P
1 Carpenter Foreman (out)	$16.30	$130.40	$27.25	$218.00	$13.62	$22.80
2 Carpenters	14.30	228.80	23.90	382.40		
3 Building Laborers	11.35	272.40	19.00	456.00		
2 Cement Finishers	14.05	224.80	22.50	360.00		
1 Rodman (reinf.)	15.55	124.40	28.20	225.60		
Power Tools		16.00		17.60		
1 Gas Finishing Mach.		34.80		38.30	.70	.77
72 M.H., Daily Totals		$1031.60		$1697.90	$14.32	$23.57
Crew C-16	Hr.	Daily	Hr.	Daily	Bare Costs	Incl. O&P
1 Labor Foreman (outside)	$13.35	$106.80	$22.35	$178.80	$13.46	$22.74
3 Building Laborers	11.35	272.40	19.00	456.00		
2 Cement Finishers	14.05	224.80	22.50	360.00		
1 Equip. Oper. (med.)	14.60	116.80	23.95	191.60		
2 Rodmen (reinf.)	15.55	248.80	28.20	451.20		
1 Concrete Pump (small)		514.60		566.05	7.14	7.86
72 M.H., Daily Totals		$1484.20		$2203.65	$20.60	$30.60
Crew C-17	Hr.	Daily	Hr.	Daily	Bare Costs	Incl. O&P
2 Skilled Worker Foremen	$16.70	$267.20	$28.00	$448.00	$15.10	$25.32
8 Skilled Workers	14.70	940.80	24.65	1577.60		
80 M.H., Daily Totals		$1208.00		$2025.60	$15.10	$25.32

CREWS

Crew No.		Bare Costs		Incl. Subs O & P		Cost Per Man-Hour	
Crew C-17A	Hr.	Daily	Hr.	Daily	Bare Costs	Incl. O&P
2 Skilled Worker Foremen	$16.70	$267.20	$28.00	$448.00	$15.10	$25.32
8 Skilled Workers	14.70	940.80	24.65	1577.60		
.125 Equip. Oper. (crane)	15.15	15.15	24.85	24.85		
.125 Crane, 80 Ton, & Tools		143.45		157.80		
.125 Hand Held Power Tools		1.05		1.15		
.125 Walk Behind Pwr. Tools		4.50		5.00	1.83	2.02
81 M.H., Daily Totals		$1372.15		$2214.40	$16.93	$27.34

Crew No.		Bare Costs		Incl. Subs O & P		Cost Per Man-Hour	
Crew C-17B	Hr.	Daily	Hr.	Daily	Bare Costs	Incl. O&P
2 Skilled Worker Foremen	$16.70	$267.20	$28.00	$448.00	$15.10	$25.32
8 Skilled Workers	14.70	940.80	24.65	1577.60		
.25 Equip. Oper. (crane)	15.15	30.30	24.85	49.70		
.25 Crane, 80 Ton, & Tools		275.85		303.45		
.25 Hand Held Power Tools		2.00		2.20		
.25 Walk Behind Power Tools		8.70		9.55	3.49	3.84
82 M.H., Daily Totals		$1524.85		$2390.50	$18.59	$29.16

Crew C-17C	Hr.	Daily	Hr.	Daily	Bare Costs	Incl. O&P
2 Skilled Worker Foremen	$16.70	$267.20	$28.00	$448.00	$15.10	$25.32
8 Skilled Workers	14.70	940.80	24.65	1577.60		
.375 Equip. Oper. (crane)	15.15	45.45	24.85	74.55		
.375 Crane, 80 Ton & Tools		419.30		461.20		
.375 Hand Held Power Tools		3.05		3.35		
.375 Walk Behind Pwr. Tools		13.20		14.55	5.24	5.77
83 M.H., Daily Totals		$1689.00		$2579.25	$20.34	$31.09

Crew C-17D	Hr.	Daily	Hr.	Daily	Bare Costs	Incl. O&P
2 Skilled Worker Foremen	$16.70	$267.20	$28.00	$448.00	$15.10	$25.32
8 Skilled Workers	14.70	940.80	24.65	1577.60		
.5 Equip. Oper. (crane)	15.15	60.60	24.85	99.40		
.5 Crane, 80 Ton & Tools		551.70		606.85		
.5 Hand Held Power Tools		4.00		4.40		
.5 Walk Behind Power Tools		17.40		19.15	6.82	7.50
84 M.H., Daily Totals		$1841.70		$2755.40	$21.92	$32.82

Crew C-17E	Hr.	Daily	Hr.	Daily	Bare Costs	Incl. O&P
2 Skilled Worker Foremen	$16.70	$267.20	$28.00	$448.00	$15.10	$25.32
8 Skilled Workers	14.70	940.80	24.65	1577.60		
1 Hyd. Jack with Rods		54.40		59.85	.68	.74
80 M.H., Daily Totals		$1262.40		$2085.45	$15.78	$26.06

Crew C-18	Hr.	Daily	Hr.	Daily	Bare Costs	Incl. O&P
.125 Labor Foreman (out)	$13.35	$13.35	$22.35	$22.35	$11.57	$19.37
1 Building Laborer	11.35	90.80	19.00	152.00		
1 Concrete Cart, 10 C.F.		44.00		48.40	4.88	5.37
9 M.H., Daily Totals		$148.15		$222.75	$16.45	$24.74

Crew C-19	Hr.	Daily	Hr.	Daily	Bare Costs	Incl. O&P
.125 Labor Foreman (out)	$13.35	$13.35	$22.35	$22.35	$11.57	$19.37
1 Building Laborer	11.35	90.80	19.00	152.00		
1 Concrete Cart, 18 C.F.		105.80		116.40	11.75	12.93
9 M.H., Daily Totals		$209.95		$290.75	$23.32	$32.30

Crew C-20	Hr.	Daily	Hr.	Daily	Bare Costs	Incl. O&P
1 Labor Foreman (outside)	$13.35	$106.80	$22.35	$178.80	$12.34	$20.47
5 Building Laborers	11.35	454.00	19.00	760.00		
1 Cement Finisher	14.05	112.40	22.50	180.00		
1 Equip. Oper. (med.)	14.60	116.80	23.95	191.60		
2 Gas Engine Vibrators		62.00		68.20		
1 Concrete Pump (small)		514.60		566.05	9.00	9.91
64 M.H., Daily Totals		$1366.60		$1944.65	$21.34	$30.38

Crew C-21	Hr.	Daily	Hr.	Daily	Bare Costs	Incl. O&P
1 Labor Foreman (outside)	$13.35	$106.80	$22.35	$178.80	$12.34	$20.47
5 Building Laborers	11.35	454.00	19.00	760.00		
1 Cement Finisher	14.05	112.40	22.50	180.00		
1 Equip. Oper. (med.)	14.60	116.80	23.95	191.60		
2 Gas Engine Vibrators		62.00		68.20		
1 Concrete Conveyer		118.80		130.70	2.82	3.10
64 M.H., Daily Totals		$970.80		$1509.30	$15.16	$23.57

Crew C-22	Hr.	Daily	Hr.	Daily	Bare Costs	Incl. O&P
1 Rodman Foreman	$17.55	$140.40	$31.80	$254.40	$15.84	$28.62
4 Rodmen (reinf.)	15.55	497.60	28.20	902.40		
.125 Equip. Oper. (crane)	15.15	15.15	24.85	24.85		
.125 Equip. Oper. Oiler	12.50	12.50	20.50	20.50		
.125 Hyd. Crane, 25 Ton		63.25		69.55	1.50	1.65
42 M.H., Daily Totals		$728.90		$1271.70	$17.34	$30.27

Crew C-23	Hr.	Daily	Hr.	Daily	Bare Costs	Incl. O&P
2 Skilled Worker Foremen	$16.70	$267.20	$28.00	$448.00	$14.92	$24.92
6 Skilled Workers	14.70	705.60	24.65	1183.20		
1 Equip. Oper. (crane)	15.15	121.20	24.85	198.80		
1 Equip. Oper. Oiler	12.50	100.00	20.50	164.00		
1 Crane, 90 Ton		1071.40		1178.55	13.39	14.73
80 M.H., Daily Totals		$2265.40		$3172.55	$28.31	$39.65

Crew C-24	Hr.	Daily	Hr.	Daily	Bare Costs	Incl. O&P
2 Skilled Worker Foremen	$16.70	$267.20	$28.00	$448.00	$14.92	$24.92
6 Skilled Workers	14.70	705.60	24.65	1183.20		
1 Equip. Oper. (crane)	15.15	121.20	24.85	198.80		
1 Equip. Oper. Oiler	12.50	100.00	20.50	164.00		
1 Truck Crane, 150 Ton		1387.80		1526.60	17.34	19.08
80 M.H., Daily Totals		$2581.80		$3520.60	$32.26	$44.00

Crew D-1	Hr.	Daily	Hr.	Daily	Bare Costs	Incl. O&P
1 Bricklayer	$14.80	$118.40	$24.35	$194.80	$13.12	$21.57
1 Bricklayer Helper	11.45	91.60	18.80	150.40		
16 M.H., Daily Totals		$210.00		$345.20	$13.12	$21.57

Crew D-2	Hr.	Daily	Hr.	Daily	Bare Costs	Incl. O&P
3 Bricklayers	$14.80	$355.20	$24.35	$584.40	$13.53	$22.29
2 Bricklayer Helpers	11.45	183.20	18.80	300.80		
.5 Carpenter	14.30	57.20	23.90	95.60		
44 M.H., Daily Totals		$595.60		$980.80	$13.53	$22.29

Crew D-3	Hr.	Daily	Hr.	Daily	Bare Costs	Incl. O&P
3 Bricklayers	$14.80	$355.20	$24.35	$584.40	$13.50	$22.21
2 Bricklayer Helpers	11.45	183.20	18.80	300.80		
.25 Carpenter	14.30	28.60	23.90	47.80		
42 M.H., Daily Totals		$567.00		$933.00	$13.50	$22.21

CREWS

Crew No.	Bare Costs Hr.	Daily	Incl. Subs O & P Hr.	Daily	Cost Per Man-Hour Bare Costs	Incl. O&P
Crew D-4						
1 Bricklayer	$14.80	$118.40	$24.35	$194.80	$12.90	$21.18
2 Bricklayer Helpers	11.45	183.20	18.80	300.80		
1 Equip. Oper. (light)	13.90	111.20	22.80	182.40		
1 Grout Pump		88.80		97.70		
1 Hoses & Hopper		23.20		25.50		
1 Accessories		9.80		10.80	3.80	4.18
32 M.H., Daily Totals		$534.60		$812.00	$16.70	$25.36
Crew D-5	Hr.	Daily	Hr.	Daily	Bare Costs	Incl. O&P
1 Bricklayer	$14.80	$118.40	$24.35	$194.80	$14.80	$24.35
1 Power Tool		32.00		35.20	4.00	4.40
8 M.H., Daily Totals		$150.40		$230.00	$18.80	$28.75
Crew D-6	Hr.	Daily	Hr.	Daily	Bare Costs	Incl. O&P
3 Bricklayers	$14.80	$355.20	$24.35	$584.40	$13.17	$21.66
3 Bricklayer Helpers	11.45	274.80	18.80	451.20		
.25 Carpenter	14.30	28.60	23.90	47.80		
50 M.H., Daily Totals		$658.60		$1083.40	$13.17	$21.66
Crew D-7	Hr.	Daily	Hr.	Daily	Bare Costs	Incl. O&P
1 Tile Layer	$14.40	$115.20	$22.90	$183.20	$12.87	$20.47
1 Tile Layer Helper	11.35	90.80	18.05	144.40		
16 M.H., Daily Totals		$206.00		$327.60	$12.87	$20.47
Crew D-8	Hr.	Daily	Hr.	Daily	Bare Costs	Incl. O&P
3 Bricklayers	$14.80	$355.20	$24.35	$584.40	$13.46	$22.13
2 Bricklayer Helpers	11.45	183.20	18.80	300.80		
40 M.H., Daily Totals		$538.40		$885.20	$13.46	$22.13
Crew D-9	Hr.	Daily	Hr.	Daily	Bare Costs	Incl. O&P
3 Bricklayers	$14.80	$355.20	$24.35	$584.40	$13.12	$21.57
3 Bricklayer Helpers	11.45	274.80	18.80	451.20		
48 M.H., Daily Totals		$630.00		$1035.60	$13.12	$21.57
Crew D-10	Hr.	Daily	Hr.	Daily	Bare Costs	Incl. O&P
1 Bricklayer Foreman	$16.80	$134.40	$27.60	$220.80	$13.93	$22.88
1 Bricklayer	14.80	118.40	24.35	194.80		
2 Bricklayer Helpers	11.45	183.20	18.80	300.80		
1 Equip. Oper. (crane)	15.15	121.20	24.85	198.80		
1 Truck Crane, 12.5 Ton		419.20		461.10	10.48	11.52
40 M.H., Daily Totals		$976.40		$1376.30	$24.41	$34.40
Crew D-11	Hr.	Daily	Hr.	Daily	Bare Costs	Incl. O&P
1 Bricklayer Foreman	$16.80	$134.40	$27.60	$220.80	$14.35	$23.58
1 Bricklayer	14.80	118.40	24.35	194.80		
1 Bricklayer Helper	11.45	91.60	18.80	150.40		
24 M.H., Daily Totals		$344.40		$566.00	$14.35	$23.58
Crew D-12	Hr.	Daily	Hr.	Daily	Bare Costs	Incl. O&P
1 Bricklayer Foreman	$16.80	$134.40	$27.60	$220.80	$13.62	$22.38
1 Bricklayer	14.80	118.40	24.35	194.80		
2 Bricklayer Helpers	11.45	183.20	18.80	300.80		
32 M.H., Daily Totals		$436.00		$716.40	$13.62	$22.38

Crew No.	Bare Costs Hr.	Daily	Incl. Subs O & P Hr.	Daily	Cost Per Man-Hour Bare Costs	Incl. O&P
Crew D-13						
1 Bricklayer Foreman	$16.80	$134.40	$27.60	$220.80	$13.99	$23.05
1 Bricklayer	14.80	118.40	24.35	194.80		
2 Bricklayer Helpers	11.45	183.20	18.80	300.80		
1 Carpenter	14.30	114.40	23.90	191.20		
1 Equip. Oper. (crane)	15.15	121.20	24.85	198.80		
1 Truck Crane, 12.5 Ton		419.20		461.10	8.73	9.60
48 M.H., Daily Totals		$1090.80		$1567.50	$22.72	$32.65
Crew E-1	Hr.	Daily	Hr.	Daily	Bare Costs	Incl. O&P
1 Welder Foreman	$17.65	$141.20	$33.40	$267.20	$15.73	$28.60
1 Welder	15.65	125.20	29.60	236.80		
1 Equip. Oper. (light)	13.90	111.20	22.80	182.40		
1 Gas Welding Machine		68.40		75.25	2.85	3.13
24 M.H., Daily Totals		$446.00		$761.65	$18.58	$31.73
Crew E-2	Hr.	Daily	Hr.	Daily	Bare Costs	Incl. O&P
1 Struc. Steel Foreman	$17.65	$141.20	$33.40	$267.20	$15.41	$28.16
4 Struc. Steel Workers	15.65	500.80	29.60	947.20		
1 Equip. Oper. (crane)	15.15	121.20	24.85	198.80		
1 Equip. Oper. Oiler	12.50	100.00	20.50	164.00		
1 Crane, 90 Ton		1071.40		1178.55	19.13	21.04
56 M.H., Daily Totals		$1934.60		$2755.75	$34.54	$49.20
Crew E-3	Hr.	Daily	Hr.	Daily	Bare Costs	Incl. O&P
1 Struc. Steel Foreman	$17.65	$141.20	$33.40	$267.20	$16.31	$30.86
1 Struc. Steel Worker	15.65	125.20	29.60	236.80		
1 Welder	15.65	125.20	29.60	236.80		
1 Gas Welding Machine		68.40		75.25		
1 Torch, Gas & Air		62.80		69.10	5.46	6.01
24 M.H., Daily Totals		$522.80		$885.15	$21.77	$36.87
Crew E-4	Hr.	Daily	Hr.	Daily	Bare Costs	Incl. O&P
1 Struc. Steel Foreman	$17.65	$141.20	$33.40	$267.20	$16.15	$30.55
3 Struc. Steel Workers	15.65	375.60	29.60	710.40		
1 Gas Welding Machine		68.40		75.25	2.13	2.35
32 M.H., Daily Totals		$585.20		$1052.85	$18.28	$32.90
Crew E-5	Hr.	Daily	Hr.	Daily	Bare Costs	Incl. O&P
2 Struc. Steel Foremen	$17.65	$282.40	$33.40	$534.40	$15.68	$28.97
5 Struc. Steel Workers	15.65	626.00	29.60	1184.00		
1 Equip. Oper. (crane)	15.15	121.20	24.85	198.80		
1 Welder	15.65	125.20	29.60	236.80		
1 Equip. Oper. Oiler	12.50	100.00	20.50	164.00		
1 Crane, 90 Ton		1071.40		1178.55		
1 Gas Welding Machine		68.40		75.25		
1 Torch, Gas & Air		62.80		69.10	15.03	16.53
80 M.H., Daily Totals		$2457.40		$3640.90	$30.71	$45.50

CREWS

Crew No.	Bare Costs		Incl. Subs O & P		Cost Per Man-Hour	
Crew E-6	Hr.	Daily	Hr.	Daily	Bare Costs	Incl. O&P
3 Struc. Steel Foremen	$17.65	$423.60	$33.40	$801.60	$15.68	$29.02
9 Struc. Steel Workers	15.65	1126.80	29.60	2131.20		
1 Equip. Oper. (crane)	15.15	121.20	24.85	198.80		
1 Welder	15.65	125.20	29.60	236.80		
1 Equip. Oper. Oiler	12.50	100.00	20.50	164.00		
1 Equip. Oper. (light)	13.90	111.20	22.80	182.40		
1 Crane, 90 Ton		1071.40		1178.55		
1 Gas Welding Machine		68.40		75.25		
1 Torch, Gas & Air		62.80		69.10		
1 Air Compr., 160 C.F.M.		85.40		93.95		
2 Impact Wrenches		55.60		61.15	10.49	11.54
128 M.H., Daily Totals		$3351.60		$5192.80	$26.17	$40.56
Crew E-7	Hr.	Daily	Hr.	Daily	Bare Costs	Incl. O&P
1 Struc. Steel Foreman	$17.65	$141.20	$33.40	$267.20	$15.68	$28.97
4 Struc. Steel Workers	15.65	500.80	29.60	947.20		
1 Equip. Oper. (crane)	15.15	121.20	24.85	198.80		
1 Equip. Oper. Oiler	12.50	100.00	20.50	164.00		
1 Welder Foreman	17.65	141.20	33.40	267.20		
2 Welders	15.65	250.40	29.60	473.60		
1 Crane, 90 Ton		1071.40		1178.55		
2 Gas Welding Machines		136.80		150.50	15.10	16.61
80 M.H., Daily Totals		$2463.00		$3647.05	$30.78	$45.58
Crew E-8	Hr.	Daily	Hr.	Daily	Bare Costs	Incl. O&P
1 Struc. Steel Foreman	$17.65	$141.20	$33.40	$267.20	$15.54	$28.59
4 Struc. Steel Workers	15.65	500.80	29.60	947.20		
1 Welder Foreman	17.65	141.20	33.40	267.20		
4 Welders	15.65	500.80	29.60	947.20		
1 Equip. Oper. (crane)	15.15	121.20	24.85	198.80		
1 Equip. Oper. Oiler	12.50	100.00	20.50	164.00		
1 Equip. Oper. (light)	13.90	111.20	22.80	182.40		
1 Crane, 90 Ton		1071.40		1178.55		
4 Gas Welding Machines		273.60		300.95	12.93	14.22
104 M.H., Daily Totals		$2961.40		$4453.50	$28.47	$42.81
Crew E-9	Hr.	Daily	Hr.	Daily	Bare Costs	Incl. O&P
2 Struc. Steel Foremen	$17.65	$282.40	$33.40	$534.40	$15.68	$29.02
5 Struc. Steel Workers	15.65	626.00	29.60	1184.00		
1 Welder Foreman	17.65	141.20	33.40	267.20		
5 Welders	15.65	626.00	29.60	1184.00		
1 Equip. Oper. (crane)	15.15	121.20	24.85	198.80		
1 Equip. Oper. Oiler	12.50	100.00	20.50	164.00		
1 Equip. Oper. (light)	13.90	111.20	22.80	182.40		
1 Crane, 90 Ton		1071.40		1178.55		
5 Gas Welding Machines		342.00		376.20		
1 Torch, Gas & Air		62.80		69.10	11.53	12.68
128 M.H., Daily Totals		$3484.20		$5338.65	$27.21	$41.70
Crew E-10	Hr.	Daily	Hr.	Daily	Bare Costs	Incl. O&P
1 Welder Foreman	$17.65	$141.20	$33.40	$267.20	$16.65	$31.50
1 Welder	15.65	125.20	29.60	236.80		
4 Gas Welding Machines		273.60		300.95		
1 Truck, 3 Ton		148.40		163.25	26.37	29.01
16 M.H., Daily Totals		$688.40		$968.20	$43.02	$60.51

Crew No.	Bare Costs		Incl. Subs O & P		Cost Per Man-Hour	
Crew E-11	Hr.	Daily	Hr.	Daily	Bare Costs	Incl. O&P
2 Painters, Struc. Steel	$13.95	$223.20	$27.00	$432.00	$13.28	$23.95
1 Building Laborer	11.35	90.80	19.00	152.00		
1 Equip. Oper. (light)	13.90	111.20	22.80	182.40		
1 Air Compressor 250 C.F.M.		88.80		97.70		
1 Sand Blaster		23.20		25.50		
1 Sand Blasting Accessories		9.80		10.80	3.80	4.18
32 M.H., Daily Totals		$547.00		$900.40	$17.08	$28.13
Crew E-12	Hr.	Daily	Hr.	Daily	Bare Costs	Incl. O&P
1 Welder Foreman	$17.65	$141.20	$33.40	$267.20	$15.77	$28.10
1 Equip. Oper. (light)	13.90	111.20	22.80	182.40		
1 Gas Welding Machine		68.40		75.25	4.27	4.70
16 M.H., Daily Totals		$320.80		$524.85	$20.04	$32.80
Crew E-13	Hr.	Daily	Hr.	Daily	Bare Costs	Incl. O&P
1 Welder Foreman	$17.65	$141.20	$33.40	$267.20	$16.40	$29.86
.5 Equip. Oper. (light)	13.90	55.60	22.80	91.20		
1 Gas Welding Machine		68.40		75.25	5.70	6.27
12 M.H., Daily Totals		$265.20		$433.65	$22.10	$36.13
Crew E-14	Hr.	Daily	Hr.	Daily	Bare Costs	Incl. O&P
1 Welder Foreman	$17.65	$141.20	$33.40	$267.20	$17.65	$33.40
1 Gas Welding Machine		68.40		75.25	8.55	9.40
8 M.H., Daily Totals		$209.60		$342.45	$26.20	$42.80
Crew E-15	Hr.	Daily	Hr.	Daily	Bare Costs	Incl. O&P
2 Painters, Struc. Steel	$13.95	$223.20	$27.00	$432.00	$13.95	$27.00
1 Paint Sprayer, 17 C.F.M.		25.40		27.95	1.58	1.74
16 M.H., Daily Totals		$248.60		$459.95	$15.53	$28.74
Crew F-1	Hr.	Daily	Hr.	Daily	Bare Costs	Incl. O&P
1 Carpenter	$14.30	$114.40	$23.90	$191.20	$14.30	$23.90
Power Tools		8.00		8.80	1.00	1.10
8 M.H., Daily Totals		$122.40		$200.00	$15.30	$25.00
Crew F-2	Hr.	Daily	Hr.	Daily	Bare Costs	Incl. O&P
2 Carpenters	$14.30	$228.80	$23.90	$382.40	$14.30	$23.90
Power Tools		16.00		17.60	1.00	1.10
16 M.H., Daily Totals		$244.80		$400.00	$15.30	$25.00
Crew F-3	Hr.	Daily	Hr.	Daily	Bare Costs	Incl. O&P
4 Carpenters	$14.30	$457.60	$23.90	$764.80	$14.47	$24.09
1 Equip. Oper. (crane)	15.15	121.20	24.85	198.80		
1 Hyd. Crane, 12 Ton		362.00		398.20		
Power Tools		16.00		17.60	9.45	10.39
40 M.H., Daily Totals		$956.80		$1379.40	$23.92	$34.48
Crew F-4	Hr.	Daily	Hr.	Daily	Bare Costs	Incl. O&P
4 Carpenters	$14.30	$457.60	$23.90	$764.80	$14.14	$23.49
1 Equip. Oper. (crane)	15.15	121.20	24.85	198.80		
1 Equip. Oper. Oiler	12.50	100.00	20.50	164.00		
1 Hyd. Crane, 55 Ton		727.20		799.90		
Power Tools		16.00		17.60	15.48	17.03
48 M.H., Daily Totals		$1422.00		$1945.10	$29.62	$40.52
Crew F-5	Hr.	Daily	Hr.	Daily	Bare Costs	Incl. O&P
1 Carpenter Foreman	$16.30	$130.40	$27.25	$218.00	$14.80	$24.73
3 Carpenters	14.30	343.20	23.90	573.60		
Power Tools		16.00		17.60	.50	.55
32 M.H., Daily Totals		$489.60		$809.20	$15.30	$25.28

CREWS

Crew No.	Bare Costs Hr.	Daily	Incl. Subs O & P Hr.	Daily	Cost Per Man-Hour Bare Costs	Incl. O&P
Crew F-6						
2 Carpenters	$14.30	$228.80	$23.90	$382.40	$13.29	$22.13
2 Building Laborers	11.35	181.60	19.00	304.00		
1 Equip. Oper. (crane)	15.15	121.20	24.85	198.80		
1 Hyd. Crane, 12 Ton		362.00		398.20		
Power Tools		16.00		17.60	9.45	10.39
40 M.H., Daily Totals		$909.60		$1301.00	$22.74	$32.52
Crew F-7						
2 Carpenters	$14.30	$228.80	$23.90	$382.40	$12.82	$21.45
2 Building Laborers	11.35	181.60	19.00	304.00		
Power Tools		16.00		17.60	.50	.55
32 M.H., Daily Totals		$426.40		$704.00	$13.32	$22.00
Crew G-1						
1 Roofer Foreman	$15.20	$121.60	$27.30	$218.40	$12.48	$22.41
4 Roofers, Composition	13.20	422.40	23.70	758.40		
2 Roofer Helpers	9.70	155.20	17.40	278.40		
Application Equipment		108.20		119.00	1.93	2.12
56 M.H., Daily Totals		$807.40		$1374.20	$14.41	$24.53
Crew G-2						
1 Plasterer	$14.15	$113.20	$23.20	$185.60	$12.38	$20.43
1 Plasterer Helper	11.65	93.20	19.10	152.80		
1 Building Laborer	11.35	90.80	19.00	152.00		
Grouting Equipment		230.40		253.45	9.60	10.56
24 M.H., Daily Totals		$527.60		$743.85	$21.98	$30.99
Crew G-3						
2 Sheet Metal Workers	$16.25	$260.00	$26.95	$431.20	$13.80	$22.97
2 Building Laborers	11.35	181.60	19.00	304.00		
Power Tools		25.10		27.65	.78	.86
32 M.H., Daily Totals		$466.70		$762.85	$14.58	$23.83
Crew G-4						
1 Labor Foreman (outside)	$13.35	$106.80	$22.35	$178.80	$12.01	$20.11
2 Building Laborers	11.35	181.60	19.00	304.00		
1 Light Truck, 1.5 Ton		146.00		160.60		
1 Air Compr., 160 C.F.M.		85.40		93.95	9.64	10.60
24 M.H., Daily Totals		$519.80		$737.35	$21.65	$30.71
Crew G-5						
1 Roofer Foreman	$15.20	$121.60	$27.30	$218.40	$12.20	$21.90
2 Roofers, Composition	13.20	211.20	23.70	379.20		
2 Roofer Helpers	9.70	155.20	17.40	278.40		
Application Equipment		108.20		119.00	2.70	2.97
40 M.H., Daily Totals		$596.20		$995.00	$14.90	$24.87
Crew H-1						
2 Glaziers	$14.65	$234.40	$23.80	$380.80	$15.15	$26.70
2 Struc. Steel Workers	15.65	250.40	29.60	473.60		
32 M.H., Daily Totals		$484.80		$854.40	$15.15	$26.70
Crew H-2						
2 Glaziers	$14.65	$234.40	$23.80	$380.80	$13.55	$22.20
1 Building Laborer	11.35	90.80	19.00	152.00		
24 M.H., Daily Totals		$325.20		$532.80	$13.55	$22.20

Crew No.	Bare Costs Hr.	Daily	Incl. Subs O & P Hr.	Daily	Cost Per Man-Hour Bare Costs	Incl. O&P
Crew J-1						
3 Plasterers	$14.15	$339.60	$23.20	$556.80	$13.15	$21.56
2 Plasterer Helpers	11.65	186.40	19.10	305.60		
1 Mixing Machine, 6 C.F.		33.20		36.50	.83	.91
40 M.H., Daily Totals		$559.20		$898.90	$13.98	$22.47
Crew J-2						
3 Plasterers	$14.15	$339.60	$23.20	$556.80	$13.33	$21.79
2 Plasterer Helpers	11.65	186.40	19.10	305.60		
1 Lather	14.25	114.00	22.95	183.60		
1 Mixing Machine, 6 C.F.		33.20		36.50	.69	.76
48 M.H., Daily Totals		$673.20		$1082.50	$14.02	$22.55
Crew J-3						
1 Terrazzo Worker	$14.35	$114.80	$22.80	$182.40	$12.80	$20.35
1 Terrazzo Helper	11.25	90.00	17.90	143.20		
1 Terrazzo Grinder, Electric		34.80		38.30		
1 Terrazzo Mixer		53.80		59.20	5.53	6.09
16 M.H., Daily Totals		$293.40		$423.10	$18.33	$26.44
Crew J-4						
1 Tile Layer	$14.40	$115.20	$22.90	$183.20	$12.87	$20.47
1 Tile Layer Helper	11.35	90.80	18.05	144.40		
16 M.H., Daily Totals		$206.00		$327.60	$12.87	$20.47
Crew K-1						
1 Carpenter	$14.30	$114.40	$23.90	$191.20	$13.02	$21.60
1 Truck Driver (light)	11.75	94.00	19.30	154.40		
1 Truck w/Power Equip.		390.30		429.30	24.39	26.83
16 M.H., Daily Totals		$598.70		$774.90	$37.41	$48.43
Crew K-2						
1 Struc. Steel Foreman	$17.65	$141.20	$33.40	$267.20	$15.01	$27.43
1 Struc. Steel Worker	15.65	125.20	29.60	236.80		
1 Truck Driver (light)	11.75	94.00	19.30	154.40		
1 Truck w/Power Equip.		390.30		429.30	16.26	17.88
24 M.H., Daily Totals		$750.70		$1087.70	$31.27	$45.31
Crew L-1						
1 Electrician	$16.35	$130.80	$26.45	$211.60	$16.45	$26.72
1 Plumber	16.55	132.40	27.00	216.00		
16 M.H., Daily Totals		$263.20		$427.60	$16.45	$26.72
Crew L-2						
1 Carpenter	$14.30	$114.40	$23.90	$191.20	$12.70	$21.32
1 Helper	11.10	88.80	18.75	150.00		
16 M.H., Daily Totals		$203.20		$341.20	$12.70	$21.32
Crew L-3						
1 Carpenter	$14.30	$114.40	$23.90	$191.20	$15.30	$25.30
.5 Electrician	16.35	65.40	26.45	105.80		
.5 Sheet Metal Worker	16.25	65.00	26.95	107.80		
16 M.H., Daily Totals		$244.80		$404.80	$15.30	$25.30
Crew L-4						
2 Skilled Workers	$14.70	$235.20	$24.65	$394.40	$13.50	$22.68
1 Helper	11.10	88.80	18.75	150.00		
24 M.H., Daily Totals		$324.00		$544.40	$13.50	$22.68

CREWS

Crew No.	Bare Costs Hr.	Daily	Incl. Subs O & P Hr.	Daily	Cost Per Man-Hour Bare Costs	Incl. O&P
Crew L-5						
1 Struc. Steel Foreman	$17.65	$141.20	$33.40	$267.20	$15.86	$29.46
5 Struc. Steel Workers	15.65	626.00	29.60	1184.00		
1 Equip. Oper. (crane)	15.15	121.20	24.85	198.80		
1 Hyd. Crane, 25 Ton		486.40		535.05	8.68	9.55
56 M.H., Daily Totals		$1374.80		$2185.05	$24.54	$39.01
Crew L-6						
1 Plumber	$16.55	$132.40	$27.00	$216.00	$16.48	$26.81
.5 Electrician	16.35	65.40	26.45	105.80		
12 M.H., Daily Totals		$197.80		$321.80	$16.48	$26.81
Crew L-7						
2 Carpenters	$14.30	$228.80	$23.90	$382.40	$13.75	$22.86
1 Building Laborer	11.35	90.80	19.00	152.00		
.5 Electrician	16.35	65.40	26.45	105.80		
28 M.H., Daily Totals		$385.00		$640.20	$13.75	$22.86
Crew L-8						
2 Carpenters	$14.30	$228.80	$23.90	$382.40	$14.75	$24.52
.5 Plumber	16.55	66.20	27.00	108.00		
20 M.H., Daily Totals		$295.00		$490.40	$14.75	$24.52
Crew L-9						
1 Labor Foreman (inside)	$11.85	$94.80	$19.85	$158.80	$12.97	$22.37
2 Building Laborers	11.35	181.60	19.00	304.00		
1 Struc. Steel Worker	15.65	125.20	29.60	236.80		
.5 Electrician	16.35	65.40	26.45	105.80		
36 M.H., Daily Totals		$467.00		$805.40	$12.97	$22.37
Crew M-1						
3 Elevator Constructors	$16.45	$394.80	$26.90	$645.60	$15.62	$25.55
1 Elevator Apprentice	13.16	105.28	21.50	172.00		
Hand Tools		76.00		83.60	2.37	2.61
32 M.H., Daily Totals		$576.08		$901.20	$17.99	$28.16
Crew M-2						
2 Millwrights	$14.90	$238.40	$23.95	$383.20	$14.90	$23.95
Power Tools		16.00		17.60	1.00	1.10
16 M.H., Daily Totals		$254.40		$400.80	$15.90	$25.05
Crew Q-1						
1 Plumber	$16.55	$132.40	$27.00	$216.00	$14.89	$24.30
1 Plumber Apprentice	13.24	105.92	21.60	172.80		
16 M.H., Daily Totals		$238.32		$388.80	$14.89	$24.30
Crew Q-2						
2 Plumbers	$16.55	$264.80	$27.00	$432.00	$15.44	$25.20
1 Plumber Apprentice	13.24	105.92	21.60	172.80		
24 M.H., Daily Totals		$370.72		$604.80	$15.44	$25.20
Crew Q-3						
1 Plumber Foreman (ins)	$17.05	$136.40	$27.85	$222.80	$15.84	$25.86
2 Plumbers	16.55	264.80	27.00	432.00		
1 Plumber Apprentice	13.24	105.92	21.60	172.80		
32 M.H., Daily Totals		$507.12		$827.60	$15.84	$25.86

Crew No.	Bare Costs Hr.	Daily	Incl. Subs O & P Hr.	Daily	Cost Per Man-Hour Bare Costs	Incl. O&P
Crew Q-4						
1 Plumber Foreman (ins)	$17.05	$136.40	$27.85	$222.80	$15.84	$25.86
1 Plumber	16.55	132.40	27.00	216.00		
1 Welder (plumber)	16.55	132.40	27.00	216.00		
1 Plumber Apprentice	13.24	105.92	21.60	172.80		
1 Electric Welding Mach.		39.00		42.90	1.21	1.34
32 M.H., Daily Totals		$546.12		$870.50	$17.05	$27.20
Crew Q-5						
1 Steamfitter	$16.55	$132.40	$27.00	$216.00	$14.89	$24.30
1 Steamfitter Apprentice	13.24	105.92	21.60	172.80		
16 M.H., Daily Totals		$238.32		$388.80	$14.89	$24.30
Crew Q-6						
2 Steamfitters	$16.55	$264.80	$27.00	$432.00	$15.44	$25.20
1 Steamfitter Apprentice	13.24	105.92	21.60	172.80		
24 M.H., Daily Totals		$370.72		$604.80	$15.44	$25.20
Crew Q-7						
1 Steamfitter Foreman (ins)	$17.05	$136.40	$27.85	$222.80	$15.84	$25.86
2 Steamfitters	16.55	264.80	27.00	432.00		
1 Steamfitter Apprentice	13.24	105.92	21.60	172.80		
32 M.H., Daily Totals		$507.12		$827.60	$15.84	$25.86
Crew Q-8						
1 Steamfitter Foreman (ins)	$17.05	$136.40	$27.85	$222.80	$15.84	$25.86
1 Steamfitter	16.55	132.40	27.00	216.00		
1 Welder (steamfitter)	16.55	132.40	27.00	216.00		
1 Steamfitter Apprentice	13.24	105.92	21.60	172.80		
1 Electric Welding Mach.		39.00		42.90	1.21	1.34
32 M.H., Daily Totals		$546.12		$870.50	$17.05	$27.20
Crew Q-9						
1 Sheet Metal Worker	$16.25	$130.00	$26.95	$215.60	$14.62	$24.25
1 Sheet Metal Apprentice	13.00	104.00	21.55	172.40		
16 M.H., Daily Totals		$234.00		$388.00	$14.62	$24.25
Crew Q-10						
2 Sheet Metal Workers	$16.25	$260.00	$26.95	$431.20	$15.16	$25.15
1 Sheet Metal Apprentice	13.00	104.00	21.55	172.40		
24 M.H., Daily Totals		$364.00		$603.60	$15.16	$25.15
Crew Q-11						
1 Sheet Metal Foreman (ins)	$16.75	$134.00	$27.80	$222.40	$15.56	$25.81
2 Sheet Metal Workers	16.25	260.00	26.95	431.20		
1 Sheet Metal Apprentice	13.00	104.00	21.55	172.40		
32 M.H., Daily Totals		$498.00		$826.00	$15.56	$25.81
Crew Q-12						
1 Sprinkler Installer	$17.15	$137.20	$28.00	$224.00	$15.43	$25.20
1 Sprinkler Apprentice	13.72	109.76	22.40	179.20		
16 M.H., Daily Totals		$246.96		$403.20	$15.43	$25.20
Crew Q-13						
1 Sprinkler Foreman (ins)	$17.65	$141.20	$28.85	$230.80	$16.41	$26.81
2 Sprinkler Installers	17.15	274.40	28.00	448.00		
1 Sprinkler Apprentice	13.72	109.76	22.40	179.20		
32 M.H., Daily Totals		$525.36		$858.00	$16.41	$26.81

CREWS

Crew No.	Bare Costs Hr.	Daily	Incl. Subs O & P Hr.	Daily	Cost Per Man-Hour Bare Costs	Incl. O&P
Crew Q-14	Hr.	Daily	Hr.	Daily	Bare Costs	Incl. O&P
1 Asbestos Worker	$16.05	$128.40	$27.15	$217.20	$14.44	$24.45
1 Asbestos Apprentice	12.84	102.72	21.75	174.00		
16 M.H., Daily Totals		$231.12		$391.20	$14.44	$24.45
Crew Q-15	Hr.	Daily	Hr.	Daily	Bare Costs	Incl. O&P
1 Plumber	$16.55	$132.40	$27.00	$216.00	$14.89	$24.30
1 Plumber Apprentice	13.24	105.92	21.60	172.80		
1 Electric Welding Mach.		39.00		42.90	2.43	2.68
16 M.H., Daily Totals		$277.32		$431.70	$17.32	$26.98
Crew Q-16	Hr.	Daily	Hr.	Daily	Bare Costs	Incl. O&P
2 Plumbers	$16.55	$264.80	$27.00	$432.00	$15.44	$25.20
1 Plumber Apprentice	13.24	105.92	21.60	172.80		
1 Electric Welding Mach.		39.00		42.90	1.62	1.78
24 M.H., Daily Totals		$409.72		$647.70	$17.06	$26.98
Crew Q-17	Hr.	Daily	Hr.	Daily	Bare Costs	Incl. O&P
1 Steamfitter	$16.55	$132.40	$27.00	$216.00	$14.89	$24.30
1 Steamfitter Apprentice	13.24	105.92	21.60	172.80		
1 Electric Welding Mach.		39.00		42.90	2.43	2.68
16 M.H., Daily Totals		$277.32		$431.70	$17.32	$26.98
Crew Q-18	Hr.	Daily	Hr.	Daily	Bare Costs	Incl. O&P
2 Steamfitters	$16.55	$264.80	$27.00	$432.00	$15.44	$25.20
1 Steamfitter Apprentice	13.24	105.92	21.60	172.80		
1 Electric Welding Mach.		39.00		42.90	1.62	1.78
24 M.H., Daily Totals		$409.72		$647.70	$17.06	$26.98
Crew Q-19	Hr.	Daily	Hr.	Daily	Bare Costs	Incl. O&P
1 Steamfitter	$16.55	$132.40	$27.00	$216.00	$15.38	$25.01
1 Steamfitter Apprentice	13.24	105.92	21.60	172.80		
1 Electrician	16.35	130.80	26.45	211.60		
24 M.H., Daily Totals		$369.12		$600.40	$15.38	$25.01
Crew Q-20	Hr.	Daily	Hr.	Daily	Bare Costs	Incl. O&P
1 Sheet Metal Worker	$16.25	$130.00	$26.95	$215.60	$14.97	$24.69
1 Sheet Metal Apprentice	13.00	104.00	21.55	172.40		
.5 Electrician	16.35	65.40	26.45	105.80		
20 M.H., Daily Totals		$299.40		$493.80	$14.97	$24.69
Crew Q-21	Hr.	Daily	Hr.	Daily	Bare Costs	Incl. O&P
2 Steamfitters	$16.55	$264.80	$27.00	$432.00	$15.67	$25.51
1 Steamfitter Apprentice	13.24	105.92	21.60	172.80		
1 Electrician	16.35	130.80	26.45	211.60		
32 M.H., Daily Totals		$501.52		$816.40	$15.67	$25.51
Crew Q-22	Hr.	Daily	Hr.	Daily	Bare Costs	Incl. O&P
1 Plumber	$16.55	$132.40	$27.00	$216.00	$14.89	$24.30
1 Plumber Apprentice	13.24	105.92	21.60	172.80		
1 Truck Crane, 12 Ton		362.00		398.20	22.62	24.88
16 M.H., Daily Totals		$600.32		$787.00	$37.51	$49.18
Crew R-1	Hr.	Daily	Hr.	Daily	Bare Costs	Incl. O&P
1 Electrician Foreman	$16.85	$134.80	$27.25	$218.00	$14.68	$24.01
3 Electricians	16.35	392.40	26.45	634.80		
2 Helpers	11.10	177.60	18.75	300.00		
48 M.H., Daily Totals		$704.80		$1152.80	$14.68	$24.01

Crew No.	Bare Costs Hr.	Daily	Incl. Subs O & P Hr.	Daily	Cost Per Man-Hour Bare Costs	Incl. O&P
Crew R-2	Hr.	Daily	Hr.	Daily	Bare Costs	Incl. O&P
1 Electrician Foreman	$16.85	$134.80	$27.25	$218.00	$14.75	$24.13
3 Electricians	16.35	392.40	26.45	634.80		
2 Helpers	11.10	177.60	18.75	300.00		
1 Equip. Oper. (crane)	15.15	121.20	24.85	198.80		
1 S.P. Crane, 5 Ton		208.00		228.80	3.71	4.08
56 M.H., Daily Totals		$1034.00		$1580.40	$18.46	$28.21
Crew R-3	Hr.	Daily	Hr.	Daily	Bare Costs	Incl. O&P
1 Electrician Foreman	$16.85	$134.80	$27.25	$218.00	$16.31	$26.45
1 Electrician	16.35	130.80	26.45	211.60		
.5 Equip. Oper. (crane)	15.15	60.60	24.85	99.40		
.5 S.P. Crane, 5 Ton		104.00		114.40	5.20	5.72
20 M.H., Daily Totals		$430.20		$643.40	$21.51	$32.17
Crew R-4	Hr.	Daily	Hr.	Daily	Bare Costs	Incl. O&P
1 Struc. Steel Foreman	$17.65	$141.20	$33.40	$267.20	$16.19	$29.73
3 Struc. Steel Workers	15.65	375.60	29.60	710.40		
1 Electrician	16.35	130.80	26.45	211.60		
1 Gas Welding Machine		68.40		75.25	1.71	1.88
40 M.H., Daily Totals		$716.00		$1264.45	$17.90	$31.61
Crew R-5	Hr.	Daily	Hr.	Daily	Bare Costs	Incl. O&P
1 Electrician Foreman	$16.85	$134.80	$27.25	$218.00	$14.48	$23.72
4 Electrician Linemen	16.35	523.20	26.45	846.40		
2 Electrician Operators	16.35	261.60	26.45	423.20		
4 Electrician Groundmen	11.10	355.20	18.75	600.00		
1 Crew Truck		161.20		177.30		
1 Tool Van		291.80		321.00		
1 Pick-up Truck		107.40		118.15		
.2 Crane, 55 Ton		145.45		160.00		
.2 Crane, 12 Ton		72.40		79.65		
.2 Auger, Truck Mtd.		297.50		327.25		
1 Tractor w/Winch		251.40		276.55	15.08	16.58
88 M.H., Daily Totals		$2601.95		$3547.50	$29.56	$40.30
Crew R-6	Hr.	Daily	Hr.	Daily	Bare Costs	Incl. O&P
1 Electrician Foreman	$16.85	$134.80	$27.25	$218.00	$14.48	$23.72
4 Electrician Linemen	16.35	523.20	26.45	846.40		
2 Electrician Operators	16.35	261.60	26.45	423.20		
4 Electrician Groundmen	11.10	355.20	18.75	600.00		
1 Crew Truck		161.20		177.30		
1 Tool Van		291.80		321.00		
1 Pick-up Truck		107.40		118.15		
.2 Crane, 55 Ton		145.45		160.00		
.2 Crane, 12 Ton		72.40		79.65		
.2 Auger, Truck Mtd.		297.50		327.25		
1 Tractor w/Winch		251.40		276.55		
3 Cable Trailers		370.80		407.90		
.5 Tensioning Rig		122.20		134.40		
.5 Cable Pulling Rig		723.70		796.05	28.90	31.79
88 M.H., Daily Totals		$3818.65		$4885.85	$43.38	$55.51
Crew R-7	Hr.	Daily	Hr.	Daily	Bare Costs	Incl. O&P
1 Electrician Foreman	$16.85	$134.80	$27.25	$218.00	$12.05	$20.16
5 Electrician Groundmen	11.10	444.00	18.75	750.00		
1 Crew Truck		161.20		177.30	3.35	3.69
48 M.H., Daily Totals		$740.00		$1145.30	$15.40	$23.85

CREWS

Crew No.		Bare Costs		Incl. Subs O & P		Cost Per Man-Hour	
Crew R-8	Hr.	Daily	Hr.	Daily	Bare Costs	Incl. O&P
1 Electrician Foreman	$16.85	$134.80	$27.25	$218.00	$14.68	$24.01
3 Electrician Linemen	16.35	392.40	26.45	634.80		
2 Electrician Groundmen	11.10	177.60	18.75	300.00		
1 Pick-up Truck		107.40		118.15		
1 Crew Truck		161.20		177.30	5.59	6.15
48 M.H., Daily Totals		$973.40		$1448.25	$20.27	$30.16

Crew No.		Bare Costs		Incl. Subs O & P		Cost Per Man-Hour	
Crew R-9	Hr.	Daily	Hr.	Daily	Bare Costs	Incl. O&P
1 Electrician Foreman	$16.85	$134.80	$27.25	$218.00	$13.78	$22.70
1 Electrician Lineman	16.35	130.80	26.45	211.60		
2 Electrician Operators	16.35	261.60	26.45	423.20		
4 Electrician Groundmen	11.10	355.20	18.75	600.00		
1 Pick-up Truck		107.40		118.15		
1 Crew Truck		161.20		177.30	4.19	4.61
64 M.H., Daily Totals		$1151.00		$1748.25	$17.97	$27.31

Crew No.		Bare Costs		Incl. Subs O & P		Cost Per Man-Hour	
Crew R-10	Hr.	Daily	Hr.	Daily	Bare Costs	Incl. O&P
1 Electrician Foreman	$16.85	$134.80	$27.25	$218.00	$15.55	$25.30
4 Electrician Linemen	16.35	523.20	26.45	846.40		
1 Electrician Groundman	11.10	88.80	18.75	150.00		
1 Crew Truck		161.20		177.30		
3 Tram Cars		436.80		480.50	12.45	13.70
48 M.H., Daily Totals		$1344.80		$1872.20	$28.00	$39.00

Crew No.		Bare Costs		Incl. Subs O & P		Cost Per Man-Hour	
Crew R-11	Hr.	Daily	Hr.	Daily	Bare Costs	Incl. O&P
1 Electrician Foreman	$16.85	$134.80	$27.25	$218.00	$14.95	$24.40
4 Electricians	16.35	523.20	26.45	846.40		
1 Helper	11.10	88.80	18.75	150.00		
1 Common Laborer	11.35	90.80	19.00	152.00		
1 Crew Truck		161.20		177.30		
1 Crane, 12 Ton		362.00		398.20	9.34	10.27
56 M.H., Daily Totals		$1360.80		$1941.90	$24.29	$34.67

Crew No.		Bare Costs		Incl. Subs O & P		Cost Per Man-Hour	
Crew R-12	Hr.	Daily	Hr.	Daily	Bare Costs	Incl. O&P
1 Carpenter Foreman	$14.80	$118.40	$24.75	$198.00	$13.42	$22.71
4 Carpenters	14.30	457.60	23.90	764.80		
4 Laborers	11.35	363.20	19.00	608.00		
1 Equip. Oper. (med.)	14.60	116.80	23.95	191.60		
1 Steel Worker	15.65	125.20	29.60	236.80		
1 Dozer, 200 H.P.		775.80		853.40		
1 Pick-up Truck		107.40		118.15	10.03	11.04
88 M.H., Daily Totals		$2064.40		$2970.75	$23.45	$33.75

LOCATION FACTORS

Costs shown in *Means Residential Cost Data 1991* are based on National Averages for materials and installation. To adjust these costs to a specific location, simply multiply the base cost by the factor for that city. The data is arranged alphabetically by state and postal zip code numbers. For a city not listed, use the factor for a nearby city with similar economic characteristics.

State/Zip	City	Residential	Commercial	State/Zip	City	Residential	Commercial
Alabama				**Calif. (Cont.)**			
350-352	Birmingham	.83	.84	955	Eureka	1.09	1.08
354	Tuscaloosa	.83	.81	956-958	Sacramento	1.09	1.08
355	Jasper	.83	.84	959	Marysville	1.09	1.08
356	Decatur	.82	.84	960	Redding	1.09	1.08
357, 358	Huntsville	.83	.84	961	Susanville	1.09	1.08
359	Gadsden	.81	.81	**Colorado**			
360, 361	Montgomery	.83	.81	800-802	Denver	.97	.93
362	Anniston	.81	.81	803	Boulder	.97	.93
363	Dothan	.85	.81	804	Golden	.97	.93
364	Evergreen	.87	.83	805	Fort Collins	.93	.87
365, 366	Mobile	.92	.86	806	Greeley	.93	.87
367	Selma	.87	.83	807	Fort Morgan	.91	.85
368	Phenix City	.87	.83	808, 809	Colorado Springs	.92	.90
369	Butler	.87	.83	810	Pueblo	.94	.92
Alaska				811	Alamosa	.94	.92
995, 996	Anchorage	1.26	1.27	812	Salida	.94	.92
997	Fairbanks	1.26	1.29	813	Durango	.94	.92
998	Juneau	1.26	1.27	814	Montrose	.94	.92
999	Ketchikan	1.26	1.27	815	Grand Junction	.98	.93
Arizona				816	Glenwood Springs	.98	.93
850	Phoenix	.94	.91	**Connecticut**			
852	Mesa/Tempe	.94	.91	060, 061	Hartford	.97	.98
855	Globe	.94	.91	062	Willimantic	.97	.98
856, 857	Tucson	.94	.92	063	New London	.97	.96
859	Show Low	.95	.92	064, 065	New Haven	.97	.98
860	Flagstaff	.95	.95	066	Bridgeport	.96	.99
863	Prescott	.95	.95	067	Waterbury	.96	.96
864	Kingman	.95	.95	068, 069	Stamford	.98	1.02
865	Chambers	.95	.95	**Delaware**			
Arkansas				197, 198	Wilmington	1.00	1.01
716	Pine Bluff	.84	.84	199	Dover	1.00	1.01
717	Camden	.84	.84	**District of Columbia**			
718	Texarkana	.84	.83	200-205	Washington	.94	.96
719	Hot Springs	.84	.84	**Florida**			
720-722	Little Rock	.84	.84	320, 322	Jacksonville	.86	.85
723	West Memphis	.88	.88	323	Tallahassee	.81	.83
724	Jonesboro	.88	.88	324	Panama City	.81	.83
725	Batesville	.83	.83	325	Pensacola	.82	.87
726	Harrison	.83	.83	326	Gainesville	.87	.84
727	Fayetteville	.85	.82	327, 328	Orlando	.86	.84
728	Russellville	.85	.82	329	Melbourne	.85	.84
729	Fort Smith	.85	.82	330, 331	Miami	.87	.89
California				333	Fort Lauderdale	.87	.89
900-918	Los Angeles	1.12	1.12	334	W. Palm Beach	.90	.87
920, 921	San Diego	1.12	1.09	335, 336	Tampa	.87	.89
922	Palm Springs	1.13	1.10	337	St. Petersburg	.87	.89
923, 924	San Bernardino	1.13	1.10	338	Lakeland	.84	.86
925	Riverside	1.13	1.10	339	Fort Myers	.86	.86
926, 927	Santa Ana	1.13	1.10	**Georgia**			
928	Anaheim	1.13	1.11	300-303	Atlanta	.84	.89
930	Ventura	1.13	1.12	304	Statesboro	.84	.86
931	Santa Barbara	1.15	1.13	305	Gainesville	.84	.89
932, 933	Bakersfield	1.10	1.05	306	Athens	.84	.89
934	San Luis Obispo	1.12	1.10	307	Dalton	.87	.86
935	Mojave	1.09	1.05	308, 309	August	.83	.85
936, 937	Fresno	1.10	1.07	310, 312	Macon	.84	.84
939	Salinas	1.06	1.06	313, 314	Savannah	.85	.86
940, 941	San Francisco	1.21	1.25	315	Waycross	.82	.82
943	Palo Alto	1.19	1.18	316	Valdosta	.82	.82
944	San Mateo	1.21	1.25	317	Albany	.81	.83
945, 946	Oakland	1.21	1.25	318, 319	Columbus	.80	.80
947	Berkeley	1.21	1.25	**Hawaii**			
948	Richmond	1.21	1.25	967, 968	Honolulu	1.15	1.10
948	San Rafael	1.18	1.12				
950, 951	San Jose	1.20	1.19				
952, 953	Stockton	1.12	1.08				
954	Santa Rosa	1.12	1.15				

LOCATION FACTORS

State/Zip	City	Residential	Commercial
Idaho			
832	Pocatello	.96	.95
833	Twin Falls	.96	.95
834	Idaho Falls	.96	.95
835	Lewiston	1.03	1.03
836, 837	Boise	.94	.93
838	Coeur D'Alene	1.03	1.03
Illinois			
600-606	Chicago	1.05	1.04
609	Kankakee	1.01	1.01
610-611	Rockford	1.01	1.00
612	Rock Island	1.02	.94
613	La Salle	1.01	.94
614	Galesburg	1.01	.94
615, 616	Peoria	1.00	.94
617	Bloomington	1.00	.96
618, 619	Champaign	1.00	.97
620, 622	East St. Louis	1.01	1.01
623	Quincy	.97	.95
624	Effingham	.98	.95
625-627	Springfield	.97	.93
628	Centralia	.98	.98
629	Carbondale	.98	.98
Indiana			
460-462	Indianapolis	.99	.97
463, 464	Gary	1.01	.99
465, 466	South Bend	.96	.94
467, 468	Fort Wayne	.91	.92
469	Kokomo	.94	.93
470	Lawrenceburg	.98	.95
471	New Albany	.92	.88
472	Columbus	.98	.95
473	Muncie	.93	.92
474	Bloomington	1.00	.97
475	Washington	.97	.97
476, 477	Evansville	.96	.96
478	Terre Haute	.97	.95
479	Lafayette	.95	.95
Iowa			
500-503	Des Moines	.94	.90
504	Mason City	.93	.87
505	Fort Dodge	.93	.87
506, 507	Waterloo	.92	.86
508	Creston	.91	.86
510, 511	Sioux City	.86	.84
512	Sibley	.86	.84
513	Spencer	.86	.84
514	Carroll	.93	.88
515	Council Bluffs	.94	.88
516	Shenandoah	.94	.88
520	Dubuque	.95	.85
521	Decorah	.92	.82
522-524	Cedar Rapids	.95	.87
525	Ottumwa	.95	.87
526	Burlington	.98	.92
527, 528	Davenport	.94	.92
Kansas			
660-662	Kansas City	.97	.95
664-666	Topeka	.89	.88
667	Fort Scott	.97	.95
668	Emporia	.91	.90
669	Belleville	.91	.85
670-672	Wichita	.89	.86
673	Independence	.89	.86
674	Salina	.89	.85
675	Hutchinson	.89	.85
676	Hays	.89	.85
677	Colby	.89	.85
678	Dodge City	.89	.86
679	Liberal	.89	.86

State/Zip	City	Residential	Commercial
Kentucky			
400-402	Louisville	.92	.89
403-405	Lexington	.90	.87
406	Frankfort	.92	.86
407-409	Corbin	.92	.86
410	Covington	.99	.96
411, 412	Ashland	.92	.93
413, 414	Campton	.90	.86
415, 416	Pikeville	.92	.93
417, 418	Hazard	.90	.86
420	Paducah	.92	.87
421, 422	Bowling Green	.92	.87
423	Owensboro	.92	.90
424	Henderson	.92	.90
425, 426	Somerset	.90	.86
427	Elizabethtown	.92	.88
Louisiana			
700, 701	New Orleans	.89	.88
703	Thibodaux	.89	.89
704	Hammond	.88	.87
705	Lafayette	.86	.83
706	Lake Charles	.86	.86
707, 708	Baton Rouge	.87	.86
710, 711	Shreveport	.83	.83
712	Monroe	.83	.83
713, 714	Alexandria	.83	.83
Maine			
039	Kittery	.88	.90
040, 041	Portland	.87	.89
042	Lewiston	.87	.88
043	Augusta	.88	.88
044	Bangor	.88	.88
045	Bath	.88	.88
046	Machias	.88	.88
047	Houlton	.88	.88
048	Rockland	.88	.88
049	Waterville	.89	.88
Maryland			
206	Waldorf	.97	.97
207, 208	College Park	.97	.97
209	Silver Spring	.97	.97
210-212	Baltimore	.96	.97
214	Annapolis	.96	.97
215	Cumberland	.93	.94
216	Easton	.96	.97
217	Hagerstown	.96	.94
218	Salisbury	.96	.97
219	Elkton	.96	.97
Massachusetts			
010, 011	Springfield	1.04	1.02
012	Pittsfield	1.00	1.00
013	Greenfield	1.03	1.01
014	Fitchburg	1.10	1.06
015, 016	Worcester	1.10	1.06
017	Framingham	1.11	1.12
018	Lowell	1.06	1.06
019	Lynn	1.15	1.15
020-022	Boston	1.16	1.17
023, 024	Brockton	1.04	1.06
025	Buzzards Bay	1.04	1.06
026	Hyannis	1.05	1.06
027	New Bedford	1.05	1.06
Michigan			
480	Royal Oak	1.07	1.06
480-482	Detroit	1.07	1.06
484, 485	Flint	.95	.96
486, 487	Saginaw	.91	.92
488, 489	Lansing	.98	.95
490, 491	Kalamazoo	.95	.89
492	Jackson	1.01	.96
493-495	Grand Rapids	.91	.88
496	Traverse City	.91	.88
497	Gaylord	.93	.93
498, 499	Iron Mountain	.94	.91

LOCATION FACTORS

State/Zip	City	Residential	Commercial
Minnesota			
550, 551	St. Paul	1.01	.99
553, 554	Minneapolis	1.03	1.00
556-558	Duluth	.93	.94
559	Rochester	.97	.94
560	Mankato	.98	.97
561	Windom	.98	.97
562	Willmar	.98	.97
563	St. Cloud	1.00	.93
564	Brainerd	1.00	.93
565	Detroit Lakes	.85	.91
566	Bemidji	.85	.91
567	Thief River Falls	.85	.91
Mississippi			
386	Clarksdale	.84	.80
387	Greenville	.84	.80
388	Tupelo	.82	.77
389	Greenwood	.84	.80
390-392	Jackson	.84	.80
393	Meridian	.84	.77
394	Laurel	.85	.81
395	Biloxi	.85	.81
396	Mc Comb	.82	.80
397	Columbus	.82	.77
Missouri			
630, 631	St. Louis	.99	1.02
633	Bowling Green	.99	1.02
634	Hannibal	.99	.92
635	Kirksville	.90	.94
636	Flat River	.99	1.02
637	Cape Girardeau	.99	1.02
638	Sikeston	.99	1.02
639	Poplar Bluff	.99	1.02
640, 641	Kansas City	1.01	.98
644, 645	Saint Joseph	.86	.90
646	Chillicothe	.86	.90
647	Harrisonville	1.00	.98
648	Joplin	.86	.88
650, 652	Columbia	.98	.91
651	Jefferson City	.98	.91
653	Sedalia	.98	.91
654, 655	Rolla	.98	.91
656-658	Springfield	.86	.88
Montana			
590-591	Billings	.93	.91
592	Wolf Point	.93	.91
593	Miles City	.93	.91
594	Great Falls	.93	.92
595	Havre	.93	.92
596	Helena	.93	.92
597	Butte	.93	.88
598	Missoula	.93	.88
599	Kalispell	.93	.92
Nebraska			
680, 681	Omaha	.89	.88
683-685	Lincoln	.87	.82
686	Columbus	.89	.88
687	Norfolk	.89	.88
688	Grand Island	.87	.83
689	Hastings	.87	.83
690	Mc Cook	.87	.83
691	North Platte	.87	.83
692	Valentine	.87	.83
693	Alliance	.86	.82
Nevada			
890, 891	Las Vegas	1.02	1.03
893	Ely	1.04	1.05
894, 895	Reno	1.01	1.04
897	Carson City	1.01	1.04
898	Elko	1.01	1.04

State/Zip	City	Residential	Commercial
New Hampshire			
030, 031	Manchester	.88	.89
032, 033	Concord	.88	.89
034	Keene	.88	.89
035	Littleton	.88	.89
036	Charlestown	.88	.89
037	Claremont	.88	.89
038	Portsmouth	.88	.87
New Jersey			
070, 071	Newark	1.06	1.04
072	Elizabeth	1.06	1.04
073	Jersey City	1.06	1.05
074, 075	Paterson	1.08	1.08
076	Hackensack	1.08	1.08
077	Long Branch	1.06	1.04
078	Dover	1.06	1.04
079	Summit	1.07	1.05
080, 083	Vineland	1.07	1.03
081	Camden	1.08	1.05
082, 084	Atlantic City	1.08	1.05
085, 086	Trenton	1.07	1.05
087	Point Pleasant	1.07	1.05
088, 089	New Brunswick	1.07	1.05
New Mexico			
870, 871	Albuquerque	.89	.91
873	Gallup	.89	.93
874	Farmington	.89	.93
875	Santa Fe	.89	.93
877	Las Vegas	.89	.93
878	Socorro	.89	.91
879	Truth/Conseq.	.89	.89
880	Las Cruces	.89	.89
881	Clovis	.89	.89
882	Roswell	.89	.89
883	Carrizozo	.89	.89
884	Tucumcari	.89	.93
New York			
100	Manhattan	1.27	1.27
103	Staten Island	1.27	1.27
104	Bronx	1.27	1.27
105	Mount Vernon	1.17	1.17
106	White Plains	1.17	1.17
107	Yonkers	1.17	1.17
108	New Rochelle	1.17	1.17
109	Suffern	1.17	1.17
110	Queens	1.27	1.27
111	Long Island City	1.27	1.27
112	Brooklyn	1.27	1.27
113	Flushing	1.27	1.27
114	Jamaica	1.27	1.27
115, 117, 118	Hicksville	1.27	1.27
116	Far Rockaway	1.27	1.27
119	Riverhead	1.27	1.27
120-122	Albany	.98	.98
123	Schenectady	.99	.99
124	Kingston	1.16	1.14
125, 126	Poughkeepsie	1.16	1.14
127	Monticello	1.16	1.14
128	Glens Falls	.97	.95
129	Plattsburgh	.97	.95
130-132	Syracuse	.97	.95
133-135	Utica	.88	.91
136	Watertown	.88	.91
137-139	Binghamton	.89	.89
140-142	Buffalo	1.08	1.04
143	Niagara Falls	1.08	1.04
144-146	Rochester	1.01	1.02
147	Jamestown	1.08	1.04
148-149	Elmira	.93	.91

LOCATION FACTORS

State/Zip	City	Residential	Commercial
North Carolina			
270, 272-274	Greensboro	.76	.77
271	Winston-Salem	.80	.81
275, 276	Raleigh	.80	.80
277	Durham	.78	.79
278	Rocky Mount	.80	.80
279	Elizabeth City	.83	.83
280-282	Charlotte	.79	.80
283	Fayetteville	.80	.80
284	Wilmington	.79	.81
285	Kingston	.80	.80
286	Hickory	.80	.81
287, 288	Asheville	.79	.81
289	Murphy	.80	.81
North Dakota			
580, 581	Fargo	.83	.88
582	Grand Forks	.83	.88
583	Devils Lake	.83	.88
584	Jamestown	.83	.88
585	Bismarck	.83	.87
586	Dickinson	.83	.87
587	Minot	.83	.87
588	Williston	.83	.87
Ohio			
430-432	Columbus	.99	.97
433	Marion	.97	.98
434-436	Toledo	1.01	1.00
437, 438	Zanesville	.97	.96
439	Steubenville	1.00	1.00
440, 441	Cleveland	1.14	1.07
442, 443	Akron	1.01	1.00
444, 445	Youngstown	1.00	.97
446, 447	Canton	.97	.96
448, 449	Mansfield	1.02	1.00
450-452	Cincinnati	1.02	.96
453, 454	Dayton	.99	.98
455	Springfield	.98	.96
456	Chillicothe	.99	.93
457	Athens	.98	.97
458	Lima	1.04	.93
Oklahoma			
730, 731	Oklahoma City	.87	.89
734	Ardmore	.87	.86
735	Lawton	.87	.86
736	Clinton	.87	.89
737	Enid	.86	.85
738	Woodward	.86	.85
739	Guymon	.86	.85
740, 741	Tulsa	.90	.87
743	Miami	.90	.87
744	Muskogee	.90	.87
745	McAlester	.86	.88
746	Ponca City	.90	.85
747	Durant	.86	.88
748	Shawnee	.86	.88
749	Poteau	.85	.81
Oregon			
970-972	Portland	1.03	1.01
973	Salem	1.02	1.01
974	Eugene	1.01	1.00
975	Medford	1.01	1.00
976	Klamath Falls	1.01	1.00
977	Bend	1.01	1.00
978	Pendleton	.98	.96
979	Vale	.98	.96
Pennsylvania			
150-152	Pittsburgh	1.02	1.00
153	Washington	1.02	1.00
154	Uniontown	1.02	1.00
155	Bedford	1.02	.95
156	Greensburg	1.02	1.00
157	Indiana	1.02	.95
158	Du Bois	1.02	.95
159	Johnstown	1.02	.95

State/Zip	City	Residential	Commercial
Pennsylvania (Cont.)			
160	Butler	1.04	1.01
161	New Castle	1.04	1.01
162	Kittanning	1.04	1.01
163	Oil City	.96	1.01
164, 165	Erie	.96	.95
166	Altoona	1.04	.95
167	Bradford	.96	.94
168	State College	.96	.96
169	Wellsboro	.94	.95
170, 171	Harrisburg	.96	.95
172	Chambersburg	.96	.95
173, 174	York	.96	.94
175, 176	Lancaster	.96	.94
177	Williamsport	.96	.95
178	Sunbury	.96	.95
179	Pottsville	.96	.95
180	Lehigh Valley	1.03	1.02
181	Allentown	1.03	1.02
182	Hazleton	1.03	1.02
183	Stroudsburg	1.03	1.02
184, 185	Scranton	.94	.97
186, 187	Wilkes Barre	.94	.97
188	Montrose	.94	.97
189	Doylestown	.97	1.09
190, 191	Philadelphia	1.11	1.09
193	Westchester	1.11	1.09
194	Norristown	1.11	1.09
195, 196	Reading	.96	.97
Rhode Island			
028, 029	Providence	.98	1.00
South Carolina			
290-292	Columbia	.77	.80
293	Spartanburg	.77	.80
294	Charleston	.78	.80
295	Florence	.77	.79
296	Greenville	.77	.80
297	Rock Hill	.77	.80
298	Aiken	.77	.80
299	Beaufort	.78	.80
South Dakota			
570, 571	Sioux Falls	.88	.82
572	Watertown	.88	.82
573	Mitchell	.88	.82
574	Aberdeen	.88	.82
575	Pierre	.88	.82
576	Mobridge	.89	.82
577	Rapid City	.89	.83
Tennessee			
370-372	Nashville	.84	.84
373, 374	Chattanooga	.86	.85
376	Johnson City	.85	.84
377-379	Knoxville	.84	.84
380, 381	Memphis	.87	.87
382	Mc Kenzie	.83	.83
383	Jackson	.79	.87
384	Columbia	.83	.83
385	Cookeville	.83	.83
Texas			
750	Mc Kinney	.94	.87
751	Waxahackie	.89	.89
752, 753	Dallas	.92	.88
754	Greenville	.93	.87
755	Texarkana	.96	.85
756	Longview	.96	.85
757	Tyler	.96	.85
758	Palestine	.85	.85
759	Lufkin	.85	.85
760, 761	Forth Worth	.90	.89
762	Denton	.96	.87
763	Wichita Falls	.87	.87
764	Eastland	.90	.89

LOCATION FACTORS

State/Zip	City	Residential	Commercial	State/Zip	City	Residential	Commercial
Texas (Cont.)				**West Virginia**			
765	Temple	.87	.81	247, 248	Bluefield	.97	.97
766, 767	Waco	.84	.83	249	Lewisburg	.97	.97
768	Brownwood	.84	.83	250-253	Charleston	.97	.97
769	San Angelo	.84	.80	254	Martinsburg	.94	.95
770-772	Houston	.89	.90	255-257	Huntington	.96	.98
773	Huntsville	.88	.88	258, 259	Beckley	.97	.97
774	Wharton	.91	.92	260	Wheeling	.95	.97
775	Galveston	.91	.92	261	Parkersburg	.95	.97
776, 777	Beaumont	.92	.94	262	Buckhannon	.97	.94
778	Bryan	.89	.88	263, 264	Clarksburg	.97	.94
779	Victoria	.85	.85	265	Morgantown	.97	.94
780-782	San Antonio	.84	.85	266	Gassaway	.97	.97
783, 784	Corpus Christi	.84	.83	267	Romney	.91	.91
785	Mc Allen	.85	.83	268	Petersburg	.97	.94
786, 787	Austin	.88	.87	**Wisconsin**			
788	Del Rio	.85	.85	530-532	Milwaukee	.98	.97
789	Giddings	.87	.86	534	Racine	1.02	.97
790, 791	Amarillo	.86	.86	535, 537	Madison	.94	.92
792	Childress	.83	.86	538	Lancaster	.94	.92
793, 794	Lubbock	.83	.85	539	Portage	.94	.92
795, 796	Abilene	.83	.83	540	New Richmond	.99	.91
797	Midland	.84	.80	541-543	Green Bay	.96	.93
798, 799	El Paso	.81	.80	544	Wausau	.94	.90
Utah				545	Rhinelander	.94	.90
840, 841	Salt Lake City	.92	.91	546	La Crosse	.94	.91
843, 844	Ogden	.91	.89	547	Eau Claire	.99	.91
845	Price	.92	.91	548	Superior	.99	.93
846	Provo	.92	.91	549	Oshkosh	.95	.92
Vermont				**Wyoming**			
050	White River Jct.	.86	.85	820	Cheyenne	.92	.87
051	Bellows Falls	.86	.85	821	Yellowstone Nat'l. Park	.92	.89
052	Bennington	.86	.85	822	Wheatland	.92	.87
053	Brattleboro	.86	.85	823	Rawlins	.92	.87
054	Burlington	.86	.87	824	Worland	.92	.89
056	Montpelier	.86	.87	825	Riverton	.92	.88
057	Rutland	.86	.85	826	Casper	.92	.88
058	St. Johnsbury	.86	.87	827	Newcastle	.92	.88
059	Guildhall	.86	.87	828	Sheridan	.92	.89
Virginia				829-831	Rock Springs	.92	.87
220, 221	Fairfax	.93	.94	**Canadian Factors (reflect Canadian currency)**			
222	Arlington	.93	.94	**Alberta**			
223	Alexandria	.93	.94		Calgary	1.03	1.00
224, 225	Fredericksburg	.93	.94		Edmonton	1.03	1.00
226	Winchester	.93	.94	**British Columbia**			
227	Culpeper	.93	.94		Vancouver	1.10	1.11
228	Harrisonburg	.93	.94	**Manitoba**			
229	Charlottesville	.86	.84		Winnipeg	1.02	1.01
230-232	Richmond	.86	.84	**New Brunswick**			
233-235	Norfolk	.83	.83		Saint John	.94	.92
236	Newport News	.84	.83		Moncton	.94	.92
237	Portsmouth	.83	.83	**Newfoundland**			
238	Petersburg	.87	.85		St. John's	.95	.94
239	Farmville	.87	.85	**Nova Scotia**			
240, 241	Roanoke	.83	.82		Halifax	.94	.93
242	Bristol	.84	.79	**Ontario**			
243	Pulaski	.83	.82		Hamilton	1.12	1.08
244	Staunton	.87	.85		London	1.09	1.07
245	Lynchburg	.85	.81		Ottawa	1.12	1.10
246	Grundy	.98	.98		Sudbury	1.12	1.10
Washington					Toronto	1.13	1.12
980, 981	Seattle	.98	1.03	**Prince Edward Island**	Charlottetown	.98	.96
982	Everett	.97	1.03				
983, 984	Tacoma	1.05	1.03	**Quebec**			
985	Olympia	1.05	1.03		Montreal	1.09	1.02
986	Vancouver	1.07	1.02		Quebec	1.09	1.01
988	Wenatchee	.98	1.02	**Saskatchewan**			
989	Yakima	1.04	1.02		Regina	1.06	1.06
990-992	Spokane	1.02	1.01		Saskatoon	1.06	1.06
993	Richland	1.02	1.01				
994	Clarkston	1.02	1.01				

ABBREVIATIONS

A	Area Square Feet; Ampere	C/C	Center to Center	Demob.	Demobilization
ABS	Acrylonitrile Butadiene Styrene; Asbestos Bonded Steel	Cab.	Cabinet	d.f.u.	Drainage Fixture Units
		Cair.	Air Tool Laborer	D.H.	Double Hung
A.C.	Alternating Current; Air Conditioning; Asbestos Cement	Calc	Calculated	DHW	Domestic Hot Water
		Cap.	Capacity	Diag.	Diagonal
		Carp.	Carpenter	Diam.	Diameter
A.C.I.	American Concrete Institute	C.B.	Circuit Breaker	Distrib.	Distribution
Addit.	Additional	C.C.A.	Chromate Copper Arsenate	Dk.	Deck
Adj.	Adjustable	C.C.F.	Hundred Cubic Feet	D.L.	Dead Load; Diesel
af	Audio-frequency	cd	Candela	Do.	Ditto
A.G.A.	American Gas Association	cd/sf	Candela per Square Foot	Dp.	Depth
Agg.	Aggregate	CD	Grade of Plywood Face & Back	D.P.S.T.	Double Pole, Single Throw
A.H.	Ampere Hours	CDX	Plywood, grade C&D, exterior glue	Dr.	Driver
A hr	Ampere-hour	Cefi.	Cement Finisher	Drink.	Drinking
A.H.U.	Air Handling Unit	Cem.	Cement	D.S.	Double Strength
A.I.A.	American Institute of Architects	CF	Hundred Feet	D.S.A.	Double Strength A Grade
AIC	Ampere Interrupting Capacity	C.F.	Cubic Feet	D.S.B.	Double Strength B Grade
Allow.	Allowance	CFM	Cubic Feet per Minute	Dty.	Duty
alt.	Altitude	c.g.	Center of Gravity	DWV	Drain Waste Vent
Alum.	Aluminum	CHW	Chilled Water	DX	Deluxe White, Direct Expansion
a.m.	Ante Meridiem	C.I.	Cast Iron	dyn	Dyne
Amp.	Ampere	C.I.P.	Cast in Place	e	Eccentricity
Anod.	Anodized	Circ.	Circuit	E	Equipment Only; East
Approx.	Approximate	C.L.	Carload Lot	Ea.	Each
Apt.	Apartment	Clab.	Common Laborer	E.B.	Encased Burial
Asb.	Asbestos	C.L.F.	Hundred Linear Feet	Econ.	Economy
A.S.B.C.	American Standard Building Code	CLF	Current Limiting Fuse	EDP	Electronic Data Processing
Asbe.	Asbestos Worker	CLP	Cross Linked Polyethylene	E.D.R.	Equiv. Direct Radiation
A.S.H.R.A.E.	American Society of Heating, Refrig. & AC Engineers	cm	Centimeter	Eq.	Equation
		CMP	Corr. Metal Pipe	Elec.	Electrician; Electrical
A.S.M.E.	American Society of Mechanical Engineers	C.M.U.	Concrete Masonry Unit	Elev.	Elevator; Elevating
		Col.	Column	EMT	Electrical Metallic Conduit; Thin Wall Conduit
A.S.T.M.	American Society for Testing and Materials	CO_2	Carbon Dioxide		
		Comb.	Combination	Eng.	Engine
Attchmt.	Attachment	Compr.	Compressor	EPDM	Ethylene Propylene Diene Monomer
Avg.	Average	Conc.	Concrete		
A.W.G.	American Wire Gauge	Cont.	Continuous; Continued	Eqhv.	Equip. Oper., heavy
Bbl.	Barrel	Corr.	Corrugated	Eqlt.	Equip. Oper., light
B.&B.	Grade B and Better; Balled & Burlapped	Cos	Cosine	Eqmd.	Equip. Oper., medium
		Cot	Cotangent	Eqmm.	Equip. Oper., Master Mechanic
B.&S.	Bell and Spigot	Cov.	Cover	Eqol.	Equip. Oper., oilers
B.&W.	Black and White	CPA	Control Point Adjustment	Equip.	Equipment
b.c.c.	Body-centered Cubic	Cplg.	Coupling	ERW	Electric Resistance Welded
BE	Bevel End	C.P.M.	Critical Path Method	Est.	Estimated
B.F.	Board Feet	CPVC	Chlorinated Polyvinyl Chloride	esu	Electrostatic Units
Bg. Cem.	Bag of Cement	C. Pr.	Hundred Pair	E.W.	Each Way
BHP	Boiler Horse Power; Brake Horse Power	CRC	Cold Rolled Channel	EWT	Entering Water Temperature
		Creos.	Creosote	Excav.	Excavation
B.I.	Black Iron	Crpt.	Carpet & Linoleum Layer	Exp.	Expansion
Bit.; Bitum.	Bituminous	CRT	Cathode-Ray Tube	Ext.	Exterior
Bk.	Backed	CS	Carbon Steel	Extru.	Extrusion
Bkrs.	Breakers	Csc	Cosecant	f.	Fiber stress
Bldg.	Building	C.S.F.	Hundred Square Feet	F	Fahrenheit; Female; Fill
Blk.	Block	CSI	Construction Specifications Institute	Fab.	Fabricated
Bm.	Beam			FBGS	Fiberglass
Boil.	Boilermaker	C.T.	Current Transformer	F.C.	Footcandles
B.P.M.	Blows per Minute	CTS	Copper Tube Size	f.c.c.	Face-centered Cubic
BR	Bedroom	Cu	Cubic	f'c.	Compressive Stress in Concrete; Extreme Compressive Stress
Brg.	Bearing	Cu. Ft.	Cubic Foot		
Brhe.	Bricklayer Helper	cw	Continuous Wave	F.E.	Front End
Bric.	Bricklayer	C.W.	Cool White; Cold Water	FEP	Fluorinated Ethylene Propylene (Teflon)
Brk.	Brick	Cwt.	100 Pounds		
Brng.	Bearing	C.W.X.	Cool White Deluxe	F.G.	Flat Grain
Brs.	Brass	C.Y.	Cubic Yard (27 cubic feet)	F.H.A.	Federal Housing Administration
Brz.	Bronze	C.Y./Hr.	Cubic Yard per Hour	Fig.	Figure
Bsn.	Basin	Cyl.	Cylinder	Fin.	Finished
Btr.	Better	d	Penny (nail size)	Fixt.	Fixture
BTU	British Thermal Unit	D	Deep; Depth; Discharge	Fl. Oz.	Fluid Ounces
BTUH	BTU per Hour	Dis.; Disch.	Discharge	Flr.	Floor
BX	Interlocked Armored Cable	Db.	Decibel	F.M.	Frequency Modulation; Factory Mutual
c	Conductivity	Dbl.	Double		
C	Hundred; Centigrade	DC	Direct Current	Fmg.	Framing

ABBREVIATIONS

Fndtn.	Foundation	I.P.	Iron Pipe	Mat; Mat'l.	Material
Fori.	Foreman, inside	I.P.S.	Iron Pipe Size	Max.	Maximum
Fount.	Fountain	I.P.T.	Iron Pipe Threaded	MBF	Thousand Board Feet
FPM	Feet per Minute	I.W.	Indirect Waste	MBH	Thousand BTU's per hr.
FPT	Female Pipe Thread	J	Joule	MC	Metal Clad Cable
Fr.	Frame	J.I.C.	Joint Industrial Council	M.C.F.	Thousand Cubic Feet
F.R.	Fire Rating	K	Thousand; Thousand Pounds;	M.C.F.M.	Thousand Cubic Feet per minute
FRK	Foil Reinforced Kraft		Heavy Wall Copper Tubing	M.C.M.	Thousand Circular Mils
FRP	Fiberglass Reinforced Plastic	K.A.H.	Thousand Amp. Hours	M.C.P.	Motor Circuit Protector
FS	Forged Steel	K.D.A.T.	Kiln Dried After Treatment	MD	Medium Duty
FSC	Cast Body; Cast Switch Box	kg	Kilogram	M.D.O.	Medium Density Overlaid
Ft.	Foot; Feet	kG	Kilogauss	Med.	Medium
Ftng.	Fitting	kgf	Kilogram force	MF	Thousand Feet
Ftg.	Footing	kHz	Kilohertz	M.F.B.M.	Thousand Feet Board Measure
Ft. Lb.	Foot Pound	Kip	1000 Pounds	Mfg.	Manufacturing
Furn.	Furniture	KJ	Kiljoule	Mfrs.	Manufacturers
FVNR	Full Voltage Non-Reversing	K.L.	Effective Length Factor	mg	Milligram
FXM	Female by Male	Km	Kilometer	MGD	Million Gallons per Day
Fy.	Minimum Yield Stress of Steel	K.L.F.	Kips per Linear Foot	MGPH	Thousand Gallons per Hour
g	Gram	K.S.F.	Kips per Square Foot	MH; M.H.	Manhole; Metal Halide; Man-Hour
G	Gauss	K.S.I.	Kips per Square Inch	MHz	Megahertz
Ga.	Gauge	K.V.	Kilovolt	Mi.	Mile
Gal.	Gallon	K.V.A.	Kilovolt Ampere	MI	Malleable Iron; Mineral Insulated
Gal./Min.	Gallon per Minute	K.V.A.R.	Kilovar (Reactance)	mm	Millimeter
Galv.	Galvanized	KW	Kilowatt	Mill.	Millwright
Gen.	General	KWh	Kilowatt-hour	Min.; min.	Minimum; minute
G.F.I.	Ground Fault Interrupter	L	Labor Only; Length; Long;	Misc.	Miscellaneous
Glaz.	Glazier		Medium Wall Copper Tubing	ml	Milliliter
GPD	Gallons per Day	Lab.	Labor	M.L.F.	Thousand Linear Feet
GPH	Gallons per Hour	lat	Latitude	Mo.	Month
GPM	Gallons per Minute	Lath.	Lather	Mobil.	Mobilization
GR	Grade	Lav.	Lavatory	Mog.	Mogul Base
Gran.	Granular	lb.; #	Pound	MPH	Miles per Hour
Grnd.	Ground	L.B.	Load Bearing; L Conduit Body	MPT	Male Pipe Thread
H	High; High Strength Bar Joist; Henry	L. & E.	Labor & Equipment	MRT	Mile Round Trip
		lb./hr.	Pounds per Hour	ms	Millisecond
H.C.	High Capacity	lb./L.F.	Pounds per Linear Foot	M.S.F.	Thousand Square Feet
H.D.	Heavy Duty; High Density	lbf/sq in.	Pound-force per Square Inch	Mstz.	Mosaic & Terrazzo Worker
H.D.O.	High Density Overlaid	L.C.L.	Less than Carload Lot	M.S.Y.	Thousand Square Yards
Hdr.	Header	Ld.	Load	Mtd.	Mounted
Hdwe.	Hardware	LE	Lead Equivalent	Mthe.	Mosaic & Terrazzo Helper
Help.	Helper average	L.F.	Linear Foot	Mtng.	Mounting
HEPA	High Efficiency Particulate Air Filter	Lg.	Long; Length; Large	Mult.	Multi; Multiply
Hg	Mercury	L. & H.	Light and Heat	M.V.A.	Million Volt Amperes
HIC	High Interrupting Capacity	L.H.	Long Span High Strength Bar Joist	M.V.A.R.	Million Volt Amperes Reactance
H.O.	High Output	L.J.	Long Span Standard Strength Bar Joist	MV	Megavolt
Horiz.	Horizontal			MW	Megawatt
H.P.	Horsepower; High Pressure	L.L.	Live Load	MXM	Male by Male
H.P.F.	High Power Factor	L.L.D.	Lamp Lumen Depreciation	MYD	Thousand yards
Hr.	Hour	lm	Lumen	N	Natural; North
Hrs./Day	Hours per Day	lm/sf	Lumen per Square Foot	nA	Nanoampere
HSC	High Short Circuit	lm/W	Lumen per Watt	NA	Not Available; Not Applicable
Ht.	Height	L.O.A.	Length Over All	N.B.C.	National Building Code
Htg.	Heating	log	Logarithm	NC	Normally Closed
Htrs.	Heaters	L.P.	Liquefied Petroleum; Low Pressure	N.E.M.A.	National Electrical Manufacturers Association
HVAC	Heating, Ventilating & Air Conditioning	L.P.F.	Low Power Factor	NEHB	Bolted Circuit Breaker to 600V.
Hvy.	Heavy	LR	Long Radius	N.L.B.	Non-Load-Bearing
HW	Hot Water	L.S.	Lump Sum	NM	Non-Metallic Cable
Hyd.; Hydr.	Hydraulic	Lt.	Light	nm	Nanometer
Hz.	Hertz (cycles)	Lt. Ga.	Light Gauge	No.	Number
I.	Moment of Inertia	L.T.L.	Less than Truckload Lot	NO	Normally Open
I.C.	Interrupting Capacity	Lt. Wt.	Lightweight	N.O.C.	Not Otherwise Classified
ID	Inside Diameter	L.V.	Low Voltage	Nose.	Nosing
I.D.	Inside Dimension; Identification	M	Thousand; Material; Male; Light Wall Copper Tubing	N.P.T.	National Pipe Thread
I.F.	Inside Frosted	m/hr; M.H.	Man-hour	NQOB	Bolted Circuit Breaker to 240V.
I.M.C.	Intermediate Metal Conduit	mA	Milliampere	N.R.C.	Noise Reduction Coefficient
In.	Inch	Mach.	Machine	N.R.S.	Non Rising Stem
Incan.	Incandescent	Mag. Str.	Magnetic Starter	ns	Nanosecond
Incl.	Included; Including	Maint.	Maintenance	nW	Nanowatt
Int.	Interior	Marb.	Marble Setter		
Inst.	Installation				
Insul.	Insulation				

ABBREVIATIONS

OB	Opposing Blade	R.H.W.	Rubber, Heat & Water Resistant; Residential Hot Water	T.D.	Temperature Difference
OC	On Center			T.E.M.	Transmission Electron Microscopy
OD	Outside Diameter	rms	Root Mean Square	TFE	Tetrafluoroethylene (Teflon)
O.D.	Outside Dimension	Rnd.	Round	T. & G.	Tongue & Groove; Tar & Gravel
ODS	Overhead Distribution System	Rodm.	Rodman		
O & P	Overhead and Profit	Rofc.	Roofer, Composition	Th.; Thk.	Thick
Oper.	Operator	Rofp.	Roofer, Precast	Thn.	Thin
Opng.	Opening	Rohe.	Roofer Helpers (Composition)	Thrded	Threaded
Orna.	Ornamental	Rots.	Roofer, Tile & Slate	Tilf.	Tile Layer Floor
O.S.&Y.	Outside Screw and Yoke	R.O.W.	Right of Way	Tilh.	Tile Layer Helper
Ovhd.	Overhead	RPM	Revolutions per Minute	THW.	Insulated Strand Wire
OWG	Oil, Water or Gas	R.R.	Direct Burial Feeder Conduit	THWN; THHN	Nylon Jacketed Wire
Oz.	Ounce	R.S.	Rapid Start	T.L.	Truckload
P.	Pole; Applied Load; Projection	RT	Round Trip	Tot.	Total
p.	Page	S.	Suction; Single Entrance; South	T.S.	Trigger Start
Pape.	Paperhanger			Tr.	Trade
P.A.P.R.	Powered Air Purifying Respirator	Scaf.	Scaffold	Transf.	Transformer
PAR	Weatherproof Reflector	Sch.; Sched.	Schedule	Trhv.	Truck Driver, Heavy
Pc.	Piece	S.C.R.	Modular Brick	Trlr.	Trailer
P.C.	Portland Cement; Power Connector	S.D.	Sound Deadening	Trlt.	Truck Driver, Light
		S.D.R.	Standard Dimension Ratio	TV	Television
P.C.M.	Phase Contrast Microscopy	S.E.	Surfaced Edge	T.W.	Thermoplastic Water Resistant Wire
P.C.F.	Pounds per Cubic Foot	S.E.R.; S.E.U.	Service Entrance Cable		
P.E.	Professional Engineer; Porcelain Enamel; Polyethylene; Plain End	S.F.	Square Foot	UCI	Uniform Construction Index
		S.F.C.A.	Square Foot Contact Area	UF	Underground Feeder
		S.F.G.	Square Foot of Ground	U.H.F.	Ultra High Frequency
Perf.	Perforated	S.F. Hor.	Square Foot Horizontal	U.L.	Underwriters Laboratory
Ph.	Phase	S.F.R.	Square Feet of Radiation	Unfin.	Unfinished
P.I.	Pressure Injected	S.F.Shlf.	Square Foot of Shelf	URD	Underground Residential Distribution
Pile.	Pile Driver	S4S	Surface 4 Sides		
Pkg.	Package	Shee.	Sheet Metal Worker	V	Volt
Pl.	Plate	Sin.	Sine	V.A.	Volt Amperes
Plah.	Plasterer Helper	Skwk.	Skilled Worker	V.A.C.	Vinyl Composition Tile
Plas.	Plasterer	SL	Saran Lined	VAV	Variable Air Volume
Pluh.	Plumbers Helper	S.L.	Slimline	Vent.	Ventilating
Plum.	Plumber	Sldr.	Solder	Vert.	Vertical
Ply.	Plywood	S.N.	Solid Neutral	V.F.	Vinyl Faced
p.m.	Post Meridiem	S.P.	Static Pressure; Single Pole; Self Propelled	V.G.	Vertical Grain
Pord.	Painter, Ordinary			V.H.F.	Very High Frequency
pp	Pages	Spri.	Sprinkler Installer	VHO	Very High Output
PP; PPL	Polypropylene	Sq.	Square; 100 square feet	Vib.	Vibrating
P.P.M.	Parts per Million	S.P.D.T.	Single Pole, Double Throw	V.L.F.	Vertical Linear Foot
Pr.	Pair	S.P.S.T.	Single Pole, Single Throw	Vol.	Volume
Prefab.	Prefabricated	SPT	Standard Pipe Thread	W	Wire; Watt; Wide; West
Prefin.	Prefinished	Sq. Hd.	Square Head	w/	With
Prop.	Propelled	Sq. In.	Square Inch	W.C.	Water Column; Water Closet
PSF; psf	Pounds per Square Foot	S.S.	Single Strength; Stainless Steel	W.F.	Wide Flange
PSI; psi	Pounds per Square Inch	S.S.B.	Single Strength B Grade	W.G.	Water Gauge
PSIG	Pounds per Square Inch Gauge	Sswk.	Structural Steel Worker	Wldg.	Welding
PSP	Plastic Sewer Pipe	Sswl.	Structural Steel Welder	W. Mile	Wire Mile
Pspr.	Painter, Spray	St.; Stl.	Steel	W.R.	Water Resistant
Psst.	Painter, Structural Steel	S.T.C.	Sound Transmission Coefficient	Wrck.	Wrecker
P.T.	Potential Transformer	Std.	Standard	W.S.P.	Water, Steam, Petroleum
P. & T.	Pressure & Temperature	STP	Standard Temperature & Pressure	WT, Wt.	Weight
Ptd.	Painted	Stpi.	Steamfitter, Pipefitter	WWF	Welded Wire Fabric
Ptns.	Partitions	Str.	Strength; Starter; Straight	XFMR	Transformer
Pu	Ultimate Load	Strd.	Stranded	XHD	Extra Heavy Duty
PVC	Polyvinyl Chloride	Struct.	Structural	XHHW; XLPE	Cross-Linked Polyethylene Wire Insulation
Pvmt.	Pavement	Sty.	Story		
Pwr.	Power	Subj.	Subject	Y	Wye
Q	Quantity Heat Flow	Subs.	Subcontractors	yd	Yard
Quan.; Qty.	Quantity	Surf.	Surface	yr	Year
Q.C.	Quick Coupling	Sw.	Switch	Δ	Delta
r	Radius of Gyration	Swbd.	Switchboard	%	Percent
R	Resistance	S.Y.	Square Yard	~	Approximately
R.C.P.	Reinforced Concrete Pipe	Syn.	Synthetic	∅	Phase
Rect.	Rectangle	Sys.	System	@	At
Reg.	Regular	t.	Thickness	#	Pound; Number
Reinf.	Reinforced	T	Temperature; Ton	<	Less Than
Req'd.	Required	Tan	Tangent	>	Greater Than
Resi	Residential	T.C.	Terra Cotta		
Rgh.	Rough	T & C	Threaded and Coupled		

INDEX

A

Abandon catch basin	248
ABC extinguisher	372
Abrasive floor tile	341
tread	341
ABS DWV pipe	367
Access door basement	271
door duct	379
Accessory bath	199
bathroom	340, 357
door	334
drainage	316
drywall	340
duct	379
formwork	267-268
masonry	272
plaster	336
Accordion door	324
Acid proof floor	344
Acoustical ceiling	342
sealant	319, 339
treatment	342
wallboard	339
Acrylic carpet	192
caulking	319
ceiling	342
wall coating	346
wallcovering	351
wood block	343
Adhesive cement	345
floor	345
roof	313
wallpaper	351
Adjustable shelf	356
Admixture masonry	272
Adobe brick	275
Aerial lift	245
Aggregate exposed	271
spreader	244
stone	265
Air cleaner electronic	378
compressor	245
conditioner cooling & heating	376
conditioner packaged terminal	376
conditioner receptacle	390
conditioner removal	252
conditioner rooftop	376
conditioner self-contained	376
conditioner thru-wall	376
conditioner window	376
conditioner wiring	392
conditioning	228, 230
conditioning ventilating	376, 378
conditioning wine vault	359
extractor	379
filter	378
filter roll type	378
hose	245
return grille	378
spade	246
supply register	379
tool	245
Air-conditioner portable	376
Air-conditioning ventilating	377
Alarm burglar	386
residential	391
Alteration fee	242
Aluminum ceiling tile	342
chain link	262
column	305
coping	273
diffuser perforated	378
downspout	315
ductwork	377
flagpole	355
flashing	177, 316
foil	306-307, 350
gravel stop	318
grille	378
gutter	317
louver	353
nail	284
rivet	280
roof	311
service entrance cable	381
sheet metal	315
siding	134, 311
siding accessories	311
sliding door	326
stair	282
storm door	327
tile	341
window	328
window demolition	254
Anchor bolt	267
buck	272
expansion	279

Anchor hollow wall	279
joist	284
masonry	272
nailing	279
partition	272
rigid	272
screw	279
steel	272
stone	272
Angle valve	369
Antenna system	388
T.V.	388
Appliance	198, 358
plumbing	372
residential	358, 391
Apron wood	294
Arch laminated	292
radial	292
Architect fee	400
Architectural equipment	358
fee	242
woodwork	300
Armored cable	381
Arrestor lightning	388
Asbestos felt	310
Ashlar veneer	407
Asphalt base sheet	313
block	259
block floor	259
coating	306
curb	259
driveway	88
felt	313
flood coat	313
floor tile	344
paper	306
primer	345
sheathing	291
shingle	309
sidewalk	86, 258
tile	193
Asphaltic curb	259
emulsion	266
Astragal	334
molding	295
Atomizing humidifier	375
Atrium	204
Attic stair	359
ventilation fan	377
Auger	244
hole	248
Automatic transfer switch	384
washing machine	359
Awning canvas	356
window	142, 330

B

Backfill	256-257
planting pit	265
trench	257
Backflow preventer	363
Backhoe	256
excavation	256
rental	244
Backup block	274
Baked enamel frame	321
Baluster	195, 305
birch	195
pine	195
Balustrade painting	349
Band molding	294
Bankrun gravel	256
Bar grab	357
towel	357
zee	340
Bark mulch	265
redwood	266
Barrel	246
Barricade	246
Base cabinet	300-301
carpet	346
ceramic tile	340
column	285
course	257
cove	344
gravel	257
metal	336
quarry tile	341
resilient	344
road	257
sheet	313
sink	300
stone	257
terrazzo	342
vanity	304
wood	294

Baseboard demolition	253
heater electric	387
heating	237, 374
register	379
Basement stair	195, 271
Basic meter device	383
Basketweave fence	263
Bath	370
accessory	199
communal	370
faucet	364
steam	362
whirlpool	370
Bathroom	208, 210, 212, 214, 216, 218, 220, 222, 224,
accessory	340, 357
fixture	370-371
Bathtub enclosure	353
removal	253
Batt insulation	136
Bay window	146, 330
Bead board	308-309
board insulation	309
casing	294
corner	336, 340
parting	296
Beam bondcrete	338
ceiling	298
drywall	338
hanger	284
laminated	292-293
mantel	298
plaster	337
steel	281
wood	286, 292
Bed molding	294
Bedding pipe	260
Beech tread	305
Bell & spigot pipe	365
Bench park	264
players	264
Berm paving	259
Bevel siding	312
Bi-fold door	190, 320, 323
Bi-passing closet door	324
door	190
Birch door	323-325
molding	296
paneling	297
stair	305
wood frame	322
Bituminous block	259
coating	306
expansion joint	268
fiber pipe	261
paving	402
pipe	260
Blanket insulation	308, 375
Blind	159, 360
exterior	299
venetian	360
window	360
Block asphalt	259
asphalt floor	259
backup	274
bituminous	259
concrete	274-275, 408-409
concrete bond beam	274
concrete exterior	274
concrete foundation	275
decorative concrete	274
filler	350
floor	343
glass	275
insulation	274
lintel	275
partition	274
quantities	405
reflective	275
wall	126
wall foundation	96
Blocking	285
wood	290
Blockout slab	269
Blown-in cellulose	307
fiberglass	307
insulation	307
Blueboard	338
Bluestone sidewalk	258
sill	273
step	264
Board & batten fence	263
& batten siding	312
bead	309
ceiling	342
fence	263
insulation	307
paneling	298

Board sheathing	291
siding	130
valance	301
verge	295
Boiler demolition	252
electric	373
electric steam	373
gas fired	373
gas/oil combination	373
hot water	373
oil fired	373
steam	373
Bollard light	385
Bolt	278
expansion	279
steel	284
toggle	279
Bondcrete	338
Bookcase	296, 301
Boom lift	245
Boring	248
Borrow	256
Bow window	146, 330
Bowstring truss	293
Box distribution	262
out	269
pull	382
stair	304
Boxes & wiring devices	382
Bracing	286
let-in	280
Brass hinge	333
screw	285
Breaker circuit	383
vacuum	365
Brick adobe	275
anchor	272
chimney	407
chimney simulated	354
cleaning	407
demolition	251, 255
driveway	88
edging	259
face	273
forklift	246
in place	406
molding	295
paving	259
price	406
quantities	405
removal	248
shelf	269
sidewalk	86, 259
sill	273
step	264
veneer	128, 275
veneer demolition	255
veneer in place	406
wall	128
wash	277
Bricklaying economies	405
Brickmould	294
Bridging	286
Broom cabinet	301
finish	271
Brownstone	277
Brush clearing	255
cutter	244
Buck anchor	272
rough	287
Buggy concrete	244, 271
Builder risk insurance	394
Building excavation	80, 82
greenhouse	362
hardware	333
paper	306
permit	242
pre-engineered steel	410
prefabricated	362, 410
Built-in range	358
Built-up roof	313
roofing	176
Bulkhead door	327
formwork	269
Bulldozer	245, 256
Bumper wall	333
Burglar alarm	386
Burlap curing	270
rubbing	271
Burner gas conversion	373
gun type	373
residential	373
Bush hammer concrete	271
Butyl caulking	319
BX removal	251

452

INDEX

C

C.I.P. concrete ... 270
Cabinet ... 196
  base ... 301
  broom ... 301
  casework ... 301
  demolition ... 252
  door ... 301-303
  electrical ... 382
  fuse ... 383
  hardware ... 303
  hinge ... 303
  kitchen ... 300
  medicine ... 357
  oven ... 301
  painting ... 347
  shower ... 352
  stain ... 347
  varnish ... 347
Cable armored ... 381
  electric ... 381
  heating ... 387
  jack ... 247
  sheathed nonmetallic ... 381
  sheathed romex ... 381
Cafe door ... 323
Canopy door ... 355
  framing ... 288
Cant roof ... 288, 314
Cantilever retaining wall ... 258
Canvas awning ... 356
Cap service entrance ... 381
Capacitor ... 384
Carbon dioxide extinguisher ... 372
Carpentry finish ... 294
  rough ... 285
Carpet ... 192, 345
  base ... 346
  felt pad ... 346
  floor ... 345
  nylon ... 345
  olefin ... 346
  padding ... 346
  removal ... 251
  stair ... 346
  urethane pad ... 346
  wool ... 346
Carrier ceiling ... 337
  channel ... 336
  fixture ... 364
Cart concrete ... 244, 271
Case work ... 301
Cased boring ... 248
Casement window ... 140, 330-331
Casework cabinet ... 301
  ground ... 290
  painting ... 347
  stain ... 347
  varnish ... 347
Casing bead ... 340
  door ... 340
  metal ... 336
  wood ... 294
Cast in place concrete ... 270
  iron bench ... 264
  iron damper ... 354
  iron drain ... 364
  iron pipe ... 365
  iron pipe fitting ... 365
  iron radiator ... 374
  iron stair ... 282
  iron trap ... 364
Catch basin ... 261
  basin removal ... 248
  door ... 303
Caulking ... 319
  sealant ... 319
Cavity wall reinforcing ... 272
Cedar closet ... 297
  fence ... 263
  molding ... 295
  paneling ... 298
  post ... 306
  roof deck ... 293
  roof plank ... 291
  shake siding ... 132
  shingle ... 310
  siding ... 312
  stair ... 304
Ceiling ... 180, 184
  acoustical ... 342
  beam ... 298
  board ... 342
  bondcrete ... 338
  carrier ... 337
  demolition ... 249
  diffuser ... 378

Ceiling drill ... 279
  drywall ... 338
  eggcrate ... 342
  framing ... 286
  furring ... 290, 336-337
  heater ... 358
  insulation ... 307
  lath ... 337
  luminous ... 342, 386
  molding ... 294
  painting ... 349-350
  plaster ... 337
  stair ... 359
  support ... 281
  suspended ... 136, 337, 343
  suspension system ... 336
  tile ... 343
Cellar door ... 327
Cellulose blown-in ... 307
  insulation ... 307
Cement adhesive ... 345
  flashing ... 314
  gypsum ... 272
  masonry ... 272
  masonry unit ... 274-275
  mortar ... 341, 404
  parging ... 306
Centrifugal pump ... 246
Ceramic mulch ... 266
  tile ... 193, 340-341
  tile countertop ... 297
  tile demolition ... 251
  tile floor ... 340
Chain hoist ... 247
  link fence ... 92, 262-263
  link fence removal ... 248
  saw ... 247
  trencher ... 245
Chair molding ... 295
  rail demolition ... 253
Chalkboard ... 352
Channel carrier ... 336
  furring ... 336, 340
  siding ... 313
  steel ... 336
Chase formwork ... 268
Chemical dry extinguisher ... 372
  toilet ... 247
Chime door ... 387
Chimney ... 272
  accessory ... 354
  brick ... 272, 407
  demolition ... 255
  flue ... 278
  foundation ... 270
  metal ... 354
  screen ... 354
  simulated brick ... 354
  vent ... 376
China cabinet ... 300
Chipper brush ... 244
Chipping hammer ... 245
Chlorination system ... 362
Chute rubbish ... 249
Circline fixture ... 386
Circuit breaker ... 383
  wiring ... 238
Circular saw ... 247
Circulating pump ... 371
Clamp water pipe ground ... 382
Clapboard painting ... 347
Clay pipe vitrified ... 261
  roofing tile ... 310
  tile coping ... 273
Cleaner steam ... 247
Cleaning brick ... 277, 407
  masonry ... 277
  up ... 247
Cleanout door ... 354
  pipe ... 363
  tee ... 363
Clear & grub ... 255
Clearing brush ... 255
Clip joist ... 336
  plywood ... 285
  stud ... 336
Clock timer ... 391
Closet cedar ... 297
  door ... 190, 320, 324
  pole ... 295
  rod ... 296
Clothes dryer residential ... 358
Coal tar pitch ... 314
Coat glaze ... 350
Coating bituminous ... 306
  roof ... 314
  rubber ... 306
  silicone ... 306

Coating special ... 346
  wall ... 346
  waterproofing ... 306
Coffee maker ... 357
Colonial door ... 323, 325
  wood frame ... 321
Column ... 281
  base ... 285
  bondcrete ... 338
  brick ... 273
  demolition ... 255
  drywall ... 338
  lally ... 281
  laminated wood ... 293
  lath ... 337
  pipe ... 281
  plaster ... 337
  removal ... 255
  wood ... 287, 292, 305
Combination device ... 389
  storm door ... 323, 325
Commercial gutting ... 252
Common brick ... 273
  nail ... 284
  rafter roof framing ... 108
Communal bath ... 370
Compact fill ... 257
Compaction ... 256
  soil ... 256
Compactor ... 198
  earth ... 245
  residential ... 358
Compensation workers' ... 242, 397-399
Compressor air ... 245
Concrete block ... 274-275, 408-409
  block bond beam ... 274
  block decorative ... 274
  block exterior ... 274
  block foundation ... 275
  block insulation ... 307
  block painting ... 350
  block wall ... 126
  buggy ... 271
  bush hammer ... 271
  C.I.P. ... 270
  cart ... 244, 271
  cast in place ... 270
  conveyer ... 244
  coping ... 273
  curb ... 259
  curing ... 270
  cutout ... 249
  demolition ... 249
  driveway ... 88
  finish ... 258
  float ... 244
  footing ... 270
  formwork ... 267
  foundation ... 98, 270
  furring ... 289
  lintel ... 271
  mixer ... 244
  paving ... 258
  pipe ... 261
  placing ... 270
  precast ... 271
  protection ... 271
  pump ... 244
  ready mix ... 270
  reinforcement ... 269
  removal ... 248
  retaining wall ... 258
  saw ... 244
  septic tank ... 262
  shingle ... 310
  sidewalk ... 86, 258
  sill ... 273
  slab ... 102
  stair ... 270
  trowel ... 244
  utility vault ... 260
  vibrator ... 244
  wheeling ... 271
Conductive floor ... 344
Conductor & grounding ... 381
  wire ... 381
Conduit & fitting flexible ... 380
  electrical ... 379
  fitting ... 380
  flexible metallic ... 380
  greenfield ... 380
  in-slab ... 379
  in-slab PVC ... 380
  in-trench electrical ... 380
  in-trench steel ... 380
  PVC ... 379
  rigid in-slab ... 380

Conduit rigid steel ... 379
Connection motor ... 380
Connector joist ... 284
  stud ... 280
  timber ... 284
Construction special ... 361
  time ... 242
Contract closeout ... 247
Contractor equipment ... 244
  overhead ... 243, 394
  overhead & profit ... 396
  pump ... 246
Control component ... 378
Conveyor ... 244
Cooking equipment ... 358
  range ... 358
Cooling ... 228, 230
  & heating air conditioner ... 376
  electric furnace ... 374
Coping ... 273, 277
  clay tile ... 273
  removal ... 255
  terra cotta ... 273
Copper cable ... 381
  downspout ... 315
  drum trap ... 364
  DWV tubing ... 366
  flashing ... 316
  gutter ... 317
  pipe ... 366
  rivet ... 280
  roof ... 314
  wallcovering ... 350
  wire ... 381
Core drill ... 244
Cork floor ... 344
  tile ... 344
  wall tile ... 350
Corner base cabinet ... 301
  bead ... 336, 340
  wall cabinet ... 301
Cornice ... 273
  molding ... 294-295
  painting ... 349
Corrugated roof tile ... 310
  siding ... 311-312
Cost pipe ... 420
Countertop ... 296-297
  demolition ... 253
  sink ... 371
Coupling PVC ... 368
Course base ... 257
Cove base ... 344
  base ceramic tile ... 340
  base terrazzo ... 342
  molding ... 294
  scotia molding ... 294
Cover ground ... 265
  pool ... 362
Covering wall ... 418
CPVC pipe ... 367
Crane hydraulic ... 247
Creosote lumber ... 300
Crew survey ... 243
Crown molding ... 294-295
Crushed stone sidewalk ... 258
Cubicle shower ... 371
Cupola ... 355
Curb asphalt ... 259
  asphaltic ... 259
  concrete ... 259
  edging ... 259
  formwork ... 269
  granite ... 259, 277
  inlet ... 259
  precast ... 259
  removal ... 248
  roof ... 288
  terrazzo ... 342
Curing concrete ... 270
  paper ... 306
Curtain rod ... 357
  type fire damper ... 379
Curved stair ... 304
  stairway ... 195
Cut stone trim ... 277
Cutout ... 249
  counter ... 297
Cutter brush ... 244
Cutting block ... 297
  torch ... 247
Cylinder lockset ... 333

453

INDEX

D

Damper fireplace	354
multi-blade	379
Dampproofing plaster	415
Darby finish	271
Deadbolt	333
Deciduous shrub	266
tree	267
Deck metal	282
roof	282, 290-291
wood	206, 291, 293
Decking metal	282
Decorator device	388
switch	388
Deep freeze	358
Dehumidifier	358
Demolition	248, 251, 253-255
baseboard	253
boiler	252
brick	251, 255
cabinet	252
ceiling	249
chimney	255
column	255
concrete	249
countertop	253
door	250
ductwork	252
electric	250-251
fireplace	255
flooring	251
framing	251
furnace	252
glass	254
granite	255
gutter	253
house	249
HVAC	252
joist	252
masonry	250, 255
millwork	253
paneling	253
partition	254
plaster	249, 254
plumbing	253
plywood	249, 254
post	252
rafter	252
railing	253
roofing	253
siding	253
tile	249
truss	252
window	254
wood	249
Detection system	386
Detector infra-red	386
motion	386
smoke	387
Device combination	389
decorator	388
GFI	390
receptacle	389
residential	388
wiring	383
Diaphragm pump	246
Diffuser ceiling	378
linear	378
opposed blade damper	378
perforated aluminum	378
rectangular	378
steel	378
T-bar mount	378
Dimmer switch	383, 388
Disappearing stair	359
Discharge hose	246
Disconnect safety-switch	384
Dishwasher	198, 358
Disposal	255
field	262
Disposer garbage	198, 358
Distribution box	262
Diving board	362
Door accessory	334
accordion	324
bell residential	390
bell system	387
bi-fold	320, 323
blind	299
bulkhead	327
cabinet	301-303
cafe	323
canopy	355
casing	340
catch	303
chime	387
cleanout	354

Door closet	320
demolition	250
double	320
dutch	323
dutch oven	355
entrance	323
exterior	150
fire	319
frame	320-321
frame welded	416
french	325
front	415
garage	154
glass	326
handle	303
hardware	333
hollow metal	415
kick plate	333
knocker	334
labeled	319
metal	319
mirror	335
molding	296
moulded	323
opener	327
overhead	326
painting	347
panel	323
paneled	320
passage	325
pre-hung	325
removal	250
residential	320, 322-323
rough buck	287
sauna	361
shower	353
sill	296, 321, 334
sliding	152-153
special	326
stain	347
steel	319-320
stop	333
storm	158, 327
switch burglar alarm	386
threshold	322
varnish	347
weatherstrip	334
weatherstrip garage	334
wood	188, 190, 321, 416
wood interior	416
wood residential	416
Dormer framing	120, 122
gable	289
roofing	170, 172
Double hung window	138, 330-331
Downspout	315-316
aluminum	315
copper	315
elbow	316
painting	348
steel	315
strainer	315
Dozer	245, 256
Drain cast iron	364
floor	364
Drainage accessory	316
pipe	261
site	261
trap	364
Drapery hardware	361
rings	361
Drawer	304
track	303
wood	303
Drill ceiling	279
core	244
drywall	279
hammer	246
plaster	279
rig	248
steel	246
wagon	245
wood	284
Drinking fountain support	364
Drip edge	315
Drive pin	280
Driver sheeting	246
stud	280
Driveway	88, 258
removal	248
Drop pan ceiling	342
Drum trap	364
trap copper	364
Dry kiln	300
Dryer clothes	358
receptacle	390
vent	359

Dryer wiring	238
Drywall	178, 180, 338
accessory	340
cutout	250
demolition	254
drill	279
frame	320-321
gypsum	338
nail	284
painting	349
prefinished	339
screw	340
Duck tarpaulin	244
Duct access door	379
accessory	379
flexible insulated	377
flexible noninsulated	377
humidifier	375
HVAC	377
insulation	375
liner	375
mechanical	377
Ductile iron pipe	260
Ductwork	377
aluminum	377
demolition	252
fabric coated flexible	377
fabricated	377
galvanized	377
rectangular	377
rigid	377
Dump charge	249
truck	245
Dumpster	249
Duplex receptacle	238
Dust partition	249
Dutch door	150, 323
oven door	355
DWV pipe ABS	367
PVC pipe	367
tubing copper	366

E

Earth compactor	245
vibrator	256
Earthwork	256-257
equipment	244, 256
Economies bricklaying	405
Edge drip	315
formwork	269
Edging curb	259
landscape	259
Eggcrate ceiling	342
Elbow downspout	316
Electric appliance	358
baseboard heater	387
boiler	373
cable	381
demolition	250-251
fixture	385-386
furnace	374
generator	246
generator set	385
heater	358
heating	237
lamp	386
log	354
metallic tubing	379
pool heater	373
service	236, 383
stair	359
switch	382, 384
unit heater	387
water heater	372
wire	381
Electrical cabinet	382
conduit	379
conduit greenfield	380
Electronic air cleaner	378
Elevator	363
Embossed metal door	325
print door	323
Employer liability	242
EMT	379
Emulsion adhesive	345
asphaltic	266
pavement	259
sprayer	246
Enclosure bathtub	353
shower	353
swimming pool	362
tub	353
Entrance cable service	381
door	150, 323, 325
frame	321
lock	333

Entrance weather cap	380
Epoxy grout	341
wall coating	346
Equipment	244, 357
earthwork	244, 256
insurance	242
rental	247
Erosion control	257
Estimate electrical heating	387
Evergreen shrub	266-267
tree	266
Excavate planting pit	265
Excavation	256
backhoe	256
footing	80
foundation	82
hand	256-257
septic tank	262
structural	256
trench	257
utility	84
Exhaust hood	358
vent	379
Expansion anchor	279
bolt	279
joint	268, 336
shield	279
tank	375
Expense main office	395
Exposed aggregate	271
aggregate coating	346
Exterior blind	299
concrete block	274
door	150
door frame	321
light	239
light fixture	385
molding	295
plaster	338
pre-hung door	325
residential door	323
wall framing	106
wood frame	322
Extinguisher fire	372
Extractor air	379

F

Fabric welded wire	270
Fabricated ductwork	377
Fabrication metal	282
Face brick	273
Facing stone	276
Fan	377
attic ventilation	377
house ventilation	377
paddle	392
residential	391
ventilation	392
wiring	238, 392
Fascia aluminum	311
board	287
board demolition	251
metal	317
vinyl	312
wood	295
Fastener	283
anchor bolt	272
timber	284
wood	285
Faucet & fitting	364
bath	364
Fee architect	400
architectural	242
management	242
Felt asbestos	310
asphalt	313
carpet pad	346
underlayment	344
Fence basketweave	263
board	263
board & batten	263
chain link	92
metal	262-263
painting	348
removal	248
residential	262
snow	263
wood	263
Fiberglass insulation	308
tube formwork	268
Fiberboard roof deck	309
Fiberglass blown-in	307
ceiling board	342
cupola	355
insulation	136, 307-308
panel	311

454

INDEX

F

Fiberglass planter	264
roof deck	309
septic tank	262
shower stall	352
tank	375
wool	307
Field disposal	262
office expense	242
septic	90
Fieldstone	276
Fill	256-257
gravel	256-257
Filler block	350
Film polyethylene	266
Filter air	378
mechanical media	378
swimming pool	362
Filtration equipment	363
Fine grade	265
Finish carpentry	294
concrete	258
floor	350
nail	284
steel trowel	271
Finisher floor	244
Finishing floor	343
Fir column	305
floor	343
molding	295
roof deck	293
roof plank	291
Fire call pullbox	387
damage repair	352
damper curtain type	379
door	319
door frame	321
escape disappearing	359
extinguisher	372
extinguishing system	372
horn	387
resistant drywall	338-339
retardant lumber	300
retardant plywood	300
Fireplace accessory	354
box	278
built-in	354
damper	354
demolition	255
form	355
free standing	354
mantel	298
masonry	200, 278
prefabricated	202, 354
Firestop gypsum	337
wood	287
Fitting conduit	380
pipe	363
Fixed window	148
Fixture bathroom	370-371
carrier	364
electric	385
exterior mercury vapor	385
fluorescent	385-386
incandescent	385
interior light	385
lantern	386
mirror light	385
plumbing	370-372, 420
removal	253
residential	386, 391
Fixtures light	239
Flagging	259, 344
slate	259
Flagpole	355
Flashing	316
aluminum	177
cement	314
copper	316
stainless	316
Flatbed truck	245
Flexible conduit & fitting	380
ductwork fabric coated	377
insulated duct	377
metallic conduit	380
Float concrete	244
finish	271
Floater equipment	242
Floating pin	333
Floodlight	246
Floor acid proof	344
adhesive	345
asphalt block	259
brick	344
bumper	333
carpet	345
ceramic tile	341

Floor cleanout	363
concrete	102
conductive	344
drain	364
finish	350
finisher	244
flagging	259
framing	104
framing removal	250
insulation	307
marble	276
nail	284
painting	348
plank	292
plywood	291
polyethylene	345
quarry tile	341
register	379
removal	254
resilient	418
rubber	345
stain	348
stone	258
subfloor	291
tile removal	251
tile terrazzo	342
underlayment	291
varnish	348
vinyl	345
wood	193, 343
Flooring	193
and carpet	344
demolition	251
Flourescent light	239
Flue chimney	278
chimney metal	278
lining	272, 278
screen	354
Fluorescent fixture	385-386
lamp	386
Flush door	323
Foam glass insulation	308
insulation	307
Foil aluminum	306-307, 350
back insulation	308
Folding accordion door	324
door shower	353
Footing	94
concrete	270
excavation	80
reinforcing	269
removal	254
spread	269
Forklift brick	246
Form fireplace	355
slab	282
Formwork	
accessory	267-268
chase	268
concrete	267
insert	268
plywood	269
sleeve	268
snap tie	268
Foundation	94
chimney	270
concrete	98, 270
concrete block	275
excavation	82
masonry	96
mat	270
removal	248
wall	275
wood	100
Frame door	320-321
drywall	320-321
entrance	321
hollow metal	416
labeled	321
metal	320
steel	320
welded	321
window	332
wood	301, 321
Framing anchor	284
canopy	288
demolition	251
dormer	120, 122
floor	104
laminated	292
metal	280
partition	124, 339
removal	251
roof	108, 110, 112, 114, 116, 118
timber	292
wood	286, 292
Freeze deep	358
French door	325

Front door	415
end loader	256
Furnace demolition	252
electric	374
gas fired	374
heating & cooling	374
hot air	374
oil fired	374
wiring	238
Furring ceiling	290, 336-337
channel	340
metal	336
wall	289, 336
Fuse cabinet	383

G

Gable dormer	289
dormer framing	120
dormer roofing	170
roof framing	108
Galvanized ductwork	377
Gambrel roof framing	114
Garage door	154, 326
door weatherstrip	334
Garbage disposer	198, 358
Gas conversion burner	373
fired boiler	373
fired furnace	374
fired pool heater	373
heat air conditioner	376
heating	228, 232
log	354
operated generator	385
pipe	260
service and distribution	260
vent	376
Gas-fired furnace	374
Gasoline operated generator	385
Gate door	262-263
Generator construction	246
emergency	385
gas operated	385
set	385
GFI receptacle	390
Girder wood	286, 292
Glass	335
bead molding	296
block	275
demolition	254
door	326
door shower	353
heat reflective	335
insulation fiber	308
lined water heater	359
low emissivity	335
mirror	335
shower stall	352
tempered	335
tile	335
tinted	335
window	335
Glaze coat	350
Glazed ceramic tile	340
wall coating	346
Glazing	335
Glued laminated	292-293
Grab bar	357
Gradall	244
Grade fine	265
Grader motorized	245
Grading site	256
Granite building	277
chips	266
curb	259, 277
demolition	255
paver	277
sidewalk	259
Grass	265
cloth wallpaper	351
seed	265
sprinkler	262
Grating	282
sewer	261
Gravel bankrun	256
base	257
fill	256-257
pea	266
stop	318
Gravity retaining wall	258
Greenfield conduit	380
Greenhouse	204, 362
Grid spike	285
Grille air return	378

Grille aluminum	378
decorative wood	298
painting	348
window	332
Grinder terrazzo	244
Ground	290
clamp water pipe	382
cover	265
fault	238
rod	381-382
wire	381
Grounding	381
& conductor	381
Grout	272
concrete block	272
epoxy	341
tile	340
wall	272
Guard gutter	317
Gunite pool	205
Gutter	317
aluminum	317
copper	317
demolition	253
guard	317
painting	348
stainless	317
steel	317
strainer	317
vinyl	317
wood	317
Gutting	252
Guying tree	265
Gypsum block demolition	250
board	338
cement	272
drywall	338
fabric wallcovering	351
firestop	337
lath	337
lath nail	284
plaster	337, 418
sheathing	291
weatherproof	291

H

Half round molding	295
Hammer bush	271
chipping	245
drill	246
hydraulic	246
Hand carved door	322
clearing	255
excavation	256-257
hole	260
rail	283
split shake	310
Hand-split shake	132
Handicapped lever	333
Handle door	303
Handrail oak	195
wood	295, 305
Hanger joist	284
Hardboard cabinet	300
overhead door	326
siding	313
soffit	299
tempered	298
underlayment	291
Hardware	333
cabinet	303
door	333
drapery	361
finish	333
rough	290
window	333
Hardwood floor	343
grille	298
Hauling truck	257
Hay	265
Header wood	289
Hearth	278
Heat pump	376
pump residential	392
radiant	387
reflective glass	335
Heater contractor	246
electric	358
electric baseboard	387
electric wall	387
infra-red quartz	387
sauna	361
swimming pool	373
water	359, 372
wiring	238
Heating	228, 230, 232, 373, 375

455

INDEX

H

Heating baseboard	374
cable	387
electric	237
estimate electrical	387
hot air	374
hydronic	373
panel radiant	387
solar	421
Heavy framing	292
Hemlock column	305
Hex nut	278
Highway paver	259
Hinge	417
brass	333
cabinet	303
residential	333
steel	333
Hip rafter	287
roof framing	112
Hoist contractor	247
lift equipment	247
Holddown	284
Hollow core door	324
metal	320
metal door	415
Hood range	358
Hook robe	357
Horizontal aluminum siding	311
vinyl siding	312
Horn fire	387
Hose air	245
discharge	246
suction	246
water	246
Hospital tip pin	333
Hot air furnace	374
air heating	374
tub	370
water boiler	373
water heating	373-374
Hot-air heating	228, 230
Hot-water heating	232
House demolition	249
ventilation fan	377
Housewrap	306
Humidifier	358
duct	375
Humus peat	265
HVAC demolition	252
duct	377
Hydraulic crane	247
hammer	246
jack	247
Hydronic heating	373

I

Icemaker	358
Impact wrench	246
In-slab conduit	379
Incandescent fixture	385-386
light	239
Infra-red detector	386
quartz heater	387
Inlet curb	259
Insecticide	258
Insert formwork	268
Insulation	136, 307, 309
blanket	375
blown-in	307
board	177
building	307
cavity wall	307
cellulose	307
duct	375
foam	307
insert	274
isocyanurate	308
masonry	307
perlite	309
pipe	375
roof deck	309
sheathing	308
vapor barrier	306
wall	274, 308
water heater	375
Insurance	242
builder risk	242, 394
equipment	242
public liability	242
Interior demolition door	250
door	188, 190
door frame	322
light	239
light fixture	385
Interior partition framing	124
pre-hung door	325
residential door	323
wood frame	322
Interval timer	388
Intrusion system	386
Ironing center	359
Ironspot brick	344

J

Jack cable	247
hydraulic	247
rafter	287
Jackhammer	245
Jalousie	328
Joint expansion	336
reinforcing	272
sealer	319
Joist anchor	284
clip	336
connector	284
demolition	252
hanger	284
lightgage	282
metal	282
sister	286
wood	286, 292
Jute mesh	258

K

Kennel fence	263
Keyway	268
Kick plate door	333
Kiln dried lumber	300
dry	300
Kitchen	198
appliance	358
cabinet	300
sink	371
sink faucet	364
Knocker door	334

L

Labeled door	319
frame	321
Ladder	246
fire escape	282
swimming pool	362
Lag screw	280
Lally column	281
Laminated beam	292-293
countertop	297
countertop plastic	297
framing	292
glued	293
roof deck	293
wood	292-293
Lamp fluorescent	386
post	283
Lampholder	383
Landing newel	305
Landscape	259
light	385
surface	345
Landscaping	265
Lantern fixture	386
Latch set	333
Latex caulking	319
underlayment	345
Lath and plaster	336
gypsum	337
Lattice molding	295
Lauan door	324
Laundry faucet	364
tray	370
Lavatory	208
faucet	364
support	364
vanity top	370
Lazy susan	301
Lead coated downspout	315
coated flashing	316
flashing	316
paint removal	351
Lean-to type greenhouse	362
Leeching field	90
pit	262
Ledger	288
Let-in bracing	280
Letter slot	356
Lever handicapped	333
Liability employer	242
Lift aerial	245
Light bollard	385
fixture exterior	385
fixture interior	385
fixtures	239
post	386
support	281
Lightgage joist	282
Lighting	238, 385-386
incandescent	385
outdoor	246
outlet	390
residential	391
strip	385
track	386
Lightning arrestor	388
protection	387
suppressor	388
Lights track	386
Lightweight block	274
Limestone	265, 276-277
coping	273
Linear diffuser	378
Linen wallcovering	351
Liner duct	375
Lining flue	278
Lintel	277, 281
block	275
Load bearing stud	339
Load-center indoor	383
plug-in breaker	383
rainproof	383
fabrication	383
Load-center residential	388
Loader front end	256
tractor	245
Loam	257
Lock entrance	333
Locking receptacle	390
Lockset cylinder	333
Log electric	354
gas	354
Louver	353
aluminum	353
midget	353
redwood	298
ventilation	298
wall	354
wood	298
Louvered blind	299
door	188, 190, 324-325
Low-voltage silicon rectifier	382
switching	382
switchplate	382
transformer	382
Lumber	286
core paneling	297
creosote	300
kiln dried	300
price	413-414
treatment	300
Luminous ceiling	342, 386
panel	342

M

Machine welding	247
Mahogany door	322
Mail box	356
Main office expense	395
Malleable iron pipe fitting	369
Management fee	242
Manhole removal	248
Mansard roof framing	116
Mantel beam	298
fireplace	298
Maple countertop	297
Marble base	276
chips	266
coping	273
countertop	297
floor	276
sill	273
synthetic	344
tile	344
Masonry accessory	272
anchor	272
brick	272, 344
cement	272
cleaning	277
cornice	273
demolition	250, 255
fireplace	200, 278
flashing	316
foundation	96
furring	290
insulation	307
nail	284
Masonry painting	350
point	277
reinforcing	272, 405
removal	248, 255
saw	247
sidewalk	259
sill	273
step	264
toothing	250
wall	126, 128, 258, 274
wall tie	272
Mat foundation	270
Mechanical duct	377
media filter	378
Median strip	265
Medicine cabinet	357
Melting snow	387
Membrane	177
curing	270
roofing	313
Mercury vapor exterior fixture	385
vapor fixture	239
Metal base	336
butt frame	321
chimney	354
clad window	138, 140, 142, 144, 146, 148
deck	282
decking	282
door	319
door residential	320
fabrication	282
faced door	325
fascia	317
fence	262-263
fireplace	202
flue chimney	375
frame	320
framing	280
furring	336
gate	262-263
halide fixture	239
hollow	320
joist	282
ornamental	283
overhead door	326
pipe	260
railing	92
roof	311
sheet	314
shelf	356
siding	134
soffit	317
stud	339-340
stud demolition	254
support system	336
threshold	334
tile	341
window	328
Metallic foil	307
Meter center rainproof	384
device basic	383
socket	383
water supply	372
water supply domestic	372
Microwave oven	358
Mill construction	292
Millwork	294, 301
demolition	253
Mineral fiber ceiling	342
fiber insulation	308
fiber shingle	309
roof	314
wool blown-in	307
Mirror ceiling board	342
door	335
glass	335
light fixture	385
wall	335
Miscellaneous mortar	404
Mix planting pit	265
Mixer concrete	244
mortar	244, 246
plaster	246
Mobilization	257
Module tub/shower	370
Moil point	246
Molding	294
base	294
brick	295
ceiling	294
exterior	295
hardboard	298
wood	305
Monel rivet	280
roof	314
Monitor support	281
Monolithic finish	271

456

INDEX

M

Monument survey	243
Mortar	272
cement	341, 404
miscellaneous	404
mixer	244, 246
quantities	405
thinset	341
Moss peat	266
Motion detector	386
Motor connection	380
generator	246
support	281
Moulded door	323
Mounting board plywood	290
Movable louver blind	360
Moving shrub	266
tree	266
Mulch	265
bark	265
ceramic	266
stone	266
Multi-blade damper	379
Muntin window	332

N

Nail	283
Nailers steel	287
wood	287
Neoprene expansion joint	268
Newel	195, 305
No-hub pipe	365
Non-removable pin	333
Nut hex	278
Nylon carpet	192, 345

O

Oak door frame	321
floor	193, 343
molding	296
paneling	297
stair tread	305
threshold	322
Oil fired boiler	373
fired furnace	374
heater temporary	246
heating	230, 232
water heater	372
Oil-fired furnace	374
Olefin carpet	346
Onyx	266
Open rail fence	263
Opener door	327
Operating cost equipment	244
Ornamental metal	283
Outdoor lighting	246
Outlet box plastic	382
box steel	382
lighting	390
Oven	358
cabinet	301
microwave	358
Overhaul	249
Overhead	242
& profit contractor	396
contractor	243, 394
door	154, 326

P

P trap	364
P&T relief valve	369
Padding	192
carpet	346
Paddle fan	392
Paint	419
removal	351
Painting	419
and wall covering	347
balustrade	349
cabinet	347
casework	347
ceiling	349-350
clapboard	347
concrete block	350
concrete floor	348
cornice	349
door	347
downspout	348
drywall	349
fence	348
floor	348
Painting grille	348
gutter	348
masonry	350
pipe	349
plaster	349
siding	347
sprayer	246
steel siding	347
stucco	347
swimming pool	363
trim	349
truss	349
wall	349-350
window	348
wood floor	348
Pan form stair	282
shower	316
Panel door	323
fiberglass	311
luminous	342
radiant heat	387
wall	276
Paneled door	188, 320
pine door	324
Paneling	298
board	298
cutout	250
demolition	253
plywood	297
wood	297
Paper building	306
curing	270
sheathing	306
Paperhanging	350
Pargeting	415
Parging cement	306
Park bench	264
Parquet floor	193, 343
Particle board siding	313
board underlayment	291
Parting bead	296
Partition	178, 182, 356
anchor	272
block	274
demolition	254
dust	249
framing	124, 339
shower	352
support	281
wood frame	290
Passage door	188, 324-325
Patch roof	314
Patching floor concrete	270
Patio	344
door	326
Pavement emulsion	259
Paver floor	344
highway	259
Paving and surfacing	258
berm	259
bituminous	402
brick	259
concrete	258
Pea gravel	266
Peastone	265
Peat humus	265
moss	266
Pegboard	298
Perforated ceiling	343
Perimeter insulation	307
Perlite insulation	308-309
plaster	337, 417
Permit building	242
Pickett fence	264
Pickup truck	247
Picture window	148, 331
Pier brick	273
Pilaster wood column	306
Pile sod	265
Pin floating	333
non-removable	333
Pine door	323
door frame	321
fireplace mantel	298
floor	343
molding	295
roof deck	293
shelving	296
siding	313
stair	305
stair tread	304
Pipe & fittings	366-369
bedding	260
bituminous	260
cast iron	365
cleanout	363
column	281
concrete	261
Pipe copper	366
cost	420
covering	375
covering fiberglass	375
CPVC	367
drainage	261
DWV ABS	367
DWV PVC	367
fitting	363
fitting cast iron	365
fitting copper	366
fitting DWV	368
fitting malleable iron	369
fitting no-hub	365
fitting plastic	367-368
fitting soil	365
fitting steel	369
gas	260
insulation	375
no-hub	365
painting	349
plastic	367
polyethylene	260
PVC	261
rail	282-283
removal	248
sewage	261
single hub	365
soil	365
stainless	283
steel	260-261
subdrainage	261
Piping hydrant	260
removal	253
Pit leeching	262
Pitch coal tar	314
emulsion tar	259
Placing concrete	270
Plank floor	292
roof	291
sheathing	291
Plant bed preparation	265
Planter	264
Planting	266
Plaster	182, 184
accessory	336
board	178, 180
ceiling	337
cutout	250
dampproofing	415
demolition	249, 254
drill	279
expansion joint	336
ground	336
gypsum	337, 418
mixer	246
painting	349
perlite	337, 417
thincoat	337
vermiculite	417
wall	337
Plasterboard	338
Plastic blind	159
clad window	138, 140, 142, 144, 146, 148
faced hardboard	298
laminated countertop	297
outlet box	382
pipe	367
pipe fitting	367-368
siding	134
skylight	318
trap	364-365
tubing	260
Plate shear	285
wall switch	383
Plating zinc	284
Players bench	264
Plenum silencer	379
Plugmold raceway	380
Plumbing	363
appliance	372
demolition	253
fixture	370-372, 420
Plywood	411
clip	285
demolition	249, 254
floor	291
formwork	269
joist	292
mounting board	290
paneling	297
sheathing	290
shelving	296
siding	313
soffit	299
subfloor	291
treatment	300
Plywood underlayment	291
Pocket door frame	322
Point masonry	277
moil	246
Pole closet	295
Police connect panel	387
Polyethylene film	266, 306
floor	345
pipe	260
pool cover	362
tarpaulin	244
Polystyrene blind	299
ceiling	342
ceiling panel	342
insulation	307-309
Polysulfide caulking	319
Polyurethane caulking	319
Polyvinyl soffit	317
Pool accessory	362
cover	362
heater electric	373
heater gas fired	373
swimming	205, 363, 420
Porcelain enamel frame	321
tile	341
Porch molding	295
Portable air compressor	245
air-conditioner	376
Post cap	285
cedar	306
demolition	252
lamp	283
light	386
wood	287
Poured insulation	136
Power wiring	383
Pre-engineered steel building	410
Pre-hung door	325
Precast catch basin	261
concrete	271
coping	273
curb	259
lintel	271
manhole	261
receptor	353
sill	274
stair	271
terrazzo	342
Prefabricated building	362, 410
fireplace	202
Prefinished drywall	339
floor	193, 343
Premolded expansion joint	268
Primer asphalt	345
Profile block	274
Projected window	328
Property line survey	243
Protection slope	258
termite	258
Pull box	382
door	303
Pump circulating	371
concrete	244
diaphragm	246
heat	376
rental	246
submersible	246, 372
sump	359, 372
trash	246
water	246, 260
Purlin roof	292
Push button lock	333
Putting	352
PVC conduit	379
conduit in-slab	380
coupling	368
DWV pipe	367
gravel stop	318
pipe	260-261, 367
siding	312
tee	367
waterstop	269

Q

Quarry tile	341
Quarter round molding	296
Quartz	266
heater	387

INDEX

R

Raceway	379
plugmold	380
wiremold	380
Radial arch	292
Radiant heat	387
heating panel	387
Radiator cast iron	374
Rafter	287
anchor	285
demolition	252
roof framing	108
Rail hand	283
pipe	282-283
wall	283
Railing aluminum	282
demolition	253
metal	92
steel	283
wood	295, 304-305
Railroad tie step	264
Rainproof meter center	384
Ranch plank floor	343
Range	198
circuit	238
cooking	358
hood	198, 358
receptacle	383, 390
Ready mix concrete	270
Receptacle	238
air conditioner	390
device	389
dryer	390
GFI	390
locking	390
range	383, 390
telephone	390
television	390
weatherproof	390
Receptor shower	352
Recessed light	239
Rectangular diffuser	378
ductwork	377
Rectifier low-voltage silicon	382
Redwood bark	266
cupola	355
louver	298
paneling	298
siding	130, 313
wine vault	359
Refinish floor	343
Reflective block	275
insulation	307
Refractories	277
Refrigeration residential	358
Register air supply	379
baseboard	379
Reinforcement concrete	269
Reinforcing footing	269
masonry	272, 405
wall	269
Relief valve pressure	369
Remodeling and repair	421
Removal BX	251
catch basin	248
chain link fence	248
concrete	248
curb	248
driveway	248
fence	248
masonry	248
paint	351
piping	253
romex	251
shingle	253
sidewalk	248
stone	248
tree	255
window	254
Remove sod	265
Rental equipment	247
equipment rate	243
generator	246
Repair and remodeling	421
fire damage	352
Repellent water	350
Replacement sash	332
sliding door	326
Residential alarm	391
appliance	358, 391
burner	373
closet door	320
device	388
door	320, 322-323
door bell	390
elevator	363
fan	391

Residential fence	262
fixture	386, 391
greenhouse	362
gutting	252
heat pump	392
hinge	333
lighting	391
loadcenter	388
lock	333
overhead door	326
refrigeration	358
service	388
smoke detector	391
stair	304
storm door	327
switch	388
ventilation	377
water heater	372, 392
wiring	388, 391
Resilient floor	344, 418
flooring	193
Resquared shingle	310
Restoration window	351
Retaining wall	258
Retarder vapor	306
Ribbed waterstop	269
Ridge board	288
shingle	310
shingle clay	310
shingle slate	310
vent	353
Rig drill	248
Rigid anchor	272
conduit in-trench	380
in-slab conduit	380
insulation	136, 307
Ring split	285
toothed	285
Rings drapery	361
Riser beech	195
oak	195
wood stair	305
Rivet	280
tool	280
Robe hook	357
Rod closet	296
curtain	357
ground	381-382
Roll roof	313
roofing	314
type air filter	378
Romex copper	381
removal	251
Roof adhesive	313
aluminum	311
beam	292
built-up	313
cant	288, 314
clay tile	310
coating	314
copper	314
deck	282, 291
deck insulation	309
deck laminated	293
deck wood	293
fiberglass	311
framing	108, 110, 112, 114, 116, 118
framing removal	250
metal	311
mineral	314
monel	314
nail	284
patch	314
purlin	292
rafter	287
roll	313
sheathing	290
skylight	318
slate	310, 415
tile	310
truss	292-293
truss wood	412
zinc	314
Roofing	160, 162, 164, 166, 168
built-up	176
demolition	253
gable end	160
gambrel	164
hip roof	162
mansard	166
membrane	313
roll	314
shed	168
Rooftop air conditioner	376
Rosewood door	322
Rosin paper	306
Rotary hammer drill	246
Rough buck	287

Rough carpentry	285
hardware	290
stone wall	276
Rough-in sink countertop	371
sink raised deck	371
sink service floor	371
tub	370
Round diffuser	378
Rubber base	344
coating	306
floor	345
floor tile	345
sheet	345
threshold	334
Rubbish chute	249
handling	249

S

Safety switch	384
Safety-switch disconnect	384
Salamander	246
Sales tax	242, 400
Salt treatment lumber	300
Sand fill	256
Sandblasting equipment	247
Sanding	352
floor	343
Sandstone	277
flagging	259
Sanitary cove base	340
Sash replacement	332
wood	332
Sauna	361
door	361
Saw	247
chain	247
circular	247
concrete	244
masonry	247
Scaffolding steel tubular	401
tubular	243
Scrape after damage	352
Screen chimney	354
fence	263
molding	295
security	329
squirrel and bird	355
window	329, 332
wood	332
Screw anchor	279
brass	285
drywall	340
lag	280
sheet metal	284
steel	285
wood	285
Scupper	362
Seal pavement	259
Sealant	306
acoustical	339
caulking	319
Sealcoat	259
Sealer joint	319
Sectional door	327
overhead door	326
Security screen	329
Seeding	265, 402
Self propelled crane	247
Self-contained air conditioner	376
Septic system	90
tank	262
Service electric	236, 383
entrance cable aluminum	381
entrance cap	381
residential	388
sink	371
sink faucet	364
Sewage pipe	261
Sewer grating	261
Sewerage and drainage	260
Shadow box fence	263
Shake siding	132
wood	310
Shear plate	285
wall	290
Sheathed nonmetallic cable	381
Sheathing	290
asphalt	291
gypsum	291
insulation	308
paper	306
plywood	290
roof	290
Shed dormer framing	122
dormer roofing	172
roof framing	118

Sheet base	313
metal	314
metal screw	284
rock	178, 180
Sheeting driver	246
Sheetrock	338
Shelf adjustable	356
brick	269
metal	356
Shellac door	347
Shelving wood	296
Shield expansion	279
termite	317
Shingle	160, 162, 164, 166, 168
asphalt	309
concrete	310
mineral fiber	309
removal	253
ridge	310
siding	132
stain	347
wood	310
Shower by-pass valve	364
door	353
enclosure	353
pan	316
partition	352
receptor	352
stall	371
surround	353
Shrub broadleaf evergreen	266
deciduous	266
evergreen	266-267
moving	266
Shutter	159, 360
Sidelight	322
Sidewalk	86, 258, 344
asphalt	258
removal	248
Siding aluminum	311
demolition	253
fiberglass	311
hardboard	313
metal	134
nail	284
painting	347
redwood	313
removal	253
shingle	132
stain	347
steel	312
vinyl	312
wood	130, 312
Silencer plenum	379
Silicone caulking	319
coating	306
Sill	277, 288
door	296, 321, 334
masonry	273
quarry tile	341
Sillcock	364
Single hub pipe	365
hung window	328
zone rooftop unit	376
Sink	198
base	300
countertop	371
countertop rough-in	371
laundry	370
lavatory	370
raised deck rough-in	371
removal	253
service	371
service floor rough-in	371
Siren	387
Sister joist	286
Site drainage	261
grading	256
improvement	262, 264
preparation	255
removal	248
Sitework	80
Skim coat	178, 180
Skirtboard	305
Skylight	174, 318
removal	253
roof	318
Skywindow	174
Slab blockout	269
concrete	102, 270
cutout	249
form	282
on grade	269
on grade removal	248
Slate	277
flagging	259
removal	253
roof	310, 415

458

INDEX

S

Slate shingle	310
sidewalk	259
sill	274
stair	277
tile	344
Sleeper	288
wood	193
Sleeve formwork	268
Sliding door	152-153
glass door	326
mirror	357
window	144, 328, 332
Slop sink	370-371
Slope protection	258
Slot letter	356
Small tool	242
Smoke detector	387
Snap tie formwork	268
Snow fence	263
melting	387
Soap holder	357
Social security tax	395
Socket meter	383
Sodding	265
Sodium low pressure fixture	385
Soffit	288
aluminum	311
drywall	338
metal	317
plaster	337
plywood	299
vinyl	312
wood	299
Softener water	359
Soil compaction	256
compactor	245
pipe	365
tamping	256
Solar heating	421
Solid wood door	323
Spa bath	370
Space heater rental	246
Spade air	246
Spanish roof tile	310
Special coating	346
construction	361
door	326
electrical system	386
stairway	195
systems	387
Spike grid	285
Spiral stair	282, 305
Split rib block	274
ring	285
Sprayed coating	306
Sprayer emulsion	246
Spread footing	269-270
Stain cabinet	347
casework	347
door	347
floor	348
shingle	347
siding	347
truss	349
Staining lumber	293
siding	313
Stainless flashing	316
gutter	317
pipe	283
steel bolt	279
steel gravel stop	318
steel hinge	333
steel rivet	280
Stair	305
basement	195, 271, 304
carpet	346
ceiling	359
climber	363
concrete	270
disappearing	359
electric	359
pan form	282
precast	271
railroad tie	264
removal	252
residential	304
slate	277
spiral	305
stringer	287
tread	195
tread quarry tile	341
tread wood	305
wood	304-305, 412
Stairway	194
curved	195
special	195

Stall shower	371
Standard brick	273
Starters boards & switches	383
Starting newel	305
Steam bath	362
bath residential	362
boiler	373
boiler electric	373
cleaner	247
Stearate coating	306
Steel anchor	272
bolt	278, 284
bridging	286
building pre-engineered	410
chain link	262
channel	336
conduit in-slab	380
conduit in-trench	380
conduit rigid	379
diffuser	378
door	319-320
downspout	315
drill	246
edging	259
fireplace	202
flashing	316
frame	320
framed formwork	268
furring	336
gravel stop	318
gutter	317
hinge	333
lintel	287
nailers	287
pipe	260-261
screw	285
siding	312
stud	339
tubular scaffolding	401
Steeple tip pin	333
Step masonry	264
stone	277
Stockade fence	264
Stone	276
aggregate	265
anchor	272
base	257
fill	256
floor	258, 276
ground cover	265
mulch	266
paver	259, 277
removal	248
step	277
threshold	274
trim cut	
veneer	276-277
wall	128, 258
Stool cap	296
window	274, 276
Stop door	296
gravel	318
Storm door	158, 327
window	158, 328-329
Stove wood burning	355
Strainer downspout	315
gutter	317
roof	315
wire	315
Strap tie	285
Straw	266
Stringer	195
stair	287
Strip floor	343
footing	270
lighting	385
shingle	309
Structural excavation	256
Stucco	184, 337, 418
interior	182
painting	347
wall	126
Stud clip	336
connector	280
demolition	252
driver	280
metal	339-340
partition	290
steel	339
wall	106, 290
Sub purlin	282
Subdrainage pipe	261
Subfloor	291
plywood	193, 291
Submersible pump	246, 260, 372
Submittal	243
Suction hose	246
Sump pump	359, 372

Sunroom	204
Support ceiling	281
drinking fountain	364
lavatory	364
light	281
monitor	281
motor	281
partition	281
Suppressor lightning	388
Surface landscape	345
Surround shower	353
tub	353
Survey crew	243
monument	243
property line	243
topographic	243
Suspended ceiling	186, 337, 343
Suspension system ceiling	336
Swimming pool	205, 362-363, 420
pool enclosure	362
pool heater	373
Swing check valve	369
Swing-up door	154
Switch	383
box	382
box plastic	382
decorator	388
dimmer	383, 388
electric	382, 384
general duty	384
residential	388
safety	384
time	384
toggle	383
wiring	238
Switching low-voltage	382
Switchplate low-voltage	382
Synthetic marble	344
Syphon ventilator rotary	379
System antenna	388
VHF	388

T

T & G siding	130
T-bar mount diffuser	378
Table top	297
Tamper	246
Tamping soil	256
Tank expansion	375
fiberglass	375
oil & gas	375
septic	90, 262
Tar paper	266
pitch emulsion	259
Tarpaulin	244
duck	244
polyethylene	244
Tax	242
sales	242, 400
Social Security	242, 395
unemployment	242, 395
Teak floor	193, 343
molding	294, 296
paneling	297
Tee cleanout	363
PVC	367
Telephone receptacle	390
Television receptacle	390
Temperature relief valve	369
Tempered glass	335
hardboard	298
Tempering valve	369
Temporary oil heater	246
Tennis court fence	92, 263
Terminal air conditioner packaged	376
Termite protection	258
shield	317
Terne coated flashing	316
Terra cotta coping	273
cotta demolition	250
Terrace	264
Terrazzo	342
precast	342
receptor	353
wainscot	342
Thermostat	378
integral	387
wiring	392
Thincoat	178, 180
plaster	337
Thinset ceramic tile	340
mortar	341
Threshold	334
door	322
stone	274, 276
wood	296

Thru-wall air conditioner	376
air-conditioner	377
Tie formwork snap	268
rafter	288
strap	285
wall	272
Tile	340, 345
ceiling	342-343
ceramic	340-341
concrete	310
cork wall	350
demolition	249
flue	278
glass	335
grout	340
marble	344
metal	341
porcelain	341
quarry	341
roof	310
slate	344
stainless steel	341
vinyl asbestos	345
Timber connector	284
fastener	284
framing	292
laminated	292
Time switch	384
Timer clock	391
interval	388
switch ventilator	378
Tinted glass	335
Toggle bolt	279
switch	383
Toilet bowl	371
chemical	247
Tongue and groove siding	130
Tool air	245
rivet	280
small	242
Toothed ring	285
Toothing masonry	250
Top dressing	257
table	297
Topographic survey	243
Torch cutting	247
Towel bar	357
Track drawer	303
lighting	386
lights	386
traverse	361
Tractor	245, 257
loader	245
truck	247
Trailer truck	245
Transfer switch automatic	384
Transformer low-voltage	382
Transit	247
Transom lite frame	321
Trap cast iron	364
drainage	364
plastic	364-365
Trash pump	246
Traverse	361
track	361
Travertine	276
Tray laundry	370
Tread abrasive	341
beech	195
oak	195
stone	277
wood	305
Treatment acoustical	342
plywood	300
window	360
wood	300
Tree	266
deciduous	267
evergreen	266
guying	265
moving	266
planted	267
removal	255
Trees	403
Trench backfill	257
excavation	257
Trencher	245
chain	245
Trenching	84
Trim exterior	295
metal	336
painting	349
tile	340
wood	295
Trowel concrete	244
finish	271
Troweled coating	306
Truck dump	245

459

INDEX

T

Truck flatbed	245
hauling	257
loading	256
pickup	247
rental	245
tractor	247
trailer	245
Truss bowstring	293
demolition	252
flat wood	293
painting	349
plate	285
roof	292-293
roof framing	110
stain	349
varnish	349
wood roof	412
Tub bath	370
enclosure	353
hot	370
redwood	370
rough-in	370
surround	353
Tub/shower module	370
Tubing copper	366
electric metallic	379
plastic	260
Tubular scaffolding	243
scaffolding steel	401
steel joist	292
Tumbler holder	357
Turned column	305
T.V. antenna	388
closed circuit	388

U

Undereave vent	353
Underground tank	375
Underlayment	291
felt	344
latex	345
Unemployment tax	242, 395
Unit heater electric	387
masonry	272
Urethane insulation	308
Utility	84
excavation	84
trench	257
vault	260

V

Vacuum breaker	365
cleaning	357
Valance board	301
Valley rafter	287
Valve angle	369
pressure relief	369
shower by-pass	364
swing check	369
tempering	369
water pressure	369
Vanity base	304
top lavatory	370
Vapor barrier	306
barrier sheathing	291
retarder	306
Varnish cabinet	347
casework	347
door	347
floor	348, 350
truss	349
Vault utility	260
wine	359
Veneer ashlar	407
brick	128, 275
brick in place	406
core paneling	297
removal	255
stone	276-277
Venetian blind	360
Vent chimney	375
dryer	359
exhaust	379
ridge	353
ridge strip	354
Ventilating air conditioning	376, 378
air-conditioning	377
Ventilation fan	392
louver	298
residential	377
Ventilator rotary syphon	379
timer switch	378
Verge board	295
Vermiculite insulation	307
plaster	417
Vertical aluminum siding	311
vinyl siding	312
VHF system	388
Vibrator concrete	244
earth	256
Vibratory equipment	245
Vinyl asbestos tile	345
blind	159, 299
chain link	262
composition floor	345
door trim	312
downspout	315
faced wallboard	338
floor	345
flooring	193
gutter	317
pool	205
shutter	159
siding	134, 312
siding accessories	312
wallpaper	351
window trim	312
Vitrified clay pipe	261
Volume control damper	379

W

Wagon drill	245
Wainscot ceramic tile	340
molding	296
quarry tile	341
terrazzo	342
Walk	258
Wall bumper	333
cabinet	301
ceramic tile	341
coating	346
concrete	271
covering	418
cutout	249-250
drywall	338
finish	271
formwork	269
foundation	275
framing	106
framing removal	250
furring	289, 336
grout	272
heater	358
heater electric	387
insulation	274, 307-308
interior	178, 182
lath	337
louver	354
masonry	126, 128, 258, 274
mirror	335
painting	349-350
panel	276
paneling	297
plaster	337
plate	283
rail	283
reinforcing	269
removal	254
retaining	258
shear	290
sheathing	290-291
siding	313
stucco	337
stud	290, 339
switch plate	383
tie	272
tile cork	350
Wallcovering	350
acrylic	351
Wallpaper	351, 418
Walnut door frame	321
floor	343
Wardrobe wood	301
Wash bowl	370
brick	277
Washer	285
residential	359
Washing machine automatic	359
Water closet	371
closet removal	253
closet support	364
distribution system	260
heater	359, 392
heater electric	372
heater insulation	375
heater oil	372
heater removal	253
heater wrap kit	375
Water heating hot	373-374
heating wiring	238
hose	246
pipe ground clamp	382
pressure relief valve	369
pressure valve	369
pump	246, 260, 359, 372
repellent	350
softener	359
supply domestic meter	372
supply meter	372
tempering valve	369
well	260
Waterproofing	306
coating	306
Waterstop	269
Weather cap entrance	380
Weatherproof receptacle	238, 390
Weatherstrip	334
door	334
window	334
Weathervane	283
Welded door frame	416
frame	321
wire fabric	270
Welding machine	247
Well	260
Wheelbarrow	247
Whirlpool bath	370
Window	138, 140, 142, 144, 146, 148, 318
air conditioner	376
aluminum	328
blind	299, 360
casement	330
casing	294
demolition	254
double hung	330-331
double-hung	138
frame	332
glass	335
grille	332
hardware	333
metal	328
muntin	332
painting	348
picture	331
removal	254
restoration	351
screen	329, 332
sill	273
sill marble	276
sill quarry tile	341
sliding	332
stool	274, 276
storm	158, 328-329
treatment	360
trim set	296
weatherstrip	334
wood	330-332, 417
wood and plastic	330
Wine vault	359
Winter protection	271
Wire copper	381
electric	381
fence	263
ground	382
mesh	338
strainer	315
thw	381
Wiremold raceway	380
Wiring	238
air conditioner	392
device	383
fan	392
power	383
residential	388, 391
thermostat	392
Wood base	294
beam	286
blind	159, 299, 360
block floor demolition	251
blocking	177, 290
canopy	288
casing	294
chips	266
column	287, 292, 305
cupola	355
deck	206, 291, 293
demolition	249
door	188, 190, 321, 323, 416
door interior	416
drawer	303
fascia	295
fastener	285
fence	263
fiber ceiling	343
fiber sheathing	291
fiber soffit	299
Wood fiber subfloor	291
fiber underlayment	291
floor	104, 193, 343
floor demolition	251
foundation	100
frame	301, 321
framing	286
furring	290
girder	286
gutter	317
handrail	295
joist	286, 292
laminated	292-293
louver	298
molding	305
nailers	287
overhead door	326
panel door	323
paneling	297
partition	290
planter	264
railing	305
roof deck	291
roof deck demolition	253
roof truss	412
sash	332
screen	332
screw	285
shake	310
sheathing	291
shelving	296
shingle	310
shutter	159
sidewalk	258
siding	130, 312
siding demolition	254
sill	288
sliding door	326
soffit	299
stair	304-305, 412
storm door	158, 325
storm window	158
subfloor	291
threshold	296
tread	305
treatment	300
trim	295
truss	293
veneer wallpaper	351
wall framing	106
wardrobe	301
window	330-332, 417
window demolition	254
Woodwork architectural	300
Wool carpet	192
fiberglass	307
Workers' compensation	242, 397-399
Wrench impact	246

Y

Yellow pine floor	343

Z

Z bar suspension	336
Zee bar	340
Zinc flashing	316
plating	284
roof	314
weatherstrip	334

New Publications

Avoiding and Resolving Construction Claims
by Barry B. Bramble, Esq.
Michael F. D'Onofrio, PE
John B. Stetson, IV, RA

1st Edition
NEW! Over 240 Pages • Illustrated • Hardcover

As a member of the construction management team, chances are that sooner or later you'll be involved in a construction claim.

It may relate to a design error, subsurface condition, defective installation, material, delay—any number of unexpected events which cost extra money.

How such claims are avoided and resolved is the subject of this penetrating new guide.

Each chapter addresses a different step of the process and includes a summary checklist for action, sample problems, graphic illustrations, and a few case histories to show how courts have decided disputes.

ISBN 0-87629-180-9
Book No. 67275

$59.95/copy
U.S. Funds

Means Estimating Handbook

1st Edition
NEW! Over 900 Pages • Illustrated • Hardcover

Means Estimating Handbook simplifies the task of evaluating construction plans and specs to obtain reliable quantities for pricing.

The Handbook reflects the tremendous variety of technical data required for estimating . . .

. . . questions relating to sizing, productivity, equipment requirements, codes, design standards, engineering, pressures, stresses, loads, coverages . . . and hundreds of similar factors.

The guide provides the busy estimator with every technical reference imaginable . . . tables, illustrations, definitions, examples . . . any construction factor which will help answer the key questions:

How many, how much, and how long will it take?

ISBN 0-87629-177-9
Book No. 67276

$89.95/copy
U.S. Funds

Survival in the Construction Business: Checklists for Success
by Thomas N. Frisby

1st Edition
NEW! 300 Pages • Illustrated
Index • Appendix • Hardcover

If you're wondering how to guide your company to success and profit in the decade ahead, *Survival in the Construction Business: Checklists for Success* can show you how.

In just eight concise chapters this guide details a step-by-step approach to construction company mangement. It gives you the practical tools you need to ensure that every decision you make will help you meet your goals.

Survival's method is based on a comprehensive series of construction "Checklists" that will steer you through every phase of company evaluation, for both long-range planning and day-to-day operation. Put these checklists to use, and you'll start seeing results right away!

ISBN 0-87629-153-1
Book No. 67274

$59.95/copy
U.S. Funds

HVAC Systems Evaluation
• Comparing Systems
• Solving Problems
• Efficiency & Maintenance
by Harold R. Colen, PE

1st Edition
NEW! Over 500 Pages • Illustrated • Hardcover

A virtual encyclopedia of experienced know-how for comparing, selecting, installing, and fixing HVAC equipment and systems.

HVAC Systems Evaluation is a convenient, straight-talk way for you to understand and select HVAC systems for new or retrofit construction.

It gives you direct, right-to-the-point comparisons of how each type of system works . . . installation costs . . . operating costs . . . applications by type of building.

You get experienced advice for fixing operational problems in existing HVAC systems—*everything is covered.*

ISBN 0-87629-182-5
Book No. 67281

$57.95/copy
U.S. Funds

Reference Books

Means Construction Cost Indexes 1991

(Individual and back issues available at $42.25 per copy)

The index service providing updated cost adjustment factors

Whether updating construction costs from Means cost manuals or data from other sources, the construction cost index service is the efficient way to ensure 90-day cost accuracy.

Published quarterly (January, April, July, October), this handy report provides cost adjustment factors for the preparation of more precise estimates no matter how late in the year. It's also the ideal method for making continuous cost revisions on ongoing projects as the year progresses.

The report is organized in four unique sections:
- breakdowns for 209 major cities
- national averages for 30 key cities
- five large city averages
- historical construction cost indexes

Book No. 60141 $169.00/year   U.S. Funds

Means Scheduling Manual
By F. William Horsley

2nd Edition
Over 200 Pages • Illustrated • Hardcover

For experienced schedulers and project managers as well as the uninitiated

Fast, convenient expertise for keeping your scheduling skills right in step with today's cost-conscious times.

This concisely written scheduling handbook shows you the entire scheduling process far faster than any reference of its kind.

You'll benefit from all the information provided on traditional bar charts, Pert and CPM ... and home in on the precision offered by *Precedence Scheduling*.

The book guides you through all aspects of scheduling, with fold-out spread sheets, charts, sample schedules.

ISBN 0-911950-36-2 $49.95/copy
Book No. 67152   U.S. Funds

Means Forms for Building Construction Professionals

2nd Edition
Over 325 Pages • Three-Ring Binder

Don't waste time trying to compose forms — we've done the job for you!

- Forms can be customized with your company name and reproduced on your copier or at your local instant printer.
- Forms for all primary construction activities—estimating, designing, project administration, scheduling, appraising. 
- Many optional variations—condensed, detailed versions.
- Forms compatible with Means annual cost books and other typical user systems.
- Ideal for standardizing estimating and project management functions at low cost.
- Full size forms on durable reproduction paper presented in a sturdy three-ring binder.

ISBN 0-911950-87-7 $76.95/copy
Book No. 67231   U.S. Funds

Means Labor Rates for the Construction Industry 1991

18th Annual Edition • Over 325 Pages
CITY • STATE • NATIONAL

- Detailed wage rates by trade for over 300 U.S. and Canadian cities
- Forty-six construction trades listed by local union number in each city
- Base hourly wage rates plus fringe benefit package costs gathered from reliable sources
- Dependable estimates for the trade wage rates not reported at press time 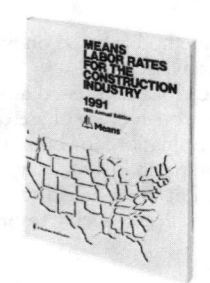
- Effective dates for newly negotiated union contracts for both 1990 and 1991
- Factors for comparing each trade rate by city, state, and national averages
- Historical 1989–1990 wage rates also included for comparison purposes
- Each city chart is alphabetically arranged with handy visual flip tabs for quick reference

ISBN 0-87629-191-4 $145.00/copy
Book No. 60121   U.S. Funds

Reference Books

Planning and Managing Interior Projects
by Carol E. Farren

1st Edition
Over 300 Pages • Illustrated • Hardcover

NOW, a clearly defined working guide to project management functions of interior installations

You can rely on the expertise in *Planning and Managing Interior Projects* because it's been tested and proved out *on the job!* The author draws upon the fruits of experience to give you a better working knowledge of each area of interior project management.

If your situation requires you to be knowledgeable in *any or all phases of carrying out interior projects*—working with the client, working with building managers, contractors, movers, telephone installers and suppliers, as well as preparing designs and plans—this book will be *the best investment you can make for doing a better, more professional job!*

ISBN 0-87629-097-7
Book No. 67245

$59.95/copy
U.S. Funds

The Facilities Manager's Reference
• Management • Building Audits
• Planning • Estimating

by Harvey H. Kaiser, Ph.D.

1st Edition
Over 240 Pages with Prototype Forms and Line Art Graphics • Hardcover

Your one-step source for the latest facilities management methods used successfully by both large and small operations

One of the nation's leading management authorities describes how to manage facilities in the "real world" of modern organizations.

The author explains the diverse "hats" a facilities manager must wear as organizer, planner, estimator, supervisor, motivator, and decision-maker, and how these roles can be managed most effectively.

Now you can have access to a huge collection of new concepts, methods, and tools that you can use *immediately* to build up your level of performance and funding!

ISBN 0-87629-142-6
Book No. 67264

$59.95/copy
U.S. Funds

Means Facilities Maintenance Standards

1st Edition
Over 575 Pages • 205 Tables, Checklists, and Diagrams • Hardcover

A definitive reference addressing thousands of facilities maintenance problems

Means Facilities Maintenance Standards is a working encyclopedia that provides solutions to almost every kind of maintenance and repair dilemma.

The book guides you to the underlying causes of material deterioration, shows you how to analyze its effects, and steps you through the appropriate methods of repair. A Man-Hours section lists estimated times to carry out various maintenance tasks.

All of the checklists in this reference are organized in the order you need them. You'll never have to worry about overlooking an important consideration or crucial step in repairs again!

ISBN 0-87629-096-9
Book No. 67246

$131.95/copy
U.S. Funds

Facilities Maintenance Management
by Gregory H. Magee, PE

1st Edition
Over 250 Pages • Illustrated • Hardcover

Provocative—instructive—you'll benefit from new ideas for planning and managing maintenance functions in your organization

This comprehensive reference will guide you through important aspects of facilities maintenance management.

It gives you ideas for staffing, estimating, budgeting, scheduling, and controlling work to produce a more efficient, cost-effective maintenance department.

No matter what your need or problem, you're sure to find direction for solving it in this authoritative book—written by a professional who's conquered every kind of challenge—*including the one on your desk right now!*

ISBN 0-87629-100-0
Book No. 67249

$59.95/copy
U.S. Funds

Reference Books

Estimating for the General Contractor
by Paul J. Cook

1st Edition
Over 225 Pages • Illustrated • Hardcover

For general contractors... breathe new life into your estimates and profits

Light on theory, heavy on practical estimating methods and ideas, here's powerful help for the contractor/estimator who wants to evaluate and polish every aspect of estimating procedures.

Estimators at all levels of experience will appreciate this comprehensive package of indispensable methods and procedures.

Through the use of clear explanations as well as detailed examples, tables, and graphs, the reader is shown how estimating may be done with *maximum efficiency*—without sacrificing *quality*.

ISBN 0-87629-110-8
Book No. 67160

$59.95/copy
U.S. Funds

Business Management for the General Contractor
by Paul J. Cook

1st Edition
Over 200 Pages • Illustrated • Hardcover

It's direct. It's current. And it's relevant to your needs.

Business Management for the General Contractor has one overriding priority—to give the contractor a basic working knowledge of all aspects of business management. With this dependable reference, you won't need bundles of cash or battalions of experts to solve your everyday problems.

You'll refer to this remarkable book again and again because the ideas it provides will be of continuous value to your career and your company's progress! You'll find efficient methods and strategies to help you handle almost any kind of management problem typical to contractors.

ISBN 0-87629-098-5
Book No. 67250

$54.95/copy
U.S. Funds

Bidding for the General Contractor
by Paul J. Cook

1st Edition
Over 225 Pages • Illustrated • Hardcover

The techniques of successful bidding and how to apply them in your own construction business

Now you can have a truly comprehensive guide for making competitive bids—methods and guidelines for all job sizes, up to multimillion-dollar projects.

It sheds new light on bidding procedures and techniques... at last you can see and compare your approach with other successful bidders. You'll have in-depth discussion and illustrations covering every step of the bid management process, beginning the first moment you get the sponsor's bid package.

ISBN 0-911950-77-X
Book No. 67180

$54.95/copy
U.S. Funds

Superintending for the General Contractor
Field Project Management
by Paul J. Cook

1st Edition
Over 220 Pages • Illustrated • Hardcover

A landmark guide to the effective on-site management of construction projects

At last there is a guide to on-site construction management that goes beyond textbook theory and simplistic discussion. Paul J. Cook's *Superintending for the General Contractor* is a fully developed, well organized working handbook. It delves deeply into every area of the superintendent's job, probing, elaborating... pointing out the do's and don'ts of managing manpower, materials, equipment, and paperwork.

Contains hundreds of valuable insights for dealing with clients, subcontractors, foremen, suppliers, and workers... anyone who works on the project... so it gets done at targeted quality, cost, and deadlines.

ISBN 0-87629-063-2
Book No. 67233

$54.95/copy
U.S. Funds

Reference Books

HVAC: Design Criteria, Options, Selection
by William H. Rowe, III, AIA, PE

1st Edition
Over 380 Pages • Illustrated • Hardcover

For a total understanding of HVAC systems . . .

If you're new to HVAC systems design, or simply want to make certain you're right in step with the newest HVAC design concepts and equipment, you'll benefit from this highly recommended resource.

HVAC: Design Criteria, Options, Selection is a masterful book, providing a thorough understanding of modern heating, ventilating, and air conditioning (HVAC) systems.

It gives you a comprehensive overview of the basic functions of HVAC, with emphasis on the design and costs of effective integrated climate control systems.

ISBN 0-87629-102-7
Book No. 67251

$59.95/copy
U.S. Funds

Hazardous Material and Hazardous Waste: A Construction Reference Manual
by F.J. Hopcroft, P.E., D.L. Vitale, M. Ed., D.L. Anglehart, Esq.

1st Edition
Over 260 Pages • Illustrated • Hardcover

With OSHA, EPA and other agencies stepping up compliance inspections at construction sites, contractors can no longer afford to put off installing programs for informing and training their workers on the proper handling and disposal of hazardous materials.

You're given a full explanation of the laws as they pertain to construction work and what you—as an employer—are expected to do.

This includes suggested methods for storing and using hazardous materials, and then disposing of hazardous wastes, all in accordance with federal and state regulations.

ISBN 0-87629-136-1
Book No. 67258

$76.95/copy
U.S. Funds

Means Electrical Estimating
Standards and Procedures

1st Edition
Over 300 Pages • Illustrated • Hardcover

Even experienced estimators applaud the countless ways this superb guidebook helps them!

This eye-opening book breaks electrical installations down into modules and explains how to estimate each of them using the *Means Electrical Cost Data* manual.

- gives you instant electrical estimating help for specific types of installations
- gives you the combined experience of the Means staff, plus top designers and electrical contractors
- covers electrical estimating in full—from takeoff to overhead and profit

80 electrical estimating modules illustrate and explain each step in the estimating process . . . units of measure for labor and materials, typical job conditions, takeoff procedures, cost modifications . . . and a great deal more!

ISBN 0-911950-83-4
Book No. 67230

$54.95/copy
U.S. Funds

Means Mechanical Estimating
Standards and Procedures

1st Edition
Over 370 Pages • Illustrated • Hardcover

For HVAC/Plumbing/Fire Protection estimating . . . from takeoff through pricing, bidding and scheduling

Means Mechanical Estimating examines each mechanical contracting activity, pointing out the best ways to predict material and installation costs. It evaluates, analyzes, and integrates every key estimating procedure from interpreting contract documents to the final minutes of the bid.

This is a comprehensive, no-nonsense reference that offers frank discussion of how to evaluate mechanical plans and estimate all cost components . . . right down to the last installed pipe hanger.

It will help you estimate better, understand mechanical work better, and develop the most cost efficient approaches to achieve your goals.

ISBN 0-87629-066-7
Book No. 67235

$54.95/copy
U.S. Funds

Reference Books

Quantity Takeoff for the General Contractor
by Paul J. Cook

1st Edition
Over 225 Pages • Illustrated • Hardcover

How to put more speed and accuracy into your quantity takeoff work

If you're new to quantity takeoff for estimating, or simply want to be sure you're using the latest and best takeoff techniques, this book is "must" reading.

It gives you a concise overview of the process—the quantity estimator's role, the tools he or she uses, how the project is broken down, and the rules to follow which help to ensure accuracy.

You will see how to evaluate plans for the site, footings, foundation, slab, floor, wall, framing, and roof, to calculate the quantity of materials and installing labor.

If you've ever had any doubts about how to do a better, faster job making quantity takeoffs—this book will help you do just that—by pointing out ways to make error-free takeoff estimates for every project.

ISBN 0-87629-141-8
Book No. 67262

$59.95/copy
U.S. Funds

Means Unit Price Estimating

1st Edition
Over 350 Pages • Hardcover

Direct, immediate help for preparing better unit cost estimates—no matter how much experience you have!

Indispensable for strengthening your unit cost estimating

Means Unit Price Estimating directs you to the right answers to your unit cost procedural questions—and directs you fast! It describes the most productive, universally-accepted ways to estimate, and uses checklists and charts to unearth shortcuts and time-savers. The strategy of bidding is explained, and up-to-date guidance is provided to assist in evaluation of your own approach.

A model estimate for a multi-story office building is included to demonstrate procedures. The book provides proven systems and special pointers to guide you through the building process.

ISBN 0-87629-027-6
Book No. 67232

$54.95/copy
U.S. Funds

Means Square Foot Estimating
by Billy J. Cox and F. William Horsley

1st Edition
Over 300 Pages • Hardcover

A new generation of techniques for conceptual and design-stage cost planning

Doing an effective job at the drawing board and estimating desk takes time. Too often, the time to carefully explore alternatives and evaluate different ideas is limited.

Means Square Foot Estimating is devoted to helping you accomplish more in less time. It steps you through the entire square foot cost process, pointing out faster, better ways to relate the design to the budgets.

In all, *Means Square Foot Estimating* provides clearer, better knowledge of how to greatly upgrade the *efficiency* and *effectiveness* of square foot cost estimating in the project's early stages.

ISBN 0-87629-090-X
Book No. 67145

$57.95/copy
U.S. Funds

Means Repair and Remodeling Estimating
by Edward B. Wetherill

Expanded New Edition
Over 450 Pages • Illustrated • Hardcover

- **Authoritative**
- **Easy to understand**
- **Follows CSI format**
- **Sample estimates**

Means Repair and Remodeling Estimating focuses on the unique problems of estimating renovations of existing structures. It helps you determine the true costs of remodeling through careful evaluation of architectural details and a site visit.

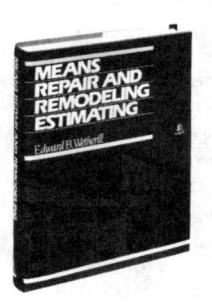

This, coupled with a CSI division-by-division discussion of potential pitfalls, and two sample estimates, gives you a real foundation for estimating remodeling work.

Although designed primarily for contractors and architects, the concepts in *Means Repair and Remodeling Estimating* apply to anyone who wants to enhance their renovation estimating skills.

ISBN 0-87629-144-2
Book No. 67265

$57.95/copy
U.S. Funds

Reference Books

Means Interior Estimating
by Alan E. Lew

1st Edition
Over 370 Pages • Illustrated • Hardcover

Four complete estimating manuals in one comprehensive reference

This book provides in-depth discussion and illustrations covering every type of interior construction ...

- **Readable.** Tightly written, easy to read.
- **Illustrated.** Dozens of easy-to-follow prototype estimating forms and diagrams of interior assemblies and building plans.
- **Answers.** Each fact-filled chapter is a gold mine of answers to your questions. 
- **Comprehensive.** Virtually anyone whose work involves interior estimating will benefit from this book.
- **Authoritative.** Authored and edited by a team of interior estimating experts, this information is based on actual experience and proven techniques.
- Hands-on application of *Means Interior Cost Data*.

ISBN 0-87629-067-5
Book No. 67237

54.95/copy
U.S. Funds

Means Landscape Estimating
by Sylvia H. Fee

1st Edition
Over 275 Pages • Illustrated • Hardcover

Answers all your questions about preparing competitive landscape construction estimates ...

Here's the important landscape estimating reference that gives you the tools you need to solve your landscape pricing problems.

Means Landscape Estimating is a thorough, easy-reading, well organized working guide that "talks you through" every step of preparing effective bids and estimates—in a minimum of time. Written by a highly respected landscape designer and contractor.

Everything you want to know about landscape estimating is right here—including marketing your services, performing the takeoff, bidding and planning the job.

ISBN 0-87629-064-0
Book No. 67239

$57.95/copy
U.S. Funds

Home Improvement Cost Guide

2nd Edition
Over 225 Pages • Illustrated • Softcover

How to plan and price home improvements quickly, easily—projects large and small

Planning a home improvement?
Maintenance project? Read this.

Prior to planning your next home improvement, wouldn't it make sense for you to talk with several expert builders who have done the same project many times before?

Suppose these professionals happily shared their insights, warned you of potential dangers, pointed out ways for you to get the most for your money ... and then provided you with a **reliable estimate** of what you'd expect to pay for the improvement—even if you did some of the work yourself?

You'd welcome this kind of advice with open arms, of course. Anyone would.

Well, that's exactly what the **Home Improvement Cost Guide** does for you.

ISBN 0-87629-173-6
Book No. 67280

$32.95/copy
U.S. Funds

Roofing: Design Criteria, Options, Selection
by R.D. Herbert, III

1st Edition
Over 200 Pages • Illustrated • Hardcover

This authoritative new guide is overflowing with fresh, practical know-how for professionals involved in roof construction—architects, contractors, owners, facilities managers, and roofing installers.

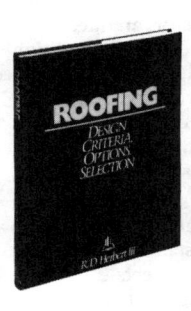

Now you can avoid roofing problems and choose the most cost-effective system—this easy-reading book helps you see the opportunities and pitfalls of modern roofing construction.

All types of roofing are covered ... built-up, singly-ply, modified bitumens, metal, sprayed-in-place, slate, tile, shingles, and shakes, as well as all types of seals and accessories.

ISBN 0-87629-104-3
Book No. 67253

$59.95/copy
U.S. Funds

Reference Books

Project Planning and Control for Construction
by David R. Pierce, Jr.

1st Edition
Over 275 Pages • Illustrated • Hardcover
Includes Sample Project

Here for the first time is a comprehensive action-guide to results-oriented project management

Project Planning and Control for Construction is designed specifically to help construction project managers work more effectively ... and profitably. It is a guide to the best, most up-to-date techniques for:

- pre-construction planning
- determining activity sequence
- scheduling
- monitoring and controlling
- managing submittal data
- managing resources
- accelerating the project
- cost control

This guide allows you to compare your current methods with those recommended by one of the nation's most highly respected scheduling and project management consultants.

ISBN 0-87629-099-3
Book No. 67247
$58.95/copy
U.S. Funds

Cost Control in Building Design
by Roger A. Killingsworth

1st Edition
Over 280 Pages • Illustrated • Hardcover

Using Square Foot and Assemblies estimating techniques to predict and control costs

Direct from the practical experience of a highly respected estimating consultant and educator, Cost Control in Building Design examines every step of the early construction planning and estimating process ... pointing out reliable new ways to budget and control costs as the design moves into sharp focus.

It explains—evaluates—integrates every key step in a total COST CONTROL SYSTEM that can help you bring projects to completion within 5% of budget.

Sample project includes mechanical and electrical estimates.

ISBN 0-87629-103-5
Book No. 67252
$58.95/copy
U.S. Funds

Cost Effective Design/Build Construction
by Anthony J. Branca, PE

1st Edition
Over 420 Pages • Illustrated • Hardcover

For contractors, architects, engineers ... any professional who wants to get into the design/build business

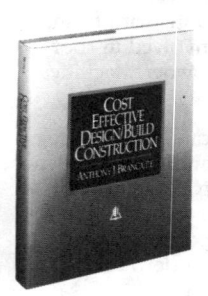

If you've been thinking about moving into design/build construction work, this book can be invaluable for helping you make your decision.

As a contractor, architect, engineer or other construction professional, perhaps you've been intrigued by the prospect of getting into design/build construction—maybe even founding your own firm.

Cost Effective Design/Build Construction takes you through every step in the business ... including what it takes to start your own firm. Learn how to market yourself, understand client needs, to prepare presentations, and how to manage projects using the design/build method. You'll find everything needed to understand exactly how design/build works.

ISBN 0-87629-088-8
Book No. 67242
$54.95/copy
U.S. Funds

The Building Professional's Guide to Contract Documents
(formerly Plans, Specs and Contracts for Building Professionals)
by Waller S. Poage, AIA, CSI, CCS

New! 2nd Edition
Over 400 Pages • Illustrated • Hardcover

Includes coverage of the latest AIA documents.

- detailed discussions of contract components ... addenda, conditions, supplements, specifications, drawings
- instructions for preparing specifications and technical requirements ... description writing, proprietary and performance specs, standards
- pointers for contract administration ... duties and responsibilities in the OPC (owner, design professional, contractor) relationship, meetings, transmittals, shop drawings, mock-ups, the punch list, payments, and more.

ISBN 0-87629-210-4
Book No. 67261
$54.95/copy
U.S. Funds

Reference Books

Bidding and Managing Government Construction
by Theodore J. Trauner, Jr., PE, PP, and Michael H. Payne, Esq.

1st Edition
Over 200 Pages • Hardcover

Learn how to win and administrate government construction contracts.

Why this book will be of immense value to you in your government construction work.

- It provides you with plain language explanations of the laws that control government construction and the complex and often inconsistent requirements of government contracts.
  - It explains the bidding process, pointing out the reasons for disqualification based on nonresponsive or irresponsible submissions.
  - It clarifies how various government agencies administer and manage construction, pointing out your rights, responsibilities and interests.
  - It describes in detail the procedures and pricing methods for changes in construction contracts.

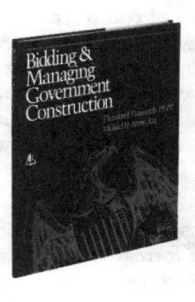

ISBN 0-87629-111-6
Book No. 67257

$58.95/copy
U.S. Funds

Understanding the Legal Aspects of Design/Build
by Timothy R. Twomey, Esq., AIA

1st Edition
Over 370 Pages • Illustrated • Hardcover

This practical design/build guide will help you:

- **Evaluate and compare** various design/build methods
- **Analyze** the strengths and weaknesses of design/build systems
- **Understand** your role, responsibilities and liabilities as contractor, designer or client
- **Gain insight** into the types of clients most likely to use these services
- **Survey** the legal issues surrounding errors, acts, and omissions
- **See how** traditional legal concepts apply differently to design/build
- **Use** prototype design/build contracts
- **Answer** insurance, bonding and licensing questions

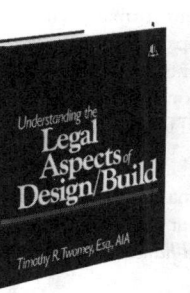

ISBN 0-87629-137-X
Book No. 67259

$71.95/copy
U.S. Funds

Risk Management for Building Professionals
by Thomas E. Papageorge, RA

1st Edition
Over 200 Pages • Illustrated • Hardcover

How well do you manage the complex risks of building design and construction?

If you've suffered losses of time, money, reputation ... harm to workers, or damage to projects because risks went unnoticed— **we have very important information for you.**

Risk Management for Building Professionals provides you with a master plan for phasing risk management functions into every department of your firm.

The goal is to provide a practical framework for recognizing potential risks and planning out how they will be handled *before* they occur.

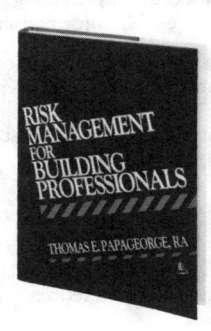

ISBN 0-87629-106-X
Book No. 67254

$54.95/copy
U.S. Funds

Contractor's Business Handbook
- Accounting • Tax Management
- Finance   • Cost Control

by Michael S. Milliner

1st Edition
Over 300 Pages • Illustrated • Hardcover

Attain new growth and profits through streamlined financial controls

This handbook is designed for contractors who want to put their business on a firmer financial footing and plan for future growth.

In plain language, the book describes and demonstrates how to use the contractor's most powerful financial management tool— *an efficient financial control system.*

The book delves deeply into accounting systems, financial analysis and forecasting, asset and debt management, tax reduction strategies, and computer-based control.

A convenient glossary defines financial terminology used in the text.

ISBN 0-87629-105-1
Book No. 67255

$58.95/copy
U.S. Funds

Reference Books

Means Man-Hour Standards for Construction

2nd Edition
Over 750 Pages • Hardcover

The "professional's choice" for uncompromised trade and labor productivity data

Here is the working encyclopedia of labor productivity information for construction professionals ... *Means Man-Hour Standards for Construction*, revised 2nd Edition.

The efficient format permits rapid comparisons of labor requirements for thousands of construction functions in the CSI MASTERFORMAT.

You'll find every bit of labor data you may need ... *all in a superb layout with "quick-find" indexes and handy visual flip tabs.*

ISBN 0-87629-089-6
Book No. 67236

$131.95/copy
U.S. Funds

Means Illustrated Construction Dictionary

1st Edition
Over 575 Pages • Illustrated • Hardcover

A working handbook of over 12,000 construction terms — explained and illustrated

Here's the on-the-job reference even the most experienced professionals can turn to for immediate answers about construction terms.

The Means Dictionary is packed with thousands of up-to-date explanations of construction terminology. It covers every area of construction from design right on through everyday lingo used by tradesmen. It's "alive" with entries covering every conceivable new technique, product.

Its no-nonsense guidance, illustrations, abbreviations, and easy-to-use format will serve you for years to come

ISBN 0-911950-82-6
Book No. 67190

$87.95/copy
U.S. Funds

Means Graphic Construction Standards

1st Edition
Over 500 Pages • Illustrated

**Create construction concepts/designs
Gain new insights and approaches**

Means Graphic Construction Standards assists you in making preliminary "audits" of your designs. It simplifies the review of construction methods, helping you sort out potential problems. You decide visually which elements are essential and which offer you the most cost-effective alternatives.

The book illustrates and discusses the relationships between various building systems. Because each construction assembly gives you extensive design data, you're able to leap from rough concepts to workable plans quickly. You don't waste time working backwards from costs to designs. The book gives you the freedom to maximize your creativity within time and budget goals.

ISBN 0-911950-79-6
Book No. 67210

$109.95/copy
U.S. Funds

Fundamentals of the Construction Process

by K.K. Bentil, AIC

1st Edition
Over 450 Pages • Illustrated • Hardcover

The first and only book designed specifically to introduce the basics of building construction

Fundamentals of the Construction Process has been prepared for executives, facilities managers, and others whose responsibilities include overseeing, budgeting, or other involvement in building or facilities construction. While construction processes are often highly technical, the book focuses on providing simplified, accessible, information.

It provides extensive coverage of the pre-construction phase, including an overview of project types, contract documents, cost estimating, contract procurement, bonding, scheduling and mobilization.

The greater part of the book is devoted to describing and illustrating the components of actual construction—materials, building methods, installation techniques—the differences between various construction "assemblies."

ISBN 0-87629-138-8
Book No. 67260

59.95/copy
U.S. Funds

Reference Books

Construction Delays:
- Documenting Causes
- Winning Claims
- Recovering Costs

by Theodore J. Trauner, Jr., PE, PP

1st Edition
NEW! 200 Pages • Illustrated • Hardcover

Learn what to look for—and what to look out for—in a construction delay case.

Whether you're a contractor or subcontractor, an owner, architect, or designer, *Construction Delays* is a detailed, fact-filled manual that can help you every step of the way—from working with your attorney to draft delay clauses in construction contracts—to learning how to document for your protection and advantage—to preparing a claim for court.

And at a time when losing a delay case could cost you thousands—even millions—of dollars, that's information you simply can't afford to be without.

Written in clear, non-legal language for construction professionals like you, *Construction Delays* takes you all the way from basic definitions and delay identification, to analysis, assessment of costs, and risk management.

ISBN 0-87629-174-4
Book No. 67278

$54.95/copy
U.S. Funds

Means Legal Reference for Design & Construction
by Charles R. Heuer, Esq., AIA

1st Edition
Over 450 Pages • Hardcover

At last—authoritative help for recognizing and understanding the legal issues in design and construction

Design and construction law is a large topic to grasp. With this in mind, the *Means Legal Reference For Design & Construction* has been prepared to enable its users to sort out and see the practical legal implications of each stage of project delivery.

Each section is illustrated and explained with examples and visuals. These make it easy for you to compare various legal documents, contracts, and situations to better understand the issues.

The large Appendix and Glossary include a comprehensive list of legal terms, names and addresses of trade associations, and samples of standard form contracts commonly used in the industry.

ISBN 0-87629-145-0
Book No. 67266

$109.95/copy
U.S. Funds

Construction Paperwork
An Efficient Management System
by J. Edward Grimes

1st Edition
Over 380 Pages • Illustrated • Hardcover

For project managers, office managers, facilities managers, design/build professionals, subcontractors . . .

Anyone responsible for using and keeping large amounts of construction documents will be delighted with this guide to controlling paperwork.

The author, J. Edward Grimes, is a project manager with 20 years of experience, and an arbitrator of construction disputes for the American Arbitration Association.

Construction Paperwork: An Efficient Management System cuts through theory to give you practical, instantly usable techniques—with immediate payback. It is the first book designed specifically to help project administrators manage paperwork more efficiently and profitably.

This book includes both manual and computer-generated formats for nearly every facet of construction documentation.

ISBN 0-87629-147-7
Book No. 67268

$65.95/copy
U.S. Funds

Insurance Repair:
Opportunities, Procedures and Methods
by Peter J. Crosa, AIC

1st Edition
Over 200 Pages • Illustrated • Hardcover

Advice for getting into the business of insurance repair—based on first-hand experience

As a contractor or subcontractor interested in expansion, you might be considering working with claims adjusters and insurance companies to repair damaged properties.

The fact is that billions of dollars are paid out annually by insurance companies . . . mostly without fierce competitive bidding. The business is also highly stable—going on in both good times and bad.

Insurance Repair: Opportunities, Procedures and Methods gives you the information you need to evaluate insurance repair, including the benefits and pitfalls—and explains what is required to be a success in this profitable business.

ISBN 0-87629-146-9
Book No. 67267

$54.95/copy
U.S. Funds

Consulting

Introducing...
MEANS CONSTRUCTION CONSULTING SERVICES

For corporate facilities departments, government agencies, architecture and engineering firms, developers, financial and investment companies

- **Project estimating and planning**
- **Construction feasibility studies/research**
- **Development and maintenance of cost databases**

R.S. Means Company now offers you the benefits of expert consulting services for individual and ongoing projects in these key areas:

Building construction estimating—planning

Control expenses, avoid cost overruns, hit budgets with Means consulting help ... including reliable estimates ... guidelines for expenses ... project duration ... cash flow projections ... resource allocation ... change order negotiations, and more.

Feasibility studies—analysis of construction options

Let the Means staff help you review and clarify the best construction approaches in terms of time, cost, use. These services include detailed analysis of technologies, lead times, materials use, and other important construction alternatives to provide facts and unbiased advice for management decision-making.

Creation of cost databases for unique or specialized construction applications

Utility companies, communications firms, energy companies, government agencies ... all can benefit from Means expertise in creating construction cost databases for unique types of construction.

**For complete information—call Robert Gair, Director—
1-800-448-8182**

Seminars

Means Construction Seminars 1991

During the year, R.S. Means offers a series of 2-day seminars oriented to a wide range of construction-related topics. All seminars include comprehensive workbooks, current Means Cost Books, plus proven techniques for estimating and scheduling.

REPAIR AND REMODELING ESTIMATING

Repair and remodeling work is becoming increasingly competitive as more professionals enter the market. Recycling existing buildings can pose difficult estimating problems. Labor costs, energy use concerns, building codes, and the limitations of working with an existing structure place enormous importance on the development of accurate estimates. Using the exclusive techniques associated with Means' widely-acclaimed *Repair & Remodeling Cost Data*, this seminar sorts out and discusses solutions to the problems of building alteration estimating. Attendees will receive two intensive days of eye-opening methods for handling virtually every kind of repair and remodeling situation . . . from demolition and removal to final restoration.

MECHANICAL AND ELECTRICAL ESTIMATING

This seminar is tailored to fit the needs of those seeking to develop or improve their skills and to have a better understanding of how mechanical and electrical estimates are prepared during the conceptual, planning, budgeting and bidding stages. Learn how to avoid costly omissions and overlaps between these two interrelated specialties by preparing complete and thorough cost estimates for both trades. Featured are order of magnitude, assemblies, and unit price estimating. In combination with the use of *Means Mechanical Cost Data*, *Means Plumbing Cost Data* and *Means Electrical Cost Data*, this seminar will ensure more accurate and complete Mechanical/Electrical estimates for both unit price and preliminary estimating procedures.

CONSTRUCTION ESTIMATING– THE UNIT PRICE APPROACH

This seminar shows how today's advanced estimating techniques and cost information sources can be used to develop more reliable unit price esimates for projects of any size. It demonstrates how to organize data, use plans efficiently, and avoid embarrassing errors by using better methods of checking.

You'll get down-to-earth help and easy-to-apply guidance for:

- making maximum use of construction cost information sources
- organizing estimating procedures in order to save time and reduce mistakes
- sorting out and identifying unusual job requirements to prevent underestimates.

SQUARE FOOT COST ESTIMATING

Learn how to make better preliminary estimates with a limited amount of budget and design information. You will benefit from examples of a wide range of systems estimates with specifications limited to building use requirements, budget, building codes, and type of building. And yet, with minimal information, you will obtain a remarkable degree of accuracy.

Workshop sessions will provide you with model square foot estimating problems and other skill-building exercises. The exclusive Means building assemblies square foot cost approach shows how to make very reliable estimates using "bare bones" budget and design information.

SCHEDULING AND PROJECT MANAGEMENT

This seminar helps you successfully establish project priorities, develop realistic schedules, and apply today's advanced management techniques to your construction projects. Hands-on exercises familiarize participants with network approaches such as Critical Path or Precedence Diagram Methods. Special emphasis is placed on cost control, including use of computer based systems. Through this seminar you'll perfect your scheduling and management skills, ensuring completion of your projects *on time* and *within budget*. Includes hands-on application of *Means Scheduling Manual* and *Building Construction Cost Data*.

THE CONSTRUCTION PROCESS– METHODS & MATERIALS

This course provides an overview of the basic construction process from the time an idea/need is identified until the final move-in. Participants will learn about the components of construction and how they are assembled to build a project.

Also provided are guidelines for reading the plans and specifications identify the key elements of a building. Attendees will achieve a thorough understanding of the construction process, from concept through completion, and with a practical overview of the methods and materials used in construction. If you are new to the construction industry or just want to know more about the complex process of converting a need for a building project into a reality, this course is for you!

AVOIDING AND RESOLVING CONSTRUCTION CLAIMS

Construction claims are a common and costly problem in the construction industry. This course provides you with insight and practical recommendations for dealing with claims. The hands-on approach focuses on recognizing and responding to problems as they arise, preparing documentation and formal reports, analyzing causation, calculating damages, evaluating responsibility and defending against unmeritorious claims. Special emphasis will be given to determining schedule and cost impact of project delays. You'll perfect your skills in negotiation to resolve disputes in order to avoid the risks of trial or arbitration. In addition, the program provides realistic approaches to minimizing and avoiding the problems which lead to claims. This course is a must for those responsible for the management and administration of construction projects.

Seminars

Means In-House Training 1991

Discover the cost savings and added benefits of bringing Means proven training programs to your facility ...

ATTENDEES
Facility, Design, and Construction Professionals who want to improve their estimating, project management, and negotiation skills

CONTENT
One or more MEANS Training Seminars (as described in Means Construction Seminar, 1991)

A two-day course running from 8 AM to 4 PM on two consecutive days

The intensive training includes conceptual work and practice exercises.

In-House Seminar (IHS) students benefit from discussion and practical work problems that are common to their particular environment.

COMPARISON
The In-House Seminar conducted at the client's facility will eliminate travel expenses and minimize time away from work.

An In-House Seminar program is more flexible and responsive to specific client needs and requirements.

IHS students improve their skills and broaden their knowledge. Students return immediate benefits to their work place.

IHS provides a standard and consistent method for preparing cost estimates.

CLASS SIZE
The cost effective break-even point is 10–12 students; most seminars have from 15 to 25 students; class size is limited to 35 students.

Occasionally, to satisfy their needs or to reduce per student training cost, clients invite outside personnel with a similar background to attend their MEANS Seminars.

SCHEDULING
Consult with Means' professional training advisor to determine the seminar that best suits your needs.

Set your training schedule immediately to assure dates that fit your calendar.

Means will make every effort to accommodate your schedule.

COMPREHENSIVE MATERIALS
Each participant receives a comprehensive workbook, Means reference books that are appropriate to the seminar, and a current Means cost book. The materials reinforce program content and serve as a valuable reference for the future.

CERTIFICATES & CEU's
A certificate of completion is awarded by R.S. Means Company, Inc. to those who complete the program. Continuing Education Units (CEU's) are also awarded through the American Association of Cost Engineers (AACE).

GUARANTEE
R.S. Means stands behind its In-House Seminars.

You will deal with real problems, not theoretical situations. If your In-House Seminar does not give you the tools you need to grow in the subject covered, just tell us why and we will give you credit toward another seminar.

Partial list of companies and organizations that have brought Mean's Training in-house:

- Army Corps of Engineers
- AT&T
- Bell Research Lab
- Bell Operating Companies
- Boston Edison
- Digital Equipment Corporation
- Eastman Kodak
- General Motors
- General Services Administration
- Housing and Urban Development
- IBM
- Internal Revenue Service
- Jacksonville Electric Authority
- Marine Corps
- National Guard
- Penn State University
- Port Authority of NY/NJ
- State of Missouri
- State of Virginia
- U.S. Air Force
- U.S. Army
- U.S. Navy
- University of Massachusetts
- Westinghouse Electric Authority

How to find out MORE—Call Joan M. Ward at (800) 448-8182

1991 Means Seminar Schedule

SPRING & SUMMER

New York City, NY	January 28–31	Denver, CO	May 13–16
Ft. Lauderdale, FL	February 4–7	Plymouth, MA	May 13–16
Las Vegas, NV	February 18–21	Los Angeles, CA	May 20–23
San Jose, CA	February 25–28	Hartford, CT	June 3–6
Atlanta, GA	March 11–14	Tarrytown, NY	June 10–13
Atlantic City, NJ	March 18–21	Indianapolis, IN	June 17–20
Washington, DC	April 15–18	Baltimore, MD	June 24–27
Seattle, WA	April 22–25	Niagara Falls, NY	July 22–25
Chicago, IL	April 29–May 2	Minneapolis, MN	August 26–29

FALL

Hyannis, MA	September 9–12	Philadelphia, PA	October 28–31
Washington, DC	September 16–19	Long Beach, CA	October 28–31
Rutherford, NJ	September 23–26	San Francisco, CA	November 4–7
Kansas City, MO	October 7–10	San Antonio, TX	December 2–5
Raleigh, NC	October 21–24	Orlando, FL	December 9–12

For a complete schedule of courses offered at each location, call our Seminar Registrar at 1-800-448-8182.

Registration Information

How to Register
To register, call our Seminar Registrar, Marcia Crosby, today. Means toll-free number for making reservations is:
1-800-448-8182.

Registration Fees
- One seminar registration — $845 per person
- Two to four seminar registrations — $745 per person
- Five or more seminar registrations — $695 per person
- Ten or more seminar registrations — call for pricing

Special Offers
Early Registration:
Sign up 45 days prior to the seminar/save $50 off each seminar registration. Payment must be in advance.

One Individual:
Sign up for two seminars in a one-year period and pay only $1345. This is a saving of 40% on the additional seminar. Payment must be received at least ten (10) days prior to seminar date to confirm this offer.

Cancellations
Cancellations will be accepted up to ten days prior to the seminar start. After that time a 2-day seminar cancellation is subject to a $150 cancellation fee. The fee may be applied to any Means seminar within one calendar year of cancellation. Substitutions can be made at any time before the session starts. No-shows are subject to the full seminar fee.

AACE Approved Courses
The R.S. Means Construction Estimating and Management Seminars described and offered to you here have each been approved for 14 hours (1.4 CEU) of credit by the American Association of Cost Engineers (AACE) Inc. Certification Board toward meeting the continuing education requirements for re-certification as a Certified Cost Engineer/Certified Cost Consultant.

Daily Course Schedule
The first day of each seminar session begins at 8:30 A.M. and ends at 4:30 P.M. The second day is 8:00–4:00. Participants are urged to bring a hand-held calculator since many actual problems will be worked out in each session.

Seminar Tuition Includes
Current Means cost manuals, appropriate Means reference manuals and seminar workbooks. Continental breakfast and coffee breaks are also provided. Each participant receives a certificate of course completion.

Hotel/Transportation Arrangements
R.S. Means has arranged to hold a block of rooms at each hotel hosting a seminar. To take advantage of special group rates when making your reservation be sure to mention that you are attending the Means Seminar. You are of course free to stay at the lodging place of your choice. (Hotel reservations and transportation arrangements should be made directly by seminar attendees.)

Important
Class sizes are limited, so please register as soon as possible.

Registration Form

Please register the following people for the Means Construction Seminars as shown here. Full payment or deposit is enclosed, and we understand that we must make our own hotel reservations if overnight stays are necessary.

- ☐ Full payment of $ _____ enclosed.
- ☐ Deposit of $ _____ enclosed.

Balance due is $ _____
U.S. FUNDS

Name of Registrant(s)
(To appear on certificate of completion)

Firm Name _____
Address _____
City/State/Zip _____
Telephone Number _____

☐ Charge our registration(s) to:
☐ American Express ☐ Visa ☐ MasterCard

Account No. _____ Expiration Date _____

CARDHOLDER'S SIGNATURE

Seminar Name   City   Dates

Please mail check to: R.S. MEANS COMPANY, INC., 100 Construction Plaza, P.O. Box 800, Kingston, MA 02364-0800 USA

Software

PULSAR
The most significant advance in construction management systems since Means invented the cost book.

A key advantage of Pulsar is its extensive database! It is derived from the *Means Facilities Cost Data* book. You can use it to estimate all types of jobs, from simple remodeling to complex new construction. A special section is included for facilities maintenance cost estimates.

You can find the unit prices you need using either of two different methods. Use CSI numbers and the convenient windowing systems take you right to the items.

You can also key in the word or phrase. It's quick and easy. For example: type "drywall" and you get a list of items associated with drywall. Make your selection and the software takes you right to that item. It's just like using the index of a book—only simpler!

Pulsar includes over 400 pre-built Assemblies. They give you the accuracy of a line-by-line estimate without the work. For example: a "wet pipe sprinkler system" lists all the components you need, quantities, materials costs, installation costs, the cost per square foot and more! You can use Assemblies as they were developed, modify them to suit your conditions, or create new ones.

"Pages" are a real Pulsar benefit! You can create, store and reuse your own original Pages — combinations of unit prices and Assemblies that form specific portions of your project. A Page can consist of just about anything you choose.

You can develop and reuse your own Assemblies for specific tasks.

And you can insert and reuse individual line items that are special to your estimate.

Your estimate can be a combination of Means data and your own costs that are adjusted for local conditions.

Means' standardized form of estimating improves your negotiating powers with outside vendors and makes it easier to work with other people in your company.

You can print reports by CSI divisions, subdivisions, and detailed line-by-line estimates. "Sort" features allow you to segment reports by floor, room, job responsibility — basically any criteria you wish to include. You decide whether to burden or unburden the job and when to add sales tax, markups, markdowns, contingencies, and bonds.

Using the Means City Cost Index, you can quickly see what a job will cost in over 200 cities in the U.S. and Canada.

You can use Pulsar estimates with popular spreadsheet, database, scheduling, project management, job cost control, and graphics packages.

"Test drive" Pulsar and experience for yourself how this comprehensive software system saves you time and gives you the tools you need for fast, reliable construction cost estimating.

Complete the order form below or call to order your Diskette Demo Package.

Software Order/Information Form

I am interested in: ☐ Astro II ☐ Pulsar

☐ Please send me the Multiple Diskette Demo Package for $50. (This cost can be credited toward your purchase of a system).*MA residents, please add state sales tax.

☐ Please tell me more about the computer services exclusively designed for the construction industry.

I have a _____ computer.   Disk Size: ☐ 3½"   ☐ 5¼"
                   make/model

* ☐ Check enclosed (save shipping & handling)
☐ Charge my Demo Package to:
  ☐ American Express   ☐ Visa   ☐ MasterCard

Your Name: _____

Company Name: _____   Account # _____

Address: _____   Expiration Date

City/State/Zip _____   ☐ Bill me (P.O.#) _____

Call toll free 1-800-448-8182, or mail this request today to:
R.S. Means Co., Inc.
100 Construction Plaza
P.O. Box 800
Kingston, MA 02364-0800

Software

The new electronic tool that lets you access over 20,000 lines of Means construction cost data right at your PC.

Means Data Source®

Accessing Means data has never been easier... or quicker. New **Means Data Source®** allows you to combine the power of your PC with the proven reliability of R.S. Means construction cost data. You're able to call up the information you need in mere seconds. Data Source enables you to:

Electronically search through the Means data base — over 20,000 cost lines in CSI MASTERFORMAT.

Select the appropriate lines for a job — either quantifying them in the Means program, or easily transferring them in ASCII format to any compatible program (including Lotus 1-2-3, dBase III and many others).

Feel the security and reassurance of using data that's formatted exactly like the data in our popular cost books.

Quickly and easily learn how to access and use Means data (with many useful on-line Help Screens available).

Generate professional reports — selecting from a menu of standard report formats in our program, or using your own format when you transfer the data to your spreadsheet.

Use the built-in quantifying program to extend quantities and calculate costs.

Perform your operations on all IBM and 100% IBM-compatible PC's (MS-DOS 2.0 or better).

With advantages like these, you'll want to be sure to order Means **Data Source** today. Just call **1-800-448-8182**, or mail the form below.

IBM is a trademark of International Business Machines Inc.
Lotus 1-2-3 is a registered trademark of Lotus Development Corp.
dBASE is a trademark of Ashton-Tate.
Means Data Source is a registered trademark of R.S. Means Co., Inc.

Please send me the following Data Source product(s):*

Quantity	Price		Total
_____ x	$395	Building Construction	$ _____
_____ x	$395	Mechanical	_____
_____ x	$395	Electrical	_____
_____ x	$395	Repair & Remodeling	_____
_____ x	$195	Light Commercial (10,000 line items)	_____
		Massachusetts residents add state sales tax:	_____
		Total	_____

Prices are for U.S. Delivery only. Canadian customers should write for current prices.

☐ Yes, please tell me more about the computer services exclusively designed for the construction industry.

I have a _____ computer.   Disk Size: ☐ 3½"   ☐ 5¼"
           make/model

Your Name: _____
Company Name: _____
Address: _____
City/State/Zip _____
Telephone _____

* ☐ Check enclosed payable to R.S. Means Company, Inc.
    (Save shipping & handling)
  ☐ Charge my order to:
    ☐ American Express   ☐ Visa   ☐ MasterCard

  Account # _____
  Expiration Date _____

  ☐ Bill me (P.O. #) _____

Call toll free 1-800-448-8182 or mail this request today to:
R.S. Means Co., Inc.
100 Construction Plaza
P.O. Box 800
Kingston, MA 02364-0800

*Discounts on Multiple Orders... starting at 25%
If you would like to order 4 or more copies of Data Source, be sure to call us at 1-800-448-8182, ext. 39. We'll provide you with complete information on multiple discounts that start at 25%.

Plug into the Means database.

Software

Means Software Systems Complement the Expertise of the Professional Estimator

No computer will ever replace years of experience and hard work! But the demands on your time are considerable. There is always pressure to get more accomplished in less time. Means Software Systems are the answer! They are the powerful tools you need for fast, accurate construction cost estimating.

Takeoff is efficient and easy! Programs are menu-driven and based on familiar "scroll, cut and paste" techniques. You quickly access specific portions of the multilevel database with the easy-to-use window and scroll operation. A single key stroke then marks ("cuts") only the items you need and sends them to a buffer file until you are ready to "paste" them into your estimate.

You can use the reliable Means figures to build your estimate, and you can adjust cost factors to fit actual job conditions. Costs can be modified in numerous ways to prepare estimates—from the smallest remodeling or repair projects to multi-story new construction.

Everything you need is readily available. Material costs, crews, equipment costs, man-hours, daily output, overhead, profit, and more! It's all in the databases included in the software.

Computerized estimating is dynamic! When costs change, even complex estimates can be rapidly adjusted. As soon as you enter a new figure, the software automatically changes all dependent calculations. With more flexible estimating procedures, you have guidelines to control costs and make more informed decisions.

You already know a lot about this outstanding software because it is arranged in the industry-standard CSI MASTERFORMAT. You have two ways to search the databases—using CSI numbers, or words and phrases.

With Means Estimating Software you build standardized estimates that are consistent and easy to understand. Standardized estimates improve communications with outside vendors and other departments within your company. They can even speed the budget approval process!

Reports cover as much detail as you need. You can get reports based on major CSI divisions and subdivisions, on a detailed item-by-item basis, for parts of the job, or for the specific job criteria that you choose.

For even more extensive manipulation and reporting, you can export all or part of your estimate to many popular spreadsheet, database, and graphics packages.

With our many years of experience in both software and publishing, *we understand the importance of support!* You can take advantage of Means superb documentation, step-by-step tutorials, on-screen help, toll-free information hot line, and optional on-site training.

With Means Annual Software Service Support Agreement, you receive updates on all your cost files for each year, continued hot line support and software enhancements as they occur.

Hardware requirements: IBM® XT™, AT®, or 100% compatible (AT is preferred; the program runs faster). Color monitor preferred, but not required. 640K main memory. One 5¼" or 3½" floppy disk drive. Hard disk with 15 mb available, MS™-DOS 2.0 or higher. IBM compatible printer.

ASTRO II
Powerful Construction Software That's Easy to Use... Even If You've Never Used a Computer for Estimating!

Manual estimating is cumbersome and time-consuming. Each item must be entered separately, and when costs or conditions change, all the figures must be recalculated. With Astro II, when you change a figure, all items it affects are automatically changed. Easy-to-read, on-screen "windows" guide you from the CSI MASTERFORMAT divisions, to the subdivisions, to the unit items you need. You can also search for items using words and phrases—it's just like using the index of a book—only simpler! Then you "mark" the items you need and "paste" them to your estimate.

R.S. Means is known for its timely and comprehensive construction cost data. With Astro II, you choose the Means Data File which best suits your estimating requirements.

As your company grows and changes, you can add other Means Cost Data Files to your existing Astro II package.

It's easy. You don't have to be a programmer. When there are items that are specific to your estimate, you can create your own user files. You can then save, change, update, and reuse them for other estimates.

Labor and equipment costs change constantly—so you can adjust specific costs where necessary to suit your area and your project.

When elements of the estimate change, you don't have to redo the estimate. You just enter new costs and line items to update the estimate as often as you like.

You may want a very detailed estimate for your use, and an overview for your customer. Reports can be generated by CSI divisions, subdivisions or as line-by-line estimates.

You can plan a construction project and then use Means City Cost Indexes to quickly see what it would cost to build in over 200 cities in the United States and Canada.

For additional reports, to test "what-if" scenarios, and to create job schedules, you can export your estimate to popular spreadsheet and project management software packages.

You can take advantage of on-screen help, a toll-free 800 hot line and superbly written documentation. The software is logical and works like you do.

**Call 1-800-448-8182
for more information**

Annual Publications

Means Open Shop Building Construction Cost Data 1991

7th Annual Edition
Over 450 Pages • Illustrated

This is "must have" information for your estimating

You depend on BCCD for union labor... now you can have the same comprehensive prices for open shop work

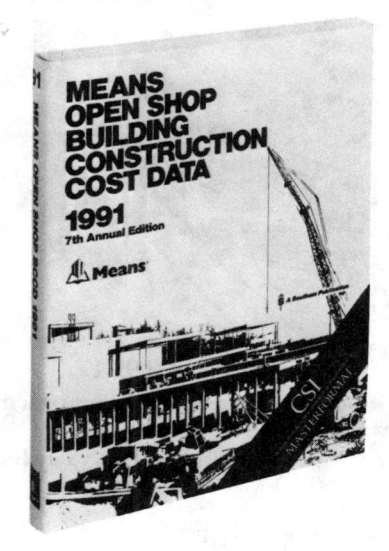

One flip through your copy of *Means Open Shop Building Construction Cost Data 1991* will convince you of its value to your estimating process.

Here at last are over 20,000 reliable unit cost entries based on non-union skilled and trade labor costs. No longer will you need to use time-consuming, inefficient ways to get these prices. The Open Shop BCCD gives you every price you need in the familiar Means layout.

The labor cost data is broken down into man-hours, daily output, crew, bare labor, equipment, overhead and profit.

You can break out labor cost facts in any way you need for substitutions, comparisons, and adjustments.

ISBN 0-87629-198-1　　　　　　$76.95/copy
Book No. 60151　　　　　　　　U.S. Funds

Building Construction Cost Data 1991
Western Edition

4th Annual Edition
Over 500 Pages • Illustrated

For western contractors, estimators, architects, engineers, builders, facilities professionals

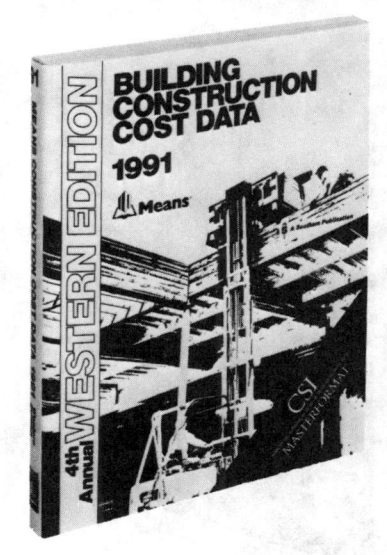

This regional edition of *Building Construction Cost Data* is specifically designed to give you more precise cost information for the West. It also provides greater information on the construction assemblies which are common in the West.

Based on western methods of construction, this edition makes unit cost information **easier to understand and use.**

Indexes are broken down into major construction components and subtrades.

The Western Edition has information regarding western practices and situations which are not found in our national edition. It helps you estimate more precisely because it has 30 different western locations, nearly **twice as many** as currently offered in our national edition!

ISBN 0-87629-188-4　　　　　　$76.95/copy
Book No. 60221　　　　　　　　U.S. Funds

Annual Publications

Means Concrete Cost Data 1991

9th Annual Edition
Over 450 Pages • Illustrated

Arranged in the CSI MASTERFORMAT

Included in the new 1991 edition of *Means Concrete Cost Data* are cost facts for almost every concrete estimating problem—from complicated formwork to lavish brickwork.

The comprehensive unit cost section shows crew, daily output, man-hour information with bare costs for materials, labor, equipment, overhead, and profit for over 10,000 individual items.

The "most-popular" assemblies cost section describes the concrete or masonry assembly with drawings, diagrams, and text.

ISBN 0-87629-189-2
Book No. 60111

$65.95/copy
U.S. Funds

Means Mechanical Cost Data 1991

14th Annual Edition
440 Pages • Illustrated

Gives you comprehensive prices for HVAC and mechanical estimating . . .

More valuable to you than ever—focused exclusively on HVAC, controls . . . all related piping, ductwork, accessories and construction

Offered in 1991

- Many prices for key materials and components used in HVAC have gone down as well as up.
- Extensive HVAC CLASSIFICATIONS including:
  - purging scoops
  - cocks and drains
  - liquid drainers—several types
  - flow check controls
  - suction diffusers
  - multi-purpose valves
  - mono-flow tee fittings
  - vacuum breakers
  - direct digital controls—expanded section
  - flue heat reclaim
  - commercial kitchen ventilation
- Plus price coverage for:
  - polyethylene foam closed cell sheet and tubing
  - gas appliance regulators
  - types of steam traps
  - air control vents
  - control system components
  - water and steam coils
  - silent check valves

ISBN 0-87629-195-7
Book No. 60021

$67.95/copy
U.S. Funds

Annual Publications

Means Assemblies Cost Data 1991

16th Annual Edition
Over 550 Pages • Illustrated

Means Assemblies Cost Data 1991 enables you to quickly compare the most desirable construction approaches using "pre-grouped" component costs called systems or assemblies—such as structure, building enclosure and interior partitions. These are expressed in an easy-to-measure element of the building such as square feet of floor area or exterior wall, linear feet of partition, or cost each.

Each assembly includes a complete grouping of the many types of materials used and their associated installation costs including the installing contractor's overhead and profit. Substitute component price selections are shown together with each assembly so it is possible to customize an assembly to meet specific use, cost goals, or for value engineering exercises.

In addition, this book contains an extensive reference section that guides the user through the actual design process. With this information one can make intelligent decisions about which method, material, or assembly to select.

ISBN 0-87629-192-2
Book No. 60061

$105.95/copy
U.S. Funds

Means Facilities Cost Data 1991

6th Annual Edition
Over 950 Pages • Illustrated

A cost planning tool for facilities construction and maintenance!

More reasons than ever to use Means Facilities Cost Data 1991 *for your facilities estimating projects!*

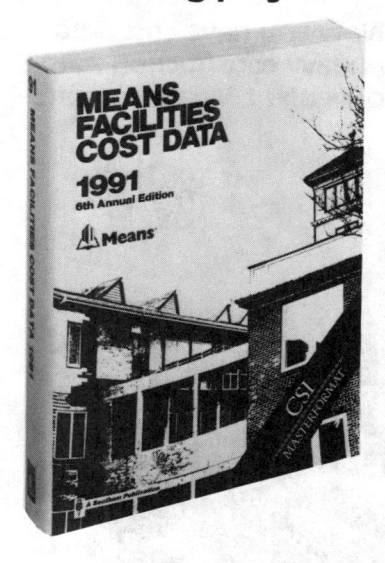

If you are involved in facilities renovations, new construction, or maintenance as a contractor bidding for jobs or a manager planning them, there is tremendous pressure on you to justify your expenditures and to make your estimates reliable.

Means Facilities Cost Data 1991 can help you do just that. This *ultra-complete reference source* makes your estimating more precise and cuts down dramatically on the time you have to spend checking other job costs and calling subs and vendors.

You can use this book to adjust national average data to specific locations.

There are hundreds of other ways you can use this guide. With well over 40,000 unit prices, assembly costs and square foot costs, it is actually four books wrapped into one.

ISBN 0-87629-194-9
Book No. 60201

$173.95/copy
U.S. Funds

Annual Publications

Means Heavy Construction Cost Data 1991

5th Annual Edition
Over 380 Pages • Illustrated

Now—heavy construction costs for utilities, public works, earthwork, roadways, airports, pipelines, sewerage, railroads, marine work and more!

Now you have cost data for heavy construction in the convenient Means format.

Means Heavy Construction Cost Data 1991 is designed for contractors and engineers responsible for estimating heavy construction projects with high reliability.

It's an estimating tool that provides prices based on painstaking research into the actual costs for heavy construction throughout North America in the past 12 months. The heavy construction unit and systems cost entries are supplemented with preparation, mobilization, and finishing costs for most projects.

The book can be used to price out an entire estimate or quickly verify estimates with cost data based on national averages, adjusted for locations in the U.S. and Canada.

The unit price entries are organized in the popular Means line item system containing crew make-up, crew productivity, man-hour data, and bare costs for materials, labor, and equipment ... with and without overhead and profit.

ISBN 0-87629-202-3 $71.95/copy
Book No. 60161 U.S. Funds

Means Site Work Cost Data 1991

10th Annual Edition
Over 400 Pages • Illustrated

Dedicated to the special problems of site work estimating...

Here are just a few of the ways
Means Site Work Cost Data 1991
will help you

- estimate crews, equipment and man-hours required for any site work operation ... earthwork hauling, underground installations
- use the price data to compare and select designs and specifications in the project's conceptual stages
- verify your prices and estimates with the manual's national averages
- use it for the hard-to-find costs and site work installations unfamiliar to you
- double-check on subcontractor bids and estimates
- get expert guidance for complicated site work estimating problems

Current data to help you
- Accurate local materials, labor and equipment price adjustment factors.
- Site work assembly cost tables for conceptual estimating.
- Reference tables for calculating quantities, pricing site work.

ISBN 0-87629-196-5 $67.95/copy
Book No. 60071 U.S. Funds

Annual Publications

Means Electrical Cost Data 1991

14th Annual Edition
Over 400 Pages • Illustrated

Complete in every way—your trusted price book for electrical estimating

Why **Means Electrical Cost Data 1991** is the "tool of choice" for your electrical estimating

Means Electrical Cost Data has become a trusted and well-used guide by your fellow electrical estimating, contracting and design professionals.

This year is no exception, particularly in light of the important price changes in recent months.

In fact, 1991 electrical estimating can hold some pricing surprises. Here's where Means value really shines. The Means staff of experts has done their homework—so you can steer clear of the pitfalls *and take advantage* of the opportunities ahead.

This is a powerful, easy-to-use resource dedicated solely to electrical estimating.

With *Means Electrical Cost Data 1991* you'll make estimates with a price source you can trust.

ISBN 0-87629-193-0 $67.95/copy
Book No. 60031   U.S. Funds

Means Electrical Change Order Cost Data 1991

3rd Annual Edition
Over 400 Pages • Illustrated

How to accurately price and document electrical change orders—making sure the costs are recoverable!

Consider the countless ways **Means Electrical Change Order Cost Data 1991** will help you . . .

As an electrical contractor, project manager, or engineer, pricing and documenting change orders is surely a key part of your job.

Change orders—or project "extras"—are the source of conflicts, lost time and sometimes serious disputes.

This guide provides you with electrical unit prices *exclusively* for pricing change orders—based on the recent, direct experience of contractors and suppliers throughout North America.

The costs are broken down into two comprehensive sections: *pre-installation* and *post-installation* changes.

For the first time, you can analyze and check your own change order estimates against the experience others have had *doing exactly the same work!*

ISBN 0-87629-205-8 $72.95/copy
Book No. 60231   U.S. Funds

Annual Publications

Means Landscape Cost Data 1991

4th Annual Edition
Over 350 Pages • Illustrated

Estimate landscape and related hard construction faster, easier—and with complete reliability

Means Landscape Cost Data 1991 is for busy landscape designers, contractors, facilities managers and other professionals needing accurate prices for landscape projects. Cost data is arranged in CSI MASTERFORMAT.

Here you have a landscape cost book that will give you direct, reliable answers for your landscape and outdoor improvements estimating.

Means Landscape Cost Data 1991 includes labor productivities and Standard Landscape Crew Tables with hourly and daily costs. Also includes a 162 City Cost Index for the U.S. and Canada showing price variations for materials and labor from region to region, hardiness zones, special plant uses and adaptability, scientific and common plant names, unit conversions, and complete subject index and appendix.

"One Stop" answers to your landscape price estimating questions

- Materials unit prices for shrubs, trees, seeding, ground covers, roads, walks, walls, fencing, underground utilities.
- Unit labor costs with crew, daily productivity, and man-hours.
- Equipment costs with equipment productivity including rental and operating cost data.
- Illustrated landscape assemblies prices with material and installation costs broken out.
- Helpful design and cost planning suggestions.
- Landscape site maintenance prices.
- Figures for the latest landscape methods, styles, construction approaches.
- Cost adjustment factors for 162 metropolitan areas in the U.S. and Canada.
- Easy-to-follow instructions for using the data.

ISBN 0-87629-203-1
Book No. 60191

$71.95/copy
U.S. Funds

Annual Publications

Means Plumbing Cost Data 1991

Piping • Fixtures • Fire Protection

14th Annual Edition
Over 400 Pages • Illustrated

Comprehensive unit and assemblies prices for every imaginable plumbing installation

Here's your all-inclusive price guide for efficiently and accurately estimating plumbing work and fire protection installations.

Tanks, filtration equipment, pipe, fittings, valves, fixtures, pumps, appliances, sprinkler and standpipe systems . . . *all related construction*

60 Illustrated Plumbing and Fire Protection Assemblies Costs

This estimating manual gives you instant access to current materials and trade labor prices for virtually all types of contemporary plumbing and fire protection installations.

One glance through this massive guide—containing thousands of "one stop" costs for piping, fittings, valves, support structures, fire protection systems, appliances—will convince you of its great value to your pricing work.

You can have plumbing prices quoted to you instantly.

Whether you use it for a complete unit price plumbing estimate, plumbing design concept, or for a sprinkler system quick price check, it will give you the estimating data you need.

Thousands of up-to-date plumbing and fire protection unit prices including:

- fixtures
- pumps
- site irrigation systems
- pipe valves and fittings
- swimming pool systems
- lawn and golf course sprinkler systems
- septic, fire hydrant and water service systems
- battery assemblies for urinals, lavatories, and water closets
- drainage and vacuum type fittings
- fire protection systems—including residential
- washing machine hook-ups
- water heaters—including point of use

Plus more graphics and illustrations of equipment and assemblies

ISBN 0-87629-204-X
Book No. 60211

$67.95/copy
U.S. Funds

Annual Publications

Means Interior Cost Data 1991

8th Annual Edition
Over 460 Pages • Illustrated

For estimating partitions, ceilings, floors, finishes, and furnishings

CSI MASTERFORMAT

Due to constantly changing styles and new design directions, thousands of new materials and hardware items for interior construction are introduced each year. Few designers and estimators can keep up with this avalanche of price options for finish work.

But now, you can keep up with—and stay ahead of—the infinite varieties of specialized materials and installation expenses involved in commercial and industrial interior construction ... thanks to Means Interior Cost Data 1991.

Here, in one all-inclusive resource, are all the prices and help you could ever hope to have for making accurate interior work estimates.

Comprehensive unit prices, illustrated assemblies costs, supplemental references—complete guidance for your interior estimating.

Estimating interior construction can be a lot easier with this new guide

13,000+ up-to-date unit price entries—with bare costs for labor, equipment, and materials.

Extensive labor and equipment productivity data—every key labor productivity, crew and cost fact helps you calculate prices for *any interior project*.

Materials, products, building techniques—updated cost information includes the latest materials and labor-saving installation methods for interior work.

Helpful 3-D illustrations where possible—materials, products, and assemblies are illustrated.

Quick-find index covers everything—nearly 5,000 listings in the index ensures that you'll find the item you're looking for fast.

Unit prices in CSI MASTERFORMAT—to speed estimates along, prices are arranged in the Construction Specifications Institute's MASTERFORMAT.

City Cost Index—enables you to adjust the prices based on costs in your local area of the U.S. or Canada.

ISBN 0-87629-190-6
Book No. 60091

$65.95/copy
U.S. Funds

Annual Publications

Means Repair & Remodeling Cost Data 1991

Commercial/Residential
12th Annual Edition
Over 450 Pages • Illustrated

Revised and updated ... the comprehensive resource for estimating commercial and residential remodeling

This is the Means cost guide that's specifically prepared for your renovation estimating.

Means Repair & Remodeling Cost Data 1991 conforms to the Construction Specifications Institute's (CSI) MASTERFORMAT so you can prepare your estimates more efficiently.

- Make your repair and remodeling estimates more reliable and precise. *Means Repair & Remodeling Cost Data 1991* is written especially to help you save time and take the worry and inconsistencies out of estimating.
- All pricing information is obtained through extensive research from contractors, builders, and suppliers throughout the country.
- PLUS ... you can get hundreds of cost and time-saving tips, hints, and advice based on the expertise and background of R.S. Means—over 48 years in the construction estimating business.

No matter what kind of renovation cost problem you face, *Means Repair & Remodeling Cost Data 1991* will give you the *special prices* you're looking for ...

- selective demolition
- gutting interiors
- debris removal
- foundation rebuilding
- supports/reinforcements
- masonry repairs
- interior replacements
- cleaning/restoration

- M/E upgrades
- interior finishes
- asbestos removal
- dust/noise protection
- testing services
- subsurface investigation
- structure moving

... plus hundreds more renovation costs

ISBN 0-87629-199-X
Book No. 60041

$67.95/copy
U.S. Funds

Annual Publications

Means Square Foot Costs 1991

Commercial/Residential Industrial/Institutional

12th Annual Edition
Over 400 Pages • Illustrated

Quoting accurate square foot prices is vital to construction planning and budgeting

Take a close look at what you get in *Means Square Foot Costs 1991*

- Highly reliable adjustments for local construction costs
- Costs for Common Additives in the commercial/industrial/institutional sections
- HVAC assemblies costs and HVAC options in the Unit-in-Place (assemblies) section
- 1991 square foot prices for all types of building construction
- Four levels of residential construction quality: economy, average, custom, and luxury
- 70 types of typical commercial, industrial and institutional buildings with illustrations
- Illustrated "building assemblies"—costs broken down by materials and installation
- Regional cost adjustment factors for local labor and materials price differences by zip code
- Helpful prototype estimating forms and worksheets
- Abundant illustrations, worked out examples

You can have reliable square foot prices for any building construction you're planning in minutes

Means Square Foot Costs 1991 is the annually updated source of cost facts that covers every situation you're likely to handle—residential, commercial, industrial and institutional construction of all types.

The convenient tables enable you to simply flip to the building type under consideration, and select an appropriate square foot price in just a few minutes.

The "Unit-in-Place" assemblies style construction prices give you the ability to prepare more detailed square foot costs through the analysis of individual construction assemblies. These pages are suited perfectly to comparing and selecting various design schemes according to predetermined budgets.

ISBN 0-87629-197-3
Book No. 60051

$76.95/copy
U.S. Funds

Annual Publications

Means Light Commercial Cost Data 1991

10th Annual Edition
Over 500 Pages • Illustrated

For the special estimating needs of light commercial contractors and architects

Easy-to-use, reliable price information about light commercial cost planning for adjusters, architects, contractors, planners, and project managers.

No better resource for estimating commercial construction with current price information

If you're still estimating commercial construction with hard-to-follow price sheets, bills for old jobs, or "guesstimates," we have good news for you.

Means new *Light Commercial Cost Data 1991* is totally dedicated to your special estimating needs as a commercial designer or builder.

It's simple to use, provides instantaneous price quotes, and is reliable for your 1991 cost planning. With a copy on your desk, you'll have the price data you need in *one convenient place*—not stacks of file folders, bills, or wrinkled computer printouts.

Yes, here in *one manual* is all the 1991 cost data you're likely to need in three estimating formats—unit prices, assemblies prices, and square foot costs.

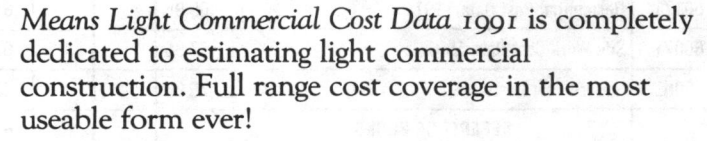

Means Light Commercial Cost Data 1991 is completely dedicated to estimating light commercial construction. Full range cost coverage in the most useable form ever!

- CSI MASTERFORMAT
- Quantity, unit, man-hour data
- Detailed descriptions
- Material and installation costs per square foot, assembly and unit price.
- Nine primary estimating divisions for each structure
- Man-hour data, materials and labor costs
- Over 20 appropriate cost modifications for each model
- Step-by-step listing of assembly components allows substitutions to fit unique needs

Means Light Commercial Cost Data 1991 covers all construction components

General requirements	Moisture thermal control	Special construction
Hourly and daily crew costs	Doors, windows and glass	Conveying systems
Site work	Finishes	Mechanical
Concrete	Specialties	Electrical
Masonry	Equipment	Square foot costs
Metals	Furnishings	Repair and remodeling
Wood and plastics		City cost indexes
		Comprehensive index

ISBN 0-87629-201-5
Book No. 60181

$65.95/copy
U.S. Funds

Order Form

Means
A Southam Company
R.S. Means Company, Inc.
100 Construction Plaza, P.O. Box 800, Kingston, MA 02364-0800

1991 ORDER FORM

CALL TOLL FREE
1-800-448-8182

QTY.	BOOK NO.	COST ESTIMATING BOOKS	UNIT PRICE	Total
	60061	Assemblies Cost Data 1991	$105.95	
	60011	Building Construction Cost Data 1991	65.95	
	60221	Building Constr. Cost Data–Western Edition 1991	76.95	
	60111	Concrete Cost Data 1991	65.95	
	60141	Construction Cost Indexes 1991	169.00	
	60141A	Construction Cost Index–January 1991	42.25	
	60141B	Construction Cost Index–April 1991	42.25	
	60141C	Construction Cost Index–July 1991	42.25	
	60141D	Construction Cost Index–October 1991	42.25	
	60231	Electrical Change Order Cost Data 1991	72.95	
	60031	Electrical Cost Data 1991	67.95	
	60201	Facilities Cost Data 1991	173.95	
	60161	Heavy Construction Cost Data 1991	71.95	
	60091	Interior Cost Data 1991	65.95	
	60121	Labor Rates for the Const. Industry 1991	145.00	
	60191	Landscape Cost Data 1991	71.95	
	60181	Light Commercial Cost Data 1991	65.95	
	60021	Mechanical Cost Data 1991	67.95	
	60151	Open Shop Building Constr. Cost Data 1991	76.95	
	60211	Plumbing Cost Data 1991	67.95	
	60041	Repair and Remodeling Cost Data 1991	67.95	
	60171	Residential Cost Data 1991	65.95	
	60071	Site Work Cost Data 1991	67.95	
	60051	Square Foot Costs 1991	76.95	
		REFERENCE BOOKS		
	67275	Avoiding and Resolving Construction Claims	59.95	
	67257	Bidding & Managing Government Construction	58.95	
	67180	Bidding for the General Contractor	54.95	
	67261	Building Profess. Guide to Contract Documents	54.95	
	67250	Business Management for the General Contractor	54.95	
	67278	Construction Delays	54.95	
	67268	Construction Paperwork	65.95	
	67255	Contractor's Business Handbook	58.95	
	67252	Cost Control in Building Design	58.95	
	67242	Cost Effective Design/Build Construction	54.95	
	67230	Electrical Estimating	54.95	
	67160	Estimating for the General Contractor	59.95	
	67276	Estimating Handbook	89.95	
	67249	Facilities Maintenance Management	59.95	
	67246	Facilities Maintenance Standards	131.95	
	67264	Facilities Manager's Reference	59.95	

QTY.	BOOK NO.	REFERENCE BOOKS (cont'd)	UNIT PRICE	Total
	67231	Forms for Building Construction Professionals	$ 76.95	
	67260	Fundamentals of the Construction Process	59.95	
	67210	Graphic Construction Standards	109.95	
	67258	Hazardous Material & Hazardous Waste	76.95	
	67280	Home Improvement Cost Guide	32.95	
	67251	HVAC: Design Criteria, Options, Selection	59.95	
	67281	HVAC Systems Evaluation	57.95	
	67190	Illustrated Construction Dictionary	87.95	
	67267	Insurance Repair	54.95	
	67237	Interior Estimating	54.95	
	67239	Landscape Estimating	57.95	
	67266	Legal Reference for Design & Construction	109.95	
	67236	Man-Hour Standards for Construction–2nd Ed.	131.95	
	67235	Mechanical Estimating	54.95	
	67245	Planning and Managing Interior Projects	59.95	
	67247	Project Planning and Control for Construction	58.95	
	67262	Quantity Takeoff for the General Contractor	59.95	
	67265	Repair & Remodeling Estimating	57.95	
	67254	Risk Management for Building Professionals	54.95	
	67253	Roofing: Design Criteria, Options, Selection	59.95	
	67152	Scheduling Manual	49.95	
	67145	Square Foot Estimating	57.95	
	67241	Structural Steel Estimating	65.95	
	67233	Superintending for the General Contractor	54.95	
	67274	Survival in the Construction Business	59.95	
	67259	Understanding the Legal Aspects of Design/Build	71.95	
	67232	Unit Price Estimating	54.95	

MA residents add state sales tax.

TOTAL (U.S. Funds)

Prices are subject to change and are for U.S. delivery only. Canadian customers should write for current prices.

Postage and handling extra when billed. Send your check with your order to save shipping and handling charges! 1991 editions available December 1990. Means will bill you or accept MasterCard, Visa, and American Express.

BC4

SEND ORDER TO:

Name (PLEASE PRINT) _____

Company _____
☐ Company
☐ Home   Address _____

_____

City/State/Zip _____

Phone # ( ) _____

P.O. # _____

(MUST ACCOMPANY ALL ORDERS BEING BILLED)

490

Annual Publications

Building Construction Cost Data 1991

49th Annual Edition
Over 450 Pages • Illustrated

America's foremost construction cost information guide with over 20,000 unit prices for labor, materials, and installation

Building Construction Cost Data, now in its 49th year of publication, offers the reliability of over 20,000 thoroughly researched unit prices, plus the efficient, easy-to-use CSI MASTERFORMAT. Even the most complicated estimates can be accurately prepared in less time than with comparable references.

Astute construction professionals prefer *Building Construction Cost Data* as their primary estimating resource. It's the original, most sought-after book of its kind . . . known and depended upon by its users for unparalleled accuracy and versatility . . . a cost resource prepared with you—the user—in mind.

Unit prices are based on the actual experience of contractors . . . coast to coast.

Price information shown in *Building Construction Cost Data 1991* is carefully gathered from the recent, actual experience of contractors throughout the United States and Canada.

Labor prices are based on union negotiated trade rates for the year.

Completely updated for 1991

- materials, fixtures, hardware, and equipment items included in each section
- all items updated to reflect 1991 costs and construction techniques
- unit prices divided into material, labor, and equipment costs with overhead and profit shown separately
- hourly and daily wage rates for installation crews and crew sizes, equipment, and average daily crew output listed
- city cost adjustment factors for material and labor costs in 19 categories for each of 162 major U.S. and Canadian metro areas
- factors to compute historical costs for all cities dating back to 1947
- square foot and cubic foot cost section showing range and medium costs for 59 common building types with plumbing, HVAC, and electrical percentages tabulated separately
- easy-to-use CSI format
- costs are the national average and can be easily adjusted for local wage scales
- over 19 index pages for quick item location and cross-reference
- helpful examples, instructions, illustrations, and explanations of how costs were developed for each major division

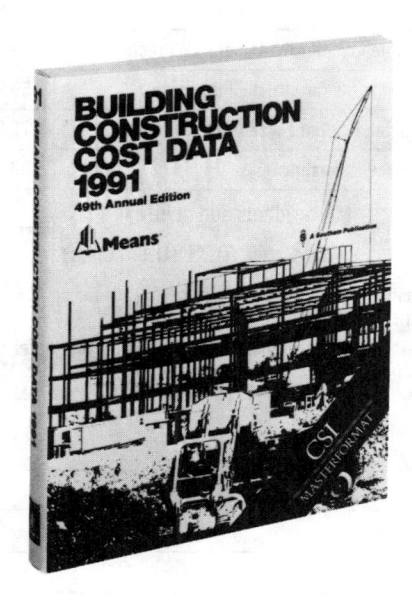

ISBN 0-87629-187-6
Book No. 60011

$65.95/copy
U.S. Funds

Order Form

Means®
A Southam Company
R.S. Means Company, Inc.
100 Construction Plaza, P.O. Box 800, Kingston, MA 02364-0800

1992 ORDER FORM

CALL TOLL FREE
1-800-448-8182

QTY.	BOOK NO.	COST ESTIMATING BOOKS	UNIT PRICE	Total
	60062	Assemblies Cost Data 1992	$115.95	
	60012	Building Construction Cost Data 1992	69.95	
	60222	Building Constr. Cost Data–Western Edition 1992	79.95	
	60112	Concrete Cost Data 1992	67.95	
	60142	Construction Cost Indexes 1992	180.00	
	60142A	Construction Cost Index–January 1992	45.00	
	60142B	Construction Cost Index–April 1992	45.00	
	60142C	Construction Cost Index–July 1992	45.00	
	60142D	Construction Cost Index–October 1992	45.00	
	60232	Electrical Change Order Cost Data 1992	79.95	
	60032	Electrical Cost Data 1992	72.95	
	60202	Facilities Cost Data 1992	179.95	
	60162	Heavy Construction Cost Data 1992	76.95	
	60092	Interior Cost Data 1992	71.95	
	60122	Labor Rates for the Const. Industry 1992	160.00	
	60192	Landscape Cost Data 1992	74.95	
	60182	Light Commercial Cost Data 1992	68.95	
	60022	Mechanical Cost Data 1992	72.95	
	60152	Open Shop Building Constr. Cost Data 1992	76.95	
	60212	Plumbing Cost Data 1992	71.95	
	60042	Repair and Remodeling Cost Data 1992	72.95	
	60172	Residential Cost Data 1992	68.95	
	60072	Site Work Cost Data 1992	71.95	
	60052	Square Foot Costs 1992	84.95	
		REFERENCE BOOKS		
	67275	Avoiding and Resolving Construction Claims	59.95	
	67257	Bidding & Managing Government Construction	62.95	
	67180	Bidding for the General Contractor	56.95	
	67261	Building Profess. Guide to Contract Documents	56.95	
	67250	Business Management for the General Contractor	58.95	
	67278	Construction Delays	61.95	
	67268	Construction Paperwork	70.95	
	67255	Contractor's Business Handbook	59.95	
	67252	Cost Control in Building Design	59.95	
	67242	Cost Effective Design/Build Construction	59.95	
	67230	Electrical Estimating	61.95	
	67160	Estimating for the General Contractor	61.95	
	67276	Estimating Handbook	89.95	
	67249	Facilities Maintenance Management	66.95	
	67246	Facilities Maintenance Standards	144.95	
	67264	Facilities Manager's Reference	67.95	

QTY.	BOOK NO.	REFERENCE BOOKS (cont'd)	UNIT PRICE	Total
	67231	Forms for Building Construction Professionals	$ 84.95	
	67260	Fundamentals of the Construction Process	64.95	
	67210	Graphic Construction Standards	114.95	
	67258	Hazardous Material & Hazardous Waste	79.95	
	67280	Home Improvement Cost Guide	35.95	
	67251	HVAC: Design Criteria, Options, Selection	64.95	
	67281	HVAC Systems Evaluation	62.95	
	67293	Illustrated Construction Dictionary, Unabridged	99.95	
	67267	Insurance Repair	58.95	
	67237	Interior Estimating	58.95	
	67239	Landscape Estimating	62.95	
	67266	Legal Reference for Design & Construction	114.95	
	67236	Man-Hour Standards for Construction–2nd Ed.	144.95	
	67235	Mechanical Estimating	62.95	
	67245	Planning and Managing Interior Projects	68.95	
	67247	Project Planning and Control for Construction	64.95	
	67262	Quantity Takeoff for the General Contractor	64.95	
	67265	Repair & Remodeling Estimating	62.95	
	67254	Risk Management for Building Professionals	54.95	
	67253	Roofing: Design Criteria, Options, Selection	59.95	
	67291	Scheduling Manual	56.95	
	67145	Square Foot Estimating	62.95	
	67241	Structural Steel Estimating	71.95	
	67233	Superintending for the General Contractor	54.95	
	67274	Survival in the Construction Business	59.95	
	67259	Understanding the Legal Aspects of Design/Build	72.95	
	67232	Unit Price Estimating	58.95	

MA residents add state sales tax.

TOTAL (U.S. Funds)

Prices are subject to change and are for U.S. delivery only. Canadian customers should write for current prices.

Postage and handling extra when billed. Send your check with your order to save shipping and handling charges! 1992 editions available December 1991. Means will bill you or accept MasterCard, Visa, and American Express.

BC4

SEND ORDER TO:

Name (PLEASE PRINT) _____

Company _____

☐ Company
☐ Home   Address _____

City/State/Zip _____

Phone # ( ) _____

P.O. # _____

(MUST ACCOMPANY ALL ORDERS BEING BILLED)